David E. Purpel
& William M. McLaurin, Jr.

Reflections
— on the —
Moral & Spiritual
Crisis in Education

PETER LANG
New York • Washington, D.C./Baltimore • Bern
Frankfurt am Main • Berlin • Brussels • Vienna • Oxford

370.11409
P985r
2004

29.95

Library of Congress Cataloging-in-Publication Data

Purpel, David E.
Reflections on the moral & spiritual crisis in education /
David E. Purpel, William M. McLaurin, Jr.
p. cm. — (Counterpoints; v. 262)
Includes bibliographical references and index.
I. Purpel, David E. Moral & spiritual crisis in education. 2. Public schools—
United States—Evaluation. 3. Education—Aims and objectives—United States.
4. Social justice—Study and teaching—United States. 5. Moral education—United States.
I. Title: Reflections on the moral and spiritual crisis in education.
II. McLaurin, Jr., William M. III. Purpel, David E. Moral & spiritual crisis in education.
IV. Title. V. Series: Counterpoints (New York, N.Y.) ; v. 262.
LA217.P874   370.11'4'0973—dc22   2004002450
ISBN 0-8204-6846-0
ISSN 1058-1634

Bibliographic information published by **Die Deutsche Bibliothek**.
Die Deutsche Bibliothek lists this publication in the "Deutsche
Nationalbibliografie"; detailed bibliographic data is available
on the Internet at http://dnb.ddb.de/.

Cover design by Lisa Barfield

The paper in this book meets the guidelines for permanence and durability
of the Committee on Production Guidelines for Book Longevity
of the Council of Library Resources.

A NOTE FROM THE PUBLISHER

It is my absolute delight to present *Reflections on the Moral and Spiritual Crisis in Education,* a significantly updated version of David Purpel's 1989 work. David has been an author of mine, as well as a friend, for many years. In this volume, he revisits the discussions from *The Moral and Spiritual Crisis in Education* from the perspective of the twenty-first century in collaboration with William M. McLaurin, Jr. whose work was introduced to me for the first time in these pages. I cannot think of a better person to have worked with David on this project, since it's obvious that he mirrors David's passion and intelligence.

I can assure you of a few things. First, these two educators are profoundly correct when they argue for the need for wisdom in our time. Second, they are themselves wise individuals who prove themselves to be up to the task of counseling us about education reform. Third, we are indeed in a crisis, one that worsens with each passing day. Although the immediate subject of this book is problems in education, the authors really talk about everything to do with modern-day life. Finally, and this is the good news, there is hope. Moral integrity, spiritual awareness and belief in real values can be the key factors in improving our lots in life.

The structure of this edition is rather unusual in that it's two books in one. After lengthy conversations, we all agreed that the 1989 edition (Part 1 of this volume) needed to be presented in its entirety. Part 2 is David and Bill's response to and analysis of David's original volume. The format allows readers to witness the development of a moral and religious framework that offers real solutions to our current educational dilemma. I hope that you will be as deeply impressed and deeply moved by the message of this book as I am.

Christopher S. Myers
Managing Director
Peter Lang Publishing

CONTENTS

PREFACE TO REFLECTIONS ON
THE MORAL AND SPIRITUAL CRISIS
IN EDUCATION

When it became apparent a few years ago that it was time for me to revise and update *The Moral and Spiritual Crisis in Education,* I have to admit that I was reluctant to take on the task. There were a number of reasons for this initial hesitation. To be sure, many of them were personal and ephemeral: my increasing fondness for indolence, my fear that I didn't have a whole lot more to say after 40 years of teaching and writing. I also began to experience a gnawing sense that perhaps it was impossible for the message of progressive educators to be heard. In those dizzying years of the 1990s there was a lot of talk about how we had learned to master our economic system and how to mitigate major geopolitical conflicts. It was a time when it became increasingly difficult (at least for me) to convince people that we were in crisis—moral, spiritual, or otherwise. Moreover, I became increasingly dispirited about a public educational policy that had hardened and coalesced into an increasingly vulgar and mindless program grounded in an obsession with competition, testing, and standardization.

However, as is obvious, I overcame my hesitations in the wake of their being overtaken by events. For one thing, I was able to convince my colleague William M. McLaurin, Jr. to cowrite the new version with me, thereby significantly reducing my workload and dramatically increasing the available talent. Second, my outrage at what had transpired over the past 10 or 12 years impelled me to reaffirm my beliefs and values and to ally myself with the voices of protest. The opening years of the 21st century have, to put it mildly, not been kind to the hopes and fantasies of the last decade of the 20th. Instead of the peace and prosperity we were assured would be the provenance of the free market and global economy, we have been beset with renewed, if not intensified, economic, social, cultural, and political crises. The threats of depression, terrorism, war, pollution, violence, disease, and hunger are surely not new; but the public sense of insecurity, danger, and vulnerability has dramatically reemerged in this post-9/11 era. And as far as educational policy and practice is concerned, the situation has become even worse as the federal government under a highly conservative administration is well on its way to imposing an extraordinarily repressive, retrogressive, and cruel regime on the public schools.

Perhaps the most serious threat of all to our hopes for a better world has been the increase in cynicism and despair about the possibilities of fundamental positive change and with it a significant loss of the energy and vitality that has fueled the impulse to create a more just and loving community. Because of this, I have become convinced that as educators and citizens, our most important and pressing educational task is to confront and overcome the paralyzing and debilitating effects of cynicism and despair.

When we carefully reread the first edition, it was clear that it needed quite a lot of copyediting and that there were a number of, by now, outmoded historical and topical allusions. However, we also came away strongly resonating with the essential thrust, analysis, and arguments of the book. Nonetheless it was also clear that the intervening years had given new meaning to some of the central elements of the book. Indeed, we found it quite instructive and interesting to note the differences in sensibility between the thinking reflected in the first edition and our present take on things. The dilemma we faced was how we could balance these varying concerns: the need to edit and update; the value of preserving the original text as well as providing new insight into the issues raised in the first edition. What we came up with seems, in retrospect, to be obvious—we would do all of the above.

Basically, this book represents both minor editing (first part) and major commentary (second part). We decided that it would be valuable to retain the original version more or less intact both in its own right as well as representing an interesting point of reference. We did not, however, want to miss the opportunity to polish some of the not-so-elegant phrases in the original edition and so we did give it a thorough cleaning without changing anything of substance. What we did do was some stylistic tweaking to improve (we hope) some awkward sentence structures and vague language as a way to clarify and reduce ambiguities. What we did not do is alter the essence of the book.

The second part of this book is in the form of a major commentary in which we affirm, modify, and extend the analyses of each of the sections of the original edition. In this way readers will have the opportunity to read both the original text with its topical and historical references intact plus our own current take on it, thereby giving readers the opportunity to go through a process similar to the one we experienced. In the first part of the book, therefore, we present the original text (as modestly copyedited) including the Introduction by Henry Giroux and Paulo Freire as well as my own Preface.

The second part contains five entirely new chapters. The first three chapters are jointly written and represent our thoughts and criticisms of each of the sections of the first edition. The last two chapters deal with the question of how we might respond to the present crisis that we both characterize as primarily spiritual in nature. (Portions of Chapter Five were previously published in *Moral Outrage in Education*, Peter Lang, 2000). However, since we both acknowledge the necessity and value of pluralism and since we have differing spiritual orientations, we decided to write to these issues from each of our own personal perspectives.

We trust that the format of the book will be as helpful to the readers as it was to the writers and very much look forward to the discussion and reactions that we hope its ideas will stimulate. The writing of this book has been a challenging and sobering task for me personally, as it has required me to reassess critical elements of my work as a teacher, student, and writer. It has also made me even more aware of the many colleagues, friends, and students who have over the years so generously helped, supported, and critiqued my scribbles. Indeed, they are so numerous that it is impossible to name them all, but I trust that they know how appreciative I am of their contributions.

However, I want to single out three individuals who were of particular help to me in this project. It was a joy to have William M. McLaurin, Jr as a coauthor, not only because of the contributions of his extraordinary vision and wisdom to the book but for his energy, kindness, and generosity—he is a true *mensch*. Connie Krosney has been a trusted colleague and good friend for many years but went far beyond the call of duty in the thorough, thoughtful, and loving way in which she read and critiqued an early draft of the book. Chris Myers of Peter Lang Publishing has made an important contribution to the field of Education by having the courage to publish controversial and critical books, often written by less well-known authors. We all owe him and his colleagues at Peter Lang a debt of gratitude for sticking out their collective necks. I want to personally extend my very deep appreciation for the help he afforded us in the preparation of this book through his professionalism and sensitivity as well as for his steadfast support and insightful suggestions.

These are very difficult and troubling times for our society and for education and, as our book indicates, difficulties that are exacerbated by a growing pessimism—even despair—among the public and the profession. However, despair simply cannot and must not be part of the arsenal of the socially responsible. As educators and citizens of a democracy, we must continue to affirm our faith in the power of robust and open debate as an essential element in the struggle to create a just, loving, and sustainable society. We must also acknowledge the necessity to be in touch with that mysterious power and energy that impels us all to engage in that excruciating and wondrous quest.

David E. Purpel

I have had immense good fortune in friends, colleagues, and family throughout my life and, as a result, there are dozens of names that belong here. For the sake of brevity, I would ask forgiveness in advance from those who have been of so much help to me in many other ways, while I acknowledge those whose help was instrumental in the present work. I would also like to echo David's acknowledgment of Chris Myers of Peter Lang and Connie Krosney for their thoughtful and insightful reading of the first draft.

David Purpel has been my dissertation advisor, mentor, coach, friend, and fellow seeker on the path that has lead us to this work together. It is with enduring gratitude and very appropriate humility that I now find myself to be his colleague. Thank you, David, for being my Teacher.

It is a rare thing for one life to include encounters with two Teachers. My gratitude for the privilege of learning from Beatrice Bruteau is profound.

When I need to demonstrate that it is possible to run a business that honors what we argue for in this book, I have the example of John Grinnell and Gerald Hutchinson, my partners at the consulting firm of Petra Leadership Solutions, Inc. I have borrowed from them shamelessly, and their patience with the time I have devoted to the present work has been indispensable.

My family is the mainstay of my life and their interest and commentary on the work that is represented here have been foundational. To Billy, to Alice and Dave, to Mac, Duke and that long line, I acknowledge my debt and good fortune. One person has paid the greatest price for the time this work has taken and has also been the source of whatever sanity I retain at the end of it—my wife and soulmate, Margaret. Thank you, Margaret, for showing me how to hear the voice from the heart, for teaching me Love.

William M. McLaurin, Jr.

BOOK I

THE MORAL AND SPIRITUAL CRISIS IN EDUCATION

PREFACE TO *THE MORAL AND SPIRITUAL CRISIS IN EDUCATION*

This is in many ways an extraordinarily exciting time for educational theorists and yet in other ways it is a particularly dreary and bleak era. The dreariness and bleakness are not very hard to locate, since they are what emerge from current mainstream educational dialogue, particularly the language of so-called educational reform. This discourse is not only trivial and distracting; it is marked also by a singular lack of imagination and daring. The criticisms made, and the solutions offered, may be important insofar as they affect current policies and programs, but they hardly stir us with wonder and awe. Beyond this hum and drone, however, there is the roar of high excitement involving enormous possibilities and dangerous risks.

I speak of two roads—the first has to do with the enormity of our present cultural, political, and economic crisis and with it the incipient possibility of catastrophe. The second general realm of energy and excitement is in the world of ideas, which is bursting with ever increasing vitality and brilliance. Virtually every scholarly and professional field is awash with significant controversies, challenges to existing canons, emerging paradigms—some of which have led to whole new areas of inquiry and new research modes. Clearly, some of this excitement is evident in the field of educational theory as we see qualitatively different discourses emerging from the invigorating effects of the newer insights, theories, and critiques. I believe that we in education do in fact need to reconceptualize mainstream educational discourse. More precisely, we need to quicken the pace of these efforts, already begun in the seminal work of such educators as Paulo Freire, James Macdonald, Henry Giroux, Maxine Greene, William Pinar, and Michael Apple.

It is my hope that this book contributes to the effort to develop a more liberating discourse on the intimate relationships among the society, culture, and education. Furthermore, I want very much to facilitate the process by which we can understand and act on the ways in which our schools might at the very least not increase the probability of social disaster. I continue to have the faith that schools can go even beyond that point and can actually contribute to the creation of a more loving, more just, saner world. My efforts toward this goal focus on the possibilities involved in enriching educational theory with a moral and religious discourse. More particularly, I have tried in this book to make a case for the necessity for educators to affirm moral and educational commitments. I believe that there is an urgency not only to be critical, not only to deconstruct, debunk, and unmask, but also simultaneously to affirm, commit, and advocate. I try in this book to confront the problematics of moral affirmation in the context of confronting the problematics of avoiding moral affirmation. I come away from these efforts more convinced than ever that we as educators have special responsibilities in this unique moment to risk positive commitment in addition to risking negative criticism. Indeed, I have come to see that one effort is not complete without the other.

The book is organized into seven chapters; the first two chapters examine the nature of recent and current mainstream educational discourse particularly in its trivial, vulgar, and technical character. These chapters present a number of explanations for this state of affairs, including a discussion of American anti-intellectualism and the fears of education. They conclude with the position that what is most lacking in current educational discourse is the inclusion of the moral and religious dimensions of society and education.

In chapter three I present a moral analysis of the current culture in a series of paradoxes and conflicts that reflect both the dangers and possibilities inherent in our present consciousness. It is an analysis that focuses most directly on middle-class life, in part because I believe that the middle class has both political and economic power and high educational potential, i.e., is in a position to inform its power with a moral and religious vision. I address in this chapter the enormous conflicts, contradictions, and divisions within our society, as well as our pride in pluralism and diversity. It is my strong belief that we both need and are capable of creating an overarching belief system (I call it a mythos) that can accommodate both our affirmation and skepticism of them.

In chapter four I spell out such a moral and religious framework or vision that speaks to meaning, purpose, and ultimacy. It is a framework that borrows from two ancient traditions—the Socratic and the Prophetic—and two current theological movements—Liberation Theology and Creation Theology. The major emphasis, however, is on Prophecy, conceptualized as the voice that in Walter Brueggemann's phrase combines "energy and criticism" and a consciousness which, says Abraham Heschel, "has the ability to hold God and man in a single thought." Prophecy holds us to our deepest commitments, chides us when we do not meet them, and provides hope for us when we think we cannot.

The fifth chapter describes how educators might internalize this voice and thereby provide themselves with purpose and direction. The chapter concludes with a credo focusing on the goal of education being that which facilitates love, justice, community, and joy.

The concluding two chapters deal with how a curriculum primarily directed at social justice and compassion might look. The chapter includes a list of specific educational goals and objectives, and the book ends with a discussion of issues of implementation and of overcoming sabotage and cooptation.

I certainly hope lots of people read this book, and if they do I certainly expect that there will be criticisms and disagreements. I hope and expect that there will be questions and eyebrows raised. I expect that flaws will be found in my reasoning; that some will point to contrary findings; and that some will find my analysis insufficient and unpersuasive. Such criticism is legitimate and required, just as vital if not more so than the work itself, and can only serve to advance our understanding. What I ask of critical readers, however, is that they not only point out faulty analysis or misreading—this surely must be done—but that they also address the issue of affirmation in general and the particular affirmations I make. This is because my strongest hope for this book is that it will stimulate others to reflect on and engage in the struggle involved in clarifying our convictions. My challenge to critics is to confront the question of what it is that we are working hard to make happen. If the convictions are unclear as stated, how and in what ways ought they be clarified? If they are insufficient, which should be added, which should be deleted? If creedal statements are more problematic that liberating, what should we say about developing evaluative criteria for judging cultural and educational policy? I look forward to this dialogue and to continued excitement and vitality in educational theory, for I continue to have faith that education can indeed help us to overcome the demons.

David E. Purpel
1989

ACKNOWLEDGMENTS

It is, of course, impossible to acknowledge fully all those who have helped and supported me in this effort. Surely family, friends, colleagues, and students have given much to me in their energy, encouragement, ideas, and criticisms. I will always be indebted to my first real teacher—Don Oliver—who overwhelmed me with his genius and who, much to my surprise, encouraged me to think that I had something to say. There are other colleagues who have been significant teachers for me—certainly Jim Macdonald, Ralph Mosher, Henry Giroux, Bob O'Kane, Fritz Mengert, and Svi Shapiro are among them.

I am happy to acknowledge the vital importance to the work of this book of the research leave granted me by the School of Education and the University of North Carolina at Greensboro. The Graduate School at UNCG also provided valuable assistance in the preparation of the manuscript. The development of my writing was also greatly helped by my participation in the Coolidge Colloquium, particularly through my interaction with Ben Beliak and Carol Ochs.

I very much appreciate the careful and thorough editing provided by Carolyn Steele and the editors at Bergin and Garvey. Joyce Sloop and Becky Blomgren read an early draft and gave me helpful reactions. A special thanks to the loving, patient, valiant, and tireless way in which Jeannette Dean has prepared the manuscript.

Henry A. Giroux & Paulo Freire

INTRODUCTION TO *THE MORAL AND SPIRITUAL CRISIS IN EDUCATION*

We must abandon completely the naïve faith, that school automatically liberates the mind and serves the cause of human progress; in fact, we know that it may serve any cause. [It] may serve tyranny as well as freedom, ignorance as well as enlightenment, falsehood as well as truth, war as well as peace, death as well as life. It may lead men and women to think they are free even as it rivets them in chains of bondage. Education is indeed a force of great power, particularly when the word is made to embrace all the agencies and organized processes for molding the mind, but whether it is good or evil depends, not on the laws of learning, but on the conception of life and civilization that gives it substance and direction. In the course of history, education has served every purpose and doctrine contrived by man [sic]. If it is to serve the cause of human freedom, it must be explicitly designed for that purpose.
George S. Counts[1]

You must know who is the object and who is the subject of a sentence in order to know if you are the object or subject of history. If you can't control a sentence you don't know how to put yourself into history, to trace your own origin in the country, to vocalize, to use voice.
Nelida Pinon[2]

There is a volatile debate in social theory taking place over what constitutes the relationship among knowledge, power, desire, and subjectivity. Within the humanities, social sciences, and educational theory there is an ongoing criticism being waged over the ideological nature and social function of the canons, the status of grand theories, the boundaries that define disciplines, the meaning of history, and the role of intellectuals. In the reaches of higher education, the major thrust to reform has come from the various discourses of poststructuralism and postmodernism. Declaring war on the categories of transcendence, certainty, and foundationalism, exponents of contemporary social theory have reconstituted the meaning and method of critical inquiry and radically challenged the dominant modes of authority and social practice. In fact, many of the new critical voices have forcefully proclaimed that there exists no "objective reference point, separate from culture and politics, available to distinguish truth from ideology, fact from opinion, or representation from interpretation."[3]

What is particularly valuable about this new mode of critical inquiry is its insistence that interpretation cannot be situated outside of ideology, that is, outside of the considerations of power, historical struggle, and human interests. The importance of this work, especially for educators, is reflected in its powerful dismantling of the resurgent discourse of the New Right,[4] whose claim to objectivity and scientism in defense of its policies has been revealed as inextricably enmeshed in the language of ideology, politics, and power. While acknowledging the important contributions of postmodern social theory, it is also crucial to recognize its serious limitations. For instance, it has not sufficiently addressed the central issue of how identities and subjectivities are constructed within different moral experiences and relations, nor has it pursued with enough analytical rigor how power produces, accommodates, and challenges not simply the discourses but also the material relations of dominant political life. In other words, it has failed to develop a substantive ethical discourse and public morality that is necessary for overcoming existing forms of exploitation and subjugation. In addition, its methods of analysis and critique have not been posed as pedagogical issues. Thus, as a mode of critique, much of what constitutes postmodern social theory has not fully appreciated the critical value of engaging its methods of analysis and inquiry as forms of pedagogical practice that bring into critical relief the relationships that obtain among teaching, knowledge/texts, and learning. One result has been that this work has had only a minor influence among critical educational theorists or within the educational reform movement presently being debated in the United States and elsewhere.

Now, as before, the debate over the reform of public schooling in the United States is being principally set by the right wing. The emphasis on character education and moral fundamentalism currently trumpeted by New Right critics such as William Bennett and Chester Finn, Jr., have served primarily to legitimate forms of authority and social discipline that undermine the very principles of democratic community and social responsibility. Similarly, this ideological thrust has been instrumental in framing the public questions related to how one should conceive of ethics, power, and history in present-day social reality and what role these should play as part of the language of educational reform. For example, public schooling and higher education are analyzed by New Right critics within what could be called a crisis of authority approach, one which abstracts equity from excellence and social responsibility from achievement. Central to this view is the claim that what constitutes the crisis in schooling is the breakdown of traditional forms of authority and moral regulation. Concerns such as those expressed above by George Counts have been largely subverted by the New Right in the current debates over schooling.[5] Under the guise of attempting to revitalize the language of morality, right-wing educators and politicians have, in reality, launched a dangerous attack on some of the most fundamental aspects of democratic public life and the obligations of socially responsible, critical citizenship. What has been valorized in this ideological discourse is not the issue of reclaiming public schools as agencies of social justice and critical democracy, but an elitist view of schooling based on a celebration of cultural uniformity, a rigid view of authority, an uncritical support for remaking school curricula in the interest of labor-market imperatives, and a return to the old transmission and acculturation model of teaching.[6]

The current crisis in educational reform is more than a crisis of authority to be resolved primarily through the language of means and technique—developing better ways to promote the same old content and social relations—it is, in fact, a crisis of morality and political nerve. This is evident both in the New Right's attempt to subordinate questions of ethics and power to the discourse of authority and rigid social discipline and in its attempt to reconstruct history as part of a wider political project. In this case, history is fashioned within a particular interpretation referred to by Christopher Lasch as arising "from a need to forget."[7] Lost from this perspective are the voices and struggles of oppressed groups fighting to transform the ideological and material conditions which support forms of subjugation and exploitation. It is a history without a language of moral responsibility, a history characterized by an impoverished civic discourse that celebrates freedom as a form of possessive individualism and treats the concept of democracy as if it were at odds with the notion of community and the call for collective social possibilities that enhance rather than demean civic and public culture. In its right-wing version, history is offered up as narrative cleansed of social conflict and struggle, reconstructed around the tenets of a mythical past dominated by republican virtues such as those expressed in the McGuffey Eclectic Readers and in an insular reading of the traditions of Western civilization.[8] Of course, there is more at work here than the abuse of history; there is an ideology and politics that denies the importance of forms of pedagogy that allow people to speak out of their own histories, cultures, experiences, and traditions.

In *The Moral and Spiritual Crisis in Education,* David Purpel takes up the challenge presented by poststructuralism and postmodernism and the threat to democracy and schooling currently posed by the New Right. He begins with the assumptions that educational reform cannot be debated or understood outside of the space of politics and social power and that central to the language of reform is the need to rethink and remake our social meanings and social relations as part of our effort as public intellectuals. From this stance, Purpel not only criticizes the New Right's attempt to undermine the democratic and moral dimensions of schooling, he also brilliantly argues for the rebirth of a moral culture from which to recon-struct and reconnect the spheres of politics, ethics, and education.

For Purpel, the reform period of the last decade exemplifies in its language and philosophy not simply the narrow political and economic interests of the Age of Reagan; more lamentably, it points to the emergence of a public philosophy which in its refusal to confront the basic moral paradoxes and contradictions that shape the ongoing relations between public schooling and the wider society constitutes a crisis of democracy and moral courage. In Purpel's terms, educational discourse has been trivialized through its neglect of larger social and political issues along with its willingness to define the task of reform as a technical rather than ethical, social, and cultural enterprise. If Purpel were to stop here his message would be important but far from new. What is both unique and inventive about his analysis is that he not only convincingly argues for the importance of recognizing the crisis in education as a crisis in meaning, but he defines what he thinks should be done about it both in terms of reconstructing a new public philosophy of education and in developing a set of pedagogical practices consistent with such a vision. Simi-larly, Purpel steps outside of the existing Left and progressive analyses of school-ing by aiming both his criticism and programs for reform at a much wider audi-ence than that usually addressed by current radical school critics. In this case, Purpel speaks both to and against the attitudes and beliefs frequently held by the middle class in this country. Rather than limiting his message to the marginal and excluded, Purpel has chosen to speak to the issues, attitudes, and values that are familiar to mainstream Americans. He does this in order to widen the possibility for change and to clarify how the challenge of empowerment is not restricted to the disenfranchised and disadvantaged.

Drawing upon a wide variety of theoretical resources and traditions, Purpel combines the languages of critique, hope, risk, and vision in offering new possibil-ities for the direction of public schooling and for the examination of political and moral responsibilities that both shape and result from our various interventions as administrators, teachers, students, and parents. Purpel's voice is not that of the technician, ideologue, or prophet. It is the voice of the engaged intellectual reflect-ing on his or her own historical presence and that of the institutions and social practices that position and engage one's work as a committed and caring educator and parent. Purpel seeks to recover the notion of the public good and make it a central aspect of teaching and education. But he is not content merely to deepen our understanding of the importance of ethical and social responsibility; he also succeeds in linking the enterprise of critical understanding to forms of teaching and social relations that ground our ideologies and visions in emotional attach-ments and spiritual concerns. In other words, Purpel provides theoretical dimen-sions to his public philosophy of education that are often missing from some of the most radical and critical approaches to education. He accomplishes this by situ-ating the ideological meanings, ideals, and language of public responsibility and virtue in politics of compassion and hope that makes all of us more attentive to the experiences and emotions of pain, joy, suffering, and human connectedness. If Horkheimer wants us to stare into the face of history in order to recognize both the suffering and possibilities it offers us, Purpel argues that we do this and more. He wants to create social practices and pedagogical relations that allow us once again to realize ourselves as historically connected subjects. Teachers, in Purpel's vision, do more than transmit meanings; they enact the role of social and moral agents of change; they uncover, reproduce, and produce forms of learning and social relations based on those often repressed memories, stories, and dreams that allow us to analyze and embrace schooling as part of a wider politics of solidarity, caring, and joy.[9]

In Purpel's work we see fleeting images of the compassion and pedagogies of Gandhi, Jesus, Martin Luther King, Rosa Luxembourg, and others who lived out their beliefs—and in some cases died defending them—as part of a political and pedagogical struggle that refused to separate learning and justice from compassion and hope. We know of few books that make explicit in such compelling and engaging terms both the foundation of a critical and emancipatory vision of schooling and the pedagogical practices that give it shape and substance. In many respects, this is a book that gives new meaning to linking a democratic vision with a politics of practice, that makes concrete without being dogmatic what it means for teachers and other educators to struggle with purpose and dignity. This is a risk-taking and pathfinding book that will be appreciated by all who recognize the importance of education as part of the wider practice to know, to learn, to care, and to struggle for a more just and better world.

Notes

1. George S. Counts, *Education and the Foundations of Freedom* (Pittsburgh: University of Pittsburgh Press, 1962), p. 62.
2. Nelida Pinon, "La contaminacion de La Languaje: Interview with Nelida Pinon," *13th Moon* 6 1(2): 74.
3. Gary Peller, "Reason and the Mob: The Politics of Representation," *Tikkun* 2(3): 30.
4. For an analysis of the notion of the New Right as part of a new political, cultural, and ideological formation, see Harvey Kaye, "The Use and Abuse of the Past: The New Right and the Crisis of History," *Socialist Register 1987*, eds. Ralph Miliband, Leo Panitch, and John Saville (London: The Merlin Press, 1987), pp. 332–64.
5. For a short but insightful analysis of this issue, see Steven Selden, "Character Education and the Triumph of Technique," *Issues in Education* 4(3): 301–12.
6. For an extended discussion of these issues, see Henry A. Giroux, *Schooling and the Struggle for Public for Public Life* (Minneapolis: University of Minnesota Press, 1988); see also Stanley Aronowitz and Henry A. Giroux, "Schooling for Less: Literacy in the Age of Broken Dreams," *Harvard Educational Review* (forthcoming); Peter McLaren, "Culture or Canon? Critical Pedagogy and the Politics of Literacy," *Harvard Educational Review* (forthcoming).

7. Christopher Lasch, Introduction to Russell Jacoby's *Social Amnesia* (Boston: Beacon Press, 1974), p. viii.
8. This is evident in the speeches, books, and commentaries made by right-wing spokespersons such as William Bennett, Chester Finn, Diane Ravitch, and John Silber.
9. Peter McLaren, *Schooling as a Ritual Performance* (London: Routledge & Kegan Paul, 1986).

BOOK 1

THE MORAL AND SPIRITUAL
CRISIS IN EDUCATION

1

THE CURRENT CRISIS IN EDUCATION
Professional Incompetence
or Cultural Failure?

The prophet is engaged in a battle for language, in an effort to create a different epistemology out of which another community might emerge. The prophet is not addressing behavioral problems. He is not even pressing for repentance. He has only the hope that the ache of God could penetrate the numbness of history. He engages not in scare or threat but only in a yearning that grows with and out of pain.
WALTER BRUEGGEMANN *The Prophetic Imagination*

Background: Education and Society

Historians are fond of reminding us that the notion of a cultural crisis, as reflected in serious criticism of current educational practice, is hardly new. Indeed, they are able to furnish quotations dating back hundreds, perhaps even thousands, of years that provide an astonishing resonance with contemporary displeasure, anxiety, and even horror over the present and future prospects of our educational system. That there have been crises before ours does not by itself demonstrate that our current sense of alarm is either overly harsh or needlessly worrisome. We are, I believe, very much in a cultural, political, and moral crisis and hence, ipso facto, in an educational crisis. Indeed, it is imperative that we confront the nature of this crisis or, more accurately, that we attend to how a number of critical, cultural, and educational issues and problems are perceived and interpreted. I prefer the word "crisis" to "problem" or "issue" or "concern" because I very much share the view that we as a culture, nation, people, even as a species, confront enormous and awesome threats to our most cherished notions of life, including life itself. In this age of triumphalism and relative prosperity , the dangers of nuclear war, starvation, political upheaval, totalitarianism, and ecological disaster are perhaps not as prominent in public consciousness as they were ten or so years ago. Nonetheless, however powerful the cultural denial, they remain menacing realities, and not to view them as problems of immense magnitude and consequence is to contribute to their seriousness.

I consider this book as an educator's response to this continuing crisis. Obviously, an educator is more than an educator and this seemingly trivial point can serve as a metaphor for the inevitable and intimate relationship between education and culture. In point of fact, many educators have presented their professional work in a detached, technical manner as if the educator were not more than an educator. A major theme of this book, then, is the critical importance of educators' broad responsibility for the state of the culture as it relates to their specific responsibility for the quality of the "educational program."

Indeed, it is becoming increasingly clear that the terms "education" and "educator" have become so reified that they are nearly counter-productive to the task of creating a more just and loving society. To the extent that education is seen as a technical enterprise and educators present themselves as experts, marks the degree to which we have obscured the social, cultural, moral, and political aspects of education. It may be wiser for educators to see themselves as cultural and moral leaders and critics who choose to focus their efforts on educational institution rather as technicians called upon to legitimize, implement, operate, and manage.

The current crisis among other things has served to enhance the highly suspect conception of the educator as a technical expert. It is amazing that in the face of a truism that borders on cliché—that education and culture are significantly interrelated—a great deal of the actual work done by professional educators is being done with minimal or superficial social/cultural analysis. It is not that educators are not to some degree aware of the significance of social and cultural context or of the importance of social goals and aims to the educational process. The difficulty is that when most professional educators examine the social setting they tend to use the very narrow and limited perspectives of the accessible present and of vocational preparation and economic need. The current situation is but the latest instance of the phenomenon of the trivialization of educational issues. Hence, in the waning days of this horrific century, we face major political and economic instability across the world, serious regional disputes, the proliferation of weapons of mass destruction, mass hunger, and a domestic economy and a job market of unusual volatility and cruelty. We also face a number of relatively recent crises of enormous difficulty and import, e.g., the AIDS epidemic; violence among and between children; and the emerging consequences of a global economy.

We are also in the midst of a great many exciting and fundamental intellectual debates on so-called new paradigms and breakthroughs in various academic and professional areas. In addition, we live in a time of extraordinary (and sometimes terrifying) scientific and technological discovery in such areas as astrophysics, biotechnology, and cybernetics. Yet, in the context of both enormous problems and incredible intellectual ferment, what constitutes the focus of mainstream educational concern? Apparently, such issues as closer evaluation of teachers and students (e.g., merit pay, competence tests, periodic testing) school prayer, "middle schools," computers in the classroom, "creationism" vs. evolution, and public aid to private schools. This extraordinary chasm between profound challenge and trivial response helps to frame two major questions for this chapter: How can we explain the continuing phenomena of the trivialization of educational discourse? What would constitute an appropriate and meaningful point of departure for a more serious educational conversation?

The Trivialization and Vulgarization of Education in America

When I speak of trivialization I refer to two major phenomena of educational discourse—the evasion or neglect of larger, more critical topics and the stress put on technical rather than on social, political, and moral issues. Ironically enough, the discourse on the trivial nature of education can be quite intelligent, elaborate, and sophisticated, and indeed we have seen enormous human energies focused on such relatively minor issues as merit pay and the efficacy of homework. This is by no means to say that laborious and painstaking study on organizational and pedagogical issues is not required but rather that such intense effort would be better channeled toward the most important social and cultural concerns of our time. To put it bluntly, it is the fundamental assumption of this book that given the elements of our political, economic, and cultural crises, educational discourse must focus on the urgent task of transforming many of our basic cultural institutions and belief systems. Responses that are at best ameliorative have the danger of deepening the crisis by further strengthening social and cultural policies and practices that endanger our deepest commitments. If we accept the basic proposition that we must make some drastic changes in our culture to forestall disaster and facilitate growth, then clearly educational institutions must be a part of that process. However energetic and imaginative, efforts that ignore or deny this necessity are eligible for "trivial" status.

Neither the spate of educational reports of the 1980s nor the reports of the various manifestations of the Goals 2000 project do not, for example, reflect or propose anything approaching a fundamental reconceptualization of the schooling process, much less anything in the way of a serious social/cultural critique. Instead they suggest relatively minor reforms directed at amelioration rather than transformation. It is indeed ironic that these reports are highly critical of the intellectual excellence of schools and yet themselves offer relatively superficial responses to the roots of the problem they identify. Even more significantly, none of the reports speak to the necessity for fundamental cultural and social changes even though it is well understood and accepted that schools reflect more than they shape policies and beliefs. The public is once again given the distinct message that schools and education can make serious changes without parallel changes in the basic conception of schooling and in cultural beliefs. Hence, attention is directed to the more modest issues of class electives, schedules of testing, length of school year, and mode of funding rather than to issues of moral numbness, spiritual alienation, social injustice, nuclear armaments, and terrorism.

Having said all this, let me offer another perspective on this allegation of trivialization. One can make a convincing case, ironically enough, that it is the profession that has, for the most part, chosen to view educational issues as technical and operational in nature and that it is the political and cultural leaders who fundamentally grasp the cultural and political significance of education. Certainly the Religious Right sees education as an integral element of its moral crusade and its critique of the schools is grounded in a well-formulated (however misguided) theoretical and ideological framework. Moreover, the preponderance of public dialogue on education is rooted in its instrumental value, namely for preparing people to design and operate the engines of the economy while most parents and students focus on the educational process in relation to how it can facilitate their social and economic advancement. President Clinton seemed to reflect the broad consensus of the nation when, in his State of the Union Adddress of 1992, he said:

> I support efforts to empower local school districts to experiment with chartering their schools . . . or having more public choice. Or do whatever they wish to do as long as we measure every school by one high standard: Are our children learning what they need to know to compete and win in the global economy.

Such formulations do not reflect trivialization as much as they reflect vulgarization in their rejection of the idea that education might be about the opportunity to deepen our understanding of who we are and might be or perhaps as the search for meaning and joy. Indeed, grounding education in competition, piety, and self-advancement is not trivial but tragic, not a limited concern for classroom learning but a wide-ranging concern for perpetuating a cultural blight. Meanwhile, most educators are counting columns of figures, creating overhead projections, and making surveys thereby demonstrating how the trivial becomes significant in its facilitation of vulgarity.

The Nature of Schooling

I do not subscribe to the nostalgic school of educational history that speaks of a fictional time when the culture recognized education as a vital and critical activity, when teachers were highly respected, and when educators were people of vision and daring, endowed with learning, sophistication, and wisdom. On the contrary, serious scholarly and systematic analysis of public education in America is still relatively scarce and recent, and very little of that has become part of public awareness.

Although there is a significant serious literature on education, the number of contemporary genuine educational gurus, leaders with profound insight and educational vision, is quite small. Indeed, an important assumption of this book is that public dialogue on education in the U.S. with a number of very important exceptions, has been narrow in scope, technical in nature, and naive in quality.

Surely much of this is due to the intellectual and moral dilemmas implicit in the complex questions about the nature and purpose of education. The term "education" has been defined and examined in a myriad of ways and from innumerable perspectives, resulting in genuine perplexity and unsettling uncertainties—it is a field fraught with conundrums, puzzles, mysteries. It is an area that has been addressed by virtually every major social, political, and philosophical theorist over the centuries from Plato to Rousseau to Machiavelli, from Marx to Dewey. However, the public dialogue on education in America rarely touches upon major theoretical alternatives but rather focuses on the much narrower possibilities within the perspective of existing practices. Even within this fairly narrow range there is a great deal of confusion, complexity, and controversy on the nature of the conventional educational model. Even under the superficial educational discourse we are unclear and unsure about our priorities. For example, should we emphasize vocational in contrast to general education? Should there be sex education or citizenship education in the curriculum?

In addition, the public has an enormous number of unrealistic, if not contradictory, expectations for the schools. We want our schools to discipline our children and support and encourage their independence; we want our children to learn to love their country, to honor and respect authority and tradition, and we also want them to develop initiative and critical thinking,—we want the schools to help students at least deal with, if not overcome, their difficulties with nutrition, health, sexuality, death, morality, interpersonal relations, the maturation process, and sibling rivalry; we want the schools to provide community for the student and to be a focus of community life for adults; we want the schools to teach students how to participate in sports, to be musical, to sew, cook, clean, do woodworking, printing, to paint, sculpt, and dance,—we want some decent place to send our children so that adults can work (or play) without worrying about them; we want the schools to provide psychological, vocational, and social counseling to our children; we want students to be evaluated intellectually, socially, psychologically; and we want to know how they rank with other students and what their prospects are. We want the schools to provide opportunities for exercise, celebration, play, hobbies, eating, ritual, friendship, and competition. And so on.

Obviously, we cannot have, and do not want, all of these things—nor do we want or can we have them in equal degrees of intensity and importance. This plethora of expectations certainly speaks to our confusion and uncertainty, but there is a deeper dimension to the confusion that has to do with the wider moral, political, and social aspects of these "educational" issues. Although there is some attempt to have public dialogue on what major social concerns underlie these concerns for students as individuals, much of it has been connected to current economic and foreign policy (e.g., competing in the global economy) or to moralistic concerns (e.g., character education and sex education). Parents are faced with the highly complex and frustrating challenge of trying to figure out simultaneously what is "best" for their individual children at this particular moment and how to participate in a discussion on what constitutes sound educational policy for the society. As a profession, we have not provided the public with very much in the way of conceptual and analytical tools to engage in this challenging and paradoxical dialogue.

It is clear that important public dialogue on the relationship between education and meaning over the years has not generally been conducted widely and intensely. We educators have for the most part been able (willing) to separate our concern for education from our discussion of our most serious and profound matters. What is the meaning of life? How do we relate as a family, nation, people? What is a just and fair way of distributing rights and responsibilities? How do we make appropriate moral choices? The irony here is that such questions are quintessentially reflective ones—areas that require knowledge, insight, understanding (i.e., an educated mind). However, we tend in our fragmented and highly differentiated society to equate education with particular institutions and processes, which are, if at all, only vaguely linked to deeper social, cultural, economic, and political matters.

A central question that must be addressed is why this dialogue has not expanded into broad public discussion—that is, why have intellectuals, politicians, and other members of cultural leadership maintained such a conventional and narrow attitude toward education? A clue to this phenomenon can perhaps be found in the complexities of the culture's ambivalence toward education. For example, given what we have just said about the enormous demands and expectations that we have for education, it is rather extraordinary that we provide so little in the way of resources to support this enterprise. Working conditions for public and private educators at the elementary and secondary levels are absolutely shocking. Compared to other educational institutions (colleges and universities) and to corporations, salaries of teachers are very low, opportunities to grow intellectually and professionally are extremely limited, and resources are slim and of low quality. Americans are supposed to put enormous faith and trust in education (which they do by and large), which should mean that they need to put enormous resources into the process (which, by and large, they do not).

The question then is not so much how we can get more funds for education but why it is we have such a low standard for what appears to be a commitment to provide high-quality education. Perhaps that can be explained as a failure to realize what would constitute the conditions for a truly excellent educational environment for all.

Somewhere along the line, we as a culture accepted general standards of the school budget—for example, classes should be around twenty-five or thirty, with twenty considered exemplary; teachers should teach between twenty-five and thirty hours per week (as opposed to nine to twelve hours for university professors); students should go to school for five or six hours per day (unlike college students who divide their twelve to fifteen hours per week in more flexible and individual ways). It is not clear how these standards came to be accepted, but the question is why the public has not seriously challenged these appallingly low standards. As usual, the answer to a question like this is probably a combination of inertia, lack of aware-ness, conscious acceptance, as well as deception, delusion, and avoidance. Yet, one uncomfortable possibility comes to mind, namely that we are perhaps suspicious of the intellectual process itself, and the acceptance of these low standards repre-sents our impulse to restrain the educational process.

It is certainly not a new idea that America has a significant tradition of what has been called "anti-intellectualism." America's support for schools is not the same as support for education, or at least for education defined as the develop-ment of the mind. As a culture we retain, along with our reverence for learning, a scorn, if not a suspicion, of it. The terms "intellectual" or "idealist" are more often used in our culture as epithets than as compliments. We seem to be more proud of our technical virtuosity, our engineering genius, and our pragmatic, problem-solving stance than we are of our theoretical and speculative conscious-ness. We value the new, the useful, and the applied as reflected in Henry Ford's classic putdown of thoughtful reflection, "History is bunk." This is surely not to say that the technical, the applied, and the pragmatic are not themselves worthy of instruction, nor that they do not have significant educative potential. It is to say that our strong emphasis on the pragmatic and applied at the cost of signifi-cant concern for the abstract, theoretical, and speculative does speak to a less than total commitment to a serious, thoroughgoing, and richly textured educa-tion for all people.

Part of this reservation toward serious education can be said to be rooted in our traditional aversion to elitism and aristocracy. Our history includes a conscious-ness, which associates people of "higher" learning with those who assume a sense of moral and human superiority; we are apt (rightfully) to reject the notion that such people deserve a higher station in life by dint of their intellectual excellence. Such an aversion is surely compatible with our traditions of democracy, equality, and skepticism. However, the fact remains that what is abhorrent here is that only a few have such an education and that people with such an education feel entitled to more privileges than those without this education. Surely, the proper response to the fear of elitism is to demand higher quality education for all and to be skepti-cal if not resistant to any special claim for preferential treatment. If certain educa-tion does give people certain powers (and it surely does), then it can be seen not only as having pragmatic meaning but moral and political significance as well. Therefore, in addition to the scorn for education by some, which probably is founded in a consciousness of ignorance, naiveté, and isolation, there is the lesser-known fear of education by the dominant culture, more likely founded in a rather sophisticated and thorough realization of the power of education. Presumably those who are not "well educated" fear and scorn the "well educated" because of their alienation. In like manner, many of those who *are* "well educated" are aware that their dominance is in part related to the powerlessness that is derived from a lack of education. Differences in educational potency become models of providing for political and moral differentiation.

Another aspect of the value and power of education lies in the possibility that this power could be used for both good and bad, or more specifically, the power could be used to challenge existing institutions and power arrangements. Education, if one is to believe educators, has enormous power, which not only has the effect of esthetic exhilaration but of inducing fear. The most powerful metaphor of this paradox is seen in the remarkable trial of Socrates in the fifth century B.C.E. that literally reflects the life and death significance of education. Although Socrates tries rather disingenuously to soft-pedal the importance of simply asking people to clarify what they are saying, his prosecutors are very much aware of the potential of such a process to undermine a contemporary and entrenched cultural consciousness. It is important to note that literally hundreds of Athenian citizens voted to execute Socrates, that this was a community decision, and not one imposed by a tyrannical and feared ruler. Undoubtedly, there were a variety of reasons for this action, but the very fact that the charges were presented to the community as a serious threat to the public welfare represents the recognition of the basic vulnerability of the status quo to serious reflection and examination.

This recognition persists today, albeit in somewhat more subtle form. Our society certainly does not legally execute people who ask us to reconsider our basic assumptions and to critically examine our culture. Although we are fearful of such people, and sometimes people like Abraham Lincoln, Malcolm X, and Martin Luther King are assassinated for insisting that we reexamine our way of being, more often that fear is masked by scorn, avoidance, and self-deception. It is indeed difficult to maintain the paradox of both valuing and fearing education, particularly when the only way to resolve the paradox is to address the underlying moral issues. Serious education, therefore, has a way of forcing continual confrontation with our basic moral commitments and, more unnerving, with our failures to meet those commitments. Such an education is not reflected in a curriculum focused on diplomas, certificates, and credentials.

Education and Culture

This returns us to the phenomenon of the fragmentation and isolation of education in our culture; we continue to sidestep moral paradoxes when we talk about education apart from the moral considerations of the kind of culture we wish to create. This is a way of avoiding conflict but at the price of irrationality, mediocrity, and madness. When we talk of education we are simultaneously talking about culture; when we propose changes in education, or when we propose not making changes, we are making moral statements. The people of Athens knew this as did the communities, which made the teaching of reading to American, slaves a felony. This obvious, usually unspoken, moral relationship is at the heart of such issues as school segregation, tracking, grading, and selective admission.

The silliness (or hypocrisy) of calling these issues "educational" rather than cultural or moral reveals our culture's discomfort with making moral choices.

The issue of "grading" is particularly instructive in this matter. I believe that most teachers regard grading (as opposed to evaluation) as an obstacle to the learning process. It is very difficult, and probably impossible, to develop procedures for giving grades that are valid, reliable, fair, and efficient; students come to worry more about grades than meaning; and both teachers and students respond to these problems by developing techniques (e.g., multiple choice tests, cramming, memorizing) which are at best distracting, and at worst counterproductive to serious learning. The concern for grading produces anxiety, cheating, grade grubbing, and unhealthy competition. However, even though grading may be at best of dubious value "educationally," it is absolutely vital to a culture that puts enormous stress on success, achievement, and individuality and to a system that requires social and economic inequality. The critical issues of grading are not primarily technical (though there are certainly such problems within the particular field of evaluation and grading) but moral and cultural. To value grading is to value competition and to accept a society of inequality and a psychology that posits external behavior rather than internal experience as more important. Grading is primarily a technique for promoting particular social, moral, and political goals, and it is those goals which should be debated rather than the technical and misleading questions about the value of essay vs. objective testing or whether to use grade point averages or standardized tests as the basis for college admission.

To raise the question of our culture's commitment to equality by critically examining so-called educational issues like grading is, of course, parallel to what led to the tragedy of Socrates' trial. There is a kind of conspiracy of silence, a tacit recognition, or what has been called "structured silences" about the intense relationships between moral/social concerns and formal education. The political question has always to do with who benefits from such an arrangement. It is clear that those who benefit at least in the short term are mostly those in power and those who represent dominant institutions and ideas. (Included in this group are, alas, educators who have little real power in the larger culture but are fearful of losing their modest power within the educational establishment. It also includes educators who have bought into the existing arrangements by still insisting that they are "educators" rather than politicians.) It is my contention that one way to avoid conflict and change in the basic cultural structure is to deflect such dialogue into discussion of technical problems. Professional educators have developed a concept called "educational policy" or "educational issues" which enables (or disables) us to trivialize and depoliticize cultural and moral issues into technical or partisan debates.

For example, educators spend enormous amounts of energy researching issues around the topic of equal educational opportunity. There is considerable research being done on the financial, sociological, and psychological aspects of the nature of the inequality and how to overcome unfair differences in educational opportunity for various groups and individuals. Programs like Head Start, magnet schools, and equitable financing of education are designed to respond to these problems, and with such programs come controversy and disagreements. Fundamental to these controversies is a deeper issue involving the basic question of who should and can be truly educated, who deserves the full development of their reflective and creative potential. To do technical studies on research on how to ameliorate the problems within existing arrangements serves to obscure and deflect the more basic moral and spiritual issues. Complex as they are, the technical problems are of relatively minor importance compared to the questions of our social and cultural vision. It is very likely that underlying the technical controversies are much more profoundly serious differences on the basic question of who is educable and who ought to be educated. Such differences cannot be overcome by technical studies or partisan debates, for they run to far deeper roots in our cultural psyche.

It is my belief that perhaps the most significant dimension in the conservative/progressive ideological continuum revolves around the matter of faith in the educability of humanity. At one end of the continuum is the faith that only a very small number of people can be expected either to be well educated or to deal with this education in a responsible manner. This is the position that holds that many if not most people are so selfish and vulgar that they would use the wisdom of the ages only for personal and short-run advantage and thereby undermine the fragile social structure. Hence, the position arises that we are better off with most people being acculturated and socialized, with only a carefully selected and thoroughly prepared minority being able to deal responsibly with the ambiguities and sophistication of serious learning and social leadership.

At the other end of the continuum is the idea that all people are capable and desirous of living a life of meaning and that all can be educated to be free and responsible. This is the position that refuses to accept inherent inequality of people; those individuals who present contrary evidence are said to be victims of an oppressive system and of false consciousness. It therefore becomes the task of educators to provide the conditions under which all people can express their full human potential. This basic difference in assumptions about the human condition represents a historic and continuous struggle between fundamentally different consciousnesses and orientations toward human nature and destiny.

What this means is obviously that when we talk about education the stakes are very high for we are talking ultimately about the basic and most important questions of human existence. To trivialize education by obsessing on technical or superficial, symptomatic concerns is not only illogical but harmful: it distracts us from the responsibility to engage in serious dialogue on how the educational process can facilitate a world of love, justice, and joy.

A particularly tough, anguishing, hair-pulling, brain-bending debate on education revolves around the question of freedom—that is, how much faith do we have in free expression and free inquiry as opposed to the kind of faith that leads to a view of education as acculturation? Many see the prime function of education as the transmission of the culture and the preservation of its values. One difficulty with this view is that our culture contains many varying traditions and value systems, some of which are in conflict. Our culture, for example, has a tradition, which speaks to major, even violent, change (e.g., the American Revolution and the Civil War), in spite of the understanding that, when we stress the importance of transmitting the culture, what we really mean is stability and continuity. The schools are yet another social locus for the drama of acting on these impulses toward both liberty and order. Generally speaking, organized education (schools, colleges) is oriented toward acculturation and order even though there are individual pockets where there is greater stress on free inquiry and liberty. I do not wish to simplify or polarize this issue—it is by definition impossible to talk of education without cultural considerations or without the necessity of preserving certain cultural values. It is, however, possible to speak of an education virtually and wholly in terms of acculturation and socialization. It is not a matter of choosing between acculturation and education but of choosing a path where we can educate about what our culture is while, at the same time, helping to redefine it. Education involves some combination of affiliation and skepticism, a concern both for boundaries and for the crossing of boundaries. Formal education is thus both parent and child of culture—they shape and reflect each other, even as both may share the same contradictions and anomalies. This is not to say they are the same. Many cultural values and institutions are not reflected in educational institutions. For example, there are greater opportunities for free speech and expression in certain cultural spaces than in the schools.

Moral Responsibilities of Educators

Most significant for our purposes is the importance of locating the unique and special responsibility and character of an educational institution. This book will directly speak to these issues, and with an orientation that many will find wanting or unacceptable. Such disagreement is not only inevitable but also necessary and desirable. However, I believe that every educator must as a minimum necessity for professional and cultural integrity make clear the moral, political, social, and cultural perspective of his or her educational ideas on policy practice. The public and the profession ought to (and I believe does) require educators to be thoughtful and reflective enough to realize the relationship between educational practice, policy, theory, and social, moral, political, and cultural issues. Furthermore, as public servants/leaders, educators owe it to the public to reveal their theoretical and ideological perspectives as a kind of truth-in-advertising principle. It is time for educators to end their naiveté and coyness about their social and moral principles, not only as part of their professional ethic but as a way of deepening and enriching the quality of public dialogue on education.

These strike me as minimal and essential expectations of educators, namely that they be able and willing to articulate the social, political, and moral principles, ideas, and ideals as well as the theoretical and experiential knowledge that inform their ideas on educational practices and policies. However, these are only minimal requirements, for what our society needs from its educators are not only the ability to understand but the ability to lead. We need, in addition to knowing about and reflecting on various orientations, to be able to choose from them. This requires not only knowledge and understanding by both the public and the educational profession; it also demands courage and wisdom. All concerned must be able to choose and act on wise, sane, and sensible orientations to education, an action that as we have already indicated is tantamount to making important moral decisions on the quality and nature of the culture. Educators must confront their awesome responsibilities and must give up their retreat into the myth of political neutrality based on a pseudoscientific conception of their work. Education surely requires knowledge of the learning and maturation process, knowledge of content, language skills, rhetoric, technique, and interpersonal relationships. However, these are necessary but not sufficient requirements for a true educator. What is required in addition to this knowledge and these skills is a commitment to a vision of who we are and what we should be. An educator without such a commitment is like the person who is all dressed up with no place to go. An educator, like other professionals, needs tools and skills but must have the wisdom to use these in such a way that mandate courage and passion.

The Present Moment

Although these are general expectations of educators, I must speak to the particulars of the specific realities of this moment. This is yet another critical moment in history—a time of enormous crisis, a time of great hush and anticipation. Shall it be war, destruction, desolation, and disaster, or shall we have peace, abundance, and freedom? We are faced with immense problems and opportunities—we are in another of Dickens's "best of times, worst of times" eras. At a time of great peril, in a moment when we realize humanity's gigantic capacity for horror, greed, callousness, cruelty, and stupidity, we also are experiencing the human capacity for brilliant creativity, we are in touch with the extraordinary possibilities of human nature and the opportunity to create true human community. Technology has not only provided us with hydrogen bombs and nuclear waste but also with the possibility of the global village.

Surely, there is intense and fundamental disagreement about the nature of our problems and how to solve them. There does seem to be a consensus, however, that as a culture, indeed as a species, we face very serious problems and that fundamental changes (either to radically new or radically old forms) will be required to overcome or at least substantially ease these problems. It is certainly not a time for "business as usual" nor a time for avoidance and self-deception. It is a time to make commitments and to meet these commitments in faith, trust, hope, and energy. It is a time for all of us to engage in this titanic struggle, and as educators we must accept our part of this struggle and seek to establish our commitment and reiterate our faith in what part the educational process can play in transcending the current crisis.

2

RECENT EDUCATIONAL REFORM
Delusions and Trivialization

Educators, as well as other middle-class moralists, underestimate the conflict of interest in political and economic relations, and attribute to disinterested ignorance what ought to be attributed to interested intelligence. . . . There is no educational process, which can place any class in possession of all the facts or cause it to appreciate all the feelings, which activate another class.
REINHOLD NIEBUHR, *Moral Man and Immoral Society*

The last two decades [the 1970s and 1980s] have been a time of so much energy and effort directed toward school reform that have been categorized into different "waves" of school reform. Although there are any number of particular suggested reforms, there clearly is a relatively short list of themes that have pervaded the specific suggestions and dominate the public dialogue. For the most part, the impetus for the spate of all the reports, recommendations, and legislative proposals is the widespread belief that, generally speaking, the public schools are in a state of crisis. More specifically, the criticism is focused on three general areas: low academic achievement, the failure of the schools to sufficiently prepare a work force appropriate to a global and high tech economy, and on what is perceived to be an increase in immoral behavior. These three broad areas overlap with each other in various ways, e.g., concern for academic achievement can be seen as an indicator of the lack of appropriate job skills and/or as a reflection of student laziness and self-absorption. Underneath all of these concerns lie the ever-present fears, and anxieties of parents and students of the capacity of their schools to deliver on the American dream of continuous social and economic advancement.

Much of this criticism is permeated with a sense that something has suddenly gone wrong with the schools, that earlier reforms had drastically changed the nature of the traditional (and presumably more effective) public schools. Although it is possible to point out important differences between the schools say of the 1920s and those of the 1980s, it is vitally important to note the persistence and continuity in the structure and content of American public education. Contrary to some folklore, for example, the 1960s were not a time of widespread radical changes in public education; permissiveness, anarchy, and experimentation were not rampant or even widespread. There were a number of modest, liberal (not radical), highly controlled attempts at ameliorating arbitrary, rigid, and unexamined practices, but the changes adopted were well within existing frameworks of traditional goals and objectives of the in-place system. Such "reforms" as "minicourses" and the "open classroom" did not challenge the notion of academic requirements or the importance of the disciplines but only represented minor organizational and conceptual approaches to how these requirements were to be met. The premises of the "open classroom," for example, included acceptance of traditional classroom goals (the three Rs, science, social studies) and differed from conventional schooling in basically instructional and organizational issues. Indeed much of the reform efforts of the 1960s represented serious efforts at increasing the academic and intellectual potency of the traditional school curriculum (most particularly in the science and math area).

What ultimately became threatening to the culture about the cultural and social movements of the 1960s were the few, but radical, programs that did have deeper social and political significance. These were programs that connected to and highlighted issues of existing social and economic inequalities, particularly as they affected the poor and the nonwhite (e.g., in education proposals for open admissions and preschool education for the poor). Another threat emerged from programs that seemed to threaten the conventional power structure of the schools (e.g., community involvement, school integration, student rights, and alternative schools). Although all of these movements started with a fairly modest goal of improving the quality of the local schools, the dominant culture soon realized that the implications of some of the proposed changes were particularly serious and far-reaching.

It is true that the 1960s saw the emergence of a significant challenge to how schools were to be governed and controlled and whose interests were to be served. What was not seriously challenged in the numerous reform efforts and community struggles, however, were the basic goals, purposes, and curriculum of the existing educational system. There were, instead, demands that quality education be made more accessible to the disenfranchised and for more proficient and qualified practitioners. It was argued that this was more likely to happen for more people if the political apparatus were changed to allow for greater community involvement and professional accountability. The major issues, therefore, were much more narrowly political than broadly educational, more concerned with the who and the how than with the what of educational policy and practice.

The results of these movements are well known. Even though there are important residues of these efforts, the combination of the political backlash and a serious economic recession has worked to wipe out many if not most of the very modest and mild changes of the 1960s. We now live in a time of great economic uncertainty after experiencing mass layoffs, high and continuing unemployment, serious international competition, the weakening of unionism, and the serious erosion of government's concern for human welfare. Our consciousness has reverted and regressed to one involving scarcity, survival, competition, and stagnation. The language of growth, potential, daring, and challenge has become muted: a sense of infinite possibility has been replaced by timidity, expansiveness by caution, long-range thinking by concern for the short-term bottom line, and visions by quotas.

In the wake of all this has come the renewal of harsh economic and social competition in which the metaphors and mythology of organized sports and war have been used to glorify, extol, and legitimate an ideology of "opportunity," the code word for meritocracy. In a meritocratic culture we congratulate ourselves for helping people to compete fairly (if not equally), for creating the conditions under which the competition is to be held and for offering enormous rewards to the "winners." Unfortunately, it also means that we continue to both produce and ignore the "losers." Freedom has come to mean license for the powerful rather than liberation for the weak; equality is seen as the privilege of competing rather than the right to dignity; individualism has come to mean greed rather than moral autonomy; and community has come to be oriented around terms of class rather than terms of humanity. At its worst, it is a time of revenge and reaction, and, even at its best, a time of rejection of tacit understandings involving compassion and support of the poor and weak. The dominant ideology of the moment, however, contains its own contradictions: freedom in the marketplace but not in the bedroom; relaxation of consumer protection, reduction in public legal services, curtailment of environmental controls, and the regulation of public utilities, but a steady increase in intellectual and moral intimidation through heavy doses of piety and sanctimony. There is more censorship of ideas and less of an attempt to check greed; our current administration values freedom of the marketplace more than freedom of ideas.

It must be remembered, however, that there are significant countervailing forces, some of which can be seen, as I mentioned before, as the residue and legacy of the 1960s. There is enormous energy that is at least latent, as reflected, for example, in popular music and dancing. There is the continuing impulse for real freedom, as well as resentment about the arbitrariness, impersonality, and coldness of our modernized, computerized, high-tech culture. What has so far kept these impulses under control is the fear and uncertainty about jobs and security, fears which have been manipulated and fanned by the hard-line attitudes of government and industry toward unions, social security, welfare programs, and other social programs supported by taxation.

In the context of a failing economy, energy has been diverted away from equality and justice to personal survival. As indicated in Robert Bellah's *Habits of the Heart* (1985), culturally we have been increasingly attracted to a consciousness of individual well being, which also became heightened during the 1960s and, ironically enough, has been given new legitimation and energy under the banner of free enterprise and so-called supply-side economics. What had, and has, been referred to as narcissism and self-indulgence in matters of taste and morals is transformed in the economic sphere into the exercise of individual initiative, freedom, and creativity. This reinforcement of the individual acting alone (which has among its origins existential and phenomenological thinking) as the primary unit has in the 1980s intensified competition and anxiety about survival and advancement. The operative metaphor has changed from making the pie bigger or being happy with equal shares of the pie to how to have the biggest piece of a shrinking pie.

This is expressed in educational communities by an even greater emphasis on the instrumental and functional nature of the schools' extraordinary emphasis on job training, meeting the needs of industry, and the school's relationship to American foreign policy. This emphasis is hardly new—we will remember that among the early major pieces of federal aid to education in the 1980s was the National *Defense* Education Act. What is different is the matter of emphasis and the nature of the trade-offs this new emphasis has meant. There is less concern for the arts, less emphasis on education for personal development, less demand for critical and creative thinking, less rhetoric about human growth and developing the potential of all children. Another casualty is the school's strong traditional responsibilities for the preservation and nurturance of democratic institutions—less concern about citizenship education, fewer opportunities for encouraging student responsibilities, and far less interest in genuine student governance. Instead, there is an almost obsessive concern for productivity, competition, and selectivity.

The current code word for this renewed energy for using the school to sort and weed is "excellence," and the basic technique for implementing these policies is testing. Excellence and testing have become two sides of a coin minted to exchange a once popular coin of equality and justice for the classic gold standard of hierarchy and privilege. "Excellence" has through a relentless process of reification and reductionism comes to mean high scores on normative standardized tests. Many politicians have been shrewd enough to pick up on this phenomenon and have pushed this technique by employing the rhetoric of excellence and the magic of testing as a way of making and fulfilling promises. Politicians can and do demand that the "quality" of education be raised since this is something everyone can applaud, particularly when there is the promise that this can be done without increased taxation or costs. And, both educators and politicians can demonstrate and prove "objectively" that the quality has in fact been improved by dint of the magic of test scores.

The process, absurd as it is, is simple enough. Give students and teachers a test, teach them how to pass the test, and eureka!—the test scores go up—which the public is told means that excellence has been achieved. What is particularly painful about this cynical travesty is the degree to which professionals in education, sociology, and psychology participate in such nonsense even when they know or should know better. These professionals participate, indeed contribute to and shape a public dialogue in which education is reduced to a concern for passing tests of dubious validity, thereby bypassing the serious and perplexing questions of what should be taught, for what reasons, and which model of humanity and community ought to ground educational policies and practices. When professionals neglect these serious and profound questions, it not only trivializes their work; more important, it blinds them from their responsibility to focus public dialogue on central issues.

This means that the dominant culture and the dominant professional community have committed themselves to facilitating the conception of the school as a place where students compete and where they are expected to learn the necessary formula for economic and social advancement. This concern for acculturation and accommodation does not necessarily preclude but certainly distracts us from serious reexamination of our basic premises. It certainly does not reflect a commitment to moral or esthetic excellence or a commitment to nourish the imagination or the idealism of our students. Rather, it represents a powerful affirmation of the political, social, and cultural status quo as well as a rejection of the idea of moral transformation. Thus, the schools are severely criticized for their inability to sufficiently meet the demands and values of the dominant culture—namely, individual achievement, personal success, political and economic continuity, corporate growth, and American dominance. The educational changes that are currently being urged are designed for more efficiency, sharper focus, and more directed energy at meeting predetermined (and largely unexamined) specific, concrete learning goals.

This focus is perhaps best expressed professionally in the strength of the "effective schools" concept and the strong interest in the instructional approach called "time on task." Politically, this emphasis is expressed in the widespread use of competence tests, which basically are techniques designed for continual monitoring and control of teachers and students.

Most of the elements of this approach are lifted from the vocabulary and discourse of corporate America, e.g., such concepts as "productivity," "quality control," "accountability," and "the bottom line" now flow smoothly from the mouths of educators. In addition, we find the application of many of the key concepts of logical positivism, such as the idea that the educational process is to be divided and broken down into constituent, observable, measurable parts to be used as criteria for selecting effective techniques and methods, as well as a basis for evaluation (control).

Within this framework, schools are criticized for wasting time by not focusing sufficient energy on instruction; for not having finely discriminating measures of teacher and student productivity; and for not setting high enough standards. The proposed remedies include merit pay for teachers based on the notion that not only should the more productive teachers be rewarded, but also that merit pay will provide incentive for teachers to increase their productivity. Other remedies call for closer, more frequent testing based on more sharply and concretely defined outcomes and clearly delimited expectations. Again, there is inherent in these proposals a tacit acceptance of the conventional curriculum, although there are some who speak more openly about a need to "return" to the traditions of academic excellence. However, even these ideas usually come down to proposals to rejuvenate the conventional courses in American history, science, English, foreign language, and mathematics, which stress knowledge, retention, homework, and mastery of material rather than developing intellectual curiosity and critical insight.

Here again we meet the paradox of the trivialization of American education: current educational reform efforts reflect a superficial, if not vulgar, response to the issues, *as well as* a response that emerges from intense interest in the issues. How can such a sophisticated culture have schools of such low quality (in the culture's own terms) in the first place, and second, how is it that even after increased study and awareness the culture persists in conceptualizing the crisis in such trivial and mechanical terms? There seem to be at least two interpretations. The optimistic one is that such superficial development represents insufficient attention, awareness, and application of reason, intelligence, and creativity. This is the thesis that underlies Charles Silberman's *Crisis in the Classroom* (1970), where he characterizes American education as "mindless." I say this is optimistic because such a reality is amenable to change: the schools could be improved if they were more "mindful," if educators put more thought, reflection, and care into them. There is, however, an alternative interpretation, namely that the so-called problems of the schools are not accidental and inadvertent. Indeed, there is a way in which the schools can be said to be a huge success in that they accomplish very well what the culture "really" expects them to do, namely to acculturate, socialize, sort, and indoctrinate.

This is not to say that there have not been radical critiques of American education. The most significant of these criticisms of education, alas, have not had an impact on the culture, although they are of stunning power and insight. Over the past two decades a whole generation of scholars has emerged that constitutes major revisionist perspectives on public education. These writers include, among many others, Michael Apple, Jonathan Kozol, Henry Giroux, Maxine Greene, Michael Katz, James Macdonald, William Pinar, and Paulo Freire. Although they most certainly write from different perspectives and emphases, their views constitute a broad consensus that can be characterized as follows: (1) the schools represent a powerful force of social, intellectual, and personal oppression; (2) the reasons for such oppression are rooted in the culture's history; (3) the schools represent a number of deeply held cultural values-hierarchy, conformity, success, materialism, control; and (4) what is required for significant changes in the schools amounts to a fundamental transformation of the culture's consciousness.

Some of this criticism has adopted the use of the term "the hidden or tacit curriculum" which refers to the values, attitudes, and assumptions toward learning and human relationships reflected in the school's policies and practices. A major theme of this criticism deals with the school's role in "reproducing the culture," in sorting out, through its various testing and classification systems, the students most capable of maintaining the existing class and caste system. The school's hidden curriculum also includes ways in which students learn to be obedient and passive, to work at meaningless tasks without complaining, to defer their pleasure, to value achievement and competition, and to please and respect authority figures. It is in the hidden curriculum that these social critics find cultural manifestations of sexism, racism, and elitism. This revisionist criticism is not directed at technique, organization, and curriculum in instrumental terms but rather in culturally symbolic ones. For example, the low salaries and dreadful working conditions for teachers are not seen as a kind of neglected agenda item, a problem requiring patience and understanding, but rather as aspects of a demoralized and weakened teaching force that is a required part of the basic strategy of a culture suspicious and fearful of serious public education. According to this analysis, it is in the culture's political interest in stability to have schools that *do not,* structurally and purposely, promote excitement, critical capacity, or creative potential.

Paulo Freire (1970, 1973) is perhaps the most eloquent and best known of these writers. Writing from the perspective of a Latin American culture beset by enormous inequalities and colonial oppression, Freire has vividly demonstrated the intimate relationship between human freedom and critical literacy. Indeed, he says that attempts to prevent people from acquiring these critical skills is tantamount to a "violation" of the human spirit and, hence, are acts of "violence" (1970:74). The "mindlessness" school of criticism would say that the fact that a very large number of Americans do not have significant verbal critical skills (Kozol 1985:4) is a function of neglect, or insufficient funding, or inadequate techniques. Revisionist critics see the poor quality of American education as functional and consistent with what is, at best, an American ambivalence toward education, and, at worst, a conscious effort to maintain the existing class structure.

The major issue for Freire is explicitly that of human liberation, and he deals with issues of technique in the perspective of the struggle for human liberation. In mainstream American educational criticism, the concern is on technique itself with little or superficial reflection on what the technique is to serve. The point of revisionist criticism is to sort out "the hidden curriculum," the implicit, tacit, indirect functions and goals that these techniques basically serve.

Whether we agree or not with these critics, we owe them immense gratitude not only for the brilliance of their individual analysis but more broadly for providing the language and possibility of discussing education in nontrivial terms. These writers have made explicit the immense importance of the issues involved in education and offer the culture an opportunity to reconstitute the nature of its dialogue in this area. It is also important to point out, however, that they are members of a culture as much as anyone else and, therefore, subject to the same opportunities and limitations that culture affords. What I mean to say is that sharp criticisms as well as apologetics can also be seen as reflections of the culture and hence these educational criticisms must represent the articulated concerns of a much wider and more representative group of people than a handful of educational theorists. These writers not only provide hope but also reflect deep concern and hope in the history and experiences of the wider culture.

Let us now shift for a moment to a broader cultural focus, in order to establish a contrast between public consciousness of broad social concerns and its response to the particular case of education. We live in a time when more people are more aware than perhaps at any other time in history. Our young people in particular are more psychologically hip, they have traveled more, have experienced more; they are more sophisticated about technology, drugs, the mind, the spirit, and are much more aware of the possibility for catastrophe. The culture includes not only an honor roll of problems but a matching list of programs, activities, and opportunities to raise consciousness about these horrors. We surely know a great deal more about pollution than we once did—and certainly we are more aware of the relationship between the environment, nutrition, and health. In particular we have become more sensitive to the real possibilities of disaster having experienced some direct and immediate ones such as the Vietnam War and the Chernobyl nuclear meltdown as well as dreading the ominous dangers of emerging ones such as global warming.

It is a time when it is very difficult to diagnose genuine paranoia. As a culture, we have become more suspicious, much more cautious, more likely to be skeptical about what our political leaders tell us after all the lies and deceit of Vietnam, Watergate, and Irangate. We have come into a consciousness of crisis and uncertainty, and in that consciousness we are edging closer to a stronger sense of the interrelationships among the elements of the crisis. We are taking on an ecological way of thinking and beginning to see not only how big business, big labor, and big government interrelate but also how university research is related to the military, how child abuse is related to poverty, and how the status of women relates to our economic structure and our epistemological beliefs. Surely, this consciousness is felt more strongly by some than others, and clearly it would be fatuous to suggest that a great many people have arrived at a full degree of awareness of our situation. However, it is clear that there is stir or unease in the culture, a sense of unsettlement and dissatisfaction in the awareness of serious worries about the future.

This kind of cultural unrest is also reflected in the field of education in that that there is at least a latent parallel fundamental concern about our basic educational structure. The educational revisionists have, I believe, succeeded in accurately reflecting these latent concerns, and their work stands in very sharp contrast to mainstream conventional discussion on education. The tragedy is that most of our educational leaders and virtually all of our political leaders have chosen to conceptualize those concerns into the trivial terms that we have described. The public is trying to grasp what is fundamental to life, liberty, and the pursuit of happiness, and in response educators give them more standardized tests; the culture yearns for meaning and hope, and the schools suggest more homework and a longer school year. The world teeters on the edge of a new holocaust, and our leaders urge us to consider merit pay.

Surely, we need and deserve more than nostalgic trips, pseudo-science, and school prayers to meet fundamentally new problems with fundamentally new approaches. This, above all else, is not a time for timidity, self-deception, or magical thinking. If we are to take education seriously, it means we are taking cultural concerns seriously. If we take cultural concerns seriously within the context of education, then what is required is far more structural change than the mainstream leadership is suggesting. To this extent, I believe that our current crop of educational and political leaders is out of touch with the culture's basic needs, fears, and concerns or, even worse, they have chosen to ignore the culture's impulse to transcend their parochial, short-term, narrow vision of personal success and achievement.

Thus, there would seem to be another general interpretation of why the culture has chosen to trivialize our current educational crisis, and that is because the culture is not so much mindless or clever as it is ambivalent. In this interpretation both Silberman and Freire are right in that the culture is only in part aware of what it is doing in the schools and perhaps at a preconscious level is not fully pleased with how these efforts are focused. What we are talking about is confusion as well as ambivalence: as a culture we have the impulse for both charity and greed; we value justice and hierarchy; we treasure community and individuality. The culture has developed clever and effective ways of deceiving itself into thinking that it can do all of these things, that it can have its cake and eat it too. However, given the heightened awareness within our culture, we have doubts—pangs of guilt, episodes of uncertainty, periods of confusion about who we are, where we came from, and where we are going. This severe confusion is magnified in a time when for many people God is not accessible, and neither are the stable and reassuring guidelines of a cherished church, government, or philosophy.

The educational establishment has done us all a disservice by refusing to connect our serious and fundamental cultural malaise to educational issues. Instead it is proposing solutions to other problems, problems that are neither real nor serious but at least serve as problems that fit the available solutions. Our primary task in education should not be to throw out premature, distracting, and obfuscating solutions to ill-conceived problems but is instead to clarify the questions that are of most worth. These questions need to be rooted not in the existing discourse of the education establishment but in the most vital concerns of the culture's and individual's search for meaning and fulfillment.

Our era has been described as "the age of anxiety" and has produced a number of gloomy descriptions and depictions of alienation, anomie, and angst. It is a time when we have been challenged seriously to confront suicide and the death of God. it has been called a time of spiritual and moral crisis—a time when words like "anxiety," "despair," and "absurdity" are part of everyday vocabulary, a time when suicide rates rise and when self-help books and organizations proliferate. A whole generation of psychological phobias and obsessions has been spawned—drug and chemical addiction, anorexia, compulsive gambling, and even serious new diseases (herpes, AIDS). The most popular response to the lack of meaning and the emptiness of life seems to be one of a highly intensified personal hedonism: an orgy of individual gratification in the form of consumerism; heavy reliance on sex, drugs, and music for release and distraction; a never-ending pursuit of still greater heights of pleasure—the best ice cream, the deepest orgasm, the most powerful and fastest automobiles. The popularity of *The Guinness Book of World Records* is revealing, as it has become a metaphor for the mindless pursuit of excess and vulgarity.

When one considers this kind of crisis and how the schools have responded to it, one would have to conclude that the schools are intellectually and morally bankrupt. A "soft" version of this indictment is based on a notion of bankruptcy by definition; if education is bankrupt, then the evidence of the culture's failure, ipso facto, reflects the failure of the educational process. This is still another case of the interpenetration of culture and education, where the loss of cultural meaning is the loss of educational meaning, and vice versa. The "harder" indictment of education's bankruptcy has to do less with symptoms and more to do with the likelihood that education has not merely failed to stem the erosion of meaning but has been a significant contributor to it. If education is important and if we are to take it seriously, then we must accept logically the proposition that education has serious consequences. Indeed, when we think of education as significant we are bound to consider it as a part of the solution to the cultural crisis. Typically, however, criticisms of the schools have been closer to the soft end of the dimension in that schools are typically criticized for failing to attend to certain major issues (e.g., the moral or esthetic dimension, a global consciousness) or to be unwitting instruments of some social policy (e.g., racism, elitism, sexism).

A major exception to this general rule is the criticism that comes from the political and religious Right. Their criticism does indeed take the educational system seriously, for they point their accusing fingers at the schools as active and conscious agents of what they call secular humanism, an ideology of godlessness and materialism. The Right (as the Left) sees the schools as an important ideological battleground and (as the Left) rejects the notion that the schools can be value-free and ideologically neutral In fact their criticism is that the school's attempt to be value free or to "clarify" values is itself an ideology, one involving the "idolatry" of science and secularism. This is not to say that the political and religious Right have a single consistent and coherent view in this area since, for example, they have serious differences among themselves about the importance of the traditional academic disciplines, particularly science. It is not altogether clear whether they mean to change the overt course of study (as they have spoken out only in the area of evolution and "obscene" books), but they do call for prayer in the schools, the active recognition of America as a Christian nation, and the teaching of (rather than teaching about) certain "traditional values" like respect, humility, obedience, piety, and hard work.

Although the professional educational community has tended to write off this movement as parochial and extremist, the criticisms of the Right merit serious consideration on a number of counts. First of all, their diatribes against so-called secular humanism, however simplistic and crude, do reflect a deeper awareness of the hidden curriculum than is usual in our culture. Like their ideological counterparts on the Left, the Right rejects the conception of the schools as innocent or bland centers of learning striving to be apolitical, neutral, fair, and objective. Both the Left and the Right have helped us to see more clearly the political nature of the nonpolitical stance, the morality of moral relativism, and the ideology of objectivity. More specifically, the Right has stumbled onto a reality that embarrasses those who like to think of the public schools as being divorced from religion. They are accurate insofar as they remind us that our culture is in part defined by an active and lively religious tradition, and they are insightful insofar as they (as well as others) point to the strength of a vivid, albeit tacit, civil religiosity often expressed in the schools (e.g., the veneration of democracy and patriotism and the celebration of rituals such as Thanksgiving and Memorial Day). Of course they are less sensitive to the traditions and realities of religious diversity and pluralism and less than open to the possibility of education and religion as having critical functions to play. Nonetheless, the harsh and strident criticism, which ironically enough is far less sophisticated and scholarly than the equally harsh and less strident criticism of the Left, gets far more public attention than afforded to the Left and has confronted educational leaders with a serious challenge.

This criticism has put the schools in virtually a "put up or shut up" situation. If the Right is wrong, then what do the schools stand for? If they are not godless, are they committed to any cosmology? If they reject "secular humanism," when do they do this and on what basis? Can the schools continue their claim to be innocent, nonpolitical, and non-moral? (To do so would be tantamount to admitting to vacuity.) If the schools are not to operate in a political and moral vacuum, then can they describe and affirm their informing and energizing principles? I do not believe that the school establishment is prepared to meet this challenge because it does not have a well-developed moral and spiritual language in which to respond. The primary language is the technical and bureaucratic one of control, task, and engineering; the school establishment has only a vague understanding of the language of ideology, religion, and meaning. This is a language deficiency of serious proportions with important consequences to our society, for it is a language that shows increasing signs of revival.

Another important dimension of the "thunder from the Right" is the powerful and popular base, which supports these criticisms. It is one thing to ignore a local crank or even a national "extreme" group, but the time has surely gone by when we can afford to dismiss the New Right (religious or otherwise) as ephemeral or faddish. Important as it is to register the emergence of this phenomenon, it is of even greater importance to note its more basic rather than superficial aspects. We need to be in touch with the concerns, needs, and impulses of these as well as other movements and be less obsessively dismissive with their solutions or proposals. I believe that there is much more opportunity for consensus on what the important problems and questions are than on what the solutions might be. However, whether or not consensus is possible, we must attend to the legitimacy of those who are sincerely passionate about the relationship between matters of faith and education and seek to at least understand and empathize both with the source and nature of this passion.

I am persuaded by Harvey Cox's argument that this passion can be seen at least in part as a *cri de coeur*, as the anguish and pain about our modern industrial nuclear computerized world. In *Religion and the Secular City*, Cox (1984) points out that the liberation theology movement in Latin America and the Moral Majority movement in the United States have, in addition to their obvious major differences, a number of common characteristics. Both are active political movements that work within religious boundaries and outside the conventional political apparatus. Most important, Cox asserts, is that they both (along with several other movements, notably the women's movement) represent rejection of modernism, that cluster of values centered on materialism, science, individuality, and consumerism which constitutes the basis of contemporary Western ideology.

Both represent very different responses to what they see as the crisis in modernity, but both represent *serious criticism* of the fundamental structure of contemporary society. Both are grass roots operations having built on popular unrest and dissatisfaction, and both have prospered by articulating that deep sense of cultural dis-ease into an alternative program. Cox goes on to speak more broadly about the renewed interest in religion and the question of the connection between politics and religion. His basic conclusion is that although there was a time in history when religion had to yield to secular forces, this is a time in history when the secular society needs *religious criticism*.

> "Secularization," one of the most severely chastised children of modernity, is also the unappreciated offspring of the prophets, including the prophet of Nazareth, who railed against religiously sanctioned injustice with as much fervor as any anticleric. At its best, such secularization was once a sturdy strand in the history of human freedom. It was a legitimate response to the illegitimate use of the sacred for demeaning purposes. It spoke with the same voice that cried out through heresies, "witches covens, popular agnosticism, and even, at times, atheism. If it eventually went to excess and produced its own pseudosacral devices—the goddess of Reason in Paris or the tomb of Lenin in Red Square—this means only that external vigilance is still the price we pay for the freedom God intends for all people. If freedom once required a secular critique of religion, it can also require a religious critique of the secular." (Cox 1984:170–71)

The notion of religion as social criticism is fully developed by a number of contemporary scholars (e.g., Ackermann 1985; Soelle 1974; Croatto 1981; Segundo 1976) and is a concept that intersects with education seen as serving a critical function. Indeed, the very essence of education can be seen as critical, in that its purpose is to help us to see, hear, and experience the world more clearly, more completely, and with more understanding.

Education can provide us with the critical tools—critical reading, critical thinking, critical seeing, critical hearing, and writing—that enable us to fully understand our world. Another vital aspect of the educational process is the development of creativity and imagination, which enable us not only to understand but to build, make, create, and re-create our world. Crucial to these processes are critical dimensions, standards to be employed in both the critical and creative processes, and frames of reference that give energy and direction to the criticism and creativity. We are talking about a vision that can illuminate what we are doing and what we might work to achieve. Such a vision needs to inform all aspects of our life, and naturally that includes education; in the case of education, it can also be said that the vision, in turn, is shaped by educators.

The questions of what our vision is and should be are in fact the most crucial and most basic questions that we face. They generate the complex and perplexing questions of how these visions are to be determined and reflect the conflict among competing groups eager to inform the vision with their particular wisdom. Fundamentally, the language of this vision belongs to the moral and religious family of language, for it is the function of moral and religious language to provide the essential dimension of education—a language of meaning. Our cultural crisis is a crisis in meaning, and this crisis can therefore be seen basically as moral and religious; we need to see the crisis in education as not primarily problems of technique, organization, and funding but as a reflection of the crisis in meaning. The educational bankruptcy is based on both its failure to sense and ease this crisis as well as its success in contributing to it. We therefore propose to examine the deeper and more profound educational crisis with the language of meaning, by examining the moral and religious dimensions of our culture as reflected in our educational policies and practices.

3

THE MORAL AND SPIRITUAL CRISIS
IN AMERICAN EDUCATION

*Real criticism begins in the capacity to grieve because that is the most visceral
announcement that things are not right. Only in the empire are we pressed and
urged and invited to pretend that things are all right either in the dean's office or in
our marriage or in the hospital room. And as long as the empire can keep the pretense
alive that things are all right, there will be no real grieving and no serious criticism.*
WALTER BRUEGGEMANN *The Prophetic Imagination*

We have thus far posited a number of basic assumptions to this analysis: the intimate interrelationship between culture and education; the view that education
should serve primarily to facilitate the struggle for meaning; that the key educational strategy is to nourish the critical and creative consciousness that will contribute to the creation and vitalization of a vision of meaning; and, finally, that the
failure of the educational system is both cause and effect of a crisis in the culture's
capacity to synthesize a coherent moral and spiritual order. I wish to explore the
nature of this moral and spiritual crisis more deeply, particularly as it is reflected in
educational policies and practices. I claim nothing like a definitive or even
thorough exposition of the mood, mores, or attitudes of the culture as the goal
here is much more modest. The purpose of this chapter is to suggest the broad
boundaries of the culture's moral stance, a project that, of course, runs the risk of
oversimplification and datedness. We take this risk because we believe such an anal-

ysis is critical to any examination of the educational process and, thus, I proceed with the confidence that such an overview is needed and with the caution that it is likely to be flawed and incomplete.

Modalities of American Culture

This is surely not the place to attempt an exact and thorough description of the American socio-economic class structure and its cultural landscape, but it is appropriate to sketch out my assumptions about what constitute major influences in American culture. I will be focusing primarily on the attitudes and values of an inchoate but bounded group that has been given several names—middle class, mid-America, the bourgeoisie, mainstream America. I will be addressing those attitudes and behaviors that generally characterize what is considered to be norms of American middle-class life—that which is legal, accepted, legitimate, routine, normal, and popular, what is considered to be part of "common sense," "normal expectations," and "popular culture." We are excluding in this particular analysis that which is considered esoteric, counter cultural, socially deviant, and eccentric.

There are several reasons for focusing on this aspect of American society. First, it is obviously an influential and powerful force in the larger culture, albeit it is also one that is itself significantly manipulated by other cultural, social, political, and economic forces. Second, it is a force/group in which I and almost all other professional educators have membership, and, thus, its examination can to some degree allow for self-reflection. In addition, this group has energy, intelligence, resources, and the capacity to make choices and changes given its relatively secure socioeconomic position. It is a group that has great potential for deeper education and, indeed, may be the only major group that has both the potential power and inclination to transform the culture.

Even though values and beliefs of this group cut across social, cultural, and economic groups, this consciousness is much more likely to be dominant in the middle class. Other cultural, political, and social groups are surely strongly affected by these belief systems, but their unique situations allow for significant variation and deviation from this consciousness. One such group consists of the supremely powerful and rich, a group very much isolated physically and culturally from mainstream America except in its exploitation and manipulation of it. We exclude them not because they are not important and powerful (indeed they are enormously so) but rather because, frankly, we are very dubious about our or anyone's capacity for developing an educational strategy that might significantly affect their consciousness.

For other reasons, we will not fully address in this chapter the belief system of marginal and counter cultural groups—the alienated, the poor, and the disenfranchised. Let me quickly say, however, that the book's central concern is in fact the plight of these people—they are the victims of a set of attitudes and values that are rooted in other sources. These are the oppressed of whom Freire (1970, 1973) has written so passionately and whose oppression is made all the more poignant when some of these oppressive norms and behaviors are internalized by the oppressed themselves. A major goal of this book is to develop ideas that can serve significantly to liberate people from poverty, bigotry, and alienation. As educators, we have a major responsibility to resist and overcome those policies and programs that serve to keep the poor and powerless poor and powerless. An absolutely fundamental tenet of social and educational orientation of this book is, therefore, the affirmation of the principle of the supreme importance of liberation for all—liberation from hunger, disease, fear, bigotry, war, ignorance, and all other barriers to a life of joy, abundance, and meaning for every single person in the world.

It is time for us to re-connect education with the culture's most profound moral commitments including most importantly the impulses to "do good " and to pursuit a coherent life of ultimate meaning. In doing so, I most certainly do not want to imply humans are not capable of doing evil but as an educator I simply do not know how to respond to people who knowingly and willingly try to keep people from being free. I prefer to operate on the assumption that there is a vast and influential group in America who would very much like to choose a way of life that is just, joyful, and loving. Part of the reason middle-class America has not been fully able to make such a choice has to do with the power of elitist and powerful groups (who perhaps represent evil), and no doubt part of the reason comes from choices that middle America has more or less consciously made. However, it is my firm belief that these choices represent confusion and frustration more than they represent a desire to hurt and oppress. Confusion and frustration are indeed areas in which the educational process is relevant and ameliorative. When we view our problems as being rooted in evil and sin, the only alternative to despair is prayer; but when we are able to see them based more on confusion, then we can put our hope in the liberating possibilities of a critical and enlightening education. What this chapter is designed to do is to explicate the confusion, one that can be summed up as a confusion about our losing struggle to choose a creative rather than a destructive life. It is a confusion that emerges from value conflicts and from the complex paradoxes and dilemmas inherent in the effort to inform what we do with deeply felt moral principles.

I have chosen to present this broad conception of the nature of this confusion in the form of a number of discrete yet clearly overlapping dyads of value paradoxes. These will be discussed more as dilemmas than as easy choices, more in dialectical than dualistic terms, more as points on a continuum than as either/or considerations. However, my purpose will not be to blur moral and value choices but rather to indicate that although certain values are clearly to be preferred, their choice usually involves legitimate conflicts with other attractive choices.

Paradoxes and Conflicts in American Culture

Individualism/Community

The first of these value dyads is perhaps the most basic and serious single cultural issue facing us, namely the matter of individuality/ community. This issue has to do with our impulse to define, maintain, and nourish both a self and group identity; we are interested in being unique, autonomous, independent, and in having a strong and well defined ego while at the same time, we seek strong human and symbolic relationships in which our identities are connected with those of others. Not only is there an impulse to seek group, interpersonal, and symbolic identity, but, in addition, the recognition of the social character of our lives: whether we like it or not, we are interdependent, have symbiotic relationships with others, and are by nature socially defined.

There is by now a vast and persuasive literature that reinforces the strong consensus that ours is a generation dominated by individuality, self-gratification, and narcissism (e.g., see Lasch 1979; Bellah 1985; Sennett 1977). It is also a time, not surprisingly, when there is great loneliness and when a myriad of new techniques to help people develop relationships has emerged, such as singles' bars, computer dating, support groups, and the like. The great emphasis on the desperate pursuit of individual gratification can be seen in the grim figures of rising divorce and suicide rates. It can also be seen in the steep increase in competition, greed, and crime, and in the decrease in concern for the poor and powerless. The concept of "welfare," for example, has come to be seen by many as a term for pariahs and slackers; public support for the unfortunate has come to mean government interference; and for many policy makers, unemployment is an unfortunate but necessary consequence of increasing productivity through greater efficiency.

By individualism we mean here not so much the development of autonomy and independence as much as an egocentricity grounded in the belief that the individual is the basic and most important unit of decision making. There is a sense here that from a perspective of self-gratification, self-fulfillment, self-help, and self-advancement, concerns for group, family, or culture, are irrelevant or threatening. The importance of the group is seen not so much as having the potential to be stifling but more as a setting for individual competition in which the group provides hierarchical norms. This stress on individualism is by no means free of its conformist aspects—indeed the dominant culture demands that individuals compete, that they strive for winning over and beating others; and that achievement in a broad but ultimately bounded realm constitutes success. The acquisition of materials, feeling good, and a sense of achievement become the common standards for individual pursuits.

This emphasis strains our commitment to the nurturance and development of community, public space, and shared moral values. This erosion of social consciousness is in spite of the fact that our traditions are full of images of common concerns and common struggle. The Declaration of Independence, the Constitution, and the Gettysburg Address, for example, speak of nationhood, people hood, brotherhood; of union, common purpose, and common destiny. We presumably value family and neighborhood; we are nostalgic about celebrations involving powerful bonding rituals: Christmas, the Fourth of July, Mother's Day, weddings, and graduations. Our politicians routinely use the rhetoric of patriotism, common heritage, and the special opportunities and blessings of the American people.

The schools, however, play a more powerful role in stressing an individual rather than a common vision. Individual success and achievement are greatly emphasized, as seen in the increasing stress in normative grading and correlatively in our obsessions with the idea of "cheating." Although we are aware of the individuality of knowledge, of the value of group study and interaction, and of the importance of students sharing their ideas, we actually discourage these educationally sound principles, mostly because they interfere with the practice of individual grading. Students are, in fact, urged to compete with each other in the classroom as reflected in such areas as entry into certain tracks or programs (e.g., reading groups, college track, gifted and talented programs) which is competitive and limited. The same is true, of course, for admission to programs of higher education, which is largely, determined by comparing individual standardized test scores, course grades, and personal qualities.

Competition is a key component as well for activities outside the classroom, notably in the athletic programs. However, there is an irony here because athletic programs (more so than academics) tend to promote serious concern for cooperation, interdependence, and to stress the intimate relationship between the team and the individual The emphasis in community on the sports program is, however, mitigated by at least two considerations: first, the sports program often supports the "star" orientation in which superior individual achievement often attains far more attention than that of the team; and second, the stress remains on winning and surpassing another team. In fairness, there still remain the ethics of sportsmanship, which, at least theoretically, affirms a community of competitors.

The insight that schools' prime educational approach consists of students trying to please teachers by getting the "right answer" is one that also reveals how students are put in a position of competing with each other on who can most please the teacher. In this phenomenon, individual students are singled out for praise or vilification so as to indicate the quality of their individual efforts and achievements or lack thereof. Students are said to earn their stars or smiling faces or detention notices or reprimands, not so much as students functioning within a cultural and social setting but as solitary figures acting as independent agents oblivious to each other and mindful only of being "fair" to competitors. This, no doubt, is appropriate preparation for the conventional world of real estate, stockbrokerage and professional sports. However, it is highly inappropriate preparation for an interdependent world in which the sense of justice, community, and compassion should be the overriding considerations.

Habits of the Heart, by Robert Bellah and associates (1985), documents the culture's inability to articulate its impulse for a consciousness that transcends concern for self and its losing struggle to find a larger meaning grounded in common and shared beliefs and experiences. In their study of current views of middle-class Americans toward self and group, they found

> all the classic polarities of American individualism still operating: the deep desire for autonomy and self-reliance combined with an equally deep conviction that life has no meaning unless shared with others in the context of community; a commitment to the equal right to dignity of every individual combined with an effort to justify inequality of reward, which when extreme, may deprive people of dignity; an insistence that life requires practical effectiveness and "realism" combined with the feeling that compromise is ethically fatal. The inner tensions of American individualism add up to a classic case of ambivalence. We strongly assert the value of our self-reliance and autonomy. We deeply feel the emptiness of a life without sustaining social commitments. Yet we are hesitant to articulate our sense that we need one another as much as we need to stand alone, for fear that if we did we would lose our independence altogether. The tensions of our lives would be even greater if we did not, in fact, engage in practices that constantly limit the effects of an isolating individualism, even though we cannot articulate those practices nearly as well as we can the quest for autonomy. (1985:150–51)

We thirst for true community, for a broader context to individually struggle and authentically share our joys, confessions, and heartbreaks. When we go to school, we are taught mostly to learn to be alone, to compete, to achieve, to succeed. The emphasis on individual achievement is not uniform in the schools since there, as elsewhere, the concern for community also gets expressed however modestly and infrequently. Schools sponsor parent groups and choral societies; they have school rallies, school songs, try to raise school spirit, speak sometimes of a school's tradition. They also try to support alumni groups and speak of the character of a group or student ("This year's junior class is really special"), and in times of distress the school community is often mobilized to express its collective concern. It is certainly not that the schools, like the broader culture, are not mindful of a social identity, but they clearly put much more emphasis on personal rather than social identity, especially as it relates to the obsession with personal success and achievement. This brings us to our second major value paradox—that involving how much our culture has come to blur worth with achievement.

Worth/Achievement

This particular value configuration represents, I believe, the core of our moral and spiritual crisis, for it reflects a glaring contradiction between our most deeply felt moral conviction—that which affirms the essential dignity of each person—and our most widespread social and cultural expectation—that which demands that each person must achieve (i.e., that each of us has to earn our dignity). Our most revered symbols and credos continue to urge us to love ourselves, our neighbors, and even our enemies; they tell us that all people are created equal, that we are born with certain inalienable rights, that we are all God's children, that we all have a spirit or soul within us, that each one of us is precious and sovereign. These profound expressions are elaborated and exhorted in every aspect of our culture—in homes, in the media, and yes, even in schools where these sentiments are accepted as part of our faith.

In addition, popular psychology urges us to be considerate of the feelings of others, to value empathy, and to support the well being of everyone. After all I'm O.K., you're O.K., and we're O.K. Well, that is not quite how it works or otherwise we would not need to be continually encouraged and urged to take on that outlook. We are having to be prodded to think that you and I are O.K. because we live in a culture that does not say that we are O.K. until and unless we demonstrate that we can do something well that is valued. In a word, we live in a world where personal dignity is not inherent and inalienable but is negotiable and problematic. Some would even say that we need to "motivate" students to strive for this dignity, and to use dignity as a reward (i.e., in exchange for achievement).

However, it is not just that many educators see reinforcement theory as a useful psychological construct or see extrinsic motivation as a "reality" of our being. The question that lies underneath the widespread use of the reward-punishment approach to learning is partly one of wondering why we are so strongly attracted to this way of being. The answer, I believe, lies in part in our insistence on maintaining hierarchy and privilege and on setting clear criteria for achieving and justifying them. Our democratic principles involve a rejection of the notion of ascribed hierarchy (i.e., privilege that comes with birth or position). However, our society tries to have our cake and be able to eat it in the way that we congratulate ourselves not for *rejecting* privilege but for validating it by redefining the conditions under which people may have privileges.

This has led us to a tacit acceptance of a notion of "deserving" namely, a set of connections that, at least implicitly, legitimates inequality on the basis that it is deserved or merited. The mainstream culture has in fact legitimated a number of conditions under which it approves more justice for some than others—for example, those who work hard, those who have strong educational backgrounds, and those who populate particular professions (medicine, law, professional music, professional sports). We are a culture that simultaneously celebrates equality and inequality, community and competition—one that rejects the notion of any person as having special privileges as immoral and unfair and yet at the same time actively creates and legitimates possibilities for this to occur.

It has been pointed out that a major shift in moral emphasis occurs at the point where children begin to go to school in earnest, and that is the difference in stress between affiliation and achievement. Presumably, families, while surely concerned with achievement, fully accept, support, and nurture their members simply because they are constituent family members (i.e., they belong). The constitutive rules of the schools are radically different in that *achievement,* and not affiliation, becomes the basic condition for acceptance. Students learn very quickly that the rewards that the schools provide—grades, honors, recognitions, and affection— are conditioned upon achievement and certain behaviors of respect, obedience, and docility.

This is not to say that the schools are monolithic and rigid in the areas in which they demand students to achieve, although the increasing stress on normative and standardized testing indicates a clear direction toward uniformity. Indeed, thoughtful, kind, and sensitive teachers often express their flexibility and progressiveness by widening the arenas of achievement. Such teachers will say in effect, "I so much want Cedric to have a good self-image which I know he can get if only he could be proud of what he did. Now, mind you it doesn't have to be in things like math or history—it could be in art or sports or woodworking, and I'm going to continue to look for whatever it is that Cedric can excel at."

We tend to applaud and glow when we hear such a sentiment expressed, and surely it is a well-intentioned impulse, one that expresses a teacher's strong dedication to the goal of helping students find fulfillment and a sense of well-being. However, such a sentiment and our approbation for it reveal very particular cultural standards for both fulfillment and a sense of well-being. It is, in fact, a sentiment that underscores our obsession with achievement and success, since what it says is that we do not care what Cedric does as long as he does *something well.* This standard indicates that a necessary if not sufficient condition for fulfillment and strong self-image is the ability to excel in a particular realm of achievement. This would indicate an ethic of conditional love: we will love you if you achieve. Presumably the more enlightened of us have a longer list of the significant areas of achievement, but the requirement is clearly that we still must achieve in order to be affirmed. Moreover, in this ethic, our worth is really not inherent, not sovereign, not inevitable, but continuously subject to trial, examination, and judgment. It is also possible and likely that the list of what areas are significant enough to achieve in will change, so we will have to be ever alert to shifts in the cultural requirements for affirmation and dignity.

This harshly severe requirement has clearly exacerbated injustice, pain, suffering, confusion, and doubt about our moral and spiritual ideals. Each of us, I suspect, harbors quietly, if not secretly, the convictions that "we and our loved ones are as good as anyone else," and yet we constantly engage in practices designed to demonstrate that we are "better than." This conflict and contradiction is destructive, self-fulfilling, and has the capacity to feed on itself—that is, the more we engage in the madness of demanding that we prove that we are deserving, the more it becomes entrenched in our consciousness and becomes "natural and inevitable."

Schools present students and the larger school community with the notion that an integral and vital aspect of school life involves the pursuit of affirmation and dignity. This is the moral assumption that allows them to take on responsibility for setting the conditions for this pursuit—for the competition of who will have how much dignity. Inevitably, this means that some people will emerge from the competition with *lots* of dignity, some with a little, and some with very little or even none. Ironically enough, it becomes apparent that the schools' mission includes, however it may be unwitting or unintended, that of identifying those who are of little or no worth.

It is not only that schools are competitive and that they encourage their students to succeed by competing with each other, but at an even more basic level they represent in their being and practice the morally repulsive idea of equating human worth and dignity with achievement. It is a notion that is so pervasive and routine in the schools and larger culture that it is hardly even noticed, much less questioned. Because their rhetoric of intellectual and academic excellence resonates so strongly with what we think of as noble aspirations, schools actually add a particularly strong legitimation to what is, at base, a serious variance with our deepest moral and spiritual convictions. In fact, schools are criticized by enlightened members of the upper-middle class (including so-called radicals) for not sufficiently stressing academic, or intellectual, or esthetic "excellence" (the code name for more intense competition).

This passionate embrace of "excellence" only reflects the depth of the culture's commitment to the values of competition, personal success, and achievement and with its commitment to social and cultural hierarchy. It is rare to see serious social, cultural, and educational critics confronting the issues of a hierarchy based on intellectual and professional abilities and achievements, i.e., meritocracy. This would indicate a very strong if not always articulated support for hierarchy, for privilege and ranking, but presumably one based on intellectual achievement. Are "smart" people any more deserving than "dumb" ones? Are brilliant poets any more entitled to privilege than conventional ones? Why do we single out individuals to "graduate with honor"? Does this mean that those who are not in this group are without honor? Why do we have minimum grade point averages as conditions to participate in certain activities?

The schools mirror the culture by giving its admittedly meager but powerfully symbolic rewards to those who achieve more than others. Again, the mark of a so-called progressive school is not necessarily that it rejects achievement but that it extends the realm of areas worthy of recognition; for example, the hardest working, the student who has made the most progress, or is the most congenial. All of this rests on a firm and presumably unshakable conviction that dignity and worth are to be earned. And yet this conviction, however strong and widespread, must coexist with our immense and overwhelming yearning for unconditional love—our intense desire to love others, be loved by others, to love others for who they are rather than for what they do or have.

Equality/Competition

The political consequences of the stress on individualism, competition, personal achievement, and success include an erosion of our traditional commitment to social equality. Historically we have had a strong tradition of activism for social and economic equality in which literally thousands of people have shown their willingness to risk and lose a great deal (including their lives) for these causes. We have, of course, also struggled with the dilemmas engendered by the situations in which social equality conflicts with personal freedom. Over time, various groups have worked out arrangements and understandings that, at least politically, have tried to overcome these difficulties by adopting an overriding concern for equality and justice. Tax policies, trade unions, professional associations, social welfare programs, unemployment insurance, minimum wages, collective bargaining, affirmative action, open admission, consumer protection policies, and pollution controls can all be said to restrict individual freedom, but they are intended to provide more freedom for more people, particularly for those whose freedom is limited by artificial and unnecessary barriers. Our overriding concern for social justice and equality and our impulse to be compassionate have enabled us, for the most part, to accept and tolerate practices which might not please us in our individual and private consciousness but which resonate with our social identity as a people dedicated to "liberty and justice for all."

However, it seems the 1980s are a time when these arrangements and understandings are no longer accepted as part of the basic framework for setting social policy. We seem to be to adopting a neo-Social Darwinism ethic based on the faith that the play of the free market will in the long run overcome economic anomalies and inequities by maximizing efficiency and eliminating the non-productive. In part, the new conservatism can be seen as the continuing backlash to the 1960s, to the fear and threat engendered by what was perceived to be moral excess. Perhaps even more significantly there is a concern for the stability of the existing power structure since the agenda of many of the movements 1960s included the necessity for community political development. Many groups, hitherto powerless and rendered invisible and harmless by their powerlessness, were given the know-how of how their latent power could be developed and expressed. The 1960s were, if nothing else, a time when collectivity was both celebrated as a virtue and utilized as a powerful agent for change. The poor, the minorities, and the neighborhoods were organized, as were various middle-class constituencies—school groups, support groups, groups of the afflicted (those dealing with the ravages of mental illness, retardation, physical handicaps, and the like). In fact, it was probably the politicization of many middle-class Americans, who perhaps for the first time experienced legally sanctioned horrors (e.g., the draft and police brutality), that had the greatest impact on the areas of greatest immediate political changes—the passage of civil rights legislation and ending the war in Vietnam. What threatened the power structure was not the number of individual hippies or freaks but the fear that what initially seemed to be a series of fads or a relatively harmless release of exuberance had been transformed into a serious political movement. This movement, though varied, had a number of common themes, particularly, collectivity, community, solidarity, peoplehood, and any barrier to dignity, freedom, and autonomy for all.

Interestingly enough, two significant policies on the military draft illustrate the ultimately destructive, distracting, and divisive powers of competition and individuality. The first of these policies is the one that gave exemptions to college students, clearly a way of providing the middle class with a significant advantage. This policy also reinforced the edge that came to those who so successfully competed in high school that they were admitted to colleges and were also able to meet the academic requirements of maintaining enrollment. Those "smart" and "wealthy" enough to be in college were seen as less appropriate for military service. The second policy, which I believe cleverly undermined middle-class resistance both to the Vietnam War and to an aggressive U.S. foreign policy, was the eventual elimination of the draft and its substitution with an all-volunteer professional army. Given economic realities, this effectively made the army appealing mostly to those unable to make it in the civilian economy—the poor and disadvantaged mostly drawn from minority groups. Taken together, these policies provided mechanisms of competition and division that had serious consequences; they were policies that forced people to think individually rather than collectively, to think of the consequences of acting on the basis of personal freedom rather than on the basis of social equality.

The political rhetoric of both parties in the 1984 election campaign (with the exception of Jesse Jackson) reflects the social consensus on the centrality of competition in our society. Some candidates stressed the concept of opportunity, which is only a way of legitimating competition made "fair" by equalizing opportunities to participate in the race for dignity. It is also a rhetoric that implicitly accepts the idea of inevitably scarce resources, and that discipline and self-restraint are in order because, if anything, the resources and goodies will soon be even scarcer. In this viewpoint, we can expect fewer jobs, less government involvement, and more "overqualified" people competing with each other.

Our economic policy, such as there is one, seems to accept as inevitable and desirable the need to aggressively enter the postindustrial era, involves even more efficiency, more cost-effective controls, less reliance on human labor, and avoidance of long-range commitment to higher wages. We are told that we are in a time of painful transition, that we have economic troubles largely because the high wages we pay make us unable to compete with countries where people work much harder and earn much less. We are also told that our federal deficit contributes to the economic crisis and that the roots of this defect are mostly in our social welfare or "entitlement" programs. This has led, among other things, to the most serious efforts by industry, with the active support of the government, to weaken if not break unions and professional associations since the 1920s. Current economic conditions have allowed many companies to use the stick of replacing unionized workers with non-unionized workers quite willing and eager to work, even if it means at lower wages to beat back demands for better working conditions and higher pay.

Much of the culture now accepts our economic situation as serious and highly shaky, and in this atmosphere of fear and anxiety the stress on competition and personal freedom is seen as both an intellectually sound economic policy of social salvation as well as a realistic way of responding to the necessities of personal and family survival. We have once again been put in a situation where we are driven to make a choice, however theoretically unnecessary, between equality and justice for all and survival for me. I believe that most of us find it hateful to confront such a choice, or at least that is my hope. I fear that there are those who may not resent this conflict because they have come to rationalize the competition not as corrosive to equality but as actually contributing to it in the long run. An even greater fear is that this seemingly technical argument about the best way to achieve equality masks an increasing indifference to the pain and suffering that are the concrete consequences of significant social inequality.

Caring: Compassion and Sentimentality

The concern for social equality can be said to be a correlate of the human impulse to be caring and to be concerned about the welfare of others to the point of helping and nurturing them. We are an inherently caring people which is most vividly represented in the intense concern parents have for their children, and for that matter, as Willlard Gaylin (1978) points out, we seem to be biologically programmed to be sensitive to the vulnerability of all children. Our culture, in fact, accepts a sense of deep caring as a natural and desirable aspect of family life; deep caring is not seen as an exotic and unrealizable ideal within the family structure but as an inevitable dimension and key defining aspect of the family.

The schools have traditionally encouraged the concept of caring in a variety of ways: organizing food drives for the needy; arranging for ways to comfort classmates who are ill or have suffered family loss; encouraging concern for others when the safety and well-being of others is involved, such as conduct in the cafeteria, hallways, and auditorium; and in the emphasis on caring as a positive value in the context of academic classes (e.g., as shown in the popularity of novels by Charles Dickens in English courses). However, the stress on competition and individuality narrows and undermines this impulse to care and nourish. Indeed, the culture and the schools have had to develop techniques to become immune to the kind of caring that might deflect us from competition and the pursuit of individual success and achievement. We have come to find ways in which indifference is valued—in some quarters, it is considered good to be "cool," to be stoic, to avoid feeling guilt. We have bought into a psychology that urges us to consider that we are responsible individually for our feelings and behavior and that we are responsible only to and for ourselves. While this may at one level enhance (properly) our own sense of personal responsibility, this attitude can and does serve to reduce the sense of our interdependence and our opportunities to help and support others.

When, for example, we call cooperative and collaborative acts of research and study "cheating," we insist that students take individual responsibility for what they claim to know. Students are neither asked to take very much responsibility in helping other students to learn, nor are they encouraged to note how their gains are often at the expense of their classmates. In addition, playing the competitive game of schooling means in part not allowing one to feel concern for the losers since losers are also competitors. To show sympathy for them would give one's competitors support and might sap one's resolve and determination to win.

Surely, students are likely to encounter the realities of human poverty and hunger in the formal curriculum and to study the whys and wherefores of these phenomena. When such matters are studied, however, it is typically with an emphasis on understanding the issues, gaining insight into them, and almost always on agreeing that it would be good to untangle the complexities in order to help these wretched people. However, schools are usually reluctant to encourage students to develop deep emotional attachment or to dwell on the moral obscenity of these situations. Teachers are very reluctant and careful not to "induce guilt" but rather to develop the emotional distance that can allow one to have a sober and thorough understanding. In any case, where schools do organize an annual fast day or encourage the social studies curriculum to deal with hunger and poverty, they often do so as simply one more "interesting" activity. There is seldom, if ever, a story of a school or university that sets as one of its prime continuous and long-range goals the cultivation of human caring and concern.

The tragedy of this policy is to truncate the human spirit, especially that part that yearns for human connection and social involvement. We as humans do and want to care and have shown a glorious tradition of responding heroically and selflessly in times of need. However, with our need to compete; with the feeling that our brothers and sisters are our competitors in the desperate race for scarce resources; with the recognition that a person in trouble is a less formidable rival in the struggle for receiving dignity, with the belief that caring for others may infantilize them and hook us into guilt; and with the knowledge of the problems that often beset well-meaning people who do get involved, the answer seems to be to "stay cool," to remain aloof, skeptical, and to avoid being swept away by the emotions of grief and pity. For one thing, such emotions will cloud our judgment, develop false expectations that we can rescue others, and distract us from our individual paths.

It is no surprise, therefore, that we hear of relationships without love, of joyless sexual activities becoming the norm for both men and women, of the sharp increase simultaneously in the use of surface pleasantries (e.g., "Have a nice day") and the reluctance to make serious human commitments grounded in a deep sense of caring. We yearn to care and to be cared for; yet, we work on developing callousness to these yearnings and in so doing deny ourselves, for as Abraham Heschel says, "The opposite of freedom is not determinism but hardness of heart" (Heschel 1962:191). When we shut down our impulse to care, we interfere with one of the very most precious essences of what it means to be human.

This is not to say that our culture is without "feelings." Quite the contrary, for we have seen a veritable explosion of discussion, analysis, and explanation of feelings. We are a culture that has learned to be in touch with our feelings, to express them, to consider them as real and vital aspects of being human, and above all else we have learned that it is important that we feel "good." Bellah's *Habits of the Heart* (1985) and Lasch's *The Culture of Narcissism* (1979) spell out the lengths to which we as people will go to extend this value of personal well being, as indicated by how we as individuals feel about our personal selves. The issue I wish to address here is the direction and locus of these feelings rather than the issue of the validity of feelings themselves. I believe we are beyond the point of actively avoiding and denying the reality and power of feelings, but we are still very much wrestling with issues related to their boundaries and to their relationship to other moral, political, and religious considerations.

Matthew Fox, in his *Spirituality as Compassion* (1979), has articulated an important distinction in this regard, that of the difference between compassion and sentimentality. *Compassion* to Fox represents an acknowledgment and celebration of interdependence that results in action directed toward easing or overcoming the "reign of pain." In contrast, Fox sees *sentimentality* as representing feeling by itself, alone and determinedly separate from any sense of responsibility. In this analysis Fox is able to provide insight into the political and moral nature of various feelings and their impact on human relationships. Sentimentalism certainly reflects feelings, but they are self-indulgent feelings or as Fox (quoting Ann Douglas) puts it, "sentimentalism is politically rancid" (1979:5).

Compassion, as defined by Fox, acknowledges the social reality of connectedness, the political reality of human relationships, and the moral impulse to care and nurture. Compassion represents feelings with moral meaning; its literal meaning of "suffering with" reveals profound understanding of the nature of being—that it is likely to involve pain and suffering, that the burdens are particularly severe when one is alone, and that it is part of human nature to share the burdens and efforts to ease them. It is the cluster of feelings that energizes our intellectual conceptions of justice as well as the expression of our deepest urges to love. Not to feel the connections with social and moral concerns is to locate the emotions we have in reaction to other people's woes in self-oriented, self-directed, ego-centered sentimentality. Fox puts it this way: "Sentimentalism is not only a block to social justice and a thorn in the side of love, justice—it is in fact their opposite. . . . It actually interferes with the natural flow of energy outwards that all persons are born with" (1979:5–6).

Given the heavy stress on competition, individualism, achievement, and personal success, any emotions of concern in school settings are likely to be of a more sentimental than compassionate nature. Surely, the school community will express its sorrow at a student's misfortune—they will likely send notes, flowers, even mobilize schoolwide or classwide expressions of concern. The coach will surely empathize with the pain of an athlete's injury and the teacher will say that the punishment he/she is inflicting is hurting teacher more than student. The administration surely sympathizes with difficult home/family conditions of some students (such as divorce, unemployment, and illness) and they will surely wince and shake their heads, as well as shrug their shoulders, when confronted with the pain and horrors that form the framework of these students' lives.

However, rules are rules, standards are standards, reality is reality—we didn't make these rules and standards, nor did we create this reality—life must go on, and, yes, it's possible that your teacher doesn't understand that you fell asleep in class because you worked the third shift. But it's up to you to find a way—have you tried talking to your teacher? Have you thought about getting another job? You have to learn to cope— after all when I was your age. . . .

The stress on individual achievement in school is the same for individual failure and pain: *it's your problem and you're going to have to deal with it.* The emphasis on sentimentalism is the emotional dimension of individuality, privatism, and competition in that it seriously de-emphasizes mutuality, interdependence, and the human origin of culture. Sentimentality allows the underlying problems to go unchallenged (e.g., why do some students have to make difficult choices between an education and economic survival?) by privatizing the feeling and locating the source of the problem in the person in pain. This distancing erodes social responsibility ("Yes, sometimes life isn't fair, so just go ahead and stay after school even if the punishment isn't fair"); encourages powerlessness ("Yes, I see your point, I feel bad that your teacher flunked you, but my hands are tied"); and engenders alienation ("Yes, I can feel your enthusiasm for music and that's very nice, but one has to establish priorities"). Here again we experience the phenomenon of conflict, of how we find ourselves in a place we did not plan or expect to be. We as people both value compassion and are compassionate—we do care for and with each other and we respond to those who extend their concern for us. At times of crisis, we yearn to help, to ease pain, and are often frustrated by the difficulty or impossibility of doing anything. The sense of impotency in the face of suffering vividly reflects the depths of what it means to be powerless, for one feels rage, guilt, and dehumanization when one is not afforded the opportunity to participate in the healing process and is denied the responsibility to help other people's lives become whole.

Responsibility and Guilt

We want to be responsible but not to feel guilty. Responsibility involves the celebration of social connections; guilt involves the pain of social demands. When we act responsibly, it means that we are (in Heschel's [1962 conception) "responding" to the human condition of interdependence and the mutuality of our interest, and hence responsibility is seen as the ability to respond to the challenges and demands that arise from that social consciousness. We have learned, however, to be wary of a phenomenon called "guilt," which is the term applied to an inappropriate response to social demands. Feeling guilty is bad because it makes us feel bad when we really do not have to feel bad. To act out of guilt is considered unhealthy and counterproductive since it engenders anger, resentment, and depression. No doubt there is the very real possibility of a pathological response to every human situation and it is clear that many people have been unnecessarily immobilized by neurotic responses to issues related to social and moral expectations. The danger that I see is that the concern for the individual's feeling "good" is so powerful that it has led to an over reliance on the phenomenon of guilt as a mechanism to avoid responsibility. One way of avoiding distasteful, entangling, absorbing, and risky responsibilities is to rename the impulse involved. By psychologizing moral issues we can transform from an inclination to view these tasks as rooted in our moral impulse to an impulse that is rooted in a concept of psychological guilt. This allows us to do what is "psychologically healthy" ("We mustn't act out of guilt") at the risk of not taking on a task that is considered morally right ("It is your responsibility to take on this task").

The school says, "It is your responsibility to work hard and get high grades and not to feel guilty if your friend flunks the course." The school says, "It's right to feel a sense of responsibility for the starving Ethiopians but you won't be able to help them if all you are really feeling is guilt." The school says, "Yes, it's a shame your friend won't be able to play because of her injury, but feeling guilty won't help." The school says, "It is not professional to complain about another teacher—you sound like you're projecting your guilt." The school says, "I don't know anything about college admissions—don't ask me to deal with your guilt trips." The guidance counselor says, "Maybe you feel guilty that you're getting good grades and that your friend is flunking out."

The culture and the schools have made a great deal of the dangers and perils of acting out of guilt on the grounds that it is unhealthy to do so. They have done far less about speaking to the consequences of moral irresponsibility; they seem less concerned with the "illness" of avoiding the consequences of mutuality than with the "illness" of personal anguish. Perhaps the school ought to set itself to the task of helping people to sort out their legitimate responsibilities and contribute to the development of the intellectual, psychological, and spiritual resources required to respond in a way that is fulfilling and meaningful. For not only do we strive to be responsible, we waver at the risks and burdens involved. Part of this wavering can be seen as having educational rather than strictly psychological significance: part of the reason we sometimes avoid our responsibilities is that we lack the clarity and the skills appropriate to exercising those responsibilities. We do not have to learn the impulse to be responsible, but we do have to be encouraged to accept the related challenges; moreover, we do have to learn how best to respond to this most human of all impulses—to be our brothers' and sisters' keeper.

Authority/Power/Coercion

With responsibility comes the opportunity and necessity to exercise power with all its risks, uncertainties, and dangers. Power in itself, and in its inevitability and ubiquity, is neither good nor bad. It is a force like fire and wind that is necessary and natural with as much capacity for life as for death. The moral and spiritual boundaries are the truly critical dimensions of power since it is they that give power its direction and meaning. Power can be seen as equivalent to the capacity to make decisions; one can then examine the issues surrounding the conditions under which this capacity is exercised. Perhaps the most significant of these conditions is the one which deals with the basis of the decision and, more particularly, with whether, or to what degree, the decision is based on some legitimate authority or is simply a function of coercion.

Let us refer to this distinction as that between authority and coercion, authority being used here to refer to some shared set of principles as to what constitutes the true, the good, and the beautiful. We are not talking here of agreement on specific issues but rather agreement on what generally constitutes acceptable criteria for a proper decision, be they very general criteria like empirical verification, logic, reason, research, or somewhat less abstract frameworks like Freudian theory, Marxism, Christianity, or Keynesian economics. What is crucial in this general attitude toward decision making is a reliance on general principles that have wide acceptance, and so it can be said that when we make decisions in this mode, we are trying to persuade and influence through mutually accepted moral, intellectual, professional, or spiritual criteria.

Those, on the other hand, who make decisions based on coercion brush aside these considerations and, instead, simply impose their will by dint of their power, whether it be direct brute power or the more indirect coercive power that implicitly stands behind people who have been chosen not to exercise authority. Presumably, if, for example, one refuses to go to school, one will confront sooner or later the full force of the police and the courts. This mode is classically expressed by Thrasymachus in Plato's *Republic* when he proclaims that "Might makes Right" (1985:35). (Socrates' response that reason makes right is an equally apt expression of decision making as authority.) This distinction is crucial to understanding the significance and meaning of education as representing the hope and faith in authority rather than reliance on coercion. The point of a critical education is to present and critically examine various approaches that claim authority. We need to learn about these claims, to know their language, grammar, and presuppositions, and to learn about modes of analysis designed to help us evaluate and judge such claims. The educated person hopes to decide and act as informed by a circle of authority of what is considered to be acceptable principles of morality, science, and art.

Surely, we are a people who claim to value authority over coercion. We certainly want decisions made fairly, sanely, and wisely rather than arbitrarily, and clearly we would rather influence than impose—we would rather be respected for our knowledge, skill, expertise, and wisdom than for the strength of our weaponry. Schools as educational institutions are full of the symbols and rituals of these deeply held values: there is the demand for proof and logic in mathematics and science; the concern for critical thinking in social studies and literature; and the stress on coherence, unity, and emphasis in grammar. We are asked to assemble our information and to distinguish between fact and opinion. We are told of the dangers of propaganda, of the necessity of precision and objectivity in science. We do not like bullies; we jeer and fear them as mindless brutes, on a level with wild, uncivilized, uneducated animals. We are certainly taught to be courteous and respectful, which represents both an antidote and rebuke to violence and personal insensitivity. Schools, as educational institutions, celebrate brain not brawn, the mind not the body, reason not force, dialogue not violence, character, rule of law, and all that kind of thing. Yes? No? Well, hardly.

The slide from authority can be relatively benign ("Well, I think it is time for you to go to bed even if you don't think so") or stern (e.g., the use of corporal punishment). Schools in their acculturation and socialization functions put great stress on obedience and deference to established power, which would seem to undermine their educational commitment to authority, as well as to the scholarly traditions of criticality and skepticism. Students are told generally of the value of critical thinking but quite directly that it is neither proper nor wise to be openly critical of their school environment. Moreover, this rule applies to the school itself in that there is no particular pressure placed on teachers to be any more authoritative than, say, the home gardener, and maybe less. Teachers, for example, typically not only do not try to persuade students that homework is a sound idea, they themselves typically do not have solid evidence that it is. (Indeed, they are often unaware of any evidence that it is or is not.) Schools glibly adapt and utilize grading systems of a profoundly dubious nature without a murmur of apology or regret. Indeed, a powerful and effective part of the school curriculum is to do what the teacher and administrator tell students to do and to come to see this as inevitable, necessary, and routine. For those who do not, the school has its own arsenal of coercive weaponry-suspension, verbal abuse, corporal punishment, withholding of affection, denial of "privileges" (recess, athletics, bathroom), and above all else the dreaded lower grade, or "bad" reference.

Personal exchanges and decisions in schools tend very much to be rule- and power-bound rather than negotiated agreements. The permeating assumption is that the student accepts school policies and practices and does what teacher says. Those few students who dare to ask for exceptions are barely tolerated; perhaps they may be seen patronizingly as "cute," but more often they are quashed ultimately not by persuasion and deference to principle but by the impatience of a force that has vastly superior firing power. Tanks are very effective against the slingshots of complainers, whiners, nitpickers.

How does one explain the extraordinary anomaly of an educational institution willing to surrender the very essence of its legitimacy by its ready resort to force and coercion? To do so undermines the very soul of an educational institution and renders its basic purpose highly problematic. However, the way in which the schools' reliance on concern is tolerated indicates not an institutional but a cultural confusion. The ease and regularity with which schools do this and the support they get from the culture for this behavior speak to the importance the culture attaches to control.

Our political preference, indeed our passion for control, makes our traditional commitment to democracy highly problematic. Our twin traditions of freedom and responsibility make the partnership of education (not necessarily schools) and democracy (not necessarily government) intimate, inevitable, inextricable, and symbiotic. The ideals of democracy include the belief that an informed public can in good faith create a society of liberty and justice for all. Such is not only a valid way of describing the nature of a true education; it is also an apt description of the conditions under which true education can thrive.

Control/Democracy

Perhaps because of the awesome traumas of the twentieth century world wars, holocaust, famine, economic depression, nuclear bombs, pollution, and the real possibility of even more horrors—we have extended our human impulse to control our destinies to obsessive dimensions, most graphically expressed in the totalitarian regimes of Hitler and Stalin. Certainly the ways in which we as a culture express those tendencies fall far short of the fanaticism, arbitrariness, and ruthlessness of the modern Orwellian police states on the Left or Right. However, even in America we all worry how our heavily bureaucratized, computerized culture-embedded in strong traditions of pragmatism, behaviorism, and technical and engineering brilliance—edges into the outskirts of a consciousness that values work, productivity, efficiency, and uniformity over play, flexibility, diversity, and freedom. When the stakes get higher and a crisis deepens, we are apt to become open to drastic solutions that focus sharply on the problem but are blind to other normally deeply held considerations of due process, rule of law, personal freedom, human rights. The recent example of the rather mild gasoline and fuel oil shortages in the United States indicates that it does not take much to set off a sense of panic and, with it, the cry for quick, tough, centralized controls—an example of what has been called our tendency toward friendly fascism.

The concern for control is also expressed in the microcosms of society—in the home, in the workplace, and in the schools. Schools have been captured by the concept of "accountability," which has been transformed from a notion that schools need to be responsive and responsible to community concerns to one in which numbers are used to demonstrate that schools have met their minimal requirement—a reductionism that has given higher priority to the need to control than to educational considerations. The need for control produces control mechanisms, and for the schools this has meant a proliferation of tests—a kind of quality control mechanism borrowed crudely and inappropriately from certain industrial settings. We control the curriculum, teachers, and staff by insisting on predefined minimal performances on specified tests. In this way schools continue their love affair with industrial and business metaphors: in this case it means employing metaphors like efficiency, cost-effectiveness, quality control, productivity to describe the educational process.

Another industrial concept that impinges strongly on educational institutions is the emphasis on management, particularly in the concepts of productivity, quotas, planning, and engineering. It is routine for schools to expect teachers and curriculum workers to operate within a framework of a cycle of activities determined and revised by a process of predetermined objectives and continuous testing. The so-called Tyler rationale, so resonant with our traditions of pragmatism, engineering, reductionism, and control, is so pervasive in the thinking of the educational profession that it qualifies as perhaps the most dramatic instance of cultural/professional hegemony in the field. It seems literally inconceivable to most educators to conceptualize education in any other way!

Obsession with control also gets expressed in school policy on "discipline," an interesting term that transfers an intellectual notion to a personal one in order to gain control over personal behavior. If schools do nothing else they deal with issues of personal control, and hence with political matters. Who can talk and under what conditions; when can we go to lunch and to the bathroom and under what conditions; who can use which language; who gets to decide what the rules are and who gets to interpret and enforce these rules—these are just some of the political matters that are a major part of everyday school life. The dominant and operating principle that shapes responses to these issues is one of school control; it is vital even in those times when students "win"; even then it demonstrates that it is the school that decides, the school that allows, lets, gives permission, waives, makes exceptions. It is students who petition, request, and plead. What is learned at every moment of contention and decision is that it is the school's policy to affirm the necessity for significant control and to vest that control in the school. Politics becomes equated with control, and the basic mechanism becomes mechanistic and paternal, a kind of bureaucratic monarchy, rule by fiat.

This political system sharply conflicts with our dedication to democratic principles, which stress self-determination and a process for both sustaining autonomy and adjusting conflicts. Indeed, it has been said that the public schools are the only major public institution specifically charged with the responsibility for nourishing and sustaining democracy. John Dewey's work represents and synthesizes the work of political, educational, and social leaders to integrate democracy and education. Dewey conceptualized the school as the "laboratory" of democracy where students and teachers could wrestle with the every day requirements, complexities, and challenges of the democratic project. It is this tradition that underlies programs in student government, courses in civics, programs in citizenship education, and various projects in community awareness and involvement. There have been times in our history when the issues of "social studies and citizenship education" were an important part of public debate and controversy, but alas, one of the casualties of the current public dialogue is the school's responsibility to nourish and develop democracy. We have stopped worrying about voter apathy, and we seem much less concerned about how informed our students are about important social and political matters; we are apparently not as concerned as we once were about the Jeffersonian principle that democracy can thrive only with a well-informed and powerfully literate citizen. Our concern for efficiency, productivity, competition, and individual success seems to have eclipsed our commitment to pursuing our democratic heritage. Student governance has become an inert issue following the flurry of efforts by some students in the 1960s and 1970s to allow for serious student participation in school decision-making. Courses and programs in citizenship education have less cogency than courses in computers, and worry about the responsibilities of citizenship has been overshadowed by worries about the necessity of raising test scores, or, as it is euphemistically called, "raising standards."

Ethnocentrism/Universalism

What we do see, instead, is an increased concern for patriotism, a strident cry for the inculcation of love of, and loyalty to, our country. This shift in emphasis from the principles of our nationhood to the reified nation perhaps reflects a similar shift from control to domination. There surely is a need for control in any culture. Indeed culture is in part defined by order, and the problematics of control are what are at issue rather than control itself. As we individually and collectively become more insecure, anxious, and even paranoid, our boundaries on control tend to extend into and beyond the realm of domination. With the impulse to dominate comes the rationalization of our own delusions of superiority and specialness, which helps legitimate blindness to the legitimate aspirations of others.

The increase in patriotism, more broadly defined as ethnocentrism, provides us with pride, esprit, and energy. The recent orgy of self-congratulations and self-indulgence that we experienced in the 1984 Olympics and the deep emotions stirred by the Iranian hostage situation are examples of the depths of feeling that can be touched when we decide to push our patriotic buttons. A perhaps more appealing instance of this fervor is the solidarity, discipline, and commitment shown in World War II. Yes, there was a great deal of profiteering, jingoism, and racism, and there was the reality that the war involved our battling for geopolitical advantage. Yet the nation was also inspired by rhetoric of a people united to put an end to totalitarianism, genocide, and military expansion. It was a time when we appealed to universal and human rights to justify our actions and sacrifices, and even if we insist on being cynical, we would all have to agree that the government found it expedient to include universal, transnational nature considerations in its propaganda.

We have since come as a culture to accept the rhetoric of a universal humanity and of human rights that cut across national, cultural, class, and tribal lines. Moreover, we have also come to experience much more of the world as community because of mass media and jet fueled transportation and to realize that nations are truly interdependent economically and politically. We have added to our vocabulary concepts like "the global village" and we sing songs with titles like "We Are the World." Educators have responded to this emerging awareness with ideas and programs, such as global education and international education; and many schools have adopted requirements for some exposure to non-Western history. However compelling and sensible these ideas may be, they still are seen as marginal and peripheral, comparable perhaps to programs in drug education. Not only do these efforts conflict with the movement of curriculum reductionism ("back to basics"), but they are out of sync with the current expression of our traditional isolationism and xenophobia. We rather glibly brand various political movements as "evil" or as "terrorist"; we try to repress our uneasiness about immigrants; we have significantly resisted bilingual education and have mounted campaigns to affirm English as the national language or at least as the language of instruction. Our pride in ourselves as a polyglot people turns into fear and rejection when we realize that we are on the verge of actually being a polyglot culture. Once again, we face serious conflict in profound values—here it is the clash between our genuine belief in a common humanity and a pride in our uniqueness. We want to value and affirm all cultures and peoples yet we find ourselves suspicious, envious, even resentful of others, including those who have accepted many of our own values, customs, and cultural forms (e.g., Japan).

The humiliation of the Vietnam war is instructive in this respect. First of all, the government, the military, and the nation seriously underestimated the skill, courage, audacity, resilience, and imagination of the Vietcong, a miscalculation that probably significantly contributed to the debacle. Moreover, our defeat led not to a recognition and acknowledgment, however grudging and tragic, of the brilliance of Vietcong military achievements but rather to an obsessive concern for our blunders. Better to acknowledge our mistakes than their success. More broadly, the Vietnam experience has not seemed to have had the effect of raising our awareness and appreciation of either the capacities of other peoples or of our shared values and talents, not as people of different nations but as humans on the same planet.

Humility/Arrogance/Affirmation

We entered that war with arrogance, but we did not leave it with humility. This arrogance takes many forms, one of which is an ethnocentrism or provincialism that emerges out of intense competition. Schools reflect this even in the presumably benign activity of school athletics. Pep rallies urge us emotionally and viscerally to express our "number one-ness" and to energize us to "kill" our archrivals from cross-town. Cheerleaders not only exhort the team but also inflame the fans by chants with the familiar themes of how great "we" are, how terrible "they" are, and why therefore we are bound to stomp them into humiliating defeat.

There is another kind of arrogance, that of intellectual certainty. Sometimes this is smugness; sometimes it is blindness; and sometimes it is rigidity. Nowhere is intellectual arrogance more inappropriate than in an educational setting, since the basic canons of educational inquiry include an awareness of the complex and elusive nature of truth and the vital importance of openness to and awareness of emerging consciousness. Education involves inquiry, and inquiry requires care, caution, and humility in the face of the enormity of the task. And yet, schools teach us to get the "right" answers, to take true-or-false examinations, and to rely on encyclopedias. Ironically, the educational process confronts us with intellectual blind alleys, and with confused, contradictory, and discredited theories that are as much a part of the search for truth as are the triumphs of research. Although we may not actually remember a particular right answer, we have learned that there is a right answer. It is not so much that schools invest in particular theoretical formulations but rather that they do not anguish over the validity of conflicting ones. The extraordinary sameness of the school's curriculum is a powerful lesson; at the core of every school's curriculum are five subjects—English, social studies, science, a foreign language, and mathematics. In a nation of diversity and pluralism, with fifty states and with over twenty thousand separate school districts, we could reasonably expect some variation on what constitutes the core of a curriculum. The lack of truly significant variation is another strong example of cultural hegemony, of beliefs so strongly ingrained that they are beyond examination and criticism.

Certainly, as educators we know that the more we know, the less sure we become, and that there is a high correlation between an academic's intellectual strength and humility. We are not equating humility with modesty; to be humble is not to disregard one's achievements but to be awed and amazed at the intricacies and complexities of what is being studied. Instead of teaching students of the limitations of our research techniques and the extent of our ignorance, we have grossly distorted the state of intellectual life by utilizing a curriculum that has been accepted as true and valid. We need not only to teach what we claim to know but to speak to what we know we don't know. In *On Hearing Mahler's Ninth Symphony*, Lewis Thomas speaks to this issue:

> I suggest that the introductory courses in science, at all levels from grade school through college, be radically revised. Leave the fundamentals, the so-called basics, aside for a while, and concentrate the attention of all students on the things that are not known. You cannot possibly teach quantum mechanics without mathematics, to be sure, but you can describe the strangeness of the world opened up by quantum theory. Let it be known, early on, that there are deep mysteries, and profound paradoxes, revealed in their distant outlines, by the quantum. Let it be known that these can be approached more closely, and puzzled over, once the language of mathematics has been sufficiently mastered
>
> Teach at the outset, before any of the fundamentals, the still imponderable puzzles of cosmology. Let it be known, as clearly as possible, by the youngest minds, that there are some things going on in the universe that lie beyond comprehension, and make it plain how little is known.
>
> Do not teach that biology is a useful and perhaps profitable science; that can come later. Teach instead that there are structures squirming inside all our cells, providing all the energy for living, that are essentially foreign creatures, brought in for symbiotic living a billion or so years ago, the lineal descendants of bacteria. Teach that we do not have the ghost of an idea how they got there, where they came from, or how they evolved to their present structure and function. The details of oxidative phosphorylation and photosynthesis can come later.

Teach ecology early on. Let it be understood that the earth's life is a system of interlining, interdependent creatures, and that we do not understand at all how it works. The earth's environment, from the range of atmospheric gases to the chemical constituents of the sea, has been held in an almost unbelievably improbable state of regulated balance since life began, and the regulation of stability and balance is accomplished solely by the life itself, like the internal environment of an immense organism, and we do not know how that one works, even less what it means. Teach that. (1983:151–52)

This is a formulation in which humility is an asset and a strength rather than a sign of weakness or timidity. There is another sense in which we need to consider humility as an ally to our quest for a life of meaning. We need to be humble about our accomplishments and our specialness. We have a right to be proud of ourselves as a people who have struggled for justice and freedom, as a people who have enriched our lives by technical advances such as the telephone and the automobile, and as a people who have devised a technology that has improved our health with such products as penicillin and snowplows. As a people, however, we need to be humbled by the reality that we have enslaved and tortured other humans, that we have put our health and environment in peril by dint of human effort, and that we live in a world where huge numbers of people—tens of millions of them—live the hell of starvation, pestilence, and degradation. With all our genius, with all our brilliance, and yes, with all our education, we as a people face the real possibility of extinction by several scenarios such as war, starvation, and ecological catastrophe.

There is yet another facet to the importance of humility to the educational process. It is certainly part of our faith as Americans, as pragmatists, engineers, optimists, and responsible people searching for existential meaning, that we can and should intervene in nature to create a joyful and abundant society. However, we have reason to be humbled by those efforts. We have encountered viruses which adapt to overcome antibiotics and pesticides, and we have seen disastrous ecological effects at attempts to change the natural rhythms of the life cycle.

As basic and profound as these humbling experiences are, none is more basic than the humbling that has accompanied the loss of a divine perspective. With the Enlightenment came the attempts to replace religious and spiritual frameworks with human ones. We have developed theories of natural law, elaborated a variety of orientations with humanism at the core, and have in the process created a number of paradigms of immense significance, vitality, and wisdom (e.g., Marxism, Freudian thought, and existentialism). However, as Richard Rubenstein's (1975) *The Cunning of History* so tragically demonstrates, the substitution of the state for God, and the absence of a law higher than man's, led, however inadvertently and unintendedly, to Auschwitz. Left to our devices, we have failed miserably to replace the myths of creation, meaning, and redemption that we have been so clever and brilliant in discrediting. We have become intensely aware of one of our most fiendishly clever inventions—namely, profound alienation. We first obliterated our path and now curse the fact that we are lost, although we still insist that we can create better, faster, newer paths. However, it is not only the paths that have been blurred; more important, in the frantic effort to develop new paths we have forgotten our destination.

Ironically, the only significant movement to involve religious concerns with the schools does not at all respond to the intellectual necessity for a posture of awe and reverence of the mysteries of life and of the universe.

Rather, many politicians have seized upon school prayer as an issue in the arrogance that God and America have a special relationship and that the spiritual search is to be reified by ritualistic affirmation of a particular and narrow religion. This movement is another example of our anti-intellectual impulse. Since serious spiritual inquiry is as suspect and threatening as serious intellectual inquiry, we are deflected to the formulistic, distracting, and ultimately less threatening issue of prayer. Serious religious and intellectual inquiry cannot tolerate arrogance, nor can it co-exist with the smugness and satisfaction of status quoism. Humility ought not to lead to modesty and timidity, as we have said, but quite the opposite, for it is the recognition of how little we know and have accomplished that ought to lead us to protest, to stir, to excite, and to act. It is arrogance that leads to stillness and silence (and vice versa), and humility that leads to agitation and response.

The last aspect of humility I wish to discuss does merge into the area of timidity, indecision, and fear. There is the kind of humility, more aptly called loss of faith that comes from those who are unable to find meaning and direction in life. We speak directly to the phenomenon of alienation—the term often applied to a series of feelings and attitudes involving a rejection of traditional creation and meaning myths. This tends to produce a sense of life as empty, absurd, devoid of meaning, as well as an inability to identify with natural or social forces, which brings on feelings of anxiety, loneliness, and dread. Alienation also gets expressed in the fragmentation of lives that is reflected in the concepts of role, role differentiation, and role conflict. We divide our time and consciousness into various compartments: we have work time and leisure time; attitudes toward family which are different from attitudes toward colleagues, ideals that we can express in the living room but not in the workplace. Religion is to be private and, for that matter, so probably should politics; when we do express our religious sentiments it is to be done in a particular place at a particular time, and political opinions are most appropriately expressed on Election Day. We are bored (if not appalled) by those who try to bring political and moral issues into discussion of popular culture or the fine arts.

The combination of the loss of religious faith, disenchantment in the principles and processes of the Enlightenment, and the fragmentation that emerges from industrialism and bureaucracy has led many of us searching for coherence and meaning in a state of bewilderment and frustration. We surely do not seek and value this alienation, for indeed our literature and social criticism is full of descriptions of the destructive and paralyzing effects of alienation, anomie, and despair.

Schools, however, do more to nurture than to overcome alienation as they are in fact a major source of the fragmentation and absurdity: Some of this is expressed in the way students are expected to respond to the schools' demands: "You just can't study what interests you"; "if you can't pass math you can't play basketball"; "Work hard now for your future"; "When you get into the real world. . ."; etc.

We also see alienation in the very structure of the school curriculum: The harsh separation of courses and subjects not only is of a dubious nature intellectually but tends to perpetuate the myth of hard and fast intellectual compartments. Having a separate physical education program actually accentuates the false dualism of mind and body; the separation of English and social studies serves the same process in a parallel way for "fact" and "fiction." The stress on pleasing teacher with "right answers" reifies and externalizes knowledge, which deprives students from articulating their *own personal* knowledge and their relationships with other knowledge. Urging students to work hard and to do well in areas in which they have little or no interest or ability is a way of encouraging mindless, instrumental behavior.

Alienation/Commitment

Perhaps it is more what schools do not do in this area that is more damaging and problematic than what they do. In its rigid and manic concerns with facilitating the individual pursuit of socioeconomic success and preserving the existing social and political frameworks, the schools have come to see their curriculum and other practices as instrumental to those goals. Indeed, it is the techniques themselves that have come to be revered rather than that which has ultimate significance. Most teachers and administrators will deny that material success represents their conception of the Ultimately Significant, while at the same time it is likely they will strongly defend helping students to adapt to and succeed in the current culture as realistic and reasonable. However, such discussions usually end when the question is raised of what they do believe to be of ultimate significance or when the basic issue is posited as the necessity to integrate the ultimate with educational processes.

My belief, however, is that the inability of such a conversation to go on does not mean that educators do not view these issues as important and relevant, but rather it represents conflict and confusion on the issues themselves. In fact, the major crisis for educators is the same as it is for the larger culture—namely, the reluctance or inability to make lasting and profound moral commitments that can energize and legitimize our day-to-day lives. Educators mirror the pain and anguish that are consequences of alienation; they are aware of its corrosive and corrupting potentialities and are often sensitive to historical, intellectual, and ideological dimensions of this crisis. They are also very much aware of the dangers of the glib and facile "solutions" to the problem that come mostly from the far Right. Many educators are aware of the complexities involved in finding meaning (some of them are humble), and most are conscious of the political fallout that comes from making sharp shifts in the school program (many of them are fearful).

The culture and its educators are faced with a very serious problem given their alternatives. They can go on as they have, and accept conventional notions of reality but to do so is not only to fail to stem alienation but actually to deepen and widen it. The alternative of taking active steps to overcome despair and emptiness perforce involves the search for, and the affirmation of, an overarching moral and spiritual framework that provides a center of meaning for the culture. This alternative involves serious political, personal, and intellectual risks given the division of opinion, the diversity of subcultures and religious affiliations, and the volatility and seriousness of the issues. However, it is my conviction that we as educators must address these problems as part of our professional ethic, and that our response should be one of humility not of avoidance, of courage not of arrogance, and of commitment not of alienation. We simply cannot allow the educational process, which has at its deepest roots a concern for meaning, to become a mechanism for pursuing a way of life we already know is rich with the possibilities of despair, absurdity, and destruction. Educators must come to see themselves not as apologists for this way of life, nor technicians in its service, but as moral leaders who can with others continue humanity's struggle to create a vision of meaning and fulfillment.

Displacement/Complacency

As I have indicated, such a responsibility involves great risks; although we must also remember that not accepting this responsibility is equally risky. A major problem in assuming this responsibility is that it clearly involves disrupting smugness and self-deception. In this problem we again meet paradoxical traditions and values in our culture, for although we value "peace and quiet," calmness, serenity, stability, and the status quo, we are also a culture of protest, dissent, and even revolution. We are, after all, a people who continue to be strongly influenced by the Puritans, who saw themselves in the line of the biblical prophets with the responsibility to storm against the transgressions of the culture. It is not only that our political tradition has revealed the necessity and value of disruption (recall Jefferson's comment that we needed to have a series of revolutions), but our personal experience and psychology are sensitive to the dangers of complacency and of standing pat. Our ambivalence about the importance of disruption is well described in Janet Gunn's (1984) paper on the works of Flannery O'Connor. In this paper, Gunn characterizes O'Connor as one who believes that before redemption must come the pain of displacement, the agony that is the inevitable consequence of confronting seriously and concretely the requirements of a redemptive life. These requirements include a jolting awareness of the "sin" or the gap between our highest aspirations and how we actually live. Gunn points out that the major figures in O'Connor's stories time and again are given the opportunity for redemption as a consequence of seriously disruptive events—a sudden death, a kidnapping, the intrusion of a new powerful person into a hither-to stable community/family.

Teachers also know of the educative power and significance of blowing up the ice on the lake of complacency and are also very conscious how peaceful and untroubled life on Lake Placid can be. They also know that the surrounding community does not like to have its calm interrupted by explosions, however muffled and remote. Educators must come to recognize that the unexploded ice is a menace, that it can choke the life around it by chilling the hopes for a new and refreshed life.

Faith/Reason

Making commitments not only involves disruption but also requires that we have sufficient confidence and investment in those commitments to sustain us in the difficult struggle to act on them. If we accept the vital importance of setting our work within a set of moral commitments, then we must remember why it is so difficult to make them. We must have compassion for each other and accept as part of our assumption that the matter of making such commitments is of great significance to each of us and that it is very likely that many of us have struggled mightily with this issue. Making moral commitments is not the same as deciding to get more exercise or resolving to read the newspaper more carefully. The difficulty in making such commitments stems from very deeply rooted phenomena, such as the powerful influence of the Enlightenment (e.g., faith in rationality and science, revelation of corruption in religious and moral institutions); the cynical exploitation of religious and moral beliefs; the failure of religious and moral institutions to respond to moral crises in the society); and the elaboration of the hidden forces that shape our lives (e.g., the work of Freud and Marx). It was first said by Nietzsche, and more recently by theologians, that God is dead. Michael Harrington (1983) has elaborated on that metaphor in *The Politics at God's Funeral,* in which he discusses man's effort to fill that void with humanly constructed rather than revealed cosmologies.

There are, of course, many who have experienced a revealed God, and they represent a group of increasing significance and power. There is an even larger group who are open and perhaps eager for spiritual revelation. We as a people yearn for powerful religious experiences and many of us are open to the power of the nonrational. Yet we are a stubbornly rational people and are committed to approaching truth by the path of science, logic, and rigorous thinking. In fact, our rational sophistication has developed to the point that many of us are persuaded scientifically and logically of the limitations of science and logic! We have been reminded of the necessity to make value and moral judgments that transcend scientific and technical criteria and have learned that much of science rests on a number of at least so far unverified (or even unverifiable) assumptions. It is our physicists who have become our modern mystics with their talk of mysterious forces in an expanding universe of "black holes" and "quarks" that probably began and will end not with a whimper but with a "big bang."

Schools take on the mantle of science and rationality even when they absurdly and crudely distort their essences. Their pretentiousness includes their claims for intellectual integrity and to value the rigorous demands of scholarship. It is clear that schools have botched this effort (e.g., a recent study estimates that less than 50 percent of Americans are more than marginally literate), but I want here to mention that there is another educational orientation that they have yet to botch because they have not seriously addressed it. I speak of the issue of the appropriateness of reasoning from a faith, of the possibility of helping people to consider the major question that transcends science. We are not here opposing faith to reason but rather examining the foundation and underpinnings of reason, that which provides its roots and substance. Nor do we wish to glibly equate faith with creed or a belief structure; faith here is meant to be closer to the concept of trust than to belief.

William Fowler's *Stages of Faith* is an eloquent and valuable source for the description and analysis of this phenomenon. At one point he describes faith as "a person's way of showing himself or herself in relation to others against a background of shared meaning and purpose" (1981:4). In another section of the book he cites H. Richard Niebuhr's (1960) notion that faith emerges out of an initial concern for caring and trusting and "the search for an overarching integrating and grounding trust in a center of value and power sufficiently worthy to give our lives unity and meaning" (1981.5). Thus faith has more to do with the questions of in what and to whom do we commit our trust and our loyalty. Fowler quotes Wilfred Cantwell Smith (1963) on this distinction: "Faith, at once, deeper and more personal than religion, is the person's or group's way of responding to transcendent values and power as perceived and grasped through the forms of the cumulative tradition. Faith and religion, in this view, are reciprocal" (1981:9).

Fowler posits a concept of "faithing" as a mode of knowledge and argues that people differ not so much on the basis of having faith or not having faith, but in the nature and quality of their "faithing" process. "Faith is the forming of images of and relations to that which exacts qualitatively different initiatives in our lives than those that occur in strictly human relations" (1981:33). Smith's pointed question gives further insight to this notion: "What hope and what ground of hope animate you and give shape to the force field of your life and to how you move in it?" (quoted in Fowler 1981:14).

These are clearly elusive concepts, but I believe that most people have struggled with these phenomena with or without a mediating conceptual language. However, it is not only that we want to have deep faith and find it very difficult to authentically commit ourselves to some faithing process, for many of us have difficulty in the various discourses of faith. The schools have either abandoned or ridiculed other paths to truth than conventional (if not outdated) scientific models, but more significantly they have totally ignored the search for wisdom.

We can tell a lot about a culture and its institutions by the quality of its hypocrisies. As we have stressed over and over again, it seems quite clear that the schools' major preoccupation is with perpetuating a system based on the individual, competitive struggle for material success. This goal, however, is masked in the rhetoric of concern for knowledge and truth, and hence the schools do not even pretend to seek higher truth, higher meaning, or wisdom. Indeed, the term "wise" has come to have a pejorative connotation as in the well known fact that schools that do not tolerate "wise guys."

We as a people have come to see that reason and knowledge can be used in evil ways even as we either deny the existence or are confused about the meaning of the concept of evil. We prefer wisdom and knowledge at a time when the concept of wisdom is discounted in educational institutions. There surely has been a knowledge and information explosion that, ironically enough, is presented as a problem. Sometimes this problem is defined as a technical one (e.g., access and dissemination); however, the essential problems are ones of interpretation, significance, and implications of knowledge. We search for context and yet our educational energies are directed to filling in the blanks. Schools present education less as an endeavor to create a vision of meaning than as a paint-by-numbers exercise.

This narrow approach to education surely undermines major tenets of serious scholarship such as care, precision, uncertainty, humility, awe, and passion. Scholars are often people who are very much in touch with their matter of faith, and it is that which accounts for the devotion and dedication of their work. Scholars typically do not equate scholarship with knowledge, facts, and data, but instead pursue models, theories, and schemata that give order and meaning to otherwise random observations. What the schools have done in their stress on textbooks, right answers, minimum standard performance, and external controls is more of a perversion of scholarship than a celebration of it.

If this distorted notion of education does not serve scholarship and the pursuit of truth, it does serve other, more pressing items on the school's agenda. Pseudoscience, narrowly defined academic goals, and predetermined answers are antithetical to serious educational inquiry, but they are excellent ways of facilitating the emphasis on grading and competition. They are effective control mechanisms and give a legitimate flavor to the hierarchical power structure in schools. Thus, schools are not terribly interested in faith or reason, truth or wisdom, but use them as part of the rhetoric of justifying the direction of enormous energy to the rather vulgar duty of helping people to make money and raise their status (thereby, no doubt, also helping to catch up with Taiwan and to thwart Soviet expansionism).

This, as the old saying goes, leaves the culture up the creek without a paddle. As we drift toward the currents of destruction, we search for stability and a new course. This predicament is not likely to be resolved entirely, as some suggest, by new technical or scientific breakthroughs, though they will help. The more fundamental and much more difficult task is that of setting the course, of having a clearer sense of direction that can give us the courage, the energy, and the hope to make the effort and sacrifices worthwhile.

What I have tried to present in this chapter can be described as an essay on cultural confusion, self-deception, and self-defeat. We have seen that we are confused and perplexed by the inherent dilemmas involved in making moral choices. It has been pointed out that the difficulty in moral decision making is actually less severe in choosing between right and wrong (it is clear that we want to choose right though aware that to do so may involve other negative consequences) than having to choose between and among rights. Moral confusion comes with the territory, and yet the schools have done precious little to help us to cope with the confusion. Indeed, we continue to exacerbate the confusion by our contradictory behavior—our insistence on wanting to behave righteously while not being able, willing, to do so.

Self-deception/Professional Responsibility

There is a point at which confusion and doubt intersect with self-deception or what Sartre calls "bad faith" (1956:67). Walter Brueggemann, a prominent contemporary American theologian, candidly reflects on his own personal experience of this intersection:

> As I reflect on ministry and especially my ministry, I know in the hidden places that the real restraints are not in my understanding or in receptivity of other people. Rather the restraints come from my own unsureness about this perception. I discover that I am as bourgeois and obdurate as any to whom I might minister. I like most others am unsure that the royal road is not the best and the royal community the one which governs the real "goodies." I, like most of the others, am unsure that the alternative community inclusive of the poor, hungry, and grieving is really the wave of God's future. We are indeed "like people, like priests" (Hos. 4:9). That very likely is the situation among many of us in ministry and there is no unanguished way out of it. It does make clear to us that our ministry will always be practiced through our conflicted selves. (1978:111–12)

This honest and courageous statement stands as a model for both anticipating and dealing with the human inevitability of self-deception. The phenomenon of self-deception is an intriguing and elusive one since it involves the paradox of our being aware of our own duplicity (i.e., why we knowingly deceive ourselves). Herbert Fingarette (1969) deals extensively and insightfully with this paradox in *Self Deception*. He suggests that a way out of this paradox lies in a full understanding of three major concepts: "spelling out," "engagement," and "avowal." "Spelling-out" has to do with being explicit, thorough, and forthcoming about one's beliefs and values (1969:39), while "engagement" refers to one's active participation in life (1969.40). "Avowal" is the process of explicitly defining one's self in a purposeful and responsive way (1969:70). Fingarette explains a self-deceiver as one who "will be provoked into a kind of engagement which, in part or in whole, the person cannot avow *as his* engagement, for to avow it would apparently lead to such intensely disruptive, distressing consequences as to be unmanageably destructive to the person. The crux of the matter here is the *unacceptability* of the engagement to the person" (1969:87).

Note the significance of taking responsibility and the risks that are involved, namely, to the point of considering them to be destructive. It is this fear, according to Fingarette, which leads some to self-deception, to the refusal to spell out. "The policy of refusing to spell out one's engagement is the most visible feature of self-deception. Though highly visible, it is a concomitant of a far more fundamental maneuver. The self-deceiver is one who is in some way engaged in the world but who disavows the engagement, who will not acknowledge it even to himself as his. That is, self-deception turns upon the personal identity one accepts *rather than the beliefs one has*" (1969:66–67; italics added).

Self-deception not only involves denial, fear, avoidance, and fragmentation, but it is also ultimately self-defeating. When we deceive ourselves and our community, we undermine our efforts to act upon our deepest beliefs. We can, of course, be cynical and consider our self-deception to be part of the sublimation process, i.e., we need a socially acceptable justification to cover up our self-serving needs for control, domination, greed, and lust. It is also possible to psychologize this problem, to see self-deception as neurotic or pathological. One could also despair at the extraordinary entanglements of life, shrug our collective shoulders, and press the *c'est la* vie button. However, as Fingarette points out, the consequences of self-deception are enormous:

> Purity of heart is to will one thing and to will it absolutely—it is the self as the unity of the entire individual acknowledged as self; it is thus the finding of the eternal, of that which endures change and even within change; it is the condition of the truly ethical life, and ultimately of the truly saving religious life. Insofar as the person fails even to avow, or disavows his individual engagements, he is to that extent immersed in the particular and immediate, has abdicated the harmonious unity and synthesis of the ethical, and is in despair. It is in the nature of despair that it is double-mindedness. Whether we view the self-deceiver as (inwardly) evasive in a clever way towards himself, or whether we view him externally as nothing but engagement in the temporal, the particular, the immediate, there is a fundamental multipliness in his existence. In either case, he is seen as the victim, within time, of particularity, rather than as the eternal surveyor of time and multiplicity. There is thus in self-deception a genuine subversion of personal agency and, for this reason in turn, a subversion of moral capacity. (196:141)

The Responsibility of Educators in a Time of Cultural Crisis

As educators we must have the courage to confront the human impulse and necessity for self-deception and have the wisdom to discern its destructiveness. We have special responsibilities to be sensitive to the psychological and moral pressures that push us to deny or discount the harsh realities of our professional lives.

As educators we must also confront ourselves as both oppressor and oppressed. We must have the courage not only to examine the nature and impact of the culture but also to consider how we as individuals reflect the values and norms of the culture. As educators we often are the system, even as we are both its cause and effect. As the contemporary German theologian Dorothee Soelle puts it in referring to those in the ministry:

It is not enough to criticize property rights and the import duty imposed on manufactured goods from developed countries, so long as we, as "powerless" individuals,
are not able to clarify how we are entangled in the general structures, that is, how we
profit from the structures and how we conform to the introverted norms that we regard as self-evident—for example, the norms of achievement, consumerism, reasons
of state and pass them on to others, even when we reject them privately and verbally.
A criticism of society which does not take account of this introversive mechanism,
and which therefore does not detect and give expression to the capitalist or the concentration camp guard that is in each one of us, but instead creates enemies in hostile
projections, I consider political propaganda, plain and simple, and not a political
interpretation of the gospel. (1974:92)

This is by no means to say that education is the "solution" to these problems or
that educators are the only or even the most important people in the process of
dealing with our social and cultural crises. I am saying that there is very definitely
an educational aspect to them and I am reiterating my faith that serious educational inquiry can in fact provide the necessary, if not sufficient, resources to participate in the re-creation our world. I will also insist that educators must respond
to these concerns within the canons of our professional ethics: we are educators
not indoctrinators; we persuade, we do not force; we are primarily social and
moral leaders, not partisan politicians; we examine political, religious, and moral
issues, we do not promulgate political, religious, and moral dogma.

And yet, in this matter of professional ethics we once more confront the heart
of our crisis: the difficulty of creating a vital, authentic, and energizing vision of
meaning in a context of significant diversity, pluralism, division, skepticism, dogmatism, and even nihilism. As educators we must simultaneously address these issues personally and communally as we profess to give our students insight into
these questions. To avoid the issues is to further the confusion, heighten the self-
deception, and contribute to our downfall.

The rest of this book represents one educator's effort to develop an educational
response to the issues as I have so far described and defined them. In order to
present specific educational suggestions and ideas, I have found it necessary to
offer a broader theoretical framework that informs the notions of curriculum and
instruction that are presented in the final chapters. This framework represents an
effort to develop language and concepts that can provide a working consensus
needed to facilitate creative and constructive responses, but not enough to foster
uniformity and standardization. We must, therefore, begin with the fundamental
issues of spiritual and moral values and necessarily confront this extremely sensitive, crucial, and volatile area. It is certainly a risky and dangerous zone filled with
land mines, but since it is also populated by time bombs, avoiding the area is at
least as dangerous.

4

A RELIGIOUS AND MORAL FRAMEWORK
FOR AMERICAN EDUCATION

The question . . . for any theology is whether it makes men more capable of love, whether it encourages or obstructs the liberation of the individual and the community.
DOROTHEE SOELLE, *Political Theology*

Men and women cannot decently live by demythologies alone.
MICHAEL HARRINGTON, *The Politics at God's Funeral*

Man's capacity for justice makes democracy possible; but man's inclination to injustice makes democracy necessary.
REINHOLD NIEBUHR

If God did not exist we would have to invent him.
VOLTAIRE

If God did exist we would have to abolish Him.
MIKHAIL BAKUNIN

Religious, Moral, and Mythic Language

My description and analysis of current American culture has emphasized its inter-penetration with our public schools. A great deal of this analysis has a religious and moral character to it, and in this chapter I will elaborate on the rationale and nature of our religious and moral interpretations. In addition, I will present and propose a set of religious and moral principles that I hope can serve to inform our educational policies and practices. It is my general position that education is at root a moral endeavor and that its present crisis is best seen as such in order to reflect not only on the educational process but on the larger culture as well.

The Moral and Spiritual Crisis in Education

Although this is not the place to attempt a definitive or even a thorough explication of what is meant by the terms "moral" and "religion, it is quite appropriate to deal with the ways I am using these terms. In this work I am very much aware of the powerful and varied connotative meanings these words evoke and will try to be sensitive to their inherent complexities and subtleties. For purposes of clarifying my own meaning, however, I take moral to be a term that focuses on principles, rules, and ideas that are related to human relationships, to how we deal with each other and with the world. Moral can be used prescriptively (e.g., people should love each other) as well as descriptively (e.g., she treats him with little respect). In both cases the concern is for the attitudes, values, and behaviors that constitute one's way of being with (other people). Moral questions and issues are largely people-to-people ones, and are hence of a social and political nature, but they also extend to how we deal with all our neighbors (i.e., the animal kingdom, the environment, and nature). Moral theories and codes serve to regulate and legitimize proper ways of dealing with these human relationships.

I am using religious in reference to ideas, principles, and tenets that have to do with our relations with forces beyond the known world. Religious questions are concerned with our relations with the cosmos and with the unknown or unknowable. Religions serve to explain fundamental questions of origin, meaning, and ultimacy and to generate human responses to these formulations.

Religion and moral orientations differ in how these two realms relate to each other. Some religions (e.g., Judaism) seek to strongly integrate moral and ethical behavior with basic religious belief, while others (e.g., Hinduism) put far greater stress on metaphysical and spiritual concerns. There are, of course, moral theories that are not based on a particular set of religious beliefs—for example, the notions of natural philosophy and humanism rest on assumptions that speak to the human or natural determination of ethical behaviors and norms. It is also important to note that we are for the most part using these terms heuristically to facilitate communication. We also note the ubiquity of these concepts across time and space and indeed there are those who maintain that the essential human characteristic is humanity's interest in and capacity for creating religious and moral images, metaphors, and schema.

However, their ubiquity in no way means consensus on either their meaning or their significance. It is obvious, for example, that there are formulations that reject religious inquiry as spurious and distracting ("religion is the opiate of the masses"), just as there are those who reject moral theories as magical thinking ("we need to go beyond freedom and dignity"). Indeed, as educators and citizens we must confront the possibility of moral and religious language becoming reified through the process of critical neglect and reductionism. I will be emphasizing the moral and religious dimensions of education and will urge my colleagues to celebrate certain religious and moral principles. In this process, I will not endorse or promote any particular religious sect (Judaism, Christianity, Buddhism), but will seek to support and sustain key principles and formulations that cut across religions, sects, denominations, and ideologies.

It is also important to point out the difference between "religion" as a theoretical construct and its institutional manifestations (i.e., religion is not synonymous with mosque, temple, church, synagogue). It is a difference that parallels the distinction between education and schooling, in that the institution of schools, although clearly connected to education, has an important number of organizational, political, fiscal, and cultural concerns which are at best only indirectly related to strictly educational concerns. There are people who feel strongly that schools do not provide "real" education, just as there are people who see the church, synagogue, mosque, or temple as the wrong place to find a truly religious experience. I do not in any way want to deal with a significant critique of institutionalized religion (although it will be very difficult to totally avoid this) but instead wish to focus on religious and moral ideas and images. I very much intend, however, to focus on a critique of institutional education, particularly in its congruity with "true" educational concerns. One can be passionate about the value of education and still (or because of that) be highly critical of the schools. In the same spirit, I ask that those who are highly critical of organized and institutional religion be open to the power and significance of religious ideas, metaphors, concepts, and insights.

Our culture includes in its plethora of significant ideas and orientations a number of formulations that have been named religious and moral in nature. This is a fact of cultural life: our human experience is, in part and, for better of worse, defined by its effort to formulate ideas and practices of ultimate meaning involving cosmological and metaphysical concepts. These formulations generate further formulations, as well as controversy, hostility, counter formulations, and, equally significant, indifference. We need also to point out that twentieth-century America is a culture that not only has a variety of theoretical orientations toward religious and moral issues but is also a highly diverse, pluralistic, complex society with a great number of constituencies and interest groups in perpetual conflict over the protection of their positions.

We have disagreements and disputes, some friendly, some academic, but some others are much less friendly and much more real. Even the "academic" disagreements can become volatile since they touch upon fundamental conceptions of who and how we are to be. No set of issues is as explosive, controversial, emotional, and threatening as moral and religious disputes. None is more vital.

Toward the Development of a Myth

The analysis in the first three chapters reveals contradictions and confusions over our basic values that are marked by self-deception and self-destructiveness. It is my position that our cultural and educational crises are rooted in these and other moral ambiguities and confusions, and we further point out that these moral difficulties emerge from our inability to deal with the even broader and deeper religious or metaphysical bases. Furthermore, I believe that this inability can be conceptualized as our failure to develop an overarching mythos of meaning, purpose, and ultimacy that can guide our work in the creation of a vision of the good, true, and beautiful life. It is also my position that as educators we must actively participate in the process of creating that vision as part of our professional responsibility.

As educators, however, our responsibilities are not simply to promulgate visions but to inquire into them, not just to study them but to be critical and discerning of them—to be contributor, critic, and celebrator. Hence, we cannot in good educational conscience avoid the serious and volatile disputes on religious and moral matters simply because they are controversial, complex, and outrageously perplexing. Quite the contrary: because they are so important and since they beg for awareness, understanding, clarification, and insight, they are central to significant educational inquiry.

Both the culture and educators are caught in a vicious circle: spiritual and moral doubt, confusion, and skepticism edge into despair and frustration, which leads to the fear of nihilism, which in turn leads us to hope and prayer for clear visions which are then quickly subjected to criticism and doubt. So, as educators we have the dual responsibility to examine that circle and to be part of the process that can transform that static circle into a spiral of movement. The crux of the dilemma is to paradoxically have a vision prior to having one, to be able to break the circle without a sense of direction and without breaking faith with our intellectual and political heritage.

I believe, to change the metaphor, that we educators and academics have been playing a "stalemate" game, a game that stresses "defense" where the basic strategy is to keep others from "scoring" by close and constant harassment of those on the "offensive." Such games usually have their action mostly in the middle of the field and in a narrow range of action that consists of modest efforts at developing an offense, which immediately and aggressively are undermined and disorganized by a pressing defense galvanized primarily by an intense desire to keep the "offense" out of "scoring range." When it comes to contests of alternative educational orientations, or of moral/religious frameworks, we usually wind up with a scoreless tie. The academic community has done far better with its oppositional critical capacities than with its creative responsibilities.

This is not to say that we should in any way ease or soften our efforts to be critical, skeptical, wary, precise, and thoughtful. We must, however, complement these skills with the creative and imaginative arts that can provide us with richer, truer, more satisfying schema, models, visions, and paradigms. Criticisms are by themselves necessary but not sufficient conditions for the development of such visions, theories, and orientations. In fact, in some ways the quality of our critical capacities may have been "too" effective in the sense that they have undermined some of the moral and spiritual foundations of our civilization. Our ability to provide equally powerful replacements for those foundations is heightened and perpetuated by a belief (tragically mistaken in my estimation) that it is impossible for us as a people to forge a consensus of religious and moral beliefs that is specific enough to be significantly energizing and meaningful.

Our despair becomes full when we come to believe this pessimistic view, especially when the opposite is the fundamental requirement for any hope for survival and cultural prosperity. It is my strong belief that we have exaggerated the difficulty of creating that consensus and underestimated the powerful cultural forces that seek to pursue (as opposed to impose) moral and religious community. A vital purpose of this book is to facilitate and further such a search for consensus by indicating important areas of potential convergence. I do not believe, however, that failing to note the enormity of the difficulties and perplexities in such an undertaking will at all facilitate this process. I call on colleagues to be open to both our differences and similarities, to convergence and divergence, to criticism and creation.

For me, the most promising aspect of this effort is the general, if implicit, agreement across religious orientations, classes, and ideologies that it is vital and valuable to have some kind of model of ultimate meaning—some way of conceptualizing a response to those critical questions of where did we come from, who are we, and where are we going. It is perhaps gratuitous to point out that there are enormous differences among these conceptualizations, but it is imperative to note that we very much want to, and in fact do, respond to a felt need to provide some narrative explanation of the human condition.

Some prefer to call these conceptual narratives our creation, meaning, and destiny myths, stories designed to help us connect our everyday lives to a cosmology. Myths provide us with stories of creation, meaning, and fate populated by personifications, metaphors, and parables, although some also take them literally. Myths provide bridges between the Other and us—between the absent and the present, between mystery and what is known, between heaven and earth, religion and morality, religion and politics, and so on. Another way of formulating our cultural and educational crisis is to say that we no longer have energizing myths and we seem incapable of creating or sustaining them. Furthermore, it can be said that although we differ on what constitutes a legitimate source of myth and which myths are acceptable, we must recognize that there is a great deal of agreement on the value and need to have such myths. By myth we obviously do not mean ideas that are demonstrably false or wrong but rather imaginative constructions of the meaning of universe and our place in it.

We can and should continue to debate the complexities of the concept of religion and myth, and we can and should continue to study the amazing range of mythic and religious images and beliefs. We can and should, at the same time, recognize the strength and persistence of this ancient, continuous, and ongoing impulse to create meaning systems that give order and direction to our lives. We must not deny that reality by obfuscating arguments about the nature of myths, religions, and moral theories, and neither must we be seduced by soothing and re-assuring myths that lull us into uncritical docility.

The richness of our culture means in effect that we are rich in our mythic tradi-tions, or, put another way, that many metaphysical, religious, and moral traditions have found expression in our lives. We are a polyglot nation that speaks several sub-languages and blends a number of unique histories. Cutting across the score of ethnicities, peoples, cultures, and traditions, one can sense a number of tran-scendent values that amount to elements of a broadly held common heritage, her-itage of common, if not universal, pride and aspiration. This heritage has both commonality and divergence, and, indeed, part of our heritage includes a commit-ment to such a tension. We can broadly categorize this heritage into three parts: political, moral, and intellectual.

Political Heritage

Our political heritage clearly involves a deep and enduring commitment to demo-cratic principles. As a nation we identify ourselves primarily as a democratic soci-ety, as reflected in our major celebrations and in our most cherished images. There is a common rhetoric of the American Revolution being waged on behalf of de-mocracy as enunciated in the Declaration of Independence and their epiphany ex-pressed in the Constitution of the United States of America. The powerful and enduring mythical figures of our political pantheon (e.g., Washington, Jefferson, Madison, Jackson, and Lincoln) are presented as heroic defenders and nourishers of democracy. Robert Bellah (1975) and others have singled out Abraham Lincoln (especially in his Gettysburg Address) as perhaps the one best able to conceptual-ize in mythic and religious language an image of America as the land of Democ-racy. It has often been pointed out that America was perhaps the first nation to be deliberately founded on a set of principles—principles that are primarily demo-cratic and rooted in a concern for equality, freedom, and justice.

Our democratic heritage celebrates a number of profoundly important political principles such as free speech, freedom of religion and assembly, the preservation of civil rights and, above all else, the principle of government requiring the con-sent of the governed. Here we can see most clearly the close relationship between the political and moral, since democratic principles rest primarily on a major moral principle: the dignity and autonomy of every individual.

Moral Heritage

Our moral heritage, in addition to a commitment to the sanctity of the individual, includes an intense concern for justice, equality, forgiveness, mercy, and, most important, an aspiration for a community infused with love. We are a culture that celebrates and reveres such expressions of moral principles as the Ten Commandments, the Sermon on the Mount, the Declaration of Independence, the Rights of Man, and the United Nations Declaration of Human Rights. We revere the historical Moses, Jesus, and Buddha, the lives of Gandhi, Schweitzer, and Martin Luther King, insofar as they represent the forces of love, equality, justice, compassion, and redemption. Our recent responses to African famine and oppression reflect how deeply these moral commitments lie within us and speak to our strong urge to reach out to the troubled and vulnerable.

Intellectual Heritage

The intellectual heritage that we cherish finds its roots in the Greek passion for the free pursuit of truth. We value freedom of inquiry and expression, we revere creativity and originality, and we urge ourselves to be open and tolerant in the force of conflicting and differing ideas.

We also revere careful, precise, and thorough scholarship; esteem a strong critical capacity; and cherish those who express themselves eloquently. We admire clarity as well as the provocative and the evocative and recognize that the paths to truth are many. We are aware that sometimes these paths crisscross, and that we need to challenge these paths as well as affirm them. Our culture values knowledge and the pursuit of knowledge, and indeed part of our myth (or faith) is that knowledge or truth or science or whatever it is called can help make us free. Many have come to regard the myth of science (read: knowledge) as the worthy successor to the myth of an omniscient God—that is, it is science that can unlock the mysteries of the universe, as well as science and knowledge that can provide us with a life of abundance, peace, and joy.

Here we can see the outlines of how these heritages merge into each other and evoke the outlines of a grand consensual myth. We are a culture that has as part of its heritage a commitment to the development of a life of justice, freedom, and equality that we believe can be built and sustained through love and compassion, utilizing human potential unlocked by the free and rigorous pursuit of truth. Each of these heritages depends on the others—our intellectual heritage provides inspiration for our political system, and our political heritage requires an informed and free citizenry.

Let us once again reiterate that we do not intend to gloss over serious differences and conflicts within this broad heritage. We certainly have deeply significant differences in our conceptions of key concepts such as democracy, justice, and equality as well as profoundly varying ideas on what constitutes valid knowledge. We also have enormously important differences of opinion on how best to relate these principles to specific policies and practices. Many would say persuasively that if there is a consensus that constitutes our heritage, it is so broad and at such an abstract level that the only true measure of consensus is that which can obtain in the context of practice. We must not in any way minimize or paper over these vital and important differences, and we must also be reminded of the important areas of commonality that are the convergent sources of our divergences. Perhaps most importantly of all, it is critical to test whether there is real consensus on the broad outlines of our heritage and to challenge our commitments to the heritage. It would be, for example, a bracing no-lose situation if people were to have continuous debates and contests on the best possible ways of enhancing justice, provided it was clear that justice was the goal and not the surrogate.

One way that can be used to determine the nature and strength of these basic commitments is to probe even more deeply; to seek out the nature of one's basic orientation to meaning, to human nature, and to humanity's origins and destinies. We can gain enormous insight into our political, moral, and social views by examining our metaphysical assumptions, our religious outlook, or perhaps the nature of our myths. For this reason we must now turn to the matter of our religious, mythic heritage.

Religious Heritage

Our history is one in which the terms religion and church have from time to time become intertwined with our daily lives. We say officially that we are a nation "under God," that we trust in God; yet, we constitutionally have mandated separation of church and state. We are a culture with significant religious traditions, but our society is for the most part officially secular. The reasons for this lie in our tangled historical roots, which we will briefly discuss in the knowledge that this will, at best, be a cursory glance at a complicated and highly textured set of issues and events.

From the earliest times our Puritan ancestors made no separation between church and state, and as Sacvan Bercovitch (1978) makes clear, they saw the colonization and development of the new world as an opportunity to further the Puritan revolution in a wilderness that was a nascent Eden. The Puritans were the first, but by no means the last, to see America as having a special place in the divine consciousness. As Bercovitch documents, the nation of America as the new Jerusalem, being specially graced by God, of America as having a divine destiny and a special responsibility to speak (and act) for the Almighty, is a particularly enduring myth that continues to permeate our beliefs and practices. Thus, we have as part of our religious heritage a tradition that speaks sometimes arrogantly about a sacred America, blessed and graced by God with special responsibilities and resources to do God's work, at least as some Christians saw and see it.

At the same time we have a religious heritage that strongly values religious freedom and diversity. Although the story that people came to America in the sixteenth and seventeenth centuries because it tolerated religious diversity is largely wrong (people came to practice their own religions, not to tolerate others), the early significant intolerance gave way to political realities. Given the number of different sects, each pursuing its own ways, the culture developed a modus vivendi that emphasized toleration and a live-and-let-live spirit rather than one of outright hostility and repression. The American Revolution came at the height of the Enlightenment, a cluster of viewpoints that included a harsh critique of established religions as oppressive, corrupt, and stultifying. Given the fears of both a strong central government and an established central church, it is not surprising that the famous wall of separation was built into the First Amendment of the Constitution. It is important to note that although the First Amendment built the wall around the federal government, the policy of established churches in individual states persisted until 1832.

Our history is also marked by significant and religious (as well as cultural and racial) intolerance, violence, and bigotry, most dramatically exemplified by anti-Catholic, anti-Semitic, anti-black movements such as the Ku Klux Klan. Furthermore, there continues to be deep suspiciousness of certain religious groups as organized religions become identified more strongly with volatile political issues (e.g., civil rights, abortion, and nuclear testing). Historically, then, we can safely say that our religious heritage includes, in addition to significant reverence and piety, a history of theocracy, religious intolerance, disestablishmentarianism, and religious pluralism.

Many recent sociological analyses of religion in America have focused on the essentially middle-class nature of organized religion and its role in legitimating and sustaining mainstream American culture. Bellah (1975) has written about the American civil religion as an amalgam of certain national and patriotic rituals and symbols with religious symbols, such as expressed in the holidays of Thanksgiving and Memorial Day. Herberg (1960) and Cuddihy (1978) write of a consolidation process in which it has become acceptable and expected that an American very likely will be either a Protestant, Catholic, or Jew, provided that religious views are expressed as private and personal, thus avoiding contentious cultural conflict and struggle. In these formulations religious ideals and symbols are seen as being co-opted by the secular society and serving as an important means of cultural acculturation, stabilization, and integration. Peter Berger goes further and sees the role of the church in America as part of the process of cultural denial and blindness. He puts it this way: "The churches play a key role in the elaborate social-psychological process by which unpleasant realities are suppressed. . . . But religion also reinforces in a general way, quite apart from ideological distortions, the notion that the world one lives in is essentially and ultimately all right. For lack of a better term, we could say that religion ratifies the "okay world"' (1961:120–21).

The complicated and contradictory nature of our religious heritage (only suggested and hinted at in this very brief glance) is part of the reason why so many people despair at forging an overarching framework of meaning for our culture. Religious differences are real and they are deep—a situation aggravated by the reality that there are forces that consider themselves strongly nonreligious, if not actually antireligious. In spite of these realities I believe that we can significantly narrow the gap of beliefs among these groups. An important dimension to this possibility lies in the conceptual distinction between the sacred and the profane. We here return to a key assumption, namely, that most of the culture supports the idea and value of a mythical system that provide meaning to our existence.

The Sacred and the Profane

Anthropologists and historians of religions who point to the persistence across time and space with which cultures insist on defining what is sacred and what is profane have proposed further evidence of this. Theorists as different as Mircea Eliade and Emile Durkheim have insisted that all cultures develop myths and religions to express their conception of what is ultimate, of what is beyond the boundaries of acceptable behavior, of a line between what is permissible and what is not—between what is "clean" and sacred and what is profane and "dirty." Robert Nisbet has not only noted Durkheim's interest in religion but the more widespread interest among post-Enlightenment figures in religious thought.

> In many ways this is the single most impressive aspect of 19th century interest in religion: its roots in the rationalist or utilitarian-minded who, despite personal indifference or hostility, were able to see religion's profound relation to the structure of human society and to the deepest regions of human consciousness. More than anything else, I think, it is this ethnological, historical, sociological and psychological envisagement of religion that separates the nineteenth from the eighteenth century. (1974:157)

In addressing the centrality of the sacred/profane concept in Durkheim's work, Nisbet cites the work of Fustel de Coulanges, a nineteenth-century scholar of classical civilization: "The heart of religion, Fustel emphasized, is not belief or faith or external authority, but the idea of the sacred; in its first form, the sacred fire. The sacred fire in each family hearth was, in the beginning, the very identity of the family [quoting Fustell. . . . 'It was a religious precept that this fire must always remain pure; which meant literally, that no filthy object ought to be cast upon it, and figuratively, that no blameworthy deed ought to be committed in its presence'" (Fustel, as quoted in Nisbet, p. 162). Nisbet then goes on to discuss how Durkheim came to elaborate this direction as the crux of religions across time and space, as expressed in Durkheim's definition of religion: "A religion is a unified system of beliefs and practices relative to sacred things, that is to say, things set apart and forbidden—beliefs and practices which united into one single moral community called a Church, all those who adhered to them" (quoted in Nisbet 1974:164).

Durkheim, the resolutely agnostic and super-rationalist social scientist, saw the role of religion as crucial, not as a supernatural force but rather as a vital social element in the fulfillment of cultural aspirations. Nisbet summarizes Durkheirn's strong interest in religion as having four aspects.

First religion is necessary to society, not merely in an abstract sense, but as a vital mechanism of integration of human beings and as a realm of unifying symbols. . . . Second, religion is a key element and a basic context of social change. . . . Third, religion's. . . . most fundamental and enduring elements are social. . . . The greatest power of religion lies not in what it teaches man about the after-life or about cosmology but in what are its symbols and rituals, cults and churches and sects of membership in society, the feeling of belonging to what Edmund Burke had called the partnership of the dead, the living, and the unborn. . . . Fourth, there is an unbreakable relation between religion and the origins of human language and thought. (1974:164–65)

Durkheim (as indicated by Nisbet) thus avoids the language of divine revelation and the controversies over the existence of a supernatural being. Instead, he sees religious expression as an inevitable and necessary aspect of the process of developing a society. Religion serves functions, has roles, and reflects the society's expression of what has meaning—what the society can, and wishes to, aspire to and what it can accomplish.

Religionists clearly have a far different perspective and are much more likely to speak of social and cultural processes as secondary rather than as primary concerns. From the perspective of a cosmology of universal creation, meaning, and destiny, religious considerations precede and dominate all others and provide the moral and analytical language of human behavior. Mircea Eliade sums up this perspective in this way,

Whatever the historical context in which he is placed, homo religious always believes that there is an absolute reality, the sacred, which transcends this world but manifests itself in this world, thereby sanctifying it and making it real He further believes that life has a sacred origin and that human existence realizes all of its potentialities in proportion as it is religious—that is, participates in reality. The gods created man and the world, the culture heroes completed the Creation, and the history of these divine and semi divine works is preserved in the myths. By ritualizing social history, by imitating the divine behavior, man puts and keeps himself close to the gods—that is, in the real and the significant. (1959.202)

This sharp difference, of course, represents an eternal argument in the sense that it has been going on for a very long time with every reason (if not hope) that it will continue in the furthest future we can envision. However, here again we must note an important area of consensus, namely that religion is a major part of human thought and experience, that it plays a very important role. I am concerned, as an educator in twentieth-century America, to find ways in which our schools can be energized with images and language that have force and meaning. I am not speaking here as a theologian but as an educator examining what possible efficacy religious and theological language might have for this effort. I share with Michael Harrington a hope that in spite of history, religious ideals can inform and sustain the work of making these ideals manifest and real.

I, like religious people, feel a sense of awe on the communion of the universal, but without a religious interpretation of the origin of that communion. . . . The serious atheistic humanist and the serious religious humanist are, I suspect, talking about the same reality. That these languages differ is not a minor detail to be forgotten by reducing antagonistic philosophies to a vague emotion. Such a promiscuous ecumenism is, of course, empty of content. But that common emotion does offer a common point of political departure. (1983:200)

Harrington goes on to quote Jacques Maritain to support his position on the need for "a coming together on 'common practical notions,' not in the affirmation of the same conception of the world, man, and knowledge but on the affirmation of the same sort of convictions requiring actions. This involves 'a sort of common residue, a sort of unwritten common law, at the point of practical convergence of extremely difficult theoretical ideologies and spiritual traditions' " (1983:203).

Elements of an Emerging Myth

Religion is the greatest utopia, in other words the greatest "metaphysic" that has appeared in history because it is the most grandiose attempt to reconcile in mythological form the real contradictions of historical life: indeed it states that men must have the same "nature," that man in general exists, as he was created by God, and consequently the brother of other men, equal to other men, free among other men, and like other men, and that he can see himself in God, "the auto consciousness" of humanity; but it also states that this is not of this world, but will happen in another (utopian) world. (Antonio Gramsci [as quoted in Henri Desroche 1979: 24])

As educators we can participate or not participate in that important, perplexing, immensely exciting series of debates and arguments on the existence of God, the origins of the universe, the comparative validity of different religions, and so on. Educators may or may not decide that it is appropriate to engage their students in these inquiries. However, all educators can recognize the value and necessity of examining the ways by which our culture has distinguished between the sacred and the profane.

At the very least, all educators should be aware (and reflect that awareness in their practice) of how "religion," "metaphysics," or "conceptions of the sacred" significantly influence our culture. More than that, educators should become more sensitive to the possibility of consensus on the desirability of becoming more aware of shared values and working on increasing and deepening them. Educational communities ought to meditate on the question of what it means to be sacred and how an education might facilitate the quest for what is holy. This book can be seen as an attempt to sacralize the educational process, to imbue it with a spirit of what is of ultimate significance and meaning. We are not talking here about religious education (as in Sunday school), nor about acculturation, but rather about the sacred dimensions and properties of education, of seeing the educational process not in instrumental terms (it gives us more power, status, etc.) but as endowed with those qualities we feel are sacred. I want to begin by stressing that many existing educational ideas can be seen as sacred and, indeed, seeing them in this way can illumine and heighten their significance. I have particularly in mind the centrality of careful, rational, critical, searching, and rigorous thought to the educational endeavor.

The Socratic Tradition

The tradition of intellectual criticism as central to education can be traced to Socrates, as revealed in the continuing reverence we have for what has come to be called the Socratic method. The Socratic method puts great emphasis on clarity and on the thorough examination of propositions and statements, on skepticism, and on logical analysis. Socrates presented himself as a humble person who insisted that the more he studied and learned, the less he knew. He also felt it extremely important to test out the adequacy not only of his own beliefs but those of his fellow citizens. We see in Plato's accounts of these encounters the relentless, persistent, and brilliant displays of unsettling questions and probes that often led people to a state of intellectual bewilderment and devastation (and rage). It is very important to note that this was not simply an intellectual exercise or a way of twitting and teasing, but that this process was of profound spiritual importance to Socrates. Socrates strongly believed that the rigorous study of virtue, especially in its relation to conventional thinking, is crucial to a life of rationality and meaning. He also was careful to affirm his own religious affiliation and saw his role as critical educator as a necessary aspect of fulfilling the wishes of the gods. Thus, Socrates integrated his pedagogy into an educational orientation as it emerged from a social and sacred vision. Critical thinking was not seen primarily as an esthetic or utilitarian matter but more centrally as having political and religious significance.

We are apt to think of the Socratic method as a metaphor for detached, logical, probingly critical thought, but we must remember its religious and political context: Socrates was devoutly religious and a strong supporter of democracy Athenian-style; he felt even at his execution time that his educational efforts were necessary to sustain those beliefs and institutions. The fact that he was charged with a capital offense (subversion of the youth) only accentuates the seriousness with which Athenians viewed educational orientations.

I strongly reaffirm the unquestionable importance of open, thorough, and careful inquiry as the cornerstone of the educational process. I cannot believe that there is any significant number of educators who would challenge the importance of clear and critical thinking to any educational theory. We, however, add to this area of consensus the proposition that critical thinking should be seen as sacred or, at least, as compatible with the sacred.

There is, of course, the religious notion that expression of capacities such as critical thinking reflects divine grace, or perhaps it reflects higher human aspirations.

However, a broader way of expressing the sacred nature of critical thinking is one that Robert J. Ackermann (1985) has noted, namely as that of *"religion as criticism"* (italics added). Ackermann's position is that religion has played an important role in providing critical criteria for judging the moral adequacy of a culture; in participating in the active change process of protest; organization; and in offering social and cultural alternatives. Indeed, he goes on to assert that only those religions that engage in social and cultural criticism can retain their legitimacy and vitality.

> Religions have arisen as legitimate protests against societies and ways of life, providing in the process the overpowering foundations for laying down one's life to improve the lot of humanity. . . . Religion is a perennial source of social critique, but religion . . . always retain[s] the potential of developing pungent social critique, no matter how accommodating a form they have assumed in particular institutional contexts. If religion is to provide the possibility of social critique, it can never be reduced to a set of mechanically understood dogmata, for in that form it would necessarily lose touch with changing social reality . . . Critique does not exhaust religion, but religion that cannot critique is already dead. . . . The main thread of religion may be one of potential opposition or criticism of a surrounding society by the development of a picture of life as how it should be lived. . . . What is being suggested is that the core of religion is potentially critical rather than functional or accommodating. (Ackermann 1985, ix–24)

What we see here is criticism as informed by, and in the interest of, a theory of meaning as opposed to a conception of "critical thinking" as a "skill" apart from meaning and logical procedures devoid of human context. Socrates was not teaching "critical thinking" or "cognitive development"; he would not be interested in coaching the debate team. He was a religious and political leader who took his convictions so much to heart that he was willing to give his life on behalf of an educational process he thought would enrich and sustain those spiritual and moral beliefs. In this sense, I suggest that another possible source of a religious or mythic consensus lies in the significance and value of informed and principled criticism—rigorous, precise, thorough criticism directed at and emerging from a vision of a life of purpose and meaning. It is in this sense that critical reflection can be seen as sacred.

The Prophetic Tradition

The most powerful source for Western culture of this integration of religion and criticism is surely the stirring and intense messages of the Biblical Prophets. These amazing people not only spoke to their times but set the foundations of a tradition that continues to flourish, inspire, excite, and energize. It is a tradition that consciously and passionately combines deep devotion to sacred ideals with a determination to speak out vividly and loudly on the profane—that is, a tradition that insists on crying out against discrepancies between what we value and what we actually

do. The Prophets did not specialize in predicting the future, for they were not endowed with extraordinary powers of clairvoyance. Rather, they were keenly aware
of what were understood to be divine imperatives and very much aware of human
responses to them. Their prophecy lay in their deep understanding of the severe
consequences that were in store for a people who where flaunting and rejecting
their own highest aspirations. Prophets were passionate social critics who applied
sacred criteria to human conduct and, when they found violations of these criteria
they cried out in anguish and outrage.

The most eloquent and insightful scholar of the Biblical Prophets is Abraham
Joshua Heschel (1962), and it is his work that I rely on primarily in my analysis. His
definitive two-volume work titled simply *The Prophets* is a work of soaring power
and haunting beauty written with extraordinary elegance and eloquence. I see in his
interpretation of the Biblical Prophets intriguing possibilities for an educational
framework that combines a sense of the relationship between the sacred and political and cultural realities with a strong reliance on critical consciousness. Heschel
presents the Prophets as social critics who castigate and judge their society, utilizing
the society's own highest goals and deepest values. Prophets re-mind—that is, they
demand that we return to a mindedness that we have affirmed as our vision. They
also urge, prod, dare, and encourage us to change our ways and continue the struggle to create that vision. They moan and curse, but not with despair alone: their
outrage moves us to act and change rather than to be defeated and resigned.

The prophetic voice speaks most directly to issues of justice and righteousness;
it is a voice that not only roars in protest at oppression, inequity, poverty, and hunger but cries out in pain and compassion. It is a voice that haunts us because it
echoes our own inner voice that speaks to our impulse to nourish and care for others. This partly explains why the prophetic voice often produces the anger and resentment that follow our recognition of our failure to sufficiently exercise responsibility (an emotion we sometimes call guilt). The Prophets were religious in the
sense that they were imbued with sacred beliefs on the ultimate meaning of life;
social leaders in the sense that they were keenly aware and interested in historical
and current social, economic, and political events, and educators in that they directed their energies toward increasing public awareness and insight into the ultimate significance of these events. Heschel puts it this way:

> The prophet seldom tells a story, but casts events. He rarely sings, but castigates. He
> does more than translate reality into a poetic key, he is a preacher whose purpose is
> not self-expression or the "purgation of emotion" but communication. His images
> must not shine, they must burn. The prophet is intent on intensifying responsibility,
> is impatient of excuse, contemptuous of pretense and self-pity. His tone, rarely sweet
> or caressing is frequently consoling and disburdening: his words are often slashing,
> even horrid-designed to shock rather than to edify . . . [The Prophet is concerned
> with] wrenching one's conscience from the state of suspended animation. (1962:7)

It is vitally important not to overstate the case for the value of this particular tradition to the development of an educational framework. The Biblical Prophets

must also be considered in the context of a particular history of a particular people in particular times. As educators we are not comfortable with the role of "preachers," nor do we wish to "shock" more than "edify." However, what we can value is the prophets' passion and commitment to persisting values—justice, compassion, and concern for the oppressed; the strong authority (as opposed to power) that their criticism provides; their courage in expressing their convictions so loudly; and the energy and hope that they inspire. It is important to remember that the prophetic voice is one that speaks not only to criticism; it is also a voice of transformation.

> Almost every prophet brings consolation, promise, and hope of reconciliation along with censure and castigation. He begins with a message of doom; he concludes with a message of hope. . . . [H]is essential task is to declare the word of God to the here and now; to disclose the future in order to illumine what is involved in the present. (Heschel 1962:12)

Nor do we have to accept the Prophets' own belief as to the source of their inspiration, mission, and powers (the Bible indicates that Prophets were devout and pious Jews who had direct communication with their God). We can recognize how essential aspects of this tradition have been reflected in other times and places but we can recognize that the prophetic voice has been expressed in a variety of settings either as explicitly recognized or as echoed in other traditions. Surely our history includes oppressive and excessively pietistic expressions of this tradition (e.g., the Puritan colonies). Yet, there is a corresponding theological tradition that seeks to resist religious arrogance and dogmatism. For example, in describing aspects of the work of Paul Tillich, Alvin Porteous makes this point: "The Protestant principle . . . contains the divine and human protest against any absolute claims for a relative reality even if this claim is made by a Protestant church. . . . It is the guardian against the attempts of the finite and conditioned to usurp the place of the unconditional in thinking and acting. It is the prophetic judgment against religious pride, ecclesiastical arrogance, and secular self-sufficiency and their destructive consequences" (1966:129).

When I urge educators to consider and utilize religious language and metaphors in their work, it is clearly meant to be, and must necessarily be, on a selective basis. More to the point, my view is that our work as educators can be significantly enriched by the prophetic voice that speaks not only critically but compassionately, one that also speaks of love, mercy, and forgiveness. Our history and that of our brothers and sisters in other lands and times are marked and blessed by remarkable leaders who have from time to time given full expression to that voice. Two such examples are represented in the persona and movements led by Mohandas K. Gandhi and Martin Luther King. These men emerged from very different religious traditions, but both led political movements directed at human liberation and shared a common vision of the relationship between the sacred and the temporal. They were both able to articulate the growing chasm between modem technological and materialistic society and the quest for justice. Gandhi in India and King in the

United States represented the continuity of a standard of criticism first generated by the Prophets and applied it to the specifics of their particular context. Heschel has characterized this criticism as follows:

> Modern thought tends to extenuate personal responsibility. Understanding the complexities of human nature, the interrelationships of individual and society, of consciousness and the subconscious, we find it difficult to isolate the deed from those circumstances in which it was done. But new insight may obscure essential vision, and man's conscience grows scales: excuses, pretence, self-pity . . . Above all, the prophets remind us of the moral state of a people: Few are guilty, but all are responsible. If we admit that the individual is in some measure conditioned or affected by the spirit of society, an individual's crime discloses society's corruption. (1962:14,16)

Gandhi and King had the courage to call attention to widespread social corruption and to the importance of individual responsibility in contributing to that corruption as well as to their role in bringing on transformation. Both saw the struggle for social justice as divinely willed and focused on universal themes—love, justice, kindness for all. These were holy men who fought political battles passionately and intensely; they rejected the fragmented and alienated modem consciousness in which religious and moral concerns are considered to be private and personal. Their basic approach mirrored much of the prophetic tradition: a direct, clear, ringing denunciation of the evil of the society based on higher principles; a call for direct actions against the existing power structure, utilizing techniques (nonviolence, endurance, petition, fasting, sit-ins) consistent with these high principles: and deep faith in ultimate victory. Gandhi and King represent those who dare to openly challenge the inertia and decay of a corrupt society and who have the audacity to try to hold their society to its commitments.

Such people do not sharply separate the secular and the holy, or theory and practice, but rather they see them in a dynamic dialectical relationship. Prophets like Gandhi and King are very practical people for they are not merely idealists but idealists who insist on the application and materialization of these ideals. They provide a practical answer to those who are skeptical if not contemptuous of the value of abstract ideals. King and Gandhi made us pay moral and spiritual attention to our practices and policies and gave us an opportunity to imbue them with sacred qualities.

A more general model of the prophetic tradition has been delineated by Walter Brueggemann (1978) in his book titled *The Prophetic Imagination,* in which he posits two broad cultural modes, one of which he labels "the prophetic consciousness" and the other "the royal consciousness." In his description of what he calls the "royal consciousness," he cites several examples including the regimes of the Pharaohs, the Solomonic era, and modern American culture. Brueggemann characterizes the consciousness of such cultures as having a sense of "static triumphalism," cultures smugly mired in a self-congratulatory inertness. To support and sustain this royal culture, God is co-opted to provide legitimation and protection. It is a society of affluence for a few and of oppression and exploitation for the many.

The royal consciousness becomes a dominant culture when "now and in every time, [it] is grossly uncritical, cannot tolerate serious and fundamental criticism, and will go to great lengths to stop it" (1978:14). Although it is a politically strong culture, its pietistic self-righteousness has to be propped up by military might, a conscripted God, and heavy insulation from criticism. However, this is "a wearied culture, nearly unable to be seriously energized to new promises from God" (1978:14). The royal consciousness is too proud and smug to change, yet at the same time is unable to conceive that change is possible even if necessary.

In sharp contrast to this cultural mode is what Brueggemann calls the "prophetic consciousness," in which the major emphasis is justice and compassion in a community where basic equality is the goal. In this consciousness, humanity is free to accept its responsibility to create a life of meaning for all and has a cosmology in which God is also free from entanglements with the establishment. This consciousness is energized by its devotion to its principles and its openness to transcendence (i.e., to the possibilities of a re-created world).

The quintessential prophetic image for Brueggemann is reflected in the story of Moses and his leadership of the Hebrews. The youthful Moses seems to have accepted along with both Egyptians and Hebrews, the "static triumphalism" of Pharaoh's rule as immovably entrenched. The great gift (grace) of Moses was that somehow (through what Brueggemann calls divine amazement) Moses came to be able to imagine what had hitherto been thought of as "impossible"—a vision of liberation. Here we note the second major theme of our framework, for not only is criticism vital to prophecy, but so is imagination. Moses has an inspired, highly imaginative conception as he literally creates a "new world" through his imaginative powers, The image is shaped by both moral criticism and moral imagination as Moses "sees" the horrors of captivity and oppression and "foresees" the possibility of liberation. As a prophet, his mission becomes one of raising awareness (very much like the process that Freire [1970, 1973] describes as *conscientization)* of a people who are in despair and unable to consider that the world might be otherwise. Moses tries to persuade Pharaoh peacefully to free the Hebrew slaves in what eventually becomes a battle between two different visions of the sacred.

However, Moses has to contend not only with a rigid and powerful ruler but also with a fearful and skeptical Hebrew community numbed by years of oppression into accepting their situation as tolerable by dint of its seeming permanence. Moreover, Moses is personally torn by self-doubts and a sense of inadequacy to the task. According to Brueggemann, Moses is able ultimately to assume the role of revered audaciously imaginative leader because of the spiritual inspiration (called God in the Bible) that enables him to transcend these fears, doubts, and resistances.

This vision is not limited to a conception of liberation as escape from captivity, but, more important, it imagines an alternative transformative society. Moses, moreover, is not only a dreamer who shares his dreams but a leader who urges his people to dare to make the dream a reality. He arouses, he energizes, he leads, and he participates in the long and arduous process of creating a new community, one centered in divinely inspired commitment to a way of life grounded in the pursuit of justice.

To Brueggemann, the major contribution of Moses and other great prophets is their ability to transform cultures by "holding together criticism and energizing" (1978:14). Prophets show us our deficiencies, failures, and sins, but they offer us hope and possibility by the force of their authority, passion, and commitment. Their authority is powerful to the extent that we accept the sacred quality of their concerns, the beauty of their imagined transformation, and the acuity of their criticisms. Prophets offer conceptions of life that are true, good, and beautiful, and fresh insights into what is involved in creating that life.

Although Brueggemann's book is probably written for an audience interested primarily in religion, I believe it contains a powerful message for educators. He describes a concept of "prophetic ministry," which I believe could just as well serve as a description of what might be called a "prophetic education." This mission (goal, concern, dimension) "is to nurture, nourish, and evoke a consciousness and perception alternative to the dominant culture" (1978:13). This "ministry" (education) involves the dimensions we have described—sharp criticism, dazzling imagination, a sacred perspective, commitment to justice and compassion, hope, energy, and involvement. Freedom does not come, according to the prophets, from adaptation, accommodation, and acceptance, nor does it emerge out of numbness and callousness to injustice. Freedom for the prophets emerges from caring, and lies in hope, possibility, and commitment.

Liberation Theology

The reality and vitality of this tradition is vividly seen and felt in the enormous struggles of Latin America, as expressed in the writings and activities of what has been called liberation theology. This theology emerges out of a struggle to overcome centuries of poverty and oppression rooted in colonialism and exploitation, one that reflects simultaneously how organized religion in this regime has served both as problem and response. Liberation theology is certainly controversial, and though it has deep and widespread support from many Catholic clergy and laypeople, it is often in sharp conflict with the part of the traditional Catholic Church that, if not in league with the existing power structure, is not inclined to resist it.

It is a theology which is very much rooted in the prophetic tradition and, hence, views Jesus as a prophet and the Gospels as an instrument for the deliverance of the poor and the oppressed. Jesus' humanity is stressed, at least as much as his divinity, in his compassion and concern for the poor and in the loving and tender way he relates to them. Jesus in this perspective is critical of a society that is more concerned with the accumulation of wealth and the exercise of power than with the suffering of the needy. To liberation theologists, the first priority for the Church is to feed the hungry and house those without shelter. From this perspective the spreading of the gospel is therefore most appropriately accomplished by acts of caring for the oppressed and resisting the oppressors.

Like other prophetic traditions, this movement is one in which ideals and practice are intertwined and whose basic approach is to construct alternative communities. Their concern in building these communities is less with ontology than with history, less with theory and more with praxis. Harvey Cox (1984) sees the phenomenon of what are called the Christian base communities as a manifestation of new theological thinking emerging from the "margins and fringes of society" (the poor, the Third World, women). These communities are built and developed by small groups of peasants, clergy, and volunteers who reflect on and discuss the connections of their work to biblical thought and vice versa. This process of praxis, the integration of theory and practice for purpose of change and liberation, is rooted in Marxist thought, and it is this tendency of liberation theology to attempt to blend Marxist analysis with Christian theology that helps to explain the strenuous resistance to this movement.

This resistance highlights the risks involved in the prophetic tradition since it involves fundamental criticism, demands for change, and active efforts to make changes. It is a tragic yet revealing measure of the powerful threat that prophetic movements generate to note the serious ongoing efforts to silence the leadership of the liberation theology movement as well as the violent fate of other great prophets like Socrates, Jesus, Gandhi, and Martin Luther King.

Though it is clear that we are not a Third World people, it is equally clear that we face some of the same critical issues—illiteracy, poverty, oppression, hunger, discrimination—albeit in different degrees and forms. We must confront the realities of our abundance and richness as well as the reality that in spite of our wealth (some would say because of it), our nation includes millions who live below or at near subsistence level. Our politicians love to proclaim that "one hungry, poor, unemployed person is too many." If one such person is intolerable, what concept can characterize the reality of over thirty million poor people in the U.S.A.? Liberation theologists demand that we confront this outrageous and obscene reality with our claim to be a nation rooted in the Judeo-Christian ethic of justice and love.

Liberation theology, in addition to its more particular Latin American roots, has resonance of course, with traditions common to American culture, most particularly, Christianity. It is a historical and sociological reality that we are a nation with very strong ties to Christian ideals, doctrines, and institutions. Christians constitute more than 90 percent of the religiously observant in America, and despite serious denominational and sectarian divisions, they are united in part in their reverence for the teachings of Jesus. Among those who do not consider themselves to be Christians, and those who are "nonreligious," there is also a very high percentage of people who are stirred and inspired by the historical personage and teachings of Jesus as prophet and social critic. One of the great casualties of religious wars and quarrels has been our ability to examine the power and significance of his teachings apart from their theological interpretations. I do not mean to diminish in any way the significance of the disputes regarding the divinity of

Jesus, not only to Christianity but to other religions as well. These are indeed serious matters, and they clearly will continue to be central to the development of religious thought. However, I believe that it is possible and desirable to incorporate some important aspects of his teachings into our cultural and educational myths.

Liberation theologists suggest ways in which this might be done in their rededication to love, compassion, justice, and mercy and to a profound concern for the poor. These are values that are certainly part of the American experience and we should be able to affirm them without embarrassment even if they are part of the credo of particular religious institutions. The liberation movements in Latin America also remind us that prompt and serious action is required in the face of economic desperation and political oppression. Liberation theology pictures Jesus as a daringly active leader who challenged the power elite by undermining their moral and religious authority. In true prophetic tradition, it does so by raising the consciousness of the poor and oppressed and by presenting extraordinary images for the possibility of hope and redemption.

Our situation in America is both similar and different. As is very well known, we have incredible wealth, but what is less well recognized is our astonishing poverty and deprivation, particularly when seen in the context of our wealth. America ranks ninth among 105 nations in a measure of illiteracy, tenth in longevity, seventeenth in infant mortality, and first in military expenditures. But even if some of these statistics, like most statistics, may be misleading, or even if at some time America should rank first in all positive realms, there are other unbelievably harsh realities that confront us. Two hundred million people in the world are hungry, millions do not have decent nutrition or drinking water, millions of children die every year before the age of ten, millions do not have adequate housing or education.

The message of Jesus and other major religious and moral leaders in different ages and places is that we are one people, one world, that we are our brothers' and sisters' keepers. For Americans (or any other group) to live prosperously and contently while hundreds of millions struggle for minimal existence is absurd and unacceptable. If we consider the very real possibility that our prosperity is at the expense of human misery, then the situation is obscene and outrageous. Such a state of being does more than oppress and violate the basic human rights and needs of those in misery; the obscenity of poverty dehumanizes and abases the impulse of the prosperous to love, to show compassion, and to do justice. We need an education that has this concern at its center and, at the same time, resonates with the particulars of our own culture, history, traditions, and symbols. I believe that much of the language and many of the images of the Socratic dialogues, of the prophetic tradition, and of liberation theology are of inestimable value in developing such a framework. There are of course other contemporary and energizing movements of a clearly American stamp that rise to provide moral and religious insight into our lives. A particularly intriguing and potentially very valuable movement is called creation theology, whose prime spokesman and theorist is the Christian theologian Matthew Fox.

Creation Theology

The creation theology movement appears to be a synthesis of several current strands of contemporary American thought. These strands include "new age" thinking, which has come mainly to mean an openness to spiritual experiences and a belief in the enormous latent possibilities of untapped human potential. New age thinkers tend to be optimistic about the future because of their faith in beneficent cosmic forces and in the human capacity to be in touch with those forces. These thinkers decidedly do not oppose science and religion and indeed point to the frontiers of scientific research as confirmation of their intuitive notions about the nature of the universe. They tend to urge us to supplement the recognized powers of rationality and analysis with the equally valuable powers inherent in intuitive and nonrational processes. Such thinkers see the current research in the functions of brain hemispheres as the basic metaphor for their epistemology in that so-called right-brained and left-brained functions are both valuable, that both need to be developed, and that the most important function is the one that integrates them. New age thinkers tend, however, to be less explicit on the need for change in social and political institutions that presumably are more likely to change as the underlying human consciousness changes—a kind of trickle-up theory.

The creation theology movement, however, is much more explicit in its political, moral, and economic agenda. There is major and deep concern for social justice as revealed in their serious criticism of capitalism and colonialism. Fox (1979) continually refers to the economic theories of E. F. Schumacher as being very influential in the formulation of creation theology. There is an explicit recognition that social and economic matters are integral aspects of religious thought and an explicit plea for smaller, more humane, more just communities in which equality, dignity, and compassion are the major informing principles. Creation theology also differs from many new age writings in its emphasis on collective and responsible action designed to transform and not just ameliorate. Another central tenet of creation theory is its passionate ecological concern in which the issues of reverence for nature, environmental pollution, and materialism are integrated with our current political and economic policies.

Indeed, creation theology represents itself in the terms of creating, constructing, building or, more accurately, re-creating and reconstructing. It is a movement that blends new-age cosmology with contemporary political theory rooted in important theological traditions and in the explicit rejection of certain religious ideas. It is a theology that rejects emphases on sin and guilt, and instead celebrates joy, creation, and responsibility. The title of Fox's (1983) broad statement on creative theology is Original Blessing, which he uses in opposition to the concept of original sin. Fox makes a thoroughgoing critique of conventional Christian theology and practices and offers a significant reformulation in which much more emphasis is placed on human sensuality, joy, and compassion, and much more faith (trust) is placed in the human capacity to be worthy of our responsibilities as co-creators of the world. It is a theology that also affirms the prophetic traditions, the teachings of Jesus, and on those who connect mystical with human concerns, particularly the writings of two medieval mystics, Meister Eckhart and Hildegard of Bingen.

We have already described in chapter two Fox's (1979) distinction between compassion and sentimentalism, as his strong emphasis on compassion is central to a vision of community, justice, and joy. In *A Spirituality Called Compassion* he rejects a number of traditional religious symbols, particularly one that he calls the image of Jacob's ladder. This image of verticality, of a struggle to achieve success rung by rung, of human hierarchy, evokes an ideal of people removed from human concerns and compassion and instead urges us to move closer to a contemplative consciousness of the cosmos. It is, according to Cox, an image that furthers the destructive dualisms of history and religion, of God and humanity, and of heaven and earth.

Fox suggests an alternative to this image in a metaphor he calls "laughing Sarah's dancing circle." The "laughing Sarah" is an allusion to the biblical Sarah who laughs joyously when it is revealed that she will through divine intervention give birth at the age of 102, The image of the circle stresses the horizontal quality of the life in contrast to the verticality of Jacob's ladder, and the metaphor of dance reflects human creativity and joy reacting to the demands of time and space. It is a kind of folk dance in which people are both individuals and part of a group, and in which individual variations and differences can easily be accommodated to the basic choreography. Such a dance allows not only for individual creativity but for the opportunity to help those who stumble and for the nimble to relate meaningfully with the awkward. It is an image of joy, creativity, community, and responsibility, a human dance energized by a divine presence, which erases the dualistic qualities of the Jacob's ladder image. For Fox, to "dance" in this manner is the "original blessing" which is the opportunity to act on our capacity to create with God a world of joy, love, and justice. The general direction of the dance is clear but it cannot be complete without human will, creativity, and energy.

Another major Christian image that is reexamined by Fox (1979) is the cross, typically used to represent the suffering and martyrdom of Jesus. Fox contends that the enormous reliance on this image has served to emphasize the pain rather than the joy in the life of Jesus, and that it focuses attention on death rather than life. He suggests that Christians instead elaborate the great potential inherent in the image of the burial cave of Jesus. This image can serve to heighten the consciousness of the regenerative and renewing aspects of the story, moving the forces from crucifixion to resurrection, from death to life, from despair to possibility. Fox sees the possibility of the recreation of life, of the reality of hope and transformation—even at the most tragic and despairing moment—as vital dimensions to the spreading of the gospel of renewal and hope.

Fox elaborates the image of the cave by contrasting its curved and circular properties to the severe and sharp lines of the cross, and bemoans the fact that the imagery of a cross turned on its side allows the image to be switched to that of a sword. The cross evokes the linearity of Jacob's ladder, while the cave evokes for Fox the gentleness and wholeness of the circle. The imagery of the burial cave reminds Fox of the shape of the womb and evokes feminine metaphors of birthing, nurturing, and compassion. Indeed, Fox points out the common derivation in Hebrew of the words for womb and compassion. In addition, the imagery of curve and circle facilitate metaphors of a renewing and continuous spiral of a dialectical relationship between the historical and divine responsibilities that humanity faces. Fox sees life as constant movement upward, but as a movement in which people participate joyfully and in concert with each other.

The focus of this movement is creation in a sacred mode—people inspired and energized by a sacred impulse to make a world of joy and justice. The key source of the concept is the biblical phrase "God created man in His own image," with the interpretation that man/woman is here described as imaging and echoing God the Creator. In this creation myth, man/woman is asked to assume responsibility as God's partner in the further creative and constructive processes needed to make the vision real. The original blessing, then, is the opportunity to create and re-create, and sin becomes the inability, refusal, or rejection of the invitation to continue the re-creative process. Creation is directed at life and is that which nourishes and deepens the joy of life, and, hence, it is a blessing, while sin is destructive in that it is anti-life when it blocks the possibility of joy, abundance, and justice. Creation theology celebrates creativity as that which connects God with humanity and people with people. It is a theology that has re-energized and renewed the symbolic relationship between criticism and imagination. The image of a world requiring re-creation allows us to be critical of a world that does not reflect that image, and it is this loving criticism that impels us to revise and reform the world.

This is a paradigm that has obvious implications for an attempt to fashion a consensual mythos of belief and meaning. It is also a formulation that has quite particular implications for a corresponding educational paradigm, particularly in the vital importance of the creative process and esthetics. The formulation puts esthetics and artistic concerns in a place of particular importance in that it encourages us to pursue a life of aesthetic fullness, a life of heightened, if not ecstatic, beauty and joy. Fox (1979) sees sensuality, ecstasy, and pleasure not as "sins" but as the fruits of the creative processes that we have been inspired to elaborate and develop. Rather, it is sinful not to participate in these blessings and to interfere with the imagination that makes them possible. Art becomes the process of integrating the true, the good, and the beautiful, as expressed in an esthetic of wholeness in which we are free to revel in the creations that represent this wholeness.

Art, creativity, and imagination are not, however, limited to the fine or applied or performing arts, nor to what is narrowly defined by the academy and the commercial world as music, painting, drama, dance, etc. All aspects of life have their esthetic dimensions and are to be seen as humanly constructed, works of art. By seeing civilization, culture, and social institutions as human constructions and as art not only enables us to more clearly recognize our own brilliance and failures in the adequacy of these constructions but heightens the awesomeness of our challenges and responsibilities. It also provides us with the opportunity to examine the creations from an esthetic perspective.

Critical to this emphasis on creativity is a faith in the creative process itself when seen in its constructive sense as part of the sacred responsibility to create a world of love, justice, and joy. It also puts stress on "work," on the active, ongoing engagement in the creative work necessary to meet those responsibilities. Fox captures this notion by urging us to consider concepts like peace, faith, and justice not as nouns but as verbs, since the process requires not only awareness and expression but commitment and action. "Peace . . . is something that needs to be won, fought for, and in fact is never fully achieved. Like justice, it is a verb and not a noun" (1979:78).

Two more quotations can serve to summarize the essential role of creativity in the pursuit of sacred meaning. Quoting Jose Arquelles, Fox distinguishes spiritual creativity from other art forms:

[Arquelles] insists that art as spirituality is always distinct from entertainment. Art for him is "the means by which all matter may be regenerated as spirit." Art is transformation of spirit that touches the very purpose of life that "is its transformation." The true art, he insists, "is the art of transformation" and to this transformation, both the artist and the scientist must die and be reborn. It is this death and dying and suffering that true art involves and that so distinguishes it from entertainment or titillation. William Blake also insisted on the universality of creativity. Not to be an artist is to betray one's own nature. . . . Creativity unlike entertainment, makes demands. (1979:110)

Finally, "Creativity is a way of living, a spirituality, just as compassion is. It is a way that all persons travel in responding to life and we call it 'the art of survival' Everyone who survives, we might say, has proven what an artist he or she is. But of course there are qualitative differences in the way some persons choose to survive. The fullest of the arts of survival would be the creative art of compassionate living." (1979:111)

Problematics of Mythos in America

This marks an appropriate place in which to review our analysis and to indicate the inherent difficulties and dangers of what we are proposing. We have argued that the educational crisis is rooted in the moral and spiritual crisis of the culture as reflected in the value confusions and contradictions discussed in Chapter Three. This analysis shows that certain social and cultural demands have frustrated and distracted us from our impulses to our basic commitments of love, justice, equality, community, and joy. Our culture's insistence on competition, individual success, and privatism is reflected in a school program that puts cultural considerations of achievement, order, control, and hierarchy over educational values of free inquiry, the development of a critical and creative consciousness, and the struggle for meaning. I argue that this cluster of confusions and contradictions, while certainly not new, has deepened and, in conjunction with other current cultural and international crises, has produced a condition that seriously impels us to confront the possibility of a new world or of no world.

Although this book focuses on educational processes, it takes the position that the intimate relationship between education, society, and culture requires educators to be sensitive to major fundamental social and cultural concerns. I have shown how critical moral and religious issues and ideas interpenetrate the larger culture and, hence, inevitably affect our educational institutions. Furthermore, this means that as educators we have the opportunity and responsibility to participate in the dialogue of meaning in order to ensure that education is directed toward that pursuit. It is my position that we educators must reaffirm our faith and humility in the significance of the educational process to facilitate that struggle. We are well aware of the enormous social and cultural constraints under which we work and that the difficulties are at their peak when the concerns are identified to be of a moral and religious nature. The challenge is formidable: (1) We must find ways to avoid paralytic and wishy-washy responses to the conflicting, student, and self-righteous demands of narrow interest groups; (2) at the same time we need to be responsive to the legitimate concerns of the constituents of our pluralistic, multicultural nation; (3) we need not have to choose between the rhetoric of (1) and (2); but can strive to reexamine our traditions and seek language and images that give us common direction and purpose.

In these three points we see three different formulations of the educator's political vulnerability, and it is my belief that it would be best to respond to the complexity and difficulty of the problem by engaging in a project of re-creating an overarching mythos that can energize the culture, and with it the schools. It is vital that we confront the difficult and thorny dilemmas that emerge from efforts to find common ground, and equally vital that we face the consequence of not finding or even searching for our commonality. I have tried in this chapter to sketch out some possibilities for the fashioning of a vision that might provide for more rather than less focus of concerted energy, imagination, and hope.

This process is based on the assumption that virtually all of us can accept the importance and desirability of making a basic polar distinction between what some would call natural and unnatural, sacred and profane, good and bad, etc. This extremely important and basic agreement between believers and nonbelievers, between atheists and agnostics, between theologians and sociologists, represents an apparent agreement that people do make such distinctions, that it is vital to do so to sustain a valid civilization, and also that there are enormous differences among us as to how to constitute and define the basic polar distinctions.

I also posit my basic belief that we as people not only yearn for and create systems of meaning but also in spite of the fact that we continue to cruelly violate our own standards and measures of meaning. As educators, we need to accept these assumptions as the starting point for our efforts, since we must also assume that people have the interest and capacity to become aware of these violations so as to develop responses that can overcome them.

The first set of problems then immediately becomes clear, namely the reality that there are those who would challenge the basic notion that we can or should make affirmations and are eager to act on them. Connected to this problem is the inherent difficulty that emerges from the willingness to accept and act on any assumption or any framework—that is, the reality that assumptions and conceptual frameworks can conceal hidden assumptions and political interests as well as reveal them. I cannot deny nor will I try to overcome this difficulty because it is one inherent in our present existence and underscores the dilemma, risk, and inevitability of making choices.

However, I will point out two countervailing notions that can, to some degree, mitigate, even though they cannot obviate, this serious difficulty. The first is that we also affirm the importance of a posture of humility and a critical consciousness as tools to guard against rigidity and dogmatism. Wariness, awareness, and humility are necessary in our present state of consciousness, but not to the point where they produce stalemate and paralysis. The familiar dictum that we be "whole-hearted and half-sure" is echoed by Sharon Welch's plea (1985) for "absolute conviction and infinite suspicion." Both can serve as guides to dealing with the paradox of the need for both commitment and criticism.

Thus, our second counter response to the difficulties inherent in having clear assumptions is to point to the risks and consequences involved with "objectivity," "detachment" and "neutrality" (i.e., notions that express the inability or reluctance to affirm any set of assumptions). There is of course a problem with the set of assumptions that holds that we cannot, or should not, make any assumptions except those which are incontrovertibly true (of which so far there do not seem to be very many useful ones). The difficulty with a policy of extreme caution and skepticism is that it can promote sterility, relativism, solipsism, if not nihilism. As has been pointed out, there is a difference between being open-minded and being empty-minded. It therefore becomes a matter of choosing among risks, for there is no question that our current problems are rooted in both wishy-washiness and dogmatism. It is clear to me that we can suffer from too much as well as from too little skepticism, and that there can be a penalty for having strong commitments as well as having none.

I believe, however, that there is on balance, a lot less risk in committing to a set of values and principles that inherently demand and insist on a rewarding life for all people. We must, however, recognize that such statements reflect another set of problematics that involve the dangers of sentimentalism and glibness. As educators we struggle with the problem of passion—that is, we know that living (hence education) necessarily involves intense feelings and literally requires heroism, deep devotion, and dedication in order to transcend our limitations. At the same time we are rightfully wary of how emotions can be manipulated, and we see that coolness and detachment are also required dimensions of the educational process.

It is easy enough to regard my analysis of our religious/sacred traditions as sentimental pieties that gloss over harsh realities and complex ideas. Much, if not all, of that analysis has not been "proved," nor can it be said that the validity of these ideas has been presented with overwhelmingly persuasive logic. They represent, at their core, assertions and prescriptions; not only is their "validity" problematic but there is enormous debate over whether and how such prepositions are or can be validated. To a large extent we are confronted here not only with issues of language but with basic theories of knowledge and truth as well.

Are we, for example, required to use the same language for our mythos that we use to describe our legal system? Do we have to "prove" our metaphysical assumptions in ways that parallel our assumptions about such matters as the requirements of valid nutrition? If there are different appropriate languages, how do we move among them without obfuscation, manipulation, and deception? Can we develop an esthetic of language that inspires us and points to transcendence but nevertheless disciplines and flexes our minds?

I offer these questions without expecting answers that can quiet these concerns since I do not believe they are questions that can or should be stifled. Nor do I believe that they should prevent us from taking on the risk of affirmation or of passion. We need to guard against sloganeering, glibness, and the manipulation of powerful images and intense feelings. We also need to guard against the consequences of strangling our aspirations and ideals by choking our voice of passion with the cold hand of detachment. Again, great horrors have been perpetrated because of intense passions, and many of them have been allowed to happen because of indifference and dispassionate analysis. Slogans can distort; aphorisms can also illuminate; truth can be felt as well as falsehood. Our talents and passions have led us in many, often conflicting directions: logic has led to the Peace Corps as well as to the Holocaust, there is an esthetic dimension to the Taj Mahal and to the guillotine.

Nonetheless, we must be aware of these problems in the same spirit of humility, awareness, skepticism, and criticism that we have described in our response to the problems of affirmation. We must build into our mythos the faith that our basic principles are strong enough to withstand and, indeed, require, significant criticism and are sufficiently flexible to allow for a continuous process of discovery and transformation. As American educators we must assume our critical responsibility with special care when we affirm a moral stance, given our historical tendency be arrogantly pietistic.

In his *The American Jeremiad,* Sacvan Bercovitch (1978) has elaborated on how very early in our history certain cultural themes developed and have continued strongly to influence our national ethos. More particularly, he carefully and thoroughly describes certain Puritan traditions, images, and ideals that were in the beginning explicitly recognized as the guidelines of the new colonies and which subsequently came to strongly permeate American culture. This book not only provides wonderful insight into our historic origins as a nation but also points to the enduring dangers of excessive piety, self-righteousness, and religious arrogance.

As we have already noted in the first part of this chapter, Bercovitch points out that the Puritans who came to colonize America were part of the great Puritan revolution in England that resulted in the execution of Charles I and the establishment of the English Commonwealth ruled by Oliver Cromwell. This revolution was deeply rooted in very intense religious concerns focused on the passionate belief in the need to purify and cleanse the country of cultural decadence and "popery." This revolution was itself later overthrown and the monarchy restored at about the same time that significant colonization in the new world was beginning. Those Puritans who came to America had the same zeal and passion as their European counterparts about the desperate need to change the direction of society.

Bercovitch, however, points to an important difference, one that was to continue to characterize American history. Whereas in Europe the failures and disappointments to achieve reform had encouraged an existing sense of European pessimism and a tragic sense of life, the American experience was quite different. Clearly, the colonists had a very different task than overthrowing the well-established European culture and power structure with its very long history, replete with particular traditions, heroes, images, rituals, and conventions. They did not see themselves as conquerors and invaders, intent on dispossessing the legitimate incumbent whom they arrogantly and ignorantly called "Indian," but as discoverers and developers of a "new world." By using this metaphor they brushed aside the reality that this was a very old world, new only to European consciousness. Furthermore, this metaphor could easily be extended into images of a new Garden of Eden and, hence, opened up the possibility of a New Jerusalem.

The American Puritans then, according to Bercovitch's analysis, tended to be much more optimistic about the future and their capacity to shape the boundaries of this new promised land. They indeed saw the discovery of this new world as an indication of divine providence, and with that grace came a definite divine imperative to do God's work on earth. From the very beginning, then, came the thread in the American myth that God and America have a special relationship, that America has a special responsibility in humanity's destiny, that, in a word, God has in fact blessed America. We can also see the origins of the optimism, if not euphoria, that comes with the opportunity to start freshly with a clean slate; and even when the slate has been written on, it can be disregarded because it is in a strange language. We see not only the disregard of history but the passion for social engineering with all its elitist arrogance and cruelty.

What we cannot accuse the Puritans of is timidity, humility, or tentativeness, for it was certainly not their purpose to promote diversity or pluralism. Eventually they had to accept the political realities of other competing groups, but the Puritans firmly believed that their beliefs and values were the right ones and that the leadership had a strong moral obligation to "help" others to see what is obviously so right, i.e., to impose their culture. This smugness and self-righteousness was supported by and grounded in an intense commitment to a religious perspective. In this way, they were able to justify what we in the present are likely to call dogmatism and arrogance, as only the consequences of seeking to do the true work of God. The Puritans saw themselves as the new chosen people entrusted for perhaps the last time to redeem the fall with a new pure, or at least much purer, world.

Bercovitch maintains that these tendencies continue throughout our history even though they have lost their purely Puritan rhetoric and flavor. He sees these

themes strongly repeated in major figures of nineteenth-century American literature such as Melville, Emerson, and Whitman. We can surely see their persistence
in contemporary American foreign policy, which proclaims to the world that it is
America's manifest destiny to control the New World, that it is America's responsibility to make the world safe for democracy, that the Soviet Union is an "evil empire," and America is God's greatest gift to humanity.

Our history itself represents the dangers of arrogance, self-righteousness, self-
deception, and the corruption that ensues when power and piety are integrated.
We must be aware that we have abused our power and are likely to continue that
abuse in the name of divine intentions and/or moral imperatives. We must be on
guard for the incipient tendency, grounded in our history, to be ruthlessly intoler-
ant and to take a maddeningly superior posture in the rigidity and smugness of
our self-appointed task as God's hammer.

We will not, however, serve our responsibilities by retreating into amorality and
vulgar pragmatism, or by a futile retreat into a sterile noncommitted posture. That
is not only facile but represents a counterproductive response to the struggle for a
life of equality and justice. A more promising approach, albeit a very difficult one,
would be to take on the task of confronting these problems by struggling with the
necessity of shaping a consciousness where serious moral convictions can co-exist
with skepticism and openness. The avowal of skepticism without some significant
degree of moral commitment amounts, at best, to incompleteness and evasion
and, at worst, to irresponsibility and cowardice. As much as we deplore our history
of arrogance and self-serving moralizing, we must not in the wake of this revulsion fail to affirm those generous impulses to do justice that are also part of the
American tradition. A failure to affirm what is truly noble in our efforts is to surrender to the forces of destructiveness and evil. A failure to affirm the evil and destructive forces in our culture has the same effect.

The final chapters represent an attempt to respond to these challenges as professional educators. As educators we cannot be expected to fully solve our problems
by ourselves, but it is our responsibility to help others to become aware of the
problems, to provide conceptual schema to probe and understand them, and to
share and nourish the intellectual, psychological, artistic, and experiential resources that are the sources for responding to the problem. The schools are part of
the culture's resources needed to pose the problems and questions as well as to
generate energized and wise ways of dealing with them.

Schools are not, however, only a way of dealing with cultural concerns; they
are a sub-culture in themselves in that they are places where life is not only studied
but lived. Hence, schools need also to be places where educators and students
deal with opportunities to be loci of joy, justice, and love, places where people
can be affirmed and where the pleasures of reflection, growth, and challenge can
be experienced.

I will in the remainder of this book sketch out a number of curricular and instructional implications of our analysis of the educational crisis and of the suggested element of a consensual mythos and their problematics. These chapters rep-

resent an effort not so much to posit a new pedagogy but rather to reorganize and reorient the wealth and treasure of the wisdom that is reflected in many educational writers and practitioners. My basic notion on reforming education is not essentially "technical." I believe that the problems are less in our ability and capacity to do what we sense is right and more in our willingness to do so. I have enormous respect for the ingenuity, imagination, and artistry that our gifted teachers continue to demonstrate. There is in the lore of accumulated practical genius a vast repertoire of marvelous techniques and approaches. Our task is to inform these techniques with principles that are intellectually and morally sound.

5

EDUCATION IN A PROPHETIC VOICE

The two dominant attitudes of prophetic faith are gratitude and contrition:
Gratitude for creation and contrition before judgment; or in other words, confidence
that life is good in spite of its evil and that it is evil in spite of good. In such faith both
sentimentality and despair are avoided.
    REINHOLD NIEBUHR, *An Interpretation of Christian Ethics*

A basic theme of this book is the intimate interconnection between culture and education, and in this chapter we will focus more sharply on the implications of the proceeding moral and religious analysis for educational practice. The remainder of the book is an attempt to lay out the meaning of our interpretation for the profession as well as its implications for curriculum and instruction and for broad educational policy. In this chapter we will deal primarily with issues concerning the profession itself, with particular focus on the possibilities inherent in the profession for significant cultural and educational leadership. Our basic position is that the profession must confront its possibilities, as well as its structural limitations, and that its redemption can emerge from a frank and courageous recognition of its responsibilities and capabilities. Therefore, we begin our specific analysis of educational practice with a consideration of the single most vital professional element, the profession itself.

The Education Profession

When we talk of an educational program we cannot limit ourselves to discussion of materials, techniques, course of study, etc., for, as is well known, one's educational experiences are shaped by a host of other phenomena. We have already spoken at length on how cultural, social, and moral views permeate the schools and classrooms in powerful ways, but the hidden curriculum includes not only the values and attitudes but the quality of school life, its atmosphere and tone, and the nature of human relationships. The quality of school life is, in turn, significantly influenced by the nature and background of the staff, the conditions under which they work, their values, and their professional beliefs. Clearly, what students learn is strongly related to the school's constitutive structural elements and the sum total of human experiences in that school. Although it is a cliché to say that teachers and administrators are part of the "curriculum," it is cliché because it is said so frequently and not because we pay a great deal of attention to its significance. We need, therefore, to address more sharply the nature of the profession itself, as a major constitutive and structural element of educational experience.

We are, alas, a very weak profession, captured in part by our difficulty in admitting to our condition. I believe, however, that we are not weak because of chance and that our weaknesses reflect the culture's basic ambivalence about the power and value of a truly liberating and critical education. What is maddening is that although we have been constituted to be weak, we are nonetheless brutally criticized by the culture for the consequences of our weakness. We are criticized for not being intellectually strong, yet the culture tends to channel its best and brightest students to other professions, such as law, medicine, and the sciences. We are berated for our sloppy theorizing and numbing jargon, yet scholars in older, well-established fields tend to ignore the serious study of education or insist on substituting their naiveté about educational matters for informed dialogue. Teachers are asked to perform at very high-level tasks of profound importance and yet are given resources that are absurd and insulting. Moreover, because school budgets tend to be prominent and distinguishable, they are often subjected to minute and haggling examination, which puts the educational community in the posture of beggars who ought to be content with their customary dole.

We have also been unable to stem the forces that seriously work to make our profession reluctant to take initiative and assume leadership, and this is because, at least in part, the people who want to keep down the budget, the complaints, the demands, and the quality of thinking are the same people who largely control our resources and destinies. There are, of course, exceptions, such as the case of teacher organizations and unions pressing very aggressively for somewhat better working conditions and pay. However, it is often the case that in these situations, even when the professional groups ask for quite modest changes, there is at best cool community support and often community hostility.

We are also a docile and passive profession for another basic and more troubling reason, one that we are reluctant to discuss publicly. I believe that we must confront our own inadequacies as a profession; we must deal with the reality that our members include a great many who are not very gifted intellectually, many who are timid or narrow about exercising leadership, and many who see teaching as a job requiring fairly modest technical skills and lots of hard work. Yes, there are a lot of incompetents in other professions, and yes, the culture does do a lot to keep brighter, abler, more energetic people out of our profession. It is also true that the well-known defensiveness of the profession is partly a function of the cruelty and ignorance that permeates much of the public criticism of the schools.

However, we do not do ourselves or the culture any favor by refusing to acknowledge serious deficiencies in the basic structure of the system (which includes our competence) and the culture's very significant responsibility for those deficiencies (including ours). We are feebler than we need be because we have allowed, if not encouraged, the culture to set the terms and boundaries of the debate and discussion of educational issues. Educators are typically put in a reactive posture and usually find themselves co-opted to work within a parameter of policies that many educators find fundamentally false. In this way educators become technical staff engaged to administer and execute policies set by those who are likely to have serious reservations about providing serious education for all. This has worked to let the profession off the hook of exercising its own responsibility to participate in, and enrich the process of, providing broad cultural leadership. The profession finds itself in a vicious circle—it is looked upon with disdain or perhaps indifference because it lacks the intellectual clout of genuine authority, and yet those in power see a confident, authoritative, and persuasive profession as a serious threat to existing arrangements. Our profession is further weakened by our own brand of specialization, divisiveness, and fragmentation. There are walls among and between teachers and administrators, among and between schools and universities. There is a myriad of worlds within worlds (gifted and talented; elementary; such organizational rubrics as science, middle school), a wide range of educational ideologies ranging from those that are "child-centered" to those totally loyal to institutional concerns. As professionals, we are divided and conquered.

Stanley Aronowitz and Henry Giroux (1985) have provided a concise and powerful analysis of the growing erosion of teacher autonomy and what they call the "proletarianization of teacher work." It is their position that there are steady pressures to reduce the significance of the teachers by increasing administrative controls, using such techniques as competency testing, the development of "teacher-proof" materials, and by emphasizing an increasingly technical and instrumental orientation toward instruction.

> Teachers are not simply being proleterianized; the changing nature of their roles and functions signifies the disappearance of a form of intellectual labor central to the nature of critical pedagogy itself Moreover, the tendency to reduce teachers to either high-level clerks implementing the orders of others within the school bureaucracy or to specialized technicians is part of a much larger problem within western societies, a problem marked by the increasing division of intellectual and social labor and the increasing trend toward the oppressive management and administration of everyday life. (1985:24)

In their brilliant essay on intellectualism and teaching, Aronowitz and Giroux distinguish among various forms of intellectual activities and maintain a firm view that the requirements of serious and sensitive teaching include the capacity for serious intellectual inquiry. Their commitment, however, is clearly to a kind of teacher they label as a "transformative intellectual," a concept that seems ideally fitted to the teacher as prophet.

> Central to the category of transformative intellectuals is the task of making the pedagogical more political and the political more pedagogical In the first instance, this means inserting education directly into the political sphere by arguing that schooling represents both a struggle for meaning and a struggle over power relations. Thus schooling becomes a central terrain where power and politics operate out of a dialectical relationship between individuals and groups, who function within specific historical conditions and structural constraints as well as within cultural forms and ideologies that are the basis for contradictions and struggles. Within this view of schooling, critical rejections and action become part of a fundamental social project to help students develop a deep and abiding faith in the struggle to overcome injustice and to change themselves. (1985:36)

It does not seem to be in the interest of those currently in power to encourage and empower the education profession to seek that intellectual and moral authority. On the other hand, there are educators who believe strongly that it is very much in the interest of those who struggle for a culture of love, joy, and justice to demand that our profession develop such a vision. These educators also believe that members of our profession have a basic right to pursue their calling with integrity and pride and to seek to fulfill their responsibilities to participate in the struggle to achieve those conditions. All educators must come to define their autonomy in relationship to these broader struggles rather than as a minor component of an existing bureaucratic apparatus. Individual members of the profession have the opportunity and indeed the imperative to search for their own meaning within the context of their work as calling rather than as job. Therefore, they need not see their professional interests as necessarily coinciding with those of school boards, college admission offices, personnel offices, state departments of education, nor even those of school administrators.

Professional autonomy in this sense is not to be confused with the self-serving, self-protective ethic of so-called professionalism, which translates into a consciousness of being quiet, polite, and deferential (e.g., "we mustn't wash our dirty linen in public" and "don't make waves"). It is nothing short of tragic that the concept of professionalism has become so distorted that it can connote narrow protectionism rather than dedication to high principles. We should as a profession profess our high ideals rather than being fearful to confess our shortcomings.

We must accept the responsibilities of being the kind of a profession which involves independence and autonomy, and in order to merit that independence and autonomy we must be competent; we must have a sound basis for our authority, and we must have a set of principles and ideas that can inform our professional ethic. As long as we see ourselves as employees or staff or technicians, we will not be a profession that leads but a camp that follows the parade. But we need more than power to lead; we need moral, intellectual, and professional authority that influences rather than imposes. As a profession we need to develop our own overarching professional mythos—a shared set of images and ideals that can guide and inform all our various specifications and concentrations. We suggest that the prophetic tradition provide direction for such a mythos.

Education and Prophecy

Both the culture and individual educators need a profession with a critical capacity and the courage and expertise to provide insights into cultural problems and to suggest reasonable responses to them. There are many people and institutions charged with the responsibility of noting and detecting our achievements and shortcomings and of suggesting ways of dealing with them. We urge that the education profession be one of those institutions that accepts that responsibility. In this way, educators would be working within the prophetic tradition that seeks to remind us of our highest aspirations, of our failures to meet them, and of the consequences of our responses to these situations. In order to act in this tradition, educators need to be well-equipped with intellectual powers, expertise, psychological strength, moral courage, strong convictions, and inner strength that derive from a sense of responding seriously to profoundly important issues. Again, it is not in the interest of the existing power structure to stress the extraordinary power and importance of teaching, but it is to our common interest that we all be mindful of the magnificence and nobility of those who seriously teach.

The educator as prophet does more than re-mind, re-answer, and re-invigorate—the prophet-educator conducts re-search and joins students in continually developing skills and knowledge that enhance the possibility of justice, community, and joy. His or her concern is with the search for meaning through the process of criticism, imagination, and creativity. Such a role (as Socrates found out) is in fact seriously threatening to those fearful of displacing the status quo. Most important, the educator as prophet seeks to orient the educational process toward a vision of ultimate meaning. The prophetic model, hence, does not allow the individual educator to go in individual or happenstance direction, for the great prophets like Socrates, Moses, Jesus, Gandhi, and King have performed their critical and creative functions within a broad but particular conception of the meaning and significance of human creation and destiny.

Educators who accept the concept of their profession as having a prophetic function must then affirm a set of sacred and moral principles—a mythos, a set of metaphysical or religious assumptions—or commit themselves to that which has ultimate meaning for them. As human beings we need to consciously participate in the process of both forming and being informed by these principles, and as educators we need to help our students learn how to participate in that process. We have indicated what at least some of these principles might be, and note that educators not only have a responsibility to be reflective, thoughtful, and critical about these principles but also have a responsibility to reflect on their own basic assumptions, however implicit, tacit, or preconscious they may be. A profession without a mythic dimension that provides a vision of ideals and goals is not capable of providing serious cultural leadership and instead serves as a tool that is manipulated by those who have such a vision in place.

Educators are well positioned to have a sense of how the culture is responding to its highest ideals and, consequently, ought to be able to respond to its opportunities for providing social criticism. Traditionally, however, the profession has not seen itself as an institution with such responsibilities and has tended to acquiesce to the dominant culture's self-definition of what the major problems and needs are. The profession needs to establish as its central concerns those policies that correspond to the culture's highest ideals and not those that distort them or deceive us.

Although it is reasonable to make some link between cultural/social success and failure with educational success and failure, it is crucial that the profession be free to focus on what actually constitutes success and failure. For example, schools are criticized, perhaps appropriately, when S.A.T. scores go down, but perhaps they should also be criticized when there is a war or when charitable donations drop. Educators must point out serious social and moral problems of our culture as part of their responsibility to be self-critical and as a way of setting a professional agenda for action. When brilliant economists and other social scientists say they can't control the economy, they are, at least partly, saying something about the inadequacy of their knowledge, of the limitations of their research, of their lack of imagination (i.e., of their education). Such problems should not logically lead us to intensify the very schooling that produced these difficulties but rather to seriously reconsider some of its basic assumptions about what constitutes a liberating and critical education.

As educators we must confront the public and ourselves with the harsh reality of the basic ignorance and intellectual and moral failures of those who by conventional standards have had the very best education. The fact that the best and the brightest have done very well in some areas and very poorly in others should not fill us with defensiveness or shame but with humility and determination. Our failures surely speak at least partly to the limits of our knowledge, or perhaps the political constraints on inquiry, as well as to the failure of the educational system to provide enough opportunities for greater insight and imagination. Educators must reflect on how they have contributed to major structural failures like persistent unemployment and poverty rather than focus on their inability to lower the dropout rate or keep schooling costs down.

Educators must confront our moral failure by seriously considering the relationship between the realities of hunger, poverty, and misery and the nature of existing educational programs. The culture that produces and allows any such oppression or degradation fails, and all its institutions must share in the responsibility for that failure. The profession must begin with the perspective of hunger, war, poverty, or starvation as its starting point, rather than from the perspective of problems of textbook selection, teacher certification requirements, or discipline policies. If there is no serious connection between education and hunger, injustice, alienation, poverty, and war, then we are wasting our time, deluding each other, and breaking faith. I believe, however, that there are strong connections and it is these connections that give educators purpose and enable us to see ourselves as having prophetic responsibilities.

In order for educators to accept and meet their responsibilities as social critics and leaders, they obviously will need to have sufficient resources. One of the most telling indications of the weakness and timidity of our profession is its acceptance of the basic framework of the conditions under which teachers in elementary and secondary schools are expected to work. Even though there is a consensus that teachers are grossly overworked and underpaid, efforts directed at change are almost always ameliorative rather than transformative in character. In fact, it takes enormous efforts simply to maintain workload and pay standards at their currently absurd levels, lest they become worse, as they have in many communities. As has been said, we see in this situation evidence of the dominant culture's fear of a strong educational program and its respect for the potential impact of schools populated by stimulating and imaginative teachers who have been given sufficient resources and a reasonable work load.

We must also, however, closely examine the reality that the profession has not made a serious concerted effort to convince the American public that its allocations to the schools are not merely inadequate but shocking, insane, and destructive. There is, for example, the extraordinary variance in salaries and working conditions between those who teach in grades K-12 and those who teach at the university level, private and public. Salaries in universities are two or three times what they are in the lower grades, opportunities for advancement and development are infinitely greater, and the differences in teacher load are astounding (i.e., typically twelve hours vs. thirty hours). Moreover, the differences in autonomy, respect, and status are such that it is extremely difficult to consider teachers in both institutions as being in the same profession. The profession itself has contributed to the glib and irrational belief that these differences are "natural" and perhaps even desirable. Do we really want to take the position that teaching at the elementary or high school level is less important or less taxing than university teaching? Are we prepared to defend a position that says that those who do not teach at the university do not need or want to do scholarly research? More to the point, why has the profession failed to address seriously not only this particular lunacy but broader question of what a proper, high-quality environment for serious teaching and learning would really entail?

One explanation is that, sadly enough, many members of the profession have come to accept the existing framework as reasonable (one perhaps needing adjustment from time to time) and, further, have failed to reflect seriously on its inadequacies. A related explanation speaks more clearly to the basic fear in our profession, a fear that produces our prodigious docility and passivity. What one hears regularly from many professionals' response to the pitiful working conditions for teachers is the belief that "we" should not seriously rock the boat lest "they" react in anger and retribution. This is the employer-employee, master-slave mentality in which we are reminded of our place and our powerlessness, urged to count our blessings, and warned about the consequences of protest. We are a profession, alas, that has, to a very large degree, internalized the oppressors' consciousness.

Let us contrast this posture of appeasement and passivity with that of the Biblical Prophets. Of course we cannot in any way return to those times, but we can hope that their example will help illuminate our present condition. First of all, there was, according to some scholars, a recognized role and function for prophets in ancient Israel. Prophesy as the process of reminding, criticizing, and warning was considered to be a necessary role in that society and while prophets were not always given official status, they were accepted and valued as legitimate, if sometimes difficult or troublesome, members of the quasi-formal leadership. They were often consulted by the priests and kings and sometimes, nevertheless, imprisoned for their views and their agitations. However, there seems to be strong evidence that the *prophetic function* was considered necessary even though the acceptance of individual prophets varied enormously. Buber describes their functions not as magical but as functional:

> The Israelite prophet utters his words, directing them into an actual and definite situation. Hardly ever does he foretell a plainly certain future. YHVH does not deliver into his hand a completed book of fate with all future events written in it, calling upon him to open it in the presence of his hearers. It was something of this kind the "false prophets" pretended, as when they stood up against Michaela and prophesied to the king, "Go up and prosper!" Their main "falsity" lay not in the fact that they prophesy salvation, but that what they prophesy is not dependent on question and alternative. This attitude is closer to the divination of the heathen than to true Israelite prophecy. The true prophet does not announce an immutable decree. He speaks into the power of decision lying in the moment, and in such a way that his message of disaster just touches this power. (1960:103)

The power structure no doubt paid attention to the prophets for a variety of reasons. First, like anyone else, they were particularly interested in a prophet's capacity to foretell the future, even though prophets were definitely not in the same category as sorcerers and magicians. The prophetic capacity of predicting the future is more akin to the aspirations of contemporary social science, that is, it emerges from a keen understanding of how underlying forces are affecting events. Second, prophets probably both reflected and influenced community attitudes and, hence, their views had important political meaning. Third, and not necessarily least of all, prophets claimed to have privileged communication with God, or at the very least to have special sensitivity to know God's will. The power structure, for whatever combination of reasons, would certainly want to connect their decisions and policies to what were accepted as sacred imperatives. The priests on the other hand were too closely identified with the power structure and were probably more interested in dealing with issues of ritual and observance than with political issues.

The culture apparently felt it was well served by the existence of a group whose independence, special sensitivities, and intense concerns could serve the function of actually preserving the culture by pointing out the necessity of appropriate change. Prophets were neither wholly inside nor wholly outside the system but clearly committed to the system's long-range well being, and, therefore, their criticisms and cries of outrage could not be easily dismissed (although they sometimes were) as work of cranks or subversives. This is certainly not to make a historical claim that prophecy was without its serious problems and resistances in ancient Israel, but only to point to a model of a culture's attempt to institutionalize a way of maintaining its commitments to its conceptions of the sacred through continuous criticism and affirmation.

Buber, in talking of the role of prophets in ancient Israel, speaks of the reluctance of that nation to have "kings" in the modem sense. Israel held onto the idea that the spirit of God should serve as sufficient governance, but eventually the Israelites came reluctantly to accept first "judges" and later "kings." Buber believes that the inevitable tensions created by monarchy contributed to the importance of prophecy.

> The dynastic continuity implies a continuity of responsibility to fulfill the divine commission. . . . The fundamental and practical opposition of the kings to this constitutional obligation resulted in the mission of the prophets. . . . Against the tendency of the kings frequently supported it seems by the priests with their sole concern for the autonomy of the social domain) to sublimate the commission into a divine right without any obligation, a divine right granting the kings to stand in accordance with ancient customs, as sons of the deity invested with full powers (cf. Ps. 2,7)—against this tendency the prophets set up the political realism which does not admit any "religious" subtlety. Over and against YHVH's vicegerent on the royal throne, acting unrighteously and therefore unlawful, but powerful, there stands the bearer of YHVH's word, without any power, but certain of his mission, reproving and claiming reproving and claiming in vain. (1960:152–53)

Clearly our culture is inevitably very different from that tiny society that struggled and flourished four thousand years ago. However, as cultures surely differ, they also have a great number of challenges in common—particularly those involved with the struggles for survival and fulfillment. Our culture does not formally recognize the prophetic function, although many individuals and institutions seek to perform it, and we are certainly not suggesting any formal institutionalization of it by creating something like the Department of Prophecy.

Ideally, all our institutions and every individual could incorporate those dimensions within their work, and indeed, the nourishment of those impulses should be considered as a prime goal of the educational process. In order to encourage "prophecy," educators themselves need to be "prophets" and speak in the prophetic voice that celebrates joy, love, justice, and abundance and cries out in anguish in the presence of oppression and misery. Educators share this prophetic responsibility with others in the culture, but they have special and critical roles in applying the prophetic perspective to professional issues, concerns, and standards. The educator as prophet needs to be particularly concerned about the degree to which the culture and the profession are keeping their sacred commitments.

Prophetic educators must facilitate the dialogue on what these sacred commitments are, how they are to be interpreted in the light of particular situations, and what constitutes appropriate responses to them. In this way we can respond to this challenge from Walter Brueggemann:

> The educational task of the community is to nurture some to prophetic speech. But for many others, it is to nurture an awareness that we must permit and welcome and evoke that prophetic tongue among us. Otherwise we will be diminished into the prose world of the king and, finally, without hope. Where there is no tongue for new truth, we are consigned to the coldness of the old truth. (1982:54)

Prophetic educators focus not only on the culture and the profession but on their more specialized practice. Educators have parallel responsibilities to be guided in their practice by their vision of the ultimate/sacred/holy and their responsibilities to be critical of shortcomings as well as to be responsive to them. Such educators must regard themselves and their students as holy and sacred, not as tools and mechanisms, hence as ends not means; they must be committed to the development of institutions of learning in which all those involved (teachers, administrators, staff, students) are full citizens, each of whom has the inherent right of personal and social fulfillment, each of whom has inherent and full dignity, and each of whom has the inherent right to grow, learn, and create as much as he/she possibly can. Thus, schools can be transformed from warehouses and training sites into centers of inquiry and growth where participants share their different abilities and talents in the pursuit of the common goal of creating a culture of deepest meaning.

Such a conception of the profession will, I believe, serve the culture and educators well, for although it certainly puts the profession into a service role, it does not put it in the service of pursuing the profane, but rather the sacred. Paradoxically, such a role limits the profession, yet liberates it from servility and collaboration in unworthy tasks to a role of participating in the creation of free and just society. Educators as prophets must therefore be mindful that their specialization plays a crucial moral and social role; they must be mindful of the professional and personal requirements necessary to meet these responsibilities. They must act simultaneously as citizens, professionals, technicians, and leaders. If educators are indeed to be prophets, it is obviously critical that they be aware of a vision that informs and guides their practice. It is to the delineation of this vision that I now turn.

Credo and History:
The Dialectic of Educational Grounding

We are at the point of articulating our basic orientation toward educational practice, one grounded in the dialectical relationship between a commitment to a broad vision of what is sacred and an understanding of the significance of this particular moment in history. As prophet educator in the tradition of Moses and Jesus, we must be in touch with our highest aspirations; as educator-prophets in the tradition of Socrates, Marx, and Freud, we must be aware of the problematics involved in our understanding of this vision, and as educator prophets in the tradition of Martin Luther King and Paulo Freire, we must be alert to its significance in the light of contemporary events. Education is a dynamic, ever-changing process that must be able to respond to the shifts and twists of this dialectic process, and hence I believe it both appropriate and imperative to attempt a basic statement on an educational framework that ought to guide our work for the next generation.

The historical grounds for this statement have already been discussed in prior sections of this book, but it is perhaps useful to summarize them in the form of several propositions:

1. We live in a moment of utmost precariousness, a time unlike other times, when particular cultures, nations, and groups are at risk, but when the entire civilization and planet confront the possibility of extinction.
2. We live in a time of massive injustice, ranging in severity from serious and devastating to unimaginably horrible. We confront staggering conditions of starvation, unemployment, poverty, misery, exploitation, and oppression.
3. We live in a time of estrangement and apartheid, ranging from moral and spiritual alienation, narcissism and personalism, to the legitimized structures of racial, economic, and social separation. Paul Tillich helps us to understand the relationship between this alienation and our concern for the sacred, an alienation he calls estrangement.

   Estrangement as sin has a threefold character. It is the willful turning away from the divine ground of our being (unbelief), combined with the elevation of our own selves to the center of all things, thus usurping the place of God (hubris). It expresses itself also in "concupiscence"—the lustful striving not only for sexual conquest, but for knowledge and power as well—in other words "the unlimited desire to draw the whole of reality into one's self. (quoted in Porteous 1966:113–14)

4. We live in a time of particularly dangerous self-deception and arrogance derived from our reluctance to accept the extent of our ignorance. Peter Berger has written on how organized religion (and by extension the schools) can contribute to moral numbness. In *The Precarious Vision* he has this to say:

   To reject the comforts and security of religious submission is to have the courage to admit the precariousness of existence and to face the silence of the universe. This certainly does not mean that one must resign oneself to meaninglessness or that one must give up the quest for meaning. It does mean the surrender of illusionary meanings and false reassurances. This also involves a relentless intellectual honesty that abhors bad faith and seeks always to be conscious to the fullest possible clarity. Such intellectual honesty forces the admission that there are many questions, even vital questions, of which we are ignorant. (1961:151)

5. We live in a time of increasing despair, a time when more and more people perceive themselves as victims and as powerless even in the face of the realization that "powerlessness corrupts and absolute powerlessness corrupts absolutely." More and more we have edged into a paranoiac state where the "system," however irrational and unwise, becomes ever stronger, more remote, and less responsive. Jose Miranda characterizes this view and its effect on, or commitment to, social justice and community:

> The system forces the man to surrender himself, with all his existential weight, to assuming his economic future and to regarding the problems of others as completely foreign to himself. (It forces him to surrender himself the spirit of calculation, to the ideology which says that a man's value depends on his cleverness in situating himself within the system. And he must do this because of the system itself, independently of indoctrination by propaganda or education or ideology; he must do this necessarily, to be someone, to be able to survive, in order not to be crushed by the social machinery. (1974.8–9)

6. We also live in a time of hope that emerges from increased consciousness and sensitivity, as well as from the achievements and potentials of our creative, artistic, scientific, and intellectual genius. We are experiencing enormously exciting and profound changes in our knowledge, theories, and paradigms in our arts, sciences, crafts, and professions. We continue to demonstrate our creative capacities to recreate the world with the increasing demands for justice, joy, and meaning for all as we widen the realm of possibility.

Given these possibilities as educators and citizens we must regard this moment as a time of utmost crisis and, therefore, must respond to these priorities with all our energy and imagination. We cannot disregard the horrors of misery, starvation, poverty for millions of people, nor the possibility of nuclear destruction of billions of people. Not to act or not to respond fully are acts of enormous consequence. As educator-prophets we can be guided by Heschel's precept that "it is an act of evil to accept the state of evil as either inevitable or final. Others may be satisfied with improvement, the prophets insist upon redemption" (1962: 181).

Nor can we disregard the immense human capacity and interest in continuing the struggle for a world of love and joy. We must confront our enormous capacities for both good and evil: what we have broken we surely can fix, what we have yet to create we can surely construct.

An Educational Credo: A Statement of Goals

As educators we have the specific responsibility of forging a broad educational belief system ever mindful of the problems of any such effort as well as the problems involved in not making such an attempt. The following represent an effort, therefore, to sketch out broad educational goals which reflect our cultural mythos and which, together with the just completed historical perspective, can help generate the somewhat more specific educational objectives described in the next chapter. The credo represents very basic values and assumptions that are in a sense "non-negotiable," even though we are simultaneously convinced of their "truth" and nervous about their problematics. In recognition of the twin dangers of being either dogmatic or uncommitted, we affirm that the goals of current educational practices ought to include:

1. *The examination and contemplation of the awe, wonder, and mystery of the universe.* As educators we have the responsibility to examine the world and universe we live in and to share our reactions authentically and rationally. We have a concomitant responsibility to be aware of and share with our students the process of observation and examination used by different scholars and observers. When we do so, we always find at least one common result—namely, enormously different observations, reactions, and explanations across and within time and place. Not only is there an immensely different assortment of cosmic explanations, but there is diversity even within very narrow fields of explanation. We find not only differences of opinion but also agreement that every field is extraordinarily complicated.

   We can and should confront this reality as a reflection of our comparative youth as a species in a universe that numbers its birthdays in the billions of years. Thus, we are appropriately humble as any novice would be, maintaining, however, the confidence that over time we have come to know more and more, and perhaps at an accelerating rate. However paradoxically, our knowledge explosion has also led to a deeper sense of the mystery of the most fundamental process of origin and destiny. The areas of the unknown may have been narrowed, but their mystery has been heightened. When we look at the incredible biological process within the human body, or the physical process that forms mountains and continents, or when we contemplate the immensity of space, we are struck with the sheer wonder of it all—we are left (almost) speechless in awe.

   Whatever cosmic explanations we use, it is inevitably and inherently breathtaking and incredible in scope. It is just as mind-blowing to posit a God who created the universe as it is to posit a universe created without a God. This awe and wonder need not and should not be sentimentalized, nor should it be a matter of indifference. It is surely intellectually honest to recognize the mystery and to examine ways in which to reduce the needlessly mysterious—that is, to do the research and the teaching designed to reduce ignorance. It is intellectually necessary to be honest not only about what we do know but about what we do not know. This is not humility for the sake of religious ritual, but necessary for the pursuit of truth, knowledge, and meaning.

   Educators perforce provide a basic context for their program of studies, and as part of this context we need to establish the reality of the immense mystery that is the surround of our existence of awesome complexity. This context is critical in that it locates us not only as an interested observer of the mystery but as an aspect of the mystery as well. Thus, we have to establish from the beginning our ontological dimension (i.e., that we are a people engaged in a process of defining our being). Moreover, this context helps to establish that such a process is an ongoing one, fraught with uncertainty and, hence, one that requires serious knowledge, reflection, and research. Furthermore, it is a context that posits that such a process will require that we be ever mindful of the profundity of the task and the modest nature of our progress. In this way we also catch a glimmer of our responsibilities for if humans are to survive they must respond.

2. *The cultivation and nourishment of the processes of meaning making.* With the experience of awe and mystery comes the recognition that though we as a species are required to take initiative for survival purposes (e.g., we have to build shelter and search for food), we are also a people intent on creating systems of thought that explain our past and guide our present and future. When educators examine these various thought systems, they confront the same kind of diversity and complexity of cosmic explanations. In a parallel way, educators must also deal with the context of meaning within which educational activities are to be presented. The educational goal is not so much to teach a particular meaning system but rather to teach for the process of responding to that challenge. Educators must remind themselves and their students that any civilization or any culture is a result of human construction, and it is a human responsibility to create and re-create culture; thus, it is intellectually unsound to encourage the notion that cultural institutions, values, and beliefs are a given. We are to a very significant degree, though certainly not entirely, responsible for the creation of our lives—we create our culture and our culture creates us. We live in dialectical relationship with the mystery, with nature, and with the culture. Therefore, in recognition of our important though limited role in the vast drama of existence, it is incumbent that we respond to our creative responsibilities.

Educators must help us all to be more aware of the nature of this creative process by sharpening our creative capacities and by exposing us to a variety of cultural creations. We need to create not only a culture that enables us to live but also one that needs to know that such a possibility exists and that there are others who have responded to that opportunity. The educational process is based on a very basic premise that the world makes sense and that we are involved in both determining and creating that sense. From almost the very beginning of their lives, people try to understand and control their world, and educational institutions must elaborate and nourish these impulses. This is not say that educators should in any way encourage solipsism and self-indulgence. Rather they should stress the collectively human basis of our culture, regarding subjectivity and imagination not so much as processes to be channeled only into self-expression but as necessary to the impulse to create a life of moral significance.

3. *The cultivation and nourishment of the concept of the oneness of nature and humanity, with the concurrent responsibility to strive for harmony, peace, and justice.* Here

we very definitely enter a realm of affirmation—that is, the acceptance of basic cosmological and moral principles. In this statement we accept as an assumptive belief that there is an ultimate sense in which we are essentially connected with each other, with nature, and with the universe. We posit, therefore, that our goals should include the development of a consciousness in which peace, harmony, and justice are integral. We assume that in a universe of harmony and meaning each individual human is inherently of worth and that the dignity of all elements of the universe is significantly interrelated. Harmony, therefore, by definition demands justice and peace—dignity is indivisible. As public educators we have special responsibilities to remind ourselves of this truth and to find ways in which to make this truth real. Since we have already assumed that we have a responsibility to help create a world of meaning, we can set in motion this process by affirming these very basic metaphysical assumptions-namely that we add to our educational context the notion that we are directed toward the struggle for harmony among the cosmic elements.

We are happy to reaffirm and, as educators, to commit ourselves to act upon these universal truths—that all people are created with equal worth and dignity and that it is our responsibility to sustain and nourish that initial position through our lifetimes. We would urge educators to provide the intellectual and emotional resources needed to take on the struggle that is involved in maintaining this commitment.

We must also be mindful of our place in the universe and our relationship to nature, particularly in our responsibilities to preserve and enrich our environment. We must confront without resort to hyperbole how we as species have threatened not only certain social institutions but the very existence of the planet as a living organism. Our struggle is to participate in the cosmic impulse for an ecology of natural, human, and universal joy, love and justice, or, as we sometimes call it, harmony. Indeed, we see major and exciting possibilities emerging in this area in the emergence of the extraordinary consciousness-raising efforts represented in both the women's and ecological movements. Both of these broad movements have at their center a fundamental concern for intimacy and harmony, based on the recognition of our interdependence and our vision of wholeness.

By accepting these principles, we as educators need to model and instruct in ways so that we can actually participate in this struggle. We need not only to be encouraged and supported in our impulse to love, to do justice, and to be one with our humanity and nature, but we also need to learn that we must work continuously, creatively, and intensely to act on these impulses. Educators must become aware of and share the techniques of the theory and practice of meaning making, and the making of a world. Educators must, however, also be candid about the complexities, paradoxes, and contradictions of human existence. We can celebrate harmony as a goal, but we must also recognize the enormous difficulties and serious resistance to the struggle for universal justice and peace.

As educators we must honestly and candidly share our knowledge of the plurality of modes of consciousness and of cultural variation. We must also note that our traditions, including educational ones, put undue stress on sharp divisions, as seen in the dualisms of mind and body, the individual and the group, and in the nurture vs. nature controversy. Given the mystery we have discussed, and by the same token given our assumption about the ultimate universal harmony, we can sustain our faith in the face of these dualisms by affirming the concept of the dialectic. We cannot avoid the danger of dualistic thinking by denying the power of one of the dyads (e.g., by denying that our lives have a significant degree of determinism to them, or that the body has a reality of its own).

4. *The cultivation, nourishment, and development of a cultural mythos that builds on a faith in the human capacity to participate in the creation of a world of justice, compassion, caring, love, and joy.* Educators here again are in a posture of affirmation, not only of these moral principles but also of their "sacred" quality. As public educators in an American context, we cannot and should not paint ourselves into an ideological comer by identifying ourselves totally with one of a number of sects, denominations, or movements with a religious or quasi-religious orientation. As educators we can and should confront ourselves and our students with the serious and important issues that are inherent in these matters and that offer us insight and tools of analysis to increase our understanding. However, as I have tried to demonstrate, teaching for understanding is not enough, for we must also teach for meaning.

Educators can and should include in their context of practice the broad areas of moral consensus that we have discussed in the previous chapter. Educators can and should also offer to their students the opportunity and responsibility to wrestle with the moral and religious dilemmas and paradoxes that permeate our culture. We can as educators offer and act on the wisdom that we are well advised to accept a sacred/profane distinction of some kind, leaving open of course the question of whether such a conception represents revelation or sociology. We can as educators and humans also in very good faith insist that we accept and act on the moral principles of love, justice, compassion, and joy for all. As educators we must also stress the enormous difficulties inherent in the ways in which these terms are defined, experienced, and implemented.

5. *The cultivation, nourishment, and development of the ideals of community, compassion, and interdependence within the traditions of democratic principles.* As educators we should not in the least be embarrassed by embracing and nourishing our democratic heritage, which is a political response to the moral requirements of equality and individual dignity as well as to the social realities of interdependence. Democratic theory is a pragmatic response to a culture's desire to deal with the everyday requirements of living within the moral contexts of two profound but potentially contradictory values: equality and freedom.

Democracy both affirms a moral position and offers concrete procedures and principles to allow us to work on the challenges of this contradiction.

We as a people have faith that we can at least approach building a society where every person can do as they like provided that it does not, paradoxically, interfere with what others may want to do. Our heritage calls for individual autonomy and concern for others; it speaks to individual freedom and social justice, to independence and compassion.

As educators and humans we should celebrate this tradition, and as educators we should be mindful of the problems, difficulties, and complexities that arise and will continue to do so as a consequence of this moral orientation. There is surely no contradiction in affirming the broad principles and intentions of democracy and at the same time to be mindful of their problems. It is in fact the very spirit of democracy that allows, indeed encourages, continuous critical reflection and free inquiry by free people. Let us, however, not interpret this to mean a community without boundaries; flexible and supportive as we may be, the cultural/ sacred mythos we have been sketching does not allow for oppression, injustice, and inequality. We must also be ever mindful of considering the meaning of democratic institution in the particular context of the social and political realities of specific historical moments. Indeed, democratic procedures must be examined in the light of their impact on moral and spiritual aspirations, even in the faith that they are of one piece.

6. *The cultivation, nourishment, and development of attitudes of outrage and responsibility in the face of injustice and oppression.* As educators we must in our celebration of democracy also be mindful of the extraordinary importance of individual participation in the life of the community. Democracy demands a great deal from each person and rests on the faith that an informed public will be alert to its failures and responsive to the need to overcome those failures. If we are to take the major and broad elements of our mythos seriously, then we will see that oppression, injustice, and indignity are collective concerns, even though they may be focused on individuals or groups. Educators must also recognize that passion is an inevitable part of human experience and that it needs to be seen in its constructive as well as its destructive sense. We will not do our cause of justice and love any service by being merely civil in the face of oppression (i.e., being polite and decorous are totally inappropriate in the context of misery). At the same time, we must recognize that passion by itself is no guarantee of the presence of deep moral principles.

Outrage at oppression is, however, an intelligent and rational response to a situation where our highest values are being violated. We must be wary when we pass off certain violations as minor or modest as in the concept of an "acceptable" level of unemployment or war casualties. Oppression and misery are horrid and unacceptable for one person, and when that horror extends to large numbers of people, the horror becomes more horrible. However, we cannot use the logic of reversing this process in such a way that horror for a few became less horrible than horror for many for otherwise we will become tolerant of some horror. As Heschel says, In a community not indifferent to suffering, uncompromisingly impatient with cruelty and falsehood, continually concerned for God and every man, crime would be infrequent rather than common. (1962:16)

The Issue of Indoctrination

We have to this point been discussing educational goals that are mostly those involving assumptions, beliefs, and values. The values and attitudes represented in these goals are derived from the dimensions of a broad cultural consensus that might serve as a statement of our sense of the sacred, of our mythos, and of our platform of beliefs. I offer no apologies for being explicit about the place of values and beliefs in education, since I operate under the assumption that education cannot and should not be "value-free." Indeed, concern for fairness and openness represents values, and educators need to affirm them. Another way of expressing these values is to raise a concern about indoctrination, manipulation, and the imposition of teacher values upon students.

As educators we must recognize and confront this dilemma and be mindful of the difficulties and risks involved in teaching. There is no way of avoiding this risk and attempts to deny these problems are bound to distract and deceive us and, therefore, likely exacerbate the difficulties. Educators can be more authentic by sharing the problem with the public, students, and each other. We also should be mindful that there are both gray areas and black-and-white ones in this realm. We can easily point to conditions, which we can call manipulative, and oppressive-situations in which coercion is used as a teaching technique (either crudely, as in punishment and grading, or more subtly, as in the denial of affection), or situations in which undue pressures are used (such as ridicule and ostracism).

The single most effective way to reduce the inherent political advantage of teachers is to reduce as much as possible, and as soon as possible, crucial significant gaps between teacher and student power. These gaps include differences in the amount and nature of knowledge; modes of analysis; critical and creative capacities; poise, confidence, personal strength, and stability. Educators must maintain their legitimate authority but give away all their coercive power as soon as possible, and in this way they, as well as students, can be free *to study* the problems rather than to use them as part of a struggle for power and domination. Ironically enough, teachers are also oppressed by the presence of the fear of indoctrination and manipulation, since many sensitive and caring teachers bend over backwards to avoid even the appearance of taking advantage of their political position. A casualty of this process can be a student losing out on the fully passionate consciousness of a teacher's commitments. Teachers and students need to be free of the fears of dominating and of being dominated in order to facilitate free common inquiry. For this reason alone, the primitive practice of "grading" students should be abolished. Grading degrades and dehumanizes in its inherent process of creating hierarchies. It is also anti-intellectual in its irrational and arbitrary character, and it is a serious barrier to the true educational process of inquiry, sharing, and dialogue.

The more specific educational goals to be discussed in the next chapter can be seen as not only vital to the overall purpose of education, as indicated, but also as part of the way we can help students and teachers avoid the possibilities of indoctrination and manipulation. They can be seen as intellectual equalizers, capacities that are enabling and empowering and that help us to be liberated from the oppressions of ignorance, incompetence, and powerlessness, and at the same time free us to make our moral commitments a reality.

6

A CURRICULUM FOR
SOCIAL JUSTICE AND COMPASSION

While compassion implies passion, pathos and deep caring arising from the bowel and guts, it also implies an intellectual life. Ideals come from ideas after all and are important. Just as there can be no justice without ideas and an intellectual life, so there can be no compassion without an intellectual life, for compassion involves the whole person in quest for justice and a mind with ideas in an obviously significant portion of any of us. . . . To develop compassion, then, means to develop an ever-keener awareness of the interdependence of all living things. But to develop such an awareness implies deep study, not only of books, of course, but of nature itself. It implies study as a spiritual discipline, as a means of entering more and more fully into the truth of the universe in which we live. It implies a rejoicing on the part of spiritual people at the facts of our universe that science can and has uncovered, and therefore an authentic kind of ecumenical dialogue between science and spirituality. Compassion, being so closely allied with justice making, requires a critical consciousness, one that resists all kinds of keptness, including that of kept academia and kept intellectuals. It implies a going out in search of authentic problems and workable solutions, born of deeper and deeper questions.
MATTHEW FOX, *Original Blessing*

This chapter focuses more sharply on the nature of educational experiences specially directed at the development of a culture of social justice and compassion. It is a framework that emerges from the discussion of priorities, given the nature of our moral and religious framework and present historical conditions.

I am using the term "educational" in this section in a somewhat narrower sense to refer to instructional or teaching strategies—that is, to school practices involving the what and how of teaching. However, there is no effort here at all to equate education with schooling even in the organizational sense, since other institutions such as the family, the press, the church, the synagogue, the media, and the workplace have important and substantial educative roles to play. Indeed, it is important that institutions that are constituted as primarily educative in character (e.g., schools, universities, nursery schools) be aware of each other's role and contribution. I am not inclined in this book to deal in any detail with special roles and functions for particular institutions except to say that whatever is done should be in harmony with a society's most emancipator and visionary goals. More specifically, schools do have a particular responsibility to respond to a very wide spectrum of educational goals, or at the very least the profession needs to stimulate public debate on the issues of what constitutes reasonable public expectations of an educational system.

Presently the public as we have already indicated has a great number of such expectations, that range from general acculturation to socialization; from job training to the development of hobbies; and from the three Rs to sex education. This list seems to grow as the public expresses its frustration and self-deception by adding to the schools' agenda and, paradoxically enough, simultaneously reducing the allocation of resources to the schools. The issue of what is or is not appropriate to be taught in schools is essentially moot as long as the schools' capacity to teach anything well to all students continues to be problematic. When the public asks us as educators to deal with a particular concern (e.g., global education, education for peace, "after-school" programs), our professional response must include consideration of intellectual, professional, and moral dimensions, as well as the nature of the resources required to meet the new or reconceptualized challenge.

The essential point here is that whatever the schools and the public determine to be appropriate for the schools' educational responsibilities must be addressed in such a way as to express our mythic goals, our sacred aspirations, and our moral commitments. If the schools are to be considered as preparation for work, they must do so by simultaneously being concerned with a society and an economy that is committed toward justice and dignity for all. If the schools are asked to develop a sports and athletics program, they should be required to do so in the context of the public's commitment to joy, dignity, and fairness for all. When the schools confront the inevitability of their acculturative role, they must also confront the public's expectation for serious criticism and imagination. The school that feels it appropriate to celebrate our nation should also see that such celebration would logically include an affirmation of those moral principles that affirm both the quality of human life and the importance of human freedom. Surely the schools should provide opportunities for those who have a deep commitment to research and scholarship, which need to be conducted with an eye on the moral and spiritual boundaries of research as well as on the underlying epistemological question.

In this chapter I will present a number of educational themes and dimensions directed toward the creation of a just, loving, and joyous community. The following chapter will present some ideas on how these themes can be and have been expressed within traditional, conventional, or experimental structures. I operate under the assumption that such themes can be presented in a great variety of ways and in the context of a large number of "disciplines" or "content areas." For that reason it is critical that we are clear that these themes of emphasis permeate the entire spectrum of educational activities hidden, overt, planned, implicit, or otherwise.

At this point I wish to reiterate a crucial theme of this book, that *the school experience ought to be seen as an opportunity for the growth and learning of all who dwell in a particular educational institution.* Schools are places of learning where people grow through an enhancement of their own capacities and human possibilities. Clearly, teachers will generally know more and have richer experiences than students who in turn will be able to learn a great deal from them. Moreover, educators as professionals need to arouse and sustain their own curiosity and humility over intellectual and professional questions. No set of intellectual and professional questions is as important to address, more perplexing to answer, and more anguishing to confront than those dealing with the purpose and goals of education.

Indeed, one continuing, very likely permanent, dimension of professional responsibility includes the serious reexamination of one's responses to these questions. Some of the questions have taken a classic form, e.g., "What knowledge is of most worth?"—but the essential questions have been asked in a variety of ways: What is the purpose of education? What is the value of education? What is the nature of knowledge? What can and must I know? What should be left to chance? Whatever the formulation, it is critical that educators continuously pose it for themselves, for the professions, and for the culture.

It is vital that these questions, if they are to be posed at all, not be presented with most of the answers already implicit, as in such questions as what are the purposes of teaching history? or what are the goals of elementary education?—both of which are asked within existing premises (i.e., history is to be taught and there are to be institutions of elementary education). When these are asked as open questions, we are almost sure to find ourselves confronting basic questions of human origin, meaning, and destiny. Focused questions (e.g., What are the goals of a fourth-grade reading program?) are more likely to keep our concerns technical and ameliorative rather than basic and transformative.

Professional educators tend to adopt a "goal-setting" framework in addressing these concerns, i.e., in a "problem-solving" manner, a process fraught with difficulties. First of all, goals should not be "set" as in concrete or stone, rather they should be presented and posed in such a manner that they invite continuous examination, reflection, and criticism. Such goals are historical and social constructions and, as such, need to be critically examined as part of our ongoing conversation, goals that need to be made and remade and not merely found and carried out! Secondly, educational goals are to be seen not as finite problems that have definite solutions (similar to an engineer's responsibility to figure out a way to build a bridge given a particular terrain, climate, and budget) but as inherently elusive issues, representing as they do, our beliefs about the true, the good, and the beautiful. Hence, the perplexities of discussing educational goals are parallel to the perplexities of discussing the meaning of life, and thus must be done in a context of awe, mystery, and humility.

What we present in the following section are a set of educational goals intended to be more directly concerned with our framework of a discourse directed at justice and compassion. The first of these broad general educational goals deals with concerns for personal and social empowerment.

The Impulse for Empowerment and Transformation

Within the context of assuming responsibilities of co-creation and the moral principles of equality, freedom, justice, and community, we affirm, as a major point of departure for this task, the significance of the insight of the concept of liberation/empowerment /praxis. If we are to accept our commitments seriously, educators have a special concern for helping us to be liberated from the various conditions that oppress us, particularly those of ignorance and illiteracy. Freire (1970, 1973) has shown misery, oppression, and us that ignorance and illiteracy are more than embarrassing and troublesome deficiencies in that they are necessary ingredients for maintaining poverty, hunger, and oppression. He has helped us better understand the powerful relationship between power and knowledge, how people hold on to their domination in part because the oppressed do not have the critical intellectual skills to overcome the powerful forces of acculturation that lead the weak to internalize the ideology of the strong. "Knowledge is power" is a well-known motto, but it is a bit misleading because it is clear that some knowledge is much more powerful than others. Educators have as part of their task, therefore, to be sensitive to this relationship and to pass on to their students that knowledge and those skills that tend to empower all rather than a few.

However, to be liberated from oppression is a necessary but not sufficient condition for meeting our commitments. Croatto (1981) and Walzer (1985) make this critical point by reminding us of two central points of the story of Exodus. First, the escape from Egypt represents one dimension of liberation, an escape from oppressive political, religious, and economic conditions, and symbolizes the availability of the energy required to escape. The agentic force that sets these events into motion emerges from a divinely inspired criticism of the very foundations of the oppressed society. The second act of this great drama narrates the work of finding the "promised land" a daunting task that involves the process of dialectically relating the sacred imperatives to the actual building of a worldly community. It is not until the Israelites are at least partially free from their bondage that they are ready to be in touch with the sacred.

As harrowing and dangerous as their saga of escape is, the trials and tribulations that the Israelites face as they embark on building their new life are even greater. The story of the trek to the "land of milk and honey" is replete with rebellion, counterrevolution, confusion, doubt, despair, and disarray. Walzer's retelling of the saga involves a depiction of swings in Moses' leadership modes, which ultimately results in Moses taking on the role, not of general or king, but of teacher. It is in this sense that Moses comes to see that he can best lead his people to the Promised Land by teaching them the skills required to make a just world. (This is a notion reechoed by John Dewey four millennia later in his concept of education as the process by which we can engage and make a world.)

Intellectual Processes and Forms

Even as we become increasingly aware of the limitations of the intellect, it is vital to affirm the fundamental importance of critical and imaginative rationality to an educational process directed at liberation. We need to know about the process of learning, the nature of knowledge, and the ways in which we seek and present truth. Students will need to study what has been called the structures of disciplines, not so much so that they might themselves become members of the disciplines or admirers of them but rather to gain insight into how we come to know and how we come to accept knowledge. We often pride ourselves as a society dedicated to reason, research, and science. We tend to accept the premise that there is a very strong relationship between knowledge and truth. Yet we do very little about carefully examining the epistemological issues, research paradigms, and learning theories that underlie this premise.

It is basic to one's education for liberation to have clear understanding of our system for symbol making—to understand language processes, modes of inquiry, theories of evidence, and theories of truth. We need to understand truly what is meant by such concepts as art, science, institution, proof, truth, verifiable, disciplines, logic, theory, paradigm, and the like. We need to know about knowing, think about thinking, and reflect on the meaning of meaning. I am not necessarily talking about a course in philosophy, but I am talking about the importance of gaining insight into major philosophical issues (i.e., issues often labeled as epistemological, axiological, and ontological). I am not necessarily talking about a course in the history of science or in intellectual history, but I do believe it is important that we know about the different ways we have to think and of their problems. We need in addition to be mindful of non-analytic modes of knowledge—the artistic, intuitive, body knowledge, kinesthetic, dance, etc. Learning about learning can help us learn not only more about teaching but about the learning process itself. Learning about knowledge can also give us more understanding of the boundaries of knowledge and of our frameworks of knowledge.

A Sense of Historicity

The importance of cultivating historicity as another critical educational goal is not at all to be equated with teaching courses in history, since the significance of the relationship between the past, present, and future extends much further than the discipline of history. We are a society that is very much present if not future-oriented, and our pragmatic and anti-intellectual impulses tend to promote an ahistoric consciousness. We tend to be impatient about the past because we naively believe that we can create our world unimpeded by considerations of what has already been. Our optimism, energy, and sense of agency compel us to act first and to (maybe) reflect on the significance of what we have done later on.

A critical consciousness of history actually can be more liberating, for it enables us to remember that there are origins and beginnings to the present and that their origins are rooted in human events. We come to know therefore that our problems and opportunities have been "created" and that they emerge from human interventions, human ideas, human responses, and human aspirations. This can help us escape the sense of determinism and inevitability which has the effect of putting a bogus legitimation on the status quo which itself leads to inertia and despair. History reminds us that life involves continuous opportunities to respond to change and that not standing pat is an important choice of how to respond.

We must remember that the study of history involves more than a chronicle of major political, military, and economic events. We need to be aware that child-rearing theories have histories, that the definition of work has a history, as do conceptions of math, history, music, art, and pedagogy. In other words, language and social practices are historical constructions and need to be treated as such. Knowing the changes that have occurred in our society may be very interesting to some, but it is likely to be enlightening to most. Not only do we have a buffer to a sense of inevitability and despair, but we have a built-in pressure for response and creativity. A strong sense of the past gives us the reality that we inevitably create tomorrow's past, the present, and that our response represents not only a comment on the future but on the past. When we know our past, we can maintain continuity by whatever we do, since even drastic change would represent a thoughtful and conscious concern with both past and future.

A sense of history reminds us of our commitments as well as the ways in which we have responded to them. It also urges us to be connected with the humanity that we will never personally know, our brothers and sisters who lived before us and those not yet born. We are all connected by history, and our sense of harmony derives from a sense of a common history of struggle. History is the repository of the human struggle for meaning and represents the connection between memory and response. Forgetting is also a historical phenomenon and must be seen, if not as purposeful, at least as extremely significant. What we forget in part determines our destiny. The responsibility for humanity to participate in its destiny is central to a conception of an education directed toward a loving, compassionate, and just world.

The Development of Social Skills

As I have said, it is theoretically possible to separate skills from substance, but it is a proposition that ought not to be emphasized for reasons already given. We present here a discussion of skills, not at all to reflect a separation, but rather to simplify the task of indicating the significance and interconnection of certain skills to the rest of the educational themes under discussion in this chapter. We are also aware that the distinction between knowledge and skills is problematic (like all distinctions), but again we wish only to draw attention to that vital aspect of education that involves experience and action. I believe that the relationship between theory and practice can be synergistic when thought of simultaneously and sterile when considered separately. Furthermore, I believe that we can and need to learn experientially, as well as analytically, and that an education directed toward the fulfillment of our moral commitments, by definition, includes serious concern for action.

Much of our culture teaches us not the skills of community building but rather those of individual competition. We know that democratic communities do not simply happen and that their growth is certainly not inevitable. Democratic communities need constant nurturance and attention to remain dynamic and responsive. This means more than learning *about democracy;* it also means learning *to do democracy;* it involves not just an understanding of the structure and how it works but how it works in *particular and concrete* situations. This also involves the skills of communication, of understanding one's social self in addition to one's personal self; of learning how to work with others and how to increase the probability that political and bureaucratic process and machinery will be responsive to our highest aspirations.

Much of the knowledge that translates into power is the knowledge that is acquired from the practice of power. There are a relatively small number of people who have power simply because they know how to be competent, how to operate social machinery, which political buttons to push, and which not to push. This is not particularly esoteric knowledge; it is simply not widely accessible (Newmann: 1975). Educators have a responsibility to determine those skills of practice that are critical to the defense and growth of our political and moral commitments. It would be tragic if our failure to live up to these commitments were based not on our rejection of these ideals but on our incompetence to make them happen.

I want to extend this list of educational themes with a discussion of other goals that actually penetrate all the others and have already been stressed implicitly and explicitly along the way, namely, the importance of knowledge and of a critical and creative consciousness. Again in the service of clarity and emphasis, they will be presented separately with the very clear assumption that these concerns are inextricably bound to all other educational goals. I present them last not because they are least, for I am not presenting a linear model. There is no need to frustrate ourselves with a chicken/egg paradox. The development of critical and imaginative capacities is absolutely critical to an educational program of liberation, justice, and love. They represent both conditions for, and results of, such a program.

The Assimilation of Critical Knowledge

This is a rather elaborate way of saying that education means, at least in part, that we "know" some information. When educators confront this issue of what we have to know, they inevitably raise a whole range of questions concerning purpose, direction, and destiny. In this section we will limit ourselves to the more limited and popular conception of "knowledge" that is information that is remembered or at least retained in a relatively unblurry manner. A real difficulty here, of course, is the issue of what it means to have knowledge, for even in common-sense terms we forget a lot of what we have learned very rapidly. John Holt reminded us of some of the absurdity of defining education as the accumulation of knowledge when he remarked that the real difference between "smart" and "dumb" students is that the smart student forgets the answers *after* the exam.

There are several justifications for the importance of "having knowledge." One is that certain knowledge is required for various job and work-related competencies. There is no need to belabor this point since it is obviously true, but such a criterion is by definition to be applied differentially—that is, those interested in knowing what is basic to a job or profession should (and no doubt will need no urging to) learn that knowledge. If pre-med students need to know about inorganic chemistry to gain entrance into medical school and to become physicians, well then of course they should learn inorganic chemistry. The real issue is not what is required for individuals with specific and particular needs and interests, but rather which knowledge should be held in common in order to promote both individual autonomy and a just society.

There are several arguments for learning a common body of knowledge. My position is that we need not debate the meta-question of whether there is such a body of knowledge, but rather we need to deal with the problem functionally as it relates to the larger framework we have been discussing. This would certainly allow for the possibility of maintaining that there is certain knowledge that everyone should have, but the issue would emerge from a consideration of the appropriateness of the knowledge to our framework, rather than vice versa.

For example, we have stressed the importance of developing a sense of community and universality. An argument can be made that community can be enhanced by (and indeed defined as) the possession of a common culture (i.e., a common body of knowledge). Let us then act on that hypothesis and examine the question of what common knowledge is most critical for that function. Similarly, we should be free to make a case that public solidarity can be nourished when we are all able to make allusions to paradigmatic stories, myths, events, dramas, literature. This is basically an issue of practice since it means figuring out which literary and intellectual pieces are most likely to enrich and bind us in ways that resonate with our myths and visions. Naturally professionals are certain to differ in their response, but what is important is that they struggle with the problem.

It is also critical that we at all times be sensitive to provide opportunities for personal joy and individual fulfillment. There can be no question that we should allow opportunities for people who are genuinely interested in the pursuit of knowledge for its own sake (i.e., for esthetic reasons). This is in the realm of specialized and individualized education, and it is important to affirm the legitimacy of this pursuit and provide for those who want to know simply because they want to know.

We have our own "list," however, of what everyone should know, some of which has already been indicated. I believe that we all should have solid awareness of the substance of critical and seminal statements about our moral commitments such as the Sermon on the Mount, the Ten Commandments, the Declaration of Independence, the United Nations Declaration of Human Rights, the U.S. Constitution, and the Gettysburg Address.

I obviously believe that all people should be able to read, write, and figure, but I shall deal with these "skills" later on in this chapter. It is certainly valuable for everyone to know, at least broadly, the major geopolitical features of our world and have a broad historical perspective on major worldwide political, ideological, and social events and trends. As indicated before, I believe everyone should know about basic modes of thought (mathematical, analytical, philosophical, esthetic, empirical) and about the properties of major disciplines. It is also valuable that everyone have a serious understanding of the properties of language, as I indicated above, and it is likely that this can be enhanced by learning at least one other language. Also, I am comfortable with teaching students knowledge which the culture believes gives one cachet (cultural capital); if we expect people to know the capital of the states, then perhaps we should teach it, as long as we remind ourselves and our students that this represents acculturation more than it does education.

However, the essential point is that we not start with a body of knowledge and then try to rationalize its importance. It is, on the other hand, legitimate to consider that the persistence of certain knowledge in the society may indicate an importance that needs to be discovered and articulated. What we need to say is that the educational vision that we have drawn very definitely includes the necessity for knowledge in the narrow sense. We have affirmed the value of knowledge for its own sake for *those who have that interest;* otherwise, when educators make a case for knowing this or that they will need to be persuasive that the possession of this particular information is functional to the vision. While knowledge is an end in itself for only some people, it is functional for all people. Knowledge must not be reified, nor must we become idolatrous of it.

We must respect the process of creating knowledge and the enormous importance to us of what knowledge we decide to accept as true. We must also be aware of our relationship to knowledge—how we create it, how it shapes us, and what it means to us. To go beyond that, however, and try to make specific bits of knowledge or information sacred is to move into reification and idolatry. Nonetheless, let it be understood that we as educators must not only be prophets, idealists, and creators, but we must be knowledgeable ones, people who can make knowledge holy by connecting it to sacred imperatives.

Critical Consciousness and Competence

The issue of the vivid relationship between a critical capacity and education has already been mentioned several times. Criticism here refers to two general capacities, that of rigor and that of judgment. When I speak of rigor, it is within the Socratic tradition, that begins with the commitment to precise, rigorous thinking and a simultaneous skepticism and humility about our capacity to do so. In order to resist flaccidity and self-deception, one has to be alert to the likelihood that any statement or proposition is incomplete or misleading. Rigorous criticism is an antidote to such thinking, since it attempts to thoroughly test the validity of propositions, statements, policies, and pronouncements by carefully examining their logic, assumptions, evidence, and coherence. The skepticism and modesty rest not only on a degree of suspicion and a dash of cynicism but more broadly on a sophisticated understanding of the perplexities, subtleties, and elusiveness inherent in the pursuit and articulation of truth.

Criticism as judgment refers to the application of moral and esthetic criteria to propositions, policies, events, and other phenomena. Socrates, as we have said, adopted his critical posture as a mode of helping to do what he thought his gods wished. The prophets criticized their society on the basis of the standards established by what was enunciated at Mt. Sinai. Criticism in this sense attempts to size up the quality of relationships between a set of prior standards and some specific and concrete phenomenon. When, for example, we read a movie review, we want more than a statement of whether or not it is a "good" movie. We also want to know the basis of the judgment, we want to know about the movie's believability, about its capacity to inspire, its point of view, its entertainment qualities, etc. To criticize means, among other things, the capacity to react, to respond, and to make relationships, and, hence, criticism can be seen as being opposed to passive acceptance. Moreover, its intellectual center is one of relationships—that is, the capacity to see the connection between principles, ideas, criteria, standards, and individual events.

Criticism involves us in combining rigor with judgment in attempting to integrate careful thinking with our moral and esthetic principles. This is another way of characterizing a major essence of our educational vision in which we utilize our intellectual skills to create and make manifest that vision. In this way we can possibly avoid the horrors that come from intellectual skills being used for destructive purposes and from applying principles with more sentimentality than reason. Thus, in affirming the vital role of criticism, we underscore the major responsibility for educators to help us to be aware of our need to have caution as well as convictions, to celebrate as well as complain, and to value that that connects head to heart.

Paulo Freire (1970, 1973) is perhaps the most eloquent and compelling educator to write on the centrality of this capacity. He, in effect, defines literacy not as the ability to read and write but as the ability to read and write *critically*. His notion of *conscientization* represents a pedagogy designed to liberate people from the oppression of illiteracy (i.e., an uncritical consciousness). To Freire, *conscientizao* represents "learning to perceive social, political, and economic contradictions, and to take action against the oppressive elements of reality" (1970:74). To be uncritical, according to Freire, is to be unaware of the human character of our culture, to see the world's condition as "natural" or inevitable and one's particular condition as a function of uncontrollable forces. To be uncritical one has to be ignorant of historical processes and of the nature and significance of knowledge. One can remain uncritical by maintaining a primitive language and by refusing to learn how to analyze language and to analyze with language. Moreover, Freire cautions us of the immense significance of not trying to provide this capacity:

> Any situation in which some men prevent others from engaging in the process of inquiry is one of violence. The means used are not important: to alienate people from their own decision-making is to change them into objects. (1970:74)

Critical thus takes on another connotation besides rigor and judgment—namely, it becomes a crucial component of freedom, autonomy, and justice. It is critical that people be critical in order that they can continue to be critical. To Freire, the development of critical literacy represents hope in that it provides a way in which humanity can freely and peacefully struggle for their freedom. Indeed, people have a responsibility to be critical once they decide on a life of meaning, for they must then discern the degree to which their lives are in concert with that sense of meaning. Human dignity entails responsibility, and responsibility entails being critical.

Maxine Greene (1978) puts emphasis on the critical consciousness that makes us aware of our presence in the world and of the existential reality that requires us to act upon it. She stresses the importance of questioning the "everydayness" of our lives and of becoming ever more aware of how we might be free to contemplate the possibility that "life might be otherwise." In a similar vein, Richard Shaull has this to say in his introduction to Freire's *Pedagogy of the Oppressed:*

> There is no such thing as a neutral educational process. Education either functions as an instrument which is used to facilitate the integration of the younger generation into the logic of the present system and bring about conformity to it, or it becomes "the practice of freedom, " the means by which men and women deal critically and creatively with reality and discover how to participate in the transformation of their world. The development of an educational methodology that facilitates this process will inevitably lead to tension and conflict within our society. But it could also contribute to the formation of a new man and mark the beginning of a new era in Western history. (1970:15)

Not only do we need to nourish a general quality we can call critical consciousness, we need also to develop particular critical skills. The fundamental skills of reading and writing should be taught not as disembodied mechanics and certainly not in isolation from "content." If we insist on reifying reading and writing, let us at least qualify those terms, let us emphasize *critical* reading and *critical* writing. We need to teach people what critical thinking is and about how to critique research, scientific findings, policy statements, and artistic creations. We need to know about various sets of rules of evidence, about the nature of rhetoric, and how to sort out the tangle of assumptions, beliefs, values, and assertions (i.e., the way we dialogue). We must always remember however, to be critical of our criticism, to be wary of our impulse to avoid the disciplines of either intellectual rigor or moral boundaries. We must also be careful not to idealize criticism itself lest our criticism result in stalemate or moral paralysis, since our basic goal is to connect criticism with creation.

Imagination and Creativity

We are here not talking of a conventional orientation toward art and creativity that essentially involves their objectification and reification. In our mainstream educational policies and practices, art and creativity have been consigned to fairly specialized areas, for the most part valued but given a special status that actually limits their significance as a consequence of this process of fragmentation. Art is typically characterized as a separate "subject" with its own space, teachers, materials, and traditions. Creativity has come more and more to mean a specialized talent to be technically competent as well as to be original, fresh, and unique. Moreover, both characteristics are often associated with an unusual talent that some people have and others do not. The effect of this is to minimize the possibility of an education in which creativity and art could permeate the entire curriculum and to perpetuate the myth that only a few of us can be "artists."

A very different orientation to art is expressed by Gibson Winter (1985) who believes that our culture's "dominant root metaphor" is changing from one of "machine" to one of "art." His position is that our consciousness is gradually changing from one that tends to see the world mechanically, as in a Newtonian system of regularity, order, precision, and predictability. The emerging consciousness is one in which we are putting more emphasis on human response, on subjectivity, and the dialectic between phenomenon and perception. Hence, we are less likely, Winter says, to view the world as a gigantic clock whose inner works have been set and whose operations are exact and orderly. We are more likely to see how much of our understanding of the world is mediated by our language, beliefs, values, and way of being. We are more likely, then, to become sensitive to the extraordinary importance of human constructions and to the processes and products of human imagination. We have become more and more conscious of how our perception and images of the world affect our experience of the world.

For a confirmation of the power of this insight, we need only to look at the fields of advertising and marketing as they are clearly aware of the power of images and the potential for creating not only new products but, even more significantly, creating the need for them. The film and television industries have created mythical cultures of America that do more than mirror America—they actually become our mirror. For those of us who are not clear on who we are, what we are supposed to say or do in particular situations, we can always look at an illuminated screen of people actually responding to these same situations. These artificially created reactions to real situations provide a model for the way things are—life imitating art.

Creativity can be experienced not only as an exotic and mysterious quality but also as an inevitable and inherent aspect of human experience. All people constantly create: we create meaning; we create language and the stories of our lives, we create our responses to nature and culture; in a word, we create culture. It is our images that we use to make sense out of the world, and it is our imagination that enables us to give moral and religious significance to life.

It is through play and imagination that we first encounter our world and give shape to it. The capacity to play, to imagine, and to fantasize allows us to create visions and frees us to transcend the forgotten boundaries that we once ourselves established. We have created our world, and as good artists we should be able to be critical of our work since artists know that they must continue to create or, more accurately, to re-create. Thinking of creation and re-creation as play provides us with the freedom to escape hegemonic thinking—that is, to go beyond what seems fixed and irreplaceable.

Play and Imagination

Stanley Aronowitz and Henry Giroux elaborate on their notion of the critical part that intellectual discourse plays in transformative education with a strong and eloquent plea for the importance of play.

> We learn as much by assimilating the world to the dictates of the sphere we call "imaginary" (which cannot always be adjusted to practical tasks) as we do in the so-called socialization process, one that is increasing technologically directed. By imaginary we mean the proclivities toward creating an alternative world, not representing that which is. The imaginary is the foundation of play; it is the way we make a new world as well as achieve self-hood. Play can be understood as the interaction of two imaginaries, especially among children where the activity itself is directed toward creating not only the social self but also a self that "goes beyond" the given of existing social structures. The relationship between education as socialization, which is directed toward suppressing the imaginary, and learning as a means by which the imaginary takes control of the ego is inevitable in any society that wishes to insure the adaptation of its young to prevailing norms. The point of technological direction is to make the imaginary into an instrument of the prevailing order. (1985:18–19)

Educators as prophets will surely then critically examine the creative process and products as a basis for indicating an agenda for further imaginative works. We cannot be fully satisfied with our creations thus far; surely we cannot accept an esthetics of oppression, misery, and war. As critics, educators will attempt to discern which creations are indeed beautiful and which are ugly, and help their students to learn these modes of discernment for themselves. Our analysis in this book reflects a particular esthetic orientation in which we see a history of heroic efforts and brilliant creations (ideas, principles, theories); yet as magnificent as these efforts are, they have fallen short of our own hopes. Do we need to gather any more evidence for this? How many more wars, genocides, famines, depressions, plagues, epidemics, and suicides do we need to be convinced that we require radically new thinking, new visions, new paradigms if we are to survive, never mind to prevail?

If we are to have faith in imagination, we must first be able to imagine what Maxine Greene has called the ability to "possibilize." There is extraordinary evidence of our limitless potential for creative and imaginative brilliance. Time and again our history gives us examples of intellectual breakthroughs, startling intuitive leaps, and dazzling poetic insight that have led to significant changes in consciousness.

The women's movement is but one example of a major social phenomenon with profound consequences that has been largely enabled by the power of imagination and a concomitant change in consciousness. There was a time when thoughtful and good people could not imagine a woman as a truck driver, airline pilot, or surgeon. Now such images come to many more people much more easily, and indeed for most of us they no longer constitute imagined reality. The changes in laws and policies regarding gender are reflections of this re-creation of our image of women. Similar changes in consciousness have occurred in our own generation in our images of blacks, children, and gay people. The political and social activism associated with these movements is energized by imagination, and their success depends on the ability of others to re-create their long-standing images. Change by definition involves recreation, and creation requires the full use of all imaginative capacities—play, intuition, analysis, and conceptualization utilizing the creative energies of body, mind, and spirit.

We also have ample and exciting evidence of an enormous flowering of creative and imaginative genius in our own times. Not only are more people involved in the arts than ever before, but there is more concern and interest in participating directly as composers, artists, and performers. Moreover, we see in virtually every academic discipline and profession very serious discussions about the necessity for making significant changes in basic assumptions about the nature of the various fields. For example, even the highly rigid and straight-laced field of "educational research" is caught up in a major debate over the adequacy of its conventional, empirical, quantitative experimental research paradigm. Indeed, the concept of paradigm shift has become a virtual cliché. This may create difficulty for those who are cliché phobic, but nonetheless we are surely in a different place when we consider references to shifts in paradigms as routine and commonplace. Parents and teachers continue to be amazed at the increasing sophistication and creativity of young people, even as they may deplore their lack of traditional knowledge or skill. Each generation brings with it even more interest and sensitivity to the infinite possibilities of the imagination, whether it be reflected in science fiction, computer usage, musical groups, or new art forms.

Educators, therefore, need to provide more opportunities to develop the imaginative and playful potentials of their students more deeply and more widely. We must see art not as a separate activity to be performed only by the gifted. We must avoid associating creativity with the esoteric, and regard the imagination not as weird but necessary. We must allow our students and ourselves to be in touch with and to affirm our own creative processes. Furthermore, we ought to find ways to foster these processes since they afford the possibility of possibility. They can, furthermore, enrich our lives personally and communally, for they can provide us with esthetic and moral delight. Our present and our future are reflections of our imagination and our destiny will be determined by the creative capacities that are now being formed. Our belief is that the task of educators is to encourage and guide students to an imagination that goes far beyond ours, to help them to develop a consciousness that we are unable, because of the limitations of our own education, to conceive. We must, as educators, continue our faith that we can continue to imagine that others will imagine what we cannot.

What we have presented is very likely a partial and initial statement of an educational framework that is concerned with efforts to create a community of joy, love, justice, and compassion. It is a framework that emerges from an interpretation of contemporary American culture in which we see ourselves at the edge of impending glory or destruction. We see the sources of the problem and resolution in the moral and spiritual realm; more particularly, we see our problems rooted in our inability to deliver on our highest aspirations, a difficulty we believe is at least partly based on confusion and self-deception. As educators we can accept the responsibility to make us more aware of our confusion and thus help to reduce deception and confusion. In this way, we can legitimately participate professionally in our human responsibilities to participate in the creation of a more just and loving community.

Basic to our difficulty has been our inability to develop a close and enduring sense of democratic community as we are driven by a value system oriented toward individuality, competition, and material success. We have argued that in spite of our pluralism and diversity we do in fact have the possibility of creating an overarching consensus of general aspirations and moral principles. I have also tried to show that as educators we must be part of the process of forging that vision that can also guide us in our professional policies and practices.

The focal points of such a mythos are those that converge in a vision of democracy, compassion, justice, equality, freedom, and joy. Fundamental to the fulfillment of these commitments is an acceptance of human responsibility for the creation of a culture and environment in which these possibilities can be realized. It is our faith that the educative process is a necessary though not sufficient condition for the development of such a culture. Such an educative process must obviously resonate with the vision and be designed to facilitate the process of constructing it. This means an educative process that affirms and celebrates the vision and consciously adopts its framework, always mindful of the basic professional ethic that mandates free, open, and continuous inquiry. Key to this general vision and the particular ethic is the framework's strong emphasis on criticism and creativity as the interlocking and interdependent hinges of the educational framework.

We are very much aware that the educational process involves a great deal more than theory and visions. Not only is the nature of the profession as described above to be considered, there is also the necessity to deal with the vitally important process of planning, development, and implementation. We deal with these issues in the next chapter, restressing the maxim that the principal ingredients necessary for significant change are the acceptance of the need for significant change and the will to make such changes.

A fundamental tenet of the study of education that we have discussed and affirmed is the intimate relationship between culture and organized education. It is vital then to reiterate this major concern when confronting the issues of educational reform: we must recognize that to make significant educational change requires and means significant cultural change. We cannot continue the myth that educational problems are rooted primarily in professional and technical matters. When we finally give up trivializing education, it will mean that we have taken seriously the propositions that education can make us free and wise, not just rich and smart.

7

ISSUES OF CURRICULUM PLANNING, DESIGN, AND IMPLEMENTATION

'The prophet does not ask if the vision can be implemented for questions of implementation are of no consequence until the vision can be imagined. The imagination must come before the implementation. Our culture is competent to implement almost anything and to imagine almost anything and to imagine almost nothing. The same royal consciousness that makes it possible to implement anything and everything is the one that shrinks imagination because imagination is a danger.
WALTER BRUEGGEMANN, *The Prophetic Imagination*

In this chapter we will deal with issues of implementation, of how we might actually make these ideas operational and put them into action so that they actually function in the way they are intended. We fully realize the critical importance of the process of planning and designing a specific and complete educational experience, not only because it is a practical necessity but because this process is also a vital element in the development of theory. Again, I reject the dichotomy between theory and practice, preferring to see them as dialectical and, hence, continuously dynamic. Indeed, the ideas so far presented represent such an interaction and are presented not as final but as in process. There is always much more work to be done and this curriculum framework is no exception. In this regard we wish to point out a number of particular issues involving implementation.

Aspects of Resistance

Resistance to Serious Change

We are all aware of the phenomenon of homeostasis, the tendency for people and institutions to seek and maintain continuity and stability. Whether we call this instability or inertia hardly matters in this context since we must recognize the very important impulse in individuals and groups to be wary of the risks that major change entails. As we have pointed out, even the most modest suggestions for educational change are resisted because at some level we realize we are connecting to the possibility of deeper, broader changes in the culture. The proposals sketched in the prior chapter, however, go beyond suggesting the mere possibility of fundamental change.

Our starting point is the necessity for change since we begin in the pain and anguish of the human condition. We are insisting that curriculum planners focus on the horrors of our time—misery, disease, hunger, poverty, war. We challenge our colleagues and fellow citizens to use these realities of our present state of being as the point of departure when dealing with educational practices. This is to say we need to replace existing points of departure—test scores, college admissions, competition, and the maintenance of the status quo with very different ones. We must, instead, examine the relationship between existing educational practices and policies and what we as a culture deem to be of ultimate significance. It is time to accept that we are already "in the long run," that there is surely enough data to demonstrate that there is much in our fundamental structure of values, institutions, and organizations that has failed.

It is also important that educators speak out not only on the inadequacy of technical aspects of the profession but on the inadequacy of our major cultural institutions. Educators must stop hiding from their responsibility to make clear statements on the moral and spiritual dimensions of various educational policies and practices. Yes, along with many others, I am talking about *significant* change, and our ideas will likely be resisted because of this alone. Those of us committed to fundamental change challenge other educators to try to demonstrate that there is less risk in not changing. Change is more overtly dramatic, but not changing is just as significant and momentous. Educators must therefore be pressed to go beyond their day-to-day slogging and engage also in the enormous struggles involved in the fulfillment of our sacred commitments. This brings us to another serious difficulty in following through on these ideas, or on any set of ideas directed at significant liberating change—namely, the differences and divisions within the profession.

Professional Resistance

Stalemates
We have already discussed the problem of paralysis and inaction that emerges from a position of severe caution and reluctance to affirm moral and religious

principles. Professional stalemates can result from basic disagreement on more empirical issues (i.e., issues of knowledge, research, strategy). In this context, I particularly wish to focus on the debate over strategies for educational change that usually center on where the optimum source of change resides. For example, some people argue that fundamental change must result from the slow accretion of gradual and modest reforms at the "practical" level, that is, from teachers and researchers focusing on current practice and work within the existing framework. Others insist that it is a waste of time to attempt to make significant educational changes because that can only happen after there are major shifts in other social, political, and cultural institutions. Still others take the position that significant change must be preceded by more high-quality research on the learning/teaching process and much more clarity and precision of critical cultural and educational concepts.

My answer is yes, yes, and yes. We cannot choose one or even a few reform modes of meeting our responsibilities. For example, it is critically important that teachers and other educators continue to work hard to squeeze as much humanity and sanity as can be found in existing arrangements. That is a critically important task because it is a way of dealing with a concrete reality for very real people and because it helps the process of increasing our critical and creative capacities. When we recognize that we have to make "lemonade from our lemons," we are indicating that we know something about lemons and lemonade.

We need to avoid the unnecessary infighting and competition that comes from differences on which of these approaches is the most efficacious. Instead, we can each of us concentrate on doing what each of us actually *does,* but provided that we have some reason to believe that at minimum what we do does not make matters worse, and even better, can contribute to an improvement in the quality of human life.

We need also to affirm the importance of engaging in an incredibly complex and profound struggle in a variety of manners and strategies. We need not, and should not, needlessly disparage other strategies in order to validate our own, because when we do so we dissipate valuable energy which has as its unintended consequence the continuation of the status quo This is not to say, however, that we should not critically attend to what we do, only to suggest that there are a great many battles and skirmishes involved in the war on injustice and oppression. Let us by all means continue to do basic and applied research and be ever mindful of the relationship between research projects and our basic moral commitments. Let us indeed attempt to ameliorate, cope, adapt, and keep bad situations from getting worse, as long as we do not confuse acceptance and coping with validation and legitimation. There can surely be disagreements on strategy, but if we link our strategies to broad common goals, even those strategies that are seemingly contradictory can be productive. We should become less tolerant of certain educational goals (e.g., competition, individual success, amorality, social irresponsibility) and more supportive of strategies designed to meet others (e.g., justice, love, compassion, equality).

Sabotage

Any program, set of ideas, or orientation can be sabotaged. By sabotage I mean those acts that are counterproductive and destructive to the original ideas performed by people uncommitted or only partially committed to them. This, of course, speaks to the power and importance of practice and the practical futility of trying to develop teacher-proof materials. The whole concept of "teacher-proof" is both a reproach to teachers as well as recognition of their power. One of the major lessons of the 1960s and 1970s curriculum movement was that the teachers who did not participate in the development of newly developed curriculum materials were more likely to resist their implementation in one way or another. We note this reality, but we wish to extend our considerations to another dimension of this phenomenon. Sometimes sabotage is actually appropriate, as in the case of trying to undermine policies that are harmful and wrong. We probably would call such acts creative and adaptive rather than subversive. However, there is also the more basic appropriateness to a situation where teachers are treated as objects and instruments.

We must not allow ourselves to be used or to consider teachers as simply another variable or "resource" to be manipulated and controlled like building blocks. To do so would undermine the basic moral legitimacy of our educational framework, which does not countenance people as a means to an end. In order for a framework such as the one described to become operational, we will need professionals who come to accept its basic validity for themselves. Such a commitment cannot and should not be mandated or taken for granted for it must be the result of conscious and informed choice. This, of course, echoes the signal importance of the professional attitudes and ethics described in the last chapter, and I repeat: the profession is itself a major element of the curriculum.

Co-optation

This is by far the most difficult and dangerous form of resistance because it is so seductive and comforting. Schools, mirroring the larger, dominant culture, are not only extremely skilled in resisting changes but are also adept in assimilating them into their fundamental structures. For example, just as the counterculture's attempt to establish its identity by wearing blue jeans as a symbol of simplicity and as a rejection of materialism was overcome by expensive and stylish "designer jeans," efforts to overcome an arbitrary curriculum eventually resulted in rigid Tylerian lesson planning. The culture and the school are extraordinarily gifted in their ability to absorb changes and pressures without making any significant alterations in basic attitudes and priorities. For example, we sometimes change the grading scheme from "A, B, C, D" to one in which different terms are used: "excellent, good, fair," or to "excellent, shows improvement, and needs improvement." But the assessment process remains hierarchical and summative regardless of the rubric.

Co-optation is a technique for survival, one that is flexible and tolerant to a degree but ultimately concerned less with change than with continuity. It is a technique for having your cake and eating it and has proven to be remarkably effective. Its danger, of course, is in its deception, in its propensity to give people the illusion and appearance of significant change. It is, therefore, seductive to those who very much want to change but are reluctant or unwilling to deal with the consequences of real change. Co-optation feeds the self-deception that believes, for example, that reducing class size from thirty to twenty-eight is a significant change or that more requirements will result in a more rigorous educational program. The educational system has a definite logic to it, for better or worse, and it will strive, usually successfully, to apply that logic to any suggestion for change. Even when some suggestions are accepted, they will likely be substantially transformed by the persistent, fundamental, and everlasting logic of the educational system. Cooptation represents at least some effort, however, to accommodate to suggestions and pressures. There is, of course, the resistance that takes on the more overt nature of rejection.

Forms of Rejection
There are a number of classic modes of rejecting new ideas, always keeping in mind that it is highly appropriate to closely examine new or difficult ideas and sometimes to reject them. We are here discussing forms of resistance that represent failures of serious reflection of those who are relentlessly and predictably committed to the preservation of the status quo no matter what alternatives are presented. It is certainly reasonable to assume some validity to the policies and practices of existing institutions, and it is not unreasonable for the burden of proof to be on those who are critical of them. In times such as ours, however, educators should not have to retreat into such a defensive posture and should instead be able to be affirmative and celebrative about their own beliefs and practices. It is not professional to be defensive, nor is it in the best interests of the culture for educators to wait for someone to try to guess or find out the serious problems of the field.

However, our profession and dominant culture do have some leaders who instinctively defend what is and who are prone to be suspicious of different formulations. It is to this group that we are addressing issues of resistance, not so much as resistance to serious change but as serious resistance to seriously considering serious change. This group has learned a number of clever responses or reactions that constitute apparently intellectually sound and realistic considerations. Three of these modes in particular need examination: rejections based on countercharges of "panacea promising," "exaggerated criticism," and "insufficient technology."

Panacea Promising
The charge is often made of suggestions for change (for better or worse) that their supporters are presenting them as a panacea, that they are presented as simple cure-alls for highly complex and perplexing problems. I personally have never seen a proposal for educational change that was ever so presented. I have certainly seen proposals that promised a great deal more than seemed plausible, but never one that promised to be a cure-all. Surely there are proposals that are blind to problems

other than the ones that they address, but to characterize them as promising a panacea is to create a straw man. I certainly do not offer a "panacea"; indeed what is presented here is not so much a cure as a diagnosis. The cure can come only if we accept the diagnosis, and if we do, it will still require an immense amount of hard and complicated work in many areas to develop reasonable responses to that diagnosis. The process of transforming the schools requires many and varied approaches as applied to a large number of situations and circumstances. There simply is no magic bullet and no one says there is. It is also vital to repeat our disclaimer that the schools by themselves cannot solve the problems of the world. We know that they cannot but that they can and should make a significant contribution to the creation of a good and just world.

The charge of panacea pushing is often associated with that of the charge of faddism, of which there is quite a lot in education. However, to lump together all critiques of existing forms as passing fads would be self-deceptive and counterproductive to efforts at transcending our current, unpassing fad that is our present educational system. It is vital to remember that our educational organization, policies, and traditions were not revealed at Mt. Sinai or in any other sacred place, but are rather recent and modest efforts by rather recent and modest folks.

Exaggerated Criticism

Another mode of rejection of consideration of serious change is captured by the old folk maxim, "Don't fix it till it's broke." This is to invoke the feeling of pride in our accomplishments and is meant to minimize the validity of the basic premise that structural change is needed. My answer to this criticism would be (and has been in this book) quite simply, "It *is* broke." However, when a system appears on the surface to be functioning, or at worst needs repairs rather than replacement, there is still something comforting to those who are terrified by the implications and suggestion of the destructive quality of the system. An automobile that pollutes the air can still get us to the fair even if such cars eventually destroy the fairgrounds and those who are there.

Educators must avoid the equivalence of the "naturalist fallacy" that confuses "is" with "ought." It is possible to argue that the persistence of our educational institutions means that they have met the test of time. I would argue that their persistence has failed the test of reason. Indeed, the argument that the persistence of the system is in itself evidence of its wisdom breaks down upon examination of the accomplishments of the goals of its own logic.

Insufficient Technology

This failure of the schools to deliver on its promises is reflected in the way this failure is projected on newly formulated proposals. The rejection of change often takes the form of demanding (at least as it has been leveled at some of my colleagues and me) that we should not try to replace the present system until we know what to replace it with. This knee-jerk, automatic support of the existing arrangements constitutes desperate last-ditch defensiveness. It is certainly proper to assume a show-me attitude when claims are made, but the criticism should be on the validity of the proposals per se, not on their inherent threat to the status quo. Conversely, it is possible to reject what is proposed as an alternative and still accept the criticism of the existing. We can accept someone as being truthful when he or she tells us that our house is on fire without hiring them to be our architect. Nor does it mean that if an architect's plan is inadequate the house we now live in is habitable.

The truth is that we do not know completely or even mostly how to teach the nature of what we are urging. However, neither do we know any better how to teach to the existing goals. The major difference is that the profession has chosen to struggle with the problems inherent in the existing educational agenda. We do not claim to have anywhere near the last word on how to teach people to understand algebra or be a good citizen or a team player. We have, however, applied enormous energies and resources to working on such professional concerns.

We have no doubt whatsoever that our educational agenda, however difficult and challenging, can be addressed successfully by a profession committed to its validity. We cannot logically (or morally) withhold its development until it has been developed. What we can do is decide to channel our imagination and energy toward the construction of a practice directed toward a world of peace, justice, love, and joy.

Issues of Planning

As we have already noted, current ideas about curriculum planning are heavily influenced by the so-called Tyler model (1949), which stresses a process of stating observable objectives, predetermined by a concern for social needs and an understanding of the learning process, that can be made specific enough for "objective" evaluation. There is no question that this model has made a genuine contribution to the field because of its emphasis on rationally determined criteria for how and what to teach. As obvious as this may sound, the Tyler model helped in the struggle against arbitrary and facile thinking about curriculum and instruction. It helped to restrict the impact of mere speculation and conventional theory, thereby enabling serious research and reflection on instructional issues. The model, in addition, is a very powerful tool for those primarily interested in efficiency, order, and control. However, it suffers from its pretense to be neutral and objective in two ways: first, the claim of neutrality and objectivity is itself naive and logically impossible, and second, it fails to explicitly affirm any governing moral principles, and the ones that are affirmed indirectly or implicitly are reflections of concerns for control, elitism, and the preservation of the status quo. For educators to posit neutrality is to deny their responsibility as social leaders and to cast doubts on their sophistication as thinkers.

Our framework suggests planning of a very different kind since it puts much more emphasis on a relatively explicit moral and religious framework and has more concern for architecture than engineering. We believe it is imperative that planning not be reduced to the implementation of an already decided set of objectives, but exist as an opportunity for teachers, students, administrators, and community members to participate in praxis—namely, in the dialectic of emerging theory and practice. I have suggested a framework not as a way to generate a set of measurable objectives but, rather as a significant point of departure for that dialogic process. The planning process itself should not only be functional to developing learning experiences for others but should itself be educative to the planners. Indeed, the concept of "planning" needs to be critically examined, particularly when it is seen as separate from the entire range of educational practice. Planning should be seen as a process and as a dimension of education, not as a separate skill or function. To concentrate on planning in the way the field does (e.g., texts and courses in "curriculum planning," which exists as a separate field for the "curriculum planner") serves mostly to emphasize engineering or applied concerns, brushing aside urgent concerns of architecture or fundamental structure. Curriculum planners in the existing system want to know the broad goals quickly in order to get on with their job of devising instruction strategies and material, and, hence, they are almost sure to avoid being critical of the more basic goals of the educational system. They see such an examination as something that is beyond their control, or perhaps as simply empty theorizing slowing down the "real" work of planning for tomorrow's classes.

The subtext of the current process is that the more fundamental curriculum planning tends to go on in the realm of big business and government. This planning is done in the context of considerations of broad social, political, and economic concerns such as foreign policy, industrial development, economic growth, and the job market. If, for example, there is to be a serious program for space exploration, there will be a concern for the recruitment and training for engineers and physicists. If the government or big business anticipates an expansion of the computer industry, then the schools are asked not only to help in training computer technicians but also to encourage computer consumption by adding computer-oriented materials to the curriculum. When a state goes on a serious campaign to attract industry, it will be sure to do important curriculum planning (e.g., develop community colleges that are responsive to industrial and commercial personnel needs).

Issues of Design

The basic design of the American schools has been set for nearly a hundred years; and through a number of variations, the basic themes are amazingly constant across time and space. Elementary schools tend to stress the acquisition of basic study skills and attitudes—reading, writing, arithmetic, memorizing, respect for authority and order, etc. At some level (e.g., middle school) there is a transition to a departmental organization. Sometimes this takes the form of areas of learning that suggest their strong connection to traditional disciplines, as is the case of language arts/English and social studies/history. Sometimes the transition is more organizational—students may go to specialized classes in science or art or music. At any rate, sooner or later the conventional secondary school curriculum with its sacred and eternal five subjects will appear. The mighty five are, of course, English, history, science, mathematics, and foreign languages. These are usually supplemented by electives and "extracurricular" activities such as music, athletics, and art, but the sacred five are dominant in virtually every secondary school in America.

There is an interesting and important strategic consideration involved with the persistence of this basic design. Of course there is a certain amount of variation within this design, but the hard question is whether it is prudent to propose an alternative design or to suggest an alternative variation. There are several advantages to the option of working within the conventional design, the most attractive one being that it would probably be politically a lot easier than trying to work for total change.

There is the valid argument that this basic design serves an important ritualistic function, one that maintains continuity and tradition. This design, although not really very ancient, does have a great deal of social acceptance, and symbolically it provides an image (however distorted) of rigor, scholarship, universality, and tradition. The argument is that it is prudent and wise to maintain the design, and that the design is flexible enough to meet the requirements of a variety of educational frameworks and orientations. There is also, of course, a strong educational argument that has been made for at least major elements of the basic design. However, it is very difficult nowadays to find any systematic effort to make sense out of the design as a whole or to feel willing to argue that the basic design makes theoretical and empirical sense as an entity.

The argument that is often made is that students need first to master two sets of basic intellectual skills—first, those often referred to as the three Rs, and second, those conceptual powers contained in major academic disciplines. Mastering these functions is thought to represent the essentials of an education, or at the very least they represent the critical prerequisites for "advanced learning." The further argument is that the exposure to major academic disciplines provides an opportunity to learn for the sake of learning as well as the chance to benefit from the pragmatic qualities of the various disciplines. Each discipline is said to have the capacity for inherent value, to provide esthetic satisfaction ("the love of learning") and to meet certain personal and social needs (e.g., the study of math helps us to be logical, and the study of history helps us to be good citizens).

There are many criticisms that have been directed at the basic design itself, many of which are implied in the preceding chapter of this book. For purposes of this particular section I wish to examine the basic design from the perspective of a single but critical question namely, the question of whether we should teach what is interesting or teach what is important. The intention of this question is to be seen as heuristic; as an analytical tool for probing the claims of the five sacred disciplines to be a major and dominating force of our basic curriculum design. Indeed, we can perhaps further sharpen our analysis by examining the corollary claim that students should be required to enroll in these courses.

In effect, the implicit claim is that these courses are inherently both interesting *and* important and that the challenge to the instructional program is to develop procedures that will make this potential real. If such a claim were true, it certainly would be not only convincingly persuasive but delightfully attractive. What could possibly be better than a set of experiences that will provide both benefits and satisfaction, have both pragmatic and esthetic payoffs, and unite needs and wants? Let us then examine this claim more carefully. Let me first clarify what I mean when I make the distinction between "interesting" and "important." When people say they are interested in something, they are reflecting a personal connection and resonance with that something that is of a different order than their relationship with other somethings. Their interest indicates that they are particularly attracted and personally inclined to become more involved and knowledgeable about the source of their interest. Interests are therefore personal and variable in the way that hobbies, tastes, and personal preferences are. To be interested in X is more of an esthetic consideration (i.e., X provides some personal satisfaction on its *own* terms). We expect enormous individual differences as far as interests are concerned, and our only boundary to them is that our personal interests do not interfere with the pursuit of other people's interest. Apart from that, we are more likely to be amused than threatened when we discover that our friends, colleagues, and neighbors have different interests than our *own*. We do not take offense when someone finds baseball more interesting than chess and we are not surprised when some people find Hemingway's stories more interesting than those of Updike.

I am using the concept of "important" here in its social sense of what is thought to be urgent, required, necessary, and vital. Perhaps it is necessary for individuals to have an interesting life, a proposition that provides one way of integrating the two concepts. Even in this case, however, we need to consider the importance of each concept since this involves the important question of how we are to create such a world. As educators, we eternally address the issue of what is important to teach since it involves the classic questions we mentioned in a prior chapter- What knowledge is of most worth? What knowledge or skill might be left to chance? When we decide to require or mandate certain experiences we do so because we believe they are vital and important to the culture and to students. We are likely to disagree on what constitutes "important," but we clearly agree that whatever is important should be taught, one way or another. Hence, "important" in this context should be seen in more social and moral terms in that it involves a statement of a hierarchy of values.

To claim that the five sacred disciplines are both important and interesting would seem to be fatuous and self-serving. To even claim that the five subjects are (or, even worse, can be) made interesting to all is arrogant, representing a denial of the realities of individual differences. There is, of course, a more attractive claim and that is to insist that what is important is inherently interesting. This, I believe, is both wishful thinking and another denial of the human condition. For example,

I believe without reservation that the technical aspects of nuclear energy are vitally important and that it would be highly desirable that I become much more informed about them than I am now. Furthermore, I am certainly very interested in many of the social issues that are involved in nuclear energy. However, it is also clear that I am not at all "interested" in learning about the details—that is, I find them boring in spite of their importance. I very much regret this, for it means either that I will neglect this area of study, probably relying on others to interpret for me, or that I will have to endure the boredom and pain of studying that which I would prefer not to study.

The case is similar for the opposite situation. I find historical details of professional baseball to be very fascinating and compelling. I have also come to know that most of my colleagues and friends find these details to be exceptionally uninteresting, a source of sadness and frustration for me. However interesting I find these data to be, I am still not able to make a case that they are vitally important to the commonweal. As much as I would like people to share my interest, I cannot demand or expect them to do so, although I reserve the right to entice them.

In parallel manner, there is no question that there are people who genuinely and deeply love particular academic disciplines (i.e., find them interesting), and it is quite reasonable to provide opportunities for others to become equally involved. Indeed, a central aspect of our educational framework is to work to create a world of joy, where all people could do what really attracts and interests them. Let us by all means expose students to areas of possible interest that they otherwise might not encounter. Why, however, should this be limited to the areas routinely found in the basic design? Why chemistry and not sociology? Why history and not psychology? Why algebra and not astronomy? Why English and not linguistics?

Furthermore, if the school is to provide opportunities to affirm and foster student interests, why limit the population of "interesting" to academic disciplines? Let us, for example, take the matter of chess, a game requiring rigorous, careful thinking, emotional strength, and a sturdy character. Many find the game of chess to be extraordinarily interesting to the point of deep passion and serious commitment. Many math teachers use chess to teach about mathematical concepts. Is it not just as reasonable to use mathematical concepts to teach about chess? A history of chess could give us interesting perspectives on different cultures in different times. Is algebra more or less interesting than chess? This, of course, is a rather silly question since people could be interested in either, or both, or neither.

If a curriculum then is to be built partly on the potential interest, it will by necessity have to offer a very wide range of opportunities. If it does not, then the curriculum will have to reflect some criteria or considerations for narrowing the range of potentially interesting phenomenon. Here, we begin to edge into the realm of that which is considered to be "important."

I am personally and professionally prepared to say that we should teach what is important even if it is not going to be very interesting, or not interesting at all. It would be wonderful if we could integrate the two, and we certainly ought to work very hard to do so, but we ought not to sacrifice our sense of what is important on the altar of personal preferences. At the same time we should also make every effort to make the knowledge we consider important meaningful to students. This means linking such knowledge to the stories and experiences that give meaning to students' lives.

I am also personally and professionally committed to the proposition that people have a right to live a life of personal joy, play, and excitement. It is vital that schools facilitate this right and nourish the human impulse to develop individual interests. We must, however, guard against another impulse, that of overestimating the significance of one's personal interests. Sometimes we become so attached and involved with an area of interest that we project that involvement onto others as a way of validating our own attachment. In this way personal interests are transformed into areas of social importance—the hobbies of a few can become the requirements for all. I believe this partly explains the persistence of the sacred five in the basic design; they found their place in the curriculum because the people who designed the curriculum liked them, or found those courses valuable. What's good for the captains of industry, academia, and government must, therefore, be good for the country!

Part of the significance of this analysis turns on different connotations of the word "interesting," and this difference is such that it could be considered a pun. There is "interested" in the sense of that which gives us a certain kind of pleasure and delight and then there is that which is in our interest (i.e., that which serves our own particular purposes). I believe that much of the basic design can be seen as confusion between these two different senses of "interesting." It is to the interests of those in power to convince people that what is interesting to the powerful is in the interest of the weak. Another way to keep the weak under control is to convince them that they are not interested in the truly interesting matters. I believe it to be in the interests of our major moral commitments that we allow individuals to pursue what is truly interesting to them and urge the educational community to pursue that which is in the interest of all people.

When it is claimed that certain disciplines are valuable in and of themselves, we are making an esthetic claim, and when we say that they are valuable because they are necessary for the achievement of certain goals (e.g., thinking logically, being a good citizen), we are making an empirical claim. It is this latter claim that we must address as we consider issues of designing a curriculum for social justice and compassion.

In one sense it hardly matters what the form and design are to be, provided that they facilitate and enhance the basic orientation of the framework. It is clear that a basic design that has certain disciplines as its main dimension could be and has been used to reflect a great number of different emphases. To say, for example, that the schools should teach history or math is to say very little, for the teaching of history and math could entail very different orientations. History, for example, can be taught as a structure, as chronology, as epic; it can be taught theoretically, requiring students to read original sources, do original research, and read critiques of history; it can be taught as intellectual history, political, or social history. Even this attempt to reflect the broad range of orientation inherent in the concept of history as a subject of learning does not begin to deal with the equally broad range of instructional approaches that might be used in the teaching of history (e.g., didactic, critical, mastery).

What matters fundamentally is, of course, the choice of orientation, emphasis, and direction. Thus, when one speaks to the pragmatic qualities of discipline or subject, it is clear that we can regard disciplines and subjects as techniques to be used to the degree that they show promise of enhancing the given educational orientation, direction, and emphasis. When we do this, we can cut across the emotion and sentimentality that characterize the passionate and partisan defense of certain disciplines. Those who love their disciplines need not be required to justify their passion, but when these lovers make claims for the potency of these disciplines, they indeed must be prepared to provide evidence for their claims,

Such claims can be examined in the same way we judge the claims of any proposed technique, such as the suggestion that this particular text, film, or learning technique is more effective than another. If a case can be made that the teaching goals can best be reached through the existing basic design as described, then let us by all means use it. Although it is certainly theoretically possible for this to be the case, I remain skeptical and wary about maintaining the basic design because it carries with it a great number of sacred cows and personal pets. It is a design that has been used so extensively and uncritically, and contains so much nostalgia, unverified assumptions, and unchallenged claims, that I doubt that its hegemonic character could be seriously eroded. It is hard for us to think of the study of Shakespeare and Euclid as being questioned and of conceiving of mathematics and biology as means rather than ends. Teachers have a tendency to identify closely with their subjects and, therefore, tend to make somewhat exaggerated claims for "their" field. It is this sometimes intense loyalty and devotion that clouds the vision of educators, just as any affair of the heart would. However, there must be better ways of sustaining the glory and beauty of a discipline than by exaggerating its importance and imposing it upon the unwilling.

Nonetheless, one must recognize the reality of the power and persistence of the basic design, and so I would not rule out the possibility of using it as a technical support for developing appropriate learning experiences. The key word, of course, is "appropriate," for any design above all else must deeply and thoroughly reflect in all aspects the major sacred, moral, and educational principles contained in our foundations of an orientation toward a society based on a serious and continuing commitment to peace, joy, love, social justice, equality, and community. In my view, it would take enormous work, major restructuring, and significant upheavals if the present basic design were to be the major organizational framework for such an education. Just as it is absurd to believe that the existing educational program is leading us to such a world, I believe it would be an act of self-deception to believe that modest or even major alterations of this program will bring us any closer.

The major difficulty with the basic design resides exactly in its hegemonic character and its sense of inevitability and permanence. The design has been with us so intimately that we find it difficult to imagine any other way of organizing educational experiences than through the medium of courses in disciplines and subjects. Indeed, as I have tried to show, these disciplines have led some of us to an idolatrous posture in which we are prepared to devote our lives to their exaltation and preservation. Just as it is difficult for us to think about education apart from schools, it is equally difficult for us to think about curriculum without regard to academic subjects.

This, as I have indicated, amounts to another dimension of our technological orientation in that our rhetoric speaks to an educational system focused on the study of techniques and forms. What we often find ourselves doing is engaging in post hoc rationalizations and extended apologies for the inclusion of new forms. Nothing represents the absurdity more than the pretense that we do otherwise. This pretense is manifest in our model of curriculum planning, which presumably tries to overcome irrational and conventional thinking by demanding that we establish objectives before choosing content, method, technique, and evaluation procedures. Establishing goals first would seem at the very least to require educators to reflect on the relationship between general goals and specific content. However, in practice teachers are typically not asked to state or reflect on their educational goals but rather on the *goals of their subject* (e.g., the purposes, goals, and objectives of teaching history). This is tantamount to giving a potential house builder bricks, mortar, and trowels and urging him or her to decide on what kind of house to build. Such is the persistence of the basic design that these absurdities are not seen as such but rather as rational and critical ways of insuring that goals and objectives inform technique. It is our inability to see subjects and disciplines as techniques that actually inhibits their real power to inform and educate. It is the reification and reductionism of education into the study of disciplines that make them into inert objects of adoration rather than active and vital elements in our liberation.

In addition to the possibility (remote as it may seem) of utilizing the basic design, I would like to suggest an alternative mode of organizing educational experiences to the existing skill/subject mode. This alternative involves organizing an educational program around important and key heuristic and critical questions. Instead of starting with techniques and answers, let us begin with problems and concerns that stir us to seek techniques and answers. Too much of schooling involves giving students answers to questions they do not have or understand, and too many educators are out of touch with many real questions that students do have. It would be far more responsible for teachers to educate students about what constitutes significant problems and questions than to convince them by trying to guess the questions that prompted the answers they are required to learn.

Our orientation toward education is one of active inquiry and research, as opposed to education as a process of passively accepting other people's answers to questions posed by people unknown and at an uncertain time. Inquiry is an impulse generated by need and want (i.e. we seek answers and solutions to meet needs or to satisfy curiosity). It is our urgent and felt uncertainties that lead us to inquire, seek, research, and study, and as many psychologists might say, it is important that we "own" the questions before we can accept the validity of the answers.

As one of my colleagues astutely put it, "It would make a lot more sense if we teachers and students swapped the roles of who asks and who answers questions." Would it not make more sense if schools were places where people could go to get their questions answered, clarified, and refined? We often wonder what happens to the seemingly insatiable curiosity seen in young children who have an endless number of perplexing and profound questions to ask. Parents are familiar with the discomfort that comes from trying to respond to questions like, Where does God come from? Why do I have to go to school if it makes me feel so bad? Why do I have to do what you tell me to do? One way to deal with this discomfort is to shut them off by discounting, sentimentalizing, or ignoring such questions. This process is strongly emphasized when young people learn very early that school is a place where the teachers and not the students ask the questions. The only exception is the policy that allows students to ask about materials and issues presented by teachers. Schools are places that already have the questions to which they pretend not to have all the answers, but really do.

First, there are the authentic questions that emerge from the experiences of students, and we might arrange schools such that students are encouraged to present their questions and that the educators are there to help them to find adequate answers. This may seem cumbersome and inefficient since there is very likely to be significant overlap between student questions and the ones schools traditionally posit. Here we once again enter the realm of distinguishing between interesting and important questions. Students have a right to ask and get help on questions that interest them—we call that phenomenon curiosity. In addition, students have a responsibility to engage in questions that the culture's wisdom has determined to be of fundamental significance for the individual and the community.

We have already indicated a number of such questions at different levels of our analysis. There are the questions regarding what it is that has ultimate significance for us, what we hold to be sacred, and to what we are willing to commit ourselves. There are also other educational questions related to these broad issues: How do we decide these matters? What are proper modes of understanding these questions? How do we deal with uncertainty? And so on.

There are questions of philosophy that are crucial to our culture and to education: What is the nature of knowledge of truth, of the beautiful, and of the good? How do people come to have knowledge and meaning? By what process do we discern reality? There are related questions on the nature of the cosmos—its origin, destiny, and nature. There are parallel questions about humanity and the earth. Mircea Eliade (1959) has written for example of these eternal questions for humanity: What can I know? What can I hope? What ought I to do? A similar and familiar formulation is constituted in the question, Who are we? Where are we? Where do we come from? Where are we going?

On a somewhat less abstract level there are the infinite number of questions that we have about our world: What is the nature of language? What is the origin of sickness? Why do we sleep, dream, forget, and remember? What are the causes of wars, depression, and creative genius? And so on. The list is literally limitless, as life will continue to spiral in its complexity and richness.

Fundamentally our position is that educators must particularly and concretely respond to the questions of how we can create a culture of abundance, joy, freedom, justice, and peace. That is the central cluster of questions that we as educators must confront and transmit to our students. It would perhaps be more appropriate for educators to transmit the culture's most important questions than their responses, since it seems that our questions are more pertinent and valid than our answers. It is right to ask how to build a culture of abundance, but there is little reason to believe that we have anything like that kind of clarity when it comes to answers. I would also say that we as educators are likely to find greater opportunity for consensus on what are the more important questions than on the answers. We can be united by our questions even as we are divided by our answers.

Education can then be seen as a serious endeavor and struggle to get insight into the questions of social and individual import. People involved in such a process are acting in good faith to work cooperatively on common questions, knowing from the very beginning that there will be enormously different responses to them. By organizing the curriculum around major questions, dilemmas, and issues (e.g., war and peace; equality and freedom; the nature of knowledge), we can also help break down the iron curtains among disciplines. Rigorous, thoughtful, and informed insight into, and understanding of, these problems will require language, concepts, and data from several traditional and nontraditional areas of study. When we study by mode (disciplines), we are forced to study the questions and problems that are illumined by that mode, and, hence, our problems are defined by our modes. It would be far preferable to give the disciplines and areas of study the task of responding to questions that emerge from our experience rather than having them respond to those issues designed at the convenience of existing research methodologies.

Let us inquire into what we need and want to learn, not simply learn what has already been studied. The prophetic voice in education reminds us to respond to what is asked of us and to question the adequacy of our answers, while the royal voice in education asks us to think of questions that will match our store of right answers. The royal voice asks us to develop a course on the benefits of the free enterprise system, while the prophetic voice asks us to inquire into the process of creating a society of abundance. The prophetic voice demands that we develop a calculus of social justice, while the royal voice asks us to find the age of Johnny's grandfather. The royal voice speaks of cutoff scores, competencies, tests of cultural quotients, and the knowledge explosion, while the prophetic voice asks us to ask, "If I am not for myself, What am I? If I am only for myself, Who am I?" and "For whom [does] the bell toll?"

To organize a curriculum around such questions, dilemmas, and problems would, of course, mean an enormous amount of complex, delicate, and painstaking work. It would have the advantage (and disadvantage) of giving up the basic design in that it would force us to be more selective and discriminating about content and instruction. It would also serve to test the strength of our commitment to education as serious inquiry rather than as a ritualistic and instructional process for maintaining our social, political, and cultural institutions.

Resources and Models

Our moral, spiritual, and educational framework is just that, a broad point of departure that focuses on principles, priorities, and orientation. It is our position that important and extensive work is required in order to transform this framework into concrete educational activities, a process that would also serve to inform and enrich the broad framework. Whether there is anything "new" or "original" in these foundations is frankly irrelevant, the more important consultation being the validity, not the age, of the ideas contained in the framework. Clearly this framework is quite different from the mainstream of contemporary educational practice, but the attempt has not been to create something that is different but something that is preferable. What this formulation stresses is its focus on a set of sacred and moral commitments and, hence, speaks to a major shift in our mindset and posture toward curriculum development. However, we are not talking about becoming superhuman or changing the nature of our species; what we *are* talking about is choosing to emphasize a different set of human impulses and about channeling our resources and capacities toward a set of strongly felt but neglected moral principles.

In this spirit we reiterate our faith and confidence in the profession's capacity to meet the challenges of design and implementation inherent in our framework. It is surely not for me to provide the last word on what the broad educational framework ought to be, never mind the absurdity of an expectation that I or anyone else could also provide a detailed blueprint of implementation and practice. This work builds very much on the theory and practice of other educators and theorists; practices of the past and present and, if they are of any value, will no doubt be enriched by those of the future. I wish, therefore, to illustrate and indicate (surely not definitively and exhaustively) how works of other theorists and practitioners who have already made major contributions to the ideas contained in this book can be used to guide their further development and implementation.

Clearly, the writings and life of Paulo Freire (1970, 1973) have had a profound influence on the ideas in this book, and, indeed, it can be said that these ideas represent an attempt to focus more sharply on the concept of *conscientization* to the specifics of American culture and education. It must be remembered that Freire is not "merely" a theorist but a brilliant practitioner and curriculum developer. His works are not only exhortations and analyses but also represent integration and synthesis of ideas and practice. His works on adult illiteracy are surely classics of applied educational theory and offer specific and concrete suggestions for action, ideas that are informed by moral and social principles.

There are, of course, other brilliant writers who have made similar integration of theory and practice and who are oriented toward the human responsibility to create a just and loving world. The genius of John Dewey still shines, and many of his works have as much bite, freshness, and brilliance today as they did decades ago. Maxine Greene (1978) writes eloquently and insightfully of how the humanities can help us become aware of our presence in the world and energize us to make for new possibilities. Henry Giroux offers us more than incisive and trenchant criticisms of the social and economic dimensions of educational practice. He also speaks to alternative practices and has written specifically on how we might more humanely and responsibly respond to the challenges of teacher education, social curriculum, and the teaching of reading. The cumulative works of the late James Macdonald (1974) are a gold mine of practical ideas emerging from an orientation that education provides us with the opportunity to transcend our biological as well as ideological boundaries. The theoretical as well as the applied work of Lawrence Kohlberg (1981) and Ralph Mosher (1979) offers fascinating and provocative examples of serious efforts to engage students in genuine moral discourse. These writers surely differ in substantial degrees on important theoretical matters, but they all are seriously involved in integrating moral concern, theoretical perspectives, and educational practice. Their work provides insight, exemplars, as well as highly useful conceptual formulations and, if nothing else, demonstrates the possibilities inherent in our profession to develop sound, sensible, and practical educational programs that have moral meaning.

It is important to reiterate that this is presented only as illustrative of existing major resources for those interested in developing a curriculum for justice and compassion. In a similar vein, I also wish to give a number of examples of quite specific concrete educational practices that have been actually implemented within the context of real, live, existing conditions of everyday school life. Some of these practices will be familiar, and, indeed, part of the point I am trying to make is that we are not proposing an esoteric or off-the-wall curriculum but rather are suggesting practices that already have a rich tradition in Western and American educational history. Limitations of space will serve to keep the number of these examples to a very few, but there is no question that there are many, many other examples of exciting and provocative practices that represent the work of imaginative, hard-working, courageous teachers who operate under extremely difficult situations.

One of these examples is the ideas contained in the Unified Science, Math, English, Social Studies Curriculum Projects (USMES) of the 1960s and 1970s. This program synthesized a number of ideas and practices of progressive education, particularly in its stress on dealing with real problems, experiential learning, and a cross-disciplinary approach. The program was designed for students of upper-elementary and junior-high-school ages and had as its focus learning as a function of specific responses to real, concrete, authentic problems. The curriculum materials themselves were a simple, direct, and straightforward general description of the approach, some sample problems and solutions, and suggestions on developing proper tools. The idea was to engage an entire class (including the teacher) in an as-yet-unsolved problem requiring utilization of a great many skills, ideas, and data. For example, a class decided to investigate the need and desirability of installing a traffic light near their school. In order to deal with this issue, the class was confronted with the realities of real inquiry: How does one begin? What do we have to know? How can we get the proper information? What are the dimensions of the problem? And so on. In the course of responding to this challenge, the class had to deal with intellectual issues, scientific concerns, social consideration, and political and economic realities. They learned about sampling and measuring problems involved in traffic flow, demographics, pedestrian habits, etc. Other examples of problems include the design of a student lounge and a nutritious yet tasty soft drink.

It is a curriculum where learning emerges from a real and important problem that has significant consequences. Students and teachers learn while and by doing; they also come to share, cooperate, and rely on each other and have the opportunity to experience viscerally the complexities of the search for the truth and the frustrations and rewards of taking social responsibility seriously

This curriculum is a good example of how collegiality and experiential learning can be nourished, providing insight into both the learning process and the nature of knowledge. It also shows how the disciplines can serve the needs and wants of people, rather than the reverse. It is a curriculum of elegant simplicity, straight forward in its approach—it stresses rigor and precision and has built-in, no-nonsense standards of success. Proponents claim that students not only gain in competence, confidence, and self-worth, but in the process they learn the conventional subject matter as well if not better than students in the conventional curriculum design. Given its simple ideas and modest costs relative to the potential excitement and value, it is vital that we raise the question of why this curriculum should not be more utilized. The question should be pressed even further: In what way is the conventional existing upper-elementary/middle-school/junior-high curriculum *superior* to the USMES formulation? More poignantly, why has this program been allowed to die?

A program similar to USMES, but far more ambitious, daring, and broader in scope, is Fred Newmann's (1975) curriculum for citizenship competence, which he developed and implemented in collaboration with the Madison, Wisconsin, public schools. Newman's proposals are rooted in his analysis of traditional citizenship education programs, which he criticizes for stressing understanding rather than competence and for focusing on remote national and international problems rather than more local and immediate issues. The basic purpose of this curriculum formulation is to enrich and preserve democratic traditions by teaching not only the skills of understanding, comprehension, and analysis but also the skills of democratic practice. It is a curriculum that acts on the Jeffersonian notion that democracy requires an active and informed citizenry who participate not just by voting on election day but by being involved in the day-by-day activities of community policymaking as well. Students are taught to be rigorous and thoughtful about the dimensions of a particular policy issue (preferably local ones, such as a change in the building code or a proposal to build a bicycle path). Eventually they are required, after careful research and intensive deliberation, to take a stand, and are then taught the specified skills involved in having that position adopted. Such skills include all the arduous, complicated, and necessary details that go into such efforts—writing letters, knowing how to communicate with various individuals and groups, figuring out which individuals and groups are involved in the issue, organizing, coordinating, making signs, making phone calls, raising funds, etc. In addition, students confront a number of psychological and moral issues that are inherent in such activities such as zealotry, frustration, fatigue, stress, over-identification with their particular stand, and competition.

As in the case of USMES, students deal with real problems and offer concrete responses that have real consequences for them as well as for the larger community. However, this curriculum is more far-reaching since it represents direct involvement in issues that extend far beyond the school setting. Furthermore, the curriculum explicitly and clearly celebrates a political and moral orientation that involves the dignity of the individual, the principle of government with the consent of the governed, and the responsibility for citizens to participate in good faith and on an informed basis in the decision-making process. The emphasis on developing specific competencies and skills provides a way of taking the goal of nourishing democracy seriously and avoids the conventional lip-service approach involved in stressing learning *about* the system. It is a curriculum of praxis-theory and practice and one that recognizes that democracy requires not only reverence and understanding but sweat and detail. It is also a curriculum that specifically affirms the basic framework of American political life as contained in the United States Constitution, meaning rule by law and attention to due process. It is a curriculum that specifically disavows radicalism, violence, and illegality by stressing its faith in the basic legal and constitutional framework and in the educability of people to exercise their democratic right intelligently, wisely, and responsibly.

Newmann has taken his ideas to the point of thoroughly working out the bureaucratic problems that are inherent to implementing such a program in existing school arrangements. He has devised ways of dealing with the complexities of scheduling, course credit, grading, and community involvement so well that it is impossible to discount the program as "impractical." Given that, and given the curriculum's affirmation of strong traditional American values (democracy, individual dignity, law and order, faith in process), we must again challenge the profession to justify the superiority of the conventional social studies curriculum over the Newmann curriculum. Do we not want all our citizens to participate fully in the democratic experience? Are we not obliged to pass on to all people all the skills required to have an impact on our community.? Are not the schools charged with the responsibility of empowering all individuals with the intellectual, social, and political skills demanded of an informed and active citizenry? This curriculum has been actually implemented within the context of a traditional public high school, so its practicality has been demonstrated. Educators must then confront the challenge that this curriculum poses so powerfully and forcefully. It is an excellent example of a curriculum that does not seek upheaval in the basic design but rather provides a serious and provocative variation of the basic design. It urges students to be thorough, careful, precise, and reflective and to utilize the valuable tools and knowledge contained in several disciplines and fields—history, government, sociology, social psychology, English, speech, art, communications, economics, political science. What is most striking for us, however, is its firm moral grounding that is, its affirmation of the centrality of human dignity. The concern for providing opportunities for young people to learn about what it means to be responsible has been taken even further in a striking program at Brookline High School, located in suburban Boston. What began as a pilot study in the moral development research programs directed by Ralph Mosher has blossomed into perhaps the most serious effort yet for significant student governance. Although there have been many innovative and promising experiments in this area for several decades, most student governance programs wind up as models of co-optation, trivialization, and impotence. The program introduced by Mosher in the setting of an experimental school-within-a-school involves the notion that students' level of cognitive moral development will increase if they have significant and authentic experience in actually being responsible (i.e., in real student governance). There is wisdom in the old adage that if we want to teach people to be responsible we need to give them responsibility. It is with this spirit that the basic format of the pilot program was adopted by the entire school.

Brookline High School is a large urban/suburban high school (approximately two thousand students) serving a very wide socioeconomic range of people. It is a mostly affluent community of about fifty thousand. Although affluence is certainly there, so are poverty, low income housing, and urban decay. It is also a community with a political organization that has maintained, in spite of its size, a representative Town Meeting of perhaps one hundred people elected at a precinct level as well as elected town selectmen, and an appointed town manager. The Town Meeting has essentially a legislative function but also serves to oversee the management of town services as directed by the town manager. The selectmen serve as a kind of executive committee with special responsibility for making recommendations on the budget and other town policies.

The community has recently applied aspects of this model to the governance of the high school. There is a town meeting composed of fifty people elected from the population of faculty, students, and staff. The principal of the high school acts as the executive officer, much like the town manager. The town meeting has weekly sessions and deals with all the issues that any school administration faces—attendance policies and procedures, curriculum requirements, hiring of faculty, discipline, exam schedules. A faculty member designated as friend of the meeting serves as a resource person on matters of existing laws, procedures, precedent, parliamentary matters, etc. The town meeting itself elects a presiding officer called a moderator.

In 1984, when I observed the process, forty-four of the fifty who were elected were students, four were teachers, and two were cafeteria workers. The meeting I observed was businesslike, responsible, and sensible and was no less and in some ways more sophisticated and effective than many a university faculty meeting I have attended.

This program acts on faith in young people to be responsible and provides them with a real opportunity to be adult and responsible beyond what is usually expected and required of them. It represents an affirmation of the principles of liberal democracy and a trust in the human capacity to rise to new challenges. This provides a very powerful example of the significance of the concept of the hidden curriculum, since a program like this clearly will have a significant impact on the students, faculty, and staff of the school community without any change in course offerings or in the instructional program.

This governance system is currently in operation, and there seems to be general agreement that the administration of the school is as smooth and efficient as it ever was. In effect, this new governance system is hardly noticeable in its technical role but obviously promises to have significant educational meaning to those involved. The members of the town meeting are clearly working within the system; they have not made, nor is it likely that they will seek to make drastic changes in basic policies. They endeavor to follow legal, professional, and constitutional guidelines just as any other formally constructed group does. Indeed, what is revealing is the perception that such a program is daring and unusual, a reaction that reflects doubt and suspicion of young adults' capacities to be responsible. This program is practical, inexpensive, highly pragmatic, and yet it is rooted in basic human values. It has demonstrated that it can work over a substantial period of time, although clearly there are problems and concerns. It is a program that also cries out for a justification for not providing such opportunities at other schools.

The notion of active social involvement takes a somewhat different orientation in the requirement at the Stuart County Day School, a private Catholic girls' school in Princeton, New Jersey. This school is part of a network of schools directed by the religious order of the Society of the Sacred Heart, who have adopted as part and parcel of their stated educational goals a commitment to providing opportunities to connect Christian teaching of love and justice with their academic program.

The programs within the Sacred Heart schools located across the country vary, but the one at Stuart County Day typifies the orientation. Each student at this school is required, as part of the school program, to do a significant amount of community service over a two-year period. Academic credit is given for these experiences, which involve such activities as volunteer work in a soup kitchen, working in low-income nursing homes, and extended internships in areas of Appalachian poverty. Most of these students come from middle- and upper-middle class families, but all are required to feel and experience firsthand the pain and anguish of poverty, misery, and deprivation. The message of this program is clearly that Christian education must perforce include opportunities to learn about the needs of the unfortunate and downtrodden and to learn to serve them.

These examples serve to demonstrate both the possibilities and the difficulties involved in the design of an educational program with a prophetic orientation. The ingenuity and soundness of these exciting programs are used to enhance powerful and meaningful intellectual and moral principles. They represent and mirror, therefore, the professional capacity to respond to the challenge of demands that are based on principle rather than expedience, or on principles that are more exalting than debasing. Yet, there is the harsh reality that these programs, as exciting and promising as they are, also represent the rather severe boundaries that surround our profession.

There is first of all the reality that even when we account for the many programs that we have not mentioned, and those of which we are not aware, we are still speaking of relatively very few in number compared with the overwhelming amount of conventional, mainstream educational practice. The very fact that these programs are unusual, if not unique, reveals a great deal about the norms of what happens in schools. Second, even these programs are essentially isolated and tangential to the overall educational program. They represent special aspects, not pervasive themes, of the curriculum; they are easily separated and distinguishable and, hence, fragmented. All of these schools still maintain the basic design: they all have traditional grading policies and concern themselves with examinations, college admissions, and competition. These are programs that supplement the usual diet, not ones that transform or replace it. Their isolation or quarantine not only prevents their growth and permutation, but their co-optation can lead to a deluded sense that serious change has taken place.

The modesty of the scope of these exemplary programs is not just within the parameters of the school program. Ultimately, such programs fall far short of the kind of commitment that we are suggesting, that is, a determination to transform our society into a just, loving, compassionate, and peaceful one. All of these exciting and imaginative programs implicitly accept or explicitly do not challenge the structure that sanctions basic cultural values such as materialism, competition, individual success, and hierarchy. They all represent an ameliorative rather than a transformative approach to the problems of our culture.

Let me be understood. I am not *against* such efforts. Indeed, I have presented them in praise and admiration, and I fervently hope that these and others like them flourish. Those who have developed and implemented such programs are to be congratulated for their imagination, integrity, and courage. The criticisms that I raise do not reflect on their ability or commitment but rather on the severe restrictions and pressures that prevent them and others from going further. These people deserve encouragement, support, and affirmation for their heroic efforts to extend the limits that our culture and profession have imposed.

I do not believe that such admiration and support is in any way diminished by realizing that these limitations, even when extended, are still too restrictive. We celebrate the achievement of our more courageous and imaginative colleagues and share with them the resolution to go beyond those achievements. Let us hope that there will be more celebrations for such achievements and for even greater ones.

These achievements are great and significant when measured by the standards of the existing and conventional, but they are modest by the profession's and culture's highest and noblest standards. Indeed, one of the painful aspects of professional duty is establishing standards that are valid but very difficult to meet. In education this translates to working very hard to accomplish that which is very unlikely to be accomplished in one's lifetime. This requires discipline, endurance, patience, and above all else hope, or, in negative terms, the avoidance of despair.

There is, to be blunt, plenty of reason to be in despair over the prospects of an educational program that focuses on the creation of a just world. Our history bulges with war, holocaust, poverty, greed, and barbarism. Our future contains real possibilities of disasters emerging from a present reality that contains pollution, suspicion, nuclear armament, and hatred. We seem to be in a desperate race for survival and are feeling more and more that we cannot control events. In the meantime, day to-day life continues in its relentless pressures—there is anxiety, fear, and frustration on issues of mundane survival. There is also the strong issue of disillusionment and cynicism about our leadership, and with it the sense that little or nothing can really change—the absence of hope, which is what despair means.

Although I have encountered many people who reject the assumption that fundamental change is necessary, I have met many more who agree that it is necessary but believe that it is not possible. Part of the reason for this despair lies in the difficulty of being able to continue to knock one's head against stone walls.

As indicated above, it is natural to want and expect to achieve substantial accomplishments. There are, however, two risks involved in such expectations. First, we may redefine what is "major" by limiting our expectations to whatever is easier to achieve. We can believe that the educational millennium has arrived, for example, by believing that it will be marked by the reduction of class size to twenty. The second risk is almost the opposite of the first: we will be frustrated and paralyzed by our failure to achieve our truly major goals. I believe that as professionals the first risk is far more dangerous and that taking the second risk has more possibility for a life of meaning and integrity.

We must in taking this risk utilize a different time span than is customarily used. In order to dwell in a profession that has universal and eternal dimensions, we must not be trapped by the narrow boundaries of the short or even medium run. We must recognize, whether we like it or not (and I do not), that there is such a tremendous amount of very difficult work to do that it perforce must take a very long time to accomplish it. Indeed, one way to keep this work from being accomplished is to expect that it can be done soon. It is a very significant accomplishment when we make a modest contribution to a profoundly significant goal. It is, on the other hand, counterproductive to make a profound contribution to an inane or very modest goal. Better to fail in a worthwhile project than succeed in a vulgar one. A large share of time and a large perspective can make this orientation less painful. When Buckminster Fuller was ridiculed about the astronomically high cost of his proposed plastic bubble around the earth, his answer was that the bubble would probably extend the life of the planet for a million years, and hence the pro-rated cost is ridiculously low.

Human history is barely of a ten-thousand-year duration, and the concept of justice, love, and compassion is perhaps four thousand years old. The fact that those ideas have been developed and affirmed is in itself miraculous, and the related fact that we have not nearly accomplished other commitments should not be at all surprising. A very wise person once noted that if it took millions of years to go from stone to energy (as in the example of coal), what would be a reasonable expectation for a people to go from animal-like to God-like? The unit of such expectations clearly cannot be months, years, or even decades. We are talking about individuals making lifelong commitments to age-long goals, so we must see the minor effort of our major efforts as part of a very long process. The basic way to make this meaningful is to be clear that the direction is of ultimate significance and is one that can be called sacred. We as a people have taken several of the first steps, and our successors will need to take several more in order to reach the end of our "ten thousand-mile journey."

What can sustain us on this trip is hope and a faith in the direction of our path. I am not talking of starting but continuing; not of returning to a land that never was, or of creating a world that can never be, but of insisting that we nourish and enrich that which is best in us. Our responsibility as educators is to remind us of this commitment, to help us become what is our best, by providing our students and ourselves with the knowledge, skills, imagination, energy, and hope that are required.

BOOK II

REFLECTIONS ON *THE
MORAL AND SPIRITUAL CRISIS
IN EDUCATION*

Connie Krosney

INTRODUCTION TO REFLECTIONS ON *THE MORAL AND SPIRITUAL CRISIS IN EDUCATION*

In this introduction to Reflections on *The Moral and Spiritual Crisis in Education*, I share my own response to the first edition, experiences I have had in using the book with graduate students and some of their responses, and finally, some thoughts about the new edition and my own excitement at being able to engage in dialogue about the new material. I am grateful for the invitation to share in this small way in this important and valuable project.

I have been involved in teacher education, professional teacher development, adult education, and the study of sociology, philosophy, and ethics in education for nearly twenty years. I have taught students in education at both graduate and some undergraduate levels at several institutions. My initial and continuing interest in education is as a means to building a more just and compassionate world, and I have taken this approach even more strongly as time continues its inevitable passage. For the most part, I find this work continues to feed my passion for justice, my need to "do good," and my thirst for relation and dialogue.

Meeting *The Moral and Spiritual Crisis in Education*

I was introduced to *The Moral and Spiritual Crisis in Education* as part of a Moral Education class I was taking toward my doctoral degree that focused on the Social Foundations of Education. Reading the book was, for me, like taking a really full breath, a cleansing breath, of fresh air. While I had been reading many wonderful works in social theory and ethics, Purpel's social analysis and critique of our society and culture, and the indictment not only of schools themselves, but of our expectations of schools, were amazingly powerful and poignant. Somehow, it seemed remarkable that an educator was writing (to educators yet!) that schools are not the answer. Now, of course, it seems silly to think that they could be. And yet, Purpel assured us, we are educators, and we need to work from where we are on the significant problems that face us as community members and citizens of the United States and of the world. And so, while schools are not *the* answer, they ought to and could very well play a role in creating a more just and compassionate world. As educators, it is our right, our duty, and our privilege to initiate, implement, and support these efforts, even while understanding the Catch-22-ness of attempting to change the system that employs us to maintain and reproduce the status quo.

The purpose of schools has long been a central question and topic in the "Great Conversation" of the field of Social Foundations of Education. Purpel calls upon us to frame answers to that question by calling upon that which is best within us—our ability to care, to feel compassion, to experience joy, to connect with others and the natural world, our urge and deep desire to alleviate human suffering—and then to articulate our response in the highest possible terms. If the answer to our problems is unconditional love, he suggests, and we understand and acknowledge that, then why do we not enact it?

Purpel calls upon us, as educators, as intellectuals, and as members of our communities, to create a social vision, and to see our work as embedded in that vision. We may not witness our culture's arrival at the Promised Land, but if we never allow and encourage ourselves to envision the Promised Land, we will certainly never see it. Perhaps there is some truth to the adage: no concept, no percept. And yet, it is clearly tricky to formulate a vision that allows for ambiguity, for multiple perspectives and interpretations, and that is inclusive and just. And this is our task, and the one we must undertake with our colleagues, our communities, and our students. For if we do not, we will have failed not only ourselves, but our children and grandchildren. At times like these—times of danger, confusion, violence, and hunger, of incredible human suffering—we have no choice, it seems, but to continue to seek to create justice and joy, to work to relieve suffering.

Experiences Using the First Edition in Graduate Education Classes

Over the last fourteen years, I have used the first edition countless times in graduate courses and seminars, through independent studies with students, and for my own solace and inspiration. Here I will share some of the ways I have approached the book in the hopes that others might find something useful or be able to adapt some of the ideas to their own situations.

Almost without fail, I use *The Moral and Spiritual Crisis in Education* at the end of a course, and my courses are intentionally rich with readings. I explain its placement at the end to students by sharing that I want to "leave them with hope and possibility," as many of the other readings, such as those Jonathan Kozol's *Savage Inequalities,* Myra and David Sadkers's *Failing at Fairness,* Hermann Hesse's *Beneath the Wheel,* and Alan Peshkin's *Permissible Advantage,* are considerably more likely to induce despair. As with many of the books I use to teach Social Foundations, I often begin by asking students for a first reaction. Sometimes I ask students to begin the class with a free-write to be shared (in whole or part) with the group. With *The Moral and Spiritual Crisis in Education,* I have now grown accustomed to the consistent echoes from student to student, group to group, year to year:

> I feel like finally someone is speaking to my heart . . .

> I've always felt that we weren't allowed to talk about these things in school . . .

> I didn't know anyone else was thinking about this—I have always felt so alone . . .

> I feel as though I was starving, and this is the first real meal I've eaten. Now I have the strength to grow my own nourishment and to cook it!

These comments have been made near the *end* of a course in which previous readings on parallel concerns have been abundant. Indeed, it is perhaps partially the students' new familiarity with and acquisition of some of the language of critical theory and transformation that makes *The Moral and Spiritual Crisis in Education* so readable, exciting, and relevant for them. However, they are most inspired by the coupling of clear social and political analysis with compelling and careful hope. A common reaction to the book is a sense of being in the "here and now," of knowing that there is no hiding from the truth of our dilemmas and the tangled tragedies of our times. When discussing Purpel's book, students cannot pretend that "everything is all right, things will work out if we just tweak this or that." We discuss this book with an understanding that the best and necessary approach to our challenges is in the here and now, rather than the there and then.

From these initial comments, I often ask students to consider the two major concepts of *mythos* and *prophecy*. As they begin to get a sense of these, of the power as well as the meaning of the words, either through working in small groups and then sharing with the whole group, or through a large group dialogue, they move toward recognition and development of their own mythos, which will guide their own work in education. Students' initial discomfort with the idea of *teachers as prophets* is often overtaken by a profound sense of possibility, a deepening awareness of the depth of the potential of their professional lives. It is perhaps this sense of possibility that resonates most strongly and ignites a sense of hope. Rather than being told what to do—the technical and the methodological—these prospective and practicing teachers are being told that their work is important, that they are capable of and in position to work toward justice. Very often, "final papers" in these courses are focused on the articulation of mythos, social vision, and implementation plans. I think of these as *real* action plans.

Another approach I have used to begin the discussion is to have small groups discuss one of the "democratic paradoxes," or dyads, to illuminate the positions and strive together to find a place of balance toward which to work. Each group actively presents its work to the others through a skit, a dialogue, or a visual representation. My hope here, which is often realized, is that students will call upon other parts of their beings to more deeply comprehend and communicate their understanding.

Once the group has come to an understanding of *mythos,* I often ask small groups to engage in dialogue and arrive at a consensual mythos, one that is inclusive of the various perspectives in the group as well as the perspectives they might imagine outside the group, but that is meaningful and worthy of their efforts. Perhaps not so remarkably, the mythos presented by the different groups are quite similar, always with some unique characteristics, but always based on a vision of justice, joy, love, and compassion. Students question and challenge each other, discuss what makes them uncomfortable as well as what resonates, and attempt together to uncover the sources of their discomfort and their agreement.

Together, we then list and discuss the challenges, obstacles, promises, and possibilities to a curriculum of justice and compassion. This activity always leads to a stimulating dialogue, as students and professor critique and affirm together. Indeed, since dialogue demands that each person comes to the discussion open to change, I have found that students by this time are prepared to engage authentically and with integrity and respect for one another. *The Moral and Spiritual Crisis in Education* creates a situation, a context, that encourages earnest exploration and eager engagement in the most critical issues we face as citizens and as educators. Indeed, students are honored to be called upon to contribute, once they recognize and acknowledge that they can and must.

Finally, I always require that students write a "letter of learning" at the end of the course, which serves partly as a self-evaluation and partly as information for me about what has most impressed and inspired. I include a few excerpts, relevant to *The Moral and Spiritual Crisis in Education,* from these letters:

> Purpel's book caused a mental earthquake for me. His wisdom, insight, and clarity of thought, coupled with an obvious love for humankind and passion for positive change, are inspirational.

> Noddings was the first to set me on my heels, but since then, Freire, Kozol, and especially Purpel have just made my brain dilate. Knowing that compassion, liberation, and transformation are more than just saccharine passing thoughts—they are frames and structures that make meaning out of lives. Living and working without conscious and serious commitments to furthering those goals is wasted time. (Secondary English teacher)

> The seminar introduced me to material that has converted me from unhealthy skeptic to someone who has found theory with which I not only fit but have fallen in love. In particular, I refer to the work of Purpel and Freire as both speak to the language of the sacred that is the bedrock of my belief system. Not only do they refer to the ontological task of education but they bring in the precepts of imagination

and awakening . . . I have found an ideological home. (Special Education teacher of children with mental illness)

I learned the most from Purpel. I usually cringe at the word "spirituality," because it has religious connotations . . . Now I understand it as embracing the questions of the world, like what is beyond us, or what is the unknown. (Elementary Licensure candidate)

Purpel's work has really affected me, more than I thought or realized . . . he introduced ideas for education that I never knew existed. Moral education, what is that? Now, I see. (Secondary Licensure candidate)

I didn't know that writers like David Purpel existed, however, and for that I am so thankful. The lenses he provides to see our work through have been such a relief for someone like me who is looking for a new way to understand how to work in community and effect change. Thank you so much for including his voice in our work. (Secondary Licensure candidate)

The Worth and Achievement paradox is one that educators, parents, and individuals come up against all the time. Mr. Rogers tells us that we are precious just the way we are, but the world tells us we really have to achieve something to earn our worth. (Middle Level teacher)

Purpel challenged my original assumptions and optimism by pointing out that critical thought and the pursuit of knowledge are not enough. If they were, we would not now face the time of crisis and suffering in which we live . . . If I complained . . . it was because my old answers were not holding up to examination. (Secondary Licensure candidate)

Each semester, I receive remarks similar to these, some with more specificity, some with less. By my estimates, 90% of the students specifically mention *The Moral and Spiritual Crisis in Education* as having deeply affected their thinking, being, and teaching. Clearly, students in teacher education and graduate teacher professional development take different messages away with them, yet most are profoundly moved.

The New Edition Arrives!

My reading of *Reflections on* The Moral and Spiritual Crisis in Education has moved me tremendously. McLaurin and Purpel's commentary on the first edition, and their honest sharing of their own spiritual explorations, legitimizes the inclusion of the spiritual in the academic and intellectual world of higher education. Purpel's defining of the spiritual as that which inspires and enlivens us resonates and works to invite transformative intellectuals, spiritual seekers, and social activists into a conversation that serves us all.

This is not an "easy" read—the crisis that was explicated in 1988 has grown more dire; the battles to which we were called have been lost, and the war goes on. One does not leave the reading feeling exhilarated; and yet, there is a stronger sense of empowerment and hope, a belief that it is our right and our duty to act in accordance with our deepest and best selves.

McLaurin and Purpel have each written final chapters that explore their own personal struggles and searches and their vision of "what is to be done." In doing so, they have modeled for the readers what it means to tear down, or at least make cracks in, the wall between the personal and the academic, between the intellect and the spirit, and to speak with integrity and courage.

McLaurin has brought to the new edition his own experience and understanding as a traveler through many paths. His organization around four themes—*The Perennial Question; Good and Evil; Hope, Faith, and Optimism;* and *Human Agency*—creates helpful entry points for readers to examine their own central philosophical and existential questions. From here, he moves to an explication of his own experiences with five traditions: the Sufis, Zen, the Hebrew Prophets, Christian Mysticism, and Western Buddhist mindfulness. McLaurin's connection to each of these, especially Eastern philosophy, as experienced by many of his (and my) generation, reflects our seemingly common discomfort with "God-talk," and our insistence on "spirit-talk." By recounting his own experiences with each, and connecting them back to the themes, McLaurin opens the doors for readers to jump in and muck around in their own spiritual and religious stories, hopefully gaining a similar insight and clarity, and a direction for action. He continues by reconnecting to the initial themes, sharing his own practice, looking for the implications for our culture and education, putting forth a list of ways to create change and hope. At the chapter's end are suggestions specifically for educators and other helping professionals, and a final plea to use our wisdom to "heal our world where we can, and then to be present with compassion where we cannot."

David Purpel's final chapter, entitled "A Response to the Crisis: The Love of Wisdom and the Wisdom of Love," is a masterful bringing together of the themes of the first and second editions, an articulation of the nature of our educational problems, a description of the "operational context of professional practice," and perhaps most stunningly, his own moral/spiritual orientation and recommendations for action. Purpel calls upon his own spiritual mentors—Heschel, Levinas, Neusner, West—and many others, to ground his sense of moral outrage at the suffering of so many, and sees it as necessary to move us toward "serious efforts at cultural and educational transformation". Purpel asserts that the effort we spend determining goals and rationale for our teaching may in fact be "largely disingenuous, since politically it usually adds up to a post hoc justification of what we are already doing". Further, he believes that the impulse to ask about purpose "reveals an unsettling lack of confidence in the validity of what we do and masks a deep and genuine uncertainty of moral direction as well as a suspicion that we are spiritually and morally lost".

As in previous chapters, Purpel reveals his disheartenment with the small changes that take the place of deep and meaningful transformation. Here, he puts forth what he sees as the rationale for the avoidance of major steps, for skirting all change except the gradual and trivial: "What I see in the trees of modest changes is the forest of a hidden curriculum that celebrates hierarchy and privilege." What are we to do, remembering Heschel's critical adage: "Few are guilty, all are responsible"? Purpel suggests that we must transform ourselves from technicians to prophets. We can change the reality of the educational workplace by committing ourselves to our responsibility of creating a just and loving world, and bringing this vision and commitment to our students and communities. It is the very desperate nature of our time that *demands* that we make this commitment.

When Purpel quotes the Talmud, "It is not for us to finish the task, but neither are we free to take no part in it", we are moved to act, to make of our lives a *praxis,* which Freire defines as the true union of reflection and action, and which must be grounded in faith. Many of us have found faith difficult to find and/or hold, especially in the midst of the mess of the early 21st century, and Purpel's kind words— "The best I can say is that the persistent search for meaning provides a powerful enough reason to be faithful"—allows us to know that we are not alone in our doubt, in our wavering, and that fact in itself gives us comfort and strength—another version of courage.

Each summer for the past five, we have been fortunate to have David Purpel visit the Master of Education Program at Vermont College during our summer residency. Students are regularly impressed by his humanity, his presence, and his ability and desire to connect to them. They are sometimes offended by his persistence in speaking the truth as he sees it, then engaged, then motivated to find their own truth and live it. Purpel's honesty and integrity shine along with his brilliant analysis and sharp insights. But it is his kindness and compassion that most inspire, and it is these to which he insists we must devote ourselves.

For those of us who teach, who work to help create a better society and world, I believe this book offers us opportunities for reflection and dialogue, and challenges us to locate ourselves within the tradition of prophecy, of social vision and action: to change the world, to change ourselves, to leave a legacy of peace and justice.

I am grateful to William M. McLaurin, Jr. for pursuing this project with David Purpel and bringing his own insights to bear. And I am incredibly grateful to David Purpel for the wonderful mentoring and friendship I have received, and even more so for the work to which he has dedicated his life. This new book makes abundantly clear why he has been an inspiration and leader for so many of us in the field of Education, Teacher Education, and Social Foundations, and why we must continue to share his work, and his shared work with McLaurin, with our students, colleagues, friends, and communities.

BOOK II

REFLECTIONS ON *THE*
MORAL AND SPIRITUAL CRISIS
IN EDUCATION

1

THAT WAS THEN AND THIS IS NOW:
The deepening educational and cultural crisis

The first two chapters of the first edition were designed to provide the political, social, and cultural background to the situation that was then current in educational policy and practice. In reflecting on those chapters today, we find ourselves unable to cite without reservation the familiar French proverb, "The more things change, the more they are the same." Indeed, there has been much change and yes, many things remain the same in spite of these changes, but it is also true that many things in education have become worse because of change.

David Purpel had posited in that section of the book a society in the midst of a crisis that we designated as primarily moral and spiritual in nature. If *crisis* denotes a point at which decisions critical to the future can be taken, then the crisis identified in the first edition is over. It appears in retrospect that the policy decisions made following the publication of the first edition of this book were not at all like the ones advocated and the decisions that were made actually intensified the difficulties. It is as if we had been in a war and, though not defeated, had lost a major battle, perhaps akin to what it would have been if the World War II D-Day invasion of Europe had been repulsed and our forces driven into the sea. This second edition looks back to see why this happened and what the consequences have been; it looks forward to see if those consequences can be mitigated or reversed.

Using the first edition of this book as a way of looking back to our world as Purpel saw it in the mid-eighties gives cause for both despair and hope. We in these early years of the 21st century, are tempted to despair because each of the struggles that we joined in the first edition seems, in large part, to have been lost.

However, those of us committed to an education for meaning, justice, and love have definitely not surrendered. In looking forward, we are invited to hope by the fact that today in the midst of the carnage from those lost struggles there is still some concern for the issues, as well as some appetite for books with such titles as this. In this reflection and critique of the first edition we shall be pursuing both of these strands. We shall be treading the edge of despair by attempting to be candid and honest in our appraisal of the current state of education (especially public schooling) and of the soul of a society that chooses to treat its children to that education. We shall seek hope in the survival of our capacity as human beings to be uncomfortable when we are being less human than we can be, a capacity evidenced by our need to turn our eyes from the results of much that we do. And yet, while it is good that as a society we often feel a need to look away, ashamed of the consequences of our behavior, we must also resist that impulse, remembering that denial is one of those emotional crutches that provides short-term relief but winds up producing pathological results in the long haul.

What Has Changed

In the wake of the collapse of the Soviet Union and socialism eastern European-style, a triumphal and uncontested world-view emerged, which held that all social and economic problems are to be solved through the magic of freer and freer markets, higher levels of productivity, and greater and greater consumer spending. As globalization has accelerated under the banner of free trade and the seductive power of American popular culture, the capacity and will of other cultures to resist this worldview is clearly diminishing. Seeing all the world through the filter of Western culture is transitioning from an unattractive habit to an unfortunate reality, to such an extent that much of the world's population struggles to emulate excesses that many citizens of the USA would have us move beyond. Statements that might have once been inappropriate generalizations from our culture to other parts of the world are becoming increasingly true through globalization, to the point where we will occasionally use that language ourselves when there appears to us to be little difference between American popular culture and the likely fate of much of the rest of the world.

The pervasiveness of this world-view in the USA for the solution of problems has been evidenced by the call to duty issued to the public by many of our leaders following the terrorist attacks of 9/11/01: it seemed that the only function of value that a common citizen could render was to return to the malls and automobile showrooms. This vision sees peace and prosperity to be the consequences of a minimally regulated global economy ever intent on creating new markets and new products. The impact of this global economy is powerfully evident in the emergence of huge international banking, communications, industrial, and media conglomerates with enormous power and in the Americanization of a great deal of the world. It has, moreover, produced a great deal of wealth for a large number of people who by dint of the global nature of their endeavors are less and less involved in community and local concerns. At the same time, these dividends of the end of the Cold War and the development of the global economy have not been realized for most of the world.

The resulting disparities, which any practiced apologist for free markets can easily rationalize, have had many unintended consequences, which occupy the bulk of our nightly news. In the eighties, many thoughtful people despaired of avoiding a nuclear exchange between the USSR and the USA. In the happier days of the nineties, public awareness of the dangers of global destruction faded somewhat, but today we are once again confronting the reality of a world stocked with a wide variety of weapons of mass destruction *whose use seems increasingly likely*. Because of the horrors of the attacks which began on September 11, 2001, Americans have become much more aware of these weapons; fearing their possible use by the agents of global terrorism. What is much less in the public awareness is how we might ourselves have helped to make this possible. Very few voices are to be heard to remedy that lack of awareness, because in the present war-time environment there is little tolerance for those who suggest that our own culture has played any part in setting the stage for the rise of terrorism. To the extent that such voices of self-blame might simply seek to excuse the murder of innocents for political purposes, such intolerance is quite appropriate. However, to the extent that the economic disparities of the growing global culture do provide fertile ground for recruiting terrorists, and to the extent that our indifference to the desire of many peoples to defend their cultural heritage from Americanization, we must not close our own minds and fail to listen to reasoned voices that might point the way to reducing the suffering of us all. In the absence of honest debate we even risk beginning our own "jihad," worsening the divisions that now separate us from many of our global neighbors who should be our allies. Much of our recent history is strewn with the violent wreckage of deeply felt but narrowly focused alienation, rage and hatred, ranging from Columbine High School to Oklahoma City and from Bosnia to Rwanda. Those who are the agents of today's growing threats make cynical but effective use of the fear and loathing against the prospect of a global culture, conceived as a triumphal *Pax Americana,* in their preparations for a global war of generational length. Despite the bankruptcy of their own beliefs, it is no coincidence where the terrorists go to find recruits: among those who have no chance of "competing and winning in the global economy," among those for whom poverty, desperation, and humiliation are the stuff of daily life, and among those who perceive the values of their ancestors as being swept away by alien ideas. To the extent that we do look away from the plight of so many of our neighbors, to the extent that we do substitute economic logic for meaning, justice, and love and thus do nothing to intervene in the economic system to save our neighbors from being subjected to these conditions, and to the extent that we lack the humility to allow others a real choice in the preservation of their cultures, we will not escape a historical judgment of complicity.

Much of the scientific community foresees another consequence of our propensity for basing all judgments on economic values. With apparent good reason, they fear that rapid global industrialization and development will have disastrous effects on our climate and environment. We have ignored many calls to remediate our choices, such as the *World Scientists' Call for Action at the Kyoto Climate Summit*, circulated by the Union of Concerned Scientists (1997) and endorsed by 1568 scientists including 110 Nobel Laureates and 60 U.S. National Medal of Science winners. This document starkly warns that, "If not checked, many of our current practices put at serious risk the future we wish for human society and the plant and animal kingdoms." What does it say about us that we continue our reckless behavior in the face of such possible consequences? It appears likely that we as a society are now choosing poorly between today's economic well-being and climate stability. We are making these choices without knowing where the "tipping point" is—without knowing when we shall pass the point of no return in perturbing a system about which we understand very little.

This behavior has been characterized as the first planet-sized biological experiment, and it is an experiment being run by occupants of the test-tube. The striking similarity between this incapacity to think beyond the moment and the self-destructiveness of addictive behavior should not be lost on the losers of the War on Drugs. One of the symptoms of that behavior over the past decade has been an increase in Americans' incessant, if not frantic or possessed, pursuit of material wealth. That pursuit was encouraged by the gold rush atmosphere of the "irrational exuberance" that created the tech stock boom/bust—in those heady times, many Americans could seriously consider the possibility that they themselves might grab the brass ring. Even though those dreams have largely failed, it is still the case that one of the sorry and horrifying consequences of this recent and lamented Bull Market economy has been an increasing gap between the wealthiest and poorest segments of our society. Indeed, even in the wake of stock market corrections, the U.S. has the dubious distinction of having the greatest degree of wealth disparity of the world's industrialized nations. This has been well documented by the world-renowned futurist Hazel Henderson (2000) and her colleagues, who have developed the *Calvert-Henderson Quality of Life Indicators;* a remarkable instrument intended to measure national trends. In her discussion of income inequality, she tracks a growing disparity in the ratio between family incomes in the U.S.A., indicating that the top 5% received 12 times the income of the bottom 20% in 1979, and noting an increase in that ratio reflecting that the disparity rose to 19 times as much by 1996. If the comparison is made between the compensation of CEOs and production workers within their companies, ratios of hundreds to one are common.

We now see that this addiction to the pursuit of material wealth is at the root of the current revelations of cynical corruption, plundering, deception, and exploitation in the corporate world. It is clear that this moral and economic debacle is an inevitable consequence of an obscene, cruel, and obsessive greed for ever more power and self-gratification.

There are within this American pursuit of wealth two parallel and complementary races going on. One race has to do with being in the running for getting into the winners' circle where one can expect roses and money. The other race is about being able to stay in the pack, lest one is left in the dust and degradation of poverty. (Poverty is officially defined by the federal government in absolutist terms. i.e., as a yearly salary below around $16,000 for a family of four and with that definition, the poverty level hovers around 14 or 15 per cent. Others, using a relativistic index such as national median income would estimate that the more accurate figure is likely to be double that of the official estimate).

Formal education has come to be seen as a primal element in these high stakes races concerned with getting rich and not getting poor. For corporate America, the schools' function is to provide a trained and productive workforce, one that has basic technical and communications skills and a proper set of attitudes and traits appropriate to the workplace, e.g., punctuality, loyalty, perseverance, a capacity for hard work, a willingness to perform tasks with little or no personal meaning, and the like. For worried parents, school success is seen as an absolutely crucial and necessary condition for the economic and social well being of their children. For those parents themselves, in the face of plant closings and dislocations, a mid-life detour to a community college for fresh credentials is becoming increasingly common. In such an environment, where many of those who are seeking education are doing so because they are being driven by fear of privation and by desire for material gain, schools are increasingly likely to be seen not as places of ongoing joy, inquiry, and community but rather as obstacle courses designed to sort out winners and losers.

None of these trends are in any way new in our society. However, their recent dramatic intensification has totally dominated and overwhelmed the educational arena. Although we are surprised at the rapidity and depth of these trends, we are not exactly shocked by them. Rather, education has suffered once again from one of the fundamental unresolved conflicts in the American psyche: despite our fervent protestations of love for the "greater good," our deep commitment to individualism continues unabated at the expense of our capacity to evidence compassion in our political and economic life. Our present struggle is a part of that ongoing "tragedy of the commons," a chronic failure in human societies to find a way to motivate service to the greater good that led the father of modern capitalism, Adam Smith, from the radical optimism of his *Theory of Moral Sentiments*. Smith moved to a minimalist position in *Wealth of Nations*, where he asserted that only self-interest has the strength to motivate humans to social ends. Smith's pessimism about human nature seems to find support in many areas of our present culture. Frequently it is the case that the consequences of this unresolved moral and spiritual issue are most apparent and most damaging at the economic margins, where those who suffer lack the private resources to protect themselves, such as students in under-funded public schools. Yet there are other manifestations where private resources are no protection from this neglect of the common good, such as the degradation of nursing care and the collapse of our public health infrastructure from malign neglect over the last few decades. (Garrett 2000).

This decline of the public health infrastructure at the same time that expenditures on individual medical care have risen to large percentages of our national income illustrates this conflict and the unintended consequences of neglect of the commons. Reduced availability of medical services for the unemployed and the underemployed, a consequence of an ideological commitment to delivering insurance through employers, has produced both unnecessary individual suffering and reservoirs of disease that threaten public health. Additional and serious consequences include our inadequate capacity to deal with potential global pandemics and actual bio-terrorism. At a more local level, we find ourselves without any common moral or spiritual ground to guide us when we face questions such as the proper use of antibiotics. As a consequence, medical practice is focused on the self-interested care of individuals rather than the health of the community, enabling patients to demand and receive widespread application of antibiotics simply to calm anxiety. Such inappropriate use insures that these critically important drugs become less effective with each passing day, as exemplified in Laurie Garrett's description of the alarming spread of resistant strains of tuberculosis (2000: 576). Seeing the outcomes of permitting our pursuit of self-interest to govern our stewardship of the public health should call us to ponder what unintended and unanticipated consequences might flow from our similar neglect of the educational commons.

In Disappointed Hindsight

As we began, we suggested that the crisis we described in the first edition is over. We passed a point at which decisions critical to the future were taken and now we inhabit the world that is a consequence of those decisions. Because of this, there are at least three major themes of the opening chapters of the original edition that require substantial and rueful revision. They reflect not only a personal over-optimism but also the significant shift in social attitudes that we have just chronicled. These themes must be revised not only because we might have failed to understand intellectually where the country was going in the 1980s, but also because these disheartening, even tragic turns in the social and cultural directions of the opening years of the 21st century have come together to create a different crisis in education. The educational themes we have in mind concern: (1) the importance of public awareness and dialogue; (2) the role of the profession; and (3) the nature of school reform.

Public Awareness and Dialogue

Part of our hopes for significant positive changes in education have rested on the value of heightened public awareness of and involvement in a more sophisticated discussion of the larger significance of educational policy. Ironically enough, since the time of the publication of the first edition, there has been a decided increase in the amount of public interest in educational issues. Indeed, many politicians consider education to be the domestic issue of highest priority to the voting public. The matter of educational policies and practice has, in the process of this revitalized public concern, become heavily politicized in the worst sense of that term, i.e., as a cynical effort to achieve partisan advantage by pandering to public fears. Nicholas Lemann has concisely described some of this political maneuvering in a recent article on proposals on federal testing programs:

> The politics of the standards movement are especially propitious for Republicans, because at least some of their interest groups are much more enthusiastic about it than the Democrats' interest groups are. Businesses see educational standards as a way to insure a supply of better workers. Teachers' unions and minority organizations worry that all the new tests (tests are an inevitable part of every standards regime) will be used to declare black and brown kids, and their teachers, to be sub par. So standards present Republicans with an opportunity to steal middle-class suburban voters—who overwhelmingly send their kids to public schools and who think of a good education as the best way to guarantee their economic future—from the Democrats. ("Testing Limits," *New Yorker*, 7/2/01, p. 19)

What sparked the tremendous pressure for more and more testing was the sense of alarm that was generated by the spate of reports and studies on education by the government and some foundations that declared our students to be unprepared for the changing times and our schools inadequate to the task. The overwhelming majority of these reports describe the academic achievements of American students as shameful and shocking, especially when compared to American students of another era and to students from other nations.

There is an exquisite irony here for in the same breath that students and schools are excoriated for their ignorance and low standards, we are asked to accept uncritically the validity of the statistical analysis and to ignore the problematic nature of the interpretations. Indeed, the work by a number of highly respected analysts who have examined the same sets of data but have come to very different conclusion has been virtually ignored by the pundits and public. (See Gerald Bracey; and Biddle and Berliner). This is, by no means, to say that there are not serious issues of school achievement nor to conclude that there is more truth to one set of interpretations than another. It is only to say the obvious, namely that statistical analyses and their interpretations are complex and controversial; therefore, they are subject to varying and often conflicting interpretations. In most other cases of controversial public issues, these conflicting understandings are part and parcel of public debate, as for example in the case of military defense where we are accustomed to hearing widely divergent views on how adequate our state of military preparedness really is. Where is the critical thinking and rigorous analysis for the propositions that our students are dopey, our teachers undemanding, and our schools out of touch? Why is there not, in the public sector, some measure of skepticism of the validity of the sweeping accusations or of the underlying assumptions of the conventional critique of the schools? Why has the public been heavily engaging in a dialogue about the quality of education in such a primitive and ignorant mode? Adults who ought to know better are talking ignorantly and stupidly about the problems of rampant ignorance and stupidity.

An example of over-optimism from the first edition concerns the outcome of the public dialogue about the discovery of a "hidden curriculum," that included—among many other features—the unspoken training of our children in obedience to arbitrary authority, uncritical acceptance of existing norms, and willingness to work long hours at meaningless tasks. At the time the term was gaining currency and the full meaning of what it meant was entering the consciousness of the academy, it seemed to us to be one of those potentially transformative insights that would change behavior on contact. It seemed reasonable that anyone who understood how the methods of education were having unacknowledged effects upon children would want to bring these effects out in the open for public discussion. It also seemed likely that the judgment that such a discussion would render would go against the hitherto "hidden" curriculum, since it would certainly make clear that the interests being served by such a process were not those of the children. Yet those "likely" events did not come to pass—today we find the most blatant elements of the hidden curriculum (e.g., concern for competition, advantage, and privilege) emblazoned on the banners of both political parties. The discussion has taken place in the political arena and the judgment rendered went against the progressive elements on every point. As a result, the potential for confrontation that arises when students engage questions of meaning has been defused; and education, to the extent that it is restricted to schooling, is clearly of no danger to the status quo.

In the larger society, the "opportunity culture" no longer needs quotation marks—the irony of the term is lost and the concept has become received wisdom. In the same sense that it is OK to have failures in schools so long as everyone takes the same test, it is OK to have deprivation in the marketplace, so long as the poor can be seen to be responsible for their own misfortune. The "rejection of the tacit understanding involving compassion and support for the poor and the weak" noted in the first edition has proceeded to the point where clearing the streets of the homeless before the arrival of a visiting dignitary is a routine function of city government. The values of the marketplace, having proven themselves so effective in the production of wealth, are now applied to social issues as well, so that we are housing children under bridges, subordinating community to "return on investment," creating lines of division that lead the privileged to feel the need for gates and fences, and yielding ever more outcomes from which we are compelled to avert our eyes.

School Reforms

In the original edition we characterized the nature of proposed school reforms as "trivial" because of what we called "the evasion of larger, more critical topics and the stress put on technical rather than on social, political, and moral issues" (pp. 2–3). We have to wonder, frankly, if we all would have been better off if the reforms had remained trivial, Today, a more accurate description of current school reforms would have to note their vulgar, degrading, crude, and reductionist qualities. What seemed like marginal and token efforts to change the schools through more student and teacher evaluation has been greatly enlarged to become the cruel instruments by which traditional educational principles and practices could be turned into an important way to make a buck, honest or otherwise.

Although it is certainly true that the public has seen public education as significantly related to the possibility of socioeconomic advance, it certainly was not always limited to that single concern. There has been, until very recently, strong public sentiment about the importance of education for the preservation of democracy, for the development of creativity and imagination, for the promotion of scholarship, and for cultural enrichment. All that seems to have been replaced by a single-minded, reductionist notion of schools for personal achievement and aggrandizement. Former President Clinton bluntly captured this emergent public consensus when, in his 1994 State of the Union Address, he caught the true essence of this extraordinarily brutal and vulgar educational vision with these remarkable words:

> I support efforts to empower local school boards to experiment with chartering their schools . . . or having more public school choice, or to do whatever they wish to do as long as we measure every school by one high standard: *Are our children learning what they need to know to compete and win in the global economy?* [Italics added]

Clearly, the major engine for this regimen of harsh and ruthless competition has been the very heavy reliance on standardized testing and evaluation. Standardized testing had until recently been seen mainly as a useful diagnostic tool that gave educators some help in getting an overview on the effectiveness of their programs and providing some insight into the quality of individual student progress. They tended to be used infrequently and the results were usually confidential and for professional use. Today, these tests have become "high-stakes." I.e., performance on these tests will have important and long-range consequences for students (e.g., promotion and graduation), teachers (e.g., salary and assignment), and schools (funding and control). Consequently, schools and parents put enormous stress on preparing students for these tests, resulting in a truncated, test-driven curriculum, enormous anxiety, and many instances of corruption among both students and teachers.

We have, at least for the foreseeable future, lost the battle over high-stakes testing. A few skirmishes still break out over the details of the surrender, but these are over issues such as how often to test, which tests we administer, and how we can best punish failure. The industrial metaphor of statistical process control that works quite well in fabricating computer parts is being applied to our children. What we have gained from this process is some assurance that defective products will not enter the marketplace with deceptive labeling, i.e., diplomas. This screening process is not yet totally efficient or effective, but we have repeated assurances from those concerned that the testing will become increasingly rigorous and well administered over time, so that future employers may be guaranteed that all graduates meet their specifications. In compensation for allowing this warranty—that those who do not teach or learn to specification will be sorted out and punished for poor workmanship—we have been excused from the more difficult task of questioning whether the specifications are descriptive of who we might really want to be.

The Role of the Profession

The first edition also spelled out some of what Purpel believed constitutes "the unique and special responsibility and character of an educational institution." We do not hesitate to reaffirm these ideas but the generally cowardly professional response to the political demands for more and more testing has led us to re-examine the limitations of both public schooling and the profession. It is, of course, highly probable that many in the profession are sincerely in favor of the recent changes, but by the same token, there is the same degree of probability that many educators have very serious reservations about them. The point here is simply that the vast majority of those in the second group have not been particularly vocal in their concerns. In the sanctuary of our graduate classes, we routinely hear the pain and anguish of teachers and administrators who believe that these changes violate their basic notions of what constitutes a valid and meaningful education. Yet, we also hear their equally anguished expressions of powerlessness and despair. Many, if not most, fear that reprisals will inevitably follow any show of resistance to the increasingly tighter controls. Even more disheartening is the number of professionals who have very little hope that they can effect any significant amelioration, never mind genuine, positive reform. It is in this sense that we believe that the profession as a whole has by and large violated its most fundamental ethic, that of providing the public with its informed ideas on what is best for students, whether or not this corresponds with the current political or public conventional wisdom. At the very least, the public has not heard the voices of many, if not most, professionals on the validity of current educational policies and practices. At worst, the profession's craven and cynical collaboration with the forces of repression and greed has seriously undermined the dream of a vital and dynamic profession grounded in moral principle, considered judgment, and rigorous thought.

This sad episode in the history of the profession and the schools also raises serious questions about our expectations of what they can actually accomplish within the political realities of our society. Can we really ask the very schools that have been designed to be institutions for continuity and stability to become agents of social and cultural transformation? Is it appropriate to ask school professionals who are essentially civil servants, under the direct control and supervision of the State, to have an independent and critical voice? We will in a later chapter provide our responses to these questions when we discuss our recommendations and suggestions.

However, we cannot lay the blame entirely on the profession for the debacle of school reform since, as we have argued, the ultimate sources of educational policy are to be found in social attitudes and cultural values. We must, therefore, also address even more basic issues, i.e., those relating to the deeper sources of the values that have generated the policies and practices that we have described. In other words, why do we often do what we know is wrong and often do not do what we know to be right?

Discomfort with Moral Choices and a New Thesis

We reiterate our strong belief that these issues are of an essentially moral nature, but with a greater awareness than we did at the writing of the first edition of the relevance and significance of spiritual matters. In the first edition, Purpel struggled with what he called the crux of the crisis, the "difficulty of creating . . . [a] vision of meaning in the context of diversity, division, skepticism, dogmatism, and nihilism." He lamented our, "Failure to develop an overarching mythos of meaning, purpose, and ultimacy . . . [to guide] us in creation of . . . vision." Then he spoke of the urgent need for developing a "working consensus" of spiritual and moral values to empower us to do work toward that vision. One of the great difficulties in advocating such a development is that, despite the skepticism prevalent in the academy, much of popular opinion and political rhetoric holds that such a consensus already exists, that America has a civil religion that sustains a strong moral culture for both ourselves and for the global civilization we have parented. While many may be rendered more comfortable by such insistence, the behavior chronicled in the preceding list of lost battles strongly argues that this position is either disingenuous or mistaken. In a time when we decide presidential elections in courts and at fund-raising events, our civil religion itself must now be sustained by litigation and legislation that emerges from a bidding war among special interests.

Our review offers the opportunity to observe that many of our choices clearly contradict what our society claims to want from education and for moral culture in general. Our willingness to engage in such contradictory behavior is more easily understood if taken as an attempt to avoid conflict, through pretending that these battles are over technical problems, rather than over moral choices that have to do with what kind of culture we hope to create. Whether it concerns research on testing or the quality of the science supporting the evidence for global warming, we induce internal inconsistencies by seeking technical solutions to moral problems. For example, we are more likely to amend Generally Accepted Accounting Principles in the wake of corporate corruption scandals than to question why this scandalous behavior was allowed to continue for years, concealed and abetted by the silence of many within these companies and within their auditing firms, all of whom consider themselves to be good people.

Maintaining the fiction that we already have a common operational morality produces unhelpful responses, ranging from moral ambivalence to malevolence. It leaves us with the social equivalent of cognitive dissonance. In that state, we are fortunate if our behavior is only irrational. Consider the seemingly intractable issues we have already discussed, such as: the distribution of wealth, the question of whose interest we serve as educators, the ownership of the earth's resources, and the responsibility to report corporate malfeasance. Call to mind the equally contentious questions about who should receive medical care, and who decides issues of "Choice/Right to Life" (we cannot even agree on a name for that one). In most of our public discourse, each side claims to hold the only morally tenable position. If we insist that we already have a common morality, that must mean that one side or the other is so profoundly wrong as to be outside the pale. And neither side would be likely to yield its position to any moral argument or accept any outcome that interfered with its freedom to hold the position already chosen. As James Hunter has it:

> We say we want a renewal of character in our day but we don't really know what we ask for. To have a renewal of character is to have a renewal of a creedal order that constrains, limits, binds, obligates and compels. This price is too high for us to pay. We want character but without conviction; we want strong morality but without the emotional burden of guilt or shame; we want virtue but without particular moral justifications that invariably offend; we want good without having to name evil; we want decency without the authority to insist on it; we want moral community without any limitations on personal freedom. In short, we want what we cannot possibly have on the terms that we want. (2000: xi)

Why do we tolerate this dissonance? Why do we not see that we cannot have what we want on the terms that we want; that the desires and motivations that have created and continue to sustain a consumer culture will never produce the kind of world that we claim we want? In the first edition, Purpel insisted on the possibility of a consensual moral framework and we still cling to that hope and assertion. However, we are confounded by the question of why so many of us foster the fiction that we have actually committed ourselves to a common morality? These questions frame the American discomfort in the face of moral choice and allow us to see more clearly the need to search for the roots of this dissonance. Having reflected upon those roots, we now feel that the primary emphasis on the moral dimensions of the crisis of the eighties, which characterized the first edition, must give way to a greater emphasis on an underlying spiritual crisis. America's failure to demonstrate the moral capacity to respond well to our crisis in the eighties causes us to conclude that it was an unexamined spiritual crisis that precipitated that earlier moral crisis; this spiritual crisis is still with us today and its dimensions are continuing to become both more apparent and more ominous. A successful resolution to the spiritual origin of our moral crisis is required if we are to develop the capacity to mitigate or reverse the consequences that are now cascading from our previous moral choices.

Much of the remainder of this reflection, therefore, will be an effort to expand upon that thesis in a meaningful way, identifying this spiritual crisis and venturing into the highly dangerous territory of describing some of the characteristics of a solution. Our current incapacity for sustaining a common morality must be seen in its historical context—the post-everything world in which we are skeptical of everything except skepticism. In this culture, lacking the compelling force of a common morality, the only compelling arguments are economic ones, so that the morality of the market place is now invading all other spheres by default, to the disadvantage of all, including even those "market fundamentalists" (Soros, 2000) who think they are individually advantaged by globalization and radically free capital markets. Every decision of moral import is today weighed in the market scales. We ask if "national interests" are at stake before intervening to stop genocide. We demand accountability in classrooms and hospitals, yet have no language for compassion there. In the USA and in the worldwide (mostly American) culture, there is a profound lack of the factor that has traditionally supported mass moral consensus. That factor is the social coercion of needing to exhibit behavior considered by one's peers to be indicative of holding a universally accepted set of beliefs. While it may well be liberating to free ourselves of any form of coercion, we find that we have deconstructed those traditional mechanisms without replacing them, leaving ourselves only license for radical self-interest—cloaked in hypocrisy, inviting a Hobbsean war of all against all.

This is not to suggest that the history of coercion that Hunter cites is a desirable state; rather we note its absence as an explanation for why the present political rhetoric of common values is vacuous. If a working consensus of spiritual insight and moral values without coercion were as simple as gathering up the best of a lot of traditions and negotiating until a majority of people could agree that they are good ideas, the task would have been resolved long ago. Whether one looks at the UN Declaration of Universal Human Rights, the various efforts of ecumenicalism, or the struggles of local school boards to define character, the results are invariably the same—such efforts are supported only so long as they either favor or at least do not interfere with individual, corporate, or national interests.

And why should we suggest that the foregoing descriptions of the state of our educational system, our economy, and our social contract be taken as symptoms of a spiritual crisis, instead of simply being seen as rather mundane social criticism? First, the pretense we have described is an indispensable support for a profound state of denial among most people in our culture. Very few of us would be candid enough to acknowledge that our own ideology, "centers on materialism, science, individuality, and consumerism," as the first edition has it, yet the outcomes of our everyday actions demonstrate that sad truth. Similarly, while more than willing to diagnose our peers with holding such views, few of us would be willing to see it in ourselves; rather, with a characteristic lack of humility most would claim that they have the capacity to live morally in an amoral culture. Such self-deception and lack of self-understanding we hold to be the stuff of spiritual disorder. Second, we believe that we have a moral crisis because of the lack of any support for a moral structure that would sustain better behavior; and that we have a spiritual crisis which consists of the absence of a *spiritual ground* to take the place of the recently and thankfully departed social coercion provided by rigid religious or ideological beliefs. While much of the balance of this book will attempt to provide a context within which to understand what the authors intend in using words such as *spiritual, spirituality,* and *wisdom,* it should be said here that by *spiritual ground,* we mean an order of reality beyond materialism, the perception of which has led to (among other things) the formation of institutional religions.

To fully describe a spiritual process and to expand on how such a process might, through the practice of spiritual discipline, bring about the outcomes we seek is the work of lifetimes. Fortunately, that work has already been done many times over. The main labor of this book is to seek common ground in discriminating between such a process and some of its most common unfortunate descendants: cultism, social organizations masquerading as something greater, and commercial enterprises exploiting the credulous. The origin of those unfortunate descendents of spiritual systems might be better understood by seeing them as by-products of the social structures that have historically grown up around religions. Religious organizations have frequently developed as attempts to replicate the mystical experience of extraordinarily gifted prophets for a larger group of people, attempting to preserve the revelations and insights of the founders after their departure. Our history shows us that the greatest hazard to the success of those attempts occurs once those in charge of the organization have lost personal contact with the original source of the prophet's inspiration, whether that source is conceived of as God, or enlightenment, or a profound understanding of human nature. Once that loss occurs, the organization has become a religious fossil, of only historical interest. It is quite possible for such a fossilized remnant to survive indefinitely thereafter, a social phenomenon preserving the container, if not the content that began the process. In such an end-state, these organizations can still coercively support a common moral culture, even if they lack the capacity to fulfill the validating purpose of their founders. Eventually, however, the rigidity of such orphaned organizations results in their losing credibility, so that their capacity to impose morality fails as well. The authors hold that it is the responsibility of every adherent to what might potentially be such a fossil system to open themselves to the possibility that such a fate might have befallen their own organization and to have the courage to ask the difficult questions that the testing of such a hypothesis entails. It is not necessary to take the liberty of nominating belief systems that are currently dearly held for such consideration, because we have available a very recent historical example of large numbers of people suffering from such a lag between the loss of content and the realization of that loss: the collapse of the moral ground once claimed by communist states. While avowed beliefs in the holding of property in common and the sharing of that property based upon need were potentially powerful moral strengths of these states (beliefs, incidentally, shared by the early Christian church), they were never successfully practiced. Instead, the political collapse of these systems lagged far behind the Stalinist destruction of those theoretical moral claims that had fueled their rise.

Without a compelling and vital spiritual base, profound moral concerns atrophy into a conventional morality that justifies and sustains rather than critiques and undermines the status quo. Some of these groups degenerate far beyond mere ineffectiveness—we might reasonably fear that many currently more innocuous organizations, which for the moment seem more intent on cash or sexual exploitation than on Armageddon, might follow the path taken by some of the horrors of our time. The nerve gas attacks in the Tokyo subway, the Jim Jones cult with its mass suicide in Guyana, oppression by the Taliban, and the murderous activities of Al-Qaida are tragic demonstrations of the processes by which spiritual and religious processes can cease to be living entities and become social organizations run amok.

To our good fortune, these disordered souls are not the only remnant we have from the great wisdom traditions of humanity. There are also many persons of great character and insight who operate both within and outside of formal religious traditions to struggle to call us to be something more than what we presently are. Efforts by these people of good will to either preserve or develop processes that sustain contact with that original source of spiritual inspiration that inspired formal religions are not foreign to our culture; many people who consider themselves highly religious (and many who do not) are deeply involved in attempts to do so. These people—not cultists and lunatics but rather the surest hope of humankind—are among us as well. However, it is fair to say that while not uncommon, their efforts are highly marginalized by the consumer culture and marketplace values.

Perhaps our greatest misfortune remains our incapacity to agree among ourselves as to which of these two descriptions (cultist or our surest hope) applies to a particular instance. As a culture, we seem to lack the fundamental capacity to discriminate between the worst and the best; thus, the dissonance noted earlier by Hunter and by the first edition. Moral ambivalence, cultural dissonance, wanting what we cannot have on the terms that we want it—no wonder our behavior and our pronouncements do not agree! Given such a state, we are indeed fortunate that our problems and the carnage of our lost battles are no worse than they already are.

Given the perennial nature of this problem, where are we to turn for some good sense? Once again, we have good fortune. We can avail ourselves of much that is known about what could be called the subtleties of moral and spiritual discrimination: suppose we were to be able to learn (then teach) the skill necessary to agree upon the distinction between the best and the worst of those who would be our Teachers. Then we might begin to find our way. In the following chapters, there will be some suggestions as to how we might seek these skillful means. Among the many voices that might be heard are those from our history who stood closest to those original mystical sources; but we do not lack for living voices. From among thousands, we might mention Jack Kornfield, who says that we must learn to want different things; Jeff Kane, who tells us that a spiritual concept of education may be seen as a developmental process, with dimensions of renunciation, transformation, and realization; Hazel Henderson, who wants us to look beyond economic warfare; and the Dalai Lama, who proposes a spiritual revolution, free of doctrinal divides; along with many others.

Understanding and teaching the transformative aspect of such a process, including the concept of spiritual *practice,* is a difficult and critical departure from much of what is held in our current common value system—the value system of the marketplace, of "market fundamentalism." It requires that we challenge the market's materialistic view of human nature in a fundamental way. We are willing to confront that difficulty with hope, because we believe, as we did at the time of the first edition, that education itself must somehow be changed into an enterprise with the capacity and the will, to, as Purpel wrote then, "Transform the static circle of doubt, despair, nihilism, hopelessness, doubt . . . into a spiral of movement," one actively engaged in fulfilling, ". . . the sacred responsibility to create a world of Love, Justice, and Joy."

2

THE STRUGGLE FOR MORAL AND SPIRITUAL AFFIRMATION IN AN AGE OF GREED, FANATICISM, AND CYNICISM

The middle chapters of the first edition (3, 4, and 5) built upon the positing of assumptions and diagnosis of crisis in the opening chapters, to explore the nature of the crisis in more depth, especially as it was reflected in educational policies and practices. In chapter three, the first edition found the crux of our educational crisis to lie in, ". . . the difficulty of creating a vital, authentic, and energizing vision of meaning in a context of significant diversity, pluralism, division, skepticism, dogmatism, and even nihilism." Finding that this crisis extended beyond education to the culture at large, we asked how we were to overcome despair and emptiness and enable ourselves, ". . . to make lasting and profound moral commitments that can energize and legitimate our day-to-day lives." It was clear to us then that the path toward such a state involved, ". . . the search for, and the affirmation of, an overarching moral and spiritual framework that provides a center of meaning for the culture."

These quotes also reflect an opinion about human nature, asserting a belief that most of the bad choices that have led us to the present state of our culture have derived more from confusion than from evil, surely a necessary and essential belief for educators to hold. As the first edition said, "When we look at our problems as rooted in evil and sin, then the only alternative to despair is prayer; but when we are able to see them based more on confusion then we can put our hope in education." In addition to providing the opportunity to engender faith in the educational process, such a belief serves us well in other aspects of today's world. Seeing confusion rather than evil intent at the root of the divide between those who name themselves enemies leaves some hope for reconciliation, rather than unending conflict and violence. Seeing such possibilities in each other helps us to move beyond hate-driven politics and irreconcilable differences, toward an ethic of understanding, compassion, and forgiveness.

Why has finding common moral ground been so problematic? Do we have no set of common beliefs that would lead us to such obviously beneficial ground? The majority of our citizens confess some sort of religious or ethical system that directly prohibits the practices that the opening chapters lamented. Why are these confusions so persistent and pervasive? There can be few who would propose that confusion be preserved; on the contrary, we tax ourselves heavily for the avowed purpose of minimizing it through public education. Why then do we profess so much and deliver so little?

How are we to deal with this history (both ancient and recent) that is a record of failure in our attempts to conform our behavior to what we already know, much less to go beyond and to develop "an overarching moral and spiritual framework?" Many thoughtful observers of human nature have recorded observations of this failure, among them Ovid ("I see the better way and approve it; I follow the worse"), Paul ("For the good that I would I do not; but the evil which I would not, that I do"), and Pogo ("We have met the enemy and it is us"). Even with the excuse of confusion, rather than the doom of an evil nature, we ought to be doing better; at present our efforts do not even rise to the level of our admittedly confused understanding. This chapter attempts to frame our response to that perennial failure.

Further Reflections on Paradoxes and Conflicts in American Culture

In the first edition, we attempted to present a broad conception of this confusion by examining a series of, ". . . discrete yet clearly overlapping dyads of value paradoxes." Those commentaries still seem basically sound to us, even in the light of a much-changed world. We did find, however, that in five instances, our present understanding of the nature of the crisis requires that we extend the scope of our earlier discussion. In the following section we shall briefly revisit *Individuality/ Community, Worth/Achievement, Humility/Arrogance,* and *Faith/Reason;* at the close of this chapter, we will also expand on *Self-Deception* at greater length in the hope that all this second-generation explication might yield some fresh insight into the perennial nature of our incapacity to do as we say, mitigate our confusion and help to find common ground.

Self-Interest/Common Good
(Individuality/Community in an Economic Vein)

In the previous chapters we described our society as one in which large numbers of people have unmet basic needs in the midst of great wealth; one in which the pursuit of wealth has become the central goal and in which one's success in the pursuit of wealth has come increasingly to be equated with one's entire worth. Because of these outcomes and despite the efforts of a good many people of good will to behave differently, we diagnosed our culture as already possessing a common value system, albeit not one that is flattering to tally. In looking at the allocation of food, education, medical care, and justice, we found that the culture agrees (in practice if not in words) that the final judgment on issues of equity is to be determined by the values of the marketplace. Reflecting back on the historical context of the original work during the Reagan years, it is probable that this diagnosis would have already been accurate at the time of the First Edition, if less obvious. However, the fall of the Soviet Union and the global triumph of the free market economic system have now given such an air of inevitability to the values of the market that these values are increasingly successful in putting themselves forward as the standard by which all human interactions are to be judged. There is an underlying pessimistic assumption about human beings implied in this belief system that remains largely unremarked, but it colors all that we do. What is this pessimistic assumption? It has been standard fare for cynics in all of our history and literature, but it received one of its most systematic and historically significant treatments by Adam Smith in the late eighteenth century.

Smith, the philosophical and economic prophet of the free market system, originally set out to develop a moral philosophy, and concluded in 1766 (*Theory of Moral Sentiments*) that human beings of right should develop in ways that curbed their natural inclination toward self-interest: "And hence it is, that to feel much for others, and little for ourselves, that to restrain our selfish, and to indulge our benevolent, affections, constitutes the perfection of human nature; and can alone produce among mankind that harmony of sentiments and passions in which consists their whole grace and propriety" (1966:27). However, within a decade, in his seminal work on free market economics, Smith had concluded that he could offer no hope of a common system of moral values that would serve to move the mass of human beings to act against their individual short-term economic interests for the sake of the good of others. (An interesting corollary, which was not proposed by Smith but is now supported by our environmental record, might be that humans will not sacrifice their short-term interests for their own *long term* good). Given that perception of human nature, Smith was pleased to think that he had discovered an amazing characteristic of free markets, such that if everyone acts selfishly, the outcomes are inevitably moved toward the greater good: ". . . he intends only his own gain, and he is in this, as in many other cases, led by an invisible hand to promote an end which was no part of his intention" (1994:485). Not wishing to engage the heirs of Smith on their own theoretical turf, we are quick to acknowledge that his system has had no fairer test than that of Marx (or Moses, or Jesus, or Buddha) since his disciples in the business world insist on proving the pessimistic hypothesis by cheating, avoiding free markets at every turn, seeking monopoly and unfair advantage. To see this departure from free market doctrine in action, one need only follow any anti-trust case (e.g., Microsoft v. Everyone) for a brief time.

What is interesting from the viewpoint of this discussion is not the adequacy of any of the economic arguments, but rather, the question of the validity of the pessimism that claims to render them necessary. Are all human beings who wish to survive in the globalized future required to come to see themselves as irredeemably selfish (and thus perhaps evil rather than confused)? Must we have incentives that serve either our wallets or our egos in order to do what we claim to know is the "right thing"? And, if we can find a way to be successful apologists for individuals, what shall we say of people in groups? Can corporations serve their communities without (or against) financial incentives? Can nation states act to stop aggression and genocide far from home if they see no "vital strategic interest" or avoid a war that might bring economic benefit to the electorate—and in either case, can nations find any grounds other than political bargaining and superior force upon which to make those judgments?

The systematic remedies customarily provided in answer to such questions (e.g., theologies, moral exhortation, and carefully reasoned moral philosophies) are the stock in trade of ethical systems and religions, although any claims for the efficacy of these products would find little historical support. Why? Is there some perverse bent in human beings that justifies the pessimistic hypothesis and causes such a fundamental set of problems to remain unsolved, even after occupying much of our history and most of our good fiction? Is the optimism about human nature that is necessary in order to assume the efficacy of education at risk?

Worth/Achievement (Further Thoughts)

This value conflict focuses our attention even more forcefully on the contradiction at the heart of our moral crisis. Our popular culture has found itself befuddled by cognitive dissonance when trying to believe simultaneously: (1) that all persons are—possibly by design—born with equal worth, and (2) that it is apparently the purpose of education and the economy to frustrate any such design (i.e., instead of working to reduce inequality, we seem intent on remedying that initial birth equality as rapidly as possible, using achievements in the marketplace to keep score.) While it should be clear from the first chapters that institutional education in our culture is an extension of the marketplace, given the complications of genetic and economic inheritance, it is understandable that considerable confusion has been generated by this issue in even the most erudite circles. Professional educators and theologians have woven fascinating tapestries of sophistries in apology for their patrons—the winners in this race. Whether the answers are "excellence" or "election" or "the divine right of kings" each answer carries its own burden of self-service.

Clearly the idea that each individual human being has an intrinsic worth that is the same as any other person, and that such worth is not dependent upon his or her economic contribution to the community is not a new idea; however it is an idea whose underpinnings may now be in danger of becoming a minority belief. That would almost certainly be the case if one were to require those claiming to hold such beliefs to evidence them by actions. It is difficult to find evidence in the actions of our present culture that are representative of the economics of Jesus, the debtors' jubilee of Moses, or the requirements for charity recorded by Mohammed in the Koran (or even the sympathy for our fellows previously quoted from the *Moral Sentiments* of Adam Smith).

What may be more to the point however is the fact that these exemplars needed to take such positions in the first place. The presence of protestations of individual worth in each of our widely held belief systems attests to a history of behaviors that rendered them necessary. It is not difficult to find fairly recent examples of slavery, human sacrifice, infanticide, and the like among the adherents to each of our traditions. While apologists have contributed to the longevity of such horrors by various clever delimitations of the term "human," such customs obviously have origins in a time when no apology was needed. Simply imagine an early human community, highly dependent upon the success of its hunters, gatherers, and workers of magic for survival. Imagine the difficulty of making a persuasive argument for intrinsic worth and against achievement-based hierarchy in such a world. Thus it might well be that holding a belief in the intrinsic worth of each and every individual human being is an example of real human progress, growing out of both cultural innovation and revelation, subsequently enshrined in religions, moral precepts, and legal codes. It seems to the authors that the different statements of intrinsic worth do show significant variability in the strength of their truth claim, relative to their origins. In the case of revelation, most traditions and a few cultural innovations hold some version of "all men [*sic*] are created equal, endowed by their creator . . . ," while most cultural innovations (such as economic belief systems) reserve a significant portion of worth to award to those who conform their behavior to cultural norms. Much of the history of the struggle for moral consensus might be read as the accommodation between the unconditional worth posited by revelation and the pragmatic rationing of worth thought to be required for effective economic incentives and the maintenance of social order.

In either case, as posited earlier, that we have such a concept (no matter how strongly stated and even if honored mostly in the breach) may be an indication that progress truly is possible. At the same time, our most recent history may indicate that we are regressing, that we may be chronicling yet another endangered element of human progress. The recently fashionable avowal of a belief in intrinsic worth is suffering continued erosion as we witness a regression to a standard of money-based worth. Consider David Korten's discussion of the logic of corporate downsizing:

In an economy that measures performance in terms of the creation of money, people become a major source of inefficiency—and the economy is shedding them with a vengeance. When the institutions of money rule the world, it is perhaps inevitable that the interests of money will take precedence over the interests of people. What we are experiencing might best be described as a case of money colonizing life. To accept this absurd distortion of human institutions and purpose should be considered nothing less than an act of collective, suicidal insanity (1995:247).

Humility (in Victory) / Patriotism (without Arrogance)

Following the events of 9/11/01, we encountered a social phenomenon that at first struck us as strange, but which makes sense upon reflection: dealing with cultural arrogance had become even more difficult than in the Cold War context of the first edition. When we look back with more perspective, we find that one of the casualties of the terrorist attacks may have been our national enthusiasm for honest self-criticism. Americans have often been characterized as being obsessively self-critical; however, an "awareness of the complex and elusive nature of truth" is never more likely to be absent than in war, at least among those who presume themselves to be the victors. Perhaps when we look back from an even later time, it will no longer seem remarkable to be able to hold *both* of the following: that the terrorist attacks were profoundly wrong *and* that an American foreign policy and economic system that better reflected our moral convictions might have reduced their likelihood. Despite our aspirations for human progress, it is still true today that such mental dexterity is too complex and elusive for our national psyche. Too often we seem to want only simple truths to carry into battle, and such subtleties often draw dark looks from many listeners. In our present crisis, many simply want to be assured that we are Good and that *any* opposition to our positions is an adequate definition of Evil. Seeking such simplicity here will lead us astray.

The point is that, while the risks of losing a war on terrorism are much discussed, we also need to understand that one risk of victory is that we might suffer hubris like that from our victory in the Cold War. We must remember that winning does not validate all of our assumptions. Humility is a necessary condition for the self-examination required if we are to hope for better outcomes to the problems we have been discussing. We are unlikely to change policies if we are unwilling to consider that they may have been mistaken; and we are unlikely to change beliefs that we are unwilling to question.

Faith/Reason/(Wisdom)

The Enlightenment's elevation of reason to stand ahead of faith insures that we will have a faith no better than our reason; Western culture must certainly have made this choice at least in part to avoid credulity, insisting that the foundation of "an overarching moral and spiritual framework" not lie beyond our rational understanding. Yet, if we limit our understanding to systems that have demonstrated their incapacity to remedy our history of behaving worse than we believe, how are we to improve upon our persistent incapacity "to make lasting and profound moral commitments"? This question does not arise in a culture with a viable *wisdom tradition*. In the next chapter, we will attend in detail to the question of Wisdom, but for the purpose of this section, consider how much of the best of our history—as evidenced by our religious, poetic, artistic, and intellectual labors—can be read as a record of humanity struggling against fear to find some higher order of reality, some hope that the worst of what we are is not all that we are. The best examples of such histories are those we call *wisdom traditions*. Some have survived as *living* wisdom traditions, and their proponents assert that they provide the direct experience of an order of reality higher than the one in which the ego operates.

In such a culture, Faith (or a working hypothesis, if you must) specifies that there are profound responses to the questions, "Where does the path lie and what are the requirements for traveling it?" in the possession of the Wise. Further, these traditions specify that the capacity to perceive the needs of a particular student and to provide what that student needs in order to progress on the path are defining characteristics of Wisdom in a teacher. The barrier that our culture's dedication to rational explication imposes to acting upon such a hypothesis is profound. We have chosen to forego Wisdom rather than to take the risk of credulity.

Even if we were able to take that risk, there are consequences for our culture's shallow understanding of egalitarianism if we come to believe that one human being might know something that another cannot know by reading a book. Wisdom traditions commonly teach that the capacity to understand the ground of a moral and spiritual framework must be acquired in ways that are not the ways of our culture. They also propose that, while every individual has the potential for this understanding as part of that nature that defines intrinsic individual worth, it is seldom developed: few will pass through "the narrow gate." As educators we are usually quite comfortable suggesting that there are prerequisites to understanding advanced work, yet in this case a history of abuse in the defense of various forms of aristocratic privilege causes us to be quite shy—we might well fear a charge of elitism were we to publicly defend such a belief. Also, almost none of us who live by educating have much competence in Wisdom, since it has been so little valued—there are employment issues! Yet every spiritual tradition that we remember claims to contain a mystical core that is (1) inaccessible using the tools approved by our present culture and (2) necessary to achieving our goal of an overarching moral and spiritual framework that provides a center of meaning for the culture.

The utilitarian morality that is supported by this present culture is devoid of such wisdom and differs not at all in its final pragmatic outcomes from the morality of the marketplace. Using such tools, we can have such justice as may be sustained by law, but we cannot have such mercy as would be sustained by compassion. By insisting that our options are limited to the present state of our reason, we have closed a door that the most respected figures in our history claim is the only way to what we seek. Is it possible to go back and reconsider that choice, in case it might be part of the cause of our present circumstance?

The Problematics of Our Religious and Moral Framework

We find on reflection that the opening of the fourth chapter of the First Edition needs little revision or commentary and we are comfortable in reaffirming the discussion of how the commonalities of our political, moral, and intellectual heritage are valuable resources available to us in our search for a common set of transcendent values. One key element upon which we do need to expand is what we characterized as the eternal argument over the question of the reality or lack thereof behind religious belief, illustrated with quotations from Durkheim and Eliade. The revision we believe is needed here is the addition of a category. To move toward a new mythos for our time, we shall need to make a distinction between religion (if construed as requiring acceptance of a set of rigid doctrines) and spirituality (if construed as the initial inspiration for the construction of religions). We believe that this distinction is necessary because the capacity for self-deception has historically been nowhere more apparent than when humanity has ventured into this area. As a result, the concept that spiritual insight might offer some access to truth beyond our other capacities has often been tainted by the excesses of the adherents of derivative doctrines. We will elaborate on the implication of this distinction in the next chapters in an attempt to support our conviction that the first edition needed more emphasis on the spiritual aspect of the crisis.

We still hold to the First Edition's appreciation for all the cautions and safeguards that our political, moral, and intellectual heritage provides against the dangers of "arrogance, self-righteousness, self-delusion and corruption that ensue when power and piety are integrated." At the same time, chapter four rightly concluded with a call not to allow these very appropriate concerns to drive us to a retreat into amorality and vulgar pragmatism. To that end there was an affirmation of the truly noble aspects of our common heritage and a condemnation of the evil and destructive forces in our culture, all of which pointed toward the fifth chapter and the Credo.

The Credo as an Exemplar of the Goal of Education

What we find now in looking back is that, despite the value and power of the noble aspects of our culture, they have historically failed and continue to fail the goal which we seek: an overarching moral and spiritual framework that provides a center of meaning for the culture. Our political, moral, and intellectual heritage is necessary but not sufficient—these resources alone have not, will not take us to where we want to go. They give us the capacity to describe the outcome we desire, but they have failed to find the path to get us there. Therefore in reflecting on that work today, we must affirm that the spiritual crisis which we face today will not abate until we find a way to wisdom that does not pass through arrogance, self-righteousness, self-delusion, and corruption.

The Credo, which was the centerpiece of chapter five in the first edition, is restated here in its entirety, so that it may be read as a whole (with revisions from Purpel and Shapiro, 1995:154–156). We consider the Credo to be an example of the sort of behavior to which we believe educators (and citizens) are called, the sort of behavior that would resolve many of the problems of education and of our society. The Credo is necessary; we cannot get to where we want to go without bringing to bear our political, moral and intellectual heritage, and we hold this Credo to be an exemplar of the application of that heritage to the present crisis. What we now add is the notion that the nature of human beings apparently requires something more than our political, moral and intellectual heritage to enable us to change our behavior to comply with the Credo. The following chapters will provide our response to what we think is missing.

An Educational Credo for a Time of Crisis and Urgency

Educators are primarily moral, political, and cultural agents charged with the responsibility of grounding their specialized insights in a cultural, political, and moral vision. An educator without some kind of moral and cultural grounding is either tragically alienated, cynically deceptive, or naively shallow. John Dewey reminds us that education is about learning to create a world and that our most vital and demanding task as educators is to be mindful of the kind of world that we want to create. Absolutely essential, therefore, in the ethics of education are the twin pillars of freedom, namely, responsibility and choice. As educators, we are required to respond to the challenges of life and to choose among the many moral, political, and cultural possibilities open to us.

We Choose, Celebrate, and Affirm These Propositions:

1. *We recognize the wonder, mystery, and awe that surrounds our life and that beckons us to contemplate, examine, and make meaning of it and of our part in it.* As educators, we must encourage and help students to separate mystery and awe from ignorance and superstition, but we must be careful to witness and be informed by what is beyond our present human capacity to comprehend. As educators, our responsibility is to present with respect varying interpretations of life's meaning. But our most compelling responsibility is to renew and reenergize the commitment to pursue lives of individual and communal meaning.
2. *We renew our faith in the capacity to celebrate diversity and difference while working to create a world of harmony, peace, and justice.* As educators, we must avoid the perils of pride and arrogance that emerge from a posture of cultural superiority. We recognize that meaning and fulfillment derive, in part, from cultural identity, and we must

therefore strive to revere and respect, not patronize and romanticize, the ethos of particular cultural, racial, and ethnic groups. This consciousness requires basic trust in the recognition that harmony is not synonymous with homogeneity, that peace is not to be equated with control, and that justice is not to be blurred with freedom.

As educators, we must move from a consciousness of mastery, domination, submission, and docility in which some persons are subjects and others are objects. As educators, we must strive to see our students not as black boxes, not as clay to be molded or minds to be trained, but as sentient beings deserving of dignity, love, and fulfillment. As educators, we must not require people to earn their dignity, but we must strive to celebrate the sanctity, miracle, and preciousness of life. This consciousness does not bring us to punishment, tracking, grading, and honors programs, but to an education that reveres life as sacred and inviolate. Such a consciousness does not urge us to get ahead, but to stand with; does not idealize competition, but venerates dignity; does not legitimate privilege and advantage, but rather seeks to heal the deadly quarrels that divide the human family.

3. *We renew our faith in the human impulse to seek to create a world of justice, compassion, love, and joy, and in the human capacity to create such a world.* As educators, our responsibility is to nurture these impulses that have permeated human history not only by increasing awareness and understanding of them but by confronting the equally human impulses to oppress, dominate, and objectify. As educators, we can be guided and comforted by the immensity of human intellectual, creative, and intuitive potential to re-create our world; and at the same time, we should be sobered by the human capacity to be destructive, cruel, and callous. We speak to an education that is grounded in our strongest and deepest moral traditions, which urge us to love our neighbor, to seek justice, and to pledge ourselves to a nation committed to liberty and justice for all and a government of the people, by the people, and for the people. We speak to an education based on traditions that urge us to beat swords into ploughshares, not to develop more deadly swords; a vision in which lions lie down with lambs, not one in which we train lambs to be lions; and a universal dream of milk and honey for all, not the American Dream of champagne and caviar for a few.

4. *We reaffirm our commitment to the joys of community, the profundity of compassion, and to the power of interdependence.* As educators, we must become aware of the spiritual disease of alienation, loneliness, fragmentation, and isolation and must act to reduce the perilous effects of an education directed toward success, achievement, and personalism. As educators, we have the responsibility of nurturing the impulse for meaningful and cooperative relationships and for exposing the myths and dangers of individual achievement. Education must not act to convert the uncivilized, but neither should it serve to create a myriad of individual universes. Compassion serves neither to distance nor to blur or annihilate differences, but rather seeks to share the struggles, pain, and joys that are common to us all. If we are to compete, we as educators need to confront the significance of the race not only for the winners but also for the losers. If we are to be committed to individual excellence, then we must know if it is achieved at the expense of others. More important, we as educators must participate in the process of creating a society in which people are more united than divided, where differences are not translated into hierarchy, and where pain and anguish are occasions for neither pity nor exploitation, but for compassion and solidarity.

5. *We affirm the central importance of nourishing a consciousness of moral outrage and social responsibility.* As educators, we must go far beyond informing, describing, and analyzing and must free ourselves from the destructive force of moral numbness. We must help our students to become aware of our failures to meet our moral and cultural imperatives and to help them inform their intellectual understanding with moral judgments. An education that engenders a posture of promiscuous tolerance, scholarly detachment, or cynical weariness toward unnecessary human suffering is an abomination! We must avoid the temptation to teach only what makes one feel good or to teach that social problems are only "interesting." Education is not about finding out things, but about finding ourselves. It is not enough to say further research is needed when what is needed is not more information but more justice. To know without a sense of outrage, compassion, or concern deadens our souls and significantly eases the struggle of demonic forces to capture our consciousness. We need an education that produces moral indignation and energy rather than one that excuses, mitigates, and temporizes human misery. Heschel reminds us that although only a few are guilty, all are responsible. Our task as educators is therefore to teach students to identify the guilty, to have compassion for the victims, and to exercise their responsibility to reduce, if not eliminate, injustices.

Self-deception

If the Credo exemplifies the behavior that would grow out of an overarching moral and spiritual framework that provided a center of meaning for the culture, then what is the nature of the path that would provide us with the capacity to comply with it? At the beginning of this chapter, we asserted a belief that most of the bad choices that have led us to the present state of our culture have derived more from confusion than from a fundamentally evil nature. In that same spirit we suggest that the reason such appropriate and noble sentiments as those we just offered are so incredibly difficult for human beings to honor lies in our immense capacity for self-deception, a failure that creates confusion and that neglected will often lead us to evil acts. The First Edition quoted Fingarette as saying that in self-deception, there is, ". . . a genuine subversion of personal agency and, for this reason in turn, a subversion of moral capacity." Perhaps we might now say that the confusion to which we have attributed the perversity of human behavior in opposing human aims might be explained as the result of this subversion by means of self-deception.

As an example, among the most self-deceptive assumptions of the worldview that is American Market Culture (and its associated reductionist cousins) are the ones holding that there is a single rational agent that constitutes each human consciousness and that this single agent makes all the choices that a human life entails. Yet so often, we seem to confront the consequences of some behavior that is "unlike us." Rather than always acting in a unified and coherent manner, most of us have found ourselves, at least on a few occasions astonished at our own anger or our unexpected emotion. Surely each of us has at least had the experience of deeply wishing that we could un-say some hurtful word or undo some "unintended" action.

Many people have experienced much more vivid examples, from rage and violence to unexplained debilitating fear. If it were the case that this variety of behaviors and feelings were the property of a single agent, then, in the light of the evidence provided by our behavior that clearly does not serve our announced aims, we would be forced to conclude that this agent was not only confused, but also non-rational and delusional.

There is an alternative hypothesis that both has considerable scientific support and is contained in the teachings of the major spiritual traditions. All that is required in order to understand the confused behavior we have discussed thus far (and that we experience every day of our lives) is that we give up a central concept dear to our present world view: that the "I" we each take ourselves to be is a unitary consciousness—that "I" am of one mind. Alas, unless a person has mastered a profound spiritual discipline, he or she is not employing an individual unitary consciousness. Rather, most of us probably have several "small minds," derived both from socialization and from the amazing neural leftovers of our evolutionary history, all contending at any given moment to divert our attention from the task at hand (Ornstein: 1989). Anyone who has attempted an extended period of concentrated thought, pursued a meditative technique, or struggled to get to sleep on a restless night has had a personal experience of this diversity of "minds." It may well be that our failed struggle to achieve our social goal (an overarching moral and spiritual framework) is a reflection of our abandonment of the preliminary personal *preparation* necessary for a spiritual seeker—integrating these many small selves. Wisdom traditions are quick to tell us that the goal of "being of one heart and one mind" or of "knowing ourselves" is not esoteric (not *only* esoteric), but rather the highly practical beginning of the path along which we must move if we are to get beyond the awfulness of our present situation. So long as we deceive ourselves by claiming that we already have that unitary consciousness, we cannot undertake its attainment and our confusion must continue.

If we as educators are to remedy confusion rather than sow it, then certainly among the primary professional responsibilities of one who offers to teach must be a personal quest for a path to such self-understanding. There are others who can speak much more authoritatively than the authors about self-deception, if less gently. Later we will quote many of them, including brusque Zen masters and Reb Menahem Mendl (The Kotzker), but at this point the directness of Idries Shah is illustrative. Speaking of members of current cultures, ". . . exercising their capacity to understand this patchy development of their thinking patterns," he says of any member of such a culture:

> . . . before he tries to add to his breadth of knowledge and his objectivity, the individual must ask himself whether he really does desire to do so. I say this because it is entirely obvious that most people, no matter what they imagine, do not in fact want to learn more. If they did, they would have been able to observe at least some of the absurdities and the shortcomings of their present patterns of thinking. There is no real evidence that this has occurred in the past few thousand years on any significant scale.

Nobody who tries to increase this knowledge in the human milieu can remain unaware that, among those who believe that they are trying to increase their knowledge, perceptions and awareness, only a small number are actually trying to do so. The rest are using the same words, but they are in fact demanding certain satisfactions from the enterprise: social, personal and community diversion being among the most obvious. (1998:40)

Listening to Shah (and the others) would tell us that, as educators, we must confront the possibility that we may not really *want* to exercise our capacity to see and act against the absurdities that plague institutionalized education. Adopting new "thinking patterns" and new behaviors is immensely difficult, as anyone who has ever set out to change an old habit can attest. One of those new thinking patterns might be to openly acknowledge how, as educators faced with the prospect of psychological, social and personal financial consequences, we are all under terrible pressure to rationalize our complicity with cruel and ineffective practices such as high-stakes testing that serve narrow interests at the expense of our students. As citizens, we must bring the same honesty to our appraisal of the part we play as co-conspirators in the flawed policies of our government. As participants in (and beneficiaries of) a global economy, we must not pretend innocence in the face of the suffering of the "losers" in the race for the achievement of wealth.

Earlier we quoted the first edition as saying, "When we look at our problems as rooted in evil and sin, then the only alternative to despair is prayer; but when we are able to see them based more on confusion then we can put our hope in education." Perhaps now we might say: when we look at our problems as rooted in confusion about the nature of human beings, then an alternative to despair is the kind of education that also includes self-understanding and awareness of the roots of self-deception; in effect, an education that is a preparation for spirituality. Such an education is the only preparation for spirituality that is safe from dogmatism, an education that closes the circle of understanding by understanding the problematic nature of our nature. And what does an educator need in order to offer to provide such an education? As promised, the next chapter will offer our response to that question, attempting to answer, "Why do we need wisdom?"

3

THE NEED FOR WISDOM IN AN AGE
OF UNCERTAINTY AND SKEPTICISM

In this and succeeding chapters, we turn our attention to the critical and vexing questions of how we as citizens and educators might respond to the continuing moral and spiritual crises in our society and education. A basic premise of the first edition is that the (re)affirmation of a consensual moral framework is a requirement for developing an educational program directed at promoting peace, love, joy, and a sustainable society. In the final chapters of the original book, Purpel laid out a particular curricular framework for such an education and noted a number of highly promising experimental programs that seemed resonant with that perspective. In addition, he described a number of general issues regarding the implementation of such programs including the nature of likely resistance from the public and the profession. Although we are comfortable with much of the analysis in those chapters, it is clear that the first edition did not adequately deal with a concern that now seems to us to be of overriding importance, namely the question of why people would be unwilling and/or unable to act on their most cherished moral commitments.

If it is true that a spiritual crisis underlies our incapacity to honor a common moral ground and that this incapacity underlies our failure to resolve our cultural dysfunction, then we would hope that a better understanding of that spiritual crisis would provide some indication of a way ahead, a path from where we are today to where we have said that we would choose to be. We observed earlier that developing a response to a spiritual crisis is the work of profoundly good people over many generations, and we noted our good fortune in having a global culture that still contains the remnants of such work, of such people, over such time. Because of what remains of their work, we are not condemned to despair that we lack the time needed to address our own culture's spiritual crisis, even in the face of growing evidence that we have very little time left to find the right responses to ecological collapse, global terror and the "next new thing," which we will likely discover shortly. There is good news: that which we need to know intellectually, that we already know; those behaviors for which we need examples have had their exemplars; and transcendence has been demonstrated to us in the lives of the best of those who have gone before. And there is further good news still: the "mystery of history and the history of mystery," the mystery that, despite everything, there is a long history of people wanting to do the right thing, a long history of Hope in the face of darkness, a long history that at least implies some source of energy that enables frail humanity to imagine, attempt, and sustain these impulses to goodness and Hope.

So, where is the problem? What lies behind the cultural failures we have described: our seeming incapacity to use what we claim to know; the chronic failure of humans to behave as they have promised themselves to behave; a perennial choosing of the self-serving over the self-transcendent? We said earlier (chapters 1 and 2) that our cultural wealth of spiritual insight is often rendered ineffective by our incapacity to discriminate between the worst and the best of our heritage. The record of our recent past shows us to be at the mercy of the propensity for self-deception we discussed (in chapter three).

Certainly this is not a new circumstance. Indeed, our great literature and our history can be seen as one continuing lament (and comedy) on these themes. Yes, the human condition is unchanged; but two new elements make this ancient story into a current crisis: (1) Our market-driven technologically powered culture has acquired the capacity to develop multiple means for destroying the life-carrying capacity of the planet in the short term; and (2) The cultural weaknesses discussed in the first three chapters are exacerbated by an unaccustomed absence of Wisdom. Wisdom in this sense we hold to be that state characteristic of human beings who: have developed certain skillful means, including the capacity to discriminate between real and imagined spirituality; have hope grounded in such real spiritual experience (rather than optimism or delusion), which provides them the strength to continue their struggle against self-deception in themselves and others; and thus, have the insight and capacity needed to Teach.

We will turn to the second point first, with a review of the symptoms that cause us to diagnose the absence of Wisdom.

Issues of Resistance to Doing the Right Thing

What has emerged over the past several years is the realization that the problem with the educational system's failure to fully deliver on its responsibilities to contribute to the creation of a more just and loving community is not primarily rooted in the absence of "good ideas" or of compelling visions. Rather, we have concluded, the more fundamentally troubling barrier lies not so much in the articulation or offering of such ideas and visions but in our difficulty to act on them. It is certainly true that many people do, in fact, deny the broad assumptions and orientation of the kind of education to which we and like-minded people are committed and that those who deny our assumptions offer directions based on differing perspectives. This kind of honest and open difference of outlook is, of course, what we ought to expect and celebrate in a free society with the faith that good faith dialogue can help us sort these differences. As we examine the response to our and similar proposals, however, we find, ironically enough, that it has been more perplexing to deal with those who are in general agreement with these formulations than with those who oppose them.

At the risk of oversimplification, it would be fair to characterize much, if not most, of the response to the first edition as well as to other similar and parallel orientations as something that amounts to, "I agree that we should strive to treat all people with dignity and that everyone deserves to live a life of meaning and well-being, BUT. . . ." Often the BUT is about qualms on human nature ("too many people are lazy and irresponsible, happy to be parasites of the hard-working and responsible"); and/or the hesitation reflects a sense of futility ("it sounds good in practice, but how are we ever going to be able to make such major changes in our minds and in the culture?").

What gives us hope from these kinds of responses is the degree to which so many people are happy to affirm the value of an education directed at creating a more just and loving community. What is disheartening is the realization that these reservations are not so much about the immensity of the task (at least some of which presumably can be seen as difficult but surmountable engineering problems) but more about primordial fears. Perhaps we fear that we will lose some of our hard-earned cherished possessions and prerogatives as a consequence of a Soviet style leveling process and redistribution of wealth. ("If everybody is equal, we'll all have to live in public housing and take public transportation.") Many of us no doubt fear the uncertainty and unforeseen consequences of major change of any direction, particularly one that is so threatening to those in power. ("The devil you know is better that the one you don't.") There is a pervasive fear of the futility of such a project, that it will inevitably result in failure. ("We've been down this road before, and in the end things are no better than when we started and perhaps even worse.") In addition, there is likely to be personal doubt about the depth of our individual commitment to these principles as well as uncertainty about having enough courage and stamina to sustain such a taxing struggle. ("I just don't know, if you get right down to it, if I care enough about my fellow human beings to put myself at so much risk.")

Although these fears have quite reasonable and understandable dimensions to them, we do not believe that they can be dissolved by rational discourse alone. Remember that we are here talking about those who affirm a vision based on respect and dignity for all, so the concern here is not so much about forging a moral consensus as it is about the willingness to act in accordance with that vision. We are led therefore to see our task as supplementing our efforts at providing a morally and intellectually defensible formulation by responding to those psychological and spiritual matters that inform our capacity to act. We must recognize the multi-dimensional qualities of humankind—we do not live by mind alone—and so in the following pages we will address the absolutely vital issues regarding the resistance, reluctance, and unwillingness to do what we believe is right and good.

A crucially important task of the struggle for a more just and compassionate society is to find ways in which we can overcome despair with hope, trump fear with courage, replace paralysis with agency, and overcome cynicism with idealism. These are matters that we now call psychological but could (and perhaps should be) called matters of the soul or of the spirit. Hence, we believe that efforts to heal wounded souls can be discerned in the life-giving and energizing realm of enduring wisdom. Much of our culture already has the wisdom to know that knowledge and understanding are surely necessary but clearly not sufficient in the struggle for the good society. We also need the wisdom to know how to overcome our capacity and impulse to create and sustain a destructive society.

The Origins of That Resistance

This book is focused strongly on the importance of the moral and spiritual aspects of what it means to be human; however, because one of the most obvious things about humans is that they present themselves to the world as a personality in a body, it would be foolish to fail to begin by examining the implications of that "incarnation" for understanding the origins of this resistance. In fact, it may well be that many of the problems discussed above derive from our inattention to what we have already learned of "human nature" in its most reductionist sense. There are many parallels between the preparatory work required by spiritual traditions and the simplest aspects of "mental hygiene" that we can derive from our clinical study of ourselves. Thus it may be useful in beginning to understand our resistance to "being good" by asking what the human sciences have learned about how our psychology can cause us to work against ourselves.

Although it may seem a commonplace, we seldom act as if we understand the assertion that the structure of human personality is such that our "ego" works to preserve itself, often at the expense of more selfless goals to which we claim to aspire. For example, many people will quickly recall "fight or flight" as the answer to the question, "What is a typical reflex response to threat in humans?" Yet, despite widespread knowledge about this phenomenon and the capacity to understand, on reflection, that much of our inherited behavioral repertoire in the face of threats is now inappropriate for our present environment, the vast majority of human interaction is still colored by this effect. In the absence of training in the appropriate disciplines, we are not properly prepared to be able to interrupt the hard-wired anger or fear that accompany our threat response. Cascades of stress hormones flow through our bloodstream at an imagined slight, calling us to battle or to a hasty retreat. Of course, if we are sitting in a committee meeting, neither of those choices is readily available. As a result, minor disagreements can have the effect of "life-or-death" issues and can easily escalate to heated arguments and even violence. We come home from a day at the office with a stress load more appropriate to a day of pitched battle. In short, our "standard equipment" as human beings predisposes us to respond to office politics in ways that were once appropriate for dealing with saber-tooth tigers, rather than responding with reason and compassion.

The same sort of mechanisms of habit and physiology constrain the development of the altruistic social interaction that we seem quite capable of understanding intellectually. Despite the fervent hopes of the Left for a "rational" cultural solution to the human dilemma, it is becoming increasingly apparent that humans, when acting as if they are solely organisms, are hard-wired to survive in what adaptation has taught us to see as a resource-limited environment. If we were forced to accept the materialistic position that remains in the absence of any hypothesis that humans are more than their personalities and bodies, then this would leave us with a human nature predisposed to acquisitiveness, self-serving behavior, and short-term focus. In that belief system, although there is evidence to indicate some adaptive value in altruistic behaviors, such behaviors are directed toward kinship systems, rather than to humanity in general. Thus, we would be left with a naturalist's vindication of Adam Smith's economics, and of capital markets as the best of human possibility. And, in fact, absent Wisdom, that is exactly the belief system that is evidenced by our behaviors in American Popular Culture, where we see our inherited instincts for satisfying basic needs perverted into extremes of acquisitiveness and greed.

The primary survival tools of the personality in this process are the primordial fears and their social corollaries, some of which we discussed above. It is a commonplace of most spiritual disciplines that the "ego" wants to live forever and fears death profoundly. From Christian mysticism to Sufism, Kabbalah to Zen, Teachers tell us that, to the extent that a human being believes itself to be limited to such a construct (a personality inside a body), he or she will be possessed by this fear. So long as we lead our lives from the viewpoint of the organism, without access to any higher perspective, we will struggle in vain against the force of habit and the biological dictates of our limbic systems. While we do owe a debt to these mechanisms for the part that they have played in our evolutionary survival, while being driven by such fears has served the adaptive needs of the organism and the species, the next step in our evolution may well be blocked by these very skills that have brought us here.

Fear is a treacherous weapon in any struggle. As our egos have fought their battles for survival, the residue of so much fear has colored our efforts and often betrayed us, leading to the construction of the most destructive elements of our culture. We fear that there will not be enough for all and thus we take from the weak. We fear that others will act in the same way toward us and we struggle for power. We fear that we will die and thus we struggle to grow without limit. Ironically, and despite the price paid, this struggle of the ego to avoid death is a futile task, since the ego (at least) is the part of us that dies, either at bodily death, or (we hope) in that "dying before we die" to which spiritual disciplines call us. So long as we stay at the level of defending our ego at all costs, we are far below our spiritual potential and likely to construct social systems that resemble Malthus more than Moses. From a spiritual viewpoint, living our lives in response to such fears drives out the possibility of acting selflessly. Our egos veil our souls.

Living Without Wisdom

Much of the best of our history is a record of humanity struggling through such ego-defense fears in an attempt to rise above this level of existence, as evidenced by our religious, poetic, artistic, and intellectual labors. The best of these we call the *wisdom traditions*. Living wisdom traditions provide the direct experience of an order of reality higher than the one in which the ego operates, even when employing the intellect to its limits. By definition, the final stages of such experience must be intellectually inaccessible, but our wits can show us the beginning of the path. Just as our preceding discussion of the threat response could lead us to seeing how psychology might provide a beginning point to prevent simple pathologies from keeping us stuck where we are, simply possessing a working hypothesis that Wisdom exists is the beginning of this path. Otherwise, we are certain to remain with some approximation of the social structure we have examined in the first part of this book.

What remains today of our wisdom traditions is far from our best, having largely succumbed to the worst of these fear-based distortions. Wisdom traditions with living teachers are rare and inaccessible to the vast majority of people. Intellectuals and official religious bodies often marginalize these traditions and fail to understand the implications of their absence, or worse, oppose them because they feel threatened by the iconoclastic nature of a discourse intended to free us from the *status quo*. Many of our social pathologies derive directly from our being dependent for moral community upon mere legal systems, remotely based upon some previously extant wisdom tradition, but now without the reality of a living tradition as its ground. Without such a ground a legal system (or an intellectually and politically based moral code) will inevitably lack the capacity to find resolutions to new moral dilemmas, or old ones in new terms. Thus, our culture finds itself bereft of the capacity to do the good that it says it intends, and we find ourselves sharing the previously cited (chapter 3) consternation of Ovid, Brueggemann, Pogo and St. Paul as we observe that, ". . . the good that I would I do not; but the evil which I would not, that I do."

Fearfully Borrowing from the Past

We have argued that honoring common moral ground is critical to education, to our social structure, and even to the survival of our species. Yet we see in our public discourse that there is no broadly persuasive argument about how to make that happen, no clear and widely accepted rationale for why anyone would obey a set of moral standards in the face of a conflicting individual need or want. Certainly it has proved relatively easy to get a consensus on the construction of a moral code where there is no substantive requirement for compliance—witness the current state of various national governments' conformity with such documents as the *Universal Declaration of Human Rights*. Thus, it seems important to include in any definition of a (useful) common morality that it be one to which (almost) every-one within that commons not only acknowledged some serious obligation of obe-dience, but also evidenced behavioral compliance. Instead, in our individualistic world, a description of our commitment to moral duty (modeled upon our actual behavior) might be: "A common morality consists of a description of how every-one must behave upon pain of punishment, with the understanding that I must be forgiven for disobeying, due to my unique special circumstances."

In our past we had resources and reasons for dealing with this problem that are no longer available to us today. For example, in the first edition we referred to Brueggemann's description of the mission of a prophet as, ". . . raising the aware-ness of a people who are in despair and unable to consider that the world might be otherwise." Yet the very people that the prophet addressed were driven by fear and doubt to resist his message. To sustain the prophet in his mission of raising aware-ness, Brueggemann stresses, ". . . the extremely important role of an audacious imagination inspired by very strongly felt forces (called God in the Bible) to some-how transcend these fears, doubts, and resistances." Yet, in our struggle for com-mon ground, we have chosen to avoid such specifically culture-bound language, a course that has deprived us of our cultural heritages and cost us the prophet's in-spiration.

In a time where last month's computer seems hopelessly out of date, it would seem to be impossible to credit the idea that we might need to model our tools upon those of any earlier culture (or any previous era in our own). From the view-point of the proponents of the present dominant world-view, it would certainly be a truism that none of our predecessor cultures possessed any knowledge super-ior to that which a well-structured internet search would yield. Yet we have said that we hold the single most distinguishing feature of our culture, which is cur-rently preempting all other cultures on our planet, to be this absence of wisdom. Further, we hold that this (possibly fatal) flaw in our culture is exacerbated by the vociferousness with which we not only accept the lack of the substance of wis-dom, but also disparage the very concept that wisdom might exist.

For example, one might choose to think anthropologically of that part of a cul-tural heritage that is called *wisdom* as simply a social toolbox, a set of answers to perennial questions, crafted by our predecessors as responses to the events of their lives, and refined across generations. However, those same predecessors, were we to bother to seek their opinion in the records they have left us, would smile at the narrowness of such secularism and insist that these answers are not social con-structions, but rather spiritual insights into the fundamental reality that frames our lives. Traditional societies claim to derive the content and the discipline of their respective wisdom traditions from those insights, insights that are inaccessible to the uninitiated. Another characteristic is that the contents of their toolboxes retain their usefulness over an extended period. Over time, the phrasing of some of the questions might have evolved in response to gradual changes, but most such change was so gradual as to give individuals a strong sense of permanence and continuity. Many persons living in such cultures owned ready answers to questions of ontology, epistemology, ethics, and morality that are today the exclusive province of a few unfashionable philosophers and theologians. Wisdom was local and available; not everyone mastered it, but everyone knew where to go to find it.

Through the secularization of the Enlightenment, our society has attempted to blend a large number of such traditional cultures while minimizing the levels of intolerance that lead to sectarian violence. One might think of the social history of the USA as a record of this transaction, where we have given up the hope of government support for most of our various ethnic certainties in exchange for the relative peace of our fractious politics. Contrary examples of recent failures of this sort of process are also instructive, as in the Balkans. In the process of secularization, the rate of change has stripped away the sense of permanence that long acquaintance had conveyed to the various answers we each brought to this common table. The interaction of broadly differing answers to the same question has strained (and fractured) the credibility of individual answers when they were presented without the accustomed support of religion and tradition that each had enjoyed in its parent culture. Wisdom in our culture has not only ceased to be an everyday matter of common heritage, it has devolved; first to the status of myth (either benign or malignant, depending on one's political persuasion), then to the point of sharing a category with unicorns, angels, and hobbits—a category of things that our hearts might wish were true, but our intellects discount with a world-weary smile.

The Costs of Trying to Live with Skepticism and Secular Morality

While some might be glad to be protected by such skepticism from any risk of believing something both false and old, few of us can sustain living entirely without the comfort of beliefs such as those that our ancestors took for granted. It is a most unusual human who can live and believe nothing. In *A Rumor of Angels,* Peter Berger, discussing a dichotomy between the middle ground of everydayness, ". . . and various marginal realms in which the taken-for-granted assumptions of the former realm are threatened or put into question," describes the cost of trying:

> . . . [that] which we take for granted as normality and sanity, can be maintained (that is inhabited) only if we suspend all doubt about its validity. Without this suspension of doubt, everyday life would be impossible, if only because it would be constantly invaded by the "fundamental anxiety" caused by our knowledge and fear of death.

This implies that all human societies and their institutions are, at their root, a barrier against naked terror. (1990:83)

As a result, at the end of the day, most of those who succeed in avoiding believing something old wind up believing something new. Among the intellectually fashionable, this might recently have meant facing the more modern gullibility risk of deconstructing oneself, in the fashion described by David Harvey (1990) in his discussion of the postmodern condition. Others might become cultists of a different sort, unknowingly fabricating replacements for their inherited traditions from whatever part of their world makes itself readily available, however inappropriately. While this might be most obviously the case with well-intentioned varieties of "New-Age" belief systems, less obvious but potentially more hazardous versions include the "Market Fundamentalism" of which Soros (2000:xii) speaks. In his landmark study Arthur Deikman discusses the similarity between many of the belief systems in our everyday lives in this society and the behaviors of the victims of cults:

> As I studied the psychological mechanisms that made cult experience possible, I began to recognize uncomfortably familiar processes. A little reflection provided many specific instances of my own compliance—conscious and unconscious—with the values and preferences of my peers, compliance that I had rationalized or ignored because I preferred to think of myself as very independent. Since no radical change or disruption of my life occurred and I was not acting at the behest of a charismatic leader or occult group, it had not occurred to me that I might be behaving like one who had been captured by a cult. Nevertheless, I now realize that the motivations and manipulations constituting cult behavior are present in varying degrees in my own life and that they play a role in the lives of most of us as they operate in our educational systems, the business world, religion, politics, and international relations. Just as many of the more notorious cults have proven to be costly and destructive, so ordinary cult behavior is damaging and harmful to some degree wherever it occurs, no matter how normal its outward appearance. . . . I believe that we need to bring into awareness the unconscious motivations and excluded information that influence our behavior and thought at the personal, national, and international levels. This requires that we first understand the dynamics of obvious cults and then address similar processes in ourselves and in ordinary society. . . . Although it is important that we study such groups to avoid being caught in them, it is even more important that we study such groups to become aware of the hidden cult thinking operating unnoticed in our daily lives. Cults are mirrors of ourselves. (1990:7–10)

In our present circumstance, behavior such as Deikman has described has led to the belief systems that sustain the destructive cultural dysfunctions that we have been analyzing. In the light of current events, this may be easiest to see when it occurs in the business world, where many who had only intended to flourish financially also become essentially Enron archetypes. No less a paragon of capitalism than George Soros (who has been accused by some of engaging in financial activities that made him personally responsible for the collapse of the "Asian

Tiger" economies during the last half of the previous decade) asserts that, "If we care about universal principles such as freedom, democracy, and the rule of law, we cannot leave them to the care of market forces. . . . there is a widely held creed that the markets will take care of all our needs. It used to be called "laissez-faire" in the nineteenth century, but I have found a better name for it: market fundamentalism (2000:xii)" According to Soros, this creed has extended its reach far beyond the limits within which such a system should operate, "Market fundamentalists have transformed an axiomatic, value-neutral theory into an ideology that influenced political and business behavior in powerful and dangerous ways. . . ." market values penetrate into areas of society where they do not properly belong (2000: 54). One would be hard pressed to find a better example of what Deikman might call cultic behavior.

This intrusion of market values into all areas of our lives is unlikely to be stopped or reversed if our moral resources are limited to those that are at home in an environment bereft of wisdom. As a continuation of the Enlightenment Project discussed earlier, many of our brightest minds still struggle to find a rationalist position that will allow us to continue to posit that secularization and moral consensus are not mutually exclusive. Witness the position of Michael Ignatieff (2001), who, in *Human Rights as Politics and Idolatry,* frames the problem with regard to the rationalist ethical positions (what he calls "Secular Morality") and their inevitable conflict with any morality with which one has a duty to comply because of divine command or spiritual insight. He concludes that we must be pragmatic about avoiding what he sees as the divisiveness of "intrinsically contestable" metaphysical claims:

> It may be tempting to relate the idea of human rights to propositions like the following: that human beings have an innate or natural dignity, that they have a natural and intrinsic self-worth, that they are sacred . . . The problem with these propositions is that they are not clear and they are controversial . . . they confuse what we wish men and women to be with what we empirically know them to be . . . each version of them must make metaphysical claims about human nature that are intrinsically contestable . . . Far better I would argue, to forgo these kinds of foundational arguments altogether and seek to build support for human rights on the basis of what such rights actually *do* for human beings. (2001:54)

Our history tells us that we have certainly tried to follow Ignatieff's pragmatic prescription. Even though such "metaphysical claims" are enshrined in our nation's founding documents, our commerce and our politics effectively ignore them and honor his pragmatic calculus. In fact, so thouroughly have we yielded, that those of us who might still hold to the foundational beliefs that Ignatieff finds less than useful in moral argument are likely to suffer dismissal at many points in our culture. As Stephen Carter observed in *The Culture of Disbelief,* after delivering a lecture at Duke University on the question of religious minorities in public schools, he took questions from the audience. One participant responded, ". . . that the problem was a simple one: we already had the Enlightenment and their side lost. That answer, of course, states the simple historical fact of the matter, but it is less an argument than an explanation. You lose because we win. We have the power and you don't. On such distinctions, all too often, is the modern notion of truth premised" (1993:182).

This condition of "despiritualization" is the result of what Joel Kovel (1991) calls "a profound spiritual crisis":

> *History and Spirit* is written not simply to advance a philosophy of spirit, but in response to a profound spiritual crisis. . . . a process of "despiritualization." Let us define this as the pressure or tendency in social institutions to devalue the spiritual dimension, render it irrational, or even suppress its expression entirely. From work to lovemaking, from the rearing of children to the pastimes of adults, spirituality seems decreasingly an element of modern experience than in so-called traditional society. . . . In traditional society—and the reader may want to reflect on what society was like for grandparents and great-grandparents—the communal basis of life was relatively secure, and values were relatively stable and taken for granted. The transition from traditional to modern society—characterized by a breakdown in the sense of values and the communal life underlying those values—is one entailing despiritualization, among other things. Its most remarkable feature from our standpoint has been the loss of the great world religions of traditional society as the principal vehicles of spiritual life. [People in a traditional society] . . . would not think of spirituality as such. Nor would they think of religion as such . . . That is, religion, spirit, and wilderness, or even nature as a whole, are notions which occur to people after they have already lost some part of what these words signify. Those who are immersed in a thing do not have a word for that thing, because they do not need one. However, the age of despiritualization makes us separate spirituality from the rest of existence and search for it. (1991:6,19)

In none of these efforts, neither our enlightenment project nor our cultism, neither our market fundamentalism nor our secular morality, has our skepticism led us to wisdom. Having paid the price of an effort (perhaps futile) to peacefully sustain the diversity that our merging of many peoples has provided, there is likely to be no path back to the earlier simpler comforts of those answers that we found in our ancestral cultures; nor would it be likely to be a good choice if there were. We are far too many now to sustain ourselves by the means of simpler times—far too crowded to tolerate difference by means of distance. So, does it matter? Is the loss of the very concept of wisdom from our present popular culture an issue of concern only to historical preservationists or lovers of the quaint? As is apparent from our review of the condition of education and our society in general, we would argue the contrary, that the incapacity to respond to fundamental questions, to follow through on our commitments, and to hold basic answers in common can easily be seen to underlie the horrors of unnecessary suffering that we inflict upon ourselves.

Beyond the many examples of such unnecessary horrors we have already offered, it may be illustrative at this point to revisit one that may have the capacity to render all the others moot, one that we mentioned earlier as the first of the conditions which make today's manifestation of this chronic human condition into a *crisis:* Our market-driven technologically powered culture has acquired the capacity to develop multiple means for destroying the life-carrying capacity of the planet in the short term.

Among those destructive means are our technical capacity to delay the consequences of population growth until we exceed a number that is sustainable in the long run, as exemplified by our present policies of feeding our growing numbers by maximizing agricultural yields through unsustainable practices, practices that include petroleum-based fertilizers and pesticides. The plowing that this type of farming encourages also increases erosion to such an extent that you might think of the U.S. grain belt as engaged in strip-mining topsoil. Similarly, our willingness to ignore the implications of finite resources for the sake of a philosophy of unlimited economic growth and unrestrained economic inequality is exemplified by the rapid draw-down of fossil water from ancient aquifers to support golf courses in the desert southwest. By exercising these capacities, by behaving in accordance with these beliefs, there is a real and present danger that we may devour our biosphere and leave no home for our children. At present there is a fundamental divide between what American Popular Culture approves, rewards, and otherwise teaches—between all that and the ecological behaviors that we need to exhibit in order to sustain ourselves physically over the long term. As Daley (1996) says, we have lost our nerve and declared any resolution of the two critical economic factors of population control and the moderation of wealth imbalance to be political impossibilities, while we neglect entirely the limits of planetary resources. With that capitulation, we are left to base our future on a vacuous optimism, a false hope that technological solutions as-yet unknown will arrive to save us.

These concerns are not the sole province of alarmists and amateurs. Biologists of the stature of E. O. Wilson have joined the chorus: "An Armageddon is approaching at the beginning or the third millennium. But it is not the cosmic war and fiery collapse of mankind foretold in sacred scripture. It is the wreckage of the planet by an exuberantly plentiful and ingenious humanity" (2002:xxiii).

In order to have any chance of avoiding such an Armageddon while working within the constraints of our present culture's mindset, it is important that many more people come to understand that the biosphere which sustains us is a *complex system* in the formal mathematical sense of that term, which means that we cannot precisely predict when sudden shifts (phase changes) might take place. Among the possibilities are very rapid changes in weather that could bring the cataclysms often predicted for the mid-century to bear on the present generation.

Most concerned citizens working to avoid such a cataclysm have come to feel that it is *necessary* to emphasize this point about the imminence and indeterminacy of the threat, not just because of our demonstrated tendency to think only in the short-term, but also because it is apparently necessary to engage people's self-interest directly in order to gain attention. Once people come to perceive that an issue like global warming might pose a direct threat to their safety or prosperity in the short-term, one would then be able to argue that such short-term unpredictability presents an unacceptable risk to the hearer and that no prudent businessman or property owner would ignore such a risk (or fail to insure against it), even if the statistical analysis yielded a much lower likelihood of occurrence than our science now predicts. This works—for example, it is widely reported that, in the aftermath of 9/11/01, the insurance industry is responding prudently in reallocating the risks associated with owning (or being the neighbor of) a targetable structure. In the future, the degree to which a monumental building is judged to invite a terrorist attack will be factored into its development cost or insured by the government and become no more interesting than its exposure to hurricanes or earthquakes. To do otherwise would be a repudiation of our pragmatic and utilitarian ethos.

However, while we must make such an argument about threats to the life-carrying capacity of our home being an immediate threat (rather than an equally certain but distant one) in the hope of finally gaining the attention of decision makers, the moral implications of *having* to make that argument are profound. If we cannot think of those who will come after us, but can only pursue our own self-interests even in questions of such magnitude, then we may already be lost.

Jeff Gates in *Democracy at Risk* says that we don't care about those neighbors who are downstream of our waste discharge (2000:271), and here we see an instance where we have come to the point of behaving so as to demonstrate that we regard even succeeding generations as *downstream*. Gates imagines having to explain our present choices to his child, "At the current pace, 50% of the earth's plant and animal species will vanish before my nine-year-old son turns sixty. For what purpose shall I tell him this was done? (2000:xvi)" It has become increasingly clear to the authors that it is only through Wisdom that we will be able to honor common moral ground and find our way past genocide, terror, and starving children to establish a world where we are not devouring the life-carrying capacity of our planet for the sake of greed. Whether one comes to that conclusion by a leap of faith or as a last-ditch hypothesis in defense against despair at the failure of all our other options, this seems to us our last and best hope as well as our only defensible bastion for optimism. (In the last chapter, there are further thoughts on the relationship between Faith, Hope, and optimism.)

A Door to Wisdom and Spirituality

We believe that if we are to sensibly and boldly respond to the environmental crisis (and the other issues of parallel significance) then we must ground our knowledge, skills, and ingenuity in a moral and spiritual vision. Of course there enormous difficulties involved in this process, not the least of which is the ability to put our hands around the concepts of spirituality and wisdom. We believe that it should be clear by now that there is a clear link between our culture's commitment to skepticism and our inability to solve our problems.

If we determine that we cannot afford these costs of skepticism, what are we to do? Many who are skeptical of the older paths are so because they fear a resumption of the history of oppression we have often seen when any *One Belief* held undisputed sway (and such fears are not unfounded to the extent that the older paths do not guard against the cult-like behaviors previously described by Deikman). A major barrier to overcoming the skepticism about the value of Wisdom Traditions is the complex matter of language, discourse, and meaning. Because of this history, much of the language that is needed to talk about these topics has, for many of us, too much emotional baggage to be of use. The term *Wisdom* has proven useful to us thus far because it has, to a certain extent, escaped this political contamination, as has another term, which we were highly tempted to use without further definition—*Spirituality*. Among those who are uncomfortable with the traditional approaches to wisdom, all but the most crassly materialistic seem to have at least a minimum level of comfort with the connotations of the spiritual dimension, connotations pointing toward some sort of nonmaterial reality that makes a difference in human lives. Among the more traditional believers, once again it is usually only at the extreme that the word *Spirituality* is unusable—fundamentalists and the profoundly literal representing that case, where the need for certainty outweighs the perceived need for inspiration. Perhaps there are enough who remain in the center of this distribution to constitute a quorum. Perhaps those who find the word "spirituality" useful might have a conversation about how those "skillful means" that various spiritual disciplines have developed might still serve us, to try to understand what wisdom means in terms that we can all use with at least some hope of moving toward its attainment.

In *Spirit and History,* Kovel acknowledges the multipaged entry for "spirit" in the *Oxford English Dictionary,* and he devotes entire chapters of his book to the significations of vital force, hidden being, and a higher way of being. He offers a definition that, while admittedly circular, is useful. He suggests that spirituality can be understood in the sense that he asks us to understand the topic of his book, "It is . . . about what happens to us as the boundaries of the self give way. Or we could say that it is about the 'soul,' by which we shall mean the form of 'being' taken by the spiritual self. And it is about 'spirituality,' which we may define as the ways people seek to realize spirit and soul in their lives . . . "(1991:1–2).

Also, and with a similar circularity that one must come to tolerate in applying words to the ineffable, we might think of spiritual disciplines as valid to the extent that they are productive of wisdom, as evidenced in the lives of their practitioners, using our earlier characterization of wisdom as that state characteristic of human beings who: have developed certain skillful means, including the capacity to discriminate between real and imagined spirituality; have hope grounded in such real spiritual experience (rather than optimism or delusion), which provides them the strength to continue their struggle against self-deception in themselves and others; and thus, have the insight and capacity needed to Teach.

The entire process, entered from any viewpoint on this definitional circle, is one that *transforms the human participant* in some profound sense for the better. A person who can be said to have become more spiritual or to have attained some degree of wisdom has been changed in some important way, so that their new consciousness has capacities not available to their former personality. For example, in the conversation about our culture, we might say that the effects of wisdom will have become apparent when we are able to overcome our fears and base impulses and truly dedicate ourselves to creating a sustainable and just community.

To assert such things is to strain the credulity of most in our culture, because it speaks to things outside our common frame of reference, especially when we include our earlier assertion (in Chapter One) that by *spiritual ground,* we mean an order of reality beyond materialism, the perception of which has led to (among other things) the formation of institutional religions. The path to understanding what has been asserted, well enough to form an intelligent opinion about it, requires more than intellectual assent. It requires an experiential component, an operational definition; as the proverb has it, "She who tastes, knows." To offer such an operational definition requires that we attempt to briefly describe at least the beginning of the disciplines by which various wisdom/spiritual traditions have historically introduced prospective students to their paths. In order to do so, we need to refer again to Deikman's point (cited above) about, "compliance—conscious and unconscious—with the values and preferences of [our] peers." We have said that our assertions are likely to strain our credulity because considering them requires that we stretch our concepts beyond the common frame of reference of American Popular Culture.

Let us first consider that this frame of reference has brought us to our present position on the edge of that chasm described above, in which case stepping outside of it might well be an excellent idea. Secondly, let us propose as a working hypothesis that unless we can bring the unconscious portions of that compliance into awareness, we will not have the option of deciding whether or not to continue to obey it.

Leading a participant to have an insight into the extent to which robot-like automatistic behavior substitutes for awareness in much of our daily lives is one of the initial functions of many spiritual disciplines; however, such work can also be undertaken as an intellectual process that allows (sometimes requires) us to do useful work as a precursor to actually undertaking one of these paths. There are many intellectual models of the functioning of this unconscious compliance with our frame of reverence, such as Thomas Kuhn's discussion of the "paradigm." Let us consider that beginning the task at hand requires that we share a "pre-analytic vision" in the sense that Herman Daly uses the term. Attempting to understand how unbridgeable the gap of understanding seems to be between the dominant form of economic analysis, which sees nature as an unlimited "free" resource and an economic analysis that takes account of the ecological limits to growth, he says that the two camps operate from different "pre-analytic visions." Of such fundamental mindsets, Daly says, quoting Schumpeter, ". . . suppose we did start [a science] from scratch . . . analytic effort is of necessity preceded by a pre-analytic cognitive act that supplies the raw material for the analytic effort. . . . vision of this kind not only must precede historically the emergence of analytic effort in any field, but also may reenter the history of every established science each time somebody teaches us to *see* things in a light of which the source is not to be found in the facts, methods, and results of the pre-existing state of the science" (1996:46). To emphasize how this relates to our present endeavor, consider what Daly says about the extent to which our subsequent analysis is captive to our point of beginning, ". . . pre-analytic visions share with religious ones the feature that ensures that we can never escape them by analysis: they define the terms of analysis and therefore cannot provide us with a perspective that could refute their own viewpoint. Their hold on us is in one part one of faith and commitment" (1996:219).

It is perhaps obvious, but let us belabor the point that one's pre-analytic vision is not the subject of everyday awareness. That is the reason that Daly holds that it is inescapable by analysis—the foundational assumptions from which we begin our arguments are unexamined and thus predispose our conclusions to some predetermined range of possibilities. So long as one operates within the limited intellectual frameworks characterized as pre-analytic, one can see only a conditioned, filtered, limited world. To seek those experiences that may lead one to find some other ground from which to see the truth is a quest for wisdom. While all human beings could be said to be operating within some pre-analytic vision at any given moment, perhaps it would not strain the metaphor too far to suggest that a characteristic of the Wise is that they have the human capacity to choose one (or be chosen by it!) that is appropriate for the task at hand.

So, from this point the reader whose present pre-analytic vision does not include the sort of discourse that is obviously being proposed here is invited to attempt to open him or herself to some additional possibilities. Consider for a moment what the consequences for such a person's worldview might be if he were to entertain a working hypothesis that: (1) the various wisdom traditions had indeed visited some common fount of knowledge, and that (2) these wisdom traditions consisted primarily of practical instructions for directing others to that same source. If such a reader were to be good-humored enough to undertake that effort, then we would certainly owe a more specific description of the quarry. For that, let us defer to Thomas Merton as he defines contemplation, an art to which he and his order of Christian monks have devoted centuries:

> By contemplation here we mean not necessarily mysticism pure and simple, but at least the direct intuition of reality, the *simplex intuitus veritatis,* the pure awareness which is and must be the ground not only of all genuine metaphysical speculation, but also of mature and sapiential religious experience. This direct awareness is a gift, but it also normally presupposes the knowledge and practice of certain traditional disciplines. Thus we can say that contemplation is both a "gift" (a "grace") and an "art." Unfortunately, we must also admit that it can almost be said to be a "lost art." And for this lost art there is certainly in the world today a definite nostalgia, not unmixed with vague hopes for the recovery of this awareness. But the nostalgia and the desire do not themselves suffice to make the nostalgic one a contemplative. (1967: 203–204)

Even among people who are willing to entertain the possibility that there is meaning in what Merton has said here, we are still confronted with the problem that Ignatieff (2001) posed of the intrinsically contestable nature of metaphysical claims. Within the limits of language and rationality, individual beliefs rarely succumb to logic on such topics. Yet we have proposed that language and rationality do not exhaust the possibilities for Gnosis. While it is easy to see that a conversation between Jerry Falwell and a radical Iranian Mullah would follow a course predictable by Ignatieff's logic, it is likely that a meeting between Jesus and Mohammed would rest on Merton's ground of "mature and sapiential religious experience." The hypothesis concerning the instrumental nature of wisdom traditions and spiritual disciplines that we are asking readers to entertain (see previous page) would certainly need to propose that doctrinal differences are surface manifestations of differing socialization and do not reflect actual differences in what has been learned during "the direct intuition of reality." In that case, in Schumpeter's terms, our willingness to fight to the death over doctrinal differences is explained to the extent that these doctrines are unexamineable as elements of our pre-analytic vision. Consider for example what Merton says of ecumenism across not just Christian denominations but also across religions:

> . . . let us turn to ecumenism, which implies dialogue: genuine ecumenism requires the communication and sharing, not only of information about doctrines which are totally and irrevocably divergent, but also of religious intuitions and truths which may turn out to have something in common, beneath surface differences . . . In all religions we encounter not only the claim to (divine) revelation in some form or another, but also the record of special experiences in which the absolute and final validity of that revelation is in some way attested. Furthermore, in all religions it is more or less generally recognized that this profound "sapiential" experience, call it gnosis, contemplation, "mysticism," "prophecy," or what you will, represents the deepest and most authentic fruit of the religion itself. (1967:204)

It seems that the common ground that we say we need lies on the other side of the pain that Peter Berger has told us we are incapable of sustaining! We cited him above, telling us that ". . . all human societies and their institutions are, at their root, a barrier against naked terror" (1990:83). Merton (and many others) will tell us that we must dare that terror to attain wisdom. Is it any wonder that such a hypothesis has found few who would be both interested and competent experimenters within our culture? Nevertheless, it seems that there is great hazard that anything less must yield the half-measures and triviality that we regretted in our earlier chapters. We have concluded that education must recognize that humanity's present pre-analytic vision is inadequate to the crisis before us and must put forth an alternative to our present course. We have concluded that if humanity does not change profoundly, it is increasingly likely that we will fail this adaptive test and make room for our biological successors.

How could we even begin to conceive of what would be required to provide such an education? What we will attempt in the next two chapters is to sketch two different but parallel operational definitions of that wisdom which has been suggested here. Illustrating the spiritual pluralism that we have found to underlie our own work together, we will each undertake to develop an outline of the pre-analytic vision that we feel would be required to imagine a culture that took the foregoing seriously, by bringing together others like Thomas Merton to describe some of the first steps on a few of the paths that propose to take one to the *simplex intuitus veritatis*.

A Way Ahead?

We began this chapter by noting the two new elements that we believe have rightly caused us to conclude that our perennial human condition should be perceived today as a crisis. We have recapitulated the first (the full flowering of our capacity to destroy ourselves) and argued for a greater comprehension of the disastrous effects of the second (that we have perfected this self-destructive capacity at a time when our cultural resources do not include a strong Wisdom Tradition). We have argued that it is not sufficient to find intellectual common ground upon which we might answer such questions as these: "What do we owe to each other? What is a good life and how are we to live it? What does it mean to have *enough*? Who deserves to have *enough*?" Such intellectual ground is not enough, because we have found that, even when we think we have understood these, we are disposed to act contrary to such understandings, to act as if there were no answers to questions such as: "Is there meaning to our existence and the pain that it brings us? And, if there is a larger meaning to this universe, what is the place of our humanity in that meaning—are we necessary to it, irrelevant, or irritating?" We must come to know how we are to overcome our fears, temptations, and hesitations that prevent us from doing what our hearts tell us is right, just, and loving.

We have referred to the answers that our predecessors found and the Wisdom that served different times. Yet, while we can acknowledge their successes and learn from their failures, it is a commonplace of wisdom traditions that we cannot simply imitate another age to find the answers to today's dilemmas. In that case, if there is no way back to the security and certainty of our traditional societies of origin, then is there a way ahead? Are there ways that fit our capacities and our times that will take us home? Are we going to be able to find a path to *Wisdom* in our wounded world?

In the next two chapters, each of the authors will attempt to offer his individual experience, reflections and speculations concerning what such a path might be. The fully justified disclaimers about our lack of competence to do so will be left to those pages; it is only a shared feeling of urgency and dread for an unremediated future that drives us to speak on a subject so far afield from our expertise—that, and the unfortunate conclusion growing out of the analysis thus far, that too few others are speaking, and even fewer are being heard on what we have concluded is the ground of our crisis.

4

William M. McLaurin, Jr.

A RESPONSE TO THE CRISIS:
The Quest for Wisdom in the Practice of an Everyday Life

Preface

As we indicated at the close of the preceding chapter, it is now time for the authors to speak individually to the question of, "What is to be done?" The deciding factor in selecting this format was our hope that, by emphasizing the diversity of our views in the context of our happiness with our collaboration, we might offer an example of how we envision others bridging other differences and together seeking the common moral ground to which we have so often looked in the preceding chapters.

Our professional backgrounds are an important part of that diversity. My lifetime in the world of business, lived parallel with a half a lifetime of weekends and evenings spent in seeking understanding through education as a student, gives me a significantly different perspective, as does my present practice as a consultant, working in a highly entrepreneurial educational environment to improve the senior leadership of corporations. Yet from that perspective, tempered with all too few opportunities for teaching as an adjunct faculty member, I find myself in strong agreement with Purpel as to the hazards we face and the changes that are required to remedy them.

There is a similar level of difference in our points of beginning in our spiritual paths, yet, once again, we have found that these seemingly divergent paths have led us to a common moral ground. We feel that it is critical that we situate our responses in these widely divergent spiritual paths and that we each associate our recommendations with our underlying spiritual grounding, since our experience in our work together argues for our thesis that it is only in the human capacity for wisdom through spiritual experience that we have any hope of finding the common moral ground necessary for meaningful responses to the present crisis.

Seeking Wisdom in an Everyday Life

As befits someone who is a child of this culture, a culture for which we have shown so little mercy in the last few chapters, my own quest for wisdom, although it has been long, has also been more often than not quixotic, and with less apparent result than I would have wished. The first part of my journey, from Presbyterian youth choir, through undergraduate atheist, to a rather indifferent agnosticism as a young husband, father, and businessperson was too stereotypical to bear telling. Perhaps, though, it is the very familiarity of that beginning of my quest which points to the makings of an interesting story. Perhaps others might find it useful to hear that the last third of such a life can pass through entrepreneurship mixed with stints as adjunct faculty, and come to its present station in a consultancy that seeks to bring David Purpel's vision of engaged morality into an educational process within the world of business, which seeks to foster leadership that is founded upon awareness, courage, and integrity. Having walked a long road to find my way here, there is a glad sweet irony in finding that I might be able to conclude my life as an educator, as both the teacher and the student of all whom I meet.

In chapter three we voiced our fascination with "the mystery of history," that people have continued to hope, even from the perspective of many generations of great suffering. There is a smaller corollary to this greater mystery in my own life: the refusal of some deeply seated part of myself to be satisfied with what our culture would judge to be a "good life." Despite considerably more good fortune than my efforts would justify, I have been unable to settle into the enjoyment of the rewards of citizenship in the dominant culture, no matter how pleasant, or to maintain my indifferent agnosticism, no matter how convenient it might have been to business pursuits. This is not because I have been an enthusiastic advocate for asceticism or piety—those who know me understand how much I enjoy life, comforts, and freedom from want. Rather, it is because my heart is perturbed by questions of meaning. Some of these questions arise because I cannot deny the part of myself that calls into question my right to enjoy these things at the expense of others or in circumstances where others are in profound want; others arise because that same part of myself questions me as to the importance of the "goods" defined by market fundamentalism and insists that humanity must somehow be called to be more than that. The market's definition of a "good life" rings hollow in the presence of what I hear from my heart.

Intertwined Themes

That which I hear from my heart I do not hear in words, therefore, the words that I apply to it are efforts at expressing impressions that, while a common human experience, do not fit well into the "pre-analytic vision" that constrains everyday experience in our culture. Thus the words can easily be contradictory or disjunctive, while the experience that they attempt to report is certainly not. To minimize this difficulty in what follows, I have tried to gather these impressions together around a series of four themes, such that, while they are not by the nature of language unitive (as is the initial experience), the themes at least suggest a series of intertwined strands, each of which offers support and interconnections to the others. These themes include: *The Perennial Question; Good and Evil; Hope, Faith, and Optimism;* and *Human Agency*. The organization of these themes derives from the traditions which I shall discuss in the next section.

The Perennial Question and the Ineffability of Its Answer

The initial theme is then our difficulty in communicating to each other the content of what may well be the most foundational experience of our humanity: the perennial question about meaning that arises in our hearts, perhaps asking in its early stages, "Is this all there is to life—is there not something more to being than birth and death, connected by our clinging to joy and fleeing from suffering?" In a middle stage of this question, it might ask, "Can the experience of Truth which I have encountered be validated by others, or is there a danger that I have become deluded?" The question evolves along with understanding, and the words that are used to try to convey it vary with one's tradition. Because each statement of the question and each effort at a personal response to it are transcriptions of a voice that does not speak in words, they pose a profound challenge for those who are trained in the Western philosophical traditions, operating under the requirements that they maintain a critical perspective and provide support for our cultural bias toward avoiding credulity at all cost.

   Despite the pains that our predecessors in this quest took to tell us that we must learn to use language differently in spiritual matters, much confusion surrounds such claims. Despite a perennial thirst for Truth, it is often the case that our very efforts to find and share understanding (by means that are familiar but not applicable) are often the greatest barriers to its attainment. This flaw in our efforts derives from a clearly discernable element of human nature: our determination to maintain old habits, even when they do not serve the purpose at hand. Eventually, the way in which we deal with our old habits of language in our responses to these early questions (and their more developed successors) seems to have much to do with whether we become cultists, self-deconstructionists, or continuing candidates for Wisdom.

Good and Evil—Nature and Human Nature: The Reality of Suffering and Its Cause

Any human response to those early questions (with the exception of a response which is some version of existential despair) must soon contend with the pervasiveness of suffering in our world. As we have pointed out extensively in the earlier chapters, this suffering is often the product of human action, yet there is also much that arises from what appears to be beyond human agency. This theme concerns the presence of good and evil and the way in which that presence situates itself both in human nature and in the nature of the universe that contains us. A little reflection can lead to the conclusion that the presence of both of these forces is necessary for the concept of suffering—in a world fully evil or fully good, the absence of contrast would surely shield us from the anguish that is contained in our experience of "what might have been."

With the seemingly opposed forces of Good and Evil contained within my limited self, within a finite consciousness that wants to have everything neat and orderly, arranged scientifically in the neat boxes of our pre-analytic vision, how might I comprehend this in a manner that will help me to find my way? If both our individual lives and the universe in which we live out these lives contain the forces of good and evil, such that we are immersed in the seeds of suffering, how did this come to be? What explanation do we offer ourselves for the existence side by side of these two? How am I to structure my understanding of a universe that contains both good and evil simultaneously? How am I to reconcile two profoundly different feelings resulting from my contact with the world: my being joyous when I encounter the sense of awe and wonder at the world that the perspective of spiritual experience brings; and the ache of compassion in the face of the immense suffering of the beings who inhabit that same world? What is the cause of the wonder and the suffering? Is the cause One or many? Is the cause completely beyond humanity, or do we have some agency?

Among those who attempt an answer to these questions that includes a personal God, each must add a theodicy to their theology, and seek to reconcile the Source of wonder with the Origin of suffering. At least as far back as the Book of Job, some theologians have felt compelled to practice theodicy, to offer apologies for the apparent contradictions between the moral character ascribed to God and the behavior reported of God toward human beings. In the present world this is not only still needed, but perhaps especially difficult. For those more focused on human agency, there is similarly a need for an understanding of our constant failure to behave in the manner we claim to value—there is a need for a psychology that speaks to spirituality, one that becomes an apologist for humanity's behavior toward itself.

Hope, Faith, and Optimism—Can There Be Any End to Suffering?

This theme is an excellent illustration of the first, because the truth that it tries to express leaves our rational capacity with the cognitive dissonance that comes from a need to hold contradictory beliefs simultaneously. It asks us to make heroic efforts to do the right thing, while also asking us to avoid clinging to our ego's plan. It urges us to accept any outcome with equanimity—to struggle mightily, then to greet whatever comes with neither grasping nor aversion. It asks us to fight with all our hearts and then, at the end of the day, to accept that what is truly real about us was never at risk—to accept that freedom and joy are not contingent. Let me try to explain why I feel the need to put myself to the trouble of believing such a difficult thing.

Through my acquaintances, my reading, and a few experiences, I have come to believe that the spiritual experience I have called "hearing from one's heart" is not uncommon among thoughtful people and is in fact a capacity available to all, a capacity whose cultivation is the business of wisdom traditions. If that is the case, then, despite the incredible coercive power that we have ascribed to our pre-analytic vision (including the culture of market fundamentalism), I suspect that there is more ground for optimism about our condition than I might have believed earlier in my life. It seems to me that if more of us were convinced of the need to make a practice of becoming more skillful in listening to the part of ourselves that insists on speaking to us about a basic human duty to exemplify compassion, goodness, and a thirst for truth, then we might actually find a way back from the edge of the precipice. One application of this skill will be familiar to the reader as that struggle to develop the capacity for discernment between cultism and spirituality, which we discussed at length in chapter three, in the section "The Costs of Trying to Live with Skepticism and Secular Morality."

Yet, holding to such thoughts in the context of the culture we have been discussing can be difficult; among those deprived of wisdom, cynicism would seem a more rational approach, and despair a more logical conclusion. Given the preceding litany of human fallibility and moral default, is there any point, any reason to undertake such a quest, or any real ground for optimism? Optimism is of course shorthand for a sort of ad hoc statistical analysis; in claiming grounds for being more optimistic, I mean specifically that I think that it is increasing likely that more of us will undertake such a practice. (Holding that the probability of choosing our future course wisely would actually increase if more of us undertook this behavior is about faith, a separate issue—see below). I must admit that this suspicion of "more cause for optimism" alternates with even more frequent periods of pessimism, especially when I find myself attempting to write in any detail about a path away from this precipice that passes through a future clouded by the anticipation of a generation of war against terrorism. It would seem that we face a greater challenge than any we have successfully overcome within our common memory. We are not only challenged to overcome old habits, sanctified by generations of socialization, but also genetic predispositions that are strengthened by our inattention, all in the midst of events that call to our most primal fears. So, if I were compelled to substitute some numerical value for my assertion that "there is more ground for optimism," my estimation of our chances would still be slim, would still be far enough below 50% to earn me a label of pessimist on almost anyone else's scale.

Yet I still persist in my own struggle to contribute to finding a better path and I recommend that persistence to others. In the face of bad odds, I still want to be among those who seek to continue our mysteriously hopeful history. On balance I still hold to a position developed earlier (1996) that, while optimism can be useful in energizing us, the times in which we are destined to live require the firmer ground of hope—a hope that does not require any certainty of success in order to inspire us to persevere in doing whatever we can to answer the duty to which we are called. It is the threat of destruction of our capacity to hold such hope that gives despair its sharp icy edge, an edge that wounds our willingness to listen to the voice from our hearts.

So, when I speak of being somewhat more optimistic, I need to offer some distinctions. The sort of optimism that must fade into despair unless it has its own way I would like to distinguish as "mundane optimism," in order to save another sense of the word for a more radical use later in this chapter. One reason that mundane optimism is so vulnerable to the events of our times lies in the high probability that the tragic sense of life voiced by Purpel in the subsequent chapter is an accurate view of our future. It is also certain, given the impermanence of the world, that all of the cultural outcomes which optimism today espouses will certainly pass away in the long reaches of time, if they ever come to pass at all. Therefore, I must find a path that allows my to enjoy moments of optimism without leaving my hope conditional upon specific outcomes.

In the language of listening to our hearts, I would say that the relationship of hope to faith to mundane optimism is a progression, which begins with an intuitive and ineffable experience of hope in our heart, which if attended to, will give us the grace to begin to formulate our faith. In order to remember and share what we come to understand about our faith, we attempt to express the understandings of our hearts in the language of our intellects, a helpful but necessarily imperfect doctrine. Doctrine, through analysis—rational or not—can lead toward (or away from) mundane optimism. Today, my Hope leads me to hold as an article of Faith that human beings have the potential to undertake practices that lead to the wisdom we need to comprehend and fulfill our destiny; when I am mundanely optimistic, I believe that enough of them will do so in time. Just like David Purpel and Cornel West (1989) my faith and my optimism must exist in a tragic world, and may have to yield to logic and events. By the end of this chapter, I shall have made an attempt to explain why my hope is proof against loss in that case.

Human Agency and Action in the World— A Path to the End of Suffering

The constant companion to these questions of hope, faith, and optimism is a theme about human agency in the presence (or absence) of spiritual awe. If I have found some response to the preceding questions, what does that mean for how I am to live? If our culture avoids and denies such responses, can and should that be repaired? What do the things I have learned say about my duty as a human being, about the constituents of a good life? And if we should come to some sense of the direction our path should take, where are the "skillful means" by which we are to extricate ourselves from our present quandary? Is there a place for intellection on the Path? What have human beings discovered in mapping our path through this reality that points to my hope, helps to build my faith, and fuels my occasional optimism?

If there is a single theme in which the difficulties of applying language to these questions are most obvious, perhaps it is here. At every turn there seem to be the kind of contradictions that force us to silence. No matter how we try to speak on the topic of the means by which limited beings can meaningfully intrude into cosmic issues, what we say often seems to be reduced to nonsense or worse. It sometimes seems that the more comprehensive one's doctrine becomes the less room in it there is for human beings to act, whether the question concerns some version of personal salvation or of the cultural repair needed to lovingly educate a child. Often, one can feel as some think Job did, that the best course is to cover one's eyes in awe before the mysterium and stop one's mouth with dust. Yet, when I return to the original call in my heart, I am reminded that the point is this: somehow, for some reason, it is truly important how we live our lives; what one of us chooses to do next Tuesday about the future of a child is included in a category of importance that also includes the fates of empires, species, galaxies, and even corporations.

One characteristic of wisdom traditions that bridges these contradictions is the concept of *practice*. Each of the traditions that have comprised my study is distinguished by its possession of the knowledge of some set of skillful means and of a process for preparing students to employ those means to effect a change in the human condition that is beneficial from a spiritual viewpoint. It is no semantic coincidence that this same word is applied to the professional relationship of educators, physicians and others to the *practice* of their crafts, a usage I wish to continue as a reminder of that heritage, despite some risk of confusion due to the present banality which the term has acquired. In an earlier chapter, we pointed out the absence in our culture of the skill of distinguishing archeological relics and cults from living wisdom traditions. Perhaps now we might be in a situation to suggest that living traditions are distinguished by the practice of skillful means that work.

Many Paths

There are many places to turn in seeking responses to the questions in these themes. In chapter three we spoke of our good fortune of living in a time when we have available thousands of years of human heritage, a heritage that contains a multitude of Wisdom traditions. As a result of that good fortune, we do not have to begin from zero in attempting to develop a practice that supports such responses. That heritage has certainly been generous to me, and I would like to share some of what I have borrowed for my journey from several wisdom traditions. I propose to do so not as a prescription for others but as an illustrative tale about how someone with the most mundane sort of life can find the beginnings of an individual path, providing both intimations of peace in one's own heart and a way to work in the world to serve the heart's call. At this point in my own life, it seems to me that such service in the world with a peaceful heart is the point of the quest for Wisdom. When I look back over years in business and over my experiences as an educator, hindsight makes clear that the best of my life has been characterized by those moments of service, intended or not, to the commands of my heart.

One reason that I characterized my own quest for wisdom as quixotic derives from an almost universal admonition from the wise, that one should as soon as possible find a teacher, settle down, and practice one's discipline. Doing otherwise has been likened to a fool attempting to have a well of cool water by digging a hundred one-foot-deep holes. Such settling down, however well advised, has not been my lot. Whether I am like that fool and have been too long a dilettante or whether I have been like a clever bee and have spent much of my life going from flower to flower, tasting and gathering the nectar of a hundred teachings, time will tell and the reader is welcome to judge.

In order to provide the promised moral and spiritual context of my responses to the present crisis, I need to tell you my story, in terms of the themes just mentioned, from five traditions that have dominated my study: the Sufis, Zen in its many forms, the heirs of the Hebrew Prophets, some Christian mystics, and the current manifestation of Buddhist mindfulness traditions in the West. What I have to say about them is intended only as the promised context and is definitely not intended as a summary of what they mean to other seekers or students. Nor do I make any pretense of completeness—these are but vignettes from these vast traditions, the mastery of any one of which is the work of lifetimes. As I offer them I feel that beside every sentence—beside every word—there should be another paragraph about another path or possibility, another cautionary footnote for the unwary seeker. But that is not the purpose of telling this story; rather, it is simply to attempt to shed some light upon the support that this study has given to the voice within my heart, and perhaps thereby to speak against despair, to offer support to any who feel a discomfort such as I feel with our culture's definition of a life well-lived.

If what follows seems occasionally rather artificially separated by disciplines, it is for the sake of the telling; the effects of each of these traditions upon my understanding are inextricably intertwined, appearing in my discourse as the several strands of the themes. Other traditions and many individuals are not included, some because I cannot speak briefly of them and some because I do not yet understand the story of how they have impacted my life. Also, despite the appearance imposed by the written form, this story is not really linear—it springs from reading shelves of texts over the course of decades and the *agon* of many late nights, and often—like our fool of a well digger—in several traditions simultaneously.

Time among the Sufis

In my thirties there were few structures in my own pre-analytic vision that gave comfort or support to the voice in my heart, while it spoke with a quiet murmur against my indifferent agnosticism and against my attempts to be a satisfied consumer. I had learned skepticism and deconstruction well, and the innocent traditions of my childhood were inaccessible to me. The sophomoric sophistication of my earlier rebellion was so much a part of my surrounding culture that I could not bear that earlier faith, and the alternatives that I had encountered reminded me of the lessons that my study of psychology had taught me about cults and fanaticism. It was in the context of that mindset that my reading brought me to a chance encounter with the works of Idries Shah, an extraordinary individual who was widely acknowledged to have been, among his other roles, the current exemplar of the Sufi tradition in the West.

Shah allowed me once again to give serious consideration to the *Perennial Question*. He seemed to bring together in one body of work so many of the elements that I had previously seen as mutually exclusive. In his work the juxtaposition of the disparate was not only possible, but necessary: he represented both the most effective iconoclasm I had ever encountered and a profound sense of the pivotal importance of mystical experience; as a teacher he had a pragmatic commitment to "what works" for the student along with a credible claim to *Knowledge* of how "what works" is to be constructed; and, while able to meet all of the world's criteria for success as a businessperson, he posed a profound challenge to our social constructs, a challenge that asked to be entertained not as an uncritical belief, but as a "working hypothesis." He demonstrated how we might avoid some of the destructive patterns of human behavior if we simply employed what we already know about ourselves from our own science, and even maintained that such understanding of "who we are" is both a necessary first step in successfully negotiating the evolutionary steps before us and one of the prerequisites for effective spiritual study. He asserted that we must learn to refrain from approaching truly important things (like Knowledge and "God") with our commercial mindset, as commodities, to be bought and sold; or with a mindset tied to those of our myths which can be shown to be less than useful in terms of Deikman's explication of "cult behavior" (see the earlier discussion in chapter three. His tradition refuses to sacrifice truth to politeness, referring to those who choose to avoid the duty to awaken as "the walking dead."

He fostered *Hope,* in that he gave me the opportunity to catch a glimpse of the "mental prison" that we construct for ourselves, and taught about the fundamental tools needed for the escape from that prison. He taught me how our efforts to meet basic psychological needs, such as the ego's need for attention, as well as our confounding of group dynamics with spirituality, intrude into what we think are spiritual matters, so that we remain fettered by our Western arrogance, our materialistic presumption that our intellect can span the possible. He was emphatic in insisting that most of what we take for mystical experience is only rudimentary emotionalism, while also asserting that there is something beyond both intellect and emotion that must not be confused with either.

Shah gave me Ibn Aribi's specification for a teacher, "People think that a teacher should display miracles and manifest illumination. But the requirement in a teacher is that he should possess all that the disciple needs" (1978:54). Among the many things that Shah possessed that I needed was a path that allowed me to open myself to the possibility of spirituality from the depths of my skepticism.

As an educator, I have often come back to this well. Throughout our culture, much of the skepticism that is a necessary part of careful intellectual inquiry has degenerated into the most toxic forms of cynicism. As a personal refuge from that toxicity and the despair that often accompanies it, I cherish Shah's modeling of an iconoclasm that is creates oases rather than deserts. Our students increasingly appear to us bearing the scars of cynicism at much too early an age, scars that many wear with pride as marks of the rite of passage into an adulthood where many of their parents peers, as my clients, must deal with the resultant risk of meaningless work. The sort of healthy skepticism that is armored against cynicism by the Wisdom exemplified by Shah allows a teacher to model an approach that is neither credulous nor despairing of trust, one that nurtures the beginnings of the "skillful means" we hypothesized in chapter three, to distinguish between the cultic misunderstandings of our pre-analytic vision and the path to the world we claim to want. Unfortunately, beyond reading the recommended books, it is not appropriate that one undertake this path without a teacher.

The Taste of Zen

Alan Watts had taught me some Zen in the sixties and seventies. I am not sure that I know any more of it now than what he taught me then, I just feel more at home with it after longer acquaintance. He showed me how one could encounter an assertion of the ineffability of Truth and still build on its insights to say useful things about the condition of our culture. In speaking of how Zen can serve to turn one's mind inside out and open us to different ways of seeing, he offered me a model to which I have often referred when struggling with what we have called here our common pre-analytic vision. Speaking of how those trained in Rinzai Zen take the extreme position on the issue of incommunicability, on the principle that "those who know do not speak and those who speak do not know," Watts discusses how such practitioners make approaching the path highly problematic for the skeptical Westerner, because:

> Although . . . they do not "put up," they do not completely "shut up." On the one hand, they would love to share their understanding with others. But on the other hand, they are convinced that words are ultimately futile, and are, furthermore, under an agreement not to discuss certain aspects of their training. They begin, therefore to take the characteristic Asian attitude of "Come and see for yourself." But the scientifically trained Westerner is, not without reason, a cautious and skeptical fellow who likes to know what he is "getting into." He is acutely conscious of the capacity of the mind for self-deception, for going into places where entrance is impossible without leaving one's critical perspective at the door. Asians tend so much to despise this attitude, and their Western devotees even more so, that they neglect to tell the scientific inquirer many things that are still within the possibilities of human speech and intellectual understanding. (Watts: 1957: xii–xiii)

Perhaps Watts' most telling point for our present effort is that the failure of both sides to bridge this gap leads (has led us) to a situation where, "It is both dangerous and absurd for our world to be a group of communions mutually excommunicate" (1957:xiii). His own teaching position is to attempt to provoke increased clarity by providing a neutral third point of view by being sympathetic and somewhat personally experimental, while resisting the temptation to "join the organization." He acknowledges that the most likely result is being disowned by both sides; however, he undertakes the effort seeing the, ". . . special value to us in attaining a critical perspective upon our own ideas. . . . to appreciate differences in the basic premises of thought and in the very methods of thinking . . ." (p. 3–4).

While I had only been able to see what Watts calls the Western side of this argument in my first encounter, after Shah I was able to revisit Zen and see it with new eyes. As unlikely as it seems from the viewpoint of intellectual history, these two traditions hold many teaching stories and attitudes in common, often differentiated by brevity and approach, rather than substance. The Zen masters with their short replies and lightning-quick strikes from their staffs upon the shoulders of sleepy disciples make the surly Sufis seem almost maternal in their kindness toward their students. The many teaching stories that occur in both traditions are almost invariably shorter and more cryptic in their Zen versions, more accessible if no more transparent in their Sufi form. In both they are "instrumental literature," intentionally designed and crafted to modify the consciousness of the student, bypassing the barrier that the intellect and its pre-analytic vision impose, on the way to being Awake. The Sufis specifically indicate that instrumental literature should not be used by the uninstructed for purposes other than this, and I have restrained my desire to quote them for that reason.

D. T. Suzuki is considered by many to have almost single-handedly brought the Zen tradition to the West in a form that is both authentic and accessible to those most committed to intellection. His work is voluminous and not for those lacking in determination; however, he is immensely helpful in pursuing the work that Alan

Watts outlined for us. Listen as he treats us better than did Watts's non-communicative Rinzai students, ". . . the ultimate aim of Zen discipline is to attain what is known as 'Satori' in Japanese . . . (enlightenment) . . . which is defined here as 'the state of consciousness in which Noble Wisdom realizes its own inner nature.' And this self-realization constitutes the truth of Zen, which is emancipation . . . and . . . freedom" (D. T. Suzuki, 1994:12). To make clear what he means by self-realization, he quotes a teaching dialogue from the Avatamska Sutra:

THE STUDENT: How does one come to this emancipation face to face? How does one get this realization?

THE TEACHER: A man comes to this emancipation face to face when his mind is awakened to Prajnaparamita [wisdom for crossing to the other shore] and stands in a most intimate relationship to it; for then he attains self-realization in all that he perceives and understands.

THE STUDENT: Does one attain self-realization by listening to the talks and discourses on Prajnaparamita?

THE TEACHER: That is not so. Why? Because Prajnaparamita sees intimately into the truth and reality of all things.

THE STUDENT: Is it not that thinking comes from hearing and that by thinking and reasoning one comes to perceive what Suchness is? And is this not self-realization?

THE TEACHER: That is not so. Self-realization never comes from mere listening and thinking. O son of a good family, I will illustrate the matter by analogy. Listen! In a great desert there are no springs or wells; in the spring-time or in the summer when it is warm, a traveler comes from the west going eastward; he meets a man coming from the east and asks him: I am terribly thirsty; pray tell me where I can find a spring and a cool refreshing shade where I may drink, bathe, rest and get thoroughly revived?

The man from the east gives the traveler, as desired, all the information in detail . . . Now, son of a good family, do you think that the thirsty traveler from the west, listening to the talk of the spring and the shady trees, and thinking of going to that place as quickly as possible, can be relieved of thirst and heat and get refreshed?

THE STUDENT: No, he cannot; because he is relieved of thirst and heat and gets refreshed only when, as directed by the other, he actually reaches the fountain and drinks of it and bathes in it.

THE TEACHER: Son of a good family, even so with the Bodhisattva. By merely listening to it, thinking of it, and intellectually understanding it, you will never come to the realization of any truth . . . to quench the thirst and to be relieved of the heat by drinking of the refreshing fountain means the realization of the truth by oneself. (1994:12–14)

Any intellection that stands between the disciple and "suchness" is subject to the master's swift discipline. While there is as much doctrine and as much schism among the various Zen schools as there are in religions, the reports of those who have followed the path of any of the schools to its end acknowledge that they have all arrived at a common point. If one would like a first lesson in Zen, she should find such a person and ask them about the nature of that end point of their journey—if that person were lucky enough to receive a reply, regardless of the form it takes, it would be certain to both assault the intellect and offer a tool to begin a life's work. As a teacher, I had always assumed that my capacity for intellection and the content of my course were what added value for my students. It required the abrupt manner of these masters and a few sharp (kindly) blows from their staffs to allow me to begin to see that a real teaching situation, while requiring some sort of structure in which to operate, is not about the "container" of the classroom or workshop in which it is taking place; but rather about the content, the heart-level interaction between student and teacher that has nothing to do with end-of-grade testing and everything to do with compassion and the transmission of wisdom.

In a similar dialogue of great interest—decidedly more contemporary—will follow in a later section on Christian mystics. We shall see Suzuki again, this time in conversation with Thomas Merton, as they find unlikely common ground in the work of a medieval German monk. In that discussion we will see more of how Zen demands the mastery of negation as a tool for breaking the walls of our self-imposed prison.

Heirs of the Hebrew Prophets

I needed to spend some more time in the wilderness before I could complete the first cycle of my prodigal's journey—despite the wonders of my other encounters, my heart still ached for the awe of the personal God of my childhood. Yet, despite that yearning to return, many of those who would offer to lead a prodigal back home all too readily brought to mind the reasons that I left. What I found was that there could be no better guide to lead me out of my wilderness time than the heirs of the Hebrew Prophets. Can there then be any question that I, who was struggling with my incapacity to give words to this ache, would be struck dumb to find this passage, when David Purpel, in the midst of teaching me by living his own path, introduced me to the work of Abraham Heschel?

> The attempt to convey what we see and cannot say is the everlasting theme of mankind's unfinished symphony, a venture in which adequacy is never achieved. Only those who live on borrowed words believe in their gift of expression . . . Most—and often the best—of what goes on in us is our own secret; we have to wrestle with it ourselves . . . What smites us with unquenchable amazement is not that which we grasp and are able to convey but that which lies within our reach but beyond our grasp . . . the true meaning, source and end of being, in other words, the ineffable. (1951: 4–5)

David Purpel clearly shares that view of intellectual humility in spiritual issues, even though those of us who have been fortunate enough to be his students certainly believe that he truly has a "gift of expression" worthy of being believed in. He taught me about the *agon*, the "wrestling with ourselves" of which Heschel is speaking here, and of the value (to one's life and to one's teaching practice) of being willing to live a response to really important questions, rather than disposing of them with a too ready answer. He also taught me that whatever we have to say that *is* worthy of expression comes from that struggle, and thus any writing that hopes to be worthwhile requires the courage to be self-revealing and the blessing of doing so with grace. This is especially important in the case of what I have termed the perennial question. In our times and in the context of what we have written above, it would be difficult to frame that question with greater strength than does Heschel:

> There are those who sense the ultimate question in moments of wonder, in moments of joy; there are those who sense the ultimate question in moments of horror, in moments of despair. . . . [when] The world is in flames, consumed by evil. Is it possible that there is no one who cares? (1955:367)

There can be no question that Heschel shared the present authors' concern for the state of our culture, in the context of what we have already written of materialism, environmental degradation, our apparent propensity for genocide, and the threat of terror from the weapons we have created. He said that we are in:

> . . . a situation that puts the problem of man in a new light. The issue is old, yet the perspective is one of emergency. New in this age is an unparalleled awareness of the terrifying seriousness of the human situation. Questions we ask seriously today would have seemed utterly absurd twenty years ago, such as, for example: Are we the last generation? Is this the very last hour for Western civilization? (Heschel, 1965:13)

What does this say about the nature of humanity, that we have brought ourselves to such a pass? While there is generally far too much self-congratulation in our culture and far too little meaningful self-criticism, on those occasions where we do look honestly at ourselves, our response to sudden insights into the defects of our culture tends to swing past the line that marks a prophetic call for repair and reform, and into self-hatred and violence. For small examples, one has only to consider the riotous response of well-intended people to globalization or the conviction held by some hackers that the appropriate response to a Microsoft monopoly is the authorship of viruses and the destruction of other people's work. In a much larger sense, self-criticism that becomes self-hatred can silence the voice in our hearts and allow despair to crowd out our hope. As Heschel (1965) says, our disdain for ourselves can have profound consequences if it causes us to lose sight of our spiritual relevance:

> The ambiguity of Homo Sapiens is an old triviality. Both praise and derision have been heaped profusely upon him. . . . Yet a note of compassion vibrates in the older discourses about him. Today we are fiercely articulate in deprecation and distain (p. 26). . . . The tragedy of this creeping self-disparagement is in the cultivation of the doubt whether man is worthy to be saved. Massive defamation of man may spell the doom of all of us. . . . If man is contemptible, why be upset about the extinction

of the human species? The eclipse of humanity, the inability to sense our spiritual relevance, to sense our being involved in the moral task is itself a dreadful punishment. (p. 27)

Heschel calls us to self-awareness, to understanding: "What is human about a human being?" lest we lose the capacity of being human. If we give in to the temptation of seeing the perennial question as beyond our capacity for response, we can become lost in solipsism. If we lose the ability to come to meaning through the *agon* of wrestling with ourselves (and with angels) over ultimate questions, we risk all that defines our humanity:

> One of the most frightening prospects we must face is that this earth may be populated by a race of beings which though belonging to the race Homo sapiens according to biology will be devoid of the qualities by which man is spiritually distinguished from the rest of organic creatures. To be human we must know what being human means, how to acquire, how to preserve it.
>
> Just as death is the liquidation of being, dehumanization is the liquidation of being human. What qualifies a being to be called a human being? . . . To claim that the question is unanswerable . . . would be to surrender the hope of attaining knowledge concerning significant issues, since . . . the significance of all other questions we ask depends on the answer we are ready to offer to this one. (1965:29)

To the task of theodicy which we had earlier identified, Heschel adds what he describes as an inseparable task of "anthropodicy," so that when we ask why God allows evil to exist, we must simultaneously ask , ". . . how man should aid God so that His justice and compassion prevail" (1973:298). Yet how can we expect ourselves to respond to such a question, especially in our times, when we must doubt whether any answer can, ". . . obviate the terrible agony the world is writhing in." (1973:300)

> Man's inability to understand the ways and acts of God is obviously due to an inherent inadequacy or privation in his nature, to the banishment of Truth from his life. So it is precisely the incapacity of man to share God's Truth that is both the source and the object of his pain. . . . And yet, if Truth were manifest and strong, man would lose his major task, his destiny; to search for it. He would live without reason for being. Is it not the essence of freedom to grope, to choose, to work out rather than be given Truth? (1973:296)

Who can rise to such a calling, especially among ourselves, the denizens of the benighted culture we have described? What sort of human being would it take to confront such privation and live? In his final book, Heschel (1973) tells the story of the Kotzker, Reb Mendl of Kotzk, in whom I would propose that we recognize not only a master of Hasidim but also of Zen. Reading of his stick-wielding forays into congregations, demanding Truth instead of lies, was so reminiscent of the masters of Rinzai as to make me bolt upright from my chair. Writing of how two forces had guided his life, Heschel said that he had throughout his life been torn between the joy and peace that his heart found in the compassionate teachings of the Baal Shem Tov and the ferocious authenticity that his mind saw from the lightening strikes of the Kotzker. "The Baal Shem helped me to refine my sense of immediate mystery; the Kotzker warned me of the constant peril of forfeiting authenticity. Honesty, authenticity, integrity without love may lead to the ruin of others, of oneself, or both. On the other hand, love, fervor, or exhalation alone may seduce us into living in a fool's Paradise—a wise man's Hell" (1973:xv). While there are many, including myself, who would wish that Heschel had given us a similar level of insight into the Baal Shem that he has into the Kotzker, we may well be in greater need of the gift that we have from him. Certainly the world that I see has great need of that continuing presence of the Kotzker which Heschel perceives:

> He has not fled from us by dying. Somehow his lightening persists. His words throw flames whenever they come into our orbit. They burn. Who can bear them? Yet many of us shall thereby shed our masks, our pretensions, and jealousies, our distorted notions, and then messianic redemption may approach its beginning. . . . For Truth is alive, dwelling somewhere, never weary. And all of mankind is needed to liberate it. (1973:323)

Can we have any hope of becoming such beings? Am I to presume that I might take this struggling soul that I perceive myself to be onto such heights? Do I possess the courage we must have if we are to "shed our masks?" This is exactly the task that Heschel insists is ours, and to lose our hope of doing so is to succumb to the loss of our "sense of our spiritual relevance." If I am to teach, in any of the venues that my life offers, I feel an obligation to be a student of hope. In a world where the opportunity to hold to hope (as opposed to holding to foolish optimism) seems more rare each day, I can easily imagine finding a use for the word "sin" in describing the teaching of despair to children, or the modeling of hopelessness to their parents. For me, in my practice, the bare fact that giants like Heschel have come through their lives with hope in their hearts provides a doorway onto the path toward a similar outcome, as well as a ground upon which to say to students, "There is another way." If there is to be any relationship between education and wisdom, I propose that it lies in responding to this duty to which Heschel calls us.

Heschel certainly knows what he means by hope, and while I cannot yet confess such a faith, I honor it as pointing in the direction that my heart wants to go:

> Over and above the deep sadness of our melodies, fears and experience of persecutions, rituals of mourning and memories of sorrow, hovers the power of hope.
> Hope is our power. It is a vital quality always at work within a person, anticipating freedom from misery. It is a power of perception, an intuition, a foreseeing.
> Hope cannot stand alone, It must be morally substantiated, faithfully attended. It must not lose the element of constancy and the intensity of expectancy.
> Hope is not cheerfulness, a temperamental confidence that all will turn out for the best. It is not an inclination to be guided by illusions rather than by facts. Hope is a conviction, rooted in trust, trust in Him who issued the promise; an ability to soar above the darkness that overshadows the divine. . . . Hope is the creative articulation of faith. (1967:93–94)

Christian Mystics

C. S. Lewis was among the first of the Christian writers whose works were accessible to me. At first I enjoyed Lewis because, for me, his Christianity did not get in the way of his stories. Over time, I have come to appreciate that his stories do not obstruct his Christianity. In all his fiction, from the lovely suitable-for-children Narnia novels to the Screwtape Letters and a mythopedic Space Trilogy, there is something that sends me away feeling nourished, refreshed, and strengthened for whatever battle the next day might bring. Yet, as unlikely as I might have thought it to be at the time, it was in his most unapologetic apologetics that I eventually came to treasure his work. Here, for example, he speaks to the focus of this book, ". . . we cannot help seeing that only the degree of virtue which we now regard as impracticable can possibly save our race from disaster . . . a consistent practice of virtue by the human race even for ten years would fill the earth from pole to pole with peace, plenty, health, merriment, and hearts-ease, and . . . nothing else will." (1996:56–57)

As can be seen from this, Lewis is quick to insist that the faith of which he often speaks does not require, or even permit, disengagement for the world, saying that, ". . . it would be quite false to suppose that the Christian view of [redemptive] suffering is incompatible with the strongest emphasis on our duty to leave the world . . . 'better' than we found it" (1996:101). And as an prescient ally of Soros in opposing "market fundamentalism" he observed that, "I should not have been honest if I had not told you that the three great civilizations [Greeks, Jews, and the Christianity of the Middle Ages] had agreed . . . in condemning the very thing upon which we have based our whole [economic] life" (1952:85). It certainly calls for inspiration to deal with what Heschel taught about both the difficulties and the importance of giving voice to the ineffable. As evidence that such inspiration does exist, that something useful could be put into language concerning that for which our hearts yearn, I could not do better than to offer this from Lewis, "All the things that have deeply possessed your soul have been but hints of it . . . echoes that died away just as they caught your ear. But . . . if there ever came an echo that did not die away but swelled into the sound itself—you would know it . . . it is the secret signature of each soul, the incommunicable and unappeasable want" (1996:131).

Lewis can then offer us a chance to understand what he means by Heaven and Hell, concepts both mystifying and off-putting to those not of his confession, by explaining them in terms of fulfillment or privation of that call of the heart. When he does so, there is great resonance with the insights of other traditions:

> All your life an unattainable ecstasy has hovered just beyond the grasp of your consciousness. The day is coming when you will awake to find, beyond all hope, that you have attained it, or else, that it was within your reach and you have lost it forever. This may seem a perilously private and subjective notion of the pearl of great price, but it is not. The thing I am speaking of is not an experience. You have experienced only

the *want* of it. . . . Always it has summoned you out of yourself. And if you will not go out of yourself to follow it, if you sit down to brood on the desire and attempt to cherish it, the desire itself will evade you. "The door into life generally opens behind us" and "the only wisdom" for one "haunted by the scent of unseen roses is work." This secret fire goes out when you use the bellows: bank it down with what seems unlikely fuel of dogma and ethics, turn your back on it and attend to your duties, and then it will blaze. (1996:132–133)

But how are we to follow such advice, when we can so seldom succeed in behaving in the ways we claim to want to? In several instances previously we have raised the question of why we seem to face such difficulties in treating each other decently and in behaving in ways that we acknowledge to be better rather than worse. Another of my teachers, Beatrice Bruteau, helped me to understand this behavior in terms of what she calls the "descriptive self." She shows us how we have come to believe that we *are* the various descriptions that we have of ourselves, including,

> . . . all those categories and quality or quantity ratings by which we customarily introduce ourselves: our occupation, our relation to spouse or parent or child, our nationality, our religion, our race, our wealth, our fame, our achievements; perhaps even some special feature that looms large in our social life, such as sexual orientation or some mental or physical handicap, or a drug dependency or a prison record. . . . we think that we *are* that description. And our life consists of trying to get the description valued or trying to get the valued description. (1993:78).

Bruteau explains that, in this world that is populated by those who believe themselves to *be* their "descriptive selves," the value of the descriptors is directly proportional to their scarcity and to the envy that the scarcity produces—others must be in want of what we have on order that we may value it. Having structured our system of values in this way, it is inevitable that the stakes in the ensuing Hobbesian battle come to be perceived by the combatants as vital:

> . . . the hurts of one generation of interacting persons or races or classes or nations are passed on to succeeding generations. . . . It is important to understand this if we want to work in the area of peace and justice, to lift up the poor and free the oppressed. We must understand that fighting, defeating, depriving, and oppressing are *systematic necessities of our present mentality*. We have to have the contrast in order to have the sense of value, in order to have the sense of who we are, in order to *maintain ourselves in being*. (1993:79–80)

And how are we to see ourselves any differently, if the pre-analytic vision of our culture is grounded in such "descriptive selves?" Bruteau calls us to see ourselves in an entirely different light, to see ourselves as grounded in our relationship with God. Because of that relationship, she tells us that what is truly real about us is never at risk, that we are capable of seeing our world in a profoundly better way in which we can see abundance instead of scarcity, love instead of fear. But releasing ourselves from our entrapment in scarcity and accepting the reality of abundance requires that we be freed from fear: "The one imperative that appears most often in the Bible is 'Don't be afraid.' We must first assure people and relieve them of their fears. This is 'salvation.' Then they will be fit to give themselves freely to one another" (1993:129). We have made our task seem impossible by requiring of ourselves that we love unconditionally while still convinced of our need to defend our egos. Rather than *requiring* that people love one another (an impossible and oppressive demand), the process is to, "Take away the damming walls of ego-defense and the fountain of love will spring forth naturally and pour out without restraint" (p. 130). And how are we to attain freedom from fear in this kind of world? Bruteau says that to have this freedom requires that we encounter a special kind of optimism, profoundly different from the sort that I earlier described as *mundane*: "The deepest truth is our union with the Absolute, Infinite Being, with God. That is the root of our reality. And it is from that root that my optimism is derived. That is why I have decided to call it 'radical optimism'. . . . shift our sense of identity to the root, to our 'real self' and the source of our being in God, and all looks very different" (1993:10). So, we must not mislead by maintaining that humans must behave unselfishly in the world in order to merit the absolute and unconditional love of God. Rather, Bruteau maintains that, "Our most important task . . . is, in my view, to correct this terrible error. We must preach and practice God's abundant, unconditional love. This is the truth of God's nature, the fulfillment of our own nature, and the rescue of our fellow beings" (p. 130).

This question of error with regard to the starting point of this quest is much to the point. If one were to search through traditions looking for a sequence of "steps on the path" toward wisdom, one would frequently encounter the conclusion that Bruteau opposes: that one progresses through a preparation of individual ethical development, to proficiency in a "practice," which results in the sort of changes in one's approach to life that eventually manifest in a transformative way as wisdom. Among the many reasonable arguments for this sequence, my favorite is that it is hard to settle down to meditation after a busy day of murder and mayhem. However, this linear progression is problematic if we understand Bruteau's argument that human beings need the realization of being unconditionally loved by God in order to move out of fear and into the capacity for loving our fellows. I think that what Bruteau would most oppose is the expectation that a novice should move from being a part of our present culture to manifesting unconditional love solely on the strength of ego, without the experience of unity with the source of that love. It would seem that we must find some less linear view of the path, one that I might struggle to articulate as a circle or a spiral that has us visiting each step again and again, each time with greater understanding, so that after much iteration, the original starting point becomes moot.

And what is the path to this experience? It is through the realization that comes from contemplation, a realization that affirms the ground of radical optimism—an optimism that, "is ultimately, metaphysically, true . . . coming from the root of our being, securely held in the Absolute Being" (Bruteau 1993:12). And what is contemplation? "The heart of it is insight, or what I often call 'realization.' The preparation for this is the exercises of relaxation and faculty-training, and the sequents from it are what I have called 'manifestation'—a kind of spontaneous overflow of goodness-filled being so powerful that it creates the world" (1993:12). And finally:

> Contemplation was initially a movement of consciousness *from* the world, as we were then thinking of it, *to* God, as we were then thinking of God. Now manifestation is a movement of consciousness from God, with God, in God, *as* God, out into the world, a movement in which the divine consciousness and my consciousness, flowing together stream out in love and in creative, healing, beautifying energy to create the world and to make it ever better (1973:132). . . . We get the kind of world we ourselves create by our faith. The only way to change the kind of world we experience is to change the kind of creative consciousness we have, the kind of faith we have. It is our faith that creates the world (p. 134). . . . Contemplation can't, in the end, be talked about. It has to be practiced. There are people who have practiced and who have seen and who have manifested. "Ask and it shall be given you; seek and you will find; knock and it will be opened to you (Matthew 7:7)." It is a great invitation and a great promise. Let us accept it. (p. 136)

Thomas Merton is of the same school of Christian Contemplatives as Bruteau. He also serves to link us back to Zen and D. T. Suzuki. At the conclusion of chapter three, we quoted Merton in a mode very similar to what we have just heard from Bruteau, saying, ". . . furthermore, in all religions it is more or less generally recognized that this profound 'sapiential' experience, call it gnosis, contemplation, 'mysticism,' 'prophecy,' or what you will, represents the deepest and most authentic fruit of the religion itself" (1967:204). While this sounds rather like a pleasant and much to be desired experience, I am reminded of Heschel's story of his two teachers, because, in addition to the joy and love to be found here, there is also the question of authenticity—the admission price to be paid by the ego if we are to follow this path. What is being asked of someone who might decide to accept this invitation? If one chooses Merton's path (or that of many other masters) there is a significant cost. Comparing the fruit of the most profound Christian contemplative discipline with Zen, Merton says:

> On the psychological level, there is an exact correspondence between the mystical night of St. John of the Cross and the emptiness of *sunyata*. The difference is theological: the night of St. John opens into a divine and personal freedom and is a gift of "grace." The void of Zen is the natural ground of Being—for which no theological explanation is either offered or desired. In either case, however, whether in attaining to the pure consciousness of Zen or in passing through the dark night of St. John of the Cross, there must be a death of that ego-identity or self-consciousness which is constituted by a calculating and desiring ego. (1967:242)

Since those of us who have not attained the realization that is under discussion might be said to be aware of little if any consciousness other than the desiring ego, this is not a small price—at this death, just as at the next one, all that I know of

William M. McLaurin, Jr. in the sense that Bruteau calls the "descriptive self" will pass away. A fearsome prospect indeed for those of us who have not already attained the perspective of "radical optimism." Yet, this is the "dying before you die" that is said by many traditions to be the only path that leads to liberation from the suffering that is the inevitable outcome of clinging to the plans of the ego, of grasping at the delusions of a dream that wishes to last forever. The realization that leads to that liberation is rare and hard-won, and its price is that it leaves no place for our convoluted ego-derived constructs. This chasm over which the ego cannot pass is also a moment of truth for those of us who teach on the mundane side of that divide. For teachers like me, the humility to acknowledge both that there is something priceless to be learned and that I do not personally hold the keys to that learning is often the only thing I have to offer a student who asks about such realization—to claim more skill than I have would be fraud, while denying the existence of the required wisdom would be to speak against what my heart knows to be true.

In a dialogue with Merton (1968:109), D. T. Suzuki says of Emptiness, ". . . the mind is filled with all kinds of defiled thought among which the worst is 'self.' For all evils and attachments start from our attachment to it. As Buddhists would say, the realization of emptiness is no more, no less than seeing into the non-existence of a thingish ego-substance. This is the greatest stumbling block in our spiritual discipline, which, in actuality consists not in getting rid of the self, but in realizing the fact that there is no such existence from the first."

To master the concepts that are broached here is a great labor—yet this intellectual learning is but a small taste of the matter. At the end of the day, the concepts matter only to the extent that they support a practice that can take one to the realization toward which all this tries to point. As the Zen master said to the obtuse student, "You keep staring at my finger—see instead that I am pointing toward the moon." In that same sense, the concepts of compassion and unconditional love found in these authors are foundational for my practice of education, in that they point me toward a path, through gnosis, to the ground for that sense of the intrinsic worth of each person, which we discussed at length in Chapter 2, a ground which the Enlightenment Project struggled to provide, and which in its failing, prepared our world for the crisis with which we now contend. The companion concept, that we are not the egos that we take ourselves to be, can restore hope in our educational endeavors, because it is the first step on the path to discovering that our perennial failures derive from very old habits for which remedy is possible, if painful.

Mindfulness

Among the varieties of Buddhism that have made the transition from Asia to America, those which emphasize mindfulness seem to me less culture-bound than many. Theirs is a meditative practice of mindful attention, whose elements are found in many traditions, perhaps best known within our culture in the form of the Buddhist *vipassana* tradition, and known among many of its American practitioners as Insight Meditation.

Within this tradition, Jack Kornfield has been, for me, a profoundly important teacher. Like Bruteau and Shah, he integrates what we understand intellectually of our humanness into his description of the beginnings of his path, so that we might prepare ourselves for the journey. In discussing how the stories we tell ourselves in our inner dialogue condition and limit us, his description of the "body of fear" is strongly reminiscent of Bruteau's "descriptive selves":

> The stories reflect our conditioning, personal and cultural. . . . Central to the stories we tell are the fixed beliefs we have about ourselves. It is as if we have been cast into a movie as a depressed person or a beautiful one, as a compromiser or a clown, an angry victim or a fighter whom no one will ever take advantage of again. Because these thoughts and assumptions are so powerful, we live out their energies over and over. These patterns of thought, together with the contractions of body and heart, create a limited sense of self. They are sometimes called "the body of fear." When we live from the body of fear, our life is simply one of habit and reaction (2000:36–37). . . . At the root of suffering is a small heart, frightened to be here, afraid to trust the river of change, to let go in this changing world . . . we can never know what will happen. With wisdom we allow this not knowing to become a form of trust. (p. 288–289)

Just as the other traditions have held, Kornfield tells us that this is no small undertaking. We cannot have this wisdom and an ever-expanding ego too. After describing the opening steps on his path, where we are dealing with the old repetitive habits of our bodies and our minds, he tells us that, to become what we might become will require a radical transformation, one that demands initiation:

> In undertaking the trials and hardships of a period of initiation, we can transform our view of ourselves and the world. We can awaken our spiritual authority and inner knowing, a trust that can carry us in the face of difficulties and death. Initiation forces upon us a shift of identity in which we can transcend our small sense of self, release what is called "the body of fear," and awaken an undying wisdom, love and fearlessness. (2000:39)

One of the stories that we tell in our inner dialogue that maintains our preanalytic vision has to do with tales about how remote and inaccessible the path to wisdom is. One reason that the path can seem so elusive is an all too human tendency to seek truth in places where it is not to be found. There is immense fascination in the idea of a grail quest, a trip to the orient to see great masters, or the discovery of esoteric knowledge hidden in ancient manuscripts. After telling one of a hundred variations on the story of the prodigal disciple who only attains enlightenment when he returns to his original master after long and unfruitful travels, Jack Kornfield says:

> The holy perfection we seek has been here all along. Dame Julian of Norwich described this perfection at the center of her prayers when she wrote, "And all shall be well, and all manner of things shall be well." To recognize the perfection of "things as

they are" is a radical opening of the heart, an awe of the sacred wholeness that underlies all things. It is always there and we can awaken to it in any situation

The question may arise, "Why hasn't some taste of enlightenment or perfection
revealed itself to me?" The truth is it probably has, but we have not noticed it or recognized it. It is like the invisible air that surrounds us, that sustains our life. (2000:
103–104.

Sylvia Boorstein speaks of this invisibility, which in a sense derives from the
very ordinariness of our quarry. She says that the truths about life experience that
the Buddha taught are so obvious that when she teaches them, her students complain of their everydayness:

That's right—they *are* commonplace truths, and it is true that everyone sort of knows
them. I believe the point of spiritual practice is that we get to know in a visceral way,
in a way that causes us to feel less frightened and behave more kindly. . . . Spiritual
practice offers the possibility of knowing . . . in a way that is transformative. In the
Buddhist texts, this transformation is called the development of wisdom. You can't
see wisdom, but you can see its reflection. Its reflection is happiness, fearlessness, and
kindness. (1995:113)

Sharon Salzberg taught me about the fruits of practice in a similar vein, using
the language of hope and faith. She recalled how, in the midst of her undergraduate despair, she was sustained by a "glimmer of possibility" that she might not have
to be lonely and afraid forever: "Like a subliminal message being played under the
predominant music, a sense of possibility, no matter how faint, drives a wedge
between the suffering we may wake up with each day and the hopelessness that can
try to move in with us on a permanent basis" (2002:11). She found from her own
experience, and then from the experience of her students, that the "lack of faith"
that many of us recall from those years was better thought of as having been denied the opportunity to seek and discover truth for ourselves. She speaks of how
critical it is to have a *practice* that moves us beyond having a handful of inherited or
accidental *beliefs,* and into a wholehearted *faith.* In doing this, she poses the fundamental questions about how we are to know if a belief is true, about how we are
to critically examine our beliefs without risking the premature crumbling of our
pre-analytic vision, about—if you will—epistemology:

In Buddhism, the distinction between faith and beliefs lies in testing what we are
told. "Put it into practice," the Buddha said, "and if you find that it leads to a kind of
wisdom that is like looking at a wall, and then the wall breaks open and you see in a
much more unbounded way, then you can trust it." No matter what my teachers told
me, it was still a belief until I tried it. (2002:55–56)

The most persistent enemy of such faith within the limits of our cultural
understanding is suffering. When we put the mundane optimism of our pre-
analytic vision up against even our smallest personal pain, that vision gives us
nothing back to sustain us. When confronted with the litany of awfulness that is

humanity's living memory, whole communities of faith tremble and fall. Yet we must not look away, for, as Kornfield says:

> Our hearts become tender and raw and we feel a natural kinship with all that lives. The cries of street children echo in our mind, images of terrorism and racism, ecological destruction, poverty, and slavery fill our consciousness. It is as if our consciousness has broken open to the struggles of humanity and the earth itself. We may feel that we are in a charnel ground, we may see the suffering of countless generations. And we recognize that there is no escape from this. Yet only by opening our eyes and heart to the suffering of the world can we find freedom or peace . . . each of us must look into this great question: What is the truth about suffering in human life and what is the cause of this suffering? (2000:65)

As we grow up, we all come to know from experience that the world is filled with "the ten thousand joys and the ten thousand sorrows." Yet, we all also cherish some secret foolishness that tells us we can have gain without loss, pleasure without pain, light without dark. Untutored, we think that the path to happiness lies in grasping at the joys and pushing away the sorrows. But Kornfield says that it is by means of this very struggling between the ego and the world that we entangle ourselves in "the body of fear," and that this drives us to the violence and hate that converts the inevitable pain of being human into the suffering that we sought to avoid:

> To see the truth of suffering completely is to come to freedom through the gate of suffering. We can never successfully grasp or control the changing conditions of life. We cannot possess our lover, our spouse, our homes, our work. We cannot even possess our children. Yes, we can love and care for them, but if we try to control them, we only create suffering. Pleasure and pain, praise and blame, success and failure alternate day after day, the world itself has pain and pleasure woven into it as night is woven together with day. If we resist this truth, we will inevitably suffer. (2000:65)

I said earlier that many succumb to an illusion about the path to such understanding, focusing on special experiences and the dramatic stories of distant lands. In the tradition of *vipassana*, enlightenment is our natural state, nearer to us than the "self" which maintains the pre-analytic vision, the "self" that is our prison guard. In a passage that calls to mind Thomas Merton's earlier comments on the death of the "desiring ego," Kornfield says that his teacher, Ajahn Chah taught him to find this natural state through reflection and meditation:

> All experiences are without self, without independent existence. They arise like the wind and pass away, all according to certain conditions. In any quiet moment of seeing this truth, he taught, we can step out of all the conditions we call "self," to rest in the timeless knowing, the unconditioned. Thus the difficult practice we undertake is to know the changing world and not get lost in it.
> In this teaching, the figure and ground of our experience are reversed. Illumination is our true state, and spiritual practice is a way to release our entanglements and live in the reality of the present. We are the goal. (2000:100)

This is not to be mistaken for a withdrawal from the world. Kornfield defines a mature spiritual life as one that discovers and embodies a complete world:

> . . . every major area of our experience on earth must be included in our spiritual life before freedom can blossom fully. No significant dimension can be excluded from awareness. The Buddhist Elders speak of cultivating four foundations of sacred awareness: the body, the feelings, the mind, and the governing principles of life. Then their teachings extend the same sacred attention to family, community, livelihood, and relations to the world at large. It is only through attention to each of these that we fulfill our awakening (2000:163). . . . In the mature heart there arises a deeper perfection that is not opposed to the things of this world, but holds them all in compassion (p. 165). . . . a mature teaching is more complete, recognizing that there is unhealthy attachment and healthy attachment (p. 166). . . . Renunciation brings freedom not primarily because we give up things (although we may do so) but because we give up grasping and possessiveness, we relinquish fear, anger, and delusion in the heart.(p. 167)

If it seems that there can be no reconciliation between the two visions in the last two quotations, no common ground that includes both "selflessness" and "holding all the world in compassion," it is because we are unaccustomed to the "Middle Path" which is the Buddha's teaching. Rather than becoming mired in dogmatism and religious fervor, on this middle way ". . . the heart becomes more flexible and sensitive . . . rigid qualities give way to the middle path, with a wise presence that is neither indulgent nor fearful" (Kornfield, 2000:168). In addition to kind laughter at our frustrations over apparent contradictions, there is also this explanation:

> The middle path embraces opposites. It rests between them, acknowledges both truths, caught by neither side. In this way we can see from one side that human life is suffering, with its inevitable string of losses culminating in sickness, aging, and death. Yet, from another perspective it is also grace—filled with gifts and blessings, expressing a divine beauty. Our very suffering can be seen as the grace that brings us to compassion, surrender, and humility. (2000:169)

To bring us round full circle, Kornfield (2000: 192) quotes Thomas Merton: "Life is this simple: we are living in a world that is absolutely transparent and the Divine is shining through it all the time. This is not just a nice story or a fable. It is true."

A Reprise of the Themes as a Confession of Faith

Each of the traditions I have studied offers a unique practice, and a path unlike the others; yet I am convinced that their paths have a common end, which each has struggled to articulate, all the while acknowledging the ineffable nature of the topic at hand. Their skills at voicing their experience have been of great comfort to me and, hopefully, of help on my own path, as it is certainly my intention not just to be comforted, but also to choose a way that arrives at their common end as well.

Further, while it is never my intention or my practice to presume to teach my students directly about these paths, to the extent that this work has opened my heart to a difficult student, or given me the opportunity to be present to someone in hope rather than despair, they are the foundation of any value that I might bring to a classroom or a consulting session.

My life and thought are dominated by hope and bracketed by faith, so that I certainly wish to give that faith what voice I can. I spoke earlier of the progression that I envision between hope, faith and doctrine. In order to complete the story that I have begun, I must attempt to express the present understandings of my heart in the language of my intellect, knowing that the *best* that I can expect is a helpful but necessarily imperfect doctrine—my confession of faith. Since I sincerely wish to avoid the worst that I might expect, before beginning I must remind myself of the hazards of the attempt. As we have said before, for many faith is by definition a rigid adherence to some verbal formula, some doctrinal statement about how the voice in the heart *must* be lived in the world. Departure from a set formula has often been (alas, still is) grounds for murder in many communities, including our own. The question of authority, of when one is to quit attending to the voice in the heart and adhere to such a doctrine, is the frame for the ancient antipathy between mystics and religionists. We spoke earlier about the hazards of delusion and the risks to spiritual life posed when the ego captures the search for Truth for its own purposes. The refuge from such delusion for the student has historically been the community that gives form to the formless voice. Unfortunately, because of the elements of human nature we have discussed, this community of doctrine, this necessary coming-together with others who report spiritual experiences in order to attempt to separate delusion from inspiration, is more often than not an ill-fated effort. I have suggested that the cause lies in that same absence of wisdom to which we have ascribed the failure of other aspects of our culture. While it is admittedly circular, it seems true that one may ascribe some wisdom to a path whose participants create a community with fewer of these failures than the norm. Perhaps then we close the circle by asking of any doctrine and of any community, "Does their behavior model their doctrine and does the result accord with what we know when we listen to our hearts?"

With all those cautions and with another nod to my having good cause to feel humble about what follows, here is my current attempt, using the themes from the beginning of the chapter as a frame, to voice a faith growing out of this tension between inspiration and doctrine. It is not a faith for others or a banner for proselytizing; rather, it is waypoint on my journey, a marker to look back on from wherever I might find myself at the end of another day:

The Perennial Question and the Ineffability of Its Answer

One of the graces with which humans are blessed is a small voice that speaks to us from our hearts. It is always there to remind us of who we really are and of our duty to reflect that reality in this mysteriously difficult world. It poses the Perennial Question, which we experience in many different ways: as poetry, as music, as a deep nostalgia for meaning, as compassion for our fellows—in each case, it speaks in the language of love. Because it does not speak in the language of our intellects, attending to it requires skillful means that our culture trains us to neglect. Although we have the capacity to ignore this voice, to drown it out with the fear of our self-descriptive inner dialogue, we cannot destroy it. It resides in every human being as the source of Hope and the ground of Faith, awaiting our attention. I believe that it is only in response to this call that we encounter what may truly be called wisdom, the teaching and learning of which is real education. Accepting any lesser definition contributes to the crisis we have described.

Good and Evil—Nature and Human Nature: The Reality of Suffering and Its Cause

There cannot be any doubt that each of us suffers, some seemingly to a far greater degree than others. Who among us, no matter how fortunate, has a life where there is only pleasure and no pain, where one gains and never loses, where there is only health and no sickness, where one lives and does not encounter death? Yet, one of the deceits of our culture's pre-analytic vision is to claim that we can have one without the other, that pain is optional, that we can expect a life in which we gain that which the ego desires and avoid that which the ego fears. It is illustrative of the power of that deceit that we acquiesce in it so broadly in a world where living memory includes whole new ranges of awfulness in our treatment of each other, from genocide to rapid advances in our capacity for self-destruction. Like all deceits, this one is strengthened by a half-truth: pain is inevitable in our world, what is optional is the transformation of pain into suffering by the alchemy of the ego's fearful struggle—that is what has the power to drive us to madness and evil. My faith requires that I look squarely into the face of these things, acknowledging that, like all who live, my own being contains the capacity for much of the good and all the evil that humans have ever done. Further, I believe that the duty to which I am called in my heart includes a responsibility to, ". . . trace evil to its discoverable roots and find out how to deal with it effectively" (Bruteau, 1993:74). One of those roots is certainly the fear that we feel when delusion disconnects us from our awareness of the unity of the cosmos—when we feel that we *are* a limited "self" that will die without our attention, we are likely to do much moral evil in its defense. To claim to educate and to never speak to this human propensity makes one especially complicit in the world we see before us. To the larger question of the nature of nature, the issue of theodicy, of whether or not there is moral evil that exists without our acquiescence, I have no knowledge. I can guess that if one were to be able to sustain the viewpoint of spiritual realization, then events such as the collision of galaxies and the end of the universe would be seen as magnificent, rather than as evil, as movements in the dance rather than as evil at the root of being.

Hope, Faith, and Optimism—Can There Be Any End to Suffering?

From the voice of hope in our hearts we hear the music of the Spirit and struggle to transcribe its notes into words, that we might speak a faith that resonates with that same voice in others. When the skill of our transcription grows to the point where we begin to hear such resonance, it is an affirmation and a healing balm; it can give us cause to feel that human beings might actually fulfill this duty that calls to us from our hearts—it can give us cause for optimism. And, if within the limits of the time we can see, we fail to rise to such a possibility, what is at risk—what can be lost—is only the object of the optimism, not our hope. We may be forced by our history to yield the object of our optimism, or even the words we craft to express our faith; but the voice in our hearts is always there, the "ancient and eternal law." Pain accompanies the loss of the objects of our optimism, of what-might-have-been; it is the inevitable accompaniment to life in our world. The cause of suffering is our futile clinging to those objects, our attempts at pushing away the consequences of impermanence. The end of suffering is possible and lies in awakening to reality. The beginning of the path to awakening to reality is learnable and available; it is a basic human duty to seek it—the extent to which it is within our capacity and our duty to teach it can only be discovered along the way.

Human Agency and Action in the World— A Path to the End of Suffering

If it is truly possible to come to the end of suffering then would not everyone want to know the way? It is my faith that there is a possibility for meaningful human agency here. I believe that there are "skillful means" through which our intentions and behaviors in the world can make a real difference. Some form of this belief is an important part of any tradition that offers to guide us to a life well-lived. As we have said so frequently, there are many such paths and no shortage of people who would show us the way. Unfortunately many of these are dead-ends: some are historical relics whose current practitioners no longer listen to their hearts, and many are byways that lead to interesting places other than this goal. The faith I voice today says that, despite this, not only is it possible to find the path to the end of suffering but also that this end is also the point that has so many other names: enlightenment, awakening, dying before we die, entering into the Kingdom of God, Nirvana, contemplative union, and many other words transcribed from the insights of seekers. Well read people could tell us volumes about the subtle and important distinctions that I ignore in putting together any list like the preceding. I agree that the distinctions are important to those who make them, because every path has its own integrity and to the extent that a path is useful it is poorly served by being randomly mixed together with another—thus the caution to our foolish well digger. My point is to affirm that each fruitful path is a "finger pointing toward the moon." The teachers involved would certainly prefer that we eventually look at the moon and not the various pointing fingers. In what follows, I will point toward my own current practice, not because I know whether or not anyone else should share it, but because it is the only means by which I can transcribe what my heart hears.

Practice

This faith manifests in my daily life through my *spiritual practice*. (The reader may wish to refer back to chapter three, where we discussed the usage of this term.) To attempt to describe a practice is to talk about how all this language might have some use as a "skillful means." I can tell you immediately and directly that in response to the question, "What is your practice?" I respond, "Mindfulness." But to the perfectly reasonable questions that follow, my responses are more than likely to be indirect and less than satisfactory. For example, if you were to ask, "What is mindfulness?" I might look back to the last section in answer: "A meditative practice of mindful attention, whose elements are found in many traditions and religions, perhaps best known within our culture in the form of the Buddhist *vipassana* tradition—known among many of its American practitioners as Insight Meditation." Having said those things, I might have allowed you to quickly pigeonhole the information into a known category and allowed you to feel informed; however, unless I were more qualified than I am, so that I might have taught you something of how to actually practice mindfulness as a skillful means, you would not, in reality have learned anything at all of what I speak.

Better to let an experienced teacher speak to this. Jon Kabat-Zinn is not only that, but also the founder and director of the Stress Reduction Clinic at the University of Massachusetts Medical Center, as well as a member of the medical school faculty. Some may remember him from the Bill Moyers PBS series, *Healing and the Mind*. To understand the definition of mindfulness that he offers, we need first to understand that from the perspective of his tradition, the ordinary waking state within which we spend our days is seen as, ". . . being severely limited and limiting, resembling in many respects an extended dream rather than wakefulness. Meditation helps us to wake up from this sleep of automaticity and unconsciousness, thereby making it possible for us to live our lives with access to the full spectrum of our conscious and unconscious possibilities" (1994:3). As a path to such awakening, mindfulness is a process of attending to the present, or as Kabat-Zinn says:

> Mindfulness has been called the heart of Buddhist meditation. Fundamentally, mindfulness is a simple concept. Its power lies in its practice and its applications. Mindfulness means paying attention in a particular way: on purpose, in the present moment, and nonjudgmentally. This kind of attention nurtures greater awareness, clarity, and acceptance of present-moment reality. It wakes us up to the fact that our lives unfold only in moments. If we are not fully present for many of those moments, we may not only miss what is most valuable in our lives, but also fail to realize the richness and the

depth of our possibilities for growth and transformation . . . A diminished awareness of the present moment inevitably creates other problems for us as well through our unconscious and automatic actions and behaviors, often driven by deep-seated fears and insecurities. (1994:4)

As one practices this discipline, there is a frequent experience of "coming to" from daydreaming to find that one's attention has strayed. When this happens, Kornfield says that the skill is to simply and kindly put this little puppy of a mind back on its newspaper. It will stray a thousand times — we bring it back a thousand times.

> Initiation's transforming process is not always outwardly obvious. Some experience it as a slow spiral, a steady and repetitive remaking of inner being. The heart gradually deepens in knowing, compassion and trust through the hundred thousand repeated practices and heartfelt sincerity of a regular spiritual discipline. The Buddha likened this process to the ocean floor which descends little by little to the depths of the sea. (Kornfield, 2000:39)

I have been asked, after discussions similar to the preceding, if I am a Buddhist; and similarly at other times, in other conversations, I have been asked if I am a Christian, a Kabalist, a Hindu, or a follower of the Sufi path. Once again my well-digging history requires me to demur, not because I would deny these traditions — all of which I love and appreciate — but rather because, were I to answer *their* questions honestly, none of their official bodies would wish to ordain me.

One Truth for Both Education and Commerce

Now I would ask the reader to look specifically at what all this might mean in the context of our need to repair our culture and heal the process by which we struggle to educate our children. How might these insights into the effects of the diminished awareness that our culture's pre-analytic vision imposes upon us serve to increase our chances of succeeding in making such repairs? Let us take one more look back at some of the things we have discussed about how the "hidden curriculum" works throughout our culture.

It is becoming increasingly clear that whatever we are willing to do to each other in business we will eventually do to our children in our schools, since as Purpel made clear in the first edition, education cannot be morally neutral, nor can it escape being the socializing instrument of the surrounding culture. Thus the educator's fundamental task in this culture must be to participate in a cultural repair that creates the sort of pre-analytic vision that favors, rather than opposes, an educational environment that honors what our hearts know children need. One criterion for judging our progress toward such an environment would be a Hippocratic injunction that wherever we educate, we must "first do no harm." The moral imperative for meeting this requirement is especially strong in the public schools, where the power of the state is employed to institutionalize children (often against their will), often for one-fifth of their lifespan. Another example of the criteria so freely available from our hearts: Purpel suggested that we always test any process within our schools by asking, "In whose interest is this being done?"

So, if we are to look for points of beginning, perhaps we can learn from some of those places where our culture educates beyond the walls of classrooms. When we do so, we find that the education that takes place by other means, such as the media, is as seldom in the interest of the student as is that in the test-driven classroom. By way of example, consider the ways in which our culture of consumption sustains itself by offering increasingly clever ways to satisfy (and surfeit) fundamental human cravings. Nutritionally it is clear how adaptive (in an evolutionary sense) our taste for salt and fat must have been in early environments where both were scarce and available only with the expenditure of considerable energy. Thus we found that until recently, salt could serve as a form of currency and excessive weight was seen as an accoutrement of wealth. Consider then, how technology and the education provided by the marketing of hamburger chains have used our desire for these items to succeed wildly, at the expense of the public health. By combining the technological capacity to produce vast quantities of once rare nutrients with the psychological understanding of how to manipulate hard-wired tastes, they have profited immensely and, as an incidental side-effect, reversed the socioeconomic meaning of body weight. I suggest an exercise to the reader, to reflect on other ways that our culture uses such things as our inherited traits, social history, and primal fears to strengthen the particular pre-analytic vision that is our prison.

So, how is the work of awareness and self-understanding to make a difference in the face of such coercive power? What is to be done? Jack Kornfield (2000:263) quotes Joanna Macy as saying, "We are going to have to want different things, seek different pleasures, pursue different goals than those that have been driving us and our global economy." While that can easily be seen to apply to the hamburger example, it is less obvious (and thus more dangerous) that we need to learn to see how our pre-analytic vision is driving us to political and economic behavior that benefits the few at the expense of the many, that enriches our own lives as it impoverishes the future of our grandchildren. Those who are benefiting now seldom take kindly to being asked to look with full awareness on the future consequences of their actions—and the "they" here is us! Quite simply, we must learn both to expect more of ourselves and expect less for ourselves, all while learning how to meet those expectations.

Our pre-analytic vision tells us that this is an impossible task, that human nature cannot rise to such a standard. Recall Adam Smith telling us (in chapter two) that humanity cannot successfully operate an economy on any basis other than that of narrow self-interest. Smith was able to reconcile that pessimistic conclusion (in which he took no joy) with his theory of moral sentiments (1966) by means of what may have been the greatest piece of unfounded optimism in Western history, the assumption that if we all pursue our selfish interests, all will be made well, as if ". . . led by an invisible hand" (1994:485).

We have discussed how immensely difficult it is even to conceive of acting outside of our pre-analytic vision, to say nothing of actually doing so. Yet, this is exactly what we must learn to do, and this is precisely the stock-in-trade of wisdom traditions.

What Are We to Do?

As I said at the beginning of this story, my intention in its telling has not been to prescribe for others or to offer a "Cliff Notes" version of these great traditions, but rather to attempt to convey the effect that these wisdom traditions have had upon my own capacity to stop ignoring the voice from my heart. At the same time, I would certainly be happy to know that something in this story might offer to others the chance to feel less of the despair of our present time and to hear more of their own inner voice, or to give it greater range. My faith holds that if more people were to take such an opportunity, the power of the pre-analytic vision within which we slumber would be weakened and we might turn aside from our foolishness before it is too late. It is that fragile possibility that I propose as the only bridge I have found between the inner work of these traditions and the task of cultural repair that confronts us. Looking for a way to help that happen is the only path I see to make the faith to which I have confessed live in this world. In order to help find such a way, I feel compelled to incur the risk of proposing some specific actions for like-minded educators and citizens to undertake. The safer alternatives of suggesting the need for further study or of humbly forswearing giving advice because of my lack of certainty (however appropriate) are choices for a luckier time, one in which generations of time would be available for the resolutions of problems. Because of the issues to which we have given so much attention, I do not believe we have that luxury. I suggest that we had best get to work.

To that end, I suggest another article of faith for the reader's consideration. If we were to have a Gandhiesque paraphrase of Kant's categorical imperative so that it said, "Behave today so that your actions, if typical of humankind, would create the world you claim to want," then we would have the opportunity to begin immediately on our task. We would not have to wait on legislation, or on a new budget, or hold meetings pending the conversion of whoever we consider to be today's Philistines. Because we would be willing to begin those new behaviors without insisting that we have certainty of success beforehand, there would be neither reason to wait another day, nor cause for ceasing while we draw breath.

Here then are some small things that would make a difference and that I know we can do now—they are in the range of rational optimism as I have framed it. I claim to know that we can do these things both because it is the stuff of my daily experience that I see colleagues and clients succeeding at such things and because I am presently struggling (with varying levels of success) to make them happen in the day to day practice of my craft. These are examples of helpful behaviors that we can teach in the practice of any of our roles, whether we are engaged in institutional education, business, parenting, or any other task in which there is a likelihood of modeling for others. Creating such a list for anyone except myself would of course be presumptuous—the reader should consider make a better one of her own:

- First of all, each of us can listen for the voice in his heart and allow it to guide us in our search for a path to wisdom. Attempts at cultural repair by persons fully in the grip of the current pre-analytic vision have produced the tortured history of reform of which we have all seen too much and about which Shah (1998) wrote so well. I believe that the particular path chosen is less an issue that the determination to find a practice that allows one to spend as little as possible of one's remaining life lost in sleep and delusion. If a path is a good one, it will eventually provide to the follower the courage and wisdom needed to act from a personal version of the paraphrased categorical imperative.
- We can model hope rather than despair. Each of us (especially educators) has a responsibility to ourselves and to our fellows, to search for a faith that not only sustains us individually but also brings light rather than darkness to those who learn from us. One such way is to seek a path to Bruteau's "Radical Optimism."
- We can work to understand how our possibilities are truncated by the pre-analytic vision of our culture. As we teach, we can open other minds to, "The prisons we choose to live inside" (Lessing, 1987).
- We can resist the pressure to be too clever at skepticism. We have enough cynics—in fact they are in oversupply. The Western denial of even the possibility of wisdom is a cornerstone of our difficulty. It is within our capacity come to agree with Heschel (1951) that *Man Is Not Alone.*
- Even within the world we have described, we can find work to do that helps rather than hinders each of these points. We can conclude with Korten (1995) that there are some jobs in our culture that should go undone.
- We can find and associate with those who seek wisdom. We can struggle like Salzberg (2002) to find/build a community of faith that honors what we hear from our own hearts. This is not an easy path and the company of others is beyond price.
- As we begin to feel some mastery of these steps, it becomes possible to develop and implement projects in our own day-to-day worlds that rise to the standards such work requires. We can each begin to model some version of the paraphrased categorical imperative so that we, "Behave today so that your actions, if typical of humankind, would create the world you claim to want." The following section is an illustration of a real project that begs to be undertaken in every institutional venue of which I am aware:

Caring for Our Wounded

Practitioners of teaching, nursing, and other professions that are often characterized by their capacity for caring and nurturance are particularly in need of wisdom for survival. We fail our students when we do not teach them this. If we allow them to enter the world assuming that the pre-analytic vision of our culture will sustain them in the face of the tragic world in which they will work, then those who do not have the good fortune to happen upon a path to wisdom for themselves (very difficult in a materialistic world) will be likely to fall victim to despair or cynicism. And, in fact, those of us who have watched the thinning ranks of the foot soldiers we have graduated from schools of education know that the carnage has been awful as these well-intended souls struggled to hang on, to spend at least as long in their practice as they had invested in their training. Unfortunately, many have learned cynicism or despair from their encounter with these "helping professions." Whether they have stayed or are searching for greener fields in the business world, they deserve better from us. In many cases we did not equip them with the wisdom that they needed to survive the world they entered—now it is time for us to make amends by helping to tend their wounds.

Certainly many people and organizations have recognized this problem. There are probably a dozen professional synonyms for "burn out" by now. Our efforts at enrichment for practitioners and remedies for burnout, even if sometimes trivial or ineffective, at least acknowledged the problem and our responsibility for it. But the many varieties of in-service solutions put forward in response have generally fallen victim to budget cuts, been co-opted into test-taking preparation, or missed the mark by being treatments for the stress response symptoms of the underlying problem. What is required is direct action by those willing to acknowledge that the absence of wisdom lies at the core of the problem. Those who decide to give some effort to their own version of the preceding list would find themselves at least better able to mitigate symptoms. Once again, I know that we can:

- Act individually to mentor the wounded, among both students and colleagues.
- Work to make our own curriculum one that helps our students to enter the world better prepared to find hope rather than despair. (We used to be in the Wisdom business, after all.)
- Use our individual influence with those who make policy for grants and budgets, not only to help to get funding for programs that use these ideas, but also to protect the process from being co-opted by our egos, into the games of status that consume so much of our lives.
- Seek new and morally sound ways to serve these ends by utilizing the entrepreneurial capacity of our economy for the creation of wealth.
- Learn how to make successful pragmatic arguments for good things.

And, beyond addressing symptoms, beyond the specifics of this example, those who share these views and these sorts of paths can work to address a fundamental cause of this and many other problems: the dissonance between what is set forth in our Credo and the reality that we allow our culture to enforce. Such people can take the personal risk of affirming their faith and claiming a place for wisdom in those parts of our culture where the causes manifest: in the curriculum, in the deliberations of the Academy, in political discourse, and in the governance of the economy. The best of educators and the best of my business clients each exemplify many of these behaviors already—these are not super-human traits, they are simply human traits that are far too rare because they are malnourished as a result of our culture's spiritual impoverishment.

Every effort needs a place of beginning, such as the preceding lists of small things, and such beginnings need little in the way of funding or grant programs. Each of my lists could be vastly improved by those who know much more than I do about the realities surrounding the specific examples. And, even as they stand now, each is significantly better than doing nothing. Some version of each is a beginning within the capacity of anyone who has read this far.

In Closing

I have spoken of the hope that my heart voices; yet, it also voices an anguish over the proximity of our possible failure as a people, perhaps as a species. If we are to avoid a fall over the precipice to which our lack of awareness has brought us, we can no longer dither with the timid half-measures and equivocations we now employ in our public discourse, with the false hope that our cultural problems will self-repair or just go away. The time is already late. We do not know whether or not it is too late to change, and in either case, the answer to that does not change our duty. The nature of the task that has fallen to our time may be to act with courage in the face of small faith and less optimism. We may be called to use what wisdom we can gather, first to heal our world where we can, and then to be present with compassion where we cannot. Then, if enough choose that path, we shall move one more step toward what we might yet become; if too few choose, it will still be better to have tried. And in either case, even if at the end we are bereft of any cause for optimism, hope need not fail.

5

David E. Purpel

A RESPONSE TO THE CRISIS:
The love of wisdom and the wisdom of love

Preface

In these last two chapters we address the very difficult and vital issues regarding what can be done to alleviate the enormous difficulties in our educational system that we have enumerated. We have argued that the issues involved with our capacity (or lack of it) to respond to these difficulties are at base of a spiritual and moral nature. We also maintain that it is possible to address these issues with a vision that has a significant degree of commonality but does not at all sacrifice the value or necessity of diverse traditions and perspectives. It is therefore incumbent on each of us to test the soundness of this proposition by setting forth our own individual modes of response in the hope that they will not only be helpful but will also stimulate others to add their own individual voices to the project of coping with the crises of our time. In this chapter, I will lay out my ideas on what the nature of our educational problems are and describe what I believe to be the operational context of professional practice. In addition, I will offer my personal moral/spiritual orientation and discuss the matter of "what is to be done" from that perspective.

The Context of Practice

Human Nature

In dealing with the questions of what is possible and what educators can do to respond to our crises, I must necessarily begin with a confession that I take the tragic view of life, that is, I see human endeavors as being fated to involve heroic and virtuous struggles that ultimately end in failure. I resonate with the Sisyphean experience of meaning and dignity deriving from continuous and never-ending engagement in the task of creating a better world in the face of an awareness of its futility. This is based not only on my own perhaps impoverished inner spirit but also on an analysis of the effects of various social movements for reform and political struggles for genuine revolution and transformation. The story of such efforts certainly contains many truly inspiring sagas of courage and determination as well as solid and enduring successes. Yet many of the gains are short-lived and even if some problems are resolved, new even more difficult ones appear. The story of public education in America is surely a case in point, for in spite of the imagination and perseverance of thousands of dedicated and talented educators and the availability of any number of wonderful ideas and programs, the sad reality of the matter is that in general the schools are less creative, less playful, less joyful, and less stimulating than they were ten or fifteen years ago. Our economists seem, in spite of their brilliance, unable either to understand or manage an economy that is cruel and relentless. Welfare programs seem to be counter productive, pesticides turn out to be deadly to humans, and antibiotics produce ever stronger, more dangerous viruses.

I do not see this view as necessarily cynical or despairing because for me it is very strongly tempered by the majesty of human persistence in the teeth of this storm of resistance to our earnest efforts. I joyfully join with those who would damn the torpedoes, light candles, fight the good fight, or who use any other familiar metaphor that celebrates the human impulse to participate in the covenant of creation. Indeed, I scorn the view that pessimism is a justification for passivity and inaction. However, having said that, I need also to confess my parallel antipathy to sentimentality, that is, a consciousness of mindless optimism that is a product of blindness, denial, wishful thinking, and fear. My position is that we must not be daunted by the magnitude of the task of creating a just and joyful community, but we must not add to its difficulty by underestimating what is involved.

The Social and Cultural Context

The task of creating cultural and social transformation is greatly magnified by two powerful, if not embarrassing, realities: (1) in spite of all our crises and fears, the dominant ideology of growth, achievement, success, privilege, individualism, and conquest is extremely alive and well and thrives in most if not all of us; and

(2) there are no broad alternative ideologies that are accessible and compelling to the public that could compete with the dominant ideology. The spirit of free enterprise and the sanctity of the concept of market are triumphant, virtually uncontested (especially with the collapse of the Soviet system and the weakening of the social democratic movements in the West), and venerated not only as ultimate truth but as a thing of beauty. There can be no greater indictment of our entire culture and particularly our entire educational program than this shocking state of affairs—that with all our knowledge and with all our creativity, imagination, and sensibilities, we find ourselves without a serious competitor to a system that is killing us with its popularity. If nothing else, this speaks to an immense failure in imagination but at a deeper level, it represents the triumph of one set of spirits over another. The spirits of individual gain, self-gratification, hedonism, competition, and possessiveness are beating the pants off the spirits of interdependence, peace, joy, and love. Our culture demands ever more products, thrills, innovations, titillations, scandals, sensations, derring-do, outrageousness; it is ever more mean-spirited and vengeful, increasingly paranoid, violent, and destructive.

What is clearly required of us, then, is an accounting of our moral vision, of what constitutes our notion of an ideal society, of a direction and path that we should follow, and a confession of the spirit that guides us on that path. To paraphrase Martin Luther King, we need to be judged not by the texture of our résumés but by the quality of our character, and by the same token, the quality of our educational programs need to be judged not by test scores or the number of rich and famous alumni but by the moral character of the community it has participated in fashioning.

Let us then examine, briefly, something of the moral visions contained in some educational formulations, something of the character of the world we are making and reproducing, and some educational implications of alternative moral visions. A charitable view would be that as a people we are mightily confused; a less charitable interpretation would be that we live a life of industrial strength contradiction verging on hypocrisy, if not madness. In a nation founded on a belief that all people are created equal, we have created a social structure that requires and legitimates inequality; in a culture rooted in a passion for life and a commitment to dignity for all, we have produced a discourse of hierarchy, privilege, and elitism. Tragically, we find ourselves engaged in maintaining and revitalizing a social structure in the form of a social triage in which some flourish, many struggle, and far too many perish. In a civilization energized by a spirit of love and justice, we are captured by a spirit of competition, achievement, success, mastery that pits people against people, group against group, nation against nation, culture against culture. We enjoin each other to love our neighbor, but we are very selective about where we live, never mind the kind of neighbor we choose to tolerate. We read that the poor are blessed and that the meek will inherit the earth, yet we as a culture find ourselves increasingly indignant, impatient, and inconvenienced by the presence and persistence of the homeless and altogether disgusted at those on welfare.

We live in a time of increasing racial tensions and divisiveness, of cultural polarization, escalating violence, of increasing suicide and prostitution among teenagers, of pollution, environmental catastrophes, of enormous alienation, despair, and cynicism. As a culture, it can be said that we have a crisis of faith.

We are rapidly losing our faith in our political system, and our faith in the capacity of science and technology to solve our problems has surely been shaken. We indeed have very serious doubts about every social and cultural institution, including religious and educational ones. In the face of such loss of connection and meaning, much of the culture finds itself mired in the self-indulgence of personal or institutional narcissism or both. There is a growing gap in incomes, a widening gap of trust among racial and ethnic groups, increasing homophobia, xenophobia, and whatever phobia it is that covers fear and loathing of the other. A dismal record indeed for a talented and enterprising people and a shameful state of affairs for a powerful and wealthy nation that claims sacred status, one explicitly founded on the principles of liberty and justice for all.

Professional Limits

The added shame of this situation is that our educational system has contributed to and colluded with much, if not all, of this. Our most powerful and influential leaders call upon education to meet the demands of a cruel economy and a meritocratic culture. The great bulk of formal educational policies and practices reflect and facilitate structured inequality, rationed dignity, rationalized privilege, and self-righteous hierarchy. Moreover, much of the rhetorical justification for this violation of our commitment to a vision of liberty and justice for all comes from the ranks of the school and academy. Perhaps most disturbing of all is the realization that the movers and shakers in government, business, communications, advertising, banking, et al., that is to say those institutions that shape our lives in critical ways, are people who almost surely have had what we have come to accept as a "good education." It is the very people who have brought us to our present plight who are among the brightest, most articulate, most creative, most imaginative, and most reflective people in the land. It would seem that at the very least, we need to re-consider what we mean by a "good education."

Moreover, the professional educational community has largely responded to our crises with characteristic opportunism, timidity, and accommodation, exercising their skills to meet the ever shifting demands of the dominant political forces. What would seem to be required is a pedagogy of moral and spiritual transformation but instead our profession has fashioned a pedagogy of control and standardization focused on technology, competitiveness, and materialism. There is, however, in spite of the overwhelming dreariness and blandness of the present professional educational discourse, some extremely encouraging work that is being done that has great power, hope, imagination, and daring. I have in mind the work being done in what I would call a pedagogy of transformation and meaning. educational ideas directed at the search for social justice and personal meaning. Among the prominent writers in this mode are Henry Giroux, Michael Apple, Svi Shapiro, Nel Noddings, Wlliam Pinar, Ron Miller, C. A. Bowers, Jane Roland Martin, and James Moffett, all of whom address basic issues of cultural and existential meaning as the necessary framework for developing educational policies and practices. It is work, which at least holds out the possibility of challenging the dominant educational discourse of achievement, competition, and standardization and of stimulating the public and profession to reexamine the relationship between our highest aspirations and prevailing notions of schooling.

I want very much to affirm and celebrate this work even as I speak to how its very insights and analyses testify to the limitations of some of our most valued educational traditions and public schooling. What this work does in its affirmation of serious reflection on fundamental issues of justice meaning in a context of their complexity, ambiguity, and perplexity is, among other critically important things, to highlight the problemmatics of detachment, independent thinking, and critical rationality. It must be pointed out that I am lumping together educational orientations that have important differences among them, e.g., the difference in the emphasis put on social, political, and economic concerns as opposed to writers who emphasize personal development and human growth. However, among the very important connections are their commitment to social and cultural transformation and their reliance on critical rationality, personal reflection, openness and respect for varying perspectives, and good faith dialogue.

I certainly would not want to quarrel with these educational approaches, and indeed I am proud to be part of an intellectual tradition and professional community that is deeply committed to them. However, I increasingly find that such an orientation, necessary as it is, is not anywhere near being sufficient to respond to our present set of existential, social, political, economic, moral and spiritual crises. Obviously, these ideas and formulations have failed to make much of a dent in the public sphere and represent only a marginal element of the profession. But, I have serious doubts about the viability of these ideas beyond this sobering reality. The twin roots of this doubt are in the sense of moral outrage that I share with many people at the depth of unnecessary pain and suffering in the world and simultaneously in the absence of moral outrage of so many people. Not only do I affirm the validity of this outrage, I consider it an absolute requisite to serious efforts at cultural and educational transformation. I am also very much aware of the problematics of a pedagogy of moral outrage, not least of which is the psychological reality of the resistance and hostility to it when it is perceived to be guilt inductive. People simply do not want to hear constant messages of disaster, gloom, and suffering and are wont to tune out jeremiads as hysterical if not counter-productive—the perfect defense mechanism. In addition, there is the frustration that comes with the awareness of the depth, enormity, and scope of the problems that engenders helplessness if not despair. Yet it is difficult for me to see in the absence of a passionate commitment to the plight of the suffering how we can seriously address the really vital issues that threaten our existence as a caring people without raising disturbing questions.

I believe it is time to question the broader notion that we can significantly effect social and cultural transformation primarily or even largely through serious study and dialogue. It is more than a little disquieting when we consider the poignant effects of critical rationality on our struggle to find meaning and create a morally sound and spiritually satisfying path to personal fulfillment, cultural richness, and social justice. This process has inevitably confronted us with enormously diverse perspectives, incredibly perplexing dilemmas, extraordinarily complex ideas, and a fathomless set of paradoxes. Because of these realities, many of us have learned to be cautious of generalizations, suspicious of certainty, reverential toward difference, and wary of affirmation. Many of us have learned a great deal about the historical, political, and subjective nature of knowledge and have had to respond with critical and skeptical detachment lest we be seduced by self-serving rhetoric masked as universal truths. We have become so smart that we find it extremely difficult to believe in anything except the contingency of knowledge and the inevitability of conflict. Our critical studies have taken us to spiritual and moral inarticulateness if not silence; our detachment has led us to the emptiness of marginally interested but paralyzed bystanders; and our tolerance has forced us into the slimy swamp of moral relativity.

Part of my skepticism is directed at the whole notion of there being such a thing as an educational enterprise, i.e., the difficulty of the effective reification of education, of separating out certain processes and phenomena from a larger framework of meaning and labeling them as "educational." I have come to believe that such a reductionism serves to blur the intimate relationships among critical cultural, political, and social phenomena and education and to nourish a myth of an objectivity based on technical expertise. Perhaps it is time to tell ourselves that Education is an emperor without clothes and that we need to return to the realms of the fully clothed. It seems rather ludicrous to me to have this vast array of sophisticated, well trained, and creative people called "educators," sitting around in their offices and classrooms with nothing to do except to define and solve "educational problems." Where do these educational problems come from? Do they exist as such, in a conceptual vacuum, outside of any larger context? Educational problems, per se, would seem to be of a secondary (no pun intended) nature; they necessarily arise as a consequence of other issues and concerns, e.g., the efforts to teach literacy emerges from a variety of motivations: to facilitate productivity, to strengthen democracy, for personal empowerment, to name a few.

Indeed one of the prime activities of educators is to determine objectives and goals in an Alice in Wonderland effort to figure out the reasons we're doing what we're doing! To me it is quite extraordinary that we are constantly being asked to state our goals (a process which, incidentally, rarely, if ever, results in changing what we do). If there is uncertainty about our educational goals, then how could we possibly continue to teach what we do? How could such uncertainty arise in the first place? Presumably, if we do not know our goals, then we should stop whatever it is we are doing and restart only when we know what the goals are. Of course, much of the goal-stating effort is largely disingenuous, since politically it usually adds up to a post-hoc justification of what we are already doing. However, beyond the cynicism and ritual, I believe that the impulse to ask the question of educational purpose reveals an unsettling lack of confidence in the validity of what we do and masks a deep and genuine uncertainty of moral direction as well as a suspicion that we are spiritually and morally lost.

Amelioration / Transformation

What is partly reflected in the past few pages is the struggle over what ought to be the proper goal of social and educational change, i.e., the debate over whether we should be striving for amelioration or for transformation. By amelioration, I mean efforts to make changes gradually, step by step, situation by situation, problem by problem. This orientation is rooted in notions of optimistic realism and sensible pragmatism in which changes will necessarily have to be incremental in the confidence that good sense, patience, and perseverance will eventually triumph. There have been, of course, any number of curricular, instructional, and administrative reforms that have been introduced that operate within the basic existing school structure. To be sure, many of these have been salubrious—e.g., public kindergarten classes, the basic elimination of corporal punishment, after-school programs, more course electives, and expanded athletics programs. (It must also be said that many of these gains have been eroded in recent times).

In this setting, I am using the term transformation to indicate much more structural and constitutive changes without regard to the necessity to be concerned with the preservation of what are currently perceived as indispensable components. This is a much more radical perspective in that changes would be based on a number of basic and fundamental cultural and social premises at significant variance from existing ones. For example, we might assume that equality and cooperation ought to be starting points of educational policies instead of meritocracy and competition. If this were to happen it would have very powerful consequences on such relatively uncontested school practices as grading and grouping.

Like many of my colleagues, I am torn between emphasizing transformation or amelioration (they are to be seen as being on a continuum rather than polarized) of one or the other of these approaches. The advantages of amelioration are clear enough—the possibilities of making gradual changes are far greater; the society and the profession are much more oriented toward pragmatism and incrementalism than to radical change; the possibility of achieving important, doable, and practical goals is very attractive to those frustrated by inertia and resistance; and it can improve the day-to-day lives of teachers and students now in the system. The difficulty with amelioration is that it ultimately serves to strengthen and solidify the status quo particularly when the changes are erroneously perceived to be fundamental in nature. This provides only for the appearance of significant change, a process that can generate further possibilities of denial, smugness, and sentimentality.

The difficulties of working for transformation are equally clear for reasons obverse to the advantages of amelioration—there is far greater resistance and fear for fundamental change; there is little realistic possibility that changes of this magnitude can be made in the foreseeable future; and few people have the stomach to engage in causes that seem futile. The value of pursuing transformation to me, however, is that it is just this kind of sweeping change that is required!

A good part of my early career (in teacher education and curriculum development) represented a commitment to an ameliorative approach but in my later years, I have become increasingly disenchanted with the cumulative effects of decades of so-called reforms. Indeed, I have at times been disdainful of the arguments for incremental change for reasons noted above. What I see in the trees of modest changes is the forest of a hidden curriculum that celebrates hierarchy and privilege. However, I am also mindful of the need to support embattled educators, in very difficult circumstances, struggling to provide students with experiences that are more nurturing and meaningful. This is a dilemma that continues to trouble me as well as many other educators who worry about shirking their responsibilities for the current as well as for the longer run. Of course, running through all these issues is the most important concern of all, namely, the value of the particular changes that are being advocated. It is not change by itself that is needed, but rather the changes that resonate with a vision of a just and loving world. Furthermore, we believe that the sources for both the vision and the capacity to pursue that vision reside in the spiritual realm

Spirituality and Me

Starting Points

The task of connecting educational issues to the realms of spirituality and to matters of ultimate concern has been and continues to be a difficult and confounding struggle that has certainly not led me to a resolution but clearly has led me to a source of authority. Some years ago I came to a place in my work when I realized that I would not be able to respond in depth to the question "to what should we be committed?" unless I was willing at some basic level to accept a starting place, a point of departure, a fundamental frame of reference where I could be comfortable; or, to put in more contemporary terms, I wanted to be part of an interpretive community based on religious principles. It was at this point that I truly encountered capital M Mystery for I came to this conclusion in part because I realized that what I was looking for involved a process that gives life to existence, which animates, energizes, and gives direction, or as it is written, that which represents the spirits that reside within our midst. Perhaps this is in part what is meant by the term, spiritual—literally, that which inspires and gives breath to. The first Mystery then has to do with the source of this energizing spirit; although I am prepared to accept, albeit gingerly and hesitantly, the importance and reality of these spirits, I remain among the baffled about what they are, where they come from, how one finds them, and what does one do with them when one does.

The second Mystery for me has to do with the reality that I find myself generally drawn to religious issues, and particularly and increasingly so, to the study of Jewish religious traditions. At first, I saw my interest as part of the way to provide further justification and validation for my work on an educational orientation that focused on equality and social justice and found powerful support for this in such traditions as the writings of the Biblical prophets. However, I quickly realized that what was going on was more than the usual kind of academic scrambling for post hoc rationalization that passes for carefully considered inquiry. I was astonished to find that much of this material was simultaneously familiar and fresh, old and new, accessible and remote. It was as if I was revisiting an important and suspended part of my consciousness even though I do not remember ever being in that state, at least in any systematic, thorough, or direct way. My formal religious training had been minimal, perfunctory, superficial, and banal if not counter-productive and misleading and yet it would seem that my work had been significantly influenced by traditions I had largely ignored and misunderstood. I still cannot fully explain why this would be so. Nor do I entirely comprehend why I am still so strongly drawn to examining Jewish sources but I am and I find myself relying increasingly on them for that which animates and informs my work. My reactions to these materials are varied, if not contradictory—I find much that is affirming and energizing; there is a great deal that I do not accept, much I do not even understand; some that seems directly relevant to my work and much of which seems quite removed from it; some of it troubles me and all of it intrigues me.

Will Herberg points out in his book *Faith in Biblical Theology*, that it is what we remember and what we expect that shapes our quest for faith. According to Herberg, "The act of faith is double: the existential affirmation of a history as one's redemptive history and the existential appropriation of this redemptive history as one's personal background history, and therefore in a real sense the foundation of one's existence" (pp. 40–41).

Accordingly, I seek to ground my work in my hopes as they are informed by what I choose to remember and by what I want to expect. I expect and accept meaningful existence and believe that as educators we must do our work within a larger framework of meaning, that which is of utmost importance to us and constitutes the substance of our very deepest commitments, those which Paul Tillich calls matters of "faith and ultimate concern." Tillich describes faith as:

> . . . the state of being ultimately concerned: the dynamics of faith are the dynamics of man's ultimate concerns. Man . . . is concerned about many things, above all about those which condition his existence, such as food and shelter. Man in contrast to other living beings, has spiritual concerns-cognitive, aesthetic, social, political. Some of them are urgent, often extremely urgent, and each of them as well as the vital concerns can claim ultimacy for a human life or the life of a social group. If it claims ultimacy it demands the total surrender of him who accepts the claim, and it promises total fulfillment even if all other claims have to be subjected to it or rejected in its name. (p. 1)

It certainly makes sense to me that we would be wise to determine our goals, purposes, and strategies within a framework of faith and ultimate concern and it also makes sense that within this frame we are wise to study, reflect, and dialogue. Even granted the validity of this dictum we are still beset with the greatest of all difficulties, that of determining what our faith is and what it is that constitutes matters of ultimate concern. The processes of critical rationality can operate with enormous power both within and without such frames of faith and ultimate concern but by themselves they cannot bring us to affirm a faith or celebrate an ultimate concern. Detached study, reflection, and analysis cannot be at the center of an education for meaning, although they surely can and ought to be among the inevitable and valued partners in the task of naming and acting on our faith. I believe that we are living in a time when there is widespread earnest and heart-felt searching for the other critical partners.

Indeed, it may be that it is the very human desire and impulse to seek faith and ultimate meaning that is itself that other critical partner. The modern condition is one in which we seem to seek rather than express faith and one that requires that we do so in order to pursue hope, and sustain our struggle to create a just and loving community. Franz Rozensweig in describing the rationale for a center of adult Jewish education said that in an earlier time people went from the Torah into life but the present was now a time when people must go "the other way round from life . . . back to the Torah" (p. 152). I find myself going in that very direction.

The modern age is one in which many of us encounter the world not with faith and a sense of ultimate meaning but with skepticism, wariness, and suspicion, and convinced that we are better served by being armed with knowledge and critical rationality. This approach has certainly served many purposes well but it has also exacerbated our alienation and anxiety leading us to be skeptical even about our skeptical armament. Many of us indeed seek the faith and framework of meaning that can enable us to understand the evil that has befallen us and that can help to sustain the impulse to resist if not overcome it and return to traditional and sacred sources like the Torah. However, it is one thing to study sacred traditions and sources of wisdom and quite another thing to be nourished and energized by them. This generates yet another search—the search and struggle for the disposition, accessibility, and openness to faith, and the desire and willingness to be nourished by the sacred.

Abraham Heschel teaches us that we can learn to have faith only when we wonder, for only when we truly wonder will we be able to confront the awesomeness and sublimity of creation. He says in *God in Search of Man:*

> Mankind will not perish from want of information; but only for want of appreciation. The beginning of our happiness lies in the understanding that life without wonder is not worth living. What we lack is not a will to believe but a will to wonder. (Heschel 1955, 46).

It is this wonder that inevitably brings us to confronting the awesomeness of the most fundamental questions of origins, purpose, and destiny—the overwhelming and disturbing mystery of existence. Heschel says that this mystery:

. . . is not a symptom for the unknown but rather a name for meaning which stands in relationship to God . . . Ultimate meaning and ultimate wisdom are not found in the world but in God, and the only way to wisdom is through our relationship to God. That relationship is awe . . . The beginning of awe is wonder, and the beginning of wisdom is awe. . . . Awe enables us to perceive in the world intimations of the divine, to sense in small things the beginning of infinite significance, to sense the ultimate in the common and the simple; to feel in the rush of the passing the stillness of the eternal. (Heschel 1955, 74, 75)

Faith then is not a function of study, not the result of research and analysis, not the culmination of reasoned reflection but rather emerges from wonder, awe, and engagement with the infinite. Heschel is not unaware of the educational implications of such a formulation for education,

. . . Our systems of education stress the importance of enabling the student to exploit the power aspect of reality. To some degree, they try to develop his ability to appreciate beauty. But there is no education for the sublime. We teach the children how to measure, how to weigh! We fail to teach to revere, how to sense wonder and awe . . . , the sense of the sublime, [and] the sign of the inward greatness of the human soul. (Heschel 1955, 36)

It seems that an alternative response to issues of ultimate meaning is to dismiss essentialism as naive, irrelevant, or sentimental, if not stupid and dangerous. I have chosen to speak from the perspective of traditions that assume quite the opposite, namely that these questions are the only ones worth asking and moreover, from the grounding of a tradition that takes commitments very seriously. As Rabbi Heschel has said,

Socrates taught us that a life without thinking is not worth living. Now, thinking is a noble effort, but the finest thinking may end in futility . . . The Bible taught us that life without commitment is not worth living; that thinking without roots will bear flowers but no fruit. . . . (1955, 216)

I affirm traditions that not only recognize that as humans we are fated to create our world but believe that above all we are called upon to create a world resonant with divine intention—a world of peace, justice, love, community, and joy for all. These are traditions that accept as givens the potentials of human abilities as well as the limits of human fallibilities; they posit our capacity to be generous as well as to be selfish; to be angelic as well as demonic; compassionate as well as cruel; wise as well as foolish. Such traditions revere knowledge but only as it is tempered with the wisdom that advances justice and mercy; a perspective that acknowledges the enormity of the task but dismisses human despair as sinful; and one that represents a consciousness of unmitigated outrage in the wake of cruelty and injustice but always in the faith that witness, confession, and healing offer the possibilities of transcendence and redemption. What is absolutely crucial to redemption is human responsibility and human agency since these traditions require that we act as God's agents, dedicated and committed to constructing and sustaining intentional communities based on joy, love, peace, and justice.

As educators, therefore, we should not be committed merely to education, we should instead be more deeply committed to human dignity; we should not dedicate ourselves to higher learning but to a high standard of living for all; our responsibilities are not to select the best students but to eradicate privilege; our commitment must not be to the market economy but to the Golden Rule. It is idolatrous to commit oneself primarily to the preservation of History, Biology, or any other discipline or field when there is injustice, inequality, and hatred in the land. We need not be concerned with a decline in test scores; we need to be outraged and obsessed with an increase in unnecessary human suffering. As educators we must not offer justice, joy, and love as rewards or luxuries but affirm them as requirements for a life of meaning. Personal dignity is not something to be rationed and manipulated but cherished as something inherent and inviolable.

Another Look at the Prophetic Tradition

In the first edition, I put considerable emphasis on the prophetic tradition in setting forth my credo and educational framework. Although I remain steadfast in my reverence and awe of the Biblical Prophets and the tradition they have engendered, I have some further concerns about the limitations of employing this tradition as a metaphor for responding to our present conditions. In an era when horrible crimes are committed in the name of God and when some who claim to speak in a prophetic voice speak a discourse of vengeance and holy war, one becomes all too aware of the excesses of self-righteousness and the terrible dangers of dogmatism. The reality is that we must be even more mindful of our responsibility to inform our spiritual and moral commitments with critical judgment in order to help distinguish the "true" from the "false" prophets. This is no small task but a crucial one, yet we are not without resources for dealing with it. We have available to us extraordinary traditions of careful reflection, intellectual rigor, and rational modes of analysis that are of immense importance in sorting out the claims and counter-claims of competing world views. We must use our minds as well as our hearts—we can think as well as feel—and we can be critical as well as affirming.

The issue of how true prophets were to be distinguished from false prophets, has been a problem that has plagued centuries of Jewish history. This problem took on a very particular meaning when the Second Temple was destroyed in the first century C.E. marking the end of a system of Jewish religious practices rooted in Temple ritual and sacrifice. This system was eventually replaced by what has come to be called rabbinic Judaism. This latter tradition puts far greater reliance on human interpretation of sacred texts than on divine revelation for guidance and direction. Indeed, The Sages (i.e., the highly revered and influential rabbis of the time) proclaimed the end of prophecy and ruled that insight into God's will hereafter would be derived by rigorous and devoted study of the sacred texts. Such study was to be thorough, detailed, and critical. The expectation is that the findings of the studies are to be subjected to ongoing discussion and that they will usually and inevitably be ambiguous and/or tentative, subject to continuing study and deliberation. However, these discussions and findings are to be based on and justified by principles and criteria laid out in sacred scripture.

Michael Walzer, in a recent book on Jewish political thought, has offered a very helpful analysis into the nature of Biblical Prophecy as well as providing important insights into the possibilities and limitations to their applicability to contemporary times.

> Prophets are not agitators in the modern sense. They don't aim to create a political or social movement; they make no effort to organize their audience. . . . On the other hand, they are also unlike modern social critics, who sit in their studies writing books and magazine articles and can hardly be imagined speaking in the streets. The prophets are religious preachers, something like contemporary revivalists, and although they criticize the whole of society and hope for its moral transformation, their precise demand is for individual teshuvah—"repentance"; the literal meaning is a "turning back" to the law of the covenant. (p. 217)

Walzer interprets the prophets as people without a particular political program but who, instead, angrily demanded that the rich and powerful repent their failure to achieve justice and to revere God. He further points out that, in their outrage at these gross violations of the covenant, they invoke a God who is destined to inflict terrible collective punishment on the community unless the rich and powerful reaffirm their obligations to God and the powerless:

> None of the prophets takes aim at the political or social hierarchy, only at the individual men and women who occupy its high places; there is no prophetic program for a democratic program and politics, or a classless society. All that the prophets demand—but how radical they make it sound!—is that the rich stop trampling the poor and that the powerful . . . act forcefully to protect the weak (p. 218). Even if idolatry could be the sin of the whole people, great and small alike, oppression can't be— there are always guiltless victims, oppressed men and women . . . the prophets speak with enormous courage on behalf of the oppressed against the powers-that-be.

Walzer goes on to make a crucial distinction between the spirituality of Biblical Prophecy and the wisdom of Rabbinic Judaism:

> Kings are challenged by prophets . . . and counseled by wise men. Wisdom is prudent, politic, worldly, and human; prophecy is radical, impolitic, utopian, and divine. Wisdom is at home in the royal court, prophecy in the desert and then in the streets and gates of the city and the temple courtyards. Rabbinic Judaism in some sense escapes this tension with its claim to be the joint heir of the wise and the prophets. (p. 202)

> The king's counselors, known by their worldly wisdom rather than their divine calling, give their advice about this or that policy matter, they no doubt raise . . . questions about trustworthiness . . . but what they explicitly invite is a debate about the

advice itself: Is this really what prudence requires in our present circumstances? The prophet, by contrast, does not invite a debate of that sort. Indeed, if they have actually been sent by God, there is no room for any debate at all. The only way to challenge them is to call their credentials into question, not the content of their prophecies. . . . But the sages [the early highly esteemed founders of Rabbinic Judaism] call themselves wise and make room for arguments about both prudence and principle. And they do everything they can to neutralize the disruptive force of prophecy. They are as bound as the prophets were to God's word, but they are its interpreters now, not its messengers. (pp. 204–205)

I am very much intrigued by this model of praxis, i.e., a dialectical process of dealing with specific and concrete issues by integrating a divinely derived ethical system with rigor, shrewdness, and common sense. In a very striking way it resembles the educational model that is at the heart of the Critical Pedagogy movement with at least one major exception. Rabbinic Judaism does in fact "interrogate" current practices for their relevance justice, but unlike Critical Pedagogy, grounds its approach in a profound commitment to achieve what God asks of us.

The mode of rabbinic study that undergirds this process is one that could serve the schools very well—one that emphasizes serious study, reflection, and critical interaction; and is one that accepts uncertainty and ambiguity as constituent to the human condition. It strikes me as eminently suited to an educational system that is serious about addressing our moral dilemmas in a profound but realistic manner and in way that honors the power of the intellect to deepen our spiritual commitments. It is a model that applies universal commitments to the realities of changing contexts and events and one that is alert to the limitations of both ideological dogmatism and moral relativism.

"The Love of Wisdom and the Wisdom of Love"

I am currently engaged in reading and studying the work of the twentieth century French-Jewish philosopher and Talmudic scholar Emmanuel Levinas. This has been no easy task for me because I find much of his work difficult to fully understand and some of it downright impenetrable. However, I have been helped e[n]ormously by reading several secondary sources, engaging in group discussion, a[nd] the insights of colleagues. I believe that as a result of this process, I have a g[reater] sense of the outlines of his orientation, which is rooted in his lifelong w[ork] studying and teaching both philosophy and Talmudic law.

My understanding is that Levinas posits a universe in which "Justice [precedes] Ontology," one guided by transcendent love and a world where each of us has a di[-]vinely mandated a priori responsibility for the well being of each person we encounter. This responsibility is not to be considered as a reciprocal one but as a divine command directed at every individual regardless of the responses of others. The responsibility is totally to the other, not as part of a social contract or for self-serving purposes but only as an aspect of God's intentions for human destiny. This process is to operate on a person-to-person, moment-to-moment basis, regardless of the historical, social and political contexts. We are simply called upon *to be and act* as our brothers' and sisters' keepers.

Levinas goes on to say that such an arrangement will inevitably lead to broader concerns about the more general conditions of fairness and equity, i.e., social justice. The process of developing a system of social justice within the context of a culture of personal and immediate responsibility is a complex one requiring serious reflection, rigorous thought, and sensitive judgment. This process is what Levinas sees as the purpose and function of philosophy in which learned and committed people would sort out the difficulties and intricacies of providing justice within the realities of the tangled complications of everyday life. In this way philosophy, as the "love of wisdom," becomes the process we use to honor and make real our affirmation of the "wisdom of love." I regard this approach as one that integrates the ideals of unconditional love and universal justice as well as one that seeks to unite mind and spirit.

This very sketchy and vague description does not begin to give the complexity and sophistication of Levinas's work and I know that I have much to learn about it before I can fully figure out its implications for educational matters. However, even in my preliminary study, I find his approach of blending the traditions of a tradition of transcendent spirituality, Talmudic study, and Western philosophy with a passionate commitment to the creation of a just and loving world to be personally exciting and enabling. I continue to struggle with the intricacies of his writings with the hope of gaining greater insight into his teachings. Even though these intellectual barriers are serious and important, my greater concern is my ability to sustain the kind of profound hope and faith that Levinas's work represents. For I believe our greatest challenges do not lie in the difficulties of understanding but in the challenges of believing.

Implications for Practice

The Public Schools and Social Transformation

Is this an oxymoron or a cherished vision? A delusional fantasy or the stuff of dreams? Is it a useful way of distracting us from the necessity of deeper structural change or the conviction of the inevitable triumph of good sense? Much has been written and much has been expected of the possibilities of public education and of course, much has been written on how the public schools act not as agents of liberation and enlightenment but as engines of the dominant classes.

Perhaps it would be useful to pause on the term "transformation" and examine it as a neutral rather than a polemical term, i.e., surely there are all kinds of possible transformations, some of which we may like and some we may not. The common schools of the nineteenth century endeavored with a great deal of success to transform a group of largely rural, multicultural, multilingual regions into a unified, industrial, and WASP nation. The schools of today are striving to transform us in such a way that we can accommodate to a consumerist culture and multinational economy. It must be remembered that public schools are bureaucratic agencies of the state, which are required by law to follow the policies of publicly elected officials who have total fiscal control of the schools. If there are to be transformative functions assigned to the schools, the assignments will be made by those in power, i.e., by the established dominant interests. In addition, we must also confront the reality of an entrenched professional bureaucracy which largely works for self-serving inertia and stasis. Although there is an honorable and modest history of the profession calling for genuine social and cultural transformation, it is a story of very little impact. At the same time it must be said that the profession has been able to make a great many technical changes (e.g., in instruction, curriculum, and assessment), but even these are usually absorbed into the basic schooling frameworks set by the dominant power structures.

However, what I believe is meant by transformation in the context of this book has to do with a fundamental change in moral and spiritual consciousness in which we reject the excesses of individualism, materialism, competitiveness, and acquisitiveness. The kind of transformation that is required is one that energizes us to pursue personal meaning, social justice, world peace, and ecological harmony. The difficulty is that those who favor this kind of transformation do not have the political clout to direct the energies of our social and cultural institutions and hence it is quite naive to expect that the public schools can be a primary source of such a transformation. After all, public school educators are under quite strong political, professional, and community controls that work to put enormous pressure certainly not for moral and spiritual transformation but on the intensification of our present consciousness. Most teachers are overworked and underpaid; and most come out of a tradition that stresses professionalism rather than social reform.

Schools are not there to thwart the will of those in power so if we want to change society it is simply neither fair nor wise to ask the schools to be in the vanguard. This means that educators who want to work for transformation cannot limit themselves to schools, community colleges, universities and the like but need to be involved with other and larger cultural movements. What we will have to do is work harder to create the cultural and social conditions that will enable the public schools to do their part in changing consciousness. It would also indicate that we need to focus on social and cultural transformation rather than on educational transformation, an even more fanciful possibility.

This seems fanciful to me because it is poignantly if not tragically clear that much of our culture is a long way from acknowledging its responsibility for such hideous phenomena as slavery, poverty, war, racism, sexism, inequality, and hunger. This refusal to take responsibility and hence to grieve and mourn for the pain we as a community have inflicted represents to me the limitations of an education grounded primarily in critical rationality, study, and the exchange and analysis of information. Indeed, many of our most learned and reflective commentators have used their vast store of knowledge, insight, and information to celebrate a smug and intoxicated triumphalism of capitalism, consumerism, and merit-ocracy, American-style. It is obviously impossible to grieve if there is no sense of significant loss, or even more strikingly, if there is a sense of significant gain! In-stead of compassion for the suffering, we have learned to blame the victims or to make them invisible; many curse rather than bless the poor; and rather than seeing others as God's children, many of us see human beings through the lens of poten-tial customer or expendable worker. The dominant culture does not celebrate jus-tice but competition, does not value unconditional love but grooves on condi-tional rewards; its rituals are not of communal solidarity but of partisan triumphs, and its energies are not rooted in a divine impulse to seek oneness but in a frantic spirit of greed and acquisitiveness.

What I believe is required for genuine transformation is an education that em-phasizes the processes that I have been discussing, namely, awe, faith, the struggle for ultimate meaning, commitment, moral outrage, and grief. In the present po-litical and cultural realities, however, these processes cannot be a significant part of the public school experience, largely because they go counter to both public and professional expectations of the role of these schools. For the most part, par-ents want their children to succeed and look to the schools to provide them with the wherewithal to gain an edge in the struggle for privilege and advantage. Aca-demics, for the most part, want to preserve their disciplines and areas of study while school administrators are preoccupied with maintaining goodwill and stability. Moreover, the public schools are politically positioned to be as accom-modating and acutely sensitive to community pressures as possible, effectively making them hostage to the demands of zealous and determined groups. The possibility of introducing, on a widespread basis, serious spiritual and moral con-sciousness or even dialogue to educational policy and practice is extremely re-mote, given the present cultural sensitivities and political realities. The cliché that the public schools try to be all things to all people and consequently fail to fully satisfy anyone is basically true and must be accepted as a consequence of our po-litical and social structures.

The daring, intriguing, and imaginative ideas of James Moffett and Nel Nod-dings are instructive to this issue. Moffett basically attacks our culture as bankrupt and our schools as perpetuating a ruinous consciousness and argues forcefully and courageously that only an education that is primarily and radically directed at per-sonal development through various spiritual disciplines can save us from ourselves. He makes a very compelling argument for this approach and I believe with many others it merits serious public and professional dialogue. However, as attractive and creative as these ideas are, I would have to say sadly and ruefully that there is virtually no possibility that they will see very much of the light of day in the fore-seeable future of public school practice. They are far too threatening to the domi-nant thrust of those who dominate public spaces.

The ideas of Nel Noddings on teaching children to wrestle with the enduring and complex issues of fundamental belief are also quite daring for public school, al-though much less radical than those of James Moffett. Noddings urges schools to provide safe and supportive opportunities to study and discuss such ideas as theodicy, immortality, the existence of God, and the nature of evil, surely a sensible and valid idea. Her plan is not, however, to make such studies the focus of the curriculum but to introduce them as relevant spin-offs and dimensions of the traditional discipline-based curriculum (e.g., math, science, history, English, foreign language). She advocates that teachers commit themselves to teaching for understanding of varying beliefs; to an attitude of "pedagogical neutrality"; and to an approach that allows them to take a position but insists that they acknowledge and recognize differing views. All in all, I see this as a very prudent and pragmatic way for the schools to deal with such vital issues but the relative cautiousness and lines of demarcation of her proposals only emphasize the limited range of public school possibilities. It is not an approach that is designed to transform the culture or galvanize spiritual struggle, moral outrage, awe, and passionate commitment but one that hopes to stimulate students to study and reflect on the fundamental questions of existence within the traditional framework of the schools as they are. And yet even such sensible and modest proposals are, within our present context, relatively controversial and radical with little likelihood of gaining broad support in the mainstream of educational practice. If schools are, at best, reluctant to provide for serious discussion of the most important questions of human existence, then how can we expect them to be a prime mover in the struggle for cultural and social transformation? We mustn't and shouldn't.

What Can Be Done?

Accepting the educational limitations of critical rationality for changing consciousness and the political liabilities of the public schools does not in any way mean that educators are irrelevant and marginal to the struggle for a just and loving world. It does mean that we have to re-examine the claims that we have made for enlightenment education and the public schools in the context of a commitment to social and cultural transformation. It does not mean that we should accept the anti-intellectualism that denies the undeniable and absolutely essential possibilities for liberation and inspiration that can and does emerge from study, dialogue, and analysis. It does mean that we need to seek other sources for the energy, wisdom, and courage to sustain the struggle for meaning. It does not mean that we should cede and surrender the public schools to the forces of either blandness or zealotry; nor does it mean that we should not continue to engage in the public and professional struggle for a humane and liberating education. It does mean that we must give up the falsely reassuring and naive way in which we equate democratic education with public schooling.

It does mean that we as educators may have to give up some of our precious programs and pet solutions, or at least be more modest about their possibilities. There is nothing particularly sacred about whole language learning or experiential learning, nothing especially ultimate involved per se in the teaching of poetry or going on field trips or even in journaling. Indeed, it is possible to turn the teaching of imagination and critical thinking into sacrilegious acts in which people use their newly augmented imagination and criticality to make a buck at the expense of others, to exploit the environment, to find tax loopholes, or to find ways to encourage teen-agers to smoke. The use of portfolios may stimulate imagination, it is surely more sophisticated than conventional, reductionist assessment, and it no doubt will afford more opportunities for advancement to more people. At the same time, portfolios have, can, and will be used to facilitate and enhance elitism, privilege, and hierarchy. On the other hand, however dubious we may be of the value of particular educational techniques, there is something clearly sacred and very special involved in promoting human dignity and social justice and to do so as educators can transform us from technicians to prophets.

Indeed, our deepest commitments should be the same as for all other people—they cannot, should not, must not be anything less than those contained in our culture's highest aspirations and most cherished dreams. Our differences with other groups lie not in the substance and nature of our commitments but only in where and how we act on them. The struggle for creating a community of peace, love, joy, and justice must go on in every sphere, including, of course and perhaps especially in educational institutions. We are not primarily educators, we are first of all God's agents, active partners in the covenant to create a community of peace, justice, love, and joy who, parenthetically, have decided to exercise our responsibilities to this project in places called schools and universities. Educators are called upon to pursue justice, to choose life, to cherish freedom for all, and to love their neighbors as themselves, maybe more but certainly not less than anyone else. Our profession will not be ennobled by feeding the engines of material growth, personal success, intellectual mastery, or national supremacy; it is ennobled by its devotion to spiritual development, individual dignity, moral sensitivity, and universal peace.

My view is that if and when public school educators commit themselves to the task of participating in the continuing responsibility to create a just and loving world, the nature of their work would change dramatically and profoundly even within the context of severe restriction. It is possible to do at least some of what Nel Noddings suggests, that is to engage students in serious dialogue on profound issues within the existing curriculum. It is possible to do what Jane Roland Martin suggests and that is to create a more nourishing and loving classroom environment where students are affirmed as they thoughtfully probe their world. It is also possible to add some of the opportunities for spiritual growth that James Moffett suggests introducing into existing classrooms. The suggestions that William Pinar makes about the importance of aesthetic opportunities for students to reflect on their inner lives and those of Henry Giroux that students and teachers critically examine the contradictions of their lived experiences are extremely important and doable possibilities. None of these orientations may become central to the schools but that doesn't mean that they can't have some impact in some however modest way.

This is an era of increasing cynicism, despair, and helplessness and a time when many suggest that the best we can do is either ride out the storm or reduce the damage as much as possible. Still others say that the apocalypse is now and that we should abandon ship and/or learn to tread water. I take a different view, namely, that we should renew our commitment to creating a world of peace, love, justice, and joy with greater determination, passion, and vigor precisely because these are such desperate times. It is surely proper to count our blessings and to affirm our vision at times of genuine cultural and social advancement but we have an even greater responsibility to remind the community of its covenant in times of danger. This is a time when we must vigorously and passionately counteract the cynicism and despair, which only deepens and extends the danger. The times call not for capitulation or curtailment of our commitments but an affirmation, as Herberg suggests, of what we remember and what we expect. We ought to remember the enormous amount of unnecessary human suffering and we ought to remember our vows to redeem that suffering with the creation of a better world. We must expect that this requires a great deal of human agency, determination, and will, and we must have faith that these efforts will ultimately succeed. And we must always remember the magnificent acts of courage and sacrifice that millions have offered in the struggle for a just and loving world.

Let us as educators, citizens, and human beings have faith in our ultimate commitment to the creation of a just and loving community. Easy to say, hard to do. Unless we take into account our amazing human capacities and that mysterious spirit that is the source of that faith that energizes and inspires them. Each of us must search for the traditions and community of meaning that provide, protect, and enrich that source. It is in these traditions and communities that we can find the authority for our moral outrage and the energy to sustain the struggle to preserve the hope that is required to meet our responsibilities. Responsibility without a moral and spiritual framework becomes psychological guilt, the kind of meaningless and unrooted dis-ease that cripples people into deafness if not hostility to human suffering. The difficulty in recognizing, enduring, and responding to moral outrageousness is, I believe, related to spiritual alienation, i.e., the result of a failure to affirm. The reality is that our vocation needs more help in the task to create a just and loving community for all than what good intentions, critical rationality, and tolerance can provide. We and our students need to have the faith that there are such additional resources available in that realm called the spirit.

It is clear to me that the public schools are sharply limited in their capacity to be a major force in such a transformational process but whatever possibilities exist should be energetically pursued. It is also clear to me that educators need to have the courage to accept deeply cherished notions of the traditions of liberal education without in any way denying their necessity. Educators need, therefore, to be at once more modest and more bold; modest in their expectations of what public schools and critical rationality can do and bold in their hopes for the possibilities of awe, faith, confession, and spirit.

Such an enterprise, I believe, requires a commitment to a spiritually grounded moral vision. In addition, it requires the kind of prudence, patience, and tolerance, and wisdom that emergences from long experience and careful reflection as represented and expressed in the Rabbinic tradition. This tradition is deeply grounded in Jewish morality and spirituality and at the same time recognizes the importance of making decisions in the context of the particularities of time and place. Moreover, it accepts, as a given, the immense difficulty and danger of finding certainty. Hence, its strong emphasis on continuous intense study and dialogue, taking pains to validate both rendered decisions and dissents to them. This path avoids the inherent danger of ameliorative efforts of undermining basic moral and spiritual commitments as well as reducing the latent dangers in transformative movements of zealotry and dogmatism.

I offer this model as my response to the need for middle-run strategies that seek to ground educational policies and practices in a powerful spiritual and moral vision as informed by the exigencies of history and circumstance. It is definitely *not* a model for temporizing, rationalization, and denial for its nonnegotiable premise is to act in a way totally resonant with the divine imperative to seek justice and meaning. For me, it means a lifetime commitment to reflection, dialogue, and action—never relenting in one's dedication to the vision and always responding to fresh and critical thought, with, as Sharon Welsh says, "absolute conviction and infinite suspicion." It also requires the faith and courage necessary to defend the inevitability of frustration, resistance, and failure. However, it is a path that has been and can be taken and if educators opt for that path they will surely enrich their lives as well as those of their students.

What Must Be Done

This perspective on the possibilities of public education does not, of course, sufficiently address those critical problems that cannot wait for careful deliberation and patient forbearance, i.e., those that threaten our very existence. The potential horrors of the use of weapons of mass destruction and environmental calamities go beyond the intense and widespread suffering that would ensue but extend to the limits of the viability of life itself. We are thus required to revisit the haunting questions of how and if we can prevent ourselves from the kind of irrationality and stupidity that can lead to self-destruction. In other words, how can we come to decide to move single-mindedly in the direction of a loving and just society for all people?

Here, I find myself inspired and moved by a spirituality that dares to offer a "solution" to this persistent and mystifying predilection (sin) of being obsessed with the immediate and with what is self-serving at the expense of the well-being of others. It is the spirituality that speaks to me through the faith, eloquence, and passion of figures like Abraham Heschel and Emmanuel Levitas. What they offer us is the spirit that enables us to reaffirm our commitment to the values that can transcend our pettiness, jealousies, fears, and hostility, namely that of the extraordinary notions that are encapsulated in the concept of universal justice and unconditional love. That such notions have emerged from human consciousness and thrived in human history is a genuine miracle as they fly in the face of the theory of Social Darwinism.

Certainly, the ideals of justice and love have routinely been ridiculed, dismissed, and trivialized but, nonetheless, they persists in our consciousness as a vision of perfection. And indeed, definition and limits of these concepts are hardly clear and consensual but I find the following explanations of *agape*, one of several conceptions of unconditional love, to be very helpful in the quest for clarity of this vision:

> In the fullest sense, *agape* is God's love. It is generous love, not appetitive in the sense that there is need to satisfy that in oneself which is incomplete, not stimulated by or dependent upon that which is loved. It is indifferent to value, seeking to confer good, rather than to obtain it. It is therefore spontaneous and creative, and it is rooted in abundance rather in poverty. (Daly 1973, 210)

This is not the place to argue the difference between justice and love except to state my own belief that they are deeply intertwined and complementary with each other. I believe that the principles and policies of the United Nations' Universal Declaration of Human Rights are a powerful example of how justice and love are infused with each other. This is a statement that was approved unanimously by the U.N. General Assembly and which all members of the United Nations are obliged to uphold. This document is grounded in the belief that *all* humans are entitled to freedom, dignity, and justice. It goes on to spell out the political, social, and economic implications of these basic commitments. Its preamble states very boldly:

> *Whereas* recognition of the inherent dignity and of the equal and inalienable rights of all members of the human family is the foundation of freedom, justice, and peace in the world. . . . Every individual and every organ of society, keeping the declaration in mind, shall strive by teaching and education to promote respect for these rights and freedoms and by progressive measures, national and international to secure their universal and effective recognition and observance.

Although this document was developed by a secular and political institution, I believe that it is a divinely inspired universal commitment to create a world permeated with love for all people. It is also clear to me that this commitment can be expressed in a variety of modes and discourses and therefore it is for each of us to find the language that best represents this powerful, redemptive, and, I believe, miraculous vision. When we make this vision real, we will have overcome the unnecessary human pain and suffering that are the consequences of depraved human agency—poverty, hunger, inequality, pollution, and the like. It is a spiritual flame that illumines this path and spiritual energy that can sustain us to hasten the journey to a world of peace, justice, joy, and love for all.

Humility, Despair, and Hope

I certainly have the faith that a commitment to universal justice and love is the path to our salvation. However, I have to confess to a wavering faith In our capacity to make these commitments real and yearn to share in the awesome and thrilling faith that people such as Heschel and Levinas represent. I also confess to a sense of humility in the face of such awesome responsibilities even as I recognize the terrifying dangers of despair. It is, therefore, important to explore the line between humility and despair, for it is one thing to be realistic and honest about our capacities and another thing to surrender to a consciousness of determinism and fatalism. The humility I speak to is not about modesty or self-deference but to the acknowledgment of the mystery and awesomeness of the human condition as well as our present social, cultural, and personal crises. I have concluded that there is an inverse relationship between the significance of a problem and its openness to solution. Put more baldly, I often muse to myself the notion that although problems surely can and should be ameliorated, suffering and pain reduced, justice and equity increased, peace furthered, violence lessened, meaning strengthened, our most significant problems cannot be "solved." To accomplish even such limited gains is exalting and exhilarating for as the Talmud teaches, "It is not for us to finish the task but neither are we free to take no part in it."

We also know that often we are not able to achieve even modest gains and even more disheartening we sometimes make things worse. How then are we able to sustain our efforts in the face of such obstacles? How do we have the energy to maintain a struggle that promises only modest advances at best and more likely ultimate failure? My response, alas, is a cliché but an enduring one, and that is we must continue to have faith and trust. But faith and trust in what, and on what basis can we sustain that faith? The best I can say is that the persistent search for meaning provides a powerful enough reason to be faithful. My impression after a cursory examination of faith traditions is that they all involve a commitment to human compassion and social justice, although obviously the source of such faith varies enormously across cultural and religious communities. For many, there is a deep faith in the human process of settling conflicts rationally and cooperatively. For others, it is a spiritual faith that speaks to the oneness of all life. In many of us, faith is fleeting at best and its source murky and unreliable. Although, for example, I gain enormous strength from the passion and moral commitments of the prophets, I am still not able to share in their unshakable faith in the revealed word. Each of us, therefore, must struggle to find a mode of expressing the kind of faith that can sustain us in the tragedy of our so far unfulfilled efforts to create a just and loving society for all.

Cornel West as a believing Christian and a philosopher/theologian/social theorist offers, as one example, a powerful framework for addressing this dilemma. In his distinction between "penultimate and ultimate salvation," he accepts a tragic view of the world in which the struggles for peace, justice, and love are destined to fail, but those who nonetheless maintain the struggle receive penultimate salvation as genuine, however tragic, heroes. According to West, such people derive their strength and energy in this extraordinarily frustrating task from their faith in ultimate salvation, that is, through Christian redemption. Those of us who do not share but admire this particular consciousness can only continue our search for that power that can and does sustain and guide us as we struggle with our moral ambivalences and conflicts. Humanity's greatest achievements would seem to be its persistence in its aspiration for goodness in the face of the incredible pressures for mere survival and self-enhancement.

My position can be summarized as follows: we continue to live a life of danger to our basic moral project of creating a community of peace, love, justice, and joy, but the task is further seriously complicated in a time of sociopolitical triumphalism with its concomitant sterility of competing alternatives. I affiliate myself with those who have faith that inevitably historical forces and human genius will once again combine to produce fresh and liberating critiques as well as compelling and energizing alternatives. It is a faith that wavers, however, and is very much in need of support and reassurance that the prime task in this moment is to work to develop the conditions necessary for the restoration of the hope and energy out of which new vitality and imagination will emerge. (My own guess is that these "new ideas" will be a restatement of some traditional ones, but so be it.)

It is in this sense that we face a spiritual more than an intellectual crisis, i.e., a loss of hope, a failure of nerve, a pessimism and despair that sap the will and only inexorably worsen the problem. This is surely not to say that we do not also face intellectual barriers, but only to posit that the ability to overcome them requires spiritual strength, i.e., the power that comes from internal energy, hope, and animation. The kind of hope and faith I am referring to is not to be confused with romanticism or even optimism; indeed it is what we need in the face of the empirical necessity to reject optimism. In other words, we must face the problem of how to proceed when we know we should but are not clear on direction and pretty sure that if we did know where we should be headed, we wouldn't be able to get there. This is a time when our knowledge tells us that the battle appears to be lost, when it seems senseless to continue, and when, alas, optimism is a delusion. In such despairing times what is urgently required is the kind of hope and energy that is so often powerfully exemplified in our religious traditions. Miraculously enough, such faith seems to have thrived in other times of complacency, if not desperation. I believe that it is our present task to keep this miraculous tradition alive.

My own faith is rooted in the Jewish commitment to social justice and a life of meaning and in the rabbinic and prophetic tradition that emphasizes a continuous collaboration between humanity and God in which both humans and God are free but interdependent and in which people are responsible for fulfilling a divine destiny. This is not an untroubled faith as it needs to be said that, as much as I would like to do otherwise, I still find it difficult to accept the reality of a personal and accessible God figure. However, Harvey Cox has helped me in this regard by suggesting what has become a liberating formulation for me:

> "God [is]" whatever it is within the vast spectacle of cosmic evolution which inspires and supports the endless struggle for liberation, not just from tyranny but from all bondages. "God" is that power which despite all setbacks never admits to final defeat. (Cox, 1973)

With that concept of God in mind, let me close with yet another quote from a theologian, this time the eminent Jewish scholar, Jacob Neusner. Neusner has translated and written a commentary on a book from the Talmud usually titled *Sayings of Our Fathers,* but which Neusner translates as Torah from Our Sages. In a section discussing the insights of Rabbi Hillel (who died a martyr's death in the 1st century B.C.E.), Neusner points to issues of hope as he examines Hillel's insistence that over time "God corrects the imbalances of life—pays back the evil and rewards the good." Although Neusner readily admits that this is hardly a description of reality, he goes on to say:

> We, for our part, must preserve that same hope for justice, even in the face of despair. We have to believe, despite the world, that God cares. . . . But part of the meaning of having faith in God believes there is justice when we see injustice, believing there is meaning when we face what seems an empty accident. Ours is not a time for complex explanation. We cannot appeal to how things come out right in the end. We have been through too much. Ours is an age that demands simple faith—or no faith at all. All the standard explanations have proved empty. But Hillel's also was an age that gave no more evidence than it does now that God rules with justice. Yet Hillel said it, and so must we: against it all, despite it all. There is no alternative. (Neusner 1994)

BIBLIOGRAPHY

Ackermann, Robert J. 1985. *Religion as Critique*. Amherst, Mass.: University of Massachusetts Press.

Aronowitz, Stanley, and Henry A. Giroux. 1985. *Education Under Siege: The Conservative, Liberal, and Radical Debate over Schooling*. South Hacuey, Mass.: Bergin & Garvey.

Bellah, Robert N., et al. 1985. *Habits of the Heart: Individualism and Commitment in American Life*. Berkeley: University of California Press.

Bellah, Robert N. 1975. *The Broken Covenant: American Civil Religion in a Time of Trial*. New York: Seabury Press.

Bercovitch, Sacvan. 1978. *The American Jeremiad*. Madison: University of Wisconsin Press.

Berger, Peter L. 1961. *The Precarious Vision: A Sociologist Looks at Social Fictions and Christian Faith*. Garden City, N.Y.: Doubleday.

Berliner, David, and Bruce Biddle. 1995. *The Manufactured Crisis*. Boston: Addison Wesley.

Bloom, Harold. 1996. *Omens of Millennium: The Gnosis of Angels, Dreams, and Resurrection*. New York: Riverhead Books.

Bly, Robert. 1996. *The Sibling Society*. Reading, Mass.: Addison-Wesley Publishing Company.

Bok, Sissela. 1995. *Common Values*. Columbia: University of Missouri Press.

Boorstein, Sylvia. 1995. *It's Easier Than You Think: The Buddhist Way to Happiness*. San Francisco: HarperSanFrancisco.

Brown, Lester, and Hal Kane. 1994. *Full House: Reassessing the Earth's Population Carrying Capacity*. New York: W. W. Norton & Company.

Brueggemann, Walter. 1978. *The Prophetic Imagination*. Philadelphia: Fortress Press.

Brueggemann, Walter. 1982. *The Creative Word: Canon as a Model for Biblical Education*. Philadelphia: Fortress Press.

Bruteau, Beatrice. 1993. *Radical Optimism: Rooting Ourselves in Reality*. New York: Crossroad Publishing Company.

Bruteau, Beatrice. 1997. *God's Ecstasy: The Creation of a Self-Creating World*. New York: Crossroad Publishing Company.

Bstan-'dzin-rgya-mtsho, Dalai Lama XIV (Tenzin Gyatso, His Holiness The Dalai Lama). 1999. *Ethics for the New Millennium*. New York: Riverhead Books/Penguin Putnam Inc.

Bstan-'dzin-rgya-mtsho, Dalai Lama XIV (Tenzin Gyatso, His Holiness The Dalai Lama). 1999. *Imagine all the People: A Conversation with the Dalai Lama on Money, Politics, and Life as It Could Be*. Somerville, MA: Wisdom Publications.

Buber, Martin. 1960. *The Prophetic Faith*. New York: Harper & Row.

Carter, Stephen L. 1993. *The Culture of Disbelief: How American Law and Politics Trivialize Religious Devotion*. New York: Anchor Books.

Carter, Stephen L. 1996. *Integrity*. New York: Basic Books.

Carter, Stephen L. 1998. *Civility: Manners, Morals, and the Etiquette of Democracy*. New York: Basic Books.

Cohen, Richard. 1994. *Elevations: The Height of the Good in Rosenzweig and Levinas*. Chicago: University of Chicago Press.

Cox, Harvey G. 1984. *Religion in the Secular City. Toward a Postmodern Theoloni*. New York: Simon & Schuster.

Cox, Harvey. 1973. *The Seduction of the Spirit*. New York: Simon & Schuster.

Croatto, J. Severino. 1981. *Exodus: A Hermeneutics of Freedom*. Trans. Salvator Attanasio. Maryknoll, N.Y.: Orbis Books.

Cuddihy, John Martin. 1978. *No Offense: Civil Religion and Protestant Taste*. New York: Seabury Press.

Daly, Mary. 1973. "Love" in *Dictionary of Ideas*. Vol. 2. New York: Charles Scribner.

Darwin, Bernard (Ed.) 1979. *The Oxford Dictionary of Quotations (Third Edition)*. Oxford: Oxford University Press.

Deikman, Arthur J. 1982. *The Observing Self: Mysticism and Psychotherapy*. Boston: Beacon Press.

Desroche, Henti. 1979. *The Sociology of Hope*. Trans. Carol Martin-Sperry. London: Routledge & Kegan Paul.

Eliade, Mircea. 1959. *The Sacred and the Profane*. Trans. William R. Trask. New York: Harcourt, Brace & Company.

Fingarette, Herbert. 1969. *Self-Deception*. New York: Humanities Press.

Fowler, James William. 1981. *Stages of Faith: The Psychology of Human Development and the Quest for Meaning*. San Francisco: Harper & Row.

Fox, Matthew. 1979. *A Spirituality Named Compassion and the Healing of the Global Village*. Minneapolis: Winston Press.

Fox, Matthew. 1983. *Original Blessing*. Santa Fe: Bear & Co.

Fox, Matthew. 1999. *Sins of the Spirit, Blessings of the Flesh: Lessons for Transforming Evil in Soul and Society*. New York: Harmony Books.

Freire, Paulo. 1970. *Pedagogy of the Oppressed*. Trans. Myra Bergman Ramos. New York: Herder & Herder.

Freire, Paulo. 1973. *Education for Critical Consciousness*. New York: Seabury Press.

Fukuyama, Francis. 1999. *The Great Disruption: Human Nature and the Reconstitution of Social Order*. New York: Free Press.

Funk, Robert W. et al. 1993. *The Five Gospels: the Search for the Authentic Words of Jesus*. New York: Macmillan Publishing.

Galbraith, John Kenneth. 1996. *The Good Society: The Humane Agenda.* New York: Houghton Mifflin Company.

Garrett, Laurie. 2000. *Betrayal of Trust: The Collapse of Global Health.* New York: Hyperion.

Gates, Jeff. 2000. *Democracy at Risk: Rescuing Main Street from Wall Street.* Cambridge, Mass.: Perseus Publishing.

Gaylin, Willard, et al. 1978. *Doing Good: The Limits of Benevolence.* New York: Pantheon Books.

Goldstein, Joseph, and Jack Kornfield. 1987. *Seeking the Heart of Wisdom: The Path of Insight Meditation.* Boston: Shambhala Publications.

Goldstein, Joseph. 2002. *One Dharma: The Emerging Western Buddhism.* San Francisco: HarperSanFrancisco.

Green, Arthur. 1994. *Seek My Face, Speak My Name: A Contemporary Jewish Theology.* Northvale, N.J.: Jason Aronson.

Greene, Maxine. 1978. *Landscapes of Learning.* New York: Teachers College Press.

Gunn, Janet. 1986. "Flannery O'Connor and the Religious Function of Displacement," unpublished paper, presented at UNC at Greensboro, November.

Harrington, Michael. 1983, *The Politics at God's Funeral: The Spiritual Crisis of Western Civilization.* New York: Holt, Rinehart & Winston.

Hawken, Paul. 1993. *The Ecology of Commerce: A Declaration of Sustainability.* New York: HarperCollins Publishers.

Henderson, Hazel. 1996. *Building a Win-Win World: Life Beyond Global Economic Warfare.* San Francisco: Berrett-Kohler Publishers.

Henderson, Hazel, et al. 2000. *Calvert-Henderson Quality of Life Indicators: A New Tool for Assessing National Trends.* Bethesda, Md.: Calvert Group Ltd.

Herberg, Will. 1960. *Protestant, Catholic, Jew: An Essay in American Religious Sociology.* Garden City, N.Y.: Anchor Books.

Herberg, Will. 1976. *Faith in Biblical Theology.* Philadelphia: Westminster Press.

Heschel, Abraham J. 1951. *Man Is Not Alone.* New York: Farrar, Straus and Giroux.

Heschel, Abraham J. 1955. *God in Search of Man: A Philosophy of Judaism.* New York: Farrar, Straus and Giroux.

Heschel, Abraham J. 1962. *The Prophets,* 2 vols. New York: Harper & Row.

Heschel, Abraham J. 1965. *Who Is Man?* Stanford, Calif.: Stanford University Press.

Heschel, Abraham J. 1967. *Israel: An Echo of Eternity.* New York: Farrar, Straus and Giroux.

Heschel, Abraham J. 1973. *A Passion for Truth.* Farrar, Straus and Giroux.

Hunter, James D. 2000. *The Death of Character: Moral Education in an Age Without Good or Evil.* New York: Basic Books/ Perseus Books Group.

Kabat-Zinn, Jon. 1994. *Wherever You Go, There You Are: Mindfulness Meditation in Everyday Life.* New York: Hyperion.

Kohlberg, Lawrence. 1981. *Essays on Moral Development.* San Francisco: Harper & Row.

Kornfield, Jack. 1993. *A Path with Heart: A Guide through the Perils and Promises of Spiritual Life.* New York: Bantam Books.

Kornfield, Jack. 2000. *After the Ecstasy, the Laundry: How the Heart Grows Wise on the Spiritual Path.* New York: Bantam Books.

Kornfield, Jack. 2002. *The Art of Forgiveness, Lovingkindness, and Peace.* New York: Bantam Books.

Korten, David C. 1995. *When Corporations Rule the World.* San Francisco: Berrett-Kohler Publishers.

Kozol, Jonathan. 1985. *Illiterate America.* Garden City, N.Y.: Anchor Press.

Lasch, Christopher. 1979. *The Culture of Narcissism: American Life in an Age of Diminishing Expectations.* New York: Norton.

Lemann, Nicholas. 2001. "Testing Limits." *New Yorker*, 7/2/01, p.19.

Lessing, Doris. 1987. *Prisons We Choose to Live Inside.* New York: Harper & Row.

Levine, Stephen. 1997. *A Year to Live: How to Live This Year as if It Were Your Last.* Boston: Beacon Press.

Lewis, C. S. 1952. *Mere Christianity.* San Francisco: HarperCollins.

Lewis, C. S. 1956. *Till We Have Faces: A Myth Retold.* New York: Harcourt.

Lewis, C. S. 1959. *The Screwtape Letters.* New York: Macmillan.

Lewis, C. S. 1996a. *A Grief Observed.* San Francisco: HarperCollins.

Lewis, C. S. 1996b. *The Problem of Pain.* New York: Simon & Schuster.

Macdonald, James. 1974. "A Transcendental Developmental Ideology of Education," in *Heightened Consciousness, Cultural Revolution, and Curriculum Theory.* Ed. William Pinar. Berkeley: McCutchan Publishing.

MacIntyre, Alasdair. 1984. *After Virtue: A Study in Moral Theory.* Notre Dame, Ind.: University of Notre Dame Press.

McLaurin, William. 1996. *Hope: Pedagogy in a Despairing World.* Ann Arbor, Mich.: UMI Dissertation Services.

Merrell-Wolff, Franklin. 1994. *Experience and Philosophy: A Personal Record of Transformation and a Discussion of Transcendental Consciousness.* Albany: State University of New York Press.

Merrell-Wolff, Franklin. 1995. *Transformations in Consciousness: The Metaphysics and Epistemology.* Albany: State University of New York Press.

Merton, Thomas. 1960. *The Wisdom of the Desert.* New York: New Directions.

Merton, Thomas. 1965. *The Way of Chuang Tzu.* New York: New Directions.

Merton, Thomas. 1967. *Mystics and Zen Masters.* New York: Noonday Press.

Merton, Thomas. 1968. *Zen and the Birds of Appetite.* New York: New Directions.

Miller, Judith, et al. 2001. *Germs: Biological Weapons and America's Secret War.* New York: Simon & Schuster.

Miranda, Jose P. 1974. *Marx and the Bible: A Critique of the Philosophy of Oppression.* Trans. John Eagleson. Maryknoll, N.Y.: Orbis Books.

Mitchell, Stephen. 1987. *The Book of Job.* New York: HarperCollins.

Moffett, James. 1994. *The Universal Schoolhouse.* San Francisco: Jossey-Bass.

Mosher, Ralph (Ed.). 1979. *Adolescent's Education and Development: A Janus Knot.* Berkeley: McCutchan Publishing.

Needleman, Jacob. 1991. *Money and the Meaning of Life.* New York: Doubleday.

Neusner, Jacob. 1993. *Torah from Our Sages: Pirke Avot.* New York: Rossel Books.

Newmann, Fred M. 1975. *Education for Citizen Action: Challenge for Secondary Curriculum.* Berkeley: McCutchan Publishers.

Niebuhr, H. Richard. 1960. *Radical Monotheism and Western Culture.* New York: Harper & Row.

Niebuhr, Reinhold. 1935. *An Interpretation of Christian Ethics.* New York: Harper & Brothers.

Niebuhr, Reinhold. 1960. *Moral Man and Immoral Society.* N.Y.: Charles Scribner.

Nisbet, Robert. 1974. *The Sociology of Emile Durkheim.* New York: Oxford University Press.

Noddings, Nel. 1993. *Educating for Intelligent Belief or Unbelief.* New York: Teachers College Press.

Ornstein, Robert. 1989. *New World New Mind: Moving Toward Conscious Evolution.* New York: Doubleday.

Ornstein, Robert. 1991. *The Evolution of Consciousness: Of Darwin, Freud, and Cranial Fire—The Origins of How We Think*. New York: Prentice Hall Press.

Outka, Gene, and John P. Reeder, Jr. (Eds.) 1993. *Prospects for a Common Morality*. Princeton, N.J.: Princeton University Press.

Plato. 1985. *The Republic*. Trans. Richard Sterling and William Scott. New York: Norton.

Polkinghorne, John. 1998. *Belief in God in an Age of Science*. New Haven, Conn.: Yale University Press.

Porteous, Alvin G. 1966. *Prophetic Voices in Contemporary Theology. The Theological Renaissance and the Renewal of the Church*. Nashville: Abingdon Press.

Purdy, Jedediah. 2000. *For Common Things: Irony, Trust, and Commitment in America Today*. New York: Vintage Books.

Purpel, David, and Svi Shapiro. 1995. *Beyond Liberation and Excellence*. New York: Bergin & Garvey.

Purpel, David. 1989. *The Moral and Spiritual Crisis in Education: A Curriculum for Justice and Compassion in Education*. New York: Bergin & Garvey.

Quinn, Daniel. 1999. *Beyond Civilization: Humanity's Next Great Adventure*. New York: Three Rivers Press.

Reich, Charles A. 1995. *Opposing the System*. New York: Crown.

Richard, Mary Caroline. 1964. *Centering*. Middletown, Conn.: Wesleyan University Press.

Riddell, Peter, and Andrew Pierce. 10/26/2001. "World Changed Forever." London: *The Times*.

Rosenzweig, Franz. 1995. *On Jewish Learning*. New York: Schocken Press.

Salk, Jonas. 1983. *Anatomy of Reality: Merging of Intuition and Reason*. New York: Columbia University Press.

Salzberg, Sharon. 1995. *Lovingkindness: The Revolutionary Art of Happiness*. Boston: Shambhala Publications.

Salzberg, Sharon. 2002. *Faith: Trusting Your Own Deepest Experience*. New York: Riverhead Books.

Sartre, Jean-Paul. 1956. *Being and Nothingness*. Trans. Hazel Barnes. New York: Philosophical Library.

Schneider, Stephen H. 8/8/1997. "Global Warming Balance Sheet: What We Really Know." New York: *The Christian Science Monitor*.

Schwartz, Peter. 1996. *The Art of the Long View: Planning for the Future in an Uncertain World*. New York: Doubleday.

Segundo, Jan Luis. 1976. *Liberation of Theology*. Trans. John Drury. Maryknoll, NY: Orbis Books.

Sennett, Richard. 1977. *The Fall of Public Man*. New York: Knopf.

Shah, Idries. 1978. *Learning How to Learn*. New York: Harper & Row.

Shah, Idries. 1998. *Knowing How to Know: A Practical Philosophy in the Sufi Tradition*. London: Octagon Press.

Silberman, Charles E. 1970. *Crisis in the Classroom: The Remaking of American Education*. New York: Random House.

Smith, Adam. 1966. *The Theory of Moral Sentiments*. New York: Augustus M. Kelly. (Originally published 1759.)

Smith, Adam. 1994. *The Wealth of Nations*. New York: The Modern Library. (Originally published 1776.)

Smith, Wilfred Cantwell. 1963. *The Meaning and End of Religion*. New York: Macmillan.

Soelle, Dorothee. 1974. *Political Theology*. Trans. John Shelley. Philadelphia: Fortress Press.

Soros, George. 1998. *The Crisis of Global Capitalism: Open Society Endangered*. New York: Little, Brown and Company.

Soros, George. 2000. *Open Society: Reforming Global Capitalism*. New York: Public Affairs/ Perseus Books Group.

Spong, John Shelby. 1999. *Why Christianity Must Change or Die: A Bishop Speaks to Believers in Exile*. San Francisco: HarperSanFrancisco.

Suzuki, D. T. 1994. *The Zen Koan as a Means of Attaining Enlightenment*. Boston: Charles E. Tuttle.

Suzuki, Shunryu. 1999. *Zen Mind, Beginner's Mind*. New York: Weatherhill.

Suzuki, Shunryu. 2002. *Not Always So: Practicing the True Spirit of Zen*. New York: Harper-Collins.

Thomas, Lewis. 1983. *Late Night Thoughts on Listening to Mahler's Ninth Symphony*. New York: Viking Press.

Tillich, Paul. 1957. *Dynamics of Faith*. New York: Harper & Row.

Tyler, Ralph. 1949. *Principles of Curriculum and Instruction*. Chicago: University of Chicago Press.

Union of Concerned Scientists. 1997. *World Scientists' Call for Action at the Kyoto Climate Summit*. Cambridge, MA: Union of Concerned Scientists.

Walzer, Michael. 1985. *Exodus and Revolution*. New York: Basic Books.

Walzer, Michael. 2000. *Jewish Political Thought*, vol.1. New Haven: Yale University Press.

Wark, Penny. 10/26/2001. "A Fragile Planet." London: *The Times*.

Watts, Alan. 1957. *The Way of Zen*. New York: Vintage Books.

Welch, Sharon. 1985. *Communities of Resistance and Solidarity*. Maryknoll, N.Y: Orbis Books.

West, Cornel. 1982. *Prophesy Deliverance*. Philadelphia: Westminster Press.

West, Cornel. 1989. *The American Evasion of Philosophy: A Genealogy of Pragmatism*. Madison, Wisc.: The University of Wisconsin Press.

West, Cornel. 1997. *Restoring Hope: Conversations on the Future of Black America*. Boston: Beacon Press.

Winter, Gibson. 1985. "Community and Education," in *Schools and Meaning*, David Purpel and H. Svi Shapiro, Eds. Washington, D.C.: University Press of America.

INDEX

Studies in the Postmodern Theory of Education

General Editors
Joe L. Kincheloe & Shirley R. Steinberg

Counterpoints publishes the most compelling and imaginative books being written in education today. Grounded on the theoretical advances in criticalism, feminism, and postmodernism in the last two decades of the twentieth century, Counterpoints engages the meaning of these innovations in various forms of educational expression. Committed to the proposition that theoretical literature should be accessible to a variety of audiences, the series insists that its authors avoid esoteric and jargonistic languages that transform educational scholarship into an elite discourse for the initiated. Scholarly work matters only to the degree it affects consciousness and practice at multiple sites. Counterpoints' editorial policy is based on these principles and the ability of scholars to break new ground, to open new conversations, to go where educators have never gone before.

For additional information about this series or for the submission of manuscripts, please contact:

Joe L. Kincheloe & Shirley R. Steinberg
c/o Peter Lang Publishing, Inc.
275 Seventh Avenue, 28th floor
New York, New York 10001

To order other books in this series, please contact our Customer Service Department:

(800) 770-LANG (within the U.S.)
(212) 647-7706 (outside the U.S.)
(212) 647-7707 FAX

Or browse online by series:

www.peterlangusa.com

Please remember that this is a library book,
and that it belongs only temporarily to each
person who uses it. Be considerate. Do
not write in this, or any, library book.

P9-CEH-202

SIGNET (0451)

Great Reading from Irving Stone and SIGNET

THE ORIGIN	(133080—$4.95)*
ADVERSARY IN THE HOUSE	(111656—$3.50)
THE AGONY AND THE ECSTASY	(146921—$4.95)*
CLARENCE DARROW FOR THE DEFENSE	(134524—$4.95)
DEAR THEO: AN AUTOBIOGRAPHY OF VINCENT VAN GOGH	(140982—$4.95)*
THE GREEK TREASURE	(134575—$4.50)*
IMMORTAL WIFE	(111729—$3.95)
JACK LONDON—SAILOR ON HORSEBACK	(148320—$3.95)*
LOVE IS ETERNAL	(145402—$4.95)*
PASSIONS OF THE MIND	(134567—$4.95)
THE PRESIDENT'S LADY	(139909—$3.95)*
THOSE WHO LOVE	(134508—$4.95)
DEPTHS OF GLORY	(146026—$4.95)*

All edited by Jean Stone
*Prices slightly higher in Canada

Buy them at your local bookstore or use this convenient coupon for ordering.

NEW AMERICAN LIBRARY,
P.O. Box 999 Bergenfield, New Jersey 07621

Please send me the books I have checked above. I am enclosing $_____
(please add $1.00 to this order to cover postage and handling). Send check
or money order—no cash or C.O.D.'s. Prices and numbers are subject to change
without notice.

Name _____

Address_____

_____State_____ Zip Code_____
Allow 4-6 weeks for delivery.
This offer is subject to withdrawal without notice.

PASSION—AND ITS PRICE

Camille Pissarro painted what he wanted, the way he wanted, no matter what the critics and the public said. Camille Pissarro loved whom he wanted, a beautiful, voluptuous, forbidden woman who made him an outcast to his own family. He and his circle of artist friends were forced to the depths of poverty and to the brink of despair— even as they created the works that would bring them immortal greatness. This is his story, and theirs—the story of a struggle against all odds and of a triumph that still fills us with wonder today. . . .

DEPTHS OF GLORY

"Not only good reading, but a mine of authentic and often picturesque information on the birth and flowering of the most celebrated school of painting since the high Renaissance in Italy."
—*John Barkham Reviews*

"FASCINATING!" —*Philadelphia Inquirer*

More . . .

DEPTHS
OF
GLORY

A Biographical Novel of
Camille Pissarro

by

Irving Stone

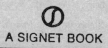

A SIGNET BOOK

NEW AMERICAN LIBRARY

Dedicated to
JEAN STONE
for the several years
of her devoted righting
of this manuscript
June 6, 1985

SIGNET TRADEMARK REG. U.S. PAT. OFF. AND FOREIGN COUNTRIES
REGISTERED TRADEMARK—MARCA REGISTRADA
HECHO EN CHICAGO. U.S.A.

SIGNET, SIGNET CLASSIC, MENTOR, ONYX, PLUME, MERIDIAN
and NAL BOOKS are published by New American Library,
1633 Broadway, New York, New York 10019

First Signet Printing, March, 1987

1 2 3 4 5 6 7 8 9

PRINTED IN THE UNITED STATES OF AMERICA

PASSION—AND ITS PRICE

Camille Pissarro painted what he wanted, the way
he wanted, no matter what the critics and the
public said. Camille Pissarro loved whom he
wanted, a beautiful, voluptuous, forbidden woman
who made him an outcast to his own family. He
and his circle of artist friends were forced to the
depths of poverty and to the brink of despair—
even as they created the works that would bring
them immortal greatness. This is his story, and
theirs—the story of a struggle against all odds and
of a triumph that still fills us with wonder today. . . .

DEPTHS
OF
GLORY

"Not only good reading, but a mine of authentic
and often picturesque information on the birth
and flowering of the most celebrated school of
painting since the high Renaissance in Italy."
—*John Barkham Reviews*

"FASCINATING!" —*Philadelphia Inquirer*

More . . .

DEPTHS OF GLORY

A Biographical Novel of
Camille Pissarro

by

Irving Stone

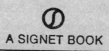
A SIGNET BOOK

NEW AMERICAN LIBRARY

Dedicated to
JEAN STONE
for the several years
of her devoted righting
of this manuscript
June 6, 1985

Contents

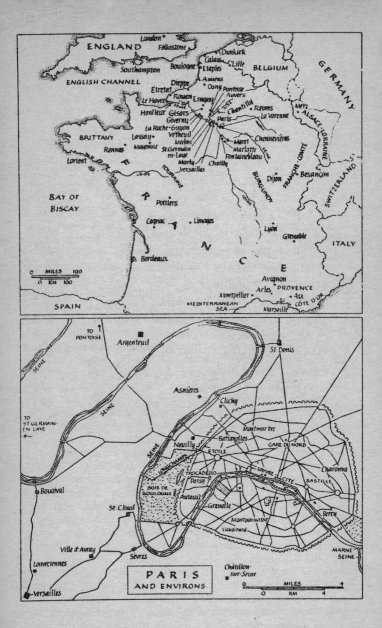

Map 1 (top)

ENGLAND

London • • Folkestone

ENGLISH CHANNEL

Southampton

Calais • • Dunkirk
Boulogne • Étaples • Lille
BELGIUM

GERMANY

Dieppe
Étretat
Le Havre
Honfleur Gisors
Giverny
La Roche-Guyon
Vétheuil
Médan
St. Germain-en-Laye
Marly
Versailles

Amiens
Osny • Pontoise
• Auvers
Ernagny
Chantilly Reims
Pontoise
Paris La Varenne
Metz
ALSACE-LORRAINE

Moret
Marlotte
Fontainebleau
Chailly

Chennevières

BRITTANY
Rennes
Lorient
Lassay
Mayenne

FRANCE

Dijon
BURGUNDY
Besançon
FRANCHE-COMTÉ
SWITZERLAND

BAY OF
BISCAY

LOIRE
TOURAINE
LOIRE

Poitiers

Cognac • • Limoges

Lyon
Grenoble

ITALY

Bordeaux

MILES 0 100
0 KM 100

SPAIN

Avignon
Arles PROVENCE
Montpellier • Aix • CÔTE D'OR
MEDITERRANEAN SEA
Marseille

Map 2 (bottom)

TO PONTOISE
Argenteuil
St. Denis
SEINE
SEINE
Asnières
Clichy
Montmartre
TO ST. GERMAIN-EN-LAYE
SEINE
Batignolles
GARE DU NORD
Neuilly
ÉTOILE
Charonne
TROCADÉRO
LOUVRE
CITÉ
BASTILLE
Passy
BOIS DE BOULOGNE
Auteuil
Bougival
Grenelle
Bercy
St. Cloud
Montparnasse
Vaugirard
MARNE
SEINE
Ville d'Avray
Sèvres
Louveciennes
Châtillon-sur-Seine
Versailles

PARIS
AND ENVIRONS

MILES 0 4
0 KM 4

BOOK ONE

Paris

1

IT TOOK HIM only a few moments to put his two leather-strapped bags through the *octroi*, customs, and carry them along the quai to the Boulogne railroad station. His heavy dark suit was still damp from the spray of the English Channel since he had preferred the open deck of the little steamer, with the salt spray in his face, to the crowded second-class salon. The crossing from Folkestone had taken less than three hours, but the Channel had been characteristically choppy. Camille Pissarro was glad to get his booted feet on terra firma, particularly after the three-week trip on the *S. S. Magdalena* from his home on the island of St. Thomas in the Lesser Antilles. He relished the brisk mid-October air, feeling his strength as he strode vigorously along the docks, a heavy portmanteau in each hand. He was twenty-five, of medium build, had broad shoulders, a slim waist and long legs. Other passengers, older or with more luggage, went by him in the carriages they had hired to transport them to the train for Paris.

He was earlier than the fifteen minutes in advance required by the stationmaster, for the Channel tide had been favorable. Pissarro walked to the black engine with its funnel protruding into the roofed station, where the engineer, dressed in a uniform similar to that of an admiral, was standing at the head of the train like a lord of the navy. He passed the open truncated coal car to the baggage car and paid a porter two sous each, two cents, for his bags, receiving claim tickets for the Gare St. Lazare. The third-class carriages were like carts, furnished with wooden benches, without roof or sides, the passengers sitting in the open air. The second-class carriages were enclosed and had a sheet-metal chimney at the back for ventilation. At the seventh of the black enclosed voitures, all riding on high wheels with a combined guardrail and step up, he found a window seat which faced forward so that he would be looking ahead at the harvested fields and thickly populated forests of the French countryside.

In 1842, when he was twelve years old and had first crossed the Atlantic on an English freighter to attend school in Passy, outside of Paris, he had had to travel several days from Bordeaux to Paris by coach. Five years later, when he returned to St. Thomas, he had been able to take the newly built railroad to Lille, where he had changed to another line whose uncompleted track had taken him much of the way to Dunkirk. He had then traveled the rest of the journey in a four-horse carriage to reach the French freighter which would carry him westward to the islands.

Now, in 1855, he had arrived in the port of Southampton, taken the train to London, then the train and boat to Boulogne. His sketching pads and the books he had brought with him to read on the ocean voyage were in his heavy valises. However he had a copy of that day's London *Times* neatly folded in his pocket. Though St. Thomas was a Danish island, the language spoken in his home in the port town of Charlotte Amalie, in the rambling flat above their prosperous haberdashery and ship victualing shop on the main street, was French. English was the commercial language of the port. Young Camille, working for his father since he had finished his preparatory education at seventeen at the Pension Savary, had picked up the language while checking incoming and outgoing cargo for the English and American ships in the harbor.

The stationmaster blew his whistle, the stoker fired up the steam engine, the engineer pulled the looped-cord whistle, the train began backing out of the yard on the way to Paris. The modest outskirts of Boulogne were soon behind them; they were traveling south down the French coast through the charming valley of the Liane, then a two-hundred-yard black tunnel during which his nostrils became infiltrated with coal dust. The train reached the abandoned port of Etaples with its two lighthouses before it turned into the desolate sand flats of the Somme River.

His mind was as filled with clashing and disparate emotions as any trunk checked with the porter at the Boulogne station. He was sorry he could not have stayed in London to study the Turner and Constable paintings. The few reproductions he had seen in the French and English newspapers which reached the island by sailing ship every few days had

2

stimulated him as much as those of the current French masters, Delacroix and Courbet. He had been reading about them for a year while waiting for his brother Alfred to return from a vacation in Paris and free him from his father's shop. His sister Emma's in-laws, the Isaacsons, had invited him to spend a week with them in London, and it would be a long time before he would have another chance to study the English school. But there had been a letter waiting for him when the *Magdalena* reached Southampton telling him to continue on to Paris immediately; his older sister, Delphine, was dying. He hoped that she would still be alive when he reached there.

The desire to draw had been born in him. When he picked up a pencil or pen it was not to write notes in his study books but to sketch the harbor of St. Thomas with its full-masted sailing ships, its little boats being rowed to the vessels to deliver or take off cargo; the green undulant hills that served as a solid and protective screen for the low-lying, wavering line of tiled houses that encircled the protected bay. On the main street, Dronningens Gade, he liked to lurk in the doorways of the shops to sketch the sailors from a dozen different countries in their colorful costumes, shopping, drinking and looking for women. He had been fortunate in his drawing master at the Pension Savary, for the instructor recognized this compulsion, even at the age of twelve, to draw everything he laid his eyes upon. He not only taught Camille the modest amount he himself knew, but had given him, when he was fourteen, an accepted text from which he could learn, Samuel Prout's *Easy Lessons in Drawing*.

The drawing master had taken his small class to the Louvre whenever they had a day in Paris, showing the youngsters the differences in the technique and subject matter of the Dutch, French, Spanish and Italian schools. During his last year he had taken Camille and one or two of the others, once a month, to the studio of Auguste Savary, a relative of the owners of the school, a respected landscape artist whose paintings of Versailles and Mayenne were frequently hung at the Salon of the Beaux-Arts. Auguste Savary was kind enough to show the young boys how to place a quarter of an inch of oil paint onto the palette, then to mix the colors before applying them to the stretched canvas, letting them feel in their hands that the oil paint at the end of the brush had a weight and a body, and was capable of infinite variations.

Camille had been enthralled but, at sixteen, knew that he would have years of drawing, sketching with pencil, charcoal and India ink, perhaps even gouache or watercolor, before he dared experiment with oil paint.

He was the only one in St. Thomas with this particular obsession. The thriving port town of Charlotte Amalie had never had or seen an artist. There was no way to conceal his activity. Because he was a good-natured lad, not handsome but with a smooth sunburned complexion and clear soft brown eyes, his idiosyncrasy was accepted. He told no one that he was determined to spend his life as an artist. He would not have been able to give his reasons coherently, yet from the beginning he had been drawn to art the way other young men were drawn to the sea, to the law, to medicine, engineering, to trade or the manipulation of money.

He took out his London *Times,* tried to concentrate but could not resist the landscape through which they were riding. He followed the valley of the Somme, its fields already harvested, the rich loam lying fallow, anticipating the winter rains, the spring plowing and planting. Before reaching Amiens there were fields where the peasant families were still gleaning. Men were working at the extensive peat excavations. The Amiens racecourse, the finest in France, came into view as his mood shifted to his anticipated excitement of returning to Paris. Paris was where painting lived. It was the art center of the world, and he was resolved to work there for the rest of his life. He was strong and healthy, he had half a century to create a body of work.

2

Though the French people had previously talked animatedly to strangers on the long, lumpy coach rides, in these new railroad carriages they were reduced to a numb silence, their expression seeming to say: "What a relief to be done with the rolling, pitching coaches crashing over mud and rock-strewn roads, locked into smelly boxes with an opaque window the size of a kerchief, and obliged to stop at still another inn for a change of horses."

Camille had been so immersed in his ricocheting emotions that he had not heard the middle-aged man next to him, with heavily pomaded hair and bilious complexion, trying to start a conversation. Men who travel alone for a long time are inclined to confide in strangers whom they are certain they will never see again.

"... name is Georges Lasch. Textiles. I represent the best in France, woolens from Lyon. Cover South America. Been gone for four months from my wife and children. *Sacrebleu!* It's been a long time sleeping in strange beds. But what a trip. Sold everywhere. Shopkeepers waiting for me with empty shelves and full pocketbooks."

Camille murmured, "*Enchanté.* I am Camille Pissarro of St. Thomas, on my way to join my mother and sisters in Paris. My sister Delphine is suffering a lingering illness; they came to France for better medical treatment. My father and brother will join us as soon as they can sell our family business. I spent two years in Caracas sketching with a painter friend, so I know the people and the Spanish language."

"What is your business?"

"I am an artist." It was the first time he had said these words aloud.

"Ah! *La vie de bohème.* Are you a good painter?"

"Not yet."

"Then when?"

"Art develops slowly."

"And you sell slowly, *n'est-ce pas?*"

"For the present."

"Better to be in textiles," Georges Lasch asserted. "Something people need. Since you know Spanish and South America, you could develop a trade for yourself."

"I've sold goods in my father's store. Enough to last me."

His mind had refused to consider the confrontation with his mother in Paris when he would announce that he would be a painter and no other. His father, Frédéric Pissarro, had been born and educated in Bordeaux. He was an enthusiast of French culture. That was why he had sent his two sons to the Pension Savary to become educated. Alfred, Camille's older brother, had been a desultory student, remaining at the school for only a year; his enthusiasm was for the violin. When Alfred came home, twelve-year-old Camille had been sent in his place. Their father needed one of his sons to help with the unloading of his supplies and the reloading on the ships. Either Camille or Alfred had directed the coal car heaped with rope, tar, holystones, victuals, ships parts, being pushed up or down the slight incline from the shore to Dronningens Gade on the one-block railroad spur, then hauled by hand across the street to the Pissarro shop.

There were two brothers and two half sisters from their

5

mother's first husband, who had died when she was only twenty-nine. There had been a public scandal when Rachel Petit became pregnant months before she was able to marry her dead husband's nephew, Frédéric Pissarro, who had come from Bordeaux to settle his uncle's estate. The Danish government had mercifully married them in a civil service before the boy, who died in infancy, was born; but the synagogue had refused to acknowledge the legitimacy of the union.

For four years Camille had worked for his father. He had been paid a good wage and been obliged by his strict parents to put most of it in a savings account. Except when he could get away in his little boat, roaming the shores of the harbor for scenes to sketch, or wandering in the deeply wooded hills above St. Thomas to find a clearing where he could attempt a watercolor of the sea below him, the years were a waste. He loved his family and wanted to serve their common interest; yet he yearned to be free of the limited island; to be free to work at the difficult and elusive technique of painting. He smoldered when his father reproved him for making drawings when he should have been looking around the busy mercantile establishment for more important things to do.

He had to get away. To another place. Where he could work at making pictures from first light to dark. But where? How justify quitting a busy and prosperous business for the nether world of art, a future of uncertainty? His parents would fight him, call it an act of betrayal.

Then he met Fritz Melbye, a young Dane who had come to St. Thomas in the summer of 1851 with a commission from the Copenhagen Academy to paint the Danish harbor of Charlotte Amalie. Camille had struck up an acquaintance with the twenty-five-year-old artist while waiting for crates and bales to be unloaded from the cargo ships, checking the manifests and using his spare time to sketch the sailing vessels, sloops, men in rowboats bringing ashore kegs and caskets; the white-winged birds swooping low to fish.

"You're the first painter I've known," he had exclaimed. "We don't produce painters on this island. Only palm trees and rum."

They had spent every hour together that Camille could get free from the shop or the supervision of the loading of provisions. Fritz Melbye had exhibited two paintings at the Copenhagen Academy at the age of twenty-two, an unusual accomplishment. He had not remained in Denmark to consolidate his success but had crossed the Atlantic, stayed in New York City a considerable while, then traveled north to the

6

Canadian border to paint a picture of Niagara Falls. He had learned a colloquial English in America, frequently, when excited, putting his verbs at the ends of his sentences.

Camille had been able to take his friend home only occasionally. The Pissarros were known for their hospitality but his mother was already alarmed by her son's fascination with drawing and looked on Fritz as a dangerous influence. Fritz had been able to find only a small, dirty room in Charlotte Amalie, using it for the few hours of sleep after his midnight talk sessions with Camille. Because he wanted to get back to Denmark he had worked furiously from every angle of the superb bay, completing a vivid watercolor of the small, gentle harbor. When he left, Fritz confided:

"I'll be next year back. Will you find me a light clean room? We can together sketch. But really we should some colorful spot in South America find. One with marvelous motifs. Can you do that? Get away?"

Camille had replied impulsively:

"I've saved enough of my salary to last for a year, perhaps two. But I'll have to leave without my parents' approval. They want me to be a businessman, not a painter." He threw back his head with its abundance of dark brown hair and laughed. ". . . Anything but a painter."

"We'll wait for a ship where we want to go, then at the last minute we'll board, a letter leave . . . ."

They had done exactly that, the following year, taking ship to La Guaira, the unprepossessing seaport of Venezuela.

He had had a whole year to decide whether he would go away with Fritz Melbye without informing his parents. There were reasons why he should not. His parents had given him five years of a wonderful education in France, depriving themselves of his company and services, and going to considerable expense. They had nurtured and loved him; had planned for him and his brother to become owners of the business when Frédéric retired. They would be badly hurt. Rachel was given to outbursts of temper and grief. It would impose a burden on his father. Yet there was no other solution.

In La Guaira Camille had immediately made a watercolor of the town, its houses lining a curving street, a family making its way, the father riding the donkey, the mother guiding a small child with one hand, carrying a heavy bundle in the other.

The train reached Clermont station, which had a buffet. Camille jumped out, bought a cut of cheese, a piece of the long narrow all-crust bread called a *ficelle*, string, and a small

7

flagon of wine produced by the nearby vines of Liancourt. He had not eaten since a hurried breakfast at the inn in London, some seven or eight hours before. He chewed hungrily on the fresh bread and cheese while the train chugged its noisy way through the pretty towns of Clermont and Liancourt, plastered along hillsides on the high chalk lands of Picardy. As he gazed at the villages with their red-tiled roofs and surrounding vineyards, delighted by the multicolored houses, he sighed:

"I wish I were able to interrupt my journey and make some studies. It would be a dream for a painter to stop en route, then continue, and stop again."

He devoured the bread and cheese, washed it down with a last draught of the wine, concluded:

"I'll do it one day."

3

Dusk came early. The train's oil lamps were lit from the outside by a worker walking along the roof of the cars. Soon they came into the Gare St. Lazare, a shanty-like shed perched above the first tunnel, built of rough stones laid in mortar and painted a pale yellow. Camille thought it ugly.

He got off on a platform exposed to the cool evening air. It was now dark; he had been en route for eleven hours. He presented his baggage tickets to a porter but had to wait a half hour until all the luggage, even that which had already been cleared at Boulogne, was laid out on tables for the customs to inspect.

Outside the station was a line of carriages. Though his mother's apartment at the base of Montmartre was close by, it was too far to carry the heavy suitcases. He approached the one-horse cab at the head of the waiting line. The horse was chewing a piece of straw attached to his hanging lips. The cabman, grumbling to himself about the wait, wore a filthy cape with several shoulder collars. His head was covered with a malformed hat, and his feet were stuffed into big sabots.

"*Combien?* How much to take me to 49 Rue Notre Dame de Lorette, on the south side of Montmartre?"

The cabman sized up this obvious foreigner who knew nothing about cab fares.

"Four francs. Eighty cents."

"Out of the question. One franc fifty is the regulation."

The cabman swore. "You're stubborn. Two francs fifty."

"Two francs. Plus some sous for a tip."

"*Je suis baba*. I am stupefied. Get in."

He climbed the two iron steps, settled himself on the Utrecht yellow velvet seat, prickly as a pack of needles. Under his feet was a bed of straw that smelled like manure. The door did not close, the window was broken, the horse of thin head and sparse tail was barely able to drag the heavy cab over the rough cobblestones.

"A regal carriage," Camille thought, amused, as they wound their way. "But Paris, at last!"

Gazing out the broken window, he realized with a start that this was not the Paris he had left almost eight years before. Whole rows of buildings had been demolished, narrow winding streets had disappeared in the rubble. He pounded on the front of the cab and shouted up to the driver:

"What has happened? It looks as though an invading army has destroyed the city."

The driver spat somewhere into the October air.

"*C'est ça*. That's right. Our crazy Emperor Napoleon III—he's an emperor like my old nag is a race horse at Amiens—with his new commissioner brought in from Poitiers. Name Haussmann. They're tearing down the whole city."

"Why?"

"*Un bonneteau*. A game easy to cheat at. The Emperor says, 'To make Paris a marble city, as beautiful as ancient Rome.' He says he wants to be another Augustus. It's a lie. He wants to get rid of the narrow streets so the people can't tear up the cobblestones and revolt like in 1848. He's going to build wide boulevards where his troops can shoot down protesters . . . ."

Camille shook his head in disbelief.

"It can't be that alone. Even as a youngster here I remember that parts of Paris were wretched slums, poverty-stricken, traps for tuberculosis.

"Nobody in power does anything good for the people. Look at my half-dead horse and rotted cab. How in a miserable lifetime—look at my mug, can you tell if I'm old or young—could I save the money for a new horse and carriage?"

The short ride took him east on the Rue St. Lazare, then left on the Rue St. Georges until they turned north to Notre Dame de Lorette, a block-square stone fortress of a church around which the neighborhood's prostitutes, called Lorettes, were already gathered in their gaudy outfits, ready for a night's commerce. The Jewish district riding uphill from Notre Dame de Lorette was a neighborhood favored by artists because of the teeming life in the open, the steep market street with stalls on the sidewalks.

"Four francs it is!" he cried as he alighted. "I apologize for bargaining with you. Buy the poor nag some oats. And put fresh hay back there. It stinks of the cowshed."

"Four francs? You're a fool. But for that kind of money I'll perfume the straw."

The Pissarro apartment was small compared to the spacious quarters above the shop in St. Thomas. The sheer bulk of their Danish West Indies furniture cluttered the rooms as badly as the French fondness for bibelots, knickknacks, plants, tables laden with bric-a-brac. But new furniture was prohibitively expensive. Each young couple was given a bed and table by parents or grandparents and waited, none too patiently, to inherit a chest of drawers or lounging chair. The entire Pissarro family, being in the process of moving to Paris, had no intention of buying furnishings for the new home. Since only Frédéric and one son, at first Camille, then Alfred, would remain in the upstairs flat in St. Thomas, they had crated their solid oversized furniture and sent it with Rachel, Emma and her three children, Delphine and Alfred on a shipping line with which the family had been doing business. They had left behind nothing but two narrow cots, a table for meals, and two less than luxurious chairs. Alfred, on his long-promised year of vacation in Paris from his duties at the Pissarro chandlering business, had helped the family settle in. Camille saw the furniture amidst which he had grown up on the tropical island transplanted to this second-story Parisian apartment. In the foyer was placed a combined coatrack, cane and umbrella stand and the small chair he had sat on while taking off wet boots.

Rachel Pissarro heard her son's footsteps, came out of her bedroom and with a happy cry enveloped him in her arms, crushing him against her substantial bosom, covering his face with emotional kisses and cries of relief.

"Camille. My dear one. At last."

He kissed his mother's cheek warmly, murmured:

"It's good to see you, Maman. I came as quickly as I could."

"I knew you would. I could always rely on you."

"Not always," Camille thought. "Not when I ran away to Venezuela for two years." But this was no time to suggest split loyalties.

He held her at arm's length. A lace cap sat on the back of her lustrous brown hair, parted sharply in the middle, side dustings of gray covering the ears; her rimless spectacles were worn low on her straight nose and ample nostrils. Her mouth was wide and sensuous, the brown eyes partly lidded and withdrawn. Tall and wide-hipped, she was now sixty. Her two-piece dress, the bodice fitted to the waist and elbows, the edges trimmed with ruching in a dark blue silk, flared out over the hips and wrists. She was an attractive woman, young or old; a fighter, a good companion to his father and partner in the growing Pissarro enterprise, for which she kept the books, maintained the credit and solvency of the firm. Their friends in St. Thomas said about her:

"Rachel Pissarro has every virtue except the ability to keep herself happy."

"Little wonder," he thought as he brushed the tears from his mother's eyes with gentle fingertips. "Two sons of her four children by her first husband died young; her husband died when she was only twenty-nine. Two of her sons from my father died, one in infancy, one at twenty. Now Delphine . . ."

She studied his large-sized head with long hair waving over the closely fitting ears, the Roman senator nose, humped slightly just below eye level, the large brown eyes that dominated the face: wideset, perceptive, friendly, yet looking out at the world a little skeptically; not to be put down or taken lightly.

"No one has ever accused me of being handsome," he laughed. "But it is a face that makes a statement."

"You've grown. You're more a man now."

"I haven't grown physically, Maman. I'm about the same, five feet nine, a hundred and sixty-five pounds. Where I've matured is inside my head, where it doesn't show."

Rachel started to ask a question, decided it was not the right time. Her eyes half closed, she murmured:

"Delphine asks for you. That is what has kept her alive, waiting for you."

His sister Emma came into the room, embraced him.

"Be forewarned, my dear brother, you cannot lie to her or bring her false hope. She knows it is a matter of days. She is resigned. She has no will to live."

Rachel broke in, her voice bitter.

"She says life has always been empty for her."

"Is that true, Emma?"

He stood gazing at his half sister, ten years older than he, who had served as a surrogate mother during the crises when Rachel had broken down, railed against her fate, cried in her anguish:

"Death must be my friend, he is so constantly by my side."

Emma was also in a two-piece dress, a high-necked cambric blouse under the bodice. She wore fewer layers of cloth over her bustle than did her mother, in partial revolt against the prosperous cloth manufacturers of France who set the style of wrapping the woman, not as tightly as a mummy, but encased in as many layers of cloth.

Camille had of course not known Emma's father, his mother's first husband, Isaac Petit; but he thought that Emma must have inherited his character: calm, steadfast, facing life with a sense of ironic humor. She and Camille were the closest members of the family, supportive of each other. Emma was not pretty, but at thirty-five and the mother of three children, she was attractive, with glossy light brown hair combed straight back, coiled in a bun and held securely in a fashionable net. She had clear, high coloring, with hazel eyes that managed to be at the same time penetrating and kindly.

"Yes," she replied quietly to Camille's question. "Because she was plain-looking, Delphine thought no one could love her. Because she lacked wit, spontaneity, she thought no one could be interested in her."

"I love her," cried Camille. "I always tried to make her laugh, to do interesting things for her. Can I go to her now? I won't dissemble; but she will see that her brother, at least, loves her."

4

Delphine's bedroom was like a whitewashed monk's cell, without decoration. She had wanted it that way. She was lying in a narrow bedstead, with thickly twirled high posts carved in the shape of a pineapple, the family's only piece of furniture manufactured in the Antilles; covered with a canopy of "Spanish work" made by the Cha-Cha women. There was a mahogany clothing cupboard and mirror attached to the wall; a small table for medications, one chair for the doctor or family watcher.

Delphine was a scant thirty-two years old, her face ashen

and furrowed. Her eyes brightened when Camille came to her side.

He took her ravaged hand, kissed it, held it tightly in his.

"Why?" he asked himself for the thousandth time. "She has no known illness. She never contracted any of the fevers that killed Maman's first husband and four of her children. The doctor says there is nothing wrong with her heart, her lungs, her blood."

Delphine answered his unspoken question.

"Emma says I was dealt a bad hand of cards. That is not true, Camille. They were blanks. No numbers; no jokers, no queens or kings. There's no possible play with blank cards. I was born that way. Maybe some other people are, too. Could that be?"

Choking back sobs, he kissed both corners of her dry lips, combed back her hair with his fingers; her brow felt feverish. Despite Emma's warning he had to try.

"Delphine, I will show you Paris. We'll share its excitement."

Delphine shook her head in denial.

"Camille, I'm content to go. It's not hard, especially with you here. You care about me . . . ."

When he left the room he found his mother outside the door. There were red spots of fury in her troubled eyes.

"It's not true. She hasn't been deprived of the good things of life. She is not dying of sadness. God gave her a fatal illness, deep inside, that no doctor can detect. Why must I be blamed for having borne a child with no will to live? It's physical, not mental. Mental may maim, but it doesn't kill."

Camille soothed her.

"Now, Maman, you've done everything a mother could do, even lived apart from your husband for this year."

His serene nature had a quieting effect upon her.

"You're a good son," she said softly. "But why must I lose five of my eight children?"

"You are religious, Maman. Ask God that question."

Emma came into the room, a short apron over her ankle-length skirt with its embroidered ruffles.

"Come into the kitchen."

It was a smallish room too far from the dining room, crowded with copper pots, skillets, skewers hanging from pegs and laid on shelves, all brought from St. Thomas.

"Have you had anything to eat?"

"Just some bread and cheese at Clermont."

"What I thought. There's plenty of soup left. I'll heat it for

13

you. We had a cook but she . . . never mind. I'll put up the teakettle.''

When he moved into the dining room he was home again in St. Thomas; he saw the mahogany extension table with which he had grown up, with its colorful inlays of light wood; the same carved cane chairs surrounded it. On one wall was the voluminous cupboard for linens and porcelains. Camille smiled as he opened one of the doors and a bell rang . . . to warn Rachel that one of her children was into the delicious West Indian jam. The sideboard on the opposite wall held their silver-shaded candlesticks, a silver ice pitcher and cut-glass decanters for rum, whiskey, cognac; flooding Camille's mind with scenes in the open gallery of their home in the islands where the family met for a cold drink and exchange of news at the end of the long hot day. All this bulky, albeit finely carved wooden furniture had had space around it in the St. Thomas rooms; here in the Parisian apartment Camille found that he had to wander through as narrow trails as he would follow in a mahogany forest.

Emma did not hover. She allowed him to eat in peace, asking no questions, affording him information about their lonely year in Paris. Their brother Alfred had acquired a mistress and had not always been at home. The Pissarro grandparents, who had taken affectionate care of Camille during his five years at the Savary boarding school, having him with them during the holidays and summer vacations, were now very old. A Pissarro uncle, Moïse, who had married his niece, came in occasionally with his young children.

''It's been a kind of isolation,'' Emma said. ''There was little we could do with Delphine so ill and dependent.''

''You made a tremendous sacrifice leaving Phineas behind.''

She shrugged. ''You brought me a packet of letters?''

''Several. He's been writing to you every day for a month.''

Camille was overjoyed to find that the many months away from her husband, with whom she had had a love-marriage relationship for seven years, had neither soured nor depressed her. It would take Phineas Isaacson, son of a solid merchant family in England who had settled in St. Thomas to capitalize on family business ventures there, a year or more to settle his affairs, part of which were interlocked with the Pissarro interest, and to move back to London where Emma and the children would join him.

''My mother needed me.'' It was a custom for the children of the family to say ''my mother'' rather than ''our mother'' or simply ''mother,'' '' . . . To set up house here, to adjust to a world capital when she had never set foot off our tiny island. Phineas has been good about it. But I also had two self-centered purposes.''

Emma had the grace of forthrightness and candor, precious gems buried so deep in the mountain of humankind's evasions.

''The first was to get my children off that pestilential island. The second was to hurry Phineas's closing of his business, even without getting the last available thousand kroner. He doesn't like living without me any more than I like being without him. We live for the day we're settled in London.''

He found his mother in the parlor, sitting like a monument in the middle of the upholstered Danish West Indies sofa. In front of it was their large circular table with its marble top and carved mahogany pedestals. There was a wall bookcase covered with glass, woven cane chairs and rockers with polished mahogany frames. He settled beside her.

''Father is well. He sends you this message: if he cannot sell the shop and the house advantageously in the next months he will come for a long stay with you in the summer.''

Rachel sighed deeply.

''How do things look?''

''Our ship chandlering is seriously hurt. The sailing vessels that had to stop for provisioning between Europe, the United States and South America are giving way to new steamships that don't need to put into port for victualing. They can go direct with their cargo.''

''The property is valuable,'' she murmured. ''One of the largest, most solid buildings on the main street . . .''

'' . . . but no buyers. My father is waiting for a favorable shift in trade. It will come.''

''But when? I need my husband with me.''

He replied gently, ''We all have needs, Maman. Don't be out of patience. We have the years ahead.''

''More for you than for me, thank God.'' She leaned toward Camille eagerly. ''Speaking of your needs . . .''

''Oh no, Maman. I've only just arrived.''

''Very well. But we have serious matters to discuss.''

''D'accord.''

Rachel trusted and felt secure only inside her own family circle. She had married her older sister's husband when her sister died young. When this inherited husband died approaching middle age, she had married her dead husband's nephew, Frédéric, seven years younger than herself, who had been sent out from Bordeaux at the age of twenty-four to settle the Isaac Petit estate to the family's advantage. She had approved Emma's marriage to Phineas because in her words:

"Phineas has been like a member of our family."

When her older brother-in-law, Moïse, married his young niece, Rachel had approved, saying:

"Keep everything in the family."

Camille asked: "Maman, do you intend to marry me inside the family as well?"

"Alas, no. There isn't an attractive cousin for you. I'll find you a nice Jewish girl from a highly placed family, with a respectable dowry."

"But don't hurry, Maman."

"Who's hurrying? I can't get you into society until you start earning a good living."

5

Paris was wearing its morning gown of dawn quietude. He awakened quickly at first light, combed his hair, put on a fresh shirt and pair of pants and went into Delphine's room. She was lying with the blanket tucked under her chin, her eyes open, staring sightlessly at the ceiling.

"Ah, good, you're awake. I'll make us some coffee. The fresh croissants should be delivered by then."

There was a tiny uplifting of Delphine's lips.

Rachel and her daughters had left for Paris immediately upon Camille's return from Venezuela. They had not had time to hear of his sojourn in South America or to see his sketchbooks and watercolors. Now he ate his breakfast off a tray as he told Delphine stories about Fritz Melbye and Caracas, the colorful life of its people, his forays into the countryside, what excitement it brought to capture their spirit on blank sheets of paper with charcoal or ink, and how difficult it was to do.

He raised her a little, her head now on a level with his, showed her his pencil sketches of handsome native women with their elaborate headcloths; a woman carrying a tray of food on her head; *Native Women Washing*. Then he turned to his China ink drawing of the marketplace with its brightly garbed men and women, a clan gathering of males in Monte

16

Avila, pen-and-ink-over-pencil studies of barefoot natives leaning on their burros. He held up his intensely alive *Carnival Dance* in sepia wash: a big darkened room in which a dozen couples were whirling to the beat of rattle gourds. And in brown wash over pencil, *The Artists' Studio* with its pair of easels for himself and Fritz Melbye, a dozen drawings and paintings decorating the walls, a young student on one side of the studio, Fritz sitting before his easel.

Delphine struggled to speak.

"I'm so happy you're here."

"Then why do you want to leave us?"

After a while she fell asleep. Emma came in quietly, wrapped in a warm robe.

"She'll sleep most of the day. Why not go for a walk? You must be hungering to get your feet on the streets of Paris. But be careful, a whole neighborhood could collapse on you."

Camille laughed.

"Anton Melbye, Fritz's brother, has a studio close by at 18 Rue de la Ferme des Mathurins. Fritz wrote asking me to drop in on him. I may do that."

He had to secure an official identity card which would prove that he was in Paris legally. When he entered the designated office he was staggered by the smell. It had to be a dead mouse between two folders; the remnants of leftover meals rotting in a corner; the sweat of long-used clothing. If, on making his way back toward the Seine, he remembered that offices in Paris stank because all windows were sealed to keep out the dread consumption, everything else seemed to have changed astonishingly. The large area between the Louvre and the Tuileries, which had formerly been a little town unto itself, with a hundred old homes of royalty in advanced stages of decay, had been knocked down and the land converted into gardens by Commissioner Haussmann and the monarch town builder, Napoleon III. On the left bank of the Seine there remained the imposing bathhouses, Les Bains Deligny, Vigier, Petit, each a floating villa anchored by the Quai d'Orsay. Although they were more expensive, he decided to indulge himself in the Chinese baths. Cleanliness had been *de rigueur* in St. Thomas, and easily achieved. The black woman who had been purchased as a slave by the Pissarros, and when freed by the act of 1848 had declared, "This my family, I stay," had bathed them once a week in a big iron tub. But most of the time he had frolicked in the waters of the bay. Here in Paris a man used the public baths

17

or went dirty. Women were not allowed in the baths on the grounds of morality. He was astonished to learn from a book he had bought for a few pennies on the quai that the majority of French women died without ever having taken a single bath. All except the well-to-do men had taken only one bath; it was compulsory before entering the army. One's hands and nails were kept scrupulously clean; but no one ever washed his hair, harrowing it relentlessly instead with a fine-toothed comb which took out the lice.

This was astonishing information for one from the tropical islands. There had to be an explanation. There was. He found it a few pages later: "Bathing is self-indulgent. It is dangerous for one's health."

Here in Paris, Rachel used the expensive method of having brawny men carry tubs of hot water up to the apartment.

From the quai he descended gently sloping stairs to a red lacquered Chinese bridge which led to the baths. The entrance was in the middle of the villa, on a wooden porch with tubs of flowers; the side of the bank was an attractive garden with poplars, willows. He walked through a gallery decorated with columns, pilasters, a painted ceiling. At the admission booth he paid twenty centimes and was ushered into a private room where hot water was run into a tub. There was a slightly used cake of soap. The oriental attendant said:

"No time limit. Call when you want warm towel."

He lingered so long he missed Rachel's dinner hour. It was no deprivation, for he could eat across the length and breadth of Paris, where all manner of food was served from street stalls, handcarts, small smoking stoves carried by women hawking their wares. Near the Pont Notre Dame he bought a bowl of soup for one sou; in an open-air kitchen at the Marché des Innocents where the farm wagons rolled in all night with freshly gathered produce, he bought a potpourri of chicken, ham and beans; coming back along the quai, he found an old woman carrying a smoking pan from whom he obtained sausages and fried potatoes wrapped in paper. The meat most eaten in Paris was pork, for sale in the dozen shops he passed, but pork had been excommunicated from their home in St. Thomas. He was walking so briskly that he never did appease his appetite. After passing an organ grinder with his instrument strapped to his chest, playing the *William Tell* overture, uniformed men passing out advertisements, and a crowd in front of a newspaper office reading the latest posted bulletins about the Crimean War, he stopped at a Swiss milk shop for a cup of hot chocolate and a *pâtisserie*.

While at the boarding school it had taken him almost three hours to cross the city from Montmartre to the Rive Gauche because of the scarcity of bridges over the Seine, and the labyrinth of alleys, blocked streets, culs-de-sac, impenetrable jungle of crazy-hatched houses that led nowhere. He recalled whole rows of small dark shops with the merchandise wrapped as though to conceal it; and with no stated price, unlike the Pissarro store in St. Thomas. French shopkeepers had not wanted to accept money; they wanted to extend credit at usurious rates.

Now all that had changed. Parisians were no longer forced to shop near their homes, they could move along the new boulevards: Strasbourg, Rue de Rennes. The shops were larger, lighter, the prices marked on everything, out in the open, and only cash was used. Two large, attractive department stores, the first in Paris, had been opened: the Bon Marché, three years before, somewhat provincial; and the year before that, the Louvre, more expensive but displaying colorfully, even dramatically, goods from all over the world.

He also found to his delight that he could ride an omnibus for six sous, making changes of vehicles. The Rue Bergère, the first asphalted street in Paris, was a marvel of smoothness. Elsewhere he saw workmen replacing old large paving stones with small sandstones that made less racket under the carriages. In the wealthy areas of the Faubourg St. Honoré there were wooden paving blocks which were even quieter and smoother to ride upon. The most popularly traveled streets were the "grand boulevards," the Boulevard des Capucines and the Boulevard des Italiens, with expensive shops for jewelry, perfumes, purses, shoes, while the rest of the city was still made up of ancient narrow streets clogged with porters, carts, strolling vendors, water carriers; wide enough for only one vehicle at a time, the sidewalks so narrow that two persons abreast had trouble keeping one foot out of a usually wet gutter. Everywhere he went he saw huge holes in the ground, sometimes where unpaved streets had collapsed. Whole areas were being torn down, new buildings going up, enroped with massive scaffoldings. What he had remembered as a quagmire of a medieval city, with the exception of the Rue de Rivoli and the Champs-Elysées, which had grown by accretion, without scheme, sense or reason, was now emerging as a modern planned metropolis.

"That cab driver was wrong," he mused. "Napoleon III

and Commissioner Haussmann are going to recast Paris into a marvel of Europe. It's good to be here." A warm glow spread over his face. "Some of us are accidentally born in the wrong port."

6

He heard the babble while mounting the several flights of dark narrow stairs at 18 Rue de la Ferme des Mathurins. There was obviously a party or a meeting going on above him. When he had climbed still one more flight he found Anton Melbye's door open. A quite astonishing sight met his eyes. The studio was filled with men, its wall shelves crammed with vases, figurines, stone axes. On oddly assorted tables under the shelves were ethnographic articles, old coins mounted in velvet-lined boxes, violins, guitars, drums of various shapes; colorful Turkish costumes and robes decorating dummy figures; large Near East water pipes, fezzes, guns, swords. Above the shelves, some of which held books kept in place by lumps of stone hieroglyphs, and fitted as neatly together as a panel of wallpaper, was a border of the painter's sketches and watercolors from Turkey. Anton Melbye himself, wearing white trousers, a white flannel coat topped by a red fez brought back from Constantinople, and thin black-rimmed spectacles, stood before an easel, painting on a large canvas a monumental sea battle while surrounded by an admiring, talking, drinking, eating, laughing entourage sitting in chairs, standing or lolling on oriental carpets on the floor. Several of the men wore artists' smocks. The others wore more formal attire, high silk hats, long coats with tapering tails, fashionably cut trousers in complimentary gray or tan, starched white shirts and collars with black bow ties. Anton contributed to the high pitch of excitement; being engulfed by what appeared to be a coterie of friends seemed to lend him a heightened vigor and perception.

No one greeted Camille. He stepped sideways into a niche where he could observe without being noticed. He was stunned.

"*Je ne sais pas sur quel pied danser,*" he murmured. "I don't know what foot to stand on. I've always believed that art was a solitary pursuit."

Obviously he had been wrong. While he and Fritz Melbye

had painted together in their studio in Caracas and out in the woods and mountains, they had done so quietly, with criticism and comment reserved for the end of the day's work. To paint in this blizzard of voices, this maelstrom of people, noise, movement! "Without missing one brush stroke!" Camille cried aloud . . . that was inconceivable. Yet that was the way Anton Melbye painted; pictures that were admired and sold at high prices.

Then came the most astonishing transition. Melbye, very like his brother Fritz, tall, broad-shouldered, with blond hair, a blond beard and gray eyes, announced in a Danish-tinged accent:

"I'm fatigued. Let's play and sing for a while."

He left his easel, picked up a guitar, sank onto a buttoned leather hassock and eased his fingers lovingly over the strings. His friends gathered around him. When Melbye started playing *"Le Bon Bourgeois, "* the men sang lustily behind him:

> "Under the celestial empire
> Of Napoleon III
> The bourgeois
> Is afraid.
> Is he hungry when he eats?
> Is he thirsty when he drinks?
> No, my word!
> His mistress is an angel
> Who often likes nothing about him
> But his money.
> Friend of routine,
> He sees in progress
> Excess.
> The word 'republic'
> Gives him in his home
> A shiver."

Melbye's respite appeared to be a kind of signal. There were hearty au revoirs, the coterie filed past Camille still singing among themselves. Camille walked across the room from his semi-hiding place by the door, introduced himself.

"Ah, you're the friend of my wandering brother. A hearty welcome. Fritz mentioned you in his letters. You had an agreeable time together, yes?"

"And productive. Fritz is an intense worker. I learned a great deal from him."

"He tells me he also learned from you."

Camille had the good grace to blush. Melbye said genially:

"Do sit down. Join me in a glass of wine. I am happy to

see you because Fritz is not an outgoing man. You are the first friend he has been willing to acknowledge. But please, tell me about Fritz's two years in Caracas. Was he happy? Was his work good?''

Camille, sipping his glass of wine, told Anton about their creative life in Venezuela. Anton cried:

"I knew you would be coming today. An inner voice told me. Do you believe in clairvoyance?''

"No. I'm having enough difficulty trying to understand the simple things I can see, hear and feel. The occult baffles me. I leave it alone, the way I do people who baffle me.''

Melbye loosened his black cravat. His fingers combed his blond hair into an attractive swash from a high point on the side, a long straight curl folded neatly under his opposite ear. His skin was fair in contrast to Camille's deep tropical tan. His eyes, magnified behind glasses, were without aggression. He radiated an aura of success, with pleased lips, as though the world tasted good. His expression said, "I have met fate genially with a *soupçon* of talent. I have made the most of it.''

"The genius of the Dane is to be able to combine the solidity of success with the ease of generous companionship. I love to work. I put in full days without push or strain. I never allow myself to feel internal rumblings of unrest or the bodily poisons of exhaustion.''

Camille noticed that he spoke without the convoluted grammar of his brother.

"Fritz says you have an inborn skill," Anton volunteered.

"We learned together, pouring our strength into the drawings. . . .''

"And into the young Venezuelan girls?''

"We had good times. Caracas was my coming-out party, so to speak.''

"How old are you?''

"Twenty-five. In St. Thomas you couldn't have a nice girl without marrying her. The only alternative for young lads like myself on a modest wage was the prostitutes who serviced the famished sailors in from long journeys at sea. Not very appetizing; and dangerous, with venereal disease brought in from every port of the world. We felt genuine affection for some of the Venezuelan girls. They were good companions on our painting forays into the country.''

"So you became a man?''

"If that's the definition of a man.''

"It's a portion. Painting is the more important portion.

What did you think of the paintings at the International Exhibition?"

"I haven't been yet. I arrived the day before yesterday."

"Then you must see it immediately. It's closing soon. I'll take you. I'm exhibited there and luckily my painting is the first one people see when they come in. It has helped my sales considerably. Be prepared! Five thousand paintings! *Ce n'est pas la mer à boire.* It's like trying to drink the sea. You're going to experience an explosion of paint and canvas you never dreamed possible."

"May I look at your work? Fritz has a high regard for it."

"Too high. He resents it. He becomes furious when people describe his work as 'Anton painting.' But there it is, master and pupil. I paint the sea, only the sea. In all weather, carrying all kinds of ships. The sea fascinates me. In my youth I wanted to become a naval officer; being nearsighted kept me out. Then I became a professional musician. When I was nineteen I went by accident to an exhibition of paintings in Copenhagen. One of them, a rendering of the sea in a violent rainstorm, so fascinated me that I registered in the Academy art school and lo! I am a seaman painter, of admiral rank."

Camille stood before the canvases, studied the storms at sea, the lighthouses lashed by furious waves, maritime battles with ships, guns, fighting men; the ocean at peace, multicolored toward the shore, reflecting sunlight or moonlight; sailing vessels and steamships in landlocked harbors. Anton Melbye was indeed a subtle observer of water and weather.

7

Their hour's walk took them past the Gare St. Lazare, then south on the Rue d'Astorg and through the Place de la Ville l'Evêque and Place Beauveau. Camille had forgotten this aspect of French architectural genius: four or five streets running into a circle, with a single rounded building occupying each corner, the rounded buildings creating a truly rounded *place,* harmonious, a joy to the eye and a dissolver of inner tensions.

When they reached the Champs-Elysées they saw the grandiose Triumphal Arc, and beyond it the Exposition Universelle.

"I think I got here at a good moment," Camille mused.

"The reconstruction of the city may lead to new ideas and new energies."

"Every painting generation is a new invention, equal to railroad cars running on tracks and gas pipes to light our apartments," Anton responded.

The Exposition Universelle loomed before them like a giant freighter suddenly bearing down upon a rowboat out of a fog-covered sea. Camille discerned four separate stone pavilions which, with their landscaping on the Champs-Elysées, covered twenty thousand square feet. A larger area than the entire main street of Charlotte Amalie.

"Do you know how its adversaries describe it?" Anton asked, having heard Camille's gasp of astonishment. "As '*d'honnêtes hangars*,' honest outhouses. But then, hostile criticism is a recognized profession in Paris."

From the Parisian newspapers *L'Illustration* and *Le Figaro*, which arrived in St. Thomas on each French packet, and the local *Tidende*, Camille had learned that Emperor Napoleon III, while he lived in exile in England, had been a great admirer of the Crystal Palace exhibition. He had determined, once he had been elected President, and more certainly after his coup d'etat in which he had himself crowned as Napoleon III, to create an ultramodern Exposition Universelle and supplant Great Britain's in importance.

"*Magnifique*," Anton cried, "*n'est-ce pas?*"

It was indeed, with four arches placed at the rear of a court centered by an overpowering chestnut tree which spread its branches high above the roof. Sheltered by the two formidable wings spreading out from the arches were the visitors coming and going, the men in high silk hats and full-cut, below-the-knee coats; the women in flowerstrewn bonnets, ground-length gowns over hoop skirts, colorful shawls decorating their shoulders.

They entered through mechanical *tourniquets* which counted the number in attendance. The turnstiles were also alleged to be able to tell the weight and age of the people entering, a false alarm which kept women out until the canard was laid to rest. Immediately inside stood officers in cocked hats, swords at their sides.

In the Palais de l'Industrie experimental machines were exhibited in a long wood-lined gallery. As they strode by Camille noted also that the French were showing the cloth from Lyon which his acquaintance on the train had been selling in South America. There was shorn wool from the north; laces, bronzes, precision instruments, the first ingots of aluminum; Sèvres vases, silver from Christofle. He passed English displays of metal and ceramics. The Americans were exhibiting hunting weapons and furniture, the Belgians sacerdotal vestments. When they entered the main hall Camille gasped; it seemed to rise at least a hundred feet, with an arched glass roof and a balcony up some sixty feet. There were staircases everywhere, huge sculptures on pedestals four times the height of the tallest man present. Individual pavilions had ornamental awnings and raised circular gardens of bushes and ferns, with cushioned seats for the comfort of tired feet. Fountains splashed and flags were hung around the tricolor of France, high up on the girders.

Camille had never imagined such a huge hall was possible. There were cafés and bars placed about for refreshments. The most popular innovation was a coffee device called a percolator, invented by a Monsieur Loysel, which could produce two thousand cups of coffee in an hour, all of which were admiringly drunk by those in attendance.

There were new locomotives and luxurious railway carriages on display; gas street lighting as a recent industry; electric batteries, exploratory light bulbs. A great stir was made by the electric telegraph, declared to be the most important invention of the century, but the Morse code, also exhibited, was not felt to be of any particular value. A major discovery was the vulcanization of rubber. Mr. Goodyear, an American, had refined a process whereby a "dazzling" display could be seen of rubber combs, toys, dogs and birds that squeaked when squeezed. A rubber mattress filled with warm water delighted the onlookers. Another novelty from America was an invention called a "sewing machine" next to which a sign read: "In the coming era nothing will be done by hand."

But the displays attracting the longest queues were the crown diamonds; the Rajah's tent in the English India exhibit; two chandeliers of rock crystal made by Baccarat; a talking doll; and a statue of God, fully dressed, exhibited by the Belgians. As far as Camille could make out, the expression on God's face was one of approval of this huge fair.

An official guide insisted upon informing them that the Exposition was a *succès fou*. Over five million visitors had attended in the two hundred days it had been open and the Exposition had taken in three million francs against an eleven million cost. However the French railroads had carted in many millions, the Paris hotels had lodged half a million guests. On Sundays, when it was free, a hundred thousand spectators trooped through. The Queen of England had visited, as had the King of Portugal. It was indeed a greater success than the 1851 Crystal Palace exhibition in London.

Half trotting through the remaining galleries, they found themselves outside in a charming garden with severely trimmed hedges, tall trees and fading flower beds. Across from them was the Beaux-Arts. Suddenly they were inside the building, with its high semicircular entrance and its two-story glass ceiling.

The smell of oil paint, varnish, canvas was ambrosia.

Camille stood transfixed before the enormous cordoned-off hall of paintings, the vast blaze of color dominating the senses. Immediately in front of him were the exhibits from Frankfurt, Denmark, Sweden, Norway, large signs above them announcing their national origin. Beyond were large squares with the Prussian and Italian displays, corridors with the Belgian, American, Spanish, Dutch, English, landscapes, portraits, still lifes, seascapes side by side, floor to high ceiling.

Anton took him by the arm and hustled him up to his own painting, *Lighthouse*. Camille's head was pounding.

"How many paintings are hung here?"

"Over five thousand."

His voice was hoarse. "It's too easy. It seems any half-wit can color a canvas. Painting is a virulent disease that has spread all over Europe."

"It's not the black plague," Anton Melbye replied sympathetically. "No one ever died from it. The Parisian argot has it, *Le mieux est l'ennemi du bien*. Better is the enemy of good. There are hundreds of good painters. You must strive to be better. Besides, you have no choice."

He led Camille through several of the national corridors and into the first of the vast French exhibits.

"I understand your reaction. You are overwhelmed. So was I when I first walked in here. After you come back a few times the individual works begin to assert themselves. When you have separated the schools you will begin to recognize the individual artists. Each is different from the other; that's one of the glories of art, the far-reaching latitudes in which each artist lives and practices."

They had ricocheted through a wide arcade containing the Piedmontese on one entire side, the Roman, Swedish and Tuscan representation on another, coming across more "school" names than he had dreamed existed: Romantic. Primitive. New Tendencies. Symbolism. Coup d'Oeil. Art Moderne. Literary movements. Progressive . . .

What did it all mean? Did the artists put themselves in

categories of this nature; or was it the literary folk who backed the painters into wolf packs?

The two extensive French pavilions held something like two thousand canvases. He slowed down, attempting to study them, to find names in the corners, and was aghast at his ignorance. Who were Glaize, Rouget, Flandrin, Yvon, Cabanel, Vignon? All qualified, apparently. Though he had avidly searched out French art magazines and Parisian papers for years, he did not recognize the names. He continued burrowing, spelled out the additional names of Jalabert, Curzon, Troyon, Français, Ziem, Gudin, Chenavard . . . hundreds. . . .

"It's impossible!" he cried aloud, causing a stare from a middle-aged couple browsing among the paintings as through a bookstall. "There must be several thousand painters in Paris alone. There's no need for more painting. Certainly not for more painters. I've been castle building!"

"Let's plow the French field first," suggested Melbye. "The selection jury is rigidly exclusive in its choices."

"*Mon Dieu!* Then how many are rejected?"

"Varies. According to the year. This spring? Several thousand, I would guess."

"Why are they refused? What happens to the poor devils who are refused?"

"First of all, there aren't walls enough for all those who paint. Secondly, a lot of the work is obviously amateurish. Other canvases have a subject matter that is unacceptable to the jury members. Some painters are taboo, for political or social or personal reasons. As for your other question, no one knows until the day before the opening who has been accepted. Those who have been hung rejoice. The other poor devils, as you call them, find their canvases stacked in an anteroom with an *R* for Rejection stamped on them. They curse or weep, pile their pictures on a small cart and trundle them home."

It was then Camille remembered two of Daumier's cartoons, in the first of which large canvases are being dashed through the streets on the shoulders of four men, while moderate-sized ones, elaborately framed, are carried on the backs of young stalwarts, the artist trailing in high-crowned, wide-brimmed hat, long uneven tresses stringing down his back, wearing a worn painter's frock and holding a palette in his left hand, eagerly putting finishing touches to the canvas with his right. They are surrounded by other artists in top hats, long dark coats and anxious expressions as they tilt forward, onrushing to the Salon. In the second, the *Marche*

27

Funèbre, the rejected painter is going home, downcast, with two younger men ahead of him carrying on a hod four canvases stamped *Refusé*.

"Which one will be a portrait of me?" he wondered.

8

Delphine was listless, failing rapidly. In Camille's supercharged state he poured out some of his bedazzlement.

"It's a whole world, Delphine, alive, vibrant, reaching out from the walls to engulf you."

His vitality brought a little color to her cheeks. She asked:
"Camille . . . ?"

"Yes, Delphine?"

"Paint a picture for me."

He kissed her on the forehead.

"Reste tranquille. I'll paint many beautiful pictures for you. A whole lifetime of them."

A glimmer of hope lighted the brown darkness of her eyes.

"Never let it happen to you as it did to me. That you wake in the morning, stare at the ceiling, ask yourself, 'What have I got to get up for today?' and answer . . . 'Nothing.' "

Delphine died just before dawn. The difference between breathing minutely and not breathing at all was barely perceptible. Camille asked himself dejectedly, "What do I paint for Delphine? She who for thirty-two years had been so blank a canvas, not even a rough sketch of life, a few dabs of color."

They did not know a rabbi to conduct the funeral service. Though they had been in Paris for a year, Rachel and Emma had felt displaced because they were women alone. They had not joined a congregation or made friends in the neighborhood. Uncle Moïse came to their aid. The rabbi from his own congregation consented, reluctantly, to perform the ritual over someone he had never known.

Père Lachaise, on the very east end of Paris, was the national cemetery. It had been founded in 1626 as a retreat by the Jesuits; been frequented by Father La Chaise, Louis XIV's confessor; and was now a monumental burial place covered with giant trees, shrubbery and resplendent tombs of France's immortals.

It was a cold and overcast day of the disagreeable kind

Paris proffers in winter. Camille helped his mother down from the carriage at the main entrance on the Rue de la Roquette. He gripped her arm firmly as they walked over the hand-sized cobblestones to a second entrance. Inside enclosed walls was the old Jewish cemetery, the greenery bent under an earlier rain. This secluded area, with its Hebrew inscriptions on the tombstones, had a calm ambience. However the sight of the prepared pit covered with a gravecloth sent Rachel into convulsive shivers.

Camille wrapped his arm around her.

"It's peaceful here, Maman. The wall keeps out noise and intrusion. There will be no more unhappiness for Delphine."

They stood at the gravesite with its suspended wooden coffin. Rachel, Camille, Emma, Uncle Moïse. The rabbi in his black robe, *tallith* and *yarmulke*, recited the Kaddish, a memorial for the dead, yet in truth an exaltation:

"*Adonai Nosan Adonai Lokach Yehee Shem Adonai Hamavorach*. The Lord giveth, the Lord hath taken away. Blessed be the name of the Lord. *Yigedal Veyiskadash Shemei Rabboh*. May His great name be exalted and glorified. *Lech Besholom*. Go thou in peace."

Camille and Emma stoically absorbed the ceremony. Not so Rachel; she moaned unrestrainedly. Once at home she lay curled on her bed, soaking towels with her tears, inconsolable over her fifth of eight children to be buried. She was a deeply emotional woman. Alfred said that her children lived in a sea of storms, with only a sometimes smooth surface. Camille remembered considerable periods of calm, demonstrated by the fact that she was a diligent bookkeeper for the St. Thomas shop from its beginning. He had not known the first sons, or understood the disappearance of the oldest Pissarro brother, Joseph Gabriel Félix, who died when Camille was only three or four. His younger brother, Aaron Gustave, had died suddenly of a pestilential fever in August of 1853, while Camille was in Caracas. The death of Delphine was the first he experienced with his family. He was stunned by his mother's total collapse. He was unaccustomed to this depth of despair and did not know how to handle it.

Emma tried to help.

"I've been through this before, with Aaron Gustave. It will last for days, then she'll fall into a fever and sleep. When she gets up she'll face the world again. Leave her to me. Go about your work."

*   *   *

When Rachel appeared to have reconciled herself that she had one daughter and two sons left, and had hired a maid who could cook and do some cleaning, Camille decided to risk setting his mother straight about his plans. It was time to begin work in earnest. He bought a used, sturdy easel, a new sketchbook, pencils, charcoal, inks and watercolors, and the next morning strapped a pack with his sketching equipment to his back. Rachel was shocked.

"Oh, Camille, not again?" she cried. "I hoped you had worked out all that foolishness on your spree in Venezuela."

"It wasn't a spree, Maman. It was a hard-working apprenticeship."

She had already spoken to two of his father's business associates in Paris about hiring her son. Since he knew the islands and South America, they had well-paying jobs to offer. He must begin to earn a living. That was the hard reality of life. Also, Uncle Moïse had two young women he wanted Camille to meet. From wealthy families. With splendid dowries. Good girls. Bright.

Camille shook his head in wonderment at the definiteness of his mother's plans.

"I won't be ready to marry for years, Maman. As a painter, you said yourself, I'm ineligible. Forgive me, *chère*. I tricked you into that."

"Just be sure you don't trick yourself. Don't forget that I have been a businesswoman all my life. I know how hard it is to earn a living, to hedge a little profit against adversity."

"I'm not ignorant of the workaday world," he said quietly.

He was not really ignorant about very much; his five years of education at the Pension Savary had been incisive and disciplined. When he entered at twelve he was introduced first to the romantic poets: Alfred de Vigny, Lamartine, Hugo. He did not understand everything he read but he grasped a good deal. The following year he was moved up to Stendhal's *The Red and the Black*, strong stuff for a thirteen-year-old. When he was fourteen he was given Montaigne's *Essays*, easy reading but hard assimilation. During this year he and his class were taken into Paris to see the French classical plays: Molière's *The Misanthrope* and *The Bourgeois Gentleman*. In his fifteenth year he was promoted to Rousseau's *The Social Contract* and Voltaire's *Candide*. He saw Racine's *Phèdre* and *Britannicus*. His last year, at seventeen, his teacher involved the class in a binge of Balzac: *Le Père Goriot, Eugénie Grandet*. To compensate for the heavy going in Plato and Herodotus in Greek, Pliny and Plutarch in

Latin, the older boys smuggled in bawdy novels. He emerged
from his five years of lycée with an ingrained love of reading
that was never to leave him, and that he found was the open
door to knowledge . . . along with his two years in Venezuela, which specialized in the realities of poverty, illiteracy,
the physical hardships of life.

"Rationally, my dear Camille," his mother was saying,
"what are the odds of your earning a decent living, or
becoming a success, known for your work?"

He did not want to deceive her or, for that matter, himself.

"Long odds, Maman. Perhaps one in a hundred."

"Or one in a thousand?"

He thought of the walls of paintings at the Exposition
Universelle.

"It could be."

"And are you a gambler?"

"Not with money at a casino table. But with my life, yes. I
can't give away my years just to fill my stomach."

"Are you St. Francis whom the birds will feed?"

He grinned sheepishly.

"I am the wrong religion to be St. Francis. Seriously,
Maman, doesn't a man have to make choices? One should
work at what gives him meaning and fulfillment."

"Is it better to be a failed painter than a successful businessman?" Rachel's voice was deeply concerned.

"For you and Father, no. For me, yes."

"How will you pay for all that paint?"

"Would you or Father spend the amount needed for five or
six years at the university for me to become a doctor or an
advocate . . . ?"

"Oh, Camille! Go to the university, become a professional
man," she interrupted. "We would support you. We would
be proud."

"That same money will secure me a place in the art world.
It's a respectable profession. You will be proud of me as a
painter."

The color drained from her face.

"If you knew how hard our families have struggled for two
to three hundred years, ever since we were Marranos in
Portugal. I beg of you, don't destroy yourself."

The tears ran down her cheeks. He brushed them off with
his fingertips, held the bulk of her against him. She murmured a half prayer:

"God protect you, Camille."

"He will. Trust us."

"I'd rather trust your father than Our Father. Frédéric gets more practical results. You know what God said to Moses on Mount Sinai. It's part of the Ten Commandments:

" 'Thou shalt not make thyself a graven image, or any likeness of anything that is in heaven above, or that is in the earth beneath, or that is in the water under the earth; you shall not bow down to them or serve them.' "

Camille knew the stricture, but he also had seen evidence of beautiful calligraphy done by Jewish artists, exquisitely wrought amulets to be used against bad fortune. These charms were kept on the walls to ward off evil, were painted on marriage agreements; were good fortune for coming babies. Sometimes, if the bride were named Rachel, out of the Bible, the artist would draw on the marriage agreement a portrait of a woman who resembled Rachel. It had nothing to do with graven images.

"Maman, the artist exalts God's creations. There can be no finer way of serving Him."

"You out-argue me, Camille, but you can't out-convince me."

Camille laughed in amused despair. She folded him in her maternal arms.

"I loved you at first sight. I fear for you. It's a mother's role to fear for her children."

"Fear, yes. But also to have confidence. Have confidence," he pleaded.

9

Camille took with him to Anton Melbye's studio a large sketchbook of his Caracas drawings, then handed him a fair-sized watercolor over pencil, *Bridge of Doña Romualda*, a group of children in front of a weather-washed pink house on top of a hill, an arched tunnel by its side leading to the sea; and *Coconut Palms by the Sea*, a small oil which he had still to complete. He explained to Melbye that he had used a thin oil paint a couple of times but didn't feel equipped to use it properly. He needed more time.

Anton Melbye expressed satisfaction with the work.

"Fritz was right. You have a strong sense of structural form. Your coloring is a bit on the vague side but you start from a firm base. Only years of hard work will tell how high you will build from that base."

When Camille mentioned that he was going back to the Beaux-Arts for a closer study, Anton offered to accompany him.

They made their way directly to the Avenue Montaigne. This entranceway was decorated with a profusion of exquisite Chinese art, folding screens inlaid with ivory and quartz; cinnabar and lacquered vases; porcelain figurines; scrolls depicting Chinese village life.

"France has recently discovered China," said Melbye cynically; "all these objects were pillaged and are now owned by the government. One way to acquire an art collection. It's been going on since Alexander the Great destroyed Persepolis and looted its treasury."

In the central court of the Beaux-Arts was the most important exhibition; a huge hall devoted to forty of Eugène Delacroix's canvases, largely religious and historical themes of visual grandeur new to European art, a gloriole of color, violence and portraiture. Delacroix was the leader of the Romantic movement, influenced by Géricault and by his own studies of Rubens and the sixteenth-century Venetians in the Louvre. Here were his *Barque of Dante*, first exhibited in the Salon of 1822, and the *Massacre at Chios* of 1824, which the highly placed academician Gros described as "the massacre of painting." However the government of France had purchased the brilliant canvas and started Delacroix on his career.

For Camille the most fascinating of the paintings were the ones that emerged from Delacroix's visit to Africa, *Women of Algiers, The Arab Family*. Wandering around the enormous room, he found intensely lifelike portraits of Chopin and George Sand. He stood in silence and wonder.

"It's truly staggering," he finally exclaimed. *"Mon Dieu*, a wall becomes a world."

"Speaking of Delacroix," Melbye said, "where did you say you lived?"

"At 49 Rue Notre Dame de Lorette."

"Delacroix has his studio just across the street from you. They tell me he's approachable. Study his self-portrait so you'll recognize him, and say *bonjour* one day when you pass each other."

Jean Auguste Dominique Ingres, Paris's second giant, had

also been allowed to hang his own show. Ingres had chosen forty-three paintings which occupied a long loggia. Now seventy-five, he was showing a retrospective of high-society portraits, but mostly there were voluptuous female nudes with flesh tones so warm and lifelike that Camille wanted to reach out and touch them: *Women Bathing, Odalisque with a Slave.* He commented:

"What wonderful flesh tones. The bodies are vibrantly alive . . . yet somehow virginal. . . . As though no man has known them."

"Not even Ingres," Anton agreed. "It's his virginal mind you're looking at. He is a painter of the exterior of human beings. Yet he is a tremendous portrait painter. Here, look at these, marvelous pictures of the painter Granet; of Comtesse d'Haussonville; of the violinist Paganini. Have you ever seen such facial perfection?"

Camille moved closer to study Ingres's technique of opening a little curtain at the rear of each portrait to reveal in the distance the church spire and buildings of a native village. He heard Melbye murmur behind him:

"Ingres and Delacroix have been staunch enemies all their professional lives because they are leaders of opposing schools, each deploring and trying to eliminate the other. They haven't exchanged a word for twenty years, though they encounter each other frequently at Academy meetings, showings. . . . Painting is a noble art, my young friend, but those who practise it are not always noble people."

Camille chewed on the thought.

"We who want to be artists have all the weaknesses of other human beings, probably magnified by the fact that we work and live outside the mainstream of normal life."

"You are a philosopher," teased Anton. "You'll need it in the Parisian art jungle."

Camille wandered among the *salles*, unmoved by the large display of Horace Vernet's military paintings, or by De-camps, a producer of oriental scenes. One by one he picked out the paintings of the group that had become known as the Fontainebleau or Barbizon School: Corot's *Evening, Memory of Marcoussy;* Millet's *Peasant Budding a Tree;* Daubigny's and Rousseau's splendid paintings of the elegant Fontaine-bleau forest and the Seine River, soft, nonaggressive, pastel landscapes. The whirling dervishes of line, color and form which had been clashing inside his vision dissolved. He felt a quietude, a sense of peace and arrival.

"This is where I belong," he thought. "But how do I get there?"

In the deepest soul-searching he had ever known, standing amidst this wealth of the world's art, he asked himself:

"Where does this hunger come from, that drives some of us to draw with a ferocity that is equaled only by the necessity to breathe, to eat, to survive? Surely it comes with birth and growth even as one's limbs or brain; a need of nature built into the organic human structure. Not a sixth toe but an index finger."

He bought a demitasse of coffee, felt the warmth descend through his chest, then found a comfortable bench in a corner near a tall fountain on which to rest.

Could he believe that those who were born to art would thrive and create superbly? That those who came to it for artificial reasons, because it looked easy or romantic or a level road to fame and fortune, might have little to contribute? The compulsion to draw and paint was a positive presence. Was it a gift or a deficiency? A blessing or a curse? Were they self-anointed or the chosen?

How did one explain this rationally to one who was not similarly afflicted? Where there was no shared language?

"To the rest of the world I may appear to be locked for life into a solitary cell," he mused, "communicating through bars."

When he returned from Caracas he had tried to explain this to his parents.

"Of what is it a residue?" they had cried. "You never had mumps or equatorial fever or consumption. You seemed happy. You appeared to love your family. What has led to this revolt? To this illegitimate child?"

Camille was confounded.

"There are no illegitimate artists, Maman; there are simply people born out of bourgeois society. They should be accepted. If there must be blame, blame it on some distant great-grandfather who bequeathed me this disturbing heritage, the way your Pommié-Manzana grandparents bequeathed you the emotional temperament you've dragged around all your life."

"Your argument is self-serving," his father had said sternly.

"It is not an argument. It is a statement of fact I must live with."

"And eat with? Put clothes on your body with? A roof over your head? *Je'en doute.*"

"Perhaps I doubt it too. But it's irrelevant. I will somehow

35

find bread, maybe even a pot roast, a shirt, a bed. My real problem will be to find money to buy brushes, canvas, watercolors, oil paints. . . .''

There had been long silences, great sighs of despair. Then his father had announced:

"I will go along. What choice do I have?"

But they had not understood . . . or believed.

He was standing before a shimmering Corot orchard when Anton Melbye rejoined him. Camille said softly:

"If I were to have a master, Corot would be my choice."

"Would you like to meet him? Papa Corot, as he is fondly called, enjoys young painters. He welcomes them at the end of a day's work. No food or drink, just welcome. Bring your latest sketches."

10

A couple of afternoons later he went with Melbye to visit Corot's studio.

"He is the most loved painter in Paris because there is no harshness in him, no fierce competitive spirit," Melbye told him. "Delacroix said about Ingres: 'He has always considered himself the world's greatest painter. In some limited ways, he is. But this overweaning conceit has led him to the fantasy that he is the Emperor Napoleon of Art.' Corot could never say anything so abrasive."

They approached the Rue Paradis Poissonnière. Corot's father, too, had been grimly determined to make him a successful merchant. He had spent six years apprenticed to a draper. Finally, at the age of twenty-six, both his employer and his father, a prosperous cloth merchant, decided he was not for trade. His father offered him his dead sister's unused dowry; three hundred dollars a year for the rest of his life. No one believed he could live on that sum, but he had a peasant's simplicity, his only luxury his daily soup.

Now approaching sixty, Corot had painted in the woods for thirty years, selling only a few canvases. He had shown at the Salon a number of times but his canvases had usually decorated hallways or been strung like cornices at the ceiling. When he was badly hung he would sigh:

"Oh dear, I am in the catacombs."

In 1833 the Salon awarded him a second-class medal for *The Forest of Fontainebleau;* in 1835 his enormous *Hagar in the Wilderness* received some praise, though it was criticized for its pale and uniform color. From the Salon of 1840 he had sold *Le Petit Berger* for fifteen thousand francs to the museum at Metz.

When it was announced in the newspaper that a Monsieur Corot had won the Légion d'Honneur, his father exclaimed:

"Why has this great honor been bestowed upon me?"

He died when Corot was fifty-one, leaving him a fortune of one hundred twenty-five thousand dollars. The painter rarely used the money, except for his charities. He did not spend even the income of the fortune and, since he had never married, distributed it to his many cousins.

They climbed the stairs up to the fourth floor of number 58. Corot's studio was a spacious room with a large sloping north-light window without draperies or carpeting. It held a few chairs and, at the far end, a table with a capacious drawer containing his account book, invitations and hundreds of sketches. On a shelf were only two books, *The Imitation of Christ* by Thomas à Kempis and *Polyeucte* by Corneille. Scattered about the room were several ancient easels, each with a painting in a state of near completion. The walls were covered with hundreds of rough, spontaneous studies of sylph-like, mist-covered trees, clouds, nature at sunrise and dusk. In an alcove over his bed hung his favorite painting, *The Bridge at Narni*. It was said of Corot:

"He needed nothing but nature, and he had her in his studies. He did not have to wander in search of his muse, for she was always with him in his neighborhood, in his pocket, where he could consult her whenever he chose."

Corot was sitting near the door, singing an aria from Gluck, a large meerschaum pipe, which he called Pipette, in his mouth. He appeared short, even sitting down, but it was evident that inside his blue peasant blouse were a powerful chest and shoulders. On his head he wore a striped, tricolored cotton cap. His hair, turning white, fringed out of the cap like tufts of hoarfrost. His eyes were of a placid blue; slight lines angling from the middle of his short nose demarcated his cheeks. His mother had exclaimed, shortly after his birth:

"*Mon Dieu,* how ordinary you look!"

For Pissarro it was no ordinary face, but one of the most unusual he had encountered: a mildness toward the outer world, and a stalwart inner force that kept him working at the only job he wanted. He received Camille cordially. All artists were his family, even the mediocre, whom he frequently helped support.

"Poor little ones," he would murmur; "to have neither ability nor money. I buy a sketch from them for a few francs. It makes them happy and puts hot soup in their bellies."

When he greeted Anton Melbye, Corot's voice came out of his barrel chest as though from a gravel pit.

"So you've brought an artist friend. That must mean you think him not without promise."

Returning Corot's firm handclasp, Camille ventured:

"Monsieur Corot, I have heard that you are not made uneasy if someone says he admires your work?"

"Uncomfortable? From honest admiration? Walk around the room with me. You see this *Sheepherders Reading* that I'm just finishing. I love it! And this nude *Marietta*. I love it! And ah, this *Spring*. A love affair!"

Camille laughed at Corot's childlike enthusiasm, studied *Spring*'s green, flowered lawn with its grass still wet with the dew of dawn, naked children dancing in a circle; trees on whose trunks were attached climbing plants rising towards the clouds. He commented:

"I have spent two days at the Exposition. While I haven't studied all five thousand paintings, your canvases are for me altogether the best drawn and painted."

Corot gazed at him shrewdly. "Why?"

Camille was taken aback. Gropingly, he attempted to present his admiration in painterly terms. Corot filled his pipe, lighted the tobacco and, after drawing on it once or twice, pointed it directly at Camille's chest.

"I see you have brought some drawings with you. Put them here on my easel. While I study them, tell me how you reached this point in your life."

Camille talked. Corot sifted the batch of drawings and color washes, looked appraisingly through the notebooks from Caracas and St. Thomas; the pencil and charcoal studies of the natives, the watercolors of La Guaira; the sepia wash of the *Carnival Dance;* the tropical forest of Monte Avila, the oil of *Coconut Palms by the Sea*, which he had just completed in Melbye's studio, at his invitation, from the dozen detailed studies he had brought with him.

"I've never had a master," he explained.

"You're fortunate," Corot replied. "Neither did I. In that way we reflect ourselves. A man can learn from passing teachers, from one's fellow artists, without violating his own instincts. *Alors*, let us go over your sketches. This one from

St. Thomas, *Route de Bussy*, is understated; but this water-color over pencil of the bridge emerges with good character. These studies of the water carriers project vitality. I like these, two women conversing on the seashore."

"I'm completing it here."

"It shows strong form and perspective, the light-colored path on which the black women are standing, and the sloping, horizontal mountains blocking in the border. But why so many coconuts?"

Camille grinned in embarrassment.

"I was advised to paint them. Native. Indigenous. I might be able to sell a suggestion of their tropical heat in a cold Paris winter."

He was half mocking himself. Corot heard the undertone.

"Forget palm trees. Paint France. The muse is in the woods. How charming the day of the landscaper is. He rises at three, before the sun. He sits beneath a tree; he looks, he waits. Nature is a white sheet upon which the vague profile of things is vaguely seen. The sky brightens. The first ray of sun. The little flowers are awakened; the birds, invisible, are singing. The landscape beyond the veil of fog is rising, revealing the blade of the silver river, the meadows, the trees, the cottages. The sun is up. The peasant is at the end of the field with his cart and oxen. There is the tinkle of sheep bells. Everything is alight. Everything burns. Noon. The sun burns the world. The earth becomes still. The hammer in the forge resounds upon the anvil."

"You paint with your words," commented Camille in admiration, "as you are a poet with your crayon and brush."

Corot stood before his own oil paintings, *Cart Fording a Stream* and *Chartres Cathedral*. He gazed at Camille with a benign sternness.

"All painting should be poetry. Nothing else. No ugliness, no vulgarity, no sordid dirt or chaos or commonness."

While talking and pulling away at his pipe, Corot kept glancing at his own study of a lake surrounded by misty trees. Suddenly he rushed forward to his palette and snatched up his brushes. Seating himself quickly at his easel, he squeezed out a tube of white and started to model on the canvas a large sunlit cloud.

"We are like crafty fishermen," he cried as he made rapid strokes with the brush; "we must seize the propitious moment to get the fish to fall into our net."

Corot worked away on the canvas in silence for some fifteen minutes. Anton and Camille stood quietly by watching his skill and intensity. Then he set down the palette, and his voice boomed forth.

"Let us continue the day of the landscapist. We go to lunch at a farm. A good slice of country bread spread over with butter fresh from the churn. Eggs, cream. I take my siesta. The sun goes down in an explosion of yellow, orange, scarlet, cherry, purple. From beneath the horizon a streak of gold and purple fringes the flying cloud. Twilight begins. The sun merges into the dark blue of the night. The breezes sigh among the leaves. A star dives from the sky into the pond. The sun is gone, but the interior sun of the soul, the sun of art has arisen. . . . Good, my picture is made."

There was silence in the room.

"At the end of my day I say, 'I must stop; my Heavenly Father has put out the lamp.' God is good. He is the original artist. All we can do is interpret. But that too is divine."

Corot turned friendly eyes on Camille.

"Monsieur Pissarro, you have an observing eye and a sensitive hand. Work every day. Work all day. Before you go, let me give you a couple of sketches off my walls. They might be of some help. Which two drawings do you like the best?"

Camille stood stunned. Then he moved about the studio, indicated one pencil and one crayon drawing of the Fontaine-bleau forest. Corot wrapped them in an old newspaper.

"Feel free to come again whenever you wish, Monsieur Pissarro, at the end of the workday. Bring your sketches. We will discuss them as confreres."

As Camille turned toward the door, Corot cried:

"One thing more. Take it as advice from an old man. Never marry. The road is too long and hard. Families, responsibilities weigh heavily; they prevent you from getting your work done. Women, yes; love, no. You are already in love with art. Remain faithful."

11

He traversed Paris not to conquer the city but to assimilate it. Sometimes he rode on the new bus system, where for thirty centimes he could sit on top in the open air, cold as it might be. He walked through the Bois de Boulogne and the Place des Vosges, sketch pad in hand, drew people, buildings, street scenes in the superb public garden of the Luxembourg; the jewel of a church, St. Germain-des-Prés, on the Left Bank, the weird and wonderful animals in the zoo of the Jardin des Plantes: elephants, tigers, zebras.

Learning that the poorest of Paris lived in the Faubourg St. Marcel, he wore his oldest boots, avoided the cesspools of the ragged alleys, inconspicuously putting on paper the falling hovels. The few inhabitants at the dead ends were pale and haggard of face, dressed in tatters: people between hunger and death. He worked all day. When night fell the remainder of the unfortunates came out of their caves, hunched over the pale lanterns to forage among the discards and alluvial garbage of better neighborhoods.

At home, late at night, having scrubbed himself in the family's iron tub and eaten the supper the domestic had set out for him, he got into his warm dressing gown and once in bed adjusted the oil lamp so that he could study the pages of his notebook. He was sick at heart at the misery they depicted. He wondered how such a majestic city as Paris could allow such dehumanizing misery to exist.

He made his way to the Cité Napoléon on the Rue de Rochechouart, one of the *cités ouvrières*, workingmen's districts, built by Napoleon III with his own money because he wanted to improve the living conditions of working families. The buildings were neat, the streets stonepaved and hosed down from horse-drawn carts; but the expressions of the people entering and leaving the lone entrance were less than enchanted.

He stopped at a corner café for a beer; stood beside a mason in jacket and cap, who complained sourly:

"The rooms are small. Cells. Better than we had, but like living in a clean prison. I earn one thousand francs a year, two hundred dollars; the rooms cost three hundred francs. If there's no work there's no pay, and no food for the three children."

A couple of changes of omnibus took him to the Place du Trône, on the southeast side of the city, where for an hour he followed the encircling wall of Paris to the Bois de Vincennes, a large landscaped park with a variety of rural scenes. Here he could draw all day, in peace of mind, for there was no human injustice to be set down, just the delightful flora of the earth's richness. For contrast he turned west the following week to the Parc de Neuilly, an undeveloped area which the French called *sauvage*, and attempted to capture the wildness of the scenery along the Seine. To get there was a chore: a long omnibus ride down the Rue St. Lazare, past the Barrière de la Roule next to the Etoile, then along the Route des Ternes until he was outside the city wall and walking along the Route de Neuilly. Every piece of Paris had its own character. The painters said rightly, "At each turn there's another picture."

As he explored and appropriated Paris, street by street, he learned the inner workings of the mazelike city. The wealthier classes lived in the heart of the town on the Boulevard des Italiens, around the Madeleine, a temple of the Roman Corinthian order; and across the Seine, on the Left Bank, in the luxurious Faubourg St. Germain. All elegant apartment houses had shops on the ground floor. The less affluent merchants lived in the backs of their shops. The wine merchant was the first to rise and the last to close up, wearing just a shirt and pants behind his polished tin counter. He learned that there were six hundred bakers in Paris, turning out some of the best, crustiest bread in the world; and numerous public fountains which ran for a number of hours each day where the poor could get free water. By razing blocks of jammed, narrow streets, Haussmann had created a number of open squares, which brought light and sun to the city.

He did a sketch of a department store, the Magasin du Grand Colbert; of the Théâtre Lyrique; of a typical confectioner's shop with luscious *gâteaux* in the window; workmen creating a new lake in the Bois de Boulogne; the Longchamp racetrack being built in the same Bois; drew the continuing construction of the Rue de Rivoli, and the completion of the Pont de l'Alma across the Seine. He followed the Seine for miles as it made its way through the city. There was always interesting traffic on the river for his pen. His room at Rachel's began to be crowded with his hundred or more sketches. She refused to allow him to tack them to the walls.

Emma was sympathetic.

"I'm having a noble time for myself," he confided. "One day this week I sketched the milk shops, another the fish and oyster market on the Pointe St. Eustache; still another, the poultry, butter and egg market on the Quai des Grands-Augustins. *Regarde*, I made separate portraits of the pheasants, turkeys, partridges, hares. . . ."

"*Parbleu!*" she cried with delight. "They're so lifelike I could eat them."

"Here, side by side, see the butchers slaughtering in their backyards, stained with blood; and the confectioners with their fluffy products."

"Camille, is it your aim to portray all of Paris?"

" . . . No. Just to understand it. Some people grasp through their ears, their nose, their eyes. I grasp through my fingers."

Emma had been looking through his pages.

"This is the best, Camille, the Marché des Innocents."

He held the sketch at arms' length before him, squinting his eyes and nodding his head.

"After midnight the farm wagons and carriages, hundreds of them, come to unload their fruit, their herbs, what they call their 'hearty' vegetables, the carrots, cabbages, lettuce, and their 'delicate' vegetables, the cauliflower, asparagus, mushrooms. Milling around are the chefs, the buying merchants. Circling the market are the all-night restaurants serving hot onion soup. And the brandy shops . . . I didn't know men could drink that much brandy."

"Would you take me one night? Are women allowed?"

"Of course. Farm wives bring in half the produce and sell it: chickens, goats, bags of corn, peas, everything Paris will be eating that day."

Emma said quietly:

"I'm beginning to understand, Camille. You want to capture life in your sketches before it disappears."

He bussed his sister on the cheek.

"*Bravo*, Emma!"

Her eyes lighted. "I received a large bank credit from Phineas today. Poor man, he thinks that if he sends me plenty of money he can compensate for our being separated." She blinked away tears. "Camille, it's hard to be alone after ten years of marriage. I don't like sleeping alone. But to whom am I going to complain? Maman? She's sleeping alone too."

She looked up at him from her diminutive height.

"Would you take me out to dinner? Now that I have all this extra money I want to go to the most elegant restaurant in Paris, the one in the Grand Hôtel du Louvre. I also want you to take me shopping on the Rue de Rivoli and the Boulevard des Italiens. For a lot of things I don't need . . . hats, fancy dresses . . ."

He laughed with her.

"*Bien*. We'll end at Ledoyen on the Champs-Elysées, sit at a sidewalk table with a raspberry sherbet and a glass of cognac."

"I'll stare at the handsome men strolling by in their high silk hats and pearl cravats, and you can ogle the pretty girls. By the by, what are you doing about pretty girls?"

"Oh, taking some and leaving others. Isn't that what a young man is supposed to do?"

43

"I couldn't say, my dear brother. I'm just an old married woman with three children, waiting in desperation for my husband to come and take me to London."

"Patience. We'll both have the lives we want."

Several late afternoons he visited with Corot, who liked particularly Camille's renderings of Montmartre, but commented:

"Pissarro, sketching is the bone of our bodies, but we also need the flesh. Oil painting is that flesh." He took off his cotton cap and shook his hair loose. "You must study the paints for your palette. Try them for effect. It is useful to draw one's picture clearly on the canvas, and then to paint the picture section by section, so that when the canvas has all been covered there is little left to retouch. I have noticed that whatever is finished at one sitting is fresher, better drawn, and profits from many lucky accidents.

"It is also very important to start by an indication of the darkest values and to continue in order to the lightest. From the darkest to the lightest I would establish twenty shades. Thus your study or picture is set up in orderly fashion. Always keep in mind the mass. Never lose sight of that first impression by which you were moved. It is logical to begin with the sky. Color and finish put charm into one's work."

"Ah, charm. There's an undefinable. Can an artist say, 'I will now make my work charming'?"

"It emerges, Pissarro, as a child of your cohabitation with nature."

"I feel . . . unprepared."

"The only way to get prepared is to begin."

12

At number 7 Avenue Montaigne, near a populous intersection and close to the Palais des Beaux-Arts, Camille came upon a substantial structure of wooden panels, with a lining of hollow brick covered in places with plaster. He recognized it as the Gustave Courbet pavilion Anton Melbye had told him about. Anton had said:

"Courbet is one of the most talked-about artists of our day. He submitted fourteen pictures to the Exposition Universelle and was enraged when three were rejected, two of which, *Burial at Ornans* and *The Atelier*, he calls his masterpieces. Any other painter would have been delighted to have eleven pictures shown. Outraged, as only Courbet can be, he decided to do what no other artist has done before him: put up his own one-man exhibition to compete with the Exposition.''

"He must sell well to have afforded it.''

"Yes. He earns large sums, but he spends them faster than they come in. Be forewarned about Courbet: as great as is his painting skill, he thrives on hostility.''

Camille moved aside the canvas door and entered the temporary structure. He bought a ticket from a half-asleep guard, paid ten centimes for a catalogue, and stood gazing at the forty forceful canvases of man and nature which confronted him. The roof of the pavilion was made of zinc-glazed skylights, the office and vestibule were covered with tarred paper, for Courbet had secured only a temporary license from the Parisian officials.

Before beginning his tour around the walls he read Courbet's manifesto:

> The appellation of Realist has been imposed upon me just as the appellation of Romanticists was imposed upon the "Men of 1830" (Corot, Millet, Rousseau, Daubigny, Diaz). At no time have labels given a correct idea of things; if they did so, the works would be superfluous.
>
> . . . To know in order to create, that was my idea. To be able to represent the customs, the ideas, the appearance of my own era according to my own valuation; to be not only a painter but a man as well; in short to create living art; this is my aim.

All extraneous thought fell away as he began his fascinated, slow, sideways movement from one picture to another. He was astonished to find himself alone. Bewildered by the outburst of demoniacal energy, he studied each picture in turn, making notes in his notebook, sketching the contours of a painting by moving his finger through the air. He was staggered by Courbet's audacity in choice of subject, the sometimes brutal reality of *The Stone Breakers*, the man and young boy smashing mountain rocks for road paving; the stark realism of the low-ceilinged kitchen and unadorned table around which the family sat in *After Dinner at Ornans*, the inner truth of the unglamorized peasants in *Return from the*

Fair, the force in *The Wrestlers*. He was certainly the equal of Ingres, Delacroix, Corot. Camille recognized the penetrating eye, accuracy, imaginative use of natural materials and sensed an underlying hardness. There was a vast amount he could learn from Courbet's technique, but it was not the concept of life he, Pissarro, wanted to portray.

It was then he saw a man come out of the little front office and, after a time, felt a pair of eyes boring into his back. Turning, he found himself face to face with Gustave Courbet, a heavy-set man of about thirty-six, wearing a black suit and blue striped shirt, with a stout torso but short neck, so that his massive head appeared to launch itself straight out of his broad shoulders. He was a fine-looking man, with bold brooding eyes, clearly chiseled features, his cheeks deep hollows in the expanse of face. His thin black hair was worn abundantly over his ears and bunched thickly behind. His beard, lined on the lower part of his jaw, was dark in color. At rest, with fingers intertwined on his capacious belly, he was an appealing man. However he was rarely at rest. He had the soul of a pugilist and the hands of a superb Renaissance craftsman.

Courbet spoke the thick guttural accent of the Franche-Comté, near the Swiss border, quite unlike that of any other area in France. After fifteen years in Paris the accent had softened, yet it was a far cry from Parisian French. So was Camille's, although his five years in the Pension Savary had given him a fair similitude.

"You are interested. Are you a critic? A collector? A painter?"

"A student of painting."

"Good. I see you have one necessary qualification: concentration. I am Gustave Courbet."

Camille shook the extended hand. It was big, warm, bony, firm.

"I recognized you, Monsieur Courbet, from your portrait in the blue striped shirt."

Courbet flashed a lightninglike smile.

"Ah, yes, my signature. Striped blue shirts. You are . . . ?"

"Camille Pissarro, lately of St. Thomas in the Antilles, now a permanent resident of France."

"I saw you come in two hours ago. You have taken each picture apart, analyzed it, and put it back together again. Tell me, Monsieur Pissarro of St. Thomas in the Antilles, what is your reaction to my corpus?"

"It is the strongest body of work I have ever seen. You are surely a 'master painter.' "

"What is it you like? As you can see, I am famished for praise, for understanding. The few critics who have deigned to visit my little exhibition have called it an absurdity, in bad taste."

"Aren't critics always a generation behind?"

Courbet glowed. "You are a perceptive young man. How old?"

"Almost twenty-six."

"Would you like to hear what the critics actually said?"

"Only if it is not painful to you."

"It is a pain I enjoy. It recharges my energies and determination. I am the kind of unfortunate artist who only glances at his occasional good review but memorizes all the bad ones. Let me quote from three of the distinguished scribblers who foul our art world.

"Maxime du Camp wrote the book *Les Beaux-Arts à l'Exposition Universelle de 1855:*

"We like artists who carry their banners high, and we feel nothing but contempt for those who wave them at street corners. Monsieur Courbet himself has chosen the place he wishes to occupy in the press; he has consigned his name and his bombast to the fourth page of the papers between the advertisements for worm-killing pills and essence of sarsaparilla. This is no longer within our province. . . .

"Eugène Loudun said:

"God save us from dwelling upon those painters who were known in Greece as rhyparographists, painters of filth. What Monsieur Courbet is trying to do is to represent people as they are, as ugly and coarse as he finds them. There is nothing noble, pure, or moral in the head that controls his hand; he invents nothing, he has no imagination; he is an artisan in painting as others are in furniture or shoemaking."

"Surely there have been good words?" Camille heard himself cry out.

"*Grâce à Dieu,* a few. From Eugène Delacroix, who is the greatest artist of the French School. He said, 'In *The Atelier,* the jury has rejected one of the most outstanding paintings of the times.' "

"Great men have the intuition to recognize greatness in others," Camille proffered. "Delacroix lives across the street from me on the Notre Dame de Lorette. I've seen him returning home from a session of sketching but I've never had the nerve to speak to him. Please tell me, Monsieur Courbet, the story behind this extraordinary exhibition. How did you get the courage . . . ?''

" . . . not to mention the money? Come into my office. So you smoke? My pipe is like a second thumb.''

"Corot's as well.''

"Ah, good old Papa Corot. Always the same imaginary scene, with the same imaginary colors, bathed in the same mythological mist. Now about this showing . . .''

It had taken him a month to persuade the officials to let him build the structure and charge an admission fee. He had hired a good architect, Isabey, a reliable contractor, Legros. The lease of the land for six months had cost four hundred dollars, the building came to seven hundred.

"The entire exhibition, as you see it,'' he threw out his arms in a gesture of fierce protective pride, "cost between ten and twelve thousand francs. I didn't have it to spend but what could I do? My pictures at the Exposition were miserably placed, the jury deliberately rejected the large ones. In short, they wanted to annihilate me. I shall save the independence of art.''

Camille knew from Melbye that this was only partly true. The Superintendent of Fine Arts, Baron de Nieuwerkerke, had invited Courbet to lunch, explained that space was at a premium, that Courbet's huge canvases would displace several other painters.

"My dearest friend and ardent collector, Alfred Bruyas of Montpellier, put up the money,'' Courbet continued. "He is the son of a wealthy father who indulges him. Alfred will become immortal because he buys so many of my paintings. Isn't it good that to be a collector is considered respectable, but not the painter who creates what makes the collector estimable?'' His lips corkscrewed into a wry grin.

"We choose our fate. *Acheté trop cher le miel qui sur les épines le lèche.* Honey is too dear if you have to lick it over thorns.''

They sat quietly for a moment. Then the sardonic smile again.

"I expected to make a hundred thousand francs and more than repay my friend Bruyas. I charged a franc admission at the beginning, and people came out of curiosity. Then the attendance fell off, and the price is now only ten cents. Bruyas will have to accept pictures for the money he put forth.''

"You have been called a Realist, as though that were an ugly thing. Yet there is beauty in your paintings. What then is Realism?''

48

Courbet responded quickly, as though he had done so many times before.

"Painting is essentially a concrete art which can exist only in the representation of real and actual things. An abstract object, invisible, nonexistent, does not lie within the domain of painting. Mythological or historical or religious subjects that abound in the supernatural are for poetry, not for canvas. . . ."

An hour went by. It was getting dark in the little room.

"Pissarro . . . That's your name, isn't it?" He broke off suddenly. "Have supper with me and my friends one night at the Brasserie Andler. I've had the same table there for years and keep open house for all who want to attend. It's close by the Cafe du Dôme at 28 Rue Hautefeuille, above which I have my studio. You'll meet our best minds, not to mention feast on the most savory sauerkraut and Bavarian beer."

13

If Paris was the art capital of the world, Camille found that it was also a facade. The externals of a home or apartment house dictated the social status of the resident. Everything was "front." Wealthy homes were faced with imposing statuary, emphasizing the upper torso, preferably female. Second-class structures could afford only the human bust. A home of the third category sported merely floral decorations. On the main boulevards all apartment houses were of a uniform height, with a wide entrance to an inner courtyard for carriages; the apartments immediately above had imposing ironwork balconies, the equivalent to a climbing French family of the red ribbon of the Legion of Honor. The first and second floors above the shops were the expensive ones, occupied by bankers and *propriétaires;* then came the *rentiers,* with small but independent incomes. The fifth to eighth floors were occupied by workers. The painters were in the *premier en descendant du ciel,* the first floor on the way down from the sky.

From across the street in the Tuileries, opposite the Rue de Rivoli, Camille sketched the shops and shoppers, the carriages entering the courtyards, the inhabitants in their social-status-revealing costumes, the nannies taking the children out for air: a dozen characters drawn on a single page.

The indigenous noises of Paris, the clonking of horses' hooves, the rattle of carts over cobblestones, the banging up of shutters, the first cries of the street vendors awoke him at five. By six he had had coffee and a brioche and was out foraging for subjects: scraps of imagery, the way hungry animals track down their prey. He drew the ragpickers' quarters, a narrow, dank dunghill of rotting houses and rotting humans, with a filthy, torn-up alley supporting a couple of bony chickens. Though sketching in the poorer sections distressed him, nowhere was the human character so deeply available to his pencil or charcoal. He learned that laborers worked a twelve-hour day; their wage, depending on their skills, was set around two and a half francs a day, fifty cents. Qualified women earned twenty cents a day. Inquiry told him that more than a hundred thousand men earned less than forty cents a day; some seventy-five thousand young girls and women earned less than twenty cents. The very poor sent their daughters into the streets as prostitutes at the age of twelve and thirteen to bring back urgent food money. Almost all prostitutes in Paris were Parisian born. Syphilis was endemic. A macabre joke declared:

"That's how the poor revenge themselves on the rich."

To get the horror out of his innards he rode out to the Bois de Boulogne to walk among the trees, meadows, man-made lakes. He recorded the parade of aristocrats in their carriages with elaborately gowned wives or mistresses; and, in good weather, the outpouring of immaculate strollers, the men in their high black hats, long cutaway coats, their trousers strapped under their boots; the women in their bonnets and hooped crinolines.

The contrast was cruel. Reviewing his studies, deepening the lines, enhancing shadows, adding detail, he asked himself: "Does each man do this to himself? Or is the condition forced upon him?"

Anton Melbye had given him permission to work in his studio in the afternoons, a privilege Rachel had denied him at home. He expressed his concern over the city's disparities when they had each finished their day's work and were having supper in a neighborhood restaurant. Melbye responded:

"Pissarro, accept the world as it is; that's the way to get your work done. The only ideals with which we should be concerned are inherent in our art. The Revolutions of 1789 and 1848 were supposed to cure these ills; they cured nothing. We are recorders, not social reformers. Confine your revolution to your paintbrush.''

He walked to the Brasserie Andler, two doors down from Courbet's studio. On entering, the blackness resembled the tunnel he had come through on the railroad from Boulogne. It was a little after six. When his eyes became accustomed to the dark he perceived that he was in a rustic tavern, not at all French, with cheeses as big as windmills, hams hanging from the rafters, ropes of colorful sausages, barrels of strong-smelling sauerkraut and kegs of Bavarian beer. There were several long tables with benches. An oil lamp stood on Madame Andler's accounting platform, where she entered the name and price of each dish as it came out of the kitchen. Camille recognized the big-faced, big-bosomed, double-chinned woman from Courbet's *Mère Grégoire*. She was Swiss; her husband, Monsieur Andler, who waited on tables, was a Bavarian.

Gustave Courbet, from his center table which housed a dozen guests crowded together, gave Camille a shouted welcome.

"So you did come. Meet my colleagues. *Soyez unis comme les doigts de la main*. Be united like the fingers of the hand. Friends, this is Camille Pissarro, lately of some tropical island. Instinct tells me he is going to be a fair painter. Proudhon, Daumier, move over. Let Pissarro join our festive board.''

He was accepted. No one doubted Courbet's intuitive judgment. Camille was particularly excited by Honoré Daumier, a painter who never showed the oils he was just beginning to paint except to a few intimates, but who was well known for his bitingly ironic cartoons. Camille had seen many of them in *Le Charivari*. The ones that had endeared him to the democrats of Paris were his *Rue Transnonain*, a working-class family murdered in its bedroom by Royalist soldiers in the Revolution of 1848; and *The Legislative Belly*. He had struck fear in Camille with his cartoons of Beaux-Arts rejections.

"Courbet hasn't seen my work,'' he murmured. "He praises me because I admire him.''

"Typical.'' Daumier's tone was slightly dour. "But I'll give him one thing: he can spot a fraud or a mediocrity as far away as that barrel of sauerkraut.''

Monsieur Andler came down the center aisle carrying a plate heavy with German food, and a heroic-sized mug of beer. He gazed toward the head of the table where Courbet was embracing everyone with his big bass voice. Camille thought:

"The human lip is so mobile as to be almost liquid. It can suck in, puff out, squiggle in half circles, lift up on one side and go down on the other, all at the same time. Watch the way a man's mouth motivates itself in action and you already know a good deal about his character."

Torn between admiration and distaste, a popular novelist across the table from Camille said:

"Look at Courbet. He chews slowly in the manner of peasants and cattle. He gurgles into his beard, stamps on the floor, lowers and raises his head while his stomach heaves and shakes violently. Yet at the same time he argues, coins witticisms, laughs. From six until eleven at night he holds forth on the arts, all the sciences, even those he knows nothing about . . . ."

"I'm lost in admiration."

"You had better be, or you won't be invited back."

"Courbet has no family, so we are his family," added Pierre Proudhon. "There at the rear is one of our foremost newspaper editors. Next to Duranty is the sculptor Byre, perhaps the best in Paris. There is Emile Montégut, who does the French translations of Shakespeare produced here. At the end are art critics Silvestre and Planche, two who favor Realism over Romanticism."

Next to Courbet was Charles Baudelaire, greatly talked of at the moment for his translation of Edgar Allan Poe's tales. The press said that the stories were not only extraordinary but extra human, that one must not take the use of the horrible or the impossible in strong doses. Baudelaire's pale face was so mobile that his painter friends despaired of capturing his image on canvas. Courbet, on the floor of whose studio Baudelaire frequently slept, had caught him as a white-skinned apprentice of the Devil, with a V of black hair coming halfway down to his eyebrows. Baudelaire hated it. Courbet had said of Baudelaire's poetry, "To write verse is dishonest; to speak differently from ordinary people is to pose as an aristocrat."

"Poor, poverty-stricken Baudelaire," murmured Daumier in response. "A victim of alcohol, cocaine, and unable to hold a mistress because of his attachment to his mother. Aristocrat, indeed! One of the unnatural damned."

"Baudelaire's own poems are superb, but detested by the authorities," Proudhon continued. "We're trying to assemble them in book form under his title *Flowers of Evil*. Do you know my work?"

"I've read *What Is Property?* I don't agree that all property

52

is theft. My father accumulated property by selling from his shop, but he always gave fair value. Nobody was robbed."

"Wait until you've lived in Paris a few years. You'll change your mind. But not publicly. I was a deputy in the republican government of 1848 but the following year, when the conservatives came back in power, I was tried for subversion and imprisoned in Ste. Pélagie and the Conciergerie for three years for my radical views of wanting a decent life for workingmen."

Proudhon blinked through his spectacles at Camille, mopped perspiration from his marble-like forehead and stroked his mild beard. "Ideas are more dangerous than acts."

A newcomer joined them, was introduced to Camille as Dr. Paul Gachet from Lille, who practiced homeopathy and immunization, and ran a one-man clinic in the Rue du Faubourg St. Denis. He dyed his hair yellow, wore a blue ambulance coat and a white cap. He loved all painters, considered them the Chosen People, treated the impecunious ones, which comprised ninety per cent of the Parisian art world, without charge, accepting drawings and paintings in lieu of a fee. Courbet confided to Camille that Dr. Gachet was a diagnostic genius.

"Ah, a new member of the group," Dr. Gachet exclaimed. "Monsieur Pissarro, let me feel the bumps in your head. Phrenology is an accepted part of science, you know. I can diagnose your character."

Sitting in circumspect silence much of the time as befitted a newcomer, full of food, warmth, comradery, relaxed, Camille sketched in his mind a group portrait as the faces, voices and personalities around the table emerged.

"We are given only a few shapes and features: eyes, nose, chin, cheeks, brow, skin, hair, skull shape; and yet the specific mix is always different," he reflected. "A chin too prominent or too receding; eyes strongly green-blue or black on the one hand, milk gray or colorless on the other. Long noses, short noses, straight noses, crooked noses, bony noses, fleshy noses; clear skin, poxed and furrowed skin; flat ears, protruding ears; choppy, stumpy teeth, regular white masklike teeth; tiny tongues, bulbous tongues . . . short brows, skull-length brows.

"No wonder portraiture is so popular. I must attempt it more seriously."

And the human voice. It was like the human face. He had noticed before from what a wide variety of locations the human voice could come. The man opposite had a high pitch, as though the sound were emerging from under his skull. The one next to him spoke through clenched lips, the words squeezed out as from a lemon. Still another garbled the words as he swished them around in his mouth. A fourth was emitting phrases like projectiles from the mass of his lower jaw. The artist beside him, Chintreuil, licked his lips after each sentence as though to eradicate the thought just expressed. Another closed his mouth as tight as a bunghole, from which emerged a thin stream of sound; another's lips quivered like a jelly mold as he uttered shapeless sentences. Then there was the barrel voice, like Corot's, rumbling up from the depths of various internal organs, sounds too much like a heavy surf to be separated into drops representing single words; and that of men who laughed in such spasms that language was engulfed. They were like the instruments of an orchestra, from the high pitch of the piccolo, the upper ranges of the clarinet and violin, through the mellow middle of the trumpet and French horn, down to the thunder of the bass viol and kettledrum of the tympana.

Newcomers continually joined the table, some dropping into chairs pulled close after a round of billiards. There was onrushing dialogue. Was Courbet's Realism the deity of the day? Was Romanticism finished, or would the convention-drenched judges of the Salon keep it alive? Were the heroes the ones of the Barbizon School, Corot, Millet, Rousseau, Daubigny, who spent quiet dedicated lives rescuing art from Academia? Or the new men who called down the wrath of the critics and the public? Gleyre, sculptor and friend of the Fontainebleau painters, cried:

"Mozart composed his first symphony at eleven. Did you ever hear of anyone painting Rembrandt's *Night Watch* at eleven? Or carving Michelangelo's *Moses* at eleven? Good painting starts late. With adults. It's a long apprenticeship."

"That means me," Camille said. "I know I have to apply for a license to copy at the Louvre. But how much time must I devote to copying? I don't seem to have the need."

A dozen diverse voices called out at once. When the hubbub died down, Courbet said:

"Pissarro, I'm frequently guilty of trying to think too fast. But I can tell you borrowing from your predecessors is slavish, learning from them is original, stimulating. By synthesis. Join your native talents to the talents of those who created before you. To be original doesn't mean to be primitive. You didn't spring whole like Athena from the brow of Zeus. Don't be afraid to have multiple parentage. Our art goes back thousands of years to the Egyptians, Greeks, the paintings on the walls of prehistoric caves, Chinese calligraphies.''

Several painters voiced a collage:

"Art's a staple. Like bread or wine or a warm coat in winter. Those who think it is a luxury have only a fragment of a mind. Man's spirit grows hungry for art in the same way his stomach growls for food. . . ."

"Artists are teachers."

"You don't know yet what is in you."

"Fill the hours with work the way you fill a pot for soup. Add stock, vegetables, spices, but never let the fire under it go out."

Camille's face became wreathed in a gargantuan smile.

Honoré Daumier leaned across the table.

"You will meet all kinds of artists: dilettantes, fakers, dawdlers. Don't reject them. They can be good companions, and together they keep a strong current moving in Paris that excites the public."

At eleven the party broke up.

"Time to get home to our girls and bed," said the painter Bonvin. "We tried bringing our mistresses at times but Madame Andler glared her rejection. She is a formidable fortification; no one of our girls has been able to breech her moral ramparts."

Camille walked home along the darkened streets until he came to the Place St. André des Arts, which led him across the Seine at the Pont St. Michel to the Ile du Palais in the center of the river. From there he made his way quickly across the silent Pont au Change to the Right Bank. On familiar ground now, walking at a fast pace from the Place du Châtelet, he passed Les Halles, not yet awakened, to the Place de la Pointe St. Eustache, which led into Notre Dame de Lorette.

He felt a happy glow. There was a brotherhood of artists in Paris, and he would have his chance to become a member. He had yearned for it over the past years but had had no idea how such a miracle could be achieved.

The future looked bright.

BOOK TWO

"The Young See Visions"

1

ANTON MELBYE offered something more practical than technical advice. He had already granted Camille the use of his studio. Now he said:

"I don't know how you are fixed for money, Pissarro, but all of us are pinched when we start. When I first came to Paris I would have starved if a friend hadn't loaned me one hundred fifty francs. Now I have more commissions than I can handle. Why not paint in the skies for me? I'll pay you well."

Camille was shocked; it showed in his expression.

Melbye chortled. "Why not? Young Michelangelo painted in skies for Ghirlandaio at the Church of the Ognissanti in Florence."

Camille realized he had been prudish.

"Forgive me, Anton. Of course I accept. It's generous of you. But I'll need instruction."

"To paint skies?"

Anton also generously bought from him two watercolors, a landscape and a holiday procession in Caracas, as well as a pen drawing of a zither player. Grateful, Camille presented him with two Venezuela pencil sketches.

He was making progress cautiously. Hardly a week passed that he did not receive some helpful instruction from Corot or Melbye. And hardly a month passed without an admonishing letter from his father in St. Thomas warning him that no success was possible unless he enrolled in a prestigious Beaux-Arts school and took the Salon-approved road to acceptance.

Toward spring of 1856 he capitulated.

"I'm registering tomorrow at François Edouard Picot's atelier," he announced to Rachel. "Monsieur Corot says it's possibly the best." What he did not add was Corot's dis-

57

claimer, " . . . if you have to submit to an academic discipline."

With the money he had earned painting skies for Anton he took Rachel and Emma to Les Frères Provençaux with its innovative new recipes from the South of France. It was the first time the family had been at a restaurant together. They enjoyed hot onion soup rich with cheese, a planked trout with a bottle of white Pouilly Fumé from the upper Loire Valley, broiled lamb chops, Lyonnaise potatoes, a salad with an herb dressing, a raspberry *bombe glacée* with macaronns, and *café brûlot*. When the cognac had stopped flaming and the waiter poured the coffee into demitasse cups, Camille grasped his mother's hand in a momentary truce.

He entered the studio of François Edouard Picot and found himself in a large rectangular room with a high ceiling, lighted by a row of windows along the north side. Bas-reliefs and dusty plaster busts stood on shelves. On the walls were equally dusty sketches. There was a message board with dates of exhibitions at the Beaux-Arts, addresses of models and the few dealers who sold pictures privately. Some of the canvases stacked facing the wall had a dealer's name on the stretcher in black letters.

There was an assortment of about twenty men in the studio from the ages of eighteen to thirty, sitting with their drawing boards on their knees or standing up at easels. They were using chalk, charcoal, lead pencils and grease crayons, drawing a nude female model standing on a platform in the center of the room, peering at her through half-closed eyes while they indicated body lines, made erasures, exhorted themselves and each other as they attempted to get the posture of the woman before them.

When Camille indicated that he wished to register as a new student, the artists gathered about him, some in shabby clothing, others in smocks, and informed him that he had to go through an initiation. He was to take off all his clothes, stand on the platform next to the model and tell the story of his sex life. He put off those who were trying to remove his trousers by effective pushes of the hard palm of his hand. Discouraged, they told him to get up on a stool and tell of his *amours*. He invented graphic details. He was then instructed to sing some of the sailor chants from the port of Charlotte Amalie. He sang enthusiastically but off key. After which he was obliged to send down for *café au lait* for everyone there. Camille ordered some cakes to go with the coffee. The students wrung his hand, clapped him on the shoulder, told him how lucky he was because an earlier novice had been tied upside down on a ladder and abandoned overnight; another had had his private parts painted Prussian blue.

When he was ready to start work he was given a corner where he could hardly see the model. He went up boldly to the redheaded *massier*, the student longest in attendance, who was in charge of the studio, its finances for models, food and drink.

"See here, I'm not an eighteen-year-old novice. I have been painting for five years."

"Oh! A master, already anointed."

"Never mind the sarcasm. I want a place where the light is good . . ."

"Or else?"

Camille simply stared the man down.

"Very well, move your chair up. Far be it from me to deprive us of a future Claude Lorrain."

Until another novice appeared to replace him, Camille found himself occupying the menial position of *rapin*, a word that applied to budding artists and unsuccessful ones as well. He had to arrive early to light the stove, to sweep the place out, get fresh water from downstairs for the jugs, run errands for the other students when they needed supplies.

He did not mind the jibes and ragging; he had been told that that was part of atelier ritual. However nobody taught him anything. None of the others appeared to be serious or burdened with talent. He considered most of the students riffraff. Not once did he hear art discussed, or an intelligent idea. Nothing but crude and stupid joking. He did not know that he was thinking almost exactly the words of an earlier painter who was describing the master Gérôme's studio.

Corot had told him what kind of teacher Ingres had been. "He corrected the drawings of his students with his thumbnail so surely and with such force that he often cut right through the paper."

He had had to pay a fifteen-franc entrance fee, and he would have to contribute about twenty francs a month, some four dollars, to the general fund, which was used to pay the master, the models, for the special soap to wash the brushes. All of this he found excessive for the services rendered.

Things changed somewhat when Picot appeared. He was a dignified man in a pince-nez and starched white shirt with a fine cutaway coat, reputed to be a good teacher who did not attempt to force his own style on his students. He was practiced in showing the pupils how to achieve the fine finish so

59

desired by the Beaux-Arts, which led to prizes and the Prix de Rome. He went from easel to easel, sketchbook to sketchbook, making pointed comments and, to Camille, cogent suggestions about his crosshatching and shadows; then vanished.

Camille was dismayed to learn that he came to the studio only once a week. For that matter, although he had appreciated the criticism, it was nothing more than he could have had from Papa Corot or Anton Melbye. When he completed his first drawing of the nude he got into an altercation with the *massier*, who saw that Camille had included the model's pubic hair.

"Pissarro, you idiot, you know there is no pubic hair on Greek and Roman casts."

"The model is not a plaster cast," he replied quietly. "She is a living human being."

"We are not sketching living humans. They're out! You'll never get into the Salon."

"I sketch what I see."

"The model is finished today anyway. It's time you started on those busts."

To himself, Camille murmured, "I'm afraid I'm not long for this academy."

He stayed the time for which his money had been paid in advance, picking up some of the argot of the artist's world: *"Gueux comme un peintre.* As poor as a painter. *Grossier comme un stulpteur.* As vulgar as a sculptor. *Bête comme un musicien.* As stupid as a musician. *Bien mis comme un architecte.* As well dressed as an architect."

Then he returned to pictorial Paris, to the shopping districts, the street voyagers, the parks, churches, the colorful Ile de la Cité in the Seine. He avoided the dark damp slums, leaving them to the ambitious Napoleon III and his commissioner to tear down.

Each day involved an intense struggle to recreate the scene before him. Sometimes he failed, returning home at dark too tired to eat his supper. There was no purpose in complaining. It was not only the artisan who had to serve a frequently frustrating apprenticeship; it was the artist as well. He tolerated the sometime hopelessness for the exhilaration of accomplishing a clean line, a quality of verisimilitude. There was no other road for the zealot.

2

It was a rainy spring; he could sketch in the streets only seldom. Nor was there any room to work in the apartment. Emma, her son and two daughters occupied two bedrooms, Rachel a third, and he the fourth. His one attempt to use the parlor, already overfilled with furniture, had sent Rachel to bed with a sick headache. With limited funds there were few alternatives. He registered at the atelier of Isidore Dagnan, where he could draw from live models. Dagnan, a respected teacher from the Beaux-Arts, was a stickler for etiquette; there was no hazing or horseplay. Dagnan dropped in each day. Calm was preserved. He gave Camille clues on how to project the inward life of the nude; but Camille did not intend to paint nudes.

Fine weather freed him. He took to the streets again, began following the Seine, one of the most picturesque rivers in Europe, with its islands, sweeps and curves through farmland and forest. His only unhappiness was at home. Rachel suffered bouts of despair that she would never see her husband or her son Alfred again; that the business and properties would never be sold. He told Emma:

"I feel guilty. If I were working at a job of which she approved; if I could bring home stories of how I'm progressing in the business world instead of color smudges on my face . . ."

"Nonsense! I've known my mother ten years longer than you have. These emotional cycles are inherent in her nature. When Father comes for his visit this summer he'll quiet her down. It's not in the power of her children to do so. Let's prop each other up. If you run short of money, let me know."

When Camille received his next sum from Anton Melbye for a month of painting skies, he showed the bank notes to Rachel, thinking it might placate her. Rachel was torn between relief and puzzlement.

"Money for painting skies? How long can that go on?"

"I don't know, Maman; possibly quite a while. It will pay for my supplies."

Frédéric Pissarro arrived for a month's visit in August. As Emma had predicted, Rachel became happy and serene. Camille had always considered his father a handsome man. So he was, even more so now in middle age, fifty-four: clean-shaven, a symmetrically shaped head with a full panoply of fine dark hair, an open pleasant face that accurately projected his amiable nature. He had protected his smooth fair skin from the tropical sun.

"He's better-looking than I am," thought Camille, "but he's such an earnest soul I can't begrudge it to him."

He was also a meticulous dresser, even in his shop: starched white shirt, black silk cravat, tailored suits that fit his broad stocky frame with admirable precision. He had cultivated a middle-range voice that was acceptable to supplier, ship's officer and resident of St. Thomas alike. Frédéric was quiet, emotionally stable; kindly but firm in his handling of the family, and not unrelenting about Camille's choice of a career; only practical.

"This is what you want?" he had demanded. "You are certain? Then you must work hard at it, travel the right roads and become successful."

Once, when Camille had passed his parents' bedroom, he heard his mother ask, solicitously:

"Do you think there's something weak in him? That he dislikes work?"

"No. There isn't a lazy limb growing out of his torso."

"Then why . . . ?"

"Because each man has his own use for his mind."

The major difference between his father's and Rachel's attitude was summed up by Camille: Frédéric believed that art could be worthwhile as a pursuit providing it succeeded. His mother felt that painting was a waste of a man's life even if he did succeed; that it was not a proper occupation for a man. It came out of her background, her family values, the fact that she had never been out of the Antilles where there was no art. Frédéric had been born and raised in Bordeaux. Though Bordeaux was an inland port on a broad river two hundred miles from Paris, it got its newspapers, books, drama, opera, politics, court, finance, mores from Paris. All of France was thus intimately connected and tightly controlled, shared Paris's opinions, culture. Bordeaux had a city council with local regulatory powers, but the laws came from Panis. Every resident of a French city believed himself to be a Parisian in absentia; and did his best to live his life as "a little Parisian." There were local styles in dress, furniture, dialect, but the differences were less than the resemblances.

Frédéric's education had been modeled after the textbooks

and customs of Paris. His family were prosperous middle-class merchants: the theater, opera, ballet, bookstore, circus were part of their lives. When he had reached St. Thomas at the age of twenty-four, Frédéric was a cultivated man. It was this influence that determined that his two boys, Alfred and Camille, be educated in France, that they be brought up in the French tradition and language. He had been able to convince Rachel of this need, but he had had to be firm, for the ship carrying Alfred to New York, where he would transship to France, had caught fire at sea. Alfred had nearly perished. Having already lost three sons, and almost losing a fourth, Rachel had been unwilling to risk Camille's departure. The thought of having him away from home for five years, even with an occasional summer visit, was also devastating. That she acquiesced spoke for her desire to see her sons get every advantage.

Alfred, though only thirteen, had shown a talent for business of his father's kind; he preferred the shop, working there and at the docks. He was bright, a quick learner, accurate in his dealings. He spoke well, studied music and gulped literature; yet obviously he was the one who was going to take over his father's affairs. Alfred considered business a game; Camille thought of it only as a way for a man to earn a living. He did whatever was required of him, but without excitement or pleasure.

When Rachel reported on Camille's activities, Frédéric said:

"This comes as no shock to me." To Camille he declared:

"I would rather have you be a good artist than a poor merchant. But mind you, by good I mean successful." And for Frédéric there was only one definition: to make a comfortable amount of money.

"Suppose I paint fine pictures and they don't sell?"

"Suppose I buy splendid merchandise and it doesn't sell?"

"*Touché.*"

"If primitive man wanted to eat, he hunted, fished, raised a crop. If modern man wants to eat he sells merchandise. Or his professional skills: doctor, advocate, engineer . . ."

". . . artist."

"On the bottom of the list. A man can't eat a painted canvas, or wear it as a coat, or sleep under its roof. In short, my young son, art is a luxury. People can do without it and not perish."

"Hunger of the mind and spirit is as strong as hunger of the belly."

"In a few, granted. Your job will be to find them. It'll be like looking for a pea in a potato field."

"*Alors*, Papa, you bequeathed me good eyesight."

3

The summer of 1856 was to be his first genuine freedom since he had left Caracas. With Frédéric in Paris the apartment was crowded; his presence not needed. Anton Melbye recommended that he go to Montmorency, nine miles north of Paris, a superb place for painting. It was a small, quiet village built around the original château of the ducal family of Montmorency, which had been razed in 1814. Little remained but low stone walls overrun by wild shrubs, brambles, trees growing in what had been the duke's enormous reception hall. He took with him, strapped to his back, a rucksack full of supplies: sketchbooks, watercolors, a palette and tubes of oil paint, on top of which he tied his collapsible easel.

He found a room in the home of the people who ran the public baths, paying the middle-aged bathkeeper and his wife thirty cents a day for his bed, plain meals and the use of the bath. The house was located on top of a hill. From his window he overlooked virgin forest, as free of trails as the ocean between St. Thomas and Boulogne. He climbed over the ruins of the once resplendent château, visited the cottage on the estate of Madame d'Epinay, where Jean Jacques Rousseau had lived until he quarreled with his woman friend; and decided to follow Papa Corot's discipline, rising in the dark, at three, stumbling through the trees until he found an opening where he could watch and draw, sometimes with color, the sun rise rhythmically over the green nightscape. He went to his small room immediately after supper, to read Rousseau's *Confessions* by candlelight. At first he was delighted to find that Rousseau, author and composer, could be so sympathetic:

I never felt sufficient longing to need to control myself. I had nothing to contend with. A single sheet of fine drawing paper tempted me more than money enough to buy a ream of it.

Then he was lost in the emotional turbulence of the Geneva-born French philosopher:

I am a man of very strong passions and while I am stirred by them nothing can equal my impetuosity. I forget all discretions, all feelings of respect, fear and decency. I am cynical, impudent, violent and fearless. In my calmer moments I am indolence and timidity itself; everything frightens and discourages me. . . .

He blew out his candle and cradled the edge of the pillow around his cheek. Rousseau's was a temperament completely foreign to him. What he was doing might prove to be wrong, but he was going to feel right doing it.

His father wrote that he would remain in Paris for four months. Camille felt released for the same period of time. He still had a modicum of the wage he had earned in his father's shop in St. Thomas, plus some of the francs from painting Anton's skies. Since he needed little except art supplies, and did not frequent Montmorency's low-ceilinged tavern, the less than two francs a day board did not seriously deplete his resources. He made no acquaintances in Montmorency; he needed none.

He attempted not so much to depict Montmorency as to understand and grasp something of its ever changing character. It was not only the city that seemed far away but the century as well. Here in the stillness he could have been living in times of the Druid; beyond that, in a mythological age before humans were born. However he had not yet arrived at the point where he could easily choose a theme or narrow down an area to be painted when the entire forest was eminently paintable.

He remembered two stories Corot had told him. In the first a companion had said, "I cannot find your composition in the landscape before us." "My foreground is a long way ahead," Corot had replied. The friend gazed intently, then exclaimed: "It's true! Amost two thousand yards away your picture rises out of the dimness of the dell, stretching beyond into a meadow."

In the second story a friend had said to Corot, "That's a great tree you are painting. But I don't see it on the landscape." "It's behind you," Corot replied. It was.

"Will I ever develop that kind of peripheral vision?" Camille asked himself.

The long hours of being alone while he searched for motifs successfully drove out of his mind the images of palm trees that had been so conspicuous in his early work; the forest of Montmorency slowly superseded the West Indies and Caracas. As the weeks passed he studied the drawings he had made of the forest with its sudden pools of water, massive boulders, some of them the shape of antediluvian monsters; he began to feel that he had made a successful transition. If he were not yet a French painter, he was at least sketching authentically an indigenous part of France.

He was totally at peace with himself, finding challenging areas for his pencil or charcoal. His drawings and watercolors were purely experimental; they had no sales value any more than had the two drawings Corot had given him off his walls. Drawings were exercises; every artist needed to exercise, perhaps the whole of his working life. He was presumptuous enough to complete one oil, *The Road of Domont at Montmorency*, which he presented as a gift to a Madame Morel who was boarding in the same house with him. His other attempts at oil painting, working at his easel deep in the woods, did not come off. He wiped the fresh paint from the canvas with a strong turpentine.

He wrote home once a week, not to announce any news, for there was none in his elemental absorption with the close-packed trees of the green forest and its natural clearings which let in bright, hot sunlight, but to assure the family that he was well and happy. The forest taught him not to copy but to develop a growing sense of selection, to rearrange the scene before him to achieve a more particular harmony. He had no need for the reaction of others, criticism or praise. As he pored over his sketches by candlelight at night, he was his own critic.

At the end of August Frédéric returned to St. Thomas to make another effort to sell his business equitably enough so that he and Rachel could retire in comfort. Rachel was devastated at being left alone again. Before he departed Frédéric took Camille aside.

"Son, you must promise me to do for the family everything necessary to make my absence painless. It will be pleasing to me to learn that you have acquitted yourself of this responsibility with zeal and good will." He frowned. It was painful for him also to face another year of separation from his wife. They had been good companions since the day he arrived in St. Thomas to liquidate his uncle's estate. He spoke more softly.

"Sleep at home as much as you can. Give your mother the attention she needs."

66

Camille gulped. Rachel's needs drained everyone around her.

"I'll do everything I can."

"And work hard, very hard, so that you can exhibit at the Salon next year and begin to sell."

Camille stared down at the carpeted floor.

"Try to do that, Camille."

When he accepted invitations to his uncle's parties he met respectable middle-class young women looking for husbands. Since he did not consider himself a prospect he made no engagements with them. Sometimes they invited him to their own *soirées*, which he enjoyed, for he was a sociable creature. But he had neither the means nor the mood for a courtship. Many painters fell into longtime relationships with their models. He had no money to hire models and no need for them. Practicing abstinence insofar as possible, he turned to the *grisettes*, young working girls who did not earn enough at their jobs to live on, and who provided a momentary love life; along with the *cocottes*, who took pleasure in becoming intimate with artists, not only for the informal gaiety of the studios but for the faint bohemian effervescence of immortality that hung suspended about them like yesterday's intriguing smells of turpentine and paint.

In mid-October Phineas Isaacson arrived in Paris for a visit. He was four years older than Emma, educated in England and, like Frédéric, had been sent to St. Thomas to represent his family's business interests there. He and Emma were married in June of 1847. Alfred frequently quarreled with Phineas during Frédéric's absence as the older businessman insisted on running the shop and making the major decisions. But Camille's casual relationship with his brother-in-law precluded any clash of interests. Phineas particularly enjoyed speaking English with Camille, which put Rachel's teeth on edge.

"Speak French," she commanded. "Even if you do splutter it. I feel like a stranger at my own board."

Camille took advantage of Phineas's presence to remain away from the apartment more often.

4

He was on the Rue Notre Dame de Lorette, returning home in the gloaming of an early fall day from transcribing a scene of people feeding pigeons in the square of the Cité before Notre Dame Cathedral, when a man overtook him carrying a folded easel box. It was Eugène Delacroix.

"From the sketch pad under your arm, and heading for the house across from mine, I would say you must be Camille Pissarro. Corot has spoken of you. He says your drawings smell of truth."

Camille blushed. "In a beginning way."

"*Alors*, we all have to begin, else how can we have a middle or an end? I've been sketching the horses in the Jardin des Plantes for a new oil. I am now free for an hour. Join me for a glass of wine."

While they walked to Delacroix's house at number 54, Camille envisioned swift line drawings of the wealthy, high-society idol beside him. He had heard that famous men and women fell silent when Delacroix spoke. He had also heard him described as "not one whom we would call handsome, but in his air of distinction he is a prince." When the great Géricault did a portrait of Delacroix at the age of twenty, Delacroix had exclaimed:

"The wickedness of my expression frightens me."

This was no longer true. His vaulting success and acceptance over thirty-five years had mellowed him; yet, as Camille observed, he still had wide flaring nostrils, sensuous lips open to life, huge eyes devastating in their stare. He was clean-shaven, with a stubborn rounded chin and black hair parted on a broad brow. As they climbed the several flights of stairs, Delacroix commented:

"I had my studio on the Left Bank for years. But now I feel Montmartre is the best area for painters. A great many are moving over."

"My friend Anton Melbye says the area is called the Mount of the Martyrs because so many painters have studios here."

Delacroix shot him a shrewd look.

"Are you expecting to become a martyr?"

"*Sacrebleu*, no. I'm planning to become one of God's gifts to French painting."

They laughed at the absurd joke as Delacroix let himself into his atelier. He poured Camille a glass of wine.

"Look around if you like. I keep on the walls examples of my drawings, etchings and oils from every period. I'm living in my own retrospective. I will excuse myself for a little while to dress for dinner."

Glass in hand, sipping, Camille was overwhelmed. The studio was a vast area, the whole upper floor of a good-sized apartment house, perhaps thirty feet wide and at least fifty feet long. There was an enormous north window extending from wainscot to the top of the thirty-foot ceiling. To ward off the winter cold, a five-foot-high, coneshaped black stove with the longest stovepipe he had ever seen rose eight feet in the air before angling into the side wall. "Truly a piece of sculpture!" Camille exclaimed.

Everything was on a heroic scale, with some fifty pictures on the walls, tight-fitted to the ceiling, as many had hung in the rooms of the Exposition Universelle. Stacks of unframed paintings leaned against the walls. Shelves in one corner were piled with antique busts. He counted five easels, some of them ten feet tall; a high, movable set of steps enabled Delacroix to work the top portion of his epic-sized canvases. A variety of worktables and benches held vases of brushes, pens, charcoal, palettes, a hundred tubes of paint. In a corner was a divan and striped linen upholstered chair. It was all meticulously clean, orderly, with oriental rugs scattered about on the scrubbed and waxed random-length plank floor. It cried out:

"I am large and imposing because I am important. All the works here are important. This is a serious *monde*."

It was an exhibition of visual grandeur. Along with the oils there were early sketches of the immense murals Delacroix had done as commissions for churches, religious subjects such as *Christ on the Sea of Galilee;* oriental subjects; lion and tiger hunts; lithographs, pen and pencil studies of people, places, gigantic battles, ancient myths, architectural renderings. In decoration he was called monumental; a projector of the spirit of classical fable, a kin of Rubens, Van Ruisdael, Watteau. He was a master illusionist. Everything he painted jumped out of the canvas, took possession of the viewer. The government had purchased his *Barque of Dante* even though the academics loathed his startling colors.

Delacroix returned, dressed in formal attire.

"I am complying with my rule of not allowing myself to finish until the effect and the tone are completely seized; and to correct things in whatever way my feeling of the moment demands. The time will come when your instinct will tell you that you have done all you can with that subject at that point in your life. Then be content, and say, '*Soit!* It is finished.' Now tell me about yourself."

Camille gave him a short recounting. Delacroix commented: "It was a mistake to return to St. Thomas when you finished school in Passy. Seventeen is by no means too young to plunge into the mainstream of Parisian art. I entered Guérin's classical studio at the age of eighteen."

"You are a native."

"Let me see your studies."

Camille handed over the sketchbook containing weeks of work. Delacroix turned the pages slowly. His lips were tightly pressed, as though he knew a secret he could not let escape; while his intense eyes, with mildly drooping lids, looked half inward, half outward, in a fiercely analytical gaze.

"Papa Corot is right. They smell authentic." He put the pad aside. "You have doubtless heard of the long quarrel between Ingres and myself. He hasn't spoken to me for more than twenty years. He seems to think art is a joust; if one man wins the other loses. No sense to that. We all win, or we all lose. He believes I am the destroyer of French art and he alone is the guardian of the fortress."

Delacroix's resolute face was that of an aristocrat yet was redeemed by good will. He was well read in English and French literature, his immense native power steadily developed through contact with the geniuses of the past and the best minds of the present. He discussed music with Chopin, literature with Balzac, took George Sand to the opening of her play, *Favilla;* was an intimate of the authors, the exquisite De Goncourt brothers. The night before he had had dinner with Dumas, who told him of his *amours* with a widow who had remained a virgin through two marriages.

"*Massacre of Chios,*" Delacroix confided, was shown in the Salon "over the dead bodies of half the jury. They called it a 'shocking, discordant composition, a lustful dwelling on horror.' Even Baudelaire, who welcomes all revolution, called it 'a terrifying hymn in honor of doom and irremedial suffering.' "

"Ah, but the painting! No one has accomplished such a miraculous outburst of color," Camille exclaimed.

This pleased Delacroix.

"For every attacker there is a defender," he added. "Remember that. It will solace you in bad moments. Baron Gros hated *Massacre of Chios,* labeled it *The Massacre of Painting.* But Adolphe Thiers, a young journalist for *Le Constitutionnel,* sang its praise so highly that the government bought it out of the Salon for two thousand francs, an immense sum for a twenty-four-year-old. From that moment on, I never looked back."

"Whom would you consider the French master I must study?" Camille asked.

Delacroix said that he had copied religiously Géricault and Meissonier. Yet in their work he had found an absence of unity. Each detail was added onto the others, and they formed only an ill-connected whole. He then advised Camille to copy in the Louvre, where he himself had learned by copying Rubens and Veronese.

"Of course a revolution helps," he added with a satiric grin. "For the uprising of 1830 I did my most popular canvas, *Liberty Leading the People,* fighters for freedom storming the barricades. Made me a national figure; but I did not become famous for my technique. Oh no, indeed! It was the propaganda value."

Delacroix rose from his chair. He was also an aficionado of the opera: Gluck, Mozart, Berlioz. That evening he was going to hear *Il Trovatore.*

"But don't envy me," he cried. "I will suffer and be bored there, and catch another cold. Nothing equals the sterility of that music; everything in it is noise. But bad music is better than none at all."

Camille remembered the line he had read about Delacroix: "He has a sun in his head and a storm in his heart; for forty years he has played on the keyboard of human emotion."

He crossed the Rue Notre Dame de Lorette at an angle to his mother's apartment. When he reached there he threw himself down on his four-poster, his hands locked behind his head, and gazed vacantly at the intricately woven canopy above as it fit snugly against the ceiling. It was his bed from St. Thomas, the richly ornamented headboard, foot panels and carved poles all of mahogany.

How many roads were there to fulfillment and success? The contrast between his own life and temperament and those of Eugène Delacroix could not be greater. Or with those of Papa Corot or Gustave Courbet.

Against the wall was one of the family desks with a pull-down leaf for writing. He began in his mind to fill its numerous pigeonholes with self-gleanings. Delacroix was a wealthy man; there was little chance he himself would ever do more than earn a living. Delacroix was the darling of the highest reaches of French society. He could be expected to be admitted only into that of bohemia. Delacroix was catholic in the range of his work: monumental murals for churches, libraries, châteaux; heroic war scenes; scenes of medieval history and fable, vibrant animal life, elaborate portraiture, ethnic travelogues. The range appeared to be endless. His own interest appeared to be in a narrow channel: people, their activities, emotions and place in the daily life around them, the streets of a city or thick green forests with a natural but unexalted beauty, rivers winding through a tranquil landscape.

But in the end did it not all come down to talent? How good was he, Camille Pissarro? How would he know?

5

At Anton Melbye's, while painting the sky of one of Anton's enormous canvases, he met a Danish friend of Anton's. David Jacobsen was a flatchested man of medium height with a slender oval face, a soft cheekbone beard and modest mustache, a creamy white skin and smallish eyes. His abundant hair was parted in the middle, curling luxuriantly behind his ears. He wore a well-made coat and vest with wide lapels, a white shirt with a starched bosom and stand-up collar, all brought from Denmark the year before. He was nine years older than Camille, unmarried. He had been admitted to the Royal Academy of Fine Arts in Copenhagen at the age of twenty-three, had studied for two years, then quickly moved into the mainstream of Danish genre painting: Danish landscape, its rural population, fishermen. He had come to Paris with a group of Danish painters to see the Exposition Universelle. The others had absorbed all they wanted and returned home. He had stayed behind.

Camille greeted him in Danish, the official though little used language of St. Thomas. Jacobsen was delighted.

"I saw that our painting was provincial in subject," Jacobsen explained. "I just had to remain and become a French painter."

"And have you? Become a French painter?"

Jacobsen smiled, shrugged.

"My family has bought some canvases, and sold a few to friends in the Jewish community of Copenhagen. But I am not happy with my work. I want to paint history."

He went off in a fierce bout of coughing. When he had apologized for the ruckus, he confided that he had suffered from tuberculosis in his earlier years.

Camille asked:

"Historical painting? Couldn't you have done that just as well in Copenhagen?"

Jacobsen's voice was soft, as was his whole manner.

"It's not our tradition. The French do it best: David, Géricault, Gros, Delacroix. I must learn from them."

"But you are a young man and that is a past tradition," thought Camille. Yes, stories from the Bible, of battles, mythology, religion were winning honors at the Salon. That was because the Salon juries belonged to the past as well.

He would not voice these sentiments. Every man must paint what he wanted to paint. He knew from Anton that David Jacobsen had had a good start in Denmark. Here he had only his cooper uncle who provided him with temporary lodging and a meal. Was he a fighter? Aggressive enough to attack overwhelming competition?

Jacobsen said morosely, "Fritz Melbye got a commission from the Danish government, though our training and talents were equal. They won't give commissions to Jewish painters."

Camille's voice was stern. "In art there is no such thing as a Jewish painter or a gentile painter. There are only good painters and mediocre painters. If your work becomes good enough, you will get commissions. You must be patient."

"Shall I wear a hair shirt like the penitents?"

"It is the native costume of the artist."

Camille laughed. Anton joined him. Jacobsen was morose.

"It's not a happy prospect."

"You chose it. Voluntarily. So did I."

He decided that David Jacobsen was a downcast character.

Jacobsen asked: "Where do you work, Pissarro?"

"In the streets, sometimes here, or at home. In an overfurnished apartment with my mother, sister and her three children. Delightful, but noisy. When one of them catches a cold I give the sick one my bedroom and sleep in a kind of closet."

A gleam came into Jacobsen's eyes.

"Would you care to see my studio? It's close by, at 56 Rue Lamartine."

"I've been longing for a studio of my own, but I simply haven't the money."

"Come along. I have an idea."

Jacobsen's studio turned out to be an L-shaped room. The longer leg was his working area, unfurnished except for an easel, one overstuffed chair and an ancient butcher-block table on which he did his drawing. In a corner were stacked canvases; sketches and drawings were tacked to the walls. In the shorter wing of the L was a cot with a bumpy mattress, a rickety wooden table on which stood a bowl and pitcher for the washing water brought up hot from the basement once a day by the cleaning woman. She also brought in coffee in the morning, accompanied by a *bâtard*, bastard, the name for the bread of medium length. There was no stove. Jacobsen had hammered nails into the walls on which to hang his spare clothing. The majority of artists in Paris lived this way.

"Do you like it?" Jacobsen asked.

"The light seems good. Why do you ask?"

"Because I desperately need someone to share the cost with me. I'm renting by the month now but the landlord is insisting on a year's lease. Four hundred francs a year is more than I can pay. At forty dollars each it would be reasonable. And I would like the company. I get very lonely; I know only a few Danes. I would never interfere with your work or private life."

Camille walked through the room with mounting excitement. He could have a studio, a place to work all day and all night if he saw fit. Undisturbed. He could hang up his sketches. Surround himself with his efforts.

Jacobsen was standing by quietly.

"I would like it very much. I haven't the money but I will ask my father for it. He's offered to help in any practical way. A studio is practical. I could start working in oils here. But the mails are slow. It will take more than a month for me to receive a reply. Can you wait?"

Jacobsen smiled with hope.

"I must. Anton has shown me some of your sketches. I won't have to be embarrassed by praising bad work."

The two men reached out and clasped hands.

"Agreed."

Frédéric's answer showed up quickly. "I understand how all the sickness in the house interferes with your work, since you have had to give up your room to the children, and that it's not good for your health to sleep in such a small room and that in order to paint you would like to rent an atelier with a friend for 400 francs a year from April onwards. *D'accord.*"

Camille was overjoyed. Those few sympathetic lines meant

a new freedom. He was too happy to be bothered by the next paragraph, which he knew his father felt an obligation to include:

" . . . But, then, you would have to work seriously to make some profit from your work. I am upset that you are doing nothing to exhibit this year at the Salon as M. Melbye was advising you. Well, let's hope that will happen next year and that then you will be strong enough to do something good which will be attractive to buyers.''

Rachel was not happy about his moving out but she was not going to see her son live uncomfortably; she agreed to let him take his bed, a chest of drawers, a nightstand and oil lamp, a small rug for the side of the bed, a washbowl and pitcher. Emma assembled sheets, blankets, a pillow and face linens and promised to bring him some bread and sugar, a traditional offering for good luck in a new home.

Before going out to hire a delivery wagon Camille kissed Rachel affectionately.

"Thank you, Maman. You won't regret your kindness. You're not losing me. I'll be home often.''

She embraced him, said dubiously, "I wish there were some way I could understand you.''

Camille helped to load the wagon, then drove off in it for the Rue Lamartine. He sat beside the driver in silence, knowing that he had come to a fork in the road.

Jacobsen had already moved his cot and table into the forward angle of the L, leaving the rear and slightly larger area, where he could have a moiety of privacy, for Camille. He was in a bright mood as he helped Camille set up his possessions.

"I hope the studio stays warm enough for you. We have no stove.''

Camille was glad to find Jacobsen cheerful. Anton Melbye had said, when told by Camille of the arrangement:

"His emotions move around in a circle like the hands of a clock. But he's always at noon or six-thirty. You'll rarely find him at a quarter to three.''

They took up their easels at opposite ends of the studio, Camille settling at the angle nearest the furnishings Rachel had afforded him. They agreed that each would come and go without comment; that they would not wait for each other at mealtimes. Jacobsen's concentration at work was as intense as Camille's; back to back, they soon forgot each other's presence, though they sometimes went down together to the Café Turc for a midday bowl of soup or stew.

Camille did not attempt to enlarge his Paris scenes into watercolors or oils; despite Corot's advice he converted several St. Thomas and Caracas sketches into large oils fairly easily, some on panel, some on canvas.

"I guess I haven't been here long enough to become a Frenchman," he said ruefully to Jacobsen over the restaurant table. "I've not yet rid my system of tropical palm trees."

He got along well with David. When Jacobsen was depressed he left him strictly alone. After a while he began to reminisce about his early years in Denmark, and his beloved brother Edvard, a managing clerk at a wallpaper factory in Copenhagen who was helping to support him.

Camille went home for dinner several nights a week. His mother still asked no questions about his work, nor did she feel she wanted to see it; if she ignored it, it was bound to go away. But Emma, who had visited the studio, liked his new versions of *Two Women Walking by the Sea, A Cove in St. Thomas, Cocoa Trees by the Shore*. When he complained about not being able to move ahead to totally new French landscapes, she replied: "You spent a lot of years in the Antilles. It will happen."

It did. The next day. Camille left the studio shortly after dawn, then did a large watercolor of a pool a couple of miles north of Montmartre. He gave it the title *Pond in the Environs of Paris*. He was so pleased with himself that he jubilantly presented it to Jacobsen. David liked it.

"How kind of you. I'll send it home to my family so they'll know what manner of artist I share my studio with."

6

A hastily scribbled message summoned him to Anton Melbye's studio where Fritz had arrived and would spend September with his brother. The two young men greeted each other with shouts of glee.

"I'm so glad you finally got here," Camille cried. "We will work in the forest at Montmorency the way we did in the countryside at the base of Avila in the Cordillera de la Costa."

Fritz glanced around his brother's studio with a touch of distaste.

"Yes, the country. I cannot here with Anton stay. This morning twenty courtiers he had."

"I know."

"In silence we paint. That is correct, no?"

"That is correct, yes."

Fritz had a curled-up face, hair coming forward from high on his forehead, curling upward about his ears and at the back of his neck, nose tucked in, strands of his cavalryman's luxuriant mustache turning up at the ends. Only his sizable eyes were straight forward in their sockets, ocean-blue, penetrating, reflecting a stability of character. Fritz knew what he wanted to do with his life. He told Camille:

"I want in Paris to paint along the Seine. A permanent stay it cannot be."

"France is superbly paintable."

"The rest of the world is also. Wherever I go, I want to be the only artist. In the Far East, China, Tibet."

Camille whistled in astonishment. "You've just made a long trek. Is it necessary to get that far away from Anton?"

"Everybody is someone fleeing: a parent, a brother, a sister, a friend, an enemy, a boss, a confrere, himself. . . ."

"But you mustn't enter Paris with one foot already crossing the border. Let's paint the hell out of Paris and the lovely woods along the Seine."

"*Soit!* Where do we start?"

"Behind Montmartre. It's still rural."

They exchanged folios of drawings, examining, probing, sometimes praising. Fritz looked up with a stern expression on his face.

"Your work is more serious. That is good."

"I have been living for a year and a half in the shadow of giant talents."

"Here it is a serious task painting."

"Oh, come, Fritz. I turned out a quantity of good work in Venezuela . . . for a beginner. Those carnival dances gave us good themes." His voice rang with enjoyment, his eyes twinkled. "You know, my old *copain,* chum, I've been wanting to do a self-portrait but could not find any justification for such egoism. Now I shall do my portrait for you as a welcome present."

"*Vous vous montez le bourrichon.* You do get carried away." He joined in the laughter. "I shall my portrait do for you."

Over beer at a sidewalk café Camille mused that Anton had come to Paris to further his career and would return in a burst of glory to become a professor at the Copenhagen Academy. Fritz was trying to forget he was a Dane; he wanted to paint all over the world. Anton basked in the light of high society as well as its extravagant finances. Fritz wanted the simple sums with which to travel and live. Fritz said grittily:

"It is good to have an older brother. He can teach you, get you commissions. But when he too much does he becomes a father."

Camille studied the scene before them. Well-dressed pedestrians hurrying to their next engagement, carriages passing each other, the horses reacting to the sound of whips cracking noisily over their heads. He raised his beer glass:

"*Salut*, Fritz. I'm taking you home for supper."

They were silent as they walked under the turquoise sky, engulfed by the harmonious noises of the closing of shops and the odors of food being prepared for the evening meal. Being with Fritz set Camille to thinking: he had been an affectionate and obedient son until he ran away to Caracas. They were a loving family. It was a long jump from boyhood to manhood. How could he have put down the strong need within him? He would have been like Rachel's other dead children.

They went to paint in the all-embracing quietude of the Montmorency woods with its myriad tangled treetops, the earth covered by a hundred-year compost of fallen leaves, branches, debris brought in by the wind and rainstorms. They rose at three in the morning, met over a cup of hot coffee and a chunk of the longest of French breads, the *parisien;* tramped through the woods looking for an open spot where they could catch the sunrise. They set their easels apart, facing in different directions but close enough so they could exchange a few words during the passing hours. Then trudged home when it became too dark to work.

Within the week he started the self-portrait in oil. He drew cautiously, careful not to flatter or romanticize himself, creating a profile as reflected in the oblong glass over his bureau. He first indicated the long hair worn over his shirt collar, waving over his close-fitting ears; the light side-of-face beard, the long, thin nose humped slightly just below eye level, veering at a mild angle to the right; then the full sensuous lips. But it was the depth of his brown eyes that dominated the face: wide-set, perceptive, looking out at the world a little skeptically, yet warm and friendly. He tested several brushes and tints to make them come alive, was grateful for the collapsible tubes of paint which were so handy to use in squeezing spots of color around the periphery of his palette.

No wonder there had been so little painting *en plein air* before his time, when artists had to mix their colors in pig bladders.

When he had finished he was not pleased with the portrait: it contained a touch of querulousness, a sideways gleam of wariness that he did not recognize. He had his hair trimmed shorter, then painted himself full face. It came out with a milder look, the eyes softer, more accepting, an uncritical, unassuming study, without protest or challenge.

Fritz Melbye liked the front view. Camille was pleased with Fritz's round-faced sketch emphasizing his own fierce, demanding eyes. They exchanged pictures at the restaurant Grand Véfour; Anton treated the younger men to several bottles of champagne, which loosened their tongues and gave them an evening of laughter.

7

The more his mother mistrusted his choice of profession, the stronger was his sister's encouragement. If Frédéric's acquiescence was less than wholehearted, his brother Alfred supported him from St. Thomas, sending him seventy-five francs, fifteen dollars, for two small commissions he had secured; and somewhat later, when Camille wanted to explore Fontainebleau, supplying enough money to spend ten days in the forest to seek out the motifs which had so deeply moved Corot, Millet, Daubigny, Rousseau. When Phineas Isaacson gave Alfred fifteen hundred francs to send to Emma to help defray the household expenses in Paris, Alfred sent the three hundred dollars on to Camille instead. Emma commented: "Maman and I already have enough to manage the apartment."

Everything in Alfred's attitude toward his younger brother was on the credit side. He had sent Camille linens he needed as well as charcoal, tubes of oil paint, pads for sketching to Caracas. Now he sent him a little money "on account," without stipulating what the account was. However, like his father, he felt compelled to write:

"I hope you can progress and earn your living. I would welcome that with so much pleasure! Try to give the lie to certain opinions being expressed by certain people who claim you are an idler . . . or that you have the profession of one that will make you die of hunger.''

Camille was pleased when he could do a small favor for Alfred in return. Alfred sent him four doubloons to buy for him the new music scores being published in Paris. When he wanted a black frock coat, some colored shirts, a pair of boots and a high silk hat, Camille went to Alfred's tailor, bootmaker, hatter, gathering up the plumage which would make Alfred one of the best-dressed men in St. Thomas. Alfred was a dashing figure with women. At the moment he was half in love with Anna Rothschild of Charlotte Amalie. The Rothschild parents did not seem charmed by this. He was also half prepared to fall in love with the Levi girl.

Camille knew that his brother was a dashing figure in his outward appearance but a quivering one inwardly, given to moodiness, bouts of melancholy. He was good at business but became bored by it; loved music but had only a mediocre talent. The shop was slow; merchandise had not arrived; he was quarreling with Phineas Isaacson since Phineas's return from Paris. ''. . . Here I have the spleen. I am bored. I am dying on my indolent feet; what monotony. I no longer go visiting, I prefer to read and play the violin. I dream only of a marriage in England or France.''

His greatest happiness had been a month in Puerto Rico where he had gone on business; in his hotel he had found several musicians and a young singer named Adelina Patti. He spent delightful days playing quartets and accompanying Mademoiselle Patti when she sang for them. Wherever he went he tried to sell Camille's work, sight unseen. '' . . . Please, tell me the price you put on your pictures. Send me a large painting like Fritz Melbye's sketch of our harbor, and I will sell it for one hundred or two hundred francs. In the meanwhile, work hard to become a success.''

Camille wrote to Alfred of his activities, new friends, the dinners at Courbet's table in the Brasserie Andler, the modest commissions that amounted to the price of a trinket. He often wondered what kind of woman Alfred would marry. Someone sympathetic to his love of music? Or would he find someone immersed in bourgeois values, with a generous dowry, who would agree with the more practical families of St. Thomas who had declared himself to be ''an idler''?

Alfred finally arrived in Paris in January of 1857 on a combined business and holiday trip. Camille met him at the Gare St. Lazare and took him home in a far better hansom cab than he himself had hired a year and a half before. He decided that Alfred was the handsomest man in the Pissarro family, favoring his father's good looks. Although his hair was beginning to recede, it was still ample, with an opulent mustache and side whiskers, fine luminous eyes under strong brows. His cravat and pearl stickpin nestled meticulously under the collar points, his velvet coat and immaculate white vest precisely fit his broad shoulders and chest.

Emma chose the moment of his arrival to announce that she was four months' pregnant . . . and feeling fine. She wanted another child, "though I imagine Phineas would like a second son instead of a third daughter." Alfred took the family to the fashionable Maison Dorée, where he ordered a festive dinner with a bottle of Alsacian Riesling with the soft-shell crabs and a champagne with the petits fours to celebrate the reunion.

He had brought his violin with him. Sometimes when Camille returned home he would hear Alfred playing in the parlor, new scores on the music rack before him. He confided to Camille:

"If I played better I might find a place in a Parisian orchestra. But I'm almost twenty-eight. If only I were a failure as a businessman, I could risk being a failure as a musician. . . ."

It took Alfred only a week to find himself a mistress, a young girl with pleasant auburn hair and hazel eyes. She, her mother and sister had come to Paris from the provinces to seek work. Antoinette was a *bonne* with a family living near the Pissarro apartment. He had met her in a *pâtisserie* when her string *bourse* spilled over.

"I've grown quite fond of her," said Alfred. "She's giving and undemanding. It's her first affair."

"Isn't that dangerous? Might she not expect you to marry her?"

"Oh, come now! Does one marry a *bonne?*"

When he left Paris he asked Camille to call on Antoinette occasionally, and to provide anything she might need.

Alfred returned to St. Thomas in a mellow mood, determined to come back to Paris for good. The first letter which reached Camille, written on April 30, 1857, was a shocker. Alfred had received a copy of Rachel's will, in which she ignored Alfred and Camille entirely, and left everything to Emma. Alfred was indignant. ". . . I am really surprised at the injustice our mother has committed in depriving us of what could come to us after her death, and all that in favor of Emma, whose husband is rich, and us poor devils."

It was true that Emma had been closest to Rachel and had

sacrificed greatly for her. In that sense Emma deserved every-thing she would possibly get. Yet to walk away from her two sons seemed hardly natural. He reflected, "She loved her little boys; perhaps we alienated her when we grew up to be men."

"What sense does it make for a mother to dispossess her two needy sons in favor of a prosperous daughter?" he asked Rachel when he next saw her.

"None!"

Emma added:

"Maman, my husband will earn all the money we'll ever need."

Rachel turned away.

"Paintings! Violins! Why should my only two sons be *démentés?*"

David Jacobsen had become so gaunt from near starvation that he was hindered in moving about. When Camille offered to lend him whatever cash he had on hand, David's pride would not allow him to accept. Only on those occasions when hunger racked him unmercifully did he bring himself to allow Camille to treat him to a meal. The crisis was resolved unwittingly by Rachel, who decided she wanted a portrait of Frédéric to hang in the parlor. When Frédéric next came to Paris she told her husband:

"I won't be so lonesome if I can see you every day."

"I have a good man for you," Camille suggested. Then he added, knowing that it would impress his parents, "He trained at the Academy in Copenhagen. Why don't I bring him to supper? You'll like him."

Frédéric and Rachel did like David, and set a fair fee for the portrait. Jacobsen came to the apartment each day for a couple of hours to sketch Frédéric, and then, after several weeks, to make the oil painting of him in his black stock, white shirt, handsomely fitted coat; a fine-looking man with a face of excellent bone structure, a full head of brown hair, and eyes that expressed both tranquillity and a sensitive puz-zlement over the peccadilloes of human nature.

Rachel was delighted. She ordered the picture framed in an oval of polished wood. When the family hung the picture tears filled her eyes.

David Jacobsen was even happier when Frédéric, express-ing his gratification over the faithful and intensely lifelike portrait, gave his artist a bonus. As they rode back to their studio Jacobsen said, "Look!" and held out the envelope full of bank notes. "I'll have money to eat on for several months."

"And we have a portrait of my father that will bring pleasure long after your money has gone to the butcher, baker and candlestick maker."

8

News in Paris was a communal affair. What appeared in the twenty and more journals spread through the arrondissements as quickly as smoke signals. Camille had been shielded during his six years at the lycée; in St. Thomas, though *Tidende* came out each afternoon at three with local news, the French and American newspapers were late in arriving and interested only those who had traveled or been educated in Europe or the United States. Now there was no escape from the daily happenings; it was collateral currency in the cafés, restaurants, theaters, concert halls, studios, the streets, shops and homes.

The Archbishop of Paris was assassinated in the Church of St. Etienne du Mont by an ex-priest barred from office for theological excesses. The British were subjecting Canton to cannon fire. There were complaints that France was Americanizing itself . . . in the worst ways. Marriage agencies began advertising. On May 9, 1857, *Madame Bovary* by Gustave Flaubert was published in book form. Camille had been reading it serially in the *Revue de Paris* and had been deeply moved by the tragic disintegration of Emma Bovary, the first time such a revealing story had been attempted in French literature. Flaubert, to the horror of the literary world, was arrested and tried on the grounds of violating public morality.

Anton Melbye took Camille and Fritz to hear *Il Trovatore* at the Théâtre Italien. Camille took Emma to a lecture by Harriet Beecher Stowe at the British Institute because they were both eager to hear English spoken.

The end of the world was predicted by a fractional religious group for June 13, 1857, owing to the approach of a comet.

On June 20 the Salon of the Beaux-Arts opened for two months. Camille waited for the second day, paid his one-franc admission, spent the hours trying to absorb the twenty-seven hundred paintings and almost five hundred sculptures in eight separate rooms. A heroic sculpted figure of the Emperor Napoleon in full regalia proudly overlooked this outburst of culture. The paintings were jammed from frame to frame up to the paneled ceiling, with a glass roof admitting a summer sunlight which washed out some of the more delicate hues. The paintings showed high proficiency in execution, but the literary, biblical, mythological subjects were for the most part banal. Camille had refused to submit a work because he did not believe he had completed an outstanding canvas.

The sculpture exhibition was criticized as having "too many plants scattered around."

This totally irrelevant jibe reminded Camille of Voltaire's comment: "It's easier to come up with insults than good reasons." However Camille had to agree with the blast of an art journal that several thousand paintings looked as though they had come from the same hand. Once again he considered the Fontainebleau-Barbizon School the most outstanding. However one of the more important reviewers went out of his way to deplore landscape painting.

The state elections proved a strong progovernment sentiment for Napoleon III, his ministers and the Chamber of Deputies. A journalist friend of Courbet's at the Brasserie Andler asked:

"Approve what government? Voltaire said it in the last century: 'The best government is that in which there are the fewest useless men.' "

Someone added: "He also said kings have the same relation with their ministers as cuckolds have with their wives. They never know what is going on."

Camille found Courbet's table at the brasserie to be the best opinion magazine in Paris. Many praised Napoleon III and Haussmann on the grounds that they were building a vast underground sewage system, Paris's first; rerouting the rivers of France, a Herculean undertaking, so that Paris would have plenty of fresh water to drink. Nearly everyone agreed. "But, ah," they exclaimed, "the fraud, the graft, the conspiracies to steal, with government officials condemning their own property at four to ten times its worth; becoming millionaires at the public's expense!"

"Greed!" added Pierre Proudhon. "When I was young I thought man's dominant sin was lust. Now I know it's greed. It will never be eradicated from human nature."

"I hope not," a cynical editor of Le Charivari retorted; "without greed as a motivating factor nothing important in this world could be accomplished. Paris is going to cost ten times what it should. *Quelle est la différence?* In a hundred years Paris will be the most beautiful capital of our world, and the waste will be forgotten.''

Frédéric had arrived for a long vacation on June 1, 1857, a few days before Emma was delivered of her fourth child, whom she named Esther. The oppressive July and August suffocation of a Paris summer with its blistering sidewalks was approaching. Phineas wrote that he wanted his family moved into the cool countryside.

"Let me look for a house in Montmorency," Camille volunteered. "I know the village."

He found a rambling wooden structure owned by a Parisian family; plain, uncluttered, but cool, and with several bedrooms. Rachel brought with them their cook and Emma her nursemaid. The family asked Camille to move in with them. He was delighted.

The first morning he left the Montmorency house before dawn to find a favorable scene, sketched until noon, returned home for dinner, had an hour's nap, and went back to the woods until, in Corot's words: "The sun merges into the dark blue of the night. The breezes sigh among the leaves. A star dives from the sky into the pond."

In the midst of the thick-packed trees there was a very old cathedral with good stained-glass windows; but it was cavernous and little used. Surrounding the forest were big walled-in estates. On one of his long walks Camille mused:

"The French always keep themselves walled in. Their private lives are their most valuable and heavily guarded possessions. Maybe that's why they love dogs so much; a dog is a companion who does not intrude his judgments into one's intimate affairs."

He invited Fritz Melbye to stay for a couple of weeks, then David Jacobsen. His two friends were happy to have the entire day to paint in the woods "where the muse is." While they did not instruct or correct each other, both men were more experienced than Camille; he learned from example and observation.

In early August Fritz bought a steamship ticket for the United States, planned to move on to China. Camille bade him an affectionate farewell, then, late in August, decided that a change of scene would refresh him also. He selected a Norman town called La Roche-Guyon, located where the Seine widened into a great stream flowing beneath a row of white stone escarpments resembling a line of forts. He had heard that it was eminently paintable. The view from the towpath overlooked ripe fields about to be harvested, rolling hills cultivated in oblong strips; stone houses with red tile roofs that had stood for centuries amidst the copse of shade trees; meandering earthen paths between farms; workmen sparsely scattered through the fields, with an occasional beginning haycock; tree-branch fences to keep the cattle grazing on their home plots; lean ascetic poplars silhouetted on the ridges against graywhite puffs of floating skies, the most enchanting he had ever seen. The luxuriant patches among the ripening fields were a dozen different shades of green.

"More than I can mix on my palette?" he wondered. "From the lightest yellow-flecked green to the darkest olive. This Seine Valley was apportioned and planted with a palette knife."

The entire village of La Roche-Guyon lay between the narrow stretch of water and limestone cliffs, with cell-like shops carved into the hills. The town was a prosperous marketplace built at the foot of an eleventh-century castle and a thirteenth- to fifteenth-century church. There was a medieval fort on the peak of the surrounding green mountains, a château just below it. The town was well kept, the inhabitants taking pride in it. Purple clusters of wisteria hung over the walls of homes, and hardy flowers, red geraniums, yellow and purple pansies, turned their faces to the sun.

He could not have found a greater contrast to the forest village of Montmorency.

He no longer had to get up at three in the morning to go searching for a motif. With the first rays of sunlight, as he moved along the towpath, he was confronted . . . "no, assailed," he told himself, by multicolored pictures.

He had essayed several tentative oil paintings in Montmorency. The work was too much like Corot's: wispy trees, gauzy skies, pastel-colored shadows and, in the clearing, a flowered carpeting. In La Roche-Guyon he wanted to do something different. It was not Corot's kind of countryside; he felt he could make it on his own.

On the traditional market day, one of the most thriving in the valley of the Seine, he encountered a genial young chap sitting on a folding stool sketching a live chicken stall attended by two enormous-hipped farm women. When the fellow saw Camille stride along with an easel on his back, he jumped up animatedly, cried:

"Welcome! We need good painters in La Roche-Guyon.

The artists we have here are grocery clerks. My name is Antoine Guillemet. With whom do I have the pleasure of shaking hands?''

Antoine Guillemet turned out to be only fifteen, the son of a wealthy wine merchant from Bercy, a family well known in Paris and respected in high places, close to official circles, including the Beaux-Arts. The Guillemets had an old family home in La Roche-Guyon, but Antoine had almost exclusive use of it.

"I've studied with Papa Corot in that informal way he has of passing on instruction; but Daubigny is my idol,'' he told Camille.

Antoine's house was small, with a lovely garden and a fountain sending up jets of spray, all in front of a limestone cliff wall; warm, fragrant and protected. After they had painted all day he sometimes invited Camille for an outdoor supper of roasted chicken and a chilled Graves.

Antoine too was largely self-taught, a realist in his work but with the happiest disposition Camille had encountered among French painters. Where Camille saw gray, Guillemet saw pink. He had been born in Chantilly and had sketched since childhood, encouraged by his father, who had set aside, in Antoine's name, sufficient income and vineyards so that he would always be wealthy.

"If there is such a thing as 'always' with money,'' Antoine said lightheartedly. "Have you noticed how it has a tendency to disappear, both from individuals and families?''

"You would laugh all day if you were poor,'' Camille replied. "You have the bright Midi sun in your nature.''

Camille quickly assessed Guillemet's work as having flair, though the results were less than superb. But he was younger than the age at which Camille had graduated from the Pension Savary. In the meanwhile here in La Roche-Guyon he was an ebullient companion, with his sparse blond mustache and brilliant eyes. In short he was young, amiable, wealthy and already acquainted with the Salon officials in Paris, a delightful change from the thorny Fritz Melbye and the depression-prone David Jacobsen.

Camille spent a fruitful month digging into the French landscape, attempting to transcribe it in oils on canvas. He loved working out in the hot sun, "like a lizard.'' The cold of Paris had brought him his first nostalgia for St. Thomas.

"Next year I'm thinking of attending the Académie Suisse,'' Guillemet said. "It's only twenty francs a month. There are no rules or instructions. Old Père Suisse is a former model who keeps the place clean, piles up wood for the fireplace and hires the male and female models. Delacroix, Courbet, Edouard Manet have worked there. Why don't you try it? You'll meet a lot of interesting painters.''

9

He sketched in the city while the good weather held up. Then, at the constant prodding of his father, entered his third atelier, that of Henri Lehmann, an ultraconservative teacher who himself had achieved distinction in 1853 with his high color and palpable surfaces on the hemispherical dome of the Hôtel de Ville. Camille enjoyed the scholarly atmosphere of the atelier more than he had the competitive aspects of his second studio, that of Isidore Dagnan, who had held monthly contests among his students, giving prizes for the work most likely to please the jury of the Salon. Lehmann was an excellent technician, and generous in sharing his knowledge with his students. However his teaching was more attuned to the painting of frescoes for churches, libraries, government buildings than to easel paintings *en plein air,* with one's feet planted firmly in the solid soil.

In October there was alternating rain and sun. The first cable was sent across the Mediterranean to Algeria, where the war was dragging on. Delhi was taken by the English. Camille took Emma to hear an opera at the Théâtre Italien and her three older children to the Winter Circus. Rachel treated them to dinner at the restaurant Les Frères Provençaux near the Palais Royal. The mail from St. Thomas was encouraging; Frédéric had begun negotiations for what looked like a satisfactory sale of their business property. Rachel greeted the news caustically:

'' '*Brebis comptées, le loup les mange*. The lambs once counted, the wolf eats them.' ''

Anton Melbye was outraged because the press was alarmed at the spread of mediums in Paris.

"They cure more illnesses than doctors do," he protested. "What's more, unlike medical men, they never kill anybody."

The newly renovated Louvre reopened with the Emperor attesting to the importance of French art. The long galleries were well lighted, and the pictures, representing the best of the last two centuries, hung at good heights and intervals so that each could be appreciated in its own right.

On November 21 there was a panic on the Bourse. Shares fell drastically; a great deal of money was lost. Paris talked of little else. The crisis was superseded in a matter of hours by the kind of story Parisians adored: a wealthy widower married a beautiful sixteen-year-old and took into his home the girl's equally beautiful mother, only thirty-two. The financier's young son fell in love with the mother and married her. He now became the father-in-law of his father; while the mother became the daughter-in-law of her daughter's husband. The French also loved to circulate funny stories which were then turned into satiric skits with bawdy dialogue for the revues. There was a farce about a young girl who was saying her prayers when an adult queried:

"Why do you ask for your daily bread?"

"Because, if I asked God for bread several days in advance, it might get stale."

Another farce grew out of the story of a young wife who took a lover who lavishly furnished an apartment for their rendezvous. The husband tracked them down, sued the lover.

"For adultery?"

"No. For the furniture."

Courbet took Camille and several others to see the one about the jumbled in-laws, but largely because he was being lampooned in a sketch on the same bill. When Camille asked him why he enjoyed being satirized, he replied with a bellowing laugh:

"Only important people are lampooned. It spreads my fame."

Camille read one newspaper each day, *Le Figaro* or *L'Evénement Illustré*. He learned of the continuing revolt in India; that the Seine was drying up; that there was an earthquake around Naples; and cab drivers were charging by the minute instead of the hour. Electricity would soon be used to light houses and apartments.

Madame Rachel, the most beloved actress of her age, whom Camille had seen in *Phèdre,* died and was mourned. An artist whose church murals had been whitewashed sued the government and lost. The established artists lined up on the government's side, Camille and his friends supported the artist. Three bombs were exploded in front of the Opera in an effort to assassinate Napoleon III and his Empress.

Camille received in the mail the announcement that Anton Melbye, at the age of thirty-nine, to the consternation of his atelier entourage, who thought they had a convivial bachelor campsite for the rest of their lives, had married an estimable Frenchwoman named Alice Dupré. The wedding was a high-society affair with Versailles well represented. A month later Camille went to Melbye's studio to congratulate him. It was still filled with his hangers-on, drinking, chattering, singing bursts of song, while Melbye in his white uniform, red fez hat, black scarf at the neck, in the midst of his Turkish costumes and shelves of ancient artifacts, stood recreating a naval battle. Yet there did not seem to be the same spontaneity; the merriment appeared forced. Melbye himself seemed damped down in his onslaught on the canvas, as was his pleasure in the hubbub about him. After a time he tired, threw down his brushes, seated himself with his guitar and played the newest satire from a Parisian revue.

"Oh, it's you, Camille," he cried, catching sight of him. *"Comment ça va?"*

"As usual. How is marriage?"

"I've settled down. Should, coming to forty. My wife is a fine person."

Neither one had heard from Fritz.

Melbye moved to a corner divan where he threw his legs up on the velvet cushions, ran a hand over his eyes.

"I'm repeating myself. It's the same canvas every time. What's expected of me. I'm a prisoner of my own success." He looked about him. "I think I will run away. The Academy in Copenhagen has offered me a teaching position. In a few years I can become a titular professor. I'll have nearly full time to paint. My wife says I'll be respectable again. She doesn't like me toadying to Napoleon and what she calls his succulents. I've had the success of Paris and Versailles. Every sailor eventually returns to his home port."

"I would miss you. You've been kind to me."

"You'll do all right, Pissarro. Eventually."

Frédéric arrived for a brief vacation in 1858, bringing the good news that the contracts were being drawn for the lease of the Pissarro business and their commodious building at 14 Dronningens Gade. He was getting out on good terms, leasing to their reliable next-door business neighbors, the Von Beverhoudts. He would return permanently by the end of the year with a comfortable fortune of between thirty and thirty-five thousand dollars. He rented a two-horse carriage and driver for several days to tour the quiet suburbs on the outskirts of Paris, looking for a permanent home. They finally selected a flat in a charming four-story house in Passy, at 12

Rue de la Pompe, on the broad, open corner of Rue Faustin-Hélie. The flat occupied the entire second floor. In addition to a large parlor and dining room there were four bedrooms, and on the top floor of the building, under the eaves, there was a row of individually locked cubicles for the servants of the flat holders.

Passy was quiet, its broad streets lined with horse chestnuts with purple blooms shaped like Christmas tree ornaments. Though the few buildings around were not entirely new, they were sturdily built. Because Rue Faustin-Hélie was a cul-de-sac there was little movement past the house, nothing to obstruct the superb view of the Seine at the rear, or the nearby park in front, allowing sun, air and privacy. The house was surrounded by a handsome black grillwork fence partly covered by green leaf hedges. Close by there were spacious gardens, walks between overhanging elms, greenswards, benches. His parents, Camille decided, when he had taken the omnibus A from the Palais Royal along the quais and the Cours la Reine, riding on the open upstairs deck to the station at the Place de Passy, had chosen one of the most delightful spots in the environs of Paris.

Most of Passy was on top of a hill, with a steep drop-off to the Seine with its parade of barges hauling sand, gravel, timber, sacks of wheat; children playing on deck as their mothers hung out the salmon-colored wash. The air had the fresh tang of the nearby Bois de Boulogne. It was a characterful small village, bourgeois, with children running noisily in the streets, irregular rooftops and, it was rumored, would soon be joined to Paris, at which time the houses would be hooked up to Baron Haussmann's main water supply from the springs of the Somme and Yonne river valleys. The inhabitants would have only to turn on a tap in a pipe. Until then they would have to have men bringing in the jugs of water each day. Camille found at 5 Rue des Eaux a thermal bath of reddish water that he promised himself he would use often.

He took Rachel shopping for her first outing. They learned that in the thirteenth century Passy had been a hamlet of woodcutters. Camille commented:

"I like to work with my hands, but not chopping wood. I'd rather stretch canvas and apply paint."

Rachel replied sardonically, "That way, you'll never raise a crop of blisters."

"No, Maman, just a crop of masterpieces."

He watched his mother thread through the merchandise on the busy shopping street, comparing prices.

"Maman, you have the soul of a shopkeeper."

"Of a bookkeeper. How else do you think we built our fortune? If you had been a girl, Papa and I could furnish a fine dowry for you. If you want to open a business with Alfred, we'll finance you. There are no artists anywhere in your father's family or mine. You're a sport."

"Like it or not, I'm on this earth because of you. Alas! There is no cure for wanting to spend a lifetime working before nature, hoping to push back man's horizon, strip veils from his eyes. For that there is neither pill nor palliative."

Rachel shook her head sorrowfully.

"You're a *verbrennte*."

"A man on fire? Yes. Without that I am nothing."

They walked down the Rue Franklin—the French loved Benjamin Franklin—and discovered Le Passy Café, its open front facing the *place*. He persuaded Rachel to sit with him on the terrace and have a cup of chocolate in the warm September sunshine. Next she took him to the Rue de l'Annonciation, a narrow cobbled street lined with shops elbowing sidewalk displays of fruits and vegetables; grocery stalls selling coffee beans, split peas, rice, lentils all in clean straw-colored sacks, each rolled neatly back like an encircling collar. There were tantalizing odors from barrels of pickled cherries, olives, cucumbers.

There was a *triperie*, which Rachel avoided because the family did not eat tripe or lights; in the wineshop window, bottles of Barsac sauterne; rows of assorted cakes in the bakery; spices in the *épicerie;* a colorful flower stand. The fruit stands were the work of design artists, with the ripe red strawberries stacked meticulously. Camille considered the fish market the most fascinating: lobsters, crabs, mussels, shrimp, mackerel, salmon, hundreds of shiny herrings and sprats. He marveled at nature's endless assortment of shapes, textures, colors. Rachel purchased at La Ferme de Passy butter, eggs, milk and cheese. Her meat she would buy in the tiny kosher market, for there were few Jews in Passy. She selected her chicken for roasting, live. The lone *shochet* would then kill and pluck it for her.

The market street was paved with smooth stones and thronged with people pinching, hefting, smelling the products. It was a colorful, noisy show that appealed to his painting instincts. Someday he wanted to create oils of markets like this. The people, the stalls, the foods, the excitement and eagerness to both buy and sell, the anticipation in every eye of enjoying the repasts all this activity would bring about.

Adjusting the purchases between them, they decided to walk home by a different route. Close by they came upon the gracious Notre Dame du Grâce, a seventeenth-century chapel and crypt. Its inscription was *"Il est mort, Il est vivant.* He is dead, He is alive."

They made their way to the bluff above the Seine, which was lined with handsome villas, and shortly came to a home set in a green lawn surrounded by trees at the base of a twenty-foot stone wall . . . to protect the privacy of Honoré de Balzac, who had hidden out there from his creditors from 1840 to 1847, writing furiously all the while and complaining of Passy's bourgeois character. Local gossip had it that the woman who owned the estate loved Balzac but that he did not return her passion, merely preferring her to his pursuing creditors. Camille wondered how the townspeople could know so much about a seven-year intimate relationship, then decided that there was no place a gossiper preferred to be more than under the blanket of the wealthy and famous.

Rachel gave her son an appraising glance.

"You admire Balzac. I saw you reading his novels when you came home from the Pension Savary."

"He was a genius. The greatest of all French novelists. He died only eight years ago and left a tremendous body of work."

"But he spent his life running from his debts. The common fate of artists. Doesn't that point a moral to you?"

"No, Maman, it points to 12 Rue de la Pompe, which is right across the street. Let's have a rum and soda with Emma to celebrate your new home; and that Phineas is offering his business at 20 Dronningens Gade for rent in the St. Thomas *Tidende* and she can look forward to taking her four children to join her husband in London."

"First we must interview the new *bonne* the agency sent out from Paris."

BOOK THREE

"*I with Trembling Soar*"

1

SHE WAS DRESSED in the work uniform provided by Rachel, a light gray cotton with a neat neckband, five buttons down the front, cut generously to cover the bustle, and falling to her shoes. Her white apron, tied in front, had a decorative pocket on either side. Camille had not visited the house in Passy since the girl was hired. He noticed her casually: trim, graceful in movement, a good country face with high complexion. When he asked, "How is she working out?" Rachel replied:

"Takes training well. Pleasant enough. We got her straight off the train from Burgundy."

Emma added, "From a bureau, actually. They had sent out untrained Grancey girls before and felt they could recommend her. For a try, at least."

"She is uncorrupted by Paris," Rachel added. "Doesn't drink or dawdle. Seems grateful for a job and a home. Can't cook, though; probably her family never had much to cook with."

"I'll introduce her the next time she comes in," Emma volunteered and, a few minutes later, "Julie, this is my brother, Monsieur Camille Pissarro. This is Julie Vellay."

The girl nodded her head. Camille nodded in return.

During dinner he told Emma about his new oil paintings of the countryside where the Bois de Boulogne was being transformed by Haussmann's engineers; of bouts of drawing and painting at Les Halles marketplace; his gouaches of the sparsely settled Montmartre mountain, of his trip downstream on the Seine with Anton Melbye to catch the flowing water effects caused by the barges of sand, gravel, coal. As he animatedly directed his words to his sister he could feel Rachel's withdrawal.

Rachel sang the praises of the new *bonne*. Julie was combing Rachel's hair, helping her to put on her endless corsets, underslips, bustles, floor-trailing layer upon layered dresses. She was immaculate in her person and kept the house clean. Emma, who hated cooking but was good at it, and their dumpy middle-aged cook, who loved food but was mediocre at preparing it, were teaching Julie how to dress poultry, to make dumplings they called matzoh balls for the chicken soup; a brisket of beef with sliced apple and caraway seeds; and pancakes of grated potato. As she moved around the table Camille observed the strong figure of the healthy peasant girl combined with a suppleness that made her movements a pleasure. He watched her come in and out of the room, her well-shaped head held high on a sturdy neck, her arms and slender but strong legs moving harmoniously as she brought in the tureen of soup, then a sweet and sour pike with raisins, lemon, gingersnaps. He was interested not only in her graceful carriage but in the look of alertness on her face; she knew what she was doing and was enjoying the task. Her features had been cast in a skilled workman's mold.

A mass of fine chestnut hair under the white cap, combed forward on a smooth modeled forehead; deep green eyes which never lingered; a smallish nose with the tiniest uplift; full lips, red with the color of robust life; small regular teeth that showed when she faced an instant of perplexity; a moderately rounded chin that matched the curve of her brow, and a smooth skin with pink coloring.

"Not a beautiful girl," he mused, "but an attractive one. She'd make an interesting character study," and then found his sister watching him as he sketched the young *bonne* with the blunt pencil of his imagination. He looked down at his plate and ate. Julie Vellay's image stayed in his mind after he left the family table.

There were close to a million personal or household servants in France. More than ninety per cent of the maids in Paris came from the provinces to work a few years and gather a dowry. Certain agencies, such as the one that had sent out Julie, represented specific districts; other areas, which had been sending girls to Paris for decades, had a *société, provinciale* through which the young women secured their jobs. Julie was a *bonne à tout faire*, maid of all work. Servant maid, house maid, nursery maid, lady's maid. In addition to her salary she received food, lodging, uniforms, light for her room in the attic, a few toilet articles, a wine allowance for meals. The specialized servant had an increasingly difficult time finding employment, while the demand for the all-purpose maid kept rising.

The French said, "One either has a servant or is one."

Rachel paid the top amount, eight dollars a month, because "I want happy people in my home."

Since Julie had come through an agency she was obliged to pay them three per cent of her annual wage within nine days of commencing work. It was a custom among the more generous families in Paris to give a starting *bonne* a bonus of from five to twenty francs upon being hired. Rachel gave Julie twenty francs, four dollars, to pay off the agency and buy a pair of soft-soled shoes which would be more comfortable to work in. By accepting the bonus and using it to pay the agency, Julie had in effect agreed to a year's contract and would be obliged to work for the Pissarro family for that length of time.

Frédéric had set aside one of the bedrooms for Camille's use because he wanted him to sleep in Passy as often as possible. Rachel was pleased that her son began coming home for dinner and spending the night more frequently than he had in the past. Perceptive Emma had an idea why but she said nothing beyond an occasional cautionary glance at her brother.

The more Camille saw of Julie the more he was intrigued by the idea of doing a full portrait, something he had not essayed except for the nudes in the ateliers. He had no great interest in nudes, nor did he care about portraiture of fully clothed, richly gowned men and women of whom he saw an abundance in the Louvre. He had populated his pictures but they were figures in a landscape: *Two Women Conversing on the Seashore* in St. Thomas; a group in miniature crossing the *Bridge of Doña Romualda* in Caracas, stated briefly but with vigor against the heavy stone bridge and the sharp-roofed buildings of the town; himself, a young student, and Fritz Melbye in front of the high wall of his studio in Venezuela, covered with framed pictures and unfinished canvases stacked on the floor. He had sketched a good many of the natives of Caracas, not as individuals, but rather as symbols at work: women washing in big tubs; selling produce in the market; walking through the streets with baskets balanced gracefully on their heads. He had seen people as part of an environment. Looking at his ambitious oil of *Coconut palms by the sea*, the palms, the land, the mountains, the sea loomed large and formidable, the two human figures walking on the path toward the bay were tiny, though they made their presence felt. Here in Paris, in his new sketches and paintings, it was the same.

However the idea of painting the youthful figure of Julie

Vellay fascinated him. He did not consider it essential to probe his motives. When an artist sees a motif that moves him he does not need rational reasons. Or so he told himself. Beyond "Good evening," and "Good morning," he had not exchanged a word with the girl. He had heard her voice when she was speaking to Rachel or Emma; it was low-pitched with a dark, rich texture and a viola-like resonance.

It was a month before he found her alone in the Passy apartment, his mother and Emma having taken the children to see a marionette show. She was waxing the heavily carved mahogany tables in the parlor.

"Good afternoon, Mademoiselle Julie."

"Good afternoon, Monsieur Camille."

"Are you enjoying Passy?"

"A good place to work."

"Your first time away from home?"

"Yes."

"I hope you have not suffered bouts of homesickness. I did, when I first left St. Thomas and came to school here in Passy."

She stood with her head down for a moment, not looking at him.

". . . since you know about it. . . . I was homesick during the first weeks. I have no one to talk to except the sister who came with me. I see her on my Sunday afternoon. There are the children but I miss the village, my friends, the plot of land where I grow things; the barnyard where I sometimes help with the birthing of the calves and colts. Mostly I miss the choir and the singing and the other young girls."

"How old are you, Julie?"

"Nineteen." She curtsied slightly, then left the room. She appeared a happy person. Camille could hear her singing as she went about her chores:

"We won't go to the woods anymore.
  The laurel trees are cut.
  The pretty ladies, will they dance?
  Enter the dance, jump, dance.
  Embrace whom you will."

A few days later he was sitting at the front window sketching the scene below. She was emboldened to peek over his shoulder.

"It's like what I see out the window," she remarked, surprised.

"It's supposed to."

"It's nice to have time to sit and do nothing."

He was amused.

"You've just suggested that I created a lifelike picture. Is that doing nothing?"

She drew up her slender eyebrows and let her eyes wonder. She was not unsympathetic; she simply had no way of understanding.

"Forgive me, Monsieur Camille, is it to work to be using a pencil? The Sisters of Providence from Langres taught us to write in Grancey when we were children."

Her voice was inquisitive, simply wanting to know. He tried to explain about sketching but, aside from some faded religious figures on the walls of the church at Grancey, she had never seen or heard of a sketch or painting. He decided to let it wait.

"I sometimes hear you humming when you go about your duties."

"Oh yes, I love to sing. I was in the Val des Dames choir in Grancey."

"Sing me a Grancey song."

She hesitated, then sang in a soft clear voice that carried the tune well:

"On the bridge of Avignon, they dance, they dance,
On the bridge of Avignon, they dance, all around.
The handsome gentlemen do thus, and then again thus.
[Salute with hats, salute with hands.]
The pretty ladies do thus, and then thus."
[Half curtsy, deep curtsy.]

When she had finished he applauded quietly.

"You have a lovely voice, Mademoiselle Julie."

Abruptly she realized that she had been overreaching her position, smiled faintly with one corner of her mouth turned up in piquant fashion and turned away, murmuring:

"I must clean the vegetables."

He watched her cross the room and thought:

"She has a charming figure. I must capture it for my notebook."

He tried but he could not. Her voice and song got in his way. He returned to his study of the houses opposite the parlor window, with iron-spiked fences and carefully tended front gardens. Immersed in the scene, he forgot her.

But not for long. He noticed her again that evening as she served dinner, in a starched white uniform, with the grace of the young girl whose body had been trimmed by outdoor work which had taught her easy control of her movements. There was a deftness with which she moved around the table, a buoyancy that became fascinating to him. He was reasonably well aware of what was beneath the uniform. Yet he sensed that, for all his studio experience and his realistic studies of the female figure, he was seeing something far more supple, symmetrically proportioned and virginal than he had known; that hidden beneath the layers of petticoats and the uniform were the most beautiful of pear-shaped breasts, lithe hips and rounded, close-knit thighs.

"Or am I romanticizing?"

Their next encounter, a week later, came when he was making a rough line drawing of her as she went about polishing silver platters on the sideboard in her work uniform, the dull gray. She gathered from his intent gaze what he was doing and asked if she might look.

"Don't I have the right to see?"

"Yes. But you won't be impressed."

"Nobody ever looked at me before . . . except the leering way country boys do."

She gazed at the few quick outlines he had drawn, shrugged.

"Don't look like anybody."

"It's just a start. Could you stand or sit still for me for a few moments when you're not busy?"

"Certainly not." Indignation flared in her cheeks. "Do you want me fired?"

"No, Julie, my mother needs you."

"And I need the work."

With which she swept out of the room, her head cocked to one side, defiantly.

"She's got spirit," he declared.

A few days later the family rode the omnibus into Paris to shop at the Bon Marché. Camille arrived at the apartment before they returned. Julie was setting the table for the midday meal.

"Mademoiselle Julie, I don't mean to intrude, but you intrigue me. You are from a town called Grancey?"

"Grancey-sur-Ource. In Burgundy."

"Tell me about the village. I've never heard of it. But then, I'm a foreigner pretending to be French. Was it pleasant for you?"

She was thoughtful, running her fingers along her cheek.

" . . . pleasant? No. Hard. For the mother. The houses were built around courtyards where the animals were kept. They smelled of manure. The father drank too much *piquette* at the inn across from Rue Massy. Came home only at night. Drunk. *Il a bu à ventre déboutonné.* He drank with an unbuttoned stomach. The father ran away when I was four. The mother support us three girls doing laundry. The mother was called 'the widow.' Monsieur the Mayor was good. He made a law. *Messieurs les Conseillers* too: 'The Commune must come to the aid of the unhappy ones abandoned by the father. It is in the spirit of the forester's code to cut wood for their winter fireplace.' ''

The council had also voted to give Julie and her two sisters six years of schooling without charge because the Vellays were indigent.

"Was your mother pretty?"

"She love us."

"Didn't her parents provide?"

"The mother digrace them with the father. The Basset grandparents give us a cow to graze along the Ource, a two-room stone house by the bank of the river. We have a poultry yard. But they don't forgive."

"It was cruel of them to allow you to be declared indigents."

"People are cruel." She studied him intently. "You are not cruel." She was quiet for a moment. Then her eyes sparkled with pride.

"Twice a year the châteaux have a washing. Clothes, linens, blankets, rugs . . . The big laundry comes in spring and autumn after field work. Around six we leave with our baskets and washers: we soap and scrub on our knees in a shed. We beat the sheets with a 'beetle,' then stretch everything on the ground around the washhouse, paved and crossed in the center by a current of water."

"Washing linen in continuously running water. Very good."

"It take a week. For washing and ironing. Half a dozen families working together. Girls from the choir, sing all day. It was *pour rire.* For fun. And money to buy things."

"Burgundy is wine country. Did you have a vineyard?"

"Had, once. After the Revolution. Council give each family a piece of land for planting. I have few vines, grow asparagus between them, and flowers. The father drink it away. But we work in others' vineyards, the mother and sisters. From when I was six. When the frost is gone, in February or first March, I help plant the young vines. Later, we cut; then we tie, prune the stalks that grow too quick or have no grapes. Then we spray. The harvest come in September or October; we crush the grapes for the barrels."

"That sounds like hard work."

She regarded him carefully to see if he were extending pity.

"We work first light to dark. But it don't seem long. We work together, families, all the young girls and boys. We gossip, sing." She quietly picked up on a little ditty:

"Say good-bye, Colin, my little brother, say bye-bye,
Papa is on the way, Mama is below sewing stockings.

"It was good. To be left out, that would be cruel."

"Burgundy must be lovely country, the French sing about it so much."

She thanked him with a smile, as though he had paid her a personal compliment.

"Burgundy soil is rich. We grow wheat, oats, barley, carrots, potatoes, cabbages, turnips. We have fruit trees: cherry, plum, apple, peach. Along the river I pick black currants and raspberries. Around us sturdy trees: oaks, beeches, dogwood. We have no francs but I bring us vegetables and fruit."

Camille found her Bourguignon accent delightful. She rolled her *r*'s, but with the end of the tongue, not as in Paris where it was done in the back of the throat. He enjoyed listening to her tale of the village of Grancey. She was animated, a fine nostalgic glint in her eye, her slim young body vigorous in its movements as she acted out her life with the choir, the neighbors, in the square of the city hall. He did not always hear what she was saying because his painter's eye was fascinated by the glow of her skin and the supple lines of her figure under the neck-to-shoetop uniform.

2

By the time he first essayed oils in St. Thomas and Caracas the collapsible tubes of paint had been invented, the oil already mixed in. Around the rim of his palette he squeezed a dozen colors, more white than anything else; the good-grade pigment, well ground, held just enough oil to work well. Ordinary colors were priced from two to three dollars a tube. It was not inexpensive to be a painter: he had to be economical, squeezing out only a quarter inch of oil paint from the tube at a time. The paint, mixed with linseed or cottonseed oil, had a substance, was capable of infinite variations; there was a tactile sensation when he applied the oil paint to canvas. Turpentine was cheap but the brushes cost a dollar each; the occasional mink brush with which he indulged himself went as high as two dollars.

When he felt prosperous he bought various-sized canvases, forty-eight to fifty-two inches being standard, some smaller, others larger, already attached securely to wooden stretchers. Frames were expensive, twenty dollars each, so he learned to buy the separate parts and assemble them himself. When he had to skimp he saved money by buying a bolt of six yards of raw unprimed canvas, cut it to different sizes, the smallest four by six inches, through a medium range of ten by fifteen inches, up to the larger twenty by thirty inches. He laid the wooden stretcher face down on his studio floor and used carpet tacks for attaching the canvas; putting the first tack in the middle of the long side, another in the middle of the short side, keeping the long side ahead of the short side. Then he primed the material with white lead, allowing several days for drying. His first pictures had been small: ten by thirteen inches; in France they went up to fourteen by eighteen for such paintings as *Picnic at Montmorency* and *Countryside in the Environs of Paris*.

Since the process of painting was costly he felt he had to justify himself by working from dawn to dusk and emerge with a viable painting even though he knew he needed far more experience, self-discipline and training. At night he joined Courbet and his brilliant, disputatious friends at the Brasserie Andler. He and Jacobsen, if they had a franc to spare, went to the Café Taranne, frequented by known painters and the famous author Gustave Flaubert, whose *Madame Bovary* had caused him to be prosecuted but later declared not guilty of immorality. Occasionally Anton Melbye took him to the Café Tortoni, patronized by the more successful painters. Once Delacroix took him for a beer at the Café Fleurus, which had been decorated by Corot.

During the working day his concentration was complete. But at night he found his thoughts drifting back to his family's flat in Passy.

He had difficulty, after he had been away on a sketching trip with Jacobsen for several weeks, engaging Julie again in conversation. It was only when he asked her about her garden in Grancey that she yielded to friendliness. She stood up tall in her resolute pride, so close to him for an instant that he caught the scent of her young skin.

"I am best with flowers: tulips, iris, lilies, asters. Never lack in the old stone house. Sometime I sell for weddings, birthdays, funerals. I raise pots of green plants, geraniums, begonias . . . the prettiest in Grancey. Some of the women are jealous of my begonias. I bring the envious ones gifts of flowers: they no longer resent."

It was the first time she had done a vaunting of self.

"What about the young Grancey men, Julie? Was there no one you cared for?"

She grimaced, but even that gesture had a captivating aspect.

"Not many boys. The forge and factories close. Young men move away. In 1852 we have the plague, doctors come from big towns, we lose a hundred of our twelve hundred people." She paused, looked at him without defiance. "Who would marry a poor girl? No dowry, not even the dozen."

"The dozen?"

"Custom of the dowry in Burgundy. The bride must bring a dozen of something: cows, sheep, horses; a dozen hundred francs or a dozen thousand francs. We don't have a dozen handkerchiefs. No chance for me or my sisters. Félicie and me, we leave Grancey."

There was no self-pity in her voice.

She eyed him intently.

"I am strong. I know how to work and make do. I don't salt the soup with tears. The mother teach us that."

"That's a good dowry, Julie."

"In Grancey they say, 'It take courage to live at all. Easier to die and end the burden.' "

"Do you believe in life after death?"

"The Bible say there is a heaven."

"I'm asking what you think, not what the Bible says."

She gazed at him hard.

"I like to find a little heaven on earth before the next world." She smiled and spoke to him directly. There was only simplicity in her manner.

"What about you, Monsieur Camille?"

"I'm in heaven when I paint and in hell at the same time because I'm not doing better. Do you understand?"

"No."

He was convinced that the years of hardship, being on the bottom of the social compost, had not hurt her, thwarted or dwarfed her. She had had six years of schooling, steady work in her beloved garden; a sharing on the little Rue Neuve where no one had much to spare. They were all in the same leaky boat; the next day's meal had to be earned by hard labor. If one family was in more straitened circumstances than another, the reverse hardship could occur in a week or month. Community survival brought equality and tranquillity. Where there was little to share, one shared.

"That's why they call Grancey a 'socialist' village," she confided.

Taxes were small. All inhabitants had been represented in the municipal council since 1750. The people of Grancey had only a minimum on which to live, but its laws provided that they be left enough to eat: milk and bread for breakfast, a thin soup for supper. There appeared to be no misery in their hearts, little resentment of the bourgeois who also had problems: death of the newborn, tuberculosis, cholera, bad crops. Everything was expensive. Baptism cost a franc, the burial of a child a franc and a half; marriage six francs; burial of an adult eighteen francs, three dollars and sixty cents.

It was not easy for them to find moments alone. Rachel or Emma and the children were usually present. Yet they managed a meeting here and there. Always Julie spoke of Grancey so that he began to see the old stone village with its inhabitants, its work and activities, the families gathered in the evening on a stoop in warm weather or in a neighbor's house before a log fire in winter, friends, neighbors, family. They played a rondo, danced the waltz, the *seuillotte*, played skittles, tourniquet, the lotteries when there were a few sous to spare. She rejoiced in these activities: their Mardi Gras, when they wore cut-out masks and a piece of colored cloth at the throat; the dressing up on Ash Wednesday. The closest city was Dijon, seventy-five miles away, so the people of Grancey amused themselves with the Saturday night markets, fairs in neighboring villages, itinerant circuses, religious and patriotic ceremonies. She had traveled to such smaller towns as Saône and Bresse with the girls' choir in lumbering farm wagons, singing as they went. He gathered that in any of these other villages she would have grown up ignorant.

She liked best when she sang at the fairs at Essoyes, Verpillières, Autricourt; she felt she was seeing the world. Camille did not point out that they were reflections of her own village, slightly enlarged. Each neighboring town experienced was another fieldstone in the structure of her life.

He could not conceive of a greater contrast with his own growing up.

He gained her confidence because she was hungry for someone to whom she could talk about home, telling him over and over about the fields in which the Vellay women worked, grew grains, hemp, vegetables raised between the long winters, the early and late frosts; bit by bit revealing the color and character of Grancey-sur-Ource, the châteaux and two large outlying farms, Le Val des Dames and Charmeronde, where the women of Grancey went to do the laundering. He listened because he watched her mobile expression, his ears responding to the timbre of her voice.

Grancey never had a notary, a bank, pharmacy; the nearest doctor was in the town of Essoyes and was rarely summoned for an individual illness, only for an epidemic. The lone store was a small window in the front room of a house. She remembered how the men dug up the cemetery, reburied the bones elsewhere, built a communal house used as a school for boys and girls which Julie and her sisters had attended. They used a *tambour*, a great bass drum, for all public announcements, which came at the same time each day, at late dusk, when work was finished, so the townspeople could assemble for the news.

"Like the journals in Paris," Camille commented, "posted in the windows. Telling of the alarm caused by the first women asking for hunting permits. Or the Donati comet bright on the horizon. That the painter Henner won the Prix de Rome for his theme, *Adam and Eve Finding the Body of Abel*."

Salvos were fired on festival days, or when newlyweds emerged from the town hall. Julie's voice was tinged with unhappiness.

"No salvo for the mother. Her belly was announcement enough."

Camille felt saddened for her.

"Why did your mother take up with your father? Were there no good men available?"

"He took her into the woods. She had a good dowry. Someone could marry her for the dowry."

She shot him a look of privity.

"She married seven months' pregnant. To an outsider, ditchdigger for the railroads. At night in the city hall. Not in the church, like it should be. He signed his wedding certificate with an X."

He did not tell her that Rachel too had been pregnant by Frédéric Pissarro when she was married by the Dutch governor in the city hall of St. Thomas after the elders of her congregation had refused her the right to be married in the synagogue.

Once, before he could know what she was about, she ran up to her little room under the roof, unlocked a drawer with the key she kept around her neck and buried deep between her breasts, and extracted a document from the wooden dresser. She held the yellow-edged paper out to him, saying:

"The mother threw it away. I saved it."

He took the paper, written in the heavy pointed pen of the town clerk, read:

Monsieur the Mayor reveals to the Council that, as a result of bad treatment exercised by the sire VELLAY on his wife and children, a judgment of the civil tribunal of Châtillon-sur-Seine condemns the conduct of VELLAY, who has abandoned his wife and children to live in a state of vagabondage since 1843. An unhappy wife and three young children, living on public charity, are deprived of the wood necessary to cook their food, and for heating in the rigorous winter season. It thinks the wife VELLAY should be considered as head of the household. Her trials, her needs, her good conduct, make it the duty of the Municipal Council to come to her aid. . . .

Camille handed back the document. "You didn't try to hear from your father after he ran away?"

"No. We wanted to throw a cat between his legs."

On May 1 there was a National Guard assembly with uniforms provided by the Commune. The Commune voted a credit to help the impoverished. The council said, "Misery speaks loud. If we can't eliminate suffering, at least we can relieve it." There were many widows and children living at a subsistence level, but the Vellay family was a rarity, cited as "poor," because of abandonment, the only abandoned family. The other "poor" had surrounding family who helped when they could.

"The men of Grancey make a living from hard labor but never a Grancey man run away from his little ones. We were

107

stuck in Grancey, but not proper Grancey. That was hard; not being poor, but being of a worthless outlander.''

''Julie, it's enough to punish ourselves for our own sins without adding those of our antecedents. Shakespeare said in his play *Othello,* 'Who steals my purse steals trash.' What is in our character cannot be taken away from us.''

She gave him an appraising study, burrowing.

''What about you, Monsieur Camille? What is your character? That cannot be stolen from you?''

He laughed, beguiled and perplexed. ''What am I at twenty-eight? That I will still be at thirty-eight or forty-eight? First of all I have to be a painter.''

''How do you know?''

''I hear a voice strong and clear: 'You must be a painter. That is what your life is for.' ''

''The voice of God?''

''I'm not so egotistical as to think that there is a Lord Jehovah who would pause long enough to plant a painter's virus in me. It just happened. Early on, when I was perhaps nine and began sketching as a means of expressing myself. I felt it.''

''You give your life to doing something when you don't know what makes you?''

''That could be a cruel question, Julie, if it weren't asked with such gentleness. It's the human predicament. Like being born with one brown eye and one blue.''

She shook her head, doggedly. ''Everything happens has a reason.''

He replied softly, ''Artists the world over have twisted and turned all their lives trying to explain why they are what they are. You would say, 'Put there by God, for a purpose.' That explanation is only acceptable if you are religious by nature.''

''I am. The sweetness was the church, music, incense, ceremonies, the sisters and the curé, who cared about our immortal souls.''

Julie loved the church on the hill, which had been built five years before she was born.

''It was the only pretty house in Grancey.''

Her voice softened, drifted, became overcome by nostalgia. Her church, dedicated to the Most Holy Virgin, so greatly honored in the area, was the Val des Dames. Built anew in 1833, it had statues of the Virgin, of St. Quentin, patron saint of the village, as well as statues of St. Nicolas, St. Sébastien, Ste. Catherine, St. Vincent.

''Now life is better. I'm no longer at the bottom of a village on the Rue Neuve.''

"You have courage . . . intelligence. . . ."

"Will that take me to my florist shop?"

"Is that what you want?"

She was smiling now, a light of hope spread over her face.

"The mother and Madame Emma have been good to me." Then shyly, "And you let me talk about Grancey." She lowered her head, added with the naturalness of the Bourgogne peasant: "You haven't . . . tried to get me into the woods. Shouldn't think you'd need to. So many girls in Paris."

"I know little more about love than you do, Julie. I've never been emotionally involved."

"Then what?"

"Amusement, relief. . . . My mother and father were close. Enjoyed each other. Theirs was a love match. Not arranged. They chose to be together . . . under considerable difficulties."

He felt this was a new concept for Julie. She would brood about unfamiliar ideas, contemplate them seriously until she achieved some clarity.

He talked about the young men and women in St. Thomas, of their freedom to be together, though the girls of the upper classes were chaperoned.

Grancey was too small for the boys and girls not to see each other in the square. But they were not allowed to be alone together. They married strangers.

"We were told love comes after marriage," she said.

"Did it?"

"Babies came."

She had arrived in Paris in a black dress, with sewn linens in two straw baskets, and found her life as a *bonne* a good one. Rachel was strict with her but kind. She missed eating pork, mainstay of the diet in Grancey. Camille replied that, alas, the agency had sent her to the wrong house. That it was against the Hebraic dietary laws. When she wrinkled her brow in quizzical fashion, declaring it delicious, he explained that in times long gone pigs were considered unsanitary. They carried the germs of trichinosis. Made people ill. Sometimes killed them. She had responded quickly:

"Not in Grancey."

When she asked why he did not eat the meat if it was clean now, couldn't the religion change? he sighed. No religion ever changed. It only became more set in its ways. The word "swine" had become a pejorative word, a bad name. Rachel had told her that pork was "*tref* . . . ," a mispronunciation.

"*Traif*," he replied. "That means nonkosher."

Rachel kept a kosher house with two sets of dishes, one for milk products, the other for meat. The same ritual applied to the pots and pans, each being defiled if used for the other. Camille pointed out that the Catholics also had dietary laws, eating fish on Friday instead of meat.

But what Julie really regretted was that there was no garden to tend. As for how long it would be before she again had flowers to raise, she answered always that she had time, an attitude similar to his own.

"You also have spunk."

She looked at him directly, studied his features in a ruminative silence he had not heard from her before.

He pieced together Julie's workday. She rose at six to light the kitchen fires, helped the silent, sixtyish cook begin breakfast and served the children. Then she dressed them and took them to the close-by kindergarten and primary school. After that she returned to serve breakfast on trays to the bedrooms, made the family beds, straightened the rooms, helped prepare the midday dinner, served, washed up. She retired then to her room in the attic for a short rest, and returned to help prepare and serve supper; again tidied the kitchen. She was through about 10 P.M.

Twice a year, in the fall and spring, there were major housecleanings to be done, including the beating of the rugs in the backyard. According to the day of the week, Julie washed, ironed, mended the linen, polished the silver and brass, cleaned one room at a time extensively. Twice a day there was the formidable task of dressing and undressing Rachel. Emma was self-sufficient and dressed more simply, eschewing some of the hoops, girdles, multiple layers of cloth.

When Camille commented that it seemed a long day, Julie replied coolly:

"In the vineyards and laundering we work from first light till dark. Then we walk home, make supper, clean up. That was hard labor, this is soft. I earn more here. I get my board and lodging. In two and a half years I'll save a thousand francs, enough for my dowry. I figured it to the centime. It will be my 'dozen' to get me a husband, not a laborer, but a clerk, or in a shop. A little more time, I have my flower stall."

It was the one subject about which she was vulnerable.

"Flowers grow beautiful for me."

"Like to like."

She snapped her eyes in anger, closed in upon herself.

"You flatter me. Will get you nothing. I am a *bonne* in the mother's flat."

"You're belittling yourself. It doesn't suit you."

"What does suit me?" Her voice was harsh.

"Being aware of your considerable qualities. Your pride. Your grasp of life. Your radiant strength, good face and figure . . . a kind of beauty."

Her defense was punctured a little. Her voice softer.

"No one ever called me that crazy word."

"Not like the beauties in the carriages in the Bois de Boulogne, that's true. Julie, let me paint you."

An ironic smile moved on her lips. She said, *"Me mettre dans la gueule du loup?* To put myself in the wolf's jaw?"

"I'm not a wolf, Julie, you have nothing to fear from me."

She put her face up into his, her eyes flaring.

"Qui se mouche trop son nez en tire du sang. Who blows his nose too much draws blood. Don't try to get too much out of something."

With which she swished her skirt about, sternly, and stalked out of the room, leaving Camille with his mouth open.

"Well, I'll be damned!" he muttered.

4

The desire grew upon him—"It's an urge, really," he decided—to do a full portrait of Julie in the long black dress he had seen her wear of a Sunday afternoon when leaving to catch the omnibus for Paris and a visit with her sister. He was fascinated by the way she walked, the tilt of her head, the rhythmical manner in which she moved her arms and hips in her work about the flat; the grace with which she lowered her head slightly when she was unwilling to meet his eyes. He had scraps of her down on paper but they were unsatisfying fragments. He needed long sessions, where he could work uninterruptedly. How could this be done? Rachel would never permit it. Where then? He did not want to invite her to his and Jacobsen's studio on her Sunday off. It was too intimate a demand.

The answer matured slowly, with considerable reluctance on his part. He would have to do the portrait in Julie's dormer bedroom when she had finished her day's work. The building's row of servants' rooms on the top floor was sacrosanct, the servants' refuge in their off hours. No one might intrude upon them for any cause whatever. How then could he persuade her to permit him this intrusion? Why should she give up her few precious hours of freedom? Particularly since "sitting for a portrait" was an inconceivable concept to her.

Yet he was obsessed by the idea, deep in the forest standing before his easel, in the sparse studio amid the stacks of finished and unfinished paintings. It gave him no rest.

It was almost Christmas before he gathered the courage to broach his idea, and his plea. He was sitting with a sketchbook on his lap.

"You want to come to my bedroom? At night? Do you think I am *folle*?"

Her eyes were blazing and, although she kept her fists clenched at her side, white-knuckled, her words almost tore his head off.

"You want to disgrace me, get me fired . . . ?"

"I have no intention of harming you."

"Words are balloons. Drift out of sight."

She shot him a glance of disdain, mingled with sympathy for his ignorance, then drew herself up proudly, her capacious chest heaving a trifle.

"You couldn't harm me!"

"Then what are you afraid of?"

"My job."

"Your free time is your own. It will be after you are through with your work. When you have gone to your room."

"With the cook in the room beside me!"

"I will be careful."

"*Il me faudrait avoir des chambres à louer dans ma tête.* I would have to have rooms to rent in my head."

He laughed.

"I like your proverbs. They constitute a book of wisdom."

She puzzled over the word "constitute," then added laconically:

"All peasant girls have."

"You are not a peasant, Julie. You read and write."

She was sidetracked for the moment.

"I do not use periods. When I write my sentences run together like the river Ource under the washhouse."

"You use periods when you speak. I can separate your sentences."

"Yes. The mother could read and write. She came from good family. The father . . ."

She made a bodily gesture of distaste, then turned around, her green eyes again blazing with wrath.

Mollified by his concentration on his sketching, she sat down for a moment in a corner of the room that gave them a sense of being alone. An element of curiosity was eating at her. Why was it so important to him to paint her portrait? He explained that getting onto canvas her mood, character, the lines of her would be a challenge.

He asked again about her plans for the future. Casually she replied:

"After I have my florist shop, I find a man. A *compère*, in a *métier*, a carpenter or mason who works steady. My sister Félicie already met one. A mechanic. Plenty work. They never starve."

"You have a practical mind, Julie."

"I remember what happened to the mother," she murmured.

"I would not take you walking in the woods."

The thought of her mother created the indignant anger he had witnessed in his first attempts to reach her, months before; she jumped up from the cane and mahogany chair, cried in a low, hurt voice:

"I'm ashamed! You are man like the rest. . . ."

"Julie, what are you saying? I meant no offense. Listen to me. I want you to sit for me in that nice black dress you brought from Grancey. The one with lace around your neck and wrists. It covers you to your shoe tops. Sitting there quietly, crocheting. . . ."

She gazed at him intently for still another moment, gold flecks irradiating her eyes.

"Do not speak to me again!"

She wanted no further communication. For his part he had no desire to embarrass or discomfort her. Since she was obviously fearful of him, or at least of his intentions, he had no wish to add to her burdens or endanger her position in the household. He liked her and would have been most happy to continue the relationship. He wanted very much to paint her. But the next move, if there was to be any, would have to come from her.

He returned to the studio on a Saturday night after an evening at the Brasserie Andler and decided to have midday Sunday dinner with the family. Julie served the roasted goose and cabbage, the noodle pudding with almonds. He chatted with his mother about her business matters, since she enjoyed that, about news of Alfred. As always they avoided any mention of his painting.

After dinner Emma bundled up her children and she and Rachel took them to the park. Camille went into the room that had been set aside for him. He became absorbed in the story of *La Cousine Bette* by Balzac and at first did not hear the gentle knocking at the door.

"Yes?"

"Monsieur Camille, may I speak to you?"

She had donned one of the soft wool sweaters she had been knitting. There was a quizzical, half-pained expression on her face, her hair was brushed back and gathered at the nape of her neck.

"Yes?"

"I meant no insult."

"I took none."

"Every other Sunday I visit my sister. But it's a long time between . . . no one to talk to . . ." She made a wry face. "Could I . . . bring you a cup of tea . . . in the parlor?"

He sat down in the big cane rocker by the front window but could no longer concentrate. He had pushed Julie out of his mind. Now she had asked for friendship in a timid, apparently long-rehearsed way. She set the tea down on a little table beside him.

"Won't you sit down, Julie?"

She sat tentatively on the edge of a chair opposite him, her catlike green eyes enormous, her lips open tremulously, famished to be near someone young. Searching for an impersonal approach, Camille asked:

"How is your sister Félicie getting on with her mechanic?"

Julie leaned forward, her hands clasped at her bosom.

"Luck has happened. Louis Estruc takes her out walking when she is free; sometimes a café or a revue. Félicie says he's serious."

Camille put down his teacup, murmured:

"Perhaps it would be better if you worked in Paris where you could meet young men, 'serious' ones. Passy is a small village."

"I must do a good job here for two years so I get the reference." She sat back in her chair. "Tell me about being a painter," she asked respectfully.

"He is a man who searches for engrossing motifs to set down on paper or paint on canvas."

"What is a motif?"

He hesitated. "I'll have to chew my cud on that."

She was amused. "Like a peasant."

"That would not be bad." He assembled his thoughts. "A motif is a composition or structure in nature. The painter looks for one that will start his creative faculties flowing, make him want to conquer it and preserve it for all to see. It is not something that is perfect. Rather it is a sight, an impression that challenges as well as it disturbs, that induces a fervor high enough to put us to work with our charcoal or brush. We know that the process will be difficult, that it will be elusive, even frightening. But it becomes the greatest desire of our life. Do you understand, Julie?"

" . . . not the words. But I want to. Your face lights up . . . so I understand what you feel. But what you mean . . . Could you say it simple?"

After thinking through the problem he said quietly, "A motif is a scene, an idea, an event that brings delight to the painter's eye and mind. Something he loves in the way that he loves a book, a building, Notre Dame de Paris, or music, Beethoven's *Pastoral*. They are the same: transliterations of nature, brought into a focus for the human brain to grasp and be enriched by. That is not being presumptuous. Any alteration or regrouping is not an artist's attempt to improve on nature, not to falsify or romanticize it; but to bring the scene into greater balance, to make it a little more orderly or, yes, meaningful. Or harmonious. It is the desire shared by all men, artists and others, to bring order out of chaos, an irrepressible desire to arrange, simplify; perhaps a little to prove his superiority over the original creation."

She smiled with a touch of sadness.

"You are talking to Monsieur Camille, not to me, Julie Vellay from Grancey."

He drew on his cup of tea, crunching the remaining bits of rough brown sugar he held between his lips, bowed his head apologetically.

"*C'est vrai*. It's what all artists do, in an effort to understand themselves. My dear Julie, a motif is a scene from nature that thrills an artist, something about which he exclaims, 'God created this on one of His better days.' "

"That's blasphemy."

"It wasn't intended. Perhaps what man is trying to do is adapt the earth to his needs."

"I see . . . a little."

"We must be patient with each other."

" . . . patient? You with me? Why?"

"Because I want us to be friends."

Looking away, thinking hard, she murmured, "Can we be?"

"We already are."

"Trying to explain all this, it means you think I can learn. It means you care. I'm not just a servant in your mother's home."

She hesitated, then asked softly:

"How many times would I have to sit?"

"For your portrait?"

"Yes. If you still want. I'm not afraid now."

"I'm happy about that, Julie. Perhaps a dozen times."

She suppressed a giggle. "At last I'll have a 'dozen'! When?"

"Tomorrow evening?"

"*Bien*. My black dress. After ten."

"I'll be there. Thank you for the confidence."

She flashed him a half-concerned smile.

5

He tried her door. She had unlatched it just a moment before. Her room was one of six small identical cubicles in a row, with the dormer window a gabled extension of the sloping roof. There was a narrow bed brought from St. Thomas with a bolster beneath her pillow to act as a backboard, and a sharply ridged coverlet, a cane chair, a four-drawer dresser holding a bowl and pitcher and, alongside, Julie's simple toilet articles. On the wall above the chest, a small mirror. The room was scrubbed clean.

In Paris the servants' dormer rooms were mere closets, badly ventilated, hot in summer, unheated in winter; breeding places for anemia. The French admitted, "The living conditions compare unfavorably with those of a prison." The Passy suburban houses had been built on a more generous scale, with some space to move around; the window opening wide to the sun and air. However there was no way to heat the room in winter. Julie placed a brick in the oven while supper was being prepared and put it, wrapped in flannel, inside the foot of her bed.

"In Grancey we say, 'Hot brick for the foot makes sleep for the head.' "

She had sponged and pressed the crepe de chine dress she had cut and sewn for herself in Grancey the year before; washed the lace collar and cuffs. The native rug from Charlotte Amalie was still damp in spots where she had bathed standing up in her basin of soapy water. Her face, freshly washed, had high color, as though she had just returned from a day in the vineyards. He considered the structure of her head good: high cheekbones, a mouth proportioned to her chin; close-fitting ears behind which she wore her gleaming dark hair and around which she had put an ornamental band.

He pushed the cane chair close to the wall and sat down with his sketchbook. He sat her at the foot of her bed.

She wriggled uncomfortably. "Do you want me to look at you?"

"Pay no attention to me. Just be natural, bending over your crocheting or needlework. I can capture you that way."

"I never been captured. I always been free."

"For a painter to 'capture' a person is simply to catch his spirit from inside out, set it down vividly. . . ." He looked up sharply. Was she teasing him?

The phrase "from inside out" did frighten her, but she decided to let it go since she had no intention of letting him know what was inside her head, let alone inside the all-embracing black dress.

He was fascinated by the guilelessness of her face and figure, unpampered and unspoiled, so different from the women he met in the ateliers, at the parties and social affairs. She wore no mask to conceal what lay beneath. It was the naturalness of a girl who had in no way been besmirched by pretension, either to protect herself or to blow up her image in public, like children carrying colored balloons.

After a few moments he said:

"It won't disturb me if you talk. Tell me more about Grancey. Happy things."

She flushed with pleasure, overcoming her feeling of being ill at ease by his concentration on her.

"Happy? Like I told you. The chorales. At church. In the square. At festivals and marriages. Walking along the street on Sunday for the feasts and ceremonies, we sang, sang, sang. . . . The *quatorze juillet* was the best. The Guard puts lanterns in the linden trees around the square, lights them at dusk on the eve, July 13. They burn all night." Her eyes brightened as she remembered the light of the candles in their blue, white and red Bengal holders. At the center an *R.F.* for République Française. The church bells tolled as they all carried lanterns in the streets, fireworks blazoning the way. They danced on the cobblestones.

On July 14 everyone wore his or her best suit or dress; the firemen their silver-buttoned uniforms. "When we are little we fight for the honor of the front row; the women sit on benches under the linden trees. There are drums, the grown-ups sing 'Song of Departure' or 'Sidi-Brahim.' The children sing, 'No bread at our house; there's some at the neighbors'.' The Mayor stands forward with his blue, white and red sash; he reads about Liberty, Equality, Fraternity. The musicians play the 'Marseillaise.' Everyone stands."

She became silent. Looked at him directly.

"It was good," she concluded, "to have something to celebrate."

When Julie asked him questions about St. Thomas he told her about the family skiff from which the boys fished and dove into the warm waters of the inlets. How they would go for all-day hikes in the rich green forests of the mountains above the port. Of his work on the docks for his father, checking in goods from the ships sailing foreign flags, loading the car and having it rolled up the track to Dronningens Gade. Of his early sketching of the sailing vessels, the native women walking with baskets on their heads; the sailors in port in their varicolored outfits. Of the private school that charged his family a monthly fee of one dollar for reading, a dollar and a half for writing, two dollars for all other subjects. How blessed he felt now that his parents had been able to afford such schooling.

The next night he talked about the palm trees and the coconuts with which he was still adorning his pictures, the yearlong tropical sun and heat; the crescent-shaped bay of Charlotte Amalie where he visited the vessels from around the world, spoke a patois of English, French and Spanish with the sailors. He pictured the languorous pace of the island, the casual attire and sandaled or bare feet, the friendliness of the polyglot inhabitants: Danes, who owned the island and governed it equitably, if not as concerned for the individual well-being as the Council in Grancey; the French, English and American merchants who flourished in the age of sail, and the prosperity of the rum and molasses trade. The affectionate family life upstairs over the shop. She could picture the apartment, furnished as it was with the same furniture she was dusting and polishing daily.

"I see it," Julie murmured. "Your St. Thomas."

Another night she told him of her first communion. Her

voice rang lyrically in his head and through his viscera as she talked with love and warmth of the three days she and the other children attended the masses, the vespers, recited the catechism and received the sacrament of the Eucharist in a heavily starched white dress with a wreath of white blossoms on her head. Her mother had hung the small gold cross around her neck that she had saved in a box since her own communion. The central aisle of the church was lined with prie-dieux, the children led to the praying stools. There were canticles, orations in Latin, a sermon given by the priest from the high altar. The tapers were lit, the children went to the baptismal font, the promises of baptism were renewed on this great day of their twelfth year; then offered their crowns to the Holy Virgin.

Her words came out so fast it was obvious she had been reliving the experience during the entire day, between sittings. She told him gratefully:

"The ceremonies, I forgot them until now. You make it good to have memories. I become more a person."

"You are a lovely person, Julie."

She flushed. " . . . that's not true. A little attractive . . . maybe. . . ."

She gazed into his eyes fiercely. "Is that what a painter does? Make a person look her best? Respect herself?"

"Perhaps that happens. But not to idealize. Not to make anything sentimental. You are what you are. I can only reflect what's in you. Painters want to preserve the color, character, vitality of a time or place, or person, so that they can never be forgotten. The artist is a lover who wants the world to see the beauty of his beloved. Whatever scene or motif of nature he falls in love with."

Julie was embarrassed at this sentiment, lowering her head over the needlework.

"Like the new *photographie?*"

"That box invented by Daguerre? No. A painter builds into his picture his own special vision. Some Sunday afternoon when you are off, we could ride to the outskirts, to the forest perhaps. Then I could find a simple picture, tell you why it attracts me, and how an artist converts the scene before him into something of his own."

Her eyes gleamed at the prospect; she missed the country. Passy was almost country, but not really. The sidewalks . . . But then she took fright. She had better not. She did not want to lose her job. She paled, picked up her crocheting, fumbled with the needle.

"I don't understand what's happening to me." Tears smarted behind her lids. She murmured:

"Better go. Getting late."

He nodded assent, keeping his distance.

"Good night, Julie."

For several days he painted at Montmorency. When he returned to the room under the eaves he brought with him his easel, palette and tubes of paint. He had had to manipulate the easel noiselessly so that he would not arouse the cook next door.

Julie said simply:

"I missed you."

"I missed you too, Julie. But I wanted to catch cold winter in the forest."

"I know. Job comes first."

"It is getting stormy now. No chance to work out of doors."

She sighed deeply, settled onto the bed and picked up an embroidery.

A few evenings later, apropos of her own interior monologue, she asked quietly:

"What is a Jew?"

Camille realized how genuine her puzzlement must be, since it was not likely that she had ever met or heard about a Jew in Grancey-sur-Ource. He hesitated for a considerable time.

"Some people call us a race, a culture, an ethic, others say we are a religion. . . ."

"How can that be? I have a real religion. Everybody knows it."

He swished thoughts around in his head. "We have a long history; the religious observance is only one of its aspects. The Jew has implicit faith in Yahweh, as told in the Old Testament, the One God. Michelangelo's beautiful white-bearded old man on the Sistine vault in Rome is the invention of fiction painters. A personal God who answers all our prayers. That's the theologian's fiction."

"You mean you're a *curé* eater? Like some of the atheists in Grancey?"

She threw her head back and laughed deep in her throat.

"No. I don't fight the synagogue. I just haven't joined."

"Can you live without faith? When there was no soup, we lived on faith that Our Lord would provide."

"There are many kinds of faith. A belief in God, the

efficacy of prayer, life after death, all that is just one kind of faith man invented to serve certain needs, to placate fear . . ."

"What other kinds of faith are there?" Belligerently.

"Faith in the order of nature. In man's ability to survive, to create, to make the world a little more decent, a little more intelligible. Faith in one's self. For myself, to paint glowing canvases that withstand time and change. You've read the Bible, haven't you?"

"Only the part the *curé* taught us. Prayers."

"You must understand that it was all written by man. Some of it, the Song of Solomon, is beautiful poetry."

"God told man what to write. It is His voice."

"Perhaps. Many think so. It doesn't matter. The Bible contains literature, history, fable, a code of ethics, the admonition to love thy neighbor as thyself. That should be enough for anyone."

"Why do you say you are not religious? You sound that way."

"Julie, all families have their problems. Yours was not alone. Jews must be married in a synagogue by the rabbi. Just like Catholics by a priest in the church. My parents were married by an officer of the Danish government in St. Thomas."

"Why?"

"Because my father was a nephew of my mother. The elders of the synagogue refused on the grounds that the Jewish law forbids marriage between nephew and aunt even if there is no blood relationship. Something about marital authority a husband is supposed to maintain, and which an aunt exercises over a nephew. The elders refused even after three sons were born. My parents fought, petitioned the chief rabbi in London, then the chief rabbi in Copenhagen. For eight years they were refused a religious blessing; they who are deeply religious. Only when their fourth son was born did the elders relent. For all those years the congregation of Charlotte Amalie, except for a few liberal members, refused them friendship. They carried their hurt with them for almost a decade. Yet it never lessened their faith in their religion. Only in the men who controlled the temple."

She leaned toward him, troubled.

"If it did not turn your parents against their religion, why did it you?"

"I did not think the sport worth the candle. That's a quotation from an early English poet, George Herbert. I learned it in school here in Passy. It means that the rewards are too little to become entrapped in a religious maze."

What he could not tell a *bonne* who could move on to another position was that the synagogue had refused the marriage on moral grounds as well. It was only a few months after her husband's death, grieving, feeling forsaken, lonely, that Rachel had fallen in love with the handsome, virile, twenty-three-year-old nephew, as he had with her. She had, as a matter of natural consequence, become pregnant. She was seven months' pregnant when they had asked to be married.

How odd that their two mothers should have shared the same fate.

6

To Julie, Camille Pissarro was a new species, like some bird or hind that had mysteriously appeared in the Bourgogne woods. Questions churned in her mind. She asked tentatively:

"Is it going to be your lifetime job, to be a painter? Like a farmer or shopkeeper or engineer?"

"It is the whole meaning of life for me."

"Men have to earn a day's wage. How do you earn a living by painting people, streets, trees?"

"People will buy my pictures. I am like a young doctor who must hang out a sign and wait for patients to seek him out."

"Doctors cure. Patients will come. What do you cure?"

"Hunger. Blindness. Boredom. The meanness of life."

"Sounds like Christ with the loaves and fishes."

He smiled indulgently. "Or Jehovah sending manna from heaven to feed the Israelites. So it is. A miracle."

"Miracles are so . . . almost never . . ."

"There is no other gamble I consider worth attempting."

Their eyes met.

"Will you put Bible stories on church walls like in Paris?"

"I don't think so." Then added, "My parents don't want me to be an artist. They want me to be a merchant. They say I will never be able to support a wife, give our mother grandchildren. It is true that it's more difficult than selling ship's stores. The painter is an outsider in the world, perhaps even despised because he's different. Yet Paris is filled with artists, England too, all Europe for that matter. I've tried to persuade my mother that a painting is at least as valuable as a lace doily on a table. To no effect. However, my father is willing, providing I am a success."

"Is success for a painter the same as for a vintner who harvests grapes and sells them for wine?"

"*Exactement.* According to my father's sentiments. But the real artist while he paints does not think of the sale, only of the need to make a beautiful living thing. In this portrait of you, you will always be young, charming, lovely."

"*Zut!* I'm just a plain country girl. When it is finished will you give it to me?"

He hesitated only for a moment. "If you want it."

"I like Madame Pissarro and Madame Emma. They are good to me. I must do my work but they treat me with respect. I think they even like Julie Vellay."

"How could we not?"

His warm smile engulfed her. He went on sketching for a considerable time, trying to catch the juxtaposition of her agile hands as they worked the crochet hook. After a while Julie broke the silence.

"You are different than the men in Grancey. More soft, gentle. You don't try to look under my petticoats the way the rough ones did, or stare at me like in Paris when I go to see my sister."

"Attractive young girls are plump fish for every young man to hook. It's part of the French way of life."

"Why am I not a plump fish for you to hook?"

He set the question aside with a quiet wave of his hand.

"Sit at rest, Julie. I'm trying to paint your picture."

"Could I see what you are doing?"

"Be patient a little longer."

Once when he had to leave the room he returned to find her studying his tentative approach to the imperatives of figure painting at which he was not greatly experienced.

She made no comment.

They found themselves to be compatible; agreeable and congenial companions. He painted her well-shaped head with its rich crown of hair as she bent over her work, determined to bring to life her mind and personality.

He was also determined to bring to life the handsomely shaped body as he perceived her under the opulent cloth, her legs crossed so as to give her a solid resting place for her crocheting hands and the doily or kerchief she was edging. The voluminous black gown was shaped by what was within it: the delicate anklebones, the linear calves, the intricate knee sockets, the fascinating inner curves of the thighs as they made their way to the crotch, the booted feet peeping out from the bottom of the dress.

He had little trouble setting down the flowing contours to his satisfaction, measuring the rounded surfaces with his eyes. He chose for his model Ingres's newly completed *The Source*, a nude young woman holding a large upside-down terra-cotta vase upon her shoulder, supported by a well-fleshed arm held over her head. Its symbolism was in the stream of water pouring from the vase; it implied that the beautifully full figure of the untouched young woman, with lovely breasts, abdomen and groin, was ready and willing to be the source of mankind. The young woman's face was serene, her eyes, though bright in anticipation, innocently unawakened. She would bear many robust children.

Julie too had the finely tuned and proportioned body, as well as the wisdom to accept her role, the same rustic durability sedately hidden beneath the cover-all dress. He did not consider that he was intruding on her privacy when he pierced the gown for the living body so that all could see that it was Julie Vellay inside those yards of material, and no other. It was an erotic experience, creation; he was caught up in the fathoming of it.

He did not express these sentiments to Julie, fearful that she would be shocked, for she had no way of knowing that no painter worth the salt on his egg is content with the superficial . . . the *photographie*. When he became unusually tense she looked up, asked:

"What is it?"

"*Rien*. Nothing. Just a technicality."

He took paper from his pad, sketched her breasts, full, with purple nipples ample enough to feed hungry infants; used his crayons for flesh tones, filling out her bosom so that it came to pulsating life under his hand, concentrating on his task with a quickening of his pace.

Julie sensed the change. She sprang up, came around to his side so quickly that there was no chance for him to obscure the drawing. She flushed crimson, turned to him with blazing eyes.

"You have undressed me." Tears came to her eyes. "You broke your promise."

He tore the sheet across in four parts, stuffed them into his coat pocket.

"Julie, it's the way portraits are made. As I paint I must make dozens of rough sketches to let me realize my subject."

"You have no right to know my bosom!"

She covered her face. He did not know how to comfort her. After a moment he proffered:

"I apologize, Julie. I meant no harm, no disrespect. Perhaps it would be better if I didn't finish."

She lifted a tearstained face.

"It was . . . the shock. I didn't understand. I thought the dress is enough."

"No. It is you inside the dress."

"I wouldn't have let you start."

"Please don't cry. No harm has been done. The drawing is destroyed."

"But how could you know so surely? As if I stood before you naked."

"I told you, Julie, I am a good painter."

"You are going to draw other parts of me too?"

"Yes, Julie. If it is to be a real portrait. But don't be frightened. Nothing will ever show but your gown, your face and busy hands."

"You can damn well be sure!" Her voice was a whiplash. "Get out of my room."

Crushed, he took out after Jacobsen, brooded over his uncompleted drawings and oils, remained away from the house in Passy.

Camille had no thought of love; neither did he have need for it, nor fear that it would strike him from behind like a hidden assailant. As far as sexuality was concerned, which he dissociated from love, he was having a scrambling time, trying to run clear of the brambles his artist friends warned him about: public women on the one hand and marriage on the other. He was not unsatisfied with the *grisettes*. The young women were not amoral: rather they were poor, earning their two francs a day on which they could barely live. Many had to contribute to their parents' support. In the evenings, in order to secure money for clothing or to put aside a few francs toward their dowries, they found a place with friends at a respectable café and took a presentable man, if one should show, to a next-door hotel where a room and a bed were rented for an hour. They were plentiful, in their twenties: pretty, nicely dressed, reasonably bright. They chose their men discreetly, charged them each the same two francs, did their best to earn the money. If the process of coupling was mechanical, at least Camille got what he had engaged for. There was no stitch of sentimentality in the sheet over their prenuptial flights to conceal the lack of personal involvement.

Then came the blond widow. Eugène Warburg, an acquaintance from St. Thomas, had written to him, "I have met a young and pretty blonde who is now a widow. She has only one desire, and that is to see you." Camille did indeed find her pretty; and accommodating; but after a time she proposed marriage, which ended the affair.

He had other friends in Paris: Raphael Herrera from Venezuela, with whom he spoke Spanish. Francisco Oller, from Puerto Rico, who had studied under Couture. Through them he met young women from good families.

"Mademoiselle Jenny Berliner is pretty, gracious and alluring," he told Emma. "We danced, played little games. It was charming. But nothing serious."

Anton Melbye continued to advise him to find an agreeable young model.

"They are not promiscuous. They stay with one lover as long as they can."

Corot continued to warn him against marriage. Courbet, Delacroix and others had also done so, some jocularly, others in deadly earnest. Their advice had been, "When you find a pleasant young girl, take her on as a steady mistress. It gives you a continuity, a sense of companionship, but use discretion before you form an alliance. Your real friends are your fellow artists. It's an unbreakable bond, a fraternity of creators which binds us together. Exercise extreme caution: if your mistress bears you a child the freedom of the relationship is disturbed; you will feel responsible."

They had advised him what to use to prevent such a happening. Only goatskin, though it was too coarse and heavy for anyone not utterly desperate. They had discussed experimenting with rubber, but there had been no results yet.

He had no wish to become familiar with Julie. He enjoyed her company, her freshness, her spontaneity, her country-air coloring, the unawakened yet perceptive greenness of her eyes, with the gold flecks that seemed to glitter when she was aroused. There had been no seduction in his mind.

After a week he received Rachel's stern note of protest about his staying away. When he saw Julie's unhappiness he was deeply sorry. He ate his dinner talking to Emma a little too loudly and distractedly. She knew something was wrong but said nothing.

It was not until the second week of his return that Julie asked shyly:

"Could I speak to you for a moment?"

She remained diffident, part of her wanting to move toward him, something holding her back.

"I had time to think. It's just that . . . well . . . I was wrong . . . to accuse you. You haven't taken advantage of me. If I hadn't surprised you I would never have known about the sketches. Would I?"

"No."

She reached out a hand to him impulsively, pulled it back. "Then we can continue?"

He did not know why his heart was beating so wildly. He was surprised to find how deeply he wanted to finish this portrait. Julie's eyes were shining.

"I'll be dressed at ten."

The relationship had changed. Even in this tiny room they had held themselves rigorously apart. There was a new ambiance, as though some affection had been germinated, some closer adherence now that they had been through a difficult transition. Because of his growing feeling for her he determined to complete the portrait as quickly as possible. He laid aside his sketches, picked up his palette. Julie flattened the folds of her dress as though to accentuate her own lines, the lean muscled stomach and long slender legs, with a complete air of acceptance. The smell of turpentine and oil permeated the room.

Julie sometimes looked up from her needlework and regarded him through half-closed eyes. But she did not leave her seat to look over his shoulder. They were comfortable with each other. Frequently it was well past midnight when he thanked her for her patience.

His sister Emma sometimes heard him leave the apartment, saw him once with his painting materials. It was quite late. One evening she confronted him as he was preparing to ascend to the servants' area under the roof.

"Where are you off to?"

He gazed at her face, so much like his own.

"From your expression I would say you know."

"Yes. And I think you are a fool. You are going to get that girl pregnant."

He flushed.

"I'm not making love to her. I'm painting her portrait."

"Ha! How long do you think you are going to be in Julie's room before you are in her bed?"

"You have no right to assume that."

"My dear brother, I'm not trying to regulate your morals. Have all the girls in Paris that you want. But it's folly to seduce a *bonne* working for your own family."

"Emma, have I ever lied to you?"

"You're basically a truthteller. You evade questions you don't want to answer."

"I have never touched Mademoiselle Julie and have no intention of doing so. I'm painting her portrait. That is all. It took me a very long time to convince her to sit for me."

"I should think so. For God's sake, Camille, do you know what Maman will do if she finds out you're going up to Julie's room? Discharge her immediately. Without a character."

"I'll be finished soon."

"I warn you, Maman will know. She'll feel the vibrations. She has a sixth sense about such things." She shook her head in despair. "Get this foolishness over with. I wouldn't put it past Maman to throw you out as well."

Camille grinned, kissed his sister lightheartedly.

"You're laughing now," said Emma. "Just be certain you don't end up in tears."

7

The weeks continued, Julie talking about Grancey, Camille responding with tales of tropical St. Thomas. She absorbed the family life of the Pissarros, every detail, experience, frustration, fulfillment, until they became an integral part of her, interwoven with her own intimate memories, so firmly implanted in the fabric of her being that she felt they were a portion of her own growing up, something she could not lose or relinquish.

The same subtle process was overtaking Camille: the abandonment by Julie's father, the struggle of the mother, the images of laboring in the vineyards, the flower garden behind the stone house on the Rue Neuve, the indulgent city council. The small village of Grancey-sur-Ource, the ingrown people who lived and died there. The pictures were burrs caught into the flesh of his mind and imagination. He saw them, suffered and enjoyed them until Julie's life by the Ource River, where she bathed in summer and walked her cow among the willows of its banks, the flowers and vegetables she grew, all became woven into the fabric of his own childhood and growing up. What he realized only dimly was that with each thought and sentence he was giving an important part of himself to her; and to that extent she was coming to possess him. His intuition told him that it also worked the other way round: as she absorbed his thinking and values, her mind, her feelings, her character were beginning to belong to him.

"I hope I'm not selling myself to her," he exclaimed aloud in his studio bed. "That would be furthest from my intentions. Yet when Julie asks about a world unknown to her I have to explain, bring my philosophy to life as she brings Grancey to life for me."

During the three years he had been in Paris he had formed not even a semialliance. Everything was in passage, his work, his home life, his means of support, his future. He had no money, no studio of his own, above all, no desire to be bound down. Among his more respectable lady friends, some insisted upon continence, allowing only embracing and kissing; others made it plain they wanted marriage. If he had refrained from many such relationships it was partly fear of the consequences but mostly of his own suspended situation. He had not found even the right techniques, the mature approach to his painting. He was without moorings or status. Not the tiniest aspect of love had surfaced.

He had not realized how emotionally starved he had been; how barren his feelings. The sexual attraction of Julie was strong. The appeal had been widened visually and emotionally by their placing themselves in each other's earlier lives, weaving the disparate strands into a harmonious cloth, stitching themselves together. It had crept upon them slowly. To each of them life now seemed to have another, deeper dimension. Perhaps by contrast; he could not be sure.

Painting Julie exclusively was a terrifying yet exhilarating experience; life-infusing strokes developing each part of her body, her head, her face, her torso, arms and legs, conquering his problems and with his paint bringing her magnificently alive on the canvas. He had created a real Julie Vellay, not a *poupée*, a doll.

After so many weeks he had come to know her face in repose, concentrated on the needlework, the pliant though not totally graceful hands; the lovely neck and slope of the shoulders. She watched his final progress, fascinated, no longer unaware of the process. There was a growing feeling between them that as he perfected each part of her figure he had created that part of her which no one had known before. As the creator, the end product became his. . . . He could only sometimes tell by her expression what she was feeling; but there was in her eyes, her gesture as she moved and spoke, liking, friendship, admiration, closeness in a hostile world.

He fulminated against himself:

"This is insane. I like Julie. I admire her, she has a fine figure that sometimes keeps me awake at night, throbbing. She is good and clean and fresh. One could easily fall in love with her, but this is all it is going to be. When this portrait is completed it will be the end."

Had he seen the same resolution in Julie's face?

He had one last chore before dressing Julie in her simple finery and calling the job finished. He had purposely stayed away from drawing her groin, as she was seated comfortably on the lower edge of the bed. He had felt it would be an impertinence; yet he had to get the basics to secure Julie's posture as she sat before him. He went about the task with intense concentration. He was determined to complete it this one night, so worked fast, first with pencil and charcoal, then with color, setting forth the muscles of Julie's abdomen, her thighs as they came together.

"Mon Dieu," he thought. "I'm violating this poor girl. She must not know it. She has her virginity. She's fought to keep it. I must not in any way diminish it."

At last the portrait had come right. The flesh pulsatingly alive, the skin smooth, soft, moistured, of good color from the hearty flow of blood within.

When he stepped back the sparse foot or two the bedroom permitted, a smile came over his face. Julie saw it.

"You're happy."

"Yes."

"Why?"

"Because now I've captured the truth."

"About me?"

"About you."

He stood looking at his canvas. He had Julie in her black crepe, the white lace ruching around the throat, the folds of her dress enhancing the torso, her chestnut hair shining, her cheeks aglow with youth and vitality . . . all instilled with love.

There was a half-throttled cry from beside him. A cry of delight.

He took her into his arms. They clung to each other, as two

humans who had been lost, now come together. It made all the difference in life.

He kissed her. Her mouth was sweet.

They made love, for love it was, passionately, joyously, inside the heart, mind, body; there was a coming together of supreme fulfillment, commitment.

"I love you, Julie. It's not just for now."

"It happened to both. I love you from the beginning."

A shiver shook both his frame and innards.

"*J'en reste baba!* I am stupefied! We have seduced each other."

BOOK FOUR

Spread Out the Heavens

1

HE WORKED every day in the streets and parks of Paris, sometimes with Jacobsen or other friends; the rural areas behind Montmartre, the nearby villages he could reach by an early morning train. He had an inner feeling of growth that kept his emotions stable. Gustave Courbet insisted that he attend his annual all-night party at his studio, with musicians, attractive girls, wine which held out until dawn. Delacroix took him to the opera or the Théâtre Français after a session analyzing Camille's work and suggesting extended themes. Yet he had a gnawing feeling that he was working alone.

"It is true that companionship can free a man in the same sense that loneliness imprisons him," he mused. "I just don't feel I've found the young people with whom I can work."

He attempted to explain this to Corot late one afternoon when both men had finished their day's chores. Corot puffed studiously on his meerschaum, emitting clouds of obscuring gray smoke, then snatched off his blue wool cap to tousle his mane of white hair. He was always hospitable, commenting on the purpose and problems of his own latest canvases, usually a newly discovered dell or hillock in Fontainebleau. Unlike Melbye, Courbet or Delacroix, he offered no succor in the form of food or drink because he himself found no need for such refreshment until his suppertime soup.

"I have a suggestion," he proffered. "The Académie Suisse. It is the farthest thing from an academy you can imagine. It's run by an old Swiss, Père Crébassolles, who was a popular model about thirty years ago. Will cost you only ten francs, two dollars, a month. For that you get nothing but a rickety stool, a male model three weeks of the month, a female model on the fourth. Père Crébassolles gives no instruction because he wouldn't know how. You're free to come and go as you like."

"Antoine Guillemet spoke to me about the Suisse."

Corot got up from his chair, walked about the studio with his strong peasant fingers laced over the tired bottom of his spine.

"It's like a club. Many of our best painters have worked there. Delacroix, Courbet, Bonington, Isabey, including a talented young man you may not yet have met, Edouard Manet. There you may find comrades of your own generation who have similar ideas. Try it."

He found the Académie Suisse close to the Pont St. Michel, on the Quai des Orfèvres. The building was badly run down; even the sign on the ground floor, SABRA, *Dentiste du Peuple*, needed a coat of paint. Camille chuckled when he remembered Corot's story of the young artist who approached the building to enroll but heard a horrendous scream from its interior where the Dentiste Sabra had just extracted an infected molar from a jaw.

"Mon Dieu," the lad had exclaimed, running away, "Père Crébassolles tortures his students!"

A similar loss was suffered by the Dentiste Sabra when a prospective patient climbed the flight of unswept stairs to the floor above and found himself staring at a nude male.

Camille was confronted with a large, plain, dusty room with thirty men sitting around on stools, their sketchbooks on their laps, a male model seated on a rough platform. The bare walls bore no sketches, unfinished oils or notices of exhibitions. There was no older student who called himself the *massier* and supervised the atelier. There was only Père Suisse, in front of a small alcove where he slept and ate his simple meals. His body had run to chunkiness, particularly in the forefront; he kept his outline concealed under a floor-length brown monk's robe. His face was battered by the furrows and random lumps of age, his head an old globe of the world that had rolled down the slope of a rocky hill.

"Père Suisse? I'm Camille Pissarro. Corot sent me. I'd like to join."

The man looked up from his book, grunted:

"Five francs to the first of the month. Ten francs a month after. Week of grace if you're strapped. Then you make way for one who can pay. Just don't burn the building down. Open six in the morning. Close ten at night."

Camille found the so-called academy a good refuge. Antoine Guillemet welcomed him. He worked there in bad weather, during the evenings, and on those afternoons when he could find no motif that stirred him. Camille guessed that most of his fellow lodgers, for that was what they considered themselves, were from sixteen years of age to about twenty-five. At twenty-nine, he was the oldest of the group. That did not bother him; for an artist, age is what ultimately shows up on the canvas. What did surprise him was that few in the loftlike barren room were drawing the model. Each day or evening as he came in and took whatever stool was empty he saw that for the most part they were landscapists. There was a good deal of boisterousness whenever another Beaux-Arts dignitary won a medal or a commission to paint a church, library or city hall.

"Funeral wreaths!" growled one. "Tributes to the dead," cried another.

Before the week was out, Camille made a friend, a nineteen-year-old who extended a boyish hand of greeting when Camille thumped down next to him.

"*Salut!* I'm Claude Monet from Le Havre. Earned my living drawing caricatures at my home port. Had a great teacher, Boudin, a painter working on the coast of Normandy. Does sea and landscapes from nature; all light and air. Earns his living by running a frame shop. Taught me a lot. One of the reasons I thought I could come to Paris and be a painter. *Comment vous appelez-vous?*"

Camille introduced himself. He was taken with Claude Monet's appealing personality, bright and vivacious. He was olive-skinned, broadly proportioned, though only of medium height. He had a genial clean-shaven face; a mass of black hair grown almost to his shoulders and looped thickly over his ears. It was a handsome face, scrubbed clean, with balanced strong features near perfect in design; enormous eyes, a finely molded slender nose. He was dressed in a blue and white turtleneck shirt, a brown jacket, light trousers, flowing cravat under the black cotton smock.

"He has an air of distinction," Camille decided. "In those deep-set eyes there lurks a look of purpose."

Claude Monet was a sociable soul; he liked to talk in a low humming voice while he worked, his head only half poised over the sketchpad.

"Have you ever watched Père Suisse reading that book? He never turns a page. It's the same book since I got here a couple of months ago. Probably the same one for years. I don't think he can read; it's just a device to let us know he's not intruding on our work. *Piquant*, don't you think? He must

135

have a hundred artists enrolled here. Good thing we don't all come at the same time. May I see your workbook? Here's mine, if you're interested."

"I am indeed. I'd like to see if you can transfer your verve to the drawing paper."

The youngster's work, shallow and uneven, had a gusto and dash to it. After studying Camille's work, Claude Monet murmured:

"I've heard you study with Corot. *Bonheur*. Lucky. My idol is Daubigny. Did you know that he lives on a houseboat, painting the Seine and Oise?"

"On a houseboat!" Camille was startled. "That explains how he manages to capture the banks of the rivers so brilliantly at dawn and dusk. I've studied his paintings and wondered how he achieved his effects."

"I'll have a houseboat like Daubigny's one day," Monet proclaimed. "Then you can come paint with me."

"One to a houseboat," Camille replied jokingly, enjoying the man's ebullience. "I'd rather paint on solid land. I feel firmer with my feet planted."

Père Suisse snapped his book with a resounding signal that it was closing time. Monet said:

"How about a *bière?* They have pretty models at the Brasserie des Martyrs. I flirt with them."

"*D'accord*. The beer, that is, not the girls."

2

There was no way to overestimate their sexual delirium. For Julie it was a world abounding with astonishment, gratification and a fulfillment of undreamed ecstasies. Camille found that everything that had gone before was a charade. Love converted this formerly casual act into a deeply emotional consummation, a conjugal and harmonious blending of mind, spirit, body into an exhaustive unity; a relationship that went through passion to an elation and exaltation, *une gaieté de coeur,* a gaiety of the heart, *un cri d'allégresse,* a joyful cheer; a lavishment of the senses that brought their lives, separately and together, a new dimension of the goodness and rightness of their little world. He had never understood the true nature of love; Julie had not even glimpsed it. All differences of religion, background, education, social position, were incinerated in its hot furnace, leaving no residue, no ash to darken it. During their quiet moments, held tenderly in embrace, they gazed at each other in awe. In the happiness they were bringing each other there was a sense that this must not end.

They got caught, of course. By Emma. Awakened early one morning by the tossing of a child, she saw Camille returning to his room. Although he and Julie had been careful not to let their eyes meet during meals or encounters in the parlor or hallways, to someone as astute as Emma, it was not difficult to perceive that the masks they attempted to wear were pathetically askew. Seizing the right moment, she said:

"Camille, I have warned you how dangerous this is."

He saw it would be useless to evade.

"It is not a casual affair, Emma. I have not seduced the parlormaid, as one does in a French farce."

"I would not have suspected you of that. No one ever thought you *mesquin,* dirt cheap."

"We harm no one."

"Camille! In the name of all that's sensible, don't let that girl become pregnant. Maman does not need that added burden."

"My relationship with Julie is clean and fine."

"I can tell from your expression that you are sincere. But as for no harm coming . . . *j'en doute.*"

He knew that Emma was right in having her doubts. Yet he felt capable of handling any problem that arose. He did not believe that being in love was the same as being reckless or irresponsible.

"I can count on your discretion, Emma?"

She stabbed him with a knife flash of fear.

"I wish I could be as certain of yours."

They finished Sunday's midday dinner by three o'clock, met without acknowledging each other at the Place Passy omnibus station. Camille sat in a distant part of the two-horse bus. At the Place Royale they changed to another omnibus which crossed a bridge of the Seine to the Left Bank where there would be no chance of their being recognized. La Rive Gauche was sparsely settled, containing only a quarter of the inhabitants of Paris. The more prominent among them were the university students, usually the poorest but most vivacious and interesting among the city's diverse groups. Camille and Julie felt at home when they sat among them as they studied in the cafés, which were considerably warmer than their unheated rooms; and where they could read their textbooks and write notes for several hours over a single cup of coffee with milk without the waiter becoming unhappy.

Julie had never seen Paris. She had gone from the railroad station to the agency, which had sent her to the Pissarros in Passy. On her alternate Sunday afternoons off she and Félicie had taken short, tentative walks or stopped in at the closest church. With Camille as her guide she now drank it all in.

"I've been here for three years," he told her. "I've roamed and sketched everywhere. I'll show you the interesting places."

She murmured her appreciation, slipped her hand into his, warm, companionable. During their first walk he led her across the Seine to the Cité and Notre Dame, where children were playing in the open square before the cathedral, feeding bread crumbs to the pigeons clustered about their feet. When he took her inside she stood trembling.

"It's the most beautiful church in the world," she whispered. "It has in . . . infin . . . ."

"Infinity? Yes. For me, as well. If anything is made divinely, it is this cathedral. I feel spiritual stirrings in the panels of stained glass, the vastness of the space. . . ."

"Everything is made by the hand of God."

"Not the evil of the world; not the cruelty or injustice."

"Those things are caused by the Devil."

"My dear Julie, the Devil is also an invention of fiction writers."

Tears welled behind her eyelids. "I don't understand."

"Must you? Your faith has sustained you. Mine will, as well."

She flashed him a smile of such brilliance and acceptance that he felt dizzy.

One Sunday he showed her his new studio, to which he and Jacobsen had been obliged to move their scant belongings, a similarly shaped room on the Rue Fontaine St. Georges; then took her to the Luxembourg Garden. It was a favorite spot for mothers and children, where the youngsters sailed their small boats in the artificial lake, played games of skip and tag, rolled hoops. They walked along the broad paths which formerly had been used as winding carriage roads, bordered by magnificent trees that had been planted by the monks who had been driven out by the uprising of 1790. Julie gazed with delight at the oblong Medici fountain similar to those in the Boboli Gardens of Florence. They accompanied families dressed in their Sunday best to the Théâtre des Marionettes.

"I've seen puppets in the country fairs," Julie confided, "but nothing so perfect. These little things look alive. See how they knock each other about.''

A sudden rain fell. They took shelter under a forest-green plane tree, each leaf as broad and water-resistant as an alpaca umbrella. When a chill wind came up he opened his spacious coat; Julie moved close to him, he folded the coat over her shoulders. He could feel the warmth of her body.

"Why are you putting your face into the rain?" she asked, her breath against his cheek.

"To get the feel of the rain on my face. . . . To keep cool," he grinned.

She freed herself from his arms.

"That's strange. I'm shivering from a chill."

"Perhaps it's the same. Come, let's make a dash for the palace."

They went through a door on the western facade of the Luxembourg Palace, mounted a modest staircase, and at the back of a little chamber saw a woman selling blue brochures, the first intimation that they were in a museum.

He led her quickly past Bouguereau's *Triumph of the Martyr* and Couture's *The Decadent Romans,* then stopped with a fine glow on his face before the superb landscapes of Daubigny, Millet, Rousseau, Corot. Julie appeared more fascinated by the ornate gold-leaf decorations on the walls and ceilings. He asked a question of the woman selling the brochures, then led Julie into the library with its paintings by Delacroix: *Dante and Virgil Walking in Limbo, Alexander Placing Homer's Poems in Darius's Gold Casket.*

"Delacroix has been kind to me. He's a great master. Let me tell you about his studio. . . ."

Next he showed her the series of twenty-four large paintings by Peter Paul Rubens, commissioned in 1621, depicting through allegory the life of Marie de Médici. He told her about Rubens's life as the leader of the Flemish School, tried to indicate what portion of the vast work had been done by Rubens's apprentices, then realized he was talking technique and she was watching, wide-eyed, his excitement and pleasure.

"You're not listening to me, are you?"

He took her to a nearby restaurant. The waiter handed them handwritten menus. Julie gazed at the listings in bewilderment.

"What is this?"

"It suggests all the foods they can prepare in the kitchen. Also dishes that are ready."

"That many?"

He laughed, amused. "They want you to have choices. To

start, you can choose among three soups: dried pea, oxtail, mulligatawny. For fish you can have halibut ring, broiled tilefish or a boiled salt mackerel with white sauce. For your meat . . ."

She put a finger impulsively across his lips.

"Please. So much food for so few people."

"It will all be eaten by the end of the day."

"*Vraiment?*"

"Let me order for you. We'll start at the top of the menu and go as far down as you like."

She was scrutinizing the list carefully.

"Hmmmm. Chocolate ice cream? I never had that. Praline kisses? Crème caramel. . . . Couldn't we start at the bottom and work our way up?"

"No, Julie, it's against the law."

"Of what?"

"Gravity. Be a conventional Granceyan and start with the soup."

"If only I could start with a frozen fig pudding. . . . Don't be angry with me, Camille. I'll do as you say."

"Waiter, bring Mademoiselle a plate of French onion soup and, at the same time, an order of frozen fig pudding. Mademoiselle has an unusual affliction. She cannot have soup unless she has a dessert along with it."

Her eyes were sparkling with pleasure.

"A sufficient reward," he thought, "for acting *fou*, crazy. What does it matter, if it makes her happy?"

3

Thrust into a den of strangers, particularly working artists, Camille had a tendency to be reserved. Claude Monet, for all his ebullience, was also on the shy side. Their friendship freed them both. They invaded the Académie Suisse as though they were a conquering army, getting on personal terms with a number of the members who had a flair for their craft and a gift of companionship. The two did together what neither would have thought to attempt alone. For Camille, as Corot had predicted, the Suisse had indeed become a personal club in a sense that the Beaux-Arts studios of Picot, Dagnan or Lehmann had not.

He enjoyed the highly stylized twenty-five-year-old American, James McNeill Whistler, whose engineer father had built the first railroad connecting St. Petersburg to Moscow; and who himself had been expelled from the United States Military Academy at West Point for defining silicon as a gas. Whistler was mischievous, droll, recognized in Paris by his two extremities; an enormous floppy straw hat covering a mass of black curls; and thin-soled ballet dancer's slippers. He was a scandalous wit, poseur, trying to live *la vie de bohème* to entertain himself and the world about him, all of which he considered his stage. He was impeccably dressed in a close-fitting black coat and a white shirt and collar which he washed every night; a dandy even when his money from his family living in London ran out, and he had to play outrageous games on restaurant keepers to fill his thin-as-a-Nile-papyrus figure, graceful as the dancer through life he conceived himself to be.

"Yet oozing talent," Claude Monet observed, almost enviously; "for drawing, printmaking, etching, watercolor. . . ."

"And under it all, he doesn't suffer fools gladly," added Camille. "His tongue can be diabolical."

The second most enjoyable companion at the Suisse was Antoine Guillemet, also with a flair for clothes, having one of the best tailors in Paris. He already showed a strong line. Camille took to Antoine's work because he adored Corot's shimmering Fontainebleau dawns and dells. Both Camille and Monet enjoyed young Fantin-Latour, born in Grenoble, and trained by his father, a portrait painter. He had a face with a foreshortened nose, soft brown hair neatly combed over a well-structured head; a ghostlike line of beard, eyes that could have dazzled a beholder except that they were turned inward. He was a visionary, not about the future of the world, but of the phantasmic moves that went on inside his own head and which he attempted to transcribe to canvas: drifting gray clouds, sea and land masses no one had ever beheld.

When he became acquainted with Camille, he asked:

"Could I do a sketch of you? I want to paint the landscape of the mind."

He had been drawn to the Venetians in the Louvre, where he had met Edouard Manet, also copying the Venetians.

No one had ever seen Fantin-Latour in a painter's smock or street coat. Even in cold weather he worked in a white shirt with a soft collar open at the throat. He behaved the same way in the neighboring cafés or in the studios of his smock-garbed friends.

Camille amused his colleagues when he appeared in the gaucho outfit Alfred had sent from South America, wide white pantaloons, black cowboy jacket and sombrero, a colorful braided sash at his waist.

The five of them, Fantin-Latour, Camille, Claude Monet, James Whistler and Antoine Guillemet, went often, after Père Suisse banged his book closed, to the Brasserie des Martyrs where there was a table reserved in a corner for artists and writers. Here they were joined by Whistler's painter friends, Chintreuil and Desbrosses; occasionally by Courbet, Daumier, Proudhon. They hung their coats on hooks in a high wooden slab; the waiters, in their dark jackets, black bow ties and white aprons wrapped tightly about their waists and extending down to their shoes, hovered without harassing their usually impecunious clients because they served as an attraction for customers who liked to feel they were in the presence of bohemia.

Camille soon learned the truth of the old adage, "If a man talks long enough he will end by talking about himself." Monet asked what it was like to grow up on a tropical island; then launched into the story of his own life, which he considered dramatic and important.

". . . which it is," Camille said to himself with an indulgent smile; "to him."

"My father wanted me in trade." Monet's voice was persuasive, as though he were selling something. "I was encouraged to draw by my mother. I've been undisciplined since I was born. All schools were to me a prison. Granted, I'm spoiled; how else to protect against the bourgeois Le Havre? My one virtue was that I was always moved by good work."

Camille was captivated by Monet's confession that he suffered from a feeling of being without a niche of his own; that in a disturbed adolescence he had the reputation of being a wandering albeit well-groomed street urchin.

"I was morose, highly critical of everyone around me. But I had the redeeming gift of the pencil, the facility to recreate precisely anything placed before me: objects in glass, metal, leather, wood, straw." He also drew caricatures of the self-important people of Le Havre, managed to get them displayed in the window of Boudin's framing shop, and began to sell them for a few francs each. At first Monet had been contemptuous of this seller of frames, then slowly realized that Boudin's canvases of Honfleur, Le Havre and Trouville were pure gems. He had come to Paris because Boudin convinced him that the move was imperative.

The soft brown eyes and Greek athlete's face glowed with determination. "I expect my sensitivity to sharpen with age. . . . I have no other wish than a close fusion with nature . . . . I'll always want to maintain the ardor of my curiosity. . . ."

Claude Monet spoke of his mother's death when he was only twelve, his escape to his mother's sister, who took him in and gave him the attic of her home as a studio. His aunt continued to send him an allowance, on which he lived.

"Thank heaven for sympathetic women," he cried. "The world would be an impossible place without them."

Camille had watched Monet draw at the Suisse for some time now. The youngster was still unable to achieve three-dimensional form.

"It's all right," he thought, "the dough has not yet risen."

Ludovic Piette de Montfoucault, called Piette, was an altogether different kind of friend. He was thirty-three, four years older than Camille, and came from the district of Mayenne, some one hundred and forty miles southwest of Paris. He seemed a little standoffish by nature, had involved himself in no relationships in the Suisse. His capitulation to Camille was the more surprising because he had done nothing extraordinary to earn Piette's regard.

Camille had noticed Piette's attention to his ongoing work. After considerable hesitation, Piette leaned over Camille's notebook, asked: "How do you achieve that effect of chiaroscuro? I can't seem to bring it off."

Camille explained his treatment of light and shade. Piette, grateful, said in a low voice:

"I've sold a few things at the shows in Bordeaux but nothing lately. To me you appear to have a solid grasp of fundamentals."

"You flatter me."

Piette was a compactly built man of average height but exceptional appearance; his head was too large for his neck and torso. His abundant upswept hair showed the attractive gray-white color he introduced so successfully into his gouaches. His neatly trimmed beard, sprouting from the youngish face with circles under its eyes, was jet black in contrast. His ash-gray eyes were often half closed protectively.

His clothing under the same kind of black paint-stained smock worn by the others seemed at odds with itself. His navy-blue jacket and lighter-colored trousers were of good cloth but routinely cut, as though he had not wanted to spend too much on the tailor. His shirt and collar were immaculate;

but he had on a pair of the soft-soled shoes such as mechanics wore to work.

"He is so tentative, he is concealing something," Camille decided.

"That word 'flatter' is the bane of my life," Piette cried. "Could you have dinner with my wife and me tomorrow evening? There's a charming little *mère et père* restaurant where they cook a *poule au pot.*"

Piette's restaurant turned out to be a former shop with only eight tables; but the mother and father who marketed, cooked and served the food had a flair for decoration, with a single flower in a slim vase on each table. Over an aperitif, Piette introduced Adèle Lévy, to whom he had been married for several years. Adèle said in a warm though unmusical voice:

"Piette has told me about you. He rarely speaks about the artists he works among. That's a compliment to you, Monsieur Pissarro."

"I can't think what I've done to deserve it."

Piette replied with a pleasant expression:

"You're quiet within yourself. I see things in you that give me confidence in you."

"I'm still looking for a formula for painting an oil canvas that has depth and conviction," Camille responded, a little embarrassed.

Adèle lifted the lid of the tureen of chicken the waitress had placed before them; the flavor of mushrooms, rice and blanched almonds steamed out.

Adèle was on the plain side, with black hair cut short, a nose that rode down her face at a slight angle, rather like Camille's. She had a good figure, full hips and full breasts, with slender legs that set off the rest of her in pleasing proportion. Her complexion was clear, a bit on the sallow side. Her eyes were her best feature: wide-set, a velvety brown, and empathy reflected in their deep pools. She had come from a middle-income Jewish family of shopkeepers. Piette had seen her in the Jewish quarter, was fascinated by her semi-oriental look and persuaded her to model for him. She was his first model and, except for the nude studies at the Suisse, his last. Nor had it taken him long to fall in love with her.

Piette ordered a bottle of dry white wine from Bordeaux.

"I'd like to drink to your visiting with us in Montfoucault. We have an agreeable house with an extra bedroom. The countryside is eminently paintable. Adèle and I are going down soon for the fruit harvest. There's a train from Paris to

Mayenne; we would meet you in our cart and carry you the seventeen kilometers to Montfoucault. We could paint out of doors together."

"Do come," urged Adèle. "Piette gets lonely being the only painter in Mayenne. The neighbors don't comment openly; his family has been at Montfoucault for too many hundreds of years. Actually, they want him to continue as mayor of the little village. They think his painting is merely a rich man's hobby."

Camille raised his eyebrows. Aside from this invitation to a moderately priced dinner he had seen no evidence that Piette was a rich man.

"Adèle, you have let the cat out of the bag," Piette gasped. "However it is a relief to let it be known. I don't want to be regarded as a stingy man, *un homme qui tondrait un oeuf,* a man who would mow an egg."

As a wealthy man in the potpourri of subsistence artists, he did not want to be exploited by the fellows at the Suisse or, what for him would be worse, dismissed by them as an idler playing games. He was also fearful of being imposed upon by people who did not really care for him. That was why he had not let it be known that he came from a long-established Catholic family in the *département* of Mayenne, or that he owned the apartment house next to this restaurant.

"I rent my studio far away from it."

Camille said quietly: "Most of us at the Suisse are troubled because we are poor. You're troubled because you have resources."

Their companionship grew. Camille persuaded Piette to accompany him to the Brasserie des Martyrs when the Suisse closed. For the first time Piette was comfortable with Claude Monet, James Whistler, Guillemet, Fantin-Latour because they were Camille's friends.

"I haven't seen Piette this happy for a long time," Adèle confided. "There are two things he'd like to ask you to do but he's afraid of imposing. First, to review his work. It's not selling. It's a matter of pride. If he sells, he's a professional, if not, he's a dilettante."

"There are very few of us selling."

"The second is for you to paint his portrait."

Camille was genuinely surprised. "Piette could find a hundred artists better equipped than I."

"You accept him. He thinks you can get that affection down on canvas."

He went to Piette's comfortable studio apartment. Adèle

served them coffee. In the studio room Piette installed Camille on a high stool and mounted, one by one on the easel, his completed gouaches, painted in opaque colors which had been ground in water and tempered with a preparation of rum; watercolors, lithographs, drawings, oils. It was a considerable body of work, done by a conscientious man.

"Your gouaches are good, Piette," Camille murmured. "You use white pigment instead of letting the paper show through. . . ."

Piette flushed with pleasure. "As for the rest . . . ?"

Piette's greatest strength was that he drew his themes from nature, not literature: the landscape around Montfoucault was populated by its natives. He made preliminary drawings and meticulous notes indicating where he must put his precise color and shadow. Yet the canvases were composed of separate groupings and figures which bore little relationship to each other. They appeared anecdotal, without a central core.

"Piette has not learned how to create an organic structure within the allotted space," Camille thought to himself.

He gave all possible praise first: Piette's sensitivity to atmosphere, his lovely skies, clearer than the ones he himself had painted for Melbye, the blue shadows he liked very much. Then he went over each canvas indicating the needed tightening of theme. Piette listened carefully, made notes. He thanked Camille heartily.

When it came to discussing the price Piette would pay for Camille's painting of his portrait, they fell into their first and last quarrel. Piette insisted that Camille was asking too little; Camille that Piette was offering too much.

"There can't be any charity in your offer, Piette. That would cripple me."

"Don't be absurd. You're worth every sou of it."

They compromised somewhere between; it was still a healthy sum for Camille, one that would ease his way for several months. He was eager to begin. Piette paid the agreed commission, then asked Camille to wait a time until he had visited Montfoucault.

"The better you know me, the truer portrait you'll do."

4

At Corot's invitation, Camille took Claude Monet and Piette out to join him for several days in Fontainebleau. Corot put them up in the family home which he had shared with his parents for many years and now occupied alone in the town of Ville d'Avray. It was a substantial stone and plaster country house hidden behind a stone wall and tall trees. There was a paved courtyard, various outbuildings, everything covered with vines. All around the house were gardens for flowers, vegetables, fruit trees.

Corot gave them an excellent dinner "without the inevitable Paris soup," Camille remarked to himself; a salad from his garden, a pheasant and wine from the neighborhood. After dinner he taught them his mother's version of bezique, and at ten sent them to their separate bedrooms. Camille commented to Monet and Piette as they climbed the stairs:

"I feel as though I were trespassing. These forests belong to the Barbizon painters. They've immortalized them . . . after a heroic struggle over thirty years."

"You're saying that there are proprietary rights in geography?" Monet demanded.

"Yes. Who is going to paint sixteenth-century Amsterdam after Rembrandt? The court of Philip IV in Madrid after Velásquez? We now see these forests through the eyes of Corot, Rousseau, Daubigny, Diaz. . . . We must find our own virgin territory."

"Where do we look?" asked Monet.

"I don't know. It will happen."

Piette was a fountain of information: about Haussmann's revolutionary new sewer system, the new boulevards streaming across the city; the torrential rains that had caused businesses and the elegant salons to suffer; the doctor who could revive the dead by pouring warm blood into their veins; the pneumatic underground cables for sending *petits bleus*, messages and letters in little metal cylinders, to terminals throughout Paris in the shortest time. He also raised issues: against the distribution agency hiring men to hand out advertisements to passersby. He did not aim to win but to prove the invasion of privacy and littering of the streets they caused.

He was an omnivorous devourer of newspapers, sitting in an easy chair in his library surrounded by the litter of half a dozen journals.

"Don't you find their contents contradictory?" Camille asked.

"Certainly. But life consists of contradictions. I'm a large property owner but I agree with a lot of Proudhon's anarchism. I approve of the monarchy but not of Napoleon III."

In spite of his ideas and arguments, which swung like a metronome, Camille found Piette to be, after Fritz Melbye, the most constant friend he had made. He also discovered that he and Adèle projected similar personalities, affectionate, perceptive, emanating an inner strength. Their voices even had some of the same tonal values and inflections though they were born some three thousand miles apart.

An entertaining thought occurred to him.

"Is that why Piette is so fond of me? Because I so closely resemble his wife?"

Piette told him of his difficulties with his family over his marriage to Adèle.

"They objected to a non-Catholic; they also wanted me to marry one of the daughters of our neighboring landowners to combine our holdings. It made sense economically but no one of the young women I grew up with made me feel so good inside myself as Adèle did. However my wealthy aunt in Le Mans, who adores me and the Church, did not take as great an exception to my marrying a Jewess—I believe she thought I would convert Adèle—as she did to my marrying a model. That word stuck in their eye like a cinder."

Flush with Piette's commission money, Camille invited them to have dinner with himself and Julie the following Sunday. Julie and Adèle insisted upon sitting close to each other, conversed animatedly, apparently starved for companionship. Julie retained the high coloring of her years in Grancey; she still seemed sun-speckled, her light brown hair, freed from the domestic cap, hung down to her shoulders, a ribbon bow tied behind. Her eyes were startled at being part of Parisian life. Adèle's short hair and introspective eyes carried an air of assurance, of belonging. Yet the two women, so different in background, slipped into a harmonious relationship with almost their first exchange. Since Camille left no doubt about the intimacy of his relationship with Julie, Adèle said to her:

"Sometime you must come out to Montfoucault with Camille."

Walking back to the omnibus at the Place Royale, Julie exulted:

"Adèle accepted me at once."

"Why should she not?"

She did not bother to answer.

Piette took Camille, Julie and Adèle to see the current successes, *Nouvelle Cendrillon* at the Gymnase; *Cartouche* at the Gaieté. He bought subscriptions for the Conservatoire concerts. At the exhibition of Spanish paintings by Murillo, Zurbarán, Herrera the elder at the Louvre, he was ecstatic with praise. Always he carried what he called his "little family" in rented, frequently hard-to-find cabs.

"Horses and carriages are the most gratuitous signs of wealth," he announced. "I do not intend to parade my assets."

Adèle looked up at the threatening skies, murmured, "They can also be mighty convenient."

Frédéric returned to Passy. His first order of business was to insist that Camille submit a work to the 1859 Salon.

"Look, son, all I ask is that you submit a painting. Not that it be accepted. That's in the discretion of the gods. Are other beginners better than you?"

"Not necessarily, Papa."

"Are you more proud than they?"

"I just don't want to submit a canvas which I myself would reject if I were on the jury."

Frédéric stated simply:

"But you will."

Camille went to see Anton Melbye, who was finally leaving with his wife the following week to teach at the Academy in Copenhagen.

"Have you heard from Fritz?" Anton demanded immediately. "Where is he? New York, Peking, Tibet? I haven't had a word. I wish I at least had an address to send money. I have more than I need, and he has less."

"Fritz is determined to be independent," Camille replied.

"Independent! Bah! An overused word signifying little more than revolt."

Camille then said, "I'm preparing an oil for the 1859 Salon, *Landscape at Montmorency*. In submitting it may I name you as my master? You told me it's *de rigueur* for a beginner to list his master, that a self-taught artist would be considered by the jury to be a primitive."

Anton threw his red fez up into the air in glee.

"I've always wanted to be someone's master! Now you have anointed me. In all truth I've taught you precious little.

Just the bric-a-brac of our trade. Papa Corot has influenced you far more.''

"I wouldn't presume to ask him. Perhaps for the next Salon. When I am doing better.''

Anton guffawed. "Ha! I am to be your master while you are half baked. By all means, use my name.''

He had done many and diverse studies of Montmorency until he was satisfied that he understood the terrain and its people. Only then did he turn to oil paint, a medium-sized picture. For the first oil he would submit to the Beaux-Arts jury he chose a particular farm with gently sloping cultivated fields in the background, a narrow curving dirt path with a peasant in straw hat and suspender-held trousers leading the viewer into the picture. In the foreground was green grass, a vegetable patch, a thin rail fence; and beyond ripening hay-fields running downhill, a tiny village of red-roofed stone houses by the bottom of the slight ravine. On the closer uphill side a patch of straw-colored haycocks stood in a harvested quadrangle. The more distant uphill fields, with dimly seen peasants in white, were a variety of softer greens against a blue sky agitated by tumultuous gray clouds.

It was a still life, with the heat of summer upon it; nothing moved except the peasant's wife or daughter coming up the path to meet him; yet it was an organic stillness with every-thing pulsing within its frame of tall straight trees. One felt that the resilient earth and the peasants who tended it were full partners, needing and respectful of the care of each other.

"Mystical perhaps,'' he thought as he worked with broad brush strokes, carefully plotting the mathematics of the scene, so that there were horizontal bands defining the front and rear of the large extent of land on either side of the ravine; and vertical in the paths leading across the valley, the angled, cultivated strips extending upward toward the distant horizon. Once into the picture, following the peasant down the curving path, there was no escape for the viewer. It was an entire world, self-contained, indigenous and compatible to man and nature; it was a homeplace, quiescent, eternal. Within the small frame there appeared to be all the pleasing colors of green and tan and blue that the eye would want to entertain and assimilate.

"Thereby being assimilated,'' he said to himself, ''*j' espère*, I hope.'' It had been difficult, but he felt that his technique was growing stronger.

He took *Landscape at Montmorency* to his older friends to judge: Corot, Courbet, Delacroix. Corot spoke about making his air more luminous; Courbet about the relation of spaces inside the architectural design; Delacroix about intensifying his colors and the drama of the scene. Jacobsen and Piette were enthusiastic. They had no criticism. All agreed that he must submit the painting to the Salon jury.

It would be an ordeal. Several thousand works would be proffered in this terminal year of the decade, 1859. Would he stand a chance in the flood?

The jury of forty men who would select the fortunate works was appointed by or composed of Academy members who worked in secrecy for a week in the massive Palais de l'Industrie where Camille had seen the marvels of modern invention four years before. The works of art being submitted were piled in its cold basement until Judgment Week when they were arranged along the walls of the Palais. On Monday at one o'clock the chairman would ring a small bell; the jury would walk past the roped-off paintings, making instantaneous dicta: "Accepted. Rejected. Discussion later."

The jury, wrapped in warm clothes to keep out the spring chill, took two hours for its first round of the gallery. Seventy white-coated attendants removed the rejects, replacing the corpses with fresh recruits while the more affluent members of the jury went to Ledoyen off the Champs-Elysées for luncheon. The rest had sandwiches, claret or chocolate at a buffet under the naked girders that supported the balcony.

At four o'clock each day they gathered in a comfortable room where they could examine the smaller paintings on the dozen easels set up on a platform covered with green baize. Again the rejects were swiftly replaced by the attendants. During the last hours of the last day they were brought back should more paintings be necessary to bring the total to the pre-established number demanded by the Emperor or the Minister of Fine Arts. Next came the "Charity Ball"; each member was allowed to choose one painting of an unfortunate friend or disciple, usually a poverty-stricken one. Thus forty more rejects, "crumbs to the beggars off the banquet table," got into the Salon. Neither the artists nor the public ever knew which were the charity cases.

"That would condemn them to a life sentence in the Bastille," Delacroix explained to Camille. "The jury is prejudiced, old-fashioned, ironclad academic; but far from stupid. Most of the accepted canvases have some quality; most of the rejected ones are amateurish. Yet there is always a mid-area of the arena that could be refought. Let's say a quarter of the accepted are dull, repetitious, worthless; a quarter of the rejects have some merit and should be shown. In our malformed world that's not too bad a ratio.''

It was a long week. He alternated between high hopes and a woebegone smile of despair.

''One painting out of several thousand? No intelligent gambler would like those odds.''

Jacobsen, himself so frequently depressed, was doing a heroic job of keeping Camille buoyed:

''No gambler is intelligent. Secondly, your chances are better than those of anyone working at the Suisse today.''

Camille threw his arms about Jacobsen's bony shoulders.

''David, it's a joy to have you be the cheerful member of our studio.''

Jacobsen muttered under his breath, ''*Un aveugle mène l'autre à la fosse*. One blind man leads another into the ditch.''

When the lists were tacked up on a wall in the Palais the artists flocked in to learn their fate. Camille felt his viscera give a great leap when he found *Landscape at Montmorency* had received an A for Accepted. James Whistler had two etchings accepted. The talented Edouard Manet, whom Camille had seen at the Brasserie des Martyrs but had not met, had his several submissions carried back to his studio by two workmen supporting them on a short-legged table.

5

The Académie des Beaux-Arts was one of the most important parts of the Institut de France, which held firmly in its hand the culture of the nation. The opening of the Beaux-Arts exhibition was one of the great social events of the year. It was a beautiful May day. The Emperor and the royal family were in attendance, as were his ministers, scholars, scientists, authors of the prestigious Académie Française; and always the world of high society, the women in four-tiered ornate gowns and bonnets of white plumage; the officers wearing side swords, tricornered hats and medals; civilians in elegantly dark coats, waistcoats crossed with gold chains, trousers held by straps nestled against the heels of shiny boots.

On the way to the Palais in the carriage Frédéric had hired for the day, Camille tried to prepare his family.

''Corot told me that in the early years he was always in the catacombs. Other times he was hung so high that he held up the ceiling. He told me not to be disappointed unless I was shown on either side of the *toilettes*. That position is fatal.''

Nothing daunted the happy Frédéric. In the February 26, 1859, St. Thomas *Tidende* he had offered his inventory of hogshead leaf tobacco, knickknacks, pork, beef, rye, flour, clothing for sale. It was purchased by the Danish Von Beverhoudt family who owned the dry-goods store, and who were already committed to paying one hundred and fifty dollars a month rent for the Dronningens Gade shop; and fifty dollars a month for the large family flat above it. They would have a rental income of twenty-four hundred dollars a year plus the return on Frédéric's investment of his capital in French bonds. At fifty-seven he was assured of financial tranquillity for the rest of his years.

It took them a long while, pushing their way through the dense crowds, its thousand throats all wanting to be heard as they engaged their friends in conversation without looking much at the paintings, to locate *Landscape at Montmorency*. When at last they did they found the picture positioned so close to the high ceiling, above four rows of frame-to-frame canvases, that it was difficult to discern the subtleties of color or the tightly knit cohesion of the scene.

Camille swallowed hard. Frédéric was jubilant.

"Come, let us have a celebration dinner," he announced. "It doesn't matter where you're hung, Camille, only that you're a part of the official Salon, certified by the Beaux-Arts to be worthy. Sales are bound to follow."

Camille did not wish to puncture his father's euphoria; the one canvas girding up the ceiling would have little chance of being noticed or of opening any golden doors. Neither ought he to disparage the accomplishment.

As they wandered through the packed crowds, Camille found Corot, Courbet, Delacroix. In the pleasantries exchanged, Rachel and Frédéric made two distinct observations: these older artists looked prosperously groomed and attired; they treated Camille with respect and liking.

For their dinner the Pissarros went to the Palais buffet, finding a table looking out into the garden shaded by tall trees and circled by statues of lions, tigers and forgotten heroes on horses. The buffet room resembled a cavern, bound by the steel beams upholding the upper floor; but the tables were cheerfully set with bowls of fruit and flowers. The diners were in a festive mood. There was a long hors d'oeuvre spread, watched over by falcon-eyed women attendants guarding their platters of stuffed eggs à la russe, pâté, cold salmon. Since Camille and Emma were having trout, while his parents had ordered the roast beef, they had bottles of both white and red wine, and in their mood of celebration drank more than was usual for them. Rachel drank two glasses of the sparkling red from Touraine, while Camille was drinking his Chenin Blanc Vouvray without bothering to count. The family touched glasses with a sense of a difficult peak having been assailed and conquered. Frédéric, after an affirmative nod from Rachel, reached out for his son's hand.

"Camille, now that you have become a professional, your mother and I have decided that you've earned the right to an allowance. We would like it to fall midway between a sum that would spoil you and one that would beggar you. We compromised on one thousand eight hundred francs a year, thirty dollars a month; and we'll continue to pay your studio rent. That should enable you to buy supplies and still have something over for a café."

Camille's breathing stopped, his ears shut out the din. His voice was husky with emotion as he thanked his parents for offering him the sustenance that meant his freedom to work.

"Bless you both! Bless the Salon jury! You will see; I will justify your generosity."

Nothing happened. Gérôme's *Caesar* was admired. Puvis de Chavannes was praised for his style but criticized for his drawing and "fakeness of his colors." Landscapes were criticized as being too easy. "Anyone can do them."

Piette said quietly, "Have you ever known a critic who could paint?"

Landscape at Montmorency had been hung in so awkward a position that no one noticed or commented on it, favorably or unfavorably. Zacharie Astruc, a critic, mentioned in his review that the painting was on the lists. The Salon catalogue read:

Pissarro (Camille), born St. Thomas (Danish colonies). Student of Anton Melbye.

But then, what more had he expected?

That summer he went with Francisco Oller, a Spaniard born in Puerto Rico who had been introduced to him by Courbet, to La Roche-Guyon, where he had first met Antoine Guillemet. Guillemet was traveling abroad and would not be there. They lived in a small inn where they took their meals but parted at daybreak, each to find his own motif. Oller was lean, olive-skinned, chipper; varied in his creations from sculptures of equestrian statues through portraits.

It was extremely hot in late June and remained that way. In July plans were announced to decorate Paris for the returning soldiers from the war against Austria in Italy. Camille wondered if he might have been employed for that purpose if he were in the city.

He spent his days drawing and painting La Roche-Guyon's river and grasslands.

When Rachel gave Julie a week's vacation at the end of her first year of work she joined Camille. They spent pleasant days in the savannas. While Camille painted she sewed under a shade tree or scampered along the riverbank, shoes and stockings off, gathering flowers for their room at the inn. In her joy at being in the country again she was like a young child, running through the meadows, climbing the shade trees bordering the orchards. To Camille she was slim and lovely, her hair loose down her back, her cheeks touched with the sun, her wide eyes dancing merrily, her arms and voice soft and loving as they lay enmeshed at night in the small bed. In the lightweight cotton dress she had sewed for herself she looked all of sixteen, a filly let out of the hay-trampled stall of a darkened barn into the sunlight and fresh green of open fields, cavorting in the delight of an almost forgotten freedom.

He worked well with her near. He was pleased about that, for he had not known whether she might be a distracting influence. It was the first time they had spent whole nights together.

"It's like a *lune de miel*, honeymoon," she murmured, lying on the bed in a light shift. Camille grunted a sleepy assent, an arm across her bountiful chest. Their lovemaking made him feel stronger and bolder as he wandered along the narrow carriage lanes, drawing the chalk cliffs, the caves, the ruins of a medieval castle on top of the mountain precipice. Oller teased and joked with Julie as they had their light evening meal of an omelet and *ficelle* with sweet butter in the rear garden.

Emma mailed him a Paris journal each week so that he and Oller were able to keep up with the news. On August 20 people lined the streets all night to cheer the soldiers returning from the Italian campaign. There was a rise in lawsuits involving painters, in which patrons refused to pay for what they deemed to be unsatisfactory portraits; as well as plagiarism suits involving paintings that had been copied or photographed for sale. There was also an important medical discovery: wounds could now be disinfected by using a mixture of plaster and coal tar.

Julie returned to Passy. When the summer was over Camille had a large folio of drawings, gouaches and watercolors which made him feel that he had grasped the La Roche-Guyon countryside, as well as the use of oils. When it came time to pay his bill at the inn he found that he owed a hundred francs . . . and had little of it. Frédéric sent him the money. Camille felt remorseful until he received a note from Emma saying, "Papa has hung your *Landscape at Montmorency* in the place of honor in the parlor."

To Oller he exclaimed, as they packed their gear to return to Paris:

"My father has just bought my first Salon painting. For twenty dollars. I hope he never feels cheated."

The fact that no one outside the perimeter of his few friends commented on his picture at the Salon, or that he had been accepted to exhibit, became a trifle disheartening. There were a few small picture shops along the Rue Laffitte but they were not taking unknowns.

He found a letter from Frédéric in the studio: "Your mother asks me to write you to come dine with us today. Because this is the evening when we celebrate *la fête de Kippur* and on this solemn occasion the whole family should be together— and tomorrow not work, we should pass that day together."

When Camille arrived at the flat the dining-room table was covered with a snowy white tablecloth. On the buffet were the *yahrzeit* candles Rachel had lighted as a memorial for their parents and the children who were gone. She had also placed candles on the table with a bowl of autumnal flowers. Julie, in a freshly starched white uniform, served a traditional fish, soup and chicken; lightly seasoned foods that would make no demands on them during the following day of fasting to atone for the year's sins. Frédéric recited a prayer which blessed the food. Rachel was radiant in a new black gown. She leaned across the table and said:

"I hope you will have a good New Year with your . . . painting, Camille." Then rose and kissed her son on the forehead.

6

The familial happiness of the New Year was short-lived.

In the beginning week of 1860 one sentence from Julie put an end to it. He had taken her to a concert at the Conservatoire, noticed that she was quiet, eyes hooded. Later, when they were sitting in a small booth at the café across from the beautiful Church of St. Germain-des-Prés, warmed by a glowing red stove and the violinist and accordionist playing Parisian ballads, he saw that she was running her fork through her food rather than eating it.

"What is it, Julie?"

"It has happened."

"What has happened?"

"I'm pregnant." In an expressionless tone.

Camille was startled at the suddenness of the statement rather than its content.

"Are you certain?"

"Yes. Five months now."

" . . . five? But you can't just have learned."

"I've known for three months."

"Why haven't you told me?"

"I wanted a peace time at Passy, as long as possible. Now I'm going to begin to show."

Though Julie had planned on marriage and family, she fortunately did not know that the odds were against her. Only a third of Paris's servants ever married and, among those, eight out of ten had no children. The plight of the single *bonne* was even more cruel. Almost four thousand a year gave birth in the city's hospitals. Many more gave birth in their dormer rooms, alone. The exigency of the unwed *bonne* bearing a child seemed to obsess the bourgeois, with frequent articles about it in the journals. The maids who became pregnant had a legitimate fear of being dismissed. The unfortunate women went to any lengths to conceal it; tight-laced corsets, work to the last possible moment; self-delivery.

He took a long soughing breath.

"Five months. That takes us back to La Roche-Guyon."

She slipped her hand into his, leaned her head on his shoulder.

"Don't be angry with me. I couldn't help it."

"Why should I be angry? We both knew it could come about."

"I'm not unhappy, *mon chéri*. I love you. I love the child. Only I'm frightened."

"Of what?"

"Your family."

"*Sacrebleu!* My parents. Of course! We have reason to be."

"What will they do? Your mother is bound to see."

"Cast us out, I suspect."

"Us? Or me?"

"It's the same."

Her voice was shaky; she began to cry.

"Oh, Camille, I'm scared. I've heard such awful stories from Félicie. The *bonnes* in Paris, when the time comes they birth themselves. Then destroy the baby."

"Julie, can that be true?"

"Félicie knows some. . . . They cut it in pieces and flush them down the toilet. The head is too large. . . . They get caught."

Camille shuddered.

"Poor creatures. How desperate they must be." He wrapped his arm securely about her, kissed her affectionately, then gripped her firmly by the shoulders.

"Julie, listen to me. We will face this together. When I took you it was not lightly; it was because I knew that I loved you. I made a commitment. The child is as much mine as yours."

She searched his face intently.

"You could tell your parents the baby is not yours. Then I would be out on the streets. I couldn't go back to Grancey. The family is gone, the house is sold. Félicie's people won't take me in. Why should they?"

He shook her. "Julie, stop it. I will never abandon you."

She dried her eyes with the back of her hand.

"For three months I've been scared . . . maybe you wouldn't want me any longer . . . with a child on the way. I believed you, but at night all kinds of ugly snakes crawl in your head."

He said hoarsely, "I'll tell my parents tomorrow. *Chien de l'enfer*. There'll be hell to pay. But it's something that has to be done. Come, eat your veal. It's delicious. Then I'll take you to the Palais Royal and put you on an early bus for Passy. You have to get a lot of sleep and take care of yourself."

Her peals of laughter rang out over the music, causing heads to turn.

It was winter. The first snows had fallen. The dining room, where the family were sitting around the mahogany table having a late supper of bread, cold meats and tea, was cold. Camille studied the cane-seated chairs with the carved mahogany backs; the rounded, highly burnished three-drawer chest, the glass-enclosed highboy. He avoided Emma's eyes. He could delay no longer. He had to tell them, but not until Julie had cleared the table and disappeared into the kitchen at the end of the hall.

"Maman, Papa, I have to tell you this. Julie is pregnant."

Rachel was shocked; her eyelids raised high, her glasses had slipped low on her nose.

"Pregnant! I would never have believed it. So shy and quiet a girl. Seemed most respectable. . . . We'll have to let her go."

This was the hard part. He was not unwilling to face up to his culpability but he knew what a devastating effect it would have on his mother.

"Maman. I am the father of Julie's child."

Rachel stared at him dumfounded, asked in an icy tone:

"How long has this been going on?"

"A year."

"In my house? You have defiled my house?"

Camille swallowed a few times before he was able to answer.

"Love never defiled anything."

"Love!" Rachel was outraged. "A young man in heat! *Penis erectus non conscientum habit.* Or any brains." Bitterly. "Those peasants, they know all the tricks, the wiles. She used her young body to trap you."

Camille knew that he had to remain calm in order to bring some sense into the revelation.

"No, Maman. We simply fell in love. Anything we did, we did together. Neither of us deceived or fooled the other. It happened gradually and honestly. I love Julie. I have for a long time."

Rachel rose, moved glacially, as though she had been struck a mortal blow. A mist blinded her eyes as she walked to the parlor and collapsed onto the St. Thomas sofa, a harbor of refuge for her over some thirty-five years of travail and tragedy. Then she broke into a torrent of sobbing, covering her face and glasses with her big hands.

Camille and Frédéric followed. Emma disappeared. Frédéric too was in shock. Camille was wretched at having imposed this gratuitous burden on his parents, who asked for little more than peaceful years to the end of their troubled lives. He watched his mother futilely trying to come to grips with the news. He ached for her. Finally, in a throttled voice, she cried:

"What's to be done? She cannot remain here. Not another day."

Frédéric, who had been standing, his head bowed, made a decision.

"We'll take care of her, Camille. A nursing home, a reputable midwife, sufficient funds until she can support herself again."

Rachel shot Camille a red-misted look of scorn.

"Weren't there enough *putains* in Paris to sleep with?"

"I don't care for them."

"What has that to do with it?"

"I care for Julie."

Rachel took a deep breath, said resolutely:

"Very well. You care about her. So, an accident happened. That doesn't mean there has to be an illegitimate child born."

Fright and anxiety cramped Camille's insides. His sun-and-wind-burned face turned white. He listened in surprise to the croaking of his voice.

"Why is the baby illegitimate if it is mine?" He hesitated, then blurted, "Were any of yours unwanted?"

"I was a married woman."

He stammered for a moment. Never before had he mentioned his mother's storm-tossed love affair and marriage to his father. Did she think he did not know when all of St. Thomas had enjoyed the gossip, spread it like fertilizer on a freshly planted field? He spoke almost inaudibly.

"Not when Joseph was conceived."

Rachel jumped as though shot.

"Are you judging your own mother?"

He went to her side, attempted to put an arm about her shoulder.

"No! No! I just don't want you to judge Julie and me!"

Again Rachel wept, shaken with distraught sobs which she made no attempt to hide. Frédéric went to his wife, comforted her. Several times he opened his mouth as though to speak. Camille cried:

"Maman, please. Have a little sympathy. I love Julie."

Rachel looked up at her son with pity.

"Sympathy for your having put yourself into an intolerable position? Or for the *bonne?* Aren't things bad enough for you already, a nonearner at thirty? You know what love is! You love the servant in our home! How long do you think that love is going to last? Six months? A year? Have your love, if that's what you call it. But somewhere else."

"Julie is a fine person. You've said so yourself. She will help me. I need her. She is innocent and fresh . . ."

" . . . was!"

Camille winced. "She has given me an inner strength. We're compatible. We'll have a beautiful baby. It will be a lasting marriage."

The room went silent.

Camille knew that Julie would be sitting at the kitchen table staring blindly into space, feeling torn to shreds while her life was being shipwrecked in a Passy apartment over-filled with Danish West Indies furniture.

Rachel pulled herself up to her full height, walked to the opposite end of the room, her shoulders back. When she spoke again her voice was restrained.

"You cannot marry a servant. No one marries a servant. Except other servants. You have your whole life before you. We will never consent. Never!"

Camille recoiled.

"She works for a living. That is not a calamity. A grandchild is not a calamity."

"You lower yourself in class. You take yourself out of the world of polite society, lose all chance of acquiring a well-grounded family that can help establish you. Is it for this we gave of our strength to earn you a fine education?"

"My work is getting better." Resolutely. "It will be salable."

"When? By what means? How will you live? Where will you live?"

"I'll scramble. The way all artists do. If I have anything worth saying my voice will be heard."

"In the wilderness."

"Maman, please. Don't torture us. It is fate that brought Julie and me together and led us to fall in love. It isn't anything I willed."

"It's senselessness, through and through."

"Isn't love a reason?"

"It never was and never will be. You've lived in France long enough to know that marriages are arranged for mutual benefit. I never gave up hope that you would make a good and sensible one. We will stop you."

"How?"

"We will disown you. Imagine if you died, our lifetime savings going to a peasant girl! The years of our hard work. I'm aghast."

"I know you've been planning for me to marry the daughter of a prosperous family and take my place in bourgeois society. That is not for me. I've tried to make it clear to you. I have to create my own life patterns."

"What patterns? Breeding, culture, social position, financial responsibility, a communal religion and background? All these are worth nothing to you? A scant village parochial education, just able to read and write, those are the patterns you mean? What dowry does she bring to her marriage? Her black dress and two baskets of petticoats and underlinens? Two penniless creatures without a job or any practicality between them. Don't sneer at it. A dowry is universal because it is sensible. It enables a man to pull himself up, to open or enlarge a business, to better his family's life."

"Julie is bright. I more and more want country life, to live and paint there. That doesn't mean peasant life."

"And what about your faith? Julie is Catholic."

"Your eight-year struggle with the synagogue has soured me on church hierarchies."

"How ironic. It didn't sour us but it took you out of your congregation. You understand that according to Catholic law any children will automatically become members of their mother's religion? The mother of your child, who walks about the house singing church hymns, songs about the Lord Jesus."

"We'll stay out of the church."

Even as he said this his voice quivered at the memory of Julie's concept of her religion as the only beautiful thing in her life; the hymns he had first heard her singing.

Rachel was pale but self-controlled.

"She will have to leave our house."

"I will take her to Jacobsen's studio to live with me."

A painful shudder went through Rachel.

"I don't ever want to see her again."

"Or the child?"

"No."

"It will be your grandchild."

"Not to me."

"You don't want to see me either?"

"You are our son. You have a duty to visit your parents . . . of a Friday . . . alone. I am heartbroken. What you are doing gives me more pain than the death of my other sons. This comes of your being an artist."

She turned to leave the room, stiff and unyielding.

"If you marry Julie you will be cut off. Completely. If you do not, Father's allowance will go on as before. . . ."

She walked down the hall, locked her bedroom door, as overcome as she had been after the burial of Delphine in the cemetery of Père Lachaise.

Camille stood looking after her. There was a burning pain in his chest. Rachel had at last accepted him as a painter, even with a little pride. Now, shocked, repulsed, deeply hurt, she connected his painting with Julie and condemned them both. It was the hardest blow: he loved his mother . . . he loved his art . . . he loved Julie. There seemed no hope for harmony.

Frédéric had long served as the conciliatory force within his family. He said to Camille:

"Son, think it over, long and hard. Don't impale yourself on a stake."

Touched by his father's softer, friendlier tone, Camille said:

"Very well, I will forget about marriage for the moment. I'm so sorry, Papa. I didn't intend to cause all this grief."

Frédéric sighed deeply.

"We fall into unexpected situations. As I did in St. Thomas almost forty years ago. Julie's a good girl. Just come in every now and then . . . alone, so Maman knows you care about her."

"I will. I do care. I love you, Papa."

"We know that, son."

BOOK FIVE

Children of Fleeting Time

1

CAMILLE HAD DECIDED that David Jacobsen must be a prototype of Shakespeare's melancholy Dane. His work was good; he was self-disciplined; he completed every painting. To no purpose. Allegorical and historical paintings done with a Danish accent might have sold if he had remained in Denmark where he had family and friends. Because he considered Camille his closest friend, and the two men got along well as studio mates, Camille was able to steer him toward more modern themes. Jacobsen completed two paintings, one of an old man with flowing white hair under a high black hat, sitting on the stone parapet of the Pont Royal, a white begging placard around his neck. The second was of a black and white cat lapping milk from a bowl. Camille thought them sensitively realized. Jacobsen lived on the small monthly check from his brother in Copenhagen, ate only one meal a day; his suit of clothes, brought from Copenhagen five years before, was threadbare. He looked more flat-chested than ever, his slender oval face had grown pinched.

He had not known what to expect in sharing a studio with David: he was neat and unobtrusive, which was to the good; but it was difficult in the L-shaped room to escape the cyclical bouts of melancholy. Camille did not realize the extent of the man's despair, since few of their young friends sold anything, had exhibitions or backers, until David left a letter to his brother Edvard on their eating table:

". . . This winter the draft has made me ill several times during the night. I have not had more to cover me in winter than in summer. As you know I do not want debt. . . . I work, but am stopped by need. Oh, I am almost tired of everything. To have to write you like this. But on the other hand it was almost a promise that you would do a little so I could pass the four months Oct., Nov., Dec., and January without worry. Maybe I would have sold 1–2 pieces here if I had had gold frames. . . . But without frames nothing can be shown. To suffer like this . . ."

He had shared the leftovers from Rachel's ample dinner table, which she had insisted Camille carry home on the omnibus in a small hand satchel. He sometimes invited David to join him at a café when he sensed that Jacobsen would see the gesture as companionship. But he had no way of knowing how Jacobsen would react to his introduction of a pregnant young woman into the studio. Would he rebel against having Julie living there? Or merely demand that Camille pay a larger part of the costs? Camille had no stomach to quarrel with David. Nor did he have anywhere else to go with Julie.

He opened the door of the room, found Jacobsen at home, and told him Julie would be living with them in his half of the studio. He was astonished to see a glow of happiness spread over Jacobsen's face.

"What a joy it will be to have a woman in my house again. There's been none since I left Copenhagen."

"I promise not to get in your way," Julie said humbly.

They hammered another hook into the stucco wall, Camille emptied one of the drawers in his chest for her underclothes, aprons. They bought a pair of curtains for which David had longed, hung them with tie-back ropes of a bright color. It would be Julie's first effort to make a home, to create a nest, no matter how modest.

Out of her savings from the Pissarro household, little more than eight hundred francs, one hundred sixty dollars, they first found a screen for their own angle of the room which would afford them a measure of privacy. Next they bought a black cast-iron stove, second hand, but in good condition; she shopped for crockery from the itinerant street vendors. They set the rickety table next to the stove, where Jacobsen happily joined them for coffee in the mornings after Camille had run down the four flights of stairs to the neighborhood *boulangerie* for freshly baked croissants. He had supper with them sometimes, and when he had a couple of francs bought a piece of meat to drop into Julie's all-embracing pot. Her presence seemed to lighten his burden.

Julie tried to find a job as a *demoiselle de boutique* but the mistresses of the florist shops did not wish to take on a pregnant woman. She became instead one of the six thousand *fleuristes* in Paris, since artificial flower making was "the Parisian industry par excellence." In St. Thomas the Pissarro shop had always imported and sold well the artificial flowers at which the French were both expert and artistic. Julie worked in a small factory where she made flowers from paper, taffeta or percale.

"A poor copy of my flowers in the garden at the bottom of the Rue Neuve," she told Camille; "but in the far-off countries where they are sent, better than no flowers at all."

Because of her nimble fingers she was able to earn two to three francs a day without working the eleven hours required of the other girls. She returned to the studio just before dark and cooked their supper.

"It's no problem. I helped the mother cook in Grancey every night after work in the vineyards, or the washing."

Occasionally they went to a neighborhood family *boîte* where they had a simple meal of a chop or a piece of boiled fish. As she got heavier she preferred to keep a soup stock on hand to which she added vegetables, sometimes pieces of meat or chicken.

It was a life of austerity and simplicity. He sold a few rough sketches for centimes rather than francs. He continued to attend the Académie Suisse and to work with the young artists there, but rarely went with them to the cafés or to Courbet's Brasserie Andler. He put in a long day tackling problems he had not known existed.

"A painter never achieves perfection, he merely strives for it," he explained to Julie.

Before, in their meetings at night in the Passy apartment or on Sunday in Paris, they were secretive, yet they had not felt that they were clandestine. It was the fate of young lovers to want each other at all costs. But they had been together only twice a week, for limited periods. Now everything was changed. And, as with all courtships that end in marriage, formal or unofficial, they were seeing each other every day, every evening, on Sundays and the frequent holidays that riddled the French calendar. He could not deny that it altered the relationship. His small world of artist friends knew that he had taken a mistress and that she was pregnant. Corot and Courbet considered it a mistake that could cripple his future. Delacroix warned him against letting the baby inveigle him into marriage. Most of the others took it as a passing phase; it had happened before to many of them, and would happen again. He must not let it deprive him of his nights with them or his attendance at the Suisse. They did not expect it to be a permanent relationship.

Camille had been in the habit of tacking up his daily

sketches for study. Julie thought it a splendid idea. She dug into his folios, covered the bare, spotted plaster walls with scenes of Paris, Montmorency, of La Roche-Guyon and Fontainebleau, some in bright watercolor. In the place of honor they put Corot's two gift drawings, as well as Anton Melbye's. By the time she had finished covering the walls, Jacobsen's drab studio bore some resemblance to an amateur art gallery, far more sightly than it had been.

"We had better ask David how he feels about this," Camille admonished her. "We have usurped his studio."

"I've left room for his sketches," Julie replied. "He never leaves them up for more than a day or two."

"Julie is right," Jacobsen agreed. "When I come home at night I like to put up my studies and admire them for a few hours. Then the reaction sets in; I begin to see the clumsy lines, the imperfections. So I tear them down. But I learn some rudiments from your drawings."

Jacobsen had become extravagantly protective of Julie's pregnancy.

"He is like a cousin from Grancey," she exclaimed. She glanced at herself in the mirror she had purchased at the flea market. "I'm beginning to bulge so far out I can watch the baby walking down the street in front of me."

When, after more than a month, he received a note from his father telling him that Rachel expected him for dinner the following Friday night, he went out to Passy drenched in anguish at the scene he feared might ensue. To his astonishment when he walked into the crowded front room, Rachel, clear-eyed, rose from her rocking chair and greeted him. She had hired a new cook and brought in a daily cleaning woman. She told him of Alfred's prospering affairs in Montevideo, their cousin Eugène's overseeing of their property in St. Thomas, remitting the monthly rent check promptly from the people who hoped to buy the Pissarro building. Phineas had finally auctioned the entire stock of his store through T. Cappe & Co., had returned to the Isaacson business in the Strand in London, and Emma looked forward to taking her four children to join him there.

The table in the dining room was set with their best silver and china. When they were seated Rachel covered her head with a starched napkin before lighting the candles, then Frédéric gave the blessing. Camille was served a dinner he remembered from his childhood: soup with small dumplings, roasted duckling with potatoes, stewed tomatoes, a mélange of cooked dried prunes and apricots, and with their tea a slice of pound cake with a wandering chocolate streak.

When Camille left the apartment, after being asked by Rachel to come back soon, Frédéric walked with him to the omnibus. Camille asked why his mother had been so relaxed. Taking a deep breath, one of the many he had gathered in during his thirty-five years of marriage, his father answered:

"Your mother has erased Julie from her mind. You don't live with her because she doesn't exist."

"How does she manage that?"

Frédéric replied compassionately. "It's a safeguard she has forced upon herself. She can go on living only if she wipes the slate clean of unfortunate fate. I wish I had the capacity to do so. Have you ever heard her mention Delphine?"

"Not since we buried her."

"In that sense, she has also buried Julie. She has done the same with your painting. You are no longer an artist."

Julie's term neared completion. Jacobsen considerately left on a sketching trip. A competent midwife was hired.

The child was stillborn.

No one knew why, including the midwife. Camille tried to comfort Julie.

"The mother's first child did not live," she told him resolutely. "It happens. She then bore three healthy girls. We will have other little ones."

Thereupon she slept.

Camille walked the streets.

"What a misfortune," he thought disconsolately, "to carry a child through heaviness and discomfort, to plan one's life around a newborn only to be left empty-handed."

When Julie awakened he wiped her face with a damp cloth, kissed her forehead. Her mind was fastened on Grancey.

"When they buried the Hermance child we followed the young parents behind the coffin. The carpenter made a 'willow cradle' for the little one. I gathered daisies and dahlias from my garden and made garlands of paper and a small cross to decorate it. Friends, neighbors, family were there, walking down the road. A second-class funeral. First class is reserved for *messieurs*. The parents had to sacrifice to pay. For the grandfather they took a third-class; he had lived out his life; we mustn't waste. But the little bell rang all the way to the cemetery, ring, ring, ring."

She began to sing, barely loud enough for him to hear the words:

"The song of the nightingale will come to wake her
And also the warbler with his sweet throat.
Cicada, my cicada, let's go, we must sing.
For the laurels of the woods are already growing again."

Frédéric came to visit, bringing her a padded *robe de matin,* and on another occasion a box of chocolates. She was touched by his attention; to her it meant that Monsieur Pissarro had accepted reality.

"Fantasy is fine when you're asleep," Frédéric had once said to Camille; "during working hours it muddles the atmosphere."

2

There was no child now to give them a feeling of urgency and need for change in their pattern of living, no crawling infant to take over the studio or dispossess Jacobsen's fat black and white cat. Even so, Camille had the feeling that he and Julie ought to live alone.

"How do we abandon David?" he asked. "He needs us to pay our share of the rent. He also needs us as family. The poor fellow is so alone. His lot is not likely to get any easier. We are none of us selling, but he is ill."

"Couldn't you persuade him to return home?"

"He would take that for rejection. He must persuade himself," Camille reasoned.

"Then we must find a larger place," Julie suggested. "A screen is not enough to divide one room."

It took a lot of looking. On the southern slope of Montmartre, on the Rue de Douai, they found a house of weather-beaten clapboard, leaning slightly, though not dangerously askew. It was surrounded by weeds, a garden patch long gone to seed; some chickens and goats who gobbled and grazed there from a farm high above. The ancient structure had once been a farmhouse, uninhabited as the city of Paris crawled up the steep flanks of Montmartre to make farming there improbable. A hallway ran down the middle of the building, dividing it into two areas of three rooms each, with two small front rooms which could serve as studios. It was a fifteen-minute walk from the Batignolles district. The rent was only a little more than they were now paying.

"It's forsaken," Camille observed, "but not necessarily forlorn. Julie, could you do something with our half?"

"Yes. Paint. You know how to use a paintbrush, *Monsieur l'artiste?* We put glass in the broken windows. I sew curtains. We need a table, some chairs, a little rug. . . . I'll help Jacobsen with his half. He can still have coffee in the morning."

Jacobsen needed no persuading. Frédéric assured Camille that he could take a two-year lease; David's sorely pressed brother Edvard guaranteed David's share.

They moved their scant possessions, borrowed buckets, mops, a scythe to cut down the overgrowth, inserted blocks under the sagging porch. If Rachel missed the round table and rug from Emma's now unoccupied room, she did not mention it. They also received from Emma a series of packages which they had to clear at the customs for a few francs: a set of English dishes, linen for their bed; two small cotton rugs for their bedside.

"Could I buy chickens and rabbits?" Julie asked. "We could build a pen."

"Wait until we're truly living in the country."

Julie had returned to the flower factory soon after the birth. She announced that the *patron* had said she could take home enough material for a week's work and deliver it on Saturday afternoons.

"I'd be sewing or crocheting anyway," she persuaded Camille.

The color had returned to her cheeks, she was again quick and graceful in her movements. She was excited at living in the country atmosphere, secure that it was a home of her own. They held hands, made love and felt part of each other.

The Beaux-Arts Academy ruled that the exhibition should be held every other year. There was to be no Salon in 1860; the painters of Paris felt this was an injustice preventing the young and the new ones from gaining an earlier foothold. They grumbled about it in the restaurants, cafés, and one another's studios, to their journalist friends, the Beaux-Arts schools.

The Académie Suisse was assuming extraordinary importance in his life because of the variety of young painters with whom he became friends; a *mélange* from all areas of society, yet motivated by one strong emotion: the belief that conventional painting was dead: the airless, the sunless, the fantasy, the allegory, the highly glazed aristocratic view of life. They wanted to tackle ordinary people, portraits unswathed in yards of costly satin and courtly lack of emotion; the city streets, the countryside.

"What will be the new art?" James Whistler asked as they gathered around a canvas which he was attempting to cover with a variety of whites, an unheard-of procedure. "We will create it even if we don't know exactly what it will become."

Whistler, who was alternately flushed with funds or flat broke, had a two-sided tongue: caustic to his opponents, sympathetic to his co-strugglers. Camille admired him because, debonair, filled with ebullient humor and seemingly indifferent to whether he had a thick bankroll or an empty pocket in the trousers he pressed each night, he gave instinctively to those who most desperately needed his effervescent nature: Paul Cézanne and the newly arrived Armand Guillaumin, who was employed as a clerk in a government office and came to the Suisse evenings and Sundays.

Guillaumin was nineteen; he had been born in Moulins in 1841 and had come to Paris originally to work in an uncle's shop. He seemed a good sort, quiet, unpretentious, freer of idiosyncrasies and protestations than any of the other students at the Académie. His weekly wage enabled him to eat sparsely, pay the Suisse its monthly fee and buy the barest amount of supplies. He occupied a back room at his uncle's and had to support his grandparents. He and Camille liked each other at once.

"I want to paint full time," he confided as they drew together from a posed male nude in a corner of the Suisse. "But I cannot until I can sell."

Camille replied consolingly, "We must all find buyers."

"Yes, but Claude Monet has his Aunt Sophie in Le Havre. Paul Cézanne his banker father in Aix. Edouard Manet comes from a wealthy family. You have your father's allowance. Whistler loves to play a character out of Murger's *La Vie de Bohème*, but he has frequent funds from London. Guillemet is wealthy. Me, I have only one way."

"What is that?" Curiously. For Guillaumin's face had lighted up.

Guillaumin drew a lottery ticket from his pocket, laid it on the palm of one hand, caressed it with two fingers of the other.

"One day I'm going to win the lottery. Enough francs to make me independent for life. Yet it costs me only a few sous a week; one day my number has to come up."

"I genuinely hope so," Camille exclaimed. "That's two gambles you're taking; they are both long odds, and one is enough. Concentrate on your painting."

Armand Guillaumin smiled, ruminated:

"Antoine Guillemet spells his name with an *e* and a *t*, and he is wealthy. I spell mine with an *au* and an *in* and I'm a pauper. Why should a few letters make such a difference?"

Camille knew Armand was having fun. He replied:

"Claude Monet and Edouard Manet are separated by only one letter; an *o* for an *a*. Manet is given a luxurious living by his parents, while Monet is dependent upon the modest charity of his aunt."

Camille had met Paul Cézanne through his Puerto Rican friend Oller, who had known him for some time. He had been at the Suisse for several months but had barricaded himself in a corner, spoken to no one except for a cursory "Yes" or "No" and obviously wanted to be left alone; a dour abrasive man from Aix-en-Provence in the south, close to the Mediterranean. He was clean-shaven except for a modest mustache, had short brown hair with the sideburns cut at the top of his ears. It was his bristling "Stay away from me!" attitude that alienated the students of the Suisse, who in private alternated between ridiculing his thick Provençal accent, with its many *s*'s: Cours becoming Coursss; and fearing his porcupine personality. He drew clumsily, was a misanthrope, suspicious of everyone and everything. Yet he attracted attention.

Paul Cézanne had been born in Aix-en-Provence in 1839, was nine years younger than Camille. His father had been a hatter, made considerable money, turned to banking and accumulated a fortune, building for his family an estate outside Aix called Jas de Bouffan. Paul and his sister had been born out of wedlock, though acknowledged by their father, who had married their mother when Paul was four, a not uncommon practice. The father had given his son the best classical education available in the area, at the Collège Bourbon. Even then Paul displayed the uncontrollable temper which was to accompany him through life. He began drawing on family walls by the age of five, with a remarkable facility, like Claude Monet, for reproducing scenes about him. Camille learned that Cézanne's distrust and near hatred of all strangers was due to his certainty that they were planning to "get their hooks" into him.

Camille encountered Cézanne early one evening while walking to the Suisse, learned that he was an admirer of Courbet and Delacroix, also went often to their studios. However Camille pointed out that he did not wish to imitate Delacroix's violent color nor Courbet's equally violent realism.

Cézanne studied Camille for a couple of long streets, trying to determine whether he was a potential enemy. Apparently the sniffing out had persuaded him that Camille Pissarro was not determined to do him harm. A couple of nights later he invited Camille to have a beer after the studio closed at a small café unknown to Camille. Camille gathered that, aside from the schoolmate in Aix, Emile Zola, with whom he had spent idyllic years roaming the hills and fields of Provence, discovering wooded valleys and rocky caves to explore, swimming and reading together, Cézanne had no friends. Though Zola had written to a childhood chum, Baptistin Baille, "To convince Cézanne of anything is like trying to persuade the towers of Notre Dame to dance a quadrille," it was later that Cézanne had turned savagely against people, become hostile to the world, without interest in politics, social justice or social graces. He seemed to Camille a sad and lonely man fighting desperately to remain aloof, with a morbid fear of entanglement.

"Most fathers want their sons to come into their businesses," Cézanne confided to Camille, "but eventually they let them go their own way. Not mine. He's granite. He forced me into the Faculté de Droit for two years. I was supposed to become a judge. For three endless years he ground me down. But at last my mother, bless her, and my sister Marie got him to turn me loose, let me come to Paris and paint. He has given me an allowance small enough to starve me back to Aix."

Then fiercely, "Why do some of the Suisse students ridicule my painting?"

Cézanne's canvases were concerned with historical and religious scenes done in a vexatious and mystic manner, alternating with large blobs of color spread aggressively with a palette knife. He called his method *couillarde*, daring; but to the others at the Suisse it reflected his own turmoil.

However, Camille replied to Cézanne amiably:

"What they really resent is your not joining in the songs and jokes. I think they know that your work is better than most but your studies of autopsies and gravesites and funerals seem morbid to them; your colors dark, surprisingly, from what I've heard of the hot Provençal sun. You have a solidity of structure that I'd like to acquire."

Cézanne almost beamed.

"You're different from the others, Pissarro. You're not trying to do me in, to manipulate me."

The two men often walked home companionably from the Suisse. Camille told stories of St. Thomas and their ships' chandlering, commented how curious it was that it was his businessman father who had given in fairly quickly to his son's desire to paint, while his mother was still not reconciled. They would stop for a coffee, sit close at the tiny circular marble table on the sidewalk. Camille had acquired an unlikely friend.

3

Love at home and exciting talk of painting at the Suisse afforded him a sense of progress. In the other accredited studios he had attended for short periods, those who were working around him had one motive: to secure government, church or private commissions, raise themselves to prosperity and respectability. There were some in the Suisse with the same ambition, but not in his own little group. They were the young artists going through what a theater enthusiast called a "prolonged rehearsal," excitedly experimenting, accepting the trial and error period as an inevitable part of their training, eager to find their own identity and means of expression. They went to the museums to re-examine and study the great painters and their excellence, but they knew instinctively that their ultimate subjects and techniques would have to come out of their own view of nature and the universe.

When he returned to the house on Butte Montmartre from the Suisse or the studio of another artist, Julie heard his footsteps on the landing, opened the door and ran to him. As he hugged and kissed her, he looked about at the sparsely furnished rooms and winced.

When Piette gave up his apartment and began a search for a new one, Camille invited him to use his own front room until he settled down again. Piette was delighted. The room was small but they managed to work without disturbing each other. After a short while he asked:

"*Mon cher ami*, might this not be an opportunity for you to paint my portrait?"

Camille painted Piette in his good black coat, lighter-colored trousers and incongruous pair of rubber-soled shoes. He sketched his friend fastidiously. Affectionately. There was Piette to the life: jet-black hair already tinged with spots of gray, the short retroussé nose that in no way conformed to his character. There was a contradiction in his heavy black eyebrows, for there was nothing heavy in his step or stature. He sat poised before his big easel, legs crossed, right arm outstretched in a graceful curve toward the canvas, left thumb hooked through the color-daubed palette.

They talked of the news in the day's journals, which managed to be at the same time interesting and irrational. In April the Paris papers reported that the Northern-held Fort Sumter in the United States had been fired upon by the South. The American Civil War had begun. There was a first call in France for compulsory education, which the members of the Académie Suisse greeted with high enthusiasm, on the parochial grounds that "Illiterates don't appreciate art." There were almost daily reports of duels causing wounds and deaths. The journals also carried a health scare about the water being distributed in certain *arrondissements*. Mental illness was being given public notice, such as the story of the man on the third floor of an apartment house who screamed, "The murderers are going to kill me," and when the neighbors summoned the police, thought they were his pursuers and jumped out of the window, killing himself.

The news heightened Piette's aspect. Camille found it a good way to observe and get down on canvas his friend's own excitements: industrial accidents were reported more frequently; a construction worker on the fifth floor of a building fell and cracked his skull; another working in the basement of a skeletal structure was killed by a falling building stone. A seventeen-year-old in a match factory had an arm cut off by a circular saw; four sewer workers remained close to death from asphyxiation when the fresh-water flow was accidentally turned off.

At the Suisse, Fantin-Latour, in a rare nonmystical vein, said as he added great dollops of creamy yellow to a bunch of outsized daffodils:

"I know why I became a painter. So I wouldn't get killed in industry."

There was sometimes good news. A scientist, Louis Pasteur, began work on the process of fermentation, which had formerly "remained in a thick veil." Henry Bessemer, an English inventor, perfected a method of manufacturing steel from cast iron.

By some queer jumble of emotions he came to the decision that he had been wrong, perhaps even lazy or careless, about not having submitted himself to the rigorous training of copying the techniques of the great ones in the Louvre. Most of his predecessors had done so. Several had advised him, "The Louvre is the School of the World. Study the masters whose works have come down to us through hundreds of years and are as shiningly beautiful as the day they were painted."

Reluctantly he applied for official permission to work in the original fortress and palace built by Philip II in 1204, extended and redecorated by centuries of succeeding monarchs of France. Napoleon, who needed space to display the fruits of his conquests, had converted the palace into an art museum. When the permit was issued he took himself down the kilometer-long corridors. One of his friends at the Académie Suisse remarked:

"Draw the people who are copying. They're more alive than the art they're trying to reproduce."

They were indeed a colorful crew: men and women from the United States, England, most of Europe and South America, each garbed in the style of his country; all meticulously neat and clothed to satisfy inspection by the Louvre officials. Because it was cold in the drafty halls all worked in heavy overcoats, woolen or fur hats, blowing on their hands to keep their fingers warm. When he looked down an endless exhibition corridor it seemed a military outpost, with sentries poised over their guns; long lines of a hundred copyists huddled over braziers, their figures leaning forward with charcoal and brush raised to attack. The pictures on the walls, well spaced, were still, very still; but the men and women copying were in constant movement. Aloud he groaned:

"*Mon Dieu*, why am I joining this brigade? *Un homme qui se noie s'attache à un brin d'herbe*. A drowning man clings to a blade of grass."

He gazed at the early Claude Lorrains with admiration, at the Chardin scenes of peasant kitchens, at the Rembrandts, Titians, Rubenses. Finally he settled his easel and took out his paints. He tried to make honest duplications, and though he had felt no affinity for the displayed sculptures of the Exposition Universelle in 1855, or the Salon exhibition of 1859, he sat on his stool in front of the superb figures of the *Victory of Samothrace* and the *Venus de Milo* with breath and blood seeming to throb inside the marble, and used charcoal to get them into his notebook. But when he returned to his studio at dusk he could rouse no enthusiasm within himself. He protested to Jacobsen:

"I don't think I'm learning anything. The masters are magnificent; but I am never going to paint like them."

Jacobsen coughed for a bit into his handkerchief.

"It's a discipline. There are attitudes to learn, perspective. . . ."

Camille found Julie easy and pleasant to live with. She was undemanding, accepted his long hours away from the house sketching in Paris or in the countryside, drawing at the Suisse many evenings. They could afford only the bare necessities, but in Grancey she had been accustomed to skimping. She was strong and rarely knew fatigue; the flower making was not a burden. It left her many hours to work in her own back garden, which she was slowly transforming from a neglected, weed-covered area. What had sustained her in the difficult years in the one-room hut at the muddy base of the Rue Neuve, her love for her mother and sisters, was what sustained her now: her love for Camille. Their sexual passion was surrounded by soft-spoken tenderness and companionship.

Julie knew that she was not the paramount love of Camille's life. Painting was, and always would be. She had no contact with his painter friends, and no need for it. They were his work companions. She was so grateful for being loved by a man she could not have aspired to that it did not occur to her to be disappointed about occupying a secondary position. She remembered her own drunken father and thanked God in her prayers every night for bringing her Camille Pissarro.

She earned her two to three francs a day, enough to supply them with food. Camille used a part of his allowance for painting supplies and his fees at the Académie Suisse; but rationed himself on all other expenditures so that there would be enough money left over to supply oil for the lamps, coal for the stove, candles, water delivered for cooking and cleaning, material for Julie to make herself underclothing or a dress. If he could not often join the others for a meal in a restaurant, he met them for coffee on the terrace of a café.

Julie was not comfortable at the Café Guerbois where Camille now met with his friends, though there were other young women present, for the most part models. The Guerbois, at 11 Grand Rue des Batignolles, was calm and quiet. At the left of the entrance were two long marble-topped tables reserved for writers, critics, illustrators, photographers, and now the young painters who met on Sundays and weekdays after five, under soft lamplight, to indulge in their *causeries*, everything from Japanese prints to the difficulty of getting a seat on the Odéon omnibus. When the animated talk among the painters had become technical, aspects of painting which were incomprehensible to her, Julie gently suggested to Camille that he go alone. Fundamentally, however, she did not think it a proper place for a respectable woman to be at night. She was intensely moral, considered herself a housewife, and was uneasy in the presence of the models. Camille pleaded their case.

"They're good people. They do no harm. They work hard for their francs."

"Posing naked before men?"

"Now, Julie, that's unsympathetic of you. It's their trade."

Fantin-Latour, in his white unbuttoned shirt, introduced Camille to Edouard Manet at the Café Guerbois, after the door had grated closed across the sand on the floor. Although two years younger than Camille, at twenty-nine Manet was the acknowledged leader of the special artists' tables of the café. He invited Camille to sit in the chair next to him.

"I've heard about you from half a dozen painters. They say you have promise."

"It's kind of them."

"Accursed word, 'promise.' They say I have it too. It's rather like an incipient epilepsy we carry around with us, bound to break out at some point in the future. Have a glass of wine."

In the glow of the café's oil lamps, Camille saw that Edouard Manet was a man of broad shoulders, yet flatly lean throughout his superb figure, and wore near white trousers trimly buttoned about his lean waist. He had what was called a Gallic head, an open and expressive face. His lustrous almost black hair was beginning to recede on both sides of the part; his soft beard and mustache were handsomely groomed. He was exuberant of nature, using many gestures to amplify his speech. For his social life among the *élégants* he wore a lavishly cut long black coat but, as a sign of independence, a brightly checkered vest; and eschewed the traditional bow tie for a long necktie of a rich fabric.

To Camille he was the most attractive man in the Guerbois, bold, self-assured, upper class, with penetrating eyes that proclaimed, "I know who I am and who I intend to become." There were no uncertainties, anxieties, repressions. He seemed warm and friendly, did not judge one's abilities yet favored the few who he thought were exceptional. Whether it was their youth, sense of fraternity, or the fact that as artists they were removed from the mainstream of society, they seemed grateful to find a common ground, readily talking about themselves.

Camille chuckled at Manet's mordant humor as he told of being one of the few artists born in Paris, having actually been baptized at St. Germain-des-Prés in an atmosphere of ancient tradition. Of his father, who was a judge of the Tribunal of the Seine, with a background of wealth and position, and his mother from the same high stratum. Of how he had been sent to the best schools to prepare him for the law and to follow the family tradition of the magistry; and had firmly planted in him the social and moral characteristics which he had inherited. He took pleasure in society and was fond of frequenting salons, where he was admired for his verve and flashing wit. It had taken a major revolt to fly in the face of so solidly prosperous and high level a family.

"My father called me refractory," he expounded. "Both parents were solidly against my corrupting the family name."

He had finally joined the naval academy to get away from home pressures, and sailed on *La Guadeloupe*, a merchant vessel plying between Le Havre and Rio de Janeiro.

"The only adventure that happened to me," he continued drolly, "was an opportunity to put into practice an innate instinct as a painter. The ship's cargo included a number of Dutch cheeses which had become discolored by the action of the salt water. The captain chose me to put the matter right. Armed with a brush and a pot of paint of bright color, I painted the cheeses so as to give the fullest satisfaction."

His parents had hoped that the hardships of freighter life would rededicate their son to luxury living as well as the need to occupy a position in the French hierarchy. They had misjudged their offspring; he was more determined than ever to devote his life to painting. By his eighteenth birthday they had decided that he was incorrigible and reluctantly gave their consent to his becoming an artist.

"But not a poverty-stricken, rumpled artist," his father decreed. "If you are going to paint, you will do so as a rich man's son."

He rented a beautiful studio for his work but continued to live at home amidst the luxury and servants of his family; and to patronize the best restaurants, always with more money in his wallet than he could use. He was a womanizer in the romantic tradition.

He asked the waiter to refill their wineglasses, then surprised Camille by saying:

"I liked your *Landscape at Montmorency* in the '59 Salon. What little I could see of it. I had no such luck. I submitted a canvas of an absinthe drinker sitting with a woman companion at a sidewalk table, but it was rejected. There's something in my work that repulses the jury. Yet I have never wanted to protest, to overthrow the art of the past, or create a new order."

Courbet had said, "Manet has a taste for reality."

Camille said quietly, "From what I've heard, you revolted against Couture, who commanded the most prestigious atelier in Paris. But don't we have to revolt to get past barricades?"

Manet smiled, showing a set of large white teeth.

"*Touché!* I spent six years at Couture's, and indeed left in open revolt against historical painting of the kind that won prizes at the Salon. Couture was furious with me; he had thought I was going to be his lifetime disciple. When I left, he cried:

" 'You'll never be anything more than the Daumier of your time. In short, a cartoonist and caricaturist.' "

"Will you submit to the 1861 Salon? I am preparing several paintings. . . ."

"Of course. The Salon is the real field of battle. It is there that one must take one's measure. I have a guitarist. I'm under the spell of the Spaniards: Velásquez, Goya, El Greco. *The Guitarist* will scare the hell out of the jury, but they'll accept it: out of fear and confusion."

Making his way home up the steep Butte Montmartre, Camille thought that Manet could not have been more friendly. It was amusing that Manet's closest friend among the painters was the bedeviled Armand Guillaumin, the poorest of the lot. Manet was also a left-wing Republican and a bitter enemy of the Second Empire under Napoleon III.

4

Despite the fact that Claude Monet considered that his chance of being called to the army was slim, Edouard Manet gave him an au revoir party when he had to return to Le Havre to participate in the military lottery, in which a given ration of young men just turned twenty had to "draw" for a seven-year service in France's army.

"My father would never buy me out," Monet cried, sitting poised on one of Edouard's delicate Louis XIV golden settees. "He's too angry with me, probably thinks the army would be good for me. But my Aunt Sophie would buy me out and send a substitute. She would never let me spend seven years in Algeria.''

Manet held open house, with two *garçons* in red-striped vests liberally passing food and drink, a three-piece orchestra playing dance music. He had suggested that the artists bring their women. It was a big party, for he had invited Monet's friends from the Suisse; Courbet and his circle from the Andler; his earlier associates from Couture's atelier; the regulars from the Café Guerbois. It was a festive group, the women in flowered gowns, the artists appearing in their best coats and trousers, many in embroidered waistcoats.

Camille insisted that Julie accompany him. Her eyes were wide at Edouard Manet's fashionably decorated studio with its colorful streamers and humorous caricatures of Claude Monet, one in a Zouave uniform, half sunk in desert sands, another amid seductive dancing girls in an Algerian harem. Camille persuaded Julie to dance with Monet and later was pleased to see that she responded sympathetically to his fellow artists as she sipped a cool wine punch.

The party lasted from late afternoon until early the next morning. Camille and Julie returned home a little tipsy. The gathering had been a great success, drawing closer the coterie of Parisian artists. However it did nothing to change Claude Monet's luck in the Le Havre "draw." His father, unalterably opened to his son's break for freedom to Paris, persuaded Aunt Sophie not to buy the boy out. Claude Monet was inducted into the French army on April 29 for a seven-year stretch.

"It's tragic," Camille mourned. "They will destroy him as an artist."

"Perhaps he can become a military painter?" Julie suggested.

"It's not in his nature." Then, after a few moments, a tiny smile twitched his mouth. "But he is a resourceful young man. He'll think of something."

For the May 1861, Salon at the Palais de l'Industrie, the group at the Académie Suisse decided, after Varnishing Day, to go together to learn the result of the jury's selection.

"We will congratulate anyone who is accepted. Those of us who are rejected will feel no envy."

Everyone at the Suisse had submitted several pieces; it was a clear advantage for the younger aspirants to do so, deciding that an *R* for rejected was better than an *O* for omission. The novices could say, as was the custom in Paris, "I submitted to the Salon but they were not yet prepared for my fresh approach."

Camille had selected three gouaches: *Plains of La Roche-Guyon*, *The Fields* and *Butte Montmartre*, all areas which he knew well and found exciting. He believed them to be the best he had done in the past two years, an advance on his 1859 oil. He was confident that he would be accepted: the jury favored those who had already shown. When they were rejected he was not only surprised but disappointed. It was one thing to be ignored in a continuous display of apathy or displeasure; it was another to be accepted and then to be cast aside. It was true that *Landscape at Montmorency* had not gained him a patron or a sale, yet it had helped to solidify his position among his confreres. His rejection now in 1861 made it appear as though his selection two years before had been an accident.

Most of those attending the Académie Suisse had also been rejected. There was no work attempted in the barren room of the atelier after what they named the "Slaughter of the Innocents."

Manet, as he had predicted, escaped the carnage. A portrait of his parents was accepted, as was *The Guitarist*, which received an honorable mention, a triumph for a man a year short of thirty.

When Camille began to scrub out the *R* stamped on his frames he was downcast. Julie put her arms about him protectively.

"It's a step back into oblivion," he cried. "*J'ai pris une colère comme un âne à qui l'on attache une fusée aux fesses.* I'm as angry as a donkey with a rocket in his rump. I'm suffering from careless optimism. I'm deflated. I thought that if the jury selected at least two of my pictures I would begin to sell. We could have a few more comforts. . . ."

She smoothed his rumpled hair as a gesture of soothing his emotional broil, said in a tremulous voice:

"We have time. Both of us."

Something in her tone sobered him. He held her from him, his hands gripping her firm round shoulders.

"How thoughtless of me. You had a rejection far more serious than mine."

"I will have babies. You will have pictures in the Salon." Then she suggested, "Join your friends at the Café Guerbois tonight. It will do you good."

A dozen young men were gathered around the corner table amidst the smoke, smell of beer and wine and high-pitched conversation.

"Let's not commiserate with each other," said Fantin-

Latour. "We have already decried the Salon's taste and judgment."

Whistler remarked with ill-concealed irony:

"It is an integral part of human nature to reject anything that is new or different. It happens in the sciences and humanities as well. Particularly if one's trough is threatened."

Nevertheless they were grazing in the rocky lowlands. They faced another two years of lack of opportunity to show their work.

Consolation came in the fact that Gustave Courbet and Jean François Millet were singled out as the masters of the year. In addition, one of the more perceptive critics of the Salon sided with the enrollees of the Académie Suisse:

> The capital sin of art today is the lack of sincerity. This is because force is lacking, which is to say, inspiration, reflection, and work. . . . The multitude, meaning mediocrity, is everywhere king. Procedure, rapid mechanism, uniformity, are tending to replace the individual strength, the spontaneous, the original. I think that art is suffering from a deep sickness now.

Frédéric enjoyed his retirement, watched the composer Rossini's house being built close by, took daily walks in the neighboring Bois. He was unhappy about the Salon rejections; art was not a straightforward business after all. Rachel appeared unknowing and unconcerned. Camille showed up for dinner often enough to keep his parents mollified. In London Emma was happy with Phineas and her now five children. She sent Camille short notes and household gifts. The house in Passy seemed empty without her. Alfred was prospering as a merchant in Montevideo, going to the opera and concerts, falling in and out of love regularly with young women from good families. Once at Alfred's insistence Camille had looked in on Antoinette. Alfred wrote him:

"I received your letter with infinite pleasure, and I see there that you are still for me the friend of yesterday. It is very bad that you have kept from me the fact that you have given money to Antoinette; she wrote me and also told me that she was very ill. So I ask you to continue for her the obliging role you have begun, certain that my thanks will be with you. . . ."

Julie carried on as a *fleuriste*. She also cultivated the land behind the house. She required little entertainment, but she loved to dance so Camille took her on occasion to an outdoor *bal* where they sat at a small table under the trees, listened to the orchestra while watching the brightly dressed women and men in black top hats waltz by; and then danced themselves.

She tied no ropes around him. When that summer Papa Corot invited him to Fontainebleau, or he went with Armand Guillaumin to sketch for a few days in the countryside north of Paris, she took the separation stoically. In the evenings he sometimes read aloud to her, the De Goncourt brothers' *Charles Demailly*, George Sand's *The Master Bell Ringers*.

He was still devoted to drawing as the foundation of all painting.

"Without drawing can there be painting? Can there be a musical composition without notes? A drama without dialogue?" he asked himself. He sometimes used colored paper, gray, light brown or pale blue. He drew with a pencil, made his hatching with a pen. From Corot he had learned how to achieve a distinction between pencil strokes and the broad use of charcoal or highlighted chalk.

He was patient in developing his technical skills; once acquired, he believed they would never be lost.

He worked out of doors every day the weather permitted, continuing to reject artificiality and sentimentality, searching for the fundamental spirit of a scene rather than its literal interpretation, feeling, "When you have trained yourself to see a tree truly, you know how to look at the human figure." He still spent considerable time composing his pictures on paper before attempting oil paint and canvas, and disciplined himself to retain nature's forms and set them down from memory. He practiced recording quickly so that his intuitive perception was the binding that held the paints together.

He went back to the Louvre to study the Great Three of French landscape painting of earlier years: Claude Lorrain, Jean Baptiste Chardin, Nicolas Poussin, of whom Corot, Millet, Daubigny and Rousseau were the legitimate descendants. He studied these masters of the past though he was determined not to reproduce them, to be faithful to their tradition without robbing them. He nodded in agreement when Cézanne said:

"We must not become intellectuals constipated by recollections of museums."

He believed with Corot that "It is not possible to look enough at nature. Get your perceptions down on canvas. That is your true voice, what your particular voice is attempting to say."

Corot had also admonished:

"Since you are an artist you don't need advice. Except for this: above all one must study values. We don't see in the same way; you see green, I see gray and blond. Work at values; they are the basis and the background of painting."

Camille had asked:

"To see colors with visual accuracy and then to grasp their relationship to each other?"

Corot nodded his white, tousled head.

"Beauty in art is truth bathed in an impression received from nature. While I strive for a conscientious imitation, I yet never for an instant lose the emotion that has taken hold of me. Before any sight and any object, abandon yourself to your first impression. If you have really been touched, you will convey to others the sincerity of your emotion."

Returning to the house in Montmartre, he set himself specific tasks: to make his brushwork supple; to portray light and shadow; to bring earth tones into harmony with white formless clouds drifting across a sky of intense blue. Intermittently he did figure drawings, both nude and clothed, so that he could introduce them into his landscapes, small figures emanating life against a village of stone houses, massive trees, cultivated fields rising to the horizon.

He had a strong feeling, an intuition, that that was the direction in which his future lay.

5

In January 1862 he joined his first protest movement: artists copying in the Louvre paid a charge for the mandatory checking of their canes or umbrellas. No such charge was made at the Salon or the Imperial Library. The copyists won. Edouard Manet, congenital opponent of bureaucracy, said acidly:

"I wish all victories against tyranny could be so easily gained. Ordinarily it takes years to move a bureaucrat from one side of his desk to another."

"It's because we acted together," Camille replied.

In February, baths for workers' children caught on for health reasons. The government voted perpetuity of copyright for literary and artistic work.

"Now, if only the government would pass a law making it obligatory for people to buy paintings!" Armand Guillaumin proposed.

In March, *L'Illustration* published news of new taxes on salt, sugar, luxury carriages. Later, the Paris papers were full of the American Civil War battle between the ironclad ships, the *Monitor* of the North and the *Merrimac* of the South, which made all wooden warships obsolete. In April the first coca or cocaine reached France from Peru. On June 7, Victor Hugo's *Les Misérables* was published to a public outcry. Opinions were passionate, both for and against. Julie shuddered at the scenes of cruelty and injustice; it did no good for Camille to explain that such matters had to be brought out into the open so they could be cured.

When the weather turned nice in late June, he took Julie for a day in the country, carrying a lunch and riding an omnibus or train to outlying villages having festivals. They watched duck races, sack races, a greased mast contest for men, ring games for young ladies; danced to a country band. As often as they could afford they went to the opera, in the inexpensive seats, or to watch the adored Emma Livry, the queen of French ballet. Paris mourned when her ballet dress caught fire from a candle flame during a rehearsal and she was burned half to death.

Piette pleaded once again that Camille and Julie come for a visit to Montfoucault, finally dropping off railroad tickets at their house.

"The countryside is superb in July. Everything coming into fruit and flower."

"Please, Camille," Julie urged.

It was a long train trip southwest to Mayenne, with many stops. Camille followed the landscape with eyes as avid as on his trip from Boulogne to Paris some seven years before. Mayenne was an ancient river port with arched stone bridges across the Mayenne River lined with high embankments of solidly fitted stone. The town was a prosperous center for agriculture, cattle and sheep raising, with a fountain in the center of a stone-paved square, an antiquated city hall and a flower market along the riverbank. The river wound placidly through the town; sailboats meandered down the peaceful valley. L'Eglise St. Martin, built of red brick, was the main church of the town, in sore need of restoration.

Piette, his face engulfed in a bright smile, took their baggage at the bottom step of the railroad car, installed them in a well-worn buggy with wheels that wobbled. Adèle reached out her hand to welcome Julie.

The ride from Mayenne to Montfoucault took two hours. The apple and peach orchards were heavy with fruit; wheat and hay crops were ripening on the green rises of low hills and level areas; sheep and black and white cattle grazed the earth under shade trees. Ancient stone houses came into view in dips of the valleys; there was uncleared forest land and, in the distance, a mountain range. The narrow winding roads, often mere trails, were picturesque as they passed through the tiny villages of Ambrières-les-Vallées, Melleray, Cigné.

"You are right, Piette. It is marvelously paintable," Camille sang out as they crossed the river again, at a château, then went through a cool stand of virgin forest. As they approached the tiny village of Montfoucault, Camille saw that at every one of the frequent crossroads there was a life-sized wooden Christ crucified, with an abundance of red paint beneath the nail wounds. The tall figures dominated the area, including the one at the little village church on a slight rise, its fieldstones encrusted with mustard-colored mildew. Camille had never seen so many "Agonies of Christ" gathered in so compact an area.

"Do all these shrines disturb you?" he asked Adèle.

"They did at first. This is an intensely religious place. In the beginning I had nightmares that I was the one being crucified. But Piette's family is the oldest in this part of the country. He comes from a long line of churchmen, university stewards, doctors, mayors, presidents of the salt granary. I was accepted. Yet I'm glad we spend half of the year in Paris."

Some of the country houses sat as daintily on the land as though balanced like a cup of tea on a crossed knee. Others looked squashed, only the second story appearing above the surface. But when they pulled up in front of Montfoucault and Piette shot the iron bolt of the cumbersome double gate, Camille exclaimed:

"What a beautiful house!"

Piette beamed at him. "Thank my ancestors, dear friend. May this be the first of many wonderful visits for you."

The house was majestically tall, of light gray and tan cut fieldstone, with a gray slate roof and chimneys on either end. On the lower floor were two large windows on each side of a high double door, the bottom half of carved wood, the upper half of glass panels. There were four equally large windows on the floor above. The windows on the lower floor had white wooden shutters to keep out the heat of summer and the cold blasts of winter.

In front of the house was a green lawn, a narrow path down its middle, and three long, separated flower beds with burgeoning blooms of tulip, iris, lilies. A ten-foot wall of gray and tan fieldstone surrounded the main house and the vegetable gardens in the back where Piette pointed out his stretches of lettuce, artichokes, onions, carrots, green beans.

"You have a good manager, Piette."

"A family. Been with us since my grandfather's time. The farm isn't doing quite as well as it did. I'm not as good a businessman as my father; and certainly not as shrewd as my grandfather."

"It is an unlikely combination, artist and businessman."

"An improbable one. That's why the farm takes in less money each year. But our income will last out our lifetime. Since we don't appear to be having any heirs, I guess that's all that counts."

"You're only thirty-six," Camille responded to lift Piette out of his momentary gloom. "You will have a harvest."

"Paintings, yes. Cattle, yes. Crops, yes. Children? We pray."

They entered through a door off a large stone-paved courtyard at the rear of the house, with barns on either side. A heavy inside door shut off the upstairs rooms; on the wall was a huge animal head with widespread antlers. The entrance hall was small. On one side it opened on to a large high-ceilinged parlor with a log-sized fireplace and three generations of oddly assorted divans, easy chairs, tables, glass-shelved *étagères* containing a century of bric-a-brac. On the left of the foyer was the kitchen with the same high ceiling. At the far end were an enormous black cook stove and a dining table under a tall window overlooking the courtyard.

There was one moderate-sized bedroom downstairs, across from the kitchen, which was used on those occasions when Adèle could find a satisfactory cook; the young women of the Mayenne district did not like to work as domestics. Upstairs there were two enormous bedrooms, the one over the parlor having an open fireplace. The kitchen chimney, on the other end of the house, did not have an opening into the second bedroom.

"I have never understood it," Piette confessed, his eyes twinkling. "Was my ancestor trying to freeze out some part of his family?" Nor had anyone over the generations bothered to build a porch, in front or back. "It's not a custom in this country," Piette explained. "When we want to sit out on a warm day I carry out chairs and a table."

Adèle and Julie cooked together. They experimented, tasted, laughed. Neither had a flair for flavor but the men were too content in their companionship to notice. They roamed the countryside, occasionally painting the identical scene. Camille spent the first two weeks sketching to get the feel of the Mayenne landscape; the geographical shift of over a hundred miles brought a startling change in topography as well as basic character from the environs he knew. Then he went into oils, painting the Montfoucault house seen from a slight rise as it sat securely on the earth; Piette's little lake in the nearby woods; the surrounding fields with their ripening crops; cross trails; animals munching; loaded carts going by.

"It's paintable country," he declared to Julie. "Nothing petty or vulgar about it."

"I never had a friend," Julie mused. "There was the mother, the sisters, then you. . . . I like this big bed and the fat quilt and the crickets chirping and the frogs croaking in the little pond and the picnics in the woods. Oh, Camille, I am so happy here."

She roamed the fields with her hair streaming behind her as she had in La Roche-Guyon, waded in a nearby creek. To Camille she seemed as young and lovely as the first day he had seen her in the apartment in Passy.

He drew her close.

"We'll move out to the country one day. But first I have to get into the Salon again. And find a dealer who will show my pictures."

Adèle was lonely in the country and worried half sick that she was barren.

"If I could have babies I would have something useful to do, raising my young. Or if I could help to manage the farm, make it more profitable. But I'm not a country girl."

"I'm a country girl," Julie said, "but I wouldn't know how to make money from the land."

They were sitting outside the front door near the flower garden, at twilight, over a supper of cold meat, fresh-baked bread and sweet butter, a salad from their vegetable garden. Piette opened a bottle of sparkling wine which had been hanging in a bucket in the well to cool. When the sky became totally dark they lighted candles. Night sounds were all around them. As they clinked glasses, murmured *"Salut!"* they somehow each sensed that this lyrical, happy moment would never be duplicated.

6

One evening in October Julie told him with a blush creeping up her cheeks that she was pregnant again. He kissed her fondly on both cheeks.

"How long?"

"Three months."

"July! At Montfoucault. I'm happy about it, *chère*. I want us to be a family. I had so many brothers and sisters, but they . . . disappeared. All I have left is Emma, far away in England; and Alfred, farther away in Montevideo."

Her eyes were diffused with a soft light.

"In Grancey we say, 'In a small field grows good wheat ' "

He patted her still lean abdomen.

"I'd like to raise many boys and girls. It would give me a sense of belonging to the world."

"Il est sûr de son bâton."

He was amused.

"After the baby is born we'll find a better place to live."

"The country." Julie was exultant. "It doesn't cost as much to live in the country. We will have a little house, raise our vegetables . . ."

Camille's thoughts had already turned that way.

"I've sketched everything I need to in Paris, enjoyed all the *écoles*, academies, cafés. I want to become part of the countryside, the fields and villages, the peasants. Everything that has happened to me tells me that I'm meant to be a landscape painter."

Their landlord would not wait for the arrival of the baby; he wanted to occupy the now renovated house himself. They found a studio on the Rue Neuve Breda, bringing them down the hill again and closer to the Notre Dame de Lorette. It was too small to accommodate David.

One day in early November, with a burnt-ash sky, Claude Monet walked into the Académie Suisse, his handsome young face wreathed in a grin.

They were all taken by surprise.

"You are supposed to be with the army in Algeria!" Camille exclaimed.

"Not any more. My father bought me out. I came home to Le Havre last May on sick leave, hovering on the brink of death!"

His friends gathered about him, hooting their derision. He did not mind; he was ecstatic at being back.

Whistler said with a straight face:

"Monet, I'm fascinated. I always like to hear the symptoms of my friends' malaises."

"I had everything but syphilis and gonorrhea; there were no Parisian models and I stayed away from the local whorehouse."

"Too bad. You could have had a discharge much earlier."

They laughed. Monet threw back his roguish head.

"I started with pneumonia which went into tuberculosis. I broke my leg in three places. I developed an insidious dysentery which reduced me to a skeleton. My body was covered with a rash of boils. Something went wrong inside my head. . . ."

"Something more than usual?" This was Antoine Guillemet.

"Much more. I imagined I was the commanding general of the fort. That's when they decided to send me home on sick leave."

"All this is documented in your dossier, of course?" asked the nonfrivolous Cézanne.

"*Exactement!* There was no other way out. Never mind. I spent the last six months working with Jongkind. The poor fellow has had several nervous breakdowns; drinks too much, has hallucinations. Tall, gaunt, rolls like a sailor, has an almost incomprehensible Dutch accent . . . but oh, when he paints! Stark clarity of tone, excitement of subject, daring use of color. . . . An even better master for me than Boudin."

"In any event, welcome back," cried Camille.

Monet's face beamed with joy.

"My father is giving me an allowance for two whole years providing I can prove that I'm working hard every day. That means Gleyre's atelier, where Gleyre will supervise me and give me testimony to send home. It is expensive, thirty francs for entrance, another thirty in advance for three months' tuition, but my father thinks it worth it because he can keep an eye on me all the way from Le Havre."

Camille worked every day, long hours. Though he remained open to ideas, particularly those of Daubigny with his diffusion of air, he was at the same time searching for an inner vision. He kept his spirit vibrantly alive, yet he was able to perceive his inadequacies. One evening when he returned from the village of Auvers-sur-Oise he painted out his day's work.

"Why do you do that?" Julie asked. "I've never seen you destroy anything."

"I was mistaken. The motif was wrong. Or I approached it from an awkward angle. My colors were murky and I'd laid on the brush strokes badly."

His devotion to nature's landscape was not shared by Baudelaire, poet genius of France whose work was largely rejected, and who was more poverty-stricken even than David Jacobsen. Visiting Camille's apartment one Sunday afternoon, his eyes feverish from the drugs he was alleged to be taking, the sharp V of his black hair making him look like a starved Satan, he told Camille, after examining his recent paintings:

"Pissarro, do you know what I answered when I was asked to contribute an essay for a book on the Barbizon-Fontainebleau School? On woods, large oak trees, verdure, insects, the sun? I am incapable of being moved by vegetation. I shall never believe that the soul of the gods resides in plants, in sanctified vegetables. I have actually always thought that in flourishing and rejuvenated nature there was something distressing. In the thick woodlands I am reminded of our astonishing cities, and the prodigious music that rolls along seems to me to be the translation of human lamentation."

Camille was as much startled as he was amused. A sensitive poet who was blind to nature? A good thing there were seven different arts!

Julie carried without discomfort. She rarely referred to the fact that there was a growing child within her. Camille took his cue from her attitude, saying little about it, but saw that she did not lift full water pails, baskets of vegetables, laundry.

"You don't have to pam . . . pamper," she protested. "It's a woman's job to carry the baby. Carrying a child is something men can't do, and never will."

He had never seen her defiant before.

"Well, I'll try to keep pace with you. I will complete three pictures for the next Salon: one landscape, one village scene, a third study of a ferry crossing the river Oise. If we sell the pictures we'll take our child to a home in the country."

He gave up the evening discussions and merriment at the cafés, kept her company, read aloud from the current novels, unobtrusively broadening her outlook and her vocabulary. Julie enjoyed the attention and applied herself diligently. The one area in which he could accomplish nothing was in trying to impose punctuation on the letters she wrote to her sister.

"Julie, my dear, you really must learn to use periods, commas and capital letters. No matter how long your notes may be you write them in one continuous flow. There are no sentences, no paragraphs. You don't end a thought or subject with a period or begin the new one with a capital letter."

"Félicie understands my letters."

"That's not the point. I will teach you what they failed to do in Grancey."

She pecked him on the cheek. "You're a fine teacher." Then, with a lightning flash of resentment, "But I can't change the way I write. It's how I think, without periods or capital letters. It will only confuse me.''

Camille did not upset her further.

Julie gave birth to a son in February of 1863, just as Camille was completing his landscape oil of La Varenne. A licensed midwife delivered her of an eight-pound boy who screamed lustily when the woman held him upside down and spanked him. They named him Lucien. Neither of them knew why.

Julie was proud that she had produced a son. It was more than her mother had done.

"Perhaps if the father had had a son instead of three daughters, he wouldn't have run away," she brooded

Camille wrote to Frédéric and Rachel about their grandchild. The letter was well punctuated with commas, periods and paragraphs. They received no reply.

7

A cyclone of energy swept through the art world. Camille and his fellow artists were caught up in it. It was eight years since the Exposition Universelle of 1855, that colossal exhibition which had brought art from dozens of countries and given an importance to painting and sculpture. It had been a watershed. Which way would the rivers run from that mountain crest? To the deep, sometimes rich ocean of the past, or into the shining seas of the future? Most of his friends had been working steadily since then, many of them breaking the patterns of light, the traditional brush strokes, the content. The work went on feverishly, artists completing the pictures they were determined to see hanging in the Salon. Unknowns had a sense that this was the year, since they had in good measure fulfilled their promises to themselves to be innovative in color, theme, composition; a giant step away from the classical past. They were no longer tyros, those with whom Camille had worked in the studios and ateliers, those he had met through the older Corot, Delacroix, Courbet.

"We're entitled to our confidence," one cried. "We've learned our craft. We've been diligent, honest. . . ."

"Alas, so are the mediocrities," said Paul Cézanne harshly.

"They won't dare turn us down," cried Claude Monet. "We've come too far."

"The jury won't like us," Whistler declared in his puckish fashion, "but they'll have to lump us . . . together."

In the last week of April 1863 three thousand aspirants converged on the entrances to the Palais de l'Industrie. For that one day the Palais storeroom was the hub of Paris. Painters poured in from the Right Bank, the Left Bank, the suburbs of Charonne and Bercy to the east, Auteuil and Grenelle to the west; artists of all ages, sizes, descriptions, carrying their pictures in carriages, on carts, on their backs; conglomerations of new and fashionable clothes, paint-spattered smocks of ancient lineage; high top hats and woolen caps, burnished boots and country clogs; the long-bearded, the clean-shaven. Camille carried his on foot, three moderate-sized ventures, paintings of the countryside villages. Manet had his *Luncheon on the Grass;* Whistler his *The White Girl;* Antoine Chintreuil three landscapes; the Desbrosses brothers, studies of autumn and evening; Jongkind, Claude Monet's newest teacher, three scenes of Holland's canals and countryside; Bracquemond and Armand Gautier finely etched prints. Fantin-Latour submitted a dreamlike skyscape in a thin gray wash. Gold frames were expensive but, being *de rigueur* for the jury, no frame, no presentation. The artists had somehow managed to buy or borrow them. Since Camille had three pictures he was eager to enter, he and Julie had scrimped during the preceding months to save the necessary money.

On all sides, setting their pictures against the walls, benches, tables, carpenters' horses, Camille saw faces he recognized out of the past eight years. Some few names came out of the mists: Cazin, Legros, Vollon, Junker, Danguy, Désiré, Cals, Bertaux, Harpignies, Lavieille, St. Marcel . . . a dozen others. Everywhere there was good cheer, cries of "This is the year. We'll make it. There'll be prizes and honors, then sales. . . ."

In 1859 Camille had been accepted; in 1861 rejected. Neither time had he felt such crackling expectancy, the high splurge of sangfroid. There was neither fear nor anxiety. Everyone had done nobly, everyone would be hung.

"In this euphoria," Whistler replied, "we're all going to Paradise; nobody is to be condemned to Purgatory."

Only Baudelaire was pessimistic. A journalist as well as a poet, most avenues of blocked information were open to him. He had gleaned, illicitly, a list of the jurors.

"The names haven't changed," he told the group at the

Brasserie des Martyrs. "The archpreservers of the past. Troglodytes. Neanderthals. They'll use their prehistoric clubs to batter your pictures into submission."

They had to wait five full days for the jury's results. Little was accomplished during that time. Paris went about its business as usual. Stores opened, salespersons displayed goods, banks extended credit, stocks were bought and sold on the Bourse. The bourgeois thought everything was normal; they did not know that the artists were tossing in bed, having dreams of glory or nightmares; that for a thousand creative hopefuls the globe was standing still.

The entire group came away with blurred *R*'s stamped on their wooden stretchers. Every last one of them. They were stunned. Each plunged into his particular version of gloom. Camille was hugely chagrined.

"Baudelaire was right," he declared. "We never had a chance . . . in spite of the fairy tales we told each other."

He joined the indignation-laden outbursts of those who had gambled and been, in their opinion, cheated; their ignominy flouted for the whole world of art to see. Nothing adequately expressed the group's detestation of the superintendent, Comte de Nieuwerkerke, or the members of the jury; among them the politer terms for him were *un Alphonse*, a pimp; *un têcheur*, a son of a bitch; *un boscard*, a parasite; *un bougre*, a bugger; *un carotteur*, a deceiver; *un escarpe*, a man who murders to steal; *un fumiste*, a bad joker; *un goujat*, a vulgar man; all the terms swept up from the lower depths of Parisian argot were helpful in relieving their passionate protest.

On the following night Camille's friends were quieter, determined to find a way out of their desperate situation. Edouard Manet said, in an unusually stern manner:

"My father, as a magistrate, has agreed to write to the Emperor."

"I'll write an article condemning the jury's choice," said Baudelaire, "and try to persuade my editor to run it."

"I'll call on Corot and Courbet to protest the rejections even though they themselves were accepted," Camille proffered.

Another man knew the Minister of Finance; he would persuade him to make demands on the government. Everyone had a friend who had a friend. . . . Many of the several thousand rejected pictures were still in the storehouse; for the first time in the history of the Beaux-Arts exhibitions offended painters had refused to move them.

"There's only one way to succeed," contributed Whistler

cynically. "Ridicule the jury and Comte de Nieuwerkerke as fools. Raise such an ungodly ruckus that all of Paris and Versailles will hear it."

Even Delacroix, deathly ill, joined his prestigious voice to the clamor. Others in the Parisian social circles contributed to the uproar. Avant-garde collectors became part of the chorus, crying:

"Paris is no longer the art capital of the world. It's become the outhouse of art."

Emperor Napoleon III heard the laments and outcries. Artists, who loathed him because he had abolished the French Republic and restored the monarchy, said:

"He doesn't want unhappiness in Paris. It's not good for his royal ass."

"He can't accomplish anything," Fantin-Latour insisted, he of the half-closed mystical eyes.

"Of course he can!" shouted Armand Guillaumin. "He's the Emperor, isn't he?"

Napoleon III arrived at the Salon in his gold carriage with the four matched bays. Comte de Nieuwerkerke had been ordered to have his assistant set up the rejected canvases still at the Salon so that the Emperor could view them from his comfortable throne chair brought in for the purpose. Baudelaire secured an accurate account of the proceedings from a Beaux-Arts workman. The Emperor spent two hours reviewing the rejects, then, after a luncheon in an apartment in the Louvre, returned to study the accepted canvases on the walls. Baudelaire reported the conversation between Napoleon III and Comte de Nieuwerkerke, his longtime friend and one of his favorites, in part because he was the adored lover of one of Napoleon III's cousins.

"*Monsieur le Comte*, the paintings that have been refused are as good as the ones that were accepted."

"Not in the opinion of the jury, Your Majesty."

"The jury be damned! They're as full of prejudices as a stray dog is of fleas."

"Doubtless so, Your Majesty. But they were chosen by the Académie as our official body to decide the fate . . ."

"Nonsense! There must be something you can do. Why else have I appointed you Superintendent of Fine Arts?"

"Your Majesty, forgive me, but there is no room in the Beaux-Arts for all these rejected ones."

"Then hang them somewhere else. I'm not going to have a revolution on my hands because a few hundred painters have been cast aside."

The Comte de Nieuwerkerke, a polished politician, knew when it was time to retreat.

"There is a building across from the Palais de l'Industrie. It is empty right now. We could hang everything there."

"Good. I knew you'd find a solution."

"We'll call it the Salon des Refusés."

The painters were elated. They had won. The Emperor had issued a royal decree in their favor. They would be shown, they would be reviewed in the press.

The only one to object to this sentiment was Corot. He sent for Camille, said to him sternly:

"Don't become part of a group. You become labeled. There is no escape."

"You are part of a group, Papa Corot. The Fontainebleau School: you, Millet, Rousseau, Daubigny, Diaz. . . ."

"With a difference," cried Corot. "We worked separately, then after twenty-five years the public linked us together as a school. We were already beginning to be established, so the group name could not hurt us. You are just starting and are self-consciously binding yourself into a sheaf under the worst possible auspices, the Rejected Ones. The public will take its hint from the name and reject you as the jury has."

"But not without looking at us! Without being seen we don't exist. Our paintings are stacked against walls. So are we."

"Take my word for it, Pissarro, you will all be destroyed."

"This is our only chance to come to life."

"I do my work and let *le bon Dieu* do the rest."

Camille said, "The good Lord has more patience than we can afford."

Corot laughed.

"*D'accord.* I will be at your opening. You're going to need someone at hand who approves your work."

The Salon de Refusés was to open on May 15, two weeks after the official Salon. An announcement was made in the *Moniteur* that the exhibition would be elective and artists who did not want to take part need only inform the administration, which would hasten to return their works to them. They had until May 7 to withdraw. Beyond that limit their pictures would be placed in the galleries.

Close to a hundred of the rejected painters met in the roomiest studio available, sitting on chairs brought in, on rugs, or on the bare floor. Because it appeared that there would not be an official catalogue, each chipped in a couple of francs. Someone knew a sympathetic printer who had agreed to do the work at cost, plus one painting drawn by lottery. A number of the more experienced painters, Chintreuil, Desbrosses, Junker, Dupuis, offered to undertake the labor of the cataloguing: 656 paintings, 27 prints and 4 architectural plans still available, listing the artists with a brief description of each. There was a serious difference when someone suggested that all of the works should not be shown; that they should insist on being their own jury.

"We must be selective," cried one. "We cannot let in bad canvases." Another shouted: "In any exhibition the worst pictures get the most attention from the critics." "We will all be tarred by the same brush," from still another.

Camille listened to the clamor. He was by no means a leader of the group but at this point found it important to speak out.

"The rejected ones acting as rejectors? Creating the same jury system that eliminated us? Oh no! We were all rejected together."

"Come, Pissarro," retorted Edouard Manet, "some of the rejected ones are hopelessly bad."

"Let the public decide that. Would you have the Emperor order a second Salon des Refusés out of this Salon des Refusés?"

There were groans and protests but the consensus was that Camille Pissarro was right: all the rejected paintings still submitted would have to be shown regardless of merit. When the meeting adjourned, a number of the artists, some of whom Camille knew only slightly, shook his hand. A few turned away.

Though he did not concern himself overly about such matters, his stand for the refused ones became known. Also the news that Comte de Nieuwerkerke had formed a special committee to hang the Refusés exhibition. Paris had heard about the additional exhibition forced upon Comte de Nieuwerkerke by Napoleon III. It was expected there would be a large attendance. Of all the artists Camille knew, only Piette was not to be represented. From Montfoucault he wrote saying that the man who had been representing his work had refused to relinquish any of the gouaches unless the Salon officially requested them . . . a request the Salon did not bother to answer.

The opening of the official Beaux-Arts Salon on April 30, 1863, was attended by the usual court coterie and several thousand Parisians interested in the social panoply of the art exhibition. The jury had been led by a man named Signol, who gave a prize to Baudry's *The Pearl and the Wave,* a young woman voluptuously extended on the bank receiving the embraces of the caressing waves. Tissot was praised. Meissonier's prodigious *Battle of Solferino* received a laudatory article. The Barbizon School was singled out for praise; Corot and Millet described by the judges as "foremost." Gustave Courbet was infuriated because he had been described as "fading and passing away." Flandrin's *Portrait of the Emperor* was judged "the most important work of the exhibit."

The critic Paul Mantz wrote:

It is an honest and prudent French school mediocrely inspired. The general effect is sleepy.

Le Figaro's critic was also disappointed with the Salon.

The two weeks preceding the Salon des Refusés dragged unmercifully. When, a couple of days prior to the opening, the Emperor announced that he and his Empress, which meant the full court, would attend the showing of the unwanted ones, a shock wave went through Paris. Everyone who had been at the opening of the official Salon would have to attend this second Salon to see and be seen by Their Majesties, as well as that part of the public which doted on such public displays. It was expected that there would be an enormous crowd.

"We'll have a great success," cried the ebullient Claude Monet.

Camille responded, "You see, to be rejected is not the same as being ignored."

On the day of the opening he and his colleagues assembled in the passageway between the Palais de l'Industrie and the adjoining building shortly before the opening hour. They found the exhibit as luxuriously mounted as that of the official Salon. Antique tapestries hung in the doorways. The walls were covered in green baize. The benches were made comfortable with red velvet cushions. The skylights were covered with white cotton screens to cut the glare. There was a long series of display rooms. All like the official Salon . . . except for the pictures. The brightness of their color, the mood, the authenticity of the figures and the presence of fresh air. The feeling of youth, of gaiety. Of innovation.

On a closer view it was seen that Comte de Nieuwerkerke and the official hanging committee had had a subtle but no less diabolical revenge: choosing what they agreed to be the most ludicrous pictures to be placed in the most prominent places in the first and major gallery, where they would be seen immediately by the viewers and would set the tone of their reaction.

In the two areas they termed "the places of dishonor" were Edouard Manet's *Luncheon on the Grass,* two gentlemen fully clothed in vests, jackets and cravats, and two women entirely naked, sitting and gathering flowers, beside them the picnic basket and its luxurious contents overflowing into the foreground. James McNeill Whistler's *The White Girl* presented a copper-haired young lady dressed in white, standing in front of an all-white curtain, a massing of white on white, telling no story as did the pictures of the time. They were the two most original canvases in the exhibition. Nothing similar had ever been painted.

Camille's three pictures were a short distance away. On the opposite wall were scenes by Claude Monet, Fantin-Latour, Antoine Guillaumin and, across from them, the oils by Paul Cézanne. The succeeding rooms represented a hundred other artists, all pictures which the Emperor had deemed as good as the ones selected by the jury. Many might be thought dull but they were reasonably safe from ridicule.

There was a smattering of the biblical, *Christ and the Woman Taken in Adultery, Jezebel Dead;* military subjects; classical myths, Greek and Roman themes.

Cézanne gazed at Camille with the closest thing to affection on that perennially suspicious face. "Pissarro, you got everybody in. When they establish a category for saints at the Académie Française, I'm going to nominate you!"

The exhibit conveyed an atmosphere of youth, determination, even the exotic odor of fanaticism. There was an equally charged expectancy on the faces of the painters, the alert, coiled-spring stance of their figures giving the exhibition rooms a feeling of buoyancy.

For a time after the noon-hour opening the artists were largely alone. Emile Zola, Cézanne's schoolboy friend from Aix-en-Provence, made a tour of the exhibition, taking notes. He aspired to be an art critic and to place the article in an important journal. He observed:

The walls are covered with a mixture of the excellent and execrable. Last-ditchers of the historical school cheek by jowl with youthful fanatics of realism. Colorless mediocrity next to blatant originality. Nothing has been left out, not even medieval subjects heavily scored with bitumen. Superficially it is an incoherent jumble, but there is truth and sincerity enough about the landscapes and sufficient points of technical interest in most of the portraits to give it a healthy atmosphere of youthful passion and vigor.

The early tricklers stood in front of *Luncheon on the Grass* and *The White Girl*, saying nothing, their faces masks of doubt and confusion. It was not until three o'clock that the people began to pour in. When His Majesty arrived, the crowd grew dense. There was an increasing crush of hundreds of viewers before the Manet and the Whistler, pushing, shoving, elbowing, everyone wanting to get closer. Almost no one left the first gallery, the main stage of the entertainment as designed by the Salon hanging committee.

It grew increasingly hot; the dust from the earthen floor cogged Camille's nostrils. He was captivated by the ominous silence. Then it started: grunts, explosive expulsions of breath, expletives, followed by chortles, full-blown laughter, roars of derisive merriment, the women putting their handkerchiefs over their mouths to stifle their outbursts; the men holding in their stomachs while their shouted imprecations laced with guffaws filled the exhibition hall. It was loudest before Manet's *Luncheon on the Grass*.

"They're whores. . . . The painter is mad. . . . He's immoral! . . . We're being made fools of. It should be cut into shreds. No wonder it was rejected. . . ."

The outburst in front of *The White Girl* was not because she was profane, for the young woman was fully clothed. There was a deeper, ominous note in the ridicule and irreverent disparagement. Fear. Not the fear of their exposure to immorality, but a challenge to everything they would have known and accepted in painting. If Manet and Whistler were right, the public had been wrong. It was frightening to know that the world had passed them by and their taste was junked.

The abuse filled the hall more densely than the dust, the laughter was hysterical in an attempt to deride the new art into oblivion. The ribald derision which engulfed *Luncheon on the Grass* and *The White Girl* swept over the entire "Salon of Infamy," as it began to be called, leaving the painters bruised, bewildered, shrinking inside themselves.

Camille heard his paintings called "stillscapes." David Jacobsen, whose paintings hung high in a back room, nursed a misery different from that of Edouard Manet, James McNeill Whistler, or even Camille Pissarro. For all intents and purposes his canvases had simply not been there at all.

When Camille reached home, unaware of what route he had trudged to get there, caught in the vise of a violent loathing of the multitude that had thrashed them so mercilessly, he found Julie eagerly awaiting him.

"Tell me what happened?"

"Nothing happened. We were laughed out of court."

"All of you?"

"Those of us they thought worthy of desecration."

She picked Lucien up from his crib, fitted herself and the boy into his arms. The warm feeling of the child, the sensation of the life he and Julie had created, set his pulse beating faster. He smiled at her, a faint smile.

"As I told Cézanne, do not attempt to convince your peers. The next generation will understand you. We have only to survive."

BOOK SIX

The Sheaves and
the Stars

1

IT WAS A village house of rough fieldstone in La Varenne, built for cooking and sleeping, the kitchen serving as the family living room with a small window alcove into which was fitted the eating table. There was an open fireplace. On the side were alcove shelves which held Julie's dishes and jugs; an enclosed well with pulleys was in the corner. Camille called in the local carpenter to build them a cabinet above the stove to hold their pitchers, baskets, potagers, molds, candlesticks. For eating, reading, sewing, they had their low rush-covered seats. He gave the scuffed terra-cotta tiles a coat of wax, then painted the exposed wall a fresh gray. The remainder of the house consisted of two bedrooms, rather like nests, with a connecting door. The neglected plaster was flaking. After the walls had been sandpapered, Camille put on a coat of the light color Julie wanted.

When he found himself in the country, not just for a month's excursion but with a place of his own, he regained the youthful enchantment of his early years in Caracas where he painted the natives in their rural settings.

He told his parents about the house and the countryside. La Varenne was fifteen miles southeast of Paris, over an hour by train.

"Do you have to live like a peasant?" Rachel asked.

"No, Maman, I don't have to be a peasant to paint one. But I do have to live among them. I want to know the basic truth of the land and its people."

"Anyone with eyes can see the landscape."

"*C'est vrai.* Just as anyone with a mind can see what's

going on in human affairs. But it takes a Victor Hugo to produce a full portrait of society and bring out its meaning."

Rachel turned away. Frédéric, who had volunteered to pay the rent, which was no higher than their half of the Montmartre house, said when his wife had left the room:

"It will be better for Julie in the country, and you'll be surrounded by motifs, whatever that means. Just continue to come home for dinner often enough so your mother knows you haven't resigned from the family. The hardest thing is to stay friendly with those you love."

La Varenne was a village with a few shops and half a dozen named streets; their house was on the Rue Hyacinthe. It had in recent years ceased to be altogether provincial; two artists had lived there a few years before; painters came out from Paris to sketch the slightly harsh countryside. It was helpful for the villagers to know that there was such a breed as a painter. They would not ask, "What is your job? How do you earn a living?" A few Parisian families were beginning to spend summers there to escape the city heat. It was an ancient village but had never been prosperous; the farm owners made a living, *tout juste*. The harvest was dependable but afforded few luxuries. Camille and Julie fitted well into the marginal ambiance.

Julie was too happy to be in the country to concern herself about Camille's status. He had chosen his profession. She was being accepted by the village and farmers' wives, albeit grudgingly; in hamlets where families had lived for generations new friendships were hard come by. They recognized her as a young peasant woman from a distant area, Grancey in Burgundy, and did not know that she was unmarried. She was content to be accepted.

Julie knew how to be a country wife. For a few centimes she bought baby chicks and rabbits, put up a rabbit hutch; planted in their yard the vegetables she had raised in Grancey: carrots, cabbages, turnips, green beans.

"How much money do we have to live on a week?" she asked.

"Four dollars."

"We won't starve; there'll be chickens and rabbits and eggs and vegetables. After a while I'll have enough to swap for milk and fruit. Bread we buy cheap; a little *vin ordinaire*, a piece of meat for our soup."

There came for Camille the mystique of the country; each day brought a revelation of the subtlety and complexity of the life and landscape before him. Two subjects fascinated him.

The first he painted as *Entering a Village* with two houses and a long low barn at the rear, bright refreshing spring greens on both sides of the dirt path leading into the village; a single peasant woman in a blue blouse and green skirt walking toward the viewer as though to meet him under an overcast gray sky.

Without his realizing it there had always been, from the first days of his painting in St. Thomas, either a road or path stretching ahead so that the viewer stepped onto it and walked its length; or a figure or two walking with their backs turned so that the viewer wished to catch up or to join them; a person approaching whom one waited with curiosity to identify.

The second painting, called *Corner of a Village*, pictured the tiny social area of La Varenne, an open square where a few chickens clucked; four women in white caps chatted on a bench under a rounding stone wall, an oddly shaped gabled house just beyond. It was not a picture of singular beauty but this was a corner of every village, the women enjoying a moment of surcease from almost constant toil, a grouping that made the countryside more social and supportive.

He was painting *en plein air* in oils. Then in the kitchen, with an easel set up by the window table, he did some retouching.

"Camille, have you noticed that our food tastes slightly of turpentine?" Julie asked.

"I guess that seems natural to me; I have the smell of it in my nostrils."

"I'll never be a great cook, but chicken à la turpentine? I'm going to put the screen we used in David's studio around you and your easel."

"With a little luck our next house will be bigger. I'll have a studio away from the kitchen."

He attended Delacroix's state funeral. The entire artist colony was there. Not a soul of them but had benefited greatly from his courage, talent, dedication. There was no sadness. Eugène Delacroix had completed an enormous body of work, had had a magnificently fulfilled life. The artists spoke of their favorite paintings: *Massacre at Chios, Women of Algiers*. He would live forever.

In August Camille received a letter from Alfred in Montevideo telling him he was coming permanently to Paris:

". . . I must leave by the next English packet, so give me the pleasure of finding me a small apartment, from five to six hundred francs, in the central area, whether Rue St. Lazare or Montholon. You will immediately install my furniture. I need a rather pretty bedroom, a small sitting room and some closets. . . .''

He also implied that Camille was to meet a ''person'' at Southampton. He found an apartment within Alfred's price range and location. The ''person'' was never mentioned again.

After drawing fastidiously for weeks on the largest project he had yet envisioned, *The Ferry at La Varenne*, he grew hungry for company of his own kind. He took an early train into Paris, then the omnibus to Passy. Rachel was pleased by his healthy glow from the La Varenne sun.

''Your trips into the country are good for you, Camille,'' his mother said. ''You should go more often.''

Camille and Frédéric exchanged a glance. His mother had not accepted the fact that he was living out of Paris.

After lunch he went in search of Claude Monet, who was still working at Gleyre's atelier. He would know the news of the art world.

Camille found Gleyre's at the end of an enclosed courtyard. He climbed several flights of stairs, stood in the open doorway of a room crowded with some forty students. Large and unwashed north windows let in a hazy light. The walls were covered with caricatures of public persons, rubbed out and daubed over with unwanted paint from a hundred palettes. There was a nude model on a platform, a fire to keep him warm, about fifty low chairs, a hatchwork of easels and drawing boards. A little man in spectacles, elderly and unwell, Gleyre himself was going from easel to easel suggesting improvements, quiet, melancholic despite the fact that he had earned a late fame with his painting. He approved of his students practicing open-air landscape painting. Having been kept out of the better studios in his youth because he was too poor to pay the fees, he charged nothing for his services, letting his *massier* collect the monies necessary to pay the rent and the models, which came to two dollars a month for each student.

Camille spied Monet slashing away with charcoal on his drawing pad. He was sitting with one leg under the other on a low stool.

''Pissarro, how good to see you,'' Monet cried. ''Where have you been hiding?''

''In a landscape you have to visit and paint. How does it go?''

''Tolerably. I'm tired of this musty studio. Let's have a beer.''

They had no sooner settled at the small marble-topped table on the narrow quiet sidewalk of the Café Guerbois than Paul Cézanne walked in with a tall blond giant who looked more like a Scandinavian than a Frenchman, and who walked stooped over so that his shorter friends would not be uncomfortable. Cézanne introduced him gruffly:

"This is Frédéric Bazille, a medical student who practices painting on the side."

"Wrong!" sang out Bazille in a basso profundo voice; "I'm a painter who goes to medical school on the side. Who keeps failing his anatomy examinations."

Bazille shook hands warmly, pulled up an iron openwork chair.

"My father insisted I enter medical school. My family's house in Montpellier is across the street from Alfred Bruyas, who financed Gustave Courbet's one-man exhibition in 1855. His house is filled with Courbets and Delacroix. He is a penetrating teacher. He taught me right out of medical school and into art."

"Quelle chance," Camille murmured.

"Vraiment! I paint at Gleyre's in the morning and in the afternoon I take courses at the Faculty of Medicine. If I fail the exams a second time my father will have to be reconciled."

Over their drink, with their heads of necessity close together at the tiny table's surface, they plunged into an animated dissection of *en plein air* painting versus studio work, the bound-to-the-past juries of the Salon, how to get one's work accepted without imitating the imitators. One suggestion was that they blow up the Beaux-Arts building during a full meeting of the Academy. Another was that they burn down the Louvre. Cézanne proffered the idea that the academics be pensioned off with the Legion of Honor and five acres in Algeria. He had adopted Bazille as one of his rare friends because Bazille came from the South of France and therefore could be trusted by a Provençal. Cézanne whispered to Camille:

"He's young, only twenty-one, but he has sincerity. His work is less harsh than mine; his nature is not so intransigent."

Camille took to the blond giant with the deep, mellow voice. Bazille admired landscape painters but himself wanted to work inside for a while, group portraits mostly, showing the times through the people who made them. He was an intellectual, fascinated by the theories of literature, art, music, the theater. Camille saw that this new associate, besides being tall and athletic, with blue eyes and a roguish beard, held himself and his views in an unpretentious manner. After an hour of animated discussion Bazille cried:

"The drinks are on me. Let's go over to my studio on the Rue des Beaux-Arts. I share it with a painter who is one of a kind, Pierre Auguste Renoir, young, twenty-two, son of a tailor from Limoges. He started earning his living painting porcelain at the age of thirteen. You'll find him interesting "

Claude Monet begged off, but Cézanne and Camille, who was in Paris for just such refreshment, went along.

The studio that Bazille shared with Renoir was a small one in the Batignolles quarter. When they had trudged up the three flights of dark narrow stairs Bazille flung open a door, revealing a young man dressed in a workman's smock seated calmly at an easel. Without pause, Bazille cried out:

"I'm bringing you two recruits. Permit me to introduce Camille Pissarro of St. Thomas in the islands; and Paul Cézanne of Aix-en-Provence."

Renoir asked shyly, "Recruits for what?"

Frédéric Bazille replied, "For fresh concepts of painting."

Renoir rose, shook hands with a boyish smile, said, "I didn't know I was in a war, but if I am I'm glad to have armed foot soldiers trudging alongside me. Though I thought I was through with the army when I escaped the seven-year draft lottery."

Camille gazed with interest at the man. Slender, graceful face, light brown hair, nonintellectual eyes, a longish neck which a high starched collar could only half cover; a slender, lithe body with mildly drooping shoulders, a dark mustache to make him look more mature.

Bazille, with a bountiful allowance, brought out an expensive bottle of brandy which the four of them drank instead of supper. . . . It loosened their tongues. Camille told about his two years of sketching in Caracas; Bazille recounted his first days at Gleyre's, how homesick he had been in the gray overcast of Paris after sun-drenched Montpellier. Cézanne complained about Emile Zola, who had spent years getting him to come to Paris and now was critical of his painting. Renoir was the only one of the four who had grown up in Paris. Camille enjoyed listening to his plain, workingman's voice, as he told how the stagecoach from Limoges had taken over two weeks, that the family's first apartment in Paris was the size of a handkerchief.

"My father, a good tailor, sat cross-legged on a little wooden platform in the parlor, where he received his customers surrounded by rolls of cloth samples, scissors, a little red velvet cushion covered with needles and pins fastened on his forearm. At night he cleared the platform, brought in a mattress and bedclothes, and that's where my brother and I slept.''

"Paint it!" growled Cézanne. "I can see it vividly."

"Too mundane." Renoir continued reflectively, "I have an aversion to doing anything I don't like. I liked painting porcelain; vases, plates, copies of Sèvres and Limoges. I started painting Marie Antoinette in profile on dessert plates for three sous each. I wanted to copy Watteau and Boucher but my boss didn't allow it. For five years, from thirteen to eighteen, I made a handsome salary. It was easy, I wasn't bothered by ideas. What goes on inside my head doesn't interest me. I want to feel, to touch, to see."

Camille shook his head slowly. He himself was very much interested in what went on inside his head.

"This notion of Rousseau's that men are born knowing everything they will ever know is a literary fancy," said Renoir. "We have all sorts of possibilities in us. It took me years to discover painting; going to the Louvre. But I am just beginning, I go on making mistakes."

Renoir had visited the Louvre on his lunch hour instead of eating with his fellow workers. That was when he had fallen in love with Fragonard's portraits of good-natured bourgeoise women. The wife of his boss at the kiln, wearing a low-cut bodice, had leaned over his work while he was decorating ceramics. He declared he had been too young to be seduced; yet he had been moved.

"Don't trust anybody who doesn't get excited at the sight of a pretty breast," he pontificated.

They emptied the brandy bottle. They were exuberant. Camille, at thirty-three, was the elder of the group.

Renoir had lost his job because of the competition from machine-stamped porcelain.

"I next painted blinds, with plenty of clouds. A cloud can be daubed on with a few brush strokes. I made a lot of money. Then I met girls. You do foolish things when you are young. It doesn't matter then because you haven't yet taken on any responsibilities. But afterwards you'd be a fool to play around with cheap tarts instead of amusing yourself with painting."

He had counted his savings, decided that he could live on them frugally for a couple of years and took the plunge, registering at the Atelier Gleyre. Here he had become friends with Bazille, who admired the way he drew. Soon they were sharing this small studio.

Camille told of the hundreds of sketches he had made of Parisian street life, its buildings, markets, parks, people, when he arrived. Of how he too had painted skies, for Anton Melbye's giant maritime scenes.

He returned to La Varenne on the last train, sleepy from the brandy, to which he was not accustomed, glowing with the joy of having met Frédéric Bazille and Auguste Renoir, and their easy fellowship. Surely with Cézanne and Monet, with the wealthy Antoine Guillemet, the poor civil servant Armand Guillaumin, Whistler, Piette, Jacobsen, Edouard Manet, Fantin-Latour there was enough potential among them to make some kind of impression on the art world.

2

They had thrived through the hot summer months. Lucien, out of doors under a shade tree most of the day, grew lustily. Julie cared for her garden and poultry and, when the La Varenne potato crop was ready to be harvested, worked in the fields with the farm women, earning as her pay enough sacks of potatoes to last the family through the winter.

"Potatoes are harder to pick than grapes," she told Camille; "but I like to dig with my hands. Besides, the women are nicer to me now that I've worked with them."

Camille painted contentedly, his head under a wide-brimmed straw hat. La Varenne was not on a river but the Marne made a wide loop around the village. He was sketching avidly the river with its crude ferry, a one-man dugout; the oblong white omnibus waiting with its black and white horse team reflected in the water; a group of travelers on the bank near the coach waiting for the last passenger to be ferried; and beyond, light green hills espaliered with dark trees, yellow-tan village houses on the crest.

Other days he went farther afield to Chennevières to draw the wide expanse of the river Marne and its populated banks, the viewer gliding slowly downstream, seeing the stone-wall settlement on one bank, two-story, opulent houses on the other, the line of poplars, the falling-away green mountain slope.

"I'd like this view of the Marne to be unforgettable," he admonished himself. "Why? So that people will come back to it, walk along the banks, ride slowly down the river in a skiff, feel that they are flowing through life the way the Marne flows through the fertile countryside."

He had days of frustration when he could not get onto the canvas what his eye could so clearly see, when the oil colors seemed to have a mind of their own, the brush strokes refused to do his bidding. Then he would come home exhausted, with half a painting, not finding anything on the canvas he had meant to put there.

Camille and Julie mixed with the villagers and peasants. Most farms were modest sized, the owners middle class; all had laborers helping to clear the land, fertilize, plant, irrigate, prune, harvest. For the hired hands it was a long succession of hard-labor days from first light to dusk; but there was no poverty. People ate adequately; clothing was unimportant; there was shelter from the elements. Camille rarely invaded private property except to cross on communal paths. Mostly he painted from roads, embankments, a copse overlooking the river. The owners did not feel that he was intruding; they merely looked at him in befuddlement that a grown man could spend a whole day working with tubes of oil paint instead of farm implements.

Piette and Adèle had been urging them to visit Montfoucault. Piette was spending less and less time in Paris. The farm needed managing, and he was not happy with his studio painting or his sketches when he worked in the outskirts of Neuilly or Grenelle. Finally he had decided to give up the studio and apartment and remain permanently at Montfoucault.

In late September, with the crops gathered, Julie said:

"Why not have a month vacation? Lucien will be no trouble and you like to paint around Mayenne."

"It's flavorsome country. But Piette's farm isn't doing well. I'll offer to pay something toward our keep."

Piette replied: "It will be done to your liking concerning the little contribution that you wish to make to my household expenses since you will then feel more comfortable and extend your stay. In order to avoid gossip I must believe you are married and you must make me believe this. It is stupid but necessary."

Adèle had been ill, she was paler and thinner, but Julie's arrival revived her. Piette, grown a bit grayer with worry, had lost some of his helpers for lack of money to pay a rudimentary wage. That did not spoil their pleasure in helping to gather the apple crop, part of which Piette insisted on sending to La Varenne.

"Mashed potatoes with applesauce," Julie enthused. "Lucien will like that. Better'n *bouillie de maïs*."

"It will make me corpulent," said Camille with a grin; for nothing had ever managed to put an ounce of fat on his trim figure.

Julie helped Adèle with the housework. Doing it together proved to be more pleasure than work.

"I wish you could live here permanently," Adèle exclaimed. "We have only Piette's aunt in Le Mans, and we rarely see her."

Julie answered with what Adèle must have known, that Camille had to visit his parents, meet with his artist friends, try to find someone to sell his work.

Once the apple harvest was in the two men went out with their easel boxes each day. Camille again grasped the Mayenne countryside. One inclement day he worked in Piette's parlor on four small studies of the local flowers. He gave one to Piette, one to Georges Thouvenal, an old man who had been a friend of Piette's father; and two for the vestibule of the small church on the knoll. As they worked together Camille recognized that, although Piette was radical in his political desire to overthrow Napoleon III, he was a conventional painter. He was happy for him that he continued as mayor of the hamlet of Montfoucault.

Winter of 1863 in La Varenne began with cold, rain, snow. Camille and Julie gathered firewood before the sleet closed them down, chopped it to proper lengths for the stove and fireplace. She kept bricks in her oven during the cooking of supper, as she had for her little dormer room in Passy, putting them in their bed later to keep their feet warm. Unlike the inclement weather in Paris which had driven him indoors, Camille found the winter scene around La Varenne fascinating. He could not keep away from it. He caught cold several times. Julie laid down the law.

"You cannot go out while it's raining or snowing. You'll get pneumonia . . . and give it to Lucien."

"It's so beautiful," he protested. "Nature angry, erupting, the trees bare, the roads and paths obliterated."

When the storms stopped he bundled himself up and went into the village and countryside to draw the snow-covered fields, the rain-drenched roads and houses, the few huddling creatures making their way of necessity toward some unwanted chore. One shopkeeper spoke with him as he crouched in a doorway trying to capture the mood of the deserted village, with its silent population indoors around their fires.

"Monsieur Pissarro, the weather is abominable, the trees

are bare, the ground stiff. We have had painters here before. They went out only on good days. Why do you want to paint our winter death?''

"It's not death, Monsieur Alain. It's another part of the life cycle. The opposite side of the shield to summer. It has its own beauty: stark, drenched, frozen, yet alive and ready to be reborn.''

With spring there were peasants hoeing, spading, pushing wheelbarrows, planting, climbing terraces, tending the animals, children working in the fields at the side of their parents. Girls prattled on a town bench, washed their feet in the brook; mothers breast-fed their infants while watching their dinners being cooked in big black iron pots. Budding branches extended in a horizontal line across the flowing stream. There were women pounding their heavy clothing with rocks to beat out the winter's dirt; houses, barns, toolsheds, barnyards with animals mixing familially; bends in the river; trees swaying in the wind, the trunks each radically different; a minuscular man plowing behind a barely suggested draft animal in a sea of furrowed soil; villages with their ancient stone walls and peaked roofs pointing at each other in a haphazard mélange. A lifetime of painting!

He achieved the sun rising, the sun *couchant,* trails wandering through rolling ranges; haycocks lying in the open; groups of men threshing the grain, women winnowing it; tall shade trees standing guard over the hamlet as carpenters, stonemasons went about the craft of building. Animals grazed or lay under the trees.

When Julie saw the dozens, then hundreds, of sketches pile up she asked, as much in a quandry as in exasperation:

"Can you sell these drawings?''

"They are not made to be sold.''

"Why then?''

"They are studies for the oils.''

"Can't you make the oils right away?''

"These are the foundation stones on which to build the house.''

He leaned down and lightly kissed the breast from which she was feeding Lucien.

"Lucien is happy with you, look at him dig! So am I, albeit for different reasons. We have a roof over our heads, coats on our backs, and our bellies are almost full. What more could we ask?''

*   *   *

215

He drew and drew and drew: cows, sheep, lambs in every posture; haycocks; red-cheeked youngsters, gnarly lumpy-faced oldsters; peasants dressed for Sunday church, with hats and umbrellas; young girls in their striped blouses; young boys reading books; women combing their hair, milking the cows from low stools; cattle drinking from the river; women with bundles on their backs, leaning against a tree to rest; groups of faces listening.

His drawing skills came from sources in his youth: the popular magazines with excellent drawings which had been available to him in St. Thomas. He had learned from Fritz and then Anton Melbye, from Corot, Courbet and Delacroix, the sturdy draftsmen; Chintreuil and Desbrosses whom he first met at the Brasserie Andler; Honoré Daumier, whose slashing satiric cartoons appeared for years in the Paris press, *La Caricature* and *Le Charivari*. It was necessary to draw, draw and draw until one was no longer an outsider looking in but an integral part of the picture gazing out.

He changed from hard pencil to the softer chalks and charcoals in conjunction with a light wash. At Montmorency and La Roche-Guyon he had marked his drawings with notes: *porte lumière, lumière, ombre, ombre foncée.* Now he wrestled with the tonal variations. His new drawings were more formally constructed, more disciplined. He was concerned with draftsmanship, the oil painter's chief tool, and wanted to paint a rural world that was timeless. That which does not pass in that which passes.

3

In May Piette again urged Camille to visit Montfoucault:

"You cannot imagine how much everything has changed, what varied, tender greens nature displays. Everything has become resplendent in the last few days. You could make a well-finished masterpiece and other studies that would be precious for color and delicacy. . . ."

He was delayed by his brother Alfred's illness, which put him to bed with a high fever. Camille spent several days in Paris nursing him with cold packs and hot drinks, sleeping in Passy. When Alfred got no better Camille decided to call on the eccentric Dr. Paul Gachet, known by the artists as "an

Original" for his bizarre dress, the yellow-dyed hair, his belief in the new science of immunization of healthy patients as a form of preventive medicine. Camille had met the man at the Brasserie Andler, wearing a Russian fur hat in winter. He was supposed to have the same diagnostic nose for talent as he had for an illness. His own painting was poor but he was convinced that in some mystical way he was the one creating the good work of art when he saved the life of the better artist.

He found Dr. Gachet at his clinic in the Rue du Faubourg St. Denis and took him to Alfred's. Dr. Gachet prescribed herbs and other *outré* medications which dispelled the fever. Alfred asked, "How am I to pay Dr. Gachet?" To which Camille replied that Dr. Gachet was slightly demented. He would accept drawings, watercolors.

"I've promised him my next oil and he says I'm going to make him immortal."

His year's work was justified when the Salon jury of 1864 accepted two of his oils: a study near La Varenne and a picture of La Roche-Guyon, completed from sketches he had made there. The jury, having been rebuked by Napoleon III the year before as being rigidly exclusive, leaned over backwards. One journal commented, "Never have peasants, male and female, been so numerously represented at the Salon." Edouard Manet, Auguste Renoir, Henri Fantin-Latour had also been accepted. Paul Cézanne, as in the past, was rejected.

The younger, more radically painting artists known as the "Batignolles" group because they had earlier gravitated to the Rue des Batignolles neighborhood to live, met in its various cafés. They made the Café Guerbois their own. It was a middle-class café, the drinks were inexpensive. The artists hung their overcoats on hooks behind them but kept their hats on. The tables were attended by mustached waiters in the traditional long wraparound aprons. The group was different from Courbet's Brasserie Andler, as was the café; it was not a social eating-and-drinking gathering. Each man paid his way with common involvement. They were diverse, iconoclastic, fiercely individual, all with potential talent and power, their own nascent ideas for which they loved to battle, but different in appearance and personality, some quiet, some flamboyant. All except Manet, Bazille and Guillemet were as short on money as they were long on determination to bring their paintings to life. Many other artists drifted in, felt ill at ease in the company of the rampant egoists, fell away.

The accepted ones gathered to celebrate their Salon endorsement, drinking beer and emitting clouds of smoke. There was laughter, self-congratulation, some of them convinced they would acquire supportive critics, dealers, collectors.

Paul Cézanne walked in, head hunched between his shoulders, every feature of his face exuding rage, every pore of his body hostile, insulted, furious. The air became heavy with sympathy.

"Singled out for rejection," he growled in the thick Provençal accent. "Am I the least talented of us all? Do I not know how to paint? Am I still a hopeless amateur? *Je me vois au pied du mur sans échelle*. I'm at the foot of the wall without a ladder."

Each painter grasped his hand, expressed his contempt at the exclusion. Antoine Guillemet thrust a glass of wine into Cézanne's hand.

"Down a sweet beverage instead of salty tears. You'll have your revenge on that jury."

Camille said, "Let's go up to your studio, Paul, and see why you are not good enough for them, or are so much better than the rest of us."

Not all left the celebration, but a considerable contingent did. Those who cared little for Cézanne, finding him hypersensitive, humorless and ill-mannered, stayed behind. Only he had had the nerve to apply for admission to the Beaux-Arts School of the Salon, though he had failed to pass the tests. Besides, he frequently disrupted the Café Guerbois with outbursts out of proportion to the idea that had offended him.

Cézanne had a bleak attic room with sharply descending eaves and a dirt-covered dormer window. He said roughly:

"My father is a banker. Bankers loan money. Loaned money earns interest. His allowance to me earns no interest, it is a dead loss. That's what galls him. Why would a man leave behind an only son who will hate his memory all the years that he lives?"

The artists set about examining Cézanne's sketches and unfinished oils. There was a turgid silence in the studio, reactions, acceptances, rejections flowed about the attic room, sometimes clashing in midair, with no way for the ill-concealed emotion to get out of the sealed dormer. One group of subjectless drawings and oils seemed slashed onto the paper and canvas with a wild morbidity, the pencil, charcoal or brush stroke having a feverish intensity, Cézanne expressing his outrage at life. *The Autopsy, The Laying in the Tomb, The Funeral Cloth* were dark and gloomy. Many of the pictures contained a mysticism which Camille could not understand;

nor could he recognize it as arising from nature: wine bottles humanly misshapen. However the self-portraits, portraits of his mother and sister, of the Negro Scipio were clear and strong. So were his still lifes; tables with pears and apples and flowers, colorful and firm in the flesh, beautiful with life, quiet, almost lovingly formed. There was also a study for a canvas to be called *Bread and Eggs*.

"He hasn't made up his mind what he wants to say," Camille decided.

"*Alors*," Cézanne cried, "what do you think? Am I too good for the Salon or too bad? The time will come when a bunch of carrots truthfully and powerfully painted will create a revolution in art."

The silence could be interpreted either way.

After the others had left, Camille said:

"You don't yet care for landscape. Your attempts are halfhearted. Why not come out to the country and paint with me? We'll tackle the same scenes. Think how much we could learn from each other."

There was a backing away on Cézanne's face, then he realized that it was his friend, Camille Pissarro, who had no hooks to set into him.

"Thank you, Pissarro. We'll do it one day. But first I will return to Aix, paint the countryside around L'Estaque."

The following week, to his profound gratification and exultation, one of Paris's few dealers, Alfred Cadart of Chez Cadart et Luquet, at 79 Rue de Richelieu, informed Camille that he wanted to exhibit his two pictures from the Salon; that he had not been much impressed at first but after the Salon closed the images kept returning to his mind. Camille knew of the few small dealers, Martin, Cadart, who occasionally sold a painting for a few dollars. The older established dealers represented only the Salon favorites who won medals and brought high prices. When he called on them he never got further than a clerk on the floor. On occasion Camille's eyes had flashed with anger.

He told Julie:

"Chez Cadart et Luquet sells the Fontainebleau School quite well and thinks my work is not too radical a departure to antagonize their customers."

"He can find someone to buy?" cried Julie. "What a good thing that would be . . . now that we're going to have two children to raise."

Camille gazed at her in silence, then took her in his arms.

"It was bound to happen, wasn't it?" she queried.

Julie had heard the old wives' tale that a woman becomes pregnant again as soon as she ceases breast-feeding her earlier infant. Aside from some dubious herbal potions, it was the only way the wives of Grancey had had of limiting their offspring. Julie had not put much faith in the legend but now she knew it was true.

"I'm happy for us, Julie."

"I feed them. You teach them to read and write."

Cadart was putting the two Salon paintings in his Rue de Richelieu window. Pissarro and Manet were the only ones of the group to have pictures at a dealer.

"We've agreed on modest prices. Five to ten dollars," said Cadart.

He took Julie on the smoke-laden, puffing hour's journey into Paris. They stood before the window holding hands, gazing at the two Pissarro pictures standing alone on easels. They had a solidity, an inner strength; they glowed, were beautiful . . . for Camille at least, though he was bound to notice that the passersby on the Rue de Richelieu, scurrying elsewhere to perform tasks or keep appointments, took no notice of them, not even stopping to look idly at this transcription of the earth which spoke eloquently of the eternality of nature, its fruits, its people.

"Nothing surprising," Cadart told him. "Ninety-nine per cent of the Parisians never look at a picture, let alone buy one, except out of the Salon."

Cadart was a mild-mannered, middle-aged man who spoke with his fingers interlocked across his spacious belly. His shop was long and narrow, not well lighted except for the glowing Fontainebleau canvases on the walls, wooded dells with trees dripping a romantic mist.

"We wait for that blessed one per cent," the dealer murmured. "They walk slowly down the boulevard. They stop in front of the window, study the pictures, become interested, then excited, and ultimately they buy. These are the *Collectors,* a God-given species without whom we would all be destroyed. What would be left? Commerce. People buying and selling, consuming food, clothing, money. That is all their lives. Ah, but the Collectors! We shall find them for you."

Most of the Guerbois group had been down to the Rue de Richelieu to see Camille's canvases staring out at the world in a bold challenge, the young painters who were in revolt against stereotyped academic art, narrow and repetitious in scope. They were not imitators, they felt they had something fresh to say about contemporary life and the values which lay behind the sentimental façade of the routine Salon painting, which had been duplicating itself for decades with textbook artificiality. They were vigorous in their disdain for worn-out formulas and were in revolt against the platitudes of the status quo, held together by the view that historical and religious painting had come to an impasse; and that what was needed now was a penetrating look at the world in its honest flaming color and truthfulness about the genuine structure of the earth, the people who walked upon it and the products they brought forth. All of which was reflected in the two canvases reposing in Chez Cadart's and Luquet's window.

If being radical meant seeing without a commercial stance, painting with the brilliant hues and colored shadows that the sun cast upon formerly despised scenes and domestic objects, then so be it. Beauty was in the eyes of the beholder; truth lay in the courage and diversity of vision. To be a radical in art would cost no lives. Their revolution would guillotine only the hackneyed, the timid, and the pedagogic atmosphere surrounding them.

The group met at the Guerbois every Thursday afternoon. The artists were delighted when Camille came in with Julie, wringing his hand, ordering wine to celebrate his triumph. Claude Monet was the most enthralled.

"First Edouard Manet, second Camille Pissarro has a gallery. Soon there will be a third, then a fourth, then all of us will be represented. That great day is just around the corner."

Camille's euphoria lasted only a few weeks. Many came to Chez Cadart et Luquet, many looked. The bland, potbellied Alfred Cadart spoke passionately, sometimes even brilliantly, about the qualities of the paintings. He could get no one to regard the pictures seriously. No one would risk five dollars, less than the cost of the canvas, backing, frame, paint, brushes, varnish. No one would take one of the pictures home on trial. After a month Cadart sent for Camille.

"I'm truly sorry," he said, his mild eyes showing sadness. "Your concept of reality in nature is too brash to be acceptable. Perhaps next year. I've fallen flat on my round belly before. Don't be discouraged."

On the hour's journey to La Varenne he studied the paintings. They were not the soft romantic greens of the Fontainebleau pictures, they were more than forest and mist. There was real air in them, real people worked their soil and walked their paths. They were perhaps not pretty enough.

When he reached home with his canvases under his arm Julie burst into tears.

"If I were going to be discouraged," he told her, "I would have quit years ago. Artists have said that for centuries. Nothing has harmed the pictures by a month of rejection on the Rue de Richelieu. They will survive."

She wrapped her arms around him.

"But we are the ones who must survive," she sobbed.

4

Claude Monet and Frédéric Bazille had become close friends, going from Gleyre's studio after work each day to a café on the Rue St. Jacques for coffee. They decided to share an apartment, Bazille leaving the studio he had been occupying with Renoir. On January 15, 1865, Camille and Julie were invited to a party in the studio on the Rue de Furstenberg. There were tall windows throughout, wood paneling, chestnut trees in the garden and a view of the charming Place de Furstenberg. The apartment had two large separate rooms and a private toilet, unheard of in art circles. Camille had seen such a luxurious apartment only when invited to visit Delacroix or Edouard Manet. He knew that Bazille, and his wealthy wine-growing family in Montpellier, had the means to maintain it. Claude Monet, living on a pittance from his Aunt Sophie in Le Havre, certainly did not.

The party, to which Julie had come reluctantly, lasted all night, with an accordionist providing dance music. There was food and copious drink. The entire Gleyre studio was there, the Café Guerbois group, dozens of artists from all over Paris. Camille was not surprised to learn the next day that the landlord invited Bazille and Monet to move out. The tall, gangling, narrow-chested eccentric Bazille mollified the man with an extra month's rent.

The surprise of the party was Claude Monet's eighteen-year-old mistress, Camille Léonie Doncieux, the delicately raised daughter of a prosperous merchant. She had met Monet casually somewhere, had agreed to visit his studio to see his paintings, had awakened from an unaroused childhood, fallen in love, and promptly been seduced. She made no attempt to conceal her adoration of the handsome, volatile Monet. Camille observed that Monet was equally fascinated. The expensively gowned girl was gorgeous; tall, long-legged, her short-cut

222

hair curled under the pink bloom of youth on her cheeks, an enigmatic smile on her lips and devastating eyes.

During the evening Antoine Guillemet, talking with Camille about living in La Varenne, asked:

"Do you have a place to stay when you come into Paris?"

"I sometimes stay overnight in my family's apartment in Passy."

"Can you paint there?"

"No space. Nor would my mother allow it."

"Why not use my studio? It's spacious, and so often I'm at home in Chantilly or sketching on the coast. Work there as much as you like, store your paintings there, stay over. Bring Julie and the boy."

Antoine Guillemet was in earnest. The studio, like that of Edouard Manet, though not of the enormous size of Eugène Delacroix's, was furnished with sofas, deep easy chairs, tables piled with books and magazines. There were oriental rugs on the floor.

"That's a nice part of being rich," Camille commented wistfully to Julie. "You can buy *things*. All so pleasant to live with."

"We can live without things," Julie Vellay from the bottom of the Rue Neuve in Grancey said with clenched molars; "all we need is food and clothing and shelter."

"We have them. Barely. But we will have more in the future."

"The future," Julie echoed quietly. "It's the best land in the world. Everyone has plenty. Only it's on the other side of the ocean."

"Ships traverse oceans. I crossed the Atlantic several times."

It had been in the late spring of 1864 that his father first began to feel unwell.

"It's nothing serious," he assured Camille, "just a bit of lassitude. I'm walking a little slower in the park, on shorter trails."

Frédéric had grown portly in retirement, his abundant hair had turned white. He sported a semicircular short white beard along his jawbone and under his chin. Yet his wide, strong-featured face showed few signs of aging.

"It will pass," he said.

It did not. He slowly lost his appetite, spent more time in his big reading chair, paper in hand but not seeing the print. Alfred located a reputable doctor in Passy. Dr. Barthou was conscientious. He went about the task of examining Frédéric in a methodical way, using all the instruments and techniques available, testing Frédéric's heart, lungs, arm and leg reflexes, then prescribing several medications.

The medications neither helped nor gave any indication of what was wrong. Nor did Dr. Paul Gachet's homeopathic remedies help. Frédéric grew silent and pale. Camille came in twice a week, stayed overnight to be with him. Emma arrived from London. They afforded him company. Rachel was frightened. She seemed to weave her hair in buns held against her ears to shut out voices she did not wish to hear.

Pain took over. No one of the subsequent doctors could diagnose the illness; they could relieve the suffering only momentarily. By November Frédéric could no longer get out of bed. There appeared a swelling on the right side of his abdomen. The tumor began to spread.

He remained calm, with all his reason, until his last breath. He slipped away on January 28, 1865. Rachel was irreconcilable; yet in a moment of resignation she instructed Alfred and Camille to have a Pissarro vault erected in Père Lachaise where all the family would one day be reunited. Frédéric was drawn across the entire city of Paris in a hearse with great black feathers rising from the top of its four posts. Camille and Alfred held Rachel firmly upright in the back seat of their following carriage.

Camille was grief-stricken over his father's death. He had been the ameliorating force in the Pissarro family, the one who had supported his resolution to become a painter, the one unadulterated pleasure in visiting the house in Passy.

With the sorrow came the assumption that he would inherit a sum which would make his future, for a number of years at least, secure. Given a large enough sum, there was the possibility of buying a more suitable home and studio. He had known that Frédéric had filed a will attesting that he regarded Rachel's two daughters, Emma and Delphine, as his own. He had, however, amended the will after Delphine's death. Emma had asked that she be left only a memory gift. Rachel was to receive half of the value of the estate, Alfred and Camille each a quarter.

On the day the will was read by the family advocate, Camille was stunned. He had been disinherited. Half of Frédéric's estate had been left to Rachel, the other half to Alfred, sizable sums going to both the synagogue and the Protestant church in St. Thomas. Camille had been left absolutely nothing.

He walked for miles along the Seine, passing its numerous

bridges, his befuddlement over his father's abandonment giving way to a mounting sense of injustice. When he could no longer stand the whirling confusion in his brain he returned to Rachel's apartment to ask, in a voice hoarse as the hucksters shouting their wares in Les Halles, for an explanation. Rachel rocked in her mahogany and rattan chair. She would not meet his gaze.

"Why? Why would Father disinherit one of the only two sons remaining to him?"

"Because he did not want to see his money wasted."

"Wasted!"

"Yes. On pictures that do not sell."

"Selling is not the primary value of a painting. Its beauty and illumination are more important."

"Perhaps. But you know that your father believed in capitalism. *Eh bien!* In capitalism money earns money. What Father left to Alfred will be invested and earn more money. Money left to you would be spent on paint, earning nothing but a soiled smock."

"I work hard, I am devoted. I shred my strength to achieve a result," he cried.

"Your father did not dispute that."

"He had no faith in me?"

"In your making a living from paints, no."

Rachel's lips trembled, her hands gripped the arms of the rocker. For the first time she looked directly into her son's eyes.

"It was a heartbreaking decision for him, arrived at after long days of troubled thought. In the end he felt he had to force you . . ."

"To give up my way of life?"

" . . . to become practical. To face reality. You have a child . . .. You are now . . . what?"

"Thirty-five."

"You would be forty or forty-five before your inheritance ran out. Too late to start in a new business."

"It's not too late now?"

"No. You are adaptable."

"Wrong. I am as stubborn as a mule."

"A mule is reputed to be not only stubborn but stupid. Are you not impelled to earn a living?"

"It will come."

"When?" Rachel wept. Wept for this gentle son, soft-spoken but staunch as a mountain of solid rock when it came to his belief that he was born to paint, that he would paint a lifetime of incisive and unique pictures which would portray a world largely ignored by former artists and which would present a changed and all-encompassing way of seeing light, color, shadow, shimmering structure in the changing hours of the day.

"I must be patient."

"You've been patient for ten years now. Is there no end?"

"When my voice is heard."

She held her face in her hands, exhausted and defeated

"You're hopeless."

"All dedicated people are hopeless. And hope-filled. When spring comes the wild flowers thrust themselves through the hard crust and the earth is covered with fresh foliage."

Rachel rose from her chair, pushed her glasses up on her nose.

"I have only half the capital now. I will continue your allowance, but at only half the amount, and I cannot pay your rent."

He took her in his arms; held her gently. They were both bereaved.

Alfred would be sympathetic. The older brother who had sent him, out of his savings, linens and painting supplies to Caracas; small sums of money and warm clothing during his early days in Paris; who had attempted to sell the paintings in Montevideo; and had exclaimed, when Camille had seen him through his troublesome illness, "I'll never forget your kindness."

Alfred was in the apartment Camille had found for him. It was a modest place, overdecorated with bric-a-brac.

"Somewhat," Camille decided, "in Alfred's manner of garbing himself in high silk hat, ruffled shirts and tails."

Camille quickly felt the chill in the air. Alfred had been expecting Camille's visit and was prepared for it. He was employed at a good salary in an import-export house dealing with South America but he spent more money than he earned. Now he would be able to open his own office and work for the considerable profits he was helping to earn for others.

He gazed at his brother through uncertain eyes.

"Alfred, do you believe it is fair that I do not receive half of what you received? Father had two sons. They should be treated equally."

"Our father and mother figured everything. It's a valid will. Father was never unjust."

"But he has cast me out."

"For business purposes, to protect his estate. Money left to me will be invested and bring a good return; money left to you will be consumed in daily living and vanish."

Camille sank onto one of the small, gilt-covered chairs.

"Do you think my paintings are pointless, worthless?"

"Come, Camille, you know that I would never pass so harsh a judgment. They fulfill a need . . . for you. Not for anyone else. Let us not quarrel. Tell me what your immediate needs are. I will lend you the money. No, not a loan, just give it to you. Not a substantial sum. Everything I inherited will be invested in my business. To pull it out would be disastrous."

"The money you invest will return profits. Why am I not entitled to some part of those profits?"

Alfred put his arm about his brother's shoulder and steered him toward the door.

"You have paintings you want to show in coming exhibitions? Give me the sizes and I will pay for the gold frames."

Camille left Alfred's apartment with a crushing sadness. He felt bereft of family, like a newly born daughter set out on the cliffs for the wolves to devour. Abandoned. For what crime?

A shudder went through him as he thought of Julie. The home he wanted for her. With many windows. Surrounded by tall trees. Would it have done them an irretrievable harm to have let him have a share of their precious money to invest in his own way?

He reached the distant Pont de Grenelle, leaned over the parapet, watched the coal and grain barges drift by, the women hanging out underwear, little children playing on the prow with makeshift toys. A revulsion swept over him, a reaction against his own despair.

"Why am I feeling so bitter? Nothing has changed. I am only a little worse off than I was before."

It was not in his nature to hate. He had always had an affection for his mother and father. They had done what they thought was best. They had their own vision of fulfillment. They had earned it. They had been generous with him, more so as he now realized how far apart their philosophies had been. Alfred was not greedy; he too was part of their world.

He would not corrode his spirit with acrimony. If he did, his painting would die under his hand.

5

As Julie grew bigger Camille sometimes patted her extended belly. "It's a girl this time."

"How do you know it's a girl?"

"I can feel her lovely legs, just like her mother's."

Julie carried easily, did her round of chores, washing, cooking, tending the rabbits and chickens that embellished the vegetables she planted, watered, weeded, then picked fresh for supper.

It was indeed a girl, delivered by a La Varenne midwife with dispatch and more boiling water than fuss. A village girl came in to cook and clean for a few days. Camille was ecstatic about his Jeanne, whom he promptly nicknamed Minette, a lovely infant from the moment of being washed and wrapped in a swaddling cloth. He crowed as though he were the one who had accomplished something miraculous in this female infant. When Minette was only a few days old he put her head on his shoulder, held her back securely in his powerful hand, and sang her the Grancey songs he had heard Julie sing to Lucien.

David Jacobsen had moved to a single garret when Camille and Julie left for the country. He also vanished from the art scene. Camille hunted him down in Montmartre, in a cold, bare room without a stove to make a hot drink, a single blanket covering the narrow cot, an easel and a table to hold supplies. They greeted each other affectionately. David was hollow-chested and hollow-cheeked, his clothing turning one of the few disagreeable greens in nature's copious palette. There was fever in his eyes. Very occasionally he had managed a small sale to a Danish citizen living in Paris; when completely destitute he would go for several days to live with his uncle, a cooper in Grenelle.

It was a Thursday afternoon. Camille took David to the Café Guerbois hoping he would make friends and find supporters. David remained silent during the discussion; he was also hostile.

"I don't agree with their ideas," he cried to Camille when they left. "I can't go along with their revolutionary concepts of color, diffused light, insubstantial forms. Or their battles over the jury and the Salon. The ambition of my life is to get into the Salon. . . . I don't belong with them.''

There was a bitter silence.

"You have talent," Camille said. "Your portraits of women are excellent. You need companionship. My friends would enjoy having you dispute them."

"They despise historical painting. You do too, Camille."

He fell into a fit of coughing.

"Let me bring Dr. Gachet to examine you. He'll take payment in pictures."

"Not mine, he won't. He prefers you realists." Then his eyes brightened. "But don't despair, I'm going to Italy. Into the warm sunshine. Since 1860 I've been applying to the Academy in Copenhagen for an Italian grant. This year it looks hopeful. Anton Melbye is writing to them."

Camille took David to a restaurant for dinner, claiming he himself was hungry. He plied Jacobsen with seafood from the bouillabaisse he had ordered, until the deep bowl was empty.

Rachel, alone now, moved to the Boulevard des Martyrs not far from the apartment to which Camille had taken the cab in October of 1855, a decade before. She hung David Jacobsen's portrait of Frédéric in the parlor, along with Camille's *Landscape at Montmorency*. She gave Camille permission to store some of his paintings in a closet but never looked at them. The unframed pictures did not exist for her, any more than did Julie or her two children. After Minette was born Camille went into Paris to tell her about the baby.

"She's adorable. Can I bring her to you?"

Instead of uttering the word "No," Rachel changed the subject.

"Emma is coming for a visit. Isn't that wonderful?"

He said hoarsely: "It will be good to see Emma again."

It was indeed. Emma visited Camille, Julie and the two children, bringing them clothing and toys. She took the little ones in her arms, loved them as her niece and nephew. Of particular importance was Julie's joy at the affectionate way Emma accepted her as a member of the family.

Camille's friendship with the testy Paul Cézanne continually deepened. Each time Cézanne was rejected by the Salon he returned to Aix in a rage; after a few months of quarreling with his father he returned to Paris in a similar rage. Early in 1865 Camille received a note from him asking him to drop in at 22 Rue Beautreillis, near the Bastille; he had landscapes to show his friend, sketches of the countryside around Aix-en-Provence and Marseille, twenty miles from there.

Camille immediately recognized the authentic Provençal thrust. The harsh light and stony mountain structures of L'Estaque were different from what Camille and the others were painting in the more amiable ambiance of the Seine and Oise valleys. They still reflected Cézanne's inner turmoil but there was an affection for the scene in them.

"Pissarro, I love Aix. It is only that when I am there I am not free. I could wish with all my heart that my liberty of action were not interfered with. I should very much like to work in the Midi, where the views offer so many opportunities."

Then he exclaimed, *"Sacrebleu!* It's Emile Zola's evening for his friends. There's not that much to eat or drink; Emile is poor. But the conversation is good. He'll be insulted if I don't show up. He would be pleased to add you to his coterie."

They crossed the Place de la Bastille, then wound their way through the Left Bank to Zola's apartment on the Rue de Vaugirard. Cézanne talked about his friend from Aix.

"His mother is French. His father is Italian from an old Venetian family and studied engineering in the military school in Pavia for five years. He finally settled in Aix-en-Provence, an ancient city with a huge wall that used to be locked at night. He noticed that only one of the town's three public fountains was running and the water was brackish. He searched the surrounding mountains until he found a natural waterfall, then designed a canal to bring the fresh water to Aix. He struggled ten years to get permission to build it, then within three months of working on the site he was trapped in our icy mistral, caught cold and died. He left his wife and only son destitute. Emile grew up in poverty, his mother sacrificing to keep him in the Collège Bourbon, where he was an even poorer student than he was at the college in Marseille and the Sorbonne University in Paris."

Cézanne sighed deeply.

"I love him. We are closer than blood brothers, roamed Provence reading poetry, novels, dreaming of a romantic future. The other boys didn't like Emile; I saved him from a beating in the schoolyard once. That's when we became inseparable."

As Cézanne talked on Camille gathered that they were also blood brothers temperamentally, pensive sufferers, mistrustful, shy, gruff. After years of grinding and humiliating poverty on the Right Bank, working for some months as a customs clerk on the Napoleonic Docks, a friend of his father got Zola a job as a shipping clerk at Librairie Hachette, successful French publishers. He was promoted to the advertising department, met authors and newspaper editors, persuaded a small firm to publish his first book, *Stories for Ninon*, which was praised but did not sell. He started writing for the journals *Le Figaro* and *L'Evènement*, literary essays and criticisms, and was described by his editor at *L'Evènement* as a "scarecrow, with his suspicious and whining air, his look of hard luck, like a butler."

Zola had fallen in love with Alexandrine, his landlord's daughter. When he and Alexandrine moved into a new apartment they took Zola's mother with them. The flat on the Left Bank was small; on occasion Zola had to pawn his possessions to keep it.

When Cézanne and Camille arrived the parlor and dining room were crowded with young men arguing animatedly, drinking wine and munching Alexandrine's offering of cheese and crackers. As they stood quietly for a moment in the foyer, Cézanne said of his friend:

"He thinks of nothing but arriving."

From his vantage point Camille realized how accurate was Cézanne's painter's eye as he had described the man:

"His eyes are luminous and dark. His forehead is square. The round head tapers down to a small cloven chin. His lower lip is thick, the small nose pugnacious though with sensitive nostrils, like that of a pointer dog . . . altogether quite aesthetic."

Zola's skin was of a pallor induced by twelve to fourteen hours a day writing hundreds of pages a month for newspaper articles, trashy serialized novels and serious studies in a frenzied effort to support his mother and mistress, entertain and become famous.

Cézanne said wryly, "Look at him. He's beginning to go about in the world, even bought his first dress suit!"

Zola spied Cézanne, guided the two men to a sideboard, introduced Camille to Alexandrine Mesley, tall, striking-looking. Her eyes had been described as having that "strange blackness of a child in an old Spanish painting." She was proving to be a young woman of courage in the face of Zola's fluctuating fortunes. She also left him free to attend the absinthe hour after five in the afternoon when the fashionable world promenaded before the Café Tortoni, the Café Anglais and the Café de l'Europe, with their open terraces.

Zola said to Camille:

"Don't pay attention to anything Cézanne says about me. Paul has the genius of a great painter but he will never have the genius to become one."

"As you will become a great writer?" twitted Camille.

"Yes. I have the inner force to become another Balzac or Flaubert. Paul says I'm sucking at the breast of illusion."

Leaving Zola's apartment, Cézanne remarked acidly:

"I'm going back to Aix. I can't stand Paris and all this talk."

6

For the Salon of 1865 Camille had submitted what he thought were his two best oil canvases, framed in gold by Alfred. *At the Edge of the Water* was accepted, *The Banks of the Marne at Chennevières* rejected. Sitting at a table outside the Café de Bade close by the Salon, he tried to figure why the jury had accepted one and not the other. He even considered *The Banks of the Marne* the better realized of the two. For that matter he could not figure why the jury took any paintings of the group, though it happened occasionally that one or two unwittingly produced a picture that appeared externally to resemble the mold the jury clung to, an accidental singularity fooling the officials.

He was interrupted in his musings by a cry from Charles Baudelaire.

"*Attention*, Camille. Your second canvas is being hung, *The Banks of the Marne*."

Startled, Camille called back: "But the jury rejected it."

Baudelaire crossed the street in the bright sunlight, came and sat down beside him.

"Each member has what's known as his 'charity.' He can pick one canvas among the rejects for free admission. Daubigny chose yours."

Flabbergasted, Camille murmured:

"*Je suis aux anges*. I'm in seventh heaven. I've admired Daubigny's work enormously, but I've not met him, so this is not a friendly favor."

"On the contrary, Daubigny thinks you're the best of the young ones."

For the count of perhaps ten Camille did not take a breath.

The corners of his mouth turned up, his deep brown eyes became like velvet.

The daylight pitifully illuminated Baudelaire's haggardness. There had recently been an enlarged edition of his poems published. *Les Fleurs du Mal*. Baudelaire and his publishers were tried, convicted and fined for "outrages against the public morality." Overstrung, impoverished, though he still tried to maintain his image as a dandy, Baudelaire cried in his strained voice that the court had judged his poems piecemeal.

"Taken as a whole, it can only inspire a horror of vice. In that book I have put all my heart, all my affection, all my religion, all my hatred!"

"Why hatred?" Camille asked soberly.

"Because I've suffered a long train of catastrophes. It has bred in me a morbid desire to shock. I shall swear by all the gods that it is a book of pure art and aged emotions and dexterous imitation, but I shall be lying like a dentist. *Alors*, the agony will soon be over. I don't have much longer to live."

Edouard Manet had cause to celebrate. The jury had selected his *Olympia*, a naked whore on her bed, with her black maid presenting a bouquet of flowers from her gentleman caller. However its fate was to be worse than that of *Luncheon on the Grass* at the Salon des Refusés.

When the show opened one man tried to slash it with his pocketknife. Women spat on it. The crowds in front of the picture were dense with outraged bodies. Nobody looked at anything else. Not the miles of historical and biblical canvases, not even the Fontainebleau pictures. Emotion, outrage ran high.

Claude Monet and Camille found a quiet corner behind a fountain where they collapsed onto a purple velours settee.

"How do you explain the jury's accepting the *Olympia*," asked Monet, "aside from the fact that it's the most brilliantly painted canvas in the show? And why this sense of revulsion? Olympia is only one of thousands of high-class prostitutes plying their trade in Paris. Everybody knows about them, even the most respectable housewives, whose husbands use them for diversion."

Camille responded hesitatingly.

"Could it be that other women portrayed naked were all romantically depicted; guileless faces in idyllic surroundings? Olympia is a professional courtesan. Her face tells of her loathing for the men she must take. All sentimentality is drained away, despite the high pinks and brightly colored flowers. No longer will Paris be able to think of the thousands of prostitutes as romantic creatures, the most elegant of them. They have reacted savagely.''

Edouard Manet made his way through the crowd, spied them. He was irritated. *"Olympia* appeared to me an opportunity to get a startling contrast of flesh colors. I never wanted to become *un scandale.* I have never desired to protest.''

Edouard Manet, a year and a half younger than Camille, was the acknowledged leader of the Batignolles group. *Luncheon on the Grass* of the 1863 Salon des Refusés was on view in the window of Martinet's Gallery on the Boulevard des Italiens, where it was a center of Paris's ridicule. *Olympia* was now destined to succeed it as the most discussed painting in Paris. But he was not the leader because of these two pictures. He was the sharpest, most entertaining of the group. He had stimulating ideas about art.

"We must eliminate half tones," he decreed at one session, "the artist has a right to paint in whatever color or tonalities he wishes. A good dash of heresy is what we all need. The Salon looks as though it was all painted by one giant hand . . . without a giant brain.''

When several of the habitués of the Café Guerbois, serious painters, Legros, Fantin-Latour, spoke of the need to win honors at the Salon in order to sell, Manet replied:

"The Salon is the field of battle. But the Empire's honors are worthless.''

"Only when one doesn't need honors to feed his family," thought Camille without rancour.

One afternoon Camille accepted Manet's invitation to visit his studio in the Rue Guyot and see the sketches he was preparing for *The Fifer,* which he planned to submit to the 1866 Salon. It was an afternoon when he had come to town to replenish his painting supplies, always aghast at their cost. The elegant studio was deceptive. It was not a place to lounge in luxury but to work, which Manet did uninterruptedly from early morning until five in the afternoon when he changed and became a boulevardier leading a succession of beautiful women to bed. Camille knew his story, strictly held within the painter's group. He had fallen in love with and seduced a young Dutch musician, an attractive girl who had been brought into the Manet home to give piano lessons. He had been barely twenty when Suzanne Leenhoff bore him a son. Manet registered the boy under an assumed name. For public purposes the child was Suzanne's young brother. Manet's father died in 1862, leaving Edouard independently wealthy. After the funeral he acknowledged the boy and married Suzanne.

Manet's mother, alone now in the big family home on the Rue de St. Pétersbourg, invited her son, Suzanne and their child to live with her.

Camille was disappointed to find two circumspectly gowned women in Manet's studio, Berthe Morisot and her sister Edma. They had met Manet in the Louvre while copying before Goya and Velásquez, whom Manet had selected as his masters. Berthe Morisot was serious about her painting and worked at it full time. Her sister was keeping her company, a necessity for anyone as socially correct as Berthe Morisot, who came from an irreproachable and wealthy family. Camille appraised the woman. She was not the kind he met very often among his painter friends. She was about twenty-four, tall, meticulously tailored in patterned white voile, a narrow black belt at her slim waist, a black ribbon with a medallion around her neck and a bit of white stocking showing above black leather pumps with pompons. She had a mass of dark hair swept in two waves away from her forehead, long immaculately combed curls down the front of her white gown, and the most enormous eyes he had ever seen; the irises literally filling the sockets. Their gaze was penetrating; the look of hauteur was contradicted by a voluptuous cupid's-bow mouth. Her glance at Camille during the introduction had been anything but admiring as she took in his worn coat and scuffed shoes.

"A good-looking face, rather than beautiful," he decided. "If Whistler hadn't moved back to London he could create a symphony of black and white artfully arranged. Her expression is fierce and domineering when she looks at me; tender and reflective when she looks at Edouard."

"Berthe is kind enough to say that I have things to teach her," Manet said humbly.

She was not too patrician to blush at the veiled innuendo. She drew herself up to her full height, said regally:

"There are techniques about painting that you could teach us all, Monsieur Manet. Since that's why we came, would you be so kind as to correct my new sketches? I have some studies of mothers with children in which I'm trying to capture the relationship."

Manet became serious over a revision of her drawings. Camille watched the two of them work together while Berthe's sister-chaperone sat in a Louis XIV chair in a corner glancing through a fashion magazine. He smiled inwardly. There was no doubt about Manet's admiration for the charmingly aristocratic face and bearing, or that he meant to acquire her. Or that she believed he never would. She was much too strait-laced and respectable.

Manet's *garçon* served coffee and pastries. Berthe Morisot, exultant over her lesson, remembered her manners. She turned to Camille to ask cordially:

"Have you met Rosa Bonheur? No? Neither have I. Nor has anyone else I know. She won a first prize as early as the Salon of 1848 and is now famous, selling very well in England and the United States. She is the best painter of animals in Europe; everyone agrees. She has a large studio with an adjoining barn where she keeps the animals she paints. It is strange she should remain so unknown amongst us. She is the best example that a woman can take a first-rate place in art. Each century produces only a few women painters."

"You also have a natural talent, my dear Berthe Morisot," Manet responded, "and a compulsive drive. I doubt anyone will stop you."

Camille excused himself, feeling uncomfortable. As he thumped down Edouard Manet's carpeted stairs, he ruminated:

"There's a lethal battle emerging there. I'd put my money, if I had any, on Mademoiselle Morisot. I suspect she has more pride than passion. Manet will never get her into his bed. She's not going to put herself in the class of his other women."

If he had not gotten to see and discuss Manet's painting for the next Salon, he had reflected on the story of Manet's receptive mother. There arose in his mind a glimmer of hope that, now that Rachel was alone, a similar arrangement might be made with her. When he was in Paris next, he took Rachel to lunch.

"Maman, you are alone, wouldn't you like me to move back with you? I wouldn't leave the country, but during the long cold winter. . . ?"

"Oh, Camille, would you? I so long for your company and comfort."

"Julie and the children would be included, of course. With your permission we will be married."

A jarring shudder went through his mother's frame as it would a freighter struck by a giant wave.

"No."

"Edouard Manet's mother took in her son's former mistress and son out of wedlock. Why can you not be reconciled?"

236

"Manet's . . . companion . . . came from a good Dutch family. Yours . . . is a *bonne*."

"She has been my . . . companion . . . for seven years. We could be a loving family."

Not even with her husband dead, her older son often out of the country, her daughter in faraway London, would Rachel accept Julie. He remembered the description of his mother from St. Thomas:

"Rachel Pissarro has every virtue except the ability to make herself happy."

He gave a long sigh of resignation.

7

Camille called on Charles François Daubigny in Auvers-sur-Oise to thank him for his kindness. Daubigny was a man of forty-nine, possessed of wanderlust and superb talent. He had married at twenty-five, now had a daughter and two sons, a home and a studio where he spent part of his summers painting with Corot, his closest friend. He had first exhibited at the Salon at the age of twenty-one, in 1838, when he entered Delaroche's studio, and had received all the Salon's medals, First, Second and Third Class; been made a Knight of the Legion of Honor and given generous commissions by the administration of the Beaux-Arts. He rarely showed less than four or five major oils painted in Fontainebleau, or the rivers of the Seine and Oise, or the landscapes of Normandy and Picardy.

By 1857 he had purchased a small boat with a square covered stern to contain his painting equipment and a bed wide enough for two. He spent weeks on end drifting alone down the rivers of France, cooking his simple meals and coffee on the open deck, tying up at night to sleep. He caught the shimmering light of dawn and dusk on the water, the foliage of the banks, as no one had done before. He was considered by the Beaux-Arts an innovator, though not a radical.

Daubigny's international reputation was established in 1857, when the French government bought *View of the Seine;* and Louis Napoleon purchased *Pond of Gylieu.* He traveled frequently to London, showed successfully at the Royal Academy there, had a book published, *Voyage by Boat,* of his sketches and studies of French river scenes.

Camille walked along the towpath watching longsuffering horses trudge past him pulling heavily loaded barges up the Oise. He found Daubigny's house in a clearing with tall trees at the borders and flower patches cared for by his wife, the plain, matronly Marie Sophie.

Daubigny's studio, a distance behind the house, had an open door and sunlight streaming through overhead windows. Camille observed Daubigny at his easel: his scraggy hair retreating in front and on the sides; a mild scraggy beard that had not grown a scintilla since the age of twenty-five, a face dominated by a pair of all-seeing, nonjudgmental eyes. He was a mild-mannered man with a low, soft voice bouncing off steel innards. He did not think anything worth fighting about except painting; then he had the teeth of a tiger. There was no mistaking his expression: try not to be any more stupid than is necessary.

He was dressed in a sagging pair of workman's pants and a faded shirt. Camille introduced himself. Daubigny grasped his hand warmly.

"Ah, Pissarro. It's a pleasure."

"I came to thank you for having hung *The Marne at Chennevilères* in your 'charity basket.' "

There was a wide grin on Daubigny's face.

"I love peace and quiet. With my family, friends, associates. But not when that *tot-toc* jury squats on its haunches." Daubigny crinkled his ordinary face in a winsome gesture. "Your entire Café Guerbois group has promise. The way our Fontainebleau School did. By the by, I had luncheon in Whistler's home in London earlier this year. He has decorated his house the way he dresses: staggering, to put out your eye. He's fighting with everyone there with that daggerlike wit of his; but he is painting in his own peculiar way, breaking the rules and making his mark. He's planning to do a series on the Thames, the way I do the Oise.

"Come. I'll show you my boat. You may want one someday to paint the rivers. Sometimes I take my wife, occasionally a friend comes along to paint. Mostly I'm alone, rowing with the current to find my scenes."

They made their way to the riverbank; on board they sipped the local wine Daubigny poured from a large jug. He murmured, raising his glass:

"To young painters! I've entered the lists on their side."

*   *   *

Camille's latest painting in La Varenne was a scene of a large open meadow bounded by hills, a river on the right and in the center two elegantly clad youngsters on ponies, facing each other head on, attended by a fashionably dressed mother. At the rear were a young boy and girl from a neighboring farm or village, shabbily clothed. He titled it *Donkey Ride at La Roche-Guyon*. He had been intrigued by the pictorial contrasts. That Thursday he stopped by the Guerbois before taking the canvas to Guillemet's for storage. One of Proudhon's fiery disciples, editor of a minuscule as well as anarchist newspaper, cried:

"At last! You've recognized the class war! With this picture you've exemplified the difference between the rich and the poor. It's uncivilized that rich children should ride their own ponies while ragged children have nothing. The earth's property has been stolen from them."

"I didn't mean . . ."

Emile Zola interrupted.

"Whether you meant it or not, it's a proletarian tract."

Edouard Manet objected. "It's a pictorial scene Pissarro wanted to set down, and it's well painted. We have sufficient troubles handling paint without being thrashed by the critics over our themes."

Claude Monet cried:

"We must get away from subject matter altogether; paint pure color, light, form."

The editor threw up his hands in exasperation.

"Why are you all defaulting? Are you frightened that the authorities will put you in jail for your revolutionary ideas? Painters can't escape social injustice; they're a part of it."

"No," said Antoine Guillemet firmly; "that would ruin us. We can't paint from an ideology; only from inner conviction of what should go onto the canvas. Besides, to say that no government is better than bad government would bring chaos."

Armand Guillaumin, the government clerk who had been closest to Proudhon in background, added:

"We're going to paint what we want to paint without every picture raising a storm."

The battle rose to a high crescendo, unusual for the closely knit group. The smoke got thicker, the beer was drunk more rapidly; voices were raised so that the rest of the café fell silent.

"Damn," Camille murmured, "what have I unleashed here? There's trouble enough in trying to capture the quiet eternity of nature without bringing in the class war."

Occasionally he was conscious of being the oldest, along with Manet, of the lot, and of being of a different religion. Neither of these differences affected his relationship with the eager youngsters with whom he was becoming deeply involved. He was attracted to some more than others; he felt an affinity for the most *outré* of the group such as Cézanne, but since there was no member who was not loaded with both talent and protest, he got along pleasantly with them all, extending his natural warmth, friendliness, trusting and outgoing nature. He spoke his mind freely, sometimes had his leg pulled by the jokers in the muster; but that was part of the companionship. He never got into the kind of raucous argument that caused Edouard Manet to challenge the critic Duranty to a duel. Because of his origin in St. Thomas and years in Venezuela he was considered to know something of the outside world. He was happy for this first fraternity and looked forward to the meetings and discussions, arguments about *plein air* versus the steady north light of a studio; and regretted it when he could not spare the train fare to go into Paris for the get-together.

He had never intended to settle permanently in La Varenne. Now, after two and a half years, he felt that he had exhausted its painterly possibilities. He would search the Seine and Oise valleys carefully to find the area that would be indigenous to his particular vision. His friends made suggestions; he went on exploratory trips to proposed sites. Then he found what he wanted, an area so filled with superb motifs that everywhere his eye looked there was another and original arrangement of landscape. The kind he wanted to paint. He could think of nobody who had put this singular terrain down on canvas. It would be his, exclusively his, a scene in which to lose himself and find himself. While he worked he would be away from the talk of art, the comradery of friends. There would be only himself and the scene before him.

On New Year's Day, 1866, he moved his family into the peasant hamlet of L'Hermitage in the Vexin region, at the base of the town of Pontoise, first settled by the Gauls because of its advantageous location on the river Oise as a port and defensible spot; then conquered and colonized by the Romans, both of whom had used the same rough road along the river into the Ile de la Cité and Paris.

Since it was winter, and the farmers were not using their equipment, he was able to hire a big farm wagon and driver to transport their furnishings from La Varenne to the house he had rented at 1 Rue du Fond-de-l'Hermitage, traveling over a meandering series of dirt roads.

The Hermitage up to a few months before had been isolated by its steep terrain, occupied by gardeners, small farmers and growers for the Pontoise wine market, without a connecting road to the town of Pontoise above. It was considered a stark, undesirable area below the social status of the people of Pontoise. The extension of Pontoise's Avenue Victor Hugo to L'Hermitage now made the little village at the foot of the city an expanding *banlieue,* suburb. New houses were going up with bright tile roofs. The older houses huddled together with small barns abutting the streets.

The house Camille rented clung to the edge of the hillside, without the gas lamps of the town above, across the dirt road from the rivulet Viosne. It was a commodious, square box of a house without adornment, with discolored and some peeling plaster, but it had six rooms.

"We are fortunate, the rent is still cheap," he explained to Julie.

He could barely wait to place their few pieces of furniture, to be off, sketchbook or easel under his arm.

Once again they were strangers; knowing not another soul, in a neighborhood which did not have another artist. For Julie the continual moving was difficult. She had been raised in a sharing community. It was one thing to be poor in the company of other poor people; it was another to be poor alone, with no one with whom she could share her plight. Camille did not like her to discuss their near poverty; it upset his calm acceptance that most painters lived on the margin of destitution. It was their fate, one they accepted with a minimum of complaint or even discussion. When he said, as he so often had to: "Haven't a sou," it was without bitterness or self-reproach. There were worse fatalities than being hungry. There was, for example, being kept from painting or sculpting or writing or composing.

Nothing of this comfort rubbed off on Julie. She was a convivial soul; she liked company. Her neighbors on the Rue du Fond-de-l'Hermitage were uncommunicative. They distrusted strangers. And the Pissarros were more than strangers. They did not go to church, did not join religious or patriotic festivals, did not earn their living by Camille's working in one of the granaries or in the chemical water factory; or by tilling the soil on a piece of rented land outside of town. They were hardly respectable; for although they had two children and gave the impression of being married, Julie did not wear the traditional thick wedding band. She would not wear a ring until she had an official ceremony and a stamped paper with legal signatures on it.

She stoically examined the tiny bit of land around the house, found a shovel and began to dig for the flower and vegetable gardens which would make this unwelcoming place home.

Camille had only to step out the door and walk a few yards over the winding paths and adjoining fields to find himself a superb picture to paint.

8

Edouard Manet introduced a new member to the Guerbois; Edgar de Gas, who hated his name and changed it to Edgar Degas. He came from a wealthy conservative family. During the Revolution of 1789 his grandfather had fled to Naples where he had founded a bank and intermarried with Italian nobility. Degas leaned heavily on his noble ancestors, combined with the wealthy ones who made him, in his own eyes, a superior being. Manet had met him at Salon openings, a rather tall man with a powerfully engineered head and a round childlike face, seemingly genial but capable of delivering sharp witticisms that were more hurtful than funny. To James Whistler, visiting Paris, garbed in his usual outlandish fashion, Degas said:

"You dress as though you had no talent."

To Berthe Morisot, who came from his own wealthy class and whom everyone thought he would treat genteelly, he muttered:

"You paint with your hands in your pockets."

Camille studied the man carefully. He was in his mid-thirties, almost as old as himself, had an abrupt nose, wide eyes, clear skin, a wispy beard and razor-thin mustache. He wore a rounded hat with turned-up brim that revealed his face as nakedly as his expression concealed the frequently hostile nature. There was a slim line of white collar showing above the tightly buttoned coat, even as he displayed a buttoned personality. He kept his eyebrows plucked; they were large and arched, cynical about everything they saw. Behind the face was a sharp intellect. To Camille he seemed a perfectionist who despised anyone who was not as gifted as he conceived himself to be.

Camille had seen his drawings of horses at racetracks and youngsters at ballet classes. He asked him, across the table:

"Where did you learn to draw so well?"

"From Ingres, my god. I managed to get his *Bathers* from a reluctant owner for the retrospective he was assembling. In return he taught me to 'Draw lines, young man, many lines, either from memory or from nature; that way you will become a good artist.' During my frequent visits to my family in Italy I studied the line drawings of the masters in Florence, Rome, Naples. Fortunately, I have natural talent for pure outline."

Since he was a newcomer all attention centered on him. When Claude Monet asked why he did not paint *en plein air* instead of taking his studies back to the dim light of a studio, he replied:

"I am indifferent to nature in the open country. When we love nature, we can never be sure she loves us in return."

Antoine Guillemet retorted:

"Nonsense, Degas. If we had to be sure we were loved in return, the human race would die out."

Degas grimaced. "Don't speak to me of those fellows who clutter up the fields with their easels. I would have the gendarmes shoot painters doing landscapes from nature. Just a little dose of bird shot as a warning. I like to look at life through a keyhole."

Whistler, stung by Degas's comment on his costume, said:

"You mean your anus instead of your eyes?"

There was a moment's silence.

"You're in good form, Whistler." Degas turned to him, a sensitive face, deep-set eyes, pouting sensual lips, determined chin and admiration for cruelty. "I find movement and color for my brush at the racetrack, opera, ballet. The workingman does not attract me. My atmosphere has no need to be breathable."

"You are making a virtue of your limitations." Edouard Manet could be a fierce antagonist.

"Everyone does," Degas answered him calmly, "because art is a painful search. I've gone into several blind alleys: historical paintings, war scenes; at one point I even admired brown-gravy Bouguereau. In my Realist period I was a prisoner of form. Now, I've turned to Japanese prints and they have freed me."

He hardly stopped talking to take a breath.

"I have a liking for the difficulties of art; and the difficulties of life as well. No art is as lacking in spontaneity as mine. As for inspiration, temperament, I know nothing of them. Art is vice. It is not to be embraced in lawful wedlock but raped."

Frédéric Bazille, a social equal, dared to bait him.

"That is the only thing you do rape. Your models say you don't *foutre* them on the divan after their sittings. Or any other women."

"I hate women. That's why I paint them so often."

Degas was a bachelor and a misanthrope. He had money at his disposal but refused to use it, living and working in a cramped studio, loaded with pictures and books, with one old women to serve him. He had few friends, only painters he considered his equal in talent and wealth. Manet leaned toward Camille and said quietly:

"Don't believe his self-portrait. It's not *fidèle*. He took care of his painter friends in Italy; persuaded his family to help them. If you knew his portraits of his aunt, uncle and female cousins, the Bellelli family, strong-willed, unamiable, dour, you'd see the way he thinks the aristocratic class should behave. He's only thirty-two; he'll outgrow it."

In a discussion about the best shops in which to buy pure unabsorbent canvas and mink brushes, Armand Guillaumin mentioned a shop where he could get the best deals. Degas cried:

"What! Do you patronize Jews?"

Again there was a hush.

It was the first time in his association with the painters of Paris that an anti-Semitic remark had been uttered in his presence. Camille sat stunned, a cascade of thoughts ripping through his mind. What could be wrong with Degas that he could harbor such an ugly infection, such a shameful prejudice? He was an educated man, he had to know that the Jews had a learned and civilized culture that went back almost five thousand years and fathered his own Christianity? That it had enriched the world with great moral values and the literary heritage of the Old Testament? Judaism was one of the most venerable and enlightened religions to emerge since the evolution of man. Even though he, Camille, did not participate in its ritual, in some unformulated fashion he knew that he had vital roots; that the verities of his ancestors permeated his brain and nature and work. He remembered his father quoting to him, in some distant past, a proverb from the Talmud:

"The righteous of all people have an inheritance in the world to come."

That there was a substratum of anti-Semitism underlying the surface of French civilization was well known; but this from a fellow artist made him a little sick at his stomach.

When several of the group had left, Degas came around the table, sat down next to Camille.

"I'm happy to meet you at last. I have a particular sympathy for you; you are so delightful in your order and your faith in landscape. I particularly admired *Banks of the Marne at Chennevières.*"

Camille could only splutter, ". . . but, Monsieur Degas, you said we painters clutter up the fields. You would like to shoot us."

Degas grinned.

"Only the amateurs who turn out a landscape with a plate of soup and three brushes. Your work is authentic, it blazes a new path for landscape painting. Let us be friends."

"I am a Jew."

"I know."

"How can you want to be my friend and be anti-Semitic?"

"Oh, that. It popped out. Pay it no mind. I inherited it from my grandparents and parents. It will never come between us. You will be my one landscape painter."

Camille remembered Degas's delightful *Woman with Chrysanthemums.*

"He's so good! I must accept him," he thought.

Pontoise itself had not attracted him, though Julie would find more conveniences in the larger community struggling tortuously up the side of a mountain which was in effect an amphitheater hollowed out by nature. It overlooked the river Oise on its right bank from the top of its limestone cliffs where most of the town's houses had been built, and from which steep embankment he could see over the valley of Montmorency, where he had painted, and the forests of St. Germain all the way to Paris. Down from the ancient plateau barges were bringing wheat, grain, rye to the prosperous granaries of Pontoise; going upstream on the Viosne and Oise were horse-drawn barges from Paris carrying manufactured goods to the prosperous agricultural country.

But it was L'Hermitage about which he told Julie:

"I think I've come home."

"Home? Another strange house, strange village, nobody to talk to. . . ."

"The Hermitage speaks to me more strongly than any place I've ever known. No one else has wanted to paint this area.

It's too untamed, too unknown. There's a thrill about pioneering here."

He waltzed her around the large front room.

"Julie, everywhere, a hundred yards from our house in any direction, there is a stimulating prospect. Not beautiful, not sacred, but deeply moving. There is a sense of time yet a sense of the eternal. I must grasp its meaning and render it on a flat piece of canvas. Not the way Monsieur Nadar does with photographs, what the camera sees. I move things around, a house, a line of trees, a path which upsets my composition. I plant trees on the opposite side of the road, put a path alongside with tiny peasants walking down it, when what I've seen is the path in the middle of the field, nothing on it but a goat. I burrow deep to get to the interior meaning of a scene. . . ."

He knew he was talking to himself but felt impelled to go on.

"I'm seeing from two points of view: what the eye records, and my inner vision. I throw off the transitional changes of the earth, get down to my own fundamental truth. That's the function of the artist. Presumptuous, isn't it?"

"I don't understand."

"You don't need to understand," he laughed. "I love you."

Though she had borne three children, her figure was slender, her face fresh. It had an optimistic glow of acceptance. She was rarely out of an apron but that was what she had been wearing when he fell in love with her in Passy. It could have been a formal gown, so gracefully did she move about the house in it. He kissed her on the mouth, held her tight.

He did a charcoal sketch of himself, wanting to compare it with the one he had done for Fritz Melbye. He had changed from the questioning youth of that self-portrait at the age of twenty-seven. It was 1866 and he was approaching thirty-six, a good time to review the things that had happened to him during the decade. Which things had been important then, and which had fallen away. He had attended four professional studios, each bringing a modest improvement in technique. He had exhibited several times at the Salon; been rejected twice; sold little. He had found a master, Papa Corot. His father was dead; his mother suffering over his affair with Julie and the illegitimate children he had sired. He had been disinherited. He had met hundreds of painters, some masters of the art, old and successful, others young and struggling as he was himself, many talented and innovative, some without a modicum of creativity. They came into Paris and the academies by the hundreds; most of them soon forgotten.

He had become part of the art community, first at Andler's with Courbet, then at the Brasserie des Martyrs, then at the Café Guerbois. He had drunk beer and wine and argued personalities and talent and painting with the friendliest of them and with the most obnoxious. He had made deep relationships and shallow. He had even for a brief few weeks had a dealer.

Most important, he had found a robust group of artists who were bound together by the fact that they were the unwanted, abused rebels trying to remake the intentions of painting. There was a bond of affection, loyalty, helpfulness among them that made the struggle viable; a group effort that would one day bring results and justify their fanatical belief that the Fontainebleau romantic aura no longer fit the times. Any more than did a hard and naked realism that attested only to man's cruelty to man. That somewhere between lay the truth of man's relationship to his universe, to nature and to his fellows. It was a faith that gave them courage through the years of hardship, rejection, invective and, for most of them, an anxiety about the next day's food, rent, canvas, tubes of paint.

He looked older, he felt older; but by way of compensation his work had matured at least a decade's worth. Perhaps at L'Hermitage and in ancient Pontoise he would reach his goal.

He had been trimming his dark beard hollow at the center so that it looked orderly and disciplined. Now he decided to let it run its course without interference or fashionable shaping, though he would trim his mustache neatly about his lips; a person listening should be able to see one speak, as well as hear. It made for clarity. He was not fearful that his beard would dwarf his face, for the longer it grew, the more enormous his deep brown eyes appeared, the stronger became his well-modeled bony nose with its slight hump so reminiscent of his mother's.

"If I ever need to wear spectacles," he confided to Julie, "they will slip down my nose just as Rachel's do. I'll be forever pushing them back up."

He wandered along the banks of the Viosne. The Viosne and Oise had been flowing there for thousands of years. Aeons. Perhaps not the identical river bed; rivers changed their courses with flood, landslide, earthquake, natural damming. But there was water long before there was a Pontoise. Were the fields across the Viosne cultivated in Celtic times? Roman? What about the pictures he would paint of the Hermitage? Would they still be alive in another decade? Another century? Can man create for eternity?

"Easy question. Impossible to answer. One does one's job and sleeps on an easy conscience for a pillow."

He tried to enunciate for himself the reasons why the Hermitage moved him so tremendously, convinced him he could do his best work there. Why he was so challenged to make this land without surface appeal accepted and understood. It would be a Hermitage strained through his own concept of its strength and beauty. He would capture its essence rather than its bulk, dig down to its indigenous beauty.

He sketched the riverbank, the peasants working in the fields, the houses of soft *moellon*, stone, pigeons dumping on the roofs, green lichen growing up their sides, the hillsides, the cultivated patches and the wild ones, the few mills and lone smokestack in the distance, until they became part of his being.

"Or have I become part of them?" he asked himself. "Is it possible for a man to become so much a part of an area that he belongs as surely as the boulders along the road? Or the bushes on the riverbank? Is it part of every man's hunger to have a small spot on earth where he can plant his feet? Say, 'This is where I belong'?"

Paris! He had never intended to be a city painter. But it had been a magnificent place to learn to use his tools, to sharpen his eye to man's incredible diversity, to experiment with the human figure, young and old, overworked or pampered, to expand his concept of what was paintable . . . the range of life all available in the streets, all laid out for him. He had had no intention of converting his hundreds of sketches into oil paintings, only to learn to get down on paper with pen and pencil, charcoal or pastel crayon what his eye was beginning to observe and his mind to understand. Having come from a limited island life, he had been excited by the multitude of people, the constant movement.

He had learned in Montmorency, La Roche-Guyon, La Varenne that he responded deeply to the earth and its fruits; that he felt an affinity with a growing field of hay, an orchard in bloom, a copse of pine with red-tiled houses seen through autumnal foliage, that he preferred the forest, the loam of fertile soil underfoot to the macadam of the Boulevard des Capucines. He was not passing judgment on their comparative importance; it was just that, as a painting man, a country pond reflecting on its surface the colors of the sky and the overhanging foliage moved him deeply.

After several months of hard painting around the Hermitage his first impetus had spent itself. When Claude Monet invited him to go with Renoir, himself and a new young painter named Alfred Sisley, with a burgeoning talent, to Mother Anthony's Inn in Fontainebleau, he was delighted to do so. The inn was a weathered building standing back from the hard-beaten dirt road that wandered through the village of Marlotte, mercifully surrounded by shade trees.

He would go to Marlotte with the artists and Julie would invite her sister Félicie and her daughter Nini out to the country.

In Alfred Sisley, Camille met a delightful man with a jolly nature and a rambunctious background of English ancestors whom he bragged about. At twenty-six he was nine years younger than Camille; they had seen each other casually at Gleyre's where Sisley had become a friend of Monet and Bazille, but no sparks had ignited between them. Now, at the round table in the corner of Madame Anthony's little dining room, they eased into an amiable relationship. Sisley was bilingual; Camille encouraged him to chat in English but Sisley liked to talk of himself in a droll French.

"My ancestors were sheep farmers in Romney Marsh in Kent; actually they made their money smuggling gold guineas into France, then French lace back into England."

Camille took in Sisley's tall, handsome figure in his expensive clothes, attractive features, smartly barbered wavy brown hair. He had the aloof eyes of a genteel observer rather than the hot inquiring gaze of the artist.

"My great-greats took good care of me. My great-grandfather became a Frenchman, married a Frenchwoman, served in the

Republican Guard and became a wealthy merchant from silks and paisley shawls. My grandmother was French, though my father married an Englishwoman. I was brought up as a Frenchman, but at seventeen my father sent me to England to learn his trade. I had to stay for five years but I learned more about Turner and Constable than I did about business. When I returned to Paris my father said, 'You want to paint? Paint! Just be happy and don't bring me any problems.' ''

"He didn't demand that you become a success?" asked Camille.

"Why should he? He'd made a fortune producing and selling artificial flowers."

Camille heard himself utter an amused groan. Artificial flowers! The kind Julie worked at. Perhaps in the Sisley factory. And how many hundreds of Sisley's father's artificial flowers had he sold in their shop in St. Thomas? How many boxes had he taken off the ships from France, loading them in the little car up the rails to Dronningens Gade! Small world.

To Sisley, he said:

"I follow Papa Corot's advice and go into the woods before sunrise. Would you care to accompany me?"

"I came to Marlotte to do just that."

In the dark before dawn they had hot coffee, bread, a confiture and sweet butter, then stumbled through the woods to a clearing. At the first intimation of coral on the horizon they set up their easels, a bit apart. To Camille's astonishment, Alfred Sisley in a smudged painter's smock was a totally different person from the one who had so gaily talked about Felicia Sell, his English mother, from whom he felt he had inherited his height and his penchant for art, coming as she did from an old and cultured London family with a love of music and society. At work he was reserved, almost timid. When after a couple of hours they took a breather and examined each other's canvas, Sisley said:

"For the present I don't intend to pursue the Salon jury or look for a dealer. I have so much to learn from you and Monet and Renoir and Guillemet. I want to paint the way you fellows do."

He gave off no odor of anxiety. There were other painters from wealthy families: Manet, Guillemet, Degas, Bazille, who had no need to sell their work, yet for all the pleasantries of their circumstances were determined to create a place for themselves as painters. They could be witty, fun-loving, gregarious; but at the same time they were grimly competitive, struggled to be accepted. In Sisley Camille felt no mortal conflict. He seemed to wear an inner lining of protection against a mundane world.

Camille found a touch of poetry in his sketches but was surprised at the dark palette, the landscape done in somber browns, heavy greens, hard blues . . . all out of character.

"Who are you trying to imitate?" he asked.

Sisley blushed, then grinned.

"*Alors,* Courbet, Gleyre . . ." He toyed with a branch he had picked up from the forest floor.

"Every painter regurgitates his masters," Camille admonished. "You will have to lighten your colors to match your own buoyant personality."

Back at Madame Anthony's, Alfred Sisley donned his fashionable clothes and laid siege to Madame Anthony's waitress Nana, a neighboring farm girl with a full country face, large deep blue eyes, a flawless skin, in a starched black uniform with a white collar and cuffs. Renoir confided:

"She is a superb girl. I painted her, and she posed like an angel. But Sisley isn't going to be satisfied just painting her."

His two weeks in Marlotte were refreshing. He spent the days painting with Renoir, Monet, Sisley, comparing results, passing jovial evenings around the supper table, small, square, low-legged, not altogether steady when loaded with a tureen of corn soup or lamb stew. They argued theory, watched Sisley's progress with the buxom Nana. Mother Anthony joined them for coffee. She was a middle-aged woman with a plain but discerning face, her hair tressed tightly toward the back of her head and wrapped securely in a gray kerchief. It was decidedly her inn. It had originally been a farmhouse to which she had added a number of modest bedrooms. She was an excellent cook of plain food, dished up in abundance, which the painters appreciated. Camille never did learn whether there was a Monsieur Anthony. She cheered her artist guests when they became depressed, nursed them if they fell ill, but was by no means a sentimentalist. Her other clients paid robust rates. For painters she charged the barest costs; nor was she known to harass them if they were late in their payments. In return they painted her walls with portraits, caricatures, Parisian scenes, landscapes.

Renoir painted *Mother Anthony's Inn* during their stay, a study of the group at the table: Nana gathering the dishes, Sisley wearing his painter's smock, Camille in his one good

Sunday suit and a rakish wide-brimmed straw hat. At Camille's feet, gazing quizzically at Renoir while he painted was Toto, Madame Anthony's white, curly-haired, overlarge lapdog.

It was a period out of time.

10

Of a Sunday afternoon he took Julie for a walk through Pontoise. They followed the new boulevard along the Viosne, then started the long climb up the Rue Impériale with its monumental staircase leading to the church of St. Maclou. There was nothing rustic about Pontoise, even though it had fallen from its medieval splendor as the capital of ancient Vexin. It was an important ecclesiastical enclave with the churches of St. Maclou of the imposing towers, Notre Dame, and the convent of the Carmelites. The village had been known as a huge monastery until the Revolution, after which the Church had lost its power. The churches and early châteaux were neglected; the crazy-angled hodgepodge of unrelated houses ran uphill with the discipline of mountain goats. Its population had decreased by half, falling to five or six thousand. It was both a living and a long-dead community, moderately prosperous but dining on the memory of its former glories. The city hall, built in the fifteenth century, was still standing; the *place* in front of it had been broadened to give Pontoise one of the open squares which Haussmann had decreed imperative for a livable city. On the square were the better shops: hairdresser, creamery, *pâtisserie*, the offices of the few notaries.

It was the Hermitage that had attracted him. Now he was beginning to find Pontoise equally stimulating.

"There are no rich people here, and no poor," he observed. "Everyone has his little piece of land to cultivate outside the town, even the shopkeepers. We fit into the landscape like everyone else."

They climbed to the top of the cliff above the river Oise and saw why it had become a vantage point: here the river was at its widest, with protected coves for loading barges. Beyond the cultivated hillsides were fertile plateaus stretching for miles, as did the fields across the river.

"Simple for plowing and planting," he said, "but enormously complex from a painter's point of view. It's not only *savoir voir*, to know how to see, that has to be learned; but also to analyze how the complex elements affect each other."

Julie grew cold in the wind off the plains. Camille took her to the Place de la Gare, to the inevitable corner café. Over the steaming *café au lait* he told her about the town: how it had been at the height of its power in the thirteenth century, then declined to the status of a granary village, a maze of winding, twisting rivulets of cobblestone streets that had never known the blueprint of the architect. Not a decaying town, but one past its exuberant era. No Parisians wanted summer houses there.

"Why?"

"Perhaps it is a little forbidding."

"Why are we the exception?"

"Because I see it as paintable, the most individual and distinct I've encountered."

Julie was more intrigued than complaining.

"We are going to spend our lives where it's paintable instead of livable?"

He put his arm about her waist as they braked their knees down the steep slope back to the Hermitage.

For the April Salon of 1866 he submitted his earlier *Banks of the Marne in Winter*, which he had started in La Varenne, and *La Maison du Père Gallien*. In *Banks of the Marne in Winter* he had captured the bare, stark, cold loneliness of winter. There was a trail on the viewer's left leading him into the scene with the suggested images of a woman with a small child; the path bordered by leafless trees. There was a green mount sloping toward the river, as did the solidly planted fields that looked as though there would be hard earth beneath them a hundred miles in depth. The only habitation was a compact group of houses and the blank side of a barn. There was no fantasy here, just harsh winter reality; and an eternally searing beauty.

He took the painting into Paris to Corot to secure permission to use the older man's name as his master in the catalogue. It was a while since he had climbed to the bare, spacious studio on the fourth floor of 54 Rue Paradis Poissonnière. Several canvases were drying on their easels. Corot, in his faded blue smock and blue wool cap, puffed away on his Pipette, humming a tune from Offenbach's opera *La Belle Hélène*. The same books, *The Imitation of Christ* and *Polyeucte*, occupied the shelves; *The Bridge at Narni*, the favorite of his paintings, still hung over his bed in the alcove. He welcomed Camille with his gravelly voice.

"Ah, Pissarro, you've brought your Salon entry for this year."

"How are you, Papa Corot?"

"Aging miraculously, thank you. Never a day without a drawing or a few dabs of oil on a canvas. That's how to stay alive forever."

"I believe you. There isn't a new wrinkle in your face."

"Why should there be? I am not a penitent who beats himself with the thorny branches of theory. I learned early how to paint and I've never changed."

He gave Camille a mellow smile.

"We are only simple mortals, subject to error; so listen to the advice of others, be firm, be meek, but follow your own convictions. When one follows another, one is always behind.
. . . You want to use my name in the catalogue? Why not! I've known your work now for a full decade."

Camille handed him *Banks of the Marne in Winter*. Almost instantly the atmosphere in the studio froze. Corot laid down his meerschaum and took a long stride to the big north window. When he turned back to Camille his face was expressionless.

"Why?" he demanded coldly.

"Why what?"

"Such flatness."

"It's a winter scene."

"Is winter ugly? Repulsive?"

"It is beautiful."

"But not on your canvas."

"Particularly on this canvas."

"There is no delicacy here, no charm."

"There isn't any on the banks of the Marne in winter."

"Then why waste your time painting it?"

"Because it's a scene of intense character."

"The composition is good. The rest estranges me. You're using Courbet's harsh tones."

"I had not meant to. The painting is not derivative."

"Certainly not of me!"

Corot went back to his stool before the easel, relighted his pipe.

"It won't be accepted, you know. You have strayed too far."

"From what?"

"A harmonious glow. A joyous impression."

"I took joy from the painting."

"It's not enough to take joy. You have to give it. This is a gloom-filled world. Ah! Modern artists, the good God is not happy at all. He shows you the most beautiful things to see, the most beautiful things to render, and you alter them, you spoil them. *Eh bien*, my little friend, God, to punish you, makes of your heart a heart of cork.''

With which he turned back to his own canvas, began to hum and apply paint. Camille saw that he had been dismissed.

He went down the four flights of stairs more slowly than he had gone up, his painting under his arm. There was no question now of putting Corot's name in the catalogue.

Banks of the Marne in Winter was rejected by the jury. Once again his picture was rescued for showing by Daubigny's "charity." Daubigny also fought to have Renoir's and Cézanne's pictures admitted, only to be outnumbered. A Cézanne portrait was rejected on the grounds that it was painted with a pistol. Daubigny replied in a last failing shot, "I prefer pictures full of boldness to the nullities that appear in every Salon."

Charles François Daubigny, a calm contemplative man, became the hero of the young painters of Paris.

Though Camille had exhibited several times now in the Salon he had never received any attention in the press. This time two articles were published, Emile Zola's in *L'Evènement*, and Jean Rousseau's in *L'Univers Illustré*. Zola said:

. . . Thank you, Monsieur (Pissarro), your winter landscape refreshed me for a good half hour during my trip through the great desert of the Salon. I know that you were admitted only with great difficulty and I congratulate you on that. Besides which, you ought to know that you please nobody and that your painting is thought to be too bare, too black. So why the devil do you have the arrant awkwardness to paint solidly and study nature so honestly! . . . You are a clumsy blunderer, sir—you are an artist that I like.

Rousseau's compliment also carried a sting:

Surely there is nothing more vulgar than this view and nevertheless I challenge you to pass by without noticing it. It becomes original by the abrupt energy of execution which underlines these uglinesses, instead of seeking to conceal them. One sees that Monsieur Pissarro is not banal by inability to be picturesque. On the contrary, he employs a robust and exuberant talent to reveal the vulgarities of the contemporary world.

Tempering the delight at his recognition was his reaction to the word *vulgaire*, a piercing sword in his innards. Of all the pejorative terms in the language this was the last one he thought he deserved. He felt himself to be a sensitive man, with only worship for the exquisite earth, the stars, the rivers, trees, fields, human habitation. Nature was his religion. It was not possible that he would desecrate that which he loved most. When he joined his friends at the Guerbois the following Thursday and Monet pulled Rousseau's clipping out of his pocket, Degas cried bitterly:

"No, Claude, don't read it. The more you move garbage the worse it stinks."

He drew hoots of sardonic laughter.

They had responded to Camille's landscapes for their lack of the sentimentality which had dominated French landscape painting for a long time; for the change in depth; the land did not sit superficially on a thin shelf. They had applauded the lightening of his palette, as indeed they had lightened their own, to show the effect of the sun on the surface of river, field, house: his introduction of multicolored shadows, reflected in nature, but anathema to the blacks and browns of the Salon's academic painters; the dignifying of peasants working in the fields without idealizing them. They did not rebel against his picturing of the harsh nature of winter, to which man accommodates in order to survive.

Camille took comfort from the vehement reaction of his friends to the reviews. Bazille and Guillemet offered to stand the table to a round of drinks.

11

His move into the Hermitage and Pontoise was an ongoing love affair, the virginity of the area no longer its major excitement. The finding of a unique milieu consonant with one's talent and temperament was so necessary to the painter that he searched for it all of his life. Even as had the painters of the Fontainebleau School been fortunate, in the poverty and neglect of their early years, to have found a place they loved within boundaries they could contain, without the need to trudge and pant, easel on back, looking for a spot that moved them to expression.

Julie sensed the depth of his emotion.

"You love it here."

"I never intend to leave."

" . . . more than you do me and the little ones?"

He held her against him, felt her palpitant anxiety.

"Now, *ma petite femme*, you're comparing olive trees with grain fields. I love you and the children. I also love all the painting to be done here. The two feelings do not oppose each other."

She murmured, "My father didn't love his family or his work. Only to wander."

"I am a daft painter who will be with you all my life. For better or being broken." He laughed quietly.

"I can stand that. As long as our needs come ahead of your oil and varnish."

His voice hardened.

"Julie, this is not a horse race. Neither of us wins or loses separately. I know I move forward so slowly it appears I'm standing still. But I'm not."

Money. It was an eternal harassment. Better men than he had been poor; yes, and with youngsters to raise. Emma sent gifts of food and clothing for the children, sometimes modest sums to Julie to buy things she urgently needed. He could rely on Rachel for his sixteen dollars a month to cover the rent and basic needs. Occasionally a friend bought a sketch or a small oil for a few francs. Alfred still volunteered to pay for the expensive gold frames needed to show his pictures at the Salon. Dr. Gachet happily accepted paintings for his services when Lucien or Minette came down with a fever.

The one luxury of which he would not deprive himself, now that his trips into Paris must be curtailed, was a daily newspaper. The journals were brought to Pontoise each morning on the train. He felt a need to know what was going on in the outside world, the international news of war and uprisings, as well as the movements in science, industry, all the peccadilloes of the human race. A health measure called vaccination was being widely practiced in Paris; should they expose their children to it or wait for results? Richardson's local anesthetic had been imported from London and was now used for surgery. Chocolate was recommended for stomach ailments. They would try it. There was a preoccupation with sticking pins and flags into maps of Europe in order to follow the Austro-Prussian War. Stuttering was becoming popular as a method of avoiding army service. Duels were more frequent. An inexperienced lawyer defended a robber very poorly. The prosecuting attorney rose, proved the robber guilty, then, "immediately changing tone and gesture, indicated with heated eloquence the way in which he would have managed the defense." The result was the acquittal of the accused.

Courbet had exhibited aquatints at Cadart et Luquet. The critics said, "What temperament! What verve! Yet he wrecks, as if willfully, the most marvelous artistic talent!" There was also a first exhibition of the paintings of lunatics, with great curiosity in the capital as to their meaning.

"And they claim we are the demented ones," Camille remarked with a sardonic grin.

He was pleased to see that Julie picked up the journals whenever she had a few spare moments during the day; or in the evening after the children were asleep. He could not persuade her to read a book; she had neither analytical nor philosophical bent, nor the free hours one needed to concentrate. She did enjoy Camille's reading to her a chapter of the De Goncourt brothers' new novel *Manette Salomon,* and discussing with her its dramatic dilemmas. He bought Emile Zola's second novel, *The Confessions of Claude.* Julie was sympathetic because Zola had received her cordially at his evenings at home. She grew angry when Camille read her the criticism of the book:

> "Monsieur Zola is an artist. We like his style, his ardent nature. When he seeks subjects outside unhealthy impressions, no doubt his work will satisfy his friends and critics."

There were some who considered Zola fortunate to get the attention.

When the winter became too cold and wet, the house inadequate to protect them from the icy winds and rains, he knew he would have to have an apartment in Paris for the worst months. He could not impose on Guillemet's hospitality for long stretches. After a hard search he found one on the Boulevard Rochechouart. The space was cramped but they were able to remain warm during the wettest and coldest part of the winter.

They took into Paris only their beds, tables and chairs. Their landlord in Pontoise permitted them to leave their other belongings there without charge. Camille worked at home and in the studios of his friends to give Julie and the children breathing room. He slashed a still life of her kitchen onto a canvas with his palette knife: two large serving spoons hanging on the wall, on the table a garden salad, a half loaf of bread, a pitcher of red wine, one glass between three ripe apples.

As soon as the icy winds died down he moved his family back to L'Hermitage.

Eighteen sixty-six had been a fruitful year, five oils of Salon potential. His confreres at the Café Guerbois declared them the perfect matching of a man and his environs.

Artists paid scant attention to Easter, the *quatorze juillet*, All Saints, or the New Year. Their date was the opening of the official Salon, one toward which they worked to perfect canvases that would get them admitted, hung, honored with medals. It kept them busy, inventive, disciplined.

In 1867 it was announced that Napoleon III was staging another Exposition Universelle, even bigger than the one Camille had visited when he arrived in Paris twelve years before. With a larger area to fill, the jury would be obliged to show more work of the artists knocking so clamorously on its hobnailed door. They clutched at optimism. After a while Julie too caught the fever of expectancy. She had been dispirited; they had run out of all available cash and Camille had had to visit the *mont-de-piété* to borrow money from the official pawnbroker on his gold watch, a gift from his father, and one of Julie's copper saucepans provided early on by Emma. Julie had turned away to conceal her tears and feed the children. She and Camille would share what was left.

Camille, Monet, Cézanne, Sisley, Whistler, again spending a season in Paris, Renoir, Degas, Bazille, Guillemet, Guillaumin, all selected their best canvases. The men around the two tables at the Café Guerbois were joined by critic and sculptor Zacharie Astruc; novelists Emile Zola and Léon Claudel; the critics Duranty and Armand Silvestre; Bracquemond and Constantin Guys, engravers; the collector Théodore Duret, son of a wealthy family and a prosperous brandy merchant with an extraordinarily keen eye. They formed a solid front against a world that had become too indifferent to be hostile. Camille cherished his secure position within the group.

Then, instead of accepting more artists to show because of the international aspect of the exposition, the jury decided to be ultracautious and selected fewer. Only Fantin-Latour's portrait of Edouard Manet was accepted, and Whistler's *At the Piano*. Obviously the jury wanted the visitors to see

France as solid, sober and respectable; believed that if the Salon exhibited any of its wild men the foreigners would think France had become unreliable, might even refuse to buy the new machinery being shown in the Palais de l'Industrie.

Camille turned to Emile Zola and Charles Baudelaire.

"It's more serious than that, isn't it? They see us as basically immoral. France has always been considered immoral sexually by puritan England, Germany and the United States. Is the jury afraid the foreigners will see our paintings as a further extension of their sins?"

Only Paul Cézanne enjoyed being part of the lost sheep.

Despite his disappointment Camille took Julie to see the World's Fair on the Champ-de-Mars. A branch of the suburban railroad was brought into Paris, as well as a flotilla of small steamboats which carried visitors from Sèvres and St. Cloud. The structure, roofed in zinc and glass, and its huge display surfaces, caused Victor Hugo to comment:

"It brings to mind the Colosseum, like a circus built by a student of Barnum."

Around two hundred thousand visitors a day trooped through the building, divided into concentric galleries, each reserved for a different nation, including the Russian Tsar, the kings of Greece and Belgium, the Viceroy of Egypt, Octave of Sweden, Bismarck, with the face of a bulldog, in his pointed helmet, applauded by the crowds as their idol. They examined the balloon called *Le Géant*, the Krupp cannon of five hundred tons from Prussia; thronged around the first steam automobile, walked through an Austrian village, a mosque with minaret, a palace of the Bey of Tunis.

"The French Empire is at the height of its glory," the press gloated. Baron Haussmann was admired for creating a superb jewel of a city; everyone sang *La Belle Hélène*.

The Salon exhibition was divided into two parts: one in the Champs-Elysées, the other on the Left Bank in the Champ-de-Mars. Gustave Courbet leased a plot halfway between the two, on the banks of the Seine near the Pont de l'Alma, and built a gallery to house his own exhibition for the rest of his life, crying:

"I shall send nothing more to the exhibitions of the government, by whom I have been so badly treated."

It cost him ten thousand dollars. He was using his own money, and showing one hundred and fifteen paintings broken into nine generic groups: a staggering quantity of work.

He received less space in the press than he had for his 1855 exhibition; the reviews were halfhearted at best, vitriolic at worst. The public was uninterested; few came. Two pictures were stolen and auctioned in London. His ticket seller, a former Zouave, learned how to cheat at the turnstile, stealing a thousand dollars. The income barely covered the daily costs. He did sell two canvases, *Stone Breakers* for three thousand two hundred dollars and *Poverty in the Village* for eight hundred; but his investment was largely lost.

Edouard Manet also used his own capital to build a personal gallery, a more modest pavilion. He showed fifty of his works, sold nothing. People came, but only to amuse themselves, not to evaluate the paintings.

Totally frustrated, the Batignolles group decided as a last resort to petition Napoleon III for another Salon des Refusés. Camille, Renoir, Sisley and Bazille wrote the paper in proper form, then dispatched it to Versailles.

Napoleon III saw no reason for another painterly outburst.

Gustave Courbet summoned the group to supper at the Brasserie Andler. There were stout kegs of Bavarian beer and smoked sausage. After treating his guests to dinner, he exclaimed:

"I hear you've been rejected as Refusés. Very well. Use my pavilion. Your only costs will be for printing catalogues, paying for guards."

Pandemonium broke loose. Courbet, in his generous fashion, had saved their year.

The group then estimated they would need over a thousand dollars to mount and maintain their Refusés exhibition for a month. Claude Monet, Berthe Morisot, Fantin-Latour, Bazille, Guillemet, Sisley, Degas offered their francs immediately. Courbet pledged a modest sum, as did Daubigny. To Camille's surprise Corot also offered a contribution.

They were able to raise a little over half the money. No one could spare any more: most of them had nothing to give. The Salon des Refusés number two was gone. It had been a wonderful opportunity.

Gustave Courbet's pavilion was also soon gone. Neglected, the roof began to fall in. The city of Paris declared it a dangerous nuisance, ordered it torn down. Leaning against the wrought-iron railing over the Pont de l'Alma watching the wrecking crew demolish Courbet's "lifetime" pavilion, Camille thought:

"Perhaps we're all dangerous nuisances and should be razed."

Ingres died at the age of eighty-seven. He was mourned by all France. When Baudelaire died in August, at the age of forty-six, he was mourned only by his artist friends at the Brasserie Andler and the Café Guerbois.

The next time Camille and his confreres gathered, Frédéric Bazille had a fighting gleam in his eye. Catching a pause in the conversation, he proffered:

"We have not been able to get exhibited. If we are going to show our work we'll have to do it ourselves."

"What are you talking about?" Cézanne growled.

"A cooperative effort. We must save our money and rent a suitable hall."

Manet dismissed the idea with a regal wave of his hand.

"No one will come."

"They'll come . . . after a while. If we persist, year after year."

"The Salon would make hash out of such an independent exhibition," Degas contributed.

"Is that any worse than being rejected by them?"

"Yes," said Manet. "If we're rejected for one Salon we can submit pictures for the next. If we go into opposition we'll be barred for life."

"Their life. Not ours. They're old. We're young. It's only reasonable that we'll outlive them and take over."

It was a strange suggestion coming from Bazille; heresy.

"We will become the art establishment." His whole gangly frame was emphatic. "Since the Salon refuses to absorb us, it's our obligation to replace them."

Guillemet cried:

"Versailles would declare us illegal."

"Not so long as we pay our bills and don't incite to riot."

Guillaumin grumbled, "The sight of our pictures incites to riot."

No one took Bazille seriously. Even Camille, who had absorbed Proudhon's concept of small communal cooperatives, murmured:

"The Salon is our only Colosseum. The jury will tire of throwing us to the lions."

Bazille bowed out of the contest.

"Obviously you're not ready for independence yet. For our own show on our own terms."

BOOK SEVEN

Cape of Tempests

1

ONCE WHEN THE tradesmen of Pontoise were pressing for payment Camille swallowed his pride and asked his mother for help. She declined: although her St. Thomas affairs were being managed by her nephew, there were constantly increasing charges against her rental income for taxes, repairs, special assessments. Some of Frédéric's French securities had fallen in value. Alfred refused to take responsibility for her remaining bonds.

"Suppose I made a bad choice?" he demanded. "I would never forgive myself. We'll have to stay with Papa's decisions."

"Even if they are getting less valuable?" his mother asked. "You're a businessman. Couldn't you make recommendations?"

"Only when I have enough money to repay you for any possible losses."

Rachel had to husband her resources.

Her hair was totally white but it was as abundant as ever, still parted severely in the center. She had found a way to tighten her spectacles; they no longer slid over her nose in moments of stress. An intricate web of wrinkles expanded outward from the corners of her eyes; there were deep lines in her cheeks on either side of her mouth. Her skin was still clear, her longsuffering eyes large as they observed the miseries of those about her.

"If only she could give her love to Julie and the children she would be happier," Camille insisted to himself. "And if only I could earn some money, not a lot, just some . . ."

Rachel was doing with one all-purpose maid, shopped herself to keep the cost down, stopped going to her dressmaker.

"Maman, is it necessary for you to live so frugally?" he asked.

"I must live on what comes in. I would be stupid to undermine my capital. I'm only seventy. I could live another ten years. I will never allow myself to become dependent on Emma or Alfred."

Camille noted with a shrinking feeling that his mother had not included him as a possible means of support.

"Maman, I feel badly about taking that allowance from you when you need it."

"I put that aside the first thing. I will not let a son of mine starve."

There was no question that his mother loved him. She was making sacrifices; she could use that two hundred dollars a year on new clothes, outings at the theater or restaurant. She did not mention Julie, Lucien or Minette, whom her sixteen dollars a month was also helping to keep from starving.

Emma had written to Camille, "Tell me if you go to dine with Maman and if you sleep there sometimes or if it is Alfred who stays with her, and if she has a good servant. I am worried about her because she doesn't know how to make herself happy."

Julie, stolid with the almost phlegmatic nature of one who knew nothing but marginal living, began to drift into a depression over the seeming dead end of his work. The drawings, watercolors, were piling up to no apparent purpose. He sold nothing. There were oil paintings in Rachel's apartment and Guillemet's studio in Paris, as well as in the Pontoise house. The cost of canvas, tubes of paint, brushes, turpentine, charcoal, sketchbooks, all drained away from their meager funds. She indicated Hermitage oils leaning against her kitchen wall.

"Today you have a dozen. In a few years you'll have a hundred. At the end of your life, how many? A thousand? What good will they do if no one wants them? They'll be burned on a dump."

"They will be wanted," he replied, wounded. "Good work finds its audience. Always has. In music, painting, sculpture. . . ."

"Sometimes I feel so low." Her voice was barely discernible.

"Thanks to your gardening we have enough to eat. The children are strong. We have a roof over our heads, clothes on our backs."

She heard the quality of hurt in his voice, crept into his arms, repentant.

"I shouldn't beat you like you was a mule. You never promised me anything . . . only love."

"I do love you, Julie. You must be patient. There are many of us in the same boat."

Another cause of her anxiety was the fact that they were not married and she had two children. Though they were not actually lying, they were putting up a pretense to deceive here in Pontoise as they had in Montfoucault. It was not an unshoulderable burden, many Parisian artists had mistresses and children by them. Yet, with Rachel's unyielding disposition and Camille's inability to support them without her aid, would he ever be able to marry her? Would she have other children, with Camille recognizing them in a statement at the city hall, but their never being legitimate? Would she have to wait for Rachel to die? The curé in Grancey had had to manipulate her father but, worthless as he was, he had married her mother. In Camille's eyes they were married, she knew that. When he went into Paris for a couple of days and wrote notes to her, he opened with, *"Ma chère petite femme*, My dear little wife"; and closed with, "Very dear Julie, believe me always your husband who loves you."

She had been a proud young woman, earning her way. Rachel's refusal to see her, talk to her, visit her grandchildren burned like a hot coal in her bosom, something she had never experienced in the most grinding years in Grancey. The grieving hurt flashed up through the depths of her feelings when she least expected it.

Camille weathered the sometime storms as quietly as he could, suffering for her. His own faith was unshaken that he would begin to sell, they would be married officially, their children would flourish, that his work would earn him the position in the art world which he was convinced one day it would deserve. He had been born to paint; in this resolution he stood on rock.

He had a marvelous sense of fulfillment with each day's work, no matter how baffling or complex the motif. To be working with the tools of his craft, with increased perception as the weeks and months passed, what greater fulfillment could a man ask? He felt the sense of the completeness of life that had been enjoyed by craftsmen who worked in metal, leather, wood, stone; the consummate worker who took joy from the production he alone created and rounded out to perfection. Were there not hazards in every walk of life? Had not even ship chandlering gone bad when sail changed to steam and ships no longer were obliged to stop at St. Thomas for refueling? But there were moments of discouragement, even as Julie had rare moments of understanding.

"Ah, that's pretty," she exclaimed of a new oil. "Like Burgundy . . . almost."

For the most part Julie derived her contentment from Camille's, offering prayers of thanks to a God she could no longer see, hear, touch, smell the incense of, since she did not go to church. She sorely missed her religion, not only for its comforts but for its joys. Early on she had asked Camille if it was proper for her to pray to God since she no longer went to confession or took the sacrament. Camille quoted an old French proverb:

"Près de l'église est souvent loin de Dieu. Near to the church is often far from God."

Many of her happiest hours while growing up had been spent in the church high on the hill, with its ceremonials, its music, its choir of which she had been a part. She comforted herself by telling Camille:

"That was when I was a child. Now I'm a grown woman. Since I am a mother, and as you say I am a wife, that will have to be my religion."

"Can you be happy with that?" His tone was light.

"You gave yourself a new religion. Painting. Can you be happy with that?" she mimicked.

He kissed her soundly.

"As they say in Caracas, it fries no bananas to question life."

Eighteen sixty-seven was again a productive year, including many large canvases. It was a year of ecstasy in which he felt he was striding seven feet above the earth, when he and nature, his palette, canvas, brushes and colors became one. When he cried with each painting, "This is it! This is what I've been trying to say." He did not believe in inspiration, a meaningless mystical word denoting some power beyond one's functioning faculties. Yet if there were such a thing as total creativity he felt that he achieved it in the canvases of *The Hermitage at Pontoise* and the *Hillside of Jallais near Pontoise,* extraordinarily complex arrangements of form and color that came so throbbingly to life they appeared to represent man's best effort in all of the fertile countrysides of the world.

He led his viewer into the hillside of Jallais by a wide mottled path on which two women, one young in white, one with a pink parasol, were approaching; beyond lay an intimate valley with its scattered stone houses and vertical green patches in a series of short comma-like brush strokes, the cultivated oblongs reaching toward the crest, and higher up the lightest pale blue sky festooned with amorphous white clouds.

Here was nature at its most verdant and man's work at its most accomplished. Cyprus trees on the horizon extended the height and deepened the tree-gorged valley.

Exhausted but exultant, he felt that this one canvas alone justified all of his years of disappointment and struggle. He was nonetheless astonished at Julie's reaction when she knelt before the painting where Camille had placed it on a chair. Her eyes were sparkling.

"It's divine," she murmured.

Happy with her extraordinary reaction, twitting her, he said:

"Only the Lord is divine. This painting was made by man."

"God created man."

"So God made this painting?"

"Yes. May I have it?"

"You have them all."

"No, I mean for my own. To keep on the bedroom wall. It makes me . . . feel good, like when the choir sang in Grancey."

He held her in a buoyant embrace.

"It's yours, Julie."

She picked up the picture, prepared to take it into the bedroom. Camille shook his head in amazement.

" *'Ventre affamé n'a pas d'oreille*. A hungry stomach has no ears.' But it has eyes."

She put down the painting, crept back into his arms.

"Oh, Camille, why do we have to be outcasts?"

He stroked her hair with his supple fingers.

"Julie, this world isn't kind, it's cruel. That's why we have love, you and I, to sustain us in the maelstrom so that we don't go under."

She put her cheek against his. He felt the wetness of her tears.

2

Within a short walk of his home was a variety of nature's self-portraiture: rolling hills, fertile fields, meandering roads for animal and human, crossing and interlocking to make the terrain navigable. The area was not lyrical as was Fontaine-

bleau or Montmorency or La Varenne, but it had a trenchant
voice: the small peasant gardens, vineyards, irregular paths
winding among the houses, each with its backyard for vegetables. The motifs existed all around him; it was a matter of
choosing the best from amidst the better. Yet Pontoise had
never produced a native-born or even a transplanted painter.
The artists of Paris roving the countryside had passed through
without attempting to seize its nature. Théodore Rousseau of
the Barbizon School had done a couple of oils around Pontoise
in the 1850s, but neither Camille nor anyone else had seen
them. Berthe Morisot, disciple of Edouard Manet, had visited
Pontoise several years earlier but had left in a matter of
weeks.

The Viosne, within reach of their front windows, was
crawling with the laden barges down from the northern country or being pulled upcountry by ropes attached to aging
horses on the banks, the bargemaster calling out instructions
to his bargemen to row and steer into the center of the stream.

He had told his mother that it was not necessary to live like
a peasant to paint them; but in fact he did. He rose at first
light, was out of the house at dawn, a rucksack on his back.
Julie cooked for the children, fed them, put them out to play,
then tilled her garden, tended her chickens and rabbits, scrubbed her kitchen, went across the road to the Viosne to pound
out her wash in the cold water of the stream. Both worked as
hard as the peasants around them. She was not looked down
upon so much as not spoken to; sensed that her neighbors did
not believe her to be married. Camille could and sometimes
did escape into the bright intellectual milieu of his friends at
the Café Guerbois. On occasion he went into Paris for the
Thursday evening at Emile Zola's and stayed overnight with
his mother. The next day he dropped in on a dealer he had
found on the Rue Laffitte called Martin the Elder, a member
of the Society of Eclectics who had a reputation for having "a
perceptive nose" for young painters and an advanced taste. A
bit of a poet who had had the wisdom to launch Corot and
who handled Jongkind, the superb but unrecognized painter
who had trained Claude Monet at Honfleur outside Le Havre.
Martin bought canvases instead of taking them on consignment, but he paid only four dollars for the smaller sizes, eight
dollars for the larger.

"I will ask triple," Martin confided, "but accept less if
necessary to make a sale. I've bought some Cézannes for
even less; for Claude Monet I've added an extra few francs
because he is so desperately in debt."

Camille was humiliated by the offer.

"Those prices don't cover my costs," he protested.

"They are that much more than nothing. I'm paying Alfred Sisley the same amount. I'll raise them as I find collectors."

Every now and then Paul Cézanne took the early morning train to spend the day with them. He had developed a special rapport with Julie. He also had a mistress, Hortense Fiquet, but kept her hidden from his associates. He felt he could talk to Julie about her, for she would be sympathetic. Cézanne and Camille painted side by side in the fields.

Claude Monet sometimes came with his companion, Camille Léonie Doncieux, whom they began to call Léonie to avoid confusion with Camille. She and Julie became close in spite of the difference in their cultural backgrounds and social positions.

Others came out for a day of painting and companionship in the country: Alfred Sisley, Antoine Guillemet, Armand Guillaumin on a weekend, amusing Frédéric Bazille, whose hair brushed the low ceilings. Renoir abandoned his beloved Paris for a day to sketch on Camille's Fond de l'Hermitage. Julie cooked a midday meal, made them comfortable.

"When the painters come to visit I feel as though they're family."

"They are our family," he assured her. "Even Alfred doesn't come to see us."

Pontoise, the town, was a way point between Paris and the Vexin countryside, a center of interlocking canals, stone quais and docks. It handled ten million bushels of wheat a year, another five million tons of cereals; had a sugar beet factory on the Viosne, a cannery, a small factory for making mineral water. It had advanced to the eighteenth century and was struggling to reach modern times. The entangling maze of shabby streets wandering aimlessly up the hillside was beginning to feel Haussmann's influence. Rows of rickety houses were being torn down to make room for tree-shaded *places*. There was a public park in front of the town's only hospital, the Hôtel Dieu. The newly completed Rue Imperiale connected the new railroad station and St. Maclou.

"When you walk from the modern railroad station to the medieval church you span four centuries in a few minutes," Camille told his visitors. "Pontoise lived in an earlier and less complicated century. The railroads will change everything but not for a number of years. The countryside is mine to portray as it has been since the Romans. The industrial development may corrupt all life here. But not in my time."

It was a robust market town: Tuesday in the Place du Grand Martroy, Thursday in front of Notre Dame. But the big market day was on Saturday in the Place de l'Hôtel de Ville. The peasants, wagon drivers, buyers from Les Halles in Paris crowded the noisy square: hawkers, housewives, peasant women patiently displaying their veal and cabbages, for which the area was famous; rough tables with spreads of peas, beans, potatoes, carrots, wheat. From their orchards they brought in pears and apples to be turned into cider. On Saturday there were marionette shows, acrobats, pony rides. Camille took Julie and the children to the market, where she bargained for her few centimes' worth of rice, flour, fish.

Peasants sold their wares from stands: flowers, clothing, sweets, toys, ducks, geese, pigs, meats: a constantly moving crowd beckoning, bargaining, shouting out their wares; weighing, exchanging money; with strolling musicians, red-nosed clowns in baggy pantaloons; an exciting noisy mélange of shoppers, sellers, starting at dawn and dribbling out, exhausted of energy and merchandise, by midafternoon.

Here Julie met the operators of cottage industries. They began to give her work crocheting doilies, trimming tea towels, pillowcases; knitting scarves, mittens, bed socks, sewing aprons, men's handkerchiefs. She made only a few francs but kept her hands busy and the extra cash bought a delicious veal chunk or a beef shank bone with some meat on it for her soup stock.

They were a detached family, playing no part in the agricultural or commercial life of Pontoise. They could not afford leather shoes, except for trips into Paris, and so the children wore wooden clogs, which brought them a measure of ridicule. Julie sewed Lucien's and Minette's clothing, an occasional work dress for herself. She put pots of water on her stove, held Camille's pants and coat over the steam to freshen them, and tried to keep him from spending their full sixteen dollars a month so that they could have a reserve for emergencies.

In good weather he found a secluded spot on the river Oise with a sandy beach where he could take the children into the water and hold them against his chest until he taught them to swim in the current, less delightful than the Charlotte Amalie bay of St. Thomas where he had been able to swim the year round in the warmth of the Lesser Antilles. Since they were both up at dawn they did not stay awake very long after the supper dishes were washed, the pots scoured, the kitchen swept. The bed was small, they fell asleep in each other's arms, enjoyed the same union of desire and flesh they had discovered in Julie's room under the eaves in Passy. Neither time nor tribulation wore away their fascination in loving each other, though fatigue sometimes did.

They decided again to spend the severe winter months out of the drafty, damp building of the Hermitage, rented an acquaintance's modest studio at 108 Boulevard Rochechouart where they had had an apartment the year before. *L'Illustration* of January 11, 1868, reported that the Seine had frozen over for the first time in twenty years and was immobile, its solid white coat decorated with ice formations, the boats locked into a vise. Drink stands were set up in the middle of the stream and under the arches of the bridges, lined solid with Parisians watching people skate and pull each other on sleds under the cold light of the winter sun. At night moving black silhouettes of men and women dotted the whiteness like shadows behind a screen. Camille took Julie and the children to see the sight. They walked to the Place Dauphine to look at the engineer Chevalier's thermometer to see how cold it was, but the mercury in the long tube had plummeted so far they could not measure how cold they felt. He borrowed skates, took Lucien to the Bois de Boulogne to teach him how to unwobble his ankles, then pulled Minette around the lake on a neighbor's sleigh.

That was the end of their fun. As the cold got worse they developed coughs.

"The children need warmer clothing," Julie warned; "we must get the freeze off the rooms. This fireplace isn't enough."

"Armand Guillaumin told me yesterday about a manufacturer who needs painters to decorate his blinds. He says we can start any morning. I'll go with him tomorrow."

Julie breathed a sigh of relief. She thought, "If the money is good he'll stay with it. We'll live better."

Camille and Guillaumin, on vacation from his job at the government bureau, made their way to the big bare warehouse in the factory district. The owner hired them at once. He tried to set a daily wage but the men, taking their cue from Renoir, insisted on a piece rate. There were young art students and Louvre copyists working in three corners. Camille and Guillaumin were assigned the fourth. In the center of the room was a fat-bellied stove and a boy stoking the fire with dried branches. It threw off good heat; still they had to work in their hats, coats and heavy trousers. They had expected slotted-lath Venetian blinds but found solid canvas rollers.

First they had to surface the canvas, then they were free to make any design they liked; an easy task for a man with a thousand images in his mind. In their corner Camille and Guillaumin tacked up their own rough sketches to make them feel at home. Their fellow workers were highly respectful; Camille Pissarro had actually exhibited at the Salon!

They worked fast and expertly and got good results, better than the proprietor had seen before. They also turned out more blinds in a day because Camille remembered Renoir's stricture:

"Put in plenty of clouds. They go fast and cover a lot of canvas."

He murmured to Guillaumin:

"As long as we have to do this job let's have *drôlerie*. Pretend you're painting for exhibition. Sign your name in the lower right-hand corner."

"We'll get fired."

"Not when the owner sees our work."

Everyone was happy. The owner, who was getting more orders because of the quality of the painting. Julie, because Camille was earning money. Rachel, because Camille was "working." Camille and Guillaumin because they were paid a little extra. They satirized each other's landscapes. One day Guillaumin announced:

"Pissarro, I'm going to paint your portrait painting a blind."

"Are you going to sell it to the boss?"

"I'm going to give it to you in return for your helping me enjoy this drudgery."

They worked six days a week, each laying by some savings. Julie observed:

"You told me, 'Love of money is the root of all evil.' *Quelle blague*. Money is the root of all good things in the shops."

They bought coal to heat the apartment, warm undergarments and wool scarves for the children, cough medicine. Julie did the shopping with the craftiness of her early training; then went to Les Halles to buy meat and dairy products to build up their resistance against the biting cold.

Along with the freeze came fires. Paris watched the Théâtre Belleville burn down. A conflagration at the stables of the omnibus company on the Rue d'Ulm, highly flammable because of its hay and fodder stocks, drove some three hundred crazed horses into the streets and pounding down the cobblestones.

For a little pleasure, Camille took Julie to hear the five

hundredth performance of Rossini's *William Tell,* the melodic score enchanting her; and then to see the theatrical success of the early 1868 season, *Paul Forestier* by Emile Augier, which proved to be a mistake, for the play dramatized the relative merits of wives and mistresses, a subject on which Julie was justifiably sensitive. She said:

"I hope we can get married before I get pregnant again. Three children are too much for a mistress. They should be for a wife."

He did not mind the work on the blinds. Corot had complained that his work had no charm. Now he found that charm had its purpose; it was quite easy to achieve and was highly salable. The last time he had been paid a wage was in the family store in St. Thomas; aside from his books and painting supplies, there had been nothing he wanted to buy. On his way home from work he treated himself to a copy of *Saturnian Poems,* by a twenty-four-year-old named Paul Verlaine.

Along with the winter freeze came turmoil with violent protests in the streets, and Napoleon III issuing harsh measures of suppression. Official permission was needed for all meetings, in particular labor meetings. There were complaints of police being everywhere watching for what they called "subversive gatherings." Seventeen liberal newspapers were indicted for subversion. The voters gained the right to elect their own legislature, but Napoleon III kept its meetings secret. The newspaper that printed its "complete and exact transcript" was shut down. Over coffee and beer in their secluded corner of the Café Guerbois, a disciple of Proudhon proclaimed:

"I can feel the cobblestones rising in the streets."

The artists around the Guerbois tables loathed the inept monarch, a third rinsing of the bottle of his illustrious ancestor; as well as the corruption in the wasteful court that surrounded him. Camille glanced with curiosity at Edouard Manet, Guillemet, Bazille and Edgar Degas, all of whom had sizable estates to lose in an upheaval. He saw no doubt whatever on their faces that they too desired a more republican form of government.

3

The message from London fell upon him like a blow from a heavy instrument: Emma had died in her sleep. She had retired the night before, apparently feeling well. Her heart had stopped beating during the night. She was only forty-eight years old. Camille had loved his half sister, who had served so loyally as surrogate mother when Rachel was in an emotional crisis; who had supported his choice of profession as well as his relationship with Julie.

"I must go and tell my mother," he told Julie, who grieved over the loss of her only friend among the Pissarros.

He sent a *petit bleu* to Alfred to meet him at Rachel's apartment. He would need his brother's help, for he feared what this unexpected disaster would do to her. Alfred took the news with relative calm; he had never been close to Emma. But when Camille told his mother, the words choking in his throat, Rachel fainted. The two remaining sons of her original eight children picked her up, carried her to her bedroom. When she recovered consciousness after Camille administered the smelling salts of carbonate ammonia which Dr. Gachet had recommended for her recurrent faintness, she broke into uncontrollable sobbing.

"Why couldn't it have been me?" she moaned. "I'm old and useless. She's young, with all those children. She left her husband in St. Thomas to come to Paris and settle me, to take care of Delphine. She's the only one who cared for her aging mother. Now I won't have anybody to give me comfort."

Alfred said quietly, "Now, Maman, you know that's not true. I visit once a week."

Rachel's sobbing allowed for no contradiction.

"What comfort can we be?" Camille asked himself. "Emma was a devoted daughter. Sons are busy, making their way. I hurt her with Julie. I'm sorry she's hurt; but I'm not sorry I have my family."

Alfred stayed late. Camille slept over. Rachel wept unceasingly. Dr. Paul Gachet came and gave her a sedative, then said quietly to Camille:

"Do not worry. Your mother has the nervous system of a fragile butterfly but the physical stamina of a white ox."

At noon when Alfred returned from his office Rachel said:

"One of you must go to London to attend the funeral. I couldn't bear to see my last daughter buried."

Alfred stammered, "My business, the next few days . . . I have large shipments . . ."

Rachel cast stricken eyes on Camille.

"You must go. Emma loved you foolishly."

"I have no money. . . ."

Alfred interrupted.

"I'll give you half. Maman will pay the rest. You have nothing else to do."

Camille overlooked the insult. He wanted to be with Emma at the last.

"I'll get the next train to Boulogne."

The Isaacson family was grateful that Camille made the crossing in time but there was little, aside from the eulogizing of Emma, that had any consolation value. The children were distraught; Phineas benumbed. He was trying to adjust to his religious belief that "The Lord giveth, and the Lord taketh away."

Camille wrote to Julie:

> My dear little wife,
>
> I am writing you early this morning because I won't have time to do it tonight before going with Rodolphe, Emma's oldest son, to the synagogue. I didn't dare refuse to do it. It's miserably cold here. It isn't freezing, it's the fog that envelops you, that chills you. . . . I will have to wait till the eight first days of mourning are over to come back to you. Perhaps three of Emma's girls will leave with me. . . .
>
> Au revoir, my dear wife, I embrace you a thousand times. Give two kisses to my dear children. *A bientôt. Tout à toi.*

He remained in London two weeks. Rachel greeted Emma's children with cries of joy. She was all energy and bustle, hiring a second maid for the time they would be with her, buying them Parisian coats, scarves and shoes, planning outings. She was so grateful to Camille for bringing her grandchildren to her that she turned over to him the sixteen-dollar monthly allowance a couple of weeks in advance.

Bitterness filled his throat at the thought of her lack of love or welcome for his own two offspring.

*   *   *

275

Spring came early to the Pontoise area. They returned to find the wheat fields green, the wild flowers surfacing on the hillsides. Camille's passion also burst into new growth. He painted in succession a landscape at Ennery near Pontoise, the mill of Pâtis, the entrance to Pontoise, a small factory, and the banks of the Seine at Bougival, the oil paintings a verisimilitude of life on earth: the multicolored houses planted like eternal boulders against the azure sky; women stooping in their sprouting cabbage patches; the winding paths through the hills edged with budding foliage; a minuscule family group against the eternal range of mountains, both indestructible.

He painted all day under a big gray umbrella, standing for hours unaware of the passage of time, watching the scene emerge slowly from the blank canvas as though he were the actual creator of the earth, its fruits, its high hills and deep valleys, its prolific stands of trees and verdant vegetable gardens. He was aflame with vision, a consanguine relationship with the forces of nature in which he was evolving as interpreter of its solidity and rhythm. The pictures reflected his sense of joy.

His companions at the Cafe Guerbois were stunned at his output. Their eyes glowed as they pored over the unframed canvases.

He took four of his 1867 paintings to Varnishing Day at the depot in Paris. Hundreds of painters were milling about, putting last-moment touches to their work. Camille had only to await Judgment Day. Two of the paintings were accepted, *Hill of Jallais* and *The Hermitage, A Landscape,* but only after Daubigny had waged another battle for them not to be hung as "charity cases" but as regular entries. Daubigny's strength and eloquence were also sufficiently persuasive to get Monet, Renoir, Bazille and Degas admitted. Once again he failed to get Cézanne accepted. Thanks to Daubigny, also, there were almost fourteen hundred more works shown than at the previous Salon, most of them by younger, unknown artists. The critic Castagnary wrote:

> In this overflow of free painting, official State painting has made a rather poor showing. . . . Daubigny is not only a great artist, but a decent man as well, one who remembers the hardships of his own youth and would wish to spare others the severe trials to which he himself submitted.

*   *   *

Camille's two canvases were hung up against the ceiling; but they had an inner glow that dazzled those spectators willing to look.

The painter-critic Redon wrote of Camille:

> . . . What a singular talent, which seems to brutalize nature! He treats it with a technique which in appearance is very rudimentary, but this denotes, above all, his sincerity. Monsieur Pissarro sees things simply: as a colorist, he makes sacrifices which allow him to express more vividly the general impression; and this impression is always strong because it is simple.

Emile Zola wrote in *L'Evènement Illustré* of May 19, 1868:

> There is no other painter who is so conscientious, so exact. He is one of the naturalists who confronts nature head on. And yet his canvases always have a character which is quite their own: a note of austerity and a truly heroic grandeur. They are quite unlike any others.
> . . . The originality here is deeply human. . . . Here you can listen to the deep voices of the soil and imagine the strength of the trees growing. . . .

There was more in the same vein. It could not have been a more beautiful eulogy. Camille was filled with joy.

"These reviews will surely lead to collectors," he assured Julie.

Julie had witnessed his burst of energy that spring. She had taken solicitous care of his needs and stayed out of his way.

"I like to believe," she said somberly; "but my cupboard is bare. You have friends with *argent?* They will lend you until your money comes?"

"No, Julie, that is my private affair."

"In Grancey we shared. Sometimes one had food, sometimes another."

"I'll pawn my watch again."

He decided the following Sunday that he would take his two attractive youngsters, Lucien, five years old, looking very like Julie, and three-year-old Minette, with his own eyes and coloring, to visit Rachel.

"Once she lays eyes on them she will never be able to give them up," he told Julie.

"And forgive them?"

"For what?"

"For being my children."

"Julie, you must not hurt yourself. They are my children too."

"Not in your mother's eyes."

He took them inside the omnibus, for the weather was cool; Lucien seated next to him, the girl in his arms. A middle-aged maid answered the door on the Boulevard des Martyrs.

"Your mother is in the bedroom."

"Would you tell her that I'm here?"

Rachel heard a child's voice through her open door as the sound rang through the hall. She quickly closed it and locked it. Camille knocked repeatedly. She remained silent. After several more attempts he gathered his young and departed. Julie had been right.

They scratched. They went without. They lived in a moneyless world, existing on Julie's vegetables, chickens, rabbits. Camille had a cup of weak coffee before setting out at dawn, and one light meal a day. He did not mind, for his painting frenzy continued unabated; full-size oils of the apple gatherers, the village across from the trees, the countryside at Ennery and the locks at Pontoise. He completed each canvas, allowed it to dry and took it into Paris, trudging the streets because he did not have fare for the omnibus, going from dealer to dealer because Martin already had several of his paintings and had sold nothing; visiting the paint-supply and frame merchants, attempting to sell for a few dollars, or at least to have the pictures put on display. Everywhere the answer was the same:

"Times are bad. Collectors are not buying. When they do, they want the state painters. With reputations."

He exploded:

"You can't show me because I have no reputation. But I can't acquire a reputation until I'm shown."

"C'est vrai," an elderly dealer agreed. "But when has it been different? To sell a manuscript, sculpture, play, opera score, you must first be successful. But how to be successful if you can't get anything accepted? It is a dilemma, with both horns piercing your *derrière.*"

He could no longer afford the few sous for a daily paper, picking up old issues wherever he found them. Parliament had at last voted the right of free assembly. For the first time in more than twenty years workmen met at the Salle Pilodo, though the July 4 *L'Illustration* showed more police there than workingmen. In July also a large section of Les Halles burned down; later, the Pereire brothers of the Crédit Mobilier scandal were tried and convicted of the misuse of public investments. The banking firm had been the financial source of public construction monies inside France and externally.

In late August the river Seine fell to such a low level that the boats and barges docked at the quais, the washing houses and bathhouses lay aground on the bottom. Pillagers searched in the mud for treasure. This was also the year of the bicycle. Women with a pretty leg, the journals alleged, "went out to ride on their *vélocipèdes,* just as their grandmothers had played the harp to show off a pretty arm."

In October a meteor flashed over Paris just past midnight, leaving a trail of light. *L'Illustration* commented, "For a few seconds the city seemed illuminated as it would have been by an immense electric lantern."

Camille read aloud to Julie, " 'In the past, the elegant French were Anglomaniacs. Today all the French have their eyes fixed on the Yankees.' "

What was it about North America that the French had come to admire so extravagantly? Their vitality? Rich resources? Egalitarian society?

When he had finished his round of fruitless visits to dealers he stored his paintings at Guillemet's studio and wandered the city. The workingmen's new housing now centered on the outskirts of the city. Little else had changed since he had roamed the streets ten years before. He recalled the line from the Gospel According to John. "The poor always ye have with you." Was some part of humanity doomed to poverty for all eternity? Was John saying that this was God's will? He could not believe it.

"You should have equal compassion for the bourgeois," the iconoclastic Cézanne commented; "they lead such dull lives, buying and selling cloth or shoes or counting money in banks. Where is their *joie de vivre?*"

"They're well fed and housed."

"So are prize Guernseys."

As the children grew older he became more conscious of their needs. There was a public school in Pontoise, independent of the Church, for all children over six years of age. Camille suggested to Julie:

"We will send Lucien to school there."

"He will learn to use periods and start new sentences?"

"You are pulling my leg."

In good weather there was a Sunday promenade in the gardens in front of the Pontoise city hall or on the quais along the Hôtel Dieu. Julie insisted they participate because of the Sunday promenades in Grancey which had given her such pleasure. She also began to protest his working on Sunday.

"It says in the Bible, 'On the seventh day God finished His work and He rested. So God blessed the seventh day and hallowed it.' "

She had her way . . . almost. Around four o'clock on Sunday afternoons he stopped work and cleaned up. Lucien and Minette were scrubbed and dressed. They walked through the town along the Oise, gazing at the residents of whom they knew only the shopkeepers they patronized. Both children had been raised with affection. They had been wanted. He found it good to hear their prattle, to kiss their baby faces, to play "horse" with Lucien until the seats and knees of their pants were worn out. He gave Lucien a drawing lesson every day.

"Don't teach him to draw too good," said Julie. "One artist in the family is enough. He'll have to get a job and help support us when he grows up."

"I want all of our children to become artists."

Julie shook her head in despair.

Lucien was an energetic child, running from one end of the house to the other. He hit his little sister when she provoked him, for which Julie gave him a solid Grancey clout on the behind. Camille used bribery to keep him in control: "Tell him if he is good I will bring him a cake." Minette was more delicate. Camille adored her, fed her from his lap at suppertime, held her, constantly reassured her that all was well and that he loved her.

He was never far away, out sketching or painting from early morning. He came home for the midday meal, sometimes napped for an hour, then returned to the outdoors. Julie toiled straight through the day. She complained only when there was nothing to work with: no soap to wash the clothes, no clothes to replace those that were worn out, no supplementary foods from the shop. Camille was only aware of missing painting supplies; brushes still cost one dollar each, a canvas of six feet four inches by four feet four inches set him back more than six dollars. Alfred was spending about two hundred dollars a year for the frames.

Winter fell early, with severe winds and cold. They were enveloped by a wet fog arising from the river Oise and the rivulet Viosne. Both children suffered from heavy colds; Minette ran a fever. They found refuge with a painter in Paris at 23 Rue Chappe.

"Being right on the river, the climate is too damp in the Hermitage," Dr. Gachet later told Camille. "The children will have intermittent illnesses. You are going to have to find a drier climate, away from the water."

It was a wrench to think of living away from his beloved Hermitage but the children had to come first. He would search for a place farther inland until they had grown a bit. Meanwhile he completed several oils from his Pontoise sketches, the entrance to the forest of Marly, a snow effect of the countryside of Pontoise.

The 1869 Salon accepted only one of the canvases. In the catalogue he gave the address of his dealer, P. F. Martin. When he went to a preview of the Salon he saw that once again he had suffered the reverse of Corot's lament, "I am hung in the catacombs." He wrote the Beaux-Arts a semijocular, deadly-in-earnest note:

Messieurs,

I call your attention to a joke the *service boys* played on me by placing my picture atop a door, and at an impossible height. I can't attribute this decision to the administration; these gentlemen will think along with me that it's already enough for an artist to be at the mercy of whatever jury, without still suffering from the judgment of the boys charged with hanging the canvases!

I have the honor to greet you.

C. Pissarro

4

Alfred Pissarro married twenty-four-year-old Marie May, from a prosperous family of Besançon. He had been courting her for a considerable time before the marriage contract and the dowry were notarized. Camille was not invited to the wedding. Alfred explained that, while he held against Julie only that she had caused disruption in the family, Marie's family were rigidly moral bourgeois and thought of Camille as a "disinherited vagabond." That Rachel would not attend if Julie were there.

After a painful silence Camille said:

"I wish you the best. I shall not even tell her you are being married."

Claude Monet, living in a ramshackle house in Bougival, a suburb of Paris, took Camille to 22 Route de Versailles in Louveciennes and showed him the unoccupied Maison Retrou. The house, a large sturdy one, had been built for Louis XIV's Captain of the Guard with royal funds. It was a hundred and seventy years old. Opposite the front door, inside a cobbled gateway, was a structure which had served as a carriage house.

"You could use this as your studio," Monet suggested. "It will give you seclusion from the family."

Camille gazed at the well-built Maison Retrou with yearning eyes.

"I couldn't afford it."

"Should be only a little more than your Pontoise house."

Camille uttered a startled, "For what reason?"

"The owners, Monsieur and Madame Ollivon, say it's too far out of Paris for anyone working in the city every day, and too big for a summer cottage for vacationing Parisians. It's noisy on this main road, which carries stagecoaches and lumbering farm wagons, and is not fashionable. It has remained empty. So the fates, perhaps, have saved it for you."

The spacious parlor and dining room faced the road; the large kitchen and what had originally been a small library looked out on an ample garden walled in by the remains of a high stone fourteenth-century aqueduct that had brought water to Versailles. It would cut some of the summer heat, but it prevented them from entering the woods from the rear of the property. There was room for a large vegetable patch, a flower garden, rabbit hutches and chicken coops. Upstairs there were four bedrooms, in one of which Camille could put a desk on which to teach the children their lessons in reading, writing, arithmetic.

He did not allow himself to think about leaving the landscape he had made his own.

"Let us go to the owner," he declared. "I'll sign for the rent starting May 1."

Once again they moved their rudimentary furniture. Julie was enchanted with the substantial house. It was the largest kitchen she had ever known. Camille arranged his novels, plays, volumes of poetry and essays on the already installed library shelves. He decided that the next time he could afford it he would buy the inexpensive paperbound classics which the reign of *L'Etat, c'est moi,* had engendered: Corneille, Racine, Molière, La Fontaine, La Rochefoucauld. He cleaned out the carriage house with its interior of rough stone. Julie would have no further occasion to complain of the smell of his tubes of paint or turpentine. It was with a sense of joy that he fitted up some rough shelves for his sketches, racks for his completed canvases, a workbench to hold his paints, palettes, jar of brushes.

"A place of my own!" he exclaimed. "Where I can lock the door behind me at night and everything will still be where I put it in the morning."

He set out to explore the area. Half a mile down the road he turned into the carriage road that had been used by Louis XIV and his courtiers to reach the imposing château, Marly-le-Roi, which had been completely destroyed by a later owner who had offered it to the original Napoleon and, when the Emperor refused to accept it, blew it up and used it as a quarry for its hand-cut stones. All that remained was a pond and a fountain surrounded by short stone pillars, a handsome stone wall with a broad entrance through which the royal horses had entered and drunk. A Sunday market was held on the grounds. Families drove in from miles away to bargain for their week's supplies and cool drinks as they enjoyed the traditional market acrobats, jugglers, clowns. It would become Lucien's and Minette's entertainment of the week.

The landscape along this tan dirt road to Versailles differed greatly from that of the Hermitage. The imposing houses on the Pissarro side and the more modest ones opposite, all strung along the connecting highway between Paris and the legendary palace of its kings, formed neither town nor village. The collection of shops that made up Louveciennes was a distance away. There was no kinship with the earth; but for his sacrifice he was being offered abundant forests, the Seine with characterful surrounding villages, dry air for his children, and an easy one-hour, sixteen-mile train trip into Paris.

If the move had been a deep wrench, an aura of success seemed to surround it from the beginning. A painter named Félix Vuillefroy, whom he had seen casually at Gleyre's when visiting his friends there, and who lived nearby, came to see him. Vuillefroy was a big-stomached man with fiery red hair covering his head and chest. He explained that he had just received a large commission, more than he wanted to handle by himself, decorating the inn of Monsieur Barbey at Chailly.

"We have to paint a bar, dining room, sitting room. Country scenes. Much color. Any themes we want to work up from our sketches. Pay is good, a hundred dollars. We'll split the work and the money."

Camille accepted instantly. Fifty dollars was three times his month's allowance.

"Monsieur Vuillefroy, you are an angel, straight from heaven."

The artist emitted an amiable growl that sounded vaguely like a chuckle. "Mistress Dominique tells me I'm a devil, straight from hell."

They worked well together, side by side in each room, making the walls bright with color. They completed the task in a little over a month. The owner of the inn was delighted, treated them to a beer at his bar, and paid the agreed sum.

"Come back any time," he told them at parting. "Beer is on the house just so long as those colors don't fade."

"They won't," Camille assured him. "I learned this mural technique at Mother Anthony's Inn at Marlotte."

With the francs stacked in a library drawer Camille was freed from worry for the next several months. The freedom released a surge of activity. Over the hot summer he painted a dozen canvases of the countryside at Louveciennes, with its white houses, the view of Mont Valérien, the environs in summer. He did a large canvas of a bouquet of chrysanthemums in a Chinese vase.

The Maison Retrou had belonged to the Retrou family for a considerable time; the name sticking even after they had sold it to the Ollivon family and moved into the house next door. Only a picket fence separated the narrow front yards planted with shrubbery and a hedge of flowers.

Monsieur and Madame Retrou were friendly. Julie sometimes chatted with Madame Retrou but more frequently with their young pretty maid when they had a few moments of leisure. Camille painted them in the yard fronting the road: Julie with her back to the viewer, in a black dress down to the ground, pinched in at her slender waist, a blue ribbon tied around her hair; Minette with golden hair, in a straw bonnet and green dress with a yellow collar; the Retrous' *bonne* in a starched gray uniform and white domestic's bonnet. A mother, father, child walked down the quiet Versailles road dappled with the shadows of trees opposite a row of modest red-tiled houses. It was a painting as tranquil, accepting and lyrical as a sunlit day in the countryside. In preparation he had done a study in black chalk of Julie and Minette in the front garden.

He frequently sketched the interior of the house, particularly the kitchen when Julie was preparing dinner, or the two children were sitting at the table eating or playing dominoes. He rarely sat with idle hands; he sketched and drew the way Julie sewed or crocheted. Drawing was for him as natural as breathing, and as lifegiving.

Julie was no longer isolated. She found the less provincial occupants along the thoroughfare to Versailles friendly and communicative, as were the shopkeepers and residents of Louveciennes. It was as if by some alchemy of the thinking process Louveciennes assumed that any family living in so prestigious a house as that of Louis XIV's Captain of the Guard was acceptable. Aided by the extra francs on hand, this brought her a kind of security she had not known in her years with Camille.

Frequently on a Sunday he walked with Julie the two miles to the boating resort of La Grenouillère to paint with Monet and Renoir, who had their women with them. Young people gaily dressed were alive with holiday pleasure, a day free of work, care, difficulty. They enjoyed each other and the beauty of the sun-glazed river.

La Grenouillère was for painters the most delightful spot on the Seine, right out of the Garden of Eden. The river was clear, gently moving. There was a densely wooded ridge behind, an island in the middle, a country road between the Seine and the nearby wooded estates. Along the bank there was dogwood, willow, water chestnut. Alfred Sisley, who lived nearby, observed:

"The Seine sings here."

While Monet and Renoir painted the holiday travelers at the bargelike restaurant, Fournaise, Camille turned to the opposite shore and a more quiet landscape, with a small factory and a chimney trailing a mist of white smoke. He did not show this canvas at the Guerbois for fear one of the followers would exclaim triumphantly:

"Ah, you have returned to the class war."

Useless to tell that vertical chimneys with their sometime wind-driven horizontal smoke effusions intrigued him for their painterly values.

They were blessed Sundays for Julie; she loved being with Léonie and with Renoir's mistress, Lise. Alfred Sisley had suffered the fate of most womanizers; he met a young girl of impeccable character, with a quiet face dominated by a pair of astonishingly large innocent eyes, and married her. They had two children, a son and a daughter. Sisley came frequently to paint with Camille. He had progressed amazingly since Camille had first met him at Mother Anthony's Inn at Marlotte. He had absorbed something from every painter at the Guerbois; then added something of his own ebullient spirit to his canvas. The critics of the 1866 and 1868 Salons had called his work "harmonious, decorative and timid."

5

In the fall a second miracle befell Camille. He acquired his first collector, independently of a gallery. Jean Baptiste Faure was one of the most popular singers of the Paris Opera, famous for his portrayal of Hamlet, a handsome bravura type of man who looked well flourishing a sword. He had been attracted by Camille's *The Hermitage, A Landscape* in the Salon and asked Edouard Manet to introduce him. They met at the Guerbois.

"I'm honored to meet you," Faure said in his rich baritone voice. "I'd like to acquire one of your Pontoise paintings. The one I saw moved me deeply."

Camille took him to Guillemet's studio. Faure studied the paintings carefully, then chose one.

"Speaks to me," he said. "How much shall I pay you?"

Camille reflected. He could not conceal from Faure that he could find canvases at Martin's for from twelve to sixteen dollars each. He told Faure about them, then added:

"That is a beggar's price. The price that would satisfy me is forty dollars."

"I'll pay it," said Faure. "You are not a man who should be bargained down. I want harmony between us so that I will be happy every time I look at your painting. Besides, I'm sure it's a good investment. I plan to acquire a Manet as well."

Camille was speechless.

Incredibly there was more good news to come. Guillemet took him to dinner at the home of Gustave Arosa, a banker who had heard about Faure's purchase and seen Camille's canvases at Guillemet's. He also wanted a painting.

"My brother Achille will want one too. Not just now; perhaps next year. Faure told me the price you consider fair. I will pay it for this scene of Louveciennes."

Next, a friend from the Académie Suisse, Lecreux by name, had interested some people in his home town of Lille, north toward the Belgian border, in Camille's St. Thomas paintings. Could Camille come quickly to Lille with two of his oils on panels? He took the train the next morning, found that Lecreux had done a splendid sales job and received cash for his two paintings of 1855 and 1856, *Coconut Palms by the Sea* and *Two Women Conversing on the Seashore*.

Julie was stunned by the news and the envelope of bank notes.

"I don't know what foot to dance on! You'll keep selling?"

"In Caracas they say: 'Good fortune is no more permanent than bad.'"

If Camille was having a run of luck, the times were hard for the other artists of the Café Guerbois. Claude Monet had improved the battered old house in Bougival for Léonie and their son but his situation was desperate. His sole means of support was Frédéric Bazille who, out of kindness, had offered to send him ten dollars a month against the purchase of *Woman in the Garden,* in which Monet's lovely young mistress posed in each of her four brilliantly striped and tailored gowns brought over from a better day with her parents. Monet confessed to Camille what he had been forced to write to Bazille:

"Dear friend, do you want to know in what situation I am, and how I live during the week I have waited for your letter? Well, ask Renoir who brings us bread from his mother's house so that we don't die of hunger. For a week, no bread, no wine, no fire for cooking, no light. It's atrocious."

Yet when Monet set up his easel with Camille on the road to Versailles, each painting the same scene from differing angles, all deprivation fell away. The canvases exploded with color, with the short vibrant brush strokes which brought a sense of palpitant reality to his painting.

Renoir was so destitute that he had to go with his model Lise to live with her parents in their country cottage.

Camille received a letter from Anton Melbye in Hamburg informing him that Fritz Melbye had died in Shanghai, at the age of forty-three. A number of his Chinese and Japanese paintings had found their way back to Copenhagen. Shortly after, Camille learned that Anton himself had had a stroke which left him nearly paralyzed. David Jacobsen also fell ill. A Danish doctor visiting Paris raised the money to send him to the warmer climate of Italy, which the Copenhagen Academy had never voted to do. Camille accompanied him to the railroad station. David was weak of knee and white of color, but his spirits were high.

"I'll recover in Florence, Rome, Naples. I'll paint beautifully there."

As he left the railroad station Camille slipped a few bank notes into Jacobsen's pocket; the Danish doctor had been able to raise little more than the train fare and a month's board.

A new rule for the selection of a jury for the 1870 Salon caused excitement at the Guerbois. This year the jury would be selected by a vote of those artists who had shown at former Salons. No one knew whose idea it was but, once launched, the Guerbois group entered into it with enthusiasm.

"If we elect our jury," they told each other, "all of our people will exhibit."

The group chose its jury, campaigned to have their friends elected: Daubigny, Millet, Corot of the older school; Manet, Daumier, Courbet, Gautier of the newer. Emile Zola published two articles in the newspapers asking all Salon artists to vote for the Guerbois selection.

Of their list Daubigny and Corot were elected; but they had also been backed by the Beaux-Arts Institute. Nevertheless the Salon was an outstanding success for the Guerbois or Batignolles group. Camille exhibited two canvases, *Autumn* and *Landscape*, Degas had one, but of a startling beauty. Bazille exhibited his *Summer Scene* and *Bathers;* Renoir a luscious female nude *Bather;* Sisley, *The Canal St. Martin in Paris;* Fantin-Latour, *A Lecture;* Berthe Morisot, *The Artist's Sister Edma and Their Mother;* Manet, a portrait of the gorgeous Eva Gonzalès, his student and mistress, which drove Berthe Morisot into an icy jealousy.

Claude Monet and Paul Cézanne were rejected categorically. Daubigny fought hard for Monet but could not get him admitted. Furious, he resigned from the jury saying:

"From the moment I liked this picture, *Madame Monet in a Red Cap*, I wouldn't allow my opinion to be contradicted. As well say that I don't know my trade."

Corot, who had no more liking for Monet's canvases than he had for Camille's, resigned from the jury out of loyalty to Daubigny.

Théodore Duret, Guerbois regular, art critic and brandy distributor, published his feelings about Camille's work:

> . . . If Pissarro is a realist in his determination to reproduce exactly the scene before him, he is not a

thoroughgoing realist in the sense that certain other painters are, who see no more than the externals of nature, without fathoming its soul and its innermost meaning. On the contrary, he stamps his every canvas with a feeling for life.

Théodore Duret, a tall, slim, handsomely garbed and bewhiskered man with a sensitive oval face, then purchased two of Camille's Louveciennes paintings. The exhibition, the praise, the sale, the fact that Martin was still enthusiastic as his dealer, brought Camille a sense of well-being.

Julie, contented in her large comfortable house on the Route de Versailles, became pregnant again.

The Paris journals of the early months of 1870 had been filled with the question of an impending war with Prussia. The problem had arisen in 1861 when the French sided with Poland in its demand for national identity. Bismarck of Prussia sided with the Tsar of Russia, crushing the Poles and diminishing French prestige. Prussia and Austria then invaded the Danish provinces of Schleswig and Holstein and, in 1866, Prussia subdued the Austrians, becoming the dominant force in Europe. Napoleon III asked Bismarck to cede to France the left bank of the Rhine. This was considered an act of aggression against Prussia. France became isolated. When in 1870 Bismarck attempted to install a distant cousin of the Prussian royal family on the Spanish throne, the French were outraged. They declared war on Prussia on July 19, 1870, confident that their army would be victorious.

In *L'Univers*, Camille read:

The war in which we are about to engage is, on the part of France, neither the work of a party nor an adventure imposed by the sovereign. The nation undertakes it willingly.

La Liberté wrote:

For several days we have not ceased to call for war. We have asked for it in all our prayers. The future . . . our soul and our conscience tell us that, in acting thus and in demanding war, we have obeyed the duty which, outside of all other considerations, the dignity and the honor France imposes upon us.

*   *   *

In the streets of Paris dense crowds forced the omnibuses off their usual routes; the "Marseillaise" was sung at café concerts. An observer noted:

"Not only the capital, but every city, every village of France, was seized with military enthusiasm; and there were but few Frenchmen who were not carried away by the popular excitement."

The South German states, considering France the aggressor, joined Bismarck and the North German states, putting their armies under the military genius of the German Von Moltke. Despite the wild displays of patriotism, the French armies were neither equipped nor prepared for a major war. On August 4 the Germans crossed the border into Alsace. One French army was defeated at Wissembourg, followed by a disaster at Sedan in which Napoleon III and one hundred thousand of his troops were captured. Napoleon III's regime was overthrown and a citizens' government formed. By mid-August Paris was besieged by the German army.

It was then that Camille heard the first artillery fire. Manet, Degas and Bazille enlisted; Manet and Degas in the Home Guard. Alfred fled to London with his wife Marie and their infant son Frédéric.

"What about us?" Julie demanded, close to term. "Don't we have to get the children away?"

"Perhaps we'd better go to Piette's at Montfoucault."

While Julie packed a couple of valises, Camille set his studio in order, putting drawings, watercolors, oils, painting equipment in their proper niches. As he was finishing he heard carriage wheels scream to a stop before his gate. Claude Monet rushed in, a bundle of rolled canvases under each arm.

"Pissarro, may I store these paintings with you? I'm getting out before the Prussians cut the railroad lines. One year in the army is enough for me. I'm not going to be caught and pressed into military service. I'm due to be called up November 1."

Camille looked quickly at the new canvases. They were brightly colored scenes of a fashionable resort beach.

"Where did you paint these?"

"At Trouville."

"That's an expensive *plage*."

Monet blushed.

"When I married Léonie in June her father tricked us out of her dowry. But we did get the interest on it, two hundred and forty dollars. We had a regal honeymoon."

"Where will you go now?"

"To London. I can't take Léonie or the boy. There's only enough money for one ticket. I'm sending them to Brittany, near Boudin. I've asked him to watch over them. I'm taking my own particular hell across the Channel with me. I'll land in London without friends or a way to eat. They'll be better off than I."

Eleven years before, when Camille had first met him at the Académie Suisse, Claude Monet had been the handsomest young man of the painters' group; now he looked beaten, stooped under a burden of nonsuccess too heavy for his sloping shoulders. His eyes were one moment bold and haughty, the next cringing. In Paris it was said of him that his principle was to have no principle. Though his cheeks above the black beard were unlined, his spirit showed rifts and gullies.

"Stack your paintings. They'll be safe here unless the Prussians occupy the area."

6

Piette met them at the Mayenne station. When they reached Montfoucault they were shocked to see how run down the farm and house were. The wartime moratorium on rents applied to Piette's apartment house in Paris, and Piette was deprived of the money he had been using to pay for his farm help. Some of the workers had joined the army, others had moved to jobs where wages were paid.

"I've been left alone on a farm which needs half a dozen hands. I can barely take care of the animals, let alone harvest the fields and orchards. The only cash I have is borrowed from the bank."

Piette was forlorn. The meticulous beard was untrimmed and straggly, the upswept curl at the forehead gray. Camille remembered him as he had painted his portrait nine years before. Now, at forty-four, the eyes seemed to have retreated into their sockets and to burn dimly.

"You have to have an inner force to paint," Piette cried. "I work all day as a laborer on my farm, watching it go to hell. Am I a bad painter because I have had to be a farmer? Or am I a bad farmer because I want to be a painter?"

"You are my closest friend," responded Camille, hugging

the man. "That makes you, in my eyes at least, a great human being in this self-destructive world."

The years appeared to lift off Piette's shoulders.

"Why can't we all live here together? Adèle could be a second mother to Lucien and Minette. We'd have time to paint together and work the farm only enough to pay the bills. Then I would no longer feel as though I'm betraying my generations of ancestors who built Montfoucault."

Adèle had been in bed for several weeks, unable to care for the house. A layer of dust overlay the tables in the parlor. The kitchen where Piette had ineptly been trying to cook for the two of them was an unbelievable field of battle: unwashed skillets, open jars of jellies showing a green mold, the stove discolored with streaks of grease. When Camille and Julie were led into Adèle's bedroom they found her olive skin pallid, a smoldering fever in her eyes. When she saw them she burst into tears, whether of joy or despair they could not fathom. Heavy as she was with child, Julie put on an apron, scrubbed the neglected stove, washed the pots and dishes, then lighted a fire of kindling and dead branches and put up the largest tub she could find and filled it with water. When it boiled she ordered the men to carry it upstairs.

When the two women reappeared Adèle had been scrubbed "like a little child," Julie whispered to Camille, "with rough toweling." She had washed Adèle's hair, combed it into a neat coiffure. Adèle was fully dressed. There was a touch of color in her cheeks.

"Piette," she cried, "go kill us a pullet. Bring in some fruit and vegetables, some cheese. Julie's going to help me cook a celebration dinner."

Later, when they went to bed warmed by a fire that Piette had laid and lighted, Camille thanked Julie for what she had done for Adèle.

"What was the illness that kept her in bed?" Julie asked.

"Unhappiness, I guess. Loneliness, like she told you. The failing farm. Being unable to conceive. Piette's being unable to paint. . . ."

"It was the ugly war that brought us here. But I think God knew they needed us."

Piette painted Camille's portrait in gouache, out in the cold sun, with defoliated trees behind him. Camille was dressed in a floppy felt hat jammed down over his ears, a warm wool scarf knotted at his throat, standing a few feet from his easel analyzing the components of the countryside before him. Piette caught him to the life: sturdy legs spread apart, right arm holding his palette at stomach height, trunk poised to react from his palette onto canvas the instant he made his decision.

When Piette finished his *Pissarro at His Easel*, the four were triumphant. Camille announced:

"It's good, Piette. Vivid, balanced, true. You caught the core of me. Why do you say you can't paint anymore?"

Piette flushed. "Affection mixes well with gouache. With anything."

There was no question of Piette's enlisting.

"If I left the farm now the animals would be stolen or die. No crops planted in the spring."

"Raising food is more important," Camille agreed. He looked anxiously at Julie. "But I really should return to Paris and enlist in the Home Guard, if they'll take a Danish citizen."

Julie looked at him with troubled eyes.

"You can't leave with the baby coming."

Rumor had it that Paris was suffering: its supplies depleted; the Prussians demanding a surrender. He wrote to his mother that he intended to enlist once the baby was born. Rachel's reply came quickly:

"You know that I absolutely have need of you so don't do anything imprudent."

He had already made out his will before leaving for London for Emma's funeral, "bequeathing all I possess of worldly goods to Mademoiselle Julie Vellay." He had no worldly goods aside from his paintings. As his patriotism to France's new republican government grew he realized that there was one thing more he must do: marry Julie so that their three children would become legitimate. He wrote to his mother with care and zeal the most eloquent letter he had ever written. It must have been, for by return mail Rachel gave her tentative permission:

"I don't approve of your marriage. I never shall. But if I must have three grandchildren they should be legitimate. Marry, if you must. Then let me hear no more about it."

Camille was jubilant. . . . After twelve years!

"I'm still the mayor here," Piette told them; "but I don't have the authority to marry people. The mayor of Mayenne is an old friend of my father's. I'll ask him to perform the ceremony. We'll ask our neighbor Georges Thouvenal to cosign the marriage certificate with me."

Julie was filled with song:

> "There was a lady Tartine [Bread]
> In a fine palace of fresh butter.
> The walls were of flour,
> The floor was of biscuits,
> Her bedroom was of wheat,
> Her bed of pastry:
> It's very good at night."

Adèle planned a picnic for the day.

Then came a second letter.

Rachel had written it the morning following her consent. Camille opened it with quivering fingers, read the first few lines, moaned, "Oh no!" and sank into the middle of the russet-colored sofa.

"My mother has changed her mind," he cried out.

Julie burst into tears. Adèle sat her down, then crouched before her, attempting to comfort her. Julie took the blow as though a knife had been thrust through her.

Camille read in a monotone:

" 'As a mother, to make you happy, and without reflection I have answered yes. That caused me to be ill the night long and I have decided to write to say that this consent distresses me very much. I rely on you then and if you have some consideration for me you will send me back the letter because I had it written without sufficient thought for a matter of importance. Wait until all these events are over, then you could go to London and there marry without my consent and without anyone knowing about it.' "

Piette suggested weakly that they pretend the second letter never reached them. "There's a war on. . . . Your wedding will be a *fait accompli.*"

Camille could see Julie trembling across the room. He turned to Piette:

"We must not complicate our problem with deceit."

He rose, paced the floor, ended in front of Julie.

"We will go to England and be married there. After the baby is born, after the war."

The baby was born, a girl, on October 21, 1870. They named her Adèle Emma. It was a difficult birth; the midwife was a practiced one but Julie became ill. She did not have sufficient milk for the infant. Rachel, when she received Camille's news, responded generously, sending a layette for the infant and an extra hundred francs. She wrote:

"Hire the best wet nurse in the neighborhood. Use the

extra money for that purpose. After a couple of months you'll be able to put her on a bottle."

It was the first break in Rachel's solid rejection.

Piette scoured the countryside and succeeded in finding a young mother who would have enough milk for her own child and Adèle Emma as well. The infant sucked robustly for a few days, then began to fail. Piette brought out their family doctor from Mayenne. He examined the child, questioned the young wet nurse. When he came from Julie's bedroom he was shaking his leonine head in anger and despair.

"The wet nurse has an intestinal infection. She has most likely passed it on to the child."

Camille asked numbly, "What can we do?"

The doctor shook his head in grim frustration.

"I don't know. Get a new wet nurse, if it's not too late."

It was. Adèle Emma lived only two weeks. Julie was crushed.

The four of them buried the infant behind the house. Piette asked solicitously:

"Would you like me to drive you into Mayenne to register the birth and death?"

"What purpose?" Julie asked bitterly. "She's come and gone as though she was never here."

Camille put his arms about her shoulders, walked her back to the house.

"It was an accident of fate. We'll do better next time."

Piette drove Camille in his carriage to the *mairie* of the neighboring village of Lassay where he signed the death certificate.

7

Paris was under heavy bombardment from enemy artillery. The battalions of the Garde Nationale were trying to relieve the siege of the city. Unlike the previous rumor, the *Revue des Deux Mondes,* which reached Piette by mail, declared that Paris had been self-sufficient for a month and a half. However:

> Our situation is beginning to become strange. . . . Paris, locked in its armor of iron, goes to sleep each evening,

and each morning awakens, taking up ordinary life again . . . it forms a state by itself, a society, a world limited for the moment by St. Denis and Clamart, by St. Cloud and Vincennes. Beyond this horizon . . . is Prussia encamped and immobilized before the guns of our forts.

Paris had prepared itself for a siege in spite of the fact that its Premier had declared war "with a light heart." The city was stocked with animals for slaughter; the Luxembourg Garden was filled with sheep. In the Bois de Boulogne there were forty thousand oxen and another quarter million sheep. A flour mill was set up in the Gare du Nord, the Louvre became an armament workshop, the Gare d'Orléans an observation balloon factory, the Gare de Lyon a cannon factory.

Rachel escaped to London. The Isaacsons found a home for her to share with Alfred's family in Norwood. They offered to locate a flat for Camille.

"My whole family is in England," Camille told Julie. "A lot of French painters are already there."

"They hate me. If Emma was still alive, yes. I've read her daughter Amélie's letters to you. She never mentions my name."

"Now, Julie, Amélie liked you when she was a child."

She gave him a pitying look, then shrugged slightly.

"The three of us are yours. Do what you will."

He needed train fare and boat fare across the English Channel. The midwife, doctor and wet nurse had been paid the last of his francs.

"Je suis désolé," Piette murmured. "I haven't a dozen francs to give you."

The following evening the elderly Georges Thouvenal came to see how they were faring. When he learned that Camille could not take his family to England because of lack of money, he asked:

"Camille, your mother said that in London you can marry Julie?"

"Yes."

"How much will that require?"

"About sixty dollars."

"Very well, I will lend you the money. Name your next son after me. That's my interest rate."

It would have been a shorter distance to go directly to Le Havre from Mayenne, but there was no railroad line connecting the two points. Travel by carriage or coach would have taken a number of days. Since the Gare St. Lazare was still open Camille took his family into Paris, then boarded the first train for Le Havre. They reached there in the early afternoon only to find there was no steamer crossing that night. One would leave Dieppe at midnight. They caught the coach to Dieppe, boarded the steamer and, after a long night huddled together in the smoke-laden salon, reached the shores of England.

Emma's oldest son, twenty-one-year-old Rodolphe, met them at the railroad station with a carriage. He had been Camille's companion during the period of Emma's funeral and mourning, renewing the friendship built in the Pissarro apartments in Montmartre and Passy. He greeted Julie shyly, then drove them slowly to the London suburb of Lower Norwood.

"I can paint this countryside," Camille declared, his eyes on the passing landscape. "Julie, don't you find it charming?"

Julie did not reply. She found it charming that she was soon to be married . . . if she was.

Their flat was upstairs of Canham's Dairy. The rooms were adequate, the windows admitting the dull winter light. The furniture had been scuffed by a series of transients. But the Thouvenal loan would cover the rent.

The home occupied by Rachel and Alfred and his family was a short distance away; but neither Rachel nor Marie visited Julie. Camille was welcome to bring the children, without Julie, to visit in Rachel's half of the house only, a concession on her part. Alfred was doing business through Isaacson's commission merchant's firm in the Strand six days a week. When Camille visited his mother, Rachel sometimes sent home treats she had bought for the children at the greengrocer.

Julie commented, "I don't like an *R* burned into my behind the way you didn't like an *R* stamped on the back of your pictures."

"When we marry there will be an *A* for Acceptance stamped on your wedding certificate."

"When?"

"As quickly as I can sell something. I want to pay for the wedding with money I earned. I will start to paint right away. I should soon have something worth selling."

"Everything's worth selling. Can you make something worth buying?"

Julie escaped the small apartment by walking with the children in the streets, taking them to the park. Without a word of English, they clung to each other, feeling completely isolated in a strange land.

"I should never have brought you into this heartless family," Camille commented. "Better to have let you go your own way. You would have found a Louis Estruc in Paris, the way your sister did. You would have married him and have had no cause for grief."

"And maybe no love." She kissed him hungrily. "A woman can't be without love."

Frédéric Bazille was killed at the battle of Beaune-la-Rolande. Since he had refused to shave off his beard the only faction of the French army that would accept him was the Zouaves. The Zouaves had engaged in the fiercest of the fighting. His father had had to search for two days among the corpses of the battlefield to find his son and take him back to Montpellier for burial. As had the others in the Guerbois group, Camille had loved this extraordinarily tall, gaunt, fun-loving, generous, enormously talented young man who, even among artist eccentrics, had stood out for his unpredictable idiosyncrasies. Along with the brokenhearted regret came an inevitable sense of guilt. While it was true that many of his close friends, younger men, Frenchmen, had not participated in the war—Monet, Sisley, Cézanne, Zola—there was still a residue at the bottom of the cup called conscience. He, Camille Pissarro, had escaped to England, allowing Frédéric Bazille to bleed to death on the battlefield.

He put on his sabots, planted his easel down the hill from the flat. It was a short road, curving and struggling uphill, covered with a thin layer of ice, the rest of the snow heaped in rows along the bank. He liked roads; they went somewhere, they connected here with there, were lines of communication. There was a little man in black garb trudging upward, the suggestion of two heavily coated women walking down. There was a leafless tree in the foreground, a few scattered houses on either side, seemingly a dead-life of winter yet alive with the implicit promise of spring. A desolate scene of no desolation whatever; only the suspended animation of the road and the people within the homes. A light trail of smoke came out of the misted pastel stucco house on the left, a fire lighted by people inside awaiting the miracle of rebirth.

Christmas was just ahead. His family paid it no heed; they celebrated Chanukah, the Festival of Lights. There was no possibility of persuading any of them to come to his flat for dinner. He bought a bunch of holly at a florist, some toys for the children, and a turkey which Julie stuffed with fresh chestnuts and veal. A black plum pudding was filled with fruit and raisins. She steamed the pudding, Camille added a half cup of the brandy Alfred had given him as a gift, set it aflame. Lucien and Minette cried their "Ohs!" and "Ahs!" Camille exclaimed:

"Now you have an English Christmas."

Julie, happy with the celebration, laughed:

"They will learn to be fire-eaters like jugglers at the fair."

She related to her young the nativity of Christ; Camille told of the restoring of the Perpetual Light in the First Temple after its desecration by the Romans. The children enjoyed both stories. Julie practiced her Catholicism silently in her prayers and remembrances of the moving rituals in the church of Val des Dames in Grancey. Neither Lucien nor Minette had been baptized. She had known from the beginning that to bring up her children as Catholics would create an even greater chasm between the little ones and their grandmother. She nourished hopes of reconciliation, for them at least.

8

In January when the painting *Lower Norwood, Effect of Snow* had dried, he took it into London, an hour's train ride. He was headed for the German Gallery of Paul Durand-Ruel at 168 New Bond Street. Paul Durand-Ruel's father had opened a gallery in the Rue de la Paix and, helped by his son, created one of the most respected galleries in Paris, selling the Fontainebleau School painters before they were established. The father had died in 1865, at which time the son took over. He was said to have an infallible eye for good and bad work. At the outbreak of the war he sent his wife and five children to his in-laws in Périgord in southwest France; then, before the railroads were cut, hastily packed up his pictures and dispatched them to London. On his arrival he arranged to show them at the German Gallery.

Camille was taking his picture to Paul Durand-Ruel because in the magazine Durand-Ruel had founded in 1869, *International Review of Art and Curiosity*, he had spoken well of Camille's canvas at the 1868 Salon. The German Gallery was more spacious and better lighted than any he had found in Paris. The pictures were hung so that neither theme nor color clashed, and were exhibited on only two levels, comfortable to the eye.

"Mon Dieu!" Camille gasped. "Durand-Ruel has nothing but masterpieces."

He went from picture to picture, studying the best work of Géricault, Corot, Millet, Courbet, Daubigny, Diaz, Dupré, magnificent watercolors by Daumier and Barye, the sculptor who had grown up with his Fontainebleau friends. To Camille's astonishment he saw on the wall a painting by Claude Monet, *Entrance to Trouville Harbor*.

"Monet must have brought that one under his arm. How did he get hung so fast?"

Durand-Ruel was out. His assistant said:

"Monsieur Daubigny brought Monsieur Monet with the painting."

"Daubigny! Is he in England?"

"He came before the war. You can find him in the French quarter, at the Hôtel de la Boule d'Or in Percy Street, or at Audinet's Restaurant in Charlotte Street."

"Would you have Monsieur Monet's address?"

"No, but Monsieur Daubigny will have it. Why not leave your painting for Monsieur Durand-Ruel to see? Monsieur Daubigny speaks of your work with high praise."

Camille received a note from Durand-Ruel almost immediately. "You have brought me a charming picture and I regret not having been at my gallery to pay my respects in person. Tell me, please, the price you would want; be kind enough to send me others as soon as you can. I must sell a lot of your work here. Your friend Monet asked me for your address. He lives at 1 Bath Place, Kensington."

He started at once on another snow effect and a view of Upper Norwood. He also decided to seek out Claude Monet in Kensington.

The two men hugged each other. Monet had little more than a rented room, with a narrow cot in a corner, an easel and a table. He had begun a couple of oils in the London parks but nothing was finished.

"How is our indestructible Julie?" Monet asked.

"Unhappy in a flat in Lower Norwood. What about Léonie?"

"She's lonely. So am I. I must get back to her. This accursed war!" His mood shifted as though the sun had darted out from a black cloud. "Paul Durand-Ruel bought a canvas I brought with me. He paid me sixty dollars. Isn't that fantastic? I sent half the money to Léonie."

"I saw the picture there. I didn't know he had bought it. Congratulations."

Camille wrung Monet's hand. Monet's face broke into a broad grin.

"He has promised to buy another as soon as I can conquer these peculiarly English parks."

"I also took Durand-Ruel a painting. He wrote asking me how much I wanted for it and asked me to show him others. Daubigny has spoken well of my work."

"Daubigny! Our *paterfamilias*. Durand-Ruel has the most progressive gallery in Paris but neither of us dared to take our paintings in to him. Why?"

"We were too awed. Would the man who sells Rembrandt, Goya, Delacroix bother with novices? He seemed to be a devout monarchist in politics and a radical in art. Can you imagine such a combination?"

They went to a small restaurant operated by an exiled French couple where they drank a toast to their dead friend, Frédéric Bazille. Then explored their chances of earning a living in London.

"We should submit to the Royal Academy exhibition," Camille suggested. "They will be judging soon."

Claude Monet visited Lower Norwood at noon on Sunday, kissed Julie affectionately on both cheeks, presented her with a winter plant. They spent the afternoon in a flow of reminiscences: Paris, Pontoise, Louveciennes.

"It's a holiday of homesickness," Camille commented.

He suggested they visit the British and South Kensington museums. "We can study Turner, Constable, Gainsborough. I wanted to do that fifteen years ago when I came from St. Thomas but my sister Delphine was dying."

"Turner's Venetian scenes are a riot of color," said Monet. "No one understood fog in London until Constable put it on canvas."

"Monet's fond of you, Julie," said Camille after he had left. "He knows what a treasure you are to me."

Julie turned her back and crossed herself.

Camille completed his painting of Upper Norwood. There were differences in the French and English countrysides, yet he felt them to be equally strong, calling forth the same truths. While the canvas dried he wrote for an appointment with Durand-Ruel and arrived at the German Gallery to find an imposing figure filling the doorway.

Paul Durand-Ruel was about forty, with a long oval face, a striking head of hair, a touch of gray at the temples, clean-shaven except for a dignified mustache; and a superb pair of smoke-gray eyes. He was squeezed into a black frock-coat topped with a new high top hat. Meeting him elsewhere, Camille might have taken him for a provincial notary or suburban solicitor: punctual, methodical, stiff. Yet his expression and personality belied his attire. He was attractive in the best French tradition.

"A likable man," Camille concluded.

Paul Durand-Ruel was also a strict Catholic, attending an eight o'clock mass every morning of his life; a rigid moralist who made no attempt to judge the personal ethics or relationships of his painters. He had traveled to Belgium, Holland, Germany, England, trumpeting the extraordinary qualities of the Fontainebleau School as well as Courbet and Delacroix, selling them for sizable prices and establishing himself as an international dealer. With his profits he had bought Rembrandt, El Greco, Velásquez, Goya, no one of whom was particularly fashionable or salable at the time. Now he was looking for the next wave of painters who would succeed Corot, Daubigny, Rousseau, Jules Dupré.

"Ah, Monsieur Pissarro, I am enchanted to meet you. You have brought me a second canvas. Let us go back to my office and set it on my easel."

With his high silk hat off, Durand-Ruel looked a little less formidable and became less so every moment as he exclaimed:

"It is the triumph of living art over academic art. Not clever, not smooth. Rough and true. Pushing out in a new direction."

"Can you sell these pictures, Monsieur Durand-Ruel?"

"What is accepted by the current fashion is always sold more easily than the work of the artists whom the public understands less the more original and personal they are. But I have a list of my early buyers here who may be willing to invest in the future rather than the past. I will slip your paintings into my exhibition . . ."

Camille's heart skipped a few beats.

". . . and I will pay you forty dollars each for the two paintings after I sell them. It should not take me long."

Camille's heart ceased beating entirely.

Durand-Ruel reached for his hat. His family had recently arrived from Périgord.

"Would you like to ride home with me to Brompton Crescent, near the South Kensington Museum? I rented a small house with a garden there."

Camille was eager to go to Julie with the news but found it impolite not to accompany the dealer.

Madame Durand-Ruel proved to be young and intelligent. Her husband leaned on her for counsel in his business affairs and her advice proved sound. Three of the children attended a Jesuit school and were old enough to sit at table. Durand-Ruel had also brought his elderly Aunt Louise to London, a *tante* for the five children.

"If my husband says that you and Claude Monet are comers, you must be," Madame Durand-Ruel volunteered.

Camille added softly, "He has also expressed an interest in others of our Guerbois group. He is unlike any other dealer. He appears to have a group vision rather than a myopic view of one canvas at a time."

Monsieur Durand-Ruel adored telling his life story.

"In my youth I wanted to become a missionary or an officer. My antecedents really determined my course. When my mother and father married they were given a paper mill worth two thousand dollars, plus four hundred dollars in cash. My father transformed the mill into a stationery store as well as a supply shop for painting materials. He accepted paintings in exchange for colors and brushes and rented them to academies for artists to copy from. In 1839 he sold the mill, opened a true gallery on the Rue de la Paix and held his first show, for which he printed a catalogue of twenty-five plates. He bought seventy paintings from Théodore Rousseau, perhaps the first time a dealer had tried to establish a 'trust,' as he described it, with a painter.

"When I took over, the gallery needed a lot of capital and willingness to stick to prices," he confided. "I did well for a time but my taste was more farsighted than immediate. I was forced to handle the easily salable, yet I knew that a dealer should back an artist in whom he has faith, acquire all his work. Even as artists must acknowledge they are a brotherhood and must support each other.

"You told me on the trip out that you came to Paris in 1855 in time to see the Exposition Universelle. Millet exhibited one canvas there, depicting a peasant grafting a tree. The press attacked it violently. Millet was destitute. His friend and neighbor, Rousseau, had just had the good fortune to come into some money. He told Millet that an art lover had directed him to purchase the *Tree Grafter* for eighty dollars. Rousseau knew that Millet would never have accepted the money if he were aware that the buyer were Rousseau himself, for frequently Rousseau was as impoverished as Millet.

That story stands for me as the symbol. Perhaps that's why artists survive in a hostile world.''

Camille left for his flat as quickly as he dared. With eighty dollars he could pay his debts, buy the children new clothing and new shoes.

He would have money with which to marry Julie!

9

Paris had held out honorably until January 28, 1871, at which time it succumbed to lack of food, ammunition, medical supplies, to superiority of numbers. Camille gathered from the English press and French journals reaching him that negotiations had begun on a treaty but there were two governments in France: one headed by Thiers as Chief Executive, who was attempting to recapture the earlier Republic; the other a spontaneous uprising of people who distrusted Thiers and his National Assembly in Versailles because it represented primarily the provinces. They believed the Assembly guilty of allowing the Prussians to tear the country apart and of rescinding the moratorium on rents. They had opposed the monarchy and now opposed any republican government from Versailles even though it was an elected one. They assembled their available arms in the city parks. When Thiers attempted to recover "weapons stolen from the state," a battle broke out. The people of Paris won, elected a municipal council named the Commune of Paris, and became known as Communards, representing all strata of Parisian life. They wanted a Republic of Paris, independent of the rest of France.

Camille went into London to see Durand-Ruel, who had just returned from France, distraught.

"My galleries, which I left in the care of one of my employees, must have been converted into a field hospital. The very morning of my arrival two generals had been assassinated in Montmartre. What sense does it make to have a Paris unrelated to the rest of France? We must become a unified country again if we are to survive."

Camille's two paintings had not yet been hung in Durand-Ruel's gallery but he continued to work, and moved his family to more spacious lodgings at 2 Chatham Terrace, near where the London Crystal Palace of 1851 had been moved from Hyde Park. Julie took the children to see the industrial exhibits and the entertainments. Camille began painting the glass structure.

He also completed oils of the church of Westow Hill and the road by Sydenham with its church bordered by an alley of green trees, against which he placed the white chapel with colors of red and blue, green and pearl gray. Then he painted the Penge Station, with the train as minuscular as the workers in a field. The curving railroad tracks in the center provided locomotion to the viewer. The train tracks seemed a natural outcropping.

When their money for food and paint began to run low he went to Alfred, asking for a loan until Durand-Ruel should pay for his pictures. Alfred told him he was sorry but he was earning only enough from the Isaacson firm to support his family.

Both Camille and Claude Monet were rejected by the Royal Academy; of the French artists the English liked only Gérôme and Rosa Bonheur. Corot and the Fontainebleau School did not yet exist for them. English painters were unsympathetic; the art market was small.

Claude Monet was bitter. He had a drink with Camille in the French quarter in Fitzroy Square.

"I'm leaving. Going to Holland. They're more hospitable there. The first day of peace I'll be back in France with my wife and son."

The snow melted, a tentative sun emerged, Camille went over to Dulwich College with his easel and canvas to paint the pond, surrounding lawns and trees in front of the main building. A couple of the trees were growing a pale green foliage, there was a thin blue sky, the college buildings were a washed brick red, the pond reflected light yellow to burnt umber. A woman's figure, vaguely indicated, stood at the near bank of the pond, put there to suggest that this was an inhabited place. It was not a realistic portrait of Dulwich College. He had done his impression of the buildings, trees, pond, woman shimmering in the uncertain light of the pre-spring day.

He had hoped that James McNeill Whistler, who had been an integral part of the group in Paris, would afford him hospitality and introduce him to a few English artists and collectors. But no one knew where Whistler was; "in the country somewhere." Alfred Sisley, who had joined his English family, was also not heard from. With the exception of stouthearted Daubigny, there was a saw-toothed edge of self-centeredness in the struggle to stay alive.

In a depressed mood he wrote to Théodore Duret: "It is only abroad that one feels how beautiful, great and hospitable France is. . . ."

Toward the end of February Prussian troops had occupied Louveciennes. He received a note from a pleasant young man named Edouard Béliard who lived across the hall from Rachel's apartment in Paris and occasionally ran an errand for her, for which he had thanked the man and made some suggestions about his drawings. Béliard wrote:

"Your blankets, suits, shoes, underclothes you may go into mourning for. Your sketches, since they are generally admired, I like to think will be ornaments in Prussian drawing rooms. The nearness of the forest will no doubt have saved your furniture."

"But it's my work I'm worrying about," Camille cried. "Hundreds of watercolors, drawings . . . my oils."

"I'm more worried about my furniture," Julie responded.

The post brought other bad news. From the Jacobsen family in Copenhagen he learned that David had taken his own life by jumping out of the window of his lodgings in Florence. His tuberculosis was fatally advanced; he owed the landlord for rent. His small stove had been given to an Italian friend who had paid for his meals during the winter. David was buried in the Jewish cemetery in Florence. His letters, drawings and paintings were sent home to his brother Edvard.

Camille was saddened; but he was not taken by surprise.

Shopping was torture for Julie. She could neither talk to the vendors nor bargain.

"In England you don't have to bargain," Camille explained. "The price is marked on everything. Use that chart I gave you converting pence and pounds into centimes and francs. You have only to look at the figures and compare. Then you'll know what things cost."

"Easy for you to say. The curious noises they make; is that a language?"

"Yes, Julie. There are dozens of different languages in the world, all of which would sound to us like 'curious noises,' as ours does to them."

He took Julie to the Isaacson home, gambling that Rachel's animosity could not have touched all of Emma's family. They were so cool that Julie wept.

"Why did you take me? I'll never go again."

When she became inconsolably homesick they went into

London for afternoon tea at the Hôtel de la Boule d'Or where other French expatriates joined them: Claude Monet, Alexandre Prevost, a painter who had shown at the Paris Salon, Charles Lecape, a refugee who had an empathy for artists. Or they went to Audinet's Restaurant for dinner with Daubigny and his friends, where Julie could hardly eat, she was so happy to be engulfed in the French language.

"Oh, Camille, when can we go home?"

"As soon as there is peace."

He took her to Covent Garden, which she compared to Les Halles, and to see a touring French company playing Molière's hilarious farce, *The Doctor in Spite of Himself*, to St. Paul's Cathedral at the head of Ludgate Hill; to Trafalgar Square; to visit the streets of the working artisans: goldsmiths, lens grinders, leather decorators, ironmongers, linen drapers. They walked along the Embankment, the docks of the river Thames with its sailing vessels and steamboats so different from the barges on the Seine.

"If only I could understand!"

"Pretend you're walking the streets of Paris. People are saying the same things."

On March 6 Durand-Ruel opened his second exhibition of French paintings, listing in his catalogue two of Camille's works, *Effect of Snow* and *Upper Norwood*. He summoned Camille, who brought with him new canvases. After a few moments the dealer declared:

"They have an inner truth. Leave them with me. I will use all the skills I've accumulated to sell them."

He then added:

"I've sold a few things, not yours unfortunately, but I do have some assets." He looked sharply into Camille's eyes. "Claude Monet was destitute; that's why I paid him his sixty dollars immediately. How are you fixed?"

"I need the money."

"Very well. I will pay you the eighty dollars for the first two canvases now. If I don't sell them here I'll take them back to Paris and find collectors there. I'll also pay you forty dollars for two more when they sell. I can't be wrong about your work."

On March 10, 1871, they received a letter from Julie's sister Félicie. The news was devastating.

"Dear Julie: I went to Louveciennes yesterday and saw your house and M. Ollivon who returned two days ago. The railroad only began operating yesterday. I caught the first train, which went only as far as the bridge. I went the rest of the way to Louveciennes on foot. . . .

"The houses are burned, the roofs broken, your front door, staircase and floor—all that has disappeared.

"When I arrived in Louveciennes I didn't even recognize your house. Monsieur Ollivon was able to save some things; your two beds but no mattresses, your wardrobe, washstand, desk, about forty paintings, the small wooden bed. The Prussians lived for nearly four months in the house and scorched it thoroughly, but they did not find the small closet on the second floor under the staircase. Your house is uninhabitable now, there is straw all over because the horses were kept on the ground floor and the Prussian soldiers lived upstairs. . . ."

Camille was stunned. "Forty paintings!"

Two weeks later, weeks of desolation and dread, the news was confirmed by their landlord's wife. Madame Ollivon wrote:

"You are asking about your house; that is not the right word for it; you should say stables. There was a good two carloads of manure in your place. In the small room, next to the living room, there were horses; the kitchen and your cellar were sheep pens, and the sheep were killed in the garden. . . .

"I was forgetting to tell you that we have some paintings well preserved. . . . There are some which these gentlemen, for fear of dirtying their feet, put on the ground in the garden to serve as a carpet. My husband picked them up and we have them, too."

Next he heard about the occupation's damage from his landlord's manager Retrou, as well as the news that the Republic had passed a law that he would have to pay the rent on the Louveciennes house for the entire time the house had been occupied by the Prussians.

He wrote in reply: " . . . You tell me that a certain quantity of my affairs were saved. Some forty pictures and I had from twelve to fifteen hundred sketches, studies, paintings, the work of twenty years of my life. I think that if there is a property that is sacred it is the product of our own intelligence and made with our own hands, and yet I don't think that at Versailles they have any intention of doing something for the losers in this category."

Julie was pregnant again. He gave her the ritualistic kiss for such announcements, then declared:

"We'll go into Croydon and be married at the register office."

"Will your family come?"

"I'll invite them."

They declined.

"It doesn't matter," he said. "I'll round up a couple of our French compatriots at the Hôtel de la Boule d'Or. They'll sign the marriage certificate for us."

Julie murmured, "As you say, 'It fries no bananas to question life.' My two children will be legitimate. The one coming. I will be too."

On May 21 Chief Executive Thiers signed a peace treaty agreeing to pay one billion dollars as indemnity and to cede Alsace and Lorraine to the Germans. The citizenry of Paris rose in revolt against the treaty, refused to disarm. Mayor Georges Clemenceau of Montmartre attempted a reconciliation but Chief Executive Thiers's troops, loyal to the newly formed Republic, entered Paris by surprise, began a week-long civil war in which seventeen thousand Parisians were killed, including women and children. The military sweep destroyed the Paris movement. Thiers prevailed and the Republic was accepted throughout France. By May 28 the Commune of Paris, which had lasted for less than two months, disappeared.

That was when calamity struck Gustave Courbet. The only artist who had been deeply involved in Parisian politics, Courbet, a month after the Commune was established, had been elected a delegate to the new governing body, then became chairman of a group of artists who managed to get some of the galleries of the Louvre reopened and dispersed pictures returned to it. They abolished the Ecole des Beaux-Arts, established a federation of artists free from government control. Before Courbet's election, the delegates had ordered the destruction of the Vendôme Column, built to celebrate Napoleon's war conquests, which the Parisian public loathed as a symbol of his creating still another monarchy. The column was duly demolished and the statue of Napoleon smashed, said the London *Times*, into splinters, a wreck, with one arm broken and the head severed from the body, while a band of the National Guard played the "Marseillaise."

Courbet was proclaimed the hero of the demolition. He was also arrested by the Republic and was awaiting trial in the Conciergerie prison, though, as he wrote to an English friend, Robert Reid:

"I am accused of having destroyed the Column Vendôme, when the fact is on the record that the decree for its destruction was voted on the 14th of April, and I was elected to the Commune on the 20th, six days afterwards!"

Julie bought some light blue silk in a draper's shop and

sewed a dress for her wedding. Camille went into London to round up his French friends, Alexandre Prevost and Charles Lecape. The English official was Edwin Bailey of the register office in Croydon. The Register went through his brief duties, everyone signed the marriage certificate. It was June 14, 1871.

"We will celebrate in Audinet's Restaurant," Camille announced. "With Reims champagne."

Julie Vellay, now Madame Pissarro, would no longer need to dissemble at Montfoucault or Louveciennes. She linked her arm affectionately through her husband's.

BOOK EIGHT

These Fragile Moments

1

DURAND-RUEL paid Camille eighty dollars for the second two canvases of the English countryside though he had sold neither of the first two.

"I assume you need money to get your family back to France," he said.

The Gare St. Lazare in Paris was bedlam, with hundreds of families awaiting the arrival of those who had taken refuge abroad. At the height of the pandemonium Julie turned to Camille and smiled.

"The curious noises they make; is that a language?"

Félicie met them at the station, taking Julie and the two children home with her. Camille rode the train to Louveciennes over tracks that had been repaired. He was filled with trepidation. His first sight of their house was a view of four workmen installing a new roof. Monsieur Ollivon, the gray-haired, parchment-wrinkled owner, had been a former town councilor for Louveciennes; he was an efficient man.

"Ah, Monsieur Pissarro. I'm glad to have you back. We're replacing the center ceiling beam in your bedroom; it burned when the soldiers set fire to the room. The government is paying for structural damage done by the cannonading and ravages of enemy troops. They'll also pay a modest sum for your stolen or damaged furniture."

Ollivon had already put on a new front door, laid a wooden ground floor to replace the one which the horses' hooves had carved into splinters, had had the carpenters rebuild the staircase to the bedroom floor. Camille made a quick check of the furniture. As Félicie and Madame Ollivon had written, the two larger beds were intact, as was a small wooden crib; the mattresses had all disappeared. The desk and tables were badly scarred. The tall clock, which Julie had hidden in the closet under the staircase, was in good order. The library room off the living room had been used as a stable but the books on the shelves were undisturbed. Would the inhabitants of the land of Goethe not harm a book?

The soldiers had moved the living-room furniture up to their bedroom quarters. Julie's big kitchen, used as a sheep pen, was empty of pots, skillets and ceramic vases, the dishes broken, the walls and floors a mess.

"I'll repair the walls and floors," Ollivon assured him. "As to Madame's kitchen utensils, you may find some of them in the garden or the surrounding woods. Consider yourself fortunate; they slaughtered the sheep in the garden instead of in the kitchen. There's one thing more, as the manager wrote you. You must pay the full rent for the months you were away."

Camille went ashen.

"That's eight months! I have no such money."

Monsieur Ollivon was a compassionate man.

"I know that. But it's still your liability. You can pay it gradually, over the next year or two."

Camille groaned as he gave Monsieur Ollivon what he had left of Durand-Ruel's eighty dollars to pay the rent for July.

"How do I pay for the past when the present is so uncertain?"

Quaking inwardly, he walked over the dead grass to the little stone building inside the wall that had been his studio and had also been used to stable the officers' horses. A layer of straw and manure two feet thick covered the floors; the smell was unbearable. His worktables were gone, as were the lower racks he had built to house his sketchbooks from St. Thomas, Caracas and Paris; his pencil and charcoal drawings, his watercolors and gouaches, his oil paintings. His knees went weak, the acid of anguish and desolation ate at his stomach. He wanted to sit down but there was nowhere to sit. He wandered out to Julie's uprooted garden; only the trees were alive. Off to one side he saw splotches of color which looked familiar. Digging around, he uncovered an oil painting from Pontoise. In a half-demented frenzy he dug out with his hands more canvases that had been subjected to scuffing, rain, mud, decomposure. He clutched the bundle to his chest, ran to the house.

"More of my paintings half buried in the garden," he cried to Monsieur Ollivon. "Destroyed as though by some pounding machine."

Ollivon did not need to look at the bedraggled canvases.

"The soldiers used them as mats on which to wipe their boots."

Camille kneeled on the new-laid floor. Tears burned in his eyes. He straightened out the canvases, one by one.

"A few can be saved," he muttered. "Retouched. There's an expert in Paris, Armand Gautier. Madame Ollivon wrote that you had saved some of these mutilated canvases. And also some that were not harmed. Where are they?"

"In my house. In a dry place. Come, we'll get them. It will cheer you."

Camille's heart leapt as he went through the canvases. Sorting them, he found undamaged seven oils, mostly from 1863; a half dozen from La Varenne and Montfoucault painted in 1864; six from La Varenne and La Roche-Guyon from 1865; from 1866 two Pontoise oils, one of them *The Banks of the Marne in Winter*, which had caused his break with Corot. For 1867 he counted eight oils from the Hermitage; for 1868 ten more of Pontoise; and wonder of wonders, a dozen unharmed paintings from Louveciennes painted just before the war. Fifty-one paintings in all!

It was only then that he thought of the canvases Claude Monet had left with him before fleeing to London. He ran back to the studio. Monet's carefully wrapped bundle rested untouched on a high recessed shelf, unseen from the floor. With them was a batch of his own paintings, stored there because they were twelve inches by twenty or less, and would fit into the aperture. The hundreds of watercolors and drawings were gone, but as he squatted on the bare floor of the living room, examining one by one the blessedly saved canvases, his spirits rose.

Two cartfuls of manure had been cleaned out of the lower floor of the house and dumped into the garden. Camille got a shovel and, standing a foot deep in droppings, began to clean out his studio. He found a number of blood-soaked canvases which had been used as aprons when the soldiers killed the sheep. When he walked to the river for a respite, some of the washerwomen were also wearing the canvases as aprons wrapped around their waists. He went among them, saying nothing but appraising each painting for damage. They were watersoaked, the moisture unfastening the sizing glue and making the paint peel off. They were mangled at the corners where they were tied with string. The women looked up at him without expression. They somehow knew they were wearing his paintings, but they had not stolen them, they had found them in the streets and the woods. When he returned to the house through the village, men who had availed themselves of his absence to loot the house and desecrate his work stared at him as though he were a stranger.

"Ravages of war," Ollivon commented when Camille told him of the unpleasantness.

"Why do they sneer? The women at the pool, the men in the streets and shops?"

"Partly because you were able to flee to safety while they had to remain here; partly because they never really accepted a man who putters with paint."

Camille gave the fire-streaked walls of their bedroom a coat of white paint, as well as Julie's kitchen and the streaked and discolored living-room walls. He scraped and varnished the tables. The paints and brushes used up his last change; how to buy a new mattress for himself and Julie, another for Lucien and Minette? How to reprovision Julie's kitchen? Replace blankets, linens . . . ?

He framed up four of what he considered his best canvases from Louveciennes and took them to Durand-Ruel in his gallery on Rue Le Peletier. The gallery had been cleaned and redecorated, some fifty paintings were hanging in the big central room, a few old masters, a goodly group of the Fontainebleau School, Camille's canvases from England as well as Monet's Trouville scene. Durand-Ruel had done well in his London gallery despite the fact that he had been unable to sell a Pissarro or Monet. Back in Paris his collectors, who had been caught up in the war for over a year, had begun returning, hungry for new acquisitions. He placed Camille's four canvases in turn on his personal viewing easel, cried out with delight at their quiet beauty.

"They are superb!" he exclaimed. Then more softly: "But I shall be prudent and buy only two. I'll take this one, *The Versailles Road,* and *The Coach at Louveciennes.*"

He used an admiring finger to trace the Louveciennes canvas, twenty-five by thirty-four inches. Two white horses pulling a traveler-coach with the barely suggested image of a driver perched on top; a man and woman waiting to board; a short stretch of wet road cobbled with splashes of yellow and green rain under leafy-topped trees. On the one side a two-story house with a front garden; on the other, the suggestion of a woman walking along a path with a raised green umbrella; and walking toward her, his umbrella rolled tight, a man with his back to the viewer.

"An ordinary scene," murmured Durand-Ruel, "a coach

in the rain, a wet road and wet white horses, a house, trees, a few small figures. Yet the world *in situ*. My dear Pissarro, looking at your painting, all the tension in my bosom is released. You make me feel as though the world is good.''

"That's how I felt while painting it."

"Ah! *The Versailles Road*. Would that be your wife and daughter in your front garden behind the picket fence?''

"It would be. Chatting with the *bonne* from the house of Madame and Monsieur Retrou next door."

"You do have the ability to draw us into the heart of a picture," the dealer commented. "A sense of man and the earth being eternal. Your paintings have God in them. It's a remarkable gift. So simple and so profound."

Camille quipped out of sheer joy:

"Monsieur Durand-Ruel, you have convinced me. I will buy both paintings from you."

Durand-Ruel smiled. This dealer who dressed like an actuary and kept the mask of an advocate on his handsome lean face, the leonine head of always meticulously brushed hair swept back from his high brow, was enraptured with art.

"Shall we say fifty dollars for each canvas?" he asked.

Camille trembled inwardly. Whom should he thank that such a good man had appeared on earth? He would be able to make the house livable again.

From the Durand-Ruel gallery he went to his mother's apartment in Montmartre. The house had been untouched by the bombing. Stored at the back of one of her closets he found several pictures from 1861, a black chalk of the Rue St. Vincent in Montmartre, among others. She had also retained his pencil sketch of her from 1856, and his *Self-Portrait as a Young Man* from the same period. He told her of his two sales that day, showed her the hundred dollars in bank notes to prove that he was telling the truth. Rachel proffered her congratulations.

"Then you won't need my allowance anymore. It must be a good feeling to be independent at last."

Camille was silent; he had not expected such a response.

"A very good feeling," he replied a little hollowly. Then added, "Julie is expecting again, in November."

Rachel had grown accustomed to Julie's frequent pregnancies.

"Alfred is too busy recovering his business to come to midday dinner. I want you to promise you'll come."

"I want a promise in return. That after the baby is born you'll come out to visit us."

It was his mother's turn to fall silent.

"So that's your price for independence!"

With the money from Durand-Ruel Camille bought mattresses for their beds, a minimum of sheets, towels. The teapot, cups and saucers Emma had brought as a gift several years before had all been destroyed, as had the tablecloths. He gave Julie money to replace the broken dishes, the ruined skillets, the kettle, spit for roasting, earthenware jugs, basket mold, candlesticks, *potager* for her soups and vegetables. They straightened and hammered out the dents in the boiling pots and cutlery.

Julie's first task was to get rid of the manure dumped in her back garden and to soak the land: that much fertilizer would burn the seeds and bulbs. She planted tomatoes, corn, zucchini, squash and pumpkin. In her flower garden she set out asters, chrysanthemums, zinnias, marigolds and dahlias from bulbs. Camille asked doubtfully, watching her:

"Can you bring them up?"

"Can you paint pictures?"

"It's July. We may get some cool days but August is a horror. That's why they lock up Paris for the month."

"If you had seen the miserable piece of ground where I raised vegetables at the bottom of the Rue Neuve you would know I can raise vegetables anywhere, any time."

Lucien was now eight. He thought leveling the garden and getting rid of the excess manure was a game. Minette was six; she trailed her mother much of the day, carrying seeds, bulbs, a sprinkling can.

He went to Guillemet's studio where he located several works from 1862, as well as one or two later ones. Félicie had his two studies of Julie: *Sewing* and *Reading*. Alfred had saved, at the bottom of a trunk, a number of sketches from Caracas. The portrait Camille had made of Piette in his Paris studio was safe in Montfoucault, as well as several of the Montfoucault countryside. Those paintings he had sold to the banker Arosa, to the opera singer Faure, to Duret, and the several canvases in Martin's shop, which had gone unbombed, were all safe. A few of his academic drawings from the ateliers came to light, the female nude whose pubic hair got him in trouble with the *massier* in François Picot's studio; Julie breast-feeding Minette from 1865. Three canvases which Julie had asked to keep for her own, *Hillside of Jallais near Pontoise*, one from La Varenne, a portrait of herself and Minette, had been securely hidden behind the clock in the closet under the stairs.

When he put everything together he found there were a full

ninety representative works. The years from 1857 to 1861 appeared to have vanished without a trace: pencil, ink and charcoal drawings, watercolors, beginning oils. He was frustrated not only by their being missing but by his memory of them. It was a staggering loss. The price he had paid for flight: for wanting to marry Julie in London, keep his children safe. Where could he have left his work that it would have been safe? He mourned the irretrievable documentation of his years, the rich source of his future.

But no invading force could take away the enormous amount he had learned through the concentrated labor. The near twenty years of hard-bitten experience in his craft were fully available for the future. He was only forty-one, in robust health, surrounded by a loving family, with stability in his determination. Good things were bound to emerge, better paintings than he had envisaged before. It would take resolution to put his loss behind him. But as the new canvases came to life the loss would fade and disappear.

Through an advocate who was handling similar claims, Camille asked the government for ten thousand francs in damages for his missing and destroyed art work. He was paid a total of one hundred and sixty-seven dollars, barely the price of a linen handkerchief or a pair of wool socks for each missing endeavor.

It was not wise to harbor bitterness. Soldiers from all nations at war looted and destroyed. Was not the Louvre filled with paintings the conquering Napoleon had taken out of Italy? Statues, ancient and inscribed monuments, out of Egypt? Frédéric Bazille's parents grieved for their tall, lovable son. What sense did it make to mourn the loss of drawings and paintings?

An end to somber regret and recriminations. Creativity was in him. He would double his output.

2

He searched out his friends, some of whom had been scattered by the war. Edouard Manet, who had become a staff officer of the National Guard, was back at work in his studio in the Batignolles district. He told Camille the war had been a humiliation for him, that he had had to serve under Meissonier, one of the most untalented and successful copiers of the Beaux-Arts who did not know that the Fontainebleau School existed, let alone the Batignolles group. The war had not destroyed any of his property yet he was fracturing his inheritance by managing to spend more than his income.

Paul Cézanne had wanted nothing to do with the war. He had spent the time at home in Aix-en-Provence painting around L'Estaque. Emile Zola had gone to Bordeaux where he had worked as a secretary to one of the government ministers. Guillaumin had continued in the Department of Bridges and Causeways. Guillemet had enlisted in the *garde mobile*. Renoir had been sent to a regiment of cuirassiers, then dispatched to a cavalry training center at Bordeaux. Degas had enlisted in the infantry but had been placed in the artillery because of a bad right eye. Piette had continued to work as a laborer on his farm to keep it producing. Claude Monet was still in Holland painting the Dutch scene.

Alfred Sisley returned from England. He and his pretty, plump-jowled wife and two children still lived close by in Louveciennes. After the bankruptcy of his father he had become destitute and for the first time in his life needed to earn a living.

Bazille alone had seen action.

Camille accompanied Durand-Ruel, who had sold Gustave Courbet successfully for years, and Boudin, Monet's mentor, to visit Courbet in prison. Camille was shocked to see how thin and haggard he had become, his hair turning white. Courbet embraced them in turn, tears in his eyes.

"Look where I am lodged," he cried, "a dark cell of dirt and vermin. I'm allowed my meals *à la pistole* from the Brasserie Laveur as long as I can pay for them, but my property and paintings have been seized against a possible fine. My hemorrhoids are causing me misery. I should be in a hospital."

Camille sat on the narrow bunk; Durand-Ruel and Boudin squatted on rickety stools.

"I did not order the column in the Place Vendôme torn down," Courbet cried. "My job was to save the art work of Paris, not destroy it."

"What can we do to get you transferred to a hospital?" Camille asked.

"Write to the Ministry of Justice. Get my case transferred to a civil tribunal instead of a military court."

Durand-Ruel said quietly, "You are going to need money for your defense. I hope this is not treason but if you have any hidden canvases I can ship them abroad for sale."

Courbet went into a spasm of revulsion.

"I haven't painted for months; I don't know that I ever will again."

When it was time to leave all three were devastated. How could they help this *rara avis,* this genius who had been so supportive of young artists of Paris?

They could not. Gustave Courbet was tried at the end of July 1871 before a Council of War "for participation in a movement designed to change the form of government and incite the citizens to take up arms against each other; complicity in the destruction of a monument, the Vendôme Column, by assisting those who committed the crime."

Camille and Sisley, whose homes were close to the court in Versailles, went to hear the verdict: six months in prison in addition to the three months he had already spent in jail; and a heavy fine. They were allowed a moment to say au revoir to Courbet, now very ill, on his way out of court to be returned to prison. Toward the end of September Camille visited him in the ancient prison of Ste. Pélagie on the Rue du Puits de l'Ermite, built in 1665 as a refuge for retired prostitutes. He was lodged in a dormitory where he had the privacy of a cubicle containing an iron bed, two tables and two chairs. He was dressed in the prison uniform of gray trousers and jacket. With an expression of disgust he described the place as "stricken by senile leprosy."

"Ah, my friend, Camille Pissarro, did you ever imagine when you saw my pavilion in 1855 and joined my friends and me at the Brasserie Andler, that I would end up here? A criminal prisoner?" Courbet smiled winsomely. "My sister Zoé will get me transferred to a nursing home. I'll go to Switzerland when my sentence is over. They're threatening to make me pay the cost of casting a new column, about one hundred thousand dollars. Better men than I have fled our charming government: Voltaire, Victor Hugo . . ."

"In the meanwhile is there something I can do to help?"

"Yes, a little paint and canvas."

Time went quickly as they resettled into the rehabilitated house on the Route de Versailles. When Rachel took ill he went into Paris to stay with her, taking Lucien with him, the first time Lucien had been received in the apartment. Dr. Gachet assured Camille that it was a passing attack of something with a medical name Camille had not heard before. Rachel was comforted by Dr. Gachet's reassurance.

In October he went to Pontoise for several days of painting

and sketching. He wrote Julie that he yearned to return permanently. That he felt Pontoise was his home place. "I love it best. And all my own." He would search for a house away from the two rivers on a higher, drier spot.

He had a keener vision of the countryside around Louveciennes for having been away in England; painted with a patient zest the orchards and banks of the Seine at Marly, an autumnal scene with a puffing boat and barge in the curving river, a tiny figure fishing with a bent pole, an anonymous couple walking along an equally curving path under the shedding trees toward the village beyond.

He providentially gained a new and experienced collector, Ernest Hoschedé, owner-manager of a department store called Gagne Petit, Save a Little, who began buying through Durand-Ruel. Hoschedé was an outsized man with a large stomach and an appetite as avid for art as it was for food and merchandising profit. He had an attractive wife, Alice, buxom, with a flock of children, who shared his enthusiasm. They were buying other members of the painting fraternity as well, for the passionately devoted Durand-Ruel had convinced the Hoschedé couple that they were buying the work of the future.

Claude Monet returned to Paris and found a studio flat for his family on the Rue de l'Isly. The exquisite Léonie, who had suffered his long absence in loneliness, was his full-time model despite having a son and flat to care for. Monet had matured considerably since his flight to London and Holland. He was still the handsomest of all Camille's painter friends; but the derring-do had vanished. Durand-Ruel bought two more of his canvases, and he sought portrait commissions. Léonie sent a message to Julie that she would like to be with her for the *accouchement*.

Julie was delivered of their second son, whom they named Georges, in November. The Monets had been staying with them for a week. Léonie managed the cooking, her affectionate companionship a considerable lift to Julie's spirits. Their son Jean, now four years old, played in the back garden with Lucien and Minette. Camille and Monet went out each day to paint in the woods of Marly, the nearby village of Voisins, on the banks of the Seine, on the road to Versailles, locating their easels close together but at different angles, learning through exploration.

"It's the light that's important, not the object underneath it," Monet commented.

"The scene has an equal importance," Camille said in

320

rebuttal. "If you lose the substance, the light becomes a glow on nothing."

Alfred Pissarro too had had a second son whom he also named Georges. He met Camille at Rachel's apartment. He had in tow a cook and a maid to install there. This done, the brothers went together for a drink at the Café de la Nouvelle Athènes on the Place Pigalle, which since the war had become the favorite café of the Guerbois group. It was the first time in years they had had a drink together. Alfred said happily:

"Congratulations to us both. We are again fathers of male heirs, and we are both prospering. The French manufacturers are importuning me to export their products. Maman told me you sold two canvases to Durand-Ruel."

"Yes. He has promised to buy as my work progresses."

"You must not deny me the pleasure of buying your gold frames. Here is twenty dollars, a nativity gift from my Georges to your Georges." He put a hand affectionately on Camille's shoulder. "You see, Camille, I was right, we each had to make our own way. Now that you are beginning to be successful we can be friends again."

Camille forced a smile. The borderline poverty, the nagging anxieties over the well-being of Julie and his children were not that easily eradicated. Nor was the fact that he and his family were unwanted in Alfred's home. Yet above all he wanted peace. Emotionally he would always be yoked to his mother and brother.

Julie was happy as Madame Camille Pissarro. The infant Georges appeared to be in good health. Lucien and Minette were doing well in the local school, walking into the village in blue smocks, book bags slung over their shoulders. Camille had an admiring dealer, was garnering collectors. For the first time she was beginning to believe that he could support his family by the simple act of painting pictures.

In mid-November the drama of fulfillment and tragedy continued to play itself out. Paul Durand-Ruel took his wife to the opera to hear *Faust*. In the middle of the performance she suffered an attack brought on by her pregnancy; subsequently she developed an inflammation of the lungs. A few days later an embolism developed. She died at two o'clock in the morning, receiving the last rites in the presence of her husband and children, the eldest of whom was only nine.

It was a shocking blow to the art dealer; his had been a harmonious marriage in which Madame Durand-Ruel was an important part of his organization. Durand-Ruel asked the elderly Aunt Louise to run the household and engaged the excellent priest of Aveyron, Abbé Fornals, to serve as tutor for his sons.

Camille considered it proper to attend the funeral at St. Louis d'Antin, the parish of their apartment in the Rue Lafayette, where the deeply religious Durand-Ruel had made his first communion. The gathering of family and friends was a desolate one. Camille and Daubigny were the only two artists present. Durand-Ruel embraced Camille but was too overcome to speak. Yet a new bond had been wrought between them.

3

The first day of 1872 was a pleasant one. Alfred Sisley and his two children came to dinner. Thanks to assiduity and decorative talent, more gentle and less revolutionary than his peers, Sisley was selling better than any of them. The happy day seemed a good omen for the coming year.

But the fates were incorrigible. The infant Georges, now three months old, began to have seizures, his eyes turning uncontrollably, his body stiffening, the blood fleeing from his face. They were terror-stricken. Dr. Gachet applied his stethoscope to Georges's chest, examined the infant's ears; found the eardrums neither hot nor red. He stroked his goatee, studied the narrow strips of flowers on the wallpaper in Georges's room above the little library, then diagnosed the problem as a convulsive fever, symptom of an infection, and advised bringing in a local doctor who could be on the scene for emergencies. He prescribed an herbal potion to be administered every hour, frequent rubdowns, a teaspoon of tea.

Julie and Camille were speechless. Of the five children Julie had birthed, the first had been stillborn, the fourth had died within two weeks from an infection caused by a wet nurse. Were they going to repeat Rachel's pattern? Camille asked himself in torment.

The crisis continued. Georges's head jerked in every direction; at times he seemed unconscious. The local doctor prescribed egg yolk, oil and orange blossom water. The attacks were so frightening that neither Camille nor Julie was able to leave the room except to spell each other for a few hours of sleep, or to prepare Lucien and Minette for school.

At the end of a month the doctor was present at a particularly violent seizure when the infant's body stiffened as though in rigor mortis. Camille accompanied him out to his carriage.

"Doctor, if Georges is saved from death will his intelligence be lost?"

"My real fear is not for his life but that he may become an epileptic."

"Epilepsy! What are their sins that little children are so cruelly punished?" he cried.

The doctor shook his head vigorously.

"The nervous system has nothing to do with rewards and punishments. You might join your wife in prayer; it's at least as effective as egg yolk, oil and orange blossom water."

The seizures lessened in intensity, then ceased altogether. Georges returned to good health, his lungs were lusty, his appetite omnivorous.

Camille changed trains in Paris for Auvers-sur-Oise to visit the house Gachet had bought in Auvers after his wife had borne a daughter and developed lung trouble. He wanted to present the doctor with two new canvases: *Sunrise* and *Snow Effect at Louveciennes*.

He followed Dr. Gachet up the stairs of the three-story structure perched on a hill, which had in earlier years been a convent and was as bizarre as Gachet's tunic, fitted at the waist, flaring to mid-thigh, with embroidered stand-up collar, epaulettes, a wide belt and gold buttons closely spaced from the neck down. The house was located in chaotic terrain, wild and picturesque. Twenty steep stone steps led to the first level of the whitish cube pierced by nine bays, topped by four different levels of roof. Under a window of the third floor was a securely nailed sign which read:

BOARDING SCHOOL FOR YOUNG GIRLS

Gachet led Camille to a studio under the eaves where he had installed an etching press on which he made mezzotints and engravings. He had tried to paint but, as he himself admitted, after a lot of the best young painters had tried to instruct him:

"I am unteachable."

But not in medicine. During the Franco-Prussian War he had pioneered the use of antiseptic solutions which had earned him praise from the medical profession, and patients who could pay in a harder currency than works of art.

Gachet put Camille's two canvases on separate easels as Camille explained they were a gift for always coming when summoned, for diagnosing the ills of the family and treating them with homeopathic potions until they were well again. Dr. Gachet stepped back from the paintings and promptly went into a frenzy of joy, waving his arms, rolling his eyes, dancing about the easels as he poured out a torrent of exultation and praise.

"Sacrebleu!" Camille cried to himself. "He's going to have a seizure."

Exhausted, Dr. Gachet sank into a canvas-backed chair, took off his fur hat and wiped the perspiration from his brow.

"Ah, no, it is too much. They are worth many times my visits. I want the two paintings, oh yes, they will enrich my life; but I must pay you something in addition."

"Please accept, my dear Doctor. It will make me easy in my mind."

The two men embraced.

The recovery of his son sent Camille out into the countryside in a paroxysm of painting: nineteen completed oils of the roads of Louveciennes, snow studies, the horse chestnut trees, the village of Voisins, the woods. He did not find the area as rich in motif as the Hermitage and Pontoise, yet there were marvelously paintable scenes close at hand. He developed his sense of what he called spatial construction, reorganized the architecture of his themes, left out the rigid borders on the top, bottom and sides used by his antecedents. He eliminated black from his palette; studied the luminous colors of shadows thrown by trees across a road; painted the simple truths he perceived of the earth and its living creatures. He was painting on good-sized canvases: the Seine at Marly, seventeen by twenty-three inches; chestnut trees of Louveciennes, sixteen by twenty-one; others twenty-four by twenty-nine, filling the space with light and shadow, using light to define form, leaving no area void. He used cream white, light brown and nature's variety of greens, a range of brush strokes to achieve diversity. He sought a balance between style and content. In front of a scene his eyes performed the function of instruments in a dissection laboratory. This done, he put the pieces together into an organic whole, assimilating the sometimes conflicting aspects of nature into his own temperament.

When he went out into the terrain with Monet or Sisley they taught each other how to reproduce on canvas the colors of nature, to keep intensity by the adroit mixing of pigments; to apply color in little strokes and patches to suggest depth. How to create meaning without spelling out detail; to portray the poetry of humble things. How to be austere, skillful, true to the spirit of the world and to one's own. They caught reflections of the winter and the luminous colors of shadows which painters had hitherto neglected.

On days of impossible weather he painted his favorite model, his winsome seven-year-old daughter. Minette adored sitting for her father; it proved that he loved her and was fascinated by her. First in school clothes, the blue smock over a red dress and red socks, a white collar-scarf, her hair tied with black ribbons, fingers intertwined in front of her. Next he painted her dressed in her pink and white striped cotton, her straw hat showing a fringed blue ribbon, holding a colorful bunch of her mother's flowers in her lap. Her face was a fine mating of her parents: Julie's regular features, broad-cheeked peasant face, dominated by Camille's large, warm brown eyes. For an artist who was not interested in portraiture, his paintings of Minette, with her long brown hair combed down over her shoulders, were sentimentally truthful.

Julie said without inflection:

"Minette is Papa's girl. You understand each other without putting commas and periods in your sentences."

Julie would not pose, though she did not object to his sketching her as she moved about her chores in the house or in her garden patches. Lucien could not sit in one place for more than a couple of minutes except for the daily drawing lesson from his father.

Durand-Ruel was buying one picture a month from Camille, Monet and Sisley. When they were in Paris together Camille and Monet took Degas and Renoir into the Durand-Ruel gallery, with several of their latest canvases. Durand-Ruel, who turned down a half dozen conventional painters a day, fell in love with Renoir's *The Pont Neuf*, buying it for enough money to enable Renoir to rent the very first studio of his own, on the Rue St. Georges. From Degas, who had never sold anything, he purchased *The Orchestra of the Opera* and *The Banker*. He told Camille:

"That was a fine thing you did, bringing in your two friends because you thought they were good enough for me to buy. It cuts down on the amount of money I have for your work and Monet's. Like Rousseau with Millet, it's an act of brotherhood. Another reason I believe your little group will not sink into the sea like thousands of painters in Paris today."

"We must all arrive together."

"So it seems." Durand-Ruel lit one of his aromatic cigars. It was a good time for Camille. Gustave Arosa commissioned four panels, Spring, Summer, Autumn, Winter, for the library of his St. Cloud home; his brother Achille acquired an English landscape. Faure bought another Louveciennes painting and Ernest Hoschedé continued to buy from Durand-Ruel.

The Beaux-Arts Salon was resumed in the spring of 1872. Camille, Monet, Sisley and Degas decided not to submit to its judging process again.

."Why should we?" Monet demanded. "We're selling outside the Salon."

Berthe Morisot, Manet, Cézanne and Renoir disagreed. All four submitted canvases. Renoir and Cézanne were summarily rejected. Morisot's brilliant study of a mother and child, painted in unorthodox colors, was accepted, as was Manet's *Combat of the Kearsarge and the Alabama*. Neither picture sold. Manet, eager to sell something, placed two of his canvases in the studio of a friend, Alfred Stevens, a Belgian who had achieved considerable success in Paris by painting society girls in opulent interiors. Stevens had a wide circle of wealthy friends; Manet was hoping that one of them would buy his pictures. One did: Paul Durand-Ruel.

Camille learned about it while sitting with friends at the Café de la Nouvelle Athènes, where they now gathered. Durand-Ruel, paying a social visit to Alfred Stevens's soigné studio, saw two of Edouard Manet's paintings, was enchanted and bought them within the hour. He asked Stevens to take him to visit Manet's studio the following day, never having met the man, and was so moved that he bought all twenty-three canvases on the walls, easels and floor, for seven thousand dollars; the first time a body of work of one of their group had been purchased as a whole; and the highest price paid. The painters were exultant.

When Camille took his next two paintings into Durand-Ruel's for his monthly sale, the dealer exclaimed:

"I marvel at my purchase; one doesn't appreciate a work of art until one possesses it and lives with it. *Luncheon on the Grass, Olympia, The Balcony, The Guitarist* appear even more beautiful to me now that I have been able to contemplate them leisurely. A few days later I returned to Manet's and bought a second lot that he had rounded up from various places."

He placed Camille's paintings on his office easels.

"Any collector wanting to acquire a Daubigny has to come to me. I have kept his prices high and steady. The same will apply to Edouard Manet. I am mounting a show for my London gallery; I will hang eleven of Manet's canvases, seven of yours, four of Sisley's, several of Claude Monet's. This exhibition should accomplish with the English collectors what I could not achieve during the war. Once I begin selling your group in Paris and London, I will buy your entire output also. Early on my father and I were regarded as a Fontainebleau gallery; now we will become known as a Batignolles gallery.''

When Camille asked offhandedly why Alfred Sisley was selling better than he was, Durand-Ruel replied:

''He paints almost as well as you and Monet. But his canvases are easier to live with, his surfaces more lyrical.''

Camille painted for a hundred days straight, drawing at his studio table far into the night, too elated by Durand-Ruel's support to give serious consideration to eating or sleep. Julie put food in front of him, enticed him into bed around midnight. He was grateful for her solicitude but rolled and pitched like a small cargo boat in a storm at sea. From his sketches he did harshly beautiful end-of-winter scenes of rain and cold, ice-cold blue and white streaks amidst barren trees. He did still lifes of Julie's emerging peonies, the surrounding farmlands sprouting bright green shoots from the chocolate-colored furrows. And he became painted out.

Exhausted. Stripped of energy and ideas. By reflex he went on painting. He took half a dozen of the canvases into Durand-Ruel.

''Ah, Pissarro, you have a batch of new work. Come, put it on the stands.''

The dealer became silent; pockets of disappointment forming at the corners of his mouth.

''These aren't of first quality,'' he declared. ''What has happened?''

Camille floundered. ''I was tired. Yet I thought I should continue. . . .''

''No. Only when you are at the top of your form.''

''I'll manage to get a few sous for them.''

''I wouldn't recommend that. You want to be represented only by your best.''

He stayed at his mother's apartment that night. He had an appointment with a dealer called Latouche for the next morning. He wrote to Julie, sending her a thousand kisses, telling her of his scene with Durand-Ruel; he did not try to hide the barking of his shins.

Latouche had a narrow store-front gallery. He bought a picture of a farm for ten dollars. Camille knew that Durand-Ruel's admonition was in season; but he could not bring himself to go home to Julie empty-handed.

4

He and Lucien gathered bundles of branches from the woods to feed their fireplaces. Though he wrote to Dr. Gachet that the family was afflicted with frightful colds and Louveciennes was no better for the children's health than Pontoise, it did not interfere with their work schedule. Lucien and Minette attended school, Julie cared for Georges, her house, vegetables and flowers. Camille painted a poetic *Entrance to the Village of Voisins*. Julie was kept content with visits from her sisters, Félicie and her daughter Nini, and Joséphine, who had married a Monsieur Daudon and moved to Paris. She had a son Jules and daughter Marie. Camille too had company. Armand Guillaumin came as often as he could get away from his job and on weekends.

"I know I'm not good yet," he confided to Camille. "That's because I have to work full time. But I'm learning from you. As soon as I win my lottery I'll be able to retire and paint seven days a week."

Claude Monet, Léonie and their son came from Argenteuil where they had found a modest house. Renoir came from his parents' cottage to share a day of painting. Even Degas, who disliked the countryside, visited, buying one of Camille's oils. Camille showed him how to achieve changing color *en plein air*.

Degas laughed. "The first time I saw you at a party in that gaucho outfit, those long white pantaloons and voluminous poncho, you looked like a Sephardic rabbi."

Piette and Adèle visited, bringing with them jams and cheeses from Montfoucault.

Because so many painters were now coming to Louveciennes, some of them obviously prosperous, the hostility of the towns-people was slowly eroded.

By July he had painted twenty complete oils, oils Durand-Ruel would not be able to fault.

"I've exhausted my interest in painting this region," he said to Julie one day.

Julie asked:

"What does that mean for the children and me?"

"That we all move."

"Where to?"

"Back to Pontoise. The Hermitage."

"Back there again?"

"Yes. I barely scratched the surface."

Dr. Gachet, close by in Auvers, found them a house in Pontoise. When they went to see it they considered it unsatisfactory, set directly on the street, sunken, inconvenient. They stayed overnight in a hotel by the Oise docks. The following day they located a small house on Rue Malbranche. It wasn't cheerful, but it was clean and roomy, and would be dry. Camille took a three-month lease; resolved to find something on higher ground, above the river mists. On the last day of July he helped a brawny driver load their furniture into a two-horse farm wagon. It was a full day's haul, starting at daybreak, using winding country roads northward through St. Germain, avoiding the Paris outskirts. Camille rode with the wagoner, protecting his packets of paintings.

They made no attempt to adorn the house, treating it as a campsite. Once installed, Julie and the children took pleasure in the big market fairs, parades on holidays, communal parks where she could sit on a bench crocheting while Georges slept in his carriage and Lucien and Minette played with other town children on the greensward. The children were back in the Pontoise school.

Camille was home again. There was no traditional period in which he had to walk and wander, familiarize himself with the vicinity. The Hermitage had not been important enough to be bombarded during the war; little if anything had changed. The peasants of the surrounding farms knew him by sight; the townspeople were accustomed to seeing him roam the hilly winding streets with a rucksack or easel on his back. They gave no appreciable sign of welcome, neither was he the stranger who incited suspicion by the oddity of his vocation. They acted as though he had never been away; after a few days of painting in the neighborhood he felt the same way.

Time was seamless. The days merged smoothly into each other as he put in long hours painting the areas that moved him so deeply, the quai at Pothuis, the streets in Pontoise, the Oise and setting sun. It was not a time without struggle and fatigue, but it was fruitful, as though his power and vision had come into focus.

Rachel became ill again during the summer of 1872. Alfred was overwhelmed by his flourishing business and could not visit her. His wife Marie did not consider it part of her matrimonial duty to nurse a sick mother-in-law. Camille could go to Paris only rarely despite her frequent emergency notes. Julie would come searching for him with the urgent messages; he would drop everything and take the next train into Paris.

He decided that the moment of truth had arrived. He could not keep rushing to Paris to comfort his mother. Neither could he continue to tolerate his mother's ignoring of his wife.

He found her propped up in bed in a robe, a book open on the blanket. Her hair was neatly combed but her skin was pale and her eyes brooding.

"This summoning me is going to stop."

Tears came into Rachel's eyes.

"You are going to abandon me."

"No. I'm going to take you home with me to Pontoise. Julie will take care of you. So will I, when my day's work is done."

"I won't go."

"Yes, you will. Or you have seen the last of me."

She sprang to attention.

"You will join my family or you will have precious little family to join."

Rachel studied her son's face, feature by feature, as though it were a freshly plastered brick wall that she had to pass through.

"At least you're married now. You're making a living. That's respectable."

"We have a bedroom for you. The country air will do you good."

Rachel felt the steel in him.

"I will come . . . until I am well."

"Stay as long as you like."

She dressed, packed a small bag. Riding out on the train they were silent.

Julie and Rachel had not seen each other since Julie had walked out of the Passy apartment almost fourteen years before. Both were ill at ease. Julie bade her mother-in-law a polite welcome, took her valise up to the bedroom in which she had put vases of flowers, several of Camille's canvases on the walls, and a new pink bedspread to match his painting of pink peonies. She helped her unpack. As she closed the door of the room behind her, she murmured:

"*Grâce à Dieu.* Now we are *unis comme les doigts de la main.*"

But Rachel had come under protest, under an ultimatum; she was not going to give in easily.

"Your house is bare. . . . You boil the vegetables too much. . . . You are too indulgent with the children. . . . You live like peasants."

"What to do?" Julie asked Camille in the privacy of their bedroom. She was near tears. "She talks to me as though I were still a *bonne*, except that when I was a *bonne* she treated me with respect."

Camille was disturbed by his mother's irascibility.

"It's her protest that I didn't marry a woman with a townhouse in Paris."

Rachel left at the end of five days. They were not exactly joined like the fingers of a hand.

In September Paul Cézanne came with Hortense Fiquet and Paul, Jr., who had been born on January 4 of that year, his birth registered at the *mairie,* with Cézanne setting down his name as the father, just as his own had been set down thirty-three years before.

"If my father found out he would cut off my allowance and we'd starve," he told them.

Camille alone among the Batignolles painters believed that Cézanne possessed a unique talent. He had not quieted during the years since his thorny nature had made him a virtual outcast at the Café Guerbois. He appeared to bristle even in repose. His head was set defensively into his shoulders as though to secure him from attack. His rounded black beard was as ferocious as his hostile dark eyes. Nine-year-old Lucien observed him with a neophyte painter's eye:

"He wears a visored cap, his hair is long, black and straggly at back and he is bald in front. He walks with a long pikestaff which frightens the peasants."

With Julie Cézanne was quiet, even docile.

"We're country people together," he said fondly. "That's one reason I asked if we could come visit you. You're like my sainted mother and sister Marie."

He pecked her on the cheek.

Julie saw beneath Cézanne's protective skin, saw his fierce hunger for affection.

"I dislike Paris; it's too crowded and agitated. I'd like to go back to Aix for a spell of painting in that dazzling clear air. But I don't dare take Hortense and the boy with me."

Paul Cézanne's affection for his son was more publicly displayed than his affection for Hortense. Julie enjoyed having Hortense Fiquet with her. Hortense had a rather phlegmatic face, with a prominent nose and brow, a small mouth and outsized chin, a smooth complexion without coloring and a thick mop of jet-black hair wrapped in a bun high in the back like the raised head of a cobra. She had been born in the small village of Saligneil but her family had moved to Paris when she was a child. Her father was a bank clerk; he had taught her to read. She was addicted to romantic novels; had earned a living sewing handmade books, was dowerless. She said she had met Cézanne while earning extra money as a model, a claim Cézanne never confirmed. It was a relationship they had fallen into by propinquity: Cézanne was not likely to have gone courting; Hortense appeared too stolid to attract passersby. She was stoical by nature, enabling her to endure Cézanne's outbursts, tirades against the way of the world, spouts of seething anger whose cause she could not determine.

Hortense asked Julie, "Do you know why they paint?"

"No. Do you?"

"They're driven. By what?"

"I don't know. Do you?"

"No," Hortense replied. "Neither do they. But there's no help for them. They chose to live with their paints, we chose to live with them. We're caught, all four of us."

Camille tried to persuade Cézanne to paint directly from nature. He knew better than to tell him what to do; but if they painted side by side for a time his resistance might falter.

"Paul, let's pack our easels and paint at the Hermitage tomorrow."

"You know I don't paint out of doors. I sketch, then go back to my studio and work under controlled light."

"Why not do an entire canvas *en plein air*? It would be exciting for both of us. We could compare values as the day moves and the light changes."

Cézanne finally gave in. When they set up their canvases just a few feet from each other, in the corner of a downhill road populated with houses hanging to its sides, Camille saw that Cézanne was painting in black, brown and heavy impastos, savagely using his palette knife instead of a brush. He puzzled over how best to handle his friend.

"Paul, look at my canvas. It's all delicate light. Look at yours. Ominous. You're painting this sun-splashed scene of vivid colors the way you did *The Autopsy* and *Murder*. There are no corpses around here, only copses. You're painting your inner mood instead of the brilliant outer mood you're gazing at."

Cézanne started to be angry, to argue, then realized that Camille had nothing to gain by his suggestions.

"You're right," he growled, "but I wouldn't take it from anyone else. Show me how you mix your colors without muddying them with emotion."

A peasant came behind them, watched them at work, then commented, pointing to Camille, "You dab," and to Cézanne, "You smear."

The men looked grim, then laughed.

"He has more perception than the critics on the Parisian journals," Cézanne commented.

They painted side by side every day for several weeks, the Cézanne family having moved to a hotel across the bridge over the Oise. Cézanne completed a couple of oils, said to Camille in a voice unused to pleasantness:

"This has been my happiest time since I roamed the fields of Provence with Emile Zola. What's more, I'm not going to destroy these oils I've done with you."

"Why should you? They're beginning to glow."

"I've destroyed half and more of my canvases. I hated them."

One day Camille walked Cézanne along the four-mile towpath to Auvers to introduce him to Dr. Gachet and the tranquillity of the thatched-roofed village overlooking the Oise. When Cézanne told him that he would like to live in Auvers, Dr. Gachet found him a home to rent. When Cézanne next walked the towpath to visit with Julie and paint with Camille, he said in an awed tone:

"Would you believe it? Dr. Gachet loves my painting. He actually paid money for two of my latest pictures."

He turned to Julie with an expression she had not seen on his face before:

"I never believed it would happen, but if I have a master, it is Camille Pissarro. To me he is *le Bon Dieu.*"

Julie exclaimed, "My Camille's a humble workman like the rest of you, painting your lives away."

"Don't be deceived, my good Julie," Cézanne replied. "Your Camille has the talent of a master."

Camille went into Paris to see Durand-Ruel. Cézanne was to join him there. He received a note instead:

I take up Lucien's pen, at an hour when the railway should be transporting me to my penates. It's to tell you in a roundabout way that I missed the train. . . . Useless to add that I'm your guest till tomorrow. Well

333

then, Madame Pissarro asks you to bring back from Paris some Nestlé's Milk Powder for little Georges, also Lucien's shirts from his aunt Félicie's.

Good evening,
Paul Cézanne

5

Toward the end of 1872, by which time Durand-Ruel had purchased close to a dozen of his paintings, Camille walked into the large gallery and began as always to study the dazzling display of venerable masters from the Italian, Spanish and Dutch schools, as well as the vigorous group of Fontainebleau painters. He was surprised to find that only one of his own oils was on the gallery wall.

"Where are the rest of my canvases?" he asked. "In the storeroom?"

Durand-Ruel glanced away. When he turned back he had made a decision.

"Many of them are in the apartment of a Monsieur Edwards, a Levantine banker."

"He couldn't have bought all of them?"

"Sit down, my friend. Light your pipe. It's a dealer's maneuver. I feel I can trust you."

Camille puffed on his pipe in puzzlement.

"Mon ami, have you ever wondered where all the money comes from to buy pictures from your group, pictures that don't sell?"

"No, monsieur. That is your private affair."

"Alors! Last year I made the acquaintance of a bronzemaker, Monsieur de Marinac, who inspired confidence in me. I told him of my wish to find a capitalist to help in the difficult campaign I had undertaken to keep the superb works I had without being pressed to sell them. He introduced me to the foreign banker Edwards, who had made a great fortune in Constantinople and who agreed to make me the advances according to my needs. I guaranteed him a sufficient number of canvases from the group I represent to cover his advances. Since he has a spacious apartment on the Boulevard Haussmann, it was decided that the pictures would hang in his salon where

it would look as though he had purchased them. At a given moment I would hold a public sale under his name. That kind of sale always succeeds best because of the great suspicion about dealers. Many of my Fontainebleau canvases are hung in his apartment as well. The auction will be a slight deception on my part, but no one will be cheated."

Camille chewed on his pipestem.

"When will you hold this auction in Monsieur Edwards's apartment?"

"In a year or two. As soon as we have been able to establish a beginning to your reputations. After the sale your positions will be secure and your prices high."

Camille felt vaguely uncomfortable, but then he was not a businessman.

"For all that time our pictures will not be seen in your gallery?"

"Oh yes, one or two of each of you. And you are of course free to sell to private collectors. I can see that you are disturbed. Please don't be. The situation is not unique."

There was only one statement Camille could make to this man who had been so kind to him.

"I have implicit confidence in your judgment."

The young artist who lived across the hall from Rachel became a frequent visitor to Pontoise. His greatest joy was painting alongside Camille. Camille liked Edouard Béliard's enthusiasm, though he was not learning much of anything.

"No matter," declared Julie; "he's good with the children. Like a young uncle."

Two more painters, Victor Vignon and Frédéric Cordey, settled in Pontoise. They came by individually to introduce themselves. It appeared that, with his flow of visitors from Paris and the nearby villages, Camille's return to Pontoise had spawned a burgeoning art colony. Ignored by painters for centuries, Pontoise and its surrounding countryside was becoming a favorite hunting ground for motifs to be painted in a new idiom. Julie welcomed them all, offered warmth and the fruits of her garden.

It was on a visit to Paris that Camille wrote a hurried note to Emile Zola, who was expecting him for dinner:

"Dear Zola, My wife asks Madame Zola to take the mother rabbit that we have for her. To hurry as she won't be long in having babies. If Madame Zola could come to Pontoise, it would make us very happy, and at the same time she could arrange with my wife to take the young mother rabbit.

"I had intended to come by your place today but I am forced to leave this morning."

The following Sunday Emile Zola and his wife Alexandrine came on the morning train to collect their mother rabbit. They had no children after eight years of being together, which frustrated Zola, though only thirty-two, because, like Camille, he wanted a large family. As he and Zola started out for a walk Alexandrine, who had been converted by marriage from a pretty girl to a beautiful woman, warned Camille:

"My husband has the habit of lecturing people on how to conduct their lives. But he never follows his own dicta."

Zola had defended Edouard Manet's work in a brilliant monograph which had brought neither him nor Manet any credit. He had abandoned the marginal life of the bohemian Left Bank for the respectability of the Rue de la Condamine in Montmartre. It was a modestly genteel house but no matter what long hours he worked at his desk there was rarely enough income from the journals to take care of himself, his wife and mother. At one point the furniture was repossessed because he could not meet the payments. At another, his mother had to take the down out of their mattresses and pawn it for money to buy bread. But poverty had only welded the three closer together, Alexandrine, a woman of growing strength and character, because she wanted to keep Zola happy; his mother because she was grateful for not being abandoned. By now Zola was deep in his third volume for a series of Rougon-Macquart novels. He was possessed by his work; some said he was a prisoner of his own planning.

"The publisher, Lacroix, has contracted to pay me one hundred dollars a month for five years. I'm going to bring Dr. Claude Bernard's 'determinism' to life. And I'm following Taine, the English philosopher, into science and naturalism. 'Vice and virtue are chemical products like sugar and vitriol.' Lamarck and Darwin have it exactly right: everything is inherited."

The fall forest was beginning to change its face from green to rose-purple.

"Forgive me, Zola, but what has this to do with literature?"

"That's what my plots are based upon, the natural and social history of the legitimate descendants of the Rougons; the illegitimate offspring of the Macquarts. Laid in the epoch of the Second Empire. It is a vast edifice but I have found the design and shall build it block by block. Balzac and Flaubert are my masters."

Zola was also at work on his ninth volume of published

prose, at the same time he was turning *Thérèse Raquin* into a play and writing articles for the journal *Corsaire*.

"But I am being brutalized by hackwork. My body aches. I go to bed every night groaning with pain. Every night I am frightened that I will die before morning."

Camille said with a wry grin:

"Zola, you know the old saw: *Qui mouche trop son nez en tire du sang*. Who blows his nose too much draws blood."

Then he realized that the aphorism applied to himself as well.

He received a message from Claude Monet in Argenteuil asking if he could come to Pontoise for an "urgent purpose."

Monet, thirty-two, had the strong regular features of an idol of the Comédie Française, cheeks of high color, huge bold eyes, a large cleancut forehead with curly hair combed forward over the brow, one of the most neatly barbered, most attractive beards to be seen on the Parisian boulevards. He also had had the most excruciating time managing to eat and buy paint, for although he had been able to wheedle a few dollars out of his father and Aunt Sophie in Le Havre, he was by nature so childishly improvident that he became known as "unfortunate Monet." If he had enough money to feed his family for the first half of the week he bought art supplies and threw himself into his painting with a wild fervor, unmindful of the fact that they would be without bread for the second half and he would be reduced once again to sending out pathetically begging letters to everyone he knew.

Léonie grew ever more beautiful, with a superb willowy figure and the face of Helen of Troy "that launched a thousand ships." Those who mistrusted Monet claimed that he had seduced her out of lust and married her for the dowry her parents then maneuvered him out of. Léonie, after almost eight years, still adored him with the single-minded devotion that should have been accorded to a saint, continuing to pose for him in her now aging gowns for endless hours every day, grateful for any kind word he might afford her. Monet treated her with a touch of condescension. Camille knew all of Claude Monet's weaknesses. As an artist he was nothing of the philosopher, had little intellect or penetrating knowledge of the world about him, the one he was painting so gloriously.

Camille told Julie, "From the viewpoint of natural talent he outstrips us all."

Cézanne exclaimed, seeing Monet's newest canvases:

"He is only an eye. But, my God, what an eye!"

After supper of rabbit stew, at dusk, Monet asked Camille if they could have a pipe by the fireplace in the living room. When the men had packed their bowls from Camille's tobacco jar and lighted them with a wooden ember from the fireplace, Monet began earnestly:

"Do you recall a few years ago, I think in 1867, that I shared a studio with Frédéric Bazille?"

Camille remembered the raucous celebration there.

"Then you will recall Bazille's suggestion that we form a society that would resemble in miniature Proudhon's concept of a 'mutualist' association and hold our own exhibitions free of governmental and Beaux-Arts regulations and prejudices."

"None of us wanted it," said Camille. "We were struggling to become Salon favorites on the road to acceptance. We had even failed to raise the funds to use Courbet's pavilion."

"Bazille insisted that the Salon would continue to reject us or keep us in inferior positions as long as they were in control."

"He was right."

Monet hitched his chair closer to Camille's, said with a radiant expression:

"The war precluded any Salon in 1871. In 1872 the new minister for the Salon was more conservative than Comte de Nieuwerkerke had ever been. Few if any of us will submit pictures or be accepted for the 1873 Salon. Instead of being the Rejected Ones, why can't we put Bazille's idea into effect now?"

Camille wrinkled his forehead.

"An exhibition of Batignolles Independents?"

"Precisely."

Camille rose, went to the window, collected his thoughts. While it was true that he had shown in seven separate Salons, he had been disrespectfully hung, had been there by the grace of Daubigny, had had an *R* stamped on his pictures three times. Realistically he agreed that the new republican jury would reject them as easily as had Napoleon III's. He also knew that if they formed an independent exhibition they would be discriminated against by the Salon forever. But none of them would get very far anyway with the self-perpetuating, convention-shackled juries. He turned back to Monet resolutely.

"The time does seem to have come. We are selling to Durand-Ruel. We have a few ardent collectors. We can afford to rent space. Durand-Ruel will back our exhibition because it will help spread our names and work. How do we begin?"

"We already have. Just now. We'll call a meeting to discuss the fundamentals. I'm sure we can convince the rest."

Camille was not that certain.

"There will be dissenters. Fearful ones. We have to be sure we're on solid ground. I'll search in Pontoise for a cooperative society whose rules of agreement we might use as a base."

Monet was jubilant. He sprang up, clapped Camille on the shoulder.

"Excellent! That's why I came to you first. You are older. You have the solidity of character. Now is the time. *Prenons la lune avec les dents.*"

Camille laughed low in his chest. "Take the moon in our teeth? I wonder if it's digestible? It looks like hard yellow rock from here."

Monet raised his eloquent eyebrows, asking, "What isn't?"

6

Camille quickly gained the cooperation of Paul Cézanne and Armand Guillaumin. He met Alfred Sisley in Durand-Ruel's and gained his consent. Durand-Ruel himself was enthusiastic.

"I like the idea," he exclaimed with the usual fervor shown to good young painters. "It's revolutionary, yet makes sense. Such an exhibition will consolidate you as a school. You can count on me. It's all to the good."

Degas, when he returned from New Orleans in the United States where he had been visiting his uncle's family, entered wholeheartedly and worked on two capable and recognized painters, Lepic and Levert, to join them.

Monet had difficulty bringing in his friend Renoir, who was painting with him in Argenteuil, until Camille promised him a position on the management committee. Monet also converted Boudin.

Piette wrote from Montfoucault: ". . . If a certain nucleus of painters plan not to exhibit at all in the Salon of 1873, and the jury is still composed of reactionaries, I also would join with pleasure."

The first serious opposition came at a meeting in Edouard Manet's studio. Manet, with a grim expression on his face, told the small assemblage:

"You cannot fly in the face of the Salon. They are the only road to recognition. If you fight, you have to throw yourself into the main arena. I will never exhibit in a place next door. It's respectability that counts."

"Manet," Camille started in a conciliatory tone. "We have all learned from you, from your talent and courage. You scandalized Paris with your magnificent *Luncheon on the Grass* and *Olympia*. Almost single-handedly you shocked the public into the modern world. Surely you wouldn't abandon us now?"

"Certainly not!" Manet's manner was acerbic. "It is you who are abandoning me. On a foolhardy venture. You will be laughed out of your underdrawers. Do you consider we were manhandled at the Salon des Refusés? Such an independent exhibition as this will be treated a hundred times more brutally. You will suffer."

"We're suffering now," said Renoir. "What have we got to lose?"

"The future."

With which he terminated the meeting. It was obvious that no one could turn him around. A few days later Camille was surprised to find Antoine Guillemet in Pontoise. Guillemet had been traveling. He had written to Camille occasionally, reaffirming their friendship and his interest in Camille's work, but was himself painting in the same manner Camille had perceived fifteen years before in La Roche-Guyon where they had first met. Guillemet launched into the purpose of his visit.

"I heard in Paris that you wanted to see me and invite me to join your society." He sat down on the sofa, pulled up his beautifully tailored trousers so they would not stretch at the knees. He had grown into an imposing figure, tall, broad, with a tanned complexion, debonair light brown mustache.

"Pissarro, you were my first friend among the artists. You introduced me to the Guerbois . . ."

Camille stood silent; these compliments forbode no good.

". . . that's why I felt I owed you a personal explanation, one I did not want to make at your next meeting. I can't join your movement. I think it unwise."

"Why do you say so?"

"It's flouting authority, it's against the proprieties. . . . Against the establishment."

"It's not against anything. It's for ourselves," Camille retorted.

Guillemet was unhappy about the encounter but by the purple flush mounting toward his eyes Camille could see that he was determined.

"Pissarro, I urge you not to go forward. Edouard Manet is right. The public is not ready for your kind of work. Stay with the Salon. Slowly you'll earn medals, commissions, sales. That's what painting is about."

Camille did not wish to argue the point. He was saddened at the loss of Antoine Guillemet and was shocked the following week to hear that Corot, upon learning of Guillemet's decision, had said:

"My dear Antoine, you have done very well to escape from that gang."

Why were they a gang, he and Monet, Sisley, Degas, Renoir, Cézanne, Boudin, Bracquemond . . . ? They were dedicated men, hard working, honest in their attempt to achieve a new color, brushwork, the light of reality and beauty combined. What had happened to the mind of the great Corot that he could dismiss contemptuously not only an idea but a whole segment of conscientious artists? Had not he and the Fontainebleau School also been revolutionaries? Did every man freeze his own revolution?

Berthe Morisot had asked if he would come to luncheon the next time he was in Paris. A *garçon* in a red-striped vest led him out to her studio built at the rear of a spacious garden behind the family town house. She received him graciously; they had been acquaintances rather than friends since there had appeared no occasion for friendship. Berthe had a long country smock over her daytime silk dress. He again realized how handsome the thirty-one-year-old woman was, tall, with a fine figure, a long dark braid on either side of her head, penetrating eyes. In Manet's group portrait, *The Balcony*, she had looked a little old and hard, but in *In Repose*, painted later, her expression was gentle, loving, as she was seated on the richly covered divan.

On her easel was a glorious canvas of a mother and child on a balcony overlooking the Seine and a view of Paris. Another canvas on an easel nearby was the quai at Lorient, "as exquisite in tone and light as anything the rest of us ever painted," Camille decided. A third oil, of a cradle, a mother fondly watching her infant sleep, was drying in a corner. Morisot's delicate touch was unsurpassed.

"Monsieur Pissarro, I heard of the society you and Monet are forming for an exhibition."

"Yes, mademoiselle. We were hoping that you would join us."

A maid in a white apron and cap summoned them to the table.

"I most certainly shall," Berthe Morisot said when they

were seated. "I think it is a splendid idea. Let us show together. Then the public will see what we are striving to accomplish. I asked you to come here specifically to tell you of my enthusiasm."

Camille stopped for a moment. It was an awkward situation. No one doubted that she was deeply in love with Edouard Manet, whom she considered her master and dearest friend, though she was unhappy about his affair with Eva Gonzalès. Did she know how vehemently Manet had opposed their movement? Should he tell her?

"Edouard Manet has informed me that he thinks you are all very wrong. He went over every one of his objections. They don't convince me. I feel that he is the one who is wrong. I told him so. Please be assured, Monsieur Pissarro, that I am my own woman. Edouard Manet can teach me painting but he cannot influence my conduct."

Camille recounted what had emerged so far, for each member of the Batignolles group was an individualist with strong opinions. They would need about thirty to pay their costs; only respected professionals would be invited.

The Morisot dining room was furnished with inlaid gold Louis XIV furniture. They were joined by Edouard Manet's younger brother, Eugène, a well-built, pleasant-appearing man more conservatively dressed than Edouard, and less dogmatic in manner. Camille gathered that he had shrewdly invested his share of the Manet fortune when his father died. He and Berthe Morisot were good friends. He had obviously graced this elegant room before.

On his way back to Pontoise, gazing absently out the window at the wintry landscape, Camille mused fleetingly:

"Her high social position will do us good. She is also by all odds the best woman painter in Paris today. In the years to come she will surpass Rosa Bonheur in public acclaim."

His occasional meetings with his confreres did not cut into his work schedule; rather the concept of a cooperative exhibition stimulated him to greater effort. In the final five months of 1872, since he had returned to his beloved Pontoise, he had completed forty-seven works, almost all of them oils; a formidable accomplishment. His portraits of Minette, and still lifes done during inclement weather, had gratifying inner harmonies. He completed the screen for Achille Arosa: the *Four Seasons* were a radiant portrait of the earth as it turned on its axis. Arosa paid him one hundred dollars. He also painted snow effects, a thaw, a fair in Pontoise, views of the

Seine, the docks, roads at the side of cultivated fields, houses in the woods. It was a period of intense fulfillment. The beauty and penetration of the canvases were attested by everyone, his dealers, the collectors, the painters who came to visit or saw the work he took into Paris. Théodore Duret told him:

"Pissarro, there is something of godlike tranquillity in your paintings. No matter how distressed I may be, when I gaze at your beautifully attuned *Fair at St. Martin* or *Road Across the Fields*, I feel a sense of peace. I maintain that rustic nature with animals is what suits your talent best. You haven't Sisley's decorative quality, nor Monet's fantastic eye, but you have an intuitive and profound feeling for nature and a powerful brush, with the result that a picture by you is something absolutely definitive."

"You give me courage to continue at this breakneck pace," Camille responded.

"You don't need more courage. All you need is canvas, stretchers and oil paint. I know those tubes of color are expensive. I'll send you a check each month until I have paid off the paintings I've purchased."

Piette and Adèle came for a visit. Each day Camille watched Piette's palette lightening in color, his brush strokes becoming shorter. Adèle was happiest when playing with the children. She was isolated from the women of Montfoucault as Julie was in Pontoise; their laughter animated their conversation, making them feel alive in a manner they could not attain alone, Adèle in Montfoucault, Julie with Camille's visiting artists who argued about art theories.

Camille was surprised to learn that Piette now opposed the cooperative effort. Not on the ground of harming themselves with the Beaux-Arts, but a distrust of artists to follow through, to remain with the organization.

The recruiting for an exhibition of independents continued, but after the first handful of their comrades there were few others who wanted to participate.

"I can't afford dues. . . ." "I won't have pictures ready. . . ." "I'm going to show in Bordeaux."

Few would admit that they were unwilling to join such a radical departure for fear of its consequences; or, more simply, they had no faith that anything could be sold out of such an unorthodox showing. Who would pay money for pictures that did not have any official stamp on them to make their investment safe?

Durand-Ruel remained steadfast. He told them to advance

without worrying about the dissenters, that the Batignolles' points of departure seemed to the conservative Beaux-Arts as dangerous as a putative uprising with political implications. But art must be a living organism; change was essential.

Camille's struggle with his own fellows came when he attempted to get Armand Guillaumin and Paul Cézanne accepted. When he proposed Guillaumin's name at a meeting at the Café de la Nouvelle Athènes, he could get no one to approve. Rejection by the only group with which Guillaumin had even a tenuous connection would be a severe blow to him, already feeling inferior to the other members because he had little education, worked as a government clerk and had laboring-class origins. Camille got to his feet, the better to communicate his feelings.

"I beg of you, don't do this to Guillaumin. It would be a public humiliation. He has trouble enough, unable to paint except on Sundays and holidays, with barely enough salary to buy supplies."

"Pissarro, his work simply is not good enough," said Degas. "He would lower the standard of our exhibition."

"He's making progress. By the time we open he will have a couple of good canvases of workmen along the Seine. Our group was not formed to brand an *R* on anyone's forehead. Not a longtime associate certainly."

All eyes turned to Degas, who shrugged assent.

"With your guarantee, we'll accept him. But you're going to have to conduct a one-man atelier for his benefit."

Camille had a far harder time with Paul Cézanne. There were two counts against Cézanne: he not only painted wildly, which would bring further derision upon them; but his abrasive personality had alienated practically everyone.

"Don't tell us you're going to teach him how to paint!" the easygoing Renoir exclaimed.

"I don't have to teach Paul Cézanne anything. He is adopting our lighter and fresher palette, giving up plastering from his palette knife. I know I'm alone in my opinion, but I am convinced that he will emerge into a truly great painter."

There was a skeptical silence. No one believed Camille; or for that matter wanted to believe him.

"He'll break up our meetings with violent outbursts," proffered Alfred Sisley, the gentlest of the group. "If we invite him we invite dissension."

"He will come to few meetings. But his *Hanged Man's House,* a picture of which we each painted in Auvers, is as good as anything we'll show."

344

No one was inclined to deny Camille anything he felt so fervently about. With Edouard Manet gone, the Batignolles painters were more and more turning to him for leadership. They knew him to be passionately devoted to their cause. Claude Monet said:

"*D'accord.* But he's on your head!"

7

At an April auction at the Hôtel Drouot for the benefit of those from the now German-owned Alsace-Lorraine who had emigrated to Algeria, Camille contributed his freshly painted *Cultivated Land*. It was bought by Duret. Later, Degas fell in love with the painting and Théodore Duret either gave or sold it to him, Camille never knew which. Nevertheless it was the ultimate compliment from one artist to another.

He was equally pleasured when Duret could not restrain himself from buying Camille's just completed *The Inundation of the Seine at Marly* for one hundred dollars, and also recommended that his friend, Madame Goblet, buy one of Camille's paintings. When Duret commissioned for himself a painting of a growing wheatfield under the coming summer sun, Camille was thoughtful:

"I will try a field of ripe wheat. But there is nothing colder than the full sun of summer. Contrary to the colorists, nature is colored in winter and cold in summer. So you must expect to find my picture very chalky and white."

On Camille's suggestion, Théodore Duret bought one of Claude Monet's Oise scenes but became disenchanted with the painting as well as with Monet's ever needful and pressing entreaties. He wanted to return the canvas to Monet; or at least not pay the second half of the eighty-dollar price. When they next met in Paris, Camille told Duret:

"Don't worry about being mistaken about Monet's talent. In my opinion it is very serious, very pure. It is a very studied oil based on observation and with an entirely new feeling. It is poetry through harmony of true colors."

Duret was not convinced. Monet, so frequently *in extremis,* asked Camille to plead for the second forty-dollar payment.

The 1873 Salon had come and gone with the Batignolles group not yet ready to open their own exhibition. The majority of them had not submitted paintings. Edouard Manet had had *The Good Bock*, after Frans Hals, accepted. It was conventional fare and consequently praised. It was not French, it was Dutch: a big-bellied burgher smoking a long-stemmed meerschaum, a fur hat on his big head, grasping fondly a glass of beer. "Pure Haarlem beer!" someone said. He was praised by the critics but his peers called it "truckling."

Just before the Salon opened, on May 5, Emile Zola's young writing protégé, Paul Alexis, had written in *L'Avenir National* that French artists existed under a rigid exclusionary system of a self-perpetuating jury, and hence "a body of artists would have much to gain by organizing immediately its own syndicate." He mentioned the names of Monet, Pissarro, Sisley, Jongkind.

The Batignolles' society was publicly born, something akin to the infant of the royal family being presented to the court. The newspaper publicity helped bring in some artists; frightened others out of any possible persuasion.

The year 1872 had been a good one for the group. Durand-Ruel's advocacy was having its effect. He began selling their canvases, slowly and at modest albeit rising prices, to adventurous collectors. He paid out to Monet twenty-seven hundred dollars; to Camille twelve hundred, to Sisley over a thousand, to Degas eighteen hundred. Renoir had been the last to sell; Durand-Ruel had paid him only one hundred dollars. Renoir had eked out the barest living possible by obtaining portrait commissions.

By May of 1873 Camille had already received six hundred dollars in monthly checks. He was now making a comfortable living. He repaid Georges Thouvenal of Montfoucault the sixty dollars he had advanced in November of 1870 to enable Camille to take his family to England and marry Julie. Julie bought new shoes and clothing, brought a wider variety of foods into the house. In the earlier years, her nerves frayed by their inadequate income, forced to give herself and Camille short rations in favor of the young; constantly worried about being unmarried after a decade and several children; rejected by Camille's mother as unworthy of being a Pissarro; faced with the constant cost of paint and canvas, she had given vent to bursts of temper. Sometimes she had been harsh. Camille had suffered the outbursts in silence. He knew that the responsibility was his. Julie, living in borderline poverty with more children sure to come, had been entitled to her fears and frustrations.

Now she felt secure. The children would be cared for. She

would not have to suffer the insolence of shopkeepers who refused her further credit when she needed to buy rice, sugar, flour. She could pay, hold her head high as she scaled the hills to shop.

Camille completed thirty-nine canvases during 1873. All the way from a bouquet of roses and a vibrant self-portrait done in his studio through dozens of outdoor motifs of winter in Pontoise: the marketplace, the convent, the heights, the valleys. Then spring along the Oise, the red and pink houses, small neighborhood factories, thatched cottages of Auvers, the roads into the small villages around the Hermitage. The summer heat as the harvest ripened. He had made up the loss of pictures in the war.

Emile Zola had told him, while researching for his Rougon-Macquart series, "Everything is findable." Camille had replied, "Everything is paintable."

No longer were there stacks of completed paintings against the walls; many were now bought by Durand-Ruel or sold to his growing group of collectors. Glorying in his work and steady income; respectably married, the children well; Rachel coming out to Pontoise for an occasional Sunday visit, Camille was not surprised when Julie cried in a burst of candor:

"You were right. All we needed was patience. Could you believe it has taken fifteen years?"

In early July Camille rented a studio at 21 Rue Berthe in Montmartre. He could afford it because Durand-Ruel was paying him a steady one hundred dollars a month. He did not use the small room for work purposes or attempt to bring in Julie and the three children. What it amounted to was a showroom for those who would not take the train out to Pontoise. He borrowed an extra easel from Degas, a couple of chairs from Durand-Ruel, on which his prospective customers could sit while he displayed canvases from Louveciennes, Norwood, Pontoise. Etienne Baudry, a small dealer and another of Duret's cousins, bought one of a Pontoise hillside, Madame Goblet bought a tranquil Louveciennes scene.

Camille was having coffee at the Brasserie des Martyrs when Monet and Renoir joined him with a young man whom they introduced as Gustave Caillebotte. He was immaculately dressed in expensive clothing, of medium height, delicate-featured, clean-shaven, with gray eyes, auburn hair and mustache. He was twenty-five, from a family of the *grande bourgeoisie*, enriched through commerce, a naval engineer and boat builder who had achieved some success in his profession.

"What's he doing with you and Renoir?" Camille asked with a satiric grin.

"That's just the point; he's a man of many interests. Not only constructs ships but loves horticulture, stamp collecting and painting. He passed the Beaux-Arts examinations and entered Bonnat's studio. I don't know how good a painter he'll become but he has an infallible eye for other people's work. He's already bought from Renoir and me, our best pictures, by the way."

Caillebotte grasped Camille's hand.

"I greet you most respectfully," he said in a pleasant voice. "I admire your work greatly. I've wanted to buy a pair of your canvases from Durand-Ruel but I hoped to meet you first so that you could guide me."

"A pair!" Camille smiled beatifically. "Paintings are usually bought, with much hand-wringing, one at a time."

Caillebotte flushed. "I know about your group. I think you are the painters of right now! The academic historical schools have had their century or two; the Fontainebleau painters are accepted."

Camille fingered his growing graying beard affectionately.

"We haven't much to throw in with. Officially we're a gaggle of struggling individuals. Before the war we were known as the Guerbois group, after the café where we met. Now we're called the Batignolles after the district we had been living in."

"I've already acquired an exquisite Edouard Manet and a charming Sisley landscape. *Regardez*, Monsieur Pissarro. I'm enchanted with your group; I want to become a part of it. *But I don't want to buy my way in*. Do you understand?"

The man's manner was impeccable, the predominant sign was modesty.

"I don't expect I will ever paint as well as any of you. Besides, I'm not giving up my naval engineering; it's a work for which I was trained and that I enjoy. I've heard about your proposed cooperative exhibition; I'm reasonably well trained in management. I am able to help."

"*Sacrebleu*, we can use help. We would never question your motives; neither should you ours."

"Now, what is the best way to acquire your paintings? Through a gallery or at your studio?" he asked.

Camille was thoughtful. Durand-Ruel's pictures were already paid for; to sell from his studio would be money in pocket. But if Durand-Ruel was to continue to buy he must also sell.

The decision was made.

"Could we meet tomorrow at the Durand-Ruel gallery? I'd be glad to discuss the merits of my canvases for whatever an artist's opinion of his own work may be worth."

"*D'accord.*"

Caillebotte, Camille found, was more than grateful; he was generous. The next day he acquired two of Camille's pictures. He also bought a Degas, a Berthe Morisot, a Cézanne. Except for the dealer Martin, and Dr. Gachet, Cézanne had never had a buyer. But Caillebotte was by no means an easy sale. He had good taste, instinctively honed in on the best work. He also had a finely tuned sense of irony.

"This picture is rejected? No one wants it? Fine. I'll take it."

8

In Pontoise Camille found a copy of the constitution of the bakers' union. The articles hardly fitted a nascent society of artists but it provided a beginning prototype. They met at the comfortable house on the Rue Pigalle that Degas now occupied, where the two lower floors were Degas's living quarters and the top floor his studio, in which there was a welter of newspapers, books, lithographs and watercolors of earlier artists; hundreds of his own studies, canvases spread about in seeming chaos. The familiar pipe smoke and smell of wine created an atmosphere in which they were accustomed to debate ideas and harangue each other with theories: Pissarro, Boudin, Monet, Sisley, Renoir, Degas. Berthe Morisot did not find it seemly to attend the meetings. She had authorized Camille to speak for her in matters that needed decision. Some of the provisions of the bakers' union were quickly voted down: a separate section for minors; a secret ballot for admission. The proposal eventually took the form of a joint stock company with shares and articles of partnership. Each member was to contribute sixty francs, at the rate of five francs a month for a year; all had equal rights, with administration to be handled by a council of fifteen elected members, one third to be renewed each year. The Société was to receive a commission of ten per cent on all sales.

Eugène Boudin, oldest of the group, approaching fifty, a student of Millet and already established for his small, exquisite scenes of the changing light of sea and sky, knew the terrors of exhibiting all too well.

"Now, we need at least twenty good conventional painters, those who have shown in the Salon once or twice, to blunt the critics' attacks. The public's as well."

Alfred Sisley agreed. "It's a way of staying out of a storm."

Renoir responded with a thin edge of sarcasm. "We can escape even better by not showing at all."

No painter would be barred because of subject matter; but they must demand professionalism and an excellence of technique. How did they set their standards? They used Daubigny's line when he fought unsuccessfully for Monet, then resigned from the 1870 Salon jury, saying:

"If I am unable to apprize excellence, I have wasted my life."

The problem became, "Not who do we keep out?" but, "How do we get painters in?"

They passed the word around that the exhibition would be open to those who qualified. They scoured the ateliers, schools, Beaux-Arts classes. The number who qualified and refused their offer became larger than the few who accepted.

The rejected ones now found themselves rejected.

"Why?" they asked each other.

It had never been done before. It could not work. It was an affront to the Beaux-Arts. They would be banned from the Salon. They did not want to be associated with revolutionary work or the Batignolles group; did not want to be labeled. It was all the fears they themselves had had, and several others.

For their next meeting Claude Monet invited everyone out to Argenteuil for a Sunday of painting the pleasure crafts moored in the Seine. Edouard Manet had secured the Monets this pleasant cottage for two hundred dollars a year, which Monet raised through Durand-Ruel's purchases and his own effective salvos on the collectors of Paris. Léonie lit her wood stove at four in the afternoon to feed her guests. Their son Jean, dressed in a suit of knitted pantaloons, rode a tricycle around the garden paths. After their years of bleak poverty there was an air of gaiety in the Monet house. Claude donned tan trousers and a brown tweed jacket which gave him the appearance of a country gentleman. The artists gathered in the studio room, their faces showing dimly in the light of an oil lamp.

They took up where they had left off.

So far eight of their own group had agreed to show, with Boudin making a ninth and Bracquemond, longtime friend of

Whistler, a tenth. Fantin-Latour, the faithful portrait painter of the group, could not make up his mind. He was important to them. He agreed with the last person to harangue him, but in the end he declined. They also lost Jean Jacques Henner, who had shown in the Salon. The outsiders who accepted were Astruc, painter-critic, Attendu, Béliard, Brandon, Bureau, Cals, Colin, Debras, Latouche, who had sold several of Camille's canvases, Lepic, Lépine, Levert, Meyer, De Molins, Mulot-Durivage, the Italian De Nittis, the sculptor Ottin, Robert, Rouart, nineteen in all, a substantial number.

Their next order of business was to name the new organization.

"Call it the Frédéric Bazille Society," said Camille. "It would be a fitting memorial to the one painter we lost in the war."

Claude Monet agreed; but the others had objections: "It would confuse the public, put the emphasis in the wrong place."

Boudin suggested they name the exhibition in honor of Gustave Courbet, whose body of work had been a guiding beacon. Courbet was only fifty-four, but his imprisonment had so undermined his health that he was no longer able to paint. His magnificent creative years from 1848 to 1868 had run their course. Another trial was impending. A testimonial was in order.

"But not our exhibition," Degas said firmly. "It will bring the police down on our heads. Courbet's shoulders are already overburdened."

Auguste Renoir gathered attention with an in-sweeping movement of his arms.

"I object to using a title with a precise meaning. If we are called 'The Somebodies' or 'The So-and-Sos' or even 'The Thirty-nine' the critics will immediately start talking of a 'new school.' I suggest Anonymous Cooperative Society of Artists, Painters, Sculptors and Engravers."

"How do you expect people to remember that?" Degas asked.

"Renoir doesn't want them to," Camille replied. "He wants the public to remember the paintings instead. Let's accept his title and have done with it."

Next they tackled the problem of how the show would be hung. Who would get the best spots? Who would be in "the catacombs"? How could they be sure they did not favor their own over the nonmembers? No. A committee always ended in a brawl. Then whose judgment would they trust? It finally came down again to Renoir.

"My father was a tailor. I should know how to stitch together an exhibition of about a hundred and fifty canvases."

During the following weeks Edouard Manet, after Durand-Ruel had sold *Le Bon Bock* to Faure for a sizable amount, tried to break up the society. He said to Berthe Morisot, Renoir and Claude Monet:

"Why don't you stay with me? You can see very well that I am on the right track." To Degas he emphasized, "Exhibit with the Salon and you may receive an honorable mention."

But he had lost his position as leader of the Batignolles painters.

At their next meeting, at the Brasserie des Martyrs, they solved the problem of where they could hold the exhibition. Félix Nadar, the most successful portrait photographer in Paris, had acquired fame during the Franco-Prussian War as a daring balloonist behind enemy lines. He was brought by Claude Monet to join them for a drink. Nadar had earlier permitted Monet to paint the Boulevard des Capucines from the front window of his reception hall. He had an enormously wide forehead with clumps of hair extended over his ears and wore his white photographer's jacket even in the cafés; his sober eyes were studious, as though under his dark cape gazing at life through the ground glass of his lens. The forehead narrowing down through a modest mustache and neat rounded chin gave his head the appearance of an upside-down pyramid.

"Why not use my studio on the Boulevard des Capucines?" he asked. "I've leased larger quarters elsewhere for next year and I'm moving out April 1."

Paul Cézanne, whom Camille had steered away from most of the meetings, asked with an edge of suspicion:

"How much will it cost us?"

"My rent is paid through May. The rooms would be standing idle. You can pay the gas bill for the month you're in, the guard and cleaning. That's all."

Camille took an omnibus to Nadar's studio. The corner of the Boulevard des Capucines and the Rue Daunou was at the very heart of Paris, in the center of the Madeleine, the fashionable shops and sidewalk cafés where much of Paris passed in the course of a day; and as Nadar had said, "That portion of Paris with money to buy luxuries."

He walked up the broad flight of stairs that led directly from the street to the entresol, entered the waiting room. It was comfortably furnished with lounge chairs, sofas, where Nadar's clients awaited their turn to be photographed. There was oblique light from the street and sufficient wall space for half a dozen medium-sized pictures. Monet and Degas were waiting for him. Together they toured the series of four large photographing rooms, each set with a different background. The walls were red-brown, without juttings or partitions, admirable for hanging framed pictures. They now had thirty painters, each of whom wanted to show between three and six works.

"Is there room?" Camille asked. "We don't want to crowd the frames or place too many above or below eye level."

Their jottings convinced them that the four rooms and reception hall would afford the wall space they would need.

Gustave Caillebotte gave them dinner in his elegant family home on the Faubourg St. Honoré to settle the remaining points of disagreement. He had already done a number of practical chores: secured a license from the police; hired two guards, a ticket salesman and the automatic turnstile used at the Palais de l'Industrie so that the Society could not be cheated as Courbet had been at his showing. He had also tracked down Nadar's gas and water bills so the group would know exactly how much expense they were incurring. He gazed at Camille over a glass of vintage wine, sifted his thoughts through a finely meshed strainer. He was eighteen years younger than Camille.

"Your group of painters is like a new-found group of brothers for me."

There was a general feeling of buoyancy and optimism. The Society of the Independents would open their first exhibition on April 15, 1874, and show for a month.

9

As he had planned, Camille searched for and found a good home at 26 Rue de l'Hermitage, above the river. One approached it by a curving path up a slight hill. The ground floor was earthen, no wood floor ever having been laid. Connecting the ground floor to the four bedrooms upstairs was a rustic winding wooden staircase with uneven steps and a narrow, loosely fitted railing of assorted branches.

"It's no more dangerous than climbing trees," said Camille when Julie looked at it askance.

Unlike the living room and dining area, the kitchen floor was of stone. It had an open fireplace for roasting meats and boiling pots of soup. The room was large enough to hold her stove, wall pegs for pans and skillets, a chopping-block table, and a corner where she could feed the children. There was a good well just outside the back door and a level area on the hillock for growing flowers and vegetables and placing her rabbit hutches. The rent was reasonable. Camille promised to lay a wood floor in the living and dining rooms before the winter rains.

Hauling the beds, wardrobe, tables up the winding staircase, which hung by some mysterious act of levitation, required a considerable engineering effort. Yet when all of the furniture had been put in its appropriate place and Camille had arranged his books on the former crockery shelves of the dining area and decorated the walls with his drawings, watercolors and oils of Louveciennes, the clean dry house was attractive. He also appropriated one of the bedrooms for a studio.

Minette became ill. Camille summoned the Pontoise physician, Dr. Menier. He diagnosed bronchitis. The following day he declared that he feared typhoid. Camille wrote a note to Dr. Gachet: ". . . Minette is sick. For four or five days, we haven't lived. We are so anxious. . . ."

Dr. Gachet arrived in Pontoise on his way to Auvers. He examined Minette carefully, prescribed an herbal potion for her sore throat, made no commitment about the possible typhoid. For weeks Minette got no better. Dr. Gachet prescribed *calcaria carbonica*. Dr. Menier still suspected typhoid. The medication seemed to help but the fever persisted. Dr. Gachet visited again.

For an entire month Camille and Julie agonized. He did not touch his paints or go into Paris. On October 30, 1873, he read that the opera house on the Rue Le Peletier was greatly damaged by fire. Fortunately there was no harm to Durand-Ruel's gallery close by, but the shops in the Rue Drouot near the Drouot auction halls had to be evacuated. The fire made it possible to start construction, at the center of the series of wide boulevards, on the new opera Baron Haussmann had proposed in 1857.

By mid-November Minette's temperature became normal. She appeared well, if not robust. Camille took up his paints and in December trudged through the snow to find meaning in its hidden barren beauty. Théodore Duret came out to Pontoise, exchanged the *Inundation* which he had bought earlier for

Springtime, giving Camille an additional forty dollars for the exchange; then bought still another painting.

"Your three little donkeys with the shepherdess is as beautiful as a Millet."

Camille's eyes sparkled.

"That's high praise. I am a longtime admirer of Millet's *Angelus* and *The Gleaners*."

"Will you guide me in buying a Cézanne? In painting I look more than ever for sheep with five legs."

"In that case I believe that Cézanne can satisfy you; he has made some studies that are very strange."

The art critic was only the fourth collector to buy a Cézanne.

On his next trip into Paris Durand-Ruel informed Camille that a financial crisis was taking place in France, with severe repercussions in the city. Stocks on the Bourse were plummeting. The gallery had not yet been seriously affected but when money became scarce art works were always the first to feel the pinch. He added reassuringly:

"I've sold several of your canvases. After the turn of the year I shall pay you a record four hundred dollars in three installments."

The small dealer, Etienne Baudry, had also sold a painting, for one hundred dollars. Camille was exultant.

The future looked bright. Although his growing family's needs, doctors' bills and painting supplies used up all the money that came in, each year would be better as his work was more widely accepted.

Camille signed the charter for the Society. On January 17, 1874, *La Chronique des Arts* announced:

> An anonymous co-operative society, of variable size and capital, has been formed by painters, sculptors, engravers and lithographers, for a period of ten years, from the 27 December last, having for its aim, (1) the organization of free exhibitions, without a jury or honorary reward, where each of the members may exhibit his work; (2) the sale of said works; (3) the publication, as soon as possible, of a journal exclusively concerned with the arts.

In late January Ernest Hoschedé, owner of the Gagne Petit department store who had bought a number of the group's paintings, was in financial straits and put up his collection at auction at the Hôtel Drouot. The Hôtel Drouot was privately owned by the Compagnie des Commissaires-Priseurs de Paris, who had built it in 1852, and was devoted only to auctions, which had before then been held at the Bourse. It was a handsome three-story building on the corner of the *rues* Drouot and Rossini, with an angled glass front where the two streets joined. The first-floor promenade was majestic, with high ceilings and wide-spaced pillars resembling an ancient monastery. The men in the promenade wore high silk hats and striped trousers. The women were in floor-length gowns and flounces, covered with large-collared cloaks.

The main auction salon was an enormous room with triple gas chandeliers, a carpeted floor, tall rostrum at the front with a large padded chair for the auctioneer. There were only a few movable stools for the buyers, which caused a jam-up among the bidders, some of whom were socializing in groups, others examining framed paintings, still others at the rear pawing over a jumbled mass of antique dressing tables and chiffoniers. All around the main salon were smaller rooms for the auctioning of porcelain faïences and all manner of objets d'art. The scene looked like pandemonium, yet somehow the auctioneer knew where his bids were coming from and pounded his gavel at the conclusion of each sale.

Camille and Monet attended the opening day to see what their paintings would bring. Though the owners were supposed to be anonymous, everyone knew it was Ernest Hoschedé's collection. They got there just before the opening hammer. Since it was a dark Parisian day, gas jets were flaring around the sides of the cream-colored room. It was filled by the time Renoir and Degas drifted in. There was a feeling of tension and excitement. People appeared eager to bid and acquire. Camille was gratified when his pictures were sold for fifty-four to nearly two hundred dollars each. Monet, Sisley and Degas were bid up to equally high prices. Camille wrote to Duret:

"The effects of the Drouot sale are felt all the way to Pontoise. People were quite surprised that one of my pictures would go for almost two hundred dollars. One gentleman here said it was a surprising price for a pure landscape!"

The best part of it for the Society members was that the auction could be trusted as a weather vane for their coming exhibition. Their work had been treated with respect. There could not be a better omen. Durand-Ruel informed them that the auction set the value level. They would get equally good prices at the Society's showing. After that, he would hold his auction in the banker Edwards's apartment on the Boulevard Haussmann. That should go even better than the Drouot.

He was painting in his studio when Duret arrived unannounced, having taken the early morning train. He was unshaven, his clothing disheveled, his voice almost hoarse as he cried:

"You mustn't. You simply must not!"

Camille was taken aback. Duret was usually a very self-possessed man. But Théodore Duret had read the announcement in the *Chronique* and had heard bad repercussions.

"I've been up all night," he cried, "wrestling with my convictions, rehearsing a speech to you. You must hear me out."

Camille put an arm about the man's shoulders. "Anything you say is in season."

"It is necessary that you resign from your Anonymous Society," Duret began. "You must not be a part of that proposed exhibition. It is a radical plan, defying criticism. You now have a small group of art lovers and collectors, your name is known to critics. After the Drouot auction you are on the verge of success, coming face to face with the big public. For that purpose there are only the auctions at the Hôtel Drouot, the established galleries and the official Salon. You cannot show at an unsponsored exhibition of a private society. . . ."

Duret paced the stonework of the studio floor. He was Camille's most ardent collector. He was genuinely concerned that Camille's work would now be associated with painters who had to contrive their own exhibitions. He would be risking his career.

Camille was upset over his friend's distress.

"We are planning a quality exhibition. We'll attract a good audience from the Boulevard des Capucines," he said.

Duret shook his head in a heavy No!

"The Hoschedé sale brought you before a fixed and numerous public. It will not accept this exhibition. You must resign."

"Mon Dieu! I am one of the organizers of the Society. We've been working together for fifteen months. You seemed to agree."

"Before. Not now."

Camille held Duret to him. "Come, take off those clothes you've wrestled in all night. A few hours' nap will refresh you. I cannot tell you how much I appreciate your concern for me."

When Duret left, Camille put on his warmest jacket, a wool cap and boots, and beat his way through the snow-covered woods. Duret was a gentle man, quiet. He must indeed have wrestled with himself before coming to the Hermitage. Could he really do himself serious damage? Manet had thought so, Guillemet had thought so. Piette had thought so. . . . So had all those who had refused to join them. Had things really changed for him? Had he been misguided, made a serious blunder just when events were beginning to go well? Was he endangering the security of Julie and the children?

He plunged through the thick woods, trying to siphon the toxicity of his mind through his legs and feet into the resilient earth. He had always found relief by walking off inner doubts. Even if his face and toes froze in the late January cold.

While it was true that his position seemed to have improved, it was equally true that all Duret's arguments had been considered when they formed their Society. They expected to be discriminated against by the established Salon and the conventional collectors. But the Salon had never done anything for them. The Nadar gallery would be a good hall; its entrance off the street would attract many people; their work would be well hung. . . .

It took an hour of plying the darkening forest before he returned home, having buried the storm of uncertainty in the soft loam of the earth which rekindles faith and courage.

10

In February Julie became certain that she was pregnant again. They took the news philosophically.

"I shan't mind," she declared. "I would like another girl to go with the boys."

Then, for no reason they or the doctors could understand, Minette took a severe turn. She complained of pain in her calves and legs; her lips were swollen. Dr. Menier thought he perceived traces of scarlet fever. Dr. Gachet gave her a potion of aconite. Each time the fever appeared they fed her orangeade and bouillon, put poultices on her stomach and *synapismes* on her chest.

Dr. Gachet became alarmed. The pains in Minette's calves and legs could mean rheumatic fever. He ordered asafetida, which they secured from a pharmacy in Pontoise, to relieve the symptoms.

Nine-year-old Minette grew steadily weaker and died on

April 6. She had succumbed, after all, to the debilitating effects of scarlet fever.

Walking to the cemetery, Julie's mind again slipped to Grancey and the burial of the Hermance child.

"We followed the young parents behind the coffin. The carpenter made a gift of a 'willow cradle,' the coffin for the little one. I gathered daisies and dahlias from my garden. We made garlands of paper and a small cross to decorate the cradle."

She began to sing:

"The song of the nightingale will come to wake her
And also the warbler with his sweet throat.
Cicada, my cicada, let's go, we must sing.
For the laurels of the woods are already growing again."

Camille was stricken. He and his daughter had been devoted to each other. They had understood from the slightest gesture or change of expression what was signified. She had posed for him, days on end, sitting admiringly while he painted her portraits, each showing the depth of his affection for the charming little girl. His world would seem empty without her. An important part of his life had been torn away. He missed her with a throbbing ache.

He was too distraught to go into Paris to see how the exhibition was coming along. He got reports of the selections from Monet, who took Camille's paintings into Paris for him. Now, in spite of his grief, he decided he must attend the opening on April 15. He must lend support to the others, particularly after Duret's attack. He told Julie that she need not attend if it would be too hard for her. She asked if the other wives would be there. They were speaking in subdued tones, as though not to disturb the now buried Minette.

"I understand so: Léonie, Hortense Fiquet, Sisley's Marie, perhaps Alexandrine Zola. You'll have plenty of company."

Though it was the kind of private showing at which Durand-Ruel would have served champagne and hors d'oeuvres, the Society decided against that; they did not have the money. Neither would they supply sitting benches; they wanted the crowds to move steadily from room to room.

Cézanne commented:

"Standing at your own exhibition waiting for a collector to buy is like standing under the guillotine waiting for a royal reprieve."

There were one hundred and sixty-five canvases. The prices

were attached unobtrusively to each, sums from forty to one hundred dollars.

Hundreds of people mounted the steps and thronged through the galleries. Some were Salon habitués, others were interested in the fringes of art; many were impelled by curiosity. The rest were passersby on the Boulevard des Capucines, attracted by the crowds going up the stairs, through the turnstile, into the entresol. They were well dressed and groomed, as one would expect in this neighborhood of the Madeleine. The six stalwarts, Camille, Monet, Sisley, Renoir, Degas and Berthe Morisot, had pictures hanging in Nadar's waiting room. They glowed like the rose-colored windows of Sainte Chapelle. Renoir had actually got the one hundred sixty-five pictures on the walls without crowding, hanging frame to frame, yet creating a harmony with few color clashes, the smaller pictures below the larger, but still at a visible height. Camille had contributed *A Morning in June, A Garden of Pontoise, The Orchard* and two others. Monet showed nine canvases, among them *Breakfast* and *Boulevard des Capucines*. Degas had ten canvases on the walls, Berthe Morisot nine, Renoir seven, Sisley five, Boudin three, Guillaumin two, Bracquemond two and Cézanne three. The others, one or two each.

When Camille and Julie arrived in midafternoon, hundreds of spectators appeared to be turning the Nadar galleries into a carnival. All four rooms were jammed with pushing, shoving, hysterical voyeurs. The noise level was staggering. It hit him like a blow in the face as they made their way through the throng from the foyer into the first gallery room. The public had gone straight as a sharp-twanged arrow to the Batignolles paintings, ignoring the conventional canvases, jeering, mocking, crying out, "Absurd! Insulting! Desecrating!" A group circled in front of Degas's *Dance Class;* Renoir's *The Loge;* Monet's *Impression: Sunrise;* Cézanne's *Hanged Man's House* from Auvers; Sisley's *The Seine at Port Marly*, his own *Hoar Frost*, even Berthe Morisot's *The Cradle*. He tried to sort out the enveloping noise but could hear only the derisive laughter, the abusive indignation, shouts of ridicule being bandied from painting to painting. It was a scene out of a ribald theatrical revue; a raucous farce.

Camille, encountering a bewildered and somewhat pale Alfred Sisley, heard himself crying out:

"How can landscapes, pictures of the theater, of ballet dancers, of laundresses, or the racetrack, arouse such bedlam? People are pointing and shouting at our canvases as though there was something indecent about them."

Sisley replied disconsolately, "It's the Salon des Refusés all over again. Worse!"

Julie and the other wives hovered in a distant corner. Only Berthe Morisot breasted the storm. Beautifully garbed, she went from one jeering encirclement to another, speaking to the women visitors, attempting to explain the new techniques and values. She could barely make herself heard. Camille gazed at the large crowd of disbelievers they had attracted when their early fear had been that few would bother to climb the outside stairs to the entresol.

"I hadn't realized hysteria was contagious," he murmured.

Opening day they sold nothing. Degas offered consolation, inviting the group to the Café de la Nouvelle Athènes, saying, "An hour of this Indian suttee immolation is more than enough. But this is the beginning, not the end. Some of these people, foundering now in mob psychology, will return and buy."

Disturbed that his clever arrangement of their provocative pictures surrounded by conventional ones had not helped, Renoir could only add:

"At least they each paid their twenty cents admission. We should take in fifty dollars today; that'll cover a week's upkeep. But why isn't anybody buying our catalogue at only ten cents?"

"Because they don't want our cast of Grand Guignol characters," Cézanne growled cynically.

Out in the street the crowds were still forming in line to climb Nadar's stairway.

Camille was grim, his back teeth clenched.

"I agree with Degas. Serious collectors will come in the quieter days ahead."

Not if the press had anything to say about it. There were appreciative words from the liberal journalists of the cafés Guerbois and Nouvelle Athènes, an understanding review by Armand Silvestre in *L'Opinion Nationale:*

. . . The landscapists Monet, Sisley and Pissarro do not at all resemble the past masters. It has a plausible side, affirmed with conviction. It is above all decorative; an effect of an impression.

Philippe Burty in *La République Française* wrote:

*   *   *

. . . even if feelings are registered that are at times as fleeting as the feeling of the freshness of the forest, a breeze of warmth from the bay, the listlessness of an autumn evening . . . one must be grateful to those young artists who have been able to pursue and catch those impressions. And this is how they have joined their work to that of the Old Masters.

But they were drowned out by vindictiveness and recrimination.

"Cézanne can only be a kind of madman, afflicted with delirium tremens while painting. . . ." "Sisley sees nature with too narrow a vision. . . ." "Degas's dancer's legs are as cottony as her gauze skirt. . . ." "Pissarro is rather crude in color . . . a still uncultivated surface. . . ." "Those are cabbages? Oh, the poor wretches. They are caricatured. I swear not to eat any more as long as I live." About Monet's *Boulevard des Capucines,* "What do those interminable black tongue-lickings in the lower part of the canvas represent? Surely not people?" And his *Breakfast,* "Two of the most absurd daubs in that laughable collection of absurdities." "Degas's *The Laundress* is badly laundered. . . ." "Berthe Morisot doesn't know how to draw. When she has a hand to paint she makes as many brush strokes lengthwise as there are fingers." "Monet, Pissarro, Berthe Morisot appear to have declared war on beauty."

Of all the Batignolles, "The coloring of shadows shows sloppiness of tone. . . ," "They are fearful daubs. . . ." "They load a pistol with several tubes of paint and fire it at the canvas. . . ." "When children amuse themselves with paper and colors, they do better. . . ." "Soon to be abandoned."

Emile Cardon wrote in *La Presse:*

The famous Salon des Refusés, about which one could not speak without laughing, that Salon where one saw women the color of Spanish tobacco, on yellow horses in the middle of forests with blue trees, that Salon was the Louvre in comparison with the exhibition at the Boulevard des Capucines.

The *coup de grâce* was delivered by Berthe Morisot's early teacher. Morisot read them the letter written to her mother by Monsieur Guichard of Lyon.

" 'I've seen Nadar's salons, and I want to give you immediately my sincere impression. Upon entrance, dear lady, I was seized by a contraction of the heart as I saw the works of your daughter in this deleterious milieu. I said to myself: "One doesn't live unscathed amidst the mad." Manet was right to obstruct his exhibit. Examining, analyzing, conscientiously, one admittedly finds here and there excellent bits, but all are more or less *soft in the head.*'"

The same comment ran through many of the articles. A critic seized on Monet's *Impression: Sunrise*, suggesting that the Batignolles artists were painting just that: *Impressions*. Monet's *Boulevard des Capucines* was labeled an Impression.

A writer in the newspaper *Le Charivari*, Louis Leroy, took a hypothetical Beaux-Arts painter through the exhibit. Leroy wrote what appeared to be satire under the heading, "Exhibition of the Impressionists."

> Very quietly, with my most naive air, I led him before *The Plowed Field [Hoar Frost]* of Monsieur Pissarro. At the sight of this astounding landscape the good man thought that the lenses of his spectacles were dirty.
>
> "What on earth is that?"
>
> "A hoar frost on deeply plowed furrows."
>
> "Those furrows? That frost? But they are palette scrapings placed uniformly on a dirty canvas. It has neither head nor tail, neither top nor bottom, neither front nor back."
>
> "Perhaps. But the impression is there."
>
> "What is this?"
>
> "An orchard by Monsieur Sisley . . . the small tree on the right; the impression . . ."
>
> "What does that canvas depict?"
>
> "It's Claude Monet's *Impression: Sunrise.*"
>
> "Impression! I was certain of it. Since I was impressed, there had to be some impression in it. Wallpaper in its embryonic state is more finished than that seascape. Oh, Corot, Corot, what crimes are committed in your name."

Through buffoonery a new name was coined: Impressionism. Thus Monet and Camille, who, sitting before Camille's fireplace in Pontoise had formed the Société Anonyme, and were responsible for the showing, were also responsible for the birth of their new name.

The journals, the critics, the commentators, the public, picked it up.

"Impressionism." A term of derision creating farcical laughter wherever mentioned. Neither were the members of the Batignolles group pleased; they objected to the word, objected to being labeled. Camille alone thought it acceptable. When a week later they met at the Brasserie des Martyrs to lick their wounds, he declared:

"We are a movement. Our efforts to disguise ourselves by bringing in conventional outsiders did not fool anyone. The critics found us instantly, and exposed us."

"Dubbing us *Impressionists,*" complained Degas. "It's an indignity and disparagement. A stick to beat a dog."

Camille remained unruffled.

"Isn't that what we are about, painting our impressions? How else do we express ourselves? Corot, the first time I was taken to his studio, told me that the muse was in the woods and I was to paint my impression of what I saw as reflected through my feelings. We're all Impressionists? Good. Let us wear the name as a badge of honor. It has meaning."

There were murmurs of *"Bravo! Entendu!"*

Nine of them were around the café table: Monet, Sisley, Degas, Renoir, Berthe Morisot, Guillaumin, Boudin. Even Cézanne. They lifted their glasses, beer mugs, coffee cups in salute.

In a subtle way the leadership of the Impressionists passed into the hands of Camille Pissarro. From now on it would be his responsibility to make the name "Impressionism" respectable; to lead the Impressionists into acceptance and prosperity. Before they had had a cohesion or a name, Edouard Manet had been their leader. Then he rejected their desire to show independently. When two of the three pictures he had submitted to the 1874 Salon were rejected, and the third, *Railroad,* was accused of being "a fearful daub cut out of sheet tin," he became thoroughly out of sorts and accused the Impressionists, a name he disdained, once again of having abandoned him.

Camille announced:

"The critics are devouring us and accusing us of not studying. I am returning to my work; that is better than reading their diatribes. One learns nothing from them."

He had been "washing the head of a donkey."

Yet if he had it all to do over again, he would follow the same path. He had no choice then, from the moment he picked up pencil and charcoal in St. Thomas at the age of ten. He had no choice now. He had to go on living, which meant painting. Loving life; loving his family; loving the world as it existed.

Life did not end.

Only painting counted.

BOOK NINE

"The Meditations of my Heart"

1

THE IMPRESSIONIST EXHIBITION had closed, after a full month. As far as visibility was concerned, the show had been successful, with thirty-five hundred viewers attending, five hundred of them in the evening. The sales had ranged from dismal to devastating. Camille sold one canvas for twenty-six dollars. Cézanne sold his *Hanged Man's House* to Comte Doria for twenty dollars. Alfred Sisley proved to be the star attraction, selling two hundred dollars' worth of canvases. Monet and Renoir sold one painting each for forty dollars. Degas and Berthe Morisot sold nothing. Neither did Boudin or Bracquemond. Nor did the conventional painters, whose canvases were ignored in the hullabaloo. The painters trundled home their pictures, a symbolic *R* provided by the public. The abuse showered upon the Society had done an effective job of souring the collectors on the so-called Impressionists. His own dealer, Martin, joined the chorus when he said publicly:

"I was wrong about Pissarro. He is doomed by his heavy approach to nature."

Durand-Ruel remained loyal. He had been suffering from the deepening downturn of the economy but had still managed to pay Camille one hundred dollars on April 17, for an earlier sale. Then one hundred and forty dollars on May 19 after the exhibition closed, from a collector who had left a sizable deposit on a Pontoise landscape. There would be no more. Because of his spirited advocacy of the "Impressionist" painters, public confidence in him fled. In order to pay his expenses he had to sell off most of his superb Fontainebleau canvases for a fraction of their worth. The banker Edwards from Constantinople, who had hung Durand-Ruel's best canvases in his Boulevard Haussmann apartment against the advances he had made to the dealer, now declared that all the pictures belonged to him; that Durand-Ruel had no further claim on them. The painters had been paid only token sums and had to consider their paintings lost.

It was a considerable time before Camille and his friends met at the Café de la Nouvelle Athènes for a session of what Degas labeled "sitting up with the corpse."

The Nouvelle Athènes on the Place Pigalle in Montmartre had a face of white paint. The glass door of the café grated on the sand floor as one opened it. The painters had privacy at the two right-hand marble tables between the front of the café and the glass partition which walled off the large coffeehouse behind it, the formal restaurant being upstairs. Frequently the group argued, debated, theorized about art until the shutters were banged closed behind them at midnight. George Moore, a waspish young English author, said to them:

"This café is the real French Academy, not the official stupidity you read of in the daily papers. The same old story: the vanquished only are the victorious."

Moore's verdict that he preferred the Café de la Nouvelle Athènes to Oxford or Cambridge for an education did not raise the painters' spirits.

"Is there anything worse than being unwanted?" Alfred Sisley asked timidly.

"Yes. Being incapable," Renoir spat out.

Gustave Caillebotte tried a philosophic approach.

"Plato said all is flux. Newton said that whatever goes up must come down. We'll rebound on the next swing."

There was agreement among the painters present that no more group exhibitions were wanted. Claude Monet was glooming into his empty beer mug. Camille alone dissented.

"The abuse will wear out faster than we will. We must train the eye of the viewer."

He convinced no one, least of all himself.

Back in Pontoise he found his words a hollow reassurance. Day by day he fell into a deeper mood. Minette was gone; every hour was filled with an inner yearning for her. The organization as such was dead; the members had taken too solid a beating. They had told him so. Théodore Duret had been an accurate prophet.

When he drummed up enough courage to visit Durand-Ruel

he found the gallery as abandoned as an old warehouse, the dealer collapsed in melancholy behind his imposing desk.

"I have been declared guilty of having presented and defended your works. Now I am feeling the backlash. I am treated as a madman and as a man of bad faith. The confidence I came to inspire has disappeared. I have become suspect with my best clients. 'How can you,' they said, 'after having been one of the first to like the School of 1830, now praise to us pictures in which there is not the shadow of quality?' I must start over again, after all these years of work converting amateurs one by one. I have neither paintings nor money nor reputation. I couldn't sell a Leonardo da Vinci as authentic. The obloquy you good people suffered from your exhibition has also brought me down."

Camille was shocked by Durand-Ruel's dismal tone. He was stricken with a feeling of guilt.

"I'm bitterly sorry that the four years you have spent supporting us has brought you only public condemnation."

Durand-Ruel's noble face and voice softened.

"It's no one's fault. I believed in you with all my heart. I still do. But there's no more help I can give you. It will be years before I will be able to buy from you again. You'll have to find other markets. I don't know where."

He turned away, not wanting Camille to see the stark hopelessness in his eyes. The incomparable Paul Durand-Ruel, who had been so life-giving to them all, would also be gone.

Back home, Camille sat in his studio, chin on his chest. He walked the cool green woods or open fields without easel or canvas on his back. He awoke each day with a dull ache. He looked at his work and found that the flair and meaning seemed to have been drained out of it. He wrote something of this to Armand Guillaumin, who came to visit the following weekend. They walked down the road in the June sunshine, the fields coming green with new life. Guillaumin clung to his clerk's job. He said sternly:

"I know that times are hard. But the utmost anarchy reigns in the opposite camp. Our enemies will tumble."

That week Duret took him to a tavern in Pontoise where, over a bottle of the same brandy he was selling throughout France, though on a lesser scale now that hard times had hit the country, he tried to ease Camille's despair.

"There are still art lovers of taste but they are not the rich patrons who pay high prices, they are the buyers in the sixty-, eighty- and one-hundred-dollar class. Very few of the people who understand your work and who brave the ridicule are millionaires. While counting on the judgment of connoisseurs you must compensate yourself for the neglect of the stupid.''

Whether it was Duret or his brandy, Camille felt a flow of warmth in his innards.

"My business is not good these days," continued Duret, "but I can afford to acquire one more of your paintings. With the purchase you have to listen to a few words of advice. Some people feel your landscapes are uninhabited. You should therefore do some genre paintings, with animals and peasants, men, women, children in full scale, not merely symbolic figures.''

The fall from grace was hardest on Julie, now thirty-five, in her eighth month of her sixth birth. She had for the most part accepted their hardships stoically, going about the business of feeding her family. She had manifestly enjoyed the respectability, the respite from gnawing anxiety, and imagined that their future was secure. Now it was gone, the optimism, the illusion that they stood on a solid base. She perceived with a terrifying clarity that their lives were like the newly invented roller skates, which would cause their legs to fly out from under them and land them on their *derrières*. They had moved again in April, from the Rue de l'Hermitage 26 to 18 *bis*, with a small stone building across from their front door which Camille would use as a studio; and a little more space.

A son, whom they named Félix, was born in late July. The birth of the boy revitalized Camille, and he again began going out at dawn. In their prosperous time he had designed a movable studio which was built by a local carpenter: a cart of two wheels with an upright frame to hold a big gray umbrella and eye-level canvas, a two-drawer structure beneath, a top drawer for his tubes of paint and brushes, the bottom for extra canvas, rags, turpentine. Every morning saw him on the maturing hillsides around Pontoise; yet there was a difference. He was not painting as though driven; rather, he was led on by the harmonious forces again working within him, achieving a landscape of superb greens, later an asymmetrical haystack with two children sitting at its base as the geometric form dominated the harvested plain. He did a plum tree in bloom, several studies of the banks of the Oise, a nearby quarry, prairies, a full sun on the countryside.

He no longer questioned whether his work was good. His companions were too busy with their own problems to make judgments. Cézanne was in Aix, hiding his mistress and son and painting the village of L'Estaque, to which he returned as to a balm; Monet was in Argenteuil with his wife and child, bitterly pressed for money, writing begging letters to his collectors. Renoir, penniless in his Paris studio, spent much of his time with the Monet family. Caillebotte, also living in Argenteuil, helped when he could. Alfred Sisley had fled to England with his wife and two children, painting around Hampton Court and recuperating from the Impressionist fiasco.

No one came to Pontoise to paint with Camille.

In the fall a letter arrived from Piette saying that he hoped that his "dear Pissarro" was not as hard up as he was. And that, if an inimical fortune was harassing him too, he should come to Montfoucault where they could make excursions in his horse-drawn buggy and find new motifs in the surroundings. Julie, recovering from the birth of Félix, was eager to go.

He could not resist her entreaty. The last of Duret's check would pay for the railroad tickets. He would have a chance to paint the genre pictures Duret had asked for, portraits of people and animals in landscapes. He told his landlord at 18 *bis* Rue de l'Hermitage that he expected to be gone about three months and did not have the money to pay in advance for that period, offering to move his furniture into storage. The landlord did not think it likely he would rent the house once winter fell, and allowed him to leave everything as it was. If he did rent it he would move their things to a barn nearby.

They closed the house, placed the baby in a basket, gave each boy a bundle to carry, changed *gares* in Paris, ate their lunch of hard-boiled eggs and slices of ham between thick-crusted bread out of Julie's large canvas market bag, turning the swaying, rattling train trip into a family picnic.

Piette and Adèle met them at the train. There was no mistaking their intense joy in seeing the Pissarros.

"We've been rattling around this big house like a couple of phantoms," Adèle cried. "I hope the boys are hellions and make lots of noise. Yes, even little Félix. Our walls need sound to keep them from moldering."

Once again she gave them the room with the fireplace and an abundant supply of wood from the forest behind the farmhouse. Julie kept the baby, now three months old, in a borrowed crib by her bedside. Lucien, eleven, and Georges, three, slept downstairs in the small room off the kitchen, whose giant stove kept it dry and moderately warm. For themselves, Piette set up a brazier, a round pan in which they burned short logs early in the evening so they would remain glowing embers through the night in the upstairs second bedroom.

Piette's apartment house in Paris, which had been shelled during the war, had been sold off for its land value. Since he had had a heavy mortgage on the property, he realized little in cash. An out-of-work farm family with two strong adolescent sons had moved into the stone building formerly occupied by Piette's overseer and were working the farm and its animals. Although prices were low, he was selling enough to give them all a precarious living. Released from manual labor, he was free to paint with Camille every day. Lucien shepherded Georges around the pond. Adèle became *Tante* to the infant. Though Julie was breast-feeding Félix, Adèle took care of him, pretending he was her own. She had not been able to afford even a village girl to help her with the housework, but now the wife of the tenant family did the laundry and heavy cleaning. Julie baked round breads in the fireplace oven. Even washing the dishes was not an unwelcome chore for the two women whose companionship made everything palatable.

During the worst of times Piette had managed not to sell off any of his land.

"It isn't that I have anyone to leave the farm to," he explained to Camille as they walked toward the natural pond where the cattle drank and the geese marched in single file. "But my great-grandfather left it to his son, who left it to my father. It's a trust."

Painting side by side, Camille saw what was still lacking in Piette's work: closer organization and a stronger statement about the reality of nature's forms. He could help him improve his composition, make a better harmony of his colors. But every man's interpretation of the universe had to be his own. In the characterful countryside of Mayenne, Camille was able to put the failure of the exhibition and the abuse behind him; the months cut out of time and torment.

"Why go back at all?" Piette asked. "There's always wood for the fireplace, milk, butter, cheese, meat from the animals and vegetables from the garden. We are so happy together."

Camille studied his friend.

"We must return to L'Hermitage and Paris. The market is there, the collectors, the exhibitions. . . ."

"You're not selling."

"Today has a tendency to become tomorrow. On all the

tomorrows I must place my paintings. There is no other way."

Julie was happy, the boys were thriving on the hearty food. Camille painted every day now, making up for the months of brooding and inactivity. Taking Duret's advice, he painted a young girl with a long branch attending cattle on the edge of the pond and half a dozen geese swimming in circles. He used broad strokes on the surface of the water surrounded by a variegated palette of deep greens through sheer pinks and fading blues. Another canvas was seen from the vantage point of Piette's backyard: a peasant woman bundling a collection of faggots, a gaggle of geese coming up the road toward her. It was an autumnal scene, the leaves yellowed, drooping branches nearly barren beyond the octagonal shapes of the blue-roofed buildings of Piette's farmhouse. He painted full-sized country people as part of the landscape in which they lived: at the well, carding wool, in the vein of the Fontaine-bleau painters, setting down the monolithic stones in their forests. When winter struck he did snow effects: the icy blue, the nakedly stripped trees, the fluffy white comforter that covered the earth and its outgrowths in a dramatic sleep.

For the first weeks he was comfortable as a guest, dropping his few remaining coins into Adèle's teapot on the shelf beside the big black stove. When he ran out of money he felt uneasy. His pride was never a swiftly surmounted obstacle. There was no one who would buy deep in this countryside far from Paris. He was not certain that his genre scenes were going well; but he was convinced that to remain here, isolated, would be creating in a vacuum.

When he told Julie that they would have to return home, her face fell.

"I must start my rounds of the dealers and collectors, try to put together another exhibition of our Independents."

"Surely you wouldn't leave us alone for *la fête de Noël?*" Adèle asked when she heard.

"No, I couldn't do that." He was humble in the face of their pleading. "I'll go out and paint the snow until it melts."

He did. Achieving a startling result by juxtaposing white upon layers of color with short impetuous strokes, creating a luminescent blanket of snow. When the weather was too howling to work out of doors he made a painting of Adèle's kitchen, a portrait of Madame Presle, a neighbor, in oil and gouache. Their days were made brighter by a note from Duret telling Camille that he had bought another Pontoise landscape

371

and would be forwarding the check as soon as his end-of-the-year accounts were paid up.

On December 11 Camille wrote to Théodore Duret: "I sent to Martin's gallery the little picture *Guardian of the Cows* with the request to give it to you on your arrival. I am thinking of returning to Pontoise and I am now asking you, if anyway it's not too inconvenient, to please send me in a registered letter twenty dollars, the price of the picture, as I will be caught short for the transportation of the entire family. You will be helping me out. . . .

"I began with figures and animals. I have several projects for pictures of the genre. I am timidly casting myself into this branch of art, so illustrated by artists of the first rank. It's really audacious. I fear making a complete mess.

"I shake hands cordially."

Next, he learned that at a membership meeting at the end of 1874 in Renoir's studio at 35 Rue St. Georges the members of the Société Anonyme Cooperative des Artistes, Peintres, Sculpteurs, Graveurs were told that with liabilities of three thousand seven hundred and thirteen francs and cash on hand amounting to two hundred and seventy-eight francs, each exhibitor owed the Société about twenty-five dollars, which only a few of them could pay. They unanimously voted to liquidate the Société and appointed Renoir and Sisley to supervise the process.

Somehow the news brought Camille to the final depth of his despair. Plunging into the woods behind Piette's home, he felt as though he were falling into an ocean in which he had only an instant to review his life before drowning. He was now forty-four years old. After almost three years of a false dawn, a time of acceptance and livelihood, he had been cast into a pit filled with venomous snakes of rejection. All the optimism was gone. Manet had been right; Guillemet; Piette; Duret, on his frantic visit to Pontoise in an attempt to rescue him from the benighted adventure.

He was back where he had started, at his first showing at the Salon in 1859, fifteen years before, with little more chance of making a living than he had had then. Perhaps less, because he had failed his best opportunity.

The familial mood held over for the month of January. But that, he knew, must be the end. Montfoucault was a wonderful haven for his wife and three children. He could raise them as Mayennes, drive them in the buggy each morning to the countryside school. It was a concept that had for him the connotation of retiring to a monastery; he was not ready to withdraw from the world.

He knew that by returning to Pontoise and Paris he was re-entering a battle zone during a war that was going badly. Ultimately, though, the forces of the opposition had to be joined, the result fought out. The Russians had defeated Napoleon by retreating, but there could be no retreat for him. Four years before he had fled to London to escape the ravages of the Franco-Prussian War. This time there was nowhere to run, except back to the barricades. To remain in this pleasant vacuum was to be annihilated.

After putting aside a month's rent out of Duret's twenty dollars, they returned to the Hermitage.

2

On his first trip into Paris, with two Montfoucault canvases under his arm, he was walking through Montmartre on the top of which an ancient church had been leveled for the base of the vast Sacré Coeur basilica, when he entered a one-block impasse connecting the Rue des Martyrs and the Rue Henri Monnier. On one side was a row of narrow shops above which were floors of apartments, white-shuttered; and a primary school for young girls. On the other Camille saw a shop painted an outrageous cobalt blue. When he read the name TANGUY above the window he remembered the owner as a peddler who had tramped the woods of Fontainebleau with a pack of oil paints and brushes on his back, selling to the painters. He had met Tanguy at Mother Anthony's Inn at Marlotte when he stayed there with Monet, Renoir and Sisley.

Tanguy stood behind a roughhewn counter, a little fellow with a pudgy face and the wistful mien of a tail-wagging puppy. He wore in all seasons a wide-brimmed straw hat which he pulled down to the level of his eyebrows. He had short arms, stubby hands, a left eye which opened twice as wide as his right. His features had been thrown together carelessly, yet because of his affectionate expression his homeliness was appealing.

They exchanged greetings. Tanguy explained that Versailles had exiled him for his work with the Communards after the Franco-Prussian War. After narrowly escaping execution, and only being reprieved a month before, he had leased this shop when the firm which manufactured the tubes of paint moved to larger quarters. He had used his savings from the four years he had labored in exile.

"May I see the two paintings you carry?" Tanguy asked in a winsome voice.

Camille showed him *Countryside with Boulders* and *The Pond at Montfoucault*. Tanguy fairly exploded with excitement; it was as though a huge beam of light had been cast upon the wistful countenance. He muttered inarticulately to himself, then began shouting his appraisal, a glob of foam forming at the corner of his mouth.

"I want to buy them. They would brighten up my life. Alas, I have no money. We live behind the store. My wife cooks a big pot of leek and potato or fish soup every day. . . . I could put them in the window."

Camille was touched by Tanguy's show of delight.

"Your window is mighty small."

"Big enough for the pictures without frames."

Camille exclaimed, "Let us put a moderate price on the paintings. If you sell you keep half. Against them, you will give me credit for colors and brushes."

"As far as I'm able. What do you need?"

Camille picked out tubes of sap green, flake white, yellow lake, Mars orange, containing himself with difficulty. Now he could go back to work in earnest, resume painting the biography of the Hermitage, Pontoise and the valley of the Oise.

While Tanguy was wrapping the tubes in newspaper, Madame Tanguy came through the parting of a floor-length cloth curtain; she was dressed in a gray-checked apron tied around her waist and ending at her shoe tops. She stepped between the two men, put out an arm to defend the already wrapped merchandise, turned to Camille and ran her thumb across the pulp of her index finger.

"I haven't money, Madame Tanguy. I've left my two paintings for sale as security."

"Security! What kind of security? Who's going to buy them? For that matter, who's going to sell them? Tanguy's no dealer. How is he to pay for all that paint?"

Madame Tanguy was a gritty little countrywoman with an angular face and a fiercely protective expression; a bony survivor who had been condemned by her husband to a life of idealism. It was she who had saved the money in exile to open this shop; a resolute creature slaving out her life to keep her husband alive on a stormy commercial sea. Anton Melbye would have painted her on the bridge of a rusty freighter in imminent danger of running aground.

Tanguy expostulated gently.

"Now, Maman, we have credit with the manufacturers."

"For how long, if we don't pay?"

"Since we get credit we can extend it to Monsieur Pissarro. He will sell."

"*Rien*. Let him sell first."

"Maman, go back into the kitchen. The soup will burn."

"If you give more credit there won't be any soup to burn." She let loose one last salvo. "You stupid artists. Share and share alike. Your creditors are not socialists, they are capitalists. They insist on being paid. You work for years to open a little shop, and now you want to give everything away. *Tu te mets dans la gueule du loup.*"

Tanguy said apologetically:

"She's right, of course. We put ourselves into the wolf's jaw. I have no business sense. I'll tell her I own your two pictures. It won't mollify her but it will sound more like a business deal."

"I dislike being the cause of a quarrel."

Tanguy had a beatific smile on his homely face.

"A squall. It will pass. I will sell something for cash this afternoon. Madame Tanguy goes to the market every morning at seven; when you are out of supplies, come at that hour. Bring more canvases."

At the Café de la Nouvelle Athènes he heard that Berthe Morisot had married Edouard Manet's brother Eugène. Since Edouard was devoted to his longtime wife and son, as well as to his beautiful mistress, how else was she to maintain a permanent place in her master's life? Camille considered this a canard. Lunching at the Morisot home with Berthe and Eugène, he had seen how close and sympatico was their relationship. Eugène was a strong, handsome man, educated, stable and wealthy. Both he and Berthe came from the same well-bred, cultured stratum of society. If Eugène looked so much like Edouard that in a sense she was marrying the two brothers in one, that did not constitute bigamy.

He also learned that on January 20, while they were in Montfoucault, Millet had died. Camille had never met him but admired his drawing. As a tribute to his passing he did a replica of Millet's peasants working in the fields.

Corot had exhibited three magnificent paintings in the 1874 Salon. Aging, and very ill, he had expected to receive the gold medal. He received a scant three votes, while Gérôme, a plodding realist workhorse, was awarded the prize. Outraged, the art world of Paris under the leadership of Marotte, friends of Ingres and Delacroix, had commissioned the sculptor Geoffroy Dechaume to create an all-Paris medal to be awarded to Corot at Durand-Ruel's gallery in the Rue Le Peletier on December 27, at a presentation ceremony.

Camille had not lost his affection for Papa Corot, respect for his work, or gratitude for his tutoring. He never understood why Corot had cast him off; did not friendship go beyond differences in technique?

The gallery had been packed with Corot's admirers. Corot had cried with emotion:

"I must go, I know. I have known health for seventy-eight years, and the love of nature and of painting. My family were fine people; I have enjoyed good friends and the belief that I have injured no one. My lot in life has been excellent. I hope with all my heart there will be painting in heaven."

Jean Baptiste Corot died on February 22, 1875.

Although there was not a whisper of a second showing of the Independents, which they preferred to call themselves, Renoir, Monet and Sisley, all as hard pressed as Camille, had organized an auction to be held at the Hôtel Drouot on March 24. Berthe Morisot had agreed to join the auction out of loyalty to her comrades. The steadfast Durand-Ruel, already mortally wounded by his Impressionist protégés, volunteered to conduct the sale, taking little for his services. The group had assembled seventy-two paintings, twenty-one by Sisley, twenty by Monet, nineteen by Renoir, twelve by Morisot. The friendly critic Philippe Burty had written an introduction to the catalogue, pleading that these Refusés from the Salon warranted serious attention and discussion. When Monet asked Camille to join them, he unhappily had to refuse. He simply did not have the francs it would take. But he was at the Hôtel Drouot to cheer for his comrades. It seemed as though all the official art circles were there; the hall was jammed with a gesticulating, noisy crowd. Camille wondered if that could be a good omen.

It was not. From the first offering of a Monet painting from Argenteuil, a Sisley from Louveciennes and a Renoir ballet rehearsal scene, pandemonium reigned. It was an echo of the Société Anonyme showing. The public had come to hoot, to jeer, to harass the auctioneer. The Arosa brothers, Faure, Duret, Dr. Paul Gachet offered serious bids. This only inflamed the crowd. Arguments arose, fists were brandished. The auctioneer, with Durand-Ruel's consent, sent for the police to quiet what had become a riot.

Camille sat with his head down, feeling shame. Not about the unspeakable conduct of what had become once again a mindless mob; but about himself. If his confreres were abused and their paintings beaten down in contempt he should somehow have been with them. He had broken ranks. At that moment he decided that, though there no longer existed a Society of Independents, he would organize a second exhibition for the following year; and persevere until they were established.

Although Berthe Morisot needed the money the least, she managed an average of fifty dollars for a few of her pastels and watercolors. Monet gained forty-seven dollars each for several of his paintings; Sisley twenty-two dollars. Renoir sold a *Pont Neuf* for an acceptable price of sixty dollars, but ten of his canvases had to be bought back by Durand-Ruel because the prices were under twenty dollars. The average price paid at the auction was thirty-two dollars, a quarter of the price for which Durand-Ruel had sold them in the prosperous years.

Camille dragged himself to the Gare St. Lazare and was somber all the way to Pontoise. The road he envisaged, as the early spring countryside of the Oise Valley sped by unviewed, would be longer and harder than any he or the others had conceived of.

But it was the only road they had.

3

By the end of April he was down to his last franc. Julie's supplies of flour, rice, beans, barley were running out. Her vegetables were just showing an iceberg top of green. He had three sons to feed; the landlord wanted his rent. No one came to see his paintings in the tiny room in the Rue Berthe which he still kept in hopes of attracting buyers. He would have to pack carefully half a dozen of his new canvases, take them into Paris and hawk them among his few possible "amateurs," a nonpejorative term used by painters to describe collectors. He felt a sense of urgency. The only money to come in was ten dollars from Duret in late March, accompanied by a note which read:

"Excuse the small amount, but I find myself at the end of this month with all sorts of debts accumulated which leave me short."

When Camille stopped briefly at Renoir's studio, Renoir told him just before dashing out:

"I must have eight dollars by noon, and all I have is sixty cents."

Monet had written to Edouard Manet, who was fond of him:

"It's getting more and more difficult. Since day before yesterday, not a cent left and no more credit, neither at the butcher nor the baker. Although I have faith in the future, you see that the present is very painful. . . . Could you not possibly send me by return mail a twenty-franc note? That would help me for a quarter of an hour."

Camille continued his rounds; not even his most ardent collectors felt they could spare any money for still one more Pissarro painting. They said kindly: "You're at the top of your form. But we'll have to wait until money eases up." Having no coins for the buses, he was on foot all day, drenched and soggy-shoed in the early spring rains. He spent a full week trudging the streets, trying the newest and smallest galleries, the list of prospects afforded by Durand-Ruel. Nothing.

He slept at his mother's, arriving late, leaving early. She asked him to come for dinner either at midday or at night, but he declined. He could not confess that he was destitute. Rachel was now eighty, growing gnarled and silent. If she perceived how exhausted and beaten he looked, she gave no sign. She had withdrawn from the contest her son had been determined to wage.

By the end of the week he had lost weight, begun to look haggard. He continued to tramp the streets, canvases lashed to his back, hoping for a release from his humiliation and anguish. He could not go back to Pontoise empty-handed, face the near desperation in Julie's eyes.

He was trudging past a government building when he recognized a customs official, Victor Chocquet, to whom he had spoken at the Hôtel Drouot debacle just a few weeks before. Chocquet, on his limited salary, for years had been collecting Delacroix and Courbet. At the Hôtel Drouot auction Chocquet had said: "I fully intended to go to your Impressionist show and buy something. Your work, and all the others', fascinates me. But at that time a friend dissuaded me.'' The man had made up for lost time by buying a Renoir, a Sisley, a Monet.

''Come, we'll have a meal at my regular restaurant,'' he exclaimed. ''We'll take a corner table and you can show me the paintings you're carrying.''

Victor Chocquet had a well-groomed head of streaked silver hair with wide-open appreciative eyes, a gentle civilized face with a neat gray beard. After he had ordered without consulting the menu, he studied Camille's paintings, two from the pond and fields around Montfoucault, two from the Hermitage houses and gardens, two from the fields around Pontoise. Camille watched his eyes as they brightened.

''Beautiful. They stir me deeply. I have a sense of utter calm, as though something divine had entered my bureaucratic life. It's hard to choose but I think I like this one best. May I buy it? What is the price?''

Camille's thoughts scrambled inside his head. Some of Renoir's paintings had been bid at less than ten dollars. Most of the Monets had gone for twenty and thirty dollars. Chocquet had been there; he knew what the prices had been. At auction his own pictures would have brought as little, or less. But this was not an auction. How could he, desperate as he was, let a major painting go for less than Durand-Ruel had paid him at his first buy in the London gallery?

''Forty dollars?'' he said tentatively.

''I'll take it,'' said Chocquet.

Camille permitted himself an enormous sigh of relief.

Julie's kitchen bins were replenished. Once again the landlord was paid two months' rent. The next time he was in Paris Camille placated Madame Tanguy with a modest amount of cash against his account . . . then left with more supplies.

Once again he ate of Julie's plain cooking. She had prepared rabbit in every way she knew how; he did not dare confess that he could barely face it again. He put back some weight, went to work with a renewed passion to set down the valley of the Oise in its spring and summer beauty. His subtle yet strong colors, his brushwork, the architectural structure he insisted on, the choice of subject were largely new to his creative mind and palette. Durand-Ruel did not spend his limited purse of praise liberally. When he had inspected the latest oils, ranging from twenty-five by thirty inches to forty-five by sixty, he exclaimed with an expressive gesture that covered his breast with outstretched fingers:

''Pissarro, my friend, these paintings are as beautiful as any you have done. They should sell.''

Camille thought, "But how do I find the collectors to buy them?" Chocquet's money was used up. How did he pay the next month's rent, buy the nux vomica for Lucien's cough and the belladonna so that Julie could breathe at night?

He endured the staggering heat of the Parisian sidewalks; the closed shutters of the stores and apartments for the month's *vacances,* walking miles every day in suffocating airlessness, perspiration flowing down his face; his clothes as wet as during the earlier rains; the pack of paintings on his back as heavy as a guilty conscience. Would they like something for their walls? The proprietors turned away; nobody bought anything in August when customers were few.

Exhausted, sleepless, he capitulated to Rachel's request that he bathe in her big tub, then have supper. At the end of the second week, having sold nothing, leaving the paintings in the studio apartment, he used the last of his coins for a third-class ticket to Pontoise. He had written to Julie confessing his failure so she was not too shocked at his frustrated expression.

Alone and forlorn at her kitchen table, her apron over her head to conceal her anguish, she demanded, half aloud:

"What do we do now?"

If ever Camille was tempted to believe in God, his own Yahweh or Julie's Lord Jesus, it was at the end of August when Edgar Degas arrived on the doorstep of 18 *bis* on a Sunday afternoon with two ladies in tow, Mary Cassatt, an American painter who had shown at the Salon, and a young friend of Miss Cassatt's, Louise Elder, nineteen years old, who had completed her course at a finishing school in France. Mary Cassatt had long held Degas's painting in esteem. They had met at a dinner party; and for some inexplicable reason Miss Cassatt, now thirty-one years old, of a wealthy, world-traveling Philadelphia family, though born in Pittsburgh, had dissolved Degas's fear of a personal relationship with a woman. They had become friends, with Degas accepting Miss Cassatt as his pupil while refusing to admit he was her master. Hard as he tried to conceal his feelings, it was obvious that he enjoyed Miss Cassatt's company.

Camille exclaimed his surprise and pleasure at seeing the three beaming faces before him. Degas explained that Louise Elder was an art enthusiast who had been introduced to the group by the admiring Miss Cassatt. He added mockingly:

"This story is self-aggrandizing but will explain our visit. Back in 1873 Miss Cassatt and her friend saw in the window of a small gallery one of my pastels, *Ballet Rehearsal*. Miss Elder rushed into the gallery and spent her full month's allowance, one hundred dollars, to buy the picture. She also bought a Monet at our exhibition last year. Now Miss Cassatt has suggested that she is ready to acquire a Pissarro.''

"Oh yes, I am," Miss Elder cried in a surprisingly mature voice. "I admired your work at Nadar's, Monsieur Pissarro, but I did not know enough to buy one."

Camille sent Lucien with a message to Julie to dress in her Sunday best and to prepare coffee for the guests, then led them across the yard to the small shed he used as a studio. Once in the little room, Degas took it upon himself to show the women Camille's paintings and explain something about the technique. It was good of him to give his wicked tongue a Sunday off and devote a day to bringing a prospective buyer out to Pontoise. In an aside he also told Camille that he had been struck by Cassatt's portrait *Ida* in the 1874 Salon, that he considered she was on the same road as he. Miss Cassatt's first love was Degas's work; she was also an enthusiast of Camille's, which enabled them all to be forthcoming as they stood in the sunlight of the late summer afternoon. Though not a portraitist, Camille's eyes broke down a person's face and figure into the elements of painting: color, planes, relation of parts to the whole. Mary Cassatt was wearing a white dress down to the floor, over a mild bustle; a poke bonnet with red flowers. She was a tallish woman with a wreath of light blond hair combed behind her ears, a robustly modeled bosom, a slender waist and what appeared to Camille to be long slender legs under the all-encompassing dress that was the custom of the day. Her eyes were small but intensely alive in a slender oval and a flawlessly smooth skin. Her expression was one of eager learning despite the fact that she had shown in four successive Salons. Along with it was a tilt of fierce independence. No one would have called her beautiful; but she had the poised charm of a doer.

She told him quite openly that her father had made a great deal of money from real estate, retired early and taken his family on a long trek through Europe. She had studied for four years at the Pennsylvania Academy of Fine Arts until she was twenty-one, returned to Philadelphia during the Franco-Prussian War, then settled permanently in Paris. Her father declared that "women were deficient in good sense," yet he had enough respect for his daughter's judgment to allow her to live alone in Paris on a liberal allowance. Camille found it ironic that Mary Cassatt had chosen as her mentor a man who had as little tolerance for women as it appeared her own father had had. It was also interesting that Degas never painted men. His ballet dancers, laundresses, modistes were all women. Mary Cassatt painted no men.

"I prefer children, and mothers with children. Or women drinking tea, bathing, combing their hair, sewing, petting the dog, listening to the opera. My hand freezes when I try to portray a male, though I have brothers whom I love. I was an admirer of Courbet, then I met the work of Edouard Manet and Edgar Degas's fabulous new pastel colors, and I began to live. I'm finishing a young bride but it's after Correggio."

Degas was angry at his father for his father's treatment of his mother. Why did Mary Cassatt find the male unpaintable? She also declared that painting was her life. She would never marry.

Louise Elder selected her painting with an assist from Degas, *Houses and Gardens of the Hermitage*. She could hardly contain her delight. She said tremulously:

"Oh dear, I do hope I can afford it. I have only my monthly allowance. How much would it be, Monsieur Pissarro?"

As always, Camille was hesitant. He had asked forty dollars from Chocquet but this painting was larger. Before the 1874 Independents' exhibition and the collapse of prices at the Hôtel Drouot auction, he had received one hundred dollars for his best canvases. He needed the money more desperately now and he was afraid of losing the sale. Before he could answer, Mary Cassatt took over the proceedings.

"Louise, two years ago you paid one hundred dollars for the Degas painting. I don't see any reason why you shouldn't pay the same sum for this exquisite Pissarro."

Louise Elder opened her lips in a gesture of relief and acceptance.

"I expected to pay that much."

She opened her small embroidered pouch and handed Camille one hundred dollars in crisp notes. His head swam. He saw himself buying Julie a dress and the boys stout winter shoes.

"Our lives are a merry-go-round," he told Julie when helping her clear the coffee cups and cake dishes from the dining-room table. "A continuous round of poverty and plenty. Or should I call it a toboggan? On top of the snowy mountain at one moment, then down in the slush at the bottom in another."

Julie could not resist asking:

"Camille, will it always be this way?"

"Apparently."

4

Paul Cézanne had returned to Paris in the spring of 1875 with
Hortense and his son, bringing his family to Pontoise to visit.
Cézanne's father had raised his thirty-six-year-old son's allowance a trifle; he still did not know that Cézanne had a
mistress or a son. Once again they painted side by side,
always learning from each other's intuitive approach to light
and the feel of the earth as the light changed. For a time they
experimented with their palette knives in an effort to achieve
a particularly thick application of paint but quickly abandoned
the idea because the impasto was alien to their gradation of color.

Gathered about the dinner table, Cézanne was flattered by
the pencil portrait Camille had done of him that day, though
to Julie it appeared pugnacious, the head set defensively deep
into the shoulders. Cézanne said, not for the first time:

"Why not come to Aix-en-Provence this winter? We could
paint in the sun."

Camille replied hesitantly, "I don't know about the Provençal
sun. The light here in the Oise Valley fits my temperament."

However he accepted Claude Monet's invitation to come
with Julie to Argenteuil for a visit and a painting spree . . .
and to bring along some baskets of food. He arranged with
Félicie to stay in Pontoise with her daughter and take care of
their boys; then wrote to Duret to pay Madame Latouche,
wife of a painter who earned part of their living selling
supplies, ten dollars for canvas he had purchased.

Edouard Manet was also staying with the Monets, as was
Renoir. Seeing Camille's surprise at his being there, Manet
commented in his cultivated way:

"You thought I deserted you last year. It's not true. I'm
still a member of the Batignolles group. I think you are all
painting better, with a verve and fresher outlook than anyone
showing in the Salon. It's just that I think the Salon is the
right milieu for me, bastards as those jury members may be.
That shouldn't put me beyond the pale."

Manet's loyalty however did not extend to Renoir, whose
choice of subjects he considered mundane and liked as little
as he did his technique. When he had Camille and Monet
alone he murmured:

"You who are close with Renoir, you ought to advise him to turn to something else. You can see that painting is not for him!"

Camille and Monet defended Renoir's portraits, many of them fleshy nudes, and his recent landscapes, which used blue, green and ivory as structural colors, the drawing fluid with broad contrasting areas of light and dark; a balanced vision of Renoir's personality.

Gustave Caillebotte's family home was nearby. He was helping Monet build a studio boat similar to Daubigny's, a shelter over the large part of an old skiff, so that Monet could paint the river in all its aspects. Caillebotte was also providing the materials for the bankrupt Monet, who was painting as omnivorously as though he were a Rothschild.

"It's the light I want to capture more than the river and its bank," he declared.

Camille had already heard that Monet was so fascinated with capturing the changing effects of light that he was beginning to lose the objects that were bathed in it. Unlike Cézanne, who that fall in Pontoise had remarked, "I'm not interested in a fleeting impression of light. I'm seeking basic structure. How much solidity of earth underlies the surface? How far down does the earth go? How does it affect the surface?"

Camille's main objective in coming to Argenteuil was to introduce the idea of a second showing of the Independents the following April before the official 1876 Salon opened. They had missed 1875 because their hides were still black and blue. He felt that if they waited longer they would be forgotten, even in their obloquy. He was convinced that their only hope was to continue the exhibitions, year after year, slowly obliterating the public's sense of shock and waiting for their most venomous critics to die off.

"Because they do, you know," he observed to Caillebotte, who had invited him for an evening meal. "Or they resign, or get fired, or find no clients to buy their reviews, leaving behind only an acrid odor while the works of art remain."

Caillebotte poured him a glass of port. He was still in his late twenties, unmarried, his cheeks flushed, moving quickly with powerful arms and chest. His longtime mistress, Charlotte Berthier, was hostess of the villa, Petit Gennevilliers, and ran it competently. Caillebotte liked to entertain both his professional and bohemian friends, mixing them casually since he was attached to both camps. She got along with the women of the industrialists and the painters. Her languid manner amused them.

"We had very poor seats for the opening of *The Power of Darkness*," she said. "Wasn't that lucky? The play bored us to death."

"I'm in total agreement with you about the necessity to show next spring," Caillebotte said across the round mahogany table. "I would like to exhibit too, if you would have me."

Camille had seen Caillebotte's paintings before supper. His work was a composite, for he had learned a little something from each of the group, particularly Monet; yet it had the stamp of his individuality as an engineer. In his *Square in Argenteuil* the trees were rigid yet the coloring and intensity of shadow showed talent.

Monet and Renoir agreed that they would exhibit, in fact Monet had said, "I'm so desperate to exhibit I'd show in a bordello." But neither man was willing to put in the hours or effort needed to organize the affair. Degas offered to help, as would Caillebotte, perhaps one or two others. They would need a gallery which the public respected. Nadar's studios had carried no prestige.

"We're referring to Durand-Ruel's gallery, of course," said Camille. "But hasn't he suffered enough for us?"

Paul Durand-Ruel still dressed in a bat-wing collar and black cravat, but he had lost his ebullience. He listened gravely, pacing the gallery with no potential customer to bump into, gazing abstractedly at the Fontainebleau paintings which no one could presently afford, the economy continuing to worsen, the Bourse staggering. He was behind in his rent.

"The only reason the landlord doesn't put me out," he explained, "is that there is no conceivable tenant to take my place."

After a few moments he responded:

"Perhaps the old adage is right. If one is going to be hanged it may as well be for murder as petty theft. The second Impressionist show shall be in my gallery."

The winter was a harsh one yet Camille went out to paint in the rain and snow, a little bridge in a deep forest, a corner of the village, the hillsides of Jallais from a new angle. All of the Independents were working steadily. Louise Elder's hundred dollars disappeared into the maw of necessity. Père Tanguy was still giving him credit, manipulating the books so that his wife would not know that Camille Pissarro now owed him several hundred dollars. Though he spent one day a week in Paris, with the soles of his wornout shoes flapping loose in the wet gutters, he sold nothing. There appeared to be no new amateurs to be discovered; his regular collectors had their walls filled, their pockets empty. In one gallery he was advised that, although there was no market for art, prosperous women were still buying the kind of fan that opened up to show a charming country or society scene. He could earn five dollars for each.

"Why not?" he demanded of himself. He had painted blinds. It was a pittance but it would put food in the mouths of his boys.

He returned to Pontoise to paint, on a fan, a farm scene of Montfoucault, of which he had brought home sketches. It was bought at once; he would do more.

The stringency and harassment did Julie's temperament no good. Camille felt the stinging blows of her wrath. He was educated, he was talented, he was disciplined; then why could he not earn a living for his family as other men of his abilities did? No one genuinely becomes accustomed to grinding poverty; it sours thin soup, pervades one's sleep. Yet Camille stubbornly held to the concept that the dedicated artist is not destroyed by deprivation, abuse or neglect; only by an inner weakening of his own resolve.

He did not count the individual days as they passed or mark off calendar dates toward a better future. The hours were a blanket under which they huddled. Not even in extreme want could he yield to Julie's pleas that he ask help from his mother. He had learned that Alfred too was struggling, the shortage of money having seeped into the import-export business. The family bond had vanished. Rachel had continued an occasional Sunday visit to see her grandchildren during their three years of prosperity. With a village girl in the house as a helper, Julie had managed to maintain a tenuous accord. With the collapse of Camille's affluence, Rachel's resigned indulgence vanished. From the back of her mind there re-emerged the concept that her son had ruined himself by marrying a housemaid; that if he had never fallen into the gully of painting as a profession he would not have been attracted to her in the first place; they were interlocking follies. When she criticized Julie's housekeeping or raising of the children Julie endured it with a bottom-of-the-Rue-Neuve phelgm. Camille excused his mother's behavior as the result of her age or illnesses, though she was using a cane for walking more as a prop than a necessity. Once she raised the cane as though to strike her daughter-in-law; Camille took it from her, said quietly, "Maman, that will be quite enough. I'll take you to the station and put you into a seat on the train. Perhaps when things get better you may want to visit again. It is not good for the children to see their grandmother want to hit their mother."

She had not been to Pontoise since. He sent her notes about the children, saw her in town when he had to remain in Paris, though he slept in the tiny exhibition room he rented in Montmartre. He acknowledged that Duret's genre painting was not his forte and abandoned the attempt, returning to essence landscape, to an earlier admonition of Duret: "Go your own way along your own path of rustic nature."

Caillebotte sent two of Camille's paintings to an exhibition in Pau, in southern France. Nothing came of it. In Paris Camille learned that Antoine Guillemet, who had abandoned them completely, was selling from the Salon, winning honors, securing state commissions, well on his way to receiving the coveted Legion of Honor for paintings that the group considered had not progressed from the first they had seen seventeen years before.

A month after the end of 1875, on February 7, he wrote to Théodore Duret:

"I haven't been able to make enough this month to pay my rent in Paris. I am forced to call upon your good friendship: if it is possible for you to give me the thirty dollars that remains due on the pictures you bought from me. That would make me very happy. I will go to Paris this week. Try to do that for me. I have only this amount to call in. Unfortunately I don't sell enough to live on."

He then turned his attention to the group's exhibition at Durand-Ruel's. The only intimate they lost was Paul Cézanne. Camille was disappointed, for his faith in Cézanne never wavered. The rest were relieved, saying: "Cézanne's painting elicits the most abusive criticism of all."

Caillebotte submitted two good scenes of the river at Argenteuil. A half dozen of the surrounding "foliage painters" from the first showing, painters the Society had hoped would mollify the critics, declined the invitation to repeat: Astruc, Bracquemond, Brandon, Colin, Latouche, several others. In their place they picked up competent conventionalists such as Legros, J. B. Millet, François, Cals, until they had accumulated a total of eighteen artists who contributed two hundred and fifty paintings. Renoir was exhibiting fifteen works, Monet eighteen, Degas twenty-four, Berthe Morisot seventeen, Sisley eight landscapes. Camille, busy organizing, decided that he would contribute only six. When Duret saw the main gallery before the opening he immediately sent a note to Camille in Pontoise, not knowing he was in Paris:

"Monet has an exhibition overwhelming in number and size of the canvases. He overwhelms everybody except Renoir who occupies an entire panel next to him. You have only six canvases there, some of which are not intended to strike and impress the public and the bourgeois.

"It seems to me that this exhibition is going to attract much attention and will be decisive for the enemy. You should come here, make a choice of your best canvases—at your collectors' or elsewhere—and like Renoir and Monet arrange a grouping that will make an impression. You occupy too little space.

"If you need any of the paintings belonging to me, they are at your disposition. But you mustn't lose time."

Julie added a note when she forwarded the letter:

"Duret is giving you good advice the future depends on it do as much as possible there is no time to lose."

Camille realized that he had been remiss. He brought in three canvases from Pontoise and the Hermitage, borrowed two older oils from Durand-Ruel and the one he had sold Chocquet.

Durand-Ruel's gallery was ablaze with color and light. The day before the show opened, arranging his twelve paintings in what to him was a meaningful design, he said to Durand-Ruel, whose own collection was in storage for the month:

"You're gambling on the same faction that hurt you so badly two years ago."

Durand-Ruel sighed.

"When I was a young man I deluded myself into thinking that there was a straight smooth road to success. There isn't. The road sometimes sinks into deep valleys. Either you eke it out with your friends or you succumb to convenient solutions. To a man of my upbringing, loyalty makes better sense than opportunism."

Camille brought Julie to the opening. For the artists and for Durand-Ruel it was an even more exhilarating display than their show at Nadar's two years before.

"I wish I were Croesus," Durand-Ruel murmured when they came in early. "I would buy them all."

The crowd that thronged in was also larger than the one of 1874. Camille thought the derisive laughter a trifle less raucous. No fights broke out. The police did not have to be called as they had at the 1875 Hôtel Drouot auction. Their few friends among the liberal journals again tried to explain what this new painting was about. The established press was lethal, led by the authoritative Albert Wolff, who pronounced their death knell in *Le Figaro*:

The Rue Le Peletier has bad luck. After the Opera fire, here is a new disaster overwhelming the district. At Durand-Ruel's there has just opened an exhibition of so-called painting . . . five or six lunatics—among them a woman. It is a frightening spectacle of human vanity gone astray to the point of madness. Try to make Monsieur Pissarro understand that trees are not violet, that the sky is not the color of fresh butter, that in no country do we see the things he paints and that no intelligence can accept such aberrations! Try indeed to make Monsieur Degas see reason; tell him that in art there are certain qualities called drawing, color, execution, control. . . . Or try to explain to Monsieur Renoir that a woman's torso is not a mass of flesh in the process of decomposition with green and violet spots which denote the state of complete putrefaction of a corpse! . . .

The exhibition, which lasted the month, had to be declared a failure, even by the romantics among the artists. Claude Monet had the one stroke of luck, he old his *Japonnerie* for four hundred dollars, a sum large enough to save him from eviction from his home in Argenteuil. Camille sold only one canvas, for less than fifty dollars. Degas, Renoir, Berthe Morisot sold one each, but at prices that gave little profit over the cost of their frames.

Had their efforts again been wasted? Gustave Caillebotte did not think so, even though he had given considerable time and money to mounting the show. He took Camille and Julie to the midday meal at Les Frères Provençaux, ordering a good bottle of dry white wine. As they clinked glasses, Caillebotte said confidently:

"You can't see any impression on the rock where the water is dripping? That's because the naked eye is limited in its vision. We will show next year, and the next and the next. Eventually the rock of opposition will be worn away."

Julie said under her breath:

"So will I."

When the official Salon opened some weeks later, in the spring of 1876, the critic Castagnary said of the Impressionists:

. . . The younger artists have flung themselves into frank simplicity to a man and, without suspecting it, the crowd acknowledges that the innovators have the right on their side.

. . . People who have been to Durand-Ruel's, who have seen the landscapes, so true and so pulsating with life, which Messieurs Monet, Pissarro and Sisley have produced, entertain no doubts as to that.

5

Camille met Dr. Georges de Bellio, a highly qualified homeopathic physician, through Claude Monet. De Bellio was a wealthy Rumanian related to the ruling dynasty of the Bibescos in his native country. He was a longtime resident of Paris and now practiced only for his friends and the artists he admired. Unlike the eccentric Dr. Paul Gachet, Dr. de Bellio was fastidiously garbed in a long black coat with wide lapels, matching waistcoat and trousers, his cravat tucked meticulously under a white collar. On the street he wore a round black hat like a parish priest's. His apartment at 66 Rue des Martyrs was filled to suffocation with sculptures and paintings of all schools, antique furniture, a Dutch chandelier, Italian terracottas, Japanese bronzes. He had started his collection by buying two paintings out of the sale at Delacroix's studio and as a frequenter of the Hôtel Drouot auctions. He was now committed to the Impressionists. In 1874 at the Society's first exhibition, he had bought Monet's ridiculed *Impression: Sunrise,* which had been savaged by the press. In 1875 he had bought a self-portrait of Renoir which Renoir had discarded but Chocquet had rescued and brought to de Bellio. He had also purchased a Sisley. He hung the paintings wherever there was space.

Now he began caring for the Pissarro family, bringing with him to Pontoise his homeopathic medicines and, like Dr. Gachet, taking a small painting in lieu of a fee.

In the summer of 1876 Léonie Monet, the loveliest and most ebullient of all the painters' wives or mistresses, became pregnant. Both Claude Monet and she feared that the future was too uncertain to support a second child; they decided she would have an abortion. Abortion had been illegal in France since 1810, the law declaring, "The aborting of a pregnant woman will be punishable by solitary confinement. The same penalty shall be imposed against a woman who induces an abortion herself, or consents to methods recommended to her.

Doctors, pharmacists who have administered these means will be condemned to hard labor."

The Monets were recommended to a local impostor without medical training. Léonie suffered a lacerated wall of the uterus which would not heal. The color drained from her cheeks; she was in severe pain. The local Argenteuil doctor saw no way of closing the wound short of a major operation. When the Pissarros learned that she could not get out of bed, they went to Argenteuil to comfort her. While Julie sat beside her friend, Monet walked Camille around and around their garden, disconsolate.

"I am riddled with guilt," he cried. "My life and little Jean's revolve about Léonie. She is terrified of an operation. Besides, we have no money for the hospital or the surgeon. We are living from day to day by begging from my amateurs."

Camille pleaded with him to turn to Dr. de Bellio. Monet had feared to approach the man because of the illegal aspect of the problem. Dr. de Bellio came instantly to Argenteuil, passed no judgment, treated Léonie with homeopathic medicines.

At the beginning of summer Camille found an even smaller, less expensive room on the Quai d'Anjou in which to store his paintings and display them. It was near the studios of Armand Guillaumin and Paul Cézanne when he was in Paris. Guillaumin offered to show the paintings to prospective buyers when Camille could not get into the city. However kind the offer, Guillaumin was unable to sell even one, and Camille soon gave up the room because he could not afford the insignificant rent.

He worked with rigid self-discipline through the autumn and winter of 1876, producing forty-three completed paintings. The orchards around Pontoise, pear trees in bloom, the streets, riverbanks, the quais in the rain, all with the vibrant colors of the changing seasons as he saw them: yellow-greens, roof-tile reds, filtered pinks and blues. His confreres told him that the new canvases were intensely alive, profoundly true; the kind that filled the bosom with a palpitant joy, awe and wonder at the creativity of the Maker.

There was no one to buy. There were those who suggested that his country scenes of peasants and working farmyards could not be hung in the elegant drawing rooms of the collectors. They went deeper into debt. Julie scrounged to get enough food for the three boys to enable them to ward off the cold of the winter snows, enough warm clothing to let the older two continue school. Camille found a job in a kiln in nearby Osny painting ceramic tiles. Unlike the window blinds he had painted years before on salary, or the fans which had had a fixed fee, he now had to gamble. He got paid only when they were sold. He painted thirty to forty of them; they brought in pennies.

He hoped for a third exhibition of the Independents at the earliest possible moment of spring. In January Monet had moved back to Paris in an apartment at 26 Rue d'Edimbourg near the Gare St. Lazare. Léonie went occasionally to his small studio nearby on the Rue Moncey to model for him, though it was difficult for her. The worst of the discomfort had passed but full recuperation would take a long time. Camille could get no encouragement from Monet for a third exhibition. The group was averse to taking still another beating for minuscular sales. Only Caillebotte emphasized the urgency of continuing the Impressionist shows to wear down the opposition. Durand-Ruel had had to lease out part of his showroom; they would have to find an empty apartment in a good location.

"How will we pay for it?" the others asked. "No one is earning except Renoir, who has a commission to paint the publisher Charpentier and his wife and young daughter."

Caillebotte located a spacious second-floor apartment at 6 Rue Le Peletier, on the site of the opera house that had burned down. He and Degas would pay the rent. With a place to show, with Caillebotte and Camille arranging for a catalogue, the seven painters who formed the core of the Impressionists responded with renewed enthusiasm and a plethora of canvases. Cézanne and Guillaumin returned, after having abstained for a year. Boudin declined. Camille added Piette; Renoir invited his friends Frank Lamy and Cordey, good Salon artists. Degas brought his friends Maureau and Tillot, conventional painters with small galleries to represent their academic work. They ended with eighteen artists and the largest exhibition of the three.

Camille had twenty-two canvases from Montfoucault, Pontoise, Auvers-sur-Oise; three lent by Caillebotte. Cézanne had several landscapes, three still lifes, a portrait of Chocquet, three watercolors. Degas showed twenty-five paintings, pastels, scenes from the opera, ballet, café concerts, women at their ablutions. Monet had thirty paintings, eight of the Gare St. Lazare, landscapes, eleven of which were lent by Hoschedé and three by Dr. de Bellio. Renoir had twenty, including his fine and remunerative portrait of Madame Charpentier and her young daughter. Sisley had seventeen landscapes, including

Flood at Marly; three were lent by Hoschedé, three by Dr. de Bellio. The hanging committee was dominated by Monet and Renoir. This time it was Piette who cried out in a throttled rage that Camille must come into Paris immediately and reorganize the hanging. That Monet and Renoir had usurped the best rooms for themselves.

Camille went into Paris, routed out Caillebotte from his naval architectural office; together they went to the Rue Le Peletier and rehung the show so that everyone had equally important space. There was no word of protest or discontent.

The day before the opening Camille went through the exhibition alone, at noon, and saw what he considered to be the most thrilling display of painting in French history. For him there was glory in it, an explosive new vision of life on earth. The display was so overwhelming, so monumental in its scope of revitalized, life-giving painting that there was no way for him to believe that it would not be a resounding success. It was now three years since their first presentation at Nadar's; the public had had ample time to be re-educated, their vision cleared for this leap ahead in every aspect of putting paint on canvas. They had carried forward the revolutions of Corot and Daubigny, the tradition of Delacroix and Courbet to an illustrious fulfillment.

It could not fail. Never had one apartment anywhere in the world been filled with so inspired a flame; color-riotous, incredibly fresh, rich, daringly avant garde in its atmospheric light, its new content: musicians, ballets, racetracks, farms, workers at labor and at leisure, a whole vital world, all barriers broken by the brilliance of what Caillebotte called "The Intransigents." The place sang with hosannahs for the earth and its fruits, man and the products of his character and talent.

Opening day brought the usual large crowd. As the viewers entered the first room they saw pictures of Monet, Renoir and Caillebotte. In the second room were two of Camille's landscapes, scenes by Sisley and Guillaumin. Cézanne and Berthe Morisot were each given a wall of the big drawing room in the middle of the apartment, along with a large Pissarro landscape and Renoir's *Dancing at the Moulin de la Galette.* Cézanne's fellow Impressionists were beginning to agree with Camille that Cézanne had a startling talent. The dining room was shared by Camille, Caillebotte, Monet, Sisley and many of the other painters because of its large area of wall. A gallery at the end of the apartment was completely Degas's, which was the way he had wanted it for concentrated viewing.

Théodore Duret, who had finally acquiesced to the need for these exhibitions, mixed with the visitors. Though the rooms were filled with derisive laughter, he told Camille:

"The majority of the visitors are of the opinion that the exhibiting artists are perhaps not devoid of talent and they might have executed good pictures if they had been willing to paint like the rest of the world; but that above all they were trying to create a rumpus to stir up the crowd."

Camille too detected less hatred, less bitterness than at the former exhibitions. There were few inflamed arguments, no red-faced vitriol or ridicule. Yet he perceived that the lack of hostility was for the wrong reason: not because the exhibit was any less a revolution in man's way of looking at the world but because the painters were now seen as harmless buffoons whose sole purpose was to afford amusement.

During the month of the exhibition the group published a small art journal called *L'Impressionniste*, largely written by a sympathetic critic, Georges Rivière, which explained and extolled what the Impressionists were trying to accomplish. No one read it except the already converted.

Cham, a disciple of the superb cartoonist Daumier, published an amusing caricature in *Le Charivari*. Under the sign: EXPOSITION DES PEINTRES IMPRESSIONNISTES, a gendarme was forcibly restraining a well-dressed, pregnant young woman: "Madame, it would be unwise to enter!"

Another critic wrote:

Stand the painting up, it's a boat on the Seine; turn it upside down and it's an orchard with a plowman.

The ultimate blow was given by Paul Mantz in the prestigious *Le Temps:*

. . . They keep their eyes closed, their hand is heavy, they show a superb disdain for execution. There is no need to discuss these visionary spirits who imagine that their carelessness might be taken for grace and their impotence for candor. There is no reason to fear that ignorance will ever become a virtue.

Camille exclaimed over coffee at the Café de la Nouvelle Athènes:

"If these critics are right we are worthless. If they are wrong, art criticism is dead."

Several thousand people thronged into 6 Rue Le Peletier,

not to evaluate and perhaps to buy, but because the Impressionists were now a *cause célèbre*. It was better than a farce at the Comédie Française.

They sold a few small still lifes by the Salon painters. The Impressionists came out empty-handed.

Durand-Ruel sent them a summons to come to his apartment on the Rue Lafayette for a conference. He had managed to keep his apartment, though it seemed barren; he had been obliged to sell off so many of the Fontainebleau paintings, the Meissen, Dresden, Spode, objets d'art he and his wife had collected for years. Aging Aunt Louise served them a cold buffet. Durand-Ruel stood before the empty mantel of the fireplace.

"I've called you here to suggest that you hold a public auction at the Hôtel Drouot when the exhibition closes. You cannot walk away from this endeavor without some canvases being sold. I have arranged with an associate, Legrand, to conduct it."

There was instantaneous and stormy dissent. Berthe Morisot said, "It will be a failure, as the last one was." Degas added, "We've had humiliation enough for one season."

"I know all that," Durand-Ruel replied grimly. "You may get back only the price of your frames. But that is better than trundling two hundred paintings home through the streets on carts."

There was an uneasy silence. Camille felt a hollow at the pit of his stomach.

"I'll put up my work," said Caillebotte, which turned the argument around; everyone knew that Caillebotte did not need the money.

Forty-five paintings survived for the auction; the others were withdrawn. The Hôtel Drouot sent out its announcement and a large audience assembled . . . to scoff as each painting was put up in turn. Yet again there was a difference. Instead of being reviled as enemies of the people, the paintings had graduated into the realm of harmless nonsense. Nevertheless Camille sold *Spring at Close* for twenty-one dollars; *Harvesters Resting* for twenty-six; *Footpath* for forty; *Pear Tree in Flower* for forty-six, *Great Pear Tree at Montfoucault* for twenty-six, a total of one hundred fifty-nine dollars.

Renoir's paintings brought between ten and fifty-seven dollars each; Sisley's between eleven and thirty-three. Caillebotte secured the highest prices for his quieter canvases. There were few new collectors. Most of the paintings were sold to adherents: Dr. de Bellio, Dr. Gachet, Duret, the Arosa brothers, Chocquet, Faure, Charpentier, the book publisher, the stockbrokers Ernest May and Paul Gauguin. Most of the pictures brought in only their cost, the average price bid being thirty-four dollars. Yet Legrand, by outmaneuvering the obstructionist crowd, managed to take in a total of fifteen hundred and twenty dollars. The Hôtel Drouot collected its percentage, but even so, the five painters took home cash instead of canvases. Caillebotte used his auction money against the rent and journal expenses; neither he nor Degas asked the others to make up the balance. The one prize the Impressionists got out of their third exhibition was a play by Halévy called *The Grasshopper,* which satirized an Impressionist. Sitting in the rattling train home to the Hermitage, Camille remembered what Courbet had told him years before:

"I'm proud to be satirized in a successful revue. It means I've arrived, that all Paris is talking about me."

6

Despite the fact that he had given each of the Pontoise merchants a few dollars and paid his landlord for back rent, by June their patience was exhausted. For the first time in all his years of hardship, Camille, at forty-seven, was threatened with bankruptcy. His creditors insisted they would seize his assets, including the furniture and all of the paintings from his studio. His landlord told him he would have to vacate by the end of the month; he had another renter who could pay steadily.

To add to their distress, Lucien became ill and the youngest, Félix, developed a cold and fever. Camille would have to go back to pounding the streets of Paris, though he was hesitant to approach the regulars who had supported the auction.

Julie's woebegone eyes were message enough. When he returned to Pontoise after five days, exhausted, he had to tell her that he had been running back and forth searching for some bits of twenty dollars, uselessly. He had not been able to locate Caillebotte in either Paris or Argenteuil. Camille wrote him a note, asking him to come out to the Hermitage on a matter of urgency.

Caillebotte arrived a couple of days before the Pissarro expulsion. He wore an expression of concern.

"My dear friend, what is it?"

Camille tried to keep his voice steady and to avoid any note of pathos as he outlined his delinquencies. Caillebotte listened carefully, then asked:

"What will it take to pay all your debts and leave you something to tide you over the summer?"

"I've added it up. Two hundred dollars."

They were in Camille's rough-stone room across the carriage path. Caillebotte shifted from one foot to the other, ran his fingers through his hair. Then a tiny smile twitched his lips.

"I can handle it."

Camille threw both arms around the big, mild-mannered man, trying to fight back tears.

"You must take home some pictures that will give you pleasure."

"Certainement! This is a purchase agreement. Show me the two paintings you think you will have the most difficulty selling."

He chose *Winter at Montfoucault* and a brilliantly hued *Sunset Effect, Pontoise.* Julie hurried to the *pâtisserie* in town for cakes, which she served in the tiny area set aside for eating. Camille had put Caillebotte's bank draft for two hundred dollars in the left-hand pocket of his shirt where he could feel it spreading warmth over his heart. Julie had difficulty restraining herself from an embarrassing profusion of gratitude.

Drinking his coffee, Caillebotte said:

"I've been thinking about the future of our Independent exhibitions. It's going to be difficult to raise money for the next one. So I've completed a will."

Camille cried: *"Sacrebleu!* You're only twenty-eight."

Julie rejoined: "God sets our time on earth."

Caillebotte went on quietly:

"I have no desire to die. I enjoy designing boats, painting, being with my friends. It's just that if I should die suddenly I want my collection to go to the state with a request that they be hung in the Louvre."

"The Louvre? We can't even get into the Salon. Your will is going to get drenched in a hailstorm of opposition."

Caillebotte handed Camille a sheet of paper covered with Caillebotte's neat hand. Camille read:

I desire that from my estate the necessary sum be taken
to arrange in 1878, under the best possible conditions,
an exhibition of the painters who are called *Les*

Intransigeants or *Les Impressionnistes*. It is rather difficult for me to fix that sum now; it may amount to thirty
or forty thousand francs, or even more. The painters to
take part in this exhibition are Degas, Monet, Pissarro,
Renoir, Cézanne, Sisley, Berthe Morisot. I name these,
not to the exclusion of others.

Camille looked over at Caillebotte.

"Are you harboring an illness?"

"Not at all."

"As a naval architect and scientist, you are not supposed to
have premonitions."

Caillebotte laughed low in his throat.

"Just remember that this paper is with my notary."

Camille walked him to the railroad station, carrying the
two canvases. When he returned to the house he took the
bank note out of his pocket, handed it to Julie as he kissed
her.

"Caillebotte has saved us from shipwreck. What a noble
creature he is!"

"I'll pray for him," responded Julie.

Everything turned around. Lucien was cured. The baby
threw off whatever had been bothering him. As Julie went
about her work in the house and garden she sang old Grancey
ballads:

> "Little nightingale in the woods,
>   Little untame nightingale,
>   Teach me your language,
>   Teach me to speak it,
>   Teach me how love is made,
>   How love is made."

The good rhythms of their family life returned: playing
with the boys, teaching them to draw; the picnics in the
woods; a unison achieved again. He set out at dawn each
morning with his wheeled cart, the big gray umbrella shading
him and his canvas while he painted the banks of the Oise, the
roads to nearby villages, portraits of Julie sewing by a window, picking vegetables in her garden, tending her rabbits; a
child with a drum, roses in a vase, poultry yards, seeking
everywhere the poetry and lyricism of country life, creating a
portrait of the Hermitage, Pontoise and the river valley so that
it would never be lost no matter the inevitable change.

He renewed his subscription to *Le Charivari* for its

iconoclastic cartoons. Daumier lethally satirized the lawyers, courts, legislature. Cham excoriated the latest news. Gavarni was a genius at portraying *grisettes* and sensuous boudoir scenes. Beaumont prodded the follies of young love. Everything was grist for *Le Charivari*'s cartoonists: the weather, bachelor peccadilloes, cuckoldry, badgered parents, tailor's bills, the Parisian in the country, the peasant in Paris, crinoline dresses on fussy ladies, holes in the roads. The cartoonists were not only delightful wits but superb draftsmen. Every issue caused Camille countless chuckles, punctured pretentious balloons, kept his perspective on the outside world finely tuned.

By the end of summer he was still unable to sell a painting. Collectors were away, the small galleries had no interest in new work. Once again he ran out of money, wondered if he had the intestinal fortitude to withstand another threat of bankruptcy.

Providence showed its face in the form of a restaurant and *pâtisserie* owner, Eugène Murer and his half sister Marie, a superb cook. Murer combed his hair long and thick at the back of his neck as the Parisian poets liked to do; but he wore the trim beard and mustache of the painter, with a soft white collar, *sans* neckpiece; and the corduroy coat of *La Bohème*. He appeared to have two sets of eyes: dark and brooding while he was thinking about poetry and art; blazing, concupiscent when he was bargaining in business. He lacked only one quality to become a Baudelaire or Delacroix: he was devoid of any suspicion of talent. Nature had played a cruel hoax, giving him only the look of the creative artist.

Recognizing this, he and his sister had set up shop on the Boulevard Voltaire. Thanks to the handy location and to Marie's cooking and pastries, the Murers were a success from the beginning.

Camille met Eugène Murer through Renoir, who patronized the small restaurant.

"I've seen your paintings at the Independents' shows," Murer told Camille. "Would you like to do a fresco for my restaurant? Renoir has already decorated the frieze. Monet has painted a wall of the bakery. A landscape of the kind you've done at Montmorency or Pontoise? I can pay you twenty dollars."

Murer was delighted with the view of the Seine at Osny with which Camille brought his restaurant to life.

"Now why not do another mural?" he asked. "I can't

offer any more money but I can give you credit for meals, fresh bread and cakes to take home when you come to Paris.''

With a half dozen of Camille's confreres working on the walls, Murer was beginning to have the most beautifully decorated restaurant in Paris. In addition he had begun buying oil paintings for his large apartment close by, evenhandedly, favoring no one, buying in succession from the Impressionists whose work he adored. But at bargain prices, paying no artist more than ten to twenty dollars even for the largest of the unframed canvases. They were all hard pressed; those who had no need for money came to Murer's for meals, late afternoon coffee, evening hot chocolate.

When the walls of the restaurant were completed Murer gave a celebration dinner for which Marie prepared her famous sole cooked with banana strips and pine nuts. Renoir, winsome eyes and plain whiskered face, arrived late, disheveled. He exclaimed to Murer, disregarding Camille's presence with Julie:

"I came to the house of a collector today, a painting under my arm, only to be told, 'Pissarro has just left, and I have taken a painting of his. It's a human consideration: he has such a large family, poor chap.' What, because I am a bachelor and have no children, am I to starve to death? I'm in just as tight a corner as Pissarro, yet when they talk of me, no one says, 'That poor Renoir!' ''

Julie replied with a touch of acerbity:

"Monsieur Renoir, get yourself married. Get yourself some children. Then people will feel sorry for you and buy your pictures.''

Murer's restaurant replaced the Café de la Nouvelle Athènes. Camille on his occasional day in Paris spent a couple of hours there, enjoying the comradeship, the political discussions, the news about possible collectors, galleries. Always he pushed for another Impressionist show. Marie Murer kept careful books on how much each artist ate or took home by way of bread and cake; but Eugène was compassionate. He never refused to feed an artist or his family if he admired his work . . . and could acquire a picture.

"But why does he take so long to pay?" Julie asked. "It's harder to get that last four dollars out of him than it is to get our Georges out of a fit of temper.''

"*Merde*. I had to pursue him ten times for every small payment for *The Bottom Lands of St. Antoine*. But he is the only one buying.''

Knowing how badly Camille needed the money, and perhaps a bit ashamed at the low prices he paid, Murer came up with an inspired idea.

"Why don't we stage a lottery for one of your paintings? I'll print a hundred tickets for twenty cents each. We should have no trouble selling them. That means you'll earn twenty dollars, or as much as eighty dollars if you're willing to raffle four. You can't lose. Do you agree?"

Camille agreed. A sale in any tortured form was good news.

"I'll bring you four canvases. We'll put them in cheap frames to make them more presentable and cover the cost by increasing the number of tickets by fifty."

Julie sold a few tickets in the Pontoise shops. Félicie's husband sold some to his fellow mechanics. The artists sold a number to friends and the suppliers of paint and canvas. However most of the tickets were sold by Murer and Marie to the servant girls around the Boulevard Voltaire. Together they managed to dispose of one hundred tickets. The young girl who had the lucky number, picked out of a flour bin, rushed in to see her prize, set up on an easel in the front bakery amidst a luscious display of pastries. She gazed at Camille's *Peasant with a Donkey* with a frown that developed into a grimace, twisted her bonnet in her hands, shuffled her feet until her toes were facing each other, then cried out:

"If it's all the same to you, I'd rather have a cream bun."

She went out happily munching the bun. There was an embarrassed silence. Murer said resignedly:

"Ah well, *de gustibus non est disputandum*. Anyway, Pissarro, here is your twenty dollars from the hundred tickets."

"I'll take my painting back, too."

"Oh no," replied Murer, removing the thinly framed canvas from its easel. "It belongs to me. I paid a month's work for it, as well as Marie's cream bun. Don't be disconsolate, my friend. Twenty dollars is better than a kick from the mule."

Julie took the money, muttered, "Let's go home. What's one painting less to a man who makes hundreds? *Un homme qui se noie s'attache à un brin d'herbe*. A drowning man clings to a blade of grass."

401

In the fall Léonie Monet became feverish and lethargic. Monet was trying to keep up the apartment, cook, take care of their son and paint. Julie suggested that Léonie and Jean be brought to the Hermitage where she could nurse Léonie better than Monet; and Dr. Gachet could stop between trains on his way home to Auvers.

Fright careened across Léonie's eyes.

"I don't want to be separated from Claude. I want to be here with him every day."

When they left the Monet apartment, Julie asked:

"Why?"

"He is her whole life," Camille replied. "It's called love, but love is not always in one's best interest."

She shot him a glance with her eyelids raised high which said clearly, "You ought to know!"

Weeks later when the two women were together Léonie confessed to Julie:

"It takes more strength and courage than I have, but what can I do? The doctor has forbidden us to make love. But we do. If I don't take care of the family, and pose for him, I may lose him."

Julie thought with peasant realism, "It's better than losing yourself."

In August Léonie became pregnant again. Both Dr. Gachet and Dr. de Bellio were aghast. It was far too dangerous for her to bear another child; the earlier malfeasance made an abortion impossible.

Temptation entered the life of Claude Monet in the form of Alice Hoschedé, wife of Ernest Hoschedé, of the Gagne Petit department store. Hoschedé was still the single most ardent collector of the Impressionists in Paris, despite the fact that he had twice found himself in financial difficulties and had had to auction off his collections. He still owned some of the best of Camille's work as well as Monet's, Manet's, Renoir's, Degas's, Sisley's and Morisot's.

Alice Hoschedé was a deep-bosomed woman, middle-aged, generous, volatile, affectionate, mother of six and disillusioned with her overweight husband. She was determined to prove that she was young, feminine, attractive; and fell wildly in love with Claude Monet, making no attempt to conceal her passion. Monet saw her frequently in the presence of his son and Léonie; and discreetly alone. The Hoschedés had a distinguished apartment in Paris. He sometimes visited their country home for weeks of painting in the country. Alice Hoschedé spent warm afternoons with Léonie, young Jean, and her own youngest, taking them to dinner, easing Léonie's lot at home, bringing in food, domestic help, friendship.

"I don't like it," said Cézanne, who appraised the situation immediately. He was visiting from Aix with Hortense and Paul, Jr., the family spending the days in Pontoise with the Pissarros, the two men painting together. "Hoschedé will hold all of us responsible, stop buying and perhaps even auction off our paintings to avenge himself."

They survived the fall and winter of 1877 only through Camille's importuning of Murer to buy more pictures and to pay the few dollars owed to him from earlier purchases. By now Murer had a first-rate collection from all the members of the Batignolles.

"He's building his own Louvre," Degas growled.

"He never pays us enough," Camille added, "but what would we do without him?"

On the last day of 1877 Camille learned that Gustave Courbet had died in exile in Bon-Port, Switzerland, at fifty-eight. He had suffered for six years under the crushing debt imposed upon him by the French government. The years had been filled with family recriminations, loneliness, heavy drinking, bloated illness, an aching for Paris.

Camille felt the loss keenly. He was indebted to Courbet for introducing him to the art world of Paris, for his encompassing hospitality at the Brasserie Andler, for teaching him by example and approval of his work right up to the day of his flight from the country. Those painters who owed a debt to Courbet gathered for an informal memorial.

"It was a cruel fate," declared Monet soberly. "Isn't that the inherent nature of fate? Ah, but Courbet's magnificent body of work! That will be remembered when the Vendôme Column story is but an obscene joke."

Shortly after the first of the year Camille began working on the next Impressionist show. Caillebotte again offered to pay the month's rent on whatever favorable rooms they could find, but suggested that they wait until June this time. Perhaps if they exhibited after the Salon closed people would appreciate the difference.

Claude Monet responded, "We ought to wait until October when the World's Fair will be open. There'll be a million people from all over, not only the Paris cynics."

Renoir abandoned them completely, running his index finger under his nose in a habitual gesture.

"There are in Paris scarcely fifteen art lovers capable of liking a painting without Salon approval. There are eighty thousand who won't buy an inch of canvas if the painter is not in the Salon. I don't want to waste my time in resentment. I believe one must do the best painting possible. That's all. My submitting to the Salon is entirely a business matter."

Acerbic Degas commented later, "The only reason he ever showed with us is that the Salon jury has been turning him down. He's been given to understand that he has a good chance of acceptance this year."

"I'd be sorry to lose him," Camille said mournfully. "He is one of our best."

Charles François Daubigny died in February at the age of sixty-one. Because of his fervent defense of the Independents and his excoriation of the fusty Salon juries, he received no official funeral. The Beaux-Arts ignored the occasion. As the artists gathered in the cemetery they extolled his vision, courage, loyalty in the face of inevitable retribution, declared that his painting would forever delight and replenish the peoples of the world.

Corot, Courbet, Daubigny. The artists clung together with a heavy sense of their mortality, the depletion of their ranks.

Théodore Duret invited Camille to visit Cognac, his parental home. He would have freedom to paint the countryside around Cognac. He also paid him twenty dollars for the purchase of "the small woman washing her linen."

Camille did not know whether the invitation included Julie and the boys, but he knew it was useless to ask since he was in fact living in a moneyless world and would not be able to round up the train fare. He was again walking the streets of Paris; "a medieval peddler." Petit, a dealer, bought a small panel for ten dollars. When Camille went to collect the money, Petit's *garçon* informed him that Petit was away on his honeymoon. He crossed the city to the Boulevard Voltaire and Murer's restaurant and bakery shop.

"I'm waiting for this drop of water like a traveler in the desert," he said to Murer plaintively. "Couldn't you advance me this sum?"

Murer loaned him the ten dollars. To Guillaumin, who

invited him to have a beer on the terrace of the Café de la Nouvelle Athènes, Camille said:

"Art is a matter of a hungry belly, an empty purse, of luckless devils. Yet it isn't me I'm feeling sorry for but my family. I've bogged them. What torment, you have no idea."

Guillaumin chose this unpropitious moment to speak his mind.

"Pissarro, I no longer have hope of winning a fortune in the lottery. I've wasted fifteen years in that Department of Bridges and Causeways. I don't want to be nothing more than a Sunday painter. I'm considering giving up my job, marrying and painting full time."

Camille studied the plain face of his thirty-seven-year-old friend and disciple, then watched the crowd in the Place Pigalle pass by, workingmen in coveralls, housewives out to market, holding tightly to their string bags. Guillaumin had learned a good deal while painting alongside Camille; he had an emerging talent. But his chances of success when the best of the Independents were living *sou* to soup? What could he say?

"Guillaumin, I agree. An artist who has worked fifteen years, having another position in hand, has wasted seven years. It is a hundred times better to send the city to the devil. But it takes a bit of character. I headed for Caracas to break the cable attaching me to bourgeois life. What I have suffered is unheard of; but I have lived."

Guillaumin gazed glumly into the last of his beer.

"I guess I'll buy more lottery tickets."

The next morning Camille sent Murer a *petit bleu* through Paris's underground *pneumatique*, which would be delivered to him within two hours by a boy riding a bicycle.

"Last night I spoke to you of a painting I have in Pontoise. You know this painting, it's a small peasant woman with a brick-red figure, head covered by a yellowish hood. If you like this canvas I will gladly sell it to you, having a desperate need to send money to Pontoise. . . . I'm throwing everything overboard, as these studies were dear to me.

"I will let you have it if you will pay me for the two small canvases ten dollars each. The Breton will have to be twenty dollars."

Murer bought the paintings but paid for them only a couple of dollars at a time.

"Enough," Julie was heard to mutter, "to keep me from killing myself."

Murer then decided he wanted Camille to paint his portrait. He had already hinted at this. His bakery shop was flourishing; he was a collector.

"How much would you charge me for the portrait?" he asked.

Camille thought for a moment.

"Thirty dollars."

Murer was aghast. "Thirty . . . But I only paid Renoir twenty dollars for his portrait of Marie."

Camille decided to hold his ground.

"It will take at least a dozen sittings. I want you to know that before quoting you a price I consulted my friend Renoir and we agreed on this price, which seems reasonable to me. Less seems impossible."

Murer desperately wanted the portrait. He yielded.

"But I'll have to pay it out so much a sitting."

Encouraged by phantoms, he took Murer's advance home to Julie, apologizing for his recent depression. Julie brushed past his apology, took the money with a wan smile.

"Now I can dare go into the shops again. They were beginning to hate my face."

He held her tight; kissed her heartily.

"It's a lovely face. I thought so at the beginning. I think so now."

BOOK TEN

Compassion

1

H<small>E MET THE</small> tall startling-looking man in the expensive black suit when visiting Gustave Arosa's estate in St. Cloud where Arosa's superb collection of Delacroix, Courbet and seemingly unfinished Daumier oil paintings had thoroughly moved him. Arosa introduced him as his godson, Paul Gauguin, whose mother had been a friend of the Arosa family. When she was dying she had extracted a promise from the Arosas that they would care for the young boy. Camille was intrigued by him; the powerful build with a bull neck, the flagrant self-assurance with which he wore his expensive clothes, the attractiveness in a brutal fashion; a broken bony nose slashed across his face, a large narrow head, narrow forehead, hooded blue-green eyes, dark hair, dramatically high cheekbones, tan mustache. A long firm chin suggested a touch of braggadocio; yet under it all perhaps a character of strong resolution.

"If you ask me who I am," Paul Gauguin said in a throaty voice, "I'll tell you I come from the Borgias of Aragon and the Viceroy of Peru. You'll say that I'm a boaster. If I tell you the Gauguins are a bunch of scavengers, you'll despise me."

"Try a few prosaic facts."

The man grinned. "I don't know any. I spent six years on South American ships as a stoker and seaman. Those six years made a man of me. Arosa says you come from St. Thomas. Of course we stopped at St. Thomas. Beautiful brown girls at Charlotte Amalie, we dreamed about them for weeks before reaching your port. I'll tell you about my conquests of women, but I'm a terrible liar!"

Camille threw his head back and laughed. True, he did walk with the rolling gait of a sailor.

When Gauguin had completed his service on the *Jérôme Napoléon* during the Franco-Prussian War he was twenty-three and needed a job. Gustave Arosa secured him a position through his son-in-law, who was a director of the Bertin stockbrokerage. They put him to work in the Rue Laffitte office. His bold, colorful assurance was perfect for a salesman. If his approach was a bit coarse it also contained a contagious conviviality. He had begun earning money at once.

Gauguin recounted to Camille that five years before he had married a young Danish girl, Mette Gad, whom he had met at a proper boardinghouse where Mette was having her first holiday in Paris. She was Gauguin's age, a tall attractive blond with a vivacious manner, china-blue eyes, the daughter of Danish civil servants. Gauguin had showed her the more respectable parts of Paris. They fell in love. He was now a successful stockbroker who could raise her out of the middle class of civil servants. Mette was broad-beamed and looked as though she would be an efficient housewife and mother. What more could an attractive young couple ask? They now had two children, Emile and Aline.

"I went to your Impressionist show and laughed with the rest of the clowns," Gauguin told him in his onrushing voice. "After a couple of sleepless nights I realized I had made a fool of myself. I want to make amends by acquiring paintings. Why don't I start with you? I have money, it's easy to make on the Bourse. I'll tell my wife the paintings are a safe investment; which they are."

Paul Gauguin came out to Pontoise the following Sunday, selected a small *Snow at Louveciennes*, the fields under a heavy covering of white, and a larger *Harvest, Pontoise* showing pickers among the fruit trees, twenty-six by thirty-two inches.

"You chose well, Gauguin."

Gauguin's sun-drenched skin flushed purple at the compliment. He confessed that he had been drawing in his spare time and studying seriously the Arosa collection.

"I have a fellow broker at Bertin's, Schuffenecker, we call him Schuff," Gauguin continued; "he is an amateur painter and enthusiast. He has guided me through the Louvre, the Luxembourg. He took me to Nadar's for the first show of the Independents. He taught me how to evaluate oil paintings and insisted I spend an evening or two a week at the Académie Collarossi. I've been sketching steadily at home."

Camille was attracted to this colorful fellow who radiated such magnetism.

"I had to deceive my wife. Told her I was out with my mistress. She would prefer that to my taking drawing lessons.

She's afraid my hobby will corrupt my drive to earn a good living."

Camille chuckled inwardly, "And so it will, so it will."

"I also had to hide that I had a small painting accepted by the 1876 Salon. It was sufficiently ignored to keep me safe."

Gauguin spent a few Sundays at Pontoise painting with Camille. Beneath the gauche beginnings Camille sensed an incipient talent.

"You're the only professional who has been willing to take the time to teach me," Gauguin said as they worked along the bank of the Oise with several green islands floating against the downsweep of the tide.

"Teaching is also learning," Camille replied to the successful thirty-year-old businessman and repressed artist who was as grateful as a schoolboy for any hint about improving his work. Camille made suggestions for strengthening Gauguin's drawing, explained the use of nature's colors without gloss or sheen, the departure from brown and black shadows to light tones. Gauguin insisted on taking Julie and the boys to a Pontoise inn for their midday meal, a hearty one in this area of France.

He also offered to sell some of Camille's paintings.

"An employee of the stock exchange wants to buy two paintings and naturally I will make him take Pissarros. Don't be annoyed at what I say, but I would like to have for this young man two paintings with the most stylish and charming subjects possible. He's a fellow who knows nothing at all but has no pretension of knowing anything, which is already good."

The sale was made. Both Camille and Julie were delighted and grateful for the francs. Julie noted Camille's growing fondness for the ebullient, sometimes boisterous younger man; she herself was more reserved. This man had no core of gentleness such as had attracted her to Camille; in fact she had a small reserve of fear of him. To her peasant mentality there was something incipiently savage in the aggressiveness his brokerage clients found so assuring.

Camille took Gauguin to the Café de la Nouvelle Athènes to meet the group. Degas took to him at once because of his rough-edged tongue. Edouard Manet glanced through his portfolio . . . drawings of the nude models at the Académie Collarossi, two studies of the Arosa house at St. Cloud, a somber winter scene, *Seine in Paris*, said, "Some of these are good."

"I'm only an amateur," Gauguin murmured.

"No," Manet replied, "the amateurs are those who make bad paintings."

Claude Monet and Renoir actively disliked him because he was a businessman, and hence to them a dilettante. They were grateful for his purchases of their work but unwilling to give friendship, suspecting that he was trying to buy their allegiance. That did not put Paul Gauguin off; he kept acquiring from Camille, Monet, Manet, Sisley, Cézanne, Jongkind, Renoir, Guillaumin, until he had spent some three thousand dollars and had the beginnings of a good collection.

Because Camille was his sponsor, he was accepted into the group.

Léonie and Claude Monet's second son, Michel Jacques, was born on March 17, 1878, the child whom the doctors had warned her against conceiving. Julie spent several days in their apartment taking care of the older Monet boy and the household. When she was obliged to return to her own family, Alice Hoschedé stepped in to care for them.

The few telegrams Camille had received over the years had contained bad news. He tore open the telegram of April 17 with trembling fingers, read to Julie:

> PIETTE DIED YESTERDAY. SUDDENLY. HEARTBROKEN.
> ADÈLE

A sense of shock swept through them. Then came grief in unmeasurable quantities. Piette had been Camille's most ardent admirer; he and Adèle had accepted Julie wholeheartedly. Over the years Camille, Julie, the children had spent enriching months in Montfoucault, whose doors were always open to them. They had lost not only their closest friend but a refuge and second home.

What had happened? True, Piette had been depressed over his failure to make a profit off the farm; or to sell his paintings; or to be able to paint in Paris. Nevertheless he had been full of life, with dozens of contradictory political ideas. He was too robust to pine away. Camille studied the telegram for a third time. The message had been delayed for more than a full day, perhaps because of the routing from Montfoucault to Mayenne through Paris to Pontoise.

"I'll have to catch the morning train to Mayenne," he said.

Julie attempted to slake her tears with her fingertips.

"Bring Adèle back with you. To become part of our family. She loves the boys."

Camille went into the village post office, sent a telegram to Adèle that he would be arriving late the next afternoon and to please hold off the funeral because he wished to be present. For the first time there was no Piette to meet him. At the Mayenne railroad station he hired a one-horse rig which he drove none too skillfully to Montfoucault. Piette's aunt from Le Mans, a tall, stick-thin lady of iron-gray hair and Piette's eyes, was working with an advocate from Mayenne. She greeted him with saddened courtesy.

"I'm sorry, Monsieur Pissarro, but we buried Piette yesterday. We had no idea you were coming."

"My telegram . . . ?"

The woman shook her head. "Probably waiting in the Mayenne office for tomorrow's postal rider."

"Where is Adèle? May I speak with her?"

The aunt shook her head in perplexity.

"Adèle is gone. Left immediately after the burial."

"To Paris?"

"I don't know. She took her clothing, some of her personal things and departed. Didn't leave an address."

Camille stared at the woman, feeling as though he must be open-mouthed.

"But surely you know whether she has a mother or father alive? I must find her, take her home to Pontoise."

The aunt sighed in resignation, then introduced him to the man working over Piette's papers.

"This is Piette's advocate. Things are worse than I could have dreamed. He would never sell off any of his land but he borrowed heavily against it. Now it must be sold so the banks can get their money back."

Camille groaned inwardly. "There will be enough for Adèle to live on?" he asked.

The advocate looked up from his papers, said grimly:

"We won't get enough through a sale to pay off the bank debts. The furniture will have to be auctioned, their paintings as well. It's a dismal view."

Camille hung his head in despair. Piette, the young man at the Suisse who had concealed his wealth so that he would not be catered to by false friends . . . to end up bankrupt. Adèle with no means of support.

The aunt said consolingly:

"Adèle did take two of her favorite Piette paintings with her. I have permission to take another pair home to Le Mans."

On the train back to Paris Camille rehearsed the obituary he would have delivered. Poor dear generous Piette, who knew he was not a good farmer or businessman. Within limits he was a capable painter but he had taken himself out of the ambience where he perhaps could have grown. If he had had sons to carry on the farm; if his apartment house in Paris had not been bombed in the Franco-Prussian War . . . He had been so full of love for Camille. Now he was gone. There was nothing to be done for him, except save Adèle and give her a home.

He could not find her. She had disappeared. He searched everywhere: in the Jewish quarter where Piette had first seen her and admired her semi-oriental beauty; at the local synagogue. He asked at the shops, inquiring about not only Adèle but her family, knocked on the front doors of dozens of apartments, checked the banks where the family might have had accounts. No one remembered anything about the Lévys; they had been gone too long. He found no trace. She had crept into some secret corner to live out her grief.

"Surely she will come to us one day?" Julie asked, when he at last abandoned the search.

An important part of their world and their past was gone.

2

He spent considerable time in Paris trying to find collectors, but most of his days were spent in the countryside seeking motifs. He was painting farther afield and no longer returned for midday dinner. Julie, pregnant once again, gave him a substatial breakfast at dawn and packed a lunch for him, hard cheese between slabs of bread, some fruit in season. He carried with him a jug of cool well water which he propped upright against a shade tree. He had been a casual pipe smoker, now each time a dead-end situation flooded over his mind he filled the bowl of the discolored clay pipe and let the tobacco smoke befog his painful predicament. But not his work. In the cold or rain he remained at his easel just short of pneumonia, returning home to warm himself before an open fire. In warm weather he sometimes fell asleep in the shade beside his painting cart, waiting out the heat. During the clement weather he was out as the sun rose, returning home at dusk when the light was failing, to have supper and spend a couple of hours teaching Lucien to draw, helping Georges with his homework and playing with four-year-old Félix.

Neither the Hermitge nor Pontoise any longer thought him an oddity. He had been there too long and worked too steadily. Nor did anyone but the shopkeepers and landlord know about his falls from monetary grace. The rest of the community knew that he sometimes sold his paintings; had he not once received some two hundred dollars for a landscape, as much as all except the landowners earned in a year? If the villagers had known about their debt-ridden existence they would not have held it against them. Who was not in debt?

Each day he went across the Pontoise countryside to Valhermeil by way of Le Chou; followed the Oise as far as Auvers, planted his easel in congenial spots; observed the land and its people; and painted. When he framed his paintings in the large white molding now called Whistler molding, which he carpentered himself, his fresh colors burst into light like fireworks.

No matter how long the workday, there was no opportunity to daydream, reminisce. Painting demanded total concentration on the task at hand. He did not carry a watch; time for him was a fluid. Except for his midday break he did not know what hour it was, nor did he care. He used his paints and brushes meticulously, spilling little, talking to no one, not even the peasants who passed, unaware of anything but the scene to be possessed in what he believed to be as immortal a medicine as man had yet devised. The town or country people who passed detected no movement, he was so inextricably one with his canvas, another tree growing in the field or along a path. He was feeling deeply, not in terms of words or intellectual concepts, only in the emotions evoked by the landscape before him and his reaction to its clarity and meaning.

When he reached home he was drained, for he had poured out everything in his consciousness. He and Julie went to sleep when their children did, between eight and nine o'clock; they were up and dressing when the cocks crowed their jubilation at sunrise.

It was a harsh spring, though the children, who were on reduced rations, were in good health, enjoying the rich deepening of color of the Oise Valley. Camille had never found money an inspiring subject; at its worst, with only Murer, Caillebotte, Duret, Chocquet and occasionally Paul Gauguin or the broker Ernest May buying, with Père Tanguy selling an occasional Cézanne but no Pissarros, and Madame Latouche, his only other dealer, failing to sell even his large canvases at twenty dollars apiece, both he and Julie felt like indentured servants. It was too late for her to go into Paris to make artificial flowers. Too late to go into Pontoise to pick up embroidery for the merchants. The job of supporting their family was too big now, the task beyond her resources. Camille would have to be the provider.

Camille remembered Dante's lines:

Turn back to view the pass that nevermore
Has left alive a single human being.

There came a dramatic event for which none of the group was prepared. Ernest Hoschedé, owner of the Gagne Petit, went bankrupt. Once again, on June 5 and 6, 1878, he placed his Impressionist paintings up for auction at the Hôtel Drouot. There was also serious trouble between Hoschedé and his wife. Madame Alice Hoschedé had been seeing far too much of Claude Monet, at the Monet apartment caring for the almost bedridden Léonie, shopping for their needs; romantically in love with Monet. Madame Hoschedé, the rumor went, was going to be on hand when Claude Monet became a widower.

It was also rumored that that was the real reason Hoschedé cared so little how much their paintings brought.

Camille's nine paintings and watercolors were bid in for a total of eighty dollars. One small oil was sold for two dollars, a gouache for one dollar forty cents. Monet's twelve paintings went for an average of thirty-seven dollars each. Berthe Morisot, Renoir, Sisley fared no better. Of the five important works by Edouard Manet, only one reached one hundred sixty dollars.

Camille was shattered. Some of his best work had gone for the price of a handmade shirt or pair of boots. During the next weeks, when Duret or Murer gave him a lead to a prospective buyer, he was told:

"I can get your things more cheaply at the Hôtel Drouot."

Murer invited him to the restaurant for supper. Marie set out his meal but he was too heartsick to eat. Murer sat down beside him.

"Your account is balanced by two dollars and forty cents in your favor if you price my portrait at thirty dollars. I don't mean to infer it's not worth that much; I would be ungrateful to dispute the sum."

Camille pulled out his pipe, remembered he had no tobacco, said in a strangulated voice:

"I have been rushing about Paris vainly trying to discover

the one man needed to buy Impressionist pictures. I ran an enthusiast to earth but the Hoschedé sale was my undoing."

He took home to Julie the two dollars and forty cents from Murer, sitting on the wooden third-class carriage bench of the train back to Pontoise surrounded on all sides by Daumier's bulbous peasant women breast-feeding their infants or eating suppers of thick-crusted bread filled with fatty ham cuts.

In rhythm with the noise of the wheels over the uneven roadbed his thoughts echoed and re-echoed in his head: "I must maintain a philosophic calm: nothing can destroy us unless we cave in. . . . What I am feeling now is common to anyone who has suffered guilt in not providing for his family. . . . I must assure Julie I am happy about the coming child. . . . Fortitude is a cement that will hold despair in place. . . ."

He must not allow his terrifying defeats to incinerate his love to paint, his view of nature and its life-giving meaning. That would turn out fragmented work. The future would be worse because he would have only crippled visions to display.

It was good to leave the train and start the long walk down the trail to the Hermitage.

Ernest Hoschedé ended the drama by abandoning the Gagne Petit, leaving his wife, children and home behind, settling in Brussels where he opened another, smaller business.

Legrand, former associate of Durand-Ruel, who had conducted the 1877 auction at the Hôtel Drouot, decided that if the French would not accept the Impressionists the Americans might. Were they not a free-spirited adventuresome people who responded to new ideas? His enthusiasm convinced Camille and his confreres, particularly since Legrand was paying all the expenses involved.

For his show in New York, Legrand chose half a dozen of Camille's paintings from Montmorency, the Hermitage, Montfoucault; Monet's scenes from Argenteuil; Degas's café concerts; Renoir's bathers in the Seine; Sisley's country scenes around Marly; Morisot's characterful oil paintings of young girls.

Julie was busy from dawn to dark cooking, cleaning the house, laundering the clothes and linens, raising food, caring for the children, among whom she sometimes included Camille. Fortunately, in a better time, they had bought a cow, and had milk; the boys churned the butter. Setting out for his day's work, Camille ruminated, "Julie works only to feed and clothe her brood. She receives no fulfillment from the painting. I cannot understand how she gets through the days. She should hate me. Perhaps she does at times. I have let her down."

Père Tanguy managed to sell another painting from his window display, sending Camille the twenty dollars instead of applying it against his account. Murer and Chocquet bought small pastels for a couple of dollars each; Caillebotte bought a large *Bouquet of Flowers;* Mary Cassatt invited him to her Sunday afternoons at home, where he met her American friends and sold an occasional drawing for five or ten dollars, since his name was unknown to them. Julie's vegetable garden flourished, her rabbits, chickens and pigeons proliferated, some of which she took to market; their fruit trees bore good crops. Whatever money Camille took in he paid to the landlord so they could continue to have a roof over their heads. He spent long days in Paris trying to interest someone, anyone, in his work, returned to Pontoise to find his wife lovingly tending her flowers or in the kitchen preparing the family's supper, straight of body, carrying her child with strength and beauty.

The fields shimmered with the heat of summer.

3

In the fall the World's Fair was held at the Champ-de-Mars, the vast garden closed in by the military school and Chaillot Hill. An exhibition of new machinery and materials, bigger than the one in the Palais de l'Industrie in 1867, it was fuel to the city's economy and spirits.

Durand-Ruel had managed to retain his gallery on the Rue Le Peletier; he borrowed some money and put up an exhibition of the group variously known as the School of 1830, the Barbizon School or the Fontainebleau School, which had become totally neglected, the artists all now dead. He hung over three hundred canvases. Camille went in to see his old friend, who had not shown or sold a picture of the Impressionists since the debacle of their group exhibition four years before. Durand-Ruel had kept up his friendships with the painters, waiting for the day when fortune would stop standing on its head and somersault back to it feet. Once again Camille was staggered by the beauty and incisiveness of the Corots, Daubignys, Rousseaus.

"It's the most gratifying group of paintings I've ever seen," he told the dealer. "They have to sell. There's nothing in the art world to equal them."

"I hope so," Durand-Ruel replied in a prayerful tone.

"Otherwise I shall be hopelessly in debt again. There's no way the press can dismiss this body of work. It's the best France has produced."

No one attacked the show. Neither did anyone display interest. The press was languid. Some viewers came, bought next to nothing.

Soon after, Camille received a letter from the painter Marcellin Desboutin asking if he could bring out to Pontoise Diego Martelli, one of Italy's most respected art historians and critics, who was collecting French paintings for an exhibit to be held in Florence. Martelli had asked to see representative canvases from each period, "to study progress and growth."

Starved for serious attention, Camille cleared the space around his best easel, put up his paintings from Montmorency, Louveciennes, the Hermitage, Pontoise. Unlike the good Dr. Paul Gachet, who had walked around them waving his arms, bubbling with excitement, Martelli sat calmly before the paintings, giving no sign except a mounting flush in his cheeks and a sharp raising of his eyebrows, confining his comments to a leather-covered pad he had drawn from an inner coat pocket.

After an hour and some fifty representative pictures, Camille sent Lucien for coffee, sat down on a stool opposite Martelli and waited for his response. The Italian spoke a fluent French, albeit accented. He rose, placed the fingers of one hand lightly on Camille's shoulder.

"Mon ami, this has been an amazing experience. These are the most realized paintings in Europe." He likened the work to the Italian Macchiaioli group, whom he was sponsoring. "I am charmed by your tonality. In your translation is reflected all the effects of nature itself; all the sensations which the soul of the artist has experienced."

Camille looked beseechingly at Desboutin. Desboutin said quietly:

"He has toured Europe looking for pictures. He knows whereof he speaks."

"Would you permit me to take these paintings of the Hermitage and Pontoise to Florence? I will of course pay all expenses and I can guarantee you the sale of both."

Camille quivered. To be shown in Florence! Where the Renaissance had flowered. Home of Michelangelo, where he had carved *David* in the Duomo workyard, painted *The Bathers* fresco in the Great Hall of the Signoria in competition with Leonardo da Vinci. To have his paintings shown in Florence and New York, surely that meant that the Parisian dealers must be in an insensible stupor? After Diego Martelli left with the two chosen canvases, he wrote to Eugène Murer:

"I have received the 20 francs you sent me by my boy Lucien. Many thanks. . . . I am still waiting for the thing that shall deliver me out of this hell of inaction. Mademoiselle Cassatt paid me a visit, also Desboutin and the Italian man of letters came to see me. He thinks so highly of my art that I am confused and can hardly bring myself to believe what he says. . . ."

Jean Baptiste Faure, returning from an operatic tour, big-voiced, big-eyed, big head of hair, also big on income, was famished for new paintings. The Pissarros were rescued. He selected two Hermitage landscapes, paying three hundred and forty dollars for both. Julie, big of belly, stared at the money dumfounded:

"Sweet Jesus."

When in Paris, now that he had a franc to spare, he would end his days at the Café de la Nouvelle Athènes where he would be likely to find Monet, Manet, Degas or the painter Desboutin, who had sat for Degas's shattering *Absinthe Drinkers;* such sympathetic critics as Paul Alexis, Georges Rivière, who had done the brochure for their 1877 catalogue; George Moore, English writer and friend of James McNeill Whistler, who was now scandalizing London by his eccentric dress, manners and decorative paintings such as *Arrangements* and *Nocturnes.*

George Moore twitted him. "Pissarro, with your white hair and flowing beard you look like Moses." Degas added:

"Carrying his canvases under his arm like the tablets of the Ten Commandments."

Laughter was precious to them. This day there was a droll tale about a musician named Cabaner who had bought a replica of the Venus de Milo. When the cast was delivered Cabaner found the Venus too tall for his ceiling. He cut off her head so that she would fit comfortably in a corner of his studio. When Monet rebelled, saying, "Her face is beautiful," Cabaner replied defensively, "I like the rest of her better."

They were no longer the tightly unified group that had coalesced at the Café Guerbois. Edouard Manet refused to show with them; Renoir had decamped; Degas had estranged several of the more sensitive souls with his coruscating humor; Claude Monet was growing reluctant, saying:

"We've taken three falls. I could possibly sustain a fourth but no more. It's not true that it's better to be hanged together than separately. Perhaps each of us has to find his own way through this miasmic swamp."

Camille and Caillebotte were again left to fight the battle for a new exhibit.

"I'll find the place," Caillebotte volunteered. "And pay the rent. You assemble the painters."

In spite of their efforts they failed to put together an Impressionist exhibition for 1878. Camille felt a sense of loss; this showing was the one opportunity all year to display a gamut of their work. The critical abuse stung, but it was better to display and be beaten than have the canvases unseen, piled against the walls and on shelves in a studio. Caillebotte comforted him:

"Don't be discouraged, Pissarro. We'll show next year."

"We'd better start organizing right now." Camille was grimly determined. "If we fail to show two years in a row the Impressionist movement will be finished."

He was forty-eight years old, too old a dog to learn new tricks. The sad truth was that he was good for nothing but painting. If he got a job, any kind of a job, there would be more security; but he would be half dead. What good was a half-dead husband and father?

Though Julie was approaching forty and had grown heavier, she was an attractive woman, her fine, dark hair worn in a long braid over her right shoulder, expressive eyes, clear smooth skin. He was deeply and irrevocably fond of her. They still enjoyed their physical love and partook of it generously. Whatever quarrels they had arose not out of their feelings for each other but from external sources: the failure of the first exhibition, Durand-Ruel's withdrawal, the near impossibility of selling anything for more than a modest sum, frequently covering only half the cost of the canvas and paint; or simply selling nothing at all. He would continue painting, and Julie was going to bear children until nature itself put a stop to the process. But deep within them they carried unfulfilled desires. Julie for the flower shop where she could display her talent and love for flowers, Camille to lose his anonymity, to be recognized, to find a place in the sun. The indication that the years had not been worthless, that one was not a victim of vanity and self-delusion.

One compensation for survival was a brochure written and published by Théodore Duret, *The Impressionist Painters*. Duret stated that the Impressionists were descended from the naturalist painters and had as their fathers Corot and Courbet, with the admirable Chardin and Watteau as earlier anteced- ents. He wrote sections on Monet, Sisley and Morisot, and then moved on to the painting of Camille Pissarro:

Pissarro, among the Impressionists, is where one finds the point of view of the purely naturalist painter. He sees nature by simplifying it, and in its permanent aspects. A painter of the rustic site, of the open countryside, he renders by solid treatment the tilled harvested fields, trees flowering or bared by winter, roads lined with pruned elms and hedges, rough paths buried under thick woods. He loves village houses with gardens around them, farmyards with domestic animals, ponds where geese and ducks splash. His canvases convey to the highest degree the sensations of space and solitude. . . .

Duret sent a message to Pontoise saying he had recom- mended Camille's *Storm Effects* to a collector, Deudon. He added that the only art criticism he had read was in *Le Temps,* castigating his monograph, and continued: ". . . It's enough to give one cholera and yellow fever. For the moment I can't add to my collection, but as soon as I have some free capital I'll think of you."

Camille had spent a good part of the month in Paris, tracking down sales and minor dealers, finding a new agent, Portier, on the Rue Lepic; visiting the aging Rachel. Julie wrote on the back of Duret's letter:

"I'm sending you Duret's letter you see he hasn't had much luck now 15 days have passed for nothing and you aren't any richer and no pictures no work really I don't understand the winter is coming and you spent all summer in Paris and you tell me yourself that everyone you know has left but what do you do you should at least tell me so I know you're not lazy I'm really tired of this life Lucien is better he's taking his medicine every morning you haven't told me if he should take it in his soup I hope as soon as you have a few sous you will come"

In October Camille again rented a small apartment, at 18 Rue des Trois Frères, to show his pictures and for Julie and the boys to live in over the winter, away from the cold of the Hermitage. Ludovic Rodolphe, named after their beloved Piette, was born there on November 21, Julie being delivered by Dr. de Bellio. As soon as she was about, she decided that the time had come to take a firm stand.

"Camille, Lucien is fifteen years old. Now that we have a fourth child, he must help support us."

Camille had known this moment would arrive and that Julie was right. He mustered his defense, swallowed hard.

"We can't put him out at a menial job. It would be a cruel injustice to our oldest son to plunge him into the working class. He needs his education. At least two more years to finish the lycée . . ."

She interrupted.

"He can finish his education later, when you are earning us a living. Right now we need his few francs."

" . . . We could condemn him . . ."

She put her hands over her ears. *"Ventre affamé n'a pas d'oreille.* A hungry stomach has no ears."

Instead of arguing further, for the first time in their relationship she sent a letter to one of his family. She asked if Alfred could come quickly to their apartment in the Rue des Trois Frères. Alfred was growing stout, had a distinguished splash of gray at the temples, sported lush sideburns to compensate for a receding hairline. His quick enveloping glance at the small barren rooms showed him all he needed to know about his brother's fortunes. Julie told Alfred her plans for Lucien in front of Camille; she would not do it behind his back. When she had finished, Alfred turned to Camille and said emphatically:

"Julie is right. And you know it. Lucien must help. I'll find him a job with a merchant with whom I do business."

Miserable, Camille hung his head.

It took Alfred only a few days to get Lucien apprenticed to a drapery shop for two dollars a week, a small sum but enough to give Julie a sense of relief. At least there would be a little something coming in for the three younger boys, two of whom were enrolled in school for the winter. Camille vowed that he would somehow paint better and sell more.

He need not have been concerned. In two weeks Lucien returned home, discharged. Alfred arrived shortly after, enraged, stringing his hand back and forth along the gold chain across his chest.

"Lucien dogged it! He wanted to be fired."

"That's not true!" Lucien cried. "I was just clumsy. No one showed me how to wrap the packages. I tied the string too tight and bunched up the cloth. The customers complained."

When Alfred had departed, and Lucien sought refuge in a bedroom, Camille said:

"The fault is mine. I brought him up to be an artist. Not to wrap draperies."

"You've condemned him to poverty, that's what you've done," Julie cried. "He'll be a drain on us, who have nothing." Her eyes emitted puffs of anger. "You'll do the same with the other boys. We're damned."

She sank to her knees, her breast heaving.

"You have defeated me. I am back on the Rue Neuve!"

4

With the arrival of 1879 Camille, from the inside of the cauldron, could see no evidence of the Impressionists being accepted, or of any extension of their collectors. Claude Monet was destitute, living off loans from Manet and the few francs he could implore by his letters, writing to Durand-Ruel: "I am obliged to solicit, almost beg for my existence, not having a penny to buy canvases and paint. . . ."

Renoir, after a brief period of being sponsored by the Charpentier family, was again without enthusiasts. Cézanne was living in Aix-en-Provence with Hortense and his son, with no one looking at his work. Degas had recovered a fraction of the money he had laid out to save his brother from bankruptcy in the New Orleans cotton market. He was happy in his relationship with Mary Cassatt, yet he was forced to make "salable" pictures which he disliked. Guillaumin was slogging along in the government office and buying lottery tickets. Sisley was "vegetating" in Paris but planning to submit to the upcoming Salon.

Even though it was deep winter and snowing Camille returned to Pontoise for bouts of work, painting the boulevards of Pontoise, the street of the Hermitage, the rabbit warren in his own back garden. When the snowfall stopped, he painted the bottomlands of St. Antoine, a view of nearby Ennery, the countryside of Auvers with a peasant mounted on a donkey, portraits of an occasional neighbor or farm girl. He was willing to let no part of it go unrecorded, the terrain or its life. Save for a visit to her sister Félicie or Joséphine, an occasional dinner at Murer's bakery shop, Julie was no less isolated in Paris than in the Hermitage, alone except for the monomaniacal painters who came to see her husband.

"I know you despise the word 'patience,' " Camille told her; "but it's the only ledge we have left to cling to. I have started work on the next Independent exhibition for April and May."

"It's *fou*. The shows failed three times already."

He had no talent for the *art populaire* which was covering the kiosks of Paris with garishly colored posters advertising the Folies-Bergère or Concert des Ambassadeurs. He had painted six or eight fans, which would bring in some francs. They were the only potboilers of which he was capable.

"I know you're trying your best," she said, succumbing, putting her arms around him. "But I added up our bills. We must get a lot of money right away."

When she stormed at him he retreated into a cool forest of self-preservation; but when she was gentle, he felt a rush of affection. He came up with a plan to ameliorate their strapped condition.

"I'll ask Caillebotte and Murer to each choose five paintings of any size, as large as thirty-five by forty-six. At a price of twenty dollars a canvas or one hundred dollars for each man."

Julie's eyes lit up with expectation.

"Will they accept?"

"It's a wealth of painting for only one hundred dollars."

Caillebotte met him in Pontoise within a couple of days of receiving Camille's summons. He had figured his finances before leaving his office, for he reasoned that Camille's message had been a cry for help. He loved Camille and knew that he would not be called except in an emergency.

By dusk Caillebotte had chosen a spectrum of village and countryside scenes. He paid over the hundred dollars Camille had asked, took the last train back to Paris, triumphantly carrying two of the canvases. Camille was to deliver the rest.

Murer also journeyed to the Hermitage, albeit reluctantly, agreed to take his favorite five paintings of Camille's redoubtable stock, then explained:

"I can't pay you a hundred dollars all at once. However I'm prepared to leave twenty dollars with you; I'll pay off the balance as I have money to spare."

Julie threw her arms about Camille's neck, cried in a combined tone of anguish and relief:

"You've pulled the fat out of the fire."

"The fire in our bellies is not so easily extinguished. But at least we're saved until the next exhibition."

*　　*　　*

Caillebotte searched for a gallery or an available apartment for their fourth show. He expected they would have greater difficulty assembling the participants. Some of the painters were adamant. Renoir was not to be persuaded, though he had been rejected at the last three Salons. Cézanne responded that he did not want to muddy his paints again with the offal of abuse. Sisley was soft, tentative.

"I'm genuinely sorry, Pissarro. It's not that I lack backbone or am afraid of *Le Figaro* or *Le Temps*. It's just that I'm not supporting my wife and two children. My English family will help only if I submit to the Salon and make my way there. They consider the Impressionist cause hopeless, that it always will be." Then, pleadingly, "You understand, don't you?"

Berthe Morisot told him:

"I simply don't have anything worthy to show this year. I'm not leaving you, I'm merely taking a recess. I haven't been painting well, perhaps because I am *enceinte*."

Camille was troubled by losing their only woman.

"Couldn't we show some of your earlier works?"

Berthe Morisot was firm.

"Things I've already shown? I think not. I'll have some good paintings for you next year."

Claude Monet, who with Camille had put together the first showing, was too weary, debt-ridden and heartsick at Léonie's declining health to agree to anything.

"I just can't face it, Pissarro. I couldn't even choose the pictures."

Camille saw the fourth exhibition slipping through his fingers.

"Could I do it for you? I'll pick those already framed so you'll have no cost."

"I'm too beaten. I couldn't stand another lashing. We don't sell enough to cover our costs. The horse is dead, Pissarro; stop trying to hitch it to a wagon."

Guillaumin had to be excused too. He had been ill for months. Camille went to visit him in his dreary room, taking him Edmond de Goncourt's recently published *La Fille Elisa*. His meager salary was being used for doctors and medicines. He had lost weight, his skin was green; there was no one to care for him.

"I should have married," the thirty-eight-year-old muttered. "At least I'd have a wife to care for me. Wives do nurse their husbands, don't they? I've been told they do."

Camille comforted his friend, thinking meanwhile, out of harsh experience:

"It's better this way. Corot was right, never marry. He doesn't have to worry about feeding hungry children."

He was instantly ashamed of his thoughts, apologized to his four sons.

Edgar Degas saved the exhibition.

"Of course I'm going to show with you. So will Mademoiselle Cassatt. I've chosen several of her best works. We decided that when we heard that Berthe Morisot wants a year's sabbatical."

Mary Cassatt brushed Degas aside with a raised eyebrow. "I choose my own paintings."

Mary Cassatt was now thirty-four, Degas forty-four. He was very much the aristocrat, sporting his silk hat while walking the boulevards of Paris, his light-colored trousers right-fitting, wearing a three-inch batwing collar and formal cravat. He still wore blue glasses and carried an umbrella in all kinds of weather. A crankily fastidious man, he never allowed crumbs to drop on his suit. To wear loose-fitting bohemian shirts, velvet jackets or smocks would have been an affront to his banker antecedents. In his studio he worked in a starched white medical coat. Mary Cassatt dressed in a long well-tailored gown, even when working Degas's newly acquired etching press.

They both lived near the Place Pigalle and the Café de la Nouvelle Athènes, the Cassatt family in an apartment house at 13 Avenue Trudaine on the Butte Montmartre. She rode horseback in the Bois de Boulogne . . . alone.

Cassatt was buying from her friends among the Impressionists out of awe and admiration. She was highly respected by the group for having gone through a rigorous academic training in Philadelphia and then turning to their movement. Early in 1878 her parents and unmarried sister Lydia had ended their journeyings and settled into Mary Cassatt's house on the Montmartre hill with a balcony overlooking the rooftops of Paris.

No one knew for sure the relationship between the woman-shy Degas and the regally independent and talented Mary Cassatt. He had never worked with or praised a woman artist before. Of Berthe Morisot, who was also a good friend, he said, "Her painting, a little vaporous, hides drawing that is of the surest."

There was no doubt that Mary Cassatt and Degas revered each other. Was it love? "Probably," the painters said. Were they having an affair? "Possibly," their group said; "but under extreme difficulties. Mary Cassatt is suffocated by her adoring family who, out of affection, have to know where she is every hour of the day and night.''

She brought Degas into her home only on a social occasion for fear her parents would ask questions. Mary Cassatt came often to Degas's studio for her painting guidance, since she considered Degas *the* master if not *her* master.

"We'll both work with you, Pissarro," Degas declared heartily. "Your insistence has earned our support."

The resourceful Gustave Caillebotte found a first-floor apartment at 28 Avenue de l'Opéra with easy access from the well-traveled street, as well as a series of large window-lighted rooms. He was elated.

"At that location we're going to get thousands of visitors," he told Camille. "I've already paid the rent for April and May and have a written lease in my pocket. Go to our regulars, tell them we have a great place to show their paintings and bring them back in."

Claude Monet said mournfully, "I've become so desperate for sales I would show in a latrine on the Boulevard Haussmann."

Of the original group labeled Impressionists in 1874, only Degas, Monet and Camille were willing to participate. Caillebotte took them to dinner, saying over a Dubonnet:

"Since we are only five we are going to have to invite back your protective foliage from the first exhibition: Bracquemond, Cals, Lebourg, Rouart. That makes nine. Not enough. We'll have to scour the town for a few more painters who have come at least part way along our lighted road."

Degas brought in his friend Tillot and a newcomer named Zandomeneghi; also a twenty-seven-year-old named Jean Louis Forain, whom Degas had been training as a printmaker. Camille contributed two of Piette's scenes from Montfoucault, as well as a good artisan painter named Somm. With Madame Bracquemond, exhibiting for the first time, they now had a total of fifteen. During the hanging Camille heard Caillebotte say in an aside to Degas:

"Pissarro is delightful in his enthusiasm and faith."

Camille and Degas hung the 1879 show in the eight large rooms of the apartment with the manual help of Caillebotte and one of the brawny designers from his office. Camille showed thirty-eight works, including three of his paintings owned by Gauguin and several acquired by Caillebotte, demonstrating to the public that Pissarro canvases had been bought by a respectable marine architect and a reputable stockbroker.

He also exhibited twelve fans and four pastels. He had begun using light-colored pastels, combined chalk and pigment, in stick form, rather like crayons; the finished work was more of a painting than a drawing.

The attendance was large. Caillebotte's ticket taker counted fifteen thousand four hundred viewers. Durand-Ruel, who spent an hour each day wandering unrecognized among them, told Camille:

"You're attracting as many as the first exhibition, but it is again an occasion of insults and jokes, surpassing in stupidity those that the first effort occasioned."

Camille disagreed. He reasoned that the scurrility had lessened. At the last Salon he had found paintings with subtle changes in subject matter, brushwork, naturalness, indicating that the Impressionists had something to say, although considered hideous in view of academic values.

"The public is not yet sure it understands our flowing form, dazzling light and shadow, our unorthodox colors. But I believe they are looking earnestly for the first time. *Le Figaro* and *Le Temps* have had their vitriolic sting damped down. Other journals are beginning to interpret our works with a new vocabulary."

The fourth exhibition took in more than two thousand one hundred dollars, leaving twelve hundred dollars after expenses. Camille received close to ninety dollars from the sale of a number of fans, a couple of watercolors, a painting to Mary Cassatt. Her work was enthusiastically received, which pleased Degas, who also sold several pieces. Fortunately Tillot and Forain, artists Caillebotte had described as "protective coloring," had each sold a piece or two. Everyone took home some francs and congratulated Camille as the leading spirit of the exhibition, though he insisted on sharing the credit with Degas and Caillebotte, who never mentioned any return of the money he had laid out for rent.

"I'll tell you one thing," Camille told the group at the Café de la Nouvelle Athènes when they met the day after the closing. "We'll show again in 1880 with a bigger and more successful exhibition."

They puffed contentedly on their pipes and drank the congratulatory wine Caillebotte also contributed.

5

That summer Paul Gauguin came out to Pontoise with his wife and three children. They stayed in the Pissarro house for a month. Mette was resentful about having her husband spend his vacation painting with Camille; she would have preferred to take her children and Paul home to her family in Copenhagen. However her major cause of concern was that Paul retain his success on the Bourse.

"He's a splendid businessman, really," she told Julie, "we must not let him incapacitate himself. He does so well, and we love him for it."

The tall blond, blue-eyed Mette was a fair companion, although more sober and unlaughing than others of the wives. She was twenty-nine, Julie forty, but they had something important in common: both considered that painting should be a hobby practiced on Sundays and holidays. About Camille, Julie could only say that he was possessed.

"But why should your husband put himself in the jaw of the wolf?" she asked Mette. "The wolf is poverty. Your husband is earning money to raise his family."

Though he still considered himself a Sunday painter, Gauguin had moved to a larger house on the Right Bank in the Rue Carcel, owned by the painter Jobbé-Duval, with a large studio separated from the rest of the residence where he could work without distraction. He had learned to sculpt from a neighbor and had shown a robust talent with wood and clay. He did not think it tactful to offer to pay Camille for room and board so he bought another two paintings, one of the Hermitage gardens, one of the sun setting over the Pontoise countryside. Julie now had enough money to feed them all; and additional cash for other needs. She was freed to enjoy the Gauguins' visit.

Camille and Gauguin left the house each day just after dawn. Camille coached him in the manner he had used with Paul Cézanne seven years before. Gauguin took the stance of student to master; all aggressiveness, braggadocio, attempts to impress were gone. He had been studying the Pissarros he owned and copying them to gain a knowledge of Camille's technique. He was a fast learner, with what Camille found to be an omnivorous appetite for instruction.

"I don't hinder you in your work, do I," he asked Camille, "when I ask how you achieve certain effects of light on foliage, or when you take the time to slash my drawings with your charcoal?"

Camille shrugged away Gauguin's fears. He had taken considerable pleasure in instructing Cézanne, Béliard, Guillaumin, Renoir, when they painted together. "Though admittedly," he told Gauguin, "I learned as much from Monet and Renoir as they did from me. Cézanne, too, in his way. Many artists are teachers. If I could not have been a painter I think I would have liked to become a teacher in a lycée. We had some wonderful ones in the Pension Savary in Passy. They enriched my life."

In 1876 Gauguin had sent to the Salon *Landscape at Viroflay*. Perhaps because it was indistinguishable from the hundreds of surrounding pictures it had been accepted. But he had judged that the Beaux-Arts was a dead end, repeating to Camille what he had heard Edouard Manet say at the Café de la Nouvelle Athènes:

"Color is a matter of taste and sensibility. However it's necessary to have something to say. Without that, good night! No one is a painter unless he loves painting more than anything else."

The three Gauguin children were all under five so it was up to the three older Pissarro boys, Lucien, Georges, Félix, to amuse them with games in the garden. There were occasional squabbles about the simple toys; tears, screams, which the two mothers quickly took care of; for the most part the seven children got along well. Mette was a relentless housekeeper and, although Julie hired a neighborhood girl for the laundry and washing of the dishes, Mette was usually behind her, wiping up. Julie was amused by Mette's meticulousness.

"It comes from being raised in Copenhagen," she explained. "My mother was fanatical on cleanliness. Paul says I go around with a magnifying glass, eagerly searching for something to be polished."

Julie was grateful for the company. She even allowed Mette to flavor the foods being cooked on the wood stove. Mette did not care much for Camille, his carelessly worn clothes, the long beard, which disoriented her. However she was delighted to be able to speak a little Danish with him. Camille's vocabulary, never large to start with, and now grown rusty, was sufficient from his years on St. Thomas to preserve some of the more common phrases. When she learned that he was still a Danish citizen she came moderately close to forgiving him for leading her husband down the garden path.

Camille Léonie Monet died in September of 1879. She was buried in the village of Vétheuil. Camille and Julie attended the funeral with other members of the Impressionist group. It was a sad ocasion. All of the artists, their wives and mistresses, had loved Léonie, who was always as cheerful as her colorful gowns. She had never been unkind and had given up a life of luxury for the exigencies of Claude Monet's unpredictable life. She had been one of the most beautiful and patiently acquiescent models in Paris.

The parish priest read the funeral service. It was the usually unsentimental Edouard Manet who pronounced the eulogy:

"She is not dead. She will never die or disappear. Monet has immortalized her glorious face and exquisite figure. *Requiescat in pace.*"

During the autumn Camille painted *Street Scene, Pontoise,* a quiet eternal pastoral: a peasant woman in a tan skirt, blue blouse and apron, and carrying a basketful of food from the market, her back to the viewer; as was the high-wheeled cart drawn by a brown horse with a peasant couple on the front seat. Gray houses with burnt umber roofs and red chimneys lined the road, with a green hillock closing in the rear. The smooth dirt passage was of a dozen subtly gradated color patterns as were the trees surrounding the houses and their shadows; on the viewer's left was a gas lantern projecting from a second-story wall of a building.

Path on a Hillside Near Pontoise portrayed a path winding mildly down the hill, a man and woman descending to their homes carrying bunches of freshly cut greens. The hillside rose sharply on their right; below them a stone-house village was scattered among rough greeneries, with a huge blue-gray sky sheltering them above. His brush strokes were shorter and gently applied. There was a fine hazy blending of the earth, the foliage, the peasants and the sky.

Toward the end of 1879 he received a letter from Durand-Ruel asking him to stop in the gallery during his next visit to Paris. Since Durand-Ruel was selling so little, Camille and the art world wondered by what series of miracles he managed to hang on.

When Camille entered the gallery he saw at once that it had a revitalized look. The dealer's desk was full of jotted notes and important-looking papers, his expressive eyes were wide with excitement.

"Good times have returned," he cried. "Recently I met Monsieur Feder, director of the famous Union Générale, the communal bank with a capital of twenty-five million francs and over two thousand shareholders. They're investing in the Balkans, Austria, Spain. Monsieur Feder is an art lover; he will put funds at my disposal for investment in various purchases."

"*Grâce à Dieu!*" Camille exclaimed. "Are we included in the 'various purchases'?"

The dealer's face was wreathed in a warm paternal smile.

"Assuredly. The Impressionists first of all! I haven't forgotten the poor artists I was forced to abandon in 1874. I am planning to organize a large exhibition of Impressionist works in the Rue St. Honoré on the old site of the Valentino concerts, most of which I intend to buy from your group, along with the best I managed to keep from earlier years."

Camille was trembling with relief, a profound thankfulness that the exacerbatingly painful past five years might be turning around.

"The results should be satisfying," he assured Camille, bunching together the papers on his desk as though he were once again an efficient businessman. "We will go back to our early schedule: I will buy one painting each month, at a higher price than before. Your days of anxiety will be over."

Camille felt a purple tinge climbing to his forehead. "We have been painfully grinding our nose against a rough stone wall. I must go home and tell Julie. Her burdens will be lifted."

Durand-Ruel laid a hand affectionately on Camille's shoulder.

"You can't know how bitter it has been for me, failing the group these years. That's over now. Bring me some canvases to choose from right after the New Year, and I will write you your first check."

Camille jumped onto the train for Pontoise. He could hardly contain his happiness.

6

He opened the envelope from Degas. Could Camille come to see him when he had a day to spare?

Camille went to Degas's tall, narrow, charming house on the Rue Pigalle. His ancient but spirited housekeeper, Sabine Neyt, led him up three flights of stairs but did not enter the studio, which was forbidden to her, as it was to all of Degas's aged housekeepers, the only kind he would employ.

As he stood in the doorway he realized why: the spacious room was a masterpiece of clutter. On the floor a neat pile of perhaps a thousand Daumier lithographs; another neat pile of all the Ingres prints Degas could afford; not so neat piles of old magazines, newspapers, colored posters, pamphlets; in a far corner a desk covered with hundreds of letters, notes, notices, largely unsorted and unanswered. There were tubes of paint, brushes, sketchbooks, half-finished canvases, articles of clothing everywhere. Degas alone understood the logic of this chaos; he could go to any desired object with the speed of a bird in flight. There were books on the shelves of one wall, on the other Mary Cassatt's newly completed oil painting of her mother and her brother Alexander's children. Camille knew about the engineer Alexander Cassatt because Mary had obliged him to buy several Pissarros "to start his modern collection." In a corner on a sturdy wooden table stood the etching press, its six spindles painted a bright red. Facing north under one gabled window was the inking stand, piles of dust-covered prints, the back copies of *Le Charivari* and *Le Figaro* stacked beneath it. Under the second window was a drawing table, and beneath it folios of safely covered drawings and watercolors. An easel with an ongoing canvas was turned to the wall.

Degas had been painting a plump nude model. When he saw Camille he called, "Welcome. I've been waiting for you." To the model he said, "You can go now. Come back on Thursday. You are a rare specimen. You have buttocks shaped like a ripe pear, like the Gioconda."

The young woman flushed with pride, dressed behind a screen and left. As she did Degas commented amusedly:

"She'll now be showing those buttocks all over Paris."

They went down to the second-floor dining room for lunch, where the furniture was as disciplined as Degas's studio was untidy. It was here and in his parlor that he kept his collection of Impressionists: Manet, Renoir, Sisley, Pissarro. He explained:

"Mary Cassatt and I are planning to start a publication to be called *Le Jour et la Nuit*. Original etchings each month; we'll also pull a few for sale purposes. We are funding the first issue. After that the subscriptions should support it; the stockbroker Ernest May has offered to help. We intend to invite Bracquemond, he's an expert, others who are qualified. You and I and Cassatt would be responsible for the main contributions. We think you are the best to help us bring Impressionism over to black and white. What do you say?"

Camille was delighted. While he ate Sabine's tender *biftec*, he told Degas:

"I enjoy printmaking. I've worked on Dr. Gachet's press, studies of Cézanne, my son Lucien."

"Good. Then it's settled." Degas chatted on, primarily about the only attachment he had apparently ever permitted himself.

"I invited Mademoiselle Cassatt to join us for lunch but her family is offended if she misses the midday meal with them. *C'est un problème*. Chains of gold are only a little less irksome than chains of brass. What she painted in the country looks very well in the studio light. It is much more firm and noble than what she did last year. She will show it in our next Impressionist exhibition."

Camille gazed up at Mary Cassatt's *Woman on a Divan* on the wall opposite. He thought it brilliantly achieved.

Degas's father had been an art collector, had frequently had painters and art historians in his home; but had thrown his son out when Edgar announced that he intended to become an artist.

"What?" screamed his cultured father. "Throw away your life on a *divertissement*, a pastime?"

Over coffee, Degas commented:

"You are a naive anarchist and I'm a hardhearted banker-family conservative. We are also the two best draftsmen among the Independents. I am a totally private man; you wear your heart on your impressionable sleeve. No art was ever less spontaneous than mine. Yet together I believe we can take etching beyond the present limited boundaries. I loathe landscape painting, but I detest even more the industrial growth that is throwing a blight of factory smoke over our countryside. Your rural paintings will be the finest set of portraits our once exquisite French countryside will have."

As they were leaving the dining room, Degas called to his housekeeper:

"I am having company for supper tonight."

The old woman replied, "No, monsieur, you will take your guests to the restaurant. I'm making marmalade this afternoon."

Camille imagined that Degas would explode. Instead he murmured contentedly:

"She makes the best marmalade in France."

Mary Cassatt arrived at three, dressed in a long beige gown with embroidery at the collar, cuffs and the shoe-length hem. She carried a neatly folded smock which she donned, covering her from neck to toe. They entered the studio and went directly to the rear of the large room. Degas began turning the six red spindles which moved one of his trial etchings through the rollers. On his left were the shelves holding containers of grounding material: acid-resistant wax, pitch, gum mastic, asphaltum with which the copper or zinc plates would be treated. On the near end of the studio he had created a small room for the acid bath into which the etched plates would be immersed. In the center of the south wall were a sink and drain but no faucet. Sabine had to carry up three gallons of water a day; but a pipe was connected to an outside downspout so that the dirty water could be drained into the courtyard. A wonderful visceral smell overlay the studio, a combination of kerosene, benzine, alcohol, charcoal, pumice and good white etching paper. The room was warm, for Degas had added a glowing brazier to his small fireplace on the entrance-door wall, saying no etching could go forward in a cold room.

Degas and Cassatt were planning to run off an etching each and invited Camille to join them. He did not know a great deal about the process but Degas was prepared to instruct him.

Degas had bought copper plates from the metal monger for the three of them. They set about polishing the surface with emery and pumice. The deeper scratches were ground out with a snakestone and charcoal block. The backside of the heavy plate was then coated with a resin that would protect it from the acid bath. Degas clamped it down to the rough table covered with old newspapers, ready to be worked.

Degas had decided to make his etching from an earlier drawing of Mary Cassatt at the Louvre. Mademoiselle Cassatt was using a drawing of her sister Lydia in her opera box. Camille chose from the portfolio he carried with him a scene of woods and undergrowth at the Hermitage. He covered the area below the intended skyline with acid-resistant liquid resin which was allowed to dry. The upper portion was then lightly sprinkled with an aquatint powder. He removed the plate from the table and held it over the brazier, causing the aquatint to melt and stick to it. The result was a finely dusted sky with bare unprotected plate showing through.

He followed Mary Cassatt to the acid bath, placing the plate in the tray containing the hydrochloric acid, and watched for a number of minutes as the solution bit down through the aquatinted area. As bubbles formed on the plate from the chemical reaction he gently brushed them away with a feather. He next pulled it from the tray, staining his fingers yellow in the process, and flooded it with water to remove the acid. The resin on the lower portion was removed with turpentine and he saw the effect of the first bath. Using a soft muslin, he rubbed black ink into the recessed areas, then carefully wiped clean the surface, leaving only the recessed ink of the sky. He was ready for his first test print.

He laid the plate in the bed of the press, took a sheet of thick trial paper from the large stack Degas had set close by. Wetting the paper, he placed it over the plate, then covered it with a heavy felt blanket. He turned the red spindles until the plate was squeezed through the press, the pressure of the top roller pushing the soft wet paper into the inked recesses of the plate. The image was transferred. Inspecting the test print, he perceived that the etching process was not an exact science. The sky was too light. He repeated the entire process several times, varying the amount of aquatint and also the length of time the plate spent in the acid bath. With each successive processing he was able to build the tone of the sky and enhance its character.

Degas had provided him with a ready-made engraving tool. Mary Cassatt used a stylus of her own. Because he was tentative about the process, Camille worked the bolder lines first, allowing them to etch in the acid bath, then scratched in the lighter lines and shadows, again pulling a copy to examine. He realized that if he had used a sharper needle he would have achieved a stronger line.

Little by little he added the undergrowth image, trees, figure, buildings, varying the amount of aquatint and ink in each pull as he became accustomed to the process. There was a mounting exaltation as, step by step, his etching became more subtle in effect and stronger in structure. As a print-maker, it was not only necessary to be a good draftsman, one had to be a good technician.

With the light of day fading and the studio growing dim, the three artists covered their plates for the night.

Camille scribbled a few lines to Julie, telling her that he would be staying over with Rachel while working with Degas on etchings for his new magazine; then bought a stamp at the Bureau de Poste and watched the clerk drop his letter into a sack designated *Oise*.

He reached Degas's at eight the following morning, with Cassatt close behind. They all set to work at once. Camille blocked out the completed area of his plate with liquid resin, covered the other portions with a soft ground made of beeswax and asphaltum, and again placed his drawing over the plate. He first used his fingernail, then a sharp pencil, pushing down onto the plate to retrace parts of the image that needed deeper incising to achieve bolder and darker shadows. Based on the previous day's work, he allowed the plate to etch in the acid bath for twenty minutes.

"Now comes the most exciting moment," they exclaimed when Camille's last pull on the rough paper had satisfied him; "the first print of the entire plate." Once more paper and plate passed through the rollers of the press. He lifted the felt blanket, peeled up the print. Degas and Mary Cassatt gathered round, delighted.

The studio was pervaded by a sense of adventure, of experimentation and discovery. The three of them had equal talent, drive and imagination. They respected and admired each other. The room resounded not only with artistic creativity but with the warmth of comradeship, the thrill of working together, praising, criticizing, suggesting as they made successive pulls. Camille's two portraits pulled off Dr. Gachet's press had been more like pencil sketches. This was a complete etching, a new and stimulating activity.

They operated with sure movements, kept out from under one another's feet, and prepared the first issue of *Le Jour et la Nuit*. It was also a revelation to observe how smoothly and affectionately Degas and Cassatt worked together, their tensions dissolved in the acid bath of workmanship. They were a superbly matched pair but grimly determined not to acknowledge it, both frightened by their attraction, held apart by a mutual horror of intimacy.

When Mary Cassatt left to rejoin her family, Degas showed Camille the portraits he and Mary Cassatt had painted of each other, commenting:

"Mademoiselle Cassatt and I work together better when

you are present because we are more relaxed. You'll come back every free day until our first issue is ready, won't you?"

It took him a month coming into Paris between surges of painting to complete his etchings for the magazine, with six versions and pulls on the press. He took to Pontoise with him two prepared zinc plates on which to work in his studio. After weeks indoors in the inclement weather he sent them in to Degas, who wrote him, after running the plates through the press:

"I hurried to Mademoiselle Cassatt with your parcel. She congratulates you, as I do. Here are the proofs. The prevailing blackish or grayish shade comes from the zinc, which is greasy in itself and retains the printer's black. . . . What did you blacken your ground with to get that bistre tone behind the drawing? It is very pretty.

"Try something a little larger with a better plate."

7

January 1880 was the beginning of a new decade. Throughout the group there was new optimism.

Since they could evoke no interest in their prints, Camille and Degas began painting women's fans, though they disdained this *art populaire*. The ordinary fans sold in the shops had ornate themes. Camille and Degas, respecting their own talents, decorated theirs with compositions made from their serious drawings; for Camille landscapes, ballet rehearsals for Degas. The fans, the first on the Paris market to be painted with professionalism, sold well for between five and eight dollars.

Edouard Manet, seemingly the most fortunate of the Batignolles, had been seized with acute pain and weakness of the legs the previous autumn. He had fallen down while leaving his studio, then begun to walk with a severe limp. One doctor diagnosed it as paralysis of a nerve center; another gave his verdict of a vascular disturbance.

"Approaching age," they commented, though Edouard Manet was just forty-eight.

His condition was pronounced incurable by a conference of his doctors. He moved with considerable difficulty but managed to get to his studio most days. When Camille stopped off for a visit he found Manet painting a large canvas, *The Bar at the Folies-Bergère,* which Camille considered surpassed the magnificence of his *Luncheon on the Grass* or *Olympia.* Manet would not discuss his illness. When they reviewed the political scene in which France was having difficulty maintaining its Republic, Manet possessed total clarity. However as the months passed his physical condition deteriorated. He became confined to a wheelchair and then to his bed, where he could handle only light projects: drawings, pastels. He received loving attention from his wife, Suzanne, his brother Eugène and Eugène's wife, Berthe Morisot. The illness put an end to his relationship with Eva Gonzalès, who married an engraver, Henri Guerard.

Camille began using even shorter brush strokes to enliven his texture, softer color to enhance the light filtering through the scene. His people had been symbolic characters, unidentified, swallowed up by the surrounding landscape. Now they took over the scene; strongly delineated men and women picking apples, peas, potatoes; a portrait of his son Georges, a neighbor woman spinning, harvesters in the fields, farm wives at the market. He had little rapport with Millet's rendering of peasants in *The Angelus* or *The Reapers;* he omitted the sentimental, sought the reality of their lives, along with the hardships of working the land. It was not that he was tired of his themes but rather that he had need of a vernal rebirth.

He also began working in fast-drying tempera and light-colored pastel chalks which could be laid on top of each other without the delay of slow-drying oils. He achieved lighter tones this way. Since he made them more quickly, he offered them more cheaply. He was now almost fifty years old, a time when fantasies begin to fade and hope is hard to come by.

He made seventeen etchings in 1880, giving them endless time. He spent long days in Degas's studio, though they pulled few copies of their work. Even those few were unsalable. It would doubtless take as long to establish Impressionist prints as it was taking for the oils. Time was not really the issue. Survival was.

From the work in Degas's studio he developed a piquant relationship with Mary Cassatt. She hung his pictures in her apartment and sang their praises to her American friends, occasionally selling one. When he came into Paris they visited the galleries together; an incongruous couple, he with his long white beard and rumpled clothing; she elegantly coiffed and tailored in gowns made for her by Parisian couturiers.

Her parents had accepted her friendship with Degas, who came from their own social class; but what was she doing with this peasant painter with whom she was seen walking the boulevards, chatting amiably, obviously enjoying his company?

Edgar Degas was amused. If he had to have a rival for her admiration, then Camille Pissarro was the right choice. It was the perfect *ménage à trois*. When Camille completed an oil painting of a busy, tumultuous market scene in Pontoise, women shoppers and sellers amidst hanging slabs of beef and pork, Degas scanned the canvas with approval, then asked:

"Are these women a bit idealized?"

"No. Neither are they brutally realistic."

"Ah!" Degas exclaimed mischievously. "Those angels who go to market."

When he took his paintings of the hills of Valhermeil, the village itself, its gardens, cottages, setting sun, to Durand-Ruel, the dealer was enthusiastic but he still had no money with which to pay for the one a month he would buy.

"The financing is assured," he reiterated. "The papers are drawn and signed by Monsieur Feder and the Union Générale, but I do not yet have the cash."

How to weather the months when he was already living marginally? His largest debt was to Père Tanguy, though Tanguy was still taking paintings as security. Each week there were a few francs for Julie from the sale of a fan or pastel.

"Durand-Ruel claims our money is guaranteed," he told her.

"Could you get a paper from him that I could show the shopkeepers saying that he is buying and the money is coming?" she asked.

Durand-Ruel's letter took off some of the pressure.

The Fifth Impressionist Exhibition was to open on April 1, 1880. He ran into instant trouble when Gauguin submitted three Pontoise landscapes. Claude Monet, angry at what he called "outrageous amateurs," cried:

"The 'little church' has become a banal school which opens its doors to the first dauber who shows up."

Camille consoled Gauguin. "The same things were said about Paul Cézanne's work when I first sought his admission. Now he is accepted."

Degas insisted on bringing in a couple of his friends who worked outside Impressionism. Caillebotte opposed the admission of Raffaëlli, whom Camille admired. Camille refused admission to a painter named Robert who had shown with them in 1874 but refused to submit paintings for the subsequent hangings.

As the dissensions grew, Caillebotte wrote to Camille:

"What is to become of our exhibition? We ought to continue only in an artistic direction, the sole direction that is of interest to us all. I ask, therefore, that a show should be composed of all those who have contributed real interest to the subject, that is, you, Monet, Renoir, Sisley, Madame Morisot, Mademoiselle Cassatt, Cézanne, Guillaumin; if you wish, Gauguin, perhaps, Cordey and myself. That's all, since Degas refuses to show on such a basis. I would rather like to know wherein the public is interested in our individual disputes. . . . Isn't it our duty to support each other and to forgive each other's weaknesses rather than to tear ourselves down?"

When Camille went to Degas's studio to urge him to remain loyal, Degas assented. On this day he was in a mellow mood. He assembled seven oil paintings and a batch of drawings and prints for the exhibition, as well as a sculptured piece called *Petite Dancing Girl of Fourteen Years*.

"Do you think I should show my sculpture?" he asked in a moment of modesty. "I'm not sure I'm ready yet."

He then called for his housekeeper to bring a jar of her marmalade as a gift for Julie.

Camille ran his hands appreciatively over the little ballet "rat."

"She's rough, but you've caught her to the life."

Renoir and Sisley defected to the official Salon. Claude Monet was not represented. Berthe Morisot and Mary Cassatt contributed their best work from the preceding year, strong individual portraits of their family and friends; women with children seen against the flowing Seine, gazing over the roofs of Paris, strolling in the park. Cézanne declined Camille's request for paintings to be shipped from Aix.

The showing at 10 Rue des Pyramides was dominated by Camille's ten oil paintings and by his, Degas's and Cassatt's etchings. Camille painted his wood frames for the prints yellow and violet to suggest sunlight and shadow. Durand-Ruel was disturbed by the showing of etchings, gouaches and watercolors, which he called "a consolation for your distress." Later he told Camille with a touch of understanding sadness:

"In popularizing yourself you saved your ability to keep producing, although perhaps at a lesser level."

Camille refrained from saying, "If you had been selling me

between 1875 and 1880 I would not have had to paint fans or make pastels.'' Neither did he ask how those few potboilers could hurt him.

He sold one picture and a fan; the others managed to sell a little something. There was no interest in the etchings. Only a handful of copies of *Le Jour et la Nuit* were purchased. Nor would anyone, including the usually generous Caillebotte or Ernest May, contribute any money toward a second issue. Discouraged, Degas abandoned the publication.

Once again they failed to make their expenses.

The spirit behind the earlier exhibitions was lacking. The élan of a glorious new adventure was gone. Instead of heady abuse or ridicule the Fifth Impressionist Exhibition was received with indifference. The Impressionists had worn out their novelty and were returned to the opaque shadows whence they had made their unwanted entrance.

Disappointed as he was, Camille told Caillebotte:

''We must exhibit again.''

But one by one the members who had participated in the exhibition informed him that they had come to the end of that particular road. They would no longer exhibit together as Impressionists.

Camille Pissarro was alone.

BOOK ELEVEN

The Depths of Glory

1

PAUL GAUGUIN came out to Pontoise to spend his summer vacation when the stock market was in the doldrums. It was six years since he had begun attending an artists' academy at night with his associate Emile Schuffenecker, training himself in the rudiments of drawing, and later working with oil paints with Camille. Camille had no doubt of Gauguin's talent, his strong hand and eye for color. Yet a deep-lying problem was coming into focus.

"I'm being torn apart," Gauguin cried. "When I am selling securities I want to be painting. When I am painting I never want to see the Bourse again."

Camille had watched Gauguin's dilemma taking shape.

"Can you afford a leave of absence?"

Gauguin snorted. "I've made a lot of money but what I've made we spent. Isn't that the normal way?"

Camille sighed. "With me it's been the other way around; I've spent before I've earned. I gather that Mette disapproves?"

"From her point of view she's right. She married an ambitious and prosperous stockbroker. She comes from government bureaucrats whose income has never been challenged. All these years we've lived very well, I've encouraged that. Now she's frightened that the money will be cut off."

"So it will be, if you give your job short shrift."

"I want to give up my job, spend full time painting. Mette says I owe her and the children an ample livelihood."

Camille was silent. After a day of work in front of a curving street lined with houses and barns buried in green trees, he glanced over at Gauguin's sure lines and masses of deep color as he caught the motif. The men filled their pipes, relaxed. Camille asked quietly:

"Could you stay with the Bertin stockbrokers another year or two, make all the money you can, and save . . . ?"

Gauguin took a swipe at his bony nose, brushing it roughly from the corner of his eye to the corner of his mouth.

"I must. But that is only postponing Judgment Day. Mette is going to have to learn to live on a painter's income. Neither she nor the children have ever known poverty."

That night after a light supper Gauguin joined Camille in guiding the four Pissarro boys in their drawing. Camille never let a day go by without giving his sons a session of instruction. Lucien was already quite good; at seventeen he had taken over the first exercises of Ludovic Rodolphe, now two years old. Camille concentrated on Georges, aged nine, and Félix, aged six. The four boys thought that converting the dining table into a large classroom desk was normal; they had never known anything else. Didn't every father train his children in drawing and the making of pastels at the end of each day? They drew, as Camille described it, "Fantastic landscapes, terrible horsemen, frightful exterminations where you see warriors fighting even without heads, a whole world of Hoffmanesque fantasy, unheard of!"

When the children had gone up to bed and Julie had retired after her long day of chores, the two men sat out in the cool of the back garden, surrounded by the night sounds of insect and forest animal foraging. Gauguin said between puffs on his pipe:

"An explosion is inevitable. Forgive me for saying so, Mette's been terrified by what she's seen of your and Julie's desperate efforts to keep afloat. She says she'll have none of it, that she has kept her promises to me, and why am I not man enough to keep my promises to her?"

They could see each other's face only in the sometime glow of the pipes. Camille said softly:

"It's a painful impasse. You'll have to resolve it according to your own character."

Gauguin flared, half rising.

"What in hell is a man of my character, descended from the Borgias of Aragon, doing with his time, selling pieces of paper to strangers who make money on them when the market rises and lose it when the market falls? My life work is painting and I'm damn well not going to waste many more of my years."

"But gently, gently. It's a hard life, friend Gauguin."

"I'm not frightened. I am a man of courage." He flexed

his biceps. "Feel how hard they are. The muscles in my head are equally powerful."

Camille tapped out the ash of his pipe on the bottom rung of his chair.

"On that exalted note let's go to bed. Sleep fast, Gauguin, for at first light we must have our easels planted in front of the blossoming orchard. Later, in the fall, we'll paint the young women picking the fruit."

The Pissarros lived off the threads of a frayed cuff. Camille had delivered a dozen oils to Durand-Ruel's gallery. The money would be forthcoming. Julie had no such faith.

"If your pictures are so good why can't he sell them and give us some francs?"

Camille shook his head in puzzlement.

He was painting well; he knew he could do better if his spirits were not so frequently depressed. He kept up a brave front but sometimes now when he was working in Pontoise or the neighboring village of Valhermeil he would be overcome by melancholy, put aside his brushes and demand of himself:

"Why am I painting still one more picture when I have a hundred stacked against my walls that nobody wants?"

It was not a permissible question. All of his life was implicit in the beginning. He had been born to paint just as Beethoven had been born to compose his symphonies and Dostoevsky to write *Crime and Punishment,* which Camille had just finished reading.

The one source of joy over the late summer was the visit of Esther Isaacson, the daughter of Camille's beloved sister Emma. Now twenty-three, she had been born in Rachel's apartment in Montmartre while Camille was living there. She was a startling replica of her mother: glossy nut-brown hair and clear, high coloring, hazel eyes, penetrating and kindly. She had been only ten when Emma died but that had been time enough to absorb her mother's values, chief of which for Camille was her love and loyalty to Camille's family. Emma's husband had never remarried; Phineas Isaacson had given his daughter as substantial an education as was available to a young woman in London. She was a treat for the Pissarro boys, spending long hours reading stories to Georges and Félix, taking them for picnics. She had a particularly quieting effect on Georges, who was frequently a menace to his young brothers but who behaved angelically when Esther paid attention to him. She liked to go through the shelves and bins in Camille's studio, studying the various phases of his work.

One afternoon after a rain squall she said:

"You've told me that no one is interested in your watercolors in Paris. Why not let me take some back to London? Watercolors sell well in England."

Camille shook his head in amazement.

"You look and sound so much like your mother that I could believe Emma is standing here in front of me. She was forever saying, 'I'd like to help.' Very well. I'll send you some."

Esther asked in a hoarse tone:

"Uncle Camille, why doesn't Grandma live here with you and Aunt Julie? She's so alone in that apartment."

Camille took his niece's hand.

"Esther dear, I've asked Maman dozens of times to come to us. Enjoy the four boys. Most grandmothers like that." He gulped. It would never be anything but a painful subject for him. "Maman doesn't get along with your Aunt Julie. . . . She has never forgiven her for what she calls 'trapping' me. Or forgiven me for marrying a *bonne*, whom she still thinks of as an ignorant girl from Grancey. And a Catholic. Maman had hopes I would marry a Jewish girl, one with a good dowry. I betrayed her."

"But that was twenty years ago. . . . Julie has been a good wife and mother."

"The only one I ever wanted."

Esther rose to her feet. "I'm going to work on Grandma. She's eighty-five, she told me. She could be happy here."

"I'd move her furniture, repaint one of the upstairs bedrooms . . .

"That would be a *mitzvah*."

Camille chuckled. "Yes, it would be a blessing. And a blessing on your head, Esther."

But when Esther suggested a reconciliation with Alfred and Marie, he replied resignedly:

"It has been ten years now that Alfred's family has treated us like strangers. Why? Have we forfeited honor? I think not. Is it because we are of a world which society reproves? It would be too bad, because we aren't so demanding."

Julie and the children took their extra vegetables and flowers by the horse-drawn omnibus into the open-air market at Gisors where they sold or bartered them for sugar, flour, rice, dried peas, condiments. Camille held off the landlord by telling him, "If you put me out now you'll lose three months' back rent. Let me stay and everything will be paid in full."

The landlord replied, "This can't go on indefinitely. I give you to the end of the year."

The boys had once more worn out their shoes. Lucien managed to keep his pair patched together but Georges and Félix were back in sabots, ridiculed by their schoolmates. Julie's heroic efforts fed them, though monotonously, but how were they to buy oil for their lamps, school supplies, replace tattered linens, medications? Her cow had fallen into the water; now she had to barter her vegetables as well with a neighbor for milk and cheese.

"This uncertainty is making me *folle*," she complained.

"The money from the Union Générale will become available. We just have to hang on."

Out of kindness for her forlorn husband she murmured:

"I guess it's no more bitter than some of those turnips we keep cool in the basement and boil for supper."

His friends would not let him suffer endlessly. Théodore Duret sent him a collector who bought *The Wool Carder*, which he had shown in the 1880 exhibition. When that money was gone, Mary Cassatt sold two small watercolors of the gardens of the Hermitage to an artist with whom she had worked at the Philadelphia Art Institute. Later, Eugène Murer brought out to Pontoise a man who bought *Peasants in the Field*. When there were simply no outside prospects, Degas or Gauguin or Berthe Morisot acquired something they liked. Camille was their paternal figure; they could not let him perish. They were also too compassionate to allow any sense of charity to enter into their purchases; they loved the man: gentle, patient, giving, but they also admired his work and knew its worth. All except Antoine Guillemet, now winning honors and medals at the Salon, getting big commissions from the state, his family income increasing from its lands and vineyards; but who no longer came around to the Café de la Nouvelle Athènes. Guillemet was running with the tide, and it was bearing him to the highest cliffs. Who could blame him for disowning a group of malcontent outsiders?

"He wants the Legion of Honor," Degas observed caustically. "The little red ribbon in his buttonhole. That's more important to him than good painting. What he doesn't understand is that the little red ribbon in his buttonhole will rot with the rest of him in his coffin, while good art is indestructible."

Camille regretted losing Guillemet, for he had liked the young man when they had been together at La Roche-Guyon, and during the companionable years when Antoine had allowed him and Julie and the children to occupy his comfortable Paris studio while he was abroad.

"Guillemet will have a good time while he's alive," Camille responded to Degas with a touch of melancholy; "we'll have ours after we're dead. *Tant pis!*"

Some twenty of his new, good-sized oil canvases remained unframed and unsold: several views of Valhermeil; a number of Pontoise. He had an added worry: his right eye was bothering him. It misted. It got cloudy. It began blinking. He disregarded it for a time but it grew worse. Should he go into Paris, oil paintings under his arm, and attempt to buy eye care with his canvases? He could not bring himself to do it. Besides, the disturbance sometimes went away. Perhaps it would cure itself? Most things did.

Lucien had become Camille's assistant, relieving him of many chores, including trips into Paris to deliver paintings, pick up supplies. He could talk to Lucien about painting: its pressures, pleasures, value. Lucien grasped most of what his father was postulating about the art and the bourgeois worlds. Since Camille could not discuss any of these artistic or social intricacies with Julie, who hated Proudhon's anarchism because she felt involuntarily trapped in it, Lucien became his father's confidant.

"It's good to have a son who understands you," Camille exulted. "Lucien has native talent, he takes training well; he'll become a fine artist."

Camille's larger paintings, forty-nine by sixty-four inches, could bring no more than twenty dollars in random selling outside a gallery; his price seemed to have settled at that figure, one from which he would have to escape if he were to survive. Yet at the moment he could not collect even one twenty-dollar payment from his dealer, who had guaranteed to pay him a good lump sum before the year was out.

He had sent a group of watercolors to Esther. Now he received several letters from Théodore Duret, who was serving in London as the art critic for the *Gazette des Beaux-Arts*. Camille had told him about the etchings he was continuing to make. Duret thought he might be able to place them in London since Paris had not recognized their value, not even the six stages of *Woods and Undergrowth at the Hermitage* which Camille had framed and displayed at the fifth exhibition. Duret wrote:

"You would have to bring me a complete series of your engravings. I need to see the baby to judge what we can do for it. . . . I lunched this morning with Whistler. He showed me a series of pastels done in Venice which are of an extraordinary charm, lightness and originality. That man is really a great artist.''

Degas had hoped to establish a society of engravers who would contribute to *Le Jour et la Nuit* but that idea was abandoned along with the magazine. Over a consolation dinner at the Café de la Paix, he asked:

''Is there any philosophy you know that says, 'A hundred failures add up to ultimate success'?''

Mary Cassatt smiled wistfully. ''You have just enunciated the universal creed of the artist.''

In mid-November Camille moved into a one-room apartment in the same building, 18 Rue des Trois Frères, where he had rented before, and where he did not have to pay any rent in advance. He brought with him oil paintings, watercolors, pastels, hoping to entice buyers. But few wanted to make the long arduous climb up steep Montmartre. Paris was cold, rainy, with a heavy gray overcast which made the location doubly difficult for potential viewers. He sold nothing. He did not attempt to bring Julie and the boys into the city. There would have been nothing for them to eat. At home they had Julie's rabbits and chickens and the vegetables and fruits she salvaged for the winter months. He ate one meal a day at Rachel's; she was always glad to feed him. Other than that he drank a cup of coffee when he needed the warm fire and bright lamp of an indoor café to drive out the chill and the dark.

His mother was using a cane to walk about. She resisted all entreaties to move out to Pontoise and ''intrude on his lordship. I've been independent too long. Alfred comes once a week, brings me medicines and gets me new maids when I need them. Which is often. I don't know what's wrong with the country girls these days.''

Toward the end of December, desperate because Durand-Ruel had not yet received his money from the Union Générale, or sold anything, he agreed to let Portier, a former clerk of Durand-Ruel's, who had now opened a shop, scour the neighborhood with his unframed oils and watercolors, taking works of art to people who would not come into his small, poorly lighted gallery; to the department stores, hotels, expensive apartment buildings. Camille considered there might be some hope in this ''traveling exhibit'' but soon found that Portier's cold temperament hindered him. He sold nothing.

It was now a full year since Durand-Ruel had guaranteed prosperity. Julie's eyes were pools of sadness with deep circles under them. Esther could find not even the smallest gallery in London to take his watercolors on consignment. Degas was laying siege to a dealer, Adrien Beugniet, at 10 Rue Laffitte. Camille did a serious watercolor of the river Oise to tempt Beugniet, writing to Duret in London:

"I hope it succeeds. I will have an outlet which will enable me to live in peace. We are working on a volcano. What a business!"

On the thirtieth of December, with the house as still as Juliet's tomb at Verona, and Camille sitting beaten and disconsolate in his cold, damp studio, there appeared Durand-Ruel, handsomely garbed in a morning coat, striped trousers and notary's black bow tie, his face broadly smiling, his hair cut fashionably.

"Ah, my dear Pissarro, you are surprised to see me. You should not be. I promised you payment for your 1880 paintings by the end of the year. Well, here is two hundred dollars, all I dared to carry. If you will come into Paris tomorrow, I have another hundred and fifty waiting for you in my safe."

Camille's mouth was dry, his tongue felt swollen. He squeezed Durand-Ruel's shoulder so hard the dealer winced.

". . . come . . . tell Julie. We are half dead. . . ."

They left the studio and walked across the driveway to the front door.

"Pissarro, you don't believe in the proper God. He takes particular care of fools, children and artists."

Camille's expression of anguish dissipated the way a heavy London fog gave way to an insistent sun.

2

On New Year's Day, 1881, with the second of Durand-Ruel's payments safely in hand, Camille and Julie went to see "Grandmother Rachel" as the boys wistfully called her. The day before they had bought her a cashmere shawl woven in soft bright colors by the women of Paisley, Scotland. After presenting the gift they persuaded her to accompany them for a New Year's dinner at the Café Helder. Rachel was both touched and flabbergasted by the shawl and the invitation. She asked quietly:

"Where did you get the money, Camille?"

"Monsieur Durand-Ruel came out to my studio two days ago and paid me a substantial sum that he owed me. He wants everything I can paint from now on, including the watercolors I sent to Esther, and has volunteered to send me a monthly bank note for two hundred and fifty dollars against my account. We came to celebrate."

Rachel's eyes were big with astonishment. She straightened up. Her voice became almost youthful.

"A celebration! I wish Alfred and Marie were here. Tomorrow morning I'll find some gifts for the children and come out on the train."

Julie murmured under her breath:

"Will wonders never cease."

Camille was the only one wanting a sixth Impressionist exhibition for 1881, convinced that the Impressionists must continue to show, to be seen, to be discussed in order to remain a viable movement. He managed to turn Caillebotte away from his former resistance and sent warm invitations to Monet, Renoir and Sisley to join the showing. Degas protested, "They're renegades. I refuse to show with them. They left us to show at the Salon . . . unsuccessfully."

"Then I refuse to exhibit with Degas!" Caillebotte cried.

Durand-Ruel's bank drafts came in regularly. Camille had covered the back rent and given Père Tanguy a fair sum on account. Julie settled her bills with the Pontoise shopkeepers. They bought clothing for the boys, provided them with school supplies and a few sous pocket money, a rarity in the Pissarro family. Julie was able to go into Paris to visit with her sisters, with Camille to attend a concert or a play, and even found some pleasure in Rachel's monthly weekend visits, arranged since their New Year's pact. She and her mother-in-law got along peaceably for the first time. Julie hired a pleasant young housemaid to help her, a laundress who took the wash down to the river every other week. Because of their newly found security Julie did not mind being pregnant again.

During the harsh winter Camille was able to afford adequate heat for the house and to work with tranquillity in his studio, converting, as Gauguin had been urging him, dozens of studies of the young peasant women of the countryside into good-sized oil paintings. When the weather cleared he went with Julie early in the morning to the market at Gisors where he sketched a woman pork butcher and painted a scene of a multitude of shoppers and strollers between a row of small stalls. It was an unusual approach for him, large groups of figures vividly realized.

His pleading with Monet, Renoir, Sisley for a sixth exhibition achieved little result. They rejected his cry for unity. Degas, Morisot, Guillaumin, Rouart, still painting academically but faithfully exhibiting each year, and Forain, who had shown with them in the fourth and fifth exhibitions, agreed. Gauguin sent his Pontoise oils. Degas's protégé Raffaëlli was again present, and many who had exhibited the year before: Tillot, Vidal, Vignon, Zandomeneghi, all of whom had moved in the direction of *plein air*, diffused light and colored shadows. The participants would each contribute a share of the expenses.

Having been the most productive of the group, Camille overwhelmed the exhibition at 35 Boulevard des Capucines, the same building in which Nadar had loaned them his photographic studio seven years before. He hung twenty-eight paintings with the most diverse statement about landscapes and peasants, penetrating portraits of Julie and the boys; their pretty young aproned maid sweeping and having a morning *café au lait*, the busy crowded market scenes of Gisors.

The sixth exhibition was, in terms of viewers and sales, a mild success. For Camille it was a triumph only for the critique of J. K. Huysmans, who was becoming a respected art observer. He wrote:

Pissarro's *The Pathway* is a landscape where a patchy sky extends to infinity, broken only by the treetops, and where a river runs, near which factory chimneys smoke and pathways cross woodlands. It is the landscape of a powerful colorist who has at last grasped and overcome the terrible difficulties of painting in full daylight in the open. . . . The true countryside at last emerges from this assembly of classically mixed colors and there is in this natural scene so bathed in air, a great calm. . . . If he can preserve his perceptive, delicate and nimble eye, we shall certainly have in him the most original landscapist of our time.

Albert Wolff, writing in *Le Figaro*, felt differently.

. . . Renoir or Claude Monet, Sisley, Caillebotte, or Pissarro, it's all the same thing; what is particularly strange about these Independents is that they are just as prone to routine as are the painters who do not belong to their brotherhood. Who has seen one picture by the Independent has seen the works of all of them. . . .

* * *

The infusion of money from Jules Feder and his Union Générale enabled Durand-Ruel to lay new carpet, acquire benches, glass skylights, matting on his walls. The gallery became almost fashionable. People who had never heard of it came to the exhibitions. He engaged two former gallery owners as his floor representatives; they were knowledgeable and persuasive. Visitors were impressed, even intimidated. Buying a painting at Durand-Ruel's, one of those color- and light-drunk canvases of the formerly disdained artists, became *comme il faut*. New "amateurs" were added, there were even celebration parties when an Impressionist painting was hung in someone's luxurious drawing room: a voluptuous pink nude by Renoir, a washerwoman or ballet scene from Degas, a light-drenched Gare St. Lazare by Monet; a peasant girl resting by a stream by Pissarro; a stone bridge over a flowing stream by Sisley; a wooden-barred cattle barge near the Pont Louis Philippe by Guillaumin. Collectors and novices bought with confidence. By the end of that year Durand-Ruel was able to pay his favorite Impressionists, after deducting his commission, the considerable sum of seventy-one thousand francs, approximately fourteen thousand two hundred dollars.

"It's almost too good to last," Camille told Julie.

Her head went back in sharp protest.

"Don't say things like that. From your mouth to the Devil's ear."

Durand-Ruel's success in relaunching the Impressionists was the ameliorating force that washed away all quarrels, past failures and divergences. The artists joined together once again in a comradery in the Café Tortoni.

It had been a grueling eighteen years since 1863's Salon des Refusés, for Camille and Julie, Claude Monet and his now dead Léonie; for Alfred Sisley, his Marie and their two children; for the government clerk Armand Guillaumin; Auguste Renoir, recently settled down with Aline Charigot, whom he had long admired. For the others with family money to back them the years had been less tortured physically; but they had all suffered from the perennial *R* burned deeply into their flesh.

Paul Cézanne had turned a deaf ear to Camille's entreaties to send paintings from Aix for the sixth exhibition. Only he of the Impressionists did not share in Durand-Ruel's revival and bounty, partly because Durand-Ruel had never cared for his work or his abrasive personality; partly because so little of it could be seen in Paris. Cézanne suffered a further blow when a friend, Victor Chocquet, wrote to Cézanne at his parents' home, Jas de Bouffan, outside Aix, saying that he had visited Hortense Fiquet and Cézanne's son Paul in Marseilles. Cézanne's father opened the letter, was outraged at the longtime concealment. Cézanne's denial helped him not at all. His father cried:

"Very well, I shall cut your allowance from forty dollars a month to twenty. That's enough for a bachelor living alone."

Emile Zola, whose Rougon-Macquart series of novels had become popular, had been supporting Hortense and Paul, Jr., for several months. Now, at the beginning of summer, Cézanne left Aix, picked up Hortense and his son and brought them to Pontoise. He sought asylum with the Pissarros in their larger house at 85 Quai du Pothuis overlooking the river. Julie was delighted. She and Hortense had always been compatible. Camille and Cézanne painted the same motifs in the neighborhood. Cézanne was using thin glazes and colors ranging from cobalt blue and red ocher to brilliant yellow, silver-white and peach-black. He was after the depth of the land, the village, the mountain, the sea, using color gradations to portray changes of surface. Camille understood why Cézanne's friends who had visited him in Aix-en-Provence reported that after a day's painting Cézanne's hands, face and smock were splotched with over a dozen different colors from his researches into the solidity of earth and its contours. He was no longer Camille's student; he had important ideas and techniques to impart to his former teacher.

The two men walked at dawn to Auvers-sur-Oise to paint the quiet village under the hospitable but excited eye of Dr. Gachet, the only collector still buying Cézanne. After a couple of weeks the Cézannes moved to their own quarters a few houses away on the same embankment.

A little Pontoise school was functioning. Guillaumin, Cézanne's longtime friend, no one knew how or why, came on weekends and holidays. He was continuing to buy lottery tickets, a fantasy of which Cézanne disapproved, the odds being too long. Paul Gauguin joined them. Inevitably Cézanne and Gauguin clashed; Cézanne, suspicious, bitterly cynical introvert; Gauguin, brash and outgoing. Neither man liked the other, or his work. When they went out to paint together they achieved a silent harmony, becoming isolated islands of energy.

"Gauguin has no talent," Cézanne insisted to Camille. "He should stick with the Bourse, selling stocks that go bad."

"Ten years ago," Camille retorted gently, "I had to defend you against that same charge. Shouldn't that make you more tolerant?"

"Tolerance is for saints like you," Cézanne growled in his guttural, Provençal accent.

"We don't have saints in the Old Testament. Only prophets."

"Then you're a prophet . . . and when it comes to Gauguin, a false one."

Gauguin, for his part, thought that Cézanne painted with a set of tricky formulas.

Camille's nine-year-old Georges, in a drawing, caught the School of Pontoise to the life: noon, outdoors, Cézanne painting at his easel, Camille and Guillaumin cutting cheese and bread while Gauguin looked on, Hortense frying eggs in a pan over a little wood fire, young Georges himself, with his long hair streaming down his back, sprawled on the ground in front of the fire. Two more easels held beginning paintings, for they were all doing the same scene, a wooded area set in front of a cave in the hillside overlooking the river and a factory smokestack on the opposite bank.

Julie, large with child, was indoors with Mette and the assorted Pissarro and Gauguin children.

3

Julie bore her child on August 27. The guests had considerately left a few days in advance. A Pontoise midwife delivered the baby, to their intense joy a girl. They named her Jeanne, after the sorely missed first Jeanne called Minette; then quickly nicknamed her Cocotte. She was a robust child from the beginning; the four boys stood around somewhat puzzled about how they were going to help raise a baby sister.

It was a good time to have a child, with the feeling of stability that Durand-Ruel's bank draft brought them at the beginning of each month. The autumn was mild, Camille painted well: studies of harvestings, gleanings, the heaping up of hay, young girls exchanging news under the trees, seated by a stream, guarding a goat; sensitive, realistic portraits caught in a natural luminous light, and in colors previously unused, violet, pale yellow, pink, yet basically true. The working people were quiet, pensive, accepting their position and their fate. They were scenes about which the English painter Walter Sickert had said: "Pissarro no more pitied the peasant than the peasant pitied himself."

Camille pitied the industrialized factory workers, all those in dull mechanical routine drudgery, but thought of the people of the fields, hard as they worked, as free. He had taught his boys not to dramatize but to have a sympathetic insight into the fields, meadows, woods and streams, and the human beings who worked them for a livelihood so that they would be in harmony with rural life and the rhythms of country labor.

His painting hand soared. He completed twenty-four major oil paintings, along with a goodly batch of watercolors, pastels, etchings, many from earlier proofs. When the heat of summer left, a bitter cold set in. Cocotte made the rough winter an enjoyable one. Camille warmed his studio room sufficiently with braziers for Julie to bring the infant to him in the well-used crib where she slept, gurgled or played with her fingers while he contentedly converted field studies into oil paintings. With still another child in the family, Julie said:

"Lucien is now eighteen, and with as much education as you had at the Pension Savary. Don't you think he should go to work?"

"He is at work . . . for me. By taking care of a hundred errands."

"But he must be given a trade, his own trade. To support himself, let alone help us."

Once again Alfred secured Lucien a job, at Niel Frères & Cie, a house well known for its cloth from Roubaix. He would live in Paris with Julie's sister, his Aunt Félicie. Julie's parting shot was, "Don't try to behave so poorly they'll fire you."

Lucien grimaced. "Maybe after a while they will let me design some fabrics."

When four-year-old Ludovic became ill with an inflammation, Camille left a note in Dr. Gachet's mailbox in Auvers: "If you pass by Pontoise I will be very grateful."

Dr. Gachet came the next day, prescribed for the boy. Seven-year-old Félix came down with a nose problem: mucus, scabs, difficulty in breathing. Dr. de Bellio came from Paris with his black bag full of medications. Camille was not a natural worrier, but illness on the part of a child made him distraught. The loss of his beloved Minette seven years before was still a fresh wound slashed across his spirit. His gratitude to the doctors Gachet and De Bellio was unbounded. He took sketches, prints, watercolors to their homes; offered them their choice of large oil paintings which they refused on the grounds that Durand-Ruel might be able to sell them. Camille priced the pictures he took to Durand-Ruel the way he valued them; two small ones, *A Rest in the Woods* and *The Royal Palace, Pontoise,* eighty dollars, two larger ones, one hundred and forty, *The Quai at Pothuis,* one hundred and sixty.

"I'm not rolling in money," he told a friend, "but I am enjoying the fruits of a moderate but regular sale. I ask only that this continue. I dread a return to the past."

Despite the continuing success of the Impressionists at Durand-Ruel's, and the bonhomie at the cafés, Camille found, at the beginning of 1882, when he started to put together the seventh exhibition, that there would still be quarreling among them. Gauguin, who had been imposed upon the Independents by Camille, wrote to him from Paris:

"Yesterday Degas told me angrily that he would sooner hand in his resignation than turn away from Raffaëlli. If I look coolly at your situation, ten years since you undertook the task of these exhibitions, I immediately see that the number of Impressionists has grown, their talent has increased and also their influence. In contrast, on Degas's side and by his doing alone, the trend has been worse and worse; every year an Impressionist has left to give way to nobodies and students of the Ecole. In another two years you alone will be left in the midst of these schemers. . . ."

Durand-Ruel rented premises at 251 Rue St. Honoré, pledging twelve hundred dollars for one month's use during each of the next three years. It was urgent that everyone be represented in the exhibition.

Gauguin agreed to exhibit. Renoir, ill with pneumonia, was in L'Estaque in the South of France, with Cézanne. He again refused to join his fellows. Durand-Ruel coddled him with good sentiments but Renoir dictated a letter to his younger brother, which the brother showed about Paris:

"To exhibit with Pissarro, Gauguin and Guillaumin is as if I were to exhibit with some sort of socialist group. A little farther and Pissarro will invite the Russian Pierre Lavrof, the anarchist, or some other revolutionary. The public doesn't like what smells of politics and I certainly don't want, at my age, to become a revolutionary. To continue with the Israelite, Pissarro—that's revolution. . . ."

When Camille heard about the letter he was stricken. Renoir had been a friend since the early days of the Salon des Refusés and knew that Camille had never introduced politics into his paintings, and assuredly not into any of their meetings. Could it be that "Israelite" was an epithet at the core of the outburst?

*   *   *

The perennially leaky roof of the French economy caved in with the collapse of the Union Générale, which lost millions of its French investors' francs in unprofitable ventures in far-off countries. Jules Feder, the director, saw his entire fortune wiped out, and with it his support of the Durand-Ruel gallery. Durand-Ruel owed Feder a large sum of money which he had advanced to the artists against future sales and profits from their works; but when Camille went into his office to console him he found that the dealer had managed to remain calm.

"It's a blow but I will survive it," he said. "Because you and your group are selling. The Union Générale bankruptcy has not yet affected the art market. Doubtless it will, but for the present I can still assure you your monthly advance."

The Seventh Impressionist Exhibition was hung in a few hectic days and was largely Camille's doing. He had been working tirelessly. Although Degas had steadfastly refused to show because the work of Raffaëlli had been rejected, Gauguin was there, and Durand-Ruel had gained Renoir's reluctant consent to allow Durand-Ruel to exhibit the paintings he already owned. There were fine displays by Sisley, Morisot, Caillebotte, Guillaumin, the painter Vignon, now influenced by the novel approaches of his friends, as well as the stalwarts Rouart and Forain. A half dozen of the "surrounding foliage," painters who Camille, Renoir, Monet and Degas had hoped would mollify the critics in the early days, declined the invitation to enter. Camille displayed nine landscapes, portraits of his family, the peasants around the Hermitage, young girls. His most admired picture was *The Harvest*, in tempera, twenty-six by forty-seven inches. In the foreground were four women in colorful kerchiefs, blouses and skirts; beyond them, four men in white and blue shirts bundling the hay, preparing to carry it to the nearest haycock, all eight of them caught in a vigorous frieze. In the distance was a gently sloping ridge, at the bottom of which were half a dozen peasant houses with the owner's château buried in the trees on top. Camille had hired the peasants, men and women alike, to pose for him: face, figure, costume, character, relation to the task at hand, all was authentic. The fields, the haystacks, the people would be there, in succession, for generations to come. It was an elegy.

Therein lay the rub. He was quickly compared to Millet and accused of trying to emulate if not to copy him. He exploded to Théodore Duret, who had become his Wailing Wall:

"They are all throwing Millet at my head but Millet was biblical! For a Hebrew, there is not much of that in me."

He feared that religion which preached resignation and a better life in the next world consistently got in the way of improvement in one's present existence. Joris Karl Huysmans, who wrote for *Art Moderne,* came to his rescue with encouragement:

> Monsieur Pissarro is entirely rid of any reminders of Millet; he paints his peasants without false grandeur, simply, as he sees them.

The seventh exhibition was judged a success because it was a cohesive display of Impressionism, with no alien or academic fence mending, with no "protective conservatives." Durand-Ruel managed the showing and sold more than enough paintings to cover the costs. The critics were less hostile. Was it fatigue or had their eyes grown accustomed to the divergence?

The worst pronouncement was by the commentator Jules Clarétie in *Le Temps:*

> . . . The group was composed of people with right ideas and wrong colors. They think well but their vision is faulty. They show the candor of children and the fervor of apostles. I am thinking of the gray-haired ones like Monsieur Pissarro. One might be tempted to admire them, these naive creatures!

Camille wrote to Esther in London:
"Our reputation grows continuously, we are definitely taking a place in the great modern artistic movement."

They closed up house and took their offspring to the Côte d'Or, near Dijon, on the river Ouche, for a vacation, boarding out so that Julie did not have to cook or clean. Camille brought no painting supplies with him. Going back to his days on the bay of Charlotte Amalie, he taught the younger boys to swim and sail a boat. Julie, who had never heard the word "vacation" in Grancey, where it would have been as esoteric a concept as a man flying through the air, rested on a rusty swing on the porch, played with her daughter Cocotte, went walking with Camille along the riverbank in the cool of the evening when the children had been bedded down after the band concert in the public square. There was a happy sparkle in her eyes. Her robust figure was attractive, her face appealing. When Camille told her so, she flushed with pleasure.

"It's because we're on our *lune de miel*," she murmured. "Can couples with five children have a honeymoon?"

He kissed her and held her to him.

Over the rest of the summer, with Gauguin, Mette and their children visiting frequently, Camille did two lyrical oils. The first was a woman at a well, a beneficent light over everything, the well, with its rounded soft red stone circle and stanchion matching the red of the woman's bonnet and the child's hair, the rich orchard foliage and roofs of houses in the distance. The space between the mother and child was eloquent with what they were ready to say to each other; the subtleness of the integrated colors and the relationship between the woman and child creating a sense of the loveliness of life.

The second was a little country maid, in which he portrayed a charming young girl sweeping noncommittally the Pissarro dining room. The boy Ludovic was seated alone at the near end of the table, which was covered with a white cloth and held a teapot, cup and saucer. On the walls were a print and an oil painting by Camille, a muted albeit multicolor carpet was on the floor, and on one side, two upholstered chairs with orange-colored frames, the color of the boy's hair. The space in the much-used dining room had an inner harmony, even with the slight broom handle sloping halfway across the room. It was a scene out of time, suggesting the continuity of domestic life.

During this same summer Durand-Ruel once again gathered the courage to stage an Impressionist exhibition in London, at 15 King's Street. He sent over half a dozen of Camille's recent landscapes and peasant girl portraits. The English press was still unfriendly; it called them uncouth.

Four years earlier John Ruskin, an Oxford professor, authority on art and architecture, had written in a journal about James McNeill Whistler's exhibition at the Grosvenor Gallery in London:

> . . . I have seen and heard much of the cockney impudence before now, but never expected to hear a coxcomb ask for two hundred guineas for flinging a pot of paint in the public's face.

Ruskin's defamatory article evoked a scandal worse than anything Albert Wolff had started in *Le Figaro*. Whistler promptly took Ruskin to court. Knowing that the eccentric, always colorful Whistler was a longtime friend of the Impressionists, Esther had sent Camille the London newspapers containing the result of the sometimes amusing trial of the lawsuit. Camille took the clippings to the Café Riche, where he and his colleagues avidly followed the progress of the case. Whistler won, and was awarded a farthing of damages, not because his painting had been traduced, but because he had unjustly been called a cockney and a coxcomb. Whistler was satisfied with the result.

At the end of September the house was already damp and the winter of 1882–83 promised to be a harsh one. Camille searched Pontoise for a better building but found nothing he could afford. He wrote to Monet that he would be obliged to leave Pontoise, to his great regret. In December they settled on an inexpensive house in the tiny village of Osny, about two and a half miles from Pontoise. If the house was small, without a backyard, the rooms cramped and the kitchen inadequate, it was dry and reasonably warm, the countryside paintable.

"Consider it a temporary stay," he told Julie consolingly; "next year we'll find a better place."

Lucien was still living with Félicie in Paris and working at Niel Frères & Cie; his pay was minimal and there was very little to take home to Pontoise. Though he was giving adequate service he was unhappy.

"I'm wasting my days, Papa. Any idiot can carry those bolts of cloth from the shelf to the counter and back again."

Camille was pained.

"It has been my promise to myself that you would have a creative life. I've nurtured an idea for some time now. Let me talk to Maman about it."

He thought it wiser to wait until he and Julie could have dinner in Paris, with a bit of holiday spirit. Over the last of their beef, and while waiting for their flaming dessert, he found the moment to make his proposal:

"Julie, I'd like you to consider the possibility of Lucien continuing his education in England. The Isaacsons have invited him to live with them while he learns English. Between Phineas and Théodore Duret, I'm sure they can find him a job to cover his side expenses. There will be no costs beyond the railroad ticket and Channel crossing. We benefit so little from what he earns here. Being bilingual will help him get a good position and an acceptable salary. What do you think?"

Julie sipped the last of her wine, gazed around the crowded restaurant, then returned her eyes to Camille.

"*Bien*. Our oldest son can do something better than unwrap bolts of Roubaix cloth."

He saw his son off at the Gare St. Lazare with the usual paternal advice and all the money he could spare. Lucien was a compact, good-looking lad with short hair and a tentative mustache and beard.

"Try to be like a well-brought-up brother to the Isaacson cousins," Camille droned. "Be tactful. Try to speak as much English as possible."

"Yes, Papa." Lucien was straining to get on the train.

"Try to find a homeopathic pharmacy in London. . . ."

"Yes, Papa." He was gone.

4

The bitter dissension that had preceded the 1882 exhibition, and the difficulty in getting it together, convinced even Camille that, for the present at least, the Impressionists should not show. Caillebotte agreed. Seven times over nine years they had displayed their work, apparently achieving little permanent effect. Yet both men felt that they must have some exposure or what modest reputation they had gained would disappear.

They took their problem to Durand-Ruel.

"I've been thinking about a plan," he responded. "You Impressionists have much in common; put together with a hundred works in one show, you overwhelm the conservative viewer. What I'd like to try is to show you quite separately."

"You mean one-man shows?" Camille was startled.

"Yes. I know it's been done before only as a retrospective; I'm convinced the time has arrived for retrospectives for living artists. You. Monet. Degas. Sisley. Renoir. When the public sees, say, fifty canvases of only one artist, covering a wide range of subjects over a period of years, it will realize that he is not a passing phenomenon. The critics will call it a commercial promotion; but what else are our huge international expositions but a promotion of the best that science and industry have evolved? Machines are going to determine our future? So is art, but more profoundly. What do you say?"

Images of Camille's favorite paintings whirled across the screen of his eyes as on a magic lantern. He murmured:

"It fills our void. Bless you."

After living and painting briefly in Dieppe, Le Havre, Poissy, Étretat, Monet and his two children, living with Madame Hoschedé and her five youngest, rented a small peasant's house in Giverny, a town near the Pissarros' Osny. They wanted to marry but no divorce was possible for the Catholic Hoschedés. When Camille, at Monet's insistence, went out to see the place he was shocked to find Giverny a barren area, the house facing the railroad tracks with a marsh beyond. The surrounding farm dwellings were dreary. He walked through the tiny rooms. There was no running water, the plumbing was outside. There was a ramshackle veranda and at a lower level a former carriage house. Camille asked:

"Why have you taken such a primitive house? The soil looks too poor to raise the flowers you want to paint, or the vegetables you have to raise for food."

"It was the only thing we could find that was big enough and cheap enough for all nine of us." Monet's handsome face was grim. "We had to quit our house at Poissy. You'd be amazed at how much clothing Alice Hoschedé's four daughters have. And our combined furniture . . . I've asked Paul Durand-Ruel for four hundred dollars in two installments. Alice and the girls are good workers; they'll make the place livable."

The Monet exhibit, first of the single-artist shows, for which Durand-Ruel rented a mezzanine at 9 Boulevard de la Madeleine, opened in March of 1883. Camille saw that Claude Monet had moved away from the transient aspects of nature into a total dazzle of light which made all objects float: the sea, the valley of the Seine, hillsides, haystacks, the Gare St. Lazare, the bridge at Argenteuil, with solids becoming blinding diaphanous textures. There were sumptuous still lifes, colors vibrantly set forth, chrysanthemums, dancing blooms in a sparkling atmosphere; luxuriant views of Vétheuil painted from across the river, achieved by short thrusts of his sable brushes. He was painting the vibrancy of light rather than landscape. Camille wrote to Lucien:

"Monet's show is a great artistic success, very well organized, not too many canvases and well spaced. He has shown some marvelous things. We shall see if the public will acclaim his show."

The gallery was almost empty. Monet was dispirited. He told the dealer:

"The show is a flop. Do not think that I aspire to see my name in the newspapers. I am very much above that, and do not care for the opinion of the press and the self-proclaimed critics of art. I know my value. But it is from the commercial point of view that we must see these things. And not to acknowledge that my exhibition has been badly announced, badly prepared, is to be unable to see the truth."

Durand-Ruel's face turned ashen at the insult. He dropped his head wearily between his shoulders. To Camille and Degas he said:

"It's Monet's way. First he cuts me to ribbons with his accusations, then he is obsequious, saying, 'I'm afraid to bother you; my demands for money are a burden on you. I know all your devotion to our cause.' " Durand-Ruel walked away a few steps, came back. "I am very annoyed the way business is going. All those whom I ask for help tell me to wait. The gallery keeps me exceedingly busy, but all I earn is trouble. I wish I were free to go live in the desert."

Whereupon he went into his office and locked the door behind him.

Degas exclaimed dramatically:

"Let us get out of here. These reflections in the water hurt my eyes. Monet's pictures always were too drafty for me. If it were any worse I would have to turn up my coat collar."

"Degas, *ne disputez jamais sur la pointe d'une aiguille.* Never quarrel on the head of a pin," Camille retorted hotly.

"I'm not quibbling. It's a poor joke."

"These exhibitions are too serious for jokes. Perhaps it is a bad idea to have a one-man show. The newspapers, knowing that a dealer is behind it, have not breathed a word."

For the second exhibition, of Renoir, Renoir and Durand-Ruel managed to raise enough money to hold a reception for the press and for a group called the "Friends of the Arts" the day before the opening. Acting on a hunch, Camille sent his brother Alfred an invitation. Alfred was flattered. He enjoyed the reception, particularly meeting some of the distinguished members of the "Friends of the Arts." He invited Camille to have lunch with him at a restaurant the following day and to attend the Colonne concert at the Châtelet. To Camille's astonishment, Alfred also invited him to his luxuriously furnished apartment at 42 Rue des Petites Ecuries for an aperitif. Marie received him coolly but correctly, then disappeared. When he was leaving, Camille said to Alfred:

"This felt like the old days when we had good times together. I enjoyed the concert. Bizet was new to me. I marvel at the 'Romeo and Juliet' of Berlioz. It's Delacroix, it's Shakespeare, the music has the mark of these men of genius. All the arts are allied.''

Alfred countered with:

"Send me an invitation to your own show. I didn't understand Renoir's work, and I probably won't understand yours any better. The whole batch of you are *outré*. But if I'm in Paris I'll come.''

Camille had been staggered by Renoir's showing. Though he displayed a number of fully clothed themes, Camille felt that voluptuousness was his driving force. Standing before Renoir's *Bathing Woman*, big-breasted, big-hipped, big-thighed, he realized that Renoir was painting out of a carnal love of the female figure: hardy, fertile, ready and eager to bear robust children.

Renoir came to his side and whispered a half apology for the slights in the letter to his brother, the deprecating of ''Israelite'' Pissarro's political views, on the grounds that his illness had depressed him. Seeing Camille's admiration before *Bathing Woman*, he said with his rolled *r*'s and drawl:

"A breast is round, warm. If God had not created a woman's beast, I do not know if I should have become a painter.''

"It's true that your flesh tones are more vibrant than Ingres's exquisite nudes,'' Camille observed. "You have an intense feeling for flesh, and your sensuality is good for your art. But I find your *Moulin de la Galette* and *Luncheon at La Grenouillère*, populated open-air scenes, equally exciting.''

"I paint flowers while looking at a nude model,'' Renoir grimaced. "Strange, isn't it, Pissarro? Yet I'm not difficult in my choice of models as long as I find a skin which does not resist the light and is not overripe like that of society ladies.''

He made a gesture of putting his arm about Camille's shoulders. Camille unconsciously stepped away.

For his own show on May 1, Camille decided to follow the example of Monet and Renoir and not exhibit more than fifty canvases, which would then be well spaced on the walls. There would be no room for what he called his ''knick-knacks,'' small drawings, pastels, prints. However he was like an indulgent father who could not resist showing off all his children, bringing canvases from home, borrowing from Julie's selection, from those still stored at Rachel's, in addition to those loaned to him by his collectors. He became so enthusiastic that he violated his resolve and hung seventy oils too close together. He had used the white frames he preferred;

the paintings were well lighted by gas lamps cleverly enhanced by reflectors which brought out his delicate wash of color.

The opening coincided with the official opening of the Salon. Many visitors came to Durand-Ruel's despite their fatigue after viewing the miles of official canvases.

Degas commented: "I am glad to see your work becoming more and more pure."

Entering the gallery, Julie exclaimed:

"It is beautiful. You should be happy."

L'Intransigeant commented:

> The Impressionists continue to give us their works. After Monet, after Renoir, it is Monsieur Pissarro's turn. Monsieur Pissarro is one of the fathers of Impressionism, and uncompromising. He has the reputation of not giving up an inch of his territory. Yet come in, and you will be stupefied—at not being stupefied at all.

The critic further claimed that they might be shocked, but they would also be enraptured.

L'Art Moderne found the same independence, liberty of interpretation, disdain for tradition and commonness in the canvases. Also that Camille sought the feeling of the open air, loved it with a great passion, then conveyed an impression of a "very great truth and accuracy. A rare quality in fleeting time."

Although half of the pictures were for sale, few were purchased. Nor had they been at the previous one-man shows. Art sales had caught up with the Union Générale debacle.

Camille missed seeing Edouard Manet frequenting his favorite restaurants, parading the boulevards in high silk hat, checkered vest and debonair clothes. He had been confined to his bed with what the doctors finally diagnosed as diabetes, a disease without known treatment or cure. He was doggedly working on drawings and pastels. Then his brother Eugène reported that gangrene had set in and the doctors talked of amputating the leg. Eugène said, "He will never allow that. He says he was born whole and he'll die whole."

The leg was amputated. Edouard Manet died eighteen days later without regaining consciousness, the first of the Refusés to pass away.

Camille went to the funeral at St. Louis d'Antin. The church walls were covered with black draperies with the initial *M*, the coffin was buried under a blanket of flowers. The pews held Edouard Manet's friends: Degas, Renoir, Monet, Guillemet, Emile Zola, Alfred Stevens, in whose home Durand-Ruel had discovered the work of Edouard Manet; poets and political figures.

The mass was said by the Abbé de Madoue, vicar of the parish. After the religious choruses and the mournful solos for the dead, the funeral procession went slowly up the Boulevard Haussmann, the Rue La Boétie and the Rue Marbeuf to the Trocadéro, then the short distance to the cemetery in Passy, where Camille and Rachel had walked when it was newly opened. There were shafts of sunshine at the entrance to the burial vault. After the eulogy, Eugène Manet took Camille aside.

"Edouard asked me to give you a message," he said. "He wanted me to tell you that he had been wrong, that he should have shown at your Impressionist exhibitions. That by all rights he should have participated in those failures and that ridicule. He owed it to you. Or to himself. It was the sole regret he expressed when he realized that death was near."

Messages brought poison, or its antidote.

5

Spring was reluctant to arrive. Georges and Félix were bedded with colds. In London, Théodore Duret had secured a job for Lucien with Stanley, Lucas, Webber and Co., music publishers. Then came the jolting information that no salary was attached. Camille assured Lucien that he would send him a few francs each month so that he would not be embarrassed by being penniless in the Isaacson home. Julie had agreed that this was proper. However Lucien now decided that the Isaacsons lived too far out, that he needed quarters closer to his work and London's activities. He wrote to his father asking for a larger allowance to cover room rent and meals. It was a violation of their agreement. No one knew it better than Camille.

"But what can I do?" he asked himself. "He needs independence. I have to give him his chance."

He asked Durand-Ruel to send Lucien a hundred and fifty francs a month out of his earnings.

When Julie learned about this from Lucien's letter of thanks, she was staggered. They were in the kitchen where, in a coverall apron, she was preparing vegetables under a cold-water tap.

"Did you actually send Lucien thirty dollars and promise to send him more?" Tight-lipped.

Camille got red in the face. He had not meant to deceive her, only to avoid a row.

"He moved first, told me afterwards."

"How could you? We need to make some savings." With the acid side of her tongue, "He must go back to his uncle's house. Where he had a bed and food. He promised. We must feed Georges, Félix, Ludovic, Cocotte."

"And me," he added with a wistful smile. "You are right, Julie. But there is a future truth which goes beyond the present one."

"Reality is today," she declared. "The future is always the same as today. Nothing changes. . . ."

"*C'est vrai*, the cycles for us have more bottoms than tops. But Lucien needs that second language. One year in England, speaking the tongue, will make him valuable here."

Julie made a derisive sound.

"Not the way you brought him up. To be an artist. Helping us to remain poverty-stricken."

"My parents helped me. It's our turn to give Lucien his chance."

"Your mother was right; you should have married a rich woman." She stared at him wide-eyed for a long moment, then threw her apron over her head and wept into it copiously as she had seen her mother do when her father had abandoned them.

"You love Lucien more than you do the rest of us put together," she sobbed.

He stopped his pacing, brought her apron down from over her face.

"We'll educate all our children. Equally."

She put her head on his shoulder, murmured:

"You try to be a good father. It's just that the money going to him could help us. We're six against his one."

"No, Julie, we're all one. That's what family means."

Julie crossed herself, something she rarely did in his presence. A look of resignation took over.

"May the Lord preserve us. No one else will."

In October Camille went for a spell of painting to Rouen, partly because he was looking for stimulating new motifs, partly because Eugène Murer and his sister Marie, erstwhile bakers and restaurateurs on the Boulevard Voltaire, had bought a controlling part of the Hôtel du Dauphin et d'Espagne and had suggested that he come to paint there. Julie's sister Joséphine would visit in Osny with Félicie's twenty-year-old daughter Nini, company for Julie. Durand-Ruel sent her one hundred dollars so she would be comfortable while Camille was away.

A large sign stood outside the hotel: *Magnificent Collection of Impressionist Paintings Which Can Be Seen Any Day Without Charge Between Ten and Six.*

When Camille stepped into the lobby and moved through the parlor to the smoking bar and restaurant he saw Murer's collection of Monets, Renoirs, Degas, Sisleys, Guillaumins, as well as half a dozen of his own works, all of which Murer had purchased with sous, croissants and omelets. Murer clasped his shoulders in an embrace. He still dressed like a Parisian bohemian, albeit a prosperous one, in a velvet coat, flowing tie, beret and fastidiously trimmed Vandyke beard.

Camille exclaimed, "Murer, you've established a *petit* museum here in Rouen."

"If the Great One in the sky did not mean for me to be an artist, at least I can be a gallery! Does Rouen understand or like the paintings? Not really. *Tant pis!* Everyone has heard about the so-called 'Impressionist' art and wants to be in the know."

Murer gave him a large room on the second foor with a view of the Cours la Reine, the waterfront boulevard on the Seine, main promenade of Rouen, planted with elms and overlooking the docks, the ships carrying cargo and passengers. There was a brown mohair sofa and lounging chair, brown and gray striped wallpaper. Murer charged him thirty dollars a month for his room and meals, "a genuine bargain." In rainy weather, of which Rouen had a good deal, Camille could paint from his windows.

After a comfortable night's sleep in a heavy wooden bed with thick bolsters, Camille set out to investigate the town. The sights were stimulating, the Seine alive with activity; the Ile Lacroix with bridges leading to it; to the north the river Aubette at the base of the mountains. Rouen was an old settlement, Celtic and Roman, which gained eminence as an archbishopric about 260 A.D. It had been sacked by the Normans, conquered by the English, made prosperous by agreements with the Hanseatic League. The great Cathedral of St. Ouen was on the Place de l'Hôtel de Ville, with the city hall on the opposite side of the vast square where Joan of Arc had been tried and burned in 1431. A fascinating part of the town was the one built by the English during their occupation, in the Elizabethan fashion with black painted wooden stripping separating sections of tan plaster. Rouen was an important center of shipbuilding, woven and dyed yarns, trade in wine, spirits, cattle, coal, timber, sand.

"And eminently paintable!" he cried after his walking tour. Murer was right.

His first picture was of the Cours la Reine, which the English painter Turner had done much earlier. He next made a drawing of the Rue de la Grosse Horloge and, when he had finished, discovered a lithograph of the same scene by Turner's countryman, Bonington, a half century earlier.

"The English got here before us," he confided to Murer a bit ruefully; "but I can capture the town in a quite different way."

While the sun was out he went on a binge, painting a near complete canvas every day, sure in his vision, sure in his strokes. When there was fog he worked from out his window in gray weather colors: the riverbank in the direction of St. Paul's Church, the houses on the quais lighted by a late morning overcast sun, in the background the stone bridge, to the left the island with its factories, boats, two-masted vessels of all colors. Everything his eye could see, his fingers could translate. He painted the square with its tramways, the coming and going of people. On a night in mid-October he wrote to Lucien: "You know that to succeed one must work hard. It is a good idea, while you are *at leisure* in London, *to keep this in mind*, for do we know how long this freedom will last?—Draw more and more often.—If you want to make copies of the primitives, there are plenty of paintings in the National Gallery, there are the Egyptians, the Holbeins. Paint the figure; and don't excuse weakness for the fear of drawing freely in public."

By the end of one week he found he had been working on nine canvases, all of which were more or less advanced. The next day he found another charming motif, a view from the balcony of a café facing the Cours la Reine. It was a small canvas, only eighteen inches by twenty-one. He knew the difficulties of working out of doors in changing weather; one had to realize the motifs in a single session. Most of the canvases needed another session in fine weather to give them firmness.

At night when he could no longer draw, he read from the

Zola novel he bought in Rouen, *The Ladies' Paradise*, which was being widely read because of its reputed open sexuality. Camille did not find it erotic. It was Zola's form of naturalism which he conceived to be the full truth about human life.

He also bought Champfleury's *History of Caricature*, an invaluable book with illustrations by Daumier, and saw at once that Daumier was the man his drawings showed him to be: a convinced, true republican. Camille felt the sweep of greatness of a man who had marched toward his goal but had not ceased to be an artist in the most profound sense; without legend or explanation his drawings conveyed their political and satiric meanings.

There was rain; he developed a cold. He had finished six of the eleven paintings in only two weeks. Of the five unfinished ones, two were passable.

One week later Paul Gauguin arrived, determined to get away from Paris and immerse himself totally in painting. He brought his family and planned to stay long enough to take the city by storm.

"There are a lot of rich people here. I'm going to sell, sell, sell," he exclaimed.

Camille helped him find a house to rent, but Gauguin's attitude about the commercial possibilities of Rouen began to be disturbing. Camille himself had no illusions about the sale of his paintings in the beautiful, conventional city. Not when a considerable part of Paris was still unaccepting of the Impressionists. Having taken a leave of absence from Bertin & Cie, with a family accustomed to living lavishly, Gauguin was insistent that Rouen was going to buy his paintings for high prices, that he would apply the commercial talent which had been successful on the Bourse.

After a couple of weeks of being pounded passionately by his erstwhile pupil, now a full-fledged pursuer of the success which had eluded Camille for most of his thirty years of work, Gauguin became difficult to be with. Camille considered the attitude not only hurtful but a waste of time. One forgot one's art and exaggerated one's value. Both he and Durand-Ruel had encouraged Gauguin to come to Rouen, but the relationship began to come apart. Gauguin no longer wanted to paint alongside Camille for fear their canvases would be too similar. Instead of talking about painting, they came close to a quarrel over France's foreign policy, the invasion of Tunis, and the French invasion of Hanoi with troops and warships.

When Gauguin insisted, "Our Foreign Minister is right.

We need protectorates in those far-off countries so we can exploit their natural resources," Camille found himself adding, "And the natives, who will extract the riches of their earth for our benefit."

"Don't be a sentimentalist," Gauguin replied. "Those natives have nothing. What we'll give them will be more than they've ever had. The opposition to our conquests is stupid and senseless."

They were diverted by news that Durand-Ruel's exhibition of Impressionists in Berlin proved to be a sensation of acceptance. The lone dissenting voice was that of a German painter, Adolf Menzel, who declared the painting to be poor. *Le Figaro*, the Independents' bête noire over the years, took up their defense, responding that the painters, some of whom were masters, were so well known in Paris that there was little point in again evaluating them. "No doubt the great Menzel is completely wrong."

Camille hooted when he had finished reading the article.

"Perhaps nationalism is good for something, after all."

Durand-Ruel wrote that he wanted him to show again in London in an Impressionist exhibit. Lucien suggested that Camille send only his best works. Camille did not take offense, but it set him to ruminating. Asking for stationery at the desk in the lobby, he replied to Lucien: "You tell me that if I have a show in London I should send my best works. That sounds simple enough, but when I reflect and ask myself: which are my best things? I am in all honesty greatly perplexed. Didn't I send to London my *Peasant Girl Taking Her Coffee*, and my *Peasant Girl with Branch?* Alas, I shall never do more careful, more finished work: however these paintings were regarded as uncouth in London. Remember that I have the temperament of a peasant. The eye of the passerby is too hasty and sees only the surface. Whoever is in a hurry will not stop for me."

Julie came for a visit with two-year-old Cocotte. She was again pregnant. They arranged with a woman at the Hôtel Dauphin to take Cocotte for airings while Camille showed Julie Rouen, walking her through the huge square, visiting the cathedral, promenading along the Cours la Reine, wandering through the Elizabethan architecture of the old town. To his surprise she was so enchanted with the city that, returning one noon to the hotel for dinner, she exclaimed over a bouillabaisse:

"Camille, I love it here. It's so pretty. And friendly. Couldn't we rent a house the way Gauguin did? We don't like Osny."

"No, Julie. I've already painted it."

He flushed. What use to tell her that the breach with Gauguin had upset him? Gauguin, who had been such a good companion, such a welcome guest in Pontoise; who had become so close to the Pissarro children, drawing with them, reading to them, making jokes.

He ate in silence for a few moments.

"Give me a little more time. I'll find a good house for us in my own part of the country."

Julie returned to Osny. Camille needed another stretch of sunshine to complete his canvases. Since it was raining he went to Petites Dalles, bringing back two large studies.

Then he got good sunlight and concluded his series of Rouen paintings, fifteen in all. He looked at them constantly, understood them only at rare moments, on days when he felt kindly disposed and indulgent to their poor maker. Sometimes he hesitated to turn round canvases which he had piled against the wall, constantly afraid of finding monsters where he believed there were precious gems. However at others he was eager to see if they were as sound as he believed while painting them, carrying his own peculiar vision. And at such moments he knew great solace, writing to Lucien, "Painting, art in general, enchants me. It is my life. What else matters? When you put all your soul into a work, all that is noble in you, you cannot fail to find a kindred soul who understands you, and you do not need a host of such spirits."

He returned to Osny on December 1, 1883. When he unpacked his studies and canvases they seemed very clear except for two versions of the waterfront. The exciting motifs had been the ships and sloops but he felt it would have taken Anton Melbye to do them justice. He settled down to convert several of his drawings to oils. During the evenings he read *Les Fleurs du Mal* by Baudelaire and *Poèmes Saturniens* by Verlaine. He did not believe those works could be appreciated by anyone who came to them with the prejudices of bourgeois tradition. Bernardin de Saint-Pierre's *Paul and Virginie* also moved him. As with Zola, De Maupassant's writing extended the movement toward sexuality in literature.

He did a portrait of Nini, Félicie's only child, who was visiting them in Osny. When Alice, one of Emma's daughters, came for a visit, they took advantage of her presence to go to Paris for a holiday outing to the Théâtre Porte-St.-Martin to see Sarah Bernhardt play Djamma in a French verse melodrama by Jean Richepin, *Nana Saïb*. Camille thought the decor too pretty, Julie found the verse incomprehensible, but both responded to the outpouring vitality and histrionics of the near forty-year-old star whom the French called "the divine Sarah."

6

He continued his search for a more satisfactory house in deep green country and stayed for three days in Gisors, an active, prosperous town northwest of Paris. He and Julie had visited its robust countryside market a number of times but they had not seen the wooded section with its extraordinary variations in terrain. Yet there was no house in Gisors he could afford to rent. In the neighboring village of L'Isle Adam he found an inexpensive house with an enormous garden in which the owner offered to build him a studio. Unfortunately it was next to a cemetery, the reason for the low rental. Camille decided that the view of the cemetery from the front windows might depress Julie or the children.

"Me, as well," he concluded.

In early March he found the house for which he had been looking; in Eragny, a small village of a few hundred inhabitants, a simple tree-lined street on the main road from Paris to Dieppe, two miles from Gisors across the narrow river Epte. The village was only a dirt road lined on each side by a dozen houses, mostly landowners, a few merchants from Gisors. There was only one store where Julie could shop in an emergency, owned by a Madame Herbie, who stocked a variety of commodities and spiced foods and barley-sugar sweets. The butcher would call at the house twice a week in his horse-drawn blue-hooded cart. Most of her buying would have to be done in Gisors, which she would reach in a horse-drawn omnibus. Because the village was without a post office, all letters would have to be carried to the market town of Gisors as well, a task assigned to the driver of the omnibus. But the village had a beautiful church, with a slim pencil-like spire. The church's garden had originally been a cemetery but only two inconspicuous headstones were still standing. The little brick *mairie* was almost opposite, next to a red brick building where a farmer named Charon kept his trotting horses.

To get from Paris to Eragny Camille would have to take the

train at the Pont de l'Arche and change at Gisors. Unfortunately the two railroad companies were rivals and determined not to facilitate train connections. The direct omnibus made the trip infrequently. The long waits between trains could be eliminated only by taking a carriage to or from Gisors. It was a two-hour journey either way.

Behind the house was an apple orchard overlooked by a raised outside porch. It consisted of seven rows or trees, five deep. Other trees, mostly peach and walnut, were enclosed by a rustic fence; and good meadowland. Alongside the orchard was an abandoned two-story barn. At the end of the long garden was a stream with pollard willows on the near bank. It was a convenient place for the family to wash its clothes.

The entrance to the house, as with the house in Louveciennes, was inside double wooden gates, with a well-designed portico over the steps leading to the front door. The two-floored building of alternating long and short red bricks, with a dormer under the sloping roof, two chimneys for fireplace heat, and at front and back four big windows symmetrically above each other, captivated him as it did Julie when he brought her to Eragny a few days later.

"Oh, Camille, this would be perfect. Lots of airy rooms. It leans a little, but I am familiar with that, and the rear garden is too big for me. Otherwise I love it."

The owner of the house, Dallemagne, asked a rent of two hundred dollars a year.

"Camille, couldn't we take it for a full year?" she pleaded. "We've always rented by the month, been behind, threatened. I've been dreaming about a home. Not to be tormented every month."

When he said that he would get the two hundred dollars from Durand-Ruel, Julie trembled with joy.

Though it was raining, spring was beginning to burgeon, the farms were green, the distant silhouette of the village of Bazincourt was a fine one on the horizon. Between the house and the barn the former occupant had built a poultry yard, which Julie said she would keep; and a pigsty which she took down to be replaced by a rabbit hutch. The farmer had left behind a substantial manure pile. Camille and the boys moved it to make way for Julie's separate gardens, one for vegetables, the other for flowers.

Durand-Ruel managed to find the money and Camille signed the year's lease. He and Julie went into Paris where they bought a Turkish rug for the bedroom; it was inexpensive but the colors were good. Downstairs she hung her curtains of faded rose with flowers and gold filigree work. The bed curtains were in green tones. There was plenty of wall space to hang the pictures they had acquired in exchanges with their fellow artists.

The house was even more spacious than Louveciennes. There were four big bedrooms upstairs. Camille and Julie took the largest one overlooking the apple orchard. Cocotte, not yet three, was installed next door with the ever changing *bonne*, the new ones hunted for by Camille in Paris. Julie had trouble with them; one drank, the next was so young as to be useless, a third could not stand the quiet of Eragny; they ran out of funds for a fourth. One of the nicer things about the house was that in pleasant weather the family could eat their meals on the back veranda overlooking Julie's newly planted tomatoes, carrots, peppers, beans, corn, squash.

When Julie learned that the Fenians, fighting for Irish independence had caused a dynamite explosion in London's Victoria Station, she became alarmed and pleaded with Lucien to come home. Returning, he once again became his father's assistant; taught his brothers and sisters English phrases. He had never held a paying job in England or helped support himself. His monthly London allowance contributed to the family pot. His plans for the future were vague; something about doing woodcuts to illustrate children's books. Julie, having fulfilled her promise to have him trained in English, now expected him to get a job where his bilingual talents would contribute to the family's income.

"I want all my sons to be artists," declared Camille. "That's how they can make their greatest contribution."

On August 8, 1884, another son, whom they named Paul Emile, was born. Julie was now forty-five. Dr. Gachet informed her that in all likelihood there would be no more children.

Camille learned that Durand-Ruel was getting severe competition from a dealer named Georges Petit, who had raised enough money to open luxurious galleries and was attracting high society. When Camille suggested that Durand-Ruel combine with Petit for an Impressionist show, Durand-Ruel declined. However when it came to the sale of Edouard Manet's body of work, the dealers cooperated amicably to show Manet's two hundred oils, pastels and drawings. The sale brought in over twenty-three thousand dollars, a respectable sum for Paris in a financial depression, during which Durand-Ruel had found himself obliged to stop all monthly advances.

Camille located a former art clerk, Achille Heymann, who had a narrow shop on a side street. He offered to accept thirty-five dollars as a cash advance from Heymann against three good-sized canvases; and was further willing to let him show a half dozen drawings for anything over two dollars each. Heymann did buy one oil, *Study of the Apple Pickers,* for a paltry sum. Camille also let other hole-in-the-wall dealers, Clauzet, Latouche, have canvases on consignment.

The reaction was immediate and violent. He had never seen Durand-Ruel in such a temper. He no longer looked like an aristocrat with a benign face and paternal manner. Gone were the calm, dawn-gray eyes. He summoned Camille to his apartment, a smaller one now that some of his children had grown and moved out. There was blood in his voice.

"Don't give anything more to this animal Heymann or anyone else who displays your pictures without frames in a dirty shop, to have them ridiculed. It is difficult to do you more wrong than by such proceedings. . . . It's a system with all these people who denigrate you; they seek to lower your prices by saying the worst they can about me."

Camille attempted a few words of explanation. Durand-Ruel waved him aside.

"I have signed for a new gallery and have some backers. Here's an envelope with sixty dollars. Work hard and make me some beautiful landscapes. Seek pretty motifs; it's a great element of success. Leave the figures a little aside for the moment, or put them in as accessories."

Camille collected his work from Heymann, returned his thirty-five dollars, retrieved his canvases from Latouche and Clauzet, and vowed that he would do no more philandering no matter how deeply *in extremis* he might be. He went back to his easel, inundated with ideas for Eragny, his own apple orchard, the village and surrounding land.

One day Lucien brought home a young man, Louis Hayet, whom he had encountered painting nearby. Hayet had long hair, a dreamy expression belied by a practical tongue. His eye sockets appeared to be on different levels. Camille asked to see the young man's picture, then cried aloud:

"Je suis étonné."

"Why are you astonished, Monsieur Pissarro?"

Hayet's canvas had no brush strokes or painted surfaces, only an enormous number of colored dots suggesting a river, people, trees, houses.

"It is a new technique. Called divisionism," said the

young man eagerly. "Have you read Chevreul's *The Principles of Harmony and Contrast of Colors?*"

"No. Tell me about it."

Hayet took a deep breath.

"Chevreul defines the primary colors as blue, red and yellow The secondary colors are green, violet and orange. The primary colors can vary only in intensity, not in hue. Hues of the secondary colors, however, may vary infinitely. . . ." He took another breath. "Chevreul sets his standard as the one supplied by nature in the prismatic spectrum; when sunshine passes through a glass prism it separates into different colors: these are the pure colors."

Camille was amused at the youth's exuberance over his academic theory.

"With respect, Monsieur Pissarro, it's a reality rather than a theory. In the mixture of color every blue pigment also contains some red or yellow; every yellow pigment contains some blue or red; and every red pigment contains some blue or yellow. . . ."

Mercifully Julie summoned the three of them to have coffee and apple cake in the dining room. When Hayet left, Lucien asked:

"What do you think, Papa? Is there anything interesting in what he says!

"Not for me, Lucien. Yet if the theories motivate him, *chacun à son goût.*"

In the growing financial deterioration in France there was widespread unemployment, thousands of prostitutes wandered the streets; the weak, ill, old were without resources and abandoned. There was a fevered collapse into depression both on the land with its bad harvest and in the cities where the industrial machine had ground to a moaning halt. The sale of paintings ceased entirely. Durand-Ruel had stamina and patience in the face of the demands on him for money. He had evolved a stance of endurance with the Impressionists. They were his children. Since the War of 1870–71 he had been their mainstay and guardian, the tentpole of their creative structure. He was determined to keep them alive and producing. Without him they might have floundered into despair and collapse. He rationed himself along with the others, contributing a few dollars to each as they reached the desperation point, never letting anyone go under. The painters suspected that he himself was begging and borrowing constantly to keep the gallery open. He was indefatigable in raising capital, organizing exhibits abroad as well as in Paris; never giving up hope, hardly providing enough sustenance but never abandoning them. He did not worry about those with family money or salaries. Those dependent upon him were Pissarro, Renoir, Sisley and Monet. He told Camille:

"Despite Proudhon's sometimes valid argument against private property, how would we survive without some rich parents to support their artist offspring? Not to mention wealthy 'amateurs' who collect paintings. *Hélas!* The other half of the Impressionists would be on my back, and we'd all sink together."

Camille apologized to the dealer for making his life miserable and wrung his hands, a gesture he deplored.

"I'm ashamed but I am still obliged to torment you for money. What to do? I need one hundred twenty dollars to keep things going and I have only sixty. Couldn't you complete the sum before the end of the month? Excuse, I beg you, my obsession, and believe that it's forced."

He was plunged into anxiety. For the first time, at the age of fifty-four, he collapsed into the cold damp valley of doubt.

Dr. Gachet of the orange hair, straw boater, admiral's gold-buttoned tunic tried to lessen the baleful mood.

"Pissarro, fifty-four is a time of self-doubt for all males. Changes take place in their bodies which affect their minds; they no longer believe their expectations of accomplishment. Of fame and fortune. The aspirations, the fantasies of success become dulled."

"What do I do about it?" Camille asked numbly.

"Outlive the period. Get a second wind."

"Do you have a homeopathic herb for me?" With a faint smile.

"Yes. One called courage. It's hard to sustain in this senseless world."

7

The mills of Camille's small art world ground exceeding fine. When he totaled up his income for 1884 he saw that Durand-Ruel had paid him one thousand eight hundred dollars, a fair sum except for the primal law of economics that income generates expenditure. Claude Monet was settled more or less comfortably into the house in Giverny; when funds ran low,

Madame Hoschedé added to her small personal income by working as a couturiere. In Aix-en-Provence, Cézanne with Hortense and their son were reconciled to a lifetime of painting without exhibition or recognition. No one was able to help unfortunate Alfred Sisley, an excellent Impressionist albeit a trifle less compulsive and penetrating, for Sisley had never learned how to cope with rejection or poverty. Degas called him "too gentle and accepting," Monet, "not sufficiently aggressive." Renoir argued that he was too much an English gentleman to beg, borrow, steal or smuggle as his ancestors from Kent had. Camille felt that the placidity in his nature was reflected in the mirror of his work; if the Fates decreed that one's family should starve, it was the will of Allah. Julie took them vegetables from her garden and fruit from the Eragny orchard whenever she went into Paris to visit her sisters.

Degas and Mary Cassatt did not suffer financially. They were companions in their work, models of discretion. Berthe Morisot mourned the death of Edouard Manet, her master and beloved, yet found contentment with his brother Eugène, and with her daughter, whom she painted from infancy on.

Despite a growing lethargy Camille went into the poultry market at Gisors, caught the enormous vitality of people testing, judging, bargaining, living more intensely than they did when they cooked the food or ate it. The market was the epitome of all class levels of hunger, desire, energy, the clearest manifestation of the surge of life in a community: its most authentic portrait. He had painted well in 1884 because of Eragny and the stimulation of fresh motifs. The first evidence of self-doubt, which had started in Rouen when he hesitated to turn his pictures from the wall for fear he would find them sterile, had grown slowly. He had painted every motif that interested him. Now he could envision only repetition, a debilitating force. An artist's mind and hand had always to be aware, believe there are new things to say about new worlds perceived, making the invisible visible. Both mind and heart seemed to have become disillusioned, closed down. For the creative artist this was a basic tragedy; he must leave center stage and wither in the wings. Were the indifference and neglect of the public getting to him? Had his small bout with prosperity and the simple joys of stability undermined his drive and belief that it would surely come? He had always felt that he had time. Had he?

Had he grown weary of what, only thirty years before, had begun to emerge as a revolution in painting which would revitalize the vision of mankind? Or had he reached the end of the road with the métier he and his companions had dug out of rock with their fingernails? Had Impressionism served its purpose and become still another phase in man's eternal need to express himself?

The brightest hours were those spent reading the recently published *Germinal*, which the increasingly successful Emile Zola had sent him. He wrote to Zola: "I read it in little bits. It is beautiful, great and terrible and it's certainly the work of a great heart. Thank you."

It was a bitter downhill road; the grade too steep; his brakes outworn. All his life he had been sanguine; no series of defeats had held him down. Now he stumbled, tore the cartilage of his knee, the soft heel of his hand on the protuberant rocks of doubt, satiety, dissatisfaction. His right eye was troubling him again. He told Durand-Ruel:

"I don't think I see enough anymore. My eyes are worn out from looking."

He was humiliated by his constant need to go into Durand-Ruel's for funds. The year before he had gone to a tailor in Paris to have a new outfit made; suit and topcoat to replace those that were growing ragged. The tailor was pressing for the balance of his money. Père Tanguy had been paid a substantial sum in January of 1883, but that was almost two years ago, and he had been painting prodigiously. Once again Madame Tanguy was demanding money to pay her own bills. But at bottom he was discontented with his expression, what he was getting on the canvas. Was it vital? Had his vision dimmed about the universality of nature? Or had it been mysticism?

He wrote to Durand-Ruel:

"My goal is to create clearly and luminously with very supple landscapes. I seek, I haven't found. That makes me sick! I am even more overwhelmed by not finishing these studies of Gisors. I am in the midst of a transformation, and I am impatiently waiting for some sort of results. I beg you to believe that it causes me great torment. It is obviously a crisis."

In the early months of 1885, perhaps by reflex, he painted a dozen canvases of the winter and spring of Eragny and Bazincourt. The summer of 1885 drifted by on uncertain wings. In July Lucien was invited to the vacation house at Villerville of his Uncle Alfred and Aunt Marie, the first hospitality ever extended by Marie. Félicie's daughter came to stay with them because her father, unable to find work, had become an alcoholic. Throughout August Camille found himself unable to finish anything. Worse, he had trouble finding scenes he was moved to paint. Julie's head was swollen from being bitten by a swarm of wasps. Camille managed the household. Lucien stopped at Pontoise for a visit with his musician friends from the lycée. He was still not home at the end of September. Durand-Ruel had promised one hundred and sixty dollars but had sent only twenty. By October Camille was thoroughly angry with Lucien, who had still not returned. Julie's expression suggested, "You get what you deserve."

While Camille was floundering, and 1885 was evaporating, Paul Durand-Ruel fell into a situation worse than his several near bankruptcies and sometimes loss of his gallery. It started with Georges Petit, owner of the luxurious gallery called the "International Exhibition," who had already lured away Monet and Renoir, whose mistress Aline Charigot had recently borne him a son, because of the success of his "blatantly commercial approach." Durand-Ruel was the world's authority on the work of Daubigny. A patron who had seen a Daubigny at Petit's gallery asked Durand-Ruel to authenticate the picture before he bought it. After a careful study of the construction, brushwork and atmosphere of the riverbank scene, Durand-Ruel declared it foreign to Daubigny's nature.

"Consequently it is false," he announced; "the work of an imitator."

Georges Petit, about to lose a handsome sale, took an oath that he had purchased the picture from Daubigny himself. Durand-Ruel, unable to refute such sworn testimony, and unwilling to call a fellow dealer a fraud, retracted his opinion. The patron bought the picture. Shortly thereafter a respected curator at the Louvre examined the painting and declared publicly that Durand-Ruel had been correct in his original judgment. It was a false Daubigny.

The scandal swept the art world of Paris. Durand-Ruel, the great authority on Daubigny, had been deceived by Petit and been willing to contradict himself. The press found it of news value and fed the public with insinuations that Paul Durand-Ruel was no longer to be trusted.

Camille took the long trip into the gallery to pledge his loyalty. As had happened several times before, he discovered the man sitting forlornly at his desk.

"*Alors*, Pissarro, welcome to another funeral."

"Monsieur Durand-Ruel, can you not expose Petit by publishing his sworn testimony that he got the picture from Daubigny?"

The dealer raised his weary face from the cradle of his supporting hands.

"I cannot. It would put him out of business permanently. I can only be hurt temporarily. The collectors who have bought from me over the years have never been misled or deceived. They will be faithful."

He swiveled in his leather chair, opened the cabinet behind him and took out a bottle of Duret's cognac. He poured them each a drink in potbellied glasses, observing:

"We have several times clinked glasses and cried *'Salut!'* There were good times and bad. My only regret is that for a limited time I may not be able to speak out for those Impressionists who have remained loyal to me." He raised his glass again: *"Salut!"*

With Lucien he dropped into Guillaumin's bare studio. Though he was still working in the government office and painting only on Sundays and holidays, he was becoming quite good.

Guillaumin grimaced. "I'm in wedlock with that bloody bureau. I've examined more bridges and embankments than any man alive. I wish they would all fall into the Seine. Then my job would disappear and I would have full time to paint. As it is, nothing but the drying up of the French rivers will save me."

"You're forgetting that million francs lottery prize you're going to win," said Camille with the first smile in many days.

"Vous vous moquez de moi. You're making fun of me. But I've had a feeling since childhood that I would win the grand prize. Such a lifetime presentiment can't be wrong."

The door opened and Paul Signac, a painter of Lucien's age, entered. Signac exclaimed genially:

"Monsieur Pissarro, I have the distinct honor of being the only one ever ejected from one of your Impressionist exhibitions."

"What were you doing, hooting derisively?"

"On the contrary. I was intently copying from your work, Monet's, Cézanne's. But Monsieur Monet informed me I had to stop. Studying from the Impressionists was not allowed."

"Of course we are to be studied by young artists," Camille exclaimed. "It's an integral part of the painter's tradition." He looked at the full-figured twenty-two-year-old; tanned and well muscled from years of sailing on the Mediterranean where he had a summer cottage in St. Tropez, and where it was known that his hobbies were sailing and fishing.

"Are you wanting to become an Impressionist?" he asked.

"I am studying with Georges Seurat. Pointillism."

In fact he had helped write the constitution for the new Pointillist group, the Société des Indépendants, headed by Seurat. Paul Signac was a fastidious man, stuck to his schedule of painting, and was perfectly at ease in a cape or homespun suit, with a spirit that insisted upon precision. A handsome chap with big expressive eyes, a well-chiseled nose and ears close to his head, clean shaven except for a slim mustache.

"Monsieur Pissarro, I want so much for you to meet Georges Seurat. His home is nearby. Won't you come with me?"

As Camille and Lucien walked to Seurat's house, Signac expounded on his master.

"Georges Seurat's Pointillism is a new approach to painting. It will revolutionize the entire concept . . ."

Camille was amused. Where had he heard those words before?

". . . the breaking down of colors to their basic elements," Signac was continuing, "by using small dots of pure color, permits them to be placed on the canvas without mixing them on the palette."

"An optical mixture instead a mixture of pigments," Camille observed doubtfully.

"Exactly. In that way the viewer's eye can distinguish every separate jot of color, achieving intense luminosity. Have you read Nicholas Rood's *Modern Chromatics?*" Signac asked.

Camille remembered the young chap Lucien had brought home.

"No. Nor Chevreul either."

"Monsieur Pissarro, I am a great admirer of your painting. But let me tell you about Rood's three constants of color: purity, luminosity and hue. . . ."

Seurat had his studio in his home at 128 *bis* Boulevard de Clichy. His mother welcomed them, acknowledged the introductions, murmuring, "All artists are welcome here. It is Georges's whole life. Paul, will you take your friends upstairs? I've been trying to persuade Georges to eat a meal and get some sleep. He says his pots of paint nourish him better than food or slumber."

Signac led them up the three flights to Seurat's studio, a big one running the full length and width of the house; for the dividing walls had been removed. As Camille stood in the doorway he saw Seurat standing high on a scaffolding before a huge unfinished picture. Tacked onto the wall were superb drawings in black Conté crayon; on an easel in one corner was an exploratory color approach for the monumental painting on which he was working, *An Afternoon on the Isle of La Grande Jatte*. Securely attached to the scaffold was a long board holding some twenty ceramic pots of differing colors in a neat circle. In his left hand Seurat held a series of small brushes, each of which he touched gently to its own pot before adding a multitude of colored dots to the canvas.

"He's hollowing out the space for a woman with an orange-topped dress and matching parasol," Signac whispered, "with her young daughter all in white beside her. He doesn't really know we're here."

Seurat finished the square he was working on, turned, saw the group below him and climbed down. Signac introduced them. Georges Seurat shook their hands warmly. He was a slender man with a long oval face, curly hair on a high brow, a beard and mustache with flowing ends. Even at work he wore a wide high-buttoned coat, a high white collar and blue ascot tie. He had been described by a contemporary as "a tall young fellow, timid as he could be, but with an energy no less extreme than his shyness. One of those peaceable but immensely obstinate people whom you expect to be frightened by everything and, in reality, nothing can deter."

It was also rumored that he had an attractive mistress and child whom he kept in a comfortable apartment nearby, visiting them each day during his afternoon walk. And that Madame Seurat knew about the arrangement and was content with it, just so long as Georges did not bring the girl home or contemplate anything so disjointing as marriage.

"It is strange that you should visit at this particular moment," Seurat said to Camille in a modulated voice. "Only the other day I was accused by Gauguin of copying your method. It's not true, of course; I have studied your shortened brush strokes and perhaps I learned more from you than anyone else, but Pointillism is my own. I've worked out every detail of the technique over the past years of application."

Camille gazed up at the huge canvas with its thirty-odd figures of all ages, sizes, modes of dress, postures: lolling on the grassy bank under tall shade trees, standing still gazing at sailboats on the river. Nothing moved; all of the people, the boats, even the dogs were statuary in airless space. Yet Camille found *La Grande Jatte* exquisitely created and deeply emotional.

"No, Monsieur Seurat, you have taken nothing from me. Pointillism, as you call it, is your own. You have invented with these thousands of dot, dot, dots a whole point of departure. It is still life, inert, breathless, yet breathing, peculiarly alive."

Seurat flushed with pleasure. Aside from his apostle, Paul Signac, he was not accustomed to praise. Unlike the Impressionists, he had not yet received abuse either, for his *Bathing Scene at Asniéres,* shown with his Société des Indépendants the year before, had been ignored. He had had no Baudelaire or Zola to praise him or Wolff to condemn him.

"In short," he told Camille, "I have not yet arrived on the Parisian art scene."

"We'll show your *Grande Jatte* at our next Impressionist exhibition, if you like, and you will have a *succès fou.*"

"I'm grateful, Monsieur Pissarro, but I'm not an Impressionist. I am a Neo-Impressionist."

"Shakespeare said, 'What's in a name?' Under any name *La Grande Jatte* will arrive. Now explain your technique to me. How and why do you dot, dot, dot?"

Seurat took a deep breath. His eyes were brilliant. He wanted Camille to understand.

"I know I'm attempting the impossible, to convert art into science. They are thought to be mutually exclusive. But with my technique I can make them compatible."

For almost an hour he explained that purity had to do with the amount of white light mixed into any color. That luminosity was a photometric problem. That what he had to determine was the degree of frangibility of wave lengths of light.

"Now," responded Camille, "please explain how Pointillism, or the dot system, enables you to put your theory into practice."

Seurat was exultant at having a qualified audience.

"Brush strokes do not achieve pure color; they change the intensity of all surrounding shades. Even large flat washes are varied in hue and hence imperfect. The dots that I take from my pure pots of white, vermilion, black, red, blue, yellow, violet, touched by totally separate unadulterated brush tips, give me fields of absolute pure color."

Walking through Paris to Rachel's apartment, Camille had two thoughts. Never had he enjoyed more the youth and enthusiasm exhibited by Georges Seurat and Paul Signac in their theories . . . and never had he been aware how old he and his companions among the Impressionists had grown over the twenty-five years since they had started out.

"I like both men a great deal," he told Lucien. "I may never understand those chromatic graphs Seurat showed us but no matter. He's the best beginning draftsman I've come across in years."

He had brought Rachel a gift for her ninetieth birthday: a warm robe against the winter's chill. A maid served them a light supper of cold meats and tea, after which Camille tucked her into bed, kissed her brow. He got into the mahogany bed in Rachel's spare room, lit the oil lamp on the side table and picked up the book Seurat had loaned him, Young's discourse, which had been published in 1802. He turned to the passage Seurat had marked:

> Each elementary portion of the retina is capable of receiving and transmitting three different sensations. One set of nerves, acted on by long light waves, produces a sensation of red. A second set of nerves, acted on by medium length waves, produces a sensation of green. A third set, acted on by short waves, produces a sensation of violet.

He paused for a moment, taking himself back to Seurat's studio and the enormous canvas in progress, with its divisionist color and muted transfusion of people and nature. In most studios there was the familiar homey astringency of oil paints coming out of tubes, turpentine, the slightly gluey smell of gouache, the faint scent of fresh canvas and strong scent of waste rags used for cleaning, the odor of paint remover for brushes, and frames. None of this was true of Seurat's antiseptic studio. Yet it was without doubt the workroom of an artist.

"He is a fascinating young man," he decided. "One of the most interesting I've met in a long time. He's not going to sell any of those huge canvases. Yet does it matter? There seemed to be enough family money to last Seurat his lifetime."

He sighed, "Ah, family money! I wonder just how God decides which artists shall be born into a fortune and which will *demander de la laine à un âne,* ask wool from a donkey?"

No answer presented itself; he fell asleep.

8

His conversion to Georges Seurat's philosophy unfolded over a period of months and a dozen hard-bitten discussions. He was caught up in Seurat's virgin excitement and enthusiasm, his belief that he was going to turn the art world around. It made him feel young, reinvigorated. Seurat's vivid personality and conviction, added to the fact that Camille believed that he had reached the end of the line with his own hard-earned technique, filled the vacuum between his discouragement and the public's lack of interest in Impressionism. He was stimulated by the completion of *La Grande Jatte*. The work, which progressed pictorially between Camille's visits to Seurat's studio, was moving and persuasive. So were Seurat's arguments as to why the gigantic painting was more than an illustration; why it was not true that all emotion had been drained out of the medium. Seurat was a good technician, both from his classical training and from his intuition. He was not going into a "static" Pointillism because he could not draw; rather he was using his indisputable draftsmanship to anchor his airless images.

"Could it be that you've never learned to draw air?" Camille asked him genially.

"On the contrary," Seurat replied, giving off sparks of intellectual denial. "I draw air first, then eliminate it, to make the boats, trees, umbrellas, people, more solid. Never wavering."

Camille had to grant that this was true.

This was a youth movement; an authentic one. In the past year he had asked himself many times, "Don't I need a new impetus? A fresh start? A more exciting approach?"

There also persisted a presentiment of dread that he would be cruelly wasting his time, negating his early work, in making so drastic a change to Pointillism. Seurat was enthusiastic about his becoming a Neo-Impressionist. He declared:

"Painting is never going to better the lot of humanity; it's time to turn to the abstract. Let's leave it to the novelists to expose injustice. Balzac in *Père Goriot*, Flaubert in *Madame Bovary*, Zola in *Germinal*. We have a different mountain to climb."

Camille asked himself, "Can it be that Seurat is insulated from the outside world by a rich and indulgent mother?"

In any event it did not lessen the beauty of his work.

A free-lance dealer sold two of Camille's fans for forty dollars each. If his paintings were not increasing in sales price, his fans were! Camille sent the money home to Julie, keeping only ten dollars to support his stay in Paris, where he tried to sell his best Gisors paintings, one done in bright sunlight, the other in a gray overcast. He did not think they were entirely happy pictures, perhaps because he had become dissatisfied with himself.

The Impressionists were trying to decide whether to risk one more group exhibition. Camille visited Mary Cassatt, pleading with her in the same vein he had used with Claude Monet:

"The crisis continues; we risk, without exhibition, finding ourselves in a more lamentable position than last summer. It demands thought, for we must sell apart from Durand-Ruel. Will we act separately? Will some succeed, perhaps, having admirers, and others enjoy nothing? Will we remain, arms crossed, waiting for admirers to ask us for pictures we have not offered them? It would be a disaster."

Julie sensed a new involvement and a growing ferment in Paris. Camille had been going into the city more frequently even though the two-hour journey from Eragny made longer stays there inevitable; but he had not been wandering the arrondissements for possible sales.

When Camille showed his first Pointillist canvas to his friends at the Café de la Nouvelle Athènes, they greeted it with an ominous silence. But when he took his first two attempts into Durand-Ruel, paintings consisting of small dabs of pigment with blank areas which he called "breathing spaces," and saw Durand-Ruel's flash of pained incredulity, he realized the extremity into which he had plunged himself. Durand-Ruel had heard of Camille's enthrallment with Seurat's Pointillism. He said in a voice caught between anger and resentment:

"So this is your idea of a fresh approach to painting?"

"It will get better, Monsieur Durand-Ruel, as I perfect the technique."

"The better it gets, the worse it will get. It's a one-man carousel. Seurat's. It's not meant for you to be a stationary horse on it."

"I can make it into something worth while. Please bear with me."

"I have. For fourteen years." Coldly. "You are walking out on your own very considerable talent."

"Then you won't represent my new pictures?"

"There's nothing to represent."

Durand-Ruel rose from his desk, put a hand on Camille's shoulder.

"It's an aberration. It will pass. I'll sell your earlier paintings whenever I can. But I will advance you nothing. Along with Monet and Degas, your paintings are the best of our age. In my opinion they will not become lesser works of art because of your present folly. You'll find one day that you have lowered yourself down a well. You will be a hermit crab living inside another creature's shell."

Camille left the gallery head down, oblivious to the passersby.

Instead of relating the bad news to Julie he began at once to organize the Eighth Impressionist Exhibition for 1886. He would persuade Seurat and Signac to exhibit. *La Grande Jatte* would be ready. It would astonish and move the art world.

BOOK TWELVE

"Plant Virtue in Every Soul"

1

In Paris in mid-January 1886 he received a note from Lucien in Eragny which would foreshadow the rest of the year:

"They've come for the rent: Mother found a pretext. If you can get the money to pay the landlord, return here. Mother claims that it's absolutely pointless for you to be in Paris and she adds that you're just annoying the people you asked to sell for you. Mother is very worried. . . ."

The dramatist poet who was to write the children's stories that Lucien's woodcuts would illustrate never wrote them. Lucien tried selling sketches to the newspapers, unsuccessfully. His association with Seurat and Signac had brought him out of his shell, given him self-confidence that he was not just the son of Camille Pissarro. On the other hand, Camille found that it was increasingly important to him to have Lucien at home, the only one in whom he could confide.

In late January Durand-Ruel paid Camille forty dollars for an early watercolor. He sent thirty dollars home to Julie. He was also commissioned by Seurat's mother to do a gouache. When Julie paid the last of her coins to an Eragny carpenter for urgent repairs, Dubois-Pillet, a painter friend of Seurat's, offered to lend Camille ten dollars, though the young man himself had little to spare. Albert Dubois-Pillet, with gray-green eyes, brush-cut auburn hair, cleft chin and oval face, was a graduate of St. Cyr, an officer of the French army. By the age of thirty he had become bored with the inactive military, finding an escape in art. Signac had helped to lighten his palette from the dark and academic. Though he was usually seen in the uniform of captain of the Garde

Républicain, decorated with frogs and a plume, and wearing a monocle, while painting he wore a blouse and outrageously large cravat to signify his independence. Camille found it exhilarating to be working in his company.

The new style and the assemblage of Seurat, Signac, Maximilien Luce, Dubois-Pillet, all Pointillists about Lucien's age, were refreshing. Luce was a Parisian, nearly thirty years younger than Camille, who had studied at the Beaux-Arts and the Académie Suisse and taken up wood engraving because his father insisted he learn a manual trade. He wore a battered hat, had a red beard, warm and melancholy golden eyes, thick lips, and was miserably poor. Seurat had converted him to Pointillism. He was using the métier to do industrial landscapes. He thought of himself as a revolutionary but his friends decided that he was a Catholic bourgeois at heart. He often visited at Eragny with his attractive, sad-eyed wife.

Lucien frequently accompanied Camille to Paris, where they had stimulating discussions not dissimilar to the ones Camille had had with his fellow Impressionists in the early years of the Café Guerbois. Paul Signac said:

"It takes great courage on your part to affiliate yourself with us. How much trouble your unselfish conduct may bring you! For us, the young, it is good fortune and a truly great support to be able to battle under your command."

Camille gulped. He had no desire to command any new movement, only to express himself once again with zest.

Often the two groups, the Impressionists and the newly labeled Neo-Impressionists, sat at adjoining tables at the Café de la Nouvelle Athènes. Camille, sitting with Seurat, was joined by Félix Fénéon, the young art critic who, along with the theorist Signac, was a spokesman for the Pointillists in Paris. There was ill will between the two tables which placed them a continent apart. Camille was disconcerted; he wanted to set forth for his longtime friends the possibilities of the exploratory technique; but the Impressionists cared not at all about the dot, believed it a ludicrous and a passing fad. When Camille proselytized about Pointillism some were amused, some angry.

Renoir, seeing Camille enter the café, called out:

"*Bonjour, Monsieur Seurat.*"

Gauguin was violently opposed to admitting Seurat and Signac to their circle. Camille retorted:

"It's only a few years since I fought for you. Why can you not fight for me?"

Gauguin pushed hard on his nose.

"Those little green chemists who pile up dots. The trouble with you, Pissarro, is that you always want to be in the vanguard. You'll sponsor any new movement, regardless of its value."

"Seurat has talent."

"He's a child playing with paint pots. But enough, I want to go and talk to Degas. He has the greatest talent among us."

"He despised you in the beginning."

"That's part of my genius, converting enemies into friends."

Camille looked about him. "You and the others are angry with me for wanting to make a change. It's all so human and so sad."

It was also human and sad, the picture of the older men at one table, resenting the youth and unmarked visages at the other. They did not wear the generous affability and indulgence of a Delacroix, Corot, Daubigny that success would have brought, but were still fighting for their own acceptance. Were they jealous for the exuberance they had lost?

Camille was hurt but by no means discouraged. He found that his "divisionism," an alternate term for Pointillism, obliged him to work much more slowly; still, he succeeded in getting considerable work done: thousands of dots of pure, unmixed color, only their juxtaposition producing the sense of depth. He had put aside his well-worn brushes, bought from Père Tanguy finely pointed ones; discarded his palette for Seurat's series of pots of color from which he tipped tentatively onto the canvas. He was painting the same peasant scenes, orchards, young girls gathering apples, with many planes of earth and foliage, but all was still. His dots were a suggestion larger than Seurat's; the colors more subtly juxtaposed; yet it was Pointillism to which he considered he had graduated. Serrated rows of cut hay, the women gleaning, the myriad dots of color and space around them creating pure light, rolling fields with planted hills on the horizon. There was no single touch of movement; but the multi-dotted landscape was the essence of reality. The peasant women in their bright headcloths, blouses and long skirts were caught in the essence of work rather than the action of toil itself.

Emile Zola, even more famous for his novels *The Dram Shop, Nana* and *Germinal*, had his new book, *The Masterpiece*, about contemporary artists, serialized in *Gil Blas*. The critical response was cautious while Pierre Loti's *An Iceland Fisherman* became the popular book of the year. *The Masterpiece* appeared to be an exposition of Impressionism and a repudiation of it. The Impressionists found it so far off key that they did not take it seriously, except to debate whether Zola's hero, Claude Lantier, was Paul Cézanne or Edouard Manet. Zola's boyhood chum, Cézanne, never spoke to him again. Claude Monet was insulted because he found his relationship with Léonie cruelly depicted. The successful Antoine Guillemet was furious because he considered himself portrayed as the painter who abandoned authentic art for richly rewarded Salon mediocrity. Camille did not find himself in the book but wondered how Emile Zola, while poor and unrecognized, had understood so well what they were attempting to create, and now, renowned and rich, missed almost the entire concept of what a painter was about. Zola's Lantier, seeking the one perfect canvas, had destroyed himself in the effort. This did not fit anyone with whom Camille had ever worked or exhibited.

The antagonism of the Independents toward him grew, but that did not deter him from resolving to put together an Impressionist exhibition in the spring of 1886, after a hiatus of four years. This time it would be even more difficult because of what they considered his apostasy. He went first to Mary Cassatt because she had always been the most considerate. Mademoiselle Cassatt had her brown hair piled on top of her head, was dressed in one of her full-length gowns covered by an unspotted gray nursing apron. When Camille was ushered into her studio she was sitting on a low hassock studying her new canvas, *Young Woman Sewing in a Garden*. She weighed the matter for a few moments, then said:

"I'll have several completed oils I'd be pleased to show. Why don't we walk over to Degas's studio; you'll need him."

An elderly housekeeper ushered them into Degas's cluttered room. Despite his deviation, Camille was still an exception to Degas's rule that he could not be interrupted at work. Mary Cassatt was never an intruder; their relationship had grown stronger. Degas listened to Camille's plea for an eighth exhibition without enthusiasm but casually agreed to go along. It was no great matter to him; he was selling, but reluctantly. He now considered his paintings eternally unfinished and did not like to part with them. However he insisted they show in May and June.

"But those are the dates of the official Salon," Camille exclaimed.

When Degas shrugged, Mary Cassatt said quietly:

"Do it his way. You are the only one who wants it desperately enough to put it together."

It was settled, Degas would participate.

It was now twenty-three years since the Salon des Refusés, yet the Impressionists had made little progress with the Parisian art aficionados, who still believed them to be a temporary aberration. Monet had gone over to the dealer Petit, hoping to convince collectors that Impressionism was not merely a whim of Durand-Ruel's. Renoir had followed on much the same grounds, leaving Durand-Ruel bereft of two of his best artists. Camille did not abandon him, he simply left works at lesser dealers, trying to avoid those Durand-Ruel most detested, and at the smaller galleries. Père Tanguy sold an occasional watercolor to apply against Camille's bill.

Camille, Mary Cassatt and Degas agreed they could have a good representation if Berthe Morisot, Gauguin, Caillebotte and Guillaumin would participate, and they would accept Seurat, Signac and Dubois-Pillet. They had almost always had to approach painters outside their own group to round out their exhibit. This time those painters, instead of being more conservative, would be more radical. Camille considered the show would be a consolidation of the two generations, appearing as a unified force.

There was little hope of attracting Monet, who was selling, though moderately. Renoir and Sisley had absented themselves years ago.

Durand-Ruel could not be approached for backing; he was still repaying a fifty-thousand-dollar debt from 1884. When Camille developed a shattering toothache and went into Durand-Ruel's to ask if he could borrow money for the dentist, the dealer had apologized that he had not the four dollars to give. A dentist, Dr. Paulin, an enthusiastic collector, extracted the abscessed molar and told Camille he could bring him a watercolor later.

Berthe Morisot and Eugène Manet had a combined fortune. Morisot was sympathetic, her husband hostile.

"Ask my wife to exhibit with the Pointillists? Never! I've had an early look at Seurat's *La Grande Jatte*. That's not painting."

Camille took a deep breath. He respected Eugène Manet for his business acumen but years of being married to the prescient Berthe Morisot had taught him little about painting.

"Seurat has something new to contribute. I am personally convinced of the progressive character of his art and certain that in time it will yield extraordinary results."

"Why not have each group show in separate rooms?" Berthe Morisot suggested. "In that way we announce to the public that we are different movements."

Camille swallowed hard. It was a halfway measure. Eugène Manet shrugged his shoulders.

"If Madame Manet wishes it that way I will finance the eighth exhibition; but it is to be clearly understood that, although the Pointillists claim to have grown out of the Impressionists, they have gone their own way and the Impressionists are not responsible for their excesses."

Trying to suppress his inner turmoil, Camille replied:

"It is also understood that I will show in the separate Neo-Impressionist room."

"It's your folly," Manet responded indifferently.

It was a disappointment when Caillebotte declined, not because he objected to Seurat, they were friends. He had visited with him on the island of the Grande Jatte while Seurat was blocking out his picture, and admired the workmanlike quality of the painting. It was just that he was too involved with his marine architecture.

"Forgive me, Pissarro," he pleaded.

When he sent Camille four concert tickets, saying he would be out of town, Camille invited Renoir and Aline to accompany him and Julie to the concert. Despite his underlying displeasure with Renoir, the man, Camille very much wanted the painter Renoir to exhibit his magnificent female nudes from what he called his "Ingres period."

"What are they playing?" Renoir asked.

"Mozart," Camille replied.

"What a relief. I thought for a moment it was that imbecile Beethoven. Beethoven is positively indecent the way he tells about himself. He doesn't spare us either the pain in his heart or his stomach. I often wished I could say to him, 'What's it to me that you're deaf? It's best for a musician to be deaf, anyway.'"

Renoir enjoyed the Mozart but not enough to agree to Camille's plan for an eighth exhibition.

"Why not?" Camille asked as the two couples sat over coffee at a café adjoining the concert hall.

"Because you are approaching art with theories. Nature knocks them to the ground. The truth is that there is not a single method that can be put into a formula."

Sisley also declined, politely.

"We're not a movement anymore," he declared.

Claude Monet was not so polite. He told Camille irascibly:

"I'm tired of hearing about your Impressionism gone scientific. It's a contradiction in terms. If you continue to harp on the subject I refuse to participate."

Camille's desire for change had created a schism between them.

Eugène Manet and Berthe Morisot found an apartment above the popular Restaurant Doré, on the corner of the Rue Laffitte and the Boulevard des Italiens, and put down the month's rent. Camille assembled a roster of seventeen painters, including old reliables and a new painter, Odilon Redon, an experimenter and seeker after an interior reality, who painted his own dream world. His remarkable lithographs were described as "going from a profound black to a blinding white." He avoided exterior reality in his work, yet he yearned for the admiration of the Impressionists.

They would have several months to prepare their show.

Durand-Ruel had received an offer from James F. Sutton of the American Art Association, with a gallery in the Madison Square Garden in New York City, to bring over a representative exhibition of some three hundred paintings of French Impressionism. He called the Impressionists together.

"This is a good opportunity—" he began.

"You sent our paintings to a Boston exhibition in 1883 with no results," Degas interrupted.

"But only a few. Compare the impact of three hundred of your finest works. They'll rock New York."

"It's an expensive business," commented Claude Monet. "Are you expecting us to pay any part of the costs?"

"Assuredly not. I've begun raising the money. There will be thousands of dollars in costs; but I'm determined."

Camille asked:

"If you take three hundred of our pictures, what would be left for our eighth exhibition here in Paris?"

"Your new work." Durand-Ruel's expression was both excited and gritty. "You people are painfully prolific."

It was a grueling task for Durand-Ruel, the assembling of the oils, watercolors, gouaches, framing them, arranging their safe crating, shipping to Le Havre for transfer to the New York-bound ship. He was resourceful and indefatigable. By March of 1886 he left with his precious cargo, which he valued around four hundred thousand dollars. He took forty Monets, thirty-nine characteristic Pissarros, thirty-five Renoirs, eighteen Boudins and eighteen Degases, eight Morisots, nine Manets, eight Caillebottes, five Guillaumins, Seurat's *The Bathing Place*, only halfway to his Pointillism; and a few conservative painters to absorb the shock. Before leaving he sent Camille one hundred twenty dollars for an unfinished

Countryside with Cows, which he said he was acquiring for himself, and which would tide the Pissarros over until his return. Although the canvas was not completed, Dr. de Bellio bought it from the gallery.

Camille left some watercolors at Clauzet's. Clauzet gave him appointments, then left him cooling his heels. Alfred Nunès, a distant cousin, sold a fan but Camille had to pursue him for weeks to get his money. He took out his feeling of humiliation by doing a series of dotted sailboats on the river.

He had let his hair grow long and thick at the back, keeping the bush down with a wide-brimmed felt hat. When he did a portrait of himself in pen and ink he found that his eyes had changed little from those in the canvas he had done for Fritz Melbye in their exchange twenty-nine years before: deep brown, observant, penetrating; yet still gentle, forgiving of all the pain he had caused and suffered. His eyebrows were still a fierce, attacking black, yet his now white mustache merged into his beard with a soft indulgent flow. He knew that his face and nature bore contradictions, perhaps inconsistencies, yet he felt that there was no way for his big strong frame to move except down a straight path.

2

The New York exhibition opened on April 10, a month before the eighth Paris show. Théodore Duret, who had grown up with the Impressionists and had defended them brilliantly for years, wrote an illuminating introduction for the catalogue. Articles from the American press began drifting in. Camille was shocked by their savagery. The *Commercial Advertiser* decried, "Gallery of Colored Nightmares. A collection of monstrosities." The New York *Times* declared:

The 300 oil and pastel pictures by the Impressionists of Paris belong to the category of Art for Art's sake, which arouses more mirth than a desire to possess it. . . . Coming suddenly upon the crude colors and the disdain of drawing, which are the traits positive and negative in the works of Renoir and Pissarro, one is likely to catch one's breath with surprise. Is this Art?

* * *

The New York *Daily Tribune* pontificated:

. . . Those who have the most to do with such conservative investments as the works of Bouguereau, Cabanel,
Meissonier and Gérôme have imparted the information
that the paintings of the Impressionists partake of the
character of a "crazy quilt," being only distinguished
by such eccentricities as blue grass, violently green
skies and water with the coloring of a rainbow. In short
it has been said that the paintings of this school are
utterly worthless.

The *Sun* declared: "Pissarro's landscapes are fantastic and
amusing; sometimes he is amusing without apparently meaning to be so." The critic of *Art Age* accused Impressionist
painting of being "communism incarnate, with the red flag of
lawless violence boldly displayed"; then achieved the non
sequitur that the landscapes of Pissarro, Monet and Sisley
were "full of a heavenly calm and wholly lovely"; that
Degas's art showed a great knowledge of life; that Renoir's
work was vigorous and virile. . . .

Camille soliloquized:

"If I'm looking for consistency I should make puddings
instead of paintings."

Among the occasional words of praise for the radical de-
parture in style, diffused color, concealed drawing, was the
New York *Herald*'s praise of Camille's eye for color and
Seurat's strong Impressionist statement in *The Bathing Place*.

Contrary to the art criticism, the answer of the American
collectors, trained for eight years by their Art Association,
was a hearty "Yea!" The New York *Daily Tribune* reported
that Durand-Ruel sold seven or eight paintings in the first two
weeks; James Sutton and Thomas Kirby of the Association
were confident that many more would be sold. By the end of
the month Monet and Renoir led the field with four sales
each; Degas and a popular American, John Lewis Brown,
were second with three. Berthe Morisot, called Morizot in the
catalogue, sold two, as did a painter unknown to Camille,
Huguet.

Camille said to Julie:

"Those seven or eight sales in two weeks could be a
beginning in America."

Julie asked:

"Will only the painters selling be paid? Or will the money
be divided evenly?"

*   *   *

Against Camille's wishes the new Paris show was called only "Eighth Exhibition of Painting," his comrades jettisoning the opprobrium attached to the word "Impressionist." There were a number of rooms in the apartment above the Restaurant Doré, giving ample space. Camille sequestered himself in two rooms with Seurat, Signac, Dubois-Pillet and Lucien. Seurat's *La Grande Jatte* occupied one whole wall; it was so enormous that it dwarfed Camille's nine oils, three watercolors, a fan, six pastels of peasant women, five etchings, only a few of them the new work. The Jablochkof Company had installed electricity as an experiment and a promotion for their new invention. The light greatly improved the later hours but the canvases were unevenly illuminated.

On the afternoon before the opening, when everything was hung, Camille met Degas in the improvised gallery. Degas was displaying two pastels of Mary Cassatt at the milliner; and a series he titled *Nudes of women bathing, washing, drying, rubbing down, combing their hair*, for which he had brought up tubs and basins to his studio. Camille led Degas through the separate rooms to Seurat's *La Grande Jatte*, then said disarmingly:

"I find Seurat's work most interesting."

With a wicked gleam in his eye Degas retorted, "I would have noticed that myself, Pissarro, except that the painting is so big."

"My dear friend, if you see no greatness in *La Grande Jatte* that simply means there is something precious that is escaping you."

Degas quipped, "Good things conspire to escape me."

Gauguin had brought in paintings from Normandy, Brittany and Denmark. When the catalogue was being prepared Berthe Morisot, who was showing a dozen paintings and additional watercolors, asked Camille:

"Shouldn't we assign you credit for being the proponent of Pointillism?"

Camille was aghast. "Oh, heavens, no! Seurat is very touchy on that point. He would be deeply offended."

Caillebotte had attended the early hanging. When he saw that Camille had sequestered himself with the Pointillists, he was disturbed.

"Pissarro, it's a mistake to align yourself exclusively with these divisionists. It amounts to renouncing your former colleagues. You should not break entirely with your past. It was too good to renounce."

George Moore crossed the Channel from England to see his old friends' eighth exhibition. He particularly studied the new element of Pointillism:

> The ten pictures of yachts in full sail were hung low, so I went down on my knees and examined the dotting in the pictures signed Seurat and the dotting in those that were signed Pissarro. After a strict examination I was able to detect some differences. Owing to a long and intimate acquaintance with Pissarro and his work, I could distinguish between him and Seurat, but to the ordinary visitor their pictures were identical.

Then, seeing Camille's *Apple Pickers*, one of the last canvases he had painted before his change of style, Moore made up for his harshness:

> The figures seem to move as in a dream: we are on the thither side of life, in a world of quiet color and happy aspiration. Those apples will never fall from the branches, those baskets that the stooping girls are filling will never be filled, that garden is the garden . . . the painter has set in an eternal dream of violet and gray.

In spite of the popularity of the Restaurant Doré and the heavy street traffic on the Boulevard des Italiens, there were few visitors. The journals were bored by the everlasting "exhibitionism" of this wild and hopeless group of aging *outrés*. Few critics bothered to attend. Seurat's canvas, as the newest innovation, received some attention but of a ridiculing nature. A few pictures were sold from the Impressionist rooms to the regular collectors; nothing of the Pointillists. Eugène Manet had to absorb the expense of the monthlong show; thanks to Berthe Morisot's loyalty to the group, he did so with good grace. Julie was not in a position to be so generous. There was nothing left of the hundred and twenty dollars Durand-Ruel had given them before he left for New York. She commented:

"You could have sold something if you had some pictures in the Impressionist rooms. You have sold in the past, one or two pieces. Some cash for my cracked coffee mug in the kitchen cupboard."

"What do you do with zealots?" he murmured.

"We are a family of eight. Do we rename all my children St. Francis? Tell them the birds will feed them?"

"I have train fare for tomorrow. I'll walk the streets until I manage to sell something."

She sighed deeply, her bosom enlarged from nursing seven children, and looked at the man before her, sitting motionless in a chair, his head in his hands, so different from the vital young man she had fallen in love with. The beard aged him. But the wide-spaced brown eyes were still luminous and warm. She knew he was not sleeping; that he was wandering the countryside, aimlessly, depressed. Commiseration overcame her.

"I don't know which is worse, being hungry when you're here or lonely when you're away."

Durand-Ruel returned to Paris on July 18, having been away for four months. At the end of the showing at the Art Association, since the gallery was committed to another exhibition, the National Academy of Design on Twenty-third Street had invited him to move the paintings to their galleries, a tremendous compliment to the Impressionists. He was allowed to keep them on the walls until the last possible sale was made, twenty-seven in all.

When Camille heard the news he was jubilant.

"Twenty-seven canvases sold. We should be getting enough to live on for the rest of the year."

He went to the gallery. The dealer was in good spirits, his handsome face uplifted, the clipped white mustache and silver-gray hair brushed back smartly. He seated Camille ceremoniously at his wide desk, stood by his side talking. Camille once again realized what a short man he was.

"There are two opposite versions of what America thinks of me, both equally exaggerated: I did not make a fortune with miraculous luck. Neither did I engage in sharp practices as the owners of some of the New York galleries charged. I am very glad I went there; and I have great hopes of possible developments, thanks to the American collectors and Art Association purchases aimed at getting a good representation for the United States. I was able to sell nothing of yours at the American Art Association but I did sell your early study of *Haystack* from Eragny to a Mr. Spencer at the National Academy of Design. He gave me a down payment. You said you were going to do a larger version next year."

It was the first word Camille had heard that he had sold anything. He felt a grudging sense of relief even as he exclaimed inwardly, "Only one picture out of thirty-nine major works!"

"Excuse a crude question, but how much will I receive?"

Durand-Ruel went to the seat behind his desk, glanced over some papers, spoke in the manner his artists had learned to trust. He had never deceived them though he had sometimes made promises of payment which he could not fulfill.

"You must realize that I had to pay back my borrowings. The packing and shipping across the Atlantic and my four months' stay in New York were expensive. I will give each of you a couple of hundred dollars. I'm preserving several thousand for our second exhibition at Madison Square Garden this fall. The American Art Association has invited us back. Now that we've broken the ice in America and I will have no loans or interest to pay, I should be able to sell four times as many canvases and bring you each back a much larger sum."

Monet and Renoir, who had sold four pictures each, were disappointed. Durand-Ruel did not reveal the differing prices paid for each picture; only that they were uniform depending on size, and that he regarded it as a group income. He did not show his books to anyone. He was not being secretive, he considered it useless to give a detailed report to an artist. As a strict religionist he would have cut off his hand before he would cheat any one of them. They were all discouraged, particularly the ones who had nothing to live on except their sales; but it would not have occurred to them to doubt his word. Even the trained business people, Eugène Manet and Gustave Caillebotte, agreed that Durand-Ruel was honest, that several thousand dollars in the bank earning interest against the second New York show would increase the painters' proportion of earnings from their second exhibit that fall, which was the best time for selling art in New York. Durand-Ruel immediately plunged into the collection of a different set of paintings, since he wanted his second show to be altogether new for the American collectors.

He put together an exciting second exhibit. When it was assembled and ready to be shipped he ran into a formidable obstacle. The New York art dealers, resenting the eight thousand dollars' worth of paintings which they felt should have been sold through them, and with a Mr. Knoedler leading the movement, so Durand-Ruel believed, caused the American Art Association to be labeled a commercial organization; even though the Association took no commission from the sales and actually spent a good deal of its own money on the educational showing of new French art. They pressured important political friends in Washington, D.C., to pass a law that Durand-Ruel could not sell anything in New York unless he paid customs duties on the entire shipment brought into the harbor. If he refused to pay the duty, every work had to be returned to France, even those that had been sold. They could then be reshipped to the United States and a customs duty paid on the sales value of each. It was an intolerable situation; no one was going to pay for a painting that he would not get back from France for months, which might perhaps be injured in the double passage, and on which there would then be a duty to be paid.

Durand-Ruel called for a meeting of the artists. They gathered in his gallery, sat around on the viewers' benches and hard chairs, smoking, drinking coffee, as he told them of the problem.

"Nevertheless we must have this second show. We've started. We have to further that process as quickly as possible. The delays have already cost us our assigned month at the Association. But the National Academy of Design will take us in the spring. Not as good a time to sell, yet we will be there to become established in the American mind. The money I saved out of the first showing will cover the cost. I'll stay only the month of the exhibition and hold expenses to the minimum."

"What do we gain if the sales will be slight in the spring?" Monet demanded.

There was the eternal optimist's gleam on Durand-Ruel's smooth-skinned face.

"I'm not figuring for the spring. I'm planning for the future. While in New York I will find an apartment, turn it into a gallery. My two sons will manage it. We'll ship in unframed, unevaluated canvases, watercolors, drawings, with minimal customs charges. Then we can frame them, stage exhibitions, sell, and return two thirds of every sales price to each of you."

"Can it work?"

"Yes. In a favorable location. With backing from our collectors there. When we gather enough money we'll move into the midst of our competition, become another American art gallery. We can sell from New York, I give you my word. It will take several years perhaps, but we all have the ability to survive."

3

He painted well, albeit slowly, finding his way for the balance of the year. Earlier he had completed four canvases, all in very short strokes, little more than Seurat's dots. He was using the color systems of Chevreul and Rood; and those of Seurat: shades of orange from bright to rust; hard blacks against blinding whites; pale gray-green for lawn and trees, subtle pinks, violets and yellows for faces, clothing, the river bed, rarely seen on canvas so pure before. He painted the prairies and the hills of Bazincourt. He carried his easel through the countryside he loved, among the stands of grass, trees, cultivation. His resolve was clear to those around him; he was painting the idyll of the Eragny-sur-Epte landscape, a portrait not only of the area but of its times. He was working as arduously as ever but was less productive. The application of the tiny touches of paint was a laborious process based on an intellectual approach rather than his more natural emotional or instinctual one. Though he mixed a little varnish with his paints to speed up the drying process, it was a painstaking task to make sure the newly added dots did not impinge on the not yet dry surrounding ones.

Meanwhile Durand-Ruel managed to sell two of the Hermitage and Pontoise paintings for sixty dollars each. Camille made no pretense of being a bookkeeper but when he added up his income from Durand-Ruel for 1886 he saw it would come to only six hundred and forty dollars. The dealer had paid him two thousand dollars in 1880, over twenty-eight hundred in 1881. Two more children had been born, Cocotte and Paul Emile, while his income had been reduced to a third of 1880's and a quarter of 1881's!

He cried in anguish to Durand-Ruel:

"Monet flourishes and I starve. Is he that much better a painter than I am?" He had cried that cry before. He refused to acknowledge, or chose not to remember, that farmyards and working peasants were not as attractive to the Parisian collector as Monet's charming, light-flooded vistas.

The dealer gritted his teeth, trying to hold down his emotion. Once again he replied, "Monet is flashier. Like that Gare St. Lazare series. He has also attracted a circle of admirers who love to be entertained at Giverny and buy his pictures.''

He often asked himself, ''How does Julie manage?'' though he knew full well the burden she carried. She was working harder than ever, needing larger vegetable and poultry runs to feed their numerous children. Her complaint that he did not do his duty was justified. It was useless to tell her that he worked hard too, that he pursued every opportunity to sell and earn money when the family was threadbare. He had tried to make it up to them with love, attention, devotion. Were they adequate substitutes? They were a happy family, here in Eragny, drawing together, writing stories about their peccadilloes, laughing at their hardships. In fact the children defended him when their mother stormed.

It was now thirty-one years since he had reached Paris and turned to painting as a full-time profession. It was inconceivable to him that after such a long and dedicated period he should not be able to support his family. Was not the workman worthy of his hire?

It was a blessing that the children were resilient. When there was plenty of food on their plates they gobbled it up. When they were on slim rations they ate what was available, then rushed out to play. They made no comment when there was plenty or when they were pauper poor. For when had it been different? They existed only because of Julie's harsh childhood in Grancey where she had learned to raise the vegetables, fruits, chickens and rabbits that enabled them to continue, and to work from morning until night. He was intensely grateful.

He was not lonely in Eragny. Paul Signac came to visit frequently, working alongside as Guillaumin, Cézanne and Gauguin had before him. In addition to becoming a good painter, Signac continued to be the brilliant theorist of Pointillism. He was of a generous nature and, backed by his prosperous merchant family, never arrived empty-handed, presenting Julie with a baked ham, a box of *pâtisseries* or a bottle of red Burgundy. Julie loved having the twenty-three-year-old in the house. When Camille went into Paris with new pictures to sell, or at least to place with a dealer who would display them, he would have dinner with Seurat, Signac, Dubois-Pillet, Luce or the young art critic, Félix Fénéon, who was writing so favorably about the Pointillists. The only limitation to his pleasure in being with these bright and spontaneous young men who revived his own youth was that Georges

Seurat, who had been overwhelmed with joy when Camille came over to Pointillism, was frequently withdrawn. Why?

Signac stroked his short, lacy beard.

"My best surmise is that Seurat is afraid that Pointillism is escaping his exclusive hold. He is prickly about having created the technique. Now he seems to be afraid that it will spread too far, that too many followers might dilute its impact." He studied Camille's face for a moment, decided that he could be honest with the beard of Moses. "I have the feeling that he doesn't want disciples."

"Including me?" Camille did not know whether to be hurt or amused at such youthful folly.

"No! He worships you. He's not afraid of your supplanting him because he feels that this is just a transitional stage for you."

"Seurat is right. I'm not tied to the stake as he is, ready for burning."

Cézanne had married Hortense Fiquet in April of 1886 and his father had welcomed her and the boy Paul into his home. Harmony having been established, Cézanne, Sr., died in a state of grace six months later. Cézanne, now the owner of the family estate, created a comfortable studio for himself in Jas de Bouffan outside Aix, settling into a lifetime of painting without any need to exhibit or sell.

The weather changed. Camille caught a winter cold. In desperation he approached a small unknown dealer, offering him drawings which he had accumulated over the past couple of years. The dealer presided over a narrow, hidden-away shop.

"I don't think your drawings are salable," he remarked. "They are too 'made' and not interesting enough. However I'll pay you twelve dollars, including the frame, for this portrait of your son Félix."

Camille shivered.

"I can't go that low. I'll take thirty dollars each, or even twenty, if you'll take four works."

"No. But I am interested in your early Impressionist oils."

"For nothing?"

He gathered his work and walked out. Julie was exasperated. Somehow he had always managed to bring home a few francs . . . or the promise of them.

"I can't make a stew out of hope; it takes meat and garlic."

He squared his shoulders.

"The truth is I constantly run after dealers and do not waste an opportunity. I am obliged to dance attendance on them; for a single rendezvous I lose five or six days. They don't show up, they forget. You don't know the embarrassment I feel, the explanations I must make; the absurd discussions I must endure. If all this led to something; but no, nothing. It's heartbreaking."

While in Paris he slept at Rachel's. She was becoming increasingly feeble. Alfred supplied her with medication and a housekeeper, who kept some food hot for Camille when he returned to the apartment at night, shredded with fatigue from the endless encounters. Rachel was always glad to have him there. She had a horror of dying alone. When Lucien was in Paris he also stayed with Rachel, who sometimes mistook him for Camille as a young man.

Lucien was jubilant when he sold his first woodcut to *La Revue Illustrée*, rushing home with the money to pay a month's back rent. Julie too sometimes identified him with the young Camille. She had come to the conclusion, after almost thirty years, that Rachel had begun with.

"It's hopeless. Find a paying job and earn a living like everyone else."

All the galleries seemed to have closed down. Camille took into Durand-Ruel his newly completed *Gray Weather*. It did not please the dealer or his son Joseph, whom he had taken into the gallery some time back. They objected to the red roof and the brick house, precisely what had inspired him to do the painting; and to the backyard, which in Camille's judgment gave character to it. He returned to Eragny penniless and travel-weary. The young ones were riding Monsieur Charon's horses, playing in the tall grain fields, bathing in the Epte. The evenings were pleasant, the six of them remaining around the dining-room table with their notebooks, stories, games. All the children were skilled at drawing; it was a way of life for them. They had grown up with artists; each had taught them a little, as well as leaving sketches and watercolors behind for their walls. Cézanne had been generous in giving the family portraits of himself and Hortense, as well as a painting *Wine Market*, all hanging in the living room, along with a Claude Monet *Effect of Snow* and several paintings by Guillaumin and Gauguin, who had stayed with them so often. On the dining-room walls there were a Degas dancer and small oil paintings by Mary Cassatt and Sisley. Scattered throughout the bedrooms were many of Camille's studies, frequently in color, interspersed with a painting and drawing by Seurat or

Signac, a Delacroix oil earned by a swap for one of his best Pontoise landscapes. On the walls of the hallways were Camille's etchings, along with those of Degas, Cassatt, Bracquemond.

Camille had recently taken young Félix, Georges and Ludovic for a tour of the Louvre. Félix commented:

"We have our own museum."

The children were also decorating the Eragny house: Georges with a variety of birds; Félix preferred rodents, which he painted on the upstairs doors. Cocotte was the only daughter amidst the five energetic and rambunctious boys. Camille took her for walks in the fields, teaching her the names of the flowers, plants, trees in his paintings. Julie taught her to sew and make her own dolls; she joined her mother at the kerosene lamp after the supper dishes had been cleared, while the boys made amusing caricatures instead of doing their schoolwork. The quiet village, the countryside and the river Epte offered endless adventure.

None of them had haircuts. Félix's rich brown hair was worn forward, covering his ears and shoulder blades. Ludovic had lighter hair parted in the middle and curling around his face like a girl's. Paul Emile, the youngest, was scragglyhaired. Cocotte had long curls over her shoulders. No one suggested that they were beautiful children, but they were appealing, defiantly individual in nature, alternately favoring Julie, then Camille. Georges, eldest after Lucien, had never fully recovered from the trauma of his early seizures and fell into hostile and querulous moods. The others learned to run away from him when he was in what they called "a bad way."

On one occasion he turned sullen and savage. Quarreling with Julie because he had no job and was not attempting to work, he shouted at her:

"You are nothing here, only a maid; Papa's mistress."

Julie blanched.

Later he apologized abjectly.

"You're not a *bonne*. You're my wonderful maman, and I love you."

For the rest they were a noisy, busy group, loved their parents, and kept them living in turmoil. Camille adored them.

Maximilien Luce came out to sketch family portraits: Camille in his spectacles and beret; Georges reading a book, Cocotte sewing, the other boys drawing, lolling. Julie was cooking dinner and did not get into the group picture but commented, more amused than caustic:

"Someone has to feed all you artists. Otherwise how will you all go down in history?" Glancing sideways at Camille, who was looking through the bottom of his spectacles and over the broad expanse of his beard, she added: "I can even get some flavor in when there's money for mustard, sugar or butter. Why couldn't I have produced one smart business-man? He could have supported us all."

4

There was absolutely no hope for a ninth exhibition of the Impressionists. Camille was distressed: he had been con-vinced from the beginning that the Impressionist shows, most of which had been failures and had lost money, were an indestructible foundation upon which they could ultimately reach the heights of the Barbizon School of the 1830s. By way of compensation he was approached by Octave Maus, the leader of a Belgian organization known as Les Vingt, an advanced group which each year invited foreign artists to show with them in Brussels. Seurat, Signac, Dubois-Pillet had also been invited. The report was that the Belgians were not as hard-crusted about change and new ideas as the French. He borrowed a couple of paintings from Julie, who disliked his change of technique because of the extreme penury into which it had plunged them, but had been captivated by his Pointillist *View from the Artist's Window in Eragmy*. Dubois-Pillet advised him to send only his new work.

"The public will be confused by two approaches."

Camille did not believe this was so; for him the one technique had grown out of the other and would be clearly discernible. But he sought harmony with his new friends and agreed.

The hostility of what he now began to call "The Romantic Impressionists" became more marked. "I am not a roman-tic!" he told himself. "I would really have no *raison d'être* if I did not pursue a considered technique which yet leaves me free to express myself."

Though the group met regularly at the Café de la Nouvelle Athènes, they no longer sent word to him to join them. To his amazement he found that Gauguin and Degas had become close friends. Gauguin went frequently to visit Degas in his studio, where Camille now felt uncomfortable. Someone told Raffaëlli, who had twice exhibited with the Impressionists, that Camille was angry with the old group. Camille retorted:

"It seems to me that they are the ones who are offended, and all because I have had the cheek to have an idea which they don't share. These authoritarians are intractable and incorrigible. But they are men of genius!"

On one occasion at the café, Guillaumin came over to shake hands with him and ask whether he was going to dine with them on Thursday. It was the first he had heard of the dinner. He had sixty cents in his pocket; he was certainly not going to hunt up two dollars for a dinner where he was not wanted.

Instead he went to Dubois-Pillet's. Seurat, Signac, Fénéon were there. These men had become his comrades, had taken the place of the Impressionists. He told them, as he had told his old comrades:

"We have the stuff to be strong," and wrote to his son from Paris: "I do not believe, my dear Lucien, that to be understood I shall have to wait as long again as I did when I made my debut. . . . One complete exhibition and we will have arrived."

But a small voice at the back of his mind queried as it never had before: "Am I indulging in fantasy?"

Durand-Ruel at last relented and accepted two small Pointillist paintings but complained that there was no firmness in the foreground. It was evening, Camille explained, and he was seeing the painting by gaslight, which neutralized the orange tones. The dealer said he would pay him later, when he sold something. Camille did not dare tell Julie but wrote to Lucien: "I am here without a cent. I shall be hard put to find a solution. Even if I wanted to leave I would not be able to do so without borrowing. I would rather lose time now, when the days are short and my paintings are drying, but this is a difficult moment. New Year's Day, 1887, is terrible for selling expensive objects, people only give sweets as gifts nowadays, this costs only a few francs and is better received."

Again he was profoundly grateful that he had Lucien for a confidant. There was no one else to whom he could pour himself out, and no man should live his years inside the rib cage of his head with no way to let out the wild animals. When words got locked inside one became a prisoner.

Dubois-Pillet volunteered to lend him a few dollars. He returned to Eragny, completed another picture for the Brussels show. He had been yoked to a canvas of the fields of Bazincourt for fifteen days and believed it much improved, more luminous, though there would always be something strange about working with points of color. If he was patient, he felt that after a while he would achieve a surprising grace.

He made a pen and ink drawing of the pig market in St. Martin. The figures came out like pitted granite statues. It was what Durand-Ruel had warned against; life had fled. He would have to be more careful.

The weather turned bad and he could not work out of doors. He completed several paintings in dots, then did two pen drawings from earlier studies. He liked the drawings and hoped he could sell them to get the family through "the terrible month of January."

Instead Durand-Ruel wrote that he had sold an earlier painting to Faure, the opera singer. Lucien sold another woodblock to *La Revue Illustrée* and placed a drawing with *La Vogue*, which brought a cautious smile to his mother's lips and noisy joy to the younger children. When the weather turned sharp and clear Camille anchored his easel in the earth, set his mind to the winding road before him, the hills in the background. He had adjusted his equipment to carry the minimum number of paint pots he would need.

The isolation and repudiation by his friends of thirty years began to corrode the basic sweetness of his nature, twisting his judgment. Seeing some paintings Monet had done the year before, he found one, in bright sunlight, which he considered incomprehensible, with great blobs of white mixed with Veronese greens and yellows, the drawing completely lost. He looked at his own *Eragny*, with its aura of calm, saw the advantage of the unmixed color, the clear and solid draftsmanship. He did not hesitate to point out the difference to Durand-Ruel, who replied that Monet pitied Camille because of the course he had taken.

When Seurat's mother learned that Camille did not have the omnibus fare to move about Paris she sent word that she would like to buy one of his dot paintings, a small canvas, for about twenty dollars.

Camille was touched by her kindness. He had a little sunset painting, *Autumn*, about sixteen inches.

He gave Julie sixteen dollars, kept four for expenses. He then went into Durand-Ruel and asked him to buy everything in his studio except the pastels and drawings. Durand-Ruel remained silent. He went to see another dealer. If he could, even at a sacrifice, get a few thousand francs he would be able to work tranquilly for a while. He would sell everything except the ones belonging to Julie, or his favorite oils hanging in the dining room.

He could find no one interested.

The year 1886 had proved longer than its number of days. By mid-January of 1887 the weather had become foul, but Lucien brought him the rumor that the dealer Petit was anxious to buy some of his earlier work. In his new pessimism he became afraid that Monet or Renoir might work against him with Petit, then admonished himself, pounding the palms of his hands against his temples:

"What is happening to me? I'm falling into such despair that I am disparaging my old friends, who would never harm me."

When he approached Petit he found the dealer uninterested.

He left a painting at a small dealer by the name of Enot in the Rue des Pyramides. He left a fan with Dr. Paulin, who was going to try to sell it. The dentist also had a friend who might want an oil painting for sixty dollars. The Arosa brothers had vanished. Murer, in his hotel in Rouen, already had a whole gallery of Impressionists. He wrote home:

"I'm trying to find a solution but the daily threatenings of war between France and Germany cry halt to everything; although paintings are the best investment."

From Les Vingt in Brussels Camille learned he was praised by a Belgian poet in *La Vie Moderne,* but sold nothing. Seurat's *La Grande Jatte* was declared scandalous by the Belgian press.

Against a stone wall, he decided the only thing left for him to do was sell his Degas pastel, a gift from Degas and his most prized possession, one that brought him continual joy. It would be painful but Degas was selling and he could get from one hundred to one hundred sixty dollars for it. Degas would be offended, but it would lighten the burden at home. Sacrifice was like the newly invented match that never went out.

He saw nothing of his fellow Impressionists except for Mary Cassatt. Degas so ridiculed Pointillism that Camille did not wish to expose himself to the biting wit. Gauguin had gone to live in Pont-Aven in Brittany, where he was leading a school of painters at the Pension La Mère Gloanec. Guillaumin had married his German cousin, a professor of letters; he then signed a contract with the dealer Clauzet and became unavailable. The days, weeks and months over the years that Gauguin and Guillaumin had spent in the Pissarro home, studying and being taught as they painted beside Camille, vanished as if they had never been. Monet, Renoir and Sisley were busy painting and being sold by the Petit gallery. It depressed him to think of how entirely he was cut off from the colleagues with whom he had worked and grown and fought. Even Dr. de Bellio, who had written him at the end of February to come and visit him, had had nothing more to say than that he did not believe that scientific research into the nature of color and light could help the arts. Nor could the law of optics. To Camille's remonstrance that the discoveries of Chevreul and other scientists had enabled him to distinguish between color and light, Dr. de Bellio had answered that Camille had always taken that into account instinctively, that art and science were fine taken separately. They made poor bedfellows. He did not buy even one small canvas.

Camille wanted to write to Julie but lacked the three cents for postage.

There was no help for it.

He got two hundred and twenty dollars for the Degas.

Julie hired a country girl for a few francs to assist with the younger four children. It would earn her a respite from the increasing drudgery and overwork of the three years since Paul Emile had been born. It lasted only a few weeks. The relative with whom the girl had left her own two children arrived without warning and deposited them on the Pissarros' doorstep.

In early March Heymann sold three watercolors. He paid Camille twelve dollars for his share but believed he was about to sell a large gouache. Camille took three Pointillist paintings into the luxurious Georges Petit gallery, whose international exposition was scheduled to open the first week in May. Monet and Renoir persuaded Petit's committee to admit Camille's work.

"It would be devilish bad luck," Camille observed to Julie, "if I did not conclude a deal which would enable me to stay in Eragny and take advantage of the good weather and sunlight."

"It's always sunny when we have the means to live," she commented dryly.

For the Petit show he had Cluzel frame an additional five of his latest landscapes with a white matting, a larger flat oak surface and a narrow gilt laurel border. In mid-March he met Théodore Duret, returned from London, who burst out with:

"Ah! You are going to exhibit, but you know you should regard this purely as a commercial affair. It is a most stupid milieu. Stupid! Nothing can be done anymore, even Zola lowers himself to earn a few cents. My dear friend, I withdraw from writing even on art. The newspapers have a horrible fear of whatever is not banal or stupid. I am content to work quietly at Cognac.''

When Duret was plying his way down the boulevard, Camille said to himself, ''That word 'commercial' has a different odor when you have no need of money.''

If, as Duret said, the Petit exhibition smelled of bourgeois values, he wanted the experience of seeing his new pictures ''hanging with those of the leaders of triumphant Impressionism.'' For the test to be decisive, he decided, he would have needed at least fifteen canvases. Nor should his works have been scattered as they were, while the Monets, Renoirs, Sisleys, Morisots, Raffaëllis, Whistlers, were shown in groups. He was enraged when Petit, to please a foreign painter, withdrew his *Plain of Eragny* and hung in its place a lesser Monet. He complained so bitterly that he was allowed to rehang it.

He sank deeper into a deprecatory mood. Monet's paintings were too lacking in the light that bathes bodies in the shade as well as the sun. Renoir was without the gift of drawing and without his former instinctive feeling for beautiful color. Sisley was adroit and delicate but false. He liked Whistler's fine sketches. Morisot had some excellent things. The new sculptor Rodin was a great artist though a little mannered. The foreign artists were inconceivably bad.

Julie did something totally unexpected; she went into Paris without informing Camille, to see Petit's international exposition, touring the gallery by herself. She made no comment.

He did not sell anything from Petit's show, took his usual shower of abuse; but received some kind words from the critic Jules Desclozeau:

> Camille Pissarro has painted a field bathed in sunlight, whose forms, colors and reflections are admirably synthesized. It is more *field* than any field we have ever seen.

5

It was at Petit's that Camille met Theo and Vincent Van Gogh. He had heard about the brothers but their paths had not crossed. Theo was a slightly built figure, with a straight nose, meticulously trimmed mustache, high brow and mass of scrupulously combed curly hair; friendly but serious eyes, pale, smooth skin. He and his brother Vincent were sons of a dominie in Brabant, Holland. Well educated, serene by nature, Theo was dressed in a fine black coat and clergyman-like stiff white collar. He had been trained as an art dealer by his Uncle Van Gogh, who had owned the Goupil Galleries in Amsterdam, London and Paris.

The two brothers, who had been close friends all their lives, could not have been a more striking contrast. Vincent, not long arrived in Paris, was an explosive iconoclast. He had red hair, a scraggly red beard, was dressed in rough clothes and square-toed boots. In his bursts of excitement the words came out of his mouth too fast. He had failed at formal studies of Latin and theology under his uncle the Reverend Mr. Stricker's guidance in Amsterdam; had volunteered to go into the poverty-stricken coal region of Belgium's Borinage as an evangelist; had reduced himself to penury and illness after an explosion in one of the mines; and been rescued from near death by Theo. He had read widely in the world's literature and had a poetic and philosophical mind. In his painting he was what the academics would have condemned, an enthusiast. He had painted for several years in The Hague and in Brabant, living with his parents, and had come to Paris at Theo's insistence.

Realizing that Vincent, who had been sketching avidly, wanted to devote his life to painting, the brothers had formed a partnership. Theo would support Vincent from his salary as manager of the former Paris Goupil Gallery, now called Boussod & Valadon; in return he would have all of Vincent's art work to place.

Theo was a successful art dealer selling conventional pictures for high prices on the ground floor of Boussod & Valadon. However he cared little for the routine paintings that supported the gallery; his heart was on the entresol where he had gained permission to show Monet, Degas, Renoir, Sisley, without any success. When Theo took Vincent up to the mezzanine on the Boulevard Montmartre on his first day in Paris and showed him the Impressionists, Vincent had exclaimed:

"Am I in a madhouse? Where has such color come from?"

Now as the brothers stood together in Petit's gallery and met Camille, Theo said, "Monsieur Pissarro, I've seen your work at Durand-Ruel's, and of course at the Impressionist exhibitions. I would not want to intrude on Durand-Ruel's exclusive . . ."

"He has no exclusion on me," Camille interrupted; "he no

longer buys outright, nor does he show more than a fraction of my work.''

Theo had a warm smile.

"Then if you have anything you would like me to show on my entresol, please bring it in. I'll do my best to make good deals for you.''

Vincent added, "Monsieur Pissarro, could I come out to your studio and study your work? Both your Impressionist and Pointillist techniques.''

"Any time. I'll meet your train in Gisors.''

Camille delivered several of his earlier landscapes to Theo Van Gogh at the Boussod & Valadon gallery. The dealer got in touch with his collectors, aroused some interest but no sales. He was not discouraged. Julie welcomed Vincent Van Gogh, who stayed several days, sleeping on a cot in Lucien's room. Camille commented:

"Julie is gracious to everyone.''

Indeed she had been hospitable to the long line of Camille's impoverished painter friends. She felt that Vincent looked battered, as though life had trod across him roughly. Yet he was gentle with the children, teaching them how to draw Dutch potato eaters, telling them stories of Brabant and the Borinage.

Theo Van Gogh quickly fulfilled his promise, selling a gouache which Camille could only vaguely remember to a young man by the name of Nélaton. Camille, in his exuberance, exclaimed:

"I'm damned lucky. That gouache brought sixty dollars. Where the devil is she now, Dame Misfortune? Can it be that she's forgotten me?''

In the fine late spring weather Camille took Vincent out into the fields around Eragny, talked about the creativity of nature, the finding of motifs, the freshly plowed and planted acres of hay and wheat, the tilt of the rolling hills, the protective copse of trees between the farms, the blossomings of the apple and pear orchards. They saw alike the varying colors of vegetable gardens extending to the banks of the river or the base of a foothill; the lilting white clouds in the bowl of blue sky overhead.

"What you say is true," Vincent exclaimed; "you must boldly exaggerate the effects of either harmony or discord which colors produce.''

In the evenings they animatedly tackled the theories of art, the philistine's ability to live comfortably without paintings, the political-social structure of Europe.

Camille exhorted Vincent, even as Corot had hammered at him, to avoid outside influence and to dig down to one's own nature and expression. As they worked side by side Camille quickly saw that he had little to teach the thirty-four-year-old Vincent about the fundamentals of drawing, adding only, "The reflection of reality in a mirror, if it could be caught, would not be a picture at all, it would be no more than a photograph."

Camille studied Vincent's work, took a sharp sidewise glance at his red-stubbled face and burning eyes, then volunteered, "I don't think Paris is the best place for you now that you have absorbed the Impressionist technique. Find yourself a countryside that you can make your own."

Back in Paris, Vincent asked Theo to show Camille his pen drawings when next he came into the gallery, and later asked, "Has Pissarro said anything about my *Sower?* I value his opinion."

Durand-Ruel summoned Camille, demanded accusingly:

"Have you given anything to Theo Van Gogh of Boussod & Valadon?"

"Yes, I have."

"You must not give pictures to a person like that!" the dealer retorted. "Bring them to me. For Van Gogh to have them is bad for my business."

"But, Monsieur Durand-Ruel, you are not able to sell my output. I desperately need the income. Theo Van Gogh is a fine gentleman and a dedicated dealer."

Durand-Ruel flushed, regained his composure.

"You're right, Van Gogh is all of those things."

At the same time that he met the Van Goghs at Petit's exhibit Camille had been introduced to Octave Mirbeau, a drama critic, novelist and severe detractor of the Impressionists. He had also been the author of the virulent "The Jewish Theatre" in the anti-Semitic publication *Les Grimaces*. To his utter astonishment Camille read Mirbeau's two favorable articles in *Gil Blas* during May 1887 about his eight pictures at Georges Petit's exposition, in which Mirbeau stated that it was not the particular technique that was important, but rather the beauty of the execution and the emotion it evoked.

During the following months Camille found out a good deal about Octave Mirbeau, including what was regarded as his complete turnaround, becoming fascinated by the Independents' paintings and abandoning his religious warp. Mirbeau was thirty-seven, twenty years younger than Camille, with a

roundish face, upturned eyebrows and mustache which reminded Camille of Fritz Melbye. His brown hair was balding
at the part, and he wore pointed white collars riding the
jawbone. It was a strong face with intelligent searching eyes.
Camille told him:

"I am very glad to find you now a sympathetic defender.
You have bound many wounds and softened many torments
for me."

Mirbeau's flawless complexion broke into a doleful smile:
"And a few remorses of my own."

Portier sold a Pontoise scene for fifty dollars. In May
Camille sold four gouaches for a modest sum. He began a
painting twenty-one by eighteen inches, with dots of cadmium
red, white and Veronese green. He started in gray weather
and then, when the sun came out, found it impossible to
continue. In addition the canvas became black in five days
because of a faulty green pigment. To console himself he did
four gouaches and then started a larger painting of the village.
It was a vivid spring scene which went well. He told his
children:

"If I didn't have so many worries the picture would paint
itself."

Georges, fifteen years old, said:

"Close your eyes so you won't see your troubles. Your
hand will paint the picture in the dark."

By mid-July of 1887 he was hoarding a dollar he needed for
train fare into Paris and back; he had also completed a large
gouache of the gathering of sweet peas. Bastille Day found
him at home, without a penny. It was only a few months
since he had asked whether Dame Misfortune had forgotten
him. Alfred volunteered to get Lucien a job on condition that
he would remain with the company and not abandon his
position the first chance he had to exhibit. Julie insisted that
Alfred was right, that he had already been embarrassed by
Lucien's flubbing a job and being discharged. Lucien told his
uncle:

"I will accept a commercial post only because it is a matter
of earning a little money for the moment. But I want to stress
that I do not want to be a shopkeeper. I think it a shortsighted
move to forgo my exhibition plans. This would compromise
my future."

Julie prevailed. Lucien took a job working in a lithography
company on the Rue du Cherche Midi, earning a little less
than three francs a day. He lived in Paris with his Aunt
Félicie.

They pawned their modest possessions at the Paris Municipal Pawnshop, *mont-de-piété*, whose method was to charge a monthly rate of interest on the money loaned. The broker would not accept works of art because no value could be placed on them, so one by one they relinquished Camille's watch, Julie's necklace from her mother, their few pieces of silver and copper pots, Camille's newer suit of clothing and overcoat, his few leather-bound books. It became a struggle to pay the couple of francs interest each month so that the *mont-de-piété* would not sell off their valuables. Camille did not go into the city with his work. Julie said:

"Maybe I can do better than you. You sold nothing on your last visits." She planted her feet solidly on the dining-room floor.

Camille let himself be persuaded. The next day he and Georges walked her to the station with two bulging portfolios, placing them on the seat beside her. She took Cocotte for company.

Two days later she returned, having stayed with her sister. Murer, visiting in Paris, had told her that Camille was lost, that when his name came up in conversation people smiled derisively. Others were equally pessimistic, feeling that Camille was falling behind in his mistaken pursuit of Pointillism. Julie came home not only empty-handed but depressed, accusing him of egoism, indifference.

Emile Zola had risen in the world. As far back as 1878 he had been able to buy a farmhouse about twenty-five miles from Paris, "hidden in a nest of verdure," he wrote, "and separated from the rest of the hamlet of Médan by a magnificent line of trees." Before long he had built a second house, many times as large as the first, with a big garden; and a large studio with windows overlooking the Seine. He was now the leading and most prosperous novelist in France. He continued his Thursday evening soirees, gathering the leading literary figures of the time, Flaubert, Guy de Maupassant, J. K. Huysmans, the De Goncourt brothers, younger aspirants. The Pissarros rarely attended. It was a complicated journey. They did not often have the train fare. Yet the two families had remained friendly.

Julie went to Médan to borrow a modest sum, walking considerable distances in the July heat between train stations. When she reached Médan, exhausted, she was refused admission by the maid. Alexandrine declined to see her on the grounds that she had not written in advance. Julie turned away from the doorstep crushed. All she could think of was the mother rabbit she had given Madame Zola, who so much wanted it. She felt humiliated in a way that their scarring poverty had not accomplished.

Julie's failures dug a hole in the bottom of her rickety barrel of life. She wrote to Lucien, who was in Paris with Camille:

"What are we to do we are eight at home to be fed every day when dinner time comes I cannot say to them 'wait'—this stupid word your father repeats and repeats I have used up anything I had put aside I am at the end of my tether and what is worse have no courage left I had decided to send the three boys to Paris and then to take the two little ones for a walk by the river you can imagine the rest everyone would have thought it an accident but when I was ready to go I lacked the courage why am I such a coward at the last moment my poor son I feared to cause you all grief and I was afraid of your remorse my poor Lucien I am terribly unhappy good-bye shall I see you again alas"

Lucien, frightened half to death, got Camille into a closed room at Rachel's, handed him the letter. Camille started to read but when he came to the suicide threat collapsed onto one of the mahogany chairs.

He was devastated.

He held his head in his hands and wept. Lucien was shattered; he had not seen his father cry since the death of Minette, thirteen years before. He put his arm about his father's shoulder, said in a hoarse voice:

"Don't cry, Papa."

Camille raised a tearstained face.

"Lucien, we have to hold our family together. Others have been poor before us."

He was trembling and ill. His head was on fire with guilt, remorse, anxiety, fear. Would Julie really kill herself, taking Cocotte and Paul Emile with her? A six-year-old girl, a three-year-old boy? His senses reeled with horror. It would destroy him and their remaining four children. If she were found dead in the river he would be dead too. There could be no further life or work. Everything would have been tragically futile.

It was an endless journey home. When he burst into the house, ran through the rooms to the kitchen, he found Julie resignedly peeling potatoes. An explosion of thankfulness burst from his lungs. He took her in his arms, wept in relief, strung broken phrases of how much he loved her and needed her. She wiped away his tears, assured him that she would never again fall so low in spirit as to contemplate suicide. She gave him a cup of coffee, with which he stumbled into the adjoining dining room and collapsed onto one of the chairs. Through the open door he could hear Lucien's voice in the kitchen.

"Maman, if both of you despair, everything will be lost."

6

That was the beginning of the end for him of Pointillism, though it took him agonizing months to make his way back. He confided to his son: "I think continually of some way of painting without the dot. I hope to achieve this but I have not been able to solve the problem of dividing the pure tone without harshness. How can one combine the purity and simplicity of the dot with the fullness and suppleness of our Impressionist art? For the dot is meager, lacking in body, diaphanous, more monotonous than simple, even in the Seurats—especially in the Seurats."

To add to his troubles, the intensity of his gaze at the thousands of individual contacts with the paper so imperative for Pointillist painting had caused him severe eyestrain. He went to see the doctor recommended by Dr. Gachet. Dr. Parenteau's office was on the street level, the front room of his dwelling, in a modest apartment house. Camille observed the good furniture and newly added washstand. There were a number of books on a wooden shelf on top of which stood Helmholtz's *Ophthalmology;* an adjustable kerosene lamp. Dr. Parenteau was swathed in an unbuttoned white coat down to his ankles. He placed Camille in what looked like an upholstered barber's chair, used a slitlamp microscope to examine the eyes, then utilized a recently developed tonometer to measure the eye pressure and search for glaucoma.

"You have an inflamed tear gland of the right eye," he pronounced eventually. "I'll give you some drops. Mostly you need to rest it. Apparently you've been giving it hard service."

Toward the end of September 1887 Theo Van Gogh sold *Gathering Sweet Peas*, in which he had extended the dot to a tiny brush stroke to bring more lifelike movement to the pickers. The deal got him out of "hot water."

The October rains lasted a week. The days were cold and gray. He was making a transition back to brush strokes but each picture took so long.

He had lunch at Murer's. Renoir and his family came by the same train. Murer said, "You knew perfectly well that the dot is impossible!" Renoir added, "You have abandoned the dot but you won't admit you were wrong."

Camille went home, studied his Pointillist canvases. After a soul-searching vigilance he said to the unresponsive walls:

"Pointillism takes life and movement out of the canvases. Durand-Ruel was right from the beginning: this is not still life, it is dead life."

Could he get out of the impasse to where he expressed himself best? Had he learned anything about the application of paint that would make his new canvases more beautiful? Had the scientific approach to painting meant that he had lost communication with nature, the richest source of his feelings about life on earth? Could he rework some of the paintings, throw the rest away?

Had he had a thirty-month misadventure?

He was only fifty-seven. He felt strong and resolute. There were many years ahead in which to feel deeply and put those feelings into paintings.

Could he?

BOOK THIRTEEN

An Artist Family

1

THEO VAN GOGH returned from a trip to Holland. Sending for Camille, the dealer told him:

"Your *Rouen* is almost sold. Your collector is anxious to have it but is not rich."

Camille sighed. "It's always the penniless who are well disposed."

Van Gogh put his hand on Camille's shoulder:

"Your etchings created a sensation. Some old man with a critic's license hurled anathema at us and predicted the end of the world. He simply cut you to pieces. Like a volley of shot came the reply from all the newspapers devoted to the renewal of art. They warmly championed you."

Camille was gratified because Lucien's woodcuts had also been well received. He went again to the Rue Le Peletier where Durand-Ruel was examining Camille's latest group of gouaches with a constrained expression.

"I don't care for this *Landscape with Cows*. It's too yellow and there is no poetry in it. Nature is not as exaggerated as you represent it to be. In this *Children Gathering Herbs*, the girl crouching is not sufficiently articulated, her body isn't felt. I do like *Two Young Girls Standing*."

Camille felt as though he had taken a whipping.

"We, the artists, have no understanding of painting?"

Durand-Ruel dropped heavily into his leather chair.

"Are you accusing me of behaving like a tradesman who disparages the goods he is to buy in order to get it at a good price?"

Camille felt the hurt in the sagging body.

"Assuredly not, Monsieur Durand-Ruel. But you said exactly the same thing to me about the gouache and painting I showed in your second exhibition in New York last year at the National Academy of Design. Yet they were among your successes.''

Durand-Ruel said wearily, ''Leave them. I'll do my best to sell them. Collectors have different tastes.''

The dealer became involved in the opening of his New York gallery. Camille took half a dozen of his freshly painted canvases to Theo Van Gogh, who was enchanted with the vibrant colors and interlaced brush strokes. He hung the paintings on his mezzanine, pleaded eloquently for them but could sell nothing. One of the reasons was the emergence of Claude Monet, putting everyone else of his group in the shadow.

''Collectors, like every other segment of society, have their fads,'' Van Gogh explained. ''It could be a trapeze artist at the Cirque d'Hiver, an actress at the Comédie Française. All Paris is talking about Monet today. Who can tell about tomorrow?''

Monet's canvases were being bought in America for eight hundred to twelve hundred dollars each. Degas declared that Monet created nothing but beautiful decorations. The critic Fénéon charged the paintings with being more vulgar than ever; Renoir found them retrograde. The Durand-Ruels declared them of poor quality, a judgment Camille suspected was caused by Monet's having given them to Theo Van Gogh to sell.

Monet extended the house in Giverny, now spacious enough to keep his two children and Madame Hoschedé's five comfortable. They hired a couple who cooked and cleaned for them and three gardeners to care for Monet's extensive plantings.

Several weeks later Camille took the train into Paris, walked from the station to the Boussod & Valadon gallery. Theo Van Gogh received him cordially. When they went up to the entresol Camille saw that all of his paintings were on the walls.

''Still no sale?'' he asked, crestfallen.

''Not yet. I have someone interested in *View of Bazincourt*. A new collector named Dupuis. He has promised to pay me eighty dollars before the end of the year.''

Camille stuttered for a moment.

''I dislike embarrassing you but since you have two paintings practically sold, could you advance me two hundred dollars? I'm that much behind.''

Van Gogh blanched. He knew he was not a good businessman; all he had was an enthusiasm for the Impressionists.

Boussod & Valadon did not care for the outrageous canvases on the mezzanine; they allowed him to continue his display only because of his sales of the Monet paintings.

"I'll get it for you," he said determinedly.

The Dutch collector paid for Camille's *Rouen;* and in November his marginally divisionist *View of Bazincourt* was bought by Dupuis, Camille receiving sixty of the eighty dollars paid for it. Van Gogh accomplished the miracle of not having Boussod & Valadon deduct these sums from the earlier advance. Camille was grateful: late in 1888 Lucien was twenty-five, Georges seventeen; Félix fourteen, and not one of them earning. Ludovic Rodolphe was ten, Cocotte seven, Paul Emile four; the expenses for his maturing family were increasing at a geometric rate.

There was unfortunate news from Arles, where Vincent Van Gogh had gone to find his own countryside. Exacerbated by vast overwork, the lashing of the mistral winds of Provence and the goadings of Paul Gauguin, who was living with him, Vincent had suffered an epileptoidal seizure, pursued Gauguin with an open razor, then cut off his own right ear through which he claimed he was hearing tormenting voices. Theo Van Gogh, terror-stricken, left immediately for Arles, where he found Vincent recovering in the local hospital under the care of young Dr. Félix Rey. Theo had shown some of Vincent's gripping paintings in a small space he had rented from Père Tanguy, but Tanguy's customers thought them demonic, even *Sunflowers* and *The Yellow House.* Camille had been deeply impressed by them.

He continued to go into Paris twice a month to see the dealers and, if he had a few francs, attend Thursday night dinners at the Café Riche, which had become a popular meeting place for Paris's journalists, critics and authors: Théodore Duret, Octave Mirbeau, Stéphane Mallarmé, Gustave Geffroy. Sometimes an Impressionist joined for the weekly clash of ideas, boisterous intellectual horseplay encased in a pleasant fog of tobacco smoke, beer suds, coffee and comradeship. Camille took Georges and Félix with him; Félix at fourteen was too young to follow the repartee and fell asleep.

They stayed with Rachel, who welcomed their visits. There was a touch of pathos in her plight; she had turned away her first daughter-in-law, Julie, while the second, Marie, had done her own rejecting.

By 1889 the ingathering of the painters had ceased. Paul Cézanne was now the master of Jas de Bouffan in Aix, attended by his wife, his mother and sister, a reclusive life that suited him. Monet was painting a series of the Creuse Valley in the south. Edgar Degas was the Paris equivalent of a Cézanne recluse, becoming increasingly irascible, perhaps because he was losing the sight of one eye. Paul Gauguin had returned from Martinique penniless, disemboweled by dysentery. He had painted some of his best-realized pictures at Pont-Aven in Brittany and was being supported by his friend Schuffenecker from his old brokerage firm. Alfred Sisley had moved to a cottage at Moret; he was selling enough through Petit to keep himself in paint, his wife and two children in food. Mary Cassatt was still living with her family, painting tender, life-teeming portraits of mothers with their children, of young women sewing, bathing; creating brilliant watercolors. Although Cassatt called Degas "my dearest friend," she went less frequently to his studio; and when Camille saw them together he sensed a growing tension.

Berthe Morisot was painting in a masterly fashion, Camille believed, but was trapped in the same "womanly" genre as Mary Cassatt, portraying mostly young girls, with swan, in a red robe, with a dog, with a basket. She, her husband Eugène and daughter Julie spent the summers in a country home near Mézy. Armand Guillaumin was presumably still working in the government bureau and investing every spare sou in the Paris lottery.

Auguste Renoir was also in Paris but rarely about. His last show had been a failure. When Camille encountered him on the boulevard near Rachel's apartment he was wearing a round straw-colored hat, a voluminous white scarf tied in a bow at his throat; his mustache was yellowed, his short scrambled beard more salt than pepper. His cheeks were ruddy, his eyes all-consuming. He launched into a dolorous monologue.

"Everybody, Durand-Ruel and my former collectors, attacks me. I don't get any more portraits to do. They deplore my attempt to go beyond my romantic period. I've grown inordinately sensitive. They say I'm imitating Ingres. . . . "

Camille had never forgiven Renoir's anti-Semitic attack, but he understood so well the dilemma of being disallowed to change one's technique, and the man's expression was so plaintive that he offered him a coffee at the Café Riche. It was no time to hold a grudge when they had all lost each other; if, in fact, there was ever a time to hold a grudge. Over their *café au lait*, poured by the waiter from a big silver pitcher in either hand, he told Renoir:

"Each of us is in search of the unity to create a solid body of work. You are achieving a line and form that only Degas's drawing can equal. If the critics could paint they would paint, but it is a God-given gift. We may have great faults but it's more intelligent and artistic to move forward as our nature and values dictate.''

Renoir banged his fist on the round marble-topped table, making the cups clatter in their saucers, gazed down at the coffee he had spilled, poured it back into the cup, then looked up shyly.

''I owe you an apology.''

Camille found no lack of exposure but sold nothing. In January he showed seven oils and twenty-two etchings at Durand-Ruel's with other artists. In early February he sent ten oil paintings and a number of sketches to Les Vingt in Brussels, then placed twelve of his Rouen watercolors at a small dealer. An American visitor offered two hundred and forty dollars for the series, about sixteen dollars each. Camille accepted. In addition he had to do a self-portrait, albeit only a sketch, to complete the deal. He gave the money to Julie, keeping only the francs needed to get good proofs of his new prints. The publishers of journals were not used to paying much for etchings; they and the collectors liked to wait for auctions where they could get rare prints for sixty to eighty cents each.

Durand-Ruel tried another group show in April, out of which Camille earned sixty dollars, the total amount the dealer was to pay him for the year 1889.

2

At ninety-four years of age, Rachel spent most of her time in bed or hobbled around painfully, dressed in a heavy robe and tight-fitting wool cap. Alfred, despite his own recurrent bouts of illness for which the doctors had no explanation, still managed to keep a servant in the apartment.

Camille came upon his mother in bed one afternoon, her eyes wide open but unseeing, her lips parted. He was alarmed; the thin white visage seemed a death mask. He put one hand on her forehead; with the other grasped her bony wrist. The pulse was there. He summoned the maid, asked her to prepare a bowl of broth, then rubbed Rachel's brow and hands gently.

When the broth was ready he slowly fed it to her. She seemed to gather strength.

He sat in a chair opposite and made a drawing of his mother as she had been when first he entered the room; the enormous draperies covering the wall in front of which she slept; the heavy blanket enveloping her; the night table with a lighted candle, a covered cylindrical container of tea. One of the curved mahogany armchairs from the parlor faced the table, close to Rachel's hand. As he sketched painstakingly a feeling of anguish overtook him. His mind pictured his early childhood, the tropical island where he had been born and where he had enjoyed life on the sun-bleached waters of Charlotte Amalie Bay; the forests of the mountains ringing the little town; their sweet-smelling, comfortable home above the ship chandlery on Dronningens Gade; her insistence that he begin early in the little private schools, at so much an hour for differing courses; her acceptance of the sacrifice of sending him to the Pension Savary in Passy for his lycée years. A highly charged woman, Rachel had showered embraces and affection on her young, giving the boys total freedom to roam the island.

He had hurt her twice, yet in both instances he had done what he thought was imperative to his own life's unfolding. First, at the age of twenty-two, impelled by something within his nature to become an artist, he had left St. Thomas secretly with Fritz Melbye to spend more than a year painting in Caracas. Then six years later, having fallen in love with the Pissarros' Catholic *bonne* and made her pregnant, he had moved with her to David Jacobsen's small studio to set up housekeeping. He thought, with the pain of contrition in his heart:

"Perhaps in time Maman would have accepted me as an impractical artist. She never found it possible to forgive me for taking Julie to wife.

"Forgive me, Maman," he murmured, "the pain I caused you."

In April a severe inflammation made his right eye puffy and painful. Dr. Parenteau declared the faulty tear duct the source of the swelling.

"You want to know why your right eye and not your left? You are a right-handed painter. Therefore your right eye is your dominant and focus eye. When looking at the canvas and holding the brush ready for color you undoubtedly squint your left, so the right eye is the one most used and hence will be the first to be affected."

He probed the lachrymal canal, explained that the tears from the tear ducts drain into two small canals and empty into a sack which is completely surrounded by bone inside the nose. The teardrops were not being discharged properly but were draining back.

"Since you favor homeopathic drugs," Dr. Parenteau said, "I'll put you on aurum. That should allow your nasal bone tissue to restore itself. But precaution must be taken; avoid wind and dust."

Camille was upset.

"That is hardly easy for a painter who has to face the elements."

The inflammation went down; Camille took himself into the fields and cross-country footpaths until spring provided sudden gusts of wind which carried its burden of seed, pollen, dust. From the middle of May the renewed inflammation and swelling caused him considerable pain. His right eye was swimming in tears. Dr. Parenteau was disturbed.

"Now you're suffering from an infection."

He slit open the canal that connected the lower tear duct to the common tear duct, cleaned out the obstruction, put a patch over the eye, tied a gauze bandage around his head.

"You may lose some depth perception. Our main concern is to keep an abscess from forming."

"Then I shall try to work with one eye. Degas does and gets good results."

After he had calmed the family's alarm over the ominous-looking bandage, he bought a pair of spectacles and went out into the warm May sunlight to paint again. Because the canvas was only two-dimensional, the lacking vision from his right eye did not appear to have any appreciable effect. He completed an oil of a footpath, set it up on his easel, took out earlier, similar work and cried:

"Ma foi! I can't detect any difference."

After two weeks he took off the bandage, which he had worn even when he slept, scrupulously avoided windy weather and wore the protective half glasses.

Rachel quietly slipped away from her storm-tossed life at the end of May, twenty-four years after Frédéric Pissarro's death. Neither Camille nor Alfred had had an opportunity to say good-bye. The funeral was modest. She was buried in the family vault in Père Lachaise, close to her husband. There would be room for Camille, Julie and their children; Alfred, Marie and their two sons. Esther Isaacson made the trip from London to be present at the brief graveside ceremony. Lucien attended with Camille. Alfred came alone. After the last words of the *kaddish* prayer for the dead, Alfred invited Camille, Lucien and Esther Isaacson back to his home. Marie gave them a comforting cup of coffee.

Rachel's sixteen-dollar-a-month allowance from her steadily decreasing funds had helped him for a lot of years. She had never thought it important that he was a painter; it puzzled her that Drs. Gachet and de Bellio accepted her son's art work in lieu of medical fees for her care, and had taken no happiness from her son's sometime success. That, he supposed, was the lot of most humans; he knew of no *corpus juris* that said man was put on earth to be happy. Rachel had had more than her share of misery; he had been one of the unsolvable dilemmas of her embattled existence. He too had been driven.

In a tortured way they had loved each other. It had been a clash of irreconcilable wills. Rachel, in spite of her severely shocked nervous system, had remained loyal to him if not to his family or his chosen job of work. The relationship between a mother and son lies precious at the back of the mind, not always shown during the gritty details of staying alive. Now that she was gone he felt a void, as though a section of terra firma had sunk into the sea. Too late to pay more attention, give more time, afford more love. Each generation suffered its own loss.

3

Life moved on.

He went to see the retrospective organized by Monet and Rodin at Petit's gallery, which showed the genesis and development of their work from 1864 to 1889. He was still bothered by Monet's idea of submerging the object in a blaze of light, felt that it was wrong, wrong as his own having abandoned the reality of movement for Pointillism. When he had a spare hour in Paris he dropped into Le Club de l'Art Social, which met once a week in the offices of the *Revue Socialiste* at 8 Rue des Martyrs, for an ongoing discussion of the politics and economics of France. He fraternized with Adolphe Tabarant, a liberal writer; Louise Michel, one of France's leading women radicals; Auguste Rodin, the sculptor who, inspired by Michelangelo's work in Florence and Rome, had by his own efforts brought sculpture back to consideration as a major art; Jean Grave, editor of *La Révolte;* agreed that serious measures were needed to right the injustices of a corrupt court system, a financial structure which kept the working classes on the edge of unemployment, hunger, cold, illness and despair. Yet, being a gentle soul, he was against the journals' advocacy of the overthrow of the government and the industrial hierarchy by violence. He knew that any uprising would bring about frightful counterviolence.

He went to see an exhibition in the Rue de Grenelle with interesting paintings by such newcomers as Toulouse-Lautrec and Anquetin, and a frightful picture by a Hyacinthe Pozier framed in straw and varnished wood. Lucien's *Road* hung between Seurat and Signac, a rugged test of competence.

Since Dr. Parenteau had advised him to stay out of the intense summer glare he worked on prints in his studio room overlooking Julie's garden, on a secondhand table he had picked up in Gisors. He used zinc and copper plates, kept a supply of acid-resistant wax, pitch, gum mastic, asphaltum. He enjoyed the smell of the chemical biting into the metal but sorely missed Degas's red-spoked printing press with its rollers and blanket cover so that he could do his own printing. He used Julie's kitchen sink for his acid bath. If she complained he responded:

"Better than the food tasting of turpentine, as it did in La Varenne."

He showed some of the prints at Durand-Ruel's for the Society of Painter-Engravers. He priced them from three to twenty-eight dollars according to size, quality and number of proofs pulled from the press. Even at these modest prices he sold only a few.

If he had lost contact with his former associates there was compensation in the growing closeness and unity between himself and his sons and daughter. He scrounged for them: sketchbooks, pens, pencils, crayons, watercolors; with Papa to encourage them, sharpen a line, adjust perspective, rearrange structure of garden, orchard, river scene; inventive and imaginary.

An artist family! That was what he had wanted, and what he had.

He and his boys created a Pissarro journal called *Le Guignol,* *Puppet Show,* an ongoing series of humorous sketches which lampooned the daily life of the family and their frequent *états de crise.* There was little privacy in the house where all upheavals and confrontations were heard by everyone. Camille tried to teach the children to laugh at their difficulties; now the young were satirizing their parents' bouts and eccentricities. They had learned their lessons from Champfleury's *History of Caricature*, as illustrated by Daumier. They adored the book, poring over it with shouts of laughter at the accuracy and cruelty of the exaggerations: too long a nose, a twisted mouth, an oddly shaped head like Napoleon III's "pear head." Julie felt there was no modicum of seclusion in her life. She could not even shout at her husband without her children gleefully recording the scene in their *Puppet Show*.

Camille contributed drawings and designed the jackets. Georges put the monthly contributions together as a book, bound in the most colorful cloth lying about the house. Their efforts were remedial; they felt masters of the situation instead of the victims of the family hardships.

Lucien had a woodcut published in the English *Dial*, which brought him into the William Morris group of handicraft artisans. Georges, at seventeen a stormy petrel, caused as much disruption as the other children put together, completed the schooling available in Eragny. What to do with him?

"He has a growing talent for design," Camille said. "He's good at woodcarving. He could be trained in the making of specially built furniture, for example."

"Is there such a place in Paris?" Julie asked.

"There is in London: the Toynbee School, run by disciples of William Morris. They teach young men to design and create furniture, stained glass, carpets, wallpaper, everything to simplify the ornate Victorian decoration. The young people trained there are sought after by the best firms."

Julie smiled happily; the prospect of her second son being prepared for a viable job instead of the capricious world of art was the best of news. They sent him off to England to live with his Uncle Phineas Isaacson and his cousins Esther, Alice and Amelie, who had converted their home in Colville Square, Bayswater, into a boardinghouse to support Phineas's failing financial position.

The summer was hot, clear, quiet. Camille was free to paint steadily: the Eragny prairies, the slopes of Gisors, the footpaths crossing the fields; peasants carrying baskets, tending the furrows, gathering their alternate crops; a deeply moving portrait of the Vexin people, their surroundings and their daily chores to provide existence, all the motifs he had searched out, loved and made his own. He did not go into Paris; there was no purpose with the collectors away. Theo

Van Gogh was the only one trying to place his pictures. The work went well, but still nothing sold. Having regained their valuables, they had to send them into the Paris pawnshop once again to borrow a few francs: the same silverware, winter coat, books, anything on which the *mont-de-piété* would lend, always struggling to pay the interest so that they would not be sold off.

He finished paintings of the harvesters, the hay gatherers, the gleaners, faintly reminiscent of Millet, in the drained colors of summer sunlight. At home he took pleasure from sketching his children as they grew, as well as simple portraits of Julie and himself.

He was aware of a constant tension growing within him. He was fifty-nine years old, rejected continually, with no money he could count on. What chance of acceptance had he, really? Nor could he sell anything in England or America, so it was not simply France that was purblind. Was his life a "tale told by an idiot, full of sound and fury, signifying nothing"? He worked feverishly, strove harder, though there was little in his thirty years of striving to give him any reassurance. How to achieve the miracle of arrival and fulfillment? He remembered the verse from Job in the Old Testament:

> For affliction does not come from the dust,
> nor does trouble sprout from the ground;
> but man is born to trouble
> as the sparks fly upward.

They received a note from the vacationing Jacob Bensusan family of Upper Norwood, whom Camille had met at the time of Emma's death, and again in 1871 during their brief refuge from the Franco-Prussian War. Camille had not much cared for Jacob Bensusan of the thick copper-red hair on his hands as well as his head. Though a knowledgeable musician, he was encased in a corset of orthodoxy in both religion and politics.

"They're connected with my family," he explained to Julie, "so we will have to invite them. Can you manage dinner?"

"I can put a chicken in the pot."

The Bensusans begged off, saying they wanted to take *bateau à vapeur* ride on the Seine. However their daughter asserted her independence by informing them that she was coming out to Eragny on the 6:10 A.M. train from Paris by herself.

"An act of mutiny!" declared Camille, having observed Jacob Bensusan's autocratic way of controlling his dependents. "Lucien, you'll have to pick her up at the station at eight-thirty in the morning."

Lucien grimaced. "She was a spindle-legged kid of about twelve when I met her at the Isaacsons'."

When he returned from the little *gare* there was a look of shock in his eyes. Camille quickly saw that Esther Bensusan, nicknamed Sterbee to distinguish her from Esther Isaacson, was now eighteen, short but with an exquisite figure. Her eyes were a warm, sensitive brown, with arching eyebrows, chestnut hair which she piled in knots at the back of a proudly held head that could have been drawn by Ingres. Camille had never seen his twenty-six-year-old son so attracted by a young woman. She in turn seemed taken by the Pissarro "family of artists."

"Father takes me to concerts," she confided after seeing many of Camille's completed works in the studio; "but for the rest I'm housebound, restricted to religious ritual four times a day, and to my reading. You people appear to be *free*."

Lucien picked up her emphasis. "We are free. Yet we are still bound by the need to have our work accepted."

"Everyone is," she replied.

She liked Lucien's drawings and woodcuts. She liked Julie's *poulet nouveau*. She chatted brightly with each of the children. Lucien was stricken; Julie did not disapprove. She too was taken by this lovely warmhearted girl who was so happy to be with them.

After midday dinner Lucien took Sterbee on the omnibus to Gisors to see the ruins of the castle of La Reine Blanche, the park with great trees and a view of the church spires in the distance. When Sterbee kissed Camille au revoir, she murmured in his ear: "Even at twelve I was taken with Lucien."

Camille promised to prepare a "family of artists" book for her nineteenth birthday.

"Love strikes like lightning," Julie murmured. But the next time Lucien was staying in Paris, she wrote to him:

"It is absolutely necessary that you earn a living business is very bad please don't waste your time to be an artist it is stupid be a businessman and leave art to those who have the money in the bank. . . ."

Camille did not know how to alleviate Julie's anxiety except to paint and pursue dealers and collectors. He was relieved when he and his wife could plead their cases through correspondence, Julie expressing her fears for the future to

Georges in England; Camille writing to his second son, who lacked faith in his own abilities: "For Maman everything finds its solution in success. She does not realize that means are never the same and that the only thing to do is to let the young man follow his sensations as much as possible. . . . Like the bee, he will know how to find the juice of the flowers on which he will live."

He might have been talking about Rachel!

Rachel's will left everything to Alfred and his family. Twenty-four years after having been disowned by his father, he was disowned by his mother. He had never been forgiven.

Julie insisted that they take the train into Paris to claim their rights. It was an unfortunate decision. Alfred was ill and his wife Marie referred them to her attorney. Camille's attorney, his cousin Alfred Nunès, agreed to handle his interest if he paid with a painting.

"It is an age of barter," Camille commented. "Too bad the shopkeepers in Eragny won't take watercolors in exchange for rice and meat."

The heavy, beautifully carved mahogany furniture from St. Thomas went to the Hôtel Drouot to be auctioned, all except the bed, chest of drawers, and nightstand Rachel had sent with Camille to Jacobsen's studio, which resided upstairs in the children's bedroom. The tables off which the Pissarros had eaten, the cabinets, wardrobes, beds in which they had slept, all the accouterments of his childhood gone into limbo; where else could childhood go?

Theo Van Gogh sold *The Gleaners* for one hundred sixty dollars. When Camille went into the gallery late in September to collect the money, Van Gogh reported that his brother Vincent had been painting in the fields around St. Rémy, where he had been hospitalized after his attack in Arles. However the intense religious atmosphere of the *maison de santé* had depressed him. After he had been in St. Rémy for three months, Dr. Peyron, young superintendent of the hospital, had allowed him to go back into Arles. The remembrance of his torments there was too much for him. He was found unconscious in a ditch between Tarascon and St. Rémy; and three months later, after completing an oil of olive groves, he was found wrapped around the trunk of a cypress. On both occasions he had lost consciousness. He was better now and wanted to come north.

Theo Van Gogh took a rumpled letter out of his inside coat pocket, reflected, then said:

"I've been carrying this around with me since September. I hesitated to show it to you because of your mother's death and your eye trouble. This is what Vincent asked me. It's for next spring."

Camille took the letter, read:

"So old Pissarro is cruelly smitten by these two misfortunes at once. As soon as I read that, I thought of asking him if there would be any way of going to stay with him. If you will pay the same as here, he will find it worth his while, for I do not need much—except work. . . . It is queer that already, two or three times before, I had had the idea of going to Pissarro's; this time, after your telling me of his recent misfortunes, I do not hesitate to ask him."

He gave Julie Theo Van Gogh's full report, adding, "I have the unhappy feeling that Vincent's seizures are recurrent."

Her eyes were wide with fright; then tears came.

"I feel so sorry for him. He would be no burden. *Mon Dieu*, we could use the extra money. But, Camille, with four young children at home . . ."

"I'll search the neighborhood for a comfortable boarding-house for him."

Julie knit her brows into a deep furrow.

"Shouldn't he have medical care . . . ?"

"*Soit!* Dr. Gachet in Auvers, of course! He loves all good painters. He'll keep Vincent under observation."

Through the efforts of a talented and popular portrait painter, John Singer Sargent, from a distinguished American family, Claude Monet sold his series *The Creuse Valley* in an American gallery, one of the pictures going for the astonishing sum of eighteen hundred dollars. This was more money than Camille had earned from his work in a number of years put together. Theo Van Gogh consoled him.

"I find your paintings very beautiful. I have a buyer for *Woman with Baskets*. I've put it in a gold frame. Soon we'll be getting as much for them as Monet does."

Camille squeezed the man's arm. It was comforting to have him as a dealer. It was not that Durand-Ruel had abandoned him but rather that he was flooded with Impressionist paintings.

A few days before Christmas, Theo Van Gogh brought his wife Jo out to Gisors where Camille met them with a carriage. Jo was almost at term; they rode slowly to Eragny to keep her comfortable. When they left, he presented her with a charmingly painted fan, *Landscape with Rainbow*, as a New Year's gift.

Edouard Manet's widow was obliged to offer up for sale

Manet's *Olympia*, which had caused a near riot at the Salon in 1865, the picture of the nude prostitute on her bed, bitter expression on her face, being handed a colorful bunch of flowers from presumably her next client. It was quickly bid for by an American. Monet and Sargent secured Madame Manet's consent to raise a fund which would acquire the painting for the Louvre. Four thousand dollars was raised, Monet, Sargent, Dr. de Bellio and Théodore Duret contributing several hundred dollars each. Camille and Renoir gave what they could, ten dollars each. Only twenty-four years before, a mob had vilified the painting, spat upon it. And now the Louvre had accepted it!

4

The decade of the 1890s opened on a note of cheer, for Theo Van Gogh began organizing a large one-man exhibition for Camille at Boussod & Valadon. He even persuaded the owners to allow him to put several of what he called Camille's "exquisite landscapes" into their window. He had started ordering the frames, white, gray wood or oak. He also considered a catalogue, with a preface, perhaps by Kahn, Geffroy or Mirbeau, which would be comprehensive; apart from what it said about Camille, it would cover the quality of his technique.

Theo Van Gogh's exhibition showed twenty-six of Camille's oils and gouaches, eighteen loaned by his collectors, including Georges Clemenceau, a rising national politico, the publisher Gallimard, Dupuis. This display of prestigious owners would have an impact on the visitors to the gallery.

Gustave Geffroy, a writer who had earlier said about the Impressionist revolution, "One step more and their paintings would have been handed over to the firing squad," wrote the introduction to the catalogue. He stated that Pissarro was in full harvest with his work, was the accepted landscapist of the Normandy fields, the sincere observer of the comings and goings of the countryside. "Everywhere, on the surface, in the demi-tints, in the shadows, he struggles to find this fluid penetrating light for which there are no hidden corners, this permanent and changing light in which the world is bathed."

Theo Van Gogh had whipped up the enthusiasm of his

collectors, spreading the word that Camille was not only the father of the Impressionist exhibitions but had literally forced the exhibitions into being. During the early crowded days of the opening week he was able to sell five of the oils for seven hundred and fifty dollars, telling his collectors:

"Pissarro has changed the way we look at the world. He has given us new eyes to see nature, fresh understanding of our earth and the people who live and work on it. The kind of beauty Pissarro has created on these canvases is immortal."

No one doubted his sincerity. Within a short time he had sold the remaining three paintings Camille owned for higher prices, which would bring the take to fifteen hundred dollars: a windfall. Theo Van Gogh also told him:

"I have not given up hope of doing better, and in any case I will always consider it an honor to arrange your exhibitions. When I see you, you always give me courage to persevere."

Camille and Julie were elated. It was a greater success than any Durand-Ruel had secured for him. He returned to work with renewed enthusiasm, painting the last effects of snow in Eragny, then the budding of the spring, his living secure. Julie again hired a country girl and earned a respite from her labors. They bought their pretty eight-year-old Cocotte a dress with a bustle in the rear, which Cocotte loved to pat.

The family had sent on Sterbee Bensusan's birthday book, an album of nine old French songs written out by Lucien in calligraphy, bound in cotton from one of Julie's discarded dresses. The frontispiece was painted by Camille while the younger boys contributed watercolors. Camille wrote that the artists of Eragny were all delighted to send the album because so few people understood them. Lucien was determined to get back to England to court the girl.

When his right eye began to tear again, Camille went to Dr. Parenteau to have the canals drained. Every few weeks the doctor put a bandage around his head to keep the eye protected; he became a usual sight on the gallery streets and in the roads of Eragny looking like a wounded soldier returned from the wars. Sometimes he thought the process was cyclical, though he kept no calendar about it; at others he believed that it was a sudden gust of wind or a bit of dust from the trails he trudged. Dr. Parenteau frequently mentioned that an operation might be necessary, but the proper moment never seemed to arrive. He continued to paint resolutely, asking his family around the dinner table:

"Why does the human species have two eyes instead of one in the middle of its forehead like Cyclops? It would have worked just as well. Nature gave us two eyes just in case one goes bad. Providential, *n'est-ce pas?*"

Félix responded:

"Papa, you should have been a philosophy professor at the Sorbonne. You have an explanation for everything that goes wrong."

He was unable to philosophize over his brother Alfred's death in late April. Alfred had been ill for a year or more; Camille had not known how seriously. Besides grief there was the eerie feeling of being the last one left of his generation. Of Rachel's four children by Isaac Petit two of the boys had died young; he had attended Delphine's funeral shortly after reaching Paris. Emma had died more than twenty years ago. Of her four boys by Frédéric Pissarro, one had died very young, the second while Camille was in Caracas, and now Alfred was gone at the age of sixty-one. He was relieved that Rachel had been saved from still another excruciating loss. He and Alfred, only one year older, were once close in temperament, for Alfred's great desire had been to become a musician, carrying his precious violin with him when he traveled and seeking company with whom to play quartets. It was the years of experience in his father's shop which had turned him into a successful merchant, one who could marry Marie May of Besançon, with her ample dowry, then support his family in comfort.

It was, Camille realized, the way of the world. Alfred had become reconciled to spending his years as an importer-exporter; had been happy watching his two sons grow up; moving to more spacious apartments as his business flourished. In the early years he had been generous with Camille, sending him painting supplies and linens to Caracas, putting money into the mail when Camille was hard pressed. He had paid for the gold frames for Camille's paintings for a long time. His refusal to share their father's estate had been a severe blow to the relationship; but Alfred had merely carried out his father's strictures and the businessman's belief that those should have money who could make it grow. He had found jobs for Camille's son, even though Lucien had not kept them.

Sometime after Alfred's death his older son Frédéric came to Eragny and proposed an amicable settlement of Rachel's will.

"Father would have wanted peace in the family," he said.

The sum they received was a modest one, but Julie was gratified that she and her children were now considered legitimate heirs to the Pissarro name.

When Vincent Van Gogh came to Paris from St. Rémy, Camille and Julie went to call on him in his brother's apartment at 8 Cité Pigalle, an *impasse* blocked by a garden court with a big black tree at the entrance. They saw with instant relief, as Vincent affectionately flung his arms about them, that he looked well, with a bright smile in his eyes. It was seventeen months since he had cut off his ear; only the healed stump of the lobe remained. Under the sofa of the living room, under the table of the dining room, under the beds of the bedroom, standing against the spare walls of the entrance, even in the kitchen, were the hundreds of completed oils and drawings from his years at Arles and St. Rémy. His brother had hung two of them, *Irises* and *Starlit Night*, at a showing in September of the previous year, which Camille had thought wonderfully painted. He had also hung a few at Tanguy's, close to Tanguy's beloved Cézannes which no one wanted. Almost the entire remaining output of the prolific artist was right here in the modest apartment. There was scarcely room to breathe but they all appeared happy. Seeing Julie's bemused expression as she looked at the monumental number of paintings, Jo said:

"They're like jewels: diamonds, emeralds and rubies filling up every inch of our home."

Vincent settled into a small back room in a modest inn, Chez Ravoux, opposite the city hall in Auvers-sur-Oise. With an expression caught between a grimace and a grin he reported:

"Each day when I finish a canvas I take it to Dr. Gachet's. He sets it up on an easel; then starts running around waving his arms and frothing. He gets as excited as though he had painted it himself."

Dr. Gachet's garden was secure and paintable, but Vincent wandered into the fields around Auvers to work.

In late May Camille crossed the Channel to England with Lucien and Maximilien Luce, his painter friend from the Pointillism days who was disconsolate because his wife had left him. Camille wanted to establish Lucien in a London studio where he could take drawing students, see how Georges was getting on, and paint more scenes of London, a city he loved. He wrote to Julie: "Museums upon museums to visit, anyone who wants to study here certainly has the material. In summer the parks are superb, one can work there without bother, the surroundings of London are also superb. This morning I worked at Chelsea."

They rented rooms in a modest hotel. Georges was struggling in the Toynbee trade school. Camille painted Charing Cross Bridge, Hampton Court green and Kensington Gardens. He spent a little time at the Phineas Isaacson home in Bayswater with the near bankrupt, querulous Phineas. His housebound and husbandless daughters welcomed him warmly.

Settling Lucien in with the Isaacsons, and exhorting Georges to work harder, he returned to Eragny.

Over the years Ernest May, the stockbroker, had accumulated five Pissarros. While Camille was in England, May suffered severe financial losses and had to give up his paintings at auction. Durand-Ruel bid them in. At first Camille felt a sense of disappointment that the dealer had not used the money to buy five new pictures instead; then realized that he had done him a service by paying a sum for each which would sustain his prices at Boussod & Valadon, who had opened a small branch at 19 Boulevard Montmartre where they allowed the Impressionists to be displayed not on a mezzanine but on the ground floor. Camille took them his London paintings. Theo Van Gogh handed him an envelope of bank notes for two additional sales.

Summer burst upon them early. Camille's eye stayed dry. Theo Van Gogh was delighted with the English pictures. Camille worked with power and joy, his eye and hand sure: women pushing a wheelbarrow, the plain of Eragny in sunlight, the setting sun in nearby Bazincourt.

When the blow fell, it was shattering. In late July Vincent Van Gogh went into the fields to paint the crows above the cornfield and in a seizure shot himself. He returned somehow to his bare hotel room, waited only long enough for his brother Theo to arrive and hold his hand, then died, murmuring:

"Ah well, my work. I risked my life for it . . . and my reason has almost foundered."

He was buried in the little cemetery in the cornfields on the hill above Auvers. A despondent Theo Van Gogh returned to Boussod & Valadon, valiantly tried to continue selling Monet and Pissarro, proposed to Camille that he pay him outright five hundred dollars for the view of the *Bridge at Charing Cross*, the *Peasants Planting Potatoes*, and the *Effect of Fog Over the Serpentine*. But he was unable to live in a world without his brother, suffered a nervous breakdown. Jo took him to a *maison de santé* in Utrecht, where he soon died, leaving his wife and son penniless, and was buried. Later, reading her Bible for comfort, Jo came across the line in Samuel:

And in their death they were not divided.

She claimed Theo's body and took it to Auvers, where she placed it by the side of his brother.

Camille was a hundredfold stricken. He had lost his friend Vincent, and Theo Van Gogh, the only dealer in Paris who was excitedly selling his work.

Maurice Joyant, son of a wealthy family, was appointed in Theo Van Gogh's place at Boussod & Valadon's Montmartre gallery. Monsieur Boussod told Joyant:

"Theo Van Gogh accumulated these horrible things of modern painters. You'll find a certain number of canvases by a landscape artist named Claude Monet who is starting to sell a little in America. As for the rest, they are horrors. Figure it out and don't ask me anything or we'll close the shop."

Maurice Joyant cared little for Camille's paintings. The five-hundred-dollar purchase Theo Van Gogh had planned evaporated. Camille murmured:

"It is not only the tides of the sea that wash away sandy beaches and rocky cliffs." He remembered the lines from Shakespeare's *Julius Caesar:*

There is a tide in the affairs of men,
Which, taken at the flood, leads on to fortune.

"There is also the tidal wave," he gloomed.

5

He had read in a November newspaper that there was a financial crash in New York and London. The Bank of France had been obliged to lend England seventy-five million francs to prevent a European disaster.

"*Parbleu!*" he thought cynically. "There is an economic crisis three thousand miles away in New York and the Paris art galleries look like morgues."

He made five landscaped fans and sold them to women who used them to keep cool. Paul Gauguin had insisted that "for every poison there is an antidote." A friend, Philippe Burty, persuaded the Ministry of Beaux-Arts to buy three of

Camille's engravings. Camille set a price of thirty dollars for the three proofs. The Ministry paid him sixteen dollars for the first two prints; the third one was misplaced. Camille wrote an indignant letter to the director of the Beaux-Arts, but his letter got as lost as the misplaced print.

Lucien had rented a large room in Cornwall Road in which to hold his classes; Sterbee was his first paid student; several others wandered in. He had been staying with the Isaacsons, taking his meals there until Phineas put him out. In addition to the studio rent of ten shillings a week Camille would have to send a pound a week to a Madame de Bouvière for Lucien's room and board. Jacob Bensusan learned that his daughter was taking lessons in Lucien's studio and promptly removed her. The two met in the British Museum for a while; when Bensusan heard about that he forbade the girl to see Lucien again. He enunciated his objections: Lucien had no money, no job, no future, in addition to which he was advocating socialism and anarchism, which Bensusan believed to be identical. Father and daughter were no longer speaking to each other. Camille wrote to Lucien "to be prudent," and, returning from Gisors, where he had posted the letter and shopped for condiments for Julie, observed wryly, "How prudent was I?"

Discouraged about his prospects, Lucien wrote dispirited letters, each of which caused a row between Julie and Camille; Julie continuing to demand that her son go to work at a proper job. Camille sat late at night sending his son philosophy in lieu of the pounds he could not afford: "Each one of us has several facets. The surface often appears more important than what is inside, hence the errors of those who judge carelessly. How many times has that not happened to me! . . . One should not think of the surface or the appearance but concentrate on what is inner."

The "Artist Family" was at odds.

Georges had done nothing in terms of serious study. He returned to Eragny. Julie and the nineteen-year-old began quarreling. He had unpleasant airs which exasperated her; the fact that he was not yet earning anything was a bone in her throat which was already punctured with poverty. She succeeded in having Camille take the untutored Félix, now sixteen, into Paris to get him a job. Camille loved his third son, gentle, doe-eyed, who had cared nothing for schoolwork but loved to draw. He could do no better than an offer for an exceedingly small wage in a factory. Camille took him back to Eragny.

"What is the point of putting the boy in a factory where he will earn little more than nothing?" he asked Julie. "Let him work with me until a good opportunity comes."

Georges and Félix began to cause turmoil; they were poorly mannered and quarreled with everyone around them. Camille did what he could to smooth over the confrontations but the upheavals were hard on Julie, who had no way of controlling her rambunctious brood. Camille had believed that within a large and loving family "union made strength"; his faith wavered.

He continued his forced march: three English landscapes sent to Brussels for an exhibition; a series of perceptive drawings called *Work in the Field* which he sent to Lucien to be made into woodcuts; five canvases of twenty-one by eighteen inches and eighteen by fifteen inches, which he carried into Paris. Camille considered his small canvases very good. Eight days before he had sent Durand-Ruel five fans; Durand-Ruel had not yet replied. Four days before Christmas Maurice Joyant informed him that one of his best collectors, young Monsieur Dupuis, had committed suicide because he believed himself bankrupt.

The year 1890 had been a Janus year, one face showing a benign generosity, the other a destructive genius.

As on the last day of 1880 when he had arrived in Pontoise with a pocketful of money from the Union Générale, Durand-Ruel now bought three of the fans and assured Camille that he would buy the three small paintings which Camille had thought to have "more liberty, more air" in them. Gustave Kahn, editor of *La Vogue*, bought a small painting. The holiday was further enlivened by Durand-Ruel informing him that there would be an article about him by Octave Mirbeau in *L'Art dans les Deux Mondes* in their January 1891 issue; a comprehensive judgment of his "body of work."

The intense cold caused his eye to swell. He made the two-hour journey into Paris. Dr. Parenteau feared erysipelas, "a serious matter. You'll have to stay in a nearby hotel so I can see you every day."

He washed out the tear sack, gave him treatments of nitric acid, argenol, tannic acid. He cut open the abscess and drained it.

Camille remained in the hotel room for a week. A second abscess formed; he was immobilized for a second week. Julie, Georges and Félix came in to vary the tedium of the "evil days." He was to pay Dr. Parenteau when he could.

Early one morning Durand-Ruel appeared with a basket of warm croissants and a portfolio of cheap reproductions of Camille's paintings.

Camille protested:

"Monsieur Durand-Ruel, these copies will make you no money and gain me no reputation. I make more than enough originals to cover any conceivable market."

Durand-Ruel lowered his leonine head. He managed the difficult combination of a sad sigh and a wistful smile.

"Not a day of my life goes by but that I try to sell a Pissarro original."

Camille was contrite.

Later that day Louis Hayet, the young man who had given Camille his first glimpse of Pointillism, came to the hotel room with its faded yellow-striped wallpaper to propose that he head up a Neo-Impressionist exhibition containing works by the newer painters. Camille declined, saying, "I am without influence. If you have qualities for leadership, the role will be thrust upon you when you are asleep."

At last he returned to Eragny, bandaged.

Camille and Mary Cassatt were excluded from membership in the Society of Painter-Engravers because they were foreigners, though they were invited to show as outsiders. Camille's lithography occupied a good part of his time. Yet there was no market for etchings. Putting together the work he had done in watercolor over the years, he found that he had a hundred and sixty *exemplaires* from the various areas in which he had painted. He mounted them on delicately colored sheets and arranged them in portfolios. The works were salable, he was sure. He wanted earnestly to exhibit them, but the white matting board would have cost him forty dollars, even though he bought it in long sheets and cut it to size. He could not spare forty dollars.

Fate played with him on the edge of its abyss. He sold two unfinished canvases, the effect of snow in Montfoucault and willows in winter in Eragny. He was also bolstered by the laudatory article by Octave Mirbeau, which declared that there were few works which had so charmed and conquered him, that there were few whose existence revealed so perfectly the narrow moral harmony that united the man to his work.

Not only does Monsieur Pissarro paint, but he knows why he paints; and what he paints; he reasons out as a technician and as a philosopher. The eye of the artist, like his thought, discovers the great aspect of things. . . .

By February he was able to remove the accursed bandage. He had fifteen beautiful days of grace during which he completed the paintings he had sold unfinished.

The abscess recurred; he returned to Dr. Parenteau, emerged with another bandage.

The emotional impact of the immobile days was one of impotence and ill-suppressed rage. He had always been passionately convinced that he had to achieve a large and diverse body of work to justify his life as an artist. Now past sixty, sensing his mortality, the inability to express himself was galling. The difficulty with his eye reappeared with the regularity of a railroad schedule. Dr. Parenteau told him he would have to operate in the spring.

Claude Monet, when he learned of Pissarro's troubles, sent him to see the publisher Charpentier, who had encouraged Renoir in the early years by commissioning him to paint a large portrait of Charpentier's wife and daughter. Charpentier bought a large-sized canvas. Degas rallied round, sent word that he loved Camille's *Field and Mill*. With the money from Charpentier's purchase, Camille bought a secondhand etching press and moved it to Eragny. Julie was furious.

His eye cleared. He made steel plates of four etchings. The little press was a poor one, parts were missing. Bracquemond, the master in the field, told him an etching would not fetch four cents in Paris. But Camille was fascinated by the technique.

In early February he exhibited in Brussels with Les Vingt, in the company of Seurat, Sisley, Gauguin, Guillaumin, some whorling Van Gogh canvases. Little to nothing was sold. At the same time he received a letter from Mette Gauguin asking whether he had any news of her husband, who she feared had abandoned her and her children.

In mid-February he had a letter from P. G. Hamerton, editor of the English magazine *Portfolio*, asking for some drawings to juxtapose to *Woman Sewing*. Later, Camille was astonished to read:

> There is Monsieur Camille Pissarro, who has some very ardent admirers, and yet who is very foreign to me. It seems to me that he admits lines and masses that a stricter taste would alter or avoid, and that he includes objects that a more scrupulous artist would reject. . . .

*   *   *

"Extraordinary ingratitude," Camille mused.

He used the money from a small sale to mount forty-two proofs of his etchings, packing them in a trunk for an English gallery. Though the state had bought only two of his prints, he sent a collection of his best proofs to the Luxembourg Museum, hoping for exposure. He heard nothing from them. Nor could Lucien place the batch of etchings in London.

6

An umbrella of happenings spread over him, offering sanctuary from neither sun, wind nor rain. Dubois-Pillet died. Camille remembered how the Pointillist artist had volunteered to lend him, from a thin purse, a little money to get him home to Pontoise. He had been a good man; that he did not have the talent to become a great painter was unfortunate. Camille and Dubois-Pillet's artist friends gave him a hearty funeral.

Ernest Hoschedé of Petit Gagne fame died in Belgium. Claude Monet and Alice Hoschedé, who had been living together for eleven years at Giverny with their assorted offspring, could, after an obligatory mourning period of nine months, be married. Monet had Hoschedé's body brought to Giverny and buried in the nearby churchyard, under a handsome monument.

"The rewards of being cuckolded," a wag slyly ventured.

At the end of March Georges Seurat died. He had been in bed only a few days with a disturbance of the throat. The illness had developed with ruinous speed. Dr. de Bellio, who was not the family doctor, diagnosed it as diphtheria. Just a few days before, Camille had seen an exhibition of his work; some delicate marines in tans and oranges, a large canvas, *The Circus*, beautifully composed, with a clown in the foreground. He had painted all the frames in dots. Signac, his disciple, was the one most deeply moved by the tragedy. He mourned that, with Seurat's death, Pointillism was also dead. Camille walked arm in arm with him from the cemetery:

"Pointillism will have consequences which will be of importance for all of us. Seurat added to our concept of the use of paint."

His eye grew better, he completed three canvases, two gouaches and several etchings no one was interested in buying.

Durand-Ruel staged the Society of Painter-Engravers show in his main salon. A conscientious man, he gave Camille and Mary Cassatt a small but nice room off the large gallery to display their prints. Camille showed twenty-four works, including his newest *Market, Breton Peasant Woman at the Well*. Mary Cassatt had made some colored engravings, "rare and exquisite," which Camille judged as beautiful as the Japanese color prints that had become the rage among Parisian artists. In terms of interest Camille and Mary Cassatt stole the show, yet there was not one offer to buy.

Two of Lucien's artist friends in London bought *La Place de la République* and *Ile Lacroix,* saying, "We definitely prefer certain of your father's etchings to Whistler's; and to find another aquafortist you have to go back to Rembrandt."

Lucien was pleased to write this good news; he was having continuing problems over Sterbee in London.

Durand-Ruel rejected his new oils, *Mowers in Repose* and *Sunset with Fog,* as unsalable. He took them to the less inviting Portier's. He was unhappy about that but the only time artists' lives had been different was in the Renaissance when they were employed as artisans, similar to stonemasons, working for wages for the Church, royalty or government. Plagued as he was, he would not have exchanged places with those of the earlier age who had danced to a harsher tune.

He took the next three completed paintings to Monsieur Montaignac's gallery. Montaignac, during his years as manager of the Petit gallery, had been reputed to have a good eye for values; but when he looked at Camille's three canvases his voice was shrill, coming out of a face dominated by a finchlike nose and large red lips.

"Frankly, I don't understand them," he enunciated in a high octave.

Trudging down the boulevard, Camille mourned:

"He wears one of Dr. Parenteau's bandages over both eyes."

Montaignac, to his surprise, sold one of the paintings. Maurice Joyant of Boussod & Valadon succeeded in placing *The Serpentime* with Gallimard, the publisher. The combined sales from the two galleries eased their lot. He started painting out of doors again, "from nature, my companion and my ally."

He also rented, after several years of being without, a room in Paris, at 12 Rue de l'Abreuvoir, Montmartre, where he could store his work and to which he could bring prospective collectors. He went to Durand-Ruel's to see Monet's new series of sunsets. He found the paintings "marvelously luminous and very masterful; in harmony they left nothing to be desired." He felt no tinge of envy when he learned that Durand-Ruel was selling Claude Monet wildly well, a series of haystacks behind Giverny bringing in thirteen thousand dollars. People were wanting nothing but Monets. Apparently he could not paint enough pictures to meet the demand. Worse, they all wanted *Haystacks in the Setting Sun*! Everything he had was going to America at prices averaging a thousand dollars. Durand-Ruel remarked:

"All this comes from not shocking the collectors. Why don't you leave your peasants and farm scenes for a while and come into Paris and paint its teeming life on the boulevards?"

Monet was preparing to purchase the house in Giverny with its surrounding land. Julie was enthralled at the idea and wanted to buy their house in Eragny. Camille was aghast.

"It would only plunge us hopelessly in debt. Besides, Eragny is too far from Paris."

Julie had not listened. She clenched her molars, defying him in silence. When he next went into Paris with two oils of the spring planting and asked Durand-Ruel for a hundred dollars for the two, Durand-Ruel declined. A smaller gallery offered forty dollars for them. He was forced to refuse and returned to Eragny, his pockets empty of francs, on the hard bench of the third-class compartment. It was twenty-eight years since the Salon des Refusés. Others of the original group were getting along. He had been culled.

He joined Mary Cassatt in deciding they would leave Durand-Ruel altogether. He appeared to be selling nothing but Monets; he already had a large stock of Pissarros, Degases, Renoirs, Sisleys which he was unable to persuade his collectors to buy. He could not buy new works until he sold some of the older ones, nor could he support all of them. But where to go? Boussod & Valadon was unsympathetic. Portier, Petit, the smaller dealers who sold conventional stock for a pittance? Then where?

When his eye troubled him again, Dr. Parenteau injected silver nitrate into the tear duct to induce inflammation and accelerate healing. He had difficulty keeping the bandage as clean as his long white beard, which swayed slightly to the right in the wind, and which he washed every day that Julie could afford him soap. However his personal problems dissolved on the day the news reached Eragny that French troops had killed ten persons at the town of Fourmies, where mine workers were demonstrating for an eight-hour day.

"It is unheard of that soldiers should allow themselves to be led into these most cowardly infamous acts," he declared to his children. "After all, they are workers too."

Maximilien Luce proposed that they launch a journal which would set forth the anarchist's concept of the role artists could play in creating a just society. Camille turned his friend off gently:

"The concept is utopian, my dear friend. In politics, as well as the outdoors, I have to keep dust out of my eye."

He went into Paris for the Arosa auction, conducted by Durand-Ruel, of the panels Camille had painted for the banker's home in St. Cloud in 1871, twenty years before. The four panels fetched two hundred and twenty dollars; a fifth canvas, *Street of Louveciennes*, went for seventy-five dollars. Durand-Ruel was pleased that the pictures had sold. At the end of the auction he came up to Camille with a broad smile.

"Monsieur Pissarro, it is your turn to have a good show."

It was the first encouraging word from the dealer in several years.

"Are you in earnest, Monsieur Durand-Ruel?" he asked, his voice a little shaky.

"My word of honor. Early next year. The entire gallery."

The rhythmical cycles continued, season following season, a new abscess forming just as regularly every couple of months, with visits to Dr. Parenteau; the inability to paint while cooped up; a rash of new work when the eye healed. He borrowed money from the affluent Claude Monet, who himself had spent many years writing begging letters: forty dollars for Julie, an installment to Dr. Parenteau; the remainder to repair a leak in the roof and a warped floorboard; a few dollars for a stay in Paris.

Julie fell ill. She sent for Dr. Avenal of Gisors, who diagnosed a uterine or cervical tumor. He told her to stay in bed and not tire herself. A pall fell over the household. Julie was submissive for a few days, letting Cocotte wait on her. Then she grew restless, dressed, took over the cooking and her work in the garden.

Madame Seurat sent Camille some of her son's drawings as a remembrance gift. Camille put them on the walls of the Eragny house. He then set about doing some of what he called "prints of character." He had meditated upon them so long during his spells of inactivity that the execution required little time. When the day's work was done he cleared away the materials from his drawing table, took out paper, pen and ink, wrote: "It is by working in the smithy that one becomes a blacksmith. It is incontestable that work in the studio is just as difficult as work outdoors, but it is entirely different from the point of view of the requirements, methods and results."

In mid-April Julie suggested that Camille take Georges into the painter Louis Hayet's studio to work and that Félix go to Contet, the framer. Neither Hayet nor Contet needed an assistant. Camille brought the boys back to Eragny, bringing Maximilien Luce along to placate Julie. What could he do? He could not leave them in Paris without a sou.

Georges was behaving better and had done some good sketches. Camille wanted to send him to London but each time they had a letter from Lucien it told of some new disappointment or failure. Camille acknowledged that the fault was his. He had decided to raise his sons to be artists without the wherewithal to pursue such a nebulous future. Georges would not take a routine factory or clerking job. Félix was unqualified for anything but manual labor. He had been wrong, but the wrong had emerged from his own character; he did not know how to put it down.

An article in *L'Echo de Paris* called attention to a Gauguin auction backed by Dr. de Bellio. Degas bought two canvases; the auction took in two thousand dollars. Gauguin left for Tahiti, abandoning Mette and the children, as she had feared he would.

"I suppose we each have our Tahiti," Camille observed thoughtfully; "mine is the French countryside, the river valleys with their fields, orchards, men and women working the land."

Mary Cassatt wanted to know if he would give lessons to some young American girls. He gave the excuse that he did not want to be tied down because his eye could become aggravated without warning. The young girls did not come out to Eragny.

"Pride," observed Julie. "You won't take pay for lessons, they won't take lessons without paying. The world is planted with idiots."

Paris's young painters, and they seemed to come in with every ship and every train, scrambled to secure a foothold. They discussed means of getting publicity for their new organizations, "come-lately, go-early," organizations, the established called them. Degas became violent about their efforts to gain space in the journals. "I have hatred for young people adventing themselves," he said. Camille felt a smile teething inside his head. How hard the Impressionists themselves had striven over the years and eight exhibitions to gain public attention for their group.

While working on a painting of two young peasant girls chatting under the trees he knew it was not a happy portrait but he had come to the conclusion that the pretty was a greater pitfall than the grotesque; what was ugly in one age became lovely in the following epoch.

"Ergo," he murmured to himself while standing before the easel on his traveling cart, "it behooves us not to paint in the style of the present generation." As he had told Cézanne, "Our peers are blind. Leave the discovery to the next generation."

Alas, that would leave the sales also.

Would scenes of farmyards and working peasants ever be purchased by city dwellers? Was Durand-Ruel right about his sophisticated collectors and their luxuriously decorated drawing rooms?

In the second half of June he did not dare undertake many pictures directly from nature for fear of not being able to continue in the heat and dust. Nevertheless he was moderately satisfied, sending Portier *Springtime in Gray Weather*, since Durand-Ruel did not want anything until the following year's retrospective. From the trunkful of etchings sent to London, a Mr. Kennedy of a New York gallery bought a group of prints for sixty dollars. Lucien was in need, so Camille told him he could keep the money. When Julie learned of it she was outraged.

"I need the money! Only a month ago you said, 'What bad luck we have, the collectors deliberate and do not buy.' You're depriving the young ones by giving to a twenty-eight-year-old who should be earning his own living."

He could think of no reply. Instead he picked up the latest copy of *l'Echo de Paris*, read an article by Charles Henry, who believed that the future would be dominated by mysticism.

"That is not the future," he grumbled. "That is going backwards."

He learned with trepidation that Durand-Ruel had had to take back a number of paintings that had been sold for a considerable sum from a collector who went bankrupt. Fortunately only a few were his. Then in the heat of summer there came a sudden wind. In two days an eye abscess had formed and broken and for two wearisome weeks he remained in a small hotel room in Paris. He reported to the family that there would be an eye operation. He was taking medication to assure its success.

The more important medication was the sale to new collectors by Joyant and Portier, enabling him to pay back the sum he owed Monet, the back rent, the Gisors merchants, his framer-dealer Clauzet, instead of giving him a major painting in lieu of the francs; Dr. Parenteau. Dr. Parenteau dressed the wound with a lint fabric; taught Félix how to change the dressing twice a day, sent him home to Eragny.

By the end of August he was out in the countryside again. For had not Durand-Ruel promised him a great show in early 1892?

7

He painted passionately the entire month of September. The Epte Valley and surrounding hayfields and ripening orchards of apples and pears were aflame with color. Octave Mirbeau was laying out a series of articles about his work. Julie was living in the future where there would be aplenty.

At the beginning of October Mirbeau bought *The Goose Girl* and *Young Peasant* for modest prices, giving Camille the money to buy passage for Georges to England with an introduction to John Singer Sargent.

He retained his showroom in the Rue de l'Abreuvoir where he occasionally managed to sell a watercolor. Julie was reading about Maeterlinck's play, *The Blind;* she asked Camille if they could go to see it.

Luck, as does misfortune, comes in bunches the way the grapes ripened in the vineyards Julie had worked in Grancey-sur-Ource. Portier sold *Little Haymakers* for ninety dollars; a new dealer, Monsieur Chéramy, in a virginal burst of enthusiasm, sold several watercolors and an orchard scene in oil. Camille, with resilient optimism, assumed that "if the money comes in as speedily as I expect, I will make over two thousand dollars this year."

He needed this reassurance; for Durand-Ruel had not set a date for his spring exhibition and was in the bargain buying in everything by Jongkind, who had died. Jongkind's prices were rising. The poor soul had sold pitifully during his lifetime.

Toward the end of October Camille decided to leave the isolation of Eragny and live nearer to Paris. He wrote to a young painter and frequent guest at Eragny, Léo Gausson, asking if he could locate a house perhaps in his own area. He needed a rather large house with a garden . . . as close as possible to the railroad and he would pay two hundred to two hundred and sixty dollars for the year. Then, because Monsieur Dallemagne, their landlord, had not replied to his earlier letter requesting needed repairs, he asked the owner for a cancellation of the lease, which had one more year to run. Dallemagne maintained a silence for which Julie was grateful. She did not want to move. Camille explained:

"When one doesn't have what it takes to attract the masses, one must be close. If we live closer I can go back and forth and not stay in Paris so much."

Julie was not impressed by this fancy footwork.

"I like this house. I can exist without repairs. Every bird needs a nest. Claude Monet bought Giverny. I want to be permanent."

Camille had once said to Lucien: "I have the sad burden of being unable to make your mother happy." She had cause enough! Years of strangulating poverty and uncertainty, the lunacy of his training his five sons to become artists. Families prayed for sons to relieve the burden of the parents' old age. Julie had had an abundance of them. But she saw plainly that they were going to have to support their offspring as long as Camille lived.

For a respite, since she rarely saw anyone except her neighbors, Père Kimir and Mère Freu, and the artists who would lock themselves up with Camille, she took Cocotte and Paul Emile into Paris for a vacation with one of her sisters, leaving Félix and Ludovic at home with Camille. A neighboring farm woman would cook their one hot meal a day. He gave her whatever money he had on hand. With it she bought her daughter and Paul Emile new wardrobes, then showed the children the same sights in Paris that their father had shown her thirty-two years before: the marionettes in the Champs-Elysées, the Luxembourg Garden, Notre Dame, the Left Bank around St. Germain-des-Prés. Camille was almost as happy as Julie for the peaceful interlude.

If Julie's life had become one of voluntary slavery, so was his own, through the compulsion to paint. He was working furiously, a woman cowherder was well advanced; he perfected an earlier *Women in the Farmyard*. There were also three new smaller canvases. He got a note from Portier informing him that his collectors did not like the smaller paintings; they were unsalable. At the same moment Mirbeau bought another two pictures, one of them for the new director of the Luxembourg Museum, a longtime friend. Mirbeau also wrote Camille a letter saying that Auguste Rodin, who had become Paris's acclaimed sculptor, was a warm admirer of Camille's work and wished to have a painting. Rodin wanted Camille to choose the canvas, but Camille told Mirbeau:

"I would like to give Rodin something, but he wants to pay. It's very charming but let him choose to his own taste. When I see something old that I've forgotten about, I become very indulgent. I look at it as the work of another. I discover qualities there and I am desolate at not having been able to continue to do so well."

He then wrote to Rodin saying that he was having Portier send him a painting, a sunset with a thick fog rising from the prairies; that he had hesitated over the choice because it happens so often that artists cherish their deformed children. The price, since Rodin insisted, was one hundred dollars.

Rodin informed Camille that his *Landscape with Effect of Fog* was splendid.

Bernheim Jeune, a dealer, bought four of Camille's paintings at auction, which he showed in his windows on the Rue Laffitte. He also told Camille that at the next auction some five or six dealers would be ready to bid at high prices; and offered to organize a show for him. Camille accepted the kind words and went off to lunch with Rodin in his high barnlike studio amidst a number of his studies for *The Gates of Hell,* including *The Kiss* and *The Thinker*. His cook spread a red and white checked cloth over a bumpy worktable and served them a hearty Normandy meal of veal made with a sauce of rich cream and Calvados. They sat opposite each other. Rodin had an extraordinarily broad head, the eyes wide-spaced, hair cropped short to accentuate the rounded forehead; and a widely flowing brown and gray beard which obviated any need to wear a collar, cravat, or even a shirt. His voice was as soft as his gaze was penetrating. When he took Camille around his studio, commenting on works in progress much as Corot had done when Camille first reached Paris, he explained that, unlike Michelangelo, he did not feel a need to cut marble; modeling in clay was sufficient for him. He seemed younger to Camille than their ten years' difference in age might have suggested; the sparks of restless energy he threw off reminded Camille of his own early years of groping toward a *modus operandi*.

"Sculpture is simply the art of depression and protuberance. The first principle is that of construction, whether the model be a human being, animal, tree or flower. Each profile is the outer evidence of the interior mass. The reality of the model must emanate from within, does it not, Monsieur Pissarro?" A slight smile came into his somber eyes and erased the vertical lines of intensity between them. "We think alike, is it not so? Your eye, grafted onto your heart, reads deeply into the bosom of nature. I must have more of your paintings to brighten my walls so that I can look into your countryside while I model on my stand."

Camille left Rodin's studio exhilarated.

In early December Maurice Joyant of Boussod & Valadon came out to Eragny and went through Camille's new paintings.

"I'd like to buy up to two hundred dollars' worth."

Camille frowned. "You can't expect to get much for so little money."

"The moment of your arrival has come. I beg you to deal with our house. We'll take old and new things. Give us preference for a big exhibition. Let me take in a half dozen of these canvases; we'll guarantee to buy two or three at your price."

Camille thought, "There's something behind this."

There was. On his Jongkind sale, Durand-Ruel had taken in sixty thousand dollars the first day, twenty thousand the second! With this money on hand, he set Camille's promised comprehensive show for January 23, 1892, and paid a good sum as a guarantee. Camille gave Joyant thirty watercolors to display.

The wind drifts of oncoming success spread out to touch others. Forces of good as well as evil feed each other. When Camille encountered Guillaumin in Paris he saw to his astonishment that Guillaumin was nattily dressed in a new suit, hat, shirt, tie, boots.

They embraced. Camille cried, "Guillaumin, good fortune has overtaken you! Did someone buy out your studio?"

Guillaumin burst into hysterical laughter. His nose was a more mobile feature than his lips. In discouragement it seemed to turn down; in normal times it was a straight and short exclamation point. Now, in his ecstasy, his nostrils quivered.

"Nothing so practical. I won the lottery last week! Twenty thousand dollars! Good-bye to poverty! My wife and I have moved into a nice apartment, bought new clothes and invested the rest in solid securities. I'll be able to live on the income and paint for the rest of my life! All the time you thought I was a hopeless dreamer."

Guillaumin moved jauntily down the boulevard. Camille stood gazing at his back in a stupor.

"One hundred thousand francs! More than I've earned in thirty-five years of painting."

8

Camille summoned Lucien from London to help him select frames and get the exhibition of the large number of canvases assembled. He then began a series of studies from his window in Eragny. It was wonderful winter weather, dry, cold, with hoarfrost and radiant sunlight. He set three different canvases on stretchers. He would have only a couple of weeks to get some five or six new paintings ready. On the day after Christmas he exulted:

"It is extraordinary how certain I am of my execution. If I finish them I will have a beautiful series of Bazincourt paintings. I was afraid that repetition of the same motif would be tiring, but the effects are so varied that everything is completely transformed."

Durand-Ruel's gallery was freshly decorated for the retrospective, which would be a graphic résumé of Camille's work, showing the transitions, changes, growth over the years. Lucien was demonstrating considerable skill in assembling the pictures. Durand-Ruel permitted him to hang them in an orderly yet continually explosive arrangement. He even agreed to pay for some of the frames. The large gallery became a cathedral with this first lifetime showing: Louveciennes, Pontoise, Eragny, London, Rouen. Everyone who wandered in during the feverish days of preparation was excited and optimistic. Lucien told his mother at home:

"The day will shortly come when you can rest easy and buy yourself beautiful dresses."

Camille said to Julie:

"If it happens, this time it will be serious."

Julie achieved a wan smile. She was praying silently and crossing herself with smooth gestures inside her head.

By mid-January Camille had been able to finish several paintings from older studies at Piette's Montfoucault and Louveciennes, done before the war. He was able to turn over to Durand-Ruel a list of twenty-five new pictures to hang with the earlier ones.

"It's now just a matter of defending myself against the wolves," he declared.

The giant show Durand-Ruel had wanted filled his high-ceilinged salon with seventy-one works, oils and gouaches, covering a period of twenty years. There were eleven paintings from the seventies, twenty-four from the eighties, eight from 1891 and five completed since New Year's of 1892. There were Julie's ten; and a number from collectors. Camille set his own prices, scaling them from one hundred sixty dollars for the smaller *Delafoli Mansion* to two hundred dollars for *Blooming Apple Tree,* and two hundred and forty dollars for *Footpath by the Court of Law, Pontoise.*

Octave Mirbeau, reporting for *Le Figaro*, was once again laudatory:

> It shows us this master who has been an eternal seeker, in all eras of his artistic life. So it is to us not only a precious aesthetic joy, but also a precious biography. . . .
>
> No one analyzes with more intelligence. I know nothing more beautiful and touching than to see Monsieur Camille Pissarro, so young under his white beard, keep all the enthusiasm of his youth; and far from the noise of coteries, juries, hideous jealousies, pursue, with the ardors of yesterday, the most beautiful, most considerable works of this time.

The attendance was large for the opening. It swelled during the week. Sales were made. When an influenza epidemic had subsided, Julie came into Paris with their youngest son, Paul Emile. She was staggered by the expanse of painting. After moving slowly from canvas to canvas, each evoking a flash of memory of the joy or pain of that particular interval, she sank onto Durand-Ruel's round leather settee in the middle of the gallery, deeply shaken. At length she murmured to Camille:

"*Je suis étonnée.* One by one each painting seemed like a hut; all together like this they are a château."

She paused, her head turning around the room, agape at the SOLD signs on the pictures.

"We haven't sold any of your pictures, Julie; though we could have." He sat down on the circular seat beside her. "It's strange, my dear wife; during the years when we could not sell anything and you rebelled against my painting, you picked out ten of my very finest for your own."

Good things continued to happen. On February 6, Alfred de Lostalot published in the *Chronique des Arts*:

> Monsieur Pissarro will remain as the precursor of a formula of art which has not yet been fixed, but whose effectiveness has already made itself felt in the production of a good part of the French School.

The public surged into Durand-Ruel's gallery. The prices became more substantial. The exhibition was a *succès formidable*. Félix Fénéon said for *L'Art Moderne* of Brussels: "He liberates nature from the accidental. . . ."

When the show closed on February 20, Durand-Ruel bought all of the unsold pictures. Julie refused to relinquish her ten, explaining:

"These paintings are my pay for an empty stomach and a heavy heart."

On February 26 Lucien helped pack his mother's canvases and returned them to Eragny. Julie led Camille to the Bon Marché, where she bought a fashionable black crepe de chine dress which enhanced her coloring and figure; and a beautiful black velvet coat and hat. When Octave Mirbeau opened the door of his Paris townhouse to them the following day, where they had been invited for luncheon, he exclaimed:

"Mais vous êtes belle!"

Julie flushed with pride.

Camille put his arm about her shoulder affectionately.

"She has also enabled us to survive."

He had been accepted back in the seventies. Been sold well by Durand-Ruel to enthusiastic amateurs, only to suffer subsequent years of neglect and shameful poverty.

They must continue to cling to each other. Enjoy this moment to the full.

BOOK FOURTEEN

Harvest

1

HE PAINTED from his second-story studio window overlooking the garden plum trees coming into flower; completing from earlier studies a shepherdess and the scenic village of Bazincourt; and took them under his arm to Portier, who went into raptures, summoning by *petits bleus* his two most ardent Parisian customers. He sold both pieces, *Shepherdress* going for two hundred dollars, the smaller *Bazincourt* for one hundred dollars.

Anarchists in such journals as *La Révolte* and *Le Père Peinard* had advocated the destruction of the oppressive French government. The building at 136 Boulevard St. Germain, where lived a magistrate who had taken part in trials in which anarchists were condemned, was blown up. A few days later a bomb exploded at Lobau barracks. Toward the end of the month a bomb destroyed another building in the Rue de Clichy. Although no lives were lost, Paris was in a state of terror. Camille was disheartened, abhorring violence in any form, and deeply regretted the blasts, believing that direct action was as destructive for the perpetrator as for the victim. He contributed to a fund to help feed the children of the men being held in the Parisian jails.

His English landscapes had sold well in France and he decided to go to England to work once again. Besides, he wanted to plead Lucien's cause with Jacob Bensusan. Lucien had sent Sterbee a proposal of marriage, the message was placed in a wooden box which Lucien had carved and painted himself. Sterbee showed the letter to her father, who declared that the day they were married he would go abroad and leave everybody. Camille proposed to approach Bensusan through his appreciation of culture. Julie declined his invitation to accompany him; at least in Eragny she knew the language and had two friendly neighbors. Besides, the landlord had told her that he must sell the house. A new owner might put them out.

"I've already written to a friend to find us something closer, perhaps in the vicinity of St. Germain-en-Laye."

Julie squared her shoulders.

"Poor as we were in Grancey, we owned our stone hut and little garden."

He filled his easel box with its collapsible legs with palette, brushes, pigments and charcoal all enclosed in a thin wooden container. He lashed several blank canvases to its side. It was heavy even when empty; full, its weight dragged painfully. He then roped together the three oil paintings on stretchers he was taking to England for sale. His suitcase too was heavy with clothing, books. When he tried to lift it all he could not. He would have to turn part of it over to the freight handlers.

In London he took a room at the bed and breakfast house, 1 Gloucester Terrace, Kew, where Lucien and Georges rented. It was opposite the gardens and over a baker's shop. They had their evening meal together at a small French restaurant. Camille wrote to Bensusan asking if he might visit Melton Lodge the following Sunday. Bensusan replied with an invitation to Sunday dinner.

Camille had never been in Bensusan's home in a luxurious Victorian suburb with large houses and evergreen shrubbery. It was a warm early June day when he walked past Dulwich College, which he had painted during his earlier stay. On top of the hill he passed the Crystal Palace, moved here after the World's Fair in Hyde Park, which he had also painted, as well as views of Upper and Lower Norwood and Sydenham, most of which Durand-Ruel had sold.

Melton Lodge was a two-story brick house with sharp-pointed dormers, curved bay windows in one wing, a carriage entrance and iron-grill fencing. His raising of the front door clapper was answered by a domestic who led him along a path bordered by spring flowers into the back garden. Jacob Bensusan of the bristling red hair, the strong nose and disciplined chin beard, held himself as erect as a British colonel, the *yarmulke* on the back of his head reinforcing his unassailable posture. He ordered glasses of seltzer to be brought out, then said in a conciliatory voice:

"I am not opposed to Lucien, only to his views. First of all to his socialism. I am a prosperous businessman; I have no stomach for such radical nonsense . . ."

Camille observed that Bensusan had a capacious stomach

covered by a heavy vest and gold chain which had a dimension sufficient to engulf all sorts of strange ideas.

". . . however, I am not worried about that. Time and the practicalities of life will convert him. It's his atheism I object to. I will have no son-in-law to be with me in the synagogue on Rosh Hashanah, on Yom Kippur, the Day of Atonement, the Yom Hadin, the Day of Judgment. Sterbee will never light the Sabbath candles for me. She and her husband will not be with me at the seder table when we thank God for saving us from Egyptian bondage. She will no longer be my child; I will think of her as dead."

"I understand," said Camille, deeply moved. "The fault is mine. I raised Lucien with art as a religion."

Bensusan frowned in disapproval.

"Judaism has made a great contribution to civilization, the belief in one God. The requirements of righteous living come from Judaism; the *mitzvoth*: the commandments to do good deeds."

"Righteous living comes from one's moral values," Camille responded. "Yours comes from Orthodoxy. Mine and Lucien's come from the beauty of the earth, which we try to transcribe for all to see. We are both right. Since you love your daughter, could you be persuaded to exercise a little less rigidity?"

The maid came out the back door to announce dinner. Bensusan rose.

"Let us break bread in peace."

He took Camille along the side path to the front of the house, ushered him into the parlor with its furniture upholstered in a heavy ribbed satin, then into the dining room with its long mahogany table set with King's pattern silver with a *B* engraved on the handles in copperplate script. They were served a noodle soup and roasted chicken. Only Bensusan's soft, plump wife, who remained silent during the meal, for in that orthodox household she had no voice, was at the table; Sterbee, Ruth and their brother Samuel were having Sunday dinner in the upstairs sitting room.

"The children are in love, they are well matched. What are your demands?" Camille asked.

"Marriage in the synagogue, after instruction by our rabbi, the children to be brought up as practicing Jews, the males circumcised. A wait of six months so that Lucien can reconsider. If he then agrees, I will give them my blessing and settle an ample dowry on Sterbee."

"If at the end of six months Lucien has not agreed?"

Fright flickered across Bensusan's eyes.

"Then I'll disinherit her."

Camille knew that Bensusan's demands were not unreasonable. Had not his own father and mother disinherited him? Given up the son they loved because they had clung to religious and social prejudices? Was there no way to innovate history? To live with nature, which did not concern itself with artificial religious or societal observances? Was there an essential pattern of frustration that dominated succeeding generations?

"I will do my best to convince Lucien to accede," he said.

Camille found Lucien pacing the street in front of their boardinghouse. He had not shaved, his hair and clothing showed hours of anxiety.

Sitting knee to knee on hard chairs by the window overlooking Kew green, Camille told his son of Bensusan's strictures and made a strong case for Lucien's acquiescence.

"I've heard that from him before," Lucien protested. "He does not doubt that we love each other; and he knows that I am not seeking Sterbee's dowry. He only wants another half year to persuade me to sign his papers and go through the ceremonies. You didn't raise me that way. Sterbee and I will be married just as quickly as we can make arrangements."

Camille sat slumped in silence. He understood Lucien's impetuosity; they had already been kept apart for more than a year. His own fear was that Lucien had never made a living, nor had he created a volume of work which showed promise of future earnings. He would have to support Lucien and Sterbee as Rachel and Frederic had supported him. His mind filled with an irony turned more against himself than against his son.

He received a bombshell from Julie. She had forstalled Monsieur Dallemagne, the owner, who had informed her that he was putting the house up at auction, by taking the first train to Giverny and borrowing three thousand dollars from Claude Monet. The total cost of the house would be something over six thousand dollars. The owner would take a mortgage at four and a half per cent for the balance, to be paid off in five years. Julie's letter arrived by registered mail because it contained a notarized deed for the purchase of the home. She told Camille in no uncertain terms, without commas, capitals or periods, that he was to write to Monet confirming his responsibility for the loan, and to send her a registered letter in which he enclosed the signed and notarized deed.

He stumbled into a chair. Julie had bought the house in Eragny! The apple orchard he did not want to own, the thousands of dollars of debt he did not want to take on.

Julie had declared doggedly: "Somehow we manage to eke out what we need before the vine louse eats the roots of the grapes."

Lucien came into the room to find Camille holding his head in his hands.

"What's wrong, Papa?"

Camille handed Lucien his mother's letter.

"She has bought the house, which is leaning to one side, with a garden too big for her to care for."

Lucien said softly:

"She has always wanted a home of her own."

Camille rose, poured some water into a wide bowl from the pitcher on the washstand, cupped the cold liquid over his face. When he had dried himself he paced the room, a picture of the abandoned two-story barn at the end of the property flashing into his mind. He had long wanted to convert it into his workplace, with an abundance of space and light, a permanent studio in which to paint in quiet. But where would the money come from?

He decided that somehow they would find what was needed. If they could pay for the house, they could pay for the studio. "The Lord takes care of His progeny," he murmured. "Particularly artists. Why else would He have put *Homo sapiens* on earth? To crop and drop? Not nearly enough for so great an accomplishment."

Claude Monet, the "abject beggar," who himself had been so brutally impoverished in his early years with Léonie, wanted no interest on his loan. With pencil and paper Camille figured out that his fixed payments would be about two hundred fifty dollars a year. He would also be required to pay off his principle by the end of five years. A portion of each sale in the future would have to go to meet that obligation. It was a sign of the intensity of Julie's desire for a permanent place that she would undertake this big debt. He stood in awe of her foolhardiness. Or was it wisdom? It would take five years to find out.

There was no help for it. He owed her that much.

He looked up the address of a notary, signed the purchase documents, had them officially embossed with a seal and dropped into the post to register the fat envelope; then resolutely put out of his mind the problem of the mortgage as well as the contretemps with Jacob Bensusan. It was an invaluable gift that when he faced his easel his mind completely concentrated on the scene before him. How else could one achieve a lifetime *oeuvre?*

He went to work at first light in the magnificent park of Kew Gardens, which had been given to the British public by the Crown in 1840, and which had been brought to maturity by the botanists William and Joseph Hooker, father and son: open swards, green copses, greenhouses, horticulture museums, miles of pathways wandering through the open labyrinth of flower and shrub. For Camille it was a treasure trove of every hue, tint, chromatic scale: rhododendrons, herbaceous borders, blue lupines at back; yellow daisies, pinks, roses, azaleas. Peonies in high tubs, jasmine amidst green leaves. Crushed gravel walks. Cedar and beech trees combining subtle shades of green. He painted them all. Ageless, he set up his easel at each different area of the gardens, found his brushes and paints fluid and fulfilling. He worked straight through the day under a wide-brimmed straw hat, drinking cool water from an earthen jug. The June weather with its cooling breeze was delicious in his nostrils; the July sun burned through his straw hat.

On August 11, 1892, Esther Bensusan and Lucien were married in a register office in Richmond, as Julie and Camille had been before them in Croydon. To replace Camille's two French witnesses, Lucien invited two artist friends to be present and sign his marriage papers. Camille stood by, happy but trepidatious. Jacob Bensusan sent a clerk from his office to make certain the ceremony was legal; but proffered no other word. The next day the newlyweds crossed the English Channel for a honeymoon in Rouen. Afterwards they were to settle into the house in Eragny where Julie would teach Sterbee how to become a capable housewife. Camille packed up his paintings and took the boat train to Dover for the crossing to Calais. His two-and-a-half-month stay in England had come off well. Again London had called out his finest efforts in capturing not only the suburb but the bridge at Charing Cross, Primrose Hill and Regent's Park: also the green, the church, the stream, the setting sun. It had not always come this easy.

"Bien fait!" he admitted to himself. "Now if only the French will continue to admire my feelings for London."

2

He walked up the main road of Eragny with its *mairie* on one side, the church with its thin steeple piercing the blue mid-August sky. Ahead of him was his home, not just the random structure into which he and Julie and their children had moved temporarily. Since the property now belonged to them, it looked and felt different. It deserved a name. The house seemed to lean more than ever but he could not call it "The Leaning Tower of Eragny." When he gazed through the open gate and saw Julie's extensive garden, he voted against "House With a Too Big Garden." Then he saw the trees heavy with bright luscious apples and he knew he had a name: "The Apple Orchard." In some mystical way, because the property now had an identity, it became more personally his. A spirit of joy flooded over him. He burst through the front door, called "Julie!" embraced her as she came running.

It was a happy reunion. Ludovic Rodolphe, Cocotte and Paul Emile swarmed over him with familial hugs and kisses. He showed them his new paintings. Julie's face flushed with joy.

"Oh, Camille, they're so *agréables*. They'll find collectors. They'll pay for our house."

Her face was tanned from the summer's outdoor work; broader and fuller than in the earlier years but still unlined, with the well-modeled features Camille loved to paint, still pleasant to look upon: high brow, lustrous hair piled on top of her head in braids; her deep green eyes accepting, white teeth intact. The years of excessive anxiety and humiliating indigence had not destroyed her inner qualities.

Julie gave Lucien and Sterbee a large bedroom facing the road, sewed a new bedspread for them, hung fresh curtains. Camille put on the walls early sketches and watercolors of Cézanne, Monet, Sisley, Caillebotte, Gauguin. For some time they were all happy together; Sterbee had a deep affection for the family into which she had married; she was eager to learn how to cook, clean, sew. Alas! She had no whit of talent for housekeeping, nor could she take it seriously enough: her timing was wrong: her vegetables were raw when the meat was ready, and her sauce not yet begun. The butter frequently browned to burning. She dusted the furniture before she had swept the floor. The Bensusan house had always been staffed with servants. Sterbee found the work time-consuming and frustrating.

Julie began to lose patience. When the costly meat burned, or clothing was still scattered about at noontime, she became upset.

"Lucien could not have married a worse housewife," she complained to Camille.

"Give her time," he responded.

Sterbee burst into tears. On a morning when Lucien had to catch the earliest train into Paris she was abruptly wakened at five in the morning by Julie banging on her door.

"Sterbee, get up. You have to walk Lucien to the station."

Sterbee made her way home disconsolate. What kind of day would she have all alone with her mother-in-law? Julie was at the stove in the kitchen. She picked up one of Lucien's shirts and tossed it on the table.

"It needs mending."

"I'm sorry, Maman. I never learned to mend."

Julie relented. "I'll show you."

When Lucien returned Camille took the two young people for a walk along the willow-lined bank of the Epte in the flaming red-purple sunset.

"Papa," Sterbee said, "I want to go home to England, find a house where Lucien and I can live alone."

"*D'accord.* I'll help you."

Julie asked, when Camille told her of the decision:

"How will Lucien survive? What sort of helpmate will she be for him when she cannot cook or take care of the house? How is she going to help him support their family?"

Camille threw his arms roughly about his wife's shoulders.

"Husbands in love get used to unmended shirts and to their wives' cooking. No man ever sought a divorce because his wife was no good in the kitchen."

At the beginning of September Octave Mirbeau invited Camille to spend a few days with him at his home, Les Damps, by the Pont de L'Arche, to catch his plantings before the dying moment of their flowering. Camille settled into a guest bedroom, then went into the color-riotous garden and began four landscapes which seemed to him superb in motif and effect. He worked steadily for two weeks, not quite having finished three of the canvases when a strong wind came up. Before he left Les Damps, Mirbeau confided that he was discouraged about his writing. Camille, old hand at bolstering one's courage, told him:

"You are discouraged at not being at the top of your work as a writer, but no matter how talented an artist is, he is never at the height he dreams of. So go to it! It's while you are desperate that you accomplish your best work." He also believed that hope was self-fulfilling, that it was the curse and salvation of the idealist.

Soon after his return Camille went to Père Tanguy's to replenish his supplies. The outside cobalt blue of the little shop had faded under Paris's lashing winter rains and burning summer suns, but inside the walls were alight with the paintings of Cézanne: apples on a table, the mountains of L'Estaque, with its stone villages and orange-tiled roofs climbing up deeply etched hillsides; Van Gogh's lashing canvases of Arles and St. Rémy. Tanguy, the aged battler for lost causes, lay thin and green-skinned in the family bed behind the beaded curtain with his equally aging but vigorous wife at the stove only a few feet away. She considered all artists to be defaulters whose debts to her husband had mired her in a life of penury. However Camille had paid up the former spring, after the Durand-Ruel show, and so she offered him a bowl of soup.

Camille drew up a cane-bottomed chair to Tanguy's bedside. Madame Tanguy muttered behind them, "The ambition of his life is to die in debt."

Tanguy lifted one hand from under the cover. Camille took it fondly. The bones were brittle in his grasp. He leaned close to Tanguy's ear, said softly:

"You provided us with pigments when we otherwise would not have been able to work. Part of our paintings are your creation."

Tanguy's illness-dulled eyes came alive. A beatific smile spread over his homely shrunken features.

"Ah! If I could believe that I would die happy."

Claude Monet and Alice Hoschedé had been married while Camille was in England, the marriage coming after twelve years of liaison. Monet had begun building greenhouses on his Giverny property and continued expanding his gardens, hiring six gardeners to keep him in the flower beds he wanted to paint. Camille visited him to say "Thank you" for his response to Julie's plea and to congratulate them.

He also called on Degas, whose cluttered fresh-paint and varnish-fragrant studio he had not seen for some time. Degas, who had told Camille early on that he would have the *gendarmerie* shoot painters doing landscapes from nature, had done a *bouleversement* and had painted outdoor scenes that conquered the critics, even those who were antagonistic to other Impressionists. Gazing at Degas's oil on the studio easel, a landscape with chimneys, Camille said wistfully:

"If they understand you, they ought to understand me."

Camille had heard a long while ago that Degas and Mary Cassatt had parted company, the rumored cause being that Degas had said something unkind about her work to a friend whom Cassatt had sent to his studio. While Camille gazed admiringly up at two Cassatt prints on the wall, Degas said sotto voce:

"My tongue bites deeper than my acid bath. But we're friends again. I found my life a soupçon flat without her. I was born without the gift of apology; it's like being born without a backside. But I managed. Mademoiselle Cassatt is the most independent woman I've ever known. And the most talented."

Camille started to put a hand approvingly on Degas's shoulder, stopped halfway. No one touched Degas's person. Instead he murmured his felicitations.

He had written to Durand-Ruel asking if he would take on his new work from London and Mirbeau's garden. When he received no reply he went into Paris to confront the dealer. Durand-Ruel had his desk piled high with correspondence, contracts, price lists. When Camille asked about his silence, he replied:

"I haven't answered you because I thought you were going to send me the pictures one of these days. As to the price, I have only one observation to make: I accept them on the condition that you don't give any to anyone else and that you don't sell them by chance to someone who doesn't want to pass through the intermediary of a frightful dealer like myself. That is the only way for me to sell your paintings conveniently. Otherwise they will start a price war against me, claiming that I am a man who sells everything for high prices."

Durand-Ruel leaned back in his chair, decided that that created too far a distance for intimate communication, came to the side of Camille, sitting rigidly on a hard-backed chair. A feeling for the dealer's dilemma seeped through Camille . . . along with the heaviness of knowing he had to support seven children. There was always this problem between a businessman, trying to stay solvent and earn a respectable profit, and the artist, who wanted only to sell his work for enough to live on.

"What I ask of you is very simple and very fair," continued Durand-Ruel. "I am prepared to take all of your pictures and that will not be costly for you as you fear. It is the only way of not having any competition and it is this competition that has prevented me for so long from supporting your prices."

Camille felt the beginning of a warm glow.

"Will that monopoly, a word that frightens me, include another big exhibition?"

"Yes. Next year. It is with this system that I managed five or six years ago to sell the Monets. It is because I have all of Renoir's pictures that I finally put him into a class worthy of him. Now that I am in a situation where I can vigorously lead my campaign without the fear of being stopped by lack of money, I must have your promise not to sell to other dealers, even at a higher price. Send me the pictures that I had counted on receiving. I told you that I would accept your prices. You know that I am very devoted."

Camille was convinced. He took a deep breath.

"Could you come out to Eragny? The Mirbeau gardens are a great success. I believe the London canvases will appeal to you even more than the four you bought when I was first in England."

The following Sunday Durand-Ruel arrived in the striped trousers and formal black coat he wore to church. He had a pleasant *café-au-lait* conversation with Julie while Camille arranged his paintings. The dealer liked everything Camille showed him.

"These twelve are worthy of presentation to the Yankees."

The next day Camille cleaned the paintings and drew up his price list. The prices ranged from one hundred twenty dollars to five hundred. The total came to something over three thousand dollars. If they sold, it would take care of the family for a considerable time and enable him to make a payment on the house.

There came a week of anxiety waiting for Durand-Ruel's approval of the figures. Toward the end of December the dealer accepted the paintings at Camille's estimates. When he went into Paris to conclude the arrangement for a comprehensive exhibition he encountered the gallery handyman, Prosper Garny, near the front entrance. Garny, who had heard most of Durand-Ruel's opinions of work at hand, congratulated him.

"You surpassed yourself. The new oils are splendid."

The wildly unexpected can be traced back to early design. Esther Isaacson had been Camille's favorite niece. She had come as often as possible to France to visit with Rachel and with Camille and Julie wherever they lived, approving of Julie and befriending her, as had her mother. She had tried to place his watercolors in a London gallery. When Georges went to London, Camille had written to her to take care of him.

Twenty-one-year-old Georges fell in love with the thirty-five-year-old motherly Esther Isaacson of the smooth skin and warm smile. Esther, fettered by Phineas Isaacson, had never been in love. She came close to Georges of the rich curly black hair waving down to his shoulders, the youthful mustache and beard; succumbed to his passionate adoration and need for her.

They were secretly married in December 1892. The fourteen-year difference in their ages was less of an obstacle than the fact that Georges had no trade, no job, no resources; that he had never accepted discipline from anyone, although his father considered that he had a growing talent.

Julie was devastated by what she called the "unsuitable union." She was inconsolable. How could they carry on their backs still another hapless couple? Phineas Isaacson was distressed by the fact that Georges and Esther were first cousins, that he did not want to lose his housekeeper, and even less to bring into the house another man after he had driven out his own two sons. He disowned his daughter. Alice, Esther's older unmarried sister, ceased speaking to her. Camille knew only one response: he had Durand-Ruel send the couple two hundred dollars to carry them over. When Mirbeau came to visit, Camille confided:

"Sometimes cycles can be tied too tightly together at the knot end. . . . Being unable to remedy an accomplished fact, I wish them happiness. My niece's only defect is in being a little disproportionate in age with her young, very young, husband. She is intelligent and devoted but we cannot help thinking of the future with fear, given the impressionable character of this boy."

He wrote to Esther, his eyes sunk deep in their sockets, that he respected their feelings because they were in the order of nature, and prayed that they would not regret the marriage.

A cup of grace appeared at Christmas, the news that Lucien had sold a picture for fifty dollars; and that Joyant was persuading Boussod & Valadon to publish the portfolio, *Work in the Field*, the informal sketches that Camille and Lucien had drawn over the years while traversing the countryside. However Julie, visiting her sister Josephine in Paris, had found her body sprawled across the bed, dead. She and Josephine had not been close, yet she suffered the special kind of grief peculiar to a family loss.

By the New Year of 1893 Georges and Esther were in Eragny to live. Georges did not look for a job but helped his father move about the countryside as far as Poissy to find stimulating motifs. The younger children thought all these marriages were great fun.

Durand-Ruel scheduled Camille's show for March 15. Julie proclaimed:

"It had better do well now that we've got four marrieds as well as four youngsters to support."

3

The entire family concentrated on setting up the exhibition. Camille was showing forty-two paintings including five of the figure, the twelve London and Mirbeau gardens, four from his studio window and ten of the countryside in the colors of the passing seasons. Durand-Ruel commented:

"I like them all, except for the hand of the *Woman in Yellow Shawl;* the sky of *Hoar Frost* is too obviously flaked."

Camille growled, "We shall see when they are framed."

The showing was well received. A number sold, after which Durand-Ruel bought thirteen of his remaining favorites and promised Camille a larger show in 1894. On April 1 there was a payment of twelve hundred dollars due. Camille was ill in bed in the Hôtel Garnier with influenza and a bad eye. Dr. Parenteau was giving him injections in the hope of avoiding another abscess. He also advised him to wear his glasses at all times. When the influenza passed, Camille painted from his window the Rue and Place St. Lazare. He found himself made surprisingly nostalgic by the scenes which had impressed him so enormously when he arrived in 1855 and had sketched from early morning to late at night. He was excited to be painting cityscapes and decided he would spend more time in Paris putting on canvas its boulevards and squares thronged with people, horse-drawn omnibuses and carriages, all enveloped in the handsome four-story buildings of distinguished architecture. During the evenings, after a light supper at the hotel's café, he read among the newly published books.

He returned home to learn that both Sterbee and Esther

were pregnant. Georges took Esther back to England, commenting:

"I never thought to let my wife be under Maman's petticoats."

Lucien and Sterbee had found a cottage in Hennell Street, Epping, surrounded by oaks and weeping willows, where Lucien fitted out a large room with deep windows as his studio. Georges and Esther moved in with them. Camille sent Esther and Sterbee forty dollars each month to support them. Georges's only complaint was that Epping was not beautiful. Camille wrote back angrily:

"Happy are those who see beauty in the modest spots where others see nothing. Everything is beautiful, the whole secret lies in knowing how to interpret."

Camille's prices got an unexpected boost in May when, at public auction, Durand-Ruel bought for an Amerian client the 1870–71 painting *The Road from St. Germain to Louveciennes* for eight hundred dollars; this despite the free silver crisis in the United States.

The July heat came on. Dr. Parenteau again operated on the eye with success. Camille began work on several compositions of peasant girls bathing, as he described it, ". . . under a shade of willows; this tropical heat suggests motifs of shaded spots on riverbanks. It seems to me that I have a sense of great poetry in this. What hampers me is the impossibility of getting a model, otherwise I could do things which would be new and rare."

A hot summer peace descended on the Apple Orchard.

Paris was shuttered for the month of August, but he sold a large painting privately, holding to Durand-Ruel's price with the dealer's permission. He then informed an architect, a Monsieur Besnard, son of a woman picture dealer, that he was ready to proceed with the remodeling of his barn. It had been built in 1839 when Camille was a nine-year-old schoolboy in St. Thomas.

Besnard came out to design the studio. He estimated the remodeling would cost about four hundred dollars. Two laborers were brought in to clean out the ten years' debris. Besnard sent out a drawing for the carpenter showing a high ceiling on the second floor, a large window on the west side, a bay window three meters wide to the north which would give good light. Camille would have preferred something more rustic but he liked the outside stairway and porch, which he planned to cover with vines. The ground floor was to be kept for storage. To the brick wall at the rear of the studio he added matting on which he could hang his paintings and thumbtack his dozens of pencil and charcoal drawings as had Corot in the first Paris studio he had ever visited. The west window had french doors which opened to the orchard. He would be able to work at his easel in the fresh and fragrant air.

Julie wrote to Lucien:

"Cocotte has a dislocation of the hip which makes her look like a hunchback I went to the dentist who fixed her teeth and Mr. de Bellio who gave me a prescription I hope that will help I really have no luck I have so little time to myself I don't have a minute to write Cocotte and Paul and the maid are out getting some butter I sent you a basket of pears friday duchesses and some butter and almonds I am very angry that master Georges left like an imbecile without thinking about what he knows about useless expenses and how he will get along if it were possible to put a plan into his head oh well too bad for them your father gave them a thousand francs in leaving would you believe it they already have nothing left and how will they get along it was supposed to last for five months and they spent everything in one month oh well too bad for you all do what you can and leave me in peace"

Esther Isaacson Pissarro gave birth to a healthy boy in her father's house at 7 Colville Square, Bayswater, at the end of August; then died two days later. Georges was inconsolable. Camille and Julie were in a state of shock. Félix left for London to join his two brothers. By the time they had received word, Esther had already been buried. Like her mother, Emma, she had died young. Camille wept. Julie said, "I will raise the little one."

"You raised seven of your own. You have more than enough to do," Camille admonished. "We'll ask Esther's sister Alice to take him. We can offer her the same forty dollars we pay the two boys."

It was done. Tommy Pissarro, as he was named, would be brought up by his Aunt Alice.

By mid-September the interior of Camille's studio was completed. He was a little frightened by its size, comfort and the aspect of its being a permanent shop of a recognized artist.

"Once I painted no matter where, in all seasons, in the worst heat, in the most frightful cold. I managed to work with enthusiasm. Will I be able to work in these new surroundings? Will my art put on gloves?"

Sterbee gave birth to a daughter whom they named Orovida.

Mother and child were well, a great relief. Jacob Bensusan accepted his daughter's marriage and would help with their support.

In the autumn, when the sensations necessary to art revive, there was wind and rain. Between setting down images, Camille kept up a barrage of instructions to his three sons in England, taking the place of those academies he had attended: Picot, Dagnan, Lehmann, the Académie Suisse. He wrote: "Let us speak of art, my boys. I look at your engravings from time to time and the more I scan them the more I become convinced that you are real chaps! I expect Félix to do something big and well studied, *based on nature*. One feels great progress in the observation of nature in Georges's engraving. Lucien's has great purity. . . ."

Nineteen-year-old Félix turned out to be a rake, promising young girls marriage in order to gain their favor. Camille extricated him from several scrapes, including one with Julie's niece. His next move was to announce his intention of marrying the daughter of a respected musician. Camille admonished:

"You blow false notes on a hunting horn and bicycle through the country hardly advancing your knowledge of values and colors."

He had Durand-Ruel send three hundred dollars to Georges, Alice and the baby Tommy. He also came down with a toothache. An artist can draw after suffering a broken leg but not with an ulcerated molar. He went into Paris to have three teeth extracted by a dentist who was happy to take his fee in drawings. He again stayed at the Hôtel Garnier. When the ache of the missing teeth abated, he sketched out five large canvases from the window of the hotel room. He would need the paintings for his forthcoming show. When he returned to Eragny, Paul Durand-Ruel's son Joseph, being trained to take over the galleries, came to see him, went through the most recent paintings and indicated which canvases he wanted for the 1894 exhibit, many of which he would buy outright.

When Joseph left, Camille ran into the house, grabbed Julie in his arms and danced her around the rooms. There was a suspicion of tears in both their eyes.

"You were right, dear Julie. Permanence has brought prosperity. The loan on the Apple Orchard, which I conceived to be a crushing burden, will be paid off in a mere year and a half. We'll have left only the money owed to Claude Monet."

"Incroyable!" Julie whispered, her heart thumping against his chest. "We've taken the moon with our teeth."

Death continued to spread its wings. Their friend and doctor, Georges de Bellio, died suddenly, and seemingly without cause, at the end of January 1894. Père Tanguy also succumbed. At the beginning of December, Gustave Caillebotte, after suffering several minor strokes, had had a "cerebral congestion." His longtime mistress advised Camille not to visit. The greathearted Caillebotte was released from his bondage without having communicated with anyone. The art world of Paris sat *shivah*, as Rachel had called the period of mourning for the dead; for Dr. de Bellio had treated the colony with affection but without charge; Père Tanguy had given them supplies when their credit, as his wife had caustically commented, *"n'existe pas!"*; Gustave Caillebotte had bought their pictures at good prices, had been an indefatigable force behind the staging of their Impressionist exhibitions; and had become a very fine artist himself. He left to the state his eighteen Pissarros, sixteen Monets, eight Renoirs, seven Degases, three Manets, two Millets, nine Sisleys and four Cézannes.

"There's bound to be a struggle to get the Beaux-Arts to accept them," Camille commented. "Can Caillebotte make us official?"

Camille had a sixty-fourth birthday. The three deaths spurred him to work harder, get his new exhibition hung, a process which took eight days. It would have a great many of his works in all the media, the largest show to date. When he had finished, he concluded:

"The wine is poured, it remains only to be drunk."

He himself would not be there to drink it. He took to his bed in the Hôtel Garnier with another case of influenza. He could not get up for the opening. As he lay glumly, half asleep, there was a sharp knock on the door. Paul Durand-Ruel entered the room, the black morning coat and white ascot a refreshing sight. There was a broad smile on his face.

"Again the mountain has come to Mohammed," he pronounced. "We sold a number of the watercolors and pastels. I have serious commitments for several of the oils. I brought you a check. Monet and Degas attended. They thought highly of your *Potato Harvest in the Setting Sun;* Gustave Geffroy is writing an article of praise, and his introduction to the catalogue was reprinted in *Le Matin.*" Geffroy had already devoted a goodly number of pages to Camille's work in his *History of Impressionism.*

In quick succession there were interesting articles in such

reputable journals as *L'Evénement*, *Le Mercure de France*, *L'Estafette* and *L'Art Français*.

Camille's cure was miraculous. He returned to Eragny immediately. Good news could be read as clearly with one eye as with two!

Toward the end of June an anarchist had assassinated President of the Republic Carnot while he was on a visit to Lyon. Three months before, the radical Auguste Vaillant had thrown a bomb into the Chamber of Deputies and been executed. By way of answer a bomb was hurled into the Café Terminus at the Gare St. Lazare. Emile Henry's arrest resulted in three more bombs being exploded in public places. Known anarchists and their sympathizers were thrown into prison. Some thirty associates of the more radical journals, called the "Thirty," were arraigned to go on trial, including the critic Fénéon and the painter Maximilien Luce. Octave Mirbeau and Pouget, editor of *Le Père Peinard*, fled the country.

So did Camille, frightened because the police had the names of all subscribers to *La Révolte* and *Le Père Peinard*. Julie left Ludovic Rodolphe, Cocotte and Paul Emile with Félicie, as well as funds to care for them. Camille told Durand-Ruel, "I'm afraid I shall be forced to stay abroad for some time. Even a concierge is allowed to open your letters, a mere denunciation can land you in prison and you are powerless to defend yourself."

He packed his easel box, two valises and took Julie to the Gare du Nord for the train to Brussels.

They were welcomed by associates from Les Vingt. Julie remained ten days, then returned to Paris. Camille left for the picturesque Dutch port of Knocke-sur-Mer, where he went on a binge painting the houses, mills, church, dunes, corners of the village. Durand-Ruel was paying him one hundred and thirty-five dollars a month but he was sending Lucien sixty, Alice and Tommy sixty, Georges and Felix forty each, a total of two hundred dollars: and he still had three younger children at home. When the emotional crisis in Paris subsided, he returned, confident that he had done a good painterly job; but Durand-Ruel ran a skeptical eye over the canvases. His voice was sharp.

"I must say that it is not what I expected from you. The motifs don't do justice to the beautiful Dutch countryside with its very particular character. One might think they were painted in France." He changed the subject. "Business has not started again. But Monday we will send one hundred dollars to you and one hundred dollars to each of your sons in London.''

In late September the terror over the anarchists had shifted to a strong wave of anti-Semitism. The connection was unclear, since France had the lowest population of Jews of any European country, two tenths of one per cent; while the bomb throwers and the murderer of President Carnot had been born into the established Church. Camille was known to his artist friends, dealers, collectors, as a Jew. He had had examples of the deep-seated prejudice in Degas and Renoir. Yet it was not in his nature to assume that attacks by critics, the failure of dealers to sell him, or indifference of the public to buying had anything to do with his religion. Only once had that thought entered his mind; he had dismissed it as unworthy.

He had also paid little attention to the accelerating abuse poured out by such writers as Edouard Drumont in his *Jewish France*, Toussenel's *Judaism and the Conversion of the Christian Peoples*. Though he began to be distressed, he nevertheless enjoyed his completed studio where he worked well by the bay window, going out in clement weather to paint the poplars, the peasants completing their harvest, bathers in the streams, another washing her feet in the river: the young women deeply felt, beautiful in their honest plainness.

Then came the worst scandal in French military history. It was discovered that an officer of the General Staff of the War Ministry had been passing secret intelligence and defense plans to the German Embassy in Paris. The November 1, 1894, issue of the anti-Semitic newspaper *La Libre Parole* named Captain Alfred Dreyfus, a Jew whose wealthy family had originated in Alsace-Lorraine. Dreyfus was a brilliant staff officer who had graduated third in his class at the War College and become the first Jew to be appointed to the prestigious General Staff. During this period he had served in the Bureau of Intelligence. He was now accused of accepting money in exchange for the French military secrets. If the charges were substantiated, anti-Semitism could sweep through France as violently as any pogrom in Russia or Poland and become a problem for every Jew in the country. The Jews had been blamed for the Panama Canal Company bankruptcy, also for the collapse of the Union Générale. There had always to be a scapegoat.

But a traitor! By the end of November *Le Figaro* published an article about Captain Dreyfus; the charges were official. There appeared to be no motivation for the treason. He had ample family wealth, did not gamble, was happily married and without a mistress, was quiet and reticent and was not known to spend lavishly. Some said it was because he had been born in Alsace-Lorraine when it was German territory; that his primary allegiance was to Germany, which he wanted to see dominant in Europe. Paris was as much scandalized as horrified; no one could talk of anything else.

At the Café Riche there were few journalists at the big round table. They spoke in swift sentences. Camille learned that the only prior charge against Dreyfus—for he had received favorable reports during his six months of training in the four departments of the General Staff—was that he was not deferential to his superiors and was therefore not popular. A dubious-looking document accompanying a set of secret papers detailing French mobilization plans, the hydraulic brake of a new gun, and troop movements, had been intercepted by the military. It was information that could be available only to the General Staff and its trainees. Dreyfus was summoned to the War Office and asked to write, as dictated, a copy of the message to the German Embassy which had been intercepted by French Intelligence. The handwriting, despite the denials of official handwriting experts, was declared to be the same. Captain Dreyfus was arrested and put in prison awaiting court-martial. Treason was an offense that could earn the death sentence. There appeared little doubt that the War Department and the majority of the journalists believed him guilty.

Camille left the café trembling. He did not know whether Captain Dreyfus was innocent or guilty. That he had been born in German Alsace-Lorraine seemed insufficient proof. But, guilty or innocent, there would be riots, bloodshed. He worried for the tiny number of Jews in France, for his own family. He read the newspapers searching for news that seeped out of the sealed tribunal. Already in Eragny people on the streets and in the markets of Gisors, peasants in the fields, turned away from him with ill-concealed distaste.

On December 22, Captain Alfred Dreyfus was condemned by a unanimous vote of the officers' court for selling military secrets to the Germans. He was to be degraded, shipped to solitary confinement on Devil's Island for the rest of his life. The military tried to keep the degradation ceremony, which was to be held in the courtyard of the Ecole Militaire, secret; but since a group of officials had been invited, as well as chosen journalists, it became known that Dreyfus's galloons were torn from his *képi*, the trefoils from his sleeves, the numbers from his collar, the buttons from his tunic, and the stripes from his trousers; his sword was broken, its scabbard thrown to the ground. He was then ordered to march before the soldiers who had formerly been under his command. Outside the walls of the Ecole the crowds shouted, "Death to the Jews."

Mobs ran through the streets for weeks pursuing known Jews and stoning their shops. Only a small segment of Parisians doubted the verdict.

For the first time Camille realized the extent of his Hebraic origins. It had taken just such a cataclysmic happening to awaken in him a realization of his heritage: everything that went on in his brain, his spirit, his values, even his perceptions. He knew the deep-seated continuity of his people, the segregation in the public mind. He reached beyond the religion with its rituals and customs to the richness and purpose Jacob Bensusan had put forth, even to the extent of forgiving the elders of the synagogue in St. Thomas who, through seven years and four sons, had refused his parents a marriage in the temple. And to acknowledge his own indebtedness of background, spirit, mind, in the Old Testament sense of the word "soul."

4

The scythe and the cycle, the rich years and the lean. This was now, at sixty-four, the pattern of his life. His son Lucien published his first book, an album called *Queen of the Fishes,* for which he did the illustrations, text and printing. Camille paid the costs.

A Dutch painter friend, who had been his host at Knocke-sur-Mer, came with his wife to Eragny. When he saw Camille's nudes he exclaimed:

"They are completely outside the formula of the schools. They have an outdoor and real peasant quality."

It was not generally commented upon that more than a quarter of Camille's etchings and lithographs were nudes. He had located a model who would pose without rousing Julie's objection. However he frequently complained of the lack of a model. Durand-Ruel did not appear interested in the etchings or lithographs. It was rewarding to have his Dutch painter comment on them now.

At the request of established dealers in Dresden and Munich Camille sent them five good-sized oil paintings. He never heard from the dealers again, except to be presented with a bill for four hundred dollars for framing; and counted himself lucky to get his canvases back.

It was only the first months of 1895, but already he had several canvases on easels. Yet the Impressionists, with the exception of Monet and Degas, seemed to be losing ground; there was a disturbing attitude of indifference. The critics and press were unconcerned; his only notice came in four pages of a book called *The Decorated, Those Who Are Not*. He had been looking forward to the opening of Caillebotte's collection at perhaps the Luxembourg, and official recognition for the Impressionists. When the state rejected the gift Caillebotte had willed to them it was a sharp blow to their pride.

Camille learned of the sudden death of Berthe Morisot from influenza at the age of fifty-four. Before going to the funeral he set down his thoughts, calling her "a distinguished woman who had such a splendid feminine talent and who brought honor to our Impressionist group. Poor Berthe Morisot, the public hardly knows her."

He returned to his studio, to a canvas on which he had been working for a year and a half, a great figure of a peasant girl crossing a brook. She filled almost the whole fifteen-by-eighteen-inch canvas. There was a luminous sky, the trees were green-blue, the execution was uneven but there was nevertheless a great unity. The picture had rather perplexed him for a long time but now he liked it. He was afraid it was terrifying but believed that time would make it a little more amiable. He also completed his *Washerwoman*, a subject Degas had made respectable by his splendid life-filled studies of big women tossing their breasts.

By a steadfast outpouring of energy he also completed thirteen canvases in early April and took them into the Rue Le Peletier. Durand-Ruel wavered, saying to Camille, surrounded by the glowing paintings he had set up around the base of the wall, "I have a million francs of your group's paintings on hand and the interest rate is high. I don't know whether it's wise to buy more of your works or attempt another exhibition."

Camille felt his breath plunge downward in his chest.

Three days later Durand-Ruel summoned him from his hotel room hell of anxiety to make him an offer. He would pay two thousand dollars for the thirteen canvases as a flat and final payment for the works. Camille cried out in anguish:

"Those terms are not wonderful. It's a great sacrifice. In fact, disastrous; bringing my prices a little over one hundred fifty dollars each. I'm going backward."

"So are the times. It's as Renoir says, we have to float like a cork on circumstances we can't control."

"I'll take the money. I'm forced to."

Claude Monet, who was spending his money faster than it came in building lily ponds, canals, a Japanese bridge, asked Camille to please pay off the balance of his debt. Camille sent the six hundred dollars still due.

In May he had gone to see a show of Monet's *Cathedrals,* a series from Rouen, and was carried away by their extraordinary deftness. To his surprise, Paul Cézanne walked into the Durand-Ruel gallery. Cézanne, now fifty-six, was as bald as marble; he had trimmed off the wild sidelocks, was wearing a tailored salt-and-pepper goatee. The pugnacious scowl was gone from his lips and eyes. He greeted Camille, spoke of their companionable times in Pontoise. Cézanne had not shown in Paris for years; but Camille had found him a dealer willing to exhibit his Aix-en-Provence canvases: Ambroise Vollard. He appeared to Camille to have no native taste but had the intelligence to listen to those who did, and was very enthusiastic. Ambroise Vollard lived in the basement under his shop at 39 Rue Laffitte, amidst his more established competitors. Yet here he entertained at gourmet Creole dinners; tall, thin, swarthy, with a narrow oval face and small eyes. He came from the West Indies, as Camille had; no one knew where his money came from but, as Renoir commented:

"With paintings the young man is as stealthy as a hunting dog on the scent of game. He also looks like Othello."

Vollard had known nothing about the Impressionists until Camille took him out to Eragny to show him his Cézanne paintings, urging Vollard to give Cézanne a retrospective. To everyone's amazement Cézanne jumped at the opportunity, sending Vollard a hundred and fifty canvases. The critics, having seen nothing of Cézanne's work, gave him a thorough whipping in print; but Camille had the last word:

"My enthusiasm was nothing compared to Renoir's. Degas is seduced by the charm of this refined savage. The only ones who are not subject to the charm of Cézanne are precisely those artists and collectors who have shown by their errors that their sensibilities are defective."

Vollard bought Cézannes, Guillaumins, a Van Gogh, ordered a "snow effect" from Camille and a watercolor, purchased three of his older sketches. Camille had brought another dealer into the marketplace.

The family assembled for the summer of 1895; only Alice and little Tommy were missing: Orovida, almost two, was the youngest, Julie fed them all with incredible frequency. Camille made a pen and crayon drawing called *The Family of the Artist*, deep in remembering his original plan for the children. Paul Emile and Cocotte were painting at easels, Lucien was instructing them. Georges was working at an etching table. Félix and Ludovic had portfolios of drawings under their arms. Camille had realized his ambition, harebrained as it might have seemed: all five of his sons were artists . . . of same sort and to a degree. Julie, who had been pictured sewing, the occupation of what she amusedly called her "leisure time," glanced at the finished sketch, asked:

"Do you truly believe that your sons are artists?"

Camille, in all honesty, had to ponder that decision as though with weights on a butcher's scale.

"Painters, no. Printmakers and woodcarvers, perhaps. But mostly they can go into the industrial arts, everything used in daily life which can be made attractive as well as utilitarian."

"Is there a living in that?"

Lucien, Sterbee and Orovida returned to England in September. Because of Julie's ardent desire to train Cocotte to be an accomplished housewife, Camille's bright fourteen-year-old daughter was getting little educational training. He felt obliged to enter her in the Ste. Catherine's boarding school in Paris. There was no religious teaching, and a number of English girls were registered. Cocotte would learn the language. When in Paris he took her on excursions to the Louvre, the Luxembourg, the historic ruins, to the privately owned galleries, and to the zoo where he called her attention to animals whose skin patterns would make beautiful tapestries. When the school was giving a party Camille showed up in time with a pretty pair of evening slippers and white gloves for her.

Degas and Monet bought some marvelous Cézannes at Vollard's exhibition. Camille traded a sketch of Louveciennes for a small picture of Cézanne's bathers and a self-portrait.

He finished five more canvases. He had sold nothing for months. On his next trip into Paris he approached Portier, as he had in the past. Portier sold his *Bather* for a price far beyond what Durand-Ruel paid him, three hundred eighty dollars. He owed the buyer, a framer by the name of Hayashi, a considerable portion of that sum for earlier framing. The balance was for Julie. Only Ludovic and eleven-year-old Paul Emile were still at home.

"Can you see us two old people alone in this great house all winter?" he asked Julie.

Soon after the turn of the year Durand-Ruel told him that he was considering an exhibition in April. He packed his supplies and went again to Rouen, where he took a room at the modest Hôtel de Paris on the quai overlooking the harbor. He paid one dollar a day. He walked through the fort and the streets of the Old Town, then set up his easel in front of his window, for he had to protect his eye from the outside cold and wind. By the first week in February he had eight paintings in varying states of completion standing against the walls waiting for the necessary light, sun or rain to be completed.

He sketched the streets of the town but mostly he painted the port, the bridges across the Seine, the busy harbor in constantly changing weather. In the painting, one of the piers of the new Boieldieu Bridge was out of alignment; when the canvas was sold the owner asked Camille to correct it. He painted the entire day: fog and mist, rain, the setting sun; a bridge near the Place de la Bourse had a stream of people crossing; cranes were at work loading and unloading the boats, some with active smokestacks. There were dockers below him working the cargo "in gray colors glistening in the rain and gray weather." What fascinated him most, he who had been a country painter, was the stir and energy he saw: the throng of hackneys, sailors, townspeople. The sense of movement gave him "fits of hope" that he had time to become a town and people-in-action painter. He found an uncommon motif from his window facing north, the whole of old Rouen seen from above the roofs, with the cathedral, St. Ouen's Church, and amazing turrets. "Extraordinary!" he exclaimed.

After some weeks Julie made a surprise visit to check on his well-being. Her first reaction on seeing his oils in process was to exclaim, "How beautiful they are!"

She worried about the cold and fog. That his eye was beginning to water. Camille was touched by her solicitude. He kissed her, told her that he would need another month to complete the pictures if Durand-Ruel was to give him the show in mid-April. She was not to worry, the heat generated by working on twelve canvases at once jumping to each as the light or rain proved exactly right, kept him warm.

He met a man named Félix François Dépeaux, a wealthy landowner and former host to Monet and Sisley in Rouen.

Dépeaux fell in love with the just completed *Roofs of Old Rouen*, proposed buying it for himself and another for his brother-in-law. Camille envisaged moving to a hotel with a fireplace. But Dépeaux never showed at their appointment.

He completed his canvases and returned home.

5

The previous July there had been a revelation that further shook Paris. Colonel Sandherr, a dedicated prosecutor of Dreyfus, was replaced as head of French Intelligence by a Lieutenant Colonel Picquart who found that military secrets were still being turned over to the German Embassy.

"Everything considered," Camille had said to his family, "Dreyfus may be innocent."

Lieutenant Colonel Georges Picquart now discovered a letter written by Schwartzkoppen, the German military attaché, addressed to a French army officer, Esterhazy. Picquart began to investigate Major Esterhazy, discovered his reputation for womanizing and extensive gambling. He also realized that Esterhazy's handwriting matched that of the incriminaing letter said to have been written by Dreyfus. For the first time Picquart saw a connection. He reported his suspicions to his superiors and was told not to proceed too hastily, not to associate the Dreyfus case with Esterhazy. Curiously, the rumor of evidence that Dreyfus had been wronged caused a new wave of anti-Semitism. Emile Zola, who had insulted Cézanne by calling him an abortive genius, and had decried his own early promoting of the Impressionists, reinstated himself with Camille by publishing the first cannonade against this reaction in *Le Figaro:*

> It is several years by now that I have been observing with increasing wonder and disgust the campaign against the Jews in France. To me it seems something monstrous, going beyond the bounds of common sense, truth and justice, something which will inevitably thrust us back several centuries or bring us to the worst, the ultimate of all horrors: religious persecution.

Camille's exhibition opened on April 15, 1896. He showed thirty-five paintings, his dozen Rouen canvases, including that of the roofs of old Rouen which he preferred to keep for himself, exclaiming, "I don't understand how I was able to get this completely gray picture to hold together." He displayed some scenes of Holland and Eragny. His friends called the exhibition a delight. Degas came to the opening to tell him that he and the other Impressionists still had the upper hand in French art. *Le Temps* wrote about his surprising new fascination with cities and the bringing to life of large groups of people, saying, "In his views of the Seine at Rouen there are bridges full of wagons, buses, and pedestrians, all pell-mell. He infallibly catches the right sense of movement."

The new canvases were also lauded by *Le Figaro*, *Le Journal des Artistes* and other well-read publications. Durand-Ruel was confident he could sell them, given time. Camille replied:

"I much prefer to sell you the pictures than wait on the caprice of collectors."

The dealer did sums in his head.

"I can give you twenty-eight hundred dollars for the eleven Rouen paintings. Will that do?"

Camille squared his shoulders.

"Yes, on condition that you take another series at the beginning of winter."

"D'accord."

Julie decided she wanted to visit Lucien, Sterbee and Orovida in London, taking Ludovic Rodolphe and Paul Emile with her. Lucien made arrangements for her to take the train to London Bridge, where he would meet her. He and Sterbee spent more than they could afford to brighten up the house in Epping as a welcoming gesture. Julie was displeased at the extravagance. Orovida had been ill with weak legs and Sterbee was taking a course as a masseuse, which cost Camille another sixty dollars. Lucien was angry with his mother for complaining. Julie's only joy was Kew Gardens. Alone with the hothouses, the splendid flowers, and shrubs she loved so deeply, she was at peace.

The bright light of Camille's summer was his successful showing at Vollard's gallery of ten prints off his ramshackle press. Another small gallery, Arnold de Dresden, sold several prints and two small oils. For stimulation he returned to Rouen. He took a more comfortable room at the Hôtel d'Angleterre on the Cours Boieldieu, with a fireplace and front windows overlooking the new iron bridge, the section of

St. Sauveur, the Gare d'Orléans, also new and shining; and a mass of chimneys from the gigantic to the diminutive with all their smoke. In the morning the light was misty and delicate. In a burst of energy he began working on ten pictures at once in which he tried to catch the life and vitality, the atmosphere of the harbor thronged with smoking ships, bridges, sections of the city in the fog and mist that he had not painted before, under the setting sun. His colors were bolder than earlier in the year, his boats with rose-colored, golden-yellow and black masts. He painted what he saw and felt.

Nine watercolors which Durand-Ruel had ordered were turned down by the dealer.

"Are you rejecting them because they're badly executed?" he asked.

"*Mon Dieu, non!* The clients who wanted them have disappeared."

He discovered that his feeling for painting the city had not been assuaged in Rouen. He longed to be in Paris to work all day amid that city's tumult, to paint the rain and snow, the biting cold on the Rue St. Lazare and Rue d'Amsterdam, the Hôtel Drouot where so many of the Impressionist paintings had been auctioned; the rounded corners of other buildings to create an open graceful *place*, frequently with fountains: the genius of architect Baron Haussmann.

He found a room in the Grand Hôtel du Louvre, on the Rue de Rivoli, with two large windows looking out on the Avenue de l'Opéra. He so enjoyed the pulsating force in his cityscapes that he hardly responded to the Vever auction at which a Monet canvas brought four thousand dollars, while his own two oils brought less than two hundred each. A painting by Daubigny was bid up to fourteen thousand dollars. He even managed to take without emotion the news that Georges and Félix had been arrested on a trip to Madrid for sketching near the fortifications and the harbor. A Spanish artillery captain with a fondness for art shipped them off to Perpignan and safety.

Durand-Ruel suggested that a series of paintings of the major boulevards would be a good idea. Camille moved to a room in the Grand Hôtel de Russie, from whose front windows he could see the whole sweep of boulevards almost as far as the Porte St. Denis. The room had two beds for a visit from Julie.

He unpacked and stretched some large canvases which would emerge as the *Rue St. Lazare* and *Boulevard des*

Italiens, Morning Effect of Sun. He prepared canvases also for the parade on Shrove Tuesday, and while waiting painted the rain on the people and carriages passing on the street below. The street was caged in shadowed dull buildings; his paintings were light, joyous, filled with the people's ardor and the love of being alive under the umbrellas or the cover of a horse-drawn carriage.

"Perhaps it is not aesthetic," he exulted, "but I am delighted to be able to paint these Paris streets that people have come to call ugly but which are so silvery, so luminous and vital."

By a rough estimate he figured that the Shrove Tuesday carnival would be the thousandth picture he had painted since he ran away to Caracas at the age of twenty-two. He could not tell whether the emotion that swept over him was one of shuddering with revulsion or shivering with joy. It was quality that was wanted, not quantity! But surely there must be many good things among that thousandfold effort?

He worked only two hours in the morning and two hours in the afternoon. Yet his concentration on the scene below him was so intense that he hammered down a full day of painting. In the evenings he paid nostalgic visits to the Brasserie Andler, the Café Guerbois, the Poulet au Pot. He learned that the rejection of the Caillebotte Impressionist paintings, due to the antipathy of the official Ecole des Beaux-Arts, had stirred such a furor that the Minister of Fine Arts had been obliged to hang part of the legacy in the Luxembourg annex, a narrow, badly lighted room. The pictures, miserably framed, hung haphazardly side by side in what was little more than a passageway. They were still in Corot's catacombs! But it was the Luxembourg nonetheless, the second most important museum in France.

Le Temps caused a stir which sent scores to see the paintings the Institut had decried: Renoir's ball at the *Moulin de la Galette*, Monet's *Railway Station*, paintings by Sisley, Camille's best canvases from Pontoise and the Hermitage. The crowds formed around the Impressionist paintings. There was no knife thrust, no raucous laughter or derision, no one spat on a canvas. Instead there were enthusiastic exclamations and discussions of what each of the Impressionist painters had achieved.

Only their denigrator, Gérôme, in an echo of the Salon des Refusés, had published a blast against them in the *Journal des Artistes* when the pictures had been accepted. His words were not new, just the surprise that the work could arouse such vehemence after over thirty years:

We are in a century of decadence and imbecility. . . .
The whole level of society is declining visibly. [This
legacy] includes the painting of Monsieur Manet, does
it not? And of Monsieur Pissarro and others? I repeat,
for the state to accept filth like this would mean a
tremendous withering of morality. . . . Anarchists!
And fools! People joke about it and say, "It's not
important—wait." But no! It's the end of the Nation
of France!

Camille, Monet, Degas, Sisley, Renoir met for a celebration at their old haunt, the Café de la Nouvelle Athènes,
toasting the good and great human being Gustave Caillebotte,
dead now for three years, who had had the wisdom when he
was quite young to leave his art works to the state. Through
the combined teaching of his artist friends, Caillebotte had
become a good painter; he would also go down in history
with Durand-Ruel and Père Tanguy as a dedicated comrade
who had enabled his confreres to survive. Degas spoke for
them all:
"In just such oblique ways does stupidity force wisdom
into recognition."
The fragmented and frequently dispersed group, a few of
whom had even disclaimed the title "Impressionist," sitting
around the white marble-topped table with its ring of brass,
raised their glasses and called:
"Salut!"

He painted the boulevard with the crowd and the march of
the Boeuf-Gras, the sun on the serpentines and the trees, the
onlookers in the shadow. There were high-built floats, vividly
colored streamers and banners; thousands of Frenchmen parading down the Boulevard Montmartre and into the Boulevard des Italiens. He worked quickly to catch the passing
pageantry, using his brush to put on large splashes of color.
He got several good-sized versions, well constructed and
vividly hued, with the stream of people seeming to be distinct
individuals: a miracle he did not quite understand himself.
While setting down the hordes of lifelike figures of the Mardi
Gras that were little more than tiny brush strokes in the vast
panorama, he reinforced what he had begun to suspect while
doing the densely peopled quais and bridges of Rouen: his
thirty months of Pointillism had not been wasted. Instead,
they were enabling him to portray the jammed-together multi-

tudes on the sidewalks and the colorful, thickly packed participants, many in the orange, green and yellow uniforms of their organizations, many holding tall banners aloft, with brass bands playing spiritedly as they came down the middle of the boulevard.

Durand-Ruel was enthralled and committed himself to a major showing the following May. He was also delighted with the exuberant articles about the Caillebotte Luxembourg exhibition. He had sent Camille's Rouen paintings of the previous year to New York, where collectors from the earlier American Art Association showing returned to buy at steadily increasing prices.

Despite the cold wet winter Camille was content with his income and his productivity; as a workman he had been worthy of his hire. In April he sent the cityscapes home to Eragny, then moved back to the less expensive Hôtel Garnier. Because of his improved status his advocate, Monsieur Teissier, who had seen him through the legalities of the acquisition of the Apple Orchard, advised that he had to have a new will that must take into account each child to whom he sent money so that a reckoning could be made with no jealousy. . . .

" . . . in case I die," Camille thought; "but that's the business of advocates: to protect the families of the deceased. Am I about to be deceased? At only sixty-six? I do not think so."

6

In April a telegram from London informed them that Lucien had suffered a stroke. Camille caught the train to Dieppe. In London he found that one arm and one side of Lucien's face were immobile. But with rest, exercise and medical treatment, the doctor assured him, Lucien would walk and recover some use of the arm and lifeless left hand. When Sterbee began taking him out in a bath chair to Bedford Park, Camille took an easel box into the square and quieted his anxiety with the anodyne of painting. However he found Félix, who had been sharing rooms with Georges, pale and coughing. Félix was the shortest and skinniest of the three older boys, with melancholy eyes usually well hidden under a peaked cap. He was earning a few pounds by hand-tooling decorated boxes.

"Just a cold," he explained.

"Hadn't we better have a doctor examine you?" Camille asked.

"You've got enough trouble with Lucien's stroke."

When Lucien was sufficiently strong to travel, Camille took him, Sterbee and Orovida home to Eragny where the clear sunshine of the coming summer would speed his recovery. Soon he was walking in the back garden. Camille enjoyed the company. Julie looked forward to their return to England.

Continuing to undergo seizures of coughing, intermittent fever and chest pains, Félix, in London, finally took to his bed. The doctor called in by Jacob Bensusan diagnosed tuberculosis. Julie threw some clothes into a portmanteau and hurried to her third son's side, as grievously stricken as Camille had been over Lucien's stroke.

Félix was moved to a sanatorium. Georges took charge, carting Julie back and forth to visit, managing their funds, sending helpful reports to his father.

The doctor reported that Félix was improving. A few days later he was dead.

Julie was prostrate. She remembered that Rachel had lost six of her eight children; the worst catastrophe that could happen to a mother.

"I'm well on my way," she grieved. Félix was the fourth of the nine she had borne.

In her mind she came to peace with her mother-in-law, now dead almost ten years.

They buried Félix in England. Georges accompanied her back to Eragny. She promptly demanded that Cocotte come home from Ste. Catherine's. Camille insisted she remain until she was graduated.

He hung one of Félix's canvases in the dining room. "Poor boy," he mourned. "What a subtle and delicate gift he had."

There were people in high positions who asserted that Dreyfus was innocent. The brochure of Bernard Lazare proved that the document the General Staff had given the press was a forgery. His contention was supported by twelve scientists of differing nationalities.

Both *Le Temps* and *Le Figaro* published letters claiming that Esterhazy was the traitor. Fifteen years before, Esterhazy had written excoriating the French: "These people are not worth the cartridges necessary to kill them."

Though the War Ministry tried to throttle the press, the

French journalists pursued the case. Esterhazy was tried but was declared innocent by a unanimous vote.

Emile Zola rose to heroic action, publishing an open letter to the President of the Republic under the headline "*J'Accuse*" in *L'Aurore*. The attack exposed the army cover-up. Zola was tried for slandering Dreyfus's accusers, was convicted, sentenced to a year of imprisonment. He fled to England.

Georges Clemenceau was next to publish a strong defense of Dreyfus. There was also an article in *Les Droits de l'Homme*.

Camille was shocked when Guillaumin, living comfortably on his lottery prize said:

"If Dreyfus had been shot at once, people would have been spared all this commotion."

Degas's virulent diatribe against Dreyfus cost him his twenty-five-year relationship with Mary Cassatt, a fervent Dreyfusard. He no longer spoke to Camille.

The more the evidence proved that Dreyfus was guiltless, the stronger the anti-Semitic sentiment became. It was no longer the anarchists who were feared, or the socialists who were condemned; for an election was coming up and Camille could sense that a *coup d'état* was being prepared by both the army and the clerics.

He took two big rooms at the Grand Hôtel du Louvre with large windows from which he could paint the Avenue de l'Opéra, "very beautiful, a real painter's motif." The weather was wretched but neither rain nor bad eye could dampen his drive. He painted a scintilliating scene of the Place du Théâtre Français. By the eleventh of April he had finished fourteen canvases of a series, the Avenue de l'Opéra and its lead-in boulevards. Except for an early Claude Monet made from the front lobby of Nadar's photographic studio, he felt it was a leap forward in transcribing what was considered to be ordinary, meaningless, into scenes of pictorial grandeur and loveliness, celebrating man's accomplishment in the creating of cities: the courageous souls walking its boulevards in the heat, rain, snow, sleet, somehow going about the business of being alive.

He sent them on to Durand-Ruel and returned to Eragny at the beginning of May, happy again to breathe the pure air there and to see green pastures and flowers. They watched a telephone line being strung through their village but did not attempt to have an instrument installed in their own house. He began tramping the fields around Eragny and Bazincourt, "so as not to lose the habit."

Durand-Ruel's May exhibition was a "decided success."

The dealer was happy with the avenue and boulevard scenes as well as the newest studies from Eragny. Camille had an entire room to himself: in adjoining rooms were the best of Monet, Renoir, Sisley and Puvis de Chavannes, an old acquaintance from the Batignolles days. The press was highly favorable. Only Arsène Alexandre, who had inherited Albert Wolff's mantle at *Le Figaro*, attacked him. As a result of the exhibition he was invited to send two paintings to the Pittsburgh Museum in the United States, with sales assured. The Pittsburgh Museum through its director also invited him to come to that city to serve on their selection jury for the annual showing. It was a temptation; the museum could help establish him in that country. But he would have to be away for a month; no painting to be done, a long distance from Julie and the children. He declined.

For a summer vacation in 1898 he and Julie visited Lyon, which he found to be "a great and beautiful city, particularly the quais of the river Saône, and the museum housing El Greco, Claude Lorrain, Tintoretto, Veronese." He then took Julie, approaching sixty, to Grancey-sur-Ource. She wanted to see the town she had left with a basket of linens on each arm, to begin her life as a domestic in the Passy apartment of the Pissarro family. He wanted to see the village that had ensnared him.

She took him for a walk along the Ource where she used to pick berries and tend the family cow; to the vineyards where she had worked with her mother and sisters trimming the vines and gathering the grapes; to the châteaux where they had joined other Grancey women in doing the biannual wash in the courtyard while singing village songs. They stood at the bottom of the Rue Neuve in front of the Vellay stone hut on the canal, in front of the washhouse over the river Ource. Her only comment was:

"Nobody's growing vegetables or flowers in the yard like I did."

They then trudged up the steep hill to the Church of Val des Dames where she had taken her first communion and whose choir had given her expression, companionship and travel around the Burgundy villages.

Here she stood in silence.

They returned to the Apple Orchard.

Camille, restless, decided to make a pilgrimage to his superiors. He spent eight days in Amsterdam. Camille studied the work of Rembrandt, Hals, Vermeer, but returned to Paris more than ever in love with the work of his confreres.

Came harsh November, with everything wet. He worried about the effect of the moisture on his freshly painted canvases. There was nothing to do but rent an apartment in Paris. They found one at 204 Rue de Rivoli facing the Tuileries, with a superb view of the park. From his front window he could see the Louvre to the left, the houses on the quais of the Seine behind the trees; to the right the Dôme des Invalides, the steeples of Ste. Clotilde behind a solid mass of chestnut trees.

They brought in enough furniture to make the apartment livable. Julie was happy to be spending the winter in the city. She designated the front room with its heroic windows as Camille's studio, establishing a comfortable dining-sitting room behind. When Sterbee sent them a batch of little Orovida's drawings, Camille was charmed.

"*Diable!* The third generation of artists. Her drawings are already full of sentiment and elegance."

He set up his easel, worked through the hours: the gardens of the Tuileries in sunshine or gray weather, early morning or afternoon, windstorm, hail or setting sun; each painting different, incandescent with a soft patina of light, each viable under his brush. The work, he knew, had to be good so that Durand-Ruel could exhibit it and sell it.

In the middle of January 1899 the weather became a continual menace. Sometimes the fog was so thick he could not see across the Rue de Rivoli. Since their arrival they had had winds that could, he said, "unhorn bulls." He was awaiting the thrust of Paris's great trees so as to get more varied effects.

He heard from Monet that Alfred Sisley had been seriously ill at Moret-sur-Loing, which he had painted so lovingly; and had died destitute. Camille brought to his mind the bright young fellow with whom he had vacationed at Mother Anthony's Inn in Marlotte, the charming romantic son of a businessman who had manufactured and sold artificial flowers to St. Thomas. Alfred Sisley had created some works of rare amplitude and beauty.

The Impressionists put together an auction for the benefit of Sisley's widow and children. Camille sent *Garden of the Tuileries on a Winter Afternoon*. It brought a good price.

By the end of March he had fourteen canvases stacked on easels and against the walls. The thick mist outside his window did not obscure his great pleasure at learning that a syndicate composed of Georges Petit; the Bernheims, who owned a prestigious gallery; and a third owner, Montaignac, had bought thirty of his pictures from Durand-Ruel, an unheard-of procedure. They next informed him that through their joint efforts they had already sold half of them and recouped their investment. He went immediately to Durand-Ruel.

"You'll be able to raise my prices, won't you, Monsieur Durand-Ruel?" The one containment on his pleasure had been that Durand-Ruel was paying him almost the same prices he had ten years before.

"*Vraiment*. We'll stage a giant show next month."

Jean Grave's journal, *Les Temps Nouveaux*, announced that in an auction to be held to help finance the publication there would be paintings by four Pissarros: Camille, Lucien, Georges and Ludovic Rodolphe. Camille had his "artist family."

Durand-Ruel's April exhibition was a noble one. Camille exhibited thirty-six paintings from 1870 to 1898. A few weeks later he showed a different twenty at Bernheim Jeune.

"How can I not be prolific when I have lived so long and worked every day?" he asked of the air around him.

Everything sold, though the critic of *La Revue Blanche* accused him of being "perpetually the ravished slave of his first impression."

The family returned to Eragny for the summer. Camille, who had now been called "a reflective visionary," went searching for visions in such villages as Argues and Varengeville near Dieppe. The country did not suit him; it was too panoramic. He wanted nooks and corners. He returned to Eragny to his own vision of fields, orchards, people picking the fruit of their plantings.

On June 3, 1899, the Court of Criminal Appeal reversed the guilty judgment against Alfred Dreyfus and ordered a new trial. Six days later he was released from his solitary cell on Devil's Island and began the long sea journey home.

The second trial was held publicly in Rennes to avoid hostile demonstrations in Paris. The papers were black with headlines. There was an attempted assassination of Dreyfus's defense lawyer, Labori. Three hundred correspondents from foreign countries sent daily dispatches home.

The President of France pardoned Dreyfus to put an end to the national turmoil. Also, it was rumored, to protect the exhibition of 1900, which was planned to surpass in scope the Exposition Universelle through which Camille had walked in 1855, thunderstruck at the thousands of paintings exhibited, intimidated and confident in turn that he could also become an artist.

Captain Dreyfus refused the pardon, demanded the restoration of his rank and command, the replacement of his military decorations and the right to march in the courtyard of the Ecole Militaire in renewed uniform and rank before the men previously under his command. It would be done.

Many of the French felt repatriated. Camille felt a resurgence of faith.

In the autumn the family moved back to the apartment on the Rue de Rivoli. He set up his easel before his front windows, grasped again the glowing portraits of immortal Paris, queen of the world's cities.

Durand-Ruel planned to organize a major room in the 1900 Great Centennial Exposition opening in April, to exhibit the finest works of all the Impressionists from the days of the Salon des Refusés through the eight Impressionist exhibitions. This gallery would come immediately after the Fontainebleau School of the 1830s: Papa Carot, Daubigny, Millet, Rousseau, to whom they were all indebted.

At the same time Camille was informed that five of his paintings had been bought for Berlin. Five were being bid for in Le Havre. Durand-Ruel was negotiating to buy nine canvases, most of them designated for New York. Portier was selling a painting to an American for the astronomical price of three thousand dollars. The prices for all of their works had risen to a respectable level. Even Cézanne, through Vollard's gallery, was receiving high prices for his long-despised canvases.

The money was not the Ultima Thule, that most distant goal of accomplishment. It was Acceptance. In the previous year there had been penetrating reviews of his work in *La Revue Blanche, Le Mercere de France*, and a second attempt at a history of Impressionism in the prestigious *Le Temps*.

He entered the vast halls of the Great Centennial Exhibition of 1900 and was immediately back in the Exposition Universelle of 1855, twenty-five years old, clean-shaven, keen-eyed, standing at Anton Melbye's side to see the galaxy of paintings that had been assembled from all over the world; confounded, astonished by the enormity of so much art; and finally exhilarated by the knowledge that painting played a universal role in the life of the human being. Confident that he too could paint, become a part of it all.

That had been the beginning, really, of the long road.

His lifetime of work was a tribute to the earth, the sky, man and his Maker. It had been inspired from the beginning by religious fervor that had made him search for the divine in the mundane. He had created steadily and devotedly for fifty years, filled with the ecstasy of expression, emblazoning the world in an eternal image.

Had it been worthwhile, the rejection, the humiliation, the suffering?

Yes! His efforts had borne luscious fruit.

He had said, early on, "If I had it to do over again, I would do it the same way. . . ."

The sun was setting over the river when he left the radiant display of the Impressionist paintings so lovingly and expertly juxtaposed by Paul Durand-Ruel on the long walls of the Great Centennial Exhibition. The Louvre, the Tuileries, the Seine were colored rose and purple. The world was glowing.

Back in the apartment he gazed out his window at the boulevard below with its young people hurrying across the Seine's bridges into the twentieth century. Had he made a scratch on the nineteenth century?

Julie summoned him to supper. Julie, who owned hundreds of his oils, watercolors, gouaches, drawings, would be secure for the rest of her life. She would never have to leave the home she had demanded for herself, the slightly leaning Apple Orchard. His four sons were well trained; they could live as skilled craftsmen, at the least. Cocotte had grown into a vivacious nineteen-year-old, nicely educated, and for whom he could now afford Julie's "dozen," a dowry.

His right eye still filled up and had to be drained by Dr. Parenteau every now and then, but he had learned to live with it. And work with it. He was certain he had another hundred paintings within him: of Paris, Bazincourt, Le Havre . . . Eragny. Perhaps another self-portrait.

He was content. In July he would celebrate his seventieth birthday. Fortunate is the artist who finds beauty in nature.

He turned away from his easel, from his window overlooking the universe, a tiny smile at the corner of his lips, his dark eyes gleaming with the memories of the decades of struggle of his Impressionist confreres.

The twentieth century might be theirs, after all.

GLOSSARY

The French Landscape

The artist was an isolated character, *outré*, exaggerated and outside the mainstream of French life whether that of the Parisian *bourgeoisie*, the conventional middle class, or the working class, and completely apart from peasant understanding. His contact with the public at *salons*, exhibits, was minimal and rare. Artists generally lived in their own *arrondissement*, district, gathering at the local café where they drank a *café au lait*, coffee with milk, a *bière*, beer, or *vin ordinaire*, an anonymous table wine. The café became their club, where they were welcome and had their own tables, not for the few *sous*, pennies, they had to spend but because they represented *la vie de bohème* and made good sightseeing for the rest of the customers. Their cries of *Bonjour*, Good day, *Salut!* Hello or Cheers, *Comment ça va?* How goes it?, as well as *Sacrebleu!* Confound it! *Parbleu!* By Jove, *Ma foi!* Really! Upon my faith!, punctuated with many an *Alors*, Well then, rang out at their constant bewilderment over fate and their rejection. Much less often were the cries *Je suis baba*, or *étonné*, I am stupefied, or *Incroyable!* Unbelievable, and *Grâce à Dieu*, Thank God, when a rare new *amateur*, collector, bought their efforts and gave them the few francs they needed for a *poulet au pot*, chicken in the pot; a *gâteau*, a cake which they bought at a *pâtissene;* their daily bread, the *ficelle*, narrow crusty string, the *bâtard*, bread of medium length, or *parisien*, longest and fattest of the long breads which they purchased at the *boulangerie* and carried through the streets under the arm, unwrapped. Francs with which to pay for a model, or the rent, to heat the *atelier*, studio, against the cold and damp of the Parisian winter. They were a poverty-stricken lot, constant visitors to the *mont-de-piété*, municipal-run pawnshop, while dreaming of a *succès fou*, a crazy wild success, and shrugging off their rejection with a *Tant pis*, That's tough, or *Chacun à son goût*, Each to his own taste.

Of companionship they had plenty, as well as girls, *grisettes*, young working girls supplementing their meager daytime salaries, *cocottes*, intimates who loved the gaiety of *la bohème*, the *joie de vivre*, exuberance of the artist's life, and of their creating.

The proverb is part of the language. It expresses what no long paragraph reveals. It is the spice and short cut of every language and, particularly among the peasants, it is the wisdom they possess. It is indicative of how universal is man's emotional response that one finds these sentiments existing in so many languages. They become commonplace, banalities, yet nothing seems to get closer to the truth. They are a constant part of dialogue. The intellectual continually searches for ways to say the same thing differently.

Un homme quise noie s'attache à un brin d'herbe. A drowning man clings to a blade of grass. *Un aveugle mène l'autre à la fosse*. One blind man leads another into the ditch. *Brebis comptées, le loup les mange*. The lambs once counted, the wolf eats them. To be foolhardy is *se mettre dans la gueule du loup*, to put one's head in the wolf's jaw. And to do that one would have rooms to rent in one's head: *chambres à louer dans la tête* . . . a hole in the head!

Stingy is the man *qui tondrait un oeuf*, who would mow an egg. A miser. And *qui se mouche trop son nez en tire du sang*, who blows his nose too much draws blood . . . pushes his luck! At the same time one is exhorted *prendre la lune avec les dents*, to take the moon with one's teeth . . . the bull by the horns. Yet *il a acheté trop cher le mel qui sur les épines le lèche*. Honey is too costly if it must be licked over thorns. Nor must one *demander de la laine à un ane*, ask wool from a donkey, blood from a stone.

Un ventre affamé n'a pas d'oreilles. A hungry stomach has no ears. Some *boivent à ventre déboutonné*, drink with an unbuttoned stomach. Others try to drink up the sea, *c'est la mer à boire*.

It is good to be *unis comme les doigts de la main*, united like the fingers of the hand. While some cry, *Je me vois au pied du mur sans échelle*. I am at the foot of the wall without a ladder. Or *Je ne sais pas sur quel pied danser*, I don't know what foot to stand on. Or, *J'ai une colère comme un âne à qui l'on attache une fussée aux fesses*, I'm as angry as a donkey with a rocket up his rump. Still others *montent le bourrichon*, get carried away, and exclaim, *Je suis aux anges*, I am in seventh heaven. Or there will be hell to pay: *chien de l'enfer*.

A more sophisticated aphorism of the pavement, not the land, is a beauty. *Le mieux est l'ennemi du bien*. Better is the enemy of good!

A *bonne* is a young servant girl, a *bonne à tout faire* is a maid of all work: a lady's maid, nursemaid, and housecleaner. A *fleuriste,* a maker of artificial flowers. A *garçon,* a waiter, or just "Boy!"

Cher is costly, or dear as in *cher ami,* dear friend, *ma chère femme,* my dear wife, *chère . . .* dearie.

Attention! means Listen! and *Regardez,* Look here. *Pour rien* is dirt cheap. *Pour rire,* it is to laugh. *Toc-tac* is phony, imitation; *tout juste . . .* by the skin of one's teeth. *Infidèle,* unfaithful; *vulgaire,* common; a *cause scandale,* a shameful scene, while *bavardage* is gossip; *drôlerie* is a jest to relieve boredom, and *un bonneteau* a game easy to cheat at.

An artist's *métier* is his craft, frequently practiced *en plein air,* out of doors. He also as frequently lives solely on *bouillie de maïs,* mush.

The Frenchman has a long list of derogatory terms: *un boscard,* a parasite, *un escarpe,* a murderer, *un goujat,* a vulgar man, *un fumiste,* a bad joker, *un Alphonse,* a pimp, *un têcheur,* a son of a bitch. But above all one hears an anguished *Merde!* Shit. No one wants to take anything *couchant,* lying down.

There would be no dialogue without *Exactement!* Exactly!; society's *de rigueur,* absolutely mandatory behavior, or the greatly to be desired *touché,* well hit, on the button.

Ironically, every conversation is peppered with *D'accord.* Agreed. For a nation that hardly ever does.

C'est vrai. It's true. *N'est-ce pas?* Isn't it?

C'est ça. That's how it is.

J.S.

Acknowledgments

My predecessors in the research and writing about Camille Pissarro have been consistently helpful and generous. John Rewald is the pioneer in the field; his edited *Letters to Lucien* (1943) first interested me in the personal life behind Pissarro's painting. Rewald's *The History of Impressionism* (1946) is the standard volume. *Pissarro* (1963) is an analysis of Pissarro's work, accompanied by excellent reproductions. Kathleen Adler's short biography, *Camille Pissarro* (1977), contains important detail. Ralph E. Shikes and Paula Harper's *Pissarro: His Life and Work* (1980) is well written and authentic. Rewald, Adler and Shikes were consistently helpful over the five years of the writing of this book.

Madame Janine Bailly-Herzberg is accomplishing the heroic task of editing *Correspondance de Camille Pissarro* (Presses Universitaires de France), the first volume of which was published in Paris in 1980. Through the cooperation of Madame Herzberg and P.U.F., I secured a photocopy of the unpublished second volume.

Christopher Lloyd, Assistant Keeper of the Ashmolean Museum, Oxford, England, published his *Camille Pissarro* (1981) with an analytical text. Lloyd was helpful at the Ashmolean; and a lucid correspondent about sticky problems of the life and technique of Camille Pissarro. Mrs. Anne Thorold of London was my guide in the Camille Pissarro archives at the Ashmolean Museum, and an indefatigable supplier of needed answers. In England I am also indebted to John Bensusan-Butt and Geoffrey Bensusan for materials about the early Bensusan family. I was also assisted by Kenneth Garlick, Keeper of Western Art, and Jean Gilliland, Pissarro archivist, at the Ashmolean. And by Christian Neffe of the JPL Fine Arts, London.

In France I am greatly indebted to Charles Durand-Ruel, who generously opened his Paul Durand-Ruel archives to me; and to Miss France Daguet, who photocopied so many of the Durand-Ruel documents. Beverly Gordey of Doubleday & Co., Paris, was indispensable. My thanks also to Elisabeth Tranié, who photocopied Madame Herzberg's second volume of Pissarro letters. Edda Maillet of the Pissarro Museum in Pontoise showed me the three homes in which Pissarro lived in Pontoise; the Directors of the Pissarro Museum permitted me to extract from the Julie Vellay and Piette de Montfoucault letters in their possession.

I am indebted to the present owners of Montfoucault, who permitted me and Mrs. Stone to sketch and photograph the interiors of Montfoucault, as well as its gardens and court.

Christiane Pluyaut, the historian and newspaper columnist of Grancey-sur-Ource, acquainted me with the village and was indefatigable in supplying answers to my many questions about the background of the Vellay family, the history and mores of Grancey.

I thank the Foundation Custodia for reprints of the twenty-five Théodore Duret letters; Michel Liflard of the Musée de la Poste, Paris; Miss Comerre of the Hôtel Drouot; and Katia Pissarro. I am also indebted to the present occupants of the Maison Retrou on the road to Versailles for permitting me to work in Pissarro's studio; and to the present owners of the Apple Orchard in Eragny.

In St. Thomas I am indebted to Corinna Gutowski for delving into the back files of newspapers of the island. Isidor Paiwonsky, pioneer, merchant and authority on St. Thomas history, was generous with his time and knowledge. John L. Loeb, Jr., American Ambassador to Denmark, provided me with authentic information about native St. Thomas furniture. Jette Kjaerboe of the Kastrupgårdsamlingen provided me with all the Fritz and Anton Melbye and David Jacobsen materials available in Denmark.

I have been particularly fortunate in my friends and associates in Southern California. Dr. Milton Heifetz was my adviser on the state of the science of medicine, 1855–1900. Dr. Ben Kagan, pediatrician, advised me in the matter of Minette's illness and death. Dr. August L. Reader III documented Pissarro's eye trouble and Dr. Parenteau's treatments. Dr. Dora Weiner of UCLA secured me information from Dr. Jean Theodorides about ophthalmology in the nineteenth century in France. Dr. Raymond Weston was always available.

Consul General François Mouton was my confrere on matters French; along with Dr. Eugene Weber of UCLA.

Ruth Weisberg, artist and Professor of Fine Arts, University of Southern California, instructed me in the use of an etching press; my son Kenneth explained the mysteries of etching and lithography.

I had considerable help on the Old Testament from Jack Skirball. Fred Shane, artist and Professor Emeritus of Fine Arts, University of Missouri, was my patient adviser on the technique of oil painting. Anna-Lee Nathan was an always willing reference on matters English. Louis and Annette Kaufman on nineteenth-century music. Our neighbors, Guilford and Diane Glazer, were the guardians of our successive chapters as the book progressed.

The Research Library and the Art Library at UCLA were, as always, generous in providing me with an endless stream of reference works.

I should like to acknowledge my indebtedness to Kacy Tebbel, my longtime copy editor at Doubleday; and to salute my two friends and editors at Doubleday, Ken McCormick and Sam Vaughan. I am grateful to my wife Jean for her patient photographing of the hundreds of scenes of Paris and the French countryside that I wanted recorded.

I am grateful to Richard Robson Brettell for permission to use his doctoral thesis (Yale University, 1978) on "Pissarro and Pontoise: The Painter in a Landscape''; and Antonia Lant for the right to consult her master's thesis, ''Pissarro, Degas and Cassatt as Print-makers in 1880'' (Leeds University, England, 1979).

Irving Stone

June 6, 1985

A Selected Bibliography

Books about Camille Pissarro

Kathleen Adler, *Camille Pissarro, A Biography*, 1977; Janine Bailly-Herzberg, *Correspondence de Camille Pissarro: 1865–1885*, 1980; Richard R. Brettell, *Pissarro and Pontoise: The Painter in a Landscape*, 1977; Richard Brettell and Christopher Lloyd, *A Catalogue of the Drawings by Camille Pissarro in the Ashmolean Museum, Oxford*, 1980; Raymond Cogniat, *Pissarro*, trans. Alice Sachs, 1975; Antonia Lant, *Pissarro, Degas and Cassatt as Print-makers in 1880*, 1979; Christopher Lloyd, *Camille Pissarro*, 1981; Lucien Pissarro and Lionello Venturi, *L'Oeuvre de Camille Pissarro*, 2 vols., 1939; John Rewald, *Camille Pissarro*, 1963; John Rewald, ed., *Camille Pissarro: Letters to His Son Lucien*, trans. Lionel Abel, 1943 (also Paul P. Appel edition, 1972); Barbara Shapiro, *Camille Pissarro: The Impressionist Printmaker*, 1973; Ralph E. Shikes and Paula Harper, *Pissarro: His Life and Work*, 1980; A. Tabarant, *Pissarro*. trans. J. Lewis May, 1925; Anne Thorold, *Artists, Writers, Politics: Camille Pissarro and His Friends*, 1980.

Articles and Monographs on Camille Pissarro

Ralph Coe, ''Camille Pissarro in Paris,'' *Gazette des Beaux-Arts*, February 1954; Frank Davis, ''Compassionate Adventurer: Camille Pissarro at the Hayward Gallery,'' *Country Life*, November 6, 1980; André Fermigier, ''Pissarro at the Grand Palais: Spreading the Good Word,'' *The Guardian*,

March 1, 1981; Jules Joets, "Unedited Letters from Pissarro to Claude Monet," *L'Amour de l'Art*, 1946; Ruth Low, "Camille Pissarro: St. Thomas' French Impressionist," *Virgin Islander*, July 1981; Octave Mirbeau, "Camille Pissarro," *L'Art dans les Deux Mondes*, January 1891; Musée Pissarro, "Pissarro & Pontoise," 1980; V. S. Pritchett, "The Poet-Logician," *The New York Review of Books*, May 14, 1981; Carter Ratcliff, "Pissarro's Distinction," *Saturday Review*, June 1981; John Rewald, "Camille Pissarro: His Work and Influence," *Burlington Magazine*, June 1938; John Rewald, "Camille Pissarro in the West Indies," *Gazette des Beaux-Arts*, October 1942; John Russell, "Pissarro: The Quiet Master," New York *Times Book Review*, July 20, 1980; Pierre Schneider, "Pissarro: l'anti-fier-à-bras," *L'Express*, February 14, 1981; Mark Stevens, "Pissarro the Patriarch," *Newsweek*, June 1, 1981; Scott Sullivan, "The Unsung Impressionist," *Newsweek*, March 16, 1981; Max Wykes-Joyce, "London Honors Pissarro," *International Herald Tribune*, December 27–28, 1980; "Pissarro," *Le petit Journal*, No. 103, 1981.

Writings about Camille Pissarro's Contemporaries

GENERAL. David Duff, *Eugenie and Napoleon III*, 1978; Paul Gachet, *Deux amis des Impressionnistes*, 1956; Robert J. Niess, *Zola, Cézanne, and Manet: A Study of L'Oeuvre*, 1968; Charles Sprague Smith, *Barbizon Days*, 1902; Wilhelm Uhde, *The Impressionists*, 1937; Paul Valéry, *Degas, Manet, Morisot,* trans. David Paul, 1960; Lionello Venturi, *Impressionists and Symbolists*, trans. Francis Steegmuller, 1950.

FRÉDÉRIC BAZILLE. J. Charensol, "Bazille and the Beginnings of Impressionism," *L'Amour de l'Art*, January 1927; François Dault, *Bazille and His Time*, 1952; Ernest Scheyer, "Jean Frédéric Bazille: The Beginnings of Impressionism," *Art Quarterly*, Spring 1942.

GEORGES DE BELLIO. Remis Niculescu, "Georges de Bellio, l'ami des Impressionnistes," *Revue roumaine de l'Histoire de l'Art*, t.I, No. 2, 1964.

GUSTAVE CAILLEBOTTE. Marie Berhaut, *Caillebotte: La vie et son oeuvre*, 1978; J. Kirk, T. Varnedoe, Thomas P. Lee, eds., *Gustave Caillebotte: A Retrospective Exhibition*, 1976; Musée Pissarro, *Gustave Caillebotte: 1848–1894*, 1984.

MARY CASSATT. George Biddle, "Some Memories of

Mary Cassatt,'' *The Arts*, August 1926; Frank Getlein, *Mary Cassatt: Paintings and Prints*, 1980; Nancy Hale, *Mary Cassatt*, 1975; Una E. Johnson, ''The Graphic Art of Mary Cassatt,'' *American Artist*, November 1945; Nancy Mowll Mathews, *Cassatt and Her Circle—Selected Letters*, 1984.

PAUL CÉZANNE. Gerstle Mack, *Paul Cézanne*, 1942; Ambroise Vollard, *Paul Cézanne*, trans. Harold L. Van Doren, 1937.

CAMILLE COROT. Everard Meynell, *Corot and His Friends*, 1892; Alfred Robaut, *L'Oeuvre de Corot*, 1905.

GUSTAVE COURBET. Georges Boudaille, *Courbet, Painter in Protest*, 1969; Charles Léger, *Courbet et son temps*, 1948; Gerstle Mack, *Gustave Courbet*, 1951.

CHARLES FRANÇOIS DAUBIGNY, Fidell-Beautort and Janine Bailly-Herzberg, *Daubigny*, 1975.

HONORÉ DAUMIER. Howard P. Vincent, *Daumier and His World*, 1968.

EDGAR DEGAS. Jeanne Fèvre, *Mon oncle Degas*, 1949; Camille Mauclair, *Degas*, 1945; Theodore Reff, *Degas: The Artist's Mind*, 1976; John Rewald, ''The Realism of Degas,'' *Magazine of Art*, January 1946; Walter Sickert, ''Degas,'' *Burlington Magazine*, November 1917; Ambroise Vollard, *Degas, an Intimate Portrait*, trans. Randolph T. Weaver, 1927; ''Unpublished Letters of Degas,'' *Art Bulletin*, March 1968; ''More Unpublished Letters of Degas,'' *Art Bulletin*, March 1969.

EUGÈNE DELACROIX. René Huyghe, *Delacroix ou le combat solitaire*, 1964; Walter Pach, ed. and trans., *The Journals of Eugène Delacroix*, 1937; Tom Prideaux, *The World of Delacroix*, 1966.

JEAN DESBROSSES. Frédéric Henriet, *Jean Desbrosses*, 1881.

ALBERT DUBOIS-PILLET. Lily Bazalgette, *Albert Dubois-Pillet*, 1976.

PAUL DURAND-RUEL. Arsène Alexandre, ''Durand-Ruel: Portrait et Histoire d'un Marchand,'' *Pan*, November 1911; Georges Lecomte, ''L'Art Impressionniste d'après la collection privée de M. Durand-Ruel,'' 1892; John Rewald, ''Durand-Ruel: 140 Years, One Man's Faith,'' *Art News*, December 1–14, 1943; ''Hommage à Paul Durand-Ruel, 1874–1974—Cent Ans de L'Impressionnisme,'' 1974.

HENRI FANTIN-LATOUR. Edward Lucie-Smith, *Fantin-Latour*, 1977.

PAUL GAUGUIN. Lawrence and Elisabeth Hanson, *Noble Savage*, 1959; Maurice Malingue, *Paul Gauguin: le peintre et son oeuvre*, 1948.

BARON HAUSSMANN. J. M. and Brian Chapman, *The Life and Times of Baron Haussmann*, 1957; Howard Saalman, *Haussmann: Paris Transformed*, 1971.

JEAN AUGUSTE INGRES. Gaëten Picon, *Ingres*, 1980.

DAVID JACOBSEN. Jette Kjaerboe, "David Jacobsen in Paris 1855–1869" (Danish monograph).

MAXIMILIEN LUCE. Jean Sutter, *Luce. Les travaux et les jours*, 1971.

EDOUARD MANET. Germain Bazin, *Edouard Manet*, 1971; Pierre Cailler, ed., *Edouard Manet and His Contemporaries*, 1953; Théodore Duret, *Manet*, trans. J. E. Crawford Flitch, 1937; Anne Coffin Hanson, *Manet and the Modern Tradition*, 1977; George Mauner, *Manet, Peintre-Philosophe: A Study of the Painter's Themes*, 1975; Robert Rey, *Manet*, 1938; John Richardson, *Edouard Manet, Paintings and Drawings*, 1958.

CLAUDE MONET. René Gimpel, "At Giverny with Claude Monet," *Art in America*, June 1927; Charles Merrill Mount, *Monet*, 1966; Walter Pach, "At the Studio of Claude Monet," *Scribner's Magazine*, 1908; Theodore Robinson, "Claude Monet," *Century Magazine*, September 1892; Louis Vauxcelles, "An Afternoon with Claude Monet," *L'Art et les Artistes*, December 1905; Daniel Wildenstein, *Monet's Years at Giverny*, 1978; "Monet at Westminster," London *Sunday Times Magazine*, September 6, 1970.

BERTHE MORISOT. Monique Angoulvent, *Berthe Morisot*, 1933; Philippe Huisman, *Morisot* (no year given).

LUCIEN PISSARRO. John Bensusan-Butt, "Recollections of Lucien Pissarro in His Seventies", 1977; W. S. Meadmore, *Lucien Pissarro*, 1962.

PIERRE AUGUSTE RENOIR. Albert Barnes and Violette de Mazia, *The Art of Renoir*, 1935; Jeanne Baudot, *Renoir; ses amis; ses modèles;* George Besson, *Renoir*, 1929; Walter Pach, "Pierre Auguste Renoir," *Scribner's Magazine*, 1912; Jean Renoir, *Renoir, My Father*, trans. Randolph and Dorothy Weaver, 1962; Ambroise Vollard, *Renoir, an Intimate Record*, trans. Harold L. Van Doren and Randolph T. Weaver, 1934.

AUGUSTE RODIN. Denys Sutton, *Triumphant Satyr—The World of Auguste Rodin*, 1966; David Weiss, *Naked Came I*, 1963.

JOHN SINGER SARGENT. Charles Merrill Mount, *John Singer Sargent, a Biography*, 1955.

ALFRED SISLEY. Raymond Cogniat, *Sisley*, 1978; François Daulte, *Alfred Sisley*, 1959; Claude Sisley, "The Ancestry of

Alfred Sisley," *Burlington Magazine*, September 1949; Forbes Watson, "Sisley's Struggle for Recognition," *The Arts*, February–March 1921.

VINCENT VAN GOGH. J. B. de la Faille, *The Works of Vincent van Gogh*, 1970; Irving Stone, *Lust for Life*, 1934; Irving Stone, *Dear Theo*, 1937.

AMBROISE VOLLARD. Ambroise Vollard, *Recollections of a Picture Dealer*, trans. Violet M. MacDonald, 1936.

JAMES MCNEILL WHISTLER. Elisabeth Luther Cary, *The Works of James McNeill Whistler*, 1913; Horace Gregory, *The World of James McNeill Whistler*, 1959; Hesketh Pearson, *The Man Whistler*, 1952; Elizabeth Robins Pennell, *Whistler: The Friend*, 1930; E. R. and J. Pennell, *The Life of James McNeill Whistler*, 1907; James McNeill Whistler, *The Gentle Art of Making Enemies*, 1890.

Art Reference Books

Jacques du Barry, *French Rainbows*, 1982; Germain Bazin, *Le Salon de 1830 à 1900;* T.S.R. Boase, *English Art, 1800—1870*, 1959; Albert Boime, *The Academy and French Painting in the Nineteenth Century*, 1971; Sheldon Cheney, *A World History of Art*, 1946; Thomas Craven, *Modern Art*, 1934; Jean Paul Crespelle, *La Vie Quotidienne des Impressionnistes*, 1981; Wynford Dewhurst, *Impressionist Painting*, 1904; Théodore Duret, *Les peintres impressionnistes*, 1878; Robert Goldwater and Marco Treves, eds., *Artists on Art*, 1945; E. H. Gombrich, *The Story of Art*, 1951; Robert L. Herbert, *Barbizon Revisited*, 1962; Robert Hughes, *The Shock of the New*, 1980; Diane Kelder, *The Great Book of French Impressionism*, 1980; Jacques Lassaigne, *Impressionism*, 1969; Gustave Lebel, *Bibliographie des revues et périodiques d'art parues en France de 1746 à 1914*, 1960; Allen Leepa, *The Challenge of Modern Art*, 1957; Jacques Lethève, *Daily Life of French Artists*, trans. Hilary E. Paddon, 1968; André Malraux, *The Voices of Silence*, trans. Stuart Gilbert, 1953; Frank Jewett Mather, Jr., *Modern Painting*, 1927; Eleanor C. Munro, *The Golden Encyclopedia of Art*, 1961; Eric Newton, *The Arts of Man*, 1960; Gabor Peterdi, *Printmaking*, 1959; John Rewald, *The History of Impressionism*, 1946; Ralph E. Shikes and Steven Heller, *The Art of Satire*. 1984; Lionello Venturi, *Les Archives de l'Impressionnisme*, 2 vols., 1939; *Handbook of Western Painting*, 1961; *McGraw-Hill Ency-*

clopedia of World Art, 1959; *The Randon House Library of Painting and Sculpture*, 4 vols., 1981.

Miscellaneous Art Articles, Monographs, Pamphlets

Maxime Du Camp, *Les Beaux-Arts à l'Exposition Universelle de 1855;* Michel Florisoone, "Individualism and Collectivism in French Nineteenth Century Art," *Burlington Magazine*, June 1938; Lloyd Goodrich, "The Impressionists Fifty Years Ago," *The Arts*, January 1927; Hans Huth, "Impressionism Comes to America," *Gazette des Beaux-Arts*, April 1946; Jette Kjaerboe, "Danish Painters, 1855–1885," 1975; Kay Larson, "History's Fickle Finger," *New York*, March 16, 1981; John Rewald, "The Future Impressionists at the Café Guerbois," *Art News*, April 1946; Tresca, *Visite à l'Exposition Universelle de Paris en 1855*, 1855; Cecilia Waern, "Some Notes on French Impressionism," *Atlantic Monthly*, April 1892; Frederick Wedmore, "The Impressionists," *Fortnightly Review*, January 1883; "Works in Oil and Pastel by the Impressionists of Paris" (introduction by Théodore Duret), 1886.

Life in Nineteenth-Century France and Paris

Jean-Paul Aron, *Le mangeur du XIXe siècle*, 1973; Jean-Paul Aron, *Misérable et glorieuse la femme du XIXe siècle*, 1980; Olivier Bernier, *Pleasure and Privilege*, 1981; Pierre Boîtard, *Guide-manuel de la bonne compagnie, du bon ton, et de la politesse*, 1853; Jean Bouvier, *Le Krach de l'Union Générale*, 1960; D. W. Brogan, *The Development of Modern France*, 1967; Robert Burnand, *La vie quotidienne en France de 1870 à 1900*, 1947; Robert Forster and Orest Ranum, eds., *Rural Society in France*, trans. Elborg Forster and Patricia Ranum, 1977; Pierre Guiral, *La vie quotidienne en France a l'âge d'or du Capitalisme 1852–1879*, 1976; J. H. Jackson, ed., *A Short History of France*, 1974; André Lefèvre, *Sous le Second Empire: Chemins de fer et politique*, 1957; André Lévêque, *L'Histoire de la civilisation française*, 1966; Philippe Perrot, *Les dessus et les dessous de la bourgeoisi*, 1981; David H. Pinkney, *Napoleon III and the Rebuilding of Paris*, 1958; Orest and Patricia Ranum, eds., *Popular Attitudes*

Toward Birth Control in Pre-Industrial France and England, 1972; Theodore Zeldin, *France: 1848–1945*, 5 vols., 1979–1981; *Dictionary of the III Republic*, 1968; *Galigani's New Paris Guide for 1856*, 1855; *Murray's Handbook, France*, 1859.

French Life as Seen Through Its Literature and Writers

CHARLES BAUDELAIRE. *Les Fleurs du Mal*, 1856; Lewis Piaget Shanks, *Baudelaire: Flesh and Spirit*, 1930.

HONORÉ DE BALZAC. *Love in a Mask*, trans. Alice M. Ivimy, 1911; *Droll Stories*, trans. Jacques Le Clercq, 1932; *Old Goriot*, trans. Ellen Marriage; *The Chouans*, trans. George Saintsbury; *Eugénie Grandet*, trans. Ellen Marriage, 1961; André Maurois, *Prometheus: The Life of Balzac*, trans. Norman Denny, 1965; Stefan Zweig, *Balzac*, trans. William and Dorothy Rose, 1946.

ALEXANDRE DUMAS (father). *The Great Lover and Other Plays*, adapted by Barnett Shaw, 1969.

ALEXANDRE DUMAS (son). *Camille*, 1956.

FÉLIX FÉNÉON. *Oeuvres*, 1948.

GUSTAVE FLAUBERT. *Madame Bovary*, trans. Francis Steegmuller, 1957.

EDMOND AND JULES DE GONCOURT. *The Goncourt Journals*, trans. Lewis Galantière, 1947.

VICTOR HUGO. *Les Misérables*, trans. Charles E. Wilbour, 1961; *The Hunchback of Notre-Dame*, trans. Walter J. Cobb, 1964.

GEORGE DE MAURIER. *Trilby*, 1894.

PROSPER MÉRIMÉE. *Tales of Love and Death*, 1948.

MICHEL EYQUEM DE MONTAIGNE. *The Essays of Montaigne*, trans. George B. Ives, 1925.

PIERRE PROUDHON. *What Is Property?*, 1876; *General Idea of the Revolution in the Nineteenth Century*, trans. John Beverly Robinson, 1972; Henri de Lubac, *The Un-Marxian Socialist: A Study of Proudhon*, trans. R. E. Scantlebury, 1948.

MARCEL PROUST. *Remembrance of Things Past*, tran. C. K. Scott-Moncrieff, 1934.

JEAN JACQUES ROUSSEAU. *Confessions;* Francis Winwar, *Jean Jacques Rousseau*, 1961.

STENDHAL. *The Red and the Black*, trans. C. K. Scott-Moncrieff, 1926.

VOLTAIRE. *Candide*, trans. Lowell Bair, 1959; Paul McPharlin, ed., *Voltaire's Alphabet of Wit*, 1945; Jean Orieux, *Voltaire*, trans. Barbara Bray and Helen R. Lane, 1979.

EMILE ZOLA. *La Curée*, trans. A. T. de Mattos, 1924; *The Masterpiece*, trans. Thomas Walton, 1950; *Germinal*, trans. Leonard Tancock, 1954;, *Thérèse Raquin*, trans. Leonard Tancock, 1962; Matthew Josephson, *Lola and His Time*, 1928; Angus Wilson, *Emile Lola: An Introductory Study of His Novels*, 1952.

General References

Theodoor De Booy and John T. Faris, *The Virgin Islands. Our New Possessions and the British Islands*, 1918; Emile Capouya and Keitha Tompkins, eds., *The Essential Kropotkin*, 1975; Germaine Carter, *The Home Book of French Cooking*, 1950; M. E. Chevreul, *The Principles of Harmony and Contrast of Colors*, 1890; Julia Child, Louisette Bertholle, Simone Beck, *Mastering the Art of French Cooking*, 1961; Peter Elman, ed., *Jewish Marriage*, 1967; M. Mielziner, *The Jewish Law on Marriage and Divorce*, 1901; Martin A. Miller, ed., *Kropotkin, Selected Writings on Anarchism and Revolution*. 1970; Nicholas Ogden Rood, *Modern Chromatics*, 1879; André L. Simon, ed., *Wines of the World*, 1962; Luther K. Zabriskie, *The Virgin Islands of the United States*, 1918.

Miscellaneous Articles, Monographs, Pamphlets

Inge Meyer Antonsen, "Researches on the Domestic Culture of the Danish West Indies," 1966; Colman Andrews, "Islands in the Seine," *TWA Ambassador*, October 1982; E. Belfort Bax, Victor Dave and William Morris, "A Short Account of the Commune of Paris," *Socialist Platform*, No. 4, 1886; Robert Borday and André Conquet, "La Mode au Parc Monceau—Epoque Napoléon III; Dolisos Laboratories, "The Basic Principles of Homeopathy"; Les Amis de Camille Pissarro, "Quatorze Lettres de Julie Pissarro," 1984; Musée Jacquemart-André, "La Vie Parisienne"; Isidor Paiewonsky, "Jewish Historical Development in the Virgin Islands, 1665–1959," 1959.

The Dreyfus Affair

Maurice Baumont, *Aux Sources de l'Affaire Dreyfus*, 1959; Bernard Blumenkranz, *Histoire des Juifs en France*, 1972; Guy Chapman, *The Dreyfus Case: A Reassessment*, 1955; Cécile Delhorbe, *L'Affaire Dreyfus et les écrivains français*, 1932; Alfred Dreyfus, *Five Years of My Life: The Diary of Captain Alfred Dreyfus*, 1977; Paula Hyman, *From Dreyfus to Vichy*, 1979; Henry Leyret, *Lettres d'un Coupable*, 1898; Douglas Johnson, *France and the Dreyfus Affair*, 1966; David L. Lewis, *Prisoners of Honor: The Dreyfus Affair*, 1973; Maurice Paléologue, *My Secret Diary of the Dreyfus Case, 1894–1899*, 1957; Louis L. Snyder, *The Dreyfus Case: A Documentary History*, 1973; Justin Vanex, *Coupable ou Non*, 1898; Nelly Wilson, *Bernard-Lazare: Antisemitism and the Problem of Jewish Identity in Late Nineteenth-Century France*, 1978.

Newspapers and Magazines

Le Corsaire, Gil Blas, La Caricature, La Chronique des Arts, La Gazette des Beaux-Arts, La Liberté, La Libre Parole, La Presse, La République Française, La Révolte, La Revue Blanshe, La Revue Ilustrée, L'Art dans Les Deux Mondes, L'Art Français, L'Art Moderne, L'Avenir National, La Vie Moderne, La Vogue, Le Charivari, L'Echo de Pans, L'Eclair, Le Constitutionnel, Le Figaro, Le Journal des Artistes, Le Matin, Le Mercure de France, Le Père Peinard, Le Prolétaire, Le Temps, L'Evènement Illustré, L'Illustration, L'Intransigeant, L'Opinion Nationale, L'Univers Illustré, Paris Illustré, Revue de Paris, Revue des Deux Mondes, Revue Socialiste.